D1326570

# THE ESSENTIAL GORE VIDAL

## Books by Gore Vidal

### Novels

*Narratives of a Golden Age*
Burr
Lincoln
1876
Empire
Hollywood
Washington, D.C.

Williwaw
In a Yellow Wood
The City and the Pillar
The Season of Comfort
A Search for the King
Dark Green, Bright Red
The Judgment of Paris
Messiah
Julian
Myra Breckinridge
Two Sisters
Myron
Kalki
Creation
Duluth
Live from Golgotha
The Smithsonian Institution

### Short Stories

A Thirsty Evil

---

### Plays

An Evening with Richard Nixon
Weekend
Romulus
The Best Man
Visit to a Small Planet

---

### Non-Fiction

Rocking the Boat
Reflections upon a Sinking Ship
Homage to Daniel Shays
Matters of Fact and of Fiction
Pink Triangle and Yellow Star
Armageddon?
At Home
Screening History
A View from the Diners Club
United States: Essays 1952–1992
Virgin Islands
Palimpsest: A Memoir

# THE ESSENTIAL GORE VIDAL

# THE ESSENTIAL GORE VIDAL

*Edited by*
*Fred Kaplan*

LITTLE, BROWN AND COMPANY

A *Little, Brown* Book

First published in the United States of America by
Random House, Inc 1999
First published in Great Britain by Little, Brown and Company 1999



A CIP catalogue record for this book
is available from the British Library.

ISBN 0 316 84806 9

*Book design by Carole Lowenstein*

Printed and bound in Great Britain by
Clays Ltd, St Ives plc

Little, Brown and Company (UK)
Brettenham House
Lancaster Place
London WC2E 7EN

# Contents

# Introduction

It is as a novelist of ideas and a satirist that Gore Vidal differs most noticeably from the other major writers of his generation. His imagination is powered by his intellect, and his high seriousness is expressed with wicked wit in an elegantly aphoristic prose style. His contemporaries—Saul Bellow, Norman Mailer, John Updike—specialize in a more Romantic prose. Bellow comes out of the picaresque novel, Rousseau, and Yiddish literature; Mailer from the dark romanticism of Carlyle, Nietzsche, and the later Dickens; Updike from an attenuated version of American Protestantism and the Richardsonian tradition of sensibility. For them the heart is the defining organ, both for life and for literature. Vidal's roots are in Petronius, Swift, Sterne, and Henry James. Intellect drives his artistry.

Vidal has been persistently involved in politics and public life, and, like Mark Twain, he has written brilliant essays on social and political topics. He also has a secondary career as a playwright and a movie script writer that echoes the preoccupations of his other writings. Its most lasting achievement is one of the few realistic plays about American politics, *The Best Man* (1960). But it is as a writer of fiction that he is most well known, and from the beginning of his career in 1946 he has published fiction in a broad range of styles and genres: short stories, collected in *A Thirsty Evil* (1956); boldly imaginative, partly surrealistic, and provocatively postmodern satirical novels, such as *Myra Breckinridge* (1968) and *Duluth* (1983); novels about the religious imagination, such as *Messiah* (1954) and *Creation* (1981); six historical novels that capture the sweep of the American experience from 1776 to 1952, among them *Burr* (1973) and *Washington, D.C.* (1967); and an extraordinary novel of the late classical world, *Julian* (1964). The range of historical and literary knowledge this represents is breathtaking.

From an early age, Vidal was, like Henry James, a serious reader, reading for life, his face buried in a book. His passion for language was inspired partly by his maternal grandfather, Senator Thomas Pryor Gore of Oklahoma, a grizzled veteran of late-nineteenth- and early-twentieth-century political wars who had an immense influence on his grandson. The Senator was a religious nonbeliever who had transformed himself from a Western populist into an anti–New Deal conservative Democrat. He was a brilliant orator, and he loved language. His grandson voraciously read books from the senator's library in Rock Creek Park in Washington, D.C., sometimes out loud to his grandfather—who was blind—sometimes to himself. Reading aloud, Vidal developed the oratorical skills that later served him well as a debater and public controversialist. Reading to himself, he expanded into literary expressiveness what was by nature a lively imagination. Though he read across genres and modes, history and literature dominated his early reading. He absorbed classical and American history and a rich variety of canonical novels and poems, and then the favorite popular novelists of his teenage years, from L. Frank Baum to Michael Arlen to Somerset Maugham. His reading for his grandfather included books and papers about political and legislative affairs, and even the *Congressional Record.*

In the spring of 1936, sitting in a window alcove of the senator's library, the ten-year-old Vidal became transfixed (and perhaps transformed) by the happenstance choice of a book with the attractive but enigmatic title *The Spartan.* Originally published under the title *Coward of Thermopylae,* it was one of many examples of a Victorian literary genre that turned Classical legend, myth, and history into exemplary moral and civic tales for Anglo-American adolescents. Written by the now obsure Caroline Dale Snedeker, *The Spartan* is the story of Aristodemos, son of Lykos of Athens, whose mother, Makaria, takes him back to her native Sparta after her husband's death. An Athenian of birth, valor, and high character, whose closest friend was the poet Pindar, Lykos had been killed in an athletic accident. Aristodemos was ten years old at the time, the same age at which Vidal read the book. The previous summer his mother, Nina Gore Vidal, had divorced his father. Later that year she married Hugh Auchincloss and took her son with her to live at Merrywood, the Auchincloss estate in Virginia. Vidal's grandfather's house in Rock Creek Park had the flavor of Athens; Merrywood was a luxurious version of Sparta, a house without intellect or art, a place of Philistines. Sixty years later, Vidal mistakenly recalled the name of the novel as *The Athenian.* Athens is the city of song and poetry. Sparta is a place where art is disdained.

*The Spartan* is a tale of the triumph of individual courage in the face of a mother's unloving rejection and a society's hostile narrow-mindedness. Aristodemos yearns for love. Then, unexpectedly, he has the deep happiness of being chosen by Leonidas, son of the king, as his companion. Leonidas teaches Aristodemos warrior skills, imparts to him information and advice, gives him emotional and physical comfort. Their union is exemplary, one of the widely encouraged tutelary and amorous relationships between young men and boys in ancient Greece.

Like Leonidas, Aristodemos becomes a patriot committed to the new and untested idea of pan-Hellenism, but, after the defeat of the Greeks at Thermopylae, he is accused of cowardice. Cursed by his mother, he flees into exile. Along the way he rescues a mistreated but noble slave boy whom, on the advice of the oracle at Delphi, he takes to Magna Graecia, to the city of Elea just south of the Amalfi coast on the Mediterranean, where the philosopher Parmenides lives and close to where Vidal himself later in life was to make his home. Parmenides is the slave boy's father. When he is reunited with his son, his joy and gratitude are so great that the curse on Aristodemos is lifted. Aristodemos is killed when he rejoins the defenders of Greece against the invading Persians at the battle of Plataea. In death he is recognized, celebrated, and thereafter remembered as the brave hero he has always been. A mother's curse is overcome by courage and accomplishment. Love between men, in an idealized and displaced form, is given cultural and personal currency. The values of Athens and of art triumph over those of militaristic Sparta. *The Spartan* is an exemplary boy's tale, but it is also, for Vidal, a paradigm of the old American republic and the new American Empire, of culture and barbarism, of art and war, of home and homelessness—the antitheses that are key to Vidal's mature work.

As an adolescent, Vidal read all of Shakespeare, and then Mark Twain, Stephen Crane, and Theodore Dreiser. An avid movie fan, he brought together in his youth, as if it were an easy combination, serious classics and popular literary and cinemagraphic culture. He matured early into the difficult ambition of writing for broad audiences. He also came to maturity as a writer at a time when the written word was king. Its only competition was the movies. His earliest essays were compositions at St. Albans School in Washington. He had his first experience of Europe on a school-conducted trip in the summer of 1939, and Rome especially gripped his intellect and imagination. European politics and the impending war became visual realities. From St. Albans he was exiled to a dismal year at the Los Alamos Ranch School in New Mexico, where his saving passion was Shakespeare. His writing life began in earnest at Phillips Exeter Academy in New Hampshire, a rigorously elite boys' school, which he attended from 1940 to 1943. It was the last stage of his formal education. Exeter challenged Vidal's intellect. It forced upon him a discipline that his iconoclastic temperament both opposed and absorbed. Intent on fashioning its boys into men and leaders, it embodied an ideology of privilege that made equals of all those who had been chosen. Vidal essentially disdained the required curriculum, pursuing what he had already decided was his own genius. He spent much of his time reading and writing: poems, essays, short stories, a number of aborted novels, and one that he finished, a story about a young man's search for vocation in literature and the arts, and the conflict of distinguishing between a man's love for men and a man's love for women. In his Exeter fiction and essays, Somerset Maugham was much on his mind. So too was Twain's comic genius. He also took himself seriously as a poet.

Reading with the aggressive energy of a young, ambitious autodidact, Vidal had another abiding passion. Unlike his literary model to be, Henry James, Vidal did not want to be "just literary." He wanted to be, like his grandfather, political also. For those attuned to politics and power, serious issues are always in the air. In the early 1940s, political issues were literally explosive. The adolescent Vidal took his domestic politics and his opinions about foreign affairs from Senator Gore, who strongly advocated resistance to the New Deal and to American involvement in the war in Europe. At Exeter, he joined one of the two main debating societies. He became a member of the school senate, and helped found the Exeter branch of America First, a group vociforously against involvement in the war. (His lifelong admiration for Senator Gore did not prevent him, a few years later, from carefully selecting from and substantially rejecting his grandfather's political views.)

When Vidal graduated from Exeter in June 1943, he enlisted in the army, and later served as first mate on a freight supply ship in the Aleutian Islands, off the coast of Alaska. While on watch, he began a short novel, *Williwaw,* that he finished in 1945, while recovering from an attack of rheumatoid arthritis at a military base in Florida. The book, which was published the following year, was written in the national literary style then so much admired. American novelists who came of age at the time of World War II took the American plain prose style as their model. Mark Twain was the nineteenth-century embodiment of its virtues, Hemingway the twentieth. Sparse, direct, syntactically simple, given more to dialogue than description, hard-bitten and unsentimental, the style minimized ornament and metaphor. It appealed particularly to writers whose first novels were based on their war experiences—Norman Mailer, James Jones, John Horne Burns, Vance Bourjaily—all of whom, as the war ended, moved from far-flung overseas theaters of military operation to New York City, now the literary capital of the world. *Williwaw,* which took its title from a native Alaskan word for an unusually violent seastorm, was a best-seller, and within the next five years Vidal wrote and published five other novels: *In a Yellow Wood* (1947), *The City and the Pillar* (1948), *The Season of Comfort* (1949), *A Search for the King* (1950), and *Dark Green, Bright Red* (1950). The result of prodigious energy, in the root sense of the adjective, each had its particular strength, each its significant resonance in its anticipation of later works.

These early novels are more ambitious than fulfilled. But all of them warrant comment. *Williwaw* evokes the yaw and pitch of exotic service and personal danger in an Alaska mostly of place and somewhat of the mind. *In a Yellow Wood* dramatizes the dislocation of an emotionless ex-serviceman moving dully through life as an office worker in New York. Its flatness captures the anomie and boredom of existential loss, of the absence of self, commitment, ambition, and ideals. Nothing could seem more gruesome and deadening to the soldier returned from the wars, the hunter from the hills, the sailor from the seas, than the prospect of a life of endless office work. Vidal's next novel, *The City and the Pillar,* published in early 1948 to a loud, mixed response, soon made the bestseller list mostly because of its notoriety. One of the first mainstream novels published by a New York trade press to deal explicitly with homosexual love, *The City and the Pillar* shocked some, pleased others, and left many bewildered. Puritanical reviewers found its very subject offensive. In flat, semi-affectless prose, it emphasized disillusionment with romantic love, especially the romantic obsession with combining sexual pleasure and love in the same object of desire. A somber, realistically devastating book, it took for granted that men have sex with men. The ending, which startled many readers, is violent, as the protagonist, a disappointed lover, murders the friend who is not willing to love him in the way that he remembered and idealized from an early encounter. In later editions, Vidal altered the ending, eliminating the murder without changing the emphasis on the destructiveness of self-deception.

*The Season of Comfort,* Vidal's next novel, brilliantly plays with modernistic narrative devices. It is his one experiment with the Joycean tradition and, like *Portrait of the Artist* almost fifty years earlier, provides a mid-twentieth-century variation on the traditional bildungsroman. Originally titled, in manuscript, *The Womb,* it dramatizes the escape from the extended womb, from a destructively willful, manipulative mother, and introduces the Washington political and social worlds, variants of which became central to Vidal's later works. As if to demonstrate his range and versatility, the next year he published a short first-person historical novel, *A Search for the King,* narrated by Blondel, King Richard the Lion-Hearted's favorite troubadour. Gracefully lyrical and humanly touching, the book combines the troubador's voice with some emerging Vidalian themes, such as male bonding and loyalty, a love between men that need not necessarily be sexual, and philosophical-religious issues. Blondel concludes that there is no controlling force in the universe, let alone a moral one; that chance plays a significant role in human life; that individual will and social circumstance rather than cosmic forces determine personal destiny.

Out of his experience in Guatemala, where he kept a writing retreat during this period, Vidal next wrote *Dark Green, Bright Red.* Too thin in its characterizations and conflicts to be fully successful, it nevertheless has the distinction of being the first post–World War II American novel to dramatize nefarious American involvement in a third-world country and, indirectly, the new American empire flexing its muscles. During the five years following the end of the war, Vidal had anticipated in his youthful fiction much of what he was to be preoccupied with in the next four decades.

With the publication, in 1952, of his seventh novel, *The Judgment of Paris,* Vidal discovered his distinctive voice as a writer of fiction. The plain prose style was no longer attractive. Having immersed himself in the classical European novel and its antecedents in Roman literature, Vidal found writers like Petronius, Apuleius, Swift, Voltaire, Peacock, Meredith, Flaubert, George Eliot, Proust, Thomas Mann, P. G. Wodehouse, and even the much neglected American novelist Dawn Powell more useful mentors. He also avidly absorbed the complete works of Henry James. In *The Judgment of Paris,* the authorial persona shares with Petronius a matter-of-fact realism about the human animal; with Swift a biting edge of satiric pessimism about the human condition; and with James a witty but essentially serious view of life as a grand comedy of clashing manners and values. It is a playfully serious novel that has intellectual texture, that uses comedy to acknowledge the seriousness of human folly, the unchangeableness of human nature, and the indeterminateness of the individual. Increasingly at home in Europe and European literature, Vidal tapped into the longstanding theme of Americans living or visiting abroad.

*Judgment* was not a commercial success. Neither was *Messiah,* which was published in 1954. With a touch of Orwell and Huxley in the background, Vidal had moved confidently into one of his major themes, a satiric indictment of Christian values and mythology. The new religion created by the American undertaker John Cave and his followers both mimics and corrects the Christian obsession with the afterlife by glorifying the finality of death, the pleasure of a totally consummated, unredeemable end. Suicide becomes a sacrament. The new religion is repressive, authoritarian, puritanical. Its brave new world is a bleak old place. For the new religion to flourish, its originator, John Cave, must be martyred so that his disciples may rule. America in the 1950s did not find this an attractive message. The sunshine of Eisenhower's smile was nowhere to be found in *Messiah.* Sales were bleak, reviews mixed and mostly unsympathetic. To bring in some cash, Vidal wrote five slim pseudonymous novels, three of them charming, modestly successful murder mysteries under the name of Edgar Box. They have a touch of Henry James as well as of Agatha Christie.

Fiction was Vidal's artistic métier. But it became increasingly apparent in the 1950s that few serious writers, especially those with countercultural messages, could make a living telling Americans what they did not want to hear. So Vidal spent much of the decade writing dramatic scenarios and scripts for live television and for Hollywood. Like Christopher Isherwood, he preferred to make his living by writing for the popular culture rather than teaching in academe. Clever and facile, he did more than fifty television plays, some of them adaptations, during the brief golden age of live television drama. Dividing his time between New York and Hollywood, he played out, sometimes perfunctorily, sometimes enthusiastically, a five-year studio contract with Metro-Goldwyn-Mayer. *Ben-Hur,* in 1958, released him from profitable bondage. He and MGM had agreed that he would get early parole in exchange for helping to rewrite the script. Writing for television and movies was, in Vidal's view, a craft, not an art, and in 1959 he did his last live television drama, *The Indestructible Mr. Gore,* based on an episode in his grandfather's youth. He himself played the onstage role of narrator-commentator. Thereafter he continued to write and/or rewrite movie scripts as he chose.

Despite the inevitable constraints of writing for the mass media, Vidal often managed to transform movie and television collaborations into vehicles for the subjects that inspired his art as well as his craft: justice, politics, power, history, self-deceit, sexuality. One of his television triumphs, *Visit to a Small Planet* (1956), was expanded the next year into a successful Broadway play. A well-crafted small farce, it dissected, with the cool comedic eye of an interplanetary anthropologist, human folly in the nuclear age. Earth is visited by extraplanetary invaders who decide that we are not worth invading. It is Swift miniaturized. *The Best Man* (1960), written for the stage and then made into a highly praised movie, was a popular success about a serious subject, a Broadway play that realistically dramatized the ruthlessness of American presidential politics. On balance, the play errs, perhaps, on the side of being too sanguine in its inference that the best man ever becomes the presidential candidate of a major political party. But it effectively reminds the audience what a political convention is actually like and how high office and low politics are inevitable bedfellows.

Eager to return to the life of the serious writer fully in control of his own art, Vidal, in the early 1960s, resumed writing novels. His success as a playwright had freed him from economic anxiety. At the same time, he began to write essays on a wide range of subjects, and they garnered almost instant praise as masterful incarnations of the genre. His voice as an essayist was on the one hand personal and autobiographical, on the other historical and authoritative. Some readers found a witty and insightful persona that they could not as easily discover in the novels of the 1940s and 1950s, and—always keenly aware of audience—Vidal found good reason to write essays. He was a frequent contributor to *The New York Review of Books,* which was founded in 1963 during a New York City newspaper strike. Suddenly, unexpectedly, there was a major new intellectual journal, specializing in review-essays, that addressed the increasingly overlapping academic and intellectual worlds. The *Review,* which was slightly left of center politically, provided Vidal with a large, responsive audience. He could choose his own subjects, and the essays could be published later in book-length collections. Though he continued to write for other journals, particularly *Esquire* and *The Nation,* his association as an essayist with *The New York Review of Books* became a signature advantage for both publisher and author. Though Vidal undoubtedly would have become a major American essayist, anyway, the timing of the appearance of *The New York Review of Books* could not have been more propitious.

For many of the essays, the hardest work for Vidal—and the greatest pleasure—was reading everything by and about the subject. Reading remained a passion, not only fiction but history, politics, memoirs, and social analysis. Vidal is probably the most engaged universal reader of any American writer of the twentieth century. His only rival as a writer who reads is Edmund Wilson, who is also his only twentieth-century competitor as an essayist. Over the years, Vidal has published several volumes of essays, one of which, *Homage to Daniel Shays* (1972), won the National Book Critics Circle Award, and a substantial volume of collected essays, *United States* (1993), which won the National Book Award. (He has been awarded no Pulitzer Prize for criticism or fiction. The three judges of the 1985 Pulitzer Prize committee for fiction selected *Lincoln,* but the general committee refused to give the award to Vidal.)

Returning, in 1964, to the novel, Vidal provided in *Julian* another variation on his fascination with the damage that Christianity has wrought. The novel is in the Victorian and modern tradition—from Tennyson, Swinburne, and Walter Pater to Robert Graves and Mary Renault—of invoking the classical past to dramatize issues and concerns of the writer's time. Whereas in *Messiah* our past is in our future, in *Julian* our future is in our past. Set in the reign of the fourth-century emperor Julian the Apostate, the novel brilliantly evokes his attempt to turn back the triumphant tide of Christianity. Julian seeks to reestablish the primacy of the old gods. A worshiper of Apollo, the god of the sun, of life, and of poetic inspiration, he opposes a religion that encourages repression and that is putting into place an oppressively bureaucratic church which will support medieval flagellations and autos-da-fé. The Christian promise (and weapon) of salvation and resurrection seems to Julian a life-defeating deception. It promises an immortality that nature can never provide and a next world that he believes does not exist. For Julian, wisdom resides in recognizing that "nothing man invents can last forever, including Christ, his most mischievous invention." The perfect Vidalian avatar, Julian succeeds—briefly—in reestablishing pagan freedom of worship, freedom to love (either or both sexes), freedom of the mind, freedom to accept death as a life-affirming finality.

In *Julian,* Vidal captures vividly, as if he had been there, the realistic details of the streets, the palaces, the military camps, the barbarities, the exoticisms, and the customs of daily life, of food, sleep, sex, and discourse in the not-so-ancient world. Though narrated within a retrospective frame, the novel has strong sense of presentness. Vidal carefully modulates multiple points of view, and balances tone and theme. The book is a long, varied, and yet tightly constructed historical novel that weighs heavily on the mind and lightly on the spirit. The language is witty, aphoristic, epigrammatic, classical in the fullness of its restraint. Its prose is both tightly and fully wrought; it gives the impression of saying all that there is to say but saying it sparely, directly, dramatically—a long book each word of which is essential. In the end, after Julian's betrayal and death, his dying teacher and friend, Libanius, meditates on both ends and beginnings:

> I have been reading Plotinus all evening. He has the power to soothe me; and I find his sadness curiously comforting. Even when he writes: "Life here with the things of earth is a sinking, a defeat, a failing of the wing." The wing has indeed failed. One sinks. Defeat is certain. Even as I write these lines, the lamp wick sputters to an end, and the pool of light in which I sit contracts. Soon the room will be dark. One has always feared that death would be like this. But what else is there? With Julian, the light went, and now nothing remains but to let the darkness come, and hope for a new sun and another day, born of time's mystery and man's love of light.

With American politics much on his mind, Vidal began *Washington, D.C.,* which he published in 1967, three years after the bestselling, critically successful *Julian.* He had himself run for office, as the Democratic candidate for Congress in 1960 from the heavily Republican upstate New York congressional district in which he resided from 1950 to 1963. He garnered more votes there than the head of the Democratic ticket, John F. Kennedy, but he nevertheless lost the election. A friend and step-relative of Kennedy's wife, he had become a slightly aloof but eagerly observant member of the Kennedy political and social world. Because of his exposure to American politics at his grandfather's knee and his extensive Washington friendships and associations during the forties and fifties, Vidal was in an unusual position for a novelist. He had a biographical and social as well as an intellectual and ideological context for the great issues of the day, the greatest of which was what direction the American Republic would take. Hovering within and between the lines of *Washington, D.C.* is a fictionally displaced dramatization of Vidal's evolution from a believer in his grandfather's political values to his gradual embrace of the post–New Deal liberalism not so much of Franklin but of Eleanor Roosevelt. Having been shaped in many crucibles, including the 1950s McCarthyite turmoil, Vidal emerged at the end of that decade as a radical who had moved so far from the combined Democratic-Republican middle that he could not be comfortable with either of the traditional parties or perhaps any party at all. Like his Victorian predecessor Thomas Carlyle, he embraced a conservatism so radical that to the conservatives he was no conservative at all. And his radicalism was so conservative, so rational, so much an expression of enlightenment utopianism, that to the doctrinaire radicals he was no radical either. An angry and disappointed utopian, with a strong practical sense, Vidal rejected the romanticism of both the right and the left.

In a series of six historical novels written over the course of twenty-three years, Vidal provided a revisionary reinterpretation of American history. *Washington, D.C.* was followed by *Burr* (1973), *1876* (1976), *Lincoln* (1984), *Empire* (1987), and *Hollywood* (1990). Vidal renders an account quite unlike the idealized semifabrications of the typical history textbook. The series embodies his understanding of how politics and power work, past and present. In this story the Founding Fathers are a brilliant but mixed lot (George Washington the dullest of them all) who create a government balanced between the big-money interests of the Federalists and the small-farm, small-money, small-government civil libertarian views of the Jeffersonians. But Jacksonian America broke the precarious balance. Land and power became the predominant concerns. The Indians east of the Mississippi were pushed westward or destroyed; slavery could not be contained, let alone abolished. Lincoln, as much villain as hero, established a nationalistic, monolithic Union, a huge industrialized anti-Jeffersonian monster. In the next fifty years, his successors, led by William McKinley and Theodore Roosevelt, transformed the United States from a Republic into an aggressive Empire. The Monroe Doctrine had established the Caribbean and South America as an American sphere of influence. Now the Pacific was going to be an American lake. World War I, into which Woodrow Wilson elected to insert America, made the United States the dominant economic power of the world. Franklin Roosevelt's New Deal retooled American government and slightly redistributed national wealth in order to make America safe for capitalism. Immediately after World War II, Harry Truman celebrated the absolute international dominance of the United States by creating for the first time a national security state whose underlying premise was that the Soviet Union was so great a menace that Americans must give up some of their freedoms in order to guard themselves against the enemy. The temporary wartime OSS was converted into the permanent peacetime CIA. Its ongoing task was to thwart the Soviet Union, whose strength was wildly exaggerated by those for whom the Cold War was an economic and ideological boon. For the first time, a huge peacetime army was put in place. The defense budget became sacred. The garrison state became permanent. Those who controlled and had always controlled wealth and political power in America remained rich and powerful. Inevitably, the Korean and Vietnam wars followed.

Vidal's fictional meditations on American history are rich in characters and ideas. As an historical novelist, he takes no liberties with fact. But, unlike the fact-bound historian, he is free to create suppositions about fact and sometimes to give these the claim of narrative truth. That is what historical novelists usually do. Vidal is particularly successful in creating credible dialogue for historical figures whose words he invents out of his rich knowledge of who they were. The supposition is that this is how they must have talked, how they would have sounded, if, like Richard Nixon, they had been taped both in public and private and then edited for clarity, emphasis, and characteristic speech patterns. As historical novelists from Scott to Stendhal, Thackeray, and Robert Graves have done, Vidal transforms minor but mostly unknown historical figures into fictional characters who dominate the narratives. Their credibility as fictional characters makes more plausible the historical figures. The novelist's art transforms history into not fiction but the super-real. Vidal stumbled into this grand historical venture with *Washington, D.C.* It gradually took on self-conscious shape, partly as a result of the organic but unplanned growth of the novelist's conception, partly as a vehicle to realize more fully his emerging ideas about power and history.

Although it was written first, *Washington, D.C.* is last in the series in terms of the time period it covers, which is contemporaneous with Vidal's youth. It captures the mood of the nation's capital during the decade that includes World War II. A brooding work, it is harshly realistic on the one hand and poignantly pessimistic on the other. Vidal's Washingtonians are victims of human and historical forces so devastating that the devastation (amid splendor) becomes the moral landscape. Success in the power game is all that counts. Those who fail are swept away, like dead leaves from the Mall. What fails most of all is American democracy. Our own domestic Evil Empire emerges, exemplified by Senator Joseph McCarthy and his brief Reign of Terror. Through the grizzled weariness of Senator Burden Day we see strong flickers of Senator Thomas P. Gore, in the elderly Blaise Sanford the great press barons William Randolph Hearst and Joseph Pulitzer. Clay Overbury embodies the dark side of John F. Kennedy. Nina Gore, Vidal's mother, makes an appearance as Enid Sanford, who lives with a frenetic willfulness that can't readily be distinguished from madness. Her self-destructiveness is punished by institutionalization when it suits her husband's and her father's political calculations. Young Peter Sanford, a version of the novelist himself, lives in places that had been homes to Vidal. As the emotional and morally interesting center of the novel, Peter embodies the touch of optimism compatible with a realistic, long-term view of the human situation:

> Loving her for this constancy, he was often able in her company to forget for long moments what he knew to be the human case: that the generations of man come and go and are in eternity no more than bacteria upon a luminous slide, and the fall of a republic or the rise of an empire—so significant to those involved—are not detectable upon the slide even were there an interested eye to behold that steadily proliferating species which would either end in time or, with luck, become something else, since change is the nature of life, and its hope.

If we are lucky, things *may* work out, *may* be transformed into something else. Peter's worldview is only slightly less despairing than that implied by Vidal in his depiction of the daily machinery of Washingtonian politics. As in *Julian,* visual concreteness and novelistic texture affirm the things of this world by allowing us to experience them vividly and fully as art. None of this is schematic. The novel is genuinely a novel, an invention, a creation, and Vidal establishes here what is to be the characteristic achievement of the series as a whole—historical fiction becomes more true than history itself and as real, as concrete, and as dramatic as are all supreme fictions.

With the publication of *Burr* (1973), Vidal made what had been a single historical novel set in the Washington of his childhood part of a wider narrative. To many readers the most artistically successful of the American history novels, *Burr* is centered on Aaron Burr, who killed Alexander Hamilton, his arch political rival, in a duel, and came as close as the vice presidency to fulfilling his highest ambition. Set in New York City in the 1830s, the novel is narrated by a fictional journalist, Charles Schuyler, who is given the diaries of the aged Aaron Burr. Past and present are woven into a story about national and individual parentage. Amid the randomness of history, Vidal finds material for the plot of a novel and fashions dramatic moments that are given a place and time. The two narrative voices, that of Charles Schuyler and Burr, have strength, resonance, and authenticity. Washington and Jefferson have real weaknesses as well as strengths, and Burr is far from the villian of his own story, although he is a foundered Founding Father. In the end, Schuyler discovers that he is Burr's illegitimate son. Once propelled into the nineteenth century, the story of Burr and his son (and Vidal's view of American history) produce inexorably the sequence and the subjects of the novels that follow.

Vidal both celebrated and undermined the American bicentennial by publishing *1876* in 1976. The novel dramatized the world of the corrupt Grant administration. Hoping to be appointed minister to France if Samuel Tilden defeats Rutherford B. Hayes, Charles Schuyler comes home after years of exile in Europe. American politics seem to him as brutal as they had been when he left, and in the end he is disappointed, for himself and for his daughter Emma, who marries the wealthy William Sanford. It remains for Emma's daughter, Caroline, to elevate the family to power and fame. Caroline Sanford emerges from the power struggles (and her rivalry with her brother Blaise Sanford, the father of the Peter of *Washington, D.C.*) during the years that span the presidencies of McKinley, Roosevelt, and Wilson. In *Empire* she becomes one of the great press lords of America, the owner of a powerful Washington newspaper, and, in *Hollywood,* under a pseudonym, one of the stars of America's newest industry, the movie business. As in all good fiction, much of the fascination of these books is in the details and in the portraiture. The cast contains invented politicians like Senator Day, whose career, like Caroline's and like Senator Gore's, begins in the nineteenth century and ends in the twentieth. The sweep is cinemagraphic. Henry Adams, Henry James, and Mark Twain make convincing cameo appearances. The ideas and conflicts that underlie American political and economic power are represented in the fictional re-creations of barons and bullies from Hearst to Theodore Roosevelt. The rise and fall of Woodrow Wilson, like that of a character in Shakespeare, has its dramatic focus in his deepest flaw, an exquisitely evil willfulness and sense of divinely sanctioned personal and intellectual superiority. America is the sum of its powerful people, and the course of American history tends toward

Empire and the Silver Screen, the alliance between Washington and Hollywood.

*Lincoln,* which was published in 1984, before *Empire* and *Hollywood,* falls between *Burr* and *1876* in the historical chronology. Lincoln is the historical character over whom Vidal has brooded most, and in this remythologizing of history he is the American Bismarck, a pragmatic and manipulative politician with one overriding desire: to save the Union and by saving it transform it into a modern, industrialized, nation state so powerful that nothing can ever tear it apart again. Lincoln is opposed to slavery, but he does not believe it is an issue worth fighting about. In favor of civil liberties, he does not hesitate to suspend them in order to wage the war more efficiently. He is sincere and incontrovertibly honest, but he knows how to dissemble, to reward friends and punish enemies, to manipulate men and money, to further his cause. In sum, he is the consummate politician. It is a controversial portrait that has touches of Vidal's Southern inheritance, his view that, just as the South should have let the slaves go, the North should have let the South go. Lincoln enthusiasts, especially professional historians, have found the depiction unsettling—formidably so, because of its vividness and credibility. Details of character and scene are rendered superbly.

If *Lincoln* suffers from a certain reductive sweep, it is because of the familiarity of many of the events. To deal with potential problems of voice and point of view, the book is narrated in the third person. The dominating consciousness is that of Lincoln's young secretary, John Hay, later to be Theodore Roosevelt's secretary of state and a prominent figure in *Empire.* Weaving a plot composed of facts about Lincoln and the war with fictional accounts of personal and political lives, Vidal both re-creates and newly creates a tapestry of conflicts that embody the issues of America's national crisis. It is John Hay, in a conversation with Charlie Schuyler, about to be resurrected for appearances in *1876* and *Empire*, who has the final word on Lincoln:

> "I think," said Mr. Schuyler . . . "We have here a subject—Lincoln and Bismarck, and new countries for old."
>
> "It will be interesting to see how Herr Bismarck ends *his* career," said Hay, who was now more than ever convinced that Lincoln, in some mysterious fashion, had willed his own murder as a form of atonement for the great and terrible thing he had done by giving so bloody and absolute a rebirth to his nation.

In 1968, Vidal published the most controversial of his novels, *Myra Breckinridge,* followed in 1974 by a sequel, *Myron.* Wildly funny, *Myra/Myron* falls into a category that Vidal has called "inventions," in contrast to novels like *Julian* and the series of novels on American history. Inventive as the historical novels are, they follow traditional narrative patterns. Their plots adhere to the laws of causality and representation associated with the realistic novel from *Tom Jones* to *Gone with the Wind.* History itself provides narrative coordinates that usually determine temporal regularity in historical fictions. With *Myra,* Vidal created a novelistic opportunity for imaginative freedom, for flights of fancy, for bright and dark humor, for satirical and inventive distortions of time, place, and character. Whereas his early fiction embraced the flatness of the American plain prose style, *Myra/Myron, Kalki* (1978), and then *Duluth* (1983) and *Live from Golgotha* (1992) have as their progenitors Sterne's *Tristram Shandy* and Swift's *Gulliver's Travels,* the former's narrative and structural freedom, the latter's bitterly satirical view of human nature. Like Sterne's novel, Vidal's inventions are uninhibitedly transgressive in regard to the novel as a genre. They are also, unlike Sterne, transgressive in their vision of human nature and the human situation. Though comedic, they are grimly serious. The comedy is in their linguistic and conceptual outrageousness, the sharply turned insights and juxtapositions of Vidal's wit. But, as with Swift, the view of human motivation is ruthlessly pragmatic. As Myra says, "It is hate alone which inspires us to action and makes for civilization. Look at Juvenal, Pope, Billy Wilder." Like Swift, Vidal has the temperament and imagination of a comparative anthropologist who travels in space and time. *Myra/Myron, Duluth,* and *Live from Golgotha* are not only human fictions but science fictions. Just as Gulliver travels to Lilliputia, Brobdingnagia, and Laputa, Myra/Myron, a modern Alice through the looking-glass, travels through a television screen to find herself/himself on the set of a Hollywood B movie.

Vidal's erudition sometimes challenges the limits of the reader's frame of reference. The allusions in *Myra/Myron* are literary and cinemagraphic, often both within the same paragraph. Myra, a transsexual who has been born Myron, has available to her the reading and movie-going experience of both her disparate selves and of the author. Just as Sterne, who is not Tristram Shandy, gave Tristram his creator's range of reference, Vidal, who is not Myra/Myron, has given them his, often for comic purposes. From Juvenal to Lévi-Strauss to American movies of the thirties and forties, the cast of supporting characters and references is encyclopedically resonant. Norman Mailer is parodied as a mad, drunk cook; Truman Capote is the smooth, effeminate, slithery slimy Maude, a movie-land facilitator; and Henry James appears as an ultra-educated black man, the sophisticated behind-the-scenes controller of the movie-set world in which Myra finds herself trapped. Narrated in the first person, *Myra/Myron* is an extended satirical dramatic monologue in which the gap between the values of the author and the monologist, sometimes smaller, sometimes greater, is the most important dramatic scale on which the novel can be interpreted. When are Myra/Myron's feelings and ideas those of the implied author? When are they not? As a character, Myra/Myron is a distortion, an extreme, and it is in that extremity that the author's meaning is to be located. But meaning is also to be found in the literature and the films that the novel makes part of its natural register. Myra, "whom no man will ever possess," is both a version of Isabel Archer in *Portrait of a Lady* and Kate Croy in *Wings of the Dove* and the "beauteous Fay Wray whom," Myra tells us, "I resemble left three-quarter profile if the key light is no more than five feet high during the close shot," and who has reduced King Kong "to a mere simian whimper."

Amid its dark and often hilarious comedy, *Myra Breckinridge* is, like all Vidal's novels, seriously engaged with philosphical and political issues. Having undergone a sex-change operation, the beautiful Myra is the unstable physical embodiment of the Myron who had found himself trapped in a man's body. Myra/Myron's instability reflects the pathology of Myron's desire to escape, at the slice of a knife, his male biology. But the underlying pathology is cultural as well, for Myra/Myron's unbalanced, self-destructive hatred for his maleness is the far side of a madness the potential for which, Vidal thinks, we are all provided by our puritanical culture. The novel is an attack on the Judeo-Christian repressive inheritance. Myra/Myron's pathology is a defensive-aggressive response to suburban homes, two cars in every garage, 2.5 children, white bread, men having sex only with women and women only with men—the style and the structure of a relentless underlying puritanism. While America temporarily flourishes, a good part of the rest of the world is overpopulated and underfed, and eventually the values and laws of Judeo-Christian moral puritanism will make the planet uninhabitable. In *Myra Breckinridge,* as in *Kalki,* Vidal's view is apocalyptic. At the conclusion of *Kalki,* the entire human race has been wiped out by a virus spread purposely by a charismatic leader who expects to repopulate the earth from his own seed with superior people like himself but who, ironically and disasterously, cannot do so. At the end of *Myra/Myron,* Myron's sex-change operation is destabilized by surgery after Myra is hit by an automobile. The deeply desired center falls apart. Myron, who has struggled with Myra in a schizophrenic battle to regain his male body, does get it back, permanently. "Since there are only a few blank lines left to this page," he concludes, "I will sign off by saying that the highly articulately silent majority to which I am darned proud to belong are happy with things as they are and that we are not going to let anybody, repeat *anybody,* change things from what they are." The sex change in

*Myra/Myron* is a literary representation of the difficulty of changing the mind-set of the culture.

By the late 1960s, Vidal had become as well known for his essays as for his fiction, especially among intellectuals and academics, although his attacks on the latter had made him somewhat unpopular in university circles. He seemed less attractive as a literary novelist to those who created college reading lists than did some of his contemporaries, such as Bellow and Mailer. Academics committed to modernism did not find Vidal readily assimilable to their categories. The variety of fictional modes and literary genres in which he worked also may have confused those looking to classify him as one kind of writer or another. Most of all, many academics, in the tradition of high modernism, were uneasy with politics as a central subject for literature, and this had become Vidal's main focus in his fiction, his essays, and a play, *An Evening with Richard Nixon,* which had a short Broadway run in 1972. The play was a withering attack on Nixon and the Vietnam War.

In 1982, still flirting with the idea of a political career, Vidal became a candidate for the Senate nomination in the California Democratic primary. He ran an unusually iconoclastic campaign, and with support from liberal Hollywood and from the gay community, he garnered enough votes to have the distinction of placing a distant second to the governor of California, Jerry Brown. Vidal was appalled by the high cost of running for office, disgusted by widespread domestic political corruption, and critical of American Cold War policies, especially the huge military budget. It was the end of any further thought of serving in political office.

What was probably Vidal's most dramatic public moment in the 1960s occurred on live television with the conservative Catholic writer, publisher, and propagandist William F. Buckley, Jr. The two men had been hired by ABC Television News to provide commentary, about fifteen prime-time minutes each night, "from the right" and "from the left," during the 1968 Republican and Democratic conventions in Miami and Chicago. Their long-standing antagonism expressed itself from the beginning of the seven telecasts in Buckley's simmering disdainfulness and Vidal's polite but argumentative condescension. In one broadcast, Buckley, with swaggering distaste, condemned Vidal as a pornographer, the author of the pernicious *Myra Breckinridge*. Vidal attacked Buckley's ultraconservative politics. The tension between the two debaters built throughout the Republican Convention. At the Democratic Convention, when demonstrators against the Vietnam War were brutally attacked by the Chicago police, Buckley was outraged by the protesters, not the police. Those who spoke against the war were traitors, and an analogy was even made to supporters of the

Nazis during World War II. This led to a shouting match in which Buckley called Vidal a "queer," thus bringing to national attention a topic that had largely been kept out of the mass media. The incident represented, among other things, the crudeness of a widespread homophobia that Vidal's novels from *The City and the Pillar* to *Julian* to *Myra Breckinridge* had been attempting to raise to a more sophisticated artistic and political discourse.

In 1970, Vidal published *Two Sisters,* "A Novel in the Form of a Memoir." The descriptive line is reversed from book jacket to title page, where it appears as "A Memoir in the Form of a Novel." Boldly cast as a synoptic narrative that alternates between "Now" and "Then," the book dramatizes, in fractured form, subjects that Vidal had long been concerned with: art, sex, gender, money, power. Anticipating, in its preoccupation with doubling or twinness, his more conventional memoir, *Palimpsest* (1995), it presents various versions of the past and investigates the relationship between past and present. At the center of the narrative is a dramatic dialogue about "The House of Lagus," a play within the exposition. The drama is putatively a screenplay created by one of the characters in the narrative, and is also for all intents and purposes a memoir. Dedicated to Vidal's half-sister, *Two Sisters* is about the family that Vidal never had, the home that he could not locate, the interaction between literature and film, between Vidal the novelist and Vidal the disaffiliated member or associate of an American tribe of writers, politicians, and first families, especially the Gores, the Auchinclosses, the Bouviers, and the Kennedys. It embodies a cryptic search for unity, for wholeness, for family, both in its themes and structure. The imaginative impulse that underlies the creation is engagingly anarchic, playfully experimental. That the experiment does not fully enough come off does not detract from the imaginativeness of the effort. *Two Sisters* is richly revealing for a reader who may have context and key, though it never is the coherent "read" that Vidal usually provides. It is probably most noteworthy for its anticipation of the more accessible autobiographical successes in the essays and in *Palimpsest.* With both the critical and commercial failure of *Two Sisters,* Vidal returned exclusively, with the exception of *Kalki,* to historical fiction for the rest of the 1970s.

In *Duluth* (1983), science fiction and the surreal are vehicles for satiric comedy. Time and space are subordinated to associative changes of scene that take their parodic tone from soap opera and popular romances. Drawing on, among other things, his long exposure to pop culture, especially of the television and movie-script variety, Vidal creates a sophisticated fiction about narrative alternatives. As in *Myra,* a part of the narrative in *Duluth* involves the narrator's awareness of self-conscious postmodernist theories of fiction. *Duluth* raises cleverness to high art of the sort that Italo Calvino had in mind when he cryptically commented that he considered Vidal "to be a master of that new form which is taking shape in world literature and which we may call the hyper-novel or the novel elevated to the square or to the cube." The new form is at least as old as *Tristram Shandy.* It is also, in recent variations, so modern that it is regularly called postmodern. In his novels of invention, Vidal is a playfully self-conscious narrator whose narrative deliberations and genre considerations are part of the story itself.

*Duluth* is beautifully bizzare. One of its subjects is, of course, itself. But that "itselfness" has a strong social conscience and includes late-twentieth-century versions of the issues that Vidal has always been interested in: justice, power, human dignity, the distribution of resources, the human condition, particularly its social and political dimensions. In the dehumanized world of *Duluth,* all narratives have been reduced to wildly popular soap operas. And the most blatantly dramatic, comedic representations of the reduction take place not only on television and in popular fiction but in class, race, and sex wars in the streets of the all-purpose, cosmopolitan city ironically called Duluth but actually a new city in a vastly rearranged American geography. It is a Duluth with palm trees, as if all American cities were inexorably slouching toward Las Vegas. It is a city of the American future made of elements of its past in which class and race warfare and widespread public and private corruption are the main legacies. In the end it is colonized by superior beings, insectlike invaders from outer space. It is of course still

> Duluth! Tricia [the outer-space "person, who belongs to a superior race of insects" and who has taken over the word processor of a popular romance novelist and is now in charge of writing the national script] taps, love it or loathe it, you can never leave it or lose it because no matter how blunt with insectivirous time your mandibles become those myriad eggs that you cannot help but lay hatch new vermiforous and myriapodal generations, forever lively in *this* present tense where you—all of you—are now at large, even though, simultaneously, you are elsewhere, too, rooted in that centripetal darkness where all this was, and where all this will be, once the bright inflorescence that is, or—now for that terminal shift, Tricia; press the lever!—*was* present-day human Duluth has come to its predestined, articulated and paginated end. Yes. *Duluth!* Loved! Loathed. Left. Lost.

For Duluth, substitute America, "love it or loathe it" (in the opening words of the novel), and now loved, loathed, left, lost. It is a disappointed lover's bitterly elegiac, wittily imaginative lament for what once was (at least in expectation) and now is no longer.

Religion is another recurrent subject in Vidal's oeuvre. He sees the three major monotheistic religions as equally destructive in their elevation and worship of a repressive "Sky-God," and his working principle is that by their fruits ye shall know them. Over the centuries they have been responsible for innumerable deaths and devastations, often of a most self-rightously brutal kind. In *Creation* (1981), a panoramic novel that adheres to the patterns and conditions of traditional storytelling, Vidal focuses on three nonmonotheistic religions that originated in the fifth century B.C.: Persian Zoroastrianism, Indian Buddhism, and Chinese Confucism. Narrated in his blind old age by the fictional Persian diplomat and traveler Cyrus Spitama, *Creation* is the story of Cyrus's engagement, as an agent of the Persian throne, with the religions and cultures of the three civilizations. As in *Julian,* Vidal evokes the details of these disparate worlds with a specificity that makes ancient history and religion compellingly real. A descendant of Zoroaster himself, Cyrus worships an early version of the same god of light that Julian attempts to reestablish as the religion of Rome a thousand years later. Traveling eastward, Cyrus meets the living Buddha and then Confucius. He is in search of an answer to the unanswerable question, What is the origin of life? By implication, he readily settles for a partial answer to an answerable question, What is the relative merit of the ethical systems of these religions? In the end, Cyrus, who becomes a materialist, most admires Confucius.

*Live from Golgotha* (1992), narrated by Saint Timothy, is Vidal's culminating deconstruction of Christianity, a parodic comic explosion of the gospels and Jesus into satiric fragments. It is also a buddy story in which Saint Paul and Timothy travel the first-century Christian religious circuit. Paul (a.k.a. "Saint"), who likes boys, and Timothy especially, leads him into hilarious adventures as he attempts to convert the heathen. Jesus' followers (or adapters) are split into two groups, those who believe that the message of Jesus is for Jews, and those who believe (as does Saint) "that Jesus had come as the messiah for everyone," that He is a big, international, multicultural business. The struggle between the competing groups is partly fought over the battleground of Timothy's attractive body, whose crucial part must be altered if the uncircumcised, non-Jewish Timothy is to be initiated. "In the beginning was the nightmare, and the knife was with Saint Paul, and the circumcision was a Jewish notion and definitely not mine." Poor Timothy! "Little did I realize when I became a Christian and met Saint and his friends that my body—specifically my whang—was to be a battleground between two warring factions within the infant church." A marketing genius, Saint eventually wins.

There is another battle in progress, so Timothy discovers when he begins to have strange extra-first-century-A.D. visitations, which include a Sony television set, network executives from the twentieth century viciously competing to televise the crucifixion live, and a master computer hack who turns out to be the man whom the world thinks was—but actually was not—crucified and who has time-traveled forward to the late twentieth century so that he can, electronically, reach back to the first to eliminate Christianity itself by erasing all records of its existence. The television networks, however, now owned by the Japanese, want their show (the crucifixion). They have no intention of allowing late-twentieth-century Christianity to be altered, let alone lost, and since the Japanese are in charge of everything, they win and Christianity is saved. Timothy watches the crucifixion on TV. The special effects are extraordinarily beautiful. The editor wins an Emmy.

With the publication of *The Smithsonian Institution* in 1998 and his memoir, *Palimpsest,* three years before, Vidal himself became a literary time-traveler. *The Smithsonian Institution,* like *Live from Golgotha,* has an intense science-fiction component, but it holds a unique place in Vidal's oeuvre. It combines the imaginative surrealism of *Duluth* and *Myra Breckinridge* with the dramatization of historical events and personalities that dominates his series of novels on American history. It also has an unmistakable autobiographical element. In *Palimpsest,* which covers his life up to the early 1960s, Vidal reveals that Jimmie Trimble, his best friend at St. Albans, was also his first sexual partner and the person he considered his lifelong Platonic twin. A fictionalized version of Trimble, referred to as "T," which also stands for "Time," is the main character in *The Smithsonian Institution.* When the scientific leaders of the Manhattan Project discover in 1939 that "T" is a mathematical genius with the ability to create formulas that will allow radical, heretofore impossible, manipulations of time and space, he is brought to the project's headquarters at the Smithsonian. There he encounters a cast of famous American historical characters, some of whom inhabit the museum's displays as waxworks during the day but come alive when the museum closes to the public. One of the figures from the Hall of Inaugural Gowns, the first wife of Grover Cleveland, becomes his lover. Lincoln appears as a museum bureaucrat in a comic turn. Brain-damaged from the assassination attempt, he has been made curator of ceramics. In the Hall of Presidents, all the previous presidents give counsel to Franklin Roosevelt. World War II is about to begin, and when "T" discovers that he will be killed in battle, he attempts to use his scientific powers to prevent the war. Transporting himself through his time-space machine to Los Alamos in the year 1943, he sees the young Gore Vidal, who is attending school there.

As always, Vidal's voice speaks vividly as a satirist and as a postmodernist writer dramatizing the breakdown of literary genres and the corruption of American political culture. The key issues are still power, politics, sex, and art, but the future seems to belong to movies and electronic media and not to books. Still, America's destiny continues to preoccupy Vidal. So too does literary art. "There will always be a certain amount of good writing," he remarked in 1992, "But who will read it? As for me, I keep writing prose because that's what I do. I'm a writer."

# EARLY FICTION

# *THE CITY AND THE PILLAR*

THE CITY AND THE PILLAR was one of the first novels about homosexual characters and experiences to be published by a mainstream New York press. After hesitantly accepting it in 1946, E. P. Dutton delayed publication for almost two years. The book appeared in January 1948, shortly before the publication of the Kinsey Report (*Sexual Behavior in the Human Male*), which presented the then startling statistic that 37 percent of American men had had at least one homosexual experience since adolescence. On one extreme, reviewers attacked the appropriateness of any novel at all on such a subject for the general reader. On the other, some welcomed it for its subject alone.

Some of the critical analysis of *The City and the Pillar* focused on its artistic awkwardness, and several otherwise sympathetic readers objected to its violent conclusion, which to them implied that homosexual relationships must always end unhappily. The two main characters, Jim Willard and Bob Ford, have an apparently mutually satisfactory late-adolescent sexual experience and then are separated by events. Willard retains an idealized remembrance of the affair, but when, much later, they meet in New York City and he attempts to renew their sexual relationship, Bob Ford finds his overtures repellent. Furious at the rejection, Willard attempts to subdue and rape Ford. In the 1948 version he kills him. In both of the revised versions (1965, 1995) Willard fights with but does not kill his former lover. In addition to the altered conclusion, the revised versions contain substantial stylistic revision.

# Preface to *The City and the Pillar and Seven Early Stories* (1995)

MUCH HAS BEEN MADE—not least by the Saint himself—of how Augustine stole and ate some pears from a Milanese orchard. Presumably, he never again trafficked in, much less ate, stolen goods, and once this youthful crime ("a rum business," snarled the unsympathetic American jurist Oliver Wendell Holmes, Jr.) was behind him, he was sainthood bound. The fact is that all of us have stolen pears; the mystery is why so few of us rate halos. I suspect that in certain notorious lives there is sometimes an abrupt moment of choice. Shall I marry or burn? Steal or give to others? Shut the door on a life longed for while opening another, deliberately, onto trouble and pain because . . . The "because" is the true story seldom told.

Currently, two biographers are at work on my sacred story, and the fact that they are trying to make sense of my life has made me curious about how and why I have done—and not done—so many things. As a result, I have begun writing what I have said that I'd never write, a memoir ("I am not my own subject," I used to say with icy superiority). Now I am reeling haphazardly through my own youth, which is when practically everything of interest happened to me, rather more soon than late, since I was force-fed, as it were, by military service in the Second World War.

My father once told me, after reviewing his unpleasant period in public office, that whenever it came time for him to make a crucial decision, he invariably made the wrong one. I told him that he must turn Churchill and write his own life, demonstrating what famous victories he had set in motion at Gallipoli or in the "dragon's underbelly" of the Third Reich. But my father was neither a writer nor a politician; he was also brought up to tell the truth. I, on the other hand, was brought up by a politician grandfather in Washington, D.C., and I wanted very much to be a politician, too. Unfortunately, nature had designed me to be a writer. I had no choice in the matter. Pears were to be my diet, stolen or homegrown. There was never a time when I did not make sentences in order to make those things that I had experienced cohere and become "real."

Finally, the novelist must always tell the truth as he understands it while the politician must never give the game away. Those who have done both comprise a very short list indeed. The fact that I was never even a candidate for the list had to do with a choice made at twenty that entirely changed my life.

At nineteen, just out of the army, I wrote a novel, *Williwaw* (1946): it was admired as, chronologically, at least, the first of the war novels. The next year I wrote the less admired *In a Yellow Wood* (1947). Simultaneously, my grandfather was arranging a political career for me in New Mexico (the governor was a protégé of the old man). Yes, believe it or not, in the greatest democracy the world has ever known—freedom's as well as bravery's home—elections can be quietly arranged, as Joe Kennedy liked to explain to you.

For someone twenty years old I was well situated in the world, thanks to two published novels and my grandfather's political skills. I was also situated dead center at a crossroads rather like the one Oedipus found himself at. I was at work on *The City and the Pillar.* If I published it, I'd take a right turn and end up accursed in Thebes. Abandon it and I'd turn left and end up in holy Delphi. Honor required that I take the road to Thebes. I have read that I was too stupid at the time to know what I was doing, but in such matters I have always had a certain alertness. I knew that my description of the love affair between two "normal" all-American boys of the sort that I had spent three years with in the wartime army would challenge every superstition about sex in my native land—which has always been more Boeotia, I fear, than Athens or haunted Thebes. Until then, American novels of "inversion" dealt with transvestites or with lonely bookish boys who married unhappily and pined for Marines. I broke that mold. My two lovers were athletes and so drawn to the entirely masculine that, in the case of one, Jim Willard, the feminine was simply irrelevant to his passion to unite with his other half, Bob Ford: unfortunately for Jim, Bob had other sexual plans, involving women and marriage.

I gave the manuscript to my New York publishers, E. P. Dutton. They hated it. One ancient editor said, "You will never be forgiven for this book. Twenty years from now you will still be attacked for it." I responded with an uneasy whistle in the dark: "If any book of mine is remembered in the year 1968, that's real fame, isn't it?"

To my grandfather's sorrow, on January 10, 1948, *The City and the Pillar* was published. Shock was the most pleasant emotion aroused in the press. How could our young war novelist . . . ? In a week or two, the book was a best-seller in the United States and wherever else it could be published—not exactly a full atlas in those days. The English publisher, John Lehmann, was very nervous. In his memoirs, *The Whispering Gallery,* he writes, "There were several passages in *The City and the Pillar,* a sad, almost tragic book and a remarkable achievement in a difficult territory for so young a man, that seemed to my travellers and the printers to go too far in frankness. I had a friendly battle with Gore to tone down and cut these passages. Irony of the time and taste: they wouldn't cause an eyebrow to be lifted in the climate of the early sixties." But only twenty years ago the book was taken from Dennis Altman as he arrived at the airport in Sydney, Australia. Altman challenged the obscenity law under which the book had been seized. The judge in the case acknowledged that under the law that he must administer the book was obscene, but then, in a famous obiter dicta, he wrote that he thought the law absurd: in due course, it was changed. Meanwhile, even today, copies of the book still fitfully blaze on the pampas and playas of Argentina and other godly countries. As I write these lines, I have just learned that the book will at last appear in Russia, where a Moscow theater group is adapting it for the stage.

What did my confreres think? I'm afraid not much. The fag writers were terrified; the others were delighted that a competitor had so neatly erased himself. I did send copies to two famous writers, fishing, as all young writers do, for endorsements. The first was to Thomas Mann. The second was to Christopher Isherwood, who responded enthusiastically. We became lifelong friends. Through Joseph Breitbach I was told that André Gide was planning to write an "appreciation," but when we finally met he spoke only of a handwritten, fetchingly illustrated pornography that he had received from an English clergyman in Hampshire.

At fourteen I had read Thomas Mann's *Joseph* books and realized that the "novel of ideas" (we still have no proper phrase in English for this sort of book or, indeed, such a genre) could work if one were to set a narrative within history. Later, I was struck by the use of dialogue in *The Magic Mountain,* particularly the debates between Settembrini and Naphta, as each man subtly vies for the favors of the dim but sexually attractive Hans Castorp. Later, there would be complaints that Jim Willard in *The City and the Pillar* was also dim. But I deliberately made Jim Willard a Hans Castorp type: what else could someone so young be, set loose in the world—the City—that was itself the center of interest? But I did give Jim something Hans lacked: a romantic passion for Bob Ford that finally excluded everything else from his life, even, in a sense, the life itself. I got a polite, perfunctory note from Thomas Mann, thanking me for my "noble work": my name was misspelled.

Contemplating the American scene in the 1940s, Stephen Spender deplored the machinery of literary success, remarking sternly that "one has only to follow the whizzing comets of Mr. Truman Capote and Mr. Gore Vidal to see how quickly and effectively this transforming, diluting, disintegrating machinery can work." He then characterized *The City and the Pillar* as a work of sexual confession, quite plainly autobiography at its most artless. Transformed, diluted, disintegrated as I was, I found this description flattering. Mr. Spender had paid me a considerable compliment; although I am the least autobiographical of novelists, I had drawn the character of the athlete Jim Willard so convincingly that to this day aging pederasts are firmly convinced that I was once a male prostitute, with an excellent backhand at tennis. The truth, alas, is quite another matter. The book was a considerable act of imagination. Jim Willard and I shared the same geography, but little else. Also, in the interest of verisimilitude I decided to tell the story in a flat gray prose reminiscent of one of James T. Farrell's social documents. There was to be nothing fancy in the writing. I wanted the prose plain and hard.

In April 1993, at the State University of New York at Albany, a dozen papers were read by academics on *The City and the Pillar.* The book has been in print for close to half a century, something I would not have thought possible in 1948, when *The New York Times* would not advertise it and no major American newspaper or magazine would review it or any other book of mine for the next six years. *Life* magazine thought that the greatest nation in the country, as Spiro Agnew used to say, had been driven queer by the young army first mate they had featured only the previous year, standing before his ship. I've not read any of the Albany papers. For one thing, it is never a good idea to read about oneself, particularly about a twenty-one-year-old self who had modeled himself, perhaps too closely, on Billy the Kid. I might be shot in the last frame, but I was going to take care of a whole lot of folks who needed taking care of before I was done.

There were those who found the original ending "melodramatic." (Jim strangles Bob after an unsuccessful sexual encounter.) When I reminded one critic that it is the nature of a romantic tragedy to end in death, I was told that so sordid a story about fags could never be considered tragic, unlike, let us say, a poignant tale of doomed love between a pair of mentally challenged teenage "heteros" in old Verona. I intended Jim Willard to demonstrate the romantic fallacy. From too much looking back, he was destroyed, an unsophisticated Humbert Humbert trying to re-create an idyll that never truly existed except in his own imagination. Despite the title, this was never plain in the narrative. And of course the coda *was* unsatisfactory. At the time it was generally believed that the publishers forced me to tack on a cautionary ending in much the same way the Motion Picture Code used to insist that wickedness be punished. This was not true. I had always meant the end of the book to be black, but not as black as it turned out. So for a new edition of the book published in 1965 I altered the last chapter considerably. In fact, I rewrote the entire book (my desire to imitate the style of Farrell was perhaps too successful), though I did not change the point of view or the essential relationships. I left Jim as he was. He had developed a life of his own outside my rough pages. Claude J. Summers recently noted that of the characters

> only Jim Willard is affecting, and he commands sustained interest largely because he combines unexpected characteristics. Bland and ordinary, he nevertheless has an unusually well-developed inner life. Himself paralyzed by romantic illusions, he is surprisingly perceptive about the illusions of others. For all the novel's treatment of him as a case history, he nevertheless preserves an essential mystery. As Robert Kiernan comments (*Gore Vidal*), Jim Willard is Everyman and yet he is l'étranger . . .* the net effect is paradoxical but appropriate for it decrees that, in the last analysis, we cannot patronize Jim Willard, sympathize with him entirely, or even claim to understand him. Much more so than the typical character in fiction, Jim Willard simply exists, not as the subject of a statement, not as the illustration of a thesis, but simply as himself.

Not long ago I received a telephone call from the biographer of Thomas Mann. Did I know, he asked, the profound effect that my book had had on Mann? I made some joke to the effect that at least toward the end of his life he may have learned how to spell my name. "But he didn't read the book until 1950, and as he read it he commented on it in his diaries. They've just been published in Germany. Get them." Now I have read, with some amazement, of the effect that Mann's twenty-one-year-old admirer had on what was then a seventy-five-year-old world master, situated by war in California.

> Wednesday 22, XI, 50
> . . . Began to read the homo-erotic novel "The City and the Pillar" by Vidal. The day at the cabin by the river and the love-play scene between Jim and Bob was quite brilliant.—Stopped reading late. Very warm night.

*Claude J. Summers in "The Cabin and the River" (*Gay Fictions,* New York: Continuum, 1990) quotes from Robert F. Kiernan's book *Gore Vidal* (New York: Frederick Ungar, 1982).

Thursday 23, XI, 50
. . . Continued "City and Pillar."
Friday 24, XI, 50
. . . In the evening continued reading "The City and the Pillar." Interesting, yes. An important human document, of excellent and enlightening truthfulness. The sexual, the affairs with the various men, is still incomprehensible to us. How can one sleep with men—[Mann uses the word *Herren,* which means not "men" but "gentlemen." Is This Mann being satiric? A rhetorical question affecting shock?].
Saturday evening 25, XI, 50
. . . in May 1943, I took out the *Felix Krull* papers only to touch them fleetingly and then turn to *Faustus.* An effort to start again must be made, if only to keep me occupied, to have a task in hand. I have nothing else, no ideas for stories; no subject for a novel. . . . Will it be possible to start [*Felix Krull*] again? Is there enough of the world and are there enough people, is there enough knowledge available? The homosexual novel interests me not least because of the experience of the world and of travel that it offers. Has my isolation picked up enough experience of human beings, enough for a social-satirical novel?
Sunday 26, XI, 50
Busy with [the *Krull*] papers, confusing.
Read more of Vidal's novel
Wednesday 29, XI, 50
. . . The *Krull* papers (on imprisonment). Always doubts. Ask myself whether this music determined by a "yearning theme" is appropriate to my years. . . . Finished Vidal's novel, moved, although a lot is faulty and unpleasant. For example, that Jim takes Bob into a Fairy Bar in New York.

I am pleased that Mann did not find the ending "melodramatic," but then what theme is more melodramatically "yearning" than *Liebestod*? In any case, the young novelist who took what seemed to everyone the wrong road at Trivium is now saluted in his own old age by the writer whom he had, in a certain sense, modeled himself on. As for Mann's surprise at how men could sleep with one another, he is writing a private diary, the most public act any German master can ever do, and though he often refers to his own "inversion" and his passions for this or that youth, he seems not to go on, like me, to Thebes but to take (with many a backward look) the high road to Delphi, and I am duly astonished and pleased that, as he read me, he was inspired—motivated—whatever verb—to return to his most youthful and enchanting work, *Felix Krull.*

Some of my short stories are almost as lighthearted as Thomas Mann in his last work. One of them, "The Ladies in the Library," is an unconscious variation on *Death in Venice.* Three variations on a theme: Mann's Hans Castorp; then my own, Jim Willard; then a further lighter, more allegro version of Jim in the guise of a character whom he appropriately called Felix—the Latin for "happy."

# From *The City and the Pillar,* 1965/1995

THEY STOOD ON THE EDGE of the cliff and looked down at the brown river, muddy from spring rains and loud where it broke up on the black rocks in midstream. Below them, the cliff dropped steeply to the river, a wall of stone, dark green with laurel and wild grapevines.

"Must be a flood upstream. That old river looks mean," said Bob.

"Maybe we'll see a house come floating down."

Bob chuckled. "Or a privy." Jim sat on a rock and plucked a piece of long grass and chewed on the white sweet-tasting stem. Bob squatted beside him. Together they listened to the roar of the river and the noise of tree frogs and the rustle of bright new leaves in the wind.

"How was Sally?"

Bob growled. "Prick-teaser, like all the rest. Leads you on so you think, *now* I can lay her and then, just as you get all hot, *she* gets scared: Oh, what're you doing to me? Oh, stop! You stop that now!" Bob sighed with disgust. "I tell you it makes a man so horny he could lay a mule, if it would just stand still." Bob contemplated mules. Then: "Why didn't you come to the dance last night? Lots of girls asked for you."

"I don't know. Don't like dancing, I guess. I don't know."

"You're too bashful."

Bob rolled up a trouser leg and removed a large black ant, which was crawling up his calf. Jim noticed how white Bob's skin was, like marble, even in the sun.

Then, to break the silence, they threw stones over the edge of the cliff. The sound of rock hitting rock was entirely satisfying. Finally Bob shouted,

"Come on!" And they crawled over the edge of the cliff and cautiously worked their way downward, holding on to bushes, finding toeholds in the rock.

The hot sun shone in a pale sky. Hawks circled while small birds flashed between trees. Snakes, lizards, rabbits all scuttled for cover as the boys made their noisy descent. At last they reached the river's muddy bank. Tall black rocks jutted from brown sand. Happily, they leapt from rock to rock, never once touching earth, stepping only on the relics of a glacier age.

Shortly after noon they came to the slave cabin, a small house with a shingled roof much perforated by weather. The interior smelled of rotted plaster and age. Yellow newspapers and rusty tin cans were scattered over the rough wood floor. On the stone hearth there were new ashes: tramps as well as lovers stayed here.

Bob set down the paper bag he had been carrying while Jim put the blankets on the cleanest part of the floor.

"Hasn't changed much." Bob looked up at the roof. The sky shone through holes. "Let's hope it don't rain."

Close to the cabin there was a large pond, bordered by willows and choked with lilies. Jim sat on the moss-covered bank while Bob undressed, throwing his clothes into a nearby tree, the trousers draped like a flag on one branch while his socks hung like pennants from another. Then he stretched happily, flexing his long muscles and admiring himself in the green smooth water. Though slim, he was strongly built and Jim admired him without envy. When Bob talked of someone who had a good build, he invariably sounded envious; yet when Jim looked at Bob's body, he felt as if he were looking at an ideal brother, a twin, and he was content. That something was lacking did not occur to him. It seemed enough that they played tennis together and Bob spoke to him endlessly of the girls he liked.

Cautiously Bob put one long foot in the water. "It's warm," he said. "Real warm. Come on in." Then, hands on knees, he leaned over and studied his own reflection. As Jim undressed, he tried to fix the image of Bob permanently in his mind, as if this might be the last time they would ever see one another. Point by point, he memorized him: wide shoulders, narrow buttocks, slim legs, curved sex.

Naked, Jim joined Bob at the water's edge. The warm breeze on his bare skin made him feel suddenly free and curiously powerful, like a dreamer who is aware that he is dreaming.

Bob looked at him thoughtfully. "You got a good tan. I sure look white. Hey!" He pointed at the water. Below the dark green surface, Jim could see the blunt slow-moving shape of a catfish. Then, suddenly, he was falling and there was a rush of water in his ears. Bob had pushed him in. Choking, he came to the surface. With a rapid movement, Jim grabbed Bob's leg and pulled him in. Grappling, they turned and twisted in the water, making the pond foam. As they wrestled, Jim took pleasure in the physical contact. So, apparently, did Bob. Not until both were exhausted did they stop.

For the rest of that day they swam, caught frogs, sunned themselves, wrestled. They talked little. Not until the light began to fail did they relax.

"It's sure nice here." Bob stretched out full length. "I guess there isn't any place as nice and peaceful as this place is." He patted his flat stomach and yawned.

Jim agreed, totally at peace; he noticed that Bob's belly quivered with the regularity of a pulse. He looked at himself: the same phenomenon. Before he could comment on it, he saw a tick heading toward his pubic hair. He pinched it hard until it popped.

"I got a tick."

Bob jumped to his feet. Ticks gave you a fever, so they examined themselves carefully, but found nothing. They got dressed.

The air was gold. Even the gray walls of the cabin looked gold in the last light of the sun. Now they were hungry. Jim built a fire while Bob made hamburgers in the frying pan. He did everything easily, expertly. At home he cooked for his father.

They ate their supper, sitting on a log facing the river. The sun had gone. Fireflies darted like yellow sparks in the green shadow of the woods.

"I'm going to miss this," said Bob finally.

Jim looked at him. In the stillness there was no sound but the rushing river. "My sister said Sally said you were going to leave right after graduation. I told her I didn't know anything about it. Are you going?"

Bob nodded and wiped his hands on his trousers. "Monday, on the Old Dominion Bus Line."

"Where are you going to go?"

"To sea."

"Like we always talked about."

"Like we always talked about. Oh, I tell you I'm fed up with this town. The old man and I don't get along at all and God knows there isn't anything to do around here. So I'm going. You know I never been out of this county, except to go over to Washington. I want to see things."

Jim nodded. "So do I. But I thought we were going to go to college first and *then* we would . . . well, you would go off on this trip."

Bob caught a firefly in his hand and let it climb up his thumb, and fly away.

"College is too much work," he said at last. "I'd have to work my way through and that means a job, which means I'd never get a chance to play around. Besides, there isn't a thing they could teach me that I want to know. All I want is to travel and to hell around."

"Me too." Jim wished that he could say what he wanted to say. "But my father wants me to go to college and I suppose I got to. Only I'd hoped we could go together . . . well, team up in tennis doubles. We could be state champions. Everybody says so."

Bob shook his head and stretched out. "I got to get moving," he said. "I don't know why but I do."

"I feel the same way, sometimes." Jim sat beside Bob on the ground and together they watched the river and the darkening sky.

"I wonder what New York is like," said Bob at last.

"Big, I guess."

"Like Washington. That sure is a big town." Bob rolled over on his side, facing Jim. "Hey, why don't you come with me? We can ship out as cabin boys, maybe even deckhands."

Jim was grateful Bob had said this, but he was cautious by nature. "I think I ought to wait till next year when I get that high-school diploma, which is important to have. Of course my old man wants me to go to college. He says I should . . ."

"Why do you pay any attention to that bastard?"

Jim was shocked and delighted. "Well, I don't really. In fact, I'd just as soon never see him again." With surprising ease, he obliterated his father. "But even so, I'm scared, going off like that."

"Nothing to it." Bob flexed the muscles of his right arm. "Why, a guy like you with brains and a good build, he can do most anything he wants. I knew these guys, they were sailors out of Norfolk, and they said there was nothing to it; easy work and when you're onshore you have a good time all the time, which is what I want. Oh, I'm tired of hanging around this town, working in stores, going out with *nice* girls. Only they're not really so damned nice, they're just afraid of getting knocked up." Fiercely he struck the ground with his fist. "Like Sally! Why, she'd do anything to you you want except the one thing you got to have. And that sure makes me mad. She makes me mad. All the girls around here make me mad!" Again he struck the dark earth.

"I know how it is," said Jim, who did not know how it was. "But aren't you scared you'll catch something from somebody you meet in New York?"

Bob laughed. "Man, I'm careful!" He turned over on his back.

Jim watched the fireflies rise from the nearby grass. It was already night. "You know," he said, "I wish I could go with you up North. I'd like to see New York and do as I please for once."

"So why don't you?"

"Like I said, I'm afraid to leave home and the family, not that I like them all that much but . . ." His voice trailed off uncertainly.

"Well, you can come with me if you want to."

"Next year, after I graduate, I'll come."

"*If* you can find me. I don't know where I'll be by then. I'm a rolling stone."

"Don't worry. I'll find you. Anyway, we'll write."

Then they walked down to the narrow boulder-strewn beach. Bob scrambled onto a flat rock and Jim followed him. The river swirled about them as they sat side by side in the blue, deep night.

One by one, great stars appeared. Jim was perfectly contented, loneliness no longer turning in the pit of his stomach, sharp as a knife. He always thought of unhappiness as the "tar sickness." When tar roads melted in the summer, he used to chew the tar and get sick. In some obscure way he had always associated "tar sickness" with being alone. No longer.

Bob took off his shoes and socks and let the river cool his feet. Jim did the same.

"I'll miss all this," said Bob for the dozenth time, absently putting his arm around Jim's shoulders.

They were very still. Jim found the weight of Bob's arm on his shoulders almost unbearable: wonderful but unbearable. Yet he did not dare move for fear the other would take his arm away. Suddenly Bob got to his feet. "Let's make a fire."

In a burst of activity, they built a fire in front of the cabin. Then Bob brought the blankets outside and spread them on the ground.

"There," he said, looking into the yellow flames, "that's done." For a long moment both stared into the hypnotically quivering flames, each possessed by his own private daydream. Bob's dream ended first. He turned to Jim. "Come on," he said menacingly. "I'll wrestle you."

They met, grappled, fell to the ground. Pushing and pulling, they fought for position; they were evenly matched, because Jim, though stronger, would not allow Bob to lose or to win. When at last they stopped, both were panting and sweating. They lay exhausted on the blanket.

Then Bob took off his shirt and Jim did the same. That was better. Jim mopped the sweat from his face while Bob stretched out on the blanket, using his shirt for a pillow. Firelight gleamed on pale skin. Jim stretched out beside him. "Too hot," he said. "Too hot to be wrestling."

Bob laughed and suddenly grabbed him. They clung to one another. Jim was overwhelmingly conscious of Bob's body. For a moment they pretended to wrestle. Then both stopped. Yet each continued to cling to the other as though waiting for a signal to break or to begin again. For a long time neither moved. Smooth chests touching, sweat mingling, breathing fast in unison.

Abruptly, Bob pulled away. For a bold moment their eyes met. Then, deliberately, gravely, Bob shut his eyes and Jim touched him, as he had so many times in dreams, without words, without thought, without fear. When the eyes are shut, the true world begins.

As faces touched, Bob gave a shuddering sigh and gripped Jim tightly in his arms. Now they were complete, each became the other, as their bodies collided with a primal violence, like to like, metal to magnet, half to half and the whole restored.

So they met. Eyes tight shut against an irrelevant world. A wind warm and sudden shook all the trees, scattered the fire's ashes, threw shadows to the ground.

But then the wind stopped. The fire went to coals. The trees were silent. No comets marked the dark lovely sky, and the moment was gone. In the fast beat of a double heart, it died.

The eyes opened again. Two bodies faced one another where only an instant before a universe had lived; the star burst and dwindled, spiraling them both down to the meager, to the separate, to the night and the trees and the firelight; all so much less than what had been.

They separated, breathing hard. Jim could feel the fire on his feet and beneath the blanket he was now uncomfortably aware of small stones and sticks. He looked at Bob, not certain of what he would see.

Bob was staring into the fire, face expressionless. But he grinned quickly when he saw Jim watching him. "This is a hell of a mess," he said, and the moment fled.

Jim looked down at himself and said as casually as he could, "It sure is."

Bob stood up, the firelight glittering on his body. "Let's wash up."

Pale as ghosts in the dark night, they walked to the pond. Through the trees they could see the light from their fire, yellow and flickering, while frogs croaked, insects buzzed, river thundered. They dove into the still black water. Not until they had returned to the fire did Bob break the silence. He was abrupt.

"You know, that was awful kid stuff we did."

"I suppose so." Jim paused. "But I liked it." He had great courage now that he had made his secret dream reality. "Did you?"

Bob frowned into the yellow fire. "Well, it was different than with a girl. And I don't think it's right."

"Why not?"

"Well, guys aren't supposed to do that with each other. It's not natural."

"I guess not." Jim looked at Bob's fire-colored body, long-lined and muscular. With his newfound courage, he put his arm around Bob's waist. Again excited, they embraced and fell back onto the blanket.

Jim woke before dawn. The sky was gray and the stars were fading. The fire was almost out. He touched Bob's arm and watched him wake up. They looked at one another. Then Bob grinned and Jim said, "You're still going Monday?"

Bob nodded.

"You'll write me, won't you? I'd like to get on the same boat with you next year."

"Sure, I'll write you."

"I wish you weren't going . . . you know, after this."

Bob laughed and grabbed him by the neck. "Hell, we got all day Sunday." And Jim was satisfied and happy to have all day Sunday with this conscious dream.

# From *The City and the Pillar,* 1948

Jim was impatient that spring. He played tennis all day, gave lessons all day; he tried to exhaust himself physically so that he would not think of Bob. He had no affairs and Maria Verlaine, who was in New York with her Argentine, was the only person he saw. He could not tell her about Bob, though, and so they talked abstractly of their lives and she tried, vainly, to help him. Jim knew that if it had not been for Bob he could have loved Maria completely. But now he was going to relive the first moment, the greatest moment in his life. He worked that spring. Peace came twice and the year ended. Reports from home told Jim that Bob was still at sea.

At last, a year late, Bob called late one afternoon. It was the end of May and the weather was warm. Jim told him to come over right away.

They shook hands as though they had seen each other just the day before.

"Nice place you've got," said Bob, looking around the apartment. "I'd think you'd hate to leave this for Virginia."

"I haven't left it yet," said Jim, smiling.

"No, you haven't." Bob sat down in a chair, his long legs stretched out in front of him on the rug. He was still in uniform.

"Are you getting out?" asked Jim.

Bob frowned and Jim saw that he was worried, that his usually clear eyes were tired. "Damned if I know. I have a chance of becoming a master. That'd be something at my age and I hate the idea of turning it down."

"But Sally?"

"That's just it . . . but Sally. I don't know what I'm going to do. She doesn't want me to take it, naturally."

"But you want to?"

"Yes, I want to."

"Well, go ahead then. You should run your own life. You should make the decisions, not Sally. If you're happier at sea then go ahead. She isn't the first woman that ever married a sailor."

Bob nodded, agreeing. "That's what I should do but she's so damned set on my staying in Virginia—her family, too. Sometimes I think it's her family more than her. She seems quite happy with the baby. I don't think she'd miss *me* particularly."

"You'll have to make up your mind," said Jim. "I think you should go to sea if you feel you should and I think Sally should want you to do what you feel you should." Jim wanted Bob to go to sea; he knew that it would take him away from him for long periods but it would also take him away from his wife. "How about dinner?" he said.

They had dinner at an Italian restaurant and they drank a large bottle of red wine. Bob got more and more cheerful and Jim could see that soon the circle would complete itself and he was glad, not jubilantly but quietly.

"Where do you want to go?" asked Jim when they had finished.

"I don't care. Any place. I think I'd like to get drunk."

"Well, we'll go to a bar I know."

They walked through the warm night air to a famous fairy bar. Jim wanted to see how Bob would react.

They took a table and ordered whiskey. The bar ran down the center of the room, and around the bar were tables. There were a few women, though not many, at the bar. There were a great many servicemen; everyone was hunting.

Bob looked about him curiously. "There're not many women in here," he said finally.

"No, not so many. Did you want one?"

"Well . . . no, not at the moment. I'm a married man, remember? Sometimes I have trouble remembering it myself." He laughed.

"I don't think there's much temptation in here," said Jim.

They drank and talked for an hour. Their old intimacy was, on the surface, resumed. Bob did most of the talking and Jim listened. The only difference was that now Jim was the one sure of himself and Bob was the one in doubt, the one as yet unresolved.

Jim watched the people in the bar. Some were very obvious. A pilot would squeeze in beside a sailor. They would have a drink together. They would talk. Jim could see their legs pressed together. Then they would leave together, their faces flushed and their eyes bright. Sometimes, however, an older man, fat and unattractive, would move in beside a soldier. The conversation would be short and the older man would go away and look for another opening, another soldier.

"That's sort of a queer-looking crowd," said Bob suddenly, motioning to the bar.

"That's New York," Jim said; he was a little frightened; he didn't know how Bob felt about these people, about themselves. It would be unfortunate if he had a feeling of guilt.

"I guess that *is* New York. There're a lot of queers here. They seem to be everywhere now. We always have a few on board ship. Once I had a skipper who was but he never bothered me. It was funny; he only liked niggers. I suppose it takes all kinds, like they say. Want another drink?" He ordered another round.

Jim knew then that Bob was not homosexual; it was better that he was not; it would give more meaning to their relationship.

They were both a little drunk now.

"You don't know many women here?" said Bob finally. "I mean just to talk to. Sally'd kill me if I ever did anything else. You know, I've only shacked up with one other woman since I married Sally. I think that's pretty good. No, I just mean girls as company."

"No," said Jim, "I don't. The ones I know who might are probably tied up tonight."

"That's so. It's pretty short notice. But I know a few girls; maybe I should call them up."

This was not according to the plan Jim had expected him to follow. He would make no protest, though; it would happen sooner or later and he did not worry. "If you like," said Jim.

Bob looked about him. "Let's go on over to my hotel," he said. "I can call from there." They paid for their drinks and left the bar. Many eyes watched them as they went out the door.

They crossed Times Square. The lights were brilliant and it was like day. People crowded through the streets and into the movies and bars. It was a hot night and the streets were full of warm people, pushing one another irritably.

Bob had a dingy room in a large, not too respectable hotel. Jim was conscious of Bob when he went into his room. It smelled of him, warm and animal and masculine. His clothes were strewn about the room; a still-damp towel was on the floor and the bed was unmade. "Sorry it's such a mess," said Bob mechanically. "I'm not very neat, I guess. Sally is always mad at me when I throw things around." He went over to the phone and called several numbers but he got no answers.

Jim sat on the bed watching him. Finally Bob put the receiver down and grinned at Jim. "I guess I was meant to be good tonight. They're all out. Well, let's get drunk; we might as well be drunk as the way we are. I've got some liquor here." He went over to his suitcase and took out a bottle. Then he got two fairly clean glasses from the bathroom and he poured two drinks. "Here's how," he said casually and he drank his at a gulp; Jim drank his more slowly.

They drank together beneath the harsh white light of an electric bulb. The room was hot and they both took their shirts off. Jim was pleased that Bob's body had not changed. It was still muscular and strong and his skin was white and smooth, not freckled as is the skin of most people with dark red hair.

Finally, Jim began to talk of what was in his mind, had been in his mind for nine years. "You remember the cabin?" he said.

"The one down by the river? Sure."

"We had a lot of fun down there, didn't we?"

"I'll say. That pond was wonderful for swimming in."

"You remember the last time we went down there?"

"The last time? . . . No, I don't think I do."

Could he have forgotten? Jim was panicky for a moment. No, he couldn't have forgotten. "You must remember. It was the weekend before you went North. After you'd graduated from school."

Bob nodded then. "Yes, I do remember now." He paused and frowned as he recalled. "We . . . we fooled around quite a bit, didn't we?"

Yes, he remembered. Now it was coming. "I guess we did," said Jim. "It was a lot of fun."

Bob chuckled. "Kids always do that, I guess. They always do that together; though it's funny I never had done it with anybody until that time."

"Neither had I," said Jim.

"I guess we were just a couple of little queers at heart," said Bob, grinning.

"Did . . . you ever do . . . that again, with anybody else?"

"Any other fellow? Hell, no. Did you?"

"N . . . no."

"Let's have another drink."

Soon they were both very drunk. Bob said that he was sleepy, that drinking made him sleepy. Jim said that he was too and that he had better go home but Bob insisted that he spend the night with him. They undressed, throwing their clothes on the floor. Bob stretched and Jim admired his long muscles. They got into bed and Bob turned out the light.

No longer thinking, but obeying his instincts, Jim reached out in the dark and took Bob in his arms.

"Hey! What's going on?" Bob sat up in bed. Jim said nothing, holding him still. Bob pushed him away. "What're you doing, anyway?" Then, when Jim didn't answer, he understood. "You're a queer," he said, "you're nothing but a damned queer! Go on and get your ass out of here!"

Then fury came to Jim, took the place of love. He threw himself at Bob;

he caught him by the shoulders. They rolled in the darkness, both drunk but both aware. It was like a nightmare. Jim was the stronger; his rage was the greater. They fell off the bed onto the floor. They fought silently.

Finally Jim had Bob by the throat; methodically he began to choke him. Bob twisted desperately on the floor but Jim was too strong. Suddenly Bob's body became rigid; then, after a long time, he went limp and Jim knew that he was dead.

Exhausted, breathing painfully, the sweat trickling off his body, Jim stood up and turned on the light. Bob lay quietly on the floor. There were red marks on his body and his face was discolored. Tenderly Jim picked him up and put him on the bed. He was very heavy. Jim arranged his arms and legs and put a pillow under his head. He kissed him.

Then, calmly, Jim got dressed. He knew what he had done. Death was unimportant but the end of his love was important. He no longer cared what might happen to him. With Bob gone there was nothing left. The dream was shattered, lay white and bruised beneath the cold electric light, and Jim was shattered, too. He left the room, leaving the light on. He went out of the hotel. He walked for a long time. Then he came to a bar and he went in. He would drink until the dream was completely over.

# From *The City and the Pillar,* 1995

THEY CROSSED TIMES SQUARE. Hot windless night. Lights flashing. People everywhere. The mood jubilant, postwar. Bob's hotel was in a side street. They went straight to his room. As Jim stepped inside, he was suddenly overwhelmed by Bob's physical reality. Clothes were strewn about the floor, a damp towel hung from the bathroom door, the bed was a tangle of sheets, and over the harsh odor of disinfectant and dust, Jim was aware of Bob's own smell, to him erotic.

"Kind of a mess," said Bob mechanically. "I'm not very neat. Sally always gets mad at the way I throw things around." He went to the telephone and placed several calls. No one was home. Finally, he put the receiver down and grinned. "I guess I was meant to be good tonight. So let's get drunk. Might as well be drunk as the way we are." He took a bottle from his suitcase and poured two drinks. "Here's how." He drank his shot at a gulp. Jim merely tasted the whiskey. He had to keep clearheaded.

As they drank beneath the harsh unshaded light of a single electric bulb, the room became stifling with summer heat. They took off their shirts. Bob's body was still muscular and strong, the skin smooth and white, not freckled, unlike most redheads.

The duet began pianissimo.

"You remember the old slave cabin?" asked Jim.

"Down by the river? Sure."

"We had a lot of fun there."

"I'll say. There was a pond, too, wasn't there? Where we swam?"

Jim nodded. "Remember the last time we were there?"

"No, I don't think I do."

Could he have forgotten? Impossible. "Sure you remember. The weekend before you went North. Right after you graduated."

Bob nodded. "Yeah, I kind of remember." He frowned. "We . . . we fooled around quite a bit, didn't we?"

Yes, he remembered. Now it would happen. "Yes. Kind of fun, wasn't it?"

Bob chuckled. "Kids always do that, I guess. Though it's funny, I never did, except that one time."

"Neither did I."

"So I guess we were just a couple of little queers at heart." Bob grinned.

"Did you ever . . . well, do *that* again, with anybody else?"

"Any other guy? Hell, no. Did you?"

"No."

"Let's have another drink."

Soon they were both drunk and Bob said that he was sleepy. Jim said that he was, too, and that he had better go home, but Bob insisted that he spend the night with him. They threw their clothes on the floor. Wearing only shorts, they tumbled onto the unmade bed. Bob lay sprawled on his back, arm across his face, apparently unconscious. Jim stared at him: was he really asleep? Boldly, Jim put his hand on Bob's chest. The skin was as smooth as he remembered. Lightly he touched the stray coppery hairs which grew below the deep-set navel. Then, carefully, like a surgeon performing a delicate operation, he unbuttoned Bob's shorts. Bob stirred, but did not wake, as Jim opened wide the shorts to reveal thick blond pubic hair from which sprouted the pale quarry. Slowly his hand closed around Bob's sex. He held him for what seemed a long time. Held him, until he looked up to find that the other was awake and watching him. Jim's heart stopped for a full beat.

"What the fuck are you doing?" The voice was hard. Jim could not speak. Obviously the world was ending. His hand remained frozen where it was. Bob pushed him. But he could not move.

"Let go of me, you queer."

Plainly a nightmare, Jim decided. None of this could be happening. But when Bob struck him hard in the face, the pain recalled him. Jim drew back. Bob leapt to his feet and stood, swaying drunkenly, fumbling with buttons. "Now will you get the hell out of here?"

Jim touched his face where he had been struck. His head still rang from the blow. Was he bleeding?

"Get out, you hear me?" Bob moved toward him, menacingly, fist ready. Suddenly, overwhelmed equally by rage and desire, Jim threw himself at Bob. They grappled. They fell across the bed. Bob was strong but Jim was stronger. Grunting and grasping, they twisted and turned, struck out with arms, legs, but Bob was no match for Jim and, at the end, he lay face down on the bed, arm bent behind him, sweating and groaning. Jim looked down at the helpless body, wanting to do murder. Deliberately he twisted the arm he held. Bob cried out. Jim was excited at the other's pain. What to do? Jim frowned. Drink made concentration difficult. He looked at the heaving body beneath him, the broad back, ripped shorts, long muscled legs. One final humiliation: with his free hand, Jim pulled down the shorts, revealing white, hard, hairless buttocks. "Jesus," Bob whispered. "Don't. Don't."

Finished, Jim lay on the still body, breathing hard, drained of emotion, conscious that the thing was done, the circle completed, and finished.

At last Jim sat up. Bob did not stir. He remained face down, clutching the pillow to his face while Jim dressed. Then Jim crossed to the bed and looked down at the body he had loved with such single-mindedness for so many years. Was this all? He put his hand on Bob's sweaty shoulder. Bob shied away from him: fear? disgust? It made no difference now. Jim touched the pillow. It was wet. Tears? Good. Without a word, Jim went to the door and opened it. He looked back once more at Bob, then he turned out the light and shut the door behind him. He left the hotel, not caring where he went. For a long time he walked aimlessly, until at last he came to one of the many bars where men looked for men. He entered, prepared to drink until the dream was completely over.

# *"THE LADIES IN THE LIBRARY"*

THOUGH THE SHORT STORY as a genre has had limited appeal to Vidal, he wrote many short stories as a schoolboy at Exeter and later published *A Thirsty Evil,* a volume of seven stories written between 1948 and 1956. The stories in *A Thirsty Evil* are notable for their clarity of style, their directness of presentation, and a delight in unusual or even bizarre characters. They are stories of character rather than plot. "The Ladies in the Library" was originally published in *New World Writing* in 1953.

# “The Ladies in the Library”

(*For Alice Bouverie*)

## I

HE SELDOM SAW his cousin Sybil and he was always ill at ease on those occasions when they did meet for she still represented the Family: a vague and now spent force which had been in a process of dissolution ever since his college days some twenty years earlier, diminishing not only as a force but as a fact until today only the two of them were left.

She lived in Baltimore and he lived in New York. Neither had married, a clear indication that nature had abandoned yet another experiment in eugenics. In other times he had occasionally tried to imagine himself as a father with numerous children in whose healthy veins his essence would be precipitated into future time, ensuring for him that posterity of blood which so appeals to those who briefly see eternity in man, but unfortunately neither the literal nor the metaphysical image ever concretized properly in his imagination, much less in life; and now, middle-aged, he assumed the conditions of his bachelor existence were fixed, the danger of serious change remote.

Sybil too had neglected to marry, and although she still made cozy allusions to weddings and Christmas parties, to Easter egg hunts and funerals, to all the beloved activities of a family’s life, in actual fact she had consigned most human relationships to pleasant memory, devoting her life instead to dogs and cats, her dealings with these dependent creatures not unlike those she might have enjoyed with the children she never bore, with the family that had died. In a sense of course all things were nearly equal: she gave Christmas parties for the dogs and she made matches for the cats, arranging their destinies with the energy of a matriarch and, certainly, with better luck than matriarchs usually enjoy in the world of people.

We have nothing in common, he thought, as he waited for her in the Union Station, the dome of the Capitol like an elaborate dessert framed in the doorway. We would never have known one another if we had not been first cousins but then, to be precise, we do not *know* each other now. With a wetted forefinger he tried to paste back one corner of a curling Excelsior Hotel sticker which threatened to tear off the way the Continental, Paris, and the El Minzah, Tangier, had, leaving his suitcase messy with shreds of bright-colored paper making no design at all, none at all.

"Ah, there you are, Walter. I'm sorry if I'm late. But then I don't think I *am* late. Here, let my porter take your bag; he's a gem." The gem took his suitcase and as they walked to the train, she asked him about New York. But he had no intention of telling her anything about New York while she, he knew, had every intention of discussing Baltimore, the dogs and the cats, and then, more soon than late, she would talk about the Family, about that race of Virginia cavaliers, the Bragnets, who, except for the two of them, had seen fit to vanish in the first half of the twentieth century leaving no monument except the house they had built near Winchester so many, many years ago when the country was new and rich and their apple orchards were still saplings, without blossoms or fruit or history. The name of Bragnet on her lips was always strange and marvelous as though she were intoning, priestesslike, the secret name of a deity, a name which could blast trees, shatter stone, separate lovers, cause twins to be born joined, curdle cream, and, best of all, re-create the house of their common memory with the graceful, long-dead figures of those Bragnets who now lay in the dust of the Episcopal cemetery at Winchester.

But she was not herself today for even after they had taken their seats in the train and he had arranged their suitcases on the rack overhead she did not pronounce the magic name. She wanted deliberately to mystify him, he decided irritably, and the only way he could retaliate was to ask no questions, to pretend that it made no difference to him that for the first time in twenty years he was returning to Winchester, at her inscrutable request.

"I've had such a busy time in Washington this week," said Sybil. "We had several really creative meetings of the Dog Society . . . oh, I know what you feel about our work. I've given up trying to convert you." She laughed heartily; she was blonde-gray, untidy, and as old, he recalled, as their splendid century but unlike the century not scarred at all. Sybil belonged to quite another time, to a world of serene country life where dogs mattered and horses were ridden, where men and women remained married despite all differences . . . a legendary age where emotion had been contained shrewdly by a formal manner which, in its turn, could only flourish in great houses, in high-ceilinged rooms with massive doors and bright brass. Sybil belonged to that world in spirit if not in fact and although she lived in a very small house in Baltimore her whole being suggested vast lawns and ordered gardens: boxwood, clipped and severe, muting the brilliance of roses; formal gardens set in wild uncharted country.

"I never knew that you knew Miss Mortimer," he said at last, forestalling a full report on the health and adventures of her animal friends in Baltimore.

"Oh, I've known her for years. As a matter of fact, I was in the house the day your mother decided to sell the place to her and I've always made it a point to keep in touch, because of the house."

Walter, at this point, was inclined to reminisce about the house (most conversations, it often seemed to him, were no more than competing monologues: a condition which he accepted as human and natural, a part of the universal strangeness) but Sybil had resolutely embarked upon Miss Mortimer: "A sweet, sweet woman. You'll adore her although people don't always, at least not at first. I'm not sure why. Perhaps because she *seems* sad and of course you never really know *what* she'll say or do . . . not that I mean she's eccentric: she's not one of those women who'll do anything for an effect. No, she's quite serious and she has her own little set in Winchester. . . . The Parker family are especially close to her. You remember the girls, don't you? the three sisters? They're all married now and all three live in Winchester . . . isn't that remarkable, keeping so close together? No, I'm really devoted to her. And I've told her so much about you. Why, she's even read one of your books. Anyway, we both decided that after all these years it was time you two got together."

Now it was out, he thought glumly. Sybil was trying to make a match, doubtless to get Bragnet House back into the family again. It was childishly clear: if he married Miss Mortimer and went to live at Bragnet, Sybil would once again have a marvelous big place to keep her dogs and cats. He looked at her suspiciously but she had again shifted the subject: she asked him about his life in New York, inquired graciously if he had written anything new.

"I'm always working." He hated to be asked what he was doing because the temptation to answer at length was so great. Briefly, he told her his plans for the season. And then, upon request, he named their mutual friends one by one and if she liked them he very subtly made them out worse than they were while if she disliked them he discovered heretofore unsuspected virtues in their characters. Neither took the ritual of this conversation very seriously; they were not half done when, like the sudden tolling of a bell, Sybil at last pronounced the name of Bragnet.

"We are the last," she said, with a rich melancholy pride, "you and I. Strange how a family dies out. There were so many Bragnets fifty years ago and now there are only two . . . and the house."

"Which is no longer ours."

"Your mother should never have sold it, never."

"It was too big for us," said Walter and then, before Sybil could embark on that line, he asked if there were to be other guests for the weekend.

"Only her nephew. He's supposed to be very bright. He's still in school. I suppose he'll inherit the house." She paused and Walter noticed she was uneasy, unlike her usual self. "Oh, you'll like her," she added, disjointedly. "I just know you will."

"Why *shouldn't* I?"

"Well, one's friends don't always like each other, do they? And she *is* a little difficult to know . . . rather unnerving at first: but that's only because she's shy."

"I promise not to be terrified."

"I'm sure you won't be." On that odd note the conversation lapsed and both for a long time studied the green countryside beyond the telephone poles which sped past with the regularity of pentameter in a blank verse tragedy.

## II

As far as the eye could see to the south the apple trees grew in ordered ranks upon the rolling land, their leaves glittering green and new and their fruit green too, not yet ripe. Among the orchards, on a hill a mile removed from the asphalt highway, stood the lawn-circled house where Walter Bragnet was born and where his family had lived for so many generations in one long golden season of comfort, untouched by the wars, made rich by their orchards, and sustained from century to century by a proud serenity which was, his cousin Sybil maintained, inspired by the earth in these parts as well as by the rose-red brick house with its Greek Revival colonnade, the last tangible expression of the Bragnet family now reduced to two travelers who, with weekend valises, were deposited by a taxicab before the front door of their old home.

As he rang the doorbell, he wondered what he should feel or, more important, what he *did* feel but as usual he could not determine . . . he would have to wait until he could safely recall this scene in memory; only in the future could he ever discover what, if anything, he had felt: he existed almost entirely in recollection, a peculiarity of considerable value to him as a writer, though disastrous in his life since no event could touch him until it was safely past, until alone in bed at night he could experience in a rush all the emotions that he had been unable to feel at the appropriate time; then he would writhe, knowing it was again too late to act.

The door opened and they were admitted by a Negro in a white jacket, an acquaintance of Sybil's. They inquired solicitously of one another, as Walter followed them up the familiar staircase. The rooms were burdened with the same odor of musty linen, of roses, and of wood smoke which he remembered from his childhood. On the walls of the upstairs corridor hung the same Gillray prints which his grandfather had brought back from England; and, finally, the room to which he was shown was the one he had lived in for nearly eighteen years. He glanced sharply at Sybil, suspecting her of stage-managing; but she only looked at him blandly and remarked, "This used to be your room, didn't it?"

He nodded and followed the servant into his old room: a four-poster bed of pale scarred wood with no canopy, a fireplace with brass phoenixes to support the logs, and, amazingly enough, his books were still on the shelves of the bookcase where he had left them the day that he went off to college. He had always presumed that when his mother sold the house she'd given them away; obviously she had not and here they were: the Oz books, the Arabian Nights, Greek mythology. . . .

As he dressed for dinner, he walked about the room, touching the books but not taking them down, repelling with a certain pleasure whatever force it was that insisted he look at them, become even more involved in Sybil's obscure plot. If she thinks that I'll try to get the house back she's mistaken, he murmured to his own image in the mirror above the chest of drawers. He noticed that his face was flushed as though he had been drinking. It was the heat, he decided, as Sybil rapped on his door and then, before he could speak, proceeded briskly into the room, plain and unfashionable in gossamer gray and wearing yellow diamonds. "I thought we would go down together since you don't know her."

"Together by all means," he said genially, and together they went down the staircase, moving decorously, tactful among their common ghosts.

In the drawing room, Miss Mortimer came forward to meet them and Walter experienced an inexplicable panic; fortunately, Sybil began to talk. "Well, here he is!" she said, embracing her hostess. "I promised I'd bring him and I did!"

"And now he's here," said Miss Mortimer with a smile; her voice was low and he found that he had to be most attentive if he wanted to hear what she said, and he did want to hear, very much. She took his hand in her cool one and drew him over to a sofa. "You have no idea how happy I am to see you at last. Sybil has talked so much about you. I've asked her many times to bring you here but you never came." They sat down, side by side.

"I've been very busy," said Walter, blushing. He paused and then repeated, "I've been very busy." He looked at Sybil, mysteriously helpless; she gave him bright succor: from her wealth of small talk, she tossed a penny to Miss Mortimer: "Where is that nephew of yours? Where's

Stephen?" And Miss Mortimer told them that her nephew would be along presently, that he had been riding all day; he had only just got home. "I am afraid at times I hardly understand him." She smiled at Walter.

"Is he so difficult?" Walter was becoming more used to her, to the situation. She was handsome with regular features, dark hair and eyes, only her mouth was bad, thin and forbidding. She was tall and she sat very straight beside him, her white hands folded in her lap.

"No, not difficult, just strange to me. Others are charmed by him. I expect he's going through a phase and of course when he's older I'll have more in common with him. At the moment he's almost too energetic. He rides horses; he writes poems."

Walter wondered if he would be asked to read the boy's poems, to advise him whether or not to pursue a career of letters. He began to rehearse in his mind his set speech on the vicissitudes of the literary life.

"Yes, Mr. Bragnet, he is at *that* stage. He even has a lady friend, a Winchester girl whom he sees every evening."

Walter looked at her with interest, wondering why she should want to discuss her nephew in such detail. There was something quite un-Virginian in her lack of reticence and he liked her a little more for this.

The nephew entered the room so quietly that Walter was not aware of him until he saw by Miss Mortimer's expression that there was someone behind him. He turned and then, as the boy approached, he rose and they shook hands. Miss Mortimer performed the introductions; then Stephen sat down in a chair between Sybil and Walter, closing the half-circle before the empty fireplace. Sybil asked him numerous questions while Walter listened to neither the questions nor the answers. The boy was uncommonly good-looking with blond hair and skin dark from the sun, the face not yet coarsened by the grain of a beard. Walter was reminded of himself at the same age, living in this house, coming home at vacation time. . . . He glanced suddenly at Miss Mortimer, who had been watching him; she nodded gravely as though she had divined his mood and wanted now to console him with truth rather than with pity: *she* knew how fine it was to be young, in this house. He wondered if he liked her any better for having understood.

Stephen was speaking: "I rode over to the Parker place this afternoon. . . ."

"Did Emily ride with you?" asked Miss Mortimer. Walter knew that Emily must be the summer beloved, traditional figure of green and yellow light.

"No, she didn't," said the boy curtly, looking at his aunt with bright cold eyes. "I went alone, and I saw old Mrs. Parker, who told me to tell you the girls will be over for lunch tomorrow."

"I'm so glad!" said Sybil. "I haven't seen them in years. You remember them, Walter?"

"Certainly." He recalled three sisters: Claudia, Alice, and . . . Laura? But they would hardly be girls now, he thought. They would be middle-aged strangers, inquisitive, tiresome. Restlessly, he shifted his position, faced Stephen more squarely, his back to Miss Mortimer. While Sybil recalled with wonder and pleasure how the girls had all managed to marry Winchester men, Stephen sat straight and polite, his brown fingers interlaced, his eyes on his aunt. Walter wondered why they disliked one another so openly. It was obvious to him that there could be little sympathy between two such dissimilar people; yet this open warfare seemed inappropriate considering the essential casualness of their relationship.

"I hope you'll show Mr. Bragnet some of your poems, Stephen. He's a writer, you know."

"Yes, I know," said Stephen smiling and Walter froze, aware that he was no longer admired, that his vogue had ended many years ago and that other writers now claimed the attention of the young and earnest.

"I should like to see them," said Walter, almost sincerely, enchanted with the boy's apparent ease, with his vitality; and he admired Stephen even more when, with an implacable grace, he faced Miss Mortimer and said, "I never show them to anyone." Then he turned quickly to Walter. "I mean I don't like to have people read them because they aren't very good and because they're private. You know what I mean, don't you?"

"Indeed I do," began Walter.

"By the way," interrupted Miss Mortimer, "why don't you ask Emily to come over for lunch tomorrow? You know I want to meet her. It would be great fun."

"Yes, it would," said Stephen, ironically, cutting short this flanking movement. "I'm sure she'd like to . . . but she can't tomorrow. She wants so much to meet *you,*" he added, grinning.

"Well, another time." And Miss Mortimer serenely accepted checkmate.

"My gracious, Stephen, aren't you awfully young to be having a lady friend?" asked Sybil with that clumsy teasing tone which she often used with the larger dogs. Walter wondered if there were some way in which he might align himself with Stephen against the two women. But his assistance was not needed. Stephen laughed and said, "No, I don't think I am." Then Miss Mortimer led them all into the dining room, where paintings of colonial Bragnets still hung upon the walls, rich by candlelight.

"We *must* get the family portraits away from you," said Sybil.

## III

The next day luncheon was dinner and though much too elaborate, too heavy for a hot day, Walter ate greedily. He had spent a restless night in the bed of his childhood and now he was tired, exhausted from lack of sleep. The Parker sisters were a further nuisance. They irritated him unreasonably. Now middle-aged, they were resolutely jolly, and appallingly confident. After lunch, still gabbling, the sisters sat side by side on a sofa in the library . . . like judges, thought Walter, loosening his belt, feeling ill. He was wondering if he should go to his room for pills (he took many pills; his heart murmured) when Miss Mortimer turned to him and they talked intimately and at length of dreams, of a particular dream he had had the night before in which he had found himself in a black sea, drowning.

Miss Mortimer appeared youthful today, even desirable, and he wondered how he could have had such a disagreeable first impression of her. During lunch she had talked to him of his books and long before the over-rich pudding had been served, he realized that she was not only intelligent but uncannily sensitive to mood, knowing when to praise, when to chide. He had not felt so easy with a new person in many years. She even divined his physical discomfort for, suddenly, she suggested he go to Stephen outside on the terrace, where she would join them presently. Both excused themselves and the Parker sisters, busy now with their knitting and their judgments, seemed not in the least annoyed, so perfectly at home were they, so used to one another's company. Even Sybil defected to observe the old stables.

The sun was hot, its light diffused by clouds; for a moment Walter stood on the terrace, dizzy and blind. Then Stephen spoke to him. "You escaped."

"Yes." The world righted itself and Walter saw the green lawn before him, bending toward orchards. "I escaped."

Stephen pulled two deck chairs together and they sat down. Walter was alarmed to find that he felt no better; could the sun be bad for him? His heart thumped irregularly. His pulses fluttered.

"You lived in this house, didn't you?"

Walter nodded. "I was about your age when I went away to college. While I was gone, my mother sold the place and we moved to Washington."

"Did you like living here?"

"Oh, very much: don't you?"

"I like the place itself," said the boy slowly. "I like to ride. . . ."

"But you don't like your aunt." He was suddenly too tired and too ill to keep to the periphery; it was easier to go to the center immediately.

"No, I don't like her, I never have." He smiled. "She says I'll understand her better when I'm older."

"Perhaps you will." Both were silent then. Neither chose to pursue this indiscreet, unchivalrous tack.

Stephen played idly with a large winged ant and Walter watched as the ant would climb the boy's thumb only to be pulled back, to begin again its laborious ascent. Little beads of perspiration gleamed on Stephen's brown forehead and his hair glittered in the sun. Finally, the ant escaped. "I'm going to take a walk. You want to come with me?"

"No, I had better stay here." Walter wanted to go but he did not dare. With a sudden, inexplicable sorrow, he watched the boy walk across the lawn. Not till he was out of sight did Walter shut his eyes and rest. Murmuring summer held him. Sharp sweet odor of new-cut grass; croaking of frogs in a distant pond. He was nearly asleep when he heard voices: the ladies in the library were discussing him. He knew that he should get up and walk away but he did not stir.

"He never married. I wonder why." Walter could identify none of the voices: the sisters spoke alike.

"Not the sort."

"I hate it when they have no children. Oh, I know it's sentimental . . ."

"Well, he has none and that's that, and we have our work to do. He's had a pleasant time."

"I should say so, and he missed all our wars. How did he manage that?"

"Heart condition."

"I suspect that *that's* our cue."

"Does he still write?"

"No, he seems to have given up."

"At fifty-one? That's rather early. Perhaps if he were to have another few years, an even sixty . . ."

"No! It *must* be now!"

They lowered their voices then and talked of knitting . . . one of them had found a knot in her yarn; they also talked of accidents and diseases and he listened less attentively, shaken by what he had heard, wondering if he might not still be dreaming: how could these women have known so much about his life? so many things not even his closest friends knew?

". . . run down by a cab in front of the Union Station."

"Oh, not that, not *that*!"

"Blood poisoning? A scratch? A fever . . . ?"

"Out of character. When in doubt, be obvious."

"The heart . . . *again*?"

"And why not? Why confect some elaborate plot when procedure is so clearly indicated? There's no reason to be bizarre."

"Very well: the heart . . . but when? Miss Mortimer is restless."

"Tomorrow on the train? as he lifts his suitcase to put it on the rack . . ."

"No, not another day. I mean, look . . . it's absolutely strung out to the end. Besides, Miss Mortimer's already on the terrace, waiting for us, poor angel."

"I'm afraid I can't get this last knot undone."

"Then use scissors. Here."

He could neither speak nor move now. He was conscious of a massive constriction in his chest. As he gasped for breath, nearly blind in the sun, Miss Mortimer appeared to him over the edge of the receding world, and he saw that she was smiling, a summer flower in her gleaming hair, an expected darkness in her lovely eyes.

# THE JUDGMENT OF PARIS

The Judgment of Paris (1952) is set in early post–World War II Europe. It dramatizes against a mythological framework the adventures of a young American law school graduate in search of vocation and self-identity. The authorial voice is sometimes satirical and aloof, but at other times the narrator is beneficently sympathetic with his hero's situation and imparts to *Judgment* some of the flavor of the traditional bildungsroman. This is the first of Vidal's novels in which he moves away from the tradition of Hemingwayesque realism that had characterized much of his earlier writing. Many of the minor characters are etched with satiric sharpness.

Philip Warren, an American abroad, brings a touch of innocence to the world of European experience. He first visits Rome, where he is thrilled by the remains of classical civilization, begins an impersonal, pleasurable love affair with Regina Durham, an American (in Rome with her powerful political husband) who wants to be his mentor in American politics, and gets involved briefly with a group of expatriate homosexuals and monarchists. Mostly through indecisiveness, partly through curiosity, he allows Lord Glenellen and Clyde Norman, who appear in the following excerpt, to involve him in their machinations to restore the monarchy. Sent on an absurd undercover mission to St. Elmo's Church in Amalfi, he discovers "the fine balance between good and evil." He soon rejects Regina's offer to help him attain a brilliant political career. From Rome, he goes to Egypt, where he engages with the second of the three ladies who represent the mythological alternatives that Philip, like the Paris of Homeric myth, must choose between. Finally, in Paris, he makes his choice.

# From *The Judgment of Paris,* Chapter One

*She wore her trauma like a plume. When she was seven an elderly man attempted to have his way with her in a telephone booth at Grand Central (her mother had been buying a ticket to Peekskill). Although she was in no way defiled, the shock was great and, to this day, she was so terrified of the telephone that she was forced always to compose innumerable messages on pale blue paper for the instruction and pleasure of those acquaintances whom she might otherwise, in a less perilous era, have telephoned.*

That was all there was to it, he thought sadly, studying this one paragraph typed neatly at the top of a sheet of fine white paper: there would be no more; he was confident of that. "She" was lost to the world, trauma and all, and the contents of those messages on blue paper would never be known. She had emerged in his mind one day, clear and precise, a lady of the highest, most Meredithean comedy, with just a trace of something more racy, vulgar even, to give her a proper contemporary relevance, but he had lost her for good after that first paragraph, watched with helpless resignation as she sank back into a limbo of unarranged words, convincing him that he would never be a man of letters: not, of course, that he had ever thought too seriously of becoming one; rather, it had seemed a pleasant way to spend a life, composing sentences day after day with a tight smile on his lips and a view of mountains, or the sea, from a study window.

His failure was complete, however, and he knew with a sad certainty that his lady of the blue notes (not a bad title, he thought, wondering if there might not be a double meaning in it: something to do with music) would remain unrevealed forever, this paragraph her *alpha* and *omega.* But that is that for now, he thought, and he gave up literature as he had given up painting and music the year before, having composed one art song to a three-line Emily Dickinson poem, and painted one nonobjective painting in the style of Mondrian. "I am not an artist," he murmured to himself with some satisfaction, putting the paper back into his suitcase and ending forever a never too urgent dream of creativity.

The problem of what to do with his life still existed, of course; but time undoubtedly would arrange all that, he decided, removing the Hotel Excelsior, Napoli, tag which had only this morning been stuck on his new suitcase by a hotel porter whom he had never seen until that moment and who expected, but never received, a large tip for this superfluous service, thus further darkening the none too bright reputation of Americans in postwar Italy. There had been a scene as he got into the taxi but he carried it off well and at the station, as an act of contrition, he gave the cab driver a thick pile of torn and dirty *lire.*

He hated scenes, he thought, looking out the train window at the green countryside rippling uncertainly beyond the solid fact of glass, shimmering in the heat of a white spring sun.

Philip Warren sighed happily. He was here at last: Italy, Europe, a year of leisure, a time for decision, a prelude to the distinguished fugue his life was sure to be, once he got really to it, once the delightful prelude had been played to its conclusion among the foreign cities.

He glanced out the window again, looking instinctively for modern ruins which he hoped would not be there: the way one reluctantly examines the remains of a dead dog on a country road. Fortunately, there were no ruins in sight, except the ancient and respectable ones. Bits of an aqueduct arched over the plains of Latium, brown-brick against the Apennines. . . . The Apennines, he murmured the name aloud, with reverence. Yes, he was on the march to Rome.

"This is your room," said the clerk, showing him a room as scrubbed and neat as the young clerk himself, a fresh-faced Swiss. A big balconied window looked out onto a quiet Roman street of tall trees against the baroque façades of seventeenth-century houses—all embassies now, remarked the clerk, opening the window and letting in the sunlit air. Then after a quick briefing on the meaning and the uses of the various bells, Philip was left alone in this handsome room with its feather bed and numerous pillows, its old-fashioned bathtub hidden, along with a bidet, behind curtains. Very happy, he unpacked.

Now then: what does he look like? What sort of man or boy or youth is Philip Warren? Well, it is much too early to draw any conclusions about his character since he is hardly yet revealed. On the other hand, there is something to be said about his appearance. The face, certainly, must be described before its owner ventures out into the Roman afternoon and as he has not yet looked into a mirror (the usual device for describing one's protagonist), let it be noted that Philip Warren is twenty-eight and fairly handsome, slim, unembarrassed by overdeveloped muscles, flat-bellied (could one ever have a protagonist who was young and stout?) and though not tall, not short (all things to all men obviously); he is, then, of middle height, his face more square than oval, his cheekbones prominent. His nose is unheroic, small and stubby, making him look even younger than he is. His eyes are a dark blue, not very interesting but, as one writer once said of another writer's eyes, interested. His skin is still boyish and taut and except for a deep line between fair brows he has no outward marks of age or experience or character in his face.

His body, for those who are interested in such things, was well formed and greatly admired by the not inconsiderable company which had, at one time or another (and on some occasions at the same time), enjoyed it. On the inside of his left thigh, near the groin, a small butterfly had been tattooed, a memento of the war when he had been a junior Naval officer on leave in Honolulu. His speaking voice was manly but marred by the faintest lisp, a defect which he hated although, unknown to him, it was his greatest charm for, instead of sounding sissy as he imagined, it made him seem very boyish and charming: a puzzled youthful man in need of a woman's protection. As a result his success with women was quite remarkable not only because of this boyishness but also because he genuinely liked them in an age and nation where, generally speaking, they were less admired than usual.

"Do you play bridge?"

"Why yes," said Philip, turning, as a stout bald man moved apologetically into the room from the hall.

"I'm so glad. I do hope you'll excuse my dropping in like this but your door was open and I live right down the hall and we do have so few people in Rome who even *play* bridge, much less *want* to play it. You do want to play?"

"Yes, not now, though. Some other time perhaps."

"Of course, of course . . . I was thinking of the future, not the present. You play it decently, I hope?"

"Rather," said Philip, meaning "rather decently" but, in the excitement of the moment, he found himself parodying the other's British accent.

"I'm so glad. Are you from home?"

"No," said Philip, already alerted. "I'm from America." He blushed as he said this unaccustomed phrase, as though he had begun suddenly to unfurl and snap, all red and white and blue in a chauvinistic breeze.

"Yes? Well, one never knows any more. The world is becoming one at last, is it not? Pleasant thought, or is it? Ah well, soon it will be a *fait accompli* and no concern of ours. My name, if I may introduce myself, is Clyde Norman." Information of this sort was formally exchanged and Mr. Norman gave him a card, a very proper sort of card which declared that Mr. Norman was a director of the Fabian Trade Mission, otherwise undefined. "I've lived in Rome almost all my life, you know. Stayed here all through the war. Very risky. Quite a story in all that, I suppose. If one likes stories, eh? But now I'm sure you have many things to do . . ."

They agreed, then, that it might be a good idea to have a drink together, to celebrate Philip's arrival.

Mr. Norman was splendidly knowing, decided Philip, as they strolled from the hotel to the Via Veneto, the fashionable street of Rome. He was able to say something amusing about almost everything mentioned, or at least he spoke as though what he said might prove amusing if one fully understood the various references.

Dingy youths stood on street corners, peddling black-market cigarettes, candy bars and currency. The streets otherwise were discouragingly familiar. The buildings were either severe and formal or baroque and formal, their stucco façades a weathered gray-gold, the color of Rome. The day was so very fine, however, that this momentary disappointment was succeeded by a sudden elation, a blitheness which he had seldom experienced since childhood. He controlled a sudden impulse to slip away from Clyde Norman, to run as fast as he could until he had reached the Forum, where he would sit among the broken marble and recall Horace and Keats and think how good it was to live, or to die, for both seemed equally desirable, the dark and the light, one meaningless without the other, twins and opposites. But he dared not mention this to Mr. Norman who was, he gathered, more concerned with details than with abstractions.

"In thirty years one picks up quite a bit, you know. One comes to know the city *behind* the city, if you get what I mean."

"I certainly do."

"England is like a foreign country to me now. I hardly know how to act when I'm there, and the climate . . . do you know English weather?"

"By reputation."

"Damp, very damp. And from September to May everyone has a cold . . . ah, here we are, the Via Veneto."

They paused for a moment, surveying this celebrated thoroughfare. Mr. Norman was somewhat proprietary while Philip found it not strange at all. The street reminded him of a minor avenue in Washington, D.C., except that it curved up a slight hill to a massive brick arch and fissured wall behind which could be glimpsed the rich green of gardens. The gardens of the Villa Borghese, according to his companion, who indicated various other sights of interest: the Excelsior Hotel, an outdoor café called Doney's where, presently, they sat in iron chairs at iron tables, the sidewalk between them and the main part of the café.

"This is the center," said Mr. Norman. "So many cities have no center. London for instance has none, or rather too many: the Strand, Westminster, Piccadilly Circus, but no place where one can go and see everybody. No cafés like this one where, sooner or later, those one wants to see will come. I have always thought London must have been like this in the days of the coffeehouses." He ordered apéritifs with unfamiliar names. Then they sat back to watch. Philip felt as though he were sitting in a theater just as the lights had begun to dim, that expectant moment before the discordancies of an orchestra trying its instruments become an overture. Mr. Norman, with a smile, figuratively tapped his music stand with an imaginary baton and the curtain rose as one of the late dictator's mistresses, a plump little woman in black, walked slowly between the crowded tables of chattering people, accompanied by a plump little chow, its sad face a doggish facsimile of her own.

"I always thought mistresses were beautiful," said Philip who had thought nothing of the kind but, having been trapped in a role—naïve, youthful, American—had the good manners not to confuse the other by assuming a character closer to his own.

"They say she used to be," said Mr. Norman, watching her as she nodded to numerous acquaintances who nodded back and then, when she was out of earshot, discussed her eagerly, her health, morals and current fortune.

"But then . . ." said Mr. Norman, solemnly, pausing as though expecting an epigram on the nature of courtesans to spring sharp and original to his thin bluish lips; but as none came he took a sip of his apéritif instead. He was, Philip decided, one of those charming men whose way of speaking is so ceremonious and shrewd that they seem to be scoring one linguistic hit after another on the all too vulnerable target of human character while, actually, they do little more than repeat the clever sayings of other men . . . which takes a good memory, decided Philip tolerantly, not to mention a sense of timing and, finally, a style which was set if not by Dr. Johnson than by Horace Walpole in the great days of aristocracy, after the perfect pearl of the Renaissance was misshapen by a rigid manner and the baroque was born of that tension between nature and artifice. Philip wondered if he would have an opportunity to tell Mr. Norman that the word "baroque" came from the Portuguese *barroco,* which meant a misshapen pearl. Later, perhaps, if they spoke of architecture (Philip was good at guiding conversations into home waters where, with infinite skill, he could scuttle the barks of others with some torpedo of esoterica, some bit of knowledge, properly timed; it was, he knew, the surest way to total unpopularity in a pretentious age).

"There are of course many different sets in Rome. The Church, the government (which isn't much these days), and the old nobility which is very fine and very distant, set apart. One hardly ever sees them. They live the way they've always lived in those *palazzi* and they are quite scornful, I suspect, of the rest of the world, of people whose ancestry does not go back to the Republic, as they maintain their own does, to the Republic and even further in some cases, to the gods."

"But then doesn't everyone go back that far?"

"Yes, but the descent is not recorded."

"Caesar traced his family back to Venus, didn't he?"

"Fully documented, too. Which proves I think that all genealogy is myth," said Mr. Norman smiling, displaying two rows of British teeth in a state of only partial repair. "But tell me why you are here, Mr. Warren, if I may ask."

"You certainly may," said Philip cordially. Then he paused awkwardly, destroying the illusion of cordiality with this ill-timed hesitation. Discreetly Mr. Norman began to murmur, to back away from the personal until Philip, the reason for his hesitation still not clear to him, said at last, "To travel. I have a year, you see."

"A year? Is that all? I mean a year for what?"

"A year to travel in, to make up my mind."

"About your future?"

"Yes, about the future."

"I wonder if one can ever do precisely that."

"You mean come to a decision about life in a given period?"

"Yes, to make a positive, irrevocable decision. I shouldn't think it could be done, or should be done."

"I would like to try, even so," said Philip vaguely, distracted by the sight of a well-known American actor who strode quickly by, scowling like Cato and carrying under one arm a new and shiny book with its provocative title in bold black letters on red: *Decadence.* The actor disappeared into the door of the Excelsior Hotel.

"Accept the moment: there is nothing else."

"Perhaps not. Still, I am nearly thirty and . . ."

"You look so young! I thought you were a college boy."

"Thank you. And I feel I must decide what to do with the rest of my life."

"Even though, terrible thought, it might be, considering the state of the world (and pardoning the impertinence of my gloom), very short?"

"Or, considering my natural cowardice and cunning, longer than the average."

"Ah, now you exaggerate. I only suggested that your life might be shortened to convince you of the very real folly of making long-range plans: they are just *not* the thing to do nowadays."

Philip appeared to ponder this pronouncement while the waiter brought them more apéritifs, pronouncing their name "Cinzano" as he slopped the glasses before them on the table.

The day, Philip decided, was perfect in every way: clouds burdened the west, preceding the golden globe of the afternoon sun as it sank rapidly through the blue to the seven hills of the city, to the sea and to the new world beyond that. The day was warm, without wind but not hot, not the way he had been warned it would be in the spring. Conscious of weather and bemused, he said yes and he said no as his pleasant companion advised him to accept what was, since there would be, for all he knew, no more. As he had already planned to do precisely that, to live as he pleased for a year, he found that he could agree with the older man and, by agreeing, could establish a tentative friendship.

"What precisely do you plan to do with this year of yours . . . this climacteric in your life?"

Philip smiled. "I haven't the slightest idea. Sit at this café, perhaps. Or go and walk in those gardens over there. Or journey up the Nile to its source."

"You have no plan?"

"None."

"Wise! Very wise . . . and then you're so fortunate."

"In what way?"

"To be young."

"One doesn't realize it at the time. I'm not conscious of any serious blessing. Perhaps I will be one day."

"You will. How extraordinary though that you should feel that way. Are you really so detached? Or like so many of the politic young men nowadays, have you merely learned the proper responses?"

"You're too quick," said Philip, taken aback, not prepared for the other's shrewdness, for of course it was true: he had learned to say many things which got him easily and with no exertion the respect of his elders, statements which he knew well in advance would amuse or shock or please and which had little or no relation to what he actually thought. It was a schoolboy's trick and he felt a sudden shame to be playing again the brightest boy with the headmaster, as though he were still fourteen and ruthless, without a heart.

Mr. Norman had the grace not to pursue his advantage; instead he remarked, "And then you are fortunate because you have money."

Philip laughed. "I have none," he said.

"But you are able to travel well . . . That's what I mean by having money. You are not caught like me in a web of chicanery, trying to make your few pounds support you by doing all the squalid black-market things."

"In that sense, yes, I'm fortunate . . . I have the correct nationality."

"Indeed you have." Mr. Norman drank his Cinzano moodily and Philip watched the street become more crowded as the golden light darkened and the evening star shone silver over the gardens. He was aware, after this discussion of currency, that he would be called upon to pay for the drinks and this thought did not sadden him for he was, after all, a young man with an income, a small one but sufficient for the traveler's purpose and he knew that he would entertain many strangers before he was done and though none of them might prove to be angels in disguise they had, he knew, a right to his hospitality since he had come among them to learn what he could.

Mr. Norman suddenly got to his feet and shook the hand of a stooped middle-aged man with a fire-red face in which, shadowed by a bird's-beak nose, two watery blue eyes danced about seemingly unable to focus (although Philip was aware that he himself had been immediately comprehended by the newcomer in one quick intense glance).

"Sit with us, Ayre," said Mr. Norman. "I want you to meet a young friend of mine, a new friend, only just arrived from America. His name is Philip Warren."

"How do you do?" said the older man in a curiously accented British voice, most of the stresses falling in unexpected places, a mock-Welsh voice as Philip later learned. "I can sit just a moment. I'm expecting Guido. I said I'd meet him here. He's late. Why is he always late? Why?"

"That's just his way."

"There is of course a possibility that *I* am late. I never know."

"I'm sure he'll be along presently," said Mr. Norman with quiet authority and then he turned to Philip and said in a voice from which every trace of pride had been resolutely banished to accord harmoniously with a Stoic attitude: "This, Mr. Warren, is Lord Glenellen." Since they were now all seated, Philip could only incline his head respectfully at the peer who was now insulting the waiter in faultless Italian, or what sounded to Philip (and to the waiter) like faultless Italian. Mr. Norman watched his countryman with some satisfaction, smiling at the more colorful epithets and frowning furiously when the waiter attempted a mild insult or two on his own.

"About the coffee," said Glenellen finally, as the waiter walked away, "coffee I had yesterday. It made me ill."

"What will you have now?"

"Not a thing. I think perhaps I'll go to the Excelsior for some decent coffee."

"And not wait for Guido?"

"He could wait for me, you know. There *are* worse fates."

"Of course, Ayre, of course."

"You're an American, aren't you?" The blue eyes, milky as though filmed by cataracts, turned on him disconcertingly, avoiding his eyes, though, concentrating instead on the line of his chin, the curve of his mouth.

"Yes, from New York, the state. . . ."

"Ah, I know. I know. Don't tell me. There's a state named that as well as a city. I was there, you see. Long, long ago. I adored Harlem. Is it still going?"

"Very much so."

"Do you visit there much?"

"No, almost never."

"Well, times change. Where do people go?"

"Nowhere in particular. There seems to be little difference now between one part of the city and another. The East Side is no different from Greenwich Village."

"Ah, I had forgotten the Village! Has it changed much? Is it still amusing?"

"I expect so. I don't live in the city, though. I live up the Hudson River, at a town called Hudson."

"All great civilizations," announced Mr. Norman, checking in, "have flourished on the banks of rivers. There has never been a civilization of any importance on a lake, for instance."

"Is that so?" Philip was polite.

"Do you plan to stay here long?" asked Glenellen.

"I have no plans."

"A gentleman of leisure," said Mr. Norman, with a father's smile.

"Fortunate boy . . . to have no plans. Now I, on the other hand, am burdened with plans. I have every day and every hour of every week outlined for months ahead. Dinner with this person and tea with that one. A week end at Ischia; a week in Vienna. I think sometimes I am overorganized because, in spite of all my activity, I have no time for work."

"Work?"

"Oh my goodness, yes."

"He composes," said Mr. Norman, giving a brother's smile this time at the lean figure beside him. "He composes music," he added, "chamber music."

"When I have time," said Glenellen uneasily. "Tell me: where are you stopping?"

"He's at my hotel," said Mr. Norman. "Isn't that a coincidence? I barged right in on him this afternoon and asked him if he played bridge. He does. Aren't you pleased?"

"I am pleased that he is here, Clyde," said the other courteously. "Besides, you know perfectly well that I seldom play cards."

"Ah, your barren life, Ayre. I had forgotten."

"I have my compensations."

"Yes, yes, indeed yes. Innumerable."

"And unmentionable!" They both laughed loudly and Philip looked from one to the other, puzzled as one always is by the private references of acquaintances newly met, the jokes which suggest vast unexplored areas of vice and virtue unrevealed to the outsider.

"But to consider you: you intend to follow your instinct, obey your whims, traveling here and there without a plan?"

"Exactly. I shall look at buildings I have heard about, absorb as much scenery as I can . . . I'm just a tourist, you know, not even a student like the rest. Then when I've had as much as I can take, I will go home and do something."

"Do something? Do what?" Glenellen leaned forward as though suddenly eager to know truth, to attend at a revelation.

But Philip was not equal to the moment nor for that matter was he in the mood to be examined, to speak of himself when for once there was so much outside himself that he wanted to see and to know: he suddenly resented the attentions of these two odd Englishmen who, for all he knew, were mocking him.

"Whatever I can," he said with a heavy attempt at lightness. "Take a job . . . I'm a lawyer, you know. I graduated from law school last June, from the one at Harvard."

"A lawyer?" Glenellen pronounced the word as though not quite sure what it meant. "How peculiar. No, I don't mean peculiar: I mean to say it seems so strange to find a personable young American who is not trying to be a painter or some such romantic thing among the ruins of our old Europe. I suppose, Clyde, that we see only the romantic ones, the ones who have got away for a time."

"I think it most impressive, his being a lawyer. Original even."

"But, my dear Clyde, does one *want* to be impressed by young men? Isn't it far more agreeable to be *pleased* by them, charmed by their freshness and impracticality?"

"*I* am charmed," said Mr. Norman, patting Philip's knee as the sun unexpectedly set: the light going from gold to gray, the air from warm to cool.

"Will you go into politics?" asked Glenellen.

"I may, yes. I've thought about it. My family is in politics, back home."

"You find it interesting?"

"Oh yes . . . but for a career, I don't know."

"And what are your politics?"

"Darkly reactionary, I suppose. In practice, however, I should, if ever in office, devote my time to staying there."

"No convictions . . . wonderful youth!" exclaimed Mr. Norman, drinking the rest of his Cinzano. "How different you are from the young men of my day. How much more sensible. Tell me, would you like an ice or something? a little cake?"

"I don't think so . . . thanks."

Glenellen looked at him thoughtfully. "I would like very much to have a chat with you one day about European politics. I have certain insights which may interest you, certain schemes which . . . but more I cannot say, for now. Though let me add that when I was your age, I, like you, was interested primarily in the progress of my own life, my time given to hobbies. . . ."

"Hobbies?"

"A joke of Lord Glenellen's, Mr. Warren," said Clyde Norman quickly, too quickly thought Philip, and he wondered what was not being said for his benefit.

"A joke, Mr. Warren, yes, a joke . . . and here is the wicked Guido. Late! You're late! Hear me?"

The wicked Guido heard and he smiled a smile like polished bone. He was a slender well-proportioned Italian boy with a head like a Michelangelo and a body, as much as could be seen through his suit (a great deal), as fine as a Donatello.

"This is Guido," said Mr. Norman urbanely as he and Philip rose and shook hands, while the high clear voice of the seated peer inveighed against the boy's character, accused him in English and Italian of monstrous crimes, denunciations which were received by the youth with a lovely smile.

"I was on my way stopped," he said, finally, when the querulous voice had paused for an instant; his English was good if original. "I find my brother has taken the only white good shirt of mine and so I went to my brother to receive the shirt once more for me. I want to look nice," he added simply, expressing his philosophy in five words.

"Shirts, suits, shoes, watches. . . ." Glenellen sighed and turned to Philip. "Those are the only things that really matter to these people."

"I like the motorcars, too," giggled Guido. "I like to drive very fast in *Alfa Romeo.* Oh good car, good car. I take cars apart. I know about things inside. Were you a soldier?" he asked all in one breath, noticing Philip as though for the first time.

"A sailor, for several years."

"In the war? In Italy?"

"In the war . . . in the Pacific."

"I knew many soldiers here. You might know some of them maybe. Nice men . . . very kind. I was fourteen years old so they gave me presents. A camera was given to me by one captain but it was stolen from me by one thief I know and he sells it."

"Come, Guido," said Glenellen, rising. "You can tell your stories to Mr. Warren another time." He turned to Philip. "I would like to see you again one day soon, if I may." They shook hands. "Do you know the Baths of Nero?"

"I'm afraid not. I've only just arrived."

"That's so. Of course you wouldn't have had a chance. . . . Well, should you have a moment to spare, do drop by tomorrow afternoon around four. I always arrive at four and leave at five, like clockwork. . . . Marvelous for the figure, I've found. Not that you need to think of that quite yet, but we could talk. I have a plan which might interest you. Now I'm off. Many thanks, my dear Clyde, for introducing this young man to me."

Farewells were made and Glenellen hurried away, followed at a more leisurely pace by Guido, immaculate in his good white shirt.

"Splendid fellow," said Mr. Norman as they watched the older man and the youth turn the corner beyond the Excelsior Hotel. "Difficult of course . . . one of the last of those eccentric peers my country used to produce with such abandon in the old days. The supply seemed inexhaustible but now of course, with currency restrictions and so on, Ayre is the last, the very last of a great line . . . and under a cloud, too."

"A cloud? But why?"

"Oh, for so many reasons. His life has been too colorful for one thing, too many hobbies. Then there was the scandal about his wife. I suppose you were too young to remember that."

"What happened to her?"

"I'm afraid he set fire to her at a party in the British Embassy at Berlin. There was the most terrible fuss made . . . relations were strained at the time and this was added fuel to the blaze, as it were. They got him out of Germany as quickly as possible. The Ambassador was furious and the party, needless to say, was ruined."

"And his wife?"

"Lady Glenellen was burned to a crisp. Fortunately they were able to get the Glenellen diamonds back . . . she had been wearing a good many of them at dinner, a number of quite important pieces too. The settings were badly melted, I believe, but Ayre had them remounted later in the Etruscan fashion, a stroke of genius as it later developed, for he started an Etruscan vogue in jewelry which lasted a number of years."

"Was he never prosecuted?"

"For making Etruscan art the vogue? Heavens no! He received a decoration from the Pope."

"I meant prosecuted for burning up his wife."

"Ah well," Mr. Norman gestured vaguely, "she was an unpopular woman, a great hypochondriac and a bit of a religious maniac, too. Then of course there was some question as to whether the fire was his fault or hers."

"Who *was* responsible?"

"Who can say? All I know is that, as the ladies were getting up from dinner to go into the drawing room, he picked up the candelabra and hurled it at her, shouting, 'Be Joan of Arc, *if you dare!*' It was the addition of the 'if you dare' which saved him from more stern consequences since the phrase implied, you see, a certain choice in the matter. That she elected of her own free will to *be* Joan of Arc demonstrated a deliberate choice on her part and, as a result, he could hardly be held responsible for an act in which she so obviously concurred, perhaps even precipitated since it was well known that she had always expected some sort of martyrdom . . . ever since the day she married Glenellen, in fact, fully aware of the extent and the nature of his hobbies. Her life was one long expiation for the original sin, as Catholics say, of having been born."

"You must tell me about his hobbies one day."

"I should be glad to, but best of all observe him yourself. He will tell you all; show you everything . . . he has no discretion, alas. You should go, by the way, to the Baths of Nero tomorrow."

"Are they interesting?"

"I have always thought so. It depends upon one's taste, of course." Mr. Norman looked at him furtively and Philip experienced a sudden weariness as he recognized the ancient pattern, traditional and obvious, revealed perfunctorily, with little hope and less ceremony. He gave it back to Mr. Norman: gently, firmly, he folded it up and placed it on the table before him; then, wiping the dust from his hands, he guided the conversation to an end.

Mr. Norman sighed. "I shall see you at the Baths then. I often go there for the health's sake . . . to lose weight. I get stout in the summer and slim in the winter, unlike the rest of the world."

"Does Lord Glenellen live in Rome or England?"

"In Rome. He isn't allowed to enter England."

"Why not?"

"They disapprove of him. At least the Home Office does. Being officials, they have no humor. They don't recognize his very real value."

"Why do they disapprove?"

"Hobbies. But now it's getting very late. Where do you plan to have dinner?"

"I hadn't thought."

"Then try the hotel. The food is very good there. I should like to dine with you but I have a function I must attend . . . dull sort of affair, part of my job, I fear." When the waiter came there was a struggle for the check which Philip won, as both knew from the beginning he would.

"Awfully good of you, really, but now of course you must allow me to take you to dinner one night this week. Until tomorrow then . . . the Baths of Nero. The hotel will direct you."

They parted and Philip made his way alone through the darkening streets to the hotel, elated and curious, aware not only of himself but of the city, too. For an instant, he was no longer separate but a part of it: an airy and fantastic bridge across the gulf challenged him and, deliberately, he moved across it, above the dark division, to the other side where strangers were.

# From Chapter Four

IN THE MIDDLE of the sky the white moon rode among black and silver clouds, blown north by the dry desert wind of Africa tempered with sea's salt but not much cooled from the long journey. The townspeople seemed more exuberant tonight than usual, as though celebrating unconsciously some old festival of the moon's fullness.

Philip paused a moment before the largest waterfront café. Inside men and women were singing and dancing. One tigerish, black-frizzy-haired woman (descendant of some Moorish or Carthaginian sailor) was doing a wild dance for the men, her skirt pulled up to her fat thighs, her legs moving like fleshy pistons in time to the music.

Philip, as unobtrusively as possible, slipped into the café and watched until, amid laughter and curses and cheering, the dancer stopped and the usual sentimental laments were wrung stickily from the fiddle and the accordion. Everyone was hot, sweating, flimsily dressed and happy, all that he'd ever imagined the joyful peasant to be. Yet he knew that if he looked close he would see what the outsider never saw: fear, antagonisms, envy, all the usual human characteristics accentuated by this summer land, the violence checked by pleasure in the evening, by piety and labor during the bedazzled day. Feeling much better, Philip left the café and turned into the street which led to the Bridge of St. Elmo.

Even these ordinarily dark streets were well lighted, for the doors that were usually sealed against the night were open and townspeople sat on their own doorsteps or lounged about the cobbled streets beneath the full moon which hung, now rich and golden, swollen with summer, among its clouds, like a lantern in the dark.

On the other side of the bridge, all was quiet. A few houses were set back against the hill on terraces above the town, accessible only by foot. Set apart from these houses was the ruin of the Church of St. Elmo, surrounded by olive trees and ilex, by giant cypresses, black and mourning in the moon's light.

But before he could get to the church he first had to climb many steps, each, it seemed to him, more steep than the one before and he was thankful for the south wind when he finally arrived, breathing heavily, at the top of the steps, where he paused a moment to rest. Amalfi was below him, its yellow light gleaming in a pattern as inscrutable as that of the white stars which shone everywhere, one beyond another, in the midnight sky. Far out to sea, a ship with blinking lights was making its way to Africa and, as he stared at the ship on the dark horizon, a star fell in the west, a delicate sudden arc of light.

He turned and walked slowly down a narrow flagstone path to the grove of trees where the church, now black and silver, stood like a ship wrecked on a sandbar, roofless, its windows empty as idiot's eyes and its towers gone. He stood for a moment looking up at the cracked stone towers. Insects whirred drily in the trees and, far far away, he heard the faint tinkle of music, the echo of laughter in the town below.

Conscious of his danger, dreading ghosts more than police or Communists, he entered the church and stood in the roofless nave surveying the shattered arch beneath which the high altar, now a mound of rubble, had once been. As he moved down the nave the noise of the cicadas abruptly ceased. He stopped then, waiting for the ordinary sounds of the night to resume, but they did not; the silence persisted. He looked up at the moon, now bone-white, no longer golden, sailing through the black and silver clouds which separated solid earth from empty sky like an antique shawl from Spain thrown over that one-half world beneath.

He waited, trembling, before the mound where the altar had been. Minutes, hours, years, eras passed and still he waited, frozen by moonlight into a pallid facsimile of his living self. He saw the church as it once was: stained glass, wine-red and cerulean, filled the empty windows and translated clear sunlight into rainbows, while figures in vivid costumes moved about in ritual attitude and celebrated the ancient Mass. Then windows shattered and the roof fell; the towers crashed down the hillside and, as he stood there, even those walls which still stood buttressed all around him fell at last and he was alone in the dust, the burnt stumps of cypress and ilex and olive around him, and the sea where the town was.

He moved. The cicadas resumed their monotonous whirring and the moon was hidden by clouds. He looked at his watch and saw by its luminous dial that he had been there ten minutes, that it was now fifteen minutes past twelve and neither conspirator nor policeman had shared with him the ghosts and the constant shadows.

"Hello!" he said in a loud voice, which frightened him; but no one answered. Resolutely, he explored the church, pushing his way past the fallen masonry into chapels where wild grapes grew. He went everywhere except down into the dark hole behind the high altar where, he knew, the illustrious dead had once been buried in ice-cold crypts, the earth of their bodies now holding, indiscriminately, nests of scorpions and the roots of flowers, in decay, as in life, the fine balance between good and evil kept. Satisfied at last that no one living was in the church, he left.

As he stepped across the stone threshold he noticed something gleaming on the lintel. He picked it up, but since the moon was hidden he could not identify it in the dark; it felt like an empty balloon or a bag. He put it in his pocket, and went down the steps to the world again, his vision lost already.

# THEATER WRITINGS

# THE BEST MAN

HAVING WRITTEN extensively in the mid-1950s for live television and for Hollywood, Vidal had the skills to compose a well-made, tightly constructed, realistically credible stage drama that would express some of the playwright's ironic vision of human nature and still be accessible to a broad audience. In 1959 he wrote his most successful drama, *The Best Man;* it ran for 520 performances, from March 1960 to July 1961, at the Morosco Theatre on Broadway. A topical play drawing on the Democratic party contest for the 1960 presidential nomination, it was, as Vidal explained in *The New Statesman* several years later, "first written as a realistic play about two men at a political convention, fighting one another for the presidential nomination. . . . When I wrote the play, the Democratic rivals for the nomination were Adlai Stevenson (who was being smeared as a homosexual—and an indecisive one to boot), John F. Kennedy (who was being smeared as an altogether too active heterosexual as well as the glad beneficiary of his wealthy father's ability to buy elections) and the majority leader of the Senate, Lyndon Johnson (who was known to take cash for any political services rendered). In the background was Harry S Truman, whose campaign for election in 1948 nearly ended before it began. . . . When I based the character of the wicked candidate in the play on Richard Nixon, I thought it would be amusing if liberal partisans were to smear unjustly that uxorious man as a homosexual." Aware that the passage of time can make theatrical topicality moot, Vidal revised *The Best Man* in the early 1980s, substituting in the topical allusions the names and references of that era for those of the early 1960s. Since time has also had its way with the changes made for the 1980 version, the 1960 text is the one reproduced here. Still, the key political characters in the play, with their invented names, are in their approach to politics and power sufficiently like most American presidential candidates of any time to make the play a viable ongoing example of a rare literary genre, theatrical political satire.

# Author's Note from the 1960 Edition

For some reason when it is ninety in the shade and the Hudson River has gone dull-gray and I cross a certain bit of lawn contained by river wall mysteriously, a train of association is set off: I brood on Henry James. I fret about Strether. I deplore the Princess and her treatment of Hyacinth, and (though ripeness is all and the rest is the madness of art) I wonder if, really, I am taken with James's way. Is he too neat? Too artificial? Too classical? Too much devoted to balance? Item: *The Tragic Muse.* Each of four characters begins at the farthest extremity of an X; they cross; each ends in an opposite position. One wonders, does a living pulse beat? Or is it only a metronome?

One day last July, the temperature went to ninety; the river turned a sullen gray; I crossed the brown lawn and started, irritably, to rethink *The Tragic Muse.* No, I did not like the method, I decided. It was all a trick, an easy parlor game. As if one were, in contemporary terms, to take . . . just, for example . . . a man of exemplary private life, yet monstrous public life, and contrast him to a man of "immoral" private life and exemplary public life. That was just the sort of thing James would take on. How he would enjoy mechanically turning the screw upon each character. For sake of argument, make the two men politicians, perhaps fighting one another for the Presidency. Then demonstrate how, in our confused age, morality means, simply, sex found out. To most Americans, cheating, character assassination, hypocrisy, self-seeking are taken quite for granted as the way things are, not pleasant perhaps but: son, you've got to look after number one because there's a lot of competition and . . . By the time I got back to the house to escape the sun and *The Tragic Muse* revisited, I had the characters for *The Best Man.* One very perceptive (if not very flattering) critic recently compared me to Sardou, remarking how I displayed the same dramatic artifice, the well-madeness, the somewhat mechanical balance . . . the critic was right in his intuition, because who did study Sardou devoutly? Disastrously? Not I, but Henry James.

I went off to Provincetown at the end of August. I never had visited the Cape before, knew no one, recalled only that Tennessee Williams once told me it was a good place to work; in fact, he composed *A Streetcar Named Desire* in Provincetown. For once, however, I did not write. I thought. I had the general line of the play clear in my head. Narrative time would be concentrated to the three days preceding a presidential convention. I planned short scenes, alternating between the candidate-suites in a Philadelphia hotel. Yet I had still to make up my mind about the two important issues on which the plot would turn. What in William Russell's past could the opportunist Senator Cantwell use at the last minute which might effectively end his candidacy? And what might Russell find in Cantwell's private life which would, first, stop Cantwell and, second, and morally more important, revolt Russell in the doing?

It was Richard Rovere who gave me the answer to the first: intimations of mental instability. It was a valuable suggestion. The *Zeitgeist* is full now of the buzz of psychoanalysis; everyone's mind is cluttered with at least a few misunderstood clinical phrases and conceptions. If William Russell had once had a nervous breakdown, and Senator Cantwell were to get his hands on Russell's case history and threaten to reveal the contents to the delegates at the convention, it was unlikely Russell could survive politically. A presidential candidate can have many faults, but even a hint of mental instability is disqualifying. The second problem I solved reluctantly. What could be brought up about Senator Cantwell? I wanted something ambiguous: it might or it might not be true but, true or not, Russell must resent having to reveal it, even to save himself. This was limiting. If Cantwell had stolen money, got a girl pregnant, run away in battle, taken dope, been a Communist or a member of the Ku Klux Klan, Russell might be reluctant to bring the matter up, but he would certainly not hesitate to save himself, especially if he were convinced the charges were true. Homosexuality was about the only thing left (no, I have not read *Advise and Consent*). It was a charge which, true or not, Russell would detest exploiting. It was also an ironic charge to bring against Cantwell, whose marriage was deliberately made in that heaven where Miss Rose Franken's Claudia and David were created. Once these two matters were decided, I was able to write the play in three weeks.

The production went smoothly. I have never been involved in any dramatic venture in which there was not at least one actor everyone wished at the end had not been hired. *The Best Man* company is unique for me: all the actors are very fine and I have no regrets, only admiration. I found Joseph Anthony an ideal director, particularly complementary to my somewhat dry style. Anthony has an extraordinary gift for opening up emotional relationships, for finding small but revelatory character points which I, intent on the argument, usually miss. I confess, somewhat sheepishly, that I can find no one to accuse of destroying my beautiful play, if only because I do not write beautiful plays. I use the theater as a place to criticize society, to satirize folly, to question presuppositions. Kenneth Tynan has remarked that I am not "adventurous" and only at my best as a destructive satirist, but who is not? It is infinitely harder to ask questions in such a way that the audience is led not to the answers (the province of the demagogue) but to new perceptions. No writer's conclusions are ever of much interest if only because wisdom, when concentrated, is proverbial. Shaw's conclusions about the Life Force (appropriated from Bergson) are not very helpful, but his method of questioning and burlesquing is his art, and at his best he teases his audiences into asking the right questions. I can think of no other reason to write plays, though other writers have other incentives, equally useful.

I should also mention that Roger L. Stevens showed considerable courage in producing *The Best Man,* shutting his ears to the wounded cries of those distinguished politicians with whom he is associated as a money-raiser for the Democratic Party. To a man they were opposed to the production—I suppose because politicians, like magicians and safe-crackers, do not enjoy being explicated.

## ACT ONE

### SCENE ONE

*A hotel suite in Philadelphia . . . perhaps July 1960. From stage right to left: a bedroom with twin beds, a connecting hall, and a living room. There is a door from living room to hall and one from bedroom to hall. At stage right, a door to the bathroom. At stage left, a door to the office part of the suite, from which can be heard telephones ringing and the buzz of talk.*

*Dominating the living room, stage left, is a television set. There is also a bar upstage and of course the usual number of chairs and sofas. The décor is early Conrad Hilton. On the wall, a poster proclaims* WILLIAM RUSSELL FOR

PRESIDENT. *The candidate, according to his portrait, is a strong, youthful-looking man of fifty. There are also various placards around the room, propped against walls and furniture:* HUSTLE WITH RUSSELL . . . , A GREAT GOVERNOR, A GREAT SECRETARY OF STATE, AND THE NEXT PRESIDENT OF THE U.S., *and similar political sentiments.*

*Since one hotel suite is apt to look very like another, this same set could be used for the opposition's suite downstairs, so that when the narrative shifts to the other suite all that would need changing would be specific props: for instance, the placards there would itemize the virtues of Senator Joe Cantwell for President:* YOU'LL DO WELL WITH CANTWELL, GO WITH JOE, *etc. Fortunately,* The Best Man*'s New York production was designed by Jo Mielziner, a crafty user of twin turntables which made it possible to have two sets which were shifted with great speed. The Cantwell suite resembled the Russell suite in layout, except that everything was reversed: the Cantwell living room was at right and the bedroom at left. The director made an amiable point in furnishing the Russell bedroom with twin beds and the Cantwell bedroom with a double bed.*

*As the curtain rises, photographers and newsmen set off a great flash of camera bulbs, aimed at* WILLIAM *and* ALICE RUSSELL, *who enter from the hall, followed by* REPORTERS, PHOTOGRAPHERS, *a* BELLBOY *and* DICK JENSEN, *Bill Russell's campaign manager.*

JENSEN *is in his late forties: intense, devoted, apprehensive by nature. There is a babble of sound: strident questions—"Any statement?" "What about California?" "The labor bill?" "Just one more, Mr. Secretary," "Red China?" "How many delegates you got?" During this* RUSSELL *tries to be heard; his wife stands rigidly beside him.* ALICE RUSSELL *is in her early forties. She is a handsome, slender, gray-haired lady of the Old American Establishment, not quite as diffident and shy as she appears.*

JENSEN

O.K., boys! O.K. Give him air! One question at a time . . .

REPORTER I

Mr. Secretary, as of today how many delegates do you have sewed up?

RUSSELL

(*Lightly*)

When it comes to delegates, we neither sow nor do we reap.

REPORTER I

(*Puzzled*)

What was that again, Mr. Secretary?

RUSSELL

I said . . .

JENSEN

Mr. Russell was making a joke, he means we . . .

REPORTER 2

(*Helpfully*)

He said neither do they sow . . .

REPORTER 3

But what about Ex-President Hockstader? Have you got his endorsement yet?

RUSSELL

In a word . . . no.

REPORTER 3

Do you think you'll get it?

RUSSELL

Ask him. There's a rumor he's in Philadelphia.

REPORTER 4

Yes. He's upstairs. He's going to make a statement tonight. He says it's between you and Senator Cantwell . . .

RUSSELL

So we'll just have to wait until tonight.

REPORTER I

Mrs. Russell, what do *you* think your husband's chances are?

ALICE

(*Uncertainly*)

Well, I . . . I don't really know. I mean, we have to wait for the convention, don't we?

REPORTER 2

Mr. Secretary, if there's a deadlock between you and Senator Cantwell, whom do you think will be the dark horse candidate?

RUSSELL

Jack Paar. (*Smiles*) I'm sorry, but I'm not about to build up a dark horse when I am doing my best to look like the light horse.

REPORTER 2

Sir, what do you think of Governor Merwin's chances?

RUSSELL

John Merwin is a very talented young man. We don't know much about him, of course, but . . .

REPORTER 4

(*Quickly*)

Would you consider Governor Merwin as a running mate?

REPORTER 3

Yes.

RUSSELL

I might. He's one of a number of capable men.

REPORTER 3

Mr. Secretary, how did you interpret the Gallup poll this morning?

RUSSELL

I didn't interpret it because I didn't see it.

REPORTER 4

Senator Cantwell's picked up two per cent from you since last week . . .

JENSEN

(*Overlapping*)

But we're still leading by nine per cent in the country with . . .

RUSSELL

But you *can* say I don't believe in polls . . .

JENSEN

(*Nervously*)

What the Secretary means is . . .

RUSSELL

(*Firmly*)

I don't believe in polls. Accurate or not. And if I may bore you with one of my little sermons: life is not a popularity contest; neither is politics. The important thing for any government is educating the people about issues, *not* following the ups and downs of popular opinion.

REPORTER 3

(*In for the kill*)

Does that mean you don't respect popular opinion? Do you think a President ought to ignore what the people want?

RUSSELL

(*Serenely*)

If the people want the wrong thing, if the people don't understand an issue, if they've been misled by the press (*Politely*)—by *some* of the press—then I think a President should ignore their opinion and try to convince them that his way is the right way.

REPORTER 2

Do you think the people mistrust intellectuals in politics?

RUSSELL

(*Smiles*)

I'm glad you asked that question. Bertrand Russell seems to think so. He once wrote that the people in a democracy tend to think they have less to fear from a stupid man than from an intelligent one.

REPORTER I

(*Lost*)

Bertrand. . . ?

RUSSELL

Bertrand Russell.

REPORTER I

(*Slow, false dawning*)

Oh, the same name . . .

RUSSELL

(*Amused*)

Yes. But no relative, unfortunately.

REPORTER 3

(*The taste of blood*)

Wasn't Bertrand Russell *fired* from City College of New York?

RUSSELL

(*Sadly*)

Yes, he was fired. But only for moral turpitude . . . *not* for incompetence as a philosopher.

REPORTER 4

What image do you feel Senator Cantwell is projecting at the moment?

RUSSELL

Image? He's behaving himself, if that's what you mean.

REPORTER 4

(*Solemnly*)

But hasn't his *basic* image changed in the last year?

RUSSELL

I'm afraid I don't know much about images. That's a word from advertising where you don't sell the product, you sell the image of the product. And sometimes the image is a fake.

REPORTER 3

(*Slyly*)

But after all, your own image . . .

RUSSELL

Is a poor thing but mine own. Paint me as I am, warts and all!

REPORTER I

What?

RUSSELL

Oliver Cromwell.

(JENSEN *starts rounding up the press*)

JENSEN

O.K., fellows, we'll have a statement for you in about an hour. Headquarters are through there. The mimeograph machine has been repaired and . . .

RUSSELL

And wisdom flows by the yard.

(JENSEN *herds the* REPORTER *off stage left. All except* REPORTER 3. *She has followed* ALICE *into the bedroom.* RUSSELL *says good-bye to the* REPORTERS *at the door*)

REPORTER 1

(*Urgently*)

Mr. Secretary . . .

(*A flood of last-minute questions and photographers shouting: "Just one more"*)

RUSSELL

(*Apologetically*)

I have a feeling Dick Jensen would like the candidate to stop talking. I'll see you all later, after the delegations. Until then, as Senator Cantwell would say, may the best man win!

(*The* REPORTERS *and* JENSEN *are gone.* RUSSELL *is relieved until he hears the cold-edged voice of* REPORTER 3 *in the bedroom*)

REPORTER 3

How do you like Philadelphia, Mrs. Russell?

ALICE

Well, I just got here . . . I used to visit here as a girl.

(RUSSELL *comes to the rescue. He propels* REPORTER 3 *to the door at stage left*)

RUSSELL

Please, *please.* Wait till we unpack.

REPORTER 3

Do you drink the tap water?

RUSSELL

I have no intention of losing Pennsylvania by admitting that I boil the local water.

(REPORTER 3 *departs with an unamused grimace.* RUSSELL *shudders.* JENSEN *returns*)

JENSEN

(*Groans*)

Bertrand Russell at a press conference.

RUSSELL

(*Placating*)

All right, Dick, all right, no more jokes. From now on we project blandness. A candidate should not mean but be. And no matter *what* happens, I shall smile: serenely, fatuously, ineluctably.

(RUSSELL, *smiling, hat in hand, marches, waving and beaming, to the bedroom*)

RUSSELL

(*Intoning*)

Floods destroy the Middle West, and the candidate smiles. Half the world is starving, and the candidate smiles. War is declared, and the candidate smiles. Is there anything more indecent than the human face when it smiles?

(ALICE *takes the hat. He returns to the connecting hall and looks into the mirror*)

RUSSELL

All these predatory teeth, reminding us of our animal descent.

JENSEN

Steady. No mention of Darwin. Evolution is out of bounds. Before the Garden of Eden was the Word. And *stop* looking in the mirror.

RUSSELL

I never pass a mirror I don't look in it. I wonder why?

(ALICE *has gone to hang a coat in the wall closet. En route, she answers him*)

ALICE

(*Briskly*)

Vanity.

(ALICE *returns to her unpacking in the bedroom*)

RUSSELL

(*Thoughtfully*)

I look to remind myself I really exist. One needs constant proofs.

ALICE

I better use the bathroom while I've got a chance.

RUSSELL

(*Genuine concern*)

Alice, *don't* drink the *water!*

(*The telephone in the living room rings*)

JENSEN

(*Answers it*)

Who? Oh, Mrs. Gamadge, good to hear your voice. . . ! Yes, ma'am. Well, he's got the Texas delegation coming in about twenty minutes, but (*Looks to* RUSSELL *for guidance.* RUSSELL *nods*) if you come over right now . . . Oh, good, you're in the hotel . . . fine. We'll see you then. (*Puts down receiver*) Our national committee woman.

RUSSELL

The only known link between the N.A.A.C.P. and the Ku Klux Klan. How does she do it? How? How?

(RUSSELL *is studying the carpet as he paces oddly downstage*)

JENSEN

(*Curiously*)

Bill . . . may I ask a very personal question?

RUSSELL

Personal? There is no other kind between us . . .

JENSEN

What the hell are you doing when you start that hopscotch thing up and down the floor?

RUSSELL

As we say at press conferences, I'm glad you asked that question. I am . . . oh, damn! (*He steps back suddenly*) The ancient Romans used to examine the entrails of animals in order to learn the future. I am told on very good authority that my rival, Senator Cantwell, goes to an astrologist in Kalorama Road, Washington, for guidance. I, lacking all superstition, study the future in multiples of threes. Put simply—and we are nothing if not experts at putting things simply, are we?—I find a carpet with workable pattern. This one's perfect. Now if I step on a leaf—see?—before I have completed three full steps *between* leaves, I will *not* get what I want. If, however, I can take three paces *without* touching that leaf, I will get what I want. I may say, I never cheat. (*Scowls*) Hell! However, I can on occasion go for the best two out of three. I also make bets with myself. For instance, if the man I'm talking to does not answer me within the count of three, I get what I want. (*He finishes his walk just short of where* JENSEN *is seated at stage left*) Ah, victory! I hope I've answered your question lucidly?

JENSEN

Yes, you have. But let's keep it *our* secret. (*A* WOMAN AID *enters with a stack of newspapers from left*) My own vice is the daily horoscope. (AID *goes*) So what did you win?

RUSSELL

The nomination. And on the first ballot, too! (*He sits on downstage sofa*) My God, I'm keyed up! I feel like I'm going to jump out of my skin. I can't sit still . . .

(JENSEN *crosses to him*)

JENSEN

Well, you won't do much sitting still between now and Wednesday. Here's today's schedule. Most of the delegations will come to us. (*Shows* RUSSELL *paper*) See? It's a tight schedule, starting with Texas at eleven-fifteen, then . . .

RUSSELL

(*Unable to attend*)

We're getting so close . . . so close! And what's going to happen?

JENSEN

You! We've got the delegates. It's yours on the first ballot. *If* you get Ex-President Hockstader's endorsement . . .

(*The door buzzer in the connecting hall sounds. There is a noise of voices from the outside corridor*)

RUSSELL AND JENSEN

(*In unison*)

Mrs. Gamadge!

(*They both cross to the hall door.* JENSEN *opens it.* MRS. GAMADGE, *small, plump, elderly, sails into view, surrounded by* NEWSMEN *and* PHOTOGRAPHERS. *She is serene in the knowledge that she is the Voice of the American Woman, by default. Her manner is an odd mixture of coziness and steeliness*)

MRS. GAMADGE

(*Beams*)

Mr. Secretary . . .

(MRS. GAMADGE *seizes* RUSSELL *for a picture. They pose, her left arm around him, her right arm raised in salute. Then* JENSEN *ushers out the press*)

RUSSELL

(*Sudden energy*)

Mrs. Gamadge, it's wonderful to see you! Come on in. Sit down. Have a drink. You know Dick Jensen, don't you? My campaign manager.

(MRS. GAMADGE *shakes* JENSEN'S *hand as she crosses to a sofa*)

MRS. GAMADGE

Such a lovely hotel for a convention. I always say the hotel you're at makes all the difference at a convention. Does Mrs. Russell like your suite?

RUSSELL

Practically a home away from home.

MRS. GAMADGE

(*Narrowly*)

She *is* here with you, isn't she?

(RUSSELL *pulls out a chair for her*)

RUSSELL

Yes. This is the good chair.

MRS. GAMADGE

I'll sit *here,* thank you.

(MRS. GAMADGE *unfurls on the sofa*)

JENSEN

I must say, I'm glad to meet you at last, Mrs. Gamadge.

MRS. GAMADGE

And I'm glad to get a chance to see you, Mr. Jensen. I love eggheads in politics.

JENSEN

(*Taken aback*)

Oh, well . . .

RUSSELL

(*Quickly*)

What can I get you to drink?

MRS. GAMADGE

I don't drink. Mr. Secretary. A Coke or a glass of soda, maybe. Anything. (*Turns to* JENSEN, *sweetly*) Professors like you give such a tone to these conventions. No, I really mean it. Of course a lot of the women don't like them but I do. Though of course I didn't like the New Deal.

(RUSSELL *gives her a glass*)

RUSSELL

Here's your soda . . .

(*She takes it with a nice smile*)

MRS. GAMADGE

A great many of the women are suspicious of you professors, Mr. Jensen. . . . You don't mind my speaking like this?

JENSEN

Certainly not, Mrs. Gamadge. After all, talking to you is like . . . well, like talking to the average American housewife. (JENSEN *is aware* MRS. GAMADGE *has frozen on "average." He stammers*) I mean *you're* not average but you speak for them . . .

MRS. GAMADGE

Very nicely put, Mr. Jensen. (*To* RUSSELL) I don't know why everyone says he's so conceited.

RUSSELL

Dick? Stuck up? Why, he's the spirit of humility . . . an old shoe, in fact! As for being intellectual, he can hardly get through the Greek Anthology without a trot.

MRS. GAMADGE

(*Nods*)

Yes. (*To business*) You see, the women like a regular kind of man, like General Eisenhower. Now he really appeals to the women. That nice smile. He has such a way with him . . . he inspires confidence because he doesn't seem like anything but *just folks.* You could imagine him washing up after dinner, listening to his wife's view on important matters.

RUSSELL

(*Quietly*)

Yes, indeed you can.

MRS. GAMADGE

Nothing pushy or aggressive or all those things we women don't like in our men. He's just grand! Now, Mr. Secretary, there is no doubt in anybody's mind you are going to get the nomination on the first ballot . . .

RUSSELL

There is doubt in *my* mind . . .

MRS. GAMADGE

(*No time for diversion*)

Yes . . . yes . . . yes . . . now let's face facts a minute. You don't mind if I talk turkey?

RUSSELL

No. By all means . . . turkey.

MRS. GAMADGE

You are not the ideal candidate for the women. You know that, I suppose.

RUSSELL

Well, what . . . what women do you have in mind?

MRS. GAMADGE

(*Coldly*)

The women don't like your trying to be funny all the time.

RUSSELL

No, no. It is a flaw, I agree.

MRS. GAMADGE

The women are *very* suspicious of a man who doesn't take things seriously. So just don't try to be smart-aleck and talk over their heads. I hope you don't mind my talking like this but there isn't much time.

RUSSELL

I am certainly grateful for your . . . candor.

(MRS. GAMADGE *rises and circles with empty glass toward the bar*)

MRS. GAMADGE

Now we want to see more of your wife. A lot more.

RUSSELL

(RUSSELL *sits stage left*)

She was sick, you know, during the primaries . . .

MRS. GAMADGE

And your two fine sons. They're very attractive and that was a nice spread of them in *Life,* at the barbecue. Very, very nice. We'll want more of that. But most important, your wife should be at your side at all times. She must *seem* to be advising you. The women must feel that there is a woman behind you (MRS. GAMADGE *has maneuvered herself into position behind* RUSSELL's *chair*), as there has been a woman behind every great man since the world began!

(RUSSELL, *aware of* MRS. GAMADGE'S *presence, rises and crosses to* JENSEN *at right*)

RUSSELL

Alice plans to campaign with me, if . . .

MRS. GAMADGE

She's a tremendous asset. I don't need to tell you. The women like the way she doesn't wear make-up and looks like a lady, and seems shy . . .

RUSSELL

She is shy.

MRS. GAMADGE

She doesn't make the women feel jealous. And that's good. Keep her with you, Mr. Secretary, at all times. It did Adlai Stevenson great harm, not having a wife, and trying to be funny all the time, too. Great harm. (MRS. GAMADGE *returns to sofa and sits down*) Now I want to ask you a blunt question: what truth is there in the rumor that there has been . . . marital discord between you and Mrs. Russell?

RUSSELL

(*Evenly*)

Mrs. Gamadge, my wife is here in Philadelphia. If I am nominated, she will do everything possible to be a helpful candidate's wife . . .

MRS. GAMADGE

Could I see her?

RUSSELL

Of course. (*Crosses to bedroom door*) Alice . . . come on out and meet Mrs. Gamadge.

(ALICE *signals* RUSSELL *to wait while she arranges her blouse*)

MRS. GAMADGE

(*To* JENSEN)

Now Mabel Cantwell is *such* a nice woman. Really one of the girls. You feel like you've known her all your life. Last time I was in Washington, Mabel gave this lovely dessert luncheon for me with four tables of canasta . . .

(*Somewhat nervously,* ALICE *enters and starts to cross to* MRS. GAMADGE, *who has risen and, to her alarm, started backing away with a speculative look, taking in everything*)

ALICE

How very nice to see you . . .

MRS. GAMADGE

(*Slowly, deliberately*)

You . . . couldn't . . . look . . . better! I mean it! I like the whole thing . . . especially the naturally gray hair, that is *such* an important point with the women. Of course Mabel Cantwell dyes her hair, but she gets away with it because she does such a bad job the women feel sorry for her.

(*A* WOMAN AID *enters from left. She gives* JENSEN *a note and goes.* JENSEN *shows the note to* RUSSELL. MRS. GAMADGE *observes this byplay*)

MRS. GAMADGE

Oh, I know you have a million things to do! Anyway, I just want you to know that I'm for you, Mr. Secretary, and I'm sure you and Mrs. Russell are a winning team. (*To* ALICE, *cozily*) When you're the First Lady just remember this: don't do too much . . . like Mrs. Roosevelt. The women didn't like that. On the other hand, don't do too little . . . like Mrs. Eisenhower. The women don't like that either. All in all, Grace Coolidge was really the best, bless her heart. My husband had such a crush on her . . .

JENSEN

How *is* Mr. Gamadge?

(RUSSELL *signals belatedly but the gaffe is made*)

MRS. GAMADGE

(*Quietly*)

Mr. Gamadge passed on in 1956. He was stricken during the New Hampshire primaries.

JENSEN

Oh, I didn't know that. I'm sorry . . .

MRS. GAMADGE

So am I. He was a fine man, though he didn't like politics. He suffered his terminal thrombosis while I was in Wisconsin, that same year. (*Hearty handclasp*) Bill, *go to it!* The women are in your corner!

RUSSELL

You don't know how much that means to me . . . Sue-Ellen.

MRS. GAMADGE

(*To* ALICE, *warmly*)

Us girls will have a get-together real soon. And that's a promise.

ALICE

I do hope so, Mrs. Gamadge.

MRS. GAMADGE

(*At the door, the knife*)

Oh, by the way! A little bird tells me Joe Cantwell has a surprise for you.

RUSSELL

A surprise?

MRS. GAMADGE

Uh-huh. He's going to smear you with something . . . so they say.

RUSSELL

(*Startled*)

Smear me?

MRS. GAMADGE

(*Gaily*)

But here I am telling you what you already know. I'm sure you can handle it. 'Bye, Bill. 'Bye, Dick!

(*In a burst of sound from the newsmen in the corridor,* MRS. GAMADGE *goes*)

ALICE

Smear you, Bill? With what?

RUSSELL

(*Frowns*)

I don't know.

(JENSEN *waves note*)

JENSEN

Well, Alice, word has come from on high. We're about to have a visit from our distinguished Ex-President.

ALICE

I must say he's one of the ones I like . . . except when he tells those long stories.

RUSSELL

Which will it be? The kiss . . . or the knife.

JENSEN

How can you miss? Like the rest of us he loves a winner.

ALICE

And he does like *you,* Bill.

RUSSELL

I don't know. He's a funny old bird.

(WOMAN AID *appears in doorway left*)

JENSEN

Yes?

AID

The "Volunteer Women for Russell" are on the mezzanine. They want to know if they can see Mrs. Russell.

RUSSELL

Are you up to it?

ALICE

Of course I am. Tell them I'll join them in a few minutes.

(ALICE *goes into bedroom to get ready.* WOMAN *gives several sheets to* JENSEN)

AID

Copies of the Secretary's speech for tonight.

JENSEN

I'll check them now.

(AID *goes, left*)

RUSSELL

(*Indicates speech*)

You might let me look at it, too. I'd like to know what I'm saying.

JENSEN

Come off it, your speech writers . . .

(RUSSELL *takes the speech and glances through it*)

RUSSELL

. . . are the best money can buy. They have written speeches for Eisenhower, Truman, Dewey, Hockstader, Roosevelt, Hoover and Harold Stassen. Which proves they are men of overpowering conviction.

JENSEN

Do you want to write four speeches a day on top of everything else?

RUSSELL

Of course I want to. But I can't. There isn't time. But it's a shameful business, speech by committee . . .

JENSEN

Not to mention *President* by committee.

(RUSSELL *hands back the speech*)

RUSSELL

Please tell the writers *again* that the word "alternative" is always singular. There is only *one* alternative per situation.

JENSEN

I will denounce them as anti-semanticists . . .

(JENSEN *goes off left.* RUSSELL, *thoughtfully, goes into bedroom*)

RUSSELL

Only one alternative per situation . . . unfortunately. That's grammar.

ALICE

(*Dryly*)

And marriage. . . . Oh, I left my handbag . . .

(ALICE *goes into bathroom.* RUSSELL *starts to unpack a suitcase. She returns*)

RUSSELL

I'm sorry we're . . . in such close quarters.

ALICE

I don't mind. If you don't.

RUSSELL

Odd, after all these years apart. Separate rooms, separate lives.

ALICE

(*Smiles*)

As someone sooner or later says: politics make strange bed-fellows.

RUSSELL

Yes.

ALICE

Certainly there's nothing stranger than the two of us in the same room.

RUSSELL

I don't suppose I'm the first candidate to be in this situation.

ALICE

Bill . . . don't apologize. I said I'd do what I could to help. And I will. Besides, I really want you to be President.

RUSSELL

Why?

ALICE

I don't know. Perhaps I'm unexpectedly ambitious. Perhaps I want to be First Lady. Or perhaps I look forward to seeing you occasionally. (*Quickly*) Don't look alarmed! Only in line of duty. You know, an unexpected meeting in the East Room, an ambiguous encounter in the Lincoln Bedroom . . .

RUSSELL

(*Amused*)

Alice . . .

ALICE

Yesterday, a woman from the press wanted to know what changes I would make when we moved into the White House. I said nothing of a *structural* nature would be changed . . . Will it?

RUSSELL

(*Awkwardly*)

You know . . . I *do* like the idea of the two of us back together again.

ALICE

(*Suddenly sharp*)

Bill, I am not a delegation from the Legion of Decency. You don't have to charm me.

(ALICE *goes to hall, hangs up a blouse*)

RUSSELL

I wasn't trying to. I mean it. I know it's tough . . .

ALICE

Tough? (*Returns to bedroom*) Only for you. You're the one who has a problem. How to get girls into the White House. Or will you have a special place on K Street where the President, in disguise of course, can meet new . . . people.

(RUSSELL *scowls and goes into bathroom with his shaving gear*)

RUSSELL

(*From the bathroom*)

Why do you say things like that?

ALICE

Obviously because I'm frustrated. Isn't that the usual excuse women give? And isn't that the usual reason?

(RUSSELL *returns to the bedroom, and his unpacking*)

RUSSELL

When the desire to make love to someone goes, it goes and nothing on earth can bring it back. Between us, it went.

ALICE

For you.

RUSSELL

I suppose what I wanted in marriage was a friend.

ALICE

And instead you got a very conventional girl who wanted a husband, who wanted . . . No. I will *not* put on that record again. I don't know why but we never manage to say anything new when we get onto the subject of my inadequacy and your . . . what shall we call it this time? Athleticism? Since according to the ground rules of our marriage we may call it anything except plain old-fashioned promiscuity.

RUSSELL

Look, if you'd rather not be with me, and have to go through with this . . . this gloomy farce, then don't. Quit! Right now.

ALICE

Quit? Certainly not. I like circuses. Besides, I'm good for you, isn't that what Dr. Artinian said? After your breakdown? You are the link, he said, between father and sons, between William Russell and the world.

RUSSELL

Dr. Artinian was right.

ALICE

But I wonder what I would have done that summer at Watch Hill, when we first met at the club, if someone had said: "The handsome young man you've just fallen in love with will always need you . . . *as a link.*" I think if I had known then what I know now I would have slashed my wrists in front of the buffet table and beautifully bled to death between the chicken salad and the lobster Newburgh.

RUSSELL

(*Smiles*)

Luckily, you are not given to melodrama.

(*Both go into living room*)

ALICE

Not yet anyway. But you are very nearly a great man and I suppose I can endure anything because of that . . . So here we are.

RUSSELL

Somewhat past our youth . . . and friends?

ALICE

It would be nice if we were, wouldn't it? Do I look all right for the "Volunteer Women for Russell"?

RUSSELL

You do.

ALICE

(*Dryly*)

I ought to. I am a founding member of that considerable body.

(ART HOCKSTADER, *a former President, in his late seventies but alert despite his years, enters from the bathroom door at right. He crosses warily to the connecting hall, where he sees* ALICE, *who is about to go*)

HOCKSTADER

Hi, honey . . .

(ALICE *is startled*)

ALICE

Oh! Mr. President!

HOCKSTADER

You look mighty pretty, Miss Alice . . . as usual!

(HOCKSTADER'S *accent is rural American*)

RUSSELL

(*Joining them*)

Mr. President!

HOCKSTADER

Just plain Art Hockstader to you . . .

ALICE

Where did you come from?

HOCKSTADER

(*Indicates right*)

Through the privy. There's a door into the next suite. I sneaked through.

ALICE

You look wonderful, after your operation!

HOCKSTADER

Ought to. Nothin but a hernia from bouncin my grandson too hard.

RUSSELL

What can I get you to drink? No, no, don't tell me . . . bourbon and branch water.

(RUSSELL *goes to the living-room bar*)

HOCKSTADER

With which I shall strike a blow for liberty. (*To the departing* ALICE) Don't let anyone know I'm here. (ALICE *nods and goes*) Well, son, how do you like politics?

RUSSELL

I like it so much I'm beginning to worry.

HOCKSTADER

Awful, ain't it? Worse than gamblin, I sometimes think. Me, I was hooked when I was no more than this high (*Indicates a child*), and a certain fourflusher named William Jennings Bryan came to town. His last campaign, I guess. . . . Well, they shot the works: torchlight parade, picnic, the works! Then finally up there on the back of an old dray, out in a field, this fellow gets up and you never heard such hollerin from a crowd. Big man he was or so he looked to me, about nine foot tall with hair sweeping over his collar and that square red face of his, and when he spoke I tell you it was like thunder on a summer evenin and everythin was still, listenin. I used to know that speech by heart, it was the famous one. (*Imitates a fustian political voice*) "You shall not press down upon the brow of labor this crown of thorns. You shall not crucify mankind upon a cross of gold!"

RUSSELL

Hurray!

(RUSSELL *gives* HOCKSTADER *his drink*)

HOCKSTADER

You betcha! Anyway, it was then and there that a certain farm boy named Art Hockstader said: I am goin to be a politician and get the folks riled up and eat plenty of barbecue and fried chicken at picnics and have all the pretty girls a-hangin on my every word.

RUSSELL

(*Carefully*)

Your endorsement, Art, is a very important thing for anybody who wants to be nominated.

HOCKSTADER

I know it is. (*Smiles*) So, indulge an old duffer! After all, gettin you fellows to listen to my stories and squirm a bit, waitin to see who I'm goin to put my money on, I tell you it's about the only pleasure I got left.

RUSSELL

I'm squirming.

HOCKSTADER

(*Gentle sadism*)

Bill, I have a fatherly feeling about you . . .

RUSSELL

And I have . . .

HOCKSTADER

(*Continues through him*)

Even though I have certain doubts about you.

RUSSELL

Doubts?

HOCKSTADER

(*Nods*)

I'm kind of responsible for your career. You were *my* Secretary of State, and you were a swell one . . . but as you know the people don't give a damn about Secretaries of State. They think the whole foreign thing's a mess anyway and the man who's got to deal with it . . . well, I'm afraid the plain folks think the Secretary of State by definition is a foreigner.

RUSSELL

(*Ruefully*)

I know. And if he doesn't like it here he better go back where he came from.

HOCKSTADER

Exactly. Of course you were a fine governor before that. Though Rhode Island is hardly what we call a king-makin state. . . . Anyway, it isn't your ability I doubt. Hell, you're ten times as well qualified as I was, and look at me! Possibly one of the greatest statesmen of all time!

RUSSELL

You were pretty good.

HOCKSTADER

I certainly was. (*Dryly*) Though it's practically our secret right now, as there has been no overpowering popular movement to add me to that rock garden at Mt. Rushmore. But that's not for me to worry about. No, my objection to you, I guess, was prejudice. For one thing you're a Fancy Dan from the East. But I am nothin if not a realist. The Age of the Great Hicks to which I belong is over. The people trust you rich boys, figurin since you got a lot of money of your own you won't go stealin theirs. I'm sure those people who like this Rockefeller are really thinkin in the back of their minds if they make him President he might decide to pay off the national debt out of his own pocket! If he would, *I'd* vote for him.

RUSSELL

What do you think of Joe Cantwell?

HOCKSTADER

(*Smiles*)

That's a leading question.

RUSSELL

Well, I *am* proposing myself as a leader.

HOCKSTADER

O.K., I'll follow. Joe Cantwell is nothin but ambition. Just plain naked ambition.

RUSSELL

And to get himself elected he will lie . . .

HOCKSTADER

(*Nods*)

Yep.

RUSSELL

He will cheat . . .

HOCKSTADER

Yep.

RUSSELL

He will destroy the reputations of others . . .

HOCKSTADER

Yep.

RUSSELL

Good. So I assume you are endorsing me for the nomination.

HOCKSTADER

Hell, no! Because he's a bastard don't mean he wouldn't be a good candidate. Or even a good President . . .

RUSSELL

Joe Cantwell a good. . . ! You're not serious.

HOCKSTADER

Well, he's got a real sense of how to operate.

RUSSELL

To operate? No. To accommodate! If the people are conservative . . .

HOCKSTADER

He'll be conservative.

RUSSELL

And if they're radical . . .

HOCKSTADER

He'll be radical. Oh, I tell you, son, he is a kind of ring-tailed wonder and don't you underestimate him.

RUSSELL

I don't.

HOCKSTADER

Of course he hasn't got your brains, but then very few of us are as bright as you.

RUSSELL

Now, Art . . .

HOCKSTADER

No, I mean it. You are a superior man of the sort we don't get very often in politics. While Joe's just another of the mediocre boys, like me . . . only smoother of course. A newer model.

RUSSELL

No, he is *not* like you. He'll do anything to win. And that makes him dangerous.

HOCKSTADER

Now I wouldn't go that far. (*The first turn to the screw*) At least he knows his own mind.

RUSSELL

And you think I don't know my own mind?

HOCKSTADER

(*Equably*)

Well, son, you got such a good mind that sometimes you're so busy thinkin how complex everything is important problems don't get solved.

RUSSELL

(*Smiles*)

No, I am not that subtle. I am not that undecided. I am not Prince Hamlet.

HOCKSTADER

(*A diversion*)

Hamlet! Lot of fine speeches in that play. Lot of fine speeches in *you,* Bill.

RUSSELL

(*Urgently*)

Art, *don't* support Cantwell!

HOCKSTADER

Now, what makes you think I'm goin to?

RUSSELL

I mean it. And I am not thinking about myself. I'm thinking about the country.

HOCKSTADER

You got to admit, Joe Cantwell ain't afraid to act.

RUSSELL

Neither am I afraid to act.

HOCKSTADER

(*Dreamily*)

Oh? Well, now, I seem to recall how once when you were at a conference with the Russians you were all set to agree to continue nuclear tests, but then when the roof fell in on my administration, I found you had gone and talked yourself up the other side of the street.

RUSSELL

I hesitated only because . . .

HOCKSTADER

I'll say you hesitated. Now you don't catch Joe Cantwell hesitatin. No, sir. He's sharp. He's tough.

RUSSELL

He is not tough. He is expedient and that's a very different thing, and I promise you if Joe were President he'd be the greatest appeaser in history.

HOCKSTADER

I would hardly call him an appeaser . . .

RUSSELL

Suppose the Chinese were to threaten to occupy India and we were faced with the possibility of a world war, the *last* world war. Now that is the kind of thing you and I understand and I think we could handle it without going to war and without losing India. But what would Joe do? He would look at the Gallup poll. And what would the Gallup poll tell him? Well, ask the average American, do you want to run the risk of being blown up to save India? And he'll say, hell, no! Joe would do the popular thing: to hell with India, and we would be the weaker for it, and that day we're all afraid of would be closer.

(HOCKSTADER *finishes his drink and rises*)

HOCKSTADER

Son, you've been reading too much of that Joe Alsop fellow. Things are never *that* bad! (*Thoughtfully*) Bill, you know it gets mighty lonely in the White House. Worse for me, I guess, than for you. I'd never lived in a big house with a lot of servants, the way you were brought up. But the worst part is, there's nobody you can believe . . . that's the awful thing: everybody's lying to you all day long. . . . Then my wife died . . . (*Sighs*) The wonder is that most of us aren't worse than we are. (*Suddenly*) Bill, do you believe in God?

RUSSELL

(*Startled*)

Do I. . . ? Well, I was confirmed in the Episcopal Church.

HOCKSTADER

Hell, that wasn't what I asked. I'm a Methodist and I'm still askin: do you believe there's a God and a Day of Judgment and a Hereafter?

RUSSELL

No. I believe in us. In man.

HOCKSTADER

(*Nods*)

I've often pretended I thought there was a God, for political purposes.

RUSSELL

(*Smiles*)

So far I haven't told a lie in this campaign. I've never used the word "God" in a speech.

HOCKSTADER

Well, the world's changed since I was politickin. In those days you had to pour God over everything, like ketchup. (*He sits on the bench downstage*) No, I don't believe there's a Hereafter. We pass this way just once. And then . . . nothing. Bill, I am dying.

RUSSELL

(*Stunned*)

What?

HOCKSTADER

That thing about the hernia was just another lie, I'm afraid. (*Dryly*) I hope you don't disapprove. . . . I got the doctors to say the operation was a great success, but it wasn't. I got cancer of the innerds and they tell me I may last just long enough to attend the next Inaugural.

(RUSSELL *rises, crosses to him*)

RUSSELL

Art, I'm. . . ! Look, isn't there . . .

HOCKSTADER

There is nothin they can do, except give me these pills to cut the pain. I tell you, son, I am scared to death. (*Laughs*) That's a phrase for you:

"Scared to death" is exactly right. I don't fancy being nothin, just a pinch of dust. No, sir, I don't like that at all.

(RUSSELL *puts his hand on* HOCKSTADER'S *shoulder*)

RUSSELL

I wish I could say something reassuring, but you wouldn't fall for it anyway.

(HOCKSTADER *shrugs away* RUSSELL'S *hand*)

HOCKSTADER

The only good thing I find is that the rest of you sons of bitches are going to join me. There's some consolation I reckon in that. (*Sighs*) Oh, I tell you if there is any point to this universe it sure as hell evades me.

RUSSELL

The whole thing's a tragedy. For all of us. (*Crosses to the sofa*) But there's hope in this: Every act we make sets off a chain of reaction which never ends. And if we are reasonably . . . good, well, there *is* some consolation in that, a kind of immortality.

HOCKSTADER

(*Dryly*)

I suggest you tell yourself that when *you* finally have to face a whole pile of nothin up ahead. (*Rises briskly*) But at the moment I'm alive. And we go into the convention hall day after tomorrow and act like life is all there is . . . which, come to think of it, is true.

(JENSEN *looks in from the office at left*)

JENSEN

The Texas Delegation is here. (*Sees* HOCKSTADER) Oh, Hello, Mr. . . .

(HOCKSTADER *motions to* JENSEN *to say nothing.* JENSEN *nods and shuts the door*)

HOCKSTADER

Bill, don't tell anybody what I told you.

RUSSELL

Of course not.

HOCKSTADER

Meanwhile, I am going to keep you in suspense, until tonight at dinner.

RUSSELL

And then?

HOCKSTADER

I will throw my support like a bridal bouquet to the lucky man. (HOCKSTADER *beams; he starts to cross to hall; he pauses*) Oh, these rumors about you and your lady friends . . . won't do you a bit of harm. *But* keep out of trouble. You haven't gone and written any letters like some fellows do?

RUSSELL

(*Smiles*)

No. No letters.

HOCKSTADER

Good boy. She's a nice girl, Alice.

RUSSELL

I think so.

HOCKSTADER

(*Slyly*)

And you never tell a lie, do you? Well, good! Glad to hear it! (*Grimaces with pain*) Christ, that upper plate of mine pinches! I was going to get a new one but they said it would take a couple of months to make. So I figured I could hold out with what I got.

(*Both men are now at the hall*)

RUSSELL

Art . . .

(*There are several whoops and rebel yells from stage left*)

HOCKSTADER

You go on in there with those crazy Texans. (*Chuckles*) I sure wish I was a fly on that wall, listening to you tell the whole *truth* about what you really think of the depletion of oil resources allowance!

RUSSELL

(*Laughs*)

Get out of here, you old bum . . .

(*Both men are now in the bedroom.* HOCKSTADER *smiles, as he crosses to the bathroom door at right*)

HOCKSTADER

Now is that a respectful way to talk to the end of an era? The last of the Great Hicks as he shuffles off the stage? By way of the privy.

(HOCKSTADER *waves as he exits.* RUSSELL *goes back into the living room.* JENSEN *enters*)

JENSEN

(*Eagerly*)

Well? What did he say?

RUSSELL

He won't let us know till tonight.

JENSEN

He's going to come out for you. I know it!

RUSSELL

(*Slowly*)

No, he's going to support Joe Cantwell.

JENSEN

(*Startled*)

What! Oh, you're out of your mind. Come on, hurry up, the natives of Texas are getting restless. Now remember on the oil issue . . .

RUSSELL

I know. I know. Double talk! (*As he follows* JENSEN *off right*) For those whom we are about to deceive, oh Lord, make us truly compassionate!

CURTAIN

## ACT ONE

### SCENE TWO

*The Cantwell suite. A few minutes later.* MABEL CANTWELL, *a blonde, pretty woman of forty in a dressing gown, lies on a sofa, watching television and drinking a martini. Around the room, placards and posters implore us to vote for Senator Joe Cantwell.*

COMMENTATOR'S VOICE

This is John Fox with the news. Well, I guess you all know this has been some day for Philadelphia, a real old-fashioned convention day, first since 1940. We got some pictures here of the candidates arriving at the Thirtieth Street station. There's the front-runner, William Russell, with Mrs. Russell . . .

MABEL

(*Perfunctorily*)

Boo!

COMMENTATOR'S VOICE

Then, just before noon, Senator Joe Cantwell arrived.

MABEL

Yea, team!

(MABEL'S *accent is Southern*)

COMMENTATOR'S VOICE

There he is getting off the train. And there's His Honor again, meeting him. The Senator's with Don Blades, his campaign manager. Oh, and there's *Mrs.* Cantwell.

(MABEL *is suddenly alert. She studies herself carefully on the screen*)

MABEL

(*Alarm*)

Oh, my Lord, that hat!

(MABEL *goes into the bedroom, picks up the offending hat and goes into bathroom to try it on. The television set continues to sound*)

REPORTER'S VOICE

Senator, do you have a statement . . . ? We're here to . . .

CANTWELL'S VOICE

All I can say is that come Wednesday I only hope that the best man wins . . .

MABEL

(*Mechanically from bathroom*)

. . . the best man wins.

(*There is a noise of* REPORTERS *as the hall door opens.* DON BLADES, *a lean gray man, ushers the smiling* JOE CANTWELL *into the living room.* CANTWELL *is in his forties. His manner is warm, plausible. Though under great tension, he suggests ease. He has a tendency not to listen when preoccupied. He poses for one more photograph, arms victoriously raised. Then* BLADES *gets the reporters out.* CANTWELL *relaxes full-length on the sofa*)

BLADES

That went well, Joe. (*Turns off set*) You better rest before dinner.

CANTWELL

About Hockstader, what did he say when you saw him? What *exactly* did he say?

BLADES

(*For the hundredth time*)

He said he hadn't made up his mind, but he would by tonight.

CANTWELL

(*Calls*)

Mabel, honey! Come on out. It's just Don Blades and me.

(MABEL *appears. She throws herself on him. They embrace warmly*)

CANTWELL

(*Laughing*)

Hey, come on! You better get dressed. We got to go down to dinner in (*Looks at watch*) thirty minutes.

MABEL

I'll be ready . . . don't you worry, baby. Fix yourself a drink, Don.

(BLADES *is at the bar upstage*)

BLADES

Can I get you anything, Mabel?

MABEL

Oh, no, I don't think so. I don't . . . well, maybe just the teeniest martini, to settle my stomach. (*Concern*) Oh, Joe, you look so tired.

CANTWELL

(*Automatically*)

Never felt better.

(CANTWELL *picks up a newspaper and reads, frowning*)

MABEL

Well, I finally got through the women's tea and I've been here watching the TV. We got awful nice coverage, Joe . . . though that new hat of mine is clearly a mistake. It looks like I have no chin, but even with no chin I certainly look better than Alice Russell. My God, she is a chilly-looking woman, just like an English teacher I had back at State College, the spittin image . . . from Boston she was and always wore her hair in this bun with no make-up and of course thought she was the cat's meow . . .

(BLADES *gives her a drink*)

BLADES

Here you go, Mabel.

MABEL

Thank you, Don.

CANTWELL

Hey, Don, that joke of yours looks pretty good.

BLADES

Oh? Which one was that?

CANTWELL

(*Reads*)

"At his press conference yesterday, Senator Cantwell quipped: 'Bill Russell has more solutions than there are problems.' "

(MABEL *tastes the martini. She sighs*)

MABEL

Don, the best martinis are made five to one, not five to four.

BLADES

I never could make a mixed drink.

MABEL

(*To* CANTWELL)

All the papers say Hockstader's going to come out for Bill Russell, heaven knows why, with your record in the Senate . . .

CANTWELL

(*Shuts his eyes*)

I am tired. (*Then he sits up, abruptly. He turns to* BLADES) I got to see Hockstader. Right now. Before that dinner.

BLADES

What are you going to tell him?

CANTWELL

Everything. The works. Maybe he won't come out for me afterwards but he'll sure drop Bill Russell.

BLADES

(*Rises*)

O.K. You're the boss.

CANTWELL

Go on up there. He's on the seventh floor. Tell him I've *got* to see him before dinner which is in (*Looks at watch*) twenty-seven minutes.

BLADES

Aye, aye, my captain.

(CANTWELL *is on his feet. He turns irritably to* MABEL)

CANTWELL

Mabel, come on, get dressed!

MABEL

I'll be ready, Joe, stop worryin . . . don't get all het up. (*She embraces him*) Why is big Poppa Bear so mean to poor little Mama Bear?

CANTWELL

Baby, I'm sorry. (*He goes into their private baby talk*) Poppa Bear is never mean to his Mama Bear, never ever. (*His own voice*) But, honey, you've *got* to get dressed!

MABEL

O.K., I will . . . I will. Joe, when are you going to spring that . . . that stuff about Bill Russell?

CANTWELL

Tomorrow.

MABEL

The *whole* thing?

CANTWELL

Pow!

(CANTWELL *goes into bedroom, searching for his electric razor*)

MABEL

(*Rapturously*)

And then we are on our way to 1600 Pennsylvania Avenue! Oh, my, it's thrilling, isn't it? Seems just like yesterday we were skimpin along hardly able to pay the bills to have Gladys's teeth straightened, and now just look at us! Poppa Bear and Mama Bear and the baby bears all in the White House!

CANTWELL

(*From bedroom*)

Where's my electric razor?

MABEL

I'll get it! (*She goes quickly into bedroom*) I'll just start putting on my clothes and . . .

(*She finds the razor and gives it to him*)

CANTWELL

Where's that last Gallup poll?

MABEL

I think Don Blades got it. Anyway, you're two per cent higher than last week with twelve per cent undecided. Merwin gained one per cent and Russell's lost two per cent.

CANTWELL

And Red China?

MABEL

(*Promptly*)

Forty-seven per cent against recognition. Twenty-three per cent in favor. Thirty per cent don't know. I'm wearing the green organza tonight, the one from Neiman Marcus, Allan Bates sent me. I think it looks real summery and nice . . .

CANTWELL

(*Frowns*)

That's not enough in favor. Russell's a fool making an issue out of China this soon . . .

(MABEL *removes her dressing gown and starts to get into her dress*)

MABEL

I had my hair done this morning by the man in the hotel; he's very nice but terribly swishy. Anyway he didn't get the curls too tight. . . . At least I don't think so. He said Alice Russell had her hair done, too. (*Unnoticed by* MABEL, CANTWELL *goes into living room, sits at desk, turns on electric razor and reads a newspaper*) He said she refuses to entertain the thought of using so much as a rinse. Well, bully for her! She looks easily ten years older than she is. (*Frowns*) Joe, do you think I've gained weight? Around the hips? Honey, you listenin to me? (*Realizing he is in the other room,* MABEL, *pouting, crosses to living-room door, the back of her dress unzipped*) No, I guess you're not . . . You never listen to poor Mama Bear any more. (*Pause*) Joe? Have you ever been unfaithful to me?

CANTWELL

(*Turns off razor*)

No. Did you see Walter Lippmann this morning? Listen to what that guy says: "The country's affairs will be in good hands should William Russell be our next President." (*Slaps the paper down*) I don't know why I don't appeal to those would-be intellectuals. My image just doesn't project to them like his does. (*Notices* MABEL *at last*) Well, look at you! Just good enough to eat . . . (*He starts to nuzzle her in a bearish way*) Mmmm—mm—

MABEL

(*Happily nuzzled*)

Now what are you doing to me? Don't muss my hair! Now come on! Stop it! And zip me up! (*She turns around. As* JOE *zips her dress, she returns to her theme*) Joe, are you sure you haven't been unfaithful to me maybe just one little time? On one of those junkets? Like that awful one to Paris you took, where the Senators got drunk and Clarence Wetlaw contracted a social disease and Helen Wetlaw was fit to be tied?

CANTWELL

Mabel, honey, there's nobody else. And even if there was, how would I have the time? I operate on a tight schedule. (*Kisses her briefly*) You know that.

(BLADES *enters from corridor door*)

BLADES

Joe, I talked to Hockstader.

CANTWELL

Well?

BLADES

He'll be right down.

CANTWELL

And?

BLADES

Not a clue.

CANTWELL

O.K. Get me that file on Russell. (*To* MABEL, *indicating bedroom*) Honey, you go in there . . . fix your face or something. The President's on his way down.

(MABEL *nods and crosses to hall*)

MABEL

Joe . . . play it cool, like the kids say now.

CANTWELL

I will.

(BLADES *gives him a manila folder*)

BLADES

This ought to do the trick.

CANTWELL

I'll say it will. (*Turns the pages*) Oh, cute. Very cute. How's the New York delegation?

BLADES

Still split down the middle.

CANTWELL

Well, they won't be split after this.

(*A sound of excited voices from corridor*)

BLADES

Here he comes. Are you ready?

(CANTWELL *nods; he takes a position at stage right*)

CANTWELL

All set. (*Warningly*) Don: remember . . . flatter him!

(BLADES *nods, opens the door.* HOCKSTADER *in evening dress pushes his way through a mob of newsmen*)

CANTWELL

Mr. President!

(CANTWELL *beams and crosses to* HOCKSTADER *as* BLADES *shuts out the press*)

HOCKSTADER

Hello, Blades . . . Hi, Joe! (HOCKSTADER *indicates the corridor door*) Well, this ought to start some rumors.

(CANTWELL *is now shaking his hand warmly*)

CANTWELL

Gosh, I'm sorry, sir. We should've arranged for you to come in the back way.

HOCKSTADER

Oh, that's all right. We're gettin near that time anyway. (*Taps coat pocket*) Got my speech right here. My teeth are in and I'm rarin to go. (*Indicates* CANTWELL) What about you? Where's your party suit?

CANTWELL

(*Seriously*)

I have it all timed. It takes me exactly three minutes to get into a tux. Two minutes for an ordinary business suit, and that's including vest.

HOCKSTADER

(*Smiles*)

Well, ain't you a ring-tailed wonder? (*Crosses to bar*) You don't mind if I strike myself a blow for liberty?

CANTWELL

Let me . . . please . . . (*Gestures to* BLADES *to help*) Don!

HOCKSTADER

(*Fixes his own drink*)

That's all right. I know Joe doesn't have the habit. People who don't drink never realize how thirsty we old bucks get long round sundown. (*Turns thoughtfully to* CANTWELL) No, sir, you don't drink, you don't smoke, you don't philander; fact, you are about the purest young man I have ever known in public life.

CANTWELL

I try to be.

(HOCKSTADER *crosses to sofa downstage*)

HOCKSTADER

Well, I am a great admirer of virtue, though a somewhat flawed vessel of grace myself.

(HOCKSTADER *sits*)

CANTWELL

Now, Mr. President . . . you're an ideal to us in the party.

(CANTWELL *sits opposite him stage left.* BLADES *is seated stage right*)

HOCKSTADER

(*Dryly*)

Sure, Joe, sure . . . Young man, you've done a remarkable job in the Senate. Most of the time.

CANTWELL

(*Quickly*)

*Most* of the time?

HOCKSTADER

(*Nods*)

There *have* been moments when I have questioned your methods.

CANTWELL

Well, you have to fight fire with fire, Mr. President.

HOCKSTADER

And the end justifies the means?

CANTWELL

Well, yes, sir. Yes. That is what I believe.

HOCKSTADER

Well, son, I have news for you about both politics and life . . . and may I say the two are *exactly* the same thing? There are no ends, Joe, only means.

CANTWELL

Well, I don't like to disagree with you, sir, but that's just sophistry. I mean . . .

HOCKSTADER

(*Amused*)

Now! None of them two-bit words on poor old Art Hockstader. I'm just an ignorant country boy. All I'm saying is that what matters in our profession . . . which is really life . . . is *how* you do things and how you treat people and what you really feel about 'em, not some ideal goal for society, or for yourself.

CANTWELL

(*His District-Attorney voice*)

Then am I to assume, Mr. President, from the statement you have just made, that you are against planning anything?

HOCKSTADER

(*Laughs*)

Oh, here it comes! I know that voice! Senator Cantwell, boy crusader, up there on the TV with these small-time hoodlums cringing before his righteousness.

BLADES

(*To the rescue*)

Now, Mr. President, Joe was *assigned* that Subcommittee. He didn't ask for it . . . and that's a fact.

HOCKSTADER

Sure. Sure. And he just fell into that big issue: how the United States is secretly governed by the Mafia.

CANTWELL

It happened to be true. Any time you want to look at my files, Mr. President . . .

HOCKSTADER

Last time somebody asked me to look at his files, it was Senator McCarthy.

CANTWELL

(*Grimly*)

I hope, sir, you're not comparing me to him.

HOCKSTADER

No . . . no, Joe. You're a much smoother article. After all, you've got an end to which you can justify your means, getting to be President. Poor old

McCarthy was just wallowing in headlines . . . sufficient to the day were the headlines thereof. No, you're much brighter, much more ruthless.

CANTWELL

I realize some of my methods upset a lot of people . . .

BLADES

(*Righteously*)

But, Mr. President, if we hadn't been tough we would never have cracked the Mafia the way we did.

(HOCKSTADER *smiles during this*)

CANTWELL

What's so funny about that, sir?

HOCKSTADER

Nothing, only you know and I know and everybody knows . . . except I'm afraid the TV audience . . . that there never was a Mafia like you said. There was no such thing. You just cooked it up.

CANTWELL

(*Dangerously*)

So we're going to get that number, are we? Well, my figures prove . . .

HOCKSTADER

(*Sharply*)

You went after a bunch of poor Sicilian bandits on the lower East Side of New York and pretended they were running all the crime in America. Well, they're not. Of course we have a pretty fair idea who is, but you didn't go after any of them, did you? No, sir, because those big rascals are heavy contributors to political campaigns.

BLADES

(*Beginning*)

Maybe Joe didn't go after all of them, sir . . .

HOCKSTADER

Just barely scratched the surface . . .

CANTWELL

But *you* should talk. J. Edgar Hoover considered you the most morally lax President in his entire career . . .

HOCKSTADER

(*Serenely*)

I reserve my opinion of J. Edgar Hoover for a posthumous memoir or maybe a time capsule to be dug up when he has finally cleansed the republic of undesirables.

CANTWELL

Hoover is a great American!

HOCKSTADER

(*Amused*)

But we're all "great Americans," Joe. (*More seriously*) No, I don't object to your headline-grabbing and crying "Wolf" all the time, that's standard stuff in politics, but it disturbs me you take yourself so seriously. It's par for the course trying to fool the people but it's downright dangerous when you start fooling yourself.

(MABEL CANTWELL, *in the bedroom, has heard voices grow angry. She crosses to the hall and listens at the living-room door*)

CANTWELL

(*Carefully*)

Mr. President, I take myself seriously. Because I am serious. This is important to me. To all of us. Which is why I don't want any little lectures from you on how to be a statesman. And if you really want to know, I think the record of your administration is one of the heaviest loads our party has to carry.

(HOCKSTADER *is on his feet, suddenly furious.* MABEL *enters*)

MABEL

Why, Mr. President! What a nice surprise, your dropping in on us like this!

(HOCKSTADER *regains his composure*)

HOCKSTADER

Well, I was invited down here by this young man for a little conference, and here he is, turning my head with flattery.

MABEL

(*Rapturously*)

Joe admires you, I guess, more than any man in public life.

CANTWELL

(*To* MABEL)

Honey, leave us alone. (*Indicates to* BLADES *that he leave, too*) Don.

(BLADES *exits right*)

MABEL

All right, but Joe, you have to get dressed soon.

CANTWELL

O.K.

MABEL

You certainly look fine, Mr. President, after your little vacation in the hospital . . .

HOCKSTADER

Fit as a fiddle. Never felt better.

(MABEL *goes into connecting hall. She shuts the door. She listens*)

CANTWELL

I'm sorry, sir, flying off the handle like that.

HOCKSTADER

(*Smiles*)

That's O.K. You just got a case of the old pre-convention jitters . . . Now I assume you didn't ask me down here to discuss the virtues of J. Edgar Hoover.

CANTWELL

No, I didn't. (*Awkwardly*) I know you don't like me . . .

HOCKSTADER

Now that you mention it, I don't. I never have.

CANTWELL

And I've never liked your kind of politician. But that's neither here nor there. I don't expect you to come out for me tonight . . .

(HOCKSTADER *crosses to the bar upstage. He fixes himself another drink*)

HOCKSTADER

I should warn you I have often endorsed men I disliked, even mistrusted, because I thought they'd do the job.

(CANTWELL *has gone to the desk. He picks up the file.* HOCKSTADER *suffers a spasm of pain at the bar. He clutches his stomach.* CANTWELL *does not notice this*)

CANTWELL

So I have something to show you about your friend William Russell. It's all here in this file. I want you to look at it and . . . (CANTWELL *looks at* HOCKSTADER; *he realizes something is wrong*) What's the matter with you?

HOCKSTADER

(*With difficulty*)

Just . . . had to take one of my pills. (*Takes a pill*) Pep me up. (CANTWELL *nods, goes downstage to sofa. He sits.* HOCKSTADER *looks at him thoughtfully*) Joe, you believe in God, don't you?

CANTWELL

(*Promptly*)

Yes, I do.

HOCKSTADER

And you believe there's a Hereafter? And a Day of Judgment?

CANTWELL

(*Sincerely*)

I do. If I didn't think there was some meaning to all of this I wouldn't be able to go on. I'm a very religious guy, in a funny way.

(CANTWELL *spreads the contents of the folder on the coffee table*)

HOCKSTADER

I'm sure you are. (*Sighs*) Times like this I wish I was. Dying is no fun, let me tell you. And that's what I'm doing.

(CANTWELL *has not been listening*)

CANTWELL

(*Briskly*)

Now it's all here. Psychiatrist reports . . . everything. And don't ask *how* I got it. My means might've been ruthless but for once I think you'll agree the end was worth it.

(HOCKSTADER *is taken aback at being ignored. He comes downstage. He indicates the papers contemptuously*)

HOCKSTADER

What is all this . . . crap?

CANTWELL

Several years ago *your* candidate, William Russell, had what is known as a nervous breakdown.

HOCKSTADER

I know that.

CANTWELL

He was raving mad for almost a year.

HOCKSTADER

He was not raving mad. It was exhaustion from overwork . . .

CANTWELL

That was the press release. The real story's right here . . .

HOCKSTADER

I know the real story.

CANTWELL

Then you know it's political dynamite. A full report on his mental state. How he deserted his wife, how their marriage has always been a phony, a political front . . .

HOCKSTADER

I won't begin to speculate on how you got hold of this . . .

CANTWELL

And all the big words are there, manic depressive, paranoid pattern, attempted suicide . . .

HOCKSTADER

He never attempted suicide.

CANTWELL

I'm sorry. It says right here that he did. See? (*Points to page*) There. Suicidal tendencies . . .

HOCKSTADER

We've all got suicidal *tendencies*. But he never tried to kill himself.

CANTWELL

But the point is he *could*.

HOCKSTADER

I thought you said he *did* try.

CANTWELL

I did not say he did. I said he could. And then all that combined with playing around with women . . .

HOCKSTADER

So what?

CANTWELL

I suppose you find promiscuity admirable?

HOCKSTADER

I couldn't care less. I was brought up on a farm and the lesson of the rooster was not entirely lost on me. A lot of men need a lot of women and there are worse faults, let me tell you.

CANTWELL

(*Suspiciously*)

What do you mean by that?

HOCKSTADER

Just that there are rumors about every public man. Why, when I was in the White House they used to say I had paresis, and how I was supposed to be keepin this colored girl over in Alexandria, silliest damn stories you ever heard but it gave a lot of people a lot of pleasure talkin about it. You know, when that Kinsey fellow wrote that book about how many men were doin this and how many men were doin that, I couldn't help but think how right along with all this peculiar activity there was a hell of a lot of *nothin* goin on!

CANTWELL

All right, leaving the moral issue out, do you think it a good idea to elect a man President who is mentally unstable?

HOCKSTADER

He is not mentally unstable and you know it.

CANTWELL

(*Inexorably*)

A manic depressive? Apt to crack up under stress?

(HOCKSTADER *gets the point*)

HOCKSTADER

So that's your little number, is it?

CANTWELL

(*Evenly*)

If Russell doesn't withdraw before Wednesday, I am going to see that every delegate gets a copy of this psychiatric report and I am going to challenge Russell openly. I'm going to ask him if he really feels that a man with his mental record should be President of the United States. Frankly, if I were he, I'd pull out before this (*Indicates papers*) hits the fan.

HOCKSTADER

Well, you are *not* Russell . . . to state the obvious. And he might say in rebuttal that after his breakdown he served a right rough period as Secretary of State and did not show the strain in any way.

CANTWELL

One of the psychiatrists reports that this pattern of his is bound to repeat itself. He is bound to have another breakdown.

HOCKSTADER

You and your experts! You know as well as I do those head-doctors will give you about as many different opinions as you want on any subject.

CANTWELL

(*Reasonably*)

I realize that, which is why I ám going to propose that he be examined, before Wednesday, by a nonpartisan group of psychiatrists to determine if he is sane.

HOCKSTADER

You know he won't submit to that.

CANTWELL

If he doesn't, that means he has something to hide.

HOCKSTADER

Wow! You sure play rough, don't you?

CANTWELL

I regard this as a public service. (*Urgently*) Look, I'm not asking you to support me. I don't even *want* your support. But I do want you to think twice before endorsing a man who is known to be psychopathic.

HOCKSTADER

You got it figured, of course, that even to hint that a man's not right in his head will be enough to knock him off? When do you plan to throw this at him?

CANTWELL

Tomorrow.

HOCKSTADER

And of course you've waited for the last minute so he won't have a chance to clear himself before the convention starts. That's right smart.

CANTWELL

(*Not listening*)

We'll have to work out some way for him to get out of the race gracefully. I thought maybe he could say . . . well, nervous exhaustion . . . doesn't feel up to the rigors of a campaign, something like that.

HOCKSTADER

And if he doesn't withdraw "gracefully"?

CANTWELL

(*Taps folder*)

This will be circulated. And I will demand he be examined by psychiatrists.

HOCKSTADER

I suppose you realize you are now open to the same kind of treatment.

CANTWELL

I have nothing to hide in my private or public life.

HOCKSTADER

Are you absolutely certain?

CANTWELL

(*Carefully*)

Just . . . try . . . anything.

HOCKSTADER

Well, looks like we're goin to have an ugly fight on our hands. Yes, sir, a real ugly fight. (*Crosses to upstage door. He turns*) So now I am going to let you have it. And when I finish with you, my boy, you will know what it is like to get in the ring with an old-time killer. I am going to have your political scalp and hang it on my belt, along with a lot of others.

CANTWELL

(*Dangerously*)

Don't mix with me, Hockstader.

HOCKSTADER

You can't touch me. But I can send you back to the insurance business. (*He removes his speech from his pocket, almost sadly*) And just think! I was going to endorse *you* for President.

CANTWELL

I don't believe you.

HOCKSTADER

It's not that I mind your bein a bastard, don't get me wrong there . . . It's your bein such a *stupid* bastard I object to.

(*Contemptuously,* HOCKSTADER *tosses the speech at* CANTWELL'S *feet. Then he turns and exits to the corridor, flinging the door open. Flash-bulbs go off. As* HOCKSTADER *disappears into the crowd of newsmen,* CANTWELL *picks up the speech and starts to read*)

CURTAIN

## ACT TWO

### SCENE ONE

*The Russell suite. The next afternoon. A delegation is being shown out by* RUSSELL *and* JENSEN. *They pump hands. Russell placards are waved. At the bar stands* SENATOR CARLIN, *a ponderous politician of the prairies.*

JENSEN

O.K., gentlemen . . . we'll see you tomorrow, in the convention hall.

DELEGATE

(*To* RUSSELL, *warmly*)

Bill, we'll nominate you on the first ballot tomorrow . . . and that's a promise . . .

RUSSELL

(*Smiles*)

If nominated, I will run. If elected, I will serve. Thanks.

JENSEN

(*To the last* DELEGATE)

We'll be in touch with you . . . (*To* RUSSELL) Well, what do you think?

RUSSELL

Looks all right. Nobody's mentioned mental health yet.

CARLIN

What *did* you fellows think of Hockstader's speech last night?

(*Both* RUSSELL *and* JENSEN *turn, startled*)

RUSSELL

Senator Carlin! I thought you'd left . . .

CARLIN

No. Just stayed to fix myself a snort, if you don't mind. Now about Hockstader's speech last night . . .

RUSSELL

Well, I was surprised as anybody.

CARLIN

You thought he was going to endorse you?

JENSEN

(*Quickly*)

We certainly did.

CARLIN

And then the old man just got up and talked plain double talk . . .

JENSEN

At least he didn't endorse Cantwell.

(JENSEN *goes off left*)

CARLIN

No. He didn't endorse *nobody.* For a minute I thought he was going to surprise us and come out for John Merwin, just to be ornery. Now I hear you were with the old man later on last night. What's he up to? My boys think a lot of old Art and they'll go along with him . . .

RUSSELL

We were having a council of war, I guess you'd call it.

CARLIN

They say Joe's got something on you, something pretty bad.

RUSSELL

Something untrue. And frankly I'm not very worried. I'm a lot more worried about the labor plank in the platform . . .

CARLIN

(*Exasperated*)

Oh, Christ, Bill! Lay off labor, will you? You got their vote now, so don't go stirring up a lot of snakes. After all, *you're* the liberal candidate . . .

RUSSELL

What is a liberal, Senator?

(RUSSELL *crosses to bedroom, picks up dictionary, returns to living room, thumbing pages*)

CARLIN

(*Groans*)

And I thought Adlai Stevenson was a pain in the neck. A liberal is a . . . well, you, Bill Russell, are a liberal, that's what a liberal is. You.

RUSSELL

According to the dictionary a liberal is one who "favors changes and reforms tending in the direction of further democracy." Well, I am in favor of further democracy for the unions' rank and file . . .

CARLIN

Bill, please . . . I'm just a poor dumb party hack . . .

RUSSELL

I'm sorry, Senator. The terrible thing about running for President is you become a compulsive talker, forever answering questions no one has asked you.

CARLIN

Well, let me ask *you* a question. Would you consider offering the Vice-President nomination to Cantwell?

RUSSELL

No.

CARLIN

(*Sourly*)

For a compulsive talker, you sure don't have much to say on that subject. (*Sighs*) Jeez, I hate an open convention. You can't ever tell what's going to happen!

RUSSELL

(*Smiles*)

They're never that open.

CARLIN

I suppose we better try for a Catholic . . . that seems to be the big thing this year . . . for *second* place, that is. (JENSEN *returns with papers*) Bill, *don't* make things tough for yourself! You got the nomination now so leave the controversial things alone.

RUSSELL

I can't help it. I am driven by a mad demon, by some imp of the perverse . . . (CARLIN *looks at him narrowly.* JENSEN *gives him a warning look*) That is, I am *compelled* to say what I think.

CARLIN

O.K., but try to lay off stuff like Red China, especially when you know Henry Luce is an absolute nut on China and you don't want to lose *Time* and *Life* when they're already behind you in the interests of good government and all that crap. . . . So keep Henry Luce happy, will you? Once you're President, you can eat with chopsticks for all anybody cares.

RUSSELL

I will be diplomatic.

CARLIN

You know, Cantwell's releasing a statement today. To all the delegates. He says it'll knock you off.

RUSSELL

We're ready for him. He may be the master of the half truth and the insinuation, but we've got the facts.

CARLIN

And the *whole* truth?

RUSSELL

(*Lightly*)

No man has the whole truth.

CARLIN

Oh, brother! Good luck, Bill. Let me know if there's anything I can do for you. I'm with you one hundred per cent, in spite of your damned dictionary.

RUSSELL

Thank you, Senator.

(CARLIN *goes.* RUSSELL *goes into the bedroom and sits wearily on the bed*)

RUSSELL

Dick, where's Dr. Artinian?

JENSEN

On his way from the airport.

(JENSEN *enters bedroom, sits on chair opposite the bed*)

RUSSELL

And Hockstader?

JENSEN

Talking to delegates. . . . Bill, I've finally got a line on Cantwell. I got some real dirt . . .

RUSSELL

Of all the stunts, this is the craziest! If you'll excuse my obsessive use of words like "mad" and "crazy."

JENSEN

You could've cut the air with a knife when you made that crack about being "driven by a mad demon" . . .

(RUSSELL *has started his walk across the carpet*)

RUSSELL

Well, they re-elected Eisenhower after a heart attack and an ileitis operation . . . didn't seem to hurt him.

JENSEN

But there was never any question about his mind or his judgment being affected. (RUSSELL *has completed his walk*) Well? What's the score?

RUSSELL

(*Smiles*)

I still get it on the first ballot but it was a near miss: I nearly stepped on that leaf, the one by the table . . . it's a bitch. (*Indicates newspaper*) What about your daily horoscope?

JENSEN

(*From memory*)

"A.M. Fine for getting apparel in order. P.M. do not quarrel with loved one." Bill, you may have to pull a Nixon.

RUSSELL

And what does "pull a Nixon" mean?

JENSEN

Go on television. And cry on the nation's shoulder. With *two* cocker spaniels.

RUSSELL

And tell them I'm not crazy? No. I admit it's possible to look directly into a camera and persuade the people I won't steal their money, but I promise you, Dick, you can't look a camera in the face and say, "Honest, I'm not crazy. I just had a nervous breakdown like any regular fellow might." No, it won't work.

JENSEN

Why not?

RUSSELL

Because it won't. And even if it did, I couldn't do it. (*Chuckles*) I might . . . laugh. It's too idiotic.

(ALICE *enters from corridor door*)

RUSSELL

How was the meeting?

ALICE

I made a speech. At least I started to read the one Dick gave me. Then halfway through I gave up and made my own speech, and do you know what? It was terrible! (*Suddenly grave*) What's happened?

RUSSELL

Dr. Artinian's on his way to Philadelphia. He's going to tell the press that I am not and never was insane.

ALICE

It gets worse and worse, doesn't it?

RUSSELL

Yes, it does.

(JENSEN *rises, crosses to connecting-hall door*)

JENSEN

I've got to get back to work. Here. (*He puts a schedule on the other twin bed*) We have Ohio in twenty minutes. Then one more go at California.

RUSSELL

Send Dr. Artinian in the second he gets here.

(JENSEN *nods, exits left*)

ALICE

Does this mean they could publish everything about us? Our marriage and . . . *everything?*

RUSSELL

Yes.

(ALICE *sits on the same twin bed as* RUSSELL; *they are back to back*)

ALICE

Will they?

RUSSELL

I don't know. I think it's just a bluff right now, to frighten me.

ALICE

It frightens me. I should hate to think of the children reading all that about us. Oh, it is filthy . . . filthy!

RUSSELL

Do you want me to quit?

ALICE
(*A pause*)

No.

(RUSSELL *puts his hand on* ALICE'S; *she smiles*)

ALICE

How very odd!

RUSSELL

What?

ALICE

Do you realize that this is the first time you've touched me when there wasn't a camera or someone in the room?

(*There is a tense moment; then he pats her hand briskly and rises; he picks up the sheet of paper* JENSEN *left on the other bed*)

RUSSELL

Well, here's your schedule. Your next appointment is . . . Oh, my God, I forgot all about this!

ALICE
(*Grimly*)

I haven't. Mabel Cantwell and I face the press together. Can I get out of it?

RUSSELL

No. Better not.

ALICE

Then I'll get ready. We're meeting in her suite. She made the point very tactfully over the phone that (ALICE *lapses into deep Mabelese*) accordin to protocol the wife of a reignin Senator outranks the wife of a former Secretary of State.

RUSSELL
(*Equally Southern*)

Well, bless my soul!

(ALICE *goes.* DR. ARTINIAN, *a distinguished-looking psychiatrist . . . the first to be depicted in the American theater without a Mittel-Europa accent . . . enters with* JENSEN *from left.* RUSSELL *crosses living room to greet him, just as the buzzer from the corridor sounds.* JENSEN *hurries to corridor door*)

RUSSELL

Robert, I'm glad you could get away like this . . .

ARTINIAN

I had to.

(JENSEN *opens corridor door to admit* HOCKSTADER, *who darts in while* JENSEN *pushes back the press*)

RUSSELL

Dr. Artinian . . . President Hockstader.

(HOCKSTADER *and* ARTINIAN *shake hands*)

HOCKSTADER

You Bill's head-doctor?

ARTINIAN

That's right. And I'm a very great admirer of yours, Mr. President.

HOCKSTADER

Well, I'm *not* an admirer of yours. Why don't you people keep your damned files where nobody can get at 'em?

ARTINIAN

We do. Or we thought we did. Apparently somebody from Cantwell's office bribed one of our nurses . . . they got the entire case history.

RUSSELL

Robert, in one hour Cantwell's releasing that file on me. Now I know this sounds silly, but when he does, I want you to meet the press and tell them I am *not* mentally unstable.

ARTINIAN

Of course I will. You don't know how guilty I feel about this.

(ARTINIAN *turns to exit left with* JENSEN)

HOCKSTADER

(*Suddenly*)

He *is* all right, isn't he?

ARTINIAN

(*Smiles*)

Mr. Russell is one of the sanest men I ever have known.

HOCKSTADER

Then what's all that stuff about suicide tendencies and manic-mania or whatever you call it?

ARTINIAN

Just technical phrases which may sound sinister to a layman. He is certainly *not* a manic depressive. Anyone's psychological profile could be made to sound . . . damaging.

RUSSELL

(*Lightly*)

In the South a candidate for sheriff once got elected by claiming that his opponent's wife had been a thespian.

JENSEN

We'll find a room for you here, Doctor. And I'll get somebody to help you with your statement.

ARTINIAN

Thank you. I also brought the Institute's lawyer with me. By way of making amends, Bill, we're filing suit against Cantwell for theft . . .

HOCKSTADER

(*Pleased*)

That's the ticket. Go to it, Doc.

ARTINIAN

(*To* RUSSELL)

I'll be ready when you want me.

RUSSELL

(*Warmly*)

Many thanks, Robert.

(ARTINIAN *and* JENSEN *go off left.* RUSSELL *is about to follow when* HOCKSTADER *stops him*)

HOCKSTADER

Bill, I want you to myself a minute. Now what's this I hear about you not goin on the TV?

RUSSELL

I can't.

HOCKSTADER

How the hell you goin to fight this thing if you don't?

RUSSELL

Dr. Artinian . . .

HOCKSTADER

(*Disgust*)

Dr. Artinian! That's just *one* doctor. They'll say he's a friend of yours. Cantwell's going to insist they have half the medical profession look you over between now and tomorrow . . . (*Pacing happily*) Oh, I tell you, Bill, I feel wonderful! Up all night . . . on the go all morning, seein delegates . . . I tell you there is *nothin* like a dirty low-down political fight to put the roses in your cheeks.

RUSSELL

(*Concerned*)

How *do* you feel?

HOCKSTADER

Immortal! Now a lot of the delegates know that somethin's up. They don't know what . . .

RUSSELL

(*Abruptly*)

Art, why didn't you endorse me last night?

HOCKSTADER

(*Awkwardly*)

Look, Bill, this isn't easy to say, but you might as well know: I came to Philadelphia to nominate Cantwell.

RUSSELL

(*Nods*)

I knew that.

HOCKSTADER

(*Taken aback*)

You did! How?

RUSSELL

(*Wryly*)

Prince Hamlet has second sight. He sees motives as well as ghosts upon the battlement.

HOCKSTADER

Guess I ain't as sly as I figured I was.

RUSSELL

Did you decide to help me now because of what Joe's doing? Bringing up that breakdown business?

HOCKSTADER

No. No. Matter of fact . . . speaking as a professional politician . . . I kind of admire what he's doing. It's clever as all hell. No, Joe Cantwell lost me because he wasn't smart. He made a mistake. He figured I was goin to back you when I wasn't. You got my message. Joe didn't. Now that's a serious error. Shows he don't understand character and a President if he don't understand anything else has got to understand people. Then he got flustered when I needled him. A President don't get flustered when a man gives him the needle. He keeps a straight face, like poker. (*Smiles*) Like you're doin right now. But what does Joe do? He don't run scared; he runs terrified. He fires off a cannon to kill a bug. And that is just plain dumb and I mean to knock him off . . . which means that you, I guess, are goin to be our next President.

RUSSELL

President . . . but by default. Because you still have your doubts about me, don't you?

HOCKSTADER

Yes, I still have my doubts. Bill, I want a strong President . . .

RUSSELL

An immoral President?

(HOCKSTADER *turns away disgustedly*)

HOCKSTADER

They hardly come in any other size.

RUSSELL

You don't believe that . . .

(JENSEN *enters with a plump, bald, nervous man of forty-odd who resembles an unmade studio couch*)

JENSEN

This is Sheldon Marcus.

HOCKSTADER

(*Irritably*)

Who the hell is Sheldon Marcus? (HOCKSTADER *turns, sees that the man is already in the room; he flashes a Presidential smile and, hand outstretched, crosses to* MARCUS) If you'll excuse me, sir?

MARCUS

That's all right. I . . . I never thought I'd meet a President. (MARCUS *rubs his shaken hand against his trouser leg*) My hands sweat. I . . . I'm nervous, I guess. You see, I just now came in from Wilmington, where I live, outside Wilmington's actually where I live, a suburb you never heard of called . . .

RUSSELL

Dick, what's this all about? I'm Bill Russell.

JENSEN

Mr. Marcus served in the army with Joe Cantwell . . .

HOCKSTADER

In the army? (*Starts to beam with anticipation*) Ah . . . ah . . . *Now* we're gettin somewhere. Well, what was it? Was he a member of the Ku Klux Klan? The Communist Party? Or did he run away when the guns went off?

MARCUS

Well, sir, Mr. President, sir, uh, we weren't anywheres around where there were guns . . .

JENSEN

They were both in the Aleutians. On the island of Adak. The Quartermaster Corps.

MARCUS

(*Nods*)

We were there for a year, well, maybe more like eighteen months for me and, oh, maybe sixteen, seventeen months for Joe, he came there February '43 and I got there . . .

RUSSELL

(*To* JENSEN)

Dick, what are you trying to prove?

HOCKSTADER

Now shush, Bill. And let's hear the dirt, whatever it is.

MARCUS

Well . . . Joe . . . (*Pauses in an agony of embarrassment*) Oh, I sure hate talking about him, telling something so awful . . .

JENSEN

I had a lead on this months ago. I finally tracked it down. . . . Tell them, Mr. Marcus.

MARCUS

Well, Joe Cantwell was a captain and I was a captain and Joe Cantwell was . . . was . . . well, he was . . . you know how it is sometimes when there's all those men together and . . . and . . .

JENSEN

And no female companionship . . .

MARCUS

That's right, though we had some nurses later on, but not enough to make much difference. I mean there were all those men . . .

JENSEN

(*Helpfully*)

And no women.

RUSSELL

(*Irritated*)

Oh, for Christ's sake, Dick, stop it, will you?

HOCKSTADER

(*Soothingly*)

Now . . . now, let's not get ahead of ourselves.

RUSSELL

You know Joe isn't that, and if he was, so what?

HOCKSTADER

I find this very interesting. Mr. Marcus . . . Captain Marcus, I should say . . .

MARCUS

(*Gabbling*)

I was a major, actually, promoted just before my discharge in '46. I'm in the reserve . . . the *in*active reserve . . . but if there was another war I would be . . .

HOCKSTADER

(*Through him*)

Major Marcus, am I to understand by the way you are beating slowly around the bush that Joe Cantwell is what . . . when I was a boy . . . we called a de-generate?

MARCUS

(*Relieved to have the word said*)

Yes, sir, Mr. President, sir, that's just what I mean . . .

RUSSELL

(*Amused in spite of himself*)

I don't believe it! Nobody with that awful wife and those ugly children could be anything but normal!

HOCKSTADER

Bill! Patience. Whether *you* believe it or not is beside the point.

RUSSELL

And even if it were true I'm damned if I'd smear him with something like that . . .

HOCKSTADER

(*Patiently and slowly*)

Bill, I, like you, am a tolerant man. I *personally* do not care if Joe Cantwell enjoys deflowering sheep by the light of a full moon. But I am interested in finding a way to stop him cold.

RUSSELL

Damn it, Art, this is exactly the kind of thing I went into politics to stop! The business of gossip instead of issues, personalities instead of policies . . . We've got enough on Cantwell's *public* life to defeat him without going into his private life which is nobody's business!

HOCKSTADER

(*Sharply*)

Any more than yours is?

RUSSELL

Any more than mine is.

HOCKSTADER

But Cantwell *is* using your private life . . .

RUSSELL

All the more reason for my *not* using his. I'm not Cantwell.

HOCKSTADER

(*Reasonably*)

But nobody's used anything *yet*.

RUSSELL

Look here, Art, you are *not* my campaign manager. I am the one running for President, not you. (*To* JENSEN, *grimly*) And as for you, Dick . . .

JENSEN

(*Growing desperate*)

Bill, at least *listen* to the man.

RUSSELL

No!

HOCKSTADER

I'm beginnin to wonder if maybe I'm tryin to help the wrong team.

RUSSELL

(*Losing control*)

Perhaps you are. Perhaps you'd be happier with Cantwell, helping him throw his mud! (*A tense silence.* HOCKSTADER *remains impassive.* RUSSELL *recovers himself quickly. He is contrite*) Art, I'm sorry. I didn't mean that.

HOCKSTADER

(*Amused*)

Observe how I kept a straight face while being insulted?

RUSSELL

You know that I only meant . . .

HOCKSTADER

(*Through him*)

Yes, I know. (*Wheedling*) Now, Bill, as a favor to an old man in his . . . sunset years, will you just listen to Major Marcus? That's all. Just listen.

RUSSELL

All right, Art. I'll listen. But only as a favor to . . . to a friend.

HOCKSTADER

That's fine, Bill. You just relax now and let events take their course. (HOCKSTADER *crosses to the dazed* MARCUS) After all, how often does a million dollars (*Pats* MARCUS) drop in your lap? Not to mention the Presidency. (*Propels* MARCUS *to a chair downstage*) Sit down, Major Marcus, sit down. Please. Make yourself comfortable. Fact, I will mix you a drink myself with these old skilled fingers, and while I do you will tell us your story. (*Crosses to bar*) Omitting no details, no matter how sordid.

(RUSSELL *turns upstage, revolted*)

MARCUS

Well, Mr. President, there was this guy up on Adak, and his name was Fenn, Bob Fenn. That is, *Robert* Fenn. (*Light starts to fade*) I don't know his middle initial but I guess it's all there in the record, how this Lieutenant Fenn . . .

CURTAIN

## ACT TWO

### SCENE TWO

*The Cantwell suite. A few minutes later.* MABEL, ALICE *and* MRS. GAMADGE *sit in a row on the sofa in the living room.* MRS. GAMADGE *is in a long evening dress with a vast corsage.* REPORTERS *and* CAMERAMEN *are winding up a press conference.* BLADES *hovers, directs.*

BLADES

All right, boys . . . come on . . . that's enough . . . our girls have got a lot to do . . .

REPORTER I

Mrs. Russell, where are your sons now?

ALICE

They . . . well, one's in Watch Hill and the other's traveling . . . he's in Europe. I wish now we had them here, for the experience.

(*A flash-bulb goes off*)

MABEL

Oh, I blinked my eyes! (*To* REPORTER 1 *gaily*) Joe and I were going to bring our girls to Philadelphia but then we decided, no, this sort of thing is just too hectic for children . . .

REPORTER 2

Mrs. Russell . . . how's *Mr.* Russell today?

ALICE

He's just fine . . .

REPORTER 3

There has been a rumor that he is not in the very best of health.

ALICE

(*Growing steely*)

I have never seen him in better health.

MABEL

My Joe just blossoms during a campaign! On the go all the time! I don't know *where* he gets the energy.

ALICE

In fact, my husband . . .

MRS. GAMADGE

(*Through her*)

Joe Cantwell is a real dynamo!

ALICE

(*A second try*)

In fact, my husband . . .

MABEL

I sometimes think Joe has got nerves of iron. Nothing ever seems to upset him.

MRS. GAMADGE

(*Nods*)

He has a great inner calm, which is almost spiritual.

ALICE

(*Gamely*)

My husband . . .

BLADES

O.K. That's it, fellows . . .

(*The* REPORTERS *start to go*)

REPORTER 3

(*To* ALICE)

What do you think's going to happen tomorrow? Do you think Mr. Russell's got it on the first ballot?

ALICE

I certainly hope so!

MABEL

(*Butter would not melt, etc.*)

Well, as for me, I just hope the best man wins! I mean for the country and everything.

MRS. GAMADGE

Amen to that!

(BLADES *follows* REPORTERS *out into corridor*)

BLADES

Good day, ladies!

(*The three women are alone.* MRS GAMADGE *sighs gustily*)

MABEL

Well, *that* was an ordeal, wasn't it, Mrs. Russell?

ALICE

I'm sure it wasn't for you. (*Afraid this sounded too sharp, amends*) I mean you've done so much of this . . . kind of thing. (*Rises*) I have to go.

(MABEL *gets to her feet quickly*)

MABEL

Oh, stay and have a drink . . . just for a minute. I don't have anything to do till (*Looks at schedule*) . . . till four-fifteen. So let's play hooky!

ALICE

I'm afraid I have an appointment in fifteen minutes.

MRS. GAMADGE

They have us girls on timetables just like trains. Will you look at me? (*She rises*) All ready to moderate the fashion show at five o'clock.

(MRS. GAMADGE *crosses to bar for a Coca Cola, which she drinks with a straw*)

MABEL

(*Cozily*)

It's a shame we couldn't do everything together, instead of first you meetin one group and then me meetin the same group . . . What can I fix you?

(MABEL *makes herself a drink*)

ALICE

Nothing, thanks. It's too early for me.

(MRS. GAMADGE *is back on the sofa, reading a newspaper*)

MRS. GAMADGE

Well, didn't Art Hockstader surprise everybody last night?

MABEL

Personally, I think he's an old meanie the way he's holding out. And you know why? (*Indicates newspaper*) Publicity! He absolutely revels in the limelight. . . . Oh, Mrs. Russell, I don't believe you've seen my children.

ALICE

I've seen pictures of them. They're very . . . pretty.

(MABEL *holds up a photograph*)

MABEL

That's Gladys there, the oldest . . . with the braces on her teeth. I'm afraid they're all going to have to have braces and Lord knows *where* they got those teeth from. Both Joe and I have perfect teeth, and oh! what a fortune it is having children's teeth straightened! Do you have a picture of your boys?

ALICE

No. Not with me . . .

MRS. GAMADGE

So good-looking . . .

MABEL

Yes! That was a nice spread on them in *Life.* Such *warm* pictures! You and Mr. Russell certainly get a lot of coverage from *Life,* much more than we do.

ALICE

Oh? I thought we were neck and neck.

MABEL

No. I'm afraid Joe and I must simply forget Mr. Luce. You're *his* candidate. For the time being. Oh, come on, sit down. (*Affectionately*) I do like the way you do your hair.

ALICE

Oh? Well . . .

MABEL

You look so like this English teacher I had at State College. A wonderful woman in every way . . .

ALICE

Thank you. But I'm afraid I'm not wonderful . . .

MABEL

Now . . . no false modesty! You are wonderful *and* courageous. I always say Alice Russell is the most courageous woman in public life, don't I, Sue-Ellen?

(MRS. GAMADGE, *immersed in her paper, nods*)

ALICE

(*Curiously*)

In what way, courageous?

MABEL

Why, that committee you were on!

MRS. GAMADGE

(*Suddenly alert*)

Committee? *What* committee?

MABEL

(*Ready for the kill*)

You know—in New York City, the one where you did all that work for *birth control.*

MRS. GAMADGE

(*Horror*)

Birth control! I didn't know that.

ALICE

Well, it *was* twenty years ago. And of course I'm not supposed to mention it now . . . (*To* MABEL) as *you* know.

MRS. GAMADGE

I should hope not! You'll have the Catholics down on us like a ton of bricks. The rhythm cycle, yes (*Makes a vague circular motion with her hand*), but anything else . . . is out.

MABEL

Of course I'm against any kind of artificial means of birth control except where it's a matter of health maybe, but believe me I think it took the courage of a lion to be in favor of people using these contraceptive things when you're in public life. Of course I guess you didn't know then your husband would be running for President one day and when you do that you just can't afford to offend a lot of nice people who vote.

ALICE

I realize that. We must offend no one. Of course, if you offend no one, you don't please anyone very much either, do you? But I suppose that is an occupational hazard in politics. We are all interchangeably inoffensive.

(*There is a pause*)

MRS. GAMADGE

Well, now!

MABEL

(*Overlapping*)

Well, hooray for Mrs. Russell! Do you know, you sounded just like your husband then? Didn't she, Sue-Ellen? Didn't she sound just like Bill Russell when he's being witty and profound and way over our poor heads!

ALICE

(*Rising*)

I'd like to think intelligence was contagious. But I'm afraid it isn't, at least in my case. Bill has the brains. I'm not awfully quick.

MABEL

Oh, yes, you are, honey!

ALICE

I've really got to go.

(ALICE *turns upstage.* MRS. GAMADGE *and* MABEL *follow her*)

MRS. GAMADGE

You girls are an absolute inspiration to the American woman, *and I meant it* . . . each in your different way.

ALICE

Thank you very much . . . for that.

MABEL

(*One last shot*)

Oh, by the way, how *is* Mr. Russell's health? I mean *really*? I thought he looked so peaked last night at the dinner and someone did say . . .

ALICE

(*Grimly*)

The reporters are gone, Mrs. Cantwell. You know as well as I do he's perfectly all right. Good-bye.

MRS. GAMADGE

'Bye.

(ALICE *goes*)

MABEL

Well . . . listen to her! "The reporters are gone, Mrs. Cantwell!" If she wasn't so high and mighty she'd take the hint and start saying right now he isn't feeling good so that when he has to pull out there'd be some preparation . . .

(MABEL *goes into bedroom and flops onto the rumpled bed*)

MRS. GAMADGE

(*Following her*)

Mabel, I don't like anything about what Joe's doing. It's plain dirty and I should warn you: I'm a loyal party worker and I'll see that the women are all behind Bill Russell.

MABEL

*Under* him is more their usual position. It's just sex, sex, sex, morning, noon and night with that Bill Russell.

MRS. GAMADGE

Now, Mabel, unless you were in the room, how would you know?

MABEL

I read that report. Bill Russell is a neurotic who has had a breakdown and his sex life is certainly not normal. Sleeping around with all those women is just plain immature. And we don't want an immature President, do we?

MRS. GAMADGE

We've had some very good Presidents who have slept around a lot more than Bill Russell ever did. And in the White House, too.

(BLADES, CANTWELL *and* CARLIN *enter living room from corridor*)

MABEL

(*Hears them*)

Here come the men!

MRS. GAMADGE

And I must get back to the women. (*She is about to leave through the corridor door when she is surprised to see* CARLIN. *She comes into the living room*) Hello, Senator Carlin. Didn't expect to see you *here.*

CARLIN

Just happened to be in the neighborhood.

(CANTWELL *comes up behind* MRS. GAMADGE *and kisses the back of her neck. She squeals*)

CANTWELL

Hi, Sue-Ellen!

MRS. GAMADGE

(*Quickly recovered*)

Joe, I hope you don't mind if I take the bull by the horns and tell you right now that anything to do with *private* lives is out in politics.

CANTWELL

I couldn't agree more.

MRS. GAMADGE

That's an unwritten law and it's a good one. Once you throw at a man that he has a mistress or an illegitimate child or something like that you get sympathy for him. (*Sadly*) I don't know why but you do. You also make yourself vulnerable because nobody's a saint. Not even you, Joe. So keep what you men do *in* bed *out* of politics. (*She goes, waving gaily*) 'Bye, Joe. 'Bye, Bill. 'Bye, Mabel.

CANTWELL

(*To* BLADES)

Photostats ready?

BLADES

All neatly bound. Six hundred copies to be released to the delegates at three-thirty P.M. Russell's doctor is in town. That means there's going to be some kind of a statement.

CANTWELL

(*Nods*)

He's going to fight.

CARLIN

Aren't you fellows afraid of getting into trouble? Stealing medical records?

BLADES

(*Quickly*)

We didn't steal them.

CANTWELL

They were given to us. *Pro bono publico.* Now just look at this . . . (CANTWELL *shows* CARLIN *the file. The phone rings in living room.* MABEL *answers it*)

MABEL

Yes? Who? Oh, Dick Jensen! Yes, Joe's here. Just a sec. You hold on now. (*To* CANTWELL, *excited*) This is it, honey! They're giving up!

CANTWELL

(*Takes phone*)

Hi, Dick. Howsa boy? Fine . . . Well, gosh, I don't see how I can delay much longer. I've told everybody three-thirty. Of course I'd sort of hoped Bill would be helpful. You know, for the Party's sake. He could back out so easily now, on this health issue . . . Yeah? Well, frankly, I don't see any point to postponing . . . Do I know who? Shel-don Mar-cus? No, I don't think so . . . *Where?* (*Harshly*) I want to see Russell. Right now . . . Well, try and fix it; I'll be right here. (*He hangs up, frowning*)

MABEL

Well, honey, what did he say? Come on now . . . give with the T.L.!

BLADES

(*Concerned*)

You aren't going to meet with Russell, are you? I thought we'd decided . . .

CANTWELL

Hold that stuff on Russell.

BLADES

Hold it? But we can't. We promised the delegates, three-thirty, we said . . .

CANTWELL

I said hold it.

MABEL

(*Alarm*)

Joe, what's happening?

(CANTWELL *takes the file from* CARLIN)

CANTWELL

Senator, if you'll excuse me . . .

CARLIN

Oh, sure . . . sure . . . Well, good-bye, Mrs. Cantwell. (*At the door, he turns to* CANTWELL) You know where to find me . . . *after* three-thirty.

(CARLIN *goes*)

CANTWELL

(*To* BLADES)

Go on. Stop that release.

BLADES

(*Bewildered*)

O.K. . . . you're the boss.

(BLADES *goes off right.* CANTWELL *goes into bedroom. He sits down on the bed, thinking hard.* MABEL *follows, panic beginning*)

MABEL

Joe, what did Russell say to you? What's he doing to you?

(CANTWELL *looks at her blankly.* MABEL *begins to understand*)

MABEL

It's not . . . it's not . . .

(MABEL *stops. Slowly,* CANTWELL *nods.* MABEL, *horrified, sits beside him on the bed, her arm around him*)

MABEL

(*Softly*)

Oh, my God!

CURTAIN

## ACT TWO

### SCENE THREE

*The Russell suite. A few minutes later.* MARCUS *has just finished his story.* RUSSELL *stands upstage, back to audience.* HOCKSTADER *starts to rise from sofa to give* MARCUS *some papers he's been studying. He sits back suddenly.* MARCUS *takes the papers from him, as* JENSEN *enters from left.*

JENSEN

(*Excitedly*)

You should've heard Cantwell's voice! First time I've ever heard him stuck! (*To* RUSSELL) He wants to see you. So I said three-thirty and he agreed without a peep. That means *no* announcement to the delegates.

(RUSSELL *turns and crosses to* MARCUS, *who rises*)

RUSSELL

Mr. Marcus, I want to thank you. I know that all this must be as . . . distasteful to you as it is to us.

(RUSSELL *shakes* MARCUS'S *hand*)

MARCUS

Well, yes, it is . . . Peggy, my wife, oh, she was fit to be tied when I said I'd talked to Mr. Jensen and was going to come here and see you. She knew the whole story of course. I tell her everything, we have no secrets, Mrs. Marcus and me . . .

(RUSSELL *talks through him as he tries to get him off stage left*)

RUSSELL

Yes . . . yes . . . well, many thanks.

JENSEN

(*To* MARCUS)

Would you wait . . . please? In my office? That's the second room, across the hall.

MARCUS

Yes, sir, Mr. Jensen. (*To* HOCKSTADER) I guess this is the biggest moment of my life, meeting you, Mr. President, sir.

(HOCKSTADER, *seated, shakes his hand*)

HOCKSTADER

I expect this *is* the biggest moment of your life, Major. You may have changed history. Excuse me for not getting up.

(MARCUS *is now beginning to enjoy the situation*)

MARCUS

I'll say one thing, I certainly never thought back in '44 when Joe Cantwell and I were on Adak that sixteen years later we'd be here in this hotel with him running for President and me talking to you, sir, who I always admired (*Confidentially*), though I didn't vote for you the second time. You see, Mrs. Marcus felt that . . .

HOCKSTADER

(*Dulcet tones*)

Let your vote, Major Marcus, remain between you and your God.

MARCUS

(*Overcome by this wisdom*)

I guess that's right. Yes. Yes! I'll remember that, sir, I really will . . . (*To* JENSEN, *at door*) I won't have to see Joe, will I?

JENSEN

We hope not.

MARCUS

He's just awful when he's mad . . . he's got this temper. It's like stepping on a snake, stepping on Joe. He can be real scary.

(JENSEN *gets him through the door at last*)

JENSEN

We'll remember that. Thanks a lot. See you in a few minutes. . . . (*To* RUSSELL) Bill, we've done it! We've stopped Joe Cantwell!

RUSSELL

(*Indicates a folder on the coffee table in front of* HOCKSTADER)

I'm not going to use this.

JENSEN

(*Quickly*)

Of course you're not. Except privately. We just take this to Joe and say: "If you make an issue out of this breakdown, *we* make an issue out of a certain bit of court-martial testimony . . ."

(ALICE *enters from corridor*)

RUSSELL

Alice, how did it go?

ALICE

My cheeks are tired from smiling for the camera. (*To* HOCKSTADER) But I must say I'm beginning to like politics, Mr. President, especially when Mrs. Gamadge tells me that I'm an inspiration to American women . . . in my way.

HOCKSTADER

You're an inspiration to me, Miss Alice. Excuse me for not getting up, but would you fetch me some branch water, some just *plain* branch water?

ALICE

Of course. (ALICE *goes to bar*) Well, first we talked about Mabel's children. Then we talked about *my* children. Then we discussed the role of women in politics. We both agreed that woman's true place was in the home.

RUSSELL

I'm sure Mrs. Gamadge was eloquent on that subject.

ALICE

Eloquent to the point of obsession. We also agreed that women should be informed about issues.

HOCKSTADER

Worst damn thing ever happened to this country, giving the women the vote. Trouble, trouble, trouble. They got no more sense than a bunch of geese. Give 'em a big smile and a pinch on the . . . anatomy and you got ten votes.

ALICE

(*Smiles*)

May I quote you, Mr. President?

HOCKSTADER

I will deny ever having made such a vile and un-American statement. (*Takes glass*) Thank you, ma'am.

ALICE

(*To* RUSSELL)

And, finally, there were some pointed references to your health . . .

RUSSELL

Which means they've started. Mentally unstable. Apt to crack up . . . already showing signs of the strain. (*Sighs*) As a matter of fact, I *am* showing signs of strain.

(JENSEN *holds up folder*)

JENSEN

Bill, you can stop them. Right now. We've got the ultimate weapon, massive retaliation as Foster Dulles used to say. (WOMAN AID *opens door at left; she whispers something to* JENSEN, *who nods. She goes.* JENSEN *beams*) We have a visitor.

(BLADES *enters, simulating jauntiness*)

BLADES

Gentlemen . . . Mr. President!

(HOCKSTADER *ignores him*)

RUSSELL

Mr. Blades, contrary to what you may have been told, I'm *not* seeing Joe Cantwell.

BLADES

Oh? But I thought you were. I thought Joe said you'd meet in his room because there aren't so many reporters down there . . .

JENSEN

(*To* RUSSELL)

That's right, Bill. I said we'd be right down . . .

RUSSELL

You did!

(BLADES *studies every nuance, trying to get a sense of what is happening*)

BLADES

So I came up to work out some way of getting the Secretary downstairs without anybody seeing him. I checked the service elevator and . . .

HOCKSTADER

Dick, you and that hatchet man there go try out the bathroom route. Through the bedroom. Into the next suite and on down.

BLADES

(*Probing*)

O.K., Mr. President, but if the Secretary *isn't* going downstairs . . .

HOCKSTADER

(*Cold command*)

Get moving, boys.

(JENSEN *indicates for* BLADES *to go with him*)

JENSEN

Come on, Don. This is the dry run.

(*Reluctantly,* BLADES *follows* JENSEN *into the bathroom by way of the bedroom*)

RUSSELL
(*To* HOCKSTADER)

I'm not going to do this.

HOCKSTADER

You have to.

ALICE

Do what?

HOCKSTADER

He's got the stuff to knock off Cantwell. Only your lily-livered husband won't go through with it.

ALICE
(*To* RUSSELL)

You can keep them from bringing up all that . . . mental business?

RUSSELL

Maybe . . .

HOCKSTADER

Definitely.

ALICE

Then do it!

RUSSELL

But you don't know what it is I have to do.

ALICE
(*Fiercely*)

I don't care! If you took a gun and shot him I'd help you if I thought that was the only way of keeping our lives . . . private.

HOCKSTADER

Atta girl! Listen to her, Bill. *She* don't run from a fight.

RUSSELL

You know I'm not afraid.

HOCKSTADER

(*Exasperation*)

Then what is wrong with you? Why are you hesitatin *this* time?

RUSSELL

Look, I'm not being righteous and I'm not being fastidious and I do want to win. But how can I, in all conscience, use . . . *this,* even against Cantwell!

HOCKSTADER

(*Furiously*)

I should've stuck with Cantwell! Because listenin to you hem and haw and talk about your conscience is turnin me against you fast. My God, what would happen if you had to make a quick decision in the White House when maybe all our lives depended on whether you could act fast . . . and you just sat there, the way you're doin now, having a high old time with your divided conscience.

RUSSELL

(*Hotly*)

I am *not* divided! I know what I should do and this is *not* it.

HOCKSTADER

Then you don't want to be king of the castle. So stay away from us. Be a saint on your own time. Because you aren't fit to lead anybody.

RUSSELL

(*Stung*)

Why? Because I don't "fire off a cannon to kill a bug"? Because I don't have that quick mindless reaction you seem to confuse with strength? Well, I promise you, there is more danger in a President who acts on animal reflex than in one who is willing to reflect before he acts, who has some vestigial moral sense that goes beyond himself. Don't you see? If I start to fight like Cantwell I lose all meaning . . .

HOCKSTADER

(*Evenly*)

If you don't start to fight, you are finished. Now I am here to tell you this: power is not a toy we give to good children; it is a weapon and the strong man takes it and he uses it and I can assure you he don't turn it on himself nor let another man come at him with a knife that he don't fight back. Well, that knife is at your throat and if you don't go down there and beat

Cantwell to the floor with this very dirty stick, then you got no business in this big league, and bastard or not I'll help Joe Cantwell take the whole damned world if he wants it, because it's not for you and never will be!

(*A long moment, broken by the return of* JENSEN *and* BLADES *from the bathroom stage right*)

JENSEN

Well, the coast is clear. We're all set.

BLADES

First, we pass through a suite containing a hosiery salesman and a woman . . . perhaps not his wife.

JENSEN

Definitely not his wife. (*To* RUSSELL) He looks forward to meeting you even though he hopes Cantwell gets the nomination. His companion betrayed no intimacy with the names of either candidate.

BLADES

Then we go down the back stairs and through a room occupied by a widow from Bangor, Maine, who is for Russell . . .

JENSEN

And from there we go to the Cantwell bathroom and then . . . they meet and make history!

BLADES

That's right! Though what's going on beats me.

(HOCKSTADER *had been eying* RUSSELL *coldly during this*)

HOCKSTADER

(*To* RUSSELL, *softly*)

Here's your chance. Your *last* chance. Take it. Go down there. I want a strong President to keep us alive a while longer.

(RUSSELL *makes his decision. He turns to* BLADES *and* JENSEN. *He motions toward the bedroom*)

RUSSELL

Wait for me in there.

BLADES

(*As he goes*)

How are you feeling, Mr. President?

HOCKSTADER

(*Grimly*)

Just fine, considering the alternative.

(*Chuckling,* BLADES *joins* JENSEN *at the bathroom door.* RUSSELL *picks up the documents*)

RUSSELL

(*Half to himself*)

And so, one by one, these compromises, these small corruptions destroy character.

HOCKSTADER

To want power is corruption already. Dear God, you hate yourself for being human.

RUSSELL

No. I only want to *be* human . . . and it is not easy. Once this sort of thing starts, there is no end to it which is why it should never begin. And if *I* start . . . well, Art, how does it end, this sort of thing? *Where* does it end?

HOCKSTADER

In the grave, son, where the dust is neither good nor bad, but just nothing.

(RUSSELL *looks first at* HOCKSTADER; *then at* ALICE. *He goes into the bedroom.* ALICE *follows him; she pauses at the door and watches as* RUSSELL *exits to the bathroom, where* JENSEN *and* BLADES *are waiting*)

ALICE

(*Slowly*)

You are a good man, Mr. President.

HOCKSTADER

I reckon I am, when all's said and done.

(HOCKSTADER, *in pain, tries to take one of his pills; he cannot get his hand to his mouth*)

ALICE

But I don't know if this is the right thing for Bill to do.

(ALICE *continues to look after* RUSSELL, *unaware of* HOCKSTADER'S *pain*)

HOCKSTADER

At least I put a fire under the candidate. I just hope it don't go out . . . Now don't you get alarmed (ALICE *turns on this, startled*) but I want you to go over and pick up that phone and ask for Dr. Latham, he's in the hotel.

Tell him I'm in here . . . tell him to come quick, through the back way. Tell him to bring a stretcher because I can't move. (ALICE, *horrified, goes quickly to the telephone*) I'm afraid the old man is just about dead.

CURTAIN

## ACT THREE

### SCENE ONE

*The Cantwell suite. A moment later.* CANTWELL *is on the telephone in the living room.* MABEL *is beside him. Both wait, nervously.*

CANTWELL

(*At last*)

Yes, that's right. The name is Conyers, General Conyers . . . C-o-n-y-e-r-s . . . Yes, this is Senator Cantwell. Yes, it's an emergency. You . . . What? Oh, no! (*To* MABEL) They can't find him!

MABEL

But he *has* to be there!

CANTWELL

(*Into telephone*)

Try his quarters, then. (*Softly, to himself*) Dammit, dammit, dammit.

MABEL

Are you sure General Conyers will back you up?

CANTWELL

He better. (*Into telephone*) Well, isn't there a phone anywhere near there? (*To* MABEL) He's playing golf! (*Into telephone*) O.K. Tell him as soon as you find him to call Senator Cantwell, in Philadelphia. The number is Walnut 8-7593 . . . Got it? Thank you.

(CANTWELL *puts receiver down; he rises, starts to pace, thinking hard*)

MABEL

But you've *got* to talk to him before they come down here.

CANTWELL

It's too late now. (*Thoughtfully*) Maybe it's just as well . . . (*Starts to plan*) Now, let's see: Conyers . . . the delegates . . . Sheldon Marcus. (*Slowly*) Yes, Sheldon Marcus . . .

MABEL

Joe, I am scared to death . . .

CANTWELL

Well, don't be. (*Soothingly*) Come here, poor Mama Bear. (*He embraces her*) And don't worry. Poppa Bear isn't going to get shot down this close to the honey-tree.

MABEL

I just don't know how they can use something like that which is so untrue, which is a dirty lie and everybody knew it was a lie even at the time . . . Oh, how I hate politics!

(*The telephone rings.* CANTWELL *breaks away to answer it*)

CANTWELL

Conyers! (*Into telephone*) Yes? Who? (*Startled*) Oh, Mrs. Russell . . . Yes, this is Joe Cantwell . . . No, Bill isn't here yet. I guess he's still on his way down . . . *What?* Oh, that's awful! And you say he's . . . Yes, of course. Of course I'll tell Bill. The second he gets here. Yes. . . . He's a great guy. Yes, thank you. Good-bye, Mrs. Russell. (*Puts down receiver*) Art Hockstader just collapsed. They've taken him to the hospital. He's dying.

MABEL

Dying? I thought he . . .

CANTWELL

That hernia stuff was a lot of bull.

MABEL

But what's this going to do to us, his dying now?

CANTWELL

Find out what hospital he's at.

(RUSSELL, BLADES *and* JENSEN *emerge from the bathroom into the bedroom.* CANTWELL *hears them. He gestures warningly to* MABEL, *who is about to exit right*)

CANTWELL

Not a word about Hockstader. I don't want anything to upset this meeting.

(MABEL *nods and goes.* CANTWELL *gets himself into position as the three men enter the living room*)

BLADES

Well, here we are!

JENSEN

Touch and go for a while there but we made it. Nobody saw us.

(RUSSELL *and* CANTWELL *stare at one another curiously. A long silence, interrupted by* MABEL'S *return*)

MABEL

(*Gaily*)

Well, now, will you look at that! I tell you they look just like two wild animals in the zoo! (*Pause*) Well, come on now . . . somebody *say* something! It's just politics, that's all, isn't like the end of the world or anything . . .

JENSEN

(*Flatly*)

Yet.

MABEL

I had such a nice visit with your wife, Mr. Russell . . . and she is getting to be a real campaigner, isn't she? (*Starts to cross to bar*) Could I fix you a drink or something? We have just about everything. Let me see, there's gin and there's Scotch and there's bourbon with branch water like President Hockstader always used to . . .

(*She stops of her own accord, remembering*)

CANTWELL

I don't think we want a drink, Mabel.

RUSSELL

No, thank you.

MABEL

(*To* BLADES)

Well, in that case I believe we must make ourselves scarce, Don.

BLADES

(*To* RUSSELL)

Let me know when you're ready to go back upstairs.

(BLADES *exits right*)

CANTWELL

(*To* RUSSELL)

Is Sheldon Marcus in the hotel?

JENSEN

Yes.

CANTWELL

Could I see him? (*To* RUSSELL) I'd like to ask him some questions . . . in front of you, if it's all right.

(RUSSELL *nods*)

JENSEN

I'll bring him down.

CANTWELL

(*Indicates office to right*)

Have him wait in there.

(JENSEN *goes off stage, left*)

MABEL

Well, I guess you two boys want to be alone. (*To* RUSSELL) Now you go easy on my Joe . . . who is the best husband that ever was, ever! Well, good-bye, now . . . (*To* CANTWELL, *nervously*) Joe honey, if you want me I'll be over in Sue-Ellen Gamadge's room, we're having a real old-time henfest this afternoon, with all the governors' wives . . .

(CANTWELL *nods to her, encouragingly.* MABEL *crosses through bedroom and exits left*)

CANTWELL

Well, Bill, here we are . . . the main event like they say.

RUSSELL

The main event. And here we stand, as Martin Luther said . . .

CANTWELL

(*Misunderstanding*)

Oh, I'm sorry . . . sit down, please . . .

RUSSELL

And it is not safe to move.

CANTWELL

Who said what?

RUSSELL

Martin Luther said: it is not safe to move. (*Explaining*) Luther was . . .

CANTWELL

(*Irritably*)

You don't need to tell me who Martin Luther was. I happen to be a Protestant. I'm a very religious kind of guy . . . Bill.

RUSSELL

(*Ironically*)

You don't need to tell *me* that . . . Joe.

(RUSSELL *sits on the sofa downstage.* CANTWELL *remains standing*)

CANTWELL

(*Stung*)

You really do think you're better than all of us, with your bad jokes, and the admiration of a lot of bleeding-heart fellow travelers and would-be intellectuals who don't mean a thing in this country!

RUSSELL

(*Appreciatively*)

That was very good, Joe. Pure Cantwell. Known as the multiple lie. Or in this case the multiple-lie-plus-confused-statement. For instance, you say that I think I'm better than the rest of you . . .

CANTWELL

(*Quickly*)

You don't deny . . .

RUSSELL

(*Chuckling*)

Excellent. Interrupt before the answer begins. That's vintage Cantwell . . .

CANTWELL

(*District Attorney's voice*)

I'm not interested in your sophistry. Your contempt. Your deliberate refusal to answer . . .

RUSSELL

(*Bangs ash tray on coffee table*)

Mr. Chairman! Mr. Chairman! Point of order! (*Laughs*) Oh, how're you going to keep them down in the Senate once they've been on TV?

CANTWELL

(*Smiles*)

Very funny. Very cute. I like that. You should have your own TV show.

RUSSELL

Thank you. I'm sure you meant that as a compliment. . . . Joe, I came down here to convince you that there are some things a man cannot do even in politics . . .

(CANTWELL *sits opposite him downstage*)

CANTWELL

(*Not listening*)

Now I have given you every hint, every opportunity in the past two days to pull out of the race. Considering your medical history, it could be done so easily . . . so logically. All you'd have to do is claim exhaustion, fatigue . . . like the last time . . . and then this ugly business would never come up and the Party could then unite behind its candidate . . .

RUSSELL

You?

CANTWELL

(*Nods*)

And we take the election in November.

RUSSELL

You make it sound so simple, but it isn't. For one thing, you'll be sued for the theft of my case history.

CANTWELL

(*Tries to interrupt*)

Bill . . .

RUSSELL

But that's not the point.

CANTWELL

(*Again*)

Bill . . .

RUSSELL

What I want you to realize . . .

CANTWELL

(*Voice of reason*)

Bill! I didn't steal it. The thing was *given* to me, unsolicited. Anyway, I'm sure your doctor won't file suit if you ask him not to.

RUSSELL

(*Taken aback*)

Why should I ask him not to?

CANTWELL

(*Promptly*)

Party unity. What's the point of smearing me when I'm the one who's got to get us into the White House?

RUSSELL

What makes you so certain *you're* going to be nominated?

CANTWELL

(*As to a child*)

Because I expect you to withdraw . . . because you've got no choice. Then who else is there? Except me.

RUSSELL

(*Stunned*)

You are . . . amazing! I came down here with enough political nitroglycerine not only to knock you out of the race but out of politics altogether, and there you sit and blandly tell me *I'm* the one to withdraw.

CANTWELL

(*Through him*)

I also promise to use you, once I'm elected. And that's a solemn promise, Bill. You can have any post in the cabinet you want, excepting Secretary of State, where I'm all hung up with somebody else. Or you can go as our first Ambassador to Red China . . . (RUSSELL *looks at him, amazed*) That's right. You'll be happy to know I intend to recognize Red China, though I won't make an issue of it until public opinion is more . . .

RUSSELL

(*Thoughtfully*)

Never defend, always attack. You're very good at this, Joe. I mean that.

CANTWELL

Another thing you ought to know since you've made such a point about it in your attacks on me: politically we are almost the same on every important issue. *Only* I am less reckless than you. I believe in timing. I don't see anything to be gained by launching a policy just to have it shot down maybe for good because the climate wasn't right.

RUSSELL

And you call that leadership?

CANTWELL

There are many ways of leading: the worst one is making brilliant speeches on the right side at the wrong time. I know how to wait . . .

RUSSELL

You are candid.

(CANTWELL, *bursting with energy and self-righteousness, starts to pace*)

CANTWELL

(*Passionately*)

And I'm right! Because I was born to this. You weren't. I know in my bones how to do this thing. I understand the people of this country. Because I'm one of them. I know how to maneuver. How to win. I knew from the time I won my first election I was going to be President and nobody was going to stop me. Not even the brilliant, witty, aristocratic, intellectual William Russell, who has no more to do with the people of this country than I have to do with the Groton Harvard Wall Street set.

RUSSELL

Well, there is no immediate need to start a class war. I am not better qualified to be President because I went to Harvard than you are because you worked your way through a state college. But as you probably know there is a certain suspicion of the self-made man these days. People aren't as naïve as you think. Any man who fights his way to the top is certainly to be admired, but the people sometimes wonder: how exactly did he do it? And whom did he hurt along the way? The self-made man often makes himself out of pieces of his victims. (RUSSELL *rises and crosses to* CANTWELL *as his own rage begins*) You are something of a Frankenstein monster, Joe, made out of the bits and pieces of Sicilian bandits . . . and your political opponents . . . all assembled before our eyes on television.

CANTWELL

(*Coldly*)

*How* I was made is not the question. What matters is, I am here.

RUSSELL

And you think that your basic public *image* has changed?

CANTWELL

It has. According to the Gallup poll only twelve per cent of the people even remember that there was a Mafia hearing.

RUSSELL

I remember.

CANTWELL

The image that they have of Cantwell is the way I am now . . .

RUSSELL

Smooth, cautious, beyond reproach . . .

CANTWELL

That is right. People forget. Nobody's going to get any mileage out of my past so let's get this Aleutian business over with. I'm going to question Sheldon Marcus now and you're going to get the surprise of your life.

(RUSSELL *turns away from him; he sits again on the sofa*)

RUSSELL

Nothing *you* do ever surprises me, Joe. What *I* do, however, is beginning to surprise me. (*He touches the folder in his jacket pocket*) I never thought I could bring up something like this against any man. It revolts me . . .

CANTWELL

(*Generously*)

Oh, come on! Don't give it a second thought. Look, I don't blame you. I'd certainly use it against you if it was there . . .

RUSSELL

That's the point; *you* would. I wouldn't. Or never thought I would.

(CANTWELL *sees a possible break in the enemy line*)

CANTWELL

Then what are you doing down here? What have you got this joker Marcus standing by for except to smear me as a homosexual which I'm not.

RUSSELL

*I* never said you were . . .

CANTWELL

(*Relentlessly*)

Then what are you doing here if you don't think I am?

RUSSELL

Had you paused at any point in your offensive, I would have told you *why* I came here and *what* I mean to do.

CANTWELL

(*Triumphantly*)

I hope you realize you have just admitted that you don't believe this accusation against me. That you are openly confessing collusion . . .

RUSSELL

(*Abruptly*)

Joe, shut up! (*Rises*) Art Hockstader was right when he said you're not very sensitive to people. You're so busy trying to win you never stop to figure out *what* it is you're winning.

CANTWELL

(*Simulated weariness*)

I am only trying to stick to the issue at hand. I don't believe in indulging in personalities.

RUSSELL

Come off it, Joe! I came here to try and convince you to drop that nonsense against me just as I mean to drop this nonsense against you. These things are irrelevant and dishonest, not to mention untrue. They cancel each other out. So I wish you would please join me by *not* indulging in personalities. (*Holds up folder*) I'll tear this up and send Sheldon Marcus back where he came from, if you drop that business against me.

CANTWELL

(*Nods*)

I see. You came here to make a deal with me.

RUSSELL

(*A sigh of exasperation*)

No! I came here to . . .

(CANTWELL *is growing confident*)

CANTWELL

(*Warmly*)

Look, Bill, it makes perfect sense, what you're doing. And I have no hard feelings. Really, I mean it. (CANTWELL *pats* RUSSELL *on the back*) So don't be apologetic.

RUSSELL

You have *no* feelings, I would say.

CANTWELL

And perhaps you have too many. Perhaps you *are* too emotional. The report on your breakdown said you might have thought of committing suicide . . .

RUSSELL

Who hasn't thought of it?

CANTWELL

I never have. And I don't think a President should. No matter how tough the going is.

RUSSELL

(*Amused*)

Am I to understand you want to save the country from me? That you are genuinely afraid I'm unstable?

CANTWELL

Yes, I am. You just admitted you thought of suicide . . .

RUSSELL

Then, Joe, if I'm so unstable, why did you offer me the ambassadorship to Red China?

CANTWELL

(*Promptly*)

The President can keep tabs on an ambassador. Nobody can keep tabs on a President.

RUSSELL

(*Nods*)

Never pause for an answer, in the best tradition of a television performer. . . . Well, let's get this dirty business over with. I won't throw my mud if you won't throw your mud.

CANTWELL

And we go into convention tomorrow and you get nominated on the first ballot? No.

RUSSELL

Well, then . . . good luck. And may "the best man" win, assuming we don't knock each other off *and* the Party.

(RUSSELL *turns to go.* CANTWELL *signals frantically*)

CANTWELL

Now wait a minute . . . Wait a minute! Bill! I realize we've got to work something out. And I'm willing to be reasonable, only you have *got* to . . .

RUSSELL

(*Exploding*)

Stop it! Either we declare a moratorium on mud or we both let fly.

(*Swiftly* CANTWELL *shifts his tack. He goes to door at right*)

CANTWELL

O.K. (*Opens door, looks through into office*) Don, send Mr. Marcus in. (*To* RUSSELL) Can I see that court-martial testimony? (RUSSELL *gives him testimony. He studies it, as* MARCUS *enters, nervously. A long moment. Then* CANTWELL *speaks, still studying documents*) Hi, Shelly, how's the boy? Long time no see.

MARCUS

Yeah . . . Joe . . . long time. . . . Hello again, Mr. Russell.

RUSSELL

Joe wants to ask you some questions . . .

MARCUS

Well, I really ought to be getting back to Wilmington, you see, my wife . . .

CANTWELL

You live in Wilmington, eh? Great town . . . used to have some cousins there named Everly, Jack and Helen Everly, maybe you know them, in real estate . . .

MARCUS

Well, it's not Wilmington proper, actually, where I live, it's a suburb where Peggy and I live. I don't think I know anybody named (*For the first time* CANTWELL *looks at* MARCUS, *who steps back in alarm*) Everly . . .

CANTWELL

(*Smiles*)

Shelly, you put on a lot of weight.

MARCUS

Well, it's Peggy . . . it's my wife Peggy's cooking, she's a wonderful cook . . . (*Close to tears*) I thought, Mr. Russell, I wouldn't have to . . . to . . .

CANTWELL

To see your old buddy? Now you know I would've been fit to be tied if I had known Shelly Marcus from Adak was in town and hadn't come to see me.

MARCUS

Well, I . . . I know how busy you are . . . *both* you men are . . . running for this President thing, and I was just . . . well, passing by.

CANTWELL

(*Pleasantly*)

And you thought you would pause just long enough to smear your old buddy?

MARCUS

Now, Joe, don't get mad at me . . . it was . . . it was my duty!

CANTWELL

To get even with me for seeing you were passed over for promotion because of incompetence. (*To* RUSSELL) Always a good idea to start with the motive.

RUSSELL

(*To* MARCUS)

Is this true?

MARCUS

(*Taken aback*)

Well, no, not really . . . I mean my efficiency report was . . .

CANTWELL

(*In for the death*)

Can be found in army records! Unsatisfactory! I was adjutant and I personally stopped his promotion *and* his transfer *and* he knew it. (*Picks up documents*) Now, on 6 April 1944 into my quonset hut at the army base on Adak there moved a Lieutenant Fenn . . .

MARCUS

That was the one, like I told you . . . that was the one . . . we all knew . . .

CANTWELL

We shared the same hut for three months.

MARCUS

Just the two of them. Like I told you. It's all in the record there . . . they were, you know . . . they were . . .

CANTWELL

(*Inexorably*)

Fenn was caught with an enlisted man *in flagrante delicto* on the afternoon of 14 June 1944 in the back of the post church. The M.P.s caught him . . .

MARCUS

(*Rapidly*)

That's right. And that's when he broke down and told about everything and everybody . . . the M.P.s laid this trap for him . . . they'd been tipped off . . .

CANTWELL

By the Advocate General . . .

MARCUS

That's right. By Colonel Conyers, he was the one finally broke up this whole ring of degenerates . . . And Fenn when he was caught gave, oh, maybe twenty, thirty names and one of those names was Joe Cantwell, his roommate . . .

CANTWELL

Correct. Now: what happened to those twenty-eight officers and men who were named at the court-martial?

MARCUS

They were all separated from the service . . . Section 8 we called it . . . for the good of the service, they were all kicked out . . .

CANTWELL

All except one.

MARCUS

That's right . . . all except you.

CANTWELL

(*Smiles at* RUSSELL)

And why wasn't I?

MARCUS

I . . . well . . . I don't know. I suppose it's in the records or something. But I know I thought then what a lot of people thought: how Joe must've pulled some pretty fancy wires to save his neck. Yes, sir, he was a real operator, he could get out of *anything,* and that's the truth . . . Anyways, it's all there in the court-martial; how he was one of them, named under oath by Lieutenant Fenn.

RUSSELL

(*To* MARCUS)

Where is Lieutenant Fenn now?

CANTWELL

He's dead.

MARCUS

That's right, he died after the war in that plane crash, you remember the one? Out in Detroit, that freak one where the lightning hit the engine and . . .

RUSSELL

(*To* CANTWELL)

If you were innocent, why did Fenn name you?

CANTWELL

(*Coldly, carefully*)

Because I was the one who turned him in.

MARCUS

(*Stunned*)

You were!

CANTWELL

This clown wouldn't know but I'm ashamed of *you,* Bill, for not doing your homework, for not checking with a certain Colonel, now Major General, Conyers who was the Advocate General up there. (*Turns on* MARCUS, *who retreats before him*) You see, Shelly, when I found out what was going on I went to Conyers and told him what I had discovered about my roommate. We laid a trap for Fenn and he fell into it. At the trial I gave secret evidence against him and that's why he named me: *in revenge,* and that's why no action was ever or could ever be taken against me. (*To* RUSSELL) I even got promoted on the strength of having helped clear those types out of our command.

MARCUS

Oh, I bet that isn't so . . . I bet you'll find he sneaked out of it like he did everything else . . . I know Joe Cantwell . . .

RUSSELL

(*To* CANTWELL)

Can you prove this?

(CANTWELL *nods. He is now upstage at desk*)

CANTWELL

A few minutes ago I talked with the Advocate General. His name is Conyers. He's in Colorado now. He told me he would back me up. In every way. (CANTWELL *gives* RUSSELL *the telephone number*) Here's his name and phone number. He's expecting a call from you, Bill. (*Like a carnivore,* CANTWELL *stalks the terrified* MARCUS *to the door*) And now, Shelly Marcus, if you ever say one word about this to anybody, I will have you up for libel, *criminal* libel . . .

MARCUS

Now, look here, Joe, don't you threaten me . . .

(MARCUS *grabs his briefcase and raincoat and tries to get to the corridor door before* CANTWELL *reaches him*)

CANTWELL

In fact, I will involve you personally in that whole mess at Adak and by the time I finish with you . . .

MARCUS

Don't you bully me, Joe, don't you try to intimidate me . . .

CANTWELL

I'll make you wish you'd never been born!

(*Just as* CANTWELL *seems about to seize him,* MARCUS *bolts into the connecting hall. He opens the corridor door. But to his horror,* NEWSMEN *and* PHOTOGRAPHERS *burst in. He is borne straight back to* CANTWELL, *who smiles and straightens* MARCUS'S *jacket. Then he turns him about for the* PHOTOGRAPHERS, *who want a picture*)

CANTWELL

Just one second . . . (*Puts arm about* MARCUS'S *shoulders*) Sure was swell to see you, Shelly. Next time when you drop by, bring the wife, bring . . . uh, Peggy. Mabel and I'd love to meet her. Love to see you both. You come see us now in Washington. (*Poses again with* MARCUS) How's that?

PHOTOGRAPHER

Hold it!

(MARCUS *goes, surrounded by* NEWSMEN. CANTWELL *shuts the corridor door after them. He pauses a moment in the connecting hall, unobserved by* RUSSELL. *He passes his hand wearily across his face. Then he pulls himself together and returns to the living room*)

CANTWELL

I'm sorry to disappoint you, Bill, but this won't work. I'm covered on every side. You won't be able to make this thing stick for two minutes. And I should also warn you: this is the kind of desperate last-minute smear that always backfires on the guy who makes it. Ask Art Hockstader. He'll tell you. (RUSSELL *stares at him with a fascinated revulsion*) Well, go on. If you don't believe me, you got General Conyers' number in your hand. Call him.

RUSSELL

True? False? We've both gone beyond the "truth" now. We're in dangerous country.

(RUSSELL *drops the paper with the telephone number on the sofa*)

CANTWELL

(*Begins*)

Every word I said was true . . .

RUSSELL

You are worse than a liar. You have no sense of right or wrong. Only what will work. (RUSSELL *picks up court-martial testimony*) Well, *this* is going to work.

CANTWELL

But you're not going to use that now!

RUSSELL

Oh, yes! Yes! I'll use *anything* against you. I can't let you be President.

(RUSSELL *crosses to bedroom.* CANTWELL *tries to block his way.* RUSSELL *pushes him aside. Both men go into bedroom*)

CANTWELL

Hey! What are you going to do? Bill, you're not really going to use that stuff. You can't. Look, it's . . . it's too dirty! Honest to God, nobody will believe it! (RUSSELL *pauses at the bathroom door. He looks at* CANTWELL; *then he turns and goes into the bathroom.* CANTWELL, *near breaking, shouts after him*) O.K. Russell, go ahead, it's your funeral. Against me, you haven't got a chance. (CANTWELL *sits down on the bed, his back to the audience. For the first time he seems exhausted, played out. Then he picks up the bedside telephone*) Send Don Blades in . . . and keep trying on that Colorado call.

(BLADES *enters living room from right. He hurries into bedroom.* CANTWELL *does not acknowledge him*)

BLADES

Well, what happened? (BLADES *peers into bathroom*) Where's Russell? Joe? (*Sudden alarm*) Hey, Joe!

(CANTWELL *is recalled from some private reverie. He looks at* BLADES*; he smiles suddenly; his tone is casual*)

CANTWELL

Oh, Don, hi.

(CANTWELL *rises and crosses to living room.* BLADES *follows*)

BLADES

What's Russell up to? What's this all about? What's he got on you?

CANTWELL

(*Thoughtfully*)

You know what that guy said just now? He said I wasn't very sensitive about other people. He said I didn't understand character . . .

BLADES

Is that what he came down here for? To give you a lecture?

CANTWELL

(*Nods*)

Yeah. Pretty much. (CANTWELL *sees the paper with* GENERAL CONYERS' *telephone number on it; he picks it up; he smiles*) Well, I have news for him.

I am a very good judge of character. (*Abruptly*) You can release that stuff on Russell now. One copy to every delegate. (*Excitement*) Don, we're home free. (*He rolls the paper into a tight wad*) And I'll make you a bet: Russell quits before the first ballot. (CANTWELL *flicks the wad across the room. The room goes dark*)

CURTAIN

## ACT THREE

### SCENE TWO

*Russell suite. The next afternoon. The television set is on.* JENSEN *watches it while going through papers at the desk. There is band music from the convention hall. In the bedroom,* ALICE *finishes packing. The telephone rings.*

JENSEN

(*Answers it*)

Who? Oh, Senator Joseph. No, he's not back yet. No, I don't know what to do. He's still over at the hospital. He's with President Hockstader and there's no way to phone . . . I guess we just stand by. How's the balloting? (*Frowns*) Oh, no!

(RUSSELL *enters from corridor, murmuring "No comment" to the press*)

JENSEN

Wait a minute, Senator. He's here. (*To* RUSSELL) Bill, it's Senator Joseph. He's in the convention hall. They're into the sixth ballot. It's still a deadlock. Cantwell's leading but nobody's got a majority. Merwin's sitting tight. Joseph says if you let him blast Cantwell now, we're in on the next ballot.

RUSSELL

What was the voting on the fifth ballot?

JENSEN

(*Looks at paper*)

Cantwell 474, Russell 386, Merwin 214 . . . all the favorite sons are gone. And nobody's budging yet.

RUSSELL

What about Merwin? If I were to get his 214 votes . . .

JENSEN

You'd win. But he's hanging on. Senator Joseph's trying to reach him now, to see if he'll take on second spot with you . . .

RUSSELL

Cantwell must be trying the same thing . . .

JENSEN

Merwin's holding out for the best possible terms.

RUSSELL

(*Smiles*)

He's showing unexpected character, isn't he?

JENSEN

(*Urgently*)

You've *got* to make up your mind! You've got to let our boys get that stuff on Cantwell to the delegates. We can ask for a recess before the seventh ballot. Then . . .

RUSSELL

Tell the Senator to wait.

JENSEN

But we *can't* wait . . .

RUSSELL

(*Firmly*)

I said, wait, Dick.

JENSEN

(*Into telephone*)

Not yet . . . (*He hangs up*) Bill, what's wrong with you? We've lost a night and a day, but one word from you and we can still wreck Joe Cantwell.

RUSSELL

I know.

JENSEN

Then why are you holding back? What have you got to lose? Joe's done his worst. Every delegation's got a copy of your case history and believe it or not we're still in business. I don't know why, but we are.

RUSSELL

Which means perhaps that dirt does not always stick . . .

JENSEN

Enough did. You lost three hundred votes because of it.

RUSSELL

But not all to Cantwell. Merwin picked up over a hundred of my votes. And that is a sign of something . . .

JENSEN

Disgust.

RUSSELL

Or human decency.

JENSEN

Decency? At a *convention?*

RUSSELL

(*Smiles*)

I am an optimist.

(RUSSELL *goes into the bedroom*)

ALICE

I packed. I thought no matter what happens, we'll be leaving tonight.

RUSSELL

Yes, we'll be leaving.

ALICE

How was Art?

RUSSELL

They wouldn't let me see him today. He's still unconscious.

(JENSEN, *who has been watching the television set, leaps to his feet and goes to the bedroom*)

JENSEN

(*Desperately*)

Bill, I don't want to press you, but will you please make up your mind. The sixth ballot's almost over and . . . (*Telephone in bedroom rings;* JENSEN *answers it*) Who? Oh, it's you . . . He does? Now? (*To* RUSSELL) It's Don Blades. Cantwell wants to see you.

RUSSELL

I'm sure he does. (*Smiles*) All right. Tell him to come up. I'd like to see Joe again.

(RUSSELL *goes into living room;* ALICE *follows*)

JENSEN

(*Into telephone*)

O.K. He'll see you. (*Puts receiver down*)

ALICE

(*To* RUSSELL)

What do you think Cantwell wants?

RUSSELL

A deal. What else does Joe Cantwell ever want. (*Picks up newspaper*) Oh, have you seen his latest statement? "The rumors about William Russell's health have been maliciously exaggerated." He's wonderful!

JENSEN

Look, before he gets here, let me call Senator Joseph . . .

RUSSELL

No, Dick.

JENSEN

But yesterday you were willing to do anything!

RUSSELL

That was yesterday. I lost my temper. And did rather a poor imitation of Joe Cantwell. I was remarkably melodramatic. I even turned my own stomach. But today I'm myself again!

JENSEN

Bill . . .

ALICE

Leave him alone, Dick.

RUSSELL

There is a certain relief to knowing that the worst has happened to you and you're still alive . . . and kicking. (*Looks at television set*) Ah . . . there's my old friend Senator Carlin. True to the end.

(RUSSELL *turns up volume*)

CARLIN'S VOICE

(*Booming*)

. . . This Sovereign State casts forty-four votes for the next Preznighstays Joe Cantwell!

(RUSSELL *turns the volume off*)

RUSSELL

(*Thoughtfully*)

Senator Carlin has every characteristic of a dog, except loyalty.

(BLADES *and* CANTWELL *enter. The press is violent in its attentions. With some difficulty, they are got out of the room*)

BLADES

Gentlemen . . .

CANTWELL

Hello, Bill . . .

RUSSELL

(*Gaily*)

Hi, Joe! What a nice surprise, your coming here like this!

CANTWELL

Yes. . . . Mrs. Russell, I'm Joe Cantwell . . . I don't think we've met.

(CANTWELL *shakes* ALICE'S *hand*)

ALICE

How do you do.

CANTWELL

(*Mechanically*)

We talked on the phone, I guess.

RUSSELL

Sit down, Joe. (CANTWELL *sits*) I thought you would be busy working on your acceptance speech. Or is it already written?

CANTWELL

(*Begins*)

Now, Bill, as I see the picture . . .

RUSSELL

I've been working for months on *my* acceptance speech, trying to strike that delicate balance between humility and confidence.

CANTWELL

Yes. Now as I see this convention . . .

RUSSELL

*You* of course have a gift for hitting the right note.

CANTWELL

Yes . . .

RUSSELL

I like the way you always manage to state the obvious with a sense of real discovery.

CANTWELL

Yes. Now, Bill . . .

RUSSELL

And that wonderful trick you have for . . .

CANTWELL

(*Exploding*)

Bill, at least let me get one word in edgewise!

RUSSELL

(*Laughs*)

I'm sorry, Joe. I couldn't resist it. (*To the others*) I was using Joe's technique: never let the other man get started. Talk right through him. Also, whenever Joe starts a sentence with "Now, Bill" . . . you know he's up to no good.

CANTWELL

(*Quickly*)

Now, Bill . . .

RUSSELL

See?

(CANTWELL *controls himself with some difficulty*)

CANTWELL

Very cute. Bill, this convention is really hung up and the way things are going we may never nominate anybody.

BLADES

And who wants to spend the next four years in Philadelphia?

CANTWELL

Believe me when I say I have given the whole thing a lot of thought: and I want you to be on my ticket.

RUSSELL

Well, that's very generous, Joe. But tell me, how can I possibly run for Vice-President when I am at this very moment suffering from one of my frequent nervous breakdowns?

CANTWELL

There was no way of keeping a report like that secret. Anyway, you've got to admit we handled the whole thing darned well. I mean look at the papers: practically no mention . . .

RUSSELL

Just as there was no mention of the fact that Art Hockstader is dying?

CANTWELL

Art didn't want anybody to know how sick he was. Did he, Mrs. Russell? He was a great old guy. You know he's dead, don't you? (RUSSELL *rises, shaken.* CANTWELL *does not notice the other man's response*) Now, as I see the picture, delegate-wise . . .

RUSSELL

I didn't know . . . Art was dead.

CANTWELL

Oh? Yeah, he died about half an hour ago. He knew it was all over last night when I saw him.

RUSSELL

(*Startled*)

You saw him?

CANTWELL

That's right. Just for a few minutes, while he was still conscious . . .

RUSSELL

Oh, no, no! Don't tell us that Art Hockstader with his dying breath said, "Bless you, Joe, go to it!" And handed on the torch.

(CANTWELL *gets to his feet, angrily*)

CANTWELL

You certainly like to jump to conclusions, don't you? If you really want to know what Art said, I'll tell you: he said, "To hell with both of you," meaning you as well as me.

BLADES

He sure was a funny old bird. Full of hell right to the end. But his day was done . . . just as well he conked out when he did.

(ALICE *goes into the bedroom*)

RUSSELL

Will you two please get out?

JENSEN

Bill!

(RUSSELL *turns to follow* ALICE)

CANTWELL

Look, Russell, for a lot of reasons we want you on the ticket and, frankly, if I were you, I'd show a little . . . well, gratitude.

(RUSSELL *wheels about, fiercely*)

RUSSELL

Gratitude! Do you realize all I have to do is call Senator Joseph . . .

BLADES

(*Quickly*)

But you know that story about Joe was a bum rap, so how could you use it?

RUSSELL

Since when has the truth been a deterrent at this convention? It is also not true that I am mentally unstable . . .

BLADES

(*Quickly*)

But it *is* true that you had a mental breakdown, and that is a fact the voters should know.

(CANTWELL *stops* BLADES *with a gesture*)

CANTWELL

Bill, I solemnly promise before these witnesses that I will give you anything you want . . . the Vice-Presidency, Secretary of State . . . commitment or no commitment . . . it's yours if you throw me your votes on the next ballot.

JENSEN

(*Delighted*)

Bill, come on, they're scared!

BLADES

Oh, no, we're not!

JENSEN

They're sweating ice!

CANTWELL

I want a united front, for the sake of the Party.

JENSEN

Look at them squirm!

BLADES

Who's squirming? Anyway, we got all the votes we need right now.

JENSEN

Where?

BLADES

Governor Merwin.

JENSEN

He won't play with you.

BLADES

He's offered to. But Joe doesn't want Merwin on the ticket. He'd rather have the Secretary here . . .

JENSEN

Merwin refused to be on the ticket with Joe and you know it . . . if he'd agreed, you wouldn't be up here, sweating!

BLADES

(*Angrily*)

I am not sweating!

JENSEN

Bill, we've got them. We've really got them. Let me call Senator Joseph?

CANTWELL

I wish you would. And tell him you'll support me, in the interest of Party unity, and that you'll accept the second spot on the ticket . . .

JENSEN

(*Overlaps*)

And tell him you're ready to lower the boom on Cantwell?

(RUSSELL *at bedroom door. He looks at* ALICE. *He decides*)

RUSSELL

All right, call him.

(ALICE *returns to the living room. She sits on the downstage sofa*)

JENSEN

Put me through to Senator Joseph. Extension 12, convention hall . . . Hello . . . that you, Senator? Well, brace yourself. This is it. Our man is about to fight . . .

(RUSSELL *comes to telephone*)

BLADES

(*Pleads*)

Russell, don't. You *can't* use that stuff. Joe's our only hope. He's the Party's only hope.

CANTWELL

Shut up, Don. We don't have to worry about Mr. Russell. He always does the right thing.

RUSSELL

(*To* CANTWELL)

Thank you. (*Into telephone*) Senator? This is William Russell. I'm coming down to the convention hall in a few minutes to make a statement. Before I do, I want you to get to the chairman of the next delegation pledged to me . . . Utah? All right. Tell the chairman to announce to the convention that I have withdrawn from the race.

JENSEN

(*Aghast*)

Bill!

BLADES

(*Ecstatic*)

Mr. Secretary, I swear you won't regret . . .

RUSSELL

And that I am releasing my 384 delegates with instructions to support Governor John Merwin.

JENSEN

Merwin!

BLADES

But . . . but you can't . . .

(RUSSELL *puts the receiver down*)

RUSSELL

I can. And I have.

JENSEN

Merwin's nobody!

RUSSELL

Well, he is now somebody . . . (*Turns to* CANTWELL, *who has sunk to a bench, his hand over his face*) Neither the angel of darkness nor the angel of light . . . if I may exaggerate my goodness . . . has carried the day. We canceled each other out.

(JENSEN *indicates the television set*)

JENSEN

(*Bitterly*)

Allowing the angel of grayness to win, as usual.

RUSSELL

The light blinds us . . . and we're all afraid of the dark. (*To* CANTWELL) I meant it, Joe, when I said I could never let you be President.

BLADES

(*Viciously*)

Well, you just cut your own throat. You are through in politics.

RUSSELL

Joe Cantwell is through in politics.

(BLADES *crosses to upstage door*)

BLADES

He had a deal! I bet he had a deal with Merwin all along, the tricky son of a . . .

(BLADES *slams the door after him.* CANTWELL *looks at* RUSSELL *for the first time; he is genuinely puzzled*)

CANTWELL

(*Slowly*)

I don't understand you.

RUSSELL

I know you don't. Because you have no sense of responsibility toward anybody or anything and that is a tragedy in a man and it is a disaster in a President! You said you were religious. Well, I'm not. But I believe profoundly in *this* life and what we do to one another and how this monstrous "I," the self, must become "we" and draw the line at murder in the games we play with one another, and try to be good even when there is no one to force us to be good.

(CANTWELL *rises. He speaks carefully, without rancor*)

CANTWELL

You don't understand me. You don't understand politics. You don't understand this country and the way it is and the way we are. You are a fool.

(CANTWELL *goes, shutting the corridor door after him.* RUSSELL *shakes his head*)

RUSSELL

We're not the way Joe thinks we are. At least not yet.

JENSEN

You don't even know Merwin. Nobody knows him. He's a man without a face.

RUSSELL

Don't underestimate him. Men without faces tend to get elected President, and power or responsibility or honor fill in the features, usually pretty well.

JENSEN

I'm afraid, Bill, your conscience is my enemy.

(JENSEN *goes off stage right.* RUSSELL *looks after him a moment, then he notices the "Hustle with Russell" placard*)

RUSSELL

(*Smiles*)

Well, everyone hustled except Russell. (*Notices television set*) Here comes Utah.

(RUSSELL *turns up volume*)

DELEGATE'S VOICE

State of Utah at the instruction of that great American and Secretary of State William Russell (*Cheering*) casts its fourteen pledged votes to the next Preznighstays that great Governor John Merwin!

COMMENTATOR'S VOICE

This is the break in the deadlock! An unexpected development! There's real excitement down on the floor . . .

(RUSSELL *turns off set*)

RUSSELL

There it is! (*To* ALICE) Well, we've got work to do. Do you want to come down to the convention? Or wait here till I get back?

ALICE

I'll go with you.

RUSSELL

What . . . do you think?

ALICE

I wish you'd been nominated.

RUSSELL

So do I.

ALICE

But I like the way you . . . really won.

RUSSELL

Thank you. Life is a choice, they say. I've made mine.

ALICE

(*Smiles*)

And without doing your one-two-three walk.

RUSSELL

You know, Alice, you don't have to stay with me, if you don't want to.

ALICE

I know I don't have to.

RUSSELL

(*Tentatively*)

But . . . *would* you like to? Even though you'll never have the chance to be another Grace Coolidge?

ALICE

Now it's *my* turn to choose? (RUSSELL *nods*) Of course I'll stay.

(ALICE *rises*)

RUSSELL

I'm glad. But I warn you: the fires of autumn burn notoriously low.

ALICE

(*Smiles*)

Well, I've been cold such a long time.

(RUSSELL *takes her arm. They start to go upstage to the corridor door when* REPORTERS *burst in from stage right. Ad-libbed cries of "Statement!" Flashbulbs go off.* RUSSELL *finally quiets them*)

RUSSELL

You may say that I think Governor Merwin will make a fine candidate, and I shall do everything I can to help him and the Party. (*Starts to go, pauses*) Oh. (*Smiles*) And I am of course happy: the best man won!

(RUSSELL *and* ALICE *followed by* REPORTERS *cross upstage, as the* CURTAIN FALLS)

# INVENTIONS

# *MYRA BRECKINRIDGE*

FIRST PUBLISHED IN 1968, *Myra Breckinridge* reflects both the decade in which it appeared and Vidal's attitude toward traditional (and especially mid-century mid-American) approaches to life and literature. Many readers at the time thought the novel was pornographic; others considered it in bad taste. Immediately notorious, *Myra Breckinridge* ascended to best-sellerdom at a time of ongoing challenges to the legal, social, and communal boundaries to public discourse. The novel was banned as obscene in Australia. Vidal was pressured to make changes to avoid indictment for obscenity and libel by his British publisher. In America, the novel was allowed to stand as written. An extended dramatic monologue, *Myra* is narrated by a larger-than-life character. It is very much about sexual politics, and as a satiric novel in the tradition of *Gulliver's Travels* its excesses are purposeful. The object is to provoke laughter, outrage, pain, and revulsion at the society that has twisted Myra's body and psyche into a representation of its views about sex and gender. In 1974, Vidal published a sequel, *Myron.*

# 1

I am Myra Breckinridge whom no man will ever possess. Clad only in garter belt and one dress shield, I held off the entire elite of the Trobriand Islanders, a race who possess no words for "why" or "because." Wielding a stone axe, I broke the arms, the limbs, the balls of their finest warriors, my beauty blinding them, as it does all men, unmanning them in the way that King Kong was reduced to a mere simian whimper by beauteous Fay Wray whom I resemble left three-quarter profile if the key light is no more than five feet high during the close shot.

# 2

The novel being dead, there is no point to writing made-up stories. Look at the French who will not and the Americans who cannot. Look at me who ought not, if only because I exist entirely outside the usual human experience . . . outside and yet wholly relevant for I am the New Woman whose astonishing history is a poignant amalgam of vulgar dreams and knife-sharp realities (shall I ever be free of the dull lingering pain that is my peculiar glory, the price so joyously paid for being Myra Breckinridge, whom no man may possess except on her . . . *my* terms!). Yet not even I can create a fictional character as one-dimensional as the average reader. Nevertheless, I intend to create a literary masterpiece in much the same way that I created myself, and for much the same reason: because it is not there. And

I shall accomplish this by presenting you, the reader (as well as Dr. Randolph Spenser Montag, my analyst friend and dentist, who has proposed that I write in this notebook as therapy), with an exact, literal sense of what it is like, from moment to moment, to be me, what it is like to possess superbly shaped breasts reminiscent of those sported by Jean Harlow in *Hell's Angels* and seen at their best four minutes after the start of the second reel. What it is like to possess perfect thighs with hips resembling that archetypal mandolin from which the male principle draws forth music with prick of flesh so akin—in this simile—to pick of celluloid, *blessed* celluloid upon which have been imprinted in our century all the dreams and shadows that have haunted the human race since man's harsh and turbulent origins (quote Lévi-Strauss). Myra Breckinridge is a dish, and never forget it, you motherfuckers, as the children say nowadays.

## 3

I shall not begin at the beginning since there is no beginning, only a middle into which you, fortunate reader, have just strayed, still uncertain as to what will be done to you in the course of our common voyage to my interior. No, to *our* interior. For we are, at least in the act of this creation, as one, each trapped in time: you later, I now, carefully, thoughtfully forming letters to make words to make sentences.

I shall begin by putting my cards on the table. At this moment (writing the word "moment"), I am not the same Myra Breckinridge who was the scourge of the Trobriand Islanders. She is a creature of fantasy, a daydream revealing the feminine principle's need to regain once more that primacy she lost at the time of the Bronze Age when the cock-worshipping Dorians enslaved the West, impiously replacing *the* Goddess with a god. Happily his days are nearly over; the phallus cracks; the uterus opens; and I am at last ready to begin my mission which is to re-create the sexes and thus save the human race from certain extinction. Meanwhile, I live no longer in the usual world. I have forsaken the familiar. And soon, by an extreme gesture, I shall cease altogether to be human and become legend like Jesus, Buddha, Cybele.

But my immediate task is to impress upon you how disturbingly beautiful I am with large breasts hanging free, for I am wearing nothing but black mesh panties in this overheated room, whose windows I have shut because it is the rush hour (6:07 P.M., Thursday, January 10) and beneath my window the Strip (Sunset Boulevard in Hollywood, California) is filled with noisy cars, barely moving through air so dark with carbon monoxide that one can almost hear in the drivers' lungs the cancer cells as they gaily proliferate like spermatozoa in a healthy boy's testicles.

## 4

From where I sit, without turning my head, I can see a window covered by venetian blinds. The fourth slat from the bottom is missing and so provides me with a glimpse of the midsection of the huge painted plaster chorus girl who holds a sombrero in one hand as she revolves slowly in front of the Château Marmont Hotel, where Greta Garbo stays on her rare visits to Hollywood. The window is set in a white wall on which a damp splotch resembles an upside-down two-leaf clover—or heart—or male scrotum as viewed from behind. But no similes. Nothing is *like* anything else. Things are themselves entirely and do not need interpretation, only a minimal respect for their precise integrity. The mark on the wall is two feet three inches wide and four feet eight and a fraction inches high. Already I have failed to be completely accurate. I must write "fraction" because I can't read the little numbers on the ruler without my glasses which I never wear.

## 5

I am certain that I can eventually capture the reality of Myra Breckinridge, despite the treachery and inadequacy of words. I must show you as I am, at this instant, seated at a small card table with two cigarette burns at the edge; one is about the size of a quarter, the other the size of a dime. The second is perhaps the result of a burning ash, while the first . . . But there is to be no speculation, only simple facts, simply stated. I sit now, perspiring freely, the odor of my lovely body is like that of new bread (just one simile, then I shall be stylistically pure), mingled with a subtle ammoniac smell that I find nearly as irresistible as all men do. In addition to my extraordinary physical presence, I studied the classics (in translation) at the New School, the contemporary French novel on my own, and I learned German last year in order to understand the films of the Thirties when UFA was a force to be reckoned with.

Now, at this arbitrary instant in time, my hand moves across the page of an oblong black notebook containing three hundred blue-lined pages. I have covered eighteen pages already; that leaves two hundred eighty-two yet to be filled, if one counts the present page of which I have used twelve of thirty-two lines—thirteen with these last words, now fourteen. The hand is small, with delicate tapering fingers and a slight golden down at the back near the wrist. The nails are exquisitely cared for (lacquered silver) except for the right index fingernail, which is cracked diagonally from the left side of the tip to the part where the flesh begins, the result of trying to pry loose an ice cube from one of those new plastic ice trays which so freeze that unless you half melt them under the hot-water tap you can never get the ice out.

There are limits, however, to describing exactly what I see as I write and you read. More to the point, one must accept the fact that there are no words to describe for you *exactly* what my body is like as I sit, perspiring freely, in this furnished room high above the Strip for which I am paying $87.50 a month, much too much, but I must not complain for a life dream has come true. I am in Hollywood, California, the source of all this century's legends, and tomorrow it has been arranged for me to visit Metro-Goldwyn-Mayer! No pilgrim to Lourdes can experience what I know I shall experience once I have stepped into that magic world which has occupied all my waking thoughts for twenty years. Yes, twenty years. Believe it or not, I am twenty-seven years old and saw my first movie at the age of seven: *Marriage Is a Private Affair,* starring Lana Turner, James Craig and the late John Hodiak; produced by Pandro S. Berman and directed by Robert Leonard.

As a small girl I used to yearn for Lana Turner to crush me against her heavy breasts, murmuring, "I love you, Myra, you perfect darling!" Fortunately this Lesbian phase passed and my desires were soon centered upon James Craig. I saw every film he ever made. I even have recordings of his voice. In Parker Tyler's masterpiece *Magic and Myth of the Movies,* he refers to James Craig's voice as "some kind of Middle Southwest drawl, a genuine lulu." I can certify that James Craig was in every way a lulu and for years I practiced self-abuse thinking of that voice, those shoulders, those powerful thighs thrust between my own and, if I may be candid, no matter what condition James Craig is in today, married or not, decrepit or not, Myra Breckinridge is ready to give him a good time for old times' sake.

## 6

Buck Loner is not the man he was when he was the Singin' Shootin' Cowboy of radio fame—movies too: he made eighteen low-budget westerns and for a time was right up there with Roy Rogers and Gene Autry. In those old movies he appeared to be lean and tough with slender hips and practically no ass at all which I don't find entirely attractive. I like a curve to the masculine buttock, on the order, say, of Tom Holt's in *The Magnificent Ambersons.* Mr. Holt, incidentally, decrepit or not, has a good time coming his way if Myra Breckinridge should happen to cross his path as she is bound to do now that Hollywood is finally, literally, at her feet (lovely feet with a high instep and naturally rosy heels, fit for any fetishist).

Today Buck Loner (born Ted Percey in Portland, Maine) is fat—no, *gross!*—with breasts even larger than mine. He is huge and disgusting and old, and obviously dying to get me into bed even though I am the recent widow of his only nephew Myron Breckinridge, the film critic, who drowned last year while crossing over to Staten Island on the ferry. Did Myron take his own life, you will ask? Yes and no is my answer. Beyond that my lips are sealed. . . . In any case, let us abandon *that* daydream in order to record the hard facts of this morning's encounter with my husband's uncle, Buck Loner.

"Never knew that boy of Gertrude's had such an eye for feminine pulchritude." This sentence drawled in the once famous Buck Loner manner was, I fear, the first thing he said to me as he helped me into a chair beside his redwood desk, one coarse redwood hand lingering for just a moment too long on my left shoulder, in order to ascertain whether or not I was wearing a bra. I was.

"Mr. Loner," I began in a careful low-pitched voice, modeled on that of the late Ann Sheridan (fifth reel of *Doughgirls*). "I will come straight to the point. I need your help."

That was the wrong thing to say. To ask for anything is always the wrong way to begin a conversation but I am not one to beat about a bush, even a bush as unappetizing as Buck Loner. He sat back in his steel and black leather chair, a very expensive item selling for about four hundred dollars at the best office supply stores. I know. I worked one entire year at Abercrombie and Fitch, and so got an idea of just how expensive nice things can be. That was the year poor Myron was trying to complete his book on Parker Tyler and the films of the Forties—a book I intend to finish one day, with or without Mr. Tyler's assistance. Why? Because Tyler's vision (films are the unconscious expressions of age-old human myths) is perhaps the only important critical insight this century has produced. Also, Tyler's close scrutiny of the films of the Forties makes him our age's central thinker, if only because *in the decade between 1935 and 1945, no irrelevant film was made in the United States.* During those years, the entire range of human (which is to say, American) legend was put on film, and any profound study of those extraordinary works is bound to make crystal-clear the human condition. For instance, to take an example at random, Johnny Weissmuller, the zahftic Tarzan, still provides the last word on the subject of soft man's relationship to hard environment . . . that glistening overweight body set against a limestone cliff at noon says the whole thing. Auden once wrote an entire poem praising limestone, unaware that any one of a thousand frames from *Tarzan and the Amazons* (1945) had not only anticipated him but made irrelevant his jingles. This was one of Myron's insights that most excited me. How I miss him.

"How I miss him, Mr. Loner. Particularly now. You see, he didn't leave a penny . . ."

"No insurance, savings account, stocks, bonds, safety deposit box maybe? Gertrude must've left the boy *something.*"

Buck fell into my trap. "No," I said, in a throaty voice with a small croak to it not unlike (but again not *really* like) that of the late Margaret Sullavan. "Gertrude, as you call her, Myron's angel mother, did not leave him one penny. All that she owned on the day she died, Christmas Eve 1966, was a set of bedroom furniture. Everything else was gone, due to a series of expensive illnesses in the family, hers, Myron's, my own. I won't bore you with the details but for the last five years we supported a dozen doctors. Now Gertrude, your sister, is gone with no one to mourn her at Frank E. Campbell's Funeral Church except Myron and me. Then he died and now I'm absolutely alone, and penniless."

During this recital Buck Loner directed toward me that same narrow-eyed gaze one detects in those scenes of Brian Donlevy whenever he is being asked a question about Akim Tamiroff. But confident in the efficacy of my ultimate weapon, I merely offered him a sad smile in return, and blinked a tear or two loose from my Max Factor Supreme eyelashes. I then looked up at the life-size photograph in color of Elvis Presley which hangs behind Buck's desk, flanked by two American flags, and began my pitch. "Mr. Loner, Gertrude, Myron's mother . . ."

"A marvelous woman . . ." he began huskily but no man alive can outdo *me* in the huskiness department.

"Gertrude," I positively *rasped* through a Niagara of tears unshed, "with her dying breath, or one of her dying breaths—we missed a lot of what she said toward the end because of the oxygen tent and the fact she could not wear her teeth—Gertrude said, 'Myron—and you too, angel girl—if anything happens to me and you ever need help, go to your Uncle Ted, go to Buck Loner and remind that son-of-a-bitch'—I am now quoting verbatim—'that the property in Westwood just outside of Hollywood where he has his Academy of Drama and Modeling was left to us jointly by our father whose orange grove it was in the Twenties, and you tell that bastard'—I'm sorry but you know how Gertrude talked, those years as a practical nurse left their toll—'that I have a copy of the will and I want my share to go to you, Myron, because that property must be worth a good million bucks by now!' " I stopped, as though too moved by my own recital to continue.

Buck Loner idly stroked the bronze bust of Pat Boone which serves as the base for his desk lamp. A long moment passed. I studied the office, admired its rich appointments, realizing that half of the ground it stood on—some fifty acres of Westwood's finest residential property—was mine. The proof was in my purse: a photostat of Buck Loner's father's will.

"Gertrude was always a high-spirited gal, ever since she was yea-high." He indicated what looked to be a Shetland pony; on one finger a huge diamond glittered. "Poor Gertrude died most horribly, Myron wrote me. Great suffering at the end." He smacked his lips, the unmitigated shit, but cool it, Myra baby, I said to myself, and half of all this will be yours. Sudden daydream: Buck Loner hanging upside down like a fat sack of potatoes while yours truly works him over with a tennis racket strung with copper wires.

"I never knew Myron," he added, as though this might somehow make spurious the relationship.

"Myron never knew you." I was deliberately redundant. "I mean he used to follow your career with interest, collected all sorts of stories about you from the old *Radio Times.* And of course you were to have figured at some length in one of the chapters of his book *Parker Tyler and the Films of the Forties; or, the Transcendental Pantheon.*"

"How about that?" Buck Loner looked pleased, as well he ought to be. "I suppose my nephew left a will?"

I was ready for that one. I told him that I possessed three wills. His father's leaving the orange grove jointly to Gertrude and himself, Gertrude's leaving her share of the Westwood property to Myron, and Myron's leaving his entire estate to me.

Buck Loner sighed. "You know," he said, "the school ain't doin' too well." Phonetically that is not exactly what he said, but it is close. I am fortunate in having no gift at all for characterizing in prose the actual speech of others and so, for literary purposes, I prefer to make everyone sound like me. Therefore I shall make no further effort to reproduce Buck Loner's speech, except when something particularly vivid stays with me. Nothing vivid was said for some minutes while he lied to me about the financial status of the Academy of Drama and Modeling. But of course everyone in show business knows that the Academy is a huge success with an enrollment of one thousand three hundred young men and women, all studying to be actors, singers, models. Some live on campus but most live elsewhere and drive to school in their jalopies (a marvelous Forties word that I heard for the first time in *Best Foot Forward*—oh, to have been an adult in those years!). The Academy mints money.

When Buck had finished his tale of woe, I crossed my legs and slowly and deliberately (my skirt was practically mini, my legs divine), and was rewarded by a noticeable increase in Buck's salivation. He swallowed hard, eyes on that triangulated darkness beneath the skirt, forever inviting the question: is it you-know-what or panties? Let him wonder! No man will ever possess Myra Breckinridge, though she will possess men, in her own good time and in ways convenient to her tyrannous lust. In any case, Buck Loner is a three-time married man whose current wife, Bobbie Dean, once sang with Claude Thornhill's band in the Forties, and is now a passionate Jehovah's Witness, forever saving sinners in back streets. Gertrude thought her common.

"Naturally, this is all quite sudden, Myra, I may call you Myra? Even though we never met but then you are my niece-in-law, and so practically kissin' kin."

There is a crash outside my window—was a crash (in the time I took to write "there is a crash" the tense changed). Two cars have collided on the Strip. I heard breaking glass. Now I hear nothing. If the accident was serious there will soon be the sound of a siren. More than ever am I convinced that the only useful form left to literature in the post-Gutenberg age is the memoir: the absolute truth, copied precisely from life, preferably at the moment it is happening . . .

Buck Loner made me an offer. While his lawyer and my lawyer work out a settlement, he would be happy to give me a job starting now and extending until the school year ends in June and all the talent scouts from TV, movie and recording companies converge upon the Academy to observe the students do their stuff. I accepted his offer. Why not? I need a place to live (as well as an entrée into the world of the movies), and so what could be better than a teaching job at the Academy? I will also enjoy meeting young men (though whether or not they will enjoy meeting me remains to be seen!), and the Academy is crawling with them, arrogant, cocky youths; several whistled at me in the corridor as I made my way to Buck Loner's office. Well, they will suffer for their bad manners! No man may jeer at Myra Breckinridge with impunity!

"Now we have an opening for you in our Acting Department—that's for movie and TV acting, we don't go in for stage-type acting, no real demand . . ."

"The theatre is finished . . ." I began.

"You can say that again." It was plain that he was not interested in my theories which reflect more or less Myron's thesis that this century's only *living* art form is the movies. I say more or less because though I agree with Myron that the films of the 1940's are superior to all the works of the so-called Renaissance, including Shakespeare and Michelangelo, I have been drawn lately to the television commercial which, though in its rude infancy, shows signs of replacing all the other visual arts. But my ideas are not yet sufficiently formulated to record them here, suffice it to say that the placing of the man in the driver's seat (courtesy of Hertz) reveals in a most cogent way man's eternal need for mastery over both space and distance, a never-ending progress that began in the caves at Lascaux and continues, even as I write, in the Apollo capsule with its mixed oxygen environment.

"Your work load will of course be light. After all, you're a member of the family and of course I'm taking into account your terrible recent loss, though it has been my experience that work distracts our attention from grief in a most extraordinary way." While he was filibustering, he was studying a chart. He then scribbled a note and gave it to me. On Monday, Thursday and Saturday mornings I am to give an hour course in Empathy. Tuesday and Friday afternoons I teach Posture.

"You seem particularly well equipped to give the course in Posture. I couldn't help but notice how you looked when you entered the room, you carry yourself like a veritable queen. As for Empathy, it is the Sign Kwa Known [*sine qua non*] of the art of film acting."

We sparred with one another, each lying to beat the band. He so pleased to have me "on the team" and me so happy to be able to work in Hollywood, California, a life's dream come true and—as they used to say in the early Sixties—all that jazz. Oh, we are a pair of jolly rogues! He means to cheat me out of my inheritance while I intend to take him for every cent he's got, as well as make him fall madly in love just so, at the crucial moment, I can kick his fat ass in, fulfilling the new pattern to which I am now irrevocably committed. Or as Diotima said to Hyperion, in Hölderlin's novel, "It was no man that you wanted, believe me; you wanted a world." I too want a world and mean to have it. This man—any man—is simply a means of getting it (which is Man).

There goes the siren. The accident was serious. I stretch my legs. The left foot's asleep. In a moment I shall put down the yellow ballpoint pen, get to my feet, experience briefly pins and needles; then go to the window and lift the blind and see if there are dead bodies in the street. Will there be blood? I dread it. Truly.

**BUCK LONER REPORTS—**
Recording Disc No. 708—
10 January

Other matters to be taken up by board in reference to purchases for new closed circuit TV period paragraph I sort of remember that Gertrudes boy was married some years ago and I recall being surprised as he was a fag or so I always thought with that sister of mine for a mother how could he not be only thing is I never knew the little bastard except one meeting in St Louis oh maybe twenty years ago when she was there with her third husband the certified public accountant and I remember vaguely this sissy kid who wanted to go to the movies all the time who I gave an autographed picture of me on Sporko that palomino horse that was and is the trademark of Buck Loner even though the origi nal palomino in question has been for a long time up there in the happy hunting ground and my ass is now too big to inflict on any other nag except maybe Myra Breckinridge period paragraph what is the true Myra Breck inridge story that is the big question you could have knocked me over with a feather when she came sashaying into the office with her skirt hiked up damn near to her chin at least when she sits down she is a good looking broad but hoteyed definitely hoteyed and possibly mentally unbalanced I must keep an eye on her in that department but the tits are keen and proba bly hers and I expect she is just hungering for the old Buck Loner Special parenthesis start taking pee-pills again to lose weight zipper keeps slipping down which makes a damned sloppy impression end parenthesis period paragraph but what I dont like one bit is the matter of the will and I guess I better put Flagler and Flagler onto it first thing tomorrow it is true that the property was left me and Gertrude jointly but she always said Ted she said she never called me Buck she was the most envious broad that ever lived especially when I was right up there biggest star of them all after Roy bigger than Gene certainly but wish I had Genes eye for real estate that man is loaded of course I dont do so bad with the Academy but Gene Autry today is capital r capital i capital c capital h rich well I was better box office Ted Gertrude said you can keep my share of that lousy orange grove that our father threw away his life savings to buy just as the bottom dropped out of the citrus fruit I never want to see or hear of it again is what she said more or less but naturally when word come to Saint Louis and later to the Island of Manhattan where she was living with that crazy picture painter that Hollywood was spilling over into nearby Brentwood and Westwood and all the other woods were filling up with lovers of the sun and fun from all parts of the USA Gertrude did ask once or twice about our mutual holding but when I told her I needed money to start the Academy and needed the orange grove to teach in and maybe put a build ing on she was very reasonable merely saying that when the time came I was to help Myron to become a movie star as he was even better looking than I was at his age and besides could act the little fag she sent me all sorts of pictures of him and he was pretty as a picture in a drippy sort of way and wrote these far out pieces about the movies that I could never get through in magazines I never heard of in England and even in French some of them were written I will say he sent them all to me including a long arti cle type piece that I did read about so help me god the rear ends of all the major cowboy stars from austere aspiring Gothic flat ass Hoot Gibson to impertinent baroque ass James Garner shit exclamation mark paragraph Flagler and Flagler will be notified first thing tomorrow morning and told to examine with a fine tooth comb the deeds to this property and also to make a careful investigation of one Myra Breckinridge widow and claimant and try to find some loophole as I have no intention at all of letting her horn in on a property that I myself increased in value from a five thousand dollar orange grove to what is now at a conservative estimate worth in the neighborhood counting buildings of course of two million dollars maybe I should lay Myra that might keep her happy for a while while we discuss the ins and outs of our business meanwhile I better see if that fag nephew of mine left a proper will this will have to be gone into in careful detail by Flagler and Flagler and their private detective meanwhile she will be working here where I can keep an eye on her period paragraph check new TV makeup equipment write President Johnson giving him my views on subsidy for the arts in line with talk I gave to Fresno Rotary before Xmas those two kids are definitely balling and I don't like that sort of thing to be too visible on the campus particularly since she lives here in the dormitory and the matron tells me she is off with that stud every chance she can get and is always coming in after midnight a beautiful little piece she is and it may well be that the Buck Loner Special could straighten her out but I must proceed cautiously like they say as she is a minor of eighteen and naturally drawn to a male minor of nineteen six feet two and built like a stone wall who wants to be a movie star with sideburns a nice kid if he stays out of jail and I hope one day he makes it but meanwhile its his making her that I mind I mean what would her mother say her worst fears about Hollywood fulfilled I better tell the matron to give her a tough talking to or back she goes to Winnepeg as an enemy alien and deflowered virgin through no fault of yours truly remember to tell masseuse to come at five instead of six am getting horny as hell talking about the dear little thing from Winnipeg whats her name Sally Sue Baby Dee Mary Ann thats it Mary Ann Pringle and shes making it with Rusty Godowski from Detroit where else a nice dumb polack who maybe has that extra some thing that makes for stardom that masseuse better be good today

## 7

I write this sitting at my desk in the office to which I have been assigned in the west wing of the main building of what must be an incredibly valuable piece of real estate. I've spent the last few days prowling about the Academy and it's a most expensive creation, worth millions I should say, and half of it's mine, or at least half the ground it stands on. I have already contacted a good lawyer and presently he will surprise Buck Loner with my claims. Our case, I am assured, is airtight.

I find Buck Loner something of an enigma. No man can be as cheerful as he seems to be, as desirous of creating love as he says he is. Yet it is true that oceans of warmth flow from him to all the students, quite indiscriminately, and they seem to adore him, even those who are known as "hippies" and mock everyone (the argot is curiously rich out here, and slightly repellent: teenagers—already a ghastly word—are known as "teeny-boppers"!). Reluctantly, I find myself admiring the man, monster though he is. But then I shall soon break him to my will. Is there a man alive who is a match for Myra Breckinridge?

## 8

I sit now in a bus on my way to Culver City—and Metro-Goldwyn-Mayer! My heart is beating so quickly that I can hardly bear to look out the window for fear that suddenly against that leaden horizon marked by oil derricks, I shall behold—like some fantastic palace of dreams—the Irving Thalberg Memorial Building and its attendant sound stages whose blank (but oh so evocative!) façades I have studied in photographs for twenty years.

Not wanting to spoil my first impression, I keep my eye on this notebook which I balance on one knee as I put down at random whatever comes into my mind, simply anything in order to save for myself the supreme moment of ecstasy when the Studio of Studios, the sublime motor to this century's myths, appears before me as it has so many times in dreams, its great doors swinging wide to welcome Myra Breckinridge to her rightful kingdom.

I was born to be a star, and look like one today: a false hairpiece gives body to my hair while the light Max Factor base favored by Merle Oberon among other screen lovelies makes luminous my face even in the harsh light of a sound stage where I shall soon be standing watching a take. Then when the director says, "O.K., print it," and the grips prepare for another setup, the director will notice me and ask my name and then take me into the commissary and there, over a Green Goddess salad (a favorite of the stars), talk to me at length about my face, wondering whether or not it is photogenic until I stop him with a smile and say: "There is only one way to find out. A screen test." To be a film star is my dearest daydream. After all, I have had some practical experience in New York. Myron and I both appeared in a number of underground movies. Of course they were experimental films and like most experiments, in the laboratory and out, they failed but even had they succeeded they could never have been truly Hollywood, truly mythic. Nevertheless, they gave me a sense of what it must be like to be a star.

This trip is endless. I hate buses. I must rent or buy a car. The distances are unbelievable out here and to hire a taxi costs a fortune. This particular section of town is definitely ratty-looking with dingy bungalows and smog-filled air; my eyes burn and water. Fortunately elaborate neon signs and an occasional eccentrically shaped building make magic of the usual. We are now passing a diner in the shape of an enormous brown doughnut. I feel better already. Fantasy has that effect on me.

What to make of the students? I have now taught four classes in Posture (how to walk gracefully and sit down without knocking over furniture) and two in Empathy (I invite them to pretend they are oranges, drinks of water, clouds . . . the results are unusual, to say the least).

Though I have nothing to do with the Speech Department, I could not help but notice what difficulty most of the students have in talking. The boys tend to bark while the girls whine through their noses. Traditional human speech seems to have passed them by, but then one must never forget that they are the first creations of that television culture which began in the early Fifties. Their formative years were spent watching pale gray figures (no blacks, no whites—significant detail) move upon a twenty-one-inch screen. As a result, they are bland and inattentive, responsive only to the bold rhythms of commercials. Few can read anything more complex than a tabloid newspaper. As for writing, it is enough that they can write their name, or "autograph" as they are encouraged to call it, anticipating stardom. Nevertheless, a few have a touch of literary genius (that never dies out entirely), witness the obscene graffiti on the men's bathroom wall into which I strayed by accident that first day and saw, in large letters over one of the urinals. "Buck Sucks." Can this be true? I would put nothing past a man who traffics so promiscuously in love, not knowing that it is hate alone which inspires us to action and makes for civilization. Look at Juvenal, Pope, Billy Wilder.

In the Posture class I was particularly struck by one of the students, a boy with a Polish name. He is tall with a great deal of sand-colored curly hair and sideburns; he has pale blue eyes with long black lashes and a curving mouth on the order of the late Richard Cromwell, so satisfyingly tortured in *Lives of a Bengal Lancer.* From a certain unevenly rounded thickness at the crotch of his blue jeans, it is safe to assume that he is marvelously hung. Unfortunately he is hot for an extremely pretty girl with long straight blonde hair (dyed), beautiful legs and breasts, reminiscent of Lupe Velez. She is mentally retarded. When I asked her to rise she did not recognize the word "rise" and so I had to ask her "to get up" which she did understand. He is probably just as stupid but fortunately has the good sense not to talk too much. When he does, however, he puts on a hillbilly accent that is so authentic that I almost melt in my drawers.

"I thank we gawn git on mahty fahn, Miz Myra" were his first words to me after class as he looked down into my upturned face, confident of his masculine primacy. He was, in fact, so close to me that I could smell the most appetizing odor of deodorant mingled with tobacco and warm boy. But before I could make a suitable answer *she* pulled him away. Poor child! She doesn't know that I shall have him in the end while

# 9

I can hardly bear it another moment! I am reborn or in the process of rebirth like Robert Montgomery in *Here Comes Mr. Jordan.*

I am seated in front of a French café in a Montmartre street on the back lot at Metro. Last year's fire destroyed many of the studio's permanent outdoor sets—those streets and castles I knew so much better than ever I knew the Chelsea area of Manhattan where Myron and I used to exist. I deeply regret the fire, mourn all that was lost, particularly the famous New York City street of brownstones and the charming village in Normandy. But, thank Heaven, this café still stands. Over a metal framework, cheap wood has been so arranged and painted as to suggest with astonishing accuracy a Paris bistro, complete with signs for BYRRH, while a striped awning shades metal tables and chairs set out on the "sidewalk." Any minute now, I expect to see Parisians. I would certainly like to see a waiter and order a Pernod.

I can hardly believe that I am sitting at the same table where Leslie Caron once awaited Gene Kelly so many years ago, and I can almost recreate for myself the lights, the camera, the sound boom, the technicians, all converged upon this one table where, in a blaze of artificial sunlight, Leslie—much too round but a lovely face with eyes like mine—sits and waits for her screen lover while a man from makeup delicately dusts those famous features with powder.

From the angle where I sit I can see part of the street in Carverville where Andy Hardy lived. The street is beautifully kept up as the shrine it is, a last memorial to all that was touching and—yes—good in the American past, an era whose end was marked by two mushroom shapes set like terminal punctuation marks against the Asian sky.

A few minutes ago I saw Judge Hardy's house with its neatly tended green lawn and windows covered with muslin behind which there is nothing at all. It is quite eerie the way in which the houses look entirely real from every angle on the slightly curving street with its tall green trees and flowering bushes. Yet when one walks around to the back of the houses, one sees the rusted metal framework, the unpainted wood that has begun to rot, the dirty glass of the windows and the muslin curtains soiled and torn. Time withers all things human; although yesterday evening when I saw Ann Rutherford, stopped in her car at a red light, I recognized immediately the great black eyes and the mobile face. She at least endures gallantly, and I could not have been more thrilled! Must find where Lewis Stone is buried.

This is the happiest moment of my life, sitting here alone on the back lot with no one in sight, for I was able to escape the studio guide by telling him that I wanted to lie down in an empty office of the Thalberg Building; then of course I flew straight here to the back lot which is separated from the main studio by a public road.

If only Myron could have seen this! Of course he would have been saddened by the signs of decay. The spirit of what used to be has fled. Most dreadful of all, NO FILM is currently being made on the lot; and that means that the twenty-seven huge sound stages which saw the creation of so many miracles: Gable, Garbo, Hepburn (Katharine), Powell, Loy, Garland, Tracy and James Craig are now empty except for a few crews making television commercials.

Yet I must write the absolute truth for I am not Myron Breckinridge but myself and despite the intensely symbiotic relationship my husband and I enjoyed during his brief life and despite the fact that I do entirely support his thesis that the films of 1935 to 1945 inclusive were the high point of Western culture, completing what began that day in the theatre of Dionysos when Aeschylus first spoke to the Athenians, I must confess that I part company with Myron on the subject of TV. Even before Marshall McLuhan, I was drawn to the gray shadows of the cathode tube. In fact, I was sufficiently *avant-garde* in 1959 to recognize the fact that it was no longer the movies but the television commercial that engaged the passionate attention of the world's best artists and technicians. And now the result of their extraordinary artistry is this new world, like it or not, we are living in: post-Gutenberg and pre-Apocalypse. For almost twenty years the minds of our children have been filled with dreams that will stay with them forever, the way those maddening jingles do (as I write, I have begun softly to whistle "Rinso White," a theme far more meaningful culturally than all of Stravinsky or even John Cage). I submitted a piece on this subject to *Partisan Review* in the summer of 1960. I believe, without false modesty, that I proved conclusively that the relationship between consumer and advertiser is the last demonstration of *necessary* love in the West, and its principal form of expression is the television commercial. I never heard from *PR* but I kept a carbon of the piece and will incorporate it into the book on Parker Tyler, perhaps as an appendix.

For almost an hour I watched a television commercial being made on the same stage where Bette Davis acted in *The Catered Affair*—that predictably unhappy result of the movies attempting to take over the television *drama* when what they should have taken over was the *spirit* of the commercials. Then I was given lunch in the commissary which is much changed since the great days when people in extraordinary costumes wandered about, creating the impression that one was inside a time machine gone berserk. Now television executives and technicians occupy all the tables and order what used to be Louis B. Mayer Chicken Soup only the name of Mayer has been, my guide told me, stricken from the menu. So much for greatness! Even more poignant as reminders of human transiency are the empty offices on the second floor of the Thalberg Building. I was particularly upset to see that the adjoining suits of Pandro S. Berman and the late Sam Zimbalist were both vacant. Zimbalist (immortal because of *Boom Town*) died in Rome while producing *Ben Hur* which saved the studio's bacon, and Pandro S. Berman (*Dragon Seed, The Picture of Dorian Gray, The Seventh Cross*) has gone into what the local trade papers refer to as "indie production." How tragic! MGM without Pandro S. Berman is like the American flag without its stars.

No doubt about it, an era has indeed ended and I am its chronicler. Farewell the classic films, hail the television commercial! Yet nothing human that is great can entirely end. It is merely transmuted—in the way that the wharf where Jeanette MacDonald arrived in New Orleans (*Naughty Marietta,* 1935) has been used over and over again for a hundred other films even though it will always remain, to those who have a sense of history, Jeanette's wharf. Speaking of history, there was something curiously godlike about Nelson Eddy's recent death before a nightclub audience at Miami. In the middle of a song, he suddenly forgot the words. And so, in that plangent baritone which long ago earned him a permanent place in the pantheon of superstars, he turned to his accompanist and said, "Play 'Dardanella,' and maybe I'll remember the words." Then he collapsed and died.

Play "Dardanella"! Play on! In any case, one must be thankful for those strips of celluloid which still endure to remind us that once there were gods and goddesses in our midst and Metro-Goldwyn-Mayer (where I now sit) preserved their shadows for all time! Could the actual Christ have possessed a fraction of the radiance and the mystery of H. B. Warner in the first *King of Kings* or revealed, even on the cross, so much as a shadow of the moonstruck Nemi-agony of Jeffrey Hunter in the second *King of Kings,* that astonishing creation of Nicholas Ray? No.

# 10

Seated at a table in the Academy cafeteria. It is three weeks to the day since I arrived. People want to sit with me, but I graciously indicate that I would rather make these notes. They respect my writing at odd times in public places. There is a rumor that I am with the CIA.

While waiting just now to be served today's lunch specialty, a chili con carne that looks suspiciously like Gravy Train, a concentrated dog food which California's poverty-stricken Mexicans mix with their beans, I noticed, as always with a certain pleasure, the way the students go about playing at stardom.

A fantastically beautiful girl called Gloria Gordon holds court at one table, wearing a silver lamé evening gown, cut to the navel, while rock-and-roll singers do an impromptu number in the center of the room, to the delight of the western stars in their boots and chaps; a pleasure not shared by the motorcyclists in their black leather, bedecked with the swastikas and chains, radiating hostility, so unlike the Easterners who are solemnly catatonic in their Brooks Brothers suits and button-down collars, each clutching an empty attaché case. The students regard the Easterners respectfully as being the farthest-out of all for they are, reputedly, the drug-takers. Of course all the students smoke pot and experiment with LSD but only a few main-line, and of those few the Easterners, to a man, are thought to be totally hooked.

As a spiritual child of the Forties, I cannot give my imprimatur to this sort of behavior. The drug-taker is a passivist. I am an activist. Yet—to be fair—how can the average person make a meaningful life for himself in an overpopulated world? There is very little of interest for him to do in the way of work, while sex is truly absorbing only for those who possess imagination as well as means. With these young people one has the sense that they know instinctively that there are plenty more where they came from and so why fuss? They'll soon be gone, their places taken by others so closely resembling them that only a mother's eye could tell the difference.

They are an anonymous blur, even to themselves which explains their fitful, mindless shuffling of roles. In the morning Gloria will wear a silver lamé gown complete with Miriam Hopkins cocktail shaker; in the evening her ensemble may consist of leotards and a sunbonnet. It is easy for these young people to be anything since they are so plainly nothing, and know it. Their metamorphoses, however, seldom involve more than a change of clothes and the affecting of certain speech mannerisms, appropriated from Western or Eastern stars of television series, liberally sprinkled with jokes told late at night on television by nightclub comedians.

Mimesis is normal, particularly in youth, and my only demur is that today's models are, by and large, debasing. In the Forties, American boys created a world empire because they chose to be James Stewart, Clark Gable and William Eythe. By imitating godlike autonomous men, our boys were able to defeat Hitler, Mussolini and Tojo. Could we do it again? Are the private eyes and denatured cowboys potent enough to serve as imperial exemplars? No. At best, there is James Bond . . . and he invariably ends up tied to a slab of marble with a blowtorch aimed at his crotch. Glory has fled and only the television commercials exist to remind us of the Republic's early greatness and virile youth.

Of all the students at the Academy, only one has sought to model himself on a Forties star: the sickest of the Easterners is currently playing Humphrey Bogart, and he is hopeless in the part. The rest are entirely contemporary, pretending to be folk singers, cowboys and English movie actors. Needless to say, all attempts at imitating Cockney or Liverpudlian accents fail. For one thing the accents are too much for them; for another, any evidence that there could be a real world *outside* Southern California tends to demoralize our students. Of course they can observe other worlds on television but then that is show business and familiar. Even the Martian landscape of Southeast Asia loses all strangeness when framed by the homey plastic of a television set, while the people involved in that war are quite plainly extras lucky enough to be called upon to fill in prime airtime with the appearance of people dying and living.

Naturally, the Vietnam exercise appeals enormously to the students. "I mean," said one of them, "if we don't stop them there—you know, where they are now—they'll be right here in L.A." To which I answered, "This city could not be worse run by the Chinese than it is by the present administration and, frankly, if the Chinese could be persuaded to take on the job—which is doubtful—I think we should let them."

Since that exchange, Myra Breckinridge has been thought by some to be a Commie, not the worst thing to be known as at the Academy since the students are scared to death of Communism (like, man, they make you *work!*), and so regard any alleged conspirator or sympathizer with awe . . . which I like. As for the theory of Communism, they have not a clue. In fact, the only book any of them has read is something called *The Green Berets,* a jingoistic work written in the spirit of Kipling with the art of Mickey Spillane. Apparently this work is a constant source of sadistic reveries. Time and again have I heard the students speak wistfully of fighting and torturing the Vietcong, or rather of other young men fighting and torturing the Vietcong on their behalf. Not only are the male students drawn to violence (at second hand), they are also quite totalitarian-minded, even for Americans, and I am convinced that any attractive television personality who wanted to become our dictator would have their full support.

As usual, I am ambivalent. On the one hand, I am intellectually devoted to the idea of the old America. I believe in justice, I want redress for all wrongs done, I want the good life—if such a thing exists—accessible to all. Yet, emotionally, I would be only too happy to become world dictator, if only to fulfill my mission: *the destruction of the last vestigial traces of traditional manhood in the race in order to realign the sexes, thus reducing population while increasing human happiness and preparing humanity for its next stage.*

No doubt this tension in me constitutes my uniqueness, and genius. Certainly everyone senses it. Students flock to my lectures. Craving my attention and advice, they giggle, fascinated and frightened, at what I say. They sense my power, particularly the boys who are drawn to it even as they fear it. Of course these students are not entirely typical of the nation. They are somewhat stupider than the average, while simultaneously rather more imaginative and prone to daydreaming. Like most members of the lower classes, they are reactionary in the truest sense: the unfamiliar alarms them and since they have had no experience outside what Dr. Montag calls their "peer group," they are, consequently, in a state of near-panic most of the time, reacting against almost everything. It was Myron who observed in 1964 that all of the male hustlers were supporting Goldwater for President. He wrote a fascinating analysis of this phenomenon and sent it to the Americans for Democratic Action, but received no reply.

## 11

There is no denying the fact that Mary-Ann Pringle of Winnipeg is an attractive girl and I plainly dislike the fact since I am jealous of all women though I do not need to be. But then envy is the nature of the human beast and one must face that fact, like all facts. For instance, is it a fact that in my Posture class I have been unnecessarily cruel to Rusty, her boyfriend? Yes. I have been cruel. One must never lie to oneself or, for that matter, to others. No truth should ever be withheld. Without precise notation and interpretation there is only chaos. Essentially, each of us is nothing but a flux of sensations and impressions that only sort themselves out as a result of the most strict analysis and precise formulation, as Robbe-Grillet has proposed but not accomplished (his efforts to revive the novel as an art form are as ineffective as his attempts to destroy the art of film are successful). Of course, a *true* naming of things is impossible. Our minds are too feeble and our sensory equipment is too mysterious and complex for us ever to do more than make approximate definitions. Yet we must continue to make the effort, no matter how inadequate the result. In fact, I have made it a rule that whatever I *consciously* experience, I promptly submit to analysis. Take Mary-Ann Pringle.

I was in my office, just after lunch, looking over my notes for tomorrow's class in Empathy, when there was a timid knock at the door (despite my vow never to make anthropomorphic references in referring to *things* there was no doubt in my mind, even as I heard that knock, that it was the result of a fist striking wood directed by a frightened i.e. timid intelligence).

Mary-Ann entered, wearing miniskirt (bright yellow) and sweater (dark green) and no bra. She is innocent, attractive, young. Her hands are those of a child, rather grubby with broken nails but marvelously smooth, like seamless gloves.

"Miss Myra, I wanted to know could I talk to you just a minute. I'm not disturbing you, am I, Miss Myra?"

As much as I dislike girls, particularly beautiful young ones, I found myself experiencing an emotion which might be called maternal. I promptly stifled it but was kind. "Of course you're not disturbing me, Mary-Ann. My door is always open to you. Sit down. A cigarette? A Coke?"

I realized too late that I was playing Gail Patrick and would have to continue flashing brilliant smiles for the remainder of the two-scene since I seldom abandon a role once I have embarked upon it. Artistic integrity demands consistency, even with the unappreciative Mary-Anns of this world. I would have been much happier playing a sad but compassionate Loretta Young but since I had begun as Gail Patrick I would so remain, grinning doggedly.

After many soft hesitancies, she came to the point: my treatment of Rusty. "You see, he's real sensitive underneath. Oh, I know he doesn't look it being so strong and playing football one year pro and everything, but he's got feelings like anybody else and when you said that he walked 'like an ape with fleas,' well, he was pretty darned upset and so was I."

I looked grave through my smile, not an easy thing to do. "Oh, I'm sorry to hear that. Truly I am. I only wanted to help. And he *does* have terrible posture."

"It's this old football accident he was too shy to tell you about which broke four ribs and when they healed he was sort of ass . . . assy . . ."

"Asymmetrical?"

"That's right, sort of curved to one side. I mean it's not noticeable except when he's nervous and trying to walk straight and you're staring at him and picking on him."

"You make me very, very ashamed, Mary-Ann." I sounded extraordinarily sincere even to my own ears. "He seems like such a strong *confident* young man that I never dreamed he was so sensitive."

"Well, he is about some things. Like that." Mary-Ann looked so forlorn, so touching, so young, so entirely attractive that it was all I could do to keep from taking her in my arms—a gesture bound to be misinterpreted!

Instead I assured her that I would try to curb my natural impatience in the future. Nevertheless, she must realize that in the teacher-student relationship one must always tell the *total* truth. In this case, though Rusty does walk like an ape with fleas, I am duty bound to add that his other bodily movements are often remarkably graceful, the result of a serene and as yet uncompromised old-fashioned virility which seems never to desert him, except in class when I draw attention to his defects. So I will, I vowed, remember in the future to mix censure with deserved praise. She was pleased and grateful. Lovely Mary-Ann. Is she as stupid as she seems?

## 12

I had just returned from Empathy II when Buck surged into my office; there is no other verb to describe his entrance. Wearing the white Stetson that is his trademark and the well-cut tweeds that reveal his true businessman's identity, Buck entirely filled the room, his smile positively scarring the air, it was so broad, so happy, so ingenuous.

"Well, li'l lady, you lookin' reel good." No, I must not attempt any further phonetic rendering of his speech which, in any case, shifts so rapidly from Cheyenne to Pomona that one could go mad trying to define its actual provenance. "The kids all love you. Honest they do. I've been getting crackerjack reports from them, particularly in Empathy, and I hope once our little business problem is ironed out, you will consider staying on." He sank into the room's only armchair and gave me a conspiratorial wink. "You got what it takes to be a fine teacher and helper to somebody like me, who's ignorant as a yellow dog."

"Not so ignorant!" Two could play at flattery. By the time I'm finished with Buck Loner, he won't have the proverbial pot to piss in or my name is not Myra Breckinridge, at whose feet the proudest men have groveled, wincing beneath the lash of her scorn, whimpering for a chance to hold in their coarse arms her—my—fragile, too lovely for this world or at least *their* world, body. *I am Woman.* "But I will say that after a week of getting to know your students, I realize at last what overpopulation means. The brains have been bred out of the current generation. They are like the local oranges, all bright appearance and no taste."

I meant to wound. I did. Buck sat back in the chair as though I had struck his great golden autumnal moon-face. "Why, that's very, *very* unfair, Myra. Very unfair indeed." He seemed at a complete loss how to begin a defense.

In any case, I did not give him time. "I realize the scandalous state of the public school system in the United States as well as the effect television has had upon the mental processes of those whose childhood was spent staring at the box, and I accept the fact that these young people are a new breed who have gone beyond linear type in their quest for experience—'knowledge' does not seem to be the right word for what they're after; perhaps the 'easy buck' says it all . . . no play on names intended. Anyway I find it extraordinarily difficult getting through to them even the simplest thought, but since I am an American brought up during the great age of film, I want to believe that our culture is still alive, still able to create a masterpiece like *Since You Went Away,* and so I must conclude that what you have assembled here are the national dregs, the misfits, the neurotics, the daydreamers, the unrealists, the—in short—fuckups who form a significant minority in our culture, witness what happened November twenty-second, 1963, at Dallas!"

Well, that took the wind out of those sails. He absolutely shrank into his chair, contracted before my eyes. The huge open face shut tight against my imperious gaze. Frankly I can think of no pleasure greater than to approach an open face and swiftly say whatever needs to be said to shut it. Myron disapproved of this trait in me but I believed then, as I do now, that if one is right, the unsayable must be said, and the faces that I temporarily shut will, in the long run, be better faces for the exercise.

Buck did not agree. "Those boys and girls are cross-section of the youth of this country, no better, no worse. What they have got that *is* unusual and which may disqualify them from attending your Business School at Harvard is the overwhelming desire to be in show business, to have their names and faces known to all the world, to see themselves beloved by strangers, and that, believe me, is the only truly gratifying life any human can have, once they get the bug, that is, like I did, and like they have."

"My dear Buck," I addressed him warmly, a husky Jean Arthur note to my voice, "*you* are unusual. Unique. You were—are—a star. You were—and through the returns of your old movies on TV, you still are, permanently—beloved. Long after these two bodies, yours and mine, have gone to dust and this room is gone, and these boys and girls have all grown old and died and their descendants come and gone, *you will live.* Buck Loner, the Singin' Shootin' Radio Cowboy, astride Sporko, will ride the ranges of the world's imagination. You are for all time. They are not and never can be."

I had him there. My famous one-two, learned from Myron: first, excessive flattery with a grain of truth swathed in cultured nacre; then the lethal puncheroo. His face reflected ecstasy and dismay. Myra's round.

"Well, honey, I see what you mean and it's a real subtle point you got there. I mean, yes, I did make eighteen feature-length oaters, that's true, and that bastard lawyer of mine never put in one word in my contracts about future resale to the TV even though I once said to him, 'Sydney, there is going to be this TV just like there was radio and when it comes the Buck Loner features are going to be worth their weight in solid platinum.' But he paid me no mind . . . But that's not what we were talking about. No. It was about the kids, yes." He frowned. "Now they are good kids who for the most part come from underprivileged homes across the length and breadth of this country, and they hitchhike to sunny California in order that they might be stars, like me. They get jobs here and there to support themselves while they study at the Academy where we do our darnedest to bring out the creative potential of each and every one . . ."

"Can the brochure, daddy-oh," I said, surprising myself by the Fifties jargon that so amused Myron but rather repelled me. "You're in business to make money, and you do."

He looked genuinely hurt. "Well, now, honey, of course I am making money or I should say *eking* out an existence, real estate taxes being what they are in this high-type residential area . . ." Noticing the scorn in my face (and realizing that I am on to his conning), he quickly got away from the ticklish subject of our mutual property.

"Anyway, I genuinely want to see these boys and girls happy because—you may laugh and probably will—I believe in Love and I try to create that sort of atmosphere here where they are as much as possible screened from the harshness of the world, which they get quite enough of working as waitresses in drive-ins and so on not to mention the unhappy often broken homes they come from. I try to give them the glamour and excitement of show business, of fame, of stardom without the pain of failure, the terrible ordeal of real-life show business where so many hearts are broken every day, needlessly, but that's the way it goes. Here at least they are able to perform on our closed-circuit TV and then read the reviews in our school paper which are always good and constructive. They can cut discs which are played on our Muzak-type system. They have special courses in how to give interviews to the press which they can then read in the school magazine. In fact, until it was recently discontinued, our late-night closed-circuit TV talk show was as good as NBC's, with our stars being interviewed by a fellow student, himself a star on the order of Johnny Carson. So with all those things, for a time, within these walls, more than a thousand young men and women with stars in their eyes are happy."

No doubt about it, he was most effective. When he spoke of hearts needlessly broken (the sort of phrase Myron would have hooted at), I confess tears came to my eyes. For he was paraphrasing Betty Hutton after one of her many failures on television. She never had any luck, that girl. Possibly because she does not realize that she is a true goddess, as a result of all those pictures she made at Paramount during the Forties; films in which she was the demonic clown, the drum majorette of Olympus or, as Parker Tyler puts it with his usual wisdom: "The Hutton comedienne is a persuasive hieroglyph that symbolizes something deeply ingrained in modern morality: the commoner man's subconscious impulse, when a girl evades or refuses a kiss, to knock her out, take it, and have done."

Never was Tyler more on the mark than when he analyzed Hutton's "epileptico-mimetic pantomime," in which he saw straight through the strenuous clowning to the hard fact that American women are eager for men to rape them and vice versa; and that in every American there is a Boston Strangler longing to break a neck during orgasm. Ours is a violent race.

Buck and I agreed to disagree. But though he is a fool, he is also a man of formidable character and persuasiveness and thus a dangerous antagonist. It will require all my genius to destroy him . . . and destroy him I must, for not only has he cheated me of Myron's proper inheritance, he represents all that I detest in the post-Forties culture: a permissive slovenliness of mind and art. It is all like, like, like . . . "like help," as the Californian said when he was drowning. They all use "like" in a way that sets my teeth on edge. Not that I am strict as a grammarian. I realize that a certain looseness of style is necessary to create that impression of spontaneity and immediacy which is the peculiar task of post-Gutenberg prose, if there is to be such a thing. But I do object to "like" because of its mindless vagueness. "What time is it, Rusty?"

"Like three o'clock, Miss Myra," he said, after looking at his watch. He knew the *exact* time but preferred to be approximate. Well, I shall teach him to tell time among other things.

**BUCK LONER REPORTS—**
Recording Disc No. 715—
5 February

Flagler and Flagler dont seem to be getting much of anywhere with the case they say that Gertrudes will is in order leaving her share of the property to Myron and Myrons will though not made by a lawyer was duly witnessed and will stand up in court leaving everything to his wife Myra so half the property is hers according to law which strikes me as perfect injustice since if it wasnt for me there wouldnt be hardly any value at all to this land even though it is Westwood the lawyers suggest I settle with her for the current going price of these acres in Westwood for land which would be in the neighborhood of two hundred thousand bucks which I am not about to pay also I got a hunch she is out for even bigger game for she has lately taken to making little jokes about what a swell team we make running the Academy I hate that woman and wish to God there was some way to get her out of my hair once and for all Flagler and Flagler are now checking up to make sure she was really mar ried to that fag nephew thats our only hope at this point proving she wasnt married or something meanwhile I cozy her along best I can period para graph the taking of drugs is frowned upon by this institution not only is it illegal and injurious to the health but it has been known to be harmful to the performances of those performing while under the influence something along those lines I must write up for the paper before the vice squad gets on my ass any more than they are now its crazy with people murdering each other from one end of L A to the other all our local storm troopers can think of is kids smoking pot which does them a lot less harm than liquor well it is a nutty world and that is for sure period paragraph dont forget to tell Hilda to send me the new French Canadian masseuse on Monday they say she gives a super around the world and also knows about massage remember to pick up chutney for Bobbie Dean whos cooking curry tonight

## 13

I have locked the bathroom door. Several people have tried to get in, including Rusty, but I call out to them, "Use the other john," and they go away, doubtless thinking that I am in here with a man when actually I am simply trying to get away from the party.

I feel very odd. I just smoked one entire marijuana cigarette, something I have never done before. In the old days Myron and I used occasionally to take a drag on someone else's joint but never an entire stick. I always thought that drugs had no effect on me but apparently I was wrong.

I feel like crying. The ring around the bathtub, no, the two rings, one light, one dark, his and hers, depress me. What am I doing? I, Myra Breckinridge, Woman, as I proceed in my long trailing robes across the desert. Suddenly I catch sight of my lover, a priest who has given up hope of Heaven for my body. I throw out my arms and run toward him across the silvery sands. . . .

I can hardly write. My eyes don't focus properly but I must put down all my impressions exactly for they are extraordinarily intense and important. The door of perception has swung open at last and now I know that what I always suspected was true is true, that time is space made fluid, that these miniskirts are too short for me; that time is a knee made fluid. That is hell.

## 14

A terrible hangover, the result of mixing gin and marijuana, though pot is supposed not to leave one with any ill effect, unless of course that is simply a legend cultivated by drug addicts. I am in my office, trying to prepare for the first class of the day. Only with the greatest effort am I able to write these lines. My hands tremble. I feel quite ill.

The party was given by one of the students in the Music Department, Clem or Clint something or other. I had never seen him before but yesterday morning Gloria Gordon (who is in my Empathy I class) told me that he gave marvelous "far-out" parties and that I would be welcome to come last night as he, Clem or Clint, had admired me from a distance.

So Laura came to Petrarch's party, to put it stylishly, and got stoned out of her head. It was too humiliating and yet during those moments when I lay in that empty bathtub with the two rings, staring up at the single electric light bulb, I did have the sense that I was at one with all creation. The notes I made under the influence do not *begin* to record what I was actually feeling, largely because I was forced to break them off when a kind of paralysis set in. Apparently I was not able to move or speak until shortly before dawn when Clem or Clint and Gloria broke the lock on the bathroom door and rescued me from my gaudy reveries.

Fortunately, they took it all as a huge joke, but I am still humiliated at having got myself in such a situation, without dignity and finally without revelation, for in the light of day I find it difficult to believe in cosmic consciousness. In fact, this terrible hangover seems to me proof that the celebrated insights of the mystics are physiological, the result of a drastic reduction of sugar in the blood that goes to the brain. *My* brain, deprived of sugar for some hours last night, now feels as if it were full of an expanding fluid on the verge of seeking desperate egress though the top of a papier-mâché skull.

I did find the party interesting, at least in its early stages. Of those present, I was one of the oldest, which did nothing for my sense of security so laboriously achieved in those long sessions with Dr. Montag. But I was a good sport, laughing and chatting and, all in all, behaving not as a teacher but as just plain Myra Breckinridge, a beautiful woman not yet thirty. As a result, several of the young men showed a sexual interest in me but though I teased them and played the flirt, I did not allow any intimacies to occur or even indicate that they might be welcomed at some future time. I preferred to be Greer Garson, a gracious lady whose compassionate breasts were more suited to be last pillow for a dying youth than as baubles for the coarse hands of some horny boy.

But sex does not appear to be the hangup with this crowd. They wear buttons which, among other things, accuse the Governor of California of being a Lesbian, the President of being God, and Frodo (a character in a fairy tale by Tolkien) of actually existing. This is all a bit fey for my taste. But one must be open to every experience and the young, in a sense, lead us since there are now more of them than there are of us. But they are peculiar creatures, particularly to one brought up within the context of the Forties. They are quite relaxed about sex; not only do they have affairs with one another, they also attend orgies in a most matter-of-fact way, so unlike my generation with its belief in the highly concentrated sort of love that Leslie Howard felt for Ingrid Bergman in *Intermezzo.* Yet despite all this athleticism, their *true* interests seem to be, in some odd way, outside sex. They like to sit for long periods doing nothing at all, just listening to music or to what they regard as music. They are essentially passive; hence the popularity of pot.

Of course, my generation (chronologically, not spiritually) began all this. We of the Fifties saw the beginning of Zen as a popular force. Certainly our Beats were nothing if not passive in their attitude to life and experience. They were always departing, never arriving. Neither Myron nor I shared their pleasures or attitudes for we were, despite our youth, a throwback to the Forties, to the last moment in human history when it was possible to possess a total commitment to something outside oneself. I mean of course the war and the necessary elimination of Hitler, Mussolini and Tojo. And I do not exaggerate when I declare that I would give ten years of my life if I could step back in time for just one hour and visit the Stage Door Canteen in Hollywood, exactly the way that Dane Clark did in the movie of the same name, and like him, meet all the great stars at their peak and perhaps even, like Dane's buddy Bob Hutton, have a romance with Joan Leslie, a star I fell hopelessly in love with while watching *Sergeant York*. But where is Joan now? Where are all those beautiful years of war and sacrifice and Pandro S. Berman films? None of this will ever come again, except in gray cloudy miniatures on the Late Show, and soon, I pray, in the sinewy prose of Myra Breckinridge as she reworks and completes her late husband's certain-to-be masterpiece *Parker Tyler and the Films of the Forties.*

But what will the current generation think of my efforts? That is the question. I find that any reference to the stars of the Forties bores them. "Who was Gary Cooper?" asked one young thing last night; to which another girl answered, "The one with the big ears," thinking he was Clark Gable! But they all find Humphrey Bogart fascinating and he may yet prove to be my bridge to them.

Conversation from last night.

"Like experience isn't everything, Myra. I mean like you also got to have *it* deep down inside you."

"But what is *it*?"

"What's deep down inside you, that's what *it* is. What you are."

"But isn't what you are what experience makes you?"

"No, it's like what you feel . . ."

Like. Like. Like! The babble of this subculture is drowning me! Although my companion was a lanky youth of the sort I am partial to, I simply shut him out and watched the group that was dancing in the center of the room, a dozen boys and girls gyrating without touching one another, each in his or her private world . . . which is the key to the game of the moment: don't touch me and I won't touch you. While the operative word is "Cool." Like fun? Like crazy!

Of the dancers, Rusty Godowski was easily the most exciting and certainly the most attractive, in his faded chinos and checked shirt, whose top two buttons were missing, revealing a smooth muscular neck at whose base, just below the hollows of the collarbone, tendrils of bronze hair curl, looking as if they would be silky to the touch, unlike the usual male Brillo. Soon I shall know for certain their texture. Poor Mary-Ann.

"He does dance well, doesn't he?" Mary-Ann sat down in the place which the metaphysician had vacated, without, I fear, my noticing his departure. Obviously she had seen me watching Rusty. She is not entirely stupid.

"I was studying him for posture." I sounded colder than I intended, but she had taken me by surprise and I dislike it when people observe me without my knowledge. "I will say he moves very well when he dances," I added with a degree of warmth which encouraged her to smile shyly.

"That's being an athlete. It's just when he walks he sort of lumbers."

"Well, we'll soon take care of that," I said briskly, and indeed I shall, poor bastard.

Mary-Ann chattered away, unaware of my designs. "We've been talking about maybe getting married in June after we finish the course—that is, if we can both get work. Of course I can always pick up a little money modeling. I'm not really crazy about a career, you know. Fact, it's just to be with Rusty that I'm taking this music course, to keep an eye on him. With all these pretty girls around and wild for him, I can't take any chances."

"You make a charming couple." I noticed again how extraordinarily attractive she is, with that fresh unclouded complexion I so love—and envy, for the *texture* of the skin of my face is not all that Helena Rubinstein would desire. In my day I have been too much a sun-worshipper and the skin must pay a price for the spirit's refreshment, and I was certainly refreshed by those long sunny afternoons at Jones Beach and amongst the Far Rockaways.

Rusty's back was to us now and I could not take my eyes off his somewhat square yet small buttocks as they made a slow grinding motion in response to the beat of an electric guitar. Though I tried to visualize what they must look like without the protective covering of cloth, I failed to come up with a satisfactory mental image. Happily, I shall soon know everything!

" 'Course we're both broke. I get a little something from the family in Winnipeg but poor Rusty's only got his uncle and aunt in Detroit who don't like him because he was kind of wild when he was a kid . . ."

"So wild that he was busted for stealing a car." The day that I first noticed Rusty in class, I went straight to Buck's office where dossiers on each student are kept. They are surprisingly thorough. Rusty's three-year suspended sentence was duly noted, as well as the cogent fact that should he ever again run afoul of the law he can be sent up for a maximum of twenty years.

Mary-Ann looked frightened. "I didn't know anybody knew about that."

"Just Uncle Buck and I." I patted her hand. "Don't worry, neither of us is going to tell."

"He's completely changed since those days, he really is. Why, in those days he used to play around with a lot of girls. You should have seen all the photographs he used to have! But after he met me he stopped all that and now he isn't interested in anything except working hard and being a star, which I'm sure he's going to be."

"He's certainly no worse than the rest of them on television." I was perfectly honest with her. "Of course he can hardly talk but neither can they."

"Oh, but he talks awfully well. It's just he has some trouble with *speaking* lines but that takes lots of practice. Anyway what is important is that he comes over so *real,* and of course so sexy. You should have seen him on the closed-circuit TV last spring when he played the part of this crazy gunman. Oh, he was *something!*"

It was at that point that I was given marijuana by Clem or Clint, and the rest of the evening took on a religious tone.

## 15

Feeling somewhat better, I gave a great deal to my Empathy II class, and though I am now exhausted, I have at least gotten over my hangover.

A letter from Dr. Montag cheered me up. He warns against depressions of the sort I have been prone to since Myron's death and so he proposes, rather obviously, that in lieu of analysis I must keep busy. Little does he dream just how busy I am! Between my plot to entrap Rusty and my efforts to obtain my rightful share of the Academy, I have hardly a moment to devote to my life's real work, completing Myron's book. Fortunately the insights gained during my visit to MGM are bound to add immeasurably to Myron's text. Meanwhile, I have had a marvelous idea for a piece on Pandro S. Berman which *Cahiers du Cinema* ought to eat up. After all, with the exception of Orson Welles and Samuel Fuller, Berman is the most important filmmaker of the Forties.

## 16

I spoke sharply to Rusty in Posture today. He shows no sign of improvement and I'm afraid I was brutal. "You simply cannot walk straight." I imitated his slouching walk which is, in its way, extremely sensual but hardly suitable for the screen.

He looked very angry and muttered something under his breath that I could not hear but assumed was uncomplimentary. Mary-Ann looked more than ever disturbed as she begged me with her eyes to desist.

"I will see you after class, Godowski." I was abrupt. "Things cannot go on as they are," I added ominously.

I then gave the class a series of exercises in how to sit down, something that did not come easily to any of them. All the while observing, out of the corner of my eye, Rusty's sullen face. My plot is working very nicely.

After class, Rusty came to my office and sat on the straight chair beside the desk, listing to one side, legs wide apart. He was not in the least nervous. In fact, he was downright defiant, even contemptuous of *me,* so secure did he think himself in his masculine superiority.

As usual, he wore a sport shirt with two missing buttons. Today, however, a T-shirt hid the chest from view. Faded blue jeans and desert boots completed the costume, and—as I have already noted—it is costumes that the young men now wear as they act out their simple-minded roles, constructing a fantasy world in order to avoid confronting the fact that to be a man in a society of machines is to be an expendable, soft auxiliary to what is useful and hard. Today there is nothing left for the old-fashioned male to do, no ritual testing of his manhood through initiation or personal contest, no physical struggle to survive or mate. Nothing is left him but to put on clothes reminiscent of a different time; only in travesty can he act out the classic hero who was a law unto himself, moving at ease through a landscape filled with admiring women. Mercifully, that age is finished. Marlon Brando was the last of the traditional heroes and, significantly, even he was invariably beaten up in the last reel, victim of a society that has no place for the ancient ideal of manhood. Since Brando, there has been nothing except the epicene O'Toole, the distracted Mastroianni, and the cheerfully incompetent Belmondo. The roof has fallen in on the male and we now live at the dawn of the age of Woman Triumphant, of Myra Breckinridge!

I began pleasantly, disarmingly. "Not long ago Mary-Ann told me that I have a tendency to pick on you, Rusty . . ."

"You sure do . . ."

"Don't interrupt, please." I was stern but pleasant, like Eve Arden. "If I have, it's because I'm trying to help you. I think you have a great *potential* talent. How great I can't decide just yet, but unless you learn to walk properly there's not a chance in this world of your ever being a major star."

The reference to his talent pleased him; the prophecy alarmed him. "Hell, Miss Myra, I don't walk that bad."

"I'm afraid you do. And look at the way you're leaning to one side right now. You look like you're about to fall out of the chair."

He straightened up and crossed his legs. "That better?" The hint of a sneer in his voice excited me. He must be built up in order that his fall be the more terrible.

"Yes. Now I realize that you have a physical problem. Mary-Ann told me about your back."

"I broke four ribs and even so finished the last half." He was inordinately proud; no doubt about it, a confident young man.

"Very admirable. Now I want you to stand up and walk first toward the door and then back here to me."

I could hear him murmur "Oh, shit" under his breath as he lumbered to his feet. Slowly he walked, or rather slouched, to the door and then returned and stood defiantly in front of me, thumbs hooked in his belt. I noted for the first time how large and strong his hands are, hairless with unusually long thumbs.

"O.K.?" he asked.

"*Not* O.K." I studied him a moment. He was so close to me that my eyes were on a level with his belt buckle. "Now, Rusty, I noticed the other night that your problem seems to go away when you dance. So, just as an exercise, I want you to do one of those stationary dances—I don't know what they're called. You know, like the one you were doing at the party."

"Dance? Here? Now?" He looked puzzled. "But there's no music."

"To be precise there never is *music* with those dances, just electronic noise. Nothing compared to the *big* sound of Glenn Miller. Anyway, all you need is a beat. You can keep time by snapping your fingers."

"I feel silly." He scowled and looked suddenly dangerous, but I knew what I was about.

"Go ahead. We haven't got all day. Start." I snapped my fingers. Half-heartedly he did the same and slowly began to gyrate his hips. I found the effect almost unbearably erotic. To have him all to myself, just three feet away, his pelvis revolving sexily. For some minutes he continued to gyrate, the snapping of fingers growing less and less precise as his hands grew sweaty. I then instructed him to turn around so that I could observe him from the rear. He did as he was told. Waves of lust made me dizzy as those strong deep buttocks slowly revolved. Have they ever been violated? I can hardly bear the suspense.

Finally, I told him he could stop. He did so, with obvious relief. When he turned back to me, I noticed the curved upper lip was beaded with perspiration. In his dense masculine way, he too had felt the tension and perhaps suspected, instinctively, its origin and so knew fear. "I can't dance so good without music," he mumbled, as if obscurely ashamed of the display he had been forced to make of himself.

"You did very well." I was brisk, even encouraging. "I think I may have a solution to our problem. All you need is something to remind you to stand straight. Where were the ribs broken?"

He touched his left side, below the heart. "Four was busted right here which is why I'm kind of pulled over to this side."

"Let me see."

At first he seemed not to understand the question. "Like this," he said, indicating the way in which he was listing to port.

"No. No." I was brusque. "Let me *see* your back. Take your shirt off."

He was startled. "But there's nothing to see. . . . I mean the ribs are all inside me that was broken."

"I know *where* the ribs are, Rusty." I was patient. "But I have to see the exact point where the muscle begins to pull you to one side."

There was no answer to this. He started to say something but decided not to. Slowly he unfastened his belt and unhooked the top button of the blue jeans. Then he unbuttoned his shirt and took it off. The T-shirt was soaked at the armpits, the result of his strenuous impromptu dance and, perhaps (do I project?), of terror.

For the first time I saw his bare arms. The skin was very white (no one out here goes to the beach in January even though it is quite sunny), with biceps clearly marked though not overdeveloped; large veins ran the length of the forearms to the hands, always an excellent sign, and not unattractive since the veins were not blue but white, indicating skin of an unusual thickness, again a good sign. On the forearms coppery straight hairs grew. He paused as though not certain what to do next. I was helpful. "The T-shirt, too. I haven't got X-ray eyes."

Glumly he pulled the T-shirt over his head. I watched fascinated by each revelation of his body. First the navel came into view, small and protruding. Just beneath it a line of dark slightly curly hairs disappeared inside the Jockey shorts which were now visible above the loosened belt. The shirt rose higher. About two inches above the navel, more hairs began (I had seen the topmost branches of this tree of life at the pot party, now I saw the narrow roots slowly widening as the tree made its way to his neck). When the chest was entirely bared, his face was momentarily hidden in the folds of the damp T-shirt and so I was able to study, unobserved, the small rose-brown breasts, at the moment concave and unaroused. Then the T-shirt was wadded up and dropped onto the floor.

Aware of my interested gaze, he blushed. Beginning at the base of the thick neck, the lovely color rose to the level of his eyes. Like so many male narcissists, he is paradoxically, modest: he enjoys revealing himself but only on his own terms.

A remark about his appearance was obviously called for and I made it. "You seem in very good condition . . ."

"Well, I work out some, not like I ought to . . . used to . . ." He hooked long thumbs into his belt, causing the smooth pectorals to twitch ever so slightly, revealing the absence of any fat or loosening of skin.

"Now will you please face the wall, arms at your sides, with your palms pressed against the wall as hard as you can."

Without a word, he did as he was told. The back was as pleasing as the front (no hairs on the shoulder, unlike poor Myron, who was forced to remove his with electrolysis). The blue jeans had begun to sag and now hung several inches below the waistline, revealing frayed Jockey shorts. Aware that the trousers were slipping, he tried to pull them up with one hand but I put a stop to that. "Hands flat against the wall!" I ordered in a sharp voice that would not take no for an answer.

"But, Miss Myra . . ." and his voice was suddenly no longer deep but a boy's voice, plaintive and frightened: the young Lon McCallister.

"Do as I say!"

He muttered something that I could not hear and did as he was told. In the process, the blue jeans cleared the curve of his buttocks and now clung precariously to the upper thighs of which a good two inches were in plain view. It was a moment to cherish, to exult in, to give a life for. His embarrassment was palpable, charging the situation with true drama since from the very beginning it has been quite plain to me that *in no way do I interest him sexually.* Since he detests me, my ultimate victory is bound to be all the more glorious and significant.

I studied my captive for some moments (the spine did indeed make an S-like curve and the thick white trapezoidal ligament was twisted to one side). Of greater interest to me, however, were the Jockey shorts and what they contained. But now I knew that I would have to proceed with some delicacy. I crossed to where he stood. I was so close to him that I could smell the horselike odor men exude when they are either frightened or in a state of rut. In this case it was fright.

Delicately I ran my hand down his spine. He shuddered at my touch but said nothing. Meanwhile I spoke to him calmly, easily, the way one does in order to soothe a nervous animal. "Yes, I can see the trouble now. It's right here, under the shoulder blade." I kneaded the warm smooth skin, and again he winced but said nothing while I continued to give my "analysis" of his condition. "Perhaps a brace in this area would help."

Now my hands were at the narrow waist. He was breathing hoarsely, arms pressed so hard against the wall that the triceps stood out like white snakes intertwined, ready to strike.

I felt something warm on the back of one hand: a drop of sweat from his left armpit. "But perhaps the trouble is lower down. Around the small of the back. Yes, of course! The lumbar region—that's just where it is!"

As I spoke, evenly, hypnotically, I gently inserted my thumbs beneath the worn elastic band of his shorts and before he was aware of what was happening, I had pulled them down to his knees. He gave a strangled cry, looked back over his shoulder at me, face scarlet, mouth open, but no words came. He started to pull away from me, then stopped, recalling that he was for all practical purposes nude. He clung now to the wall, the last protector of his modesty.

Meanwhile I continued to chat. "Yes, we can start the brace right here." I touched the end of the spine, a rather protuberant bony tip set between the high curve of buttocks now revealed to me in all their splendor . . . and splendor is the only word to describe them! Smooth, white, hairless except just beneath the spinal tip where a number of dark coppery hairs began, only to disappear from view into the deep crack of buttocks so tightly clenched that not even a crowbar could have pried them apart.

Casually I ran my hand over the smooth slightly damp cheeks. To the touch they were like highly polished marble warmed by the sun of some perfect Mediterranean day. I even allowed my forefinger the indiscretion of fingering the coppery wires not only at the tip of the spine but also the thicker growth at the back of his thighs. Like so many young males, he has a relatively hairless torso with heavily furred legs. Myron was the same. With age, however, the legs lose much of this adolescent growth while the torso's pelt grows heavier.

I had now gone almost as far as I could go with my inspection. After all, I have not yet established total mastery. But I have made a good beginning: half of the mystery has now been revealed, the rest must wait for a more propitious time. And so, after one last kneading of the buttocks (I tried and failed to pull apart the cheeks), I said, "That will do for now, Rusty. I think we've almost got to the root of the problem."

He leaned rigidly, all of a piece, to one side and grabbed the fallen trousers. Had he slightly squatted—the normal thing to do in his position—I might have caught a glimpse of the heart of the mystery from the rear, an unflattering angle which, paradoxically, has always excited me, possibly because it is in some way involved with my passion for "backstage," for observing what is magic from the unusual, privileged angle. But he kept his legs as much together as possible, pulling on clothes with astonishing speed, the only lapse occurring when something in front was caught by the ascending shorts, causing him to grunt and fumble. But then all was in order and when he finally turned around, the belt buckle had been firmly fastened. He was satisfying pale and alarmed-looking.

I was all business. "I think this has been a very useful session—yes, you can put on your shirt." His hands trembled as he buttoned his shirt. "I'll have a chat with the chiropractor Uncle Buck uses" (the "Uncle Buck" always works wonders at the Academy) "and we'll see what he can do for you."

"Yes, Miss Myra." The voice was almost inaudible. Nervously, he mopped his face with a handkerchief.

"It is stuffy in here, isn't it? I always turn the airconditioning off. It's bad for my sinus. Well, I don't want to keep you another minute from Mary-Ann. What a wonderful girl! I hope you realize how lucky you are."

"Oh, yes, Miss Myra, I sure do," he gabbled. Then, with the assurance that I had only his interest at heart, I showed him out of the room. It was, in many ways, the most exciting *sensual* moment of my life—so far. But the best is yet to come, for I mean to prove once and for all to Dr. Montag that it is possible to work out in life *all* one's fantasies, and so become entirely whole.

No sooner was Rusty out the door than I noticed he had left his T-shirt behind. I buried my face in its warm sweaty folds, a most agreeable surrogate for skin. The odor was somewhat sharp at the armpits but by no means unpleasant since fresh sweat is the greatest of aphrodisiacs as well as nature's own lubricant.

**BUCK LONER REPORTS—**
Recording Disc No. 721—
18 February

Dont know when I have ever come across a woman as awful as Myra Breckinridge she is wreaking total havoc with the program telling the students they have no talent and no chance of stardom which is downright mean not to mention bad for business so I had a talk with her in the back of the auditorium where she was holding her Empa thy class which for reasons not clear to me is double the size of any of the other classes the kids are fascinated by her because of what she says and she is a sharptongued bitch no doubt of that theres seldom a class of hers where somebody dont run out crying to beat the band but they come back for more which is downright unhealthy as I told her in no uncertain terms you are undermining all of our work here at the Academy which is to build up capital c confidence exclamation point paragraph well she just gave me that high and mighty stare of hers and said you think lying to people is good for them you think telling somebody whos got cancer that he is all right and doesnt need an operation is the right thing to do of course not I said but if he has had the operation and is a terminal case I think you must keep him as happy as possible and in a good frame of mind under the cir cumstances well she said in a voice so loud that the students on the stage who were pretending to be billboards could hear her at least you admit that these cretins are terminal cases and that its curtains for the lot of them no it is not I said wanting to crack her one against the side of her head just to take that smirk off of her face no they are carefully selected as possible candidates for future stardom every last one of them well then she inter rupts with a single swear word delivered in a hiss that I swear sent shivers down my spine like some mean old rattler out there in the sagebrush just waiting to sink his fangs into your leg well I was not about to be put down on my own Academy and so I said getting real tough you don't talk to me that way and get away with it you consider yourself warned or else Ill have you out of here so fast you wont know what hit you to which she just smiled prettily and cocked her pretty head at me and said ever so sweet you just try it you motherfucker and Ill take this whole place away from you lock stock and Empathy class well I don't think no woman has ever spoke to me like that certainly no man would dare for fear of getting hisself beat to a pulp all I could say then was well you watch your step thats all and as for taking this place away from me I need to know a whole lot more about you than I do why I dont even know whether you was ever really married to that fag Myron well I suppose I did go too far on that one for she hauled off and let me have it right in the kisser and I saw stars because this wasnt no girls slap no sir it was a goddam fist with what felt like a roll of quarters in it I nearly fell over it was such a jolt and the noise mustve been like a pis tol going off for the kids all stopped pretending to be billboards and stared at us like we was putting on a show which is the way she handled it for cool as can be she said to the kids I quote now that is the classic stage slap deliv ered in such a way that though the person being slapped really seems to be hit hard he isn't its all fake later Ill show you how its done its a trick first used on stage by Miss Patricia Collinge in The Little Foxes so thank you Uncle Buck for the demonstration unquote and with that the bitch went back to teaching her class and I come straight back here to the office and canceled my appointment for massage I am too shook up and then phoned to Flagler and Flagler to ask if theres any report on her from the detective in New York they say the only thing theyve so far found is that Myron really was a fag quite well known in what they call the underground movie set and its thought he killed hisself probably because of Myra about who they cant find out anything except there is no record of her marrying him in New York New Jersey or Connecticut they are meanwhile going to check the other forty-seven states it would be the happiest day of my life if I can find out she really wasnt married to him and put her in the damned hoosegow for fraud on the other hand the three wills are all in order worse luck for me so everything depends now on that marriage license dont for get Bobbie Deans yoghurt with prune whip

# 17

I am sitting in a booth at Schwab's drugstore in Hollywood where the young Lana Turner was discovered by an agent. Of course the present Schwab's does not in the least resemble the Schwab's of thirty years ago. Today's drugstore consists of two large rooms. The one where I am sitting contains booths while the other is occupied by drugstore, soda fountain and a large display of magazines and paperback books where out-of-work actors and actresses can be seen at any time of day or night furtively reading *Silver Screen,* or searching feverishly through the pages of novels looking for lurid passages whose crude imagery can be calculated to enliven sexual bouts with "loved ones" or, as one hippie said to another after sex, "I'll tell you who I was thinking of if you'll tell me who you were thinking of."

It is curious how often the male (and sometimes the female) needs to think of those not present in the act. Even with Myron, I was always imagining someone else, a boy glimpsed at Jones Beach or a man observed briefly at the wheel of a truck or sometimes (yes, I may as well confess it) a slender blonde girl that used to live in the brownstone next door when we lived at the corner of 11th Street and Ninth Avenue. She studied at the Art Students League and though I never once spoke to her, I was constantly aware of her and learned a good deal about her from the owner of the Ninth Avenue Delicatessen where each of us had an account, ours too seldom paid on time.

Fortunately, I am no longer susceptible to the charm of the female body. Not that a straightforward invitation from the young Lana Turner or the young Ava Gardner might not, as they say out here, "turn me on," but luckily for me there is no longer a young Lana Turner or Ava Gardner and so my lust has taken a different and quite spectacular form since Myron's death.

Rusty has been avoiding me ever since the day of his humiliation. He has even taken to cutting Posture class, which is a serious matter. This morning as I was on my way to Empathy II (held in the auditorium because of the students' desire to be taught by me: the other teachers are mad with envy!), I bumped into Rusty—literally collided with him at the turning of a corridor. I dropped my briefcase, which he swiftly retrieved.

"I'm sorry, Miss Myra." He handed me the briefcase at arm's length as though it contained a ticking bomb.

"You really should watch where you're going." I was severe and he gulped like Gary Cooper, his attractiveness greatly enhanced by a total inability to look me in the eye.

"You've missed two Posture classes in a row. That's very serious, Rusty.

Very, very serious. You know how Uncle Buck dislikes that, and how it is bound to count against your final grade."

"But I been real busy, Miss Myra. Working, see . . ."

"The garage?"

"No, with these friends, helping to start this business. Anyway, next week I'll be back in class and that's for sure, Miss Myra." He looked at me with such frightened sincerity that it was all I could do to keep my hands off him right then and there. Gone was the easy masculine arrogance that had characterized him in our early relations. Now he was jittery and profoundly hostile, and all because of *me*! Though the corridor was airconditioned to a polar temperature (like so many fat men Buck suffers from heat), a bead of sweat appearing at the tip of one sideburn reminded me to say, "I still have the T-shirt you left in my office."

Bright red at this reference to his humiliation, he said that he was sorry to be so forgetful and that, if it was all right, he would come around sometime and retrieve the garment. Then the bell rang for class and we parted. I watched him a moment as he ran down the corridor, the buttocks that once I had beheld in all their innocent naked glory covered now by thick corduroy. Soon I shall have occasion to examine them again, at leisure, as his education continues, impelling each of us inexorably toward the last degree.

The class went well until Buck decided to look in. I tolerated his presence. But then when he became critical of me I was forced to take a stern line with him. In fact, after he made a direct challenge to my authority, I struck him. All in all, it was a most satisfying thing to do and it will be some time before that keg of lard dares to cross me again.

Afterwards, in the faculty room (wall-to-wall champagne-beige carpeting, piped-in music, and a color television set), two of my colleagues joined me for coffee from the mechanical dispenser. Apparently "everyone" has heard that there was some sort of contretemps between me and the president of the Academy. But I assured them that Uncle Buck and I could never quarrel about anything. "Oh, perhaps a disagreement or two about how far one should go in telling the students whether or not they really do have talent."

Unfortunately both my colleagues share the Buck Loner philosophy. One of them is a Negro queen named Irving Amadeus. A recent convert to the Bahai religion, he lives entirely on organic foods raised in a series of pots in the backyard of a large house at Van Nuys which he shares with a number of fellow cultists. There are, incidentally, nine Negro teachers but only seven Negro students. Though I suspect that Buck dislikes our dusky cousins, he has done his best to integrate the school at the teaching level, leaning over backwards to give work to almost any show-biz-type Negro who comes his way (the Stepin Fetchit Lecture Series, however, fell through at the last moment, due to a contractual snag). But at the student level, integration has not been easy. A vocal minority are prejudiced, possibly because many young white males fear the Negro cock. Time and again I have observed white youths inadvertently clench their buttocks at the approach of a black man, as though fearful of anal penetration, not realizing that the legend of Negro size is just that—legend. The dozen or so jungle bunnies I have trafficked with were perfectly ordinary in that department . . . in fact, two were hung like chipmunks (Myron, incidentally, was larger than any of them, a fact which, paradoxically, caused him not joy but despair). The physiological origin of the myth was once explained to me by Dr. Montag. Apparently the Negro penis limp is almost the same size as it is when erect, a phenomenon which, though it causes consternation in a shower room, brings no added joy to the bedroom. Nevertheless, uneasy white males still continue to tighten their rosy sphincters at the approach of spooks.

In defense of the Buck Loner philosophy, Irving Amadeus (he pretends to have been Jewish before his conversion to Bahai) spoke of love. "It is necessary to have love for all things, particularly those young people entrusted to our care."

"Love," I said, "ought never to exclude truth."

"But love does not wound." He continued for some time in this vein. Fortunately Miss Cluff, the other teacher, has no interest in love, at least of the caritas sort. She is lean and profoundly Lesbian, forever proposing that we go to drive-in movies together in her secondhand Oldsmobile. Temporarily she is teaching the Bell Telephone Hour Course in Song in order to make enough money to pay for a concert debut in New York.

"Nonsense!" she said to Bahai, cutting him short. "We *must* wound if we are to create artists. I myself am the result of an uncle whom I hated, a teacher of piano who forced me at the age of nine to practice seven, eight, ten hours a day, striking my fingers with a stick whenever I got a note wrong. This was in Oregon." We all recognized the plot of *The Seventh Veil* and so were able to ask the right questions in order to help her complete the fantasy whose denouement was that, in spite of everything, she had come through, become an artist, after the obligatory nervous breakdown, et cetera, and she owed it all to her uncle who had been cruel but *cared.*

I found this conversation pleasing, for I am always happy when people resort to the storehouse of movie myth in order to create for themselves attractive personas. I was not prepared, however, for her next observation. "There is really only one talented student in any of my classes and that is a girl called Mary-Ann Pringle."

I sat up, almost spilling the dregs of my coffee. *Had I missed a trick?* "But I know the girl. I have her in Posture. She is a complete nothing."

"Except," said Black Beauty, "for her connection with Rusty Godowski. I have him in Atavistic Rhythm, and I am here to tell you that that ofay boy has really got sex appeal in spades!" (All in all, not a happy figure of speech, I thought.)

"I know *what* he's got," I said too quickly, and not quite accurately.

"Then you know he is absolutely total man, or, as we in Bahai believe . . ."

"What," I turned to Miss Cluff, drowning out Mother Africa, "is so talented about Mary-Ann Pringle?"

"Her *voice*! It is the pure, the white *bel canto.* Untrained, of course, like a smudged diamond, but a jewel no less. She could be a star of the same magnitude as . . ."

"Kathryn Grayson?"

Miss Cluff is too young to know from experience the Forties and too self-absorbed to attend films seriously. For her the movies are simply a pretext for getting girls onto the back seat of her secondhand Oldsmobile. "She could . . . she *must* sing opera."

But Darkness at Noon saw, perhaps rightly, another fate for Mary-Ann. "As long as that young man wants her she won't have a career. And from what I've seen of him these last two years, he shows no signs of losing interest. Every girl in Atavistic Rhythm has made a play for Rusty, and no dice."

Miss Cluff looked grim. "Women's rights are never won! Never! To think that a girl of her talent is prepared to waste her life—and genius—on a hulk, an oaf, a thing, a man!"

"A mighty *cute* thing," giggled Heart of Darkness, but then recalled himself to add, more seriously, "and talented, too, possessing a natural animal magnetism, and of course highly photogenic as we all of us saw last spring, before Myra joined us, when he acted in a Rod Serling classic on the closed-circuit TV . . ."

Although I usually collect every comment testifying to Rusty's male attractiveness, adding bit by bit to the vivid mosaic that is Rusty the Man (soon to be shattered by me into a million fragments, that I may then rearrange him along other and more meaningful lines), I suddenly found myself morbidly eager to hear about Mary-Ann. Miss Cluff, eager to tell, told. And I believed her. Though mad as a hatter, Miss Cluff is every bit as tough-minded about the arts as I am. And so I am tempted to believe her when she tells me that *Mary-Ann has star quality.*

The columnist Sidney Skolsky has just entered the main part of the drugstore. Everyone stares at him. As well they might! With Louella and Hedda gone, he is Mr. Movies. They say his office is upstairs.

# 18

I am home now. The blinds are raised and I have been staring for some minutes at the bespangled ten-times-life-size girl as she slowly turns in front of the Château Marmont Hotel. For me she is Hollywood, and mesmerizing.

No further encounter with Rusty. He attended one Posture class but we did not speak and he was more than ever nervous and sullen in my presence. His T-shirt is still in my desk drawer, which now smells of him, a musky disturbing odor that makes me quite weak since, regretfully, I am not able to smell the original, for he keeps half a room's distance between us. I must soon make operative the second phase of my plan.

Meanwhile, to my surprise, Mary-Ann has been unusually friendly. When I told her yesterday that Miss Cluff thought her very talented, she was enormously pleased. "Miss Cluff *is* nice to say that. And I do like singing but, like Rusty says, there's only room for one star in any bed . . . I mean family." She stammered, blushing deliciously at her error, which was no doubt a lovers' joke.

"I'm sure that's what he *would* say. It's the usual male view."

"But I like it. Honestly I do. I think the man's *got* to be boss so a girl knows where she is."

"I'm afraid that's a slightly outmoded point of view," I was careful, however, not to sound too sharp. "Particularly now when the relationship between the sexes is changing so rapidly, and women are becoming aggressive and men passive and . . ."

"Which I just hate!" Mary-Ann was unexpectedly vehement. Good. The subject has occurred to her before. Excellent. "I hate these boys who just drift around taking pot and trips and not caring if—well, if it's a boy or a girl they're with. It's just terrible the way so many are now, and I guess that's why I'm so hung up on Rusty. He's all man."

I thought with some amusement of "all man's" defenseless bottom, quivering at my touch. I have the power forever to alter her image of Rusty. But that is for later. Now I must win her friendship, even love. The plan requires it.

Although Dr. Montag and I write each other at least once a week, I feel somewhat guilty for not having told him what I am up to (these notes will be your introduction, dear Randolph). On the other hand, we do discuss the one topic we most disagree on, the changing relationship between the sexes. Being Jewish as well as neo-Freudian, he is not able to divest himself entirely of the Law of Moses. For the Jew, the family is everything; if it had not been, that religion which they so cherish (but happily do not practice) would have long since ended and with it their baleful sense of identity. As a result, the Jew finds literally demoralizing the normal human sexual drive toward promiscuity. Also, the Old Testament injunction not to look upon the father's nakedness is the core to a puritanism which finds unbearable the thought that the male in himself might possess an intrinsic attractiveness, either aesthetically or sensually. In fact, they hate the male body and ritually tear the penis in order to remind the man so damaged that his sex is unlovely. It is, all in all, a religion even more dreadful than Christianity.

Dr. Montag, however, is a thoughtful man, aware of the damage done him as a child growing up in the household of a kosher butcher whose wife wanted their son to be a rabbi. But even then Randolph was a nonconformist; he chose to be a dentist, that last resort of the rabbi *manqué.* But dentistry soon palled (it was the tongue, not the teeth that interested him) and so he became a psychologist, and his book, *Sexual Role and/or Responsibility* made a complete shambles of Karen Horney, among others.

Myron and I met Dr. Montag some years ago at a lecture Myron gave on "The Uterine Vision in the Films of the Forties" (this lecture is the basis for the chapter on Betty Hutton and Martha Raye in his Parker Tyler book). Needless to say, the lecture was sparsely attended. Myron was a nervous lecturer and his voice had a tendency to become shrill if he sensed any serious disagreement, and of course there was—is—always disagreement about his work as there is bound to be controversy about the work of any entirely original thinker.

On that famous night poor Myron was forced to shriek his way through the lecture in an effort to drown out the usual hecklers (this particular talk was given, like so many of his best performances, at the Blue Owl Grill on 132nd Street, a place where Happenings used to occur regularly before Happenings were known, and of course poets read). When the lecture was over and the booing had ceased, we were joined by a thickset man with blue jowls. "I am Randolph Spenser Montag," the man said, taking Myron's fragile hand into his own large one. "*Dr.* Montag," the man added but without unction or pride, merely a simple statement, "and I want you to know that you have broken new ground along lines similar to my own."

They talked until morning. I had never before known Myron to be so excited, so energized, so exalted as he was at that moment when he found for the first time in his life a masculine mind complementary to his own. This is not the place to review their joint achievements (as you know better than anyone, Randolph, and it is essentially for you and to you that I write in this notebook, a most liberating activity as well as an excellent way for me to tell you how much I admire you without any of the uneasiness caused by our usual face-to-face encounters, particularly those official ones when I am on the patient's couch and you are striding noisily about the room wheezing and gasping from emphysema). That meeting in the Blue Owl was historic not only for the three of us but for the world, since many of the insights in *Sexual Role* as well as at least four chapters of Myron's Parker Tyler book can be said to have had their genesis in our knowing one another.

But now I am troubled by something in the letter just arrived. Referring to Myron with his usual fondness (do you deliberately want to set me off?), Dr. Montag remarked: "Myron's polymorphism (quite exceptional even by contemporary standards) was coupled with a desire to surrender entirely to the feminine side of his nature, symbolized by you. Yet I cannot help but believe that his masculinity was of great intensity, as you knew best, while the sadomasochistic proportion was quite evenly balanced. That is to say, he was as apt to beat up trade as be beaten up." This is not exactly correct. For all Dr. Montag's extraordinary sensitivity, he remains at heart a dentist of the most conventional kind. Myron's masculinity was, *at times,* intense, but the feminine aspects of his nature were the controlling ones, as I knew best. He wanted men to possess him rather than the other way around. He saw himself as a woman, made to suffer at the hands of some insensitive man. Needless to say, he found partners galore. When I think of the elaborate dinners he used to cook for merchant seamen with tattoos! The continual fussing about the house, so reminiscent of the female bird preparing to lay her egg! The humiliating position he would put himself in when some piece of trade spurned him because he was not able to lay on the requisite bread! Yet, paradoxically, Myron was physically quite strong despite the seeming fragility of his body and, properly aroused, he could beat up a man twice his size; unfortunately, he took no more pleasure in this than he did in the company of lovely girls. He was a tormented creature, similar to Hart Crane, except that while it was Crane's kick to blow those sailors he encountered along the squalid waterfronts of that vivid never-to-be-recaptured prewar world, Myron invariably took it from behind. But though this was a source of great consolation to Myron, Dr. Montag always felt, in his somewhat naïve way, that Myron's obsession involved a certain amount of gratuitous perversity, not to mention just plain waste because Myron's own penis was exceptionally large and much admired (it can be seen briefly in the underground film *Lysol*). Dr. Montag never understood that Myron's sexual integrity required him to withhold that splendid penis from those who most needed it, thus exerting power over them and what, finally, are human relations but the desire in each of us to exercise absolute power over others?

It is my view that the struggle to achieve power is the underlying theme to all of Myron's work, even though he never formulated it clearly. Certainly, *I* was never able to do so until his death clarified so many things for me. At the time I wanted to die, too. But then I entered the next stage: mystical elation. I understood—or thought I understood—*everything*! Myron's restless cruising of bars was the result of a desire to draw into himself, literally, that which men possess for quite another purpose. For him to be able to take from Woman her rightful pleasure—not to mention the race's instrument of generation—became a means of exercising power over *both* sexes and, yes, even over life itself! That is why he was never drawn to homosexuals. In fact, once the man *wished* to penetrate him, Myron lost interest for then he himself would become the thing used, and so lose the power struggle. What excited him most was to find a heterosexual man down on his luck, preferably starving to death, and force him to commit an act repugnant to him but necessary if he was to be paid the money that he needed for survival. At such moments, Myron confessed, he knew ecstasy: the forbidden was his! He had conquered Man, even though to the naïve observer it was Myron who *seemed* to be the one used. But he was almost always user, and that was his glory. Yet like all appetites, the one for power is insatiable. The more one obtains, the more one wants. In the end Myron could not, living, be what he wanted to be, an all-powerful user of men, and so he ended his life, leaving me to complete as best I can not only his masterpiece but the pattern he sought to make, with Dr. Montag's reluctant help.

Yet it is now plain to me that the good Doctor preferred Myron to me, and I cannot at times avoid a certain sense of hurt and rejection. Particularly when I realize that the only way the Doctor could be made happy would be if I were to marry and settle down. Dr. Montag still believes that each sex is intended to be half of a unit, like those monsters mentioned in Plato's *Symposium.* This is the Doctor's Mosaic side overwhelming common sense, not to mention the evidence of his senses. Admittedly *some* are best served when the struggle for power narrows to but one other person and this duel endures for a lifetime as mate attempts to destroy mate in that long wrangling for supremacy which is called marriage. Most human beings, however, prefer the short duet, lasting anywhere from five minutes with a stranger to five months with a lover. Certainly the supreme moments occur only in those brief exchanges when each party, absorbed by private fantasy, believes he is achieving mastery over the other. The sailor who stands against a wall, looking down at the bobbing head of the gobbling queen, regards himself as master of the situation; yet it is the queen (does not that derisive epithet suggest primacy and dominion?) who has won the day, extracting from the flesh of the sailor his posterity, the one element in every man which is eternal and (a scientific fact) cellulary resembles not at all the rest of the body. So to the queen goes the ultimate elixir of victory, that which was not meant for him but for the sailor's wife or girl or simply Woman. Much of my interest in the capture of Rusty is the thought that he is so entirely involved with Mary-Ann. That gives value to what I mean to seize. If it were freely offered, I would reject it. Fortunately he hates me which excites me and so my triumph, when it comes, will be all the sweeter.

**BUCK LONER REPORTS—**
Recording Disc No. 736—
22 February

So decision has been made to present for the June jamboree a musical comedy based on the life story of Elvis Presley who will I am sure be present to see this show or better be since he isn't doing all that well box office wise and could use the publicity I dont know who can play the lead but we got a lot of boys capable of singing like Elvis except funnily enough I was surprised to see some objections raised from some of the kids on the ground that Elvis is old fashioned and another generation like Bing Crosby well this made me feel old but I said you got to have some traditional values and respect the show business greats even when they are over thirty years old the girl who will sing the girl lead will be Mary Ann Pringle then there will be two ninety minute closed circuit capital c color TV dramas from the old Playhouse 90 which again brings a lot of criticism down on my head from the hippies who have no respect for the classics of early television well they will learn better anyway we have a lot of speaking parts in both plays and the western lead will be Rusty Godowski who is aimed for stardom if he stays out of the clink write the Governor another letter about the Ronald Reagan festival explaining it was no joke but a serious offer for him to M C the festival and gain good exposure period good news at last from the lawyers about one Myra Breck inridge who was never repeat never married to my nephew in any one of the fifty United States now Flagler and Flagler will fix her pretty wagon and out she goes on her ass the way she is making trouble around here is like some kind of God damned plague of Egypt telling everybody how lousy they are reminder to stop by Farmers Market and buy okra Bobbie is cooking gumbo tonight

## 19

Clem Masters grows on one. At that first party when I became hopelessly stoned and passed out in the bathtub, I thought him the creep of the world. But since then I have got to know him and of all the students, he is the only one with something resembling a brain. He comes, needless to say, from the East (Buffalo, New York), and wants to be a singer but will probably settle for a career as songwriter. This morning, after Empathy, I met him in the corridor and he said, "Come on, baby, and let me play you something I just wrote."

"Wrote?" I asked. "Or stole from the Beatles like that last little number you recorded for Pop Tune IV . . ."

"You're a gas, Myra." He was not in the least distressed by my accusation of plagiarism. In fact, of all the students he alone seems not to fear me and since he interests me not at all sexually (he is weedy-looking with thick glasses and a black beard and never washes), I am able to enjoy his irreverence.

Clem took me into one of the music rooms where he promptly fell upon the piano and rushed through several loud syncopated numbers, bellowing banal lyrics at the top of his voice. When at last he stopped, I said the truth, as always, "It's just awful, Clem."

"You crazy mixed-up chick!" He laughed, he actually laughed at Myra Breckinridge! My first instinct was to slam shut the piano cover on his spidery fingers, breaking them all at once. But then I realized that his physical agony would do nothing for me, and so I laughed, too (a good sport like Carole Lombard), and said, "Why crazy? Why mixed-up?"

"Because what you heard is *music,* popular music and I am going to sell the whole mother score, piece by piece, to the Four Skins."

"What score? What skins?"

He looked at me pityingly. "The Four Skins are number four and number twenty-seven respectively in the January *Billboard.* So this score—which is for this life of Elvis Presley big Buck Loner has inflicted upon us—will make me some money."

"In that case, I think your songs are perfectly apt."

"I knew you had taste! Now listen, Myra, in some sick way you appeal to me. No, I really mean it. I dig you and I was thinking why don't we . . ."

"Clem." I was firm yet—how can I deny it?—flattered. After all, I am a woman. "I enjoy your company, you know that. You're the only student I can talk to but I could no more go to bed with you . . ."

"Baby, baby, baby . . ." He interrupted me impatiently. "Not with *me,* baby. I don't want to go to bed, the two of us. That's square, I mean a *party,* like maybe twenty cats . . ."

"*Twenty* men?" Not even my idlest daydreams of Myra Breckinridge, warrior queen, ever included a scene in which I was called upon to master twenty men at the same time. Might it not be too much, psychologically?

"Ten men and ten girls, you nit, or maybe seven of one and thirteen of the other or nine of one and eleven of the other. I mean who's *counting*? Want to make the scene?" Clem looked at me shrewdly through thick spectacles.

I was at a loss for words. On the one hand, the idea was definitely attractive. Myron sometimes enjoyed the company of four or five men at the same time but he did not believe in mixing the sexes. I of course do. Yet what pleasure, I calculated swiftly, would I extract from such a tableau? My little quirks can only be fulfilled with one man at a time.

I deliberately dithered, trying to make up my mind. "Oh, I don't think I should. Certainly not with people I know, not with the students."

"Not students, baby. I never let those cats in on anything if I can help it. No, you'll meet all five of the Four Skins and some crazy chicks . . . oh, it's your scene, I can tell . . ."

I knew that my hesitation had already betrayed my interest. "Perhaps I might just . . . *watch,* you know, and perhaps help out, in little ways . . ."

"All or nothing. No tourists allowed." He wrote an address on a slip of paper. "Tomorrow night. Ten o'clock." He goosed me, which I detest, but before I could knee him, the door was flung open and Miss Cluff looked in and blushed, for no discernible reason, and said, "Welcome to the Music Department, Myra. We've all been looking for you."

"Clem was playing me his score."

"He's so talented! Mr. Loner wants to see you right away, it's urgent."

Buck was sitting with his feet on the desk and his Stetson over one eye. Since he made no move to sit up, much less stand up, when I entered the room, I was obliged to strike his feet a blow with my stout black leather handbag; they slid off the desk and onto the floor with a crash.

"Stand up when a lady comes into the room, you son of a bitch," I said but with a sweet tone and not unlike Irene Dunne in *The White Cliffs of Dover.*

"Lady!" He snorted. I leapt upon him, handbag raised to strike again, but he managed with unexpected agility to get to his feet and put the desk once more between us. "You're nothing but some con-girl pretending to be married to my nephew when I got proof he never married nobody. Here!" He thrust a legal document at me, which I ignored. I knew that I had been careless, and have been found out. My own fault.

"No record of my marriage to Myron exists in any of the United States," I said, "for the excellent reason," I wadded up the document and threw it at him, "that we were married in Mexico."

"Whereabouts?"

"My lawyers will tell your lawyers," I said. "Meanwhile, if that settlement is not made by April first, I will take over the whole shooting match." When in doubt, double the stakes, as James Cagney used to say.

I departed regally, but I was—am—shaken by the interview. I immediately rang my lawyer to assure him that I will be able to produce the marriage license as soon as a new one is issued at Monterrey.

Meanwhile—what a mess! Suddenly I feel terribly alone and afraid. My mood was hardly improved when I learned a few moments ago from a distraught Mary-Ann that Rusty has left town. When I pressed her as to why, she burst into tears and could not or would not say. I have never liked the month of February—even when the sun shines, as it does now, and it is warm.

## 20

My ground rules for the party were respected. I would wear bra and panties, unless otherwise inspired to remove them. Clem was forced to agree to this after I pointed out to him that in spite of his assurance to me no students would be present, Gloria Gordon was not only at the party but his hostess. My compromise was accepted. Give a little, get a little, as the saying goes.

The party was held in a small house high in the Hollywood Hills. I was driven there by a stocky monosyllabic man who was once a waiter at Romanoff's and could, if he chose, tell a thousand stories about the stars he waited on but instead spoke to me only of the weather and baseball. But then I think that he was probably stoned when he came to pick me up, and not at his conversational best.

When we arrived at the house, the door was opened by Clem, who wore nothing but glasses and a large door key on a chain about his neck. He is extremely hairy, which I don't like, and though he did not have an erection and so could not be fairly judged, his prick is small and rather dismal-looking as if too many people had chewed on it, and of course he is circumcised, which I find unattractive. Naturally, like so many physically underprivileged men, Clem regards himself as irresistible (no doubt some obscure psychological law of compensation is at work). He promptly took me in goatish arms, rammed his soft acorn against my pudendum, and bit my ear.

I stepped hard on his bare toes, and was promptly freed.

"Jesus, Myra!" He hopped on one foot, holding the other in his hand, a ludicrous sight that somewhat aroused me. I was even more aroused by Gloria who came to show me into the changing room. She, too, was nude with a body almost too beautiful for this world, slender and long, somewhat on the order of the early Jinx Falkenburg. As I undressed, it was all I could do not to take delicately in my hand one of those perfect rose-nippled breasts and simple hold it, worshipfully. Although I am not a Lesbian, I do share the normal human response to whatever is attractive physically in either sex. I say *normal* human response, realizing that our culture has resolutely resisted the idea of bisexuality. We insist that there is only one *right* way of having sex: man and woman joined together to make baby; all else is wrong. Worse, the neo-Freudian rabbis (of whom Dr. Montag is still one despite my efforts at conversion) believe that what they call heterosexuality is "healthy," that homosexuality is unhealthy, and that bisexuality is a myth despite their master Freud's tentative conviction that all human beings are attracted to both sexes.

Intellectually, Dr. Montag is aware of the variety of normal human sexual response but, emotionally, no dentist from the Grand Concourse of the Bronx can ever accept the idea that a woman could or should find quite as much pleasure with her own sex as she does with men. Yet many women lead perfectly contented lives switching back and forth from male to female with a minimum of nervous wear and tear. But in the great tradition of neo-Freudian analysis, Dr. Montag refuses to accept any evidence that does not entirely square with his preconceptions. For him it is either Moses or the Golden Calf. There is no middle range. Yet he is often persuasive, even luminous, and for a time Myron fell under his spell just as Dr. Montag has since fallen under mine. Nevertheless, for all his limitations, it must never be forgotten that it was Randolph Spenser Montag who convinced Myron that one ought to live in consistent accordance with one's *essential* nature. As a result, on the Staten Island ferry, Myron acted out a dream of the absolute and like a Venetian Doge married that symbol of woman the sea but with his life, not a ring, leaving me to change the world alone.

Since that traumatic experience for us all, Randolph has been, in some ways, a new man, a changed dentist. Now he almost believes those stories his younger patients tell him of parties where sexual roles change rapidly, according to whim and in response to the moment's pleasure, stories he used to reject as wish-fulfillments. Between a beautiful girl and an unattractive man (between Gloria and Clem), I shall always be drawn, like any healthy-minded woman, to the girl, as I was last night when, very simply, I took both of Gloria's breasts in my hands and stooped to kiss the appendix scar just to the right of her navel, for all the world like a delicate dimple, so marvelously had the surgeon done his work.

"Chick, you are turning me on!" Gloria exclaimed as she flung my dress willy-nilly upon the bed with all the other clothes. Then she clutched at my panties, but I restrained her, reminding her of the agreement with Clem.

She frowned and pouted. "Not even for me?" she asked, fingering my lovely breasts already partially revealed through the lacy mesh of the bra.

"Later," I whispered, looking over Gloria's shoulder at my escort who was stripping down. It was evident that what he lacked in conversation he made up for in other ways. Beneath a not unpleasantly curved beer-belly, a large white object sprouted, as inviting to the touch as a well-wrought pitcher's handle.

On his way to the door, my hand snaked out and seized him, causing him to stop abruptly. I held him just long enough to achieve a small but exquisite sense of power (he was not able to move, so powerful is my grasp). Then I released him. Shouting "Crazy!" he vanished into the darkened room where the party was.

Impressions: varied, some pleasant, some not. All in all, *not* my sort of scene. I need one man to break down, not twenty to serve. But visually the scene was appealing. Mattresses spread at random across a tile floor. Towels hung from every lamp, giving a festive look to a room whose only light came from a single Moroccan lamp of intricately chased silver inset with red and blue glass.

Aesthetically, the decor was all that one could have wished and so were the girls; the men had seen to that. In fact, simply on circumstantial evidence, one could tell that a man had selected the guest list, for though there were several attractive young studs in the room (two of the five members of the Four Skins were present), the majority resembled Clem: physically unimpressive males forced to rely upon personality and money to get girls to bed. For my taste, they are exactly the wrong sort to have at an orgy, which, no doubt, is the reason why they are always the leading instigators of what is known locally as the "gangbang."

The party lasted four hours. That is as long as the male can hold out. Women of course can go on indefinitely if they are allowed occasional catnaps between orgasms. At one point Gloria experienced twelve orgasms in as many minutes (supplied her by the ex-waiter from Romanoff's, a really formidable man, capable of quite astonishing endurance and restraint); then she promptly fell asleep with her head in the lap of Clem, whom she had been attending to in an absentminded way. To his great alarm, she could not be awakened. Fortunately, we were able to pry her mouth open and salvage the tiny treasure before serious damage was done. Ten minutes later our Gloria was wide awake and ready for fun. This time Clem provided it. Having strapped on a formidable dildo because, as he said, "You got to have head," he was able to give her maximum pleasure with a minimum of exertion on his part.

My own participation was limited. I watched, and only occasionally helped out: a tickle here, a pull there, a lick, a bite, no more, except for one sudden rude intrusion from the rear which I did not see coming. It was one of the Four Skins, a hillbilly type who explained to me, as he was relieving himself, that he had first committed this particular act at the age of twelve with a sheep and so, to this day, he not only preferred back to front but sheep to goats, or did he say girls? Like the rest of the Four Skins his conversation is as difficult to understand as the lyrics they sing. Had there been a pair of shears at hand, I would have made a steer of him on the spot but since there were not I did not, suffering in silence and even, to be honest, deriving a certain perverse, masochistic, Myronesque enjoyment from the unlikely situation of Myra Breckinridge, victorious Amazon, laid low.

Then, having discharged himself, the Skin abandoned me and proceeded on his bully way. I shall of course take my revenge upon him some day, somehow . . . even if I must wait twenty years! Myra Breckinridge is implacable and pitiless.

These graphic notes are really for your benefit, dear Randolph. Examples of the way that the goyim you especially despise behave (of course Clem is Jewish but he has been entirely absorbed by California, that great sponge into which all things are drawn and promptly homogenized, including Judaism). Yet even you, with your prejudices, could not help but be impressed at the ease with which these young people let themselves go, without any apparent fear of commitment or of compromise. The males do not worry about acting out what the society believes to the man's role (brutal, destructive, vagina-centered); they play with one another's bodies in a sportive way, and seem to have no secret dreams they dare not act out. All is in the open, or as one of them said to me as he rested on the floor between engagements, "After a scene like this I don't need it again for a week. I've had it, and there's nothing left I want, and I never feel so good like I do after a real party." So the Dionysian is still a necessity in our lives. Certainly its absence has made the world neurotic and mad. I am positive that access to this sort of pleasure in my adolescence would have changed me entirely. Fortunately, as it turned out, I was frustrated. If I had not been, Myra Breckinridge could never have existed, and the subsequent loss to the world of Myra, the self-creation, is something we, none of us, can afford at this time.

As I write these words, I suddenly think of Myron making love to Gloria Gordon! Why? How strange . . . just the thought of such a thing makes my eyes fill suddenly with tears. Poor Myron. Yet, all in all, he is better dead.

One must not underestimate the influence of these young people on our society. It is true that the swingers, as they are called, make up only a small minority of our society; yet they hold a great attraction for the young and bored who are the majority and who keep their sanity (those that do) by having a double sense of themselves. On the one hand, they must appear to accept without question our culture's myth that the male must be dominant, aggressive, woman-oriented. On the other hand, they are perfectly aware that few men are anything but slaves to an economic and social system that does not allow them to knock people down as proof of virility or in any way act out the traditional male role. As a result, the young men compensate by *playing* at being men, wearing cowboy clothes, boots, black leather, attempting through clothes (what an age for the fetishist!) to impersonate the kind of man our society *claims* to admire but swiftly puts down should he attempt to be anything more than an illusionist, playing a part.

It is the wisdom of the male swinger to know what he is: a man who is socially and economically weak, as much put upon by women as by society. Accepting his situation, he is able to assert himself through a polymorphic sexual abandon in which the lines between the sexes dissolve, to the delight of all. I suspect that this may be the only workable pattern for the future, and it is a most healthy one . . . certainly healthier than the rigid old-fashioned masculinity of someone like Rusty whose instinct to dominate in traditional ways is bound to end in defeat or frustration, excepting perhaps in his relations with the old-fashioned Mary-Ann . . . relations which are currently at an end, for she has still not heard from him, or so she says. I suspect he has been busted. And just as I was about to make my final move. It is too unfair!

The party ended in an orgy of eating. Delicate girls devoured cold cuts as though they had not been fed in weeks, while spent youths lay snoring among tangled towels that smelled of new-made love. How Myron would have enjoyed all this! Though I'm afraid he would have paid more attention to the boys than to the girls and perhaps imitated my bull-like Skin who, waiting until one young man had assumed the classic position between a girl's legs, leapt upon him and forced his way in, to the obvious irritation of the raped youth who, nevertheless, had sufficient aplomb (and Dionysian abandon) not to break his own stride, as it were—oh, how various are the ways of true love!

**BUCK LONER REPORTS—**
Recording Disc No. 751—
27 February

Well so far she has got the jump on me this morning she came into my office and gave me this Mexican wedding license apologizing for not having got it sooner but it was mislaid Uncle Buck I tell you when she calls me Uncle Buck like that Id like to break her neck she is living hell and theres no doubt about that she also said she was getting impatient for her share of the estate and she hoped quote mean old Flagler and Flagler would soon see their way clear to the half million dollar settle ment unquote half million dollar settlement I asked it was three fifty that we finally agreed on before well she says quote that was before but I have been kept waiting and waiting while your detectives have been trying to get something on me like I was criticizing General Motors or something and so I regard the extra one fifty as damages for the mental anguish you have been causing me unquote well I controlled myself as best I could and said quote now Myra you know what lawyers are and after all we never did meet before and whats to keep a total stranger from barging in and claim ing to be married to my late nephew question mark end quote so I see your point of view she says in quotes of course I do but you must also see mine and realize just what it is I have been going through since Myron died leav ing me entirely alone in the world and broke well we kicked that around the poor defenseless widow number and then she again gave me until April one to pay up or else she goes to court and really gets mean so I do my best to soothe her putting the blame on Flagler and Flagler but the thing is still fishy even though theres no doubt she was involved deeply with Myron because though I didnt know him I sure as hell knew Gertrude and at one point Myra let slip the fact that she personally had always found Gertrude hell particularly the way she used to save worthless things like newspapers and string and keep the icebox jammed with food that had gone bad that she was too damned miserly to throw out well Myra didnt make that up and we both agreed that anybody who had a meal at Gertrudes was courting ptomaine but then when I said Gertrude really loved that boy of hers Myra frowned and said oh no she didnt Uncle Buck she just loved herself well dont we all I said no she said not to that degree unquote but she wouldnt open up any more obviously the two girls did not get on hard to say which is the worst no not hard at all Myra is the worst woman I have ever met exclamation mark paragraph she then asked me if I had had news of Rusty Godowski and I said no but that our students often disappear for a time like that and then show up again like nothings happened but she said she was concerned because of poor Mary Ann being so heartbroken Mary Ann hell Im sure Myras got her eye on that stud like half the girls on campus and is now demonstrating the edginess of a filly in heat anyway I said I would look into the matter of his disappearance beginning by calling up my friend the Sheriff a good Republican and ask him if the boy has been incarcerated in a hoosegow since he was on probation to begin with period paragraph then Myra asks me for permission to look at the medical reports on the students which are kept in my outer office and are private because quote I am doing some research on the I think she said post Rosenberg generation she is probably a Commie along with everything else but I have to handle little Miss Dynamite with kid gloves so I gave her permission after all theres nothing interesting in any of them reports just a routine physical checkup at the beginning of their academic life we did consider once taking naked pictures like they do at Yale but the girls objected or to be exact the mothers and fathers of the girls objected even though this is the era of the Playboy bunny so that very good idea came to naught period paragraph change masseuses appointment from this afternoon to tomorrow as I must go in to town for a conference with Letitia Van Allen the best actors agent in this town for young stars of tomorrow having in her pocket practically her own key to casting at Universal dont forget to pick up sour cream for Bobbies beef Stroganoff

# 21

I am sitting beside Mary-Ann at the CBS television studio on Fairfax Avenue. Though it is only a caricature of a film studio, the ultimate effect is impressive. So impressive in fact that I am more than ever certain that the movies are now a mere subsidiary to this electronic device for projecting images around the world at, literally, the speed of light. What it will mean, I have not yet worked out. But it now plain that the classic age of films has ended and will not return any more than verse drama, despite the wonder of the Jacobeans, has a chance of revival.

Of course visual narratives will always be filmed and shown if not in theatres on television. Yet the *nature* of those narratives is bound to change as television creates a new kind of person who will then create a new kind of art, a circle of creation that is only now just beginning. It is a thrilling moment to be alive! And though I yearn romantically for the classic films of the Forties, I know that they can never be reproduced since their era is as gone as the Depression, World War II and the national innocence which made it possible for Pandro S. Berman and a host of others to decorate the screens of tens of thousands of movie theatres with perfect dreams. There was a wholeness then which is lacking now and neither Alain Resnais nor Andy Warhol (the only film-makers of comparable stature today) can give us work which is not helplessly fragmented. I except always Warhol's *Sleeping Man,* which broke new ground aesthetically and proved a radical theory I had always held but dared not openly formulate: that boredom in the arts can be, under the right circumstances, significantly dull.

I find it altogether too satisfying to be sitting beside Mary-Ann in the audience that has been assembled for the Art Linkletter Show. An M.C. is trying to warm us up with bad jokes. In a few minutes we shall be on the air, performers, technicians, audience, viewers—all made one by the magic of the tube. I find this particular show absolutely unbearable, preferring as I do the *total* electronic effect of, let us say, Milton Berle. But I am here because Mary-Ann wanted me to come and I usually do what she wants me to do for we are now curiously united by Rusty's disappearance. Of course she continues to believe that I dislike him and think him an ape, and I do nothing to disabuse her of this notion. I find almost unbearable the painful sweetness of knowing that I shall one day possess, in my own way, what she believes to be entirely hers, assuming of course that Rusty ever returns.

Mary-Ann believes that if he is not in prison (the likeliest possibility since a boy with a police record is prone to constant false arrest in the Los Angeles area where only professional criminals are safe from harassment by the local police), he has gone off with some of his wild friends, possibly to Mexico. I do my best to soothe her, and we have long "girl-talks" about men and life . . . and about her career.

Unlike the other students, Mary-Ann could be professional. Miss Cluff is absolutely right and I for one would like to cut a corner or two and present her directly to an agent, instead of waiting until June, the usual time for the students to show what they can do which, traditionally, is not much. Miss Cluff tells me that in the seven years that she has been at the Academy no student has ever got a job on television or appeared in a film. This is a remarkable record. Some do get jobs modeling but that is often just plain whoring.

When I asked Buck about the dismal showing his students make in the professional world, he seemed not at all taken aback. "Honey," he said, knowing how much I hate to be called "honey," resembling, in this, at least one former First Lady, "what matters is making people happy and while the kids are here they are happy. Now there is, I am willing to admit, a real letdown come June when our kids realize that the outside world of show biz is a big cruel place with maybe no place for them. Yes, I admit that's an awful thing for them to find out and I've even toyed with the idea of never allowing any agents or professional people to come to the June exercises but of course if I really kept them away I'd go out of business, so we all have to suffer through the June Letdown which is immediately followed by the Buck Loner July Spectacular which is a series of awards based closely on the actual Academy Awards, with many Oscars (or Bucks as the kids call them) to be given out by some real-life celebrity on the order of Bobby Darin and that, let me tell you, sure as hell makes up for June."

"Yes, but sooner or later they will *have* to go out into the world . . ."

"Why?" The question was straightforward. "As long as they scrounge up enough money to pay the tuition they can stay here for life. Look at Irving Amadeus. He came here fourteen years ago as a student to become a singing star on the order of Paul Robeson and he is with us still, on the staff now as an invaluable teacher with over *three hundred recordings* to his credit. If that isn't as good as being a real star I don't know what is!"

This curiously hateful philosophy has made Buck Loner rich. But then, to be honest, all that I care about at the moment is my share of his wealth. That and Mary-Ann's career which she does not take seriously. "Only one star in the family," she keeps quoting Rusty. To which I invariably reply, "You're the star. He's the garage mechanic."

I have now got Mary-Ann to the point where she will at least audition for an agent before June, and that means I must start making the rounds myself, trying to find the best person to handle her. Although her voice has a classic tone like Jeanette MacDonald (and so of no use in the current market), she also has a second more jazzy voice not unlike that of the late

La Verne, the most talented of the Andrews Sisters. I am certain that if she were to develop her La Verne-voice she could, with her remarkable appearance acting as opening wedge, become a star.

Last night I played several Andrews Sisters records for her and though she had never before heard of the Andrews Sisters (!), she conceded that their *tone* was unusual—which is understating the matter! Their tone is unique and genuinely mythic, a part of the folklore of the best years of the American past. They really did roll out that barrel, and no one has yet rolled it back.

Mary-Ann has just nudged my arm. "Really, Miss Myra, you mustn't write like that in public!" She chides me gently, for to write in public in the electronic age is to commit an antisocial obscenity.

To please her, I shall now put away this notebook and listen to the jokes of the comedian as he responds to the sterile laughter of the studio audience of which I am a part, for we are suddenly all of us—such a pleasure—on the air!

## 22

Just as I expected, seventy-two per cent of the male students are circumcised. At Clem's party I had been reminded of the promiscuous way in which American doctors circumcise males in childhood, a practice I highly disapprove of, agreeing with that publisher who is forever advertising in the New York *Times Book Review* a work which proves that circumcision is necessary for only a very few men. For the rest, it constitutes, in the advertiser's phrase, "a rape of the penis." Until the Forties, only the upper or educated classes were circumcised in America. The *real* people were spared this humiliation. But during the affluent postwar years the operation became standard procedure, making money for doctors as well as allowing the American mother to mutilate her son in order that he might never forget her early power over him. Today only the poor Boston Irish, the Midwestern Poles and the Appalachian Southerners can be counted upon to be complete.

Myron never forgave Gertrude for her circumcision of him. In fact, he once denounced her in my presence for it. She defended herself by saying that the doctor had recommended it on hygienic grounds—which of course does not hold water since most foreskins are easily manipulated and kept clean. What is truly sinister is the fact that with the foreskin's removal, up to fifty per cent of the sensation in the glans penis is reduced . . . a condition no doubt as pleasing to the puritan American mother as it is to her co-conspirator, the puritan Jewish doctor who delights in being able to mutilate the goyim in the same vivid way that his religion (and mother!) mutilated him.

I once had the subject out with Dr. Montag, who granted me every single point and yet, finally, turned dentist and confessed, "Whenever I hear the word 'smegma,' I become physically ill." I am sure Moses is roasting in hell, along with Jesus, Saint Paul, and Gertrude Percy Breckinridge.

I was not able to find Rusty's medical report and so do not know whether or not he has been circumcised. I hope not for I prefer the penis intact . . . in order that it be raped not by impersonal surgery but by me!

## 23

In an alcove at the back of the cafeteria Buck Loner often has lunch with some notable he would like the students to observe at close hand. Today it was the famous agent Letitia Van Allen, and so I joined them, to Buck's ill-disguised fury. Miss Van Allen is a handsome vigorous woman of perhaps forty, with steely gray eyes. We got on famously, to Buck's chagrin.

"Talent is not what Uncle Buck and I deal in, Miss Van Allen," I said, lightly resting my hand on Buck's clenched fist. "We deal in *myths.* At any given moment the world requires one full-bodied blonde Aphrodite (Jean Harlow), one dark siren of flawless beauty (Hedy Lamarr), one powerful inarticulate brute of a man (John Wayne), one smooth debonair charmer (Melvyn Douglas), one world-weary corrupt lover past his prime (Humphrey Bogart), one eternal good-sex woman-wife (Myrna Loy), one wide-eyed chicken boy (Lon McCallister), one gentle girl singer (Susanna Foster), one winning stud (Clark Gable), one losing stud outside the law (James Cagney), and so on. Olympus supports many gods and goddesses and they are truly eternal, since whenever one fades or falls another promptly takes his place, for the race requires that the pantheon be always filled. So what we are looking for—and what you, Miss Van Allen, have *found* time and again—are those mythic figures who, at the right moment, can be placed upon their proper pedestal. For instance, since the death of Marilyn Monroe, no blonde voluptuous goddess has yet appeared to take her place and so, if I were creating stars, I would look for a girl who most filled that particular bill, who could be the lost Golden Girl. In fact, as in any other business, we must begin with market research. This means carefully analyzing Olympus to find out which archetypal roles are temporarily vacant and who are the contenders. At the moment the suave male seducer is in great supply while the befuddled normal man next door, filled with ludicrous fantasies, is a drug on the market, what with at least one and a half Jack Lemmon pictures a year. But the blonde goddess, the dark goddess, the singing girl and the inarticulate hero as each currently in need of someone to make of the divine spirit living flesh as well as eternal celluloid. At this very moment, perhaps in this very room, there are unknown boys and girls destined to be—for the length of a career—like gods, if only we can find and reveal them. That is why you and I, Letitia—I may call you that?—are similar to those Tibetan priests who upon the death of the Dalai Lama must seek out his reincarnation. And so, like priestesses, despite all personal hardship, we must constantly test and analyze the young men and women of America in order to find the glittering few who are immortal, who are the old, the permanent gods of our race reborn."

There was a long silence when I finished. Buck toyed with his icebox cake while Letitia Van Allen simply stared at me. Then she said, "That is the damnedest, truest thing I've ever heard said about this lousy racket. Come on, let's have a drink. Buck, give us a drink in that office of yours, you old bastard!" She took me by the arm. "He's far and away the biggest con-man in the business, but from where I sit it looks like he may have met his match. You've got quite a line and, as a fellow con-girl, I would like to give it some study." I had made, as I intended, an enormous impression.

Over a beaker of Scotch in Buck's office, Letitia told me in no uncertain terms that if I ever wanted to leave Buck there was a place in her office for a go-getter like me.

Buck brightened when he heard this. "Why, honey, that sounds just swell, don't it? This is too little a pond for a talent like yours." To which I replied demurely, "It may be a small pond but it's ours, Uncle Buck, yours and mine (you see, Letitia, I'm a half-owner of the property), and I could never let Uncle Buck down." Buck's face shut with a snap.

Miss Van Allen missed this exchange, for I had just given her some photographs of Mary-Ann Pringle. "Pretty girl. But no Marilyn Monroe." She gave the pictures back.

"It's her voice," I explained. "That's what makes her a possible immortal. She is the Singing Girl Goddess, waiting for the chance to reveal herself."

"They're not making that kind of picture right now. But maybe she could work up a nightclub act or get in the road show of some Broadway musical. Anyway, on your say-so, I'll listen to her—but not now. What about studs?" Letitia, I fear, is a monosexual. Only men arouse her.

"We got some swell kids . . ." began Buck but I cut him short. "There's one—*maybe.* Category: Inarticulate Hero. His name is Rusty Godowski . . ."

"That name has got to go and so do I." Letitia turned to me. "Come see me the first of the week, Myra . . . lunch . . . I'll pick your brains. You Easterners have all the kinky angles that are *in* right now. That's what I keep telling them at Universal: 'Don't be so California, for God's sake! California's square, while the world is full of kinks as yet undreamed of in the Greater Los Angeles Area.' " Then she was gone.

I could not help but rub it in. "Stick with me," I said to the crestfallen Buck, "and maybe some of your students will actually find work in show biz."

Before he could answer, the masseuse arrived: a spectacular Eurasian in a white nurse's uniform. As we parted, I reminded him of our deadline. Either he has paid me my share in full by April 1 or we up the ante.

**BUCK LONER REPORTS—**
Recording Disc No. 763—
4 March

Things are coming to a head at least if they dont I dont know if I can stand it much longer with the new masseuse it took over an hour which is a sign of something and that something is Myra Breckinridge archfiend Flagler and Flagler are doing their best they say to get something on Myra but so far nothing at all they are even bugging her telephone and just now sent over this tape which may be significant or so they think of her talking long distance to a New York head shrinker called Randolph Montag his tape is herewith enclosed or included or whatever you call it

The Golden State Detective Agency submits the following unedited telephone conversation with the understanding that the contents of same are highly confidential and Golden State assumes no responsibility whatsoever for having obtained said property.

OPERATOR: Los Angeles calling Dr. Rudolph Moon . . . what's the name again, dear?
MYRA: Montag, Randolph not Rudolph Montag, and why don't you . . .
OPERATOR: Los Angeles calling Dr. Moondog . . . is he there?

VOICE: Mummy [two words not audible] later [three to four words not audible] the cat's sick . . .

OPERATOR: Little boy, could you tell your daddy this is Los Angeles . . .

MYRA: Damn it, Dr. Montag is not married . . .

OPERATOR: . . . Los Angeles calling and . . .

VOICE: . . . threw up all over the floor . . .

MYRA: God damn it, operator, you've got the wrong number . . .

OPERATOR: I hear you, miss, you don't have to shout . . .

MYRA: The number is . . .

OPERATOR: . . . I will redial the number, miss.

ELECTRONIC SOUNDS: heavy breathing of operator and/or Myra.

VOICE: This is a recording. The number you have just dialed is not a working number . . .

MYRA: Operator, please I don't have all day . . .

OPERATOR: Apparently the number you gave me is not a working number . . .

MYRA: Dial it again, damn it! You silly [word not clearly audible].

VOICE: Yes?

OPERATOR: Los Angeles calling Dr. Rupert Moonman, are you him?

VOICE: Yes, yes. This is Dr. Moonman, I mean Montag, who is calling he . . . ?

MYRA: Randolph, this is Myra . . .

OPERATOR: Your party is on the line, Miss . . .

MYRA: I haven't written because I've been . . .

OPERATOR: *Dr. Moon is on the line . . .*

MYRA: I know he is, now will you kindly get off . . .

MONTAG: Who is calling him again?

MYRA: It's Myra Breckinridge, you idiot!

MONTAG: Myra! This is a real pleasure . . .

MYRA: . . . . didn't write because so much work to do . . .

MONTAG: . . . so how's the weather out there?

MYRA: . . . need your help . . .

MONTAG: . . . cold here, maybe twelve above zero which is why the ten o'clock patient missed her hour so I can talk . . .

MYRA: . . . about this damned inheritance . . .

MONTAG: . . . how is your dental health?

MYRA: Never been better, as a matter of fact we are on the verge of a real mental breakthrough which should . . .

MONTAG: I meant how are your teeth? That impacted wisdom tooth that was giving us so much trouble . . .

MYRA: For God's sake, Randolph, don't waste the three minutes talking about teeth . . . they're O.K. . . .

MONTAG: Good dental health means good mental health . . .

MYRA: . . . what I want is this: for you to say you were a witness to my marriage, in Monterrey, Mexico. And, God knows, in the truest sense you were and are . . .

MONTAG: At a certain level of course I am a witness and will gladly say so but there's also the legal aspect . . .

MYRA: . . . have to do is come out here and at a crucial moment which may or may not arise say you were present when I married Myron, which you were. . . .

MONTAG: . . . I suppose this all has to do with Gertrude's property . . .

MYRA: . . . swine Buck Loner is trying to do me out of a settlement, and so he wants to prove we were never really married . . .

MONTAG: . . . thinking about poor Myron the other day . . .

MYRA: You might think about *me* for a change. . . .

MONTAG: . . . projecting hostility again, must be careful . . .

MYRA: . . . am in trouble, Myron's dead . . .

MONTAG: Myron was a Christ figure . . .

MYRA: Luckily he found the right doctor with the two sticks of wood and the three nails . . .

MONTAG: . . . need help again. Can't you come back here for a few sessions . . .

MYRA: I'm broke and this conversation is breaking me so will you do what I ask . . .

MONTAG: Naturally only . . .

MYRA: In writing!

MONTAG: Is that necessary?

MYRA: It may have to be. Well? Cat got your tongue?

MONTAG: No, I was lighting a cigar, oral gratification is called for at moments of discomfort . . .

MYRA: Are you uncomfortable?

MONTAG: Naturally, Myra. Who wouldn't be in the spot you've put me in? After all our relationship is a good deal more than that of just analyst and patient. I am also your dentist and have your best interests at heart. Yes, of course I will *say* I was a witness to the marriage with the proviso . . .

MYRA: No proviso unless you want to have your license as a lay analyst revoked in the State of New York for gross malpractice . . .

MONTAG: I detect *a great deal* of hostility, Myra, in your voice . . .

MYRA: . . . then it's a deal. This is costing money . . .

MONTAG: Of course I'll help but . . .

MYRA: Goodbye, Randolph. . . .

End of tape.

**BUCK LONER REPORTS—**
Recording Disc No. 763—
(continued)

Something obviously fishy but what question mark Myra probably was married in Monterrey from the sound of what they were saying to each other but why is that doctor so nervous and unwilling to put his John Hancock to any sort of document I will tell Flagler and Flagler to put the heat on this doctor because I must find out the truth or die in the attempt not to mention losing half this place which I built up from nothing period paragraph well I couldve been knocked over with a feather when Letitia Van Allen who I used to boff in the old days and was also a good friend to Bobbie Dean took a shine to Myra who barged in on our lunch in the cafeteria and promptly began one of her endless speeches which drive me up the wall like they say but Letitia who is easily the toughest dame in this town with the key to casting at Universal in her pocket and not one youd think to be taken in by nutty highbrow Eastern talk well Myra did her work and the two girls are now bosom buddies which is not good for yours truly which is why everything depends now on nailing Myra Breckinridge once and for all question what about framing her with drugs maybe no she would still get the money even in jail God damn it buy chicory for Bobbie

# 24

Letitia Van Allen has heard the voice of Mary-Ann! And loved it! Yesterday I met Letitia at her offices on Melrose Avenue which occupy an entire Greek revival house, reminiscent of Tara, the late David O. Selznick's trademark. All the rooms are furnished in such a way as to suggest a gracious Southern mansion, not a talent agency. Letitia's private office (we are now on a first-name basis) is a lovely large airy second-floor bedroom-cum-boudoir, a most unusual setting for a famous agent yet somehow entirely suitable for her. Letitia works at a Dutch provincial writing desk in an alcove within view of the four-poster bed at the far end of the room. The effect is enchanting.

The salad and cottage cheese lunch was less charming (I have developed an extraordinary appetite lately and must for the first time in my life worry about becoming heavy). We talked of everything, and found many areas of agreement. She believes I would make a formidable agent and I have no doubt that she is right but I prefer to go my own solitary way as critic and mythmaker, and of course as explicator of the mind of Parker Tyler. Like Myron, I am in the tradition of Mortimer Brewster, the drama critic in *Arsenic and Old Lace,* a man for whom, as Tyler puts it so superbly, "the facts of *lunacy, virginity,* and *death,* the last a mask for *impotence,* are inseparable."

Over a dry martini *after* lunch (Letitia, I suspect, has a drinking problem), we listened to a record of Mary-Ann singing a number of songs of the Forties, selected by me and arranged by Miss Cluff. Letitia listened with eyes narrowed. When the record was finished, she again asked for photographs. I gave them to her. She studied them for a long time. "O.K.," she said, "I'll meet her. Make an appointment with my secretary, any free time next week." Then Letitia put her feet up on a Regency bench. "Why're you pushing this kid?"

"She has talent. So few people do."

"But according to your theory, that will probably count against her. Now if you don't mind my asking a personal question, you aren't perhaps involved with her on a more *personal* level?"

I blushed for the first time in some years. "If you mean am I a dyke, no. Not at all. Quite the contrary. Actually I'm interested in her because of her boyfriend who happens to have skipped town and I feel sorry for her. . . ."

"There's nothing wrong with being a dyke, you know." Letitia blew smoke rings thoughtfully. For an instant I wondered if perhaps I had not got her range. But she quickly assured me that my first impression of her had been the right one. "That bed," she said, indicating the four-poster with a swagger stick, "has held just about every stud in town who wants to be an actor. Do I shock you, Myra?"

"How can you shock me when you are just like me? The new American woman who uses men the way they used women."

"Jesus, Myra, but you are *quick*! What a team we'd make. Sure you don't want another martini? It's just water now in the shaker. Well, then I'll have it." She poured herself a full glass. "Listen, dear, if you find anything really interesting at that circus of no-talent Buck's conducting, send him over for a chat with Letitia."

"With pleasure."

"And you come along, too." Letitia flashed a brilliant smile which I answered with one equally brilliant. Two masterful women had met and there is no man alive capable of surviving our united onslaught. Like had been attracted to like from the first moment we met and though it was now plain that she expected me to supply her with studs, I was not in the least distressed at being so used. Women like ourselves owe it to one another to present a united front to the enemy. Meanwhile, as quid for my quo, she will try to find work for Mary-Ann. All in all, as satisfying an encounter as I have had since Dr. Montag first introduced himself to us at the Blue Owl Grill.

## 25

Is it possible to describe anything accurately? That is the problem set us by the French New Novelists. The answer is, like so many answers to important questions, neither yes nor no. The treachery of words is notorious. I write that I "care for" Mary-Ann. But what does that *mean*? Nothing at all because I do not care for her at all times or at any time in all ways. To be precise (the task set us in the age of science), as I sit here at the card table in my room, wearing an old dressing gown of Myron's, I can say that I like her eyes and voice but not her mouth (too small) or hands (too blunt). I could fill many pages of yes-no and still not bring the reader to any *deep* knowledge of what it is I feel at 7:10 P.M., March 12. It is impossible to sort out all one's feeling at any given moment on any given subject, and so perhaps it is wise never to take on any subject other than one's own protean but still manageable self.

What does Mary-Ann think of me? I could not begin to do more than guess nor, I suppose, could she answer this question even to herself: liking, hostility, attraction, revulsion, self-aggrandizement, self-sacrifice, all mingled together with no clear motif save the desire of each to exert power over the other. That is the one human constant, to which all else is tributary.

Dr. Montag still challenges my theory from time to time. Once he spoke of the maternal instinct as something *not* involving power. But of course it does, in the most obvious way: the teat (or bottle) is the source of life to the baby, to be given or withheld at the mother's pleasure. If there is any more fulfilling way of achieving total power over another human being, I have yet to hear of it. Of course most people successfully disguise their power drives, particularly from themselves. Yet the will to prevail is constant and unrelenting. Take that charming, seemingly unaggressive man who makes apparently idle jokes that cause others to laugh. In a sly way, he is exerting power quite as much as Hitler did: after all, his listeners were not laughing until he *made* them laugh. Thus it goes, at every level. My own uniqueness is simply the result of self-knowledge. *I know what I want and I know what I am,* a creation of my own will, now preparing for a breakthrough into an area where, until Myron's death, I could enter only in dreams. Having already destroyed subjectively the masculine principle, I must now shatter it objectively in the person of Rusty, who has reappeared.

But who am I? What do I feel? Do I exist at all? That is the unanswerable question. At the moment I feel like the amnesiac in *Spellbound,* aware that something strange is about to happen. I am apprehensive; obscurely excited

## 26

The telephone just rang. It was Mary-Ann. I have never heard her so excited. "He's back! Rusty's back!" I allowed her to think that she was telling me something that I did not know. In actual fact, late this afternoon, Irving Amadeus told me, "That beautiful creature just showed up for Atavistic Rhythm, and here we'd all given him up for lost!"

I went straight to Buck's office and checked with the secretary, who was at first reluctant to give me details, but when I threatened to take the matter up with Buck himself, she told me that Rusty had been arrested with two other young men at the Mexican border and held on suspicion of smuggling marijuana into the States. Fortunately, there was no very compelling evidence against them, and they were let go. Nevertheless, Rusty's period of probation has been extended, and the probation officer has asked Buck to keep an eye on him.

But Rusty had told Mary-Ann none of this. "You see, he was with these wild boys in Mexico and their car broke down and they were too broke to pay even for a bus ticket and so the American consul finally bailed them out, after they were practically starving to death." No doubt about it, Rusty is very much a man of his era: his fantasy life shields Mary-Ann as well as himself from the cruel disorders of reality.

Though I cannot say that the pleasure of others has ever had any effect upon me except to produce a profound melancholy, I was *almost* pleased at Mary-Ann's delight. "You must be very happy," I whispered like Phyllis Thaxter in *Thirty Seconds over Tokyo,* with wonderful Van Johnson.

"And we want to have dinner with you tonight, if that's all right. I told him how simply wonderful you've been to me while he was gone."

"I'm sure you'd rather have him all to yourself tonight. Besides, are you sure he wants to see me?"

There was a slight hesitation, followed by much protestation to the effect that Rusty was really very admiring of me since I had been such a help to him in Posture class.

## 27

It is now midnight. In many ways, a most exciting evening. I met Mary-Ann and Rusty at the Cock and Bull on the Strip; as one might guess, it is Rusty's favorite restaurant for the food is profoundly hearty. He was unusually exuberant and for once I did not seem to make him uneasy. He improvised freely about his adventures in Mexico, all the while eating scones smeared with raspberry jam. I toyed with a single slice of turkey. I am in danger of becoming fat like Gertrude, who resembled, in her last days, a spoiled pear.

"Then after we left Tijuana, we had to break up because, you see, three guys can't hitchhike together. Nobody would pick up three guys looking like us, with beards and all dirty, though there was this one fruit . . ." Rusty frowned at the pseudo-memory or, more likely, at an actual recollection transposed to flesh out the current fantasy. "He was willing to give us a lift, this funny little Mexican with shiny gold teeth and so nervous those gold teeth was chattering but he wanted us real bad, but we said hell no, I mean who wants to go that route?"

"Many do," I said casually, in such a way that I did not seem to be challenging him. Under the table I gave Mary-Ann's hand a little squeeze which she gratefully returned.

Rusty nodded wisely, mouth full. "Yeah, I know. Why there are some guys—some guys I know right at school—who'll sell their ass to some fruit for twenty bucks, just because they're too lazy to get a job."

"But wouldn't *you* do that, if you needed the money?"

"Hell, I'd starve first, and that's the truth." He pulled Mary-Ann close to him and gave her a kiss. I believed him.

In a sense, Rusty is a throwback to the stars of the Forties, who themselves were simply shadows cast in the bright morning of the nation. Yet in the age of the television commercial he is sadly superfluous, an anachronism, acting out a masculine charade that has lost all meaning. That is why, to save him (and the world from his sort), *I must change entirely his sense of himself.*

When Rusty had finally completed his story of having been down-and-out in Mexico (borrowing heavily from a recent television drama on the same theme), we spoke of Mary-Ann and the good impression that she had made on Letitia Van Allen. Even the unworldly Rusty was impressed. "Do you *really* think she likes Mary-Ann?"

"Very much."

"Oh, not that much." Although a Kathryn Grayson singing star, Mary-Ann also belongs to the Joan Leslie tradition of self-effacing good-sex woman-wife. For her it is Rusty's career that matters, not her own. "Anyway," she said, "it's all due to Miss Myra. She arranged the whole thing."

"That was a swell thing to do." Rusty's voice was deep and warm and he gave me a level gaze reminiscent of James Craig in the fourth reel of *Marriage Is a Private Affair.* "A mighty swell thing, and we're both as grateful as we can be," he added, carefully putting the two of them together on one side, leaving me alone on the other.

"Who Miss Van Allen should really see is Rusty," said Mary-Ann, predictably, to which I replied, as predictably, "Of course she'll see him, but in June. Don't worry, I've already told her about him."

"That's real nice of you. . . ." He was overcome by sincerity like James Stewart in any movie. Then the large veined hands with the blunt fingers took yet another scone and covered it with jam, and I meditated on the dark journey of those veins inside the jacket as they proceeded up the marbled forearms, coiling about the thick biceps, vanishing finally in the deep armpits.

What would Myron have thought of him? Probably not much. Myron preferred the sinister and vicious, the totally abandoned. Rusty is not only not abandoned, he would not have been available, even to Myron whose technique as a seducer was highly developed. Yet where Myron would have failed I shall succeed.

The fact that Rusty has not an inkling of my plans makes every moment we spend together in Mary-Ann's company exquisite. Also, the deliberate (on my part) manipulation of the conversation was curiously thrilling, affording me an opportunity to observe how something entirely alien behaves in its native habitat: the never-fulfilled desire of the dedicated anthropologist who realizes that the moment he arrives in a village to study its culture, that culture has already been subtly altered by the simple fact of his presence; just as the earthly microbes our astronauts are certain to let loose upon other worlds are sure to kill or change those extraterrestrial forms of life we would most like to preserve in order to understand. But then it is our peculiar fate to destroy or change all things we touch since (and let us never forget it) *we* are the constant and compulsive killers of life, the mad dogs of creation, and our triumphant viral progress can only end in a burst of cleansing solar fire, either simulated by us or thrust upon us by the self-protective mechanism of a creation that cannot for long endure too many violent antibodies within its harmonious system. Death and destruction, hate and rage, these are the most characteristic of human attributes, as Myra Breckinridge knows and personifies but soon means, in the most extraordinary way, entirely to transcend.

Yet the presence of the anthropologist (me) at the wooden table in the Cock and Bull did, eventually, alter significantly the behavior of the two natives as they lost their self-consciousness to the degree that the conversation ceased to be particular and became general, something that almost never happens among the lower orders who are, to a man, walking autobiographers, reciting their dull memoirs at extraordinary length, oblivious to the extent that they bore even others of their kind who, of course, wait impatiently to tell *their* stories.

Somehow the subject reverted to Rusty's proud rejection of the Mexican's advances, and Mary-Ann made it plain that for her part she could never consider making love to another woman. "It just . . . well, disgusts me," she said. "I mean I just *couldn't.* I think, well, a woman should act like a woman and a man should act like a man, and that's that."

"But *how* should a man act?" I was mild.

Rusty knew. "He should ball chicks, that's how he should act."

"But only if he really loves them." Mary-Ann was droll; both laughed at what was obviously a private joke.

"And *why* should he ball chicks?" I continued my gentle catechism.

"Well, because that's . . . well, Christ, it's *natural!*"

"And that's how you get babies," said Mary-Ann sagely. "I mean that's how nature intended it."

"Do you think nature intended you to have a baby each time you make love?"

Mary-Ann looked like a lapsed Catholic, trying to recall what she had been taught. But Rusty was a good Catholic Pole and knew right from wrong. "That's what you're *supposed* to do, yes. That's what we're told in church."

"But you do use contraceptives, don't you?"

Both flushed, and Rusty said, "Well, sure. I guess most Catholics do now, but that doesn't mean you don't know it's wrong."

"Then you basically believe that it's right for more and more babies to be born, even though half the people ever born in the world are now alive, and that each day twelve thousand people starve to death in India and South America?" Oh, the sly Myra Breckinridge! Nothing can escape the fine net of her dialectic!

Rusty frowned to show that he was thinking when actually, as one of the acting-students recently said of another's performance, he was only thinking he was thinking. "Well, maybe those Indians and Chinese and so on should probably practice birth control since their religion doesn't care, if they have one . . ."

"But they do have religions. And they do care. And they believe that for a man to be manly he must have as many children as possible . . ."

"Because so many of their babies die in childbirth." Mary-Ann was unusually thoughtful.

"They used to die," I said. "And that kept the population in a proper balance with the food supply. But now the children live. And starve. And all because their parents passionately believe that to be manly is to make babies and to be womanly is to bear them."

"But we're different." Rusty was dogged. "We got enough food and we also have . . ."

"Family planning." Mary-Ann looked happy. No doubt contemplating some planning of her own.

"Enough food," however, was all the cue I needed. I was brilliant. I quoted the best of the world's food authorities (famine for us all by 1974 or 1984 and forget about plankton and seaweed: not enough of it). I demonstrated that essentially Malthus had been right, despite errors of calculation. I described what happens to rats when they are crowded in too small a place: their kidneys deteriorate, and they go mad. I told how whenever the food supply of the lemmings is endangered, a majority of the race drown themselves in order that those left behind may flourish.

Then I gave statistics for the current world death rate, showing how it has drastically declined in the last fifty years due to advanced medicine. The physically and mentally weak who ordinarily would have died at birth now grow up to become revolutionaries in Africa, Asia and Harlem. As a result of miracle drugs and incontinent breeding, the world's food supply can no longer support the billions of people alive at present; there will of course be even less food for those thousands who are joining us every minute. What is to be done? How is the race to be saved (I did not go into the more profound question of whether or not it *should* be saved)? My answer was simple enough: famine and war are now man's only hope. To survive, human population must be drastically reduced. Happily, our leaders are working instinctively toward that end, and there is no doubt in my mind that nature intends Lyndon Johnson and Mao Tse-tung to be the agents of our salvation. By destroying a majority of the human race, they will preserve the breed since the survivors are bound to be not only wiser than we but racially stronger as a result of cellular mutancies caused by atomic radiation. If I say so myself, I had my listeners' eyes bugging out by the time I had sketched for them man's marvelous if fiery fate.

"But what can we do to *stop* all this from happening?" Mary-Ann was plainly alarmed.

"Don't have children. That is the best thing. A gesture of course, but better than nothing. And try to change your attitudes about what is normal." Then, in quick succession, I delivered a number of anthropological haymakers. Proper womanly behavior for an Eskimo wife is to go to bed with anyone her husband brings back to the igloo. Proper manly behavior for the Spartan warrior was to make love to a boy while teaching him how to be a soldier. I gave a rapid review of what is considered proper sexual behavior in Polynesia and along the Amazon. Everything I said came as revelation to Rusty and Mary-Ann, and they were obviously horrified by the *un*naturalness of what was considered natural in other parts of the world. I believe I planted a seed or two. Mary-Ann of course could never prostitute herself like an Eskimo wife nor could Rusty ever make love to an adolescent boy ("those teeny-boppers gave me a pain"); yet each now regards his old certainties as being, at least, relative. That is progress.

As could be expected, it was Mary-Ann who mounted the counterattack. "Maybe you're right when you say there's nothing that's really *basically* normal but when everybody tells you that they want you to behave in a certain way, like marrying one man and having only his children, isn't that the *right* thing to do because doesn't the society deep down *know* what it's doing, and is trying to protect itself?"

Unexpectedly she had made a good point. Not once in all these weeks have I suspected her of possessing a true intelligence. Obviously I have been misled by her California manner which is resolutely cretinous as well as nasal. The possibility that she might one day be a woman I could actually talk to was a revelation, and by no means an unpleasant one. Naturally, she could not be allowed to *win* her point. Even so, it will, as we academics say, count against the final grade.

I challenged her with a simple question: does any society know how to preserve itself? I then listed a number of civilizations that had destroyed themselves through upholding customs that were self-destructive. For instance, the health of the Roman state depended upon a vigorous aristocracy but that aristocracy committed suicide by insisting that their cooking be done in expensive pots made of lead. The result was acute lead poisoning which led to impotence and the literal extinction of an entire class, killed by custom. Then, superb dialectician that I am, I discussed every society's *secret* drive to destroy itself and whether or not this was a good thing, taken in the larger context of the human race's evolution. They were both shocked at the idea, particularly when I brought it home to them by suggesting that Rusty's desire to have sex only with girls and Mary-Ann's desire to have at least four children the world did not need might be considered proof that our society is now preparing to kill itself by exhausting the food supply and making nuclear war inevitable. Should this be the case, the only alternative (and a most unlikely one) would be for all the Rustys to follow the Spartan custom of making love to boys while the Mary-Anns, as lovers of women, would at least help preserve the race by bringing no more children into the world. But of course I was playing devil's advocate since I am secretly convinced that we shall soon be purged by a chiliastic fire, and so, in the long run, current behavior will best serve us by hastening our necessary end. Yet efforts must still be made to preserve life, to change the sexes, to re-create Man. There is an off chance that my mission may yet succeed.

Mary-Ann was most depressed.

I took her hand in mine. "Don't worry," I said. "What will happen will happen. Meanwhile, all I ask is that you be happy . . . and you, too, Rusty." I gave him a beautiful yet knowing smile like Ann Sothern in the first of the Maisie films. "But to be *truly* happy, I think you must both begin to think a little bit about changing your sexual attitudes, becoming more open, less limited, abandoning old-fashioned stereotypes of what is manly and what is feminine. As it is, if you, Rusty, should ever find a boy sexually interesting, you might or might not do something about it but whatever you did do or did not do you'd certainly feel guilty because you've been taught that to be a man is to be physically strong, self-reliant, and a lover of girls, one at a time."

"So what's wrong with that?" Rusty gave me a cocky grin.

"Nothing." I was patient. "Except modern man is not self-reliant as for making love to girls, that is only one aspect of his nature . . ."

"It's my only one. Why, just the thought of boffing some hairy boy makes me sick all over."

"Not all boys are as hairy as you," I said gaily, recklessly. Mary-Ann looked surprised while Rusty looked uneasy at this reminder of our old intimate encounter. I turned to Mary-Ann. "It's positively coquettish the way the top two buttons of his shirt are always missing."

She was relieved. "Men are so vain," she said, looking at him fondly.

"But in America only women are supposed to worry about their appearance. The real man never looks into a mirror. That's effeminate. . . ." I teased them.

"Well, *that's* changing, I guess." Mary-Ann brought Rusty's hands to her lips. "And I'm just as glad. I think men are beautiful."

"So does Rusty," I could not help but observe.

"Oh, shit, Miss Myra," was the boyish response. Soon. Soon. Soon.

**BUCK LONER REPORTS—**
Recording Disc No. 777—
18 March

Flagler and Flagler have come up with dyna mite or they think its dynamite but you never know with that woman apparently the Monterrey Mexican marriage certificate is a phony and there is no record from what they can find out of her being married down there but weve been burned before I said to Flagler Junior who is working on the case shell just go out and prove they lost the records or something and then that doctor friend of hers will swear he was a witness which is what it sounded like on the long distance telephone call that was bugged and what do we do then I ask you question mark well Flagler Junior seems to think they are on solid ground with the Mexicans though he admits that our little brown friends are not only kind of confused in the paper works department but if Myra thinks of it and shell think of it the bitch they can be bribed to say that there was a marriage when there wasnt so meanwhile I am biding my time until tomorrow when there should be a full final report from Mexico that there really isnt a record of this marriage in ques tion period paragraph Flagler Juniors New York man has already met once with Doctor Montag and his report is on my desk now as I dictate while being massaged by Milly who is the best masseuse in the whole business I mean that Milly you little angel thats right rub good and hard it takes time but when it comes the Buck Loner Special strike that period paragraph interesting conversation with Letitia who thinks that Mary Ann Pringle properly handled could make it as a recording star and she will make some appointments all this is Myras doing she is meddling into everything trying to force the kids out into the cold world when their place is here protected and looked after I know how well I know showbiz and all its heartbreaks and Mary Ann will end up like all the others which is nowhere a waitress some place assuming she doesnt get lucky and marry some guy who will take care of her and cherish her the way Buck Loners Academy does that guy certainly wont be Rusty whos a wild number the Sheriffs office just asked me to keep an eye on him and I told him so yesterday told him that he would have to watch his step or it was the hoosegow for him he was real shook up and asked me not to tell anybody about his scrape in Mexico and I said nobody knows but me and Myra who happened to be checking into his file and read the Sheriffs last letter to me that woman is into everything Rusty seemed upset by this I guess because he thinks Myra will tell Mary Ann well its no business of mine and thats for sure Milly you are the best ever and if you keep that up theres a big surprise coming your way strike that period paragraph Myra asked permission to use the infirmary tonight God knows why I suppose she is mixing up some poison which it is my prayer she takes Jesus Milly dont stop Milly Jesus Milly

## 28

I am sitting in the infirmary, a small antiseptic white room with glass cabinets containing all sorts of drugs and wicked-looking instruments. Against one wall is an examination table which can be raised or lowered. It is now some four feet above the floor and tilted at a slight angle. Next to it are scales and measuring instruments for both weight and body width. I am seated at a small surgical table, making notes while I wait for Rusty.

It is ten o'clock at night. The Academy building is dark. The students are gone. No one will disturb us. I am astonished at my own calm. All of my life's hunger is about to be fed. I am as serene as a great surgeon preparing to make the necessary incision that will root out the problem.

This morning, after Posture class, I took Rusty to one side. He has been friendly and smiling ever since our dinner at the Cock and Bull and now treats me in the confident condescending way that the ordinary young man treats an ordinary girl.

I put a stop to that. His grinning face went pale when I said coldly, "There's been no improvement, Rusty. None at all. You're not trying to walk straight."

"Honest to God I am, Miss Myra, why I even practiced last night with Mary-Ann, she'll tell you I did. I really am trying." He seemed genuinely hurt that I had not recognized his effort.

I was somewhat kinder in my manner, sharp but in the Eve Arden way. "I'm sure you have tried. But you need special attention and I think I can give it. I'll expect you at the infirmary at ten o'clock tonight."

"The infirmary?" He looked almost as puzzled as James Craig in the sixth reel of *Little Mister Jim.*

"I've arranged everything with Uncle Buck. He agrees with me that you need extra help."

"But what *kind* of help?" He was still puzzled but, as yet, unsuspicious.

"You'll see." I started to go.

He stopped me. "Look, I've got a date with Mary-Ann for dinner."

"Postpone it. You see her every night *after* dinner anyway."

"Well, yes. But we were invited some place at ten."

"Then go at eleven. I'm sorry. But this is more important than your social life. After all, you want to be a star, don't you?"

That was always the clincher in dealing with any of the students. They have been conditioned from childhood in the knowledge that to achieve stardom they might be called upon to do *anything,* and of course they would do anything because stardom is everything and worth any humiliation or anguish. So the saints must have felt in the early days of Christendom, as they burned to death with their eyes on heaven where the true stars shine.

I spent all afternoon making my preparations. I have the entire procedure worked out to the last detail. When I have finished, I shall have achieved in life every dream and

## 29

I must write it all down now. Exactly as it happened. While it is fresh in my memory. But my hand trembles. Why? Twice I've dropped the yellow ballpoint pen. Now I sit at the surgical table, making the greatest effort to calm myself, to put it all down not only for its own sake but also for you, Randolph, who never dreamed that anyone could ever act out *totally* his fantasies and survive. Certainly your own guilty longing to kill the nerve in each of Lyndon Johnson's twenty-odd teeth *without* the use of anesthetic can never in this life be achieved, and so your dreams must feed upon pale surrogates while mine have been made reality.

Shortly after ten, Rusty arrived. He wore the usual checked shirt with two buttons missing and no T-shirt, as well as chino trousers and highly polished cowboy boots. He looked about the infirmary curiously. "I never been in here before."

"That explains why there's no physical record of you."

"Never been sick a day in my life." Oh, he was proud! No doubt of that.

"But even so, the Academy requires a record. It's one of Uncle Buck's rules."

"Yeah. I know. And I've been meaning to drop in sometime and see the Doc."

"Perhaps that won't be necessary." I placed the physical examination chart squarely in the middle of the surgical table. "Sit down." I was pleasant. He sat in a chair so close to mine that our knees touched. Quickly he swung his legs wide so that my knees were now between his and there was no possibility of further contact. It was plain that in no way do I attract him.

We chatted a moment about Mary-Ann, and about Letitia's interest in her career. I could see that Rusty was both pleased and envious, a normal reaction. Then, delicately, I got around to the subject of Mexico; he became visibly nervous. Finally, I told him that I knew what had happened.

"You won't tell Mary-Ann, will you?" That was his first response. "It would just kill her."

"Of course I won't. And of course I'll give a good report to Mr. Martinson, your parole officer."

He was startled. "You know him?"

"Oh, yes," I lied—actually I happened to come across a letter from him to Buck. "In fact, he's asked me to keep an eye on you, and I said I would."

"I hope you tell him that I sure as hell am reformed." He was vehement.

"I will—if you really are, and behave yourself, and let me try to help you with your problem."

"Of course I will, Miss Myra. You know that." He looked entirely sincere, blue eyes round as a boy's. Perhaps he is an actor after all.

"Now then, about your back. I've talked to the chiropractor who will arrange for a special brace. He couldn't be here tonight but he asked me to take an exact tracing of your spine and then he'll know what to do. So now if you'll just slip off that shirt, we'll get to work."

Resignedly, he got to his feet. Automatically his hands went to his belt buckle in order to loosen it but then, obviously recalling our last encounter, he left the belt as it was, pulling off the shirt with a certain arrogant ease.

The belt just covered his navel; otherwise he was in exactly the same state as he had been at the beginning of our first session. I was pleased that my visual recollection of him was so precise. I remembered in exact detail the tracery design of bronze hair across the pale chest, as well as the small roselike inverted nipples.

"Stand on the scales, please." I imitated the chilliest of trained nurses. "Face to the wall and we'll measure you." He put one foot on the scales, when I stopped him. "Take off those atrocious cowboy boots! They'll break the machine."

"Oh, no they won't, why . . ." He started to argue.

"Rusty!" I was sharp. "Do *exactly* as I tell you. You don't want me to tell Mr. Martinson that you've been uncooperative, do you?"

"No . . . no." Standing first on one foot and then on the other, he awkwardly pulled off the boots. He wore white cotton socks; one had a large hole in it through which the big toe protruded. He grinned sheepishly. "Guess I'm full of holes."

"That's all right." The small room was now full of the not unpleasant odor of warm leather.

Obediently he got onto the scales exactly as I directed, face to the wall. In a most professional way, I measured the width of the chest, and then allowed myself the pleasure of running my hand down the smooth warm back, tracing the spine's curve right to the point where it vanished, frustratingly, into the white chinos as they swelled just below my hand, masking those famous inviolate buttocks.

"All right," I said, marking down figures on the physical examination chart. "Now we need your weight which is one seventy-four and your height which is six one and a quarter. The chart's filling up nicely. All right, you can get down."

He stepped off the scales. He was surprisingly at ease: obviously our dinner at the Cock and Bull had given him confidence. "This doctor can really fix me with something that will work?" He was genuinely curious.

"He thinks he can, yes. Of course, he'll have to fit you himself. This is just the preliminary examination which, while we're at it, Uncle Buck said I should turn into an ordinary physical and so kill two birds with one stone, as he put it in his colorful way."

"You mean like height and weight and that stuff?" As yet he showed no particular alarm.

"Exactly," I said, ready now to begin to shake his self-confidence. I took a small bottle. "That means a urine specimen."

The look of surprise was exquisite as he took the bottle. "Go behind that screen." I indicated a white screen in one corner of the room.

"But . . ." he began.

"But?" I repeated pleasantly. Without a word, he went behind the screen which was waist-high. He turned and faced the wall; he fumbled with his trousers. Then there was a long moment of complete silence.

"What's the matter?" I asked.

"I . . . don't know. I guess I'm what they call pee-shy."

"Don't be. Just relax. We've got plenty of time."

The thought of "plenty of time" had a most releasing effect. Water passed into the bottle with a surging sound. He then rearranged his clothes and brought me the specimen which I took (marveling at the warmth of the glass: we are furnaces inside!) and carefully placed on it a white sticker inscribed with his name. The entire affair was conducted without a false note.

"Now then we'll just do a drawing of the spine. Loosen your belt and lie face down on the table."

For the first time he seemed aware that history might repeat itself. He stalled. "Maybe we better wait till I see the doctor."

"Rusty," I was patient but firm. "I'm just following doctor's orders and you are going to follow *my* orders, or else. Is that understood?"

"Well, yes, but . . ."

"There are no 'buts' for someone on probation."

"Yes, ma'am!" He got the point. Quickly he undid the belt buckle; then he unfastened the catch to his trousers and, holding them firmly in place, lay face down on the table. It was a delicious sight, that slender muscular body stretched full length as sacrifice to some cruel goddess. His arms were at his sides, and I noticed with some amusement that he was pressing the palms hard against the table, instinctively repeating his earlier performance.

I covered his back with a large sheet of paper. Then with an eyebrow pencil, I slowly traced the spine's course from the nape of the neck to the line of his trousers.

"This is going very, very well." I sounded to my own ears exactly like Laraine Day, an all-time favorite.

"It sort of tickles," came a muffled voice. Triceps muscles writhed beneath silk-smooth skin.

"*Are* you ticklish?" This suddenly opened an unexpected vista. Fortunately my program was so designed as to include an occasional inspired improvisation.

"Well, no, not really . . ."

But I had already taken one large sweaty foot in hand (again marveling at the body heat through the thin sock) and delicately tickled the base of the toes. The effect was electric. The whole body gave a sudden twitch. With a powerful reflex, he kicked the foot from my hand, exclaiming "Cut that out!" in a masterful voice, so entirely had he forgotten his place.

I was mild. "Do that again, Rusty, and I will punish you."

"I'm sorry, Miss Myra." He was conciliatory. He looked at me over his shoulder (the tracing paper had fallen to the floor). "I guess I'm more ticklish than I thought."

"Apparently. Or perhaps I hurt you. You don't have athlete's foot, do you?"

"Oh, no. No. Not for a long time . . . in the summer, sometimes . . ."

"We'll just take a look." With some difficulty, I slipped off the damp socks. If I were a foot-fetishist like poor Myron, I would have been in seventh heaven. As it was, what excited me was his profound embarrassment, for he has the American male's horror of smelling bad. Actually, he was relatively odorless. "You must have just had a shower," I said.

He buried his face in the table. "Yeah . . . just now." Carefully I examined each toe, holding it tight as though I feared that, at any moment, one of the little piggies might decide to run all the way home. But except for a certain rigidity of the body, he did not show, in any way, distress; not even when I examined each pink toe.

"Good," I said, putting the foot down. "You're learning control. Ticklishness is a sign of sexual fear, did you know that?"

A faint "no" from the head of the table.

"That's why I was so surprised at the way you reacted when I touched your foot. From what you said at the Cock and Bull I couldn't imagine you ever being tense with a woman."

"I guess you sort of took me by surprise," was the best that he could think to say. In his present position, he obviously did not want to be reminded of his usual cockiness.

"I'm sorry," I said, deftly sliding his trousers down to his knees.

As I had anticipated, he gave a slight gasp but made no move other than to grip with both hands the sides of the trousers in an effort to keep at least his front decently covered.

On the table before me, like some cannibal banquet, the famous buttocks curved beneath frayed Jockey shorts. Below the elastic, two round holes, like eyes, revealed fair skin. Teasingly, I put my finger in one of the holes. He winced at the touch. "Doesn't Mary-Ann ever mend your clothes?"

"She . . . can't . . . sew . . ." He sounded as if he had been running hard, and could not get his breath. But at least he had steeled himself for my next move.

The total unveiling of the buttocks was accomplished in an absolute, almost religious, silence. They were glorious. Under the direct overhead light, I was able to appreciate physical details that I had missed in the office. A tiny dark mole on one cheek. An angry red pimple just inside the crack where a hair had grown in upon itself. The iridescent quality of the skin which was covered with the most delicate pale peach fuzz, visible only in a strong light and glittering now with new sweat. I could smell his fear. It was intoxicating.

I also noted that although I had pulled the Jockey shorts down to the thighs in the back, he had craftily contrived to hold them up in front, and so his honor, he believed, was only half lost.

Intimately I passed my hand over the hard buttocks, firmly locked to all intruders, and remarked, according to plan, "You aren't feverish, are you?"

"No . . . I'm O.K. . . ." The voice was barely audible. With my free hand I felt his brow; it was bathed in perspiration.

"You *are* hot. We'd better take your temperature. Besides, they want it for the chart."

As I went over to the surgical table and prepared the thermometer, he watched me dully, like a trapped animal. Then I returned to my quarry and, putting one hand on each cheek at the exact point where buttock joins thigh, I said, "Relax now."

He raised up on his arms and looked around at me, eyes suddenly bright with alarm. *"What?"*

"I've got to take your temperature, Rusty."

"But . . . *there?*" His voice broke like a teenage boy's.

"Of course. Now then . . ."

"But why can't you use the other kind, you know, in the mouth . . ." With the back of my left hand, I struck him hard across the bottom. He gasped, pulled back.

"There is more where that came from," I said coldly, noting with pleasure a certain darkening of skin where the blood had been brought to the surface by the force of my blow.

"Yes, ma'am." Defeated, the head returned to its position on the table and once again I put my hands on those firm cheeks.

"Now," I said, "relax the muscle." I could feel beneath my fingers the muscles slowly, reluctantly go slack.

I confess I was now trembling with excitement. Gently, carefully I pushed the cheeks apart until everything—secret sphincter and all—was revealed.

Normally at moments of great victory, there is a sense of letdown. But not in this case. For one thing I had half feared to find him not clean—unlike so many anal erotics I am not at all attracted by fecal matter, quite the reverse in fact. Yet had he *not* been tidy, his humiliation would have been total. So I was torn between conflicting desires. As it turned out, his shower had been thorough. The sphincter resembled a tiny pale pink tea rose, or perhaps a kitten's nose and mouth. From its circumference, like the rays of a sunburst, bronze hairs reflected the overhead light. The only disappointment was that he had craftily managed to arrange his scrotum so that it was entirely out of view, only a thick tuft of hair at the juncture of the groin indicating the direction in which it could be found. But sufficient to the moment are the revelations thereof.

I squeezed some lubricant from a tube onto my index finger and then, delicately, touched the never-used entrance. A tremor went through his whole body—the term "fleshquake" occurred to me: so Atlantis must have shuddered before the fall! Carefully, daintily, I applied the lubricant to the silky puckered surface. He held himself quite rigid, again not breathing.

Then I grew bolder. I inserted my finger into the tight hot place as far as it would go. I must have touched the prostrate for he suddenly groaned, but said nothing. Then, either deliberately or through uncontrollable reflex, he brought the full force of his youthful muscularity to bear on the sphincter muscle and for a moment it felt as though my finger might be nipped off.

With my free hand, I slapped his tight buttock smartly. "Relax!" I commanded. He mumbled something I could not hear and the sphincter again loosened. I then removed my finger and inserted the thermometer, after first teasing the virginal orifice with delicate probes that made him squirm. Once the thermometer was in, it was completely lost to sight for his buttocks are deep and since the legs were only slightly spread, his cheeks promptly came together when I let them go.

I then took up the chart and read off a list of childhood diseases. Chicken pox, measles, whooping cough . . . and he whispered "yes" or "no" or "I don't remember" in response to the catechism. When I was finished, I said, "All in all, a healthy young boy." My cold cheery manner was calculated to increase his alarm; obviously it did for not once would he look at me, preferring to stare at the wall just opposite, chin pushed hard against the table.

"Now let's see what's cooking." I pushed open the cheeks and slowly removed the thermometer. He was normal of course but I saw fit to lie: "Just as I thought, you do have a touch of fever. Well, we'll soon take care of that. Now roll over on your back."

He did as he was told, swiftly pulling up trousers and shorts in front; nevertheless, the line of his belt was two inches below the navel and could not, in his present position, be pulled higher. As a result, the timberline of pubic hair was briefly revealed, briefly because he promptly placed both hands over himself in an attempt to hide that quarry from the hunter's approach.

On his back, bare feet pointed and chest streaked with sweat, he seemed smaller than in fact he was, already more boy than man, despite the mature muscularity of the torso. The process of diminishing was well begun. He looked up at me, apprehensively. "Is there much more I got to do?"

"We must both follow the chart." I was enigmatic, as I picked up a wooden tongue depressor. "Open your mouth." He obeyed. I pressed down the pink tongue until he gagged, noting, as I did, the whiteness of the teeth and the abnormal salivation that fear sometimes creates. "You take good care of your teeth." I gave him the sort of grudging compliment the stern nurse gives a child. "Your body, too. I was happily surprised to find that you were clean in places most boys your age neglect." Carefully I was reducing his status from man to boy to child—ah, the triumph! He responded numbly to the progression, blinking with embarrassment.

"Now put your hands behind your head." Slowly he obeyed, aware that I could now see at least a quarter of an inch of dark pubic hair, surprisingly thick and in texture coarser than the fine hairs on the rest of his body. A pulse just above the navel beat rapidly, causing the entire stomach to quiver like some frightened small beast.

I let my hand rest lightly on his navel. Crisp hairs tickled my palm as I in turn tickled them. I could feel the pounding of the blood in his arteries. The sense of power was overwhelming. I felt as if, in some way, it was I who controlled the coursing of the blood in his veins and that it was at *my* command that the heart beat at all. I felt that I could do anything.

"You seem nervous, Rusty." I challenged him.

He swallowed hard. "No . . . no, Miss Myra. No, I'm not really. It's just that it's kind of hot in here . . ."

"And you're not enjoying your examination."

"Well, it's kind of strange, you know. . . ." His voice trailed off nervously.

"*What's* kind of strange?"

"Well, you know . . . I mean having a girl . . . you know, a lady, like you, do all this to a guy."

"Haven't you ever been examined by a nurse?"

"Never!" This reversion to the old masculine Rusty was promptly quelled by the sudden tug I gave to his Jockey shorts; the full bush was now visible, though nothing else for the shorts were stopped at the crucial juncture by the weight of his body.

With great thoroughness, I felt the different sections of his belly, taking pleasure in the firmness of muscles, hard rubber beneath silk. I lingered for quite some time over the pubic area taking the powerful pulse of each of the two arteries that meet at the groin. I could not, however, make out even the base of his penis.

I then took an instrument which resembled sugar tongs, used to test the thickness of the skin's subcutaneous layer. With frightened eyes, he watched as I picked away at the skin of his belly, pulling the skin as high as I could and then releasing it with a snap. "Nicely resilient," I said, pinching hard as I could a fold of his belly and causing him to cry out plaintively, "Hey, that hurts!" The return to childhood was well underway.

"Stop being such a baby!" Delicately I took one of his nipples in the tongs. He shrank from me, but the tongs pursued. I was careful, however, not to hurt him.

With feather touch, I teased the tiny inverted nipple, making him writhe at the tickling pleasure it gave him. Then, suddenly, the nipple was erect. I then teased the other nipple, manipulating the golden aureole of hairs until it, too, ceased to be concave. A glassy look came into his eyes; for the first time an erogenous zone had been explored and exploited (I do not count the probing of his sphincter which, in the context of my investigation, did not arouse him, rather the reverse). I looked at the front of his trousers to see if there was any sudden swelling but I could detect nothing.

"You had better slip off those trousers," I said. "They're getting badly creased, the way you're sweating."

"Oh, that's O.K." His voice cracked again.

"Hurry up! We haven't got all night." Grimly he sat up and pulled his trousers down over his knees. I pulled them over his feet and carefully hung them on a chair.

When I turned back to my victim, I was surprised to find him sitting up on the table, poised for flight. He had trickily used the turning of my back to restore his shorts to their normal position. Sitting as he was, bare legs dangling over the table, I could see nothing of the crotch, concealed by muscular thighs pressed close together while both hands rested protectively in his lap. He was not going to surrender the last bastion without a struggle.

"I didn't tell you to sit up, did I?" I was cold.

"But I thought you were through with me here." The timbre of the voice had become light; he sounded like a pubescent boy trying to escape punishment.

"You're not finished until I say you are. All right. Stand up. Over here. In front of me."

He got to his feet and approached to within a foot of me. There he stood, awkwardly, hands crossed in front of him, torso glittering with sweat, legs as well proportioned as the rest of him, though somewhat overdeveloped in the thighs, no doubt the result of playing football. He was so close to me that I could feel the heat of his flesh and smell the healthy earthlike aroma the young male body exudes.

"Rest your arms at your sides and at least *try* to stand straight." He obeyed. The target was now directly in front of me, at my eye's level. As I stared straight at the hidden area he clenched his fists nervously, and shifted from foot to foot. The frayed Jockey shorts were unfortunately too loose to reveal more than a large rounded area, without clear definition; they were, however, splotched with fresh urine.

"Look! You wet yourself!" I pinched the damp cloth, careful to touch nothing beneath.

He gave a start. "I guess I did. I was in a hurry."

"Boys are so careless about those things." We had gone from bowel-training to bed-wetting: such was progress! I looked at the examination card. "Oh yes! Have you ever had a venereal disease?"

"Oh, no, ma'am. Never!"

"I hope you're telling me the truth." I was ominous as I wrote "no" on the chart. "We have ways of finding out, you know."

"Honest, I never have. I always been careful . . . always."

"Always? Just exactly *when* did you begin with girls?"

"When?" He looked at me dumbly.

"How old were you?"

"Thirteen, I guess. I don't remember."

"Was she older than you?"

He nodded. "In high school. She was a Protestant," he added wildly.

"Did she make the advances?"

"Yes. Kind of. She'd show me hers if I showed her mine. You know, kid stuff."

"And you liked what you saw?"

"Oh, yes." A smile flickered for an instant across the frightened face.

"Did she like what she saw?"

The smile went, as he was reminded of his situation. "Well, there was no complaints."

"Would you say that you were well developed for your age?"

"I guess so. I don't know."

"Did you masturbate often?"

The face went red. "Well . . . maybe some. I guess all guys do."

"What about now?"

"Now? Oh, no. Why should I?"

"You mean Mary-Ann is quite enough to satisfy you?"

"Yes. And I don't cheat on her."

"How often do you come with her in a night?"

He gulped. "That's awful personal . . ."

I took the measuring stick and with a great cracking sound struck his right thigh. He yelled. Fear and reproach in his face, as he rubbed the hurt skin.

"There's more where that came from if you don't answer my questions."

He accepted defeat. "I guess I can go four or five times but mostly we just go a couple times because, you see, we have to get up so early . . ."

"Then you *are* quite a stud, as they say out here."

"Oh, I don't know . . ." He gestured helplessly.

"Would you say that your penis was larger than most boys' your age or smaller?"

He began to tremble, aware of the prey I was stalking. "Christ, I don't know. I mean *how* could I know?"

"You see the other boys in the shower, and you were an athlete, after all."

"I guess I didn't look . . ."

"But surely you must occasionally have taken a peek." I looked straight at the worn cotton which hid the subject of my inquiry. Both of his hands twitched, as though he wanted to protect himself.

"I guess I'm average. I never thought about it . . . honest." This of course was a lie since in every known society the adolescent male spends a great deal of time worriedly comparing himself with other males.

"You're unusually modest." I was dry. "Now I'm supposed to check you for hernia. So if you'll just pull down those shorts . . ."

"But I don't have hernia," he gabbled. "I was all checked out by this prison doctor in Mexico, and he said I was just fine in that department."

"But it does no harm to double-check. So if you'll slip them down . . ."

"Honest, I'm O.K." He was sweating heavily.

"Rusty, I get the impression that for some mysterious reason you don't want me to examine your genitals. Exactly what mischief are you trying to hide from me?"

"Nothing, honest! I got nothing to hide . . ."

"Then why are you so afraid to let me examine you?"

"Because—well, you're a woman and I'm a man . . ."

"A boy, technically . . ."

"A boy, O.K., and well, it's just wrong."

"Then you're shy."

"Sure. I'm shy about *that,* in front of a lady."

"But surely you aren't shy with all those girls you've—what's that word of yours?—'boffed'?"

"But that's different, when you're *both* making love, that's O.K."

"Baffling," I said. I frowned as though trying to find some way out of our dilemma. "Naturally, I want to respect your modesty. At the same time I must complete the examination." I paused; then I gave the appearance of having reached a decision. "All right. You won't have to remove your shorts . . ."

He gave a sigh of relief . . . too soon.

"However, I shall have to insert my hand inside the shorts and press each testicle as required by the chart."

"Oh." Dismay and defeat.

"I think you'll agree that's a statesmanlike compromise." On that bright note, I slid my left hand up the inside of his left thigh. He wriggled involuntarily as I forced my fingers past the leg opening of the shorts. The scrotum's heat was far greater than that of the thigh, I noticed, and the hairs were soaked with sweat.

Carefully I took his left testicle in my hand. It was unusually large and firm to the touch, though somewhat loose in the sac, no doubt due to his overheated condition. Delicately I fingered the beloved enemy, at last in my power. Then I looked up and saw that Rusty's eyes were screwed shut, as though anticipating pain. I gave it to him. I maneuvered the testicle back and forth until I had found the hole from which, in boyhood, it had so joyously descended. I shoved it back up into the hole. He groaned. Then he gagged as I held it in place. With the gagging, I could feel the entire scrotum contract like a terrified beast, seeking escape. When he gagged again and seemed on the verge of actually being sick, I let the testicle fall back into its normal place and took my hand away.

"Jesus," he whispered. "I almost threw up."

"I'm sorry. But I have to be thorough. I'll be gentler this time." Again my hand pushed past the damp cloth and seized the right testicle, which was somewhat smaller than the left. As I maneuvered it gently about, my forefinger strayed and struck the side of something thick and smooth, rooted in wiry hair. He shuddered, but continued to suffer at my hands. I slipped the right testicle into its ancient place and held it there until I sensed he was about to gag. Then I let it drop and removed my hand.

He gave a deep sigh. "I guess that's it."

"Yes, I think so." I pretended to examine the chart.

With a sigh, he sat down on the chair opposite me and clumsily pulled on one sock, tearing the flimsy material; the toes went through the tip.

"You're very clumsy." I observed.

"Yes, ma'am." He agreed, quickly pulling on the other sock, not wanting in any way to cross me, so eager was he to escape.

"Oh, here's a question we forgot." I was incredibly sunny. "Have you been circumcised?"

The foot he was holding on his knee slid to the floor. Quickly he pressed his thighs together, wadding up his shirt, and covered the beleaguered lap. "Why, no, ma'am. I never was."

"So few Polish boys are, I'm told." I made a check on the chart. "Does the skin pull back easily?"

"Oh, sure!" He was beet-red. "Sure. I'm O.K. Mary-Ann's waiting."

"Not so fast." I was cold. "I didn't give you permission to dress, you know."

"But I thought you were finished. . . ." The deep voice was now a whine.

"I was. But your jumping the gun like that makes me very suspicious."

"Suspicious?" He was bewildered.

"Yes. First, I let you talk me out of giving you the venereal disease examination, and now you're suddenly getting dressed, without permission, just when the subject once more has to do with your penis. Rusty, I am very, very suspicious."

The blue eyes filled with tears as he sensed what was approaching. "Don't be, Miss Myra. Believe me, I'm absolutely O.K. . . ."

"We have to think of Mary-Ann, too, you know. You could make her very sick just through your carelessness."

"Honest to God, I'm O.K. They even gave me the Wassermann test in the jail. . . ." He jabbered nervously.

"I'm sure they did. But what was the result?"

"Mr. Martinson will tell you. I was a hundred percent O.K."

"But Mr. Martinson isn't here while you are, and frankly I don't see how I can omit this part of the examination. Stand up please and put down that shirt."

"Oh, come on, please don't . . ." His voice broke again, close to a sob.

"Do as I say."

On that note of icy command, he stood up slowly and like a man going to his execution—or a schoolboy to his spanking—he put down the shirt and stood dumbly facing me. "Come over here." He came to within a few inches of where I was sitting; he was so close that my knees touched the warm fur of his shins.

"Now let's see what kind of stud you really are."

"Please . . ." He whispered. "I don't want to. It isn't right."

Deliberately I took the Jockey shorts by the elastic waistband and pulled them slowly, slowly down, enjoying each station of his shame. The first glimpse was encouraging. The base of the penis sprouted from the bronze bush at an angle of almost forty-five degrees, an earnest of vitality. It was well over an inch wide, always a good sign, with one large blue vein down the center, again promising. But another three inches of slow unveiling revealed Rusty's manhood in its entirety, I slid the shorts to the floor.

When I looked up at his face, I saw that once again the eyes were shut, the lips trembling. Then I carefully examined the object of my long and arduous hunt, at last captive. A phrase of Myron's occurred to me: "all potatoes and no meat." Rusty's balls were unusually large and impressive; one lower than the other, as they hung bull-like in the rather loose scrotal sac. They were all that I could desire. The penis, on the other hand, was not a success, and I could see now why he was so reluctant to let me see just how short it is. On the other hand both base and head are uncommonly thick and, as Myron always said, thickness not length is how you gauge the size of the ultimate erection. The skin was dead white with several not undecorative veins, while the foreskin covered the entire head meeting at the tip in an irregular rosy pucker, plainly cousin to the sphincter I had so recently probed.

"I'm afraid, Rusty, that you've been somewhat oversold on the campus. Poor Mary-Ann. That's a boy's equipment."

This had the desired effect of stinging him into a manly response. "Ain't been no complaints," he growled. But as he did, both testicles rose in their sac as though seeking an escape hatch in case of battle, while the penis betrayed him by visibly shrinking into the safety of the brush.

"Next you'll tell me that it's not the size that counts but what you do." I followed verbal insult with physical: I took the penis firmly in my hand.

He dared not move, or speak, or even cry out. The shock had reduced him exactly as planned. I had also confirmed an old theory that although the "normal" male delights in exposing himself to females who attract him he is, conversely, terrified to do so in front of those he dislikes or fears, as though any knowledge they might obtain of the center of his being will create bad magic and hence unman him. In any case, the grail was in my hand at last, smooth, warm, soft.

My joy was complete as I slid back the skin, exposing the shiny deep rose of the head which was impressively large and beautifully shaped, giving some credence to the legend that, in action, its owner (already Rusty had become a mere appendage to this reality) was a formidable lover. He was sweaty but clean (I was so close to him that I could smell the strong but not disagreeable fernlike odor of genitals). Delicately but firmly, I pressed the glans, making the phallic eye open. Not one tear was shed. "Apparently, you *are* all right," I observed as he looked down with horror at my hand which held him firmly in its grasp, the glans penis exposed like a summer rose.

"You're also clean but beyond that I'm afraid you're something of a disappointment." The penis again shrank in my hand. "But of course you're probably still growing." The humiliation was complete. There was nothing that he could say. In actual fact, the largeness of the head had already convinced me that what I said was untrue, but policy dictated that I be scornful.

"Now then, let's see how free the foreskin is." I slid the skin forward, then back. He shuddered. "Now, you do it a few times."

To his relief, I let him go. Clumsily he took himself in one hand as though never before had he touched this strange object, so beloved of Mary-Ann. He gave a few halfhearted tugs to the skin, looking for all the world like a child frightened in the act of masturbating.

"Come on," I said, "you can do better than that."

He changed his grip to the one he obviously used when alone. His hands worked rapidly as he pumped himself like one of those machines that extract oil from the earth, milk from the cow, water from shale. After several minutes of intense and rhythmic massage I noted, with some surprise, that though the head had become a bit larger and darker, the stem had not changed in size. Apparently he knew how to restrain himself. He continued for another minute or two, the only sound in the room his heavy breathing and the soft waterlike sound of skin slapping against skin; then he stopped.

"You see," he said. "It works O.K."

"But I didn't tell you to stop."

"But if I keep on . . . I mean . . . well, Christ, a man's going to . . ."

"A boy," I corrected.

"A boy's going to . . . to . . ."

"To what?"

"Get . . . excited."

"Go right ahead. I'd be amused to see what Mary-Ann sees in you."

Without another word, grimly, he set to work and continued for some time, sweating hard. But still we were denied the full glory. Some lengthening and thickening took place but not to the fullest degree.

"Is anything wrong?" I asked sweetly.

"I don't know." He gulped, trying to catch his breath. "It can't . . . won't . . ." He was incoherent at the double humiliation.

"Do you often have this problem with Mary-Ann?" I sounded as compassionate as Kay Francis, as warm as June Allyson.

"Never! I swear . . ."

"Five times in one night and now this! Really, you young boys are such liars."

"I wasn't lying. I just don't know what's wrong. . . ." He beat at himself as though through sheer force he could tap the well of generation. But it was no use. Finally I told him to stop. Then I took over, practicing a number of subtle pressures and frictions learned from Myron . . . all to no avail.

In a curious way the absence of an erection, though not part of the plan, gave me an unexpected thrill: to have so cowed my victim as to short-circuit his legendary powers as a stud was, psychologically, far more fulfilling than my original intention.

While I was vigorously shaking him, he made the long-expected move that would complete the drama, the holy passion of Myra Breckinridge.

"Do you . . ." He began tentatively, looking down at me and the loose-stemmed rose that I held in my hand.

"Do I what?"

"Do you want me to . . . well, to ball you?" The delivery was superb, as shy as a nubile boy requesting a first kiss.

I let go of him as though in horror. "Rusty! Do you know who you're talking to?"

"Yes, Miss Myra. I'm sorry. I didn't mean to offend you. . . ."

"What sort of woman do you think I am?" I took the heavy balls in my hand, as an offering. "These belong to Mary-Ann, and no one else, and if I ever catch you playing around with anybody else, I'll see that Mr. Martinson puts you away for twenty years."

He turned white. "I'm sorry. I didn't know. I thought maybe . . . the way you were . . . doing what you were doing. . . . I'm sorry, really." The voice stopped.

"You have every reason to be sorry." Again I let him go; the large balls swung back between his legs, and continued gently to sway, like a double pendulum. "In any case, if I had wanted you to—as you put it—'ball me,' it's very plain that you couldn't. As a stud, you're a disaster."

He flushed at the insult but said nothing. I was now ready for my master stroke. "However, as a lesson, I shall ball you."

He was entirely at sea. "Ball *me?* How?"

"Put out your hands." He did so and I bound them together with surgical gauze. Not for nothing had I once been a nurses' aide.

"What're you doing that for?" Alarm growing.

With a forefinger, I flicked the scrotal sac, making him cry out from shock. "No questions, my boy." When the hands were firmly secured, I lowered the examination table until it was just two feet from the floor. "Lie down," I ordered. "On your stomach."

Mystified, he did as he was told. I then tied his bound hands to the top of the metal table. He was, as they say, entirely in my power. If I had wanted, I could have killed him. But my fantasies have never involved murder or even physical suffering for I have a horror of blood preferring to inflict pain in more subtle ways, destroying totally, for instance, a man's idea of himself in relation to the triumphant sex.

"Now then, up on your knees."

"But . . ." A hard slap across the buttocks put an end to all objections. He pulled himself up on his knees, legs tight together and buttocks clenched shut. He resembled a pyramid whose base was his head and white-socked feet, and whose apex was his rectum. I was now ready for the final rite.

"Legs wide apart," I commanded. Reluctantly, he moved his knees apart so that they lined up with the exact edges of the table. I was now afforded my favorite view of the male, the heavy rose scrotum dangling from the groin above which the tiny sphincter shyly twinkled in the light. Carefully I applied lubricant to the mystery that even Mary-Ann has never seen, much less violated.

"What're you doing?" The voice was light as a child. True terror had begun.

"Now remember the secret is to relax entirely. Otherwise you could be seriously hurt."

I then pulled up my skirt to reveal, strapped to my groin, Clem's dildo which I borrowed yesterday on the pretext that I wanted it copied for a lamp base. Clem had been most amused.

Rusty cried out with alarm. "Oh, no! For God's sake, don't."

"Now you will find out what it is the girl feels when you play the man with her."

"Jesus, you'll split me!" The voice was treble with fear. As I approached him, dildo in front of me like the god Priapus personified, he tried to wrench free of his bonds, but failed. Then he did the next best thing, and brought his knees together in an attempt to deny me entrance. But it was no use. I spread him wide and put my battering ram to the gate.

For a moment I wondered if he might not be right about the splitting: the opening was the size of a dime while the dildo was over two inches wide at the head and nearly a foot long. But then I recalled how Myron used to have no trouble in accommodating objects this size or larger, and what the fragile Myron could do so could the inexperienced but sturdy Rusty.

I pushed. The pink lips opened. The tip of the head entered and stopped.

"I can't," Rusty moaned. "Honestly I can't. It's too big."

"Just relax, and you'll stretch. Don't worry."

He made whatever effort was necessary and the pursed lips became a grin allowing the head to enter, but not without a gasp of pain and shock.

Once inside, I savored my triumph. I had avenged Myron. A lifetime of being penetrated had brought him only misery. Now, in the person of Rusty, I was able, as Woman Triumphant, to destroy the adored destroyer.

Holding tight to Rusty's slippery hips, I plunged deeper. He cried out with pain.

But I was inexorable. I pushed even farther into him, triggering the prostate gland, for when I felt between his legs, I discovered that the erection he had not been able to present me with had now, inadvertently, occurred. The size was most respectable, and hard as metal.

But when I plunged deeper, the penis went soft with pain, and he cried out again, begged me to stop, but now I was like a woman possessed, riding, riding, riding my sweating stallion into forbidden country, shouting with joy as I experienced my own sort of orgasm, oblivious to his staccato shrieks as I delved that innocent flesh. Oh, it was a holy moment! I was one with the Bacchae, with all the priestesses of the dark bloody cults, with the great goddess herself for whom Attis unmanned himself. I was the eternal feminine made flesh, the source of life and its destroyer, dealing with man as incidental toy, whose blood as well as semen is needed to make me whole!

There was blood at the end. And once my passion had spent itself, I was saddened and repelled. I had not meant actually to tear the tender flesh but apparently I had, and the withdrawing of my weapon brought with it bright blood. He did not stir as I washed him clean (like a loving mother), applying medicine to the small cut, inserting gauze (how often had I done this for Myron!). Then I unbound him.

Shakily, he stood up, rubbing tears from his swollen face. In silence he dressed while I removed the harness of the dildo and put it away in the attaché case.

Not until he was finally dressed did he speak. "Can I go now?"

"Yes. You can go now." I sat down at the surgical table and took out this notebook. He was at the door when I said, "Aren't you going to thank me for the trouble I've taken?"

He looked at me, face perfectly blank. Then, tonelessly, he murmured, "Thank you, ma'am," and went.

And so it was that Myra Breckinridge achieved one of the great victories for her sex. But one which is not yet entirely complete even though, alone of all women, I know what it is like to be a goddess enthroned, and all-powerful.

## 30

I sit now at the card table. Through the window I can see the turning chorus girl in front of the Château Marmont Hotel; only she is not turning. A power failure? are they making repairs? or is she at last being dismantled? The question takes on symbolic importance since she is, to me, Hollywood. She must never *not* be allowed to dominate the Strip.

Rusty did not appear at school today. I would have been disappointed if he had. But what did distress me was Mary-Ann's absence from Posture. She has never before missed one of my classes.

Discouraged and uneasy, I rang Miss Cluff to see if Mary-Ann had attended the Bell Telephone Hour class. She had not, "I haven't seen hide nor hair of her. But you know how girls are. It's probably her time. . . ." Bell-like laughter from Miss Cluff. Next I rang the girls' dormitory. The matron told me that Mary-Ann had not returned the previous evening, and she had already made a report to Buck.

I confess I was terrified. Had Rusty told her what had happened? I could not believe it. Masculine pride (no matter how damaged) would have prevented him. But he still could have told her *something* which had made her leave the school . . . and me. I had a sudden vision of them together in Mexico, growing marijuana, utterly happy. The thought was too depressing. Also, I reminded myself, impractical since he is on parole and may not leave L.A., much less cross the border.

Matters were not much helped when I received a call from Buck's office to see him at five. I found him looking altogether too pleased with himself. With him was a typical California type: a bronzed empty face with clear eyes and that vapid smile which the Pacific Ocean somehow manages to impress upon the lips of almost everyone doomed to live in any proximity to those tedious waters. It is fascinating how, in a single generation, stern New England Protestants, grim Iowans and keen New York Jews have all become entirely Tahitianized by that dead ocean with its sweet miasmic climate in which thoughts become dreams while perceptions blur and distinctions are so erased that men are women are men are nothing are everything are one. Gentlemen, the desire and the pursuit of the whole ends at Santa Monica!

The typical specimen was Charlie Flagler Junior, lawyer. He gave me the whitest of smiles, the firmest of handshakes and then, at Buck's insistence, he let me have it. "Mrs. Breckinridge, as you know, in representing my client, Mr. Loner, or any client, I—we must of course try to leave no stone unturned in order to—like make it *crystal clear* what their position is."

Buck clapped his hands together, as if in applause. Then he said, "I think, Myra, you should know that Charlie's dad and me have been pals for lo! these many years, ever since he handled me when I had that big row with the Blue Network."

"I guess we value Mr. Loner's account more than almost any single non-corporate account, not only for old times' sake—like Dad says—but because Buck Loner has a *reputation* in this town"—Charlie Flagler Junior's voice became very grave and solemn—"for being like a straight-shooter."

"For Christ's sake," I said, no doubt in the same tone that Dr. Margaret

Mead must have used in trying to extract a straight bit of folklore from *her* Polynesians, "stop gassing and tell me what lousy trick you're up to now."

Buck's face half shut; he looked pained. Charlie Flagler Junior gave me a curious look. I imagined him stretched out before me the way Rusty had been; a satisfying vision except, curiously enough, so complete was last night's experience that any repetition of it would be redundant, even in fantasy. I have accomplished what nature intended me to do and except for one last turn to the screw, I am complete.

"No lousy trick, Mrs. Breckinridge." The young lawyer wanted to appear grieved but the Polynesian face has only two expressions: joy and incomprehension. He looked quite stupid. "I simply must respect my client's wishes and defend his interests which in this case are your claim to like half the value of this Westwood property, due you as the alleged widow of his nephew."

"Alleged?" I was ready for battle.

Joy filled the brown Pacific face, as though a toasted breadfruit had been offered him after a long swim with Dorothy Lamour. "Alleged. The marriage certificate you gave us is an out-and-out forgery."

I was not as prepared to answer this charge as I thought I would be. The game is now becoming most tricky and dangerous. One false move and all will come to a dead halt, like the ominously stationary ten-times-life-size chorine outside my window. "Mr. Charlie Flagler Junior and you, Buck Loner, brother of Gertrude and cheerful thief, I am the heiress to half this property, and I am going to get it. So don't think for one moment you can hold out on me."

"Honey, we're not trying to keep what's yours from you." Buck was plaintive. "That's the last thing on our minds but we've got to make sure you really are entitled to it. I mean you could be some kind of impersonator, saying you are who you are."

"Gertrude gave you two hundred dollars back in Philadelphia when you were twenty years old to pay for the abortion of the daughter of the Rexall druggist you knocked up and refused to marry."

Buck turned white. The Polynesian remained brown. Buck cleared his throat, "I'm not saying you didn't know Gertrude and the boy well. Obviously you did . . ."

"The point is like this," said Charlie Flagler Junior, "you have to *prove* you were married. That's all."

"I shall prove it." I rose to go. The men rose, too, with a new respect. At least they don't underestimate their adversary. "Proof will arrive before the end of the week. Meanwhile, Uncle Buck, I shall list all the loans Gertrude made you over the years, and I shall expect repayment, with interest." I slammed the door as I left.

I have just talked to Dr. Montag in New York. He dithered. I was firm. "Randolph, you owe this to me. You owe this to Myron. I don't want to blackmail you emotionally but you also owe it to the insights we exchanged, the three of us, at the Blue Owl Grill. We made you just as you made us. Now we are at the crunch. . . ."

"The what?" His nervous wheezing often keeps him from hearing what others say.

" 'Crunch' is a word currently favored by the keener journalists. It means the showdown, the moment of truth. Well, this is the crunch, and I am appealing to you, not only as Myron's analyst and my dentist but as our only friend. Fly out here tomorrow."

"But, Myra, I can't. Your appeal reaches me at every level, there's no doubt about that. I am touched in every department from lower id, as your husband used to say, to upper superego, but there is the problem of my other patients. They need me. . . ."

"Randolph." I was peremptory. "I'll cut you in for ten percent of the take."

There was an alarming series of wheezes and coughs at the other end of the line. Then Dr. Montag said what sounded like "Between, Myra."

"Between what?"

"Fifteen!" he shouted from the Island of Manhattan. "Fifteen percent and I'm in L.A. tomorrow."

"Answered like a true Adlerian! *Fifteen it is!*" I knew my man. Many was the night that the three of us used to sit until the Blue Owl closed discussing Randolph's inordinate greed for pastry and money. It was—is—the most likable thing about him. With that taken care of, I can now

## 31

Life continues to support Myra Breckinridge in all her schemes to obtain uniqueness. As I write this, Mary-Ann is asleep in my bed (I have fixed up the daybed in here for myself). It is three in the morning. We have talked and wept together for five hours. I have never known such delight. Last night with Rusty was religious ecstasy; tonight a rebirth.

While I was writing in this notebook, there was a rap at the door. I opened it. Mary-Ann stood in the doorway, pale, bedraggled and carrying a Pan Am overnight zipper bag. "Miss Myra, I've got to talk to you. You're the only person I can." With that she burst into tears and I took her in my arms, reveling in the full rounded warmth of that body, so reminiscent of the early Lana Turner. In a curious way, though she is so much younger and more vulnerable than I, she suggests a mother figure to me, which is madness since in our relationship I am, necessarily, the one who is wise, the one who comforts and directs. I daresay my hatred of my own mother must have had some *positive* element in it since I am now able to feel genuine warmth for another woman, and a mere girl at that. I must discuss the matter thoroughly with Randolph.

Soon the sobbing ceased, and I poured her a glass of gin which she drank neat. This seemed to steady her.

"Rusty's gone again." She sat on the daybed, and blew her nose. Her legs are every bit as beautiful as Eleanor Powell's in the last reel of *Rosalie,* on those drums.

"Gone where?" I was about to say that any boy on parole is not apt to take a long trip, but I thought better of it.

"I don't know. It happened last night." She dried her eyes.

"Yes?" I was cautious. "You were with him last night?"

She nodded. "We were supposed to have dinner but he said you wanted to see him at ten. . . ."

"A routine chat." I was casual. "I'm sorry I picked such an odd hour and ruined your dinner but I was busy with Miss Cluff and . . ."

She was, happily, not interested in his visit to me. "Anyway he didn't pick me up till after eleven, and I've never seen him in such a bad mood . . ."

"Strange," I added to the official record, "he seemed quite cheerful when he left me. In fact, he thanked me profusely for the help I'd given him."

"I know you were nice to him. You always are—now. Anyway he didn't mention you. He just picked a fight with me, over nothing, and I got angry and then he said maybe I'd better go back to the dorm and not spend the night with him. He said he was . . ." she paused, tears beginning, "sick of me, sick of women, and wanted just to go off by himself. . . ."

"Sick of you or of women in general?" This was a key point.

"I don't know exactly what he said, I was so upset. Both, I guess."

Apparently I had done my work better than I expected.

"On top of that, he said he was feeling lousy and he'd pulled a muscle or something and it hurt him to sit down . . . oh, I don't know, he was just awful. But then I told him about the date I'd made for him, and that cheered him up a bit."

"What date?"

"You won't be mad at me?" She looked so frightened, young, vulnerable that I wanted to hold her in my arms. "Of course not, dear." I was Janet Gaynor. "I could never be angry with you."

"You *are* a friend." She gave me a dim watery smile. "Well, I had got us both invited to Letitia Van Allen's rustic home at Malibu, in the Colony."

I sat up straight. *I* have never been invited to Letitia's house but then of course I have yet to be of any use to her as a purveyor of studs. Now poor Mary-Ann had fallen unwittingly into Letitia's trap. "Just how did this invitation come about?"

"Well, I was in her office and we were talking about this date she'd made for me with that record company and then, I don't know, the conversation got around to Rusty and she asked to see a picture of him, and I showed her the ones I always carry and she said he was very handsome and had star quality and I asked her if she wanted to meet him . . . oh, I know you didn't want him to talk to her until June . . ."

"It would have been better *after* his closed-circuit TV performance. Anyway the damage is done. So you took him to Malibu last night."

She nodded bleakly. "There were a dozen people there, all so successful and rich. One was a star. You know, the one who's in that television series that was just canceled by CBS, *Riptide*? He was nice but drunk. Anyway Letitia made a big fuss over Rusty, who was rude as could be to her and to everybody else. I've never seen him act like that before."

"Perhaps he had something on his mind."

"Well, whatever it is it was eating him up, for suddenly he gets up and says to Miss Van Allen. 'I got to go. This isn't my scene.' And left just like that, *without me.* I was never so embarrassed and hurt. Anyway Miss Van Allen couldn't have been nicer and said she wouldn't hold it against Rusty and since it was so late I'd better sleep over, which I did, though I didn't sleep much, with that boy from *Riptide* banging on the door all night."

I poured her more gin which she drank. Her spirits improved. "Anyway, today I called Rusty at the place where he's staying and they said he didn't come home last night, and then I called the Academy and they said he didn't go to any of his classes, and then I got scared that maybe he was killed or something so I called the police but they didn't know anything. Then I waited in the dorm all evening for him to call and when finally he didn't, I came here. . . ." Her voice had become quavery again.

"You did the right thing," I said. "And I want you to stay here with me until everything's straightened itself out."

"You're so good, Miss Myra!"

"Not at all. Now don't worry about Rusty. Nothing's happened to him. He's probably in a bad mood because of the situation he's in." Then I told her in detail about Rusty's Mexican adventures. "So you see he's on parole and that means the probation officer must always know where he is. So if Rusty ever really did disappear, Uncle Buck and I would be the first to know about it."

Mary-Ann frowned, still absorbing what I had told her. I gave her more gin which she drank as though it was her favorite drink, Seven-Up. "He promised me he was never going to see any of those boys he used to hang out with."

"Well, he's young. Let him have his fun. As long as he stays out of jail, of course."

She shook her head, suddenly grim. "It's them or me, I told him."

"And of course it will be you." I was soothing as I began to spread and arrange my net. "Don't worry. Now lie down and rest while we chat."

She gave me a grateful smile and stretched out on the daybed. It was all I could do not to sit beside her and caress those extraordinary breasts, made doubly attractive for me since they are Rusty's to do with as he likes, or so he believes. Having raped his manhood, I shall now seduce his girl. Beyond that, ambition stops and godhood begins.

We talked of everything. She is totally in love with Rusty, though shaken by what has happened as well as by my revelation of his Mexican capers. She has had only three lovers in her life, all male. Lesbianism is repulsive to her. But she did agree, after the fourth glass of gin, that she felt entirely secure and warm with me, and that one woman could offer another, under the right circumstances, great reassurance and affection.

Finally, slightly drunk, I took her into the bedroom and helped her to undress. The breasts are *better* than Lana Turner's in *They Won't Forget.* Smooth and white with large rosy nipples (in a curious way they are an exaggerated version of Rusty's own), their shape is marvelously subtle . . . at least what I could see of them, for she promptly pulled on her nightdress and only then removed her panties, hiding from me that center of Rusty's sexual being in which he has so many times (but never again if I can help it!) spent himself.

The thought that soon I shall know intimately the body *he* knew so made me tremble that I did not dare embrace her good night but instead blew her a kiss from the door, shut it, and promptly rang Mr. Martinson, who was angry at being waked up. But he did tell me that Rusty had decided to leave the Academy and take a permanent job with a firm that sells foreign cars on Melrose Avenue; however, when I asked where Rusty was staying, Mr. Martinson told me that it was none of my business. Needless to say, I told him where and how to head in, and hung up.

Now I must find some way of breaking the news to Mary-Ann. This will be tricky because under no circumstances must they be allowed to resume their love affair. That is at an end.

A miraculous omen! I just looked out the window at the enormous woman and she is again turning gaily upon her axis, beautiful and omnipotent, the very image of deity!

# 32

Dr. Montag is sitting on the daybed reading my description of the conquest of Rusty. I sit at the card table, writing these lines, waiting for his comment. Tomorrow we meet Buck and his lawyers. The showdown.

Randolph is wheezing through clouds of pipe smoke. He is frowning. I suppose he disapproves. Yet of all people he should understand what it is that I have done. He looks simply God-awful. He thinks he's in Hawaii. He is wearing a flowered short-sleeved shirt that hangs outside his shiny black rabbinical trousers and

# 33

Randolph has returned to his motel for a nap; he is still not used to the change in time and wants to be at his best for tomorrow's meeting. We have prepared two lines of attack; at the worst, one will succeed.

The description of my life's triumph did not entirely please him which, naturally, does not please *me,* and that is what matters.

"Am I to understand all this really happened?" Ashes fell upon the page which I snatched from his hand. Randolph's pipe often produces cinders as well as smoke, for he has a tendency to blow through the stem when ill at ease.

"Exactly," I said. "At least you'll have to agree that I've got him down in black and white, once and for all, every detail, every hair, every pimple."

"You've got his *outside,* yes." Judiciously he arranged a screen of smoke between us. "But that's just Rusty's skin, you haven't shown his inside."

"I haven't shown his inside, dear Randolph, because I don't know it. And, if I may say so, it is presumptuous for anyone to even pretend he can know what another person's interior is really like, short of an autopsy. The only thing we can ever know for certain is skin, and I now know his better than he does himself."

"Possibly. Possibly." Randolph still appeared distressed.

"In fact," I improvised, "nothing matters except what is visible to the eye. For me to write, as I shall when you go, that you *looked* distressed at this moment could very easily be a projection on my part, and misreading of your mood. To be accurate, I should simply write that while you were reading my notes there was a double crease between your brows, which is not usual, since . . ."

"It is *not* a projection to say that I am distressed. And up to a point we can, more or less, assume that we know what others are feeling, at least at the more accessible levels of consciousness. At this moment, I am feeling a certain distress for that young man, a certain male empathy. After all, it is a most unpleasant thing to be assaulted anally and I think we can both assume that he was not happy, no matter how mute the skin."

"I agree and that's why in my review of what happened, I not only recorded his conversation but tried to give what I believed were his feelings when he spoke. Yet I realize that at best my interpretation is entirely subjective, and perhaps false. Since I wanted to frighten and humiliate him, I chose to regard his groans and grunts as symptoms of fright and humiliation."

"Which, no doubt, they were. Although we must never rule out the possibility that he was enjoying himself."

"If that is true, my life's work has failed." I was very grave. I have never been more serious.

"Or succeeded in ways you do not yet understand. In any case, his girlfriend is living with you, isn't she?"

"Yes, she came to me. Of all the people she knows, I am the one she turned to. The irony is perfect." So is my delight!

"Does she know what you've done?"

"Of course not."

"What will happen if she finds out?"

"I have no intention of telling her. As for Rusty, I don't think either of us needs a degree in psychiatry" (Randolph looked momentarily unhappy; he has only an M.A. in psychology) "to know that he will never tell anyone what was done to him."

"Perhaps not." Randolph's pipe went off again. One bright cinder burned a hole in the carpet. "But aren't you afraid he may want compensation for what you did, particularly if he is as healthy and 'normal' as you think?"

"What sort of compensation?"

"He might take *physical* revenge on you. Do to you what you did to him."

"Rape? Not very likely. He's much too terrified. No, I've heard the last of him, except in connection with Mary-Ann . . ."

Randolph listened carefully as I told him how I planned, with every appearance of love and affection, to possess Mary-Ann in order that the cycle be completed.

"What cycle?"

"The justification of Myron's life." I was prompt. I have intellectualized everything, as I always do, to the despair of Randolph, who is, despite all his modish pretensions and quibbling subterfuges, entirely emotional, in many ways a dead ringer for Jean Hersholt. "By acting out what was done to him, I exalt him—the idea of him, anyway—and also avenge him . . ."

"*Avenge* him? In what way? The Myron I knew was hardly a victim. Rather the contrary."

"No, he was victim. I know that now. But no matter what he really was . . ."

"A marvelous man . . ."

"How you enjoy throwing that in my face!" I was stung and deeply hurt, as I always am, by reminders that Randolph worshipped Myron and cannot, at heart, bear me.

"Now, now you must not project. When I praise Myron, I praise *him.* I don't denigrate you."

"*You* are the one projecting now. But, in any case, once I have completed my seduction, I shall be free of all guilt toward Myron and for Myron. I shall be a new woman, literally new, something unique under the sun."

"But who and what will you be?"

I answered vehemently, at length, but said nothing, for, as usual, Randolph, in his blundering way, has touched upon the dilemma's horn: I have no clear idea as to my ultimate identity once every fantasy has been acted out with living flesh. All that I do know is that I shall be freed of obsession and, in this at least, be like no one else who ever lived.

Randolph then departed for his nap to be followed by a trip to Disneyland. So here I sit, making these notes. Suddenly ill at ease. Why? The telephone rings

## 34

That was Letitia. She came straight to the point. "Rusty's living with me. He's down at the beach house right now."

"Letitia!" That was the best I could do. Not even in my wildest dreams had I ever connected the two of them, particularly after Mary-Ann's description of Rusty's rudeness to Letitia on the famous night.

"All I can say, Myra, is you sure know how to pick 'em. That is the best Grade A stud I have ever had, and as rumor hath doubtless had it here at the heart of the Industry, Letitia Van Allen has made many a trip to the old corral."

I could think of nothing but Rusty's soft rose wobbling childishly in my hand. "Is he really the *very* best stud of all?"

"The very best, and I've you to thank for it. When I saw how you had conned that girlfriend of his into bringing him to my house, I said to myself: Myra Breckinridge is a *pal!*"

I was startled but delighted at being given full credit for maneuvering

Rusty into Letitia's orbit. "Of course I knew you'd enjoy meeting him." I was neutral, not wanting to betray the fact that it was Mary-Ann I had wanted Letitia to help, not Rusty.

"He's *everything* I like!" Letitia roared into the telephone. "In fact, the moment I clapped eyes on him, I said, 'God, Letitia, but that's it!' "

"But Mary-Ann told me he behaved abominably at your house."

"Natch! That's what I like. He was sullen, sneering, raging inside . . ."

"I'm sure he was." I purred with secret satisfaction.

"But I knew by the way that he insulted everybody and stormed out of the house that I'd soon be seeing him again. And I did. The next day he came to the office and apologized, still sullen, of course, but wanting to make up . . . said he'd had a fight with the girl, as if I didn't know, and could I get him work. So I said you bet I can, and signed him to a five-year representational talent contract. Then I rang up Maddox Motors and got him a job as a mechanic. He was grateful, and showed it, right then and there, on the old four-poster. That chenille bedspread will never be the same again."

"And it was really marvelous?" I was genuinely curious to see how Rusty would perform after my disciplinary session.

"I thought, Myra," Letitia's words were measured and awed, "that he would *kill* me. I have never known anyone so masterful. He threw me on the bed and struck me repeatedly. Yes, *struck* Letitia Van Allen who *never* goes that route but did this time. I'm still black and blue and totally happy, all thanks to you!"

"You exaggerate." Rusty's compensation with Letitia for what he had suffered at my hands will fascinate Randolph. "But did he . . . well, say anything about leaving school, about me?"

"Not a word, except that he was sick of being treated like a kid and wanted to get to work. He won't talk about you at all. Did you ever lay him?"

"Not in the classic way, no. But what does he say about Mary-Ann?"

"That's why I'm calling you. He feels guilty. I can tell. Now, let's put our cards on the table. I want him all to myself as long as possible which won't be very long, since once he starts making a living he'll be off with the cute young chicks, leaving poor old Letitia to her Scotch and casting couch. But for now I'm hanging on to him for dear life. So what do we do to keep Miss Pieface out of our lives?"

I told her exactly how it could be done . . . and will be done tonight! Thanking me profusely, and vowing eternal friendship, Letitia hung up.

# 35

Three in the morning again. Joy and despair, equally mixed, as I watch, hypnotized, the turning statue, and think for the first time how lonely she must be out there, ten times life-size, worshipped but not loved, like me.

As soon as Mary-Ann returned from school, I suggested that we drive down to the beach in my rented Chrysler and watch the sunset. She seemed to like the idea. Though she was plainly fretting over Rusty, she did not mention him once, as we drove along the Pacific Highway, bumper to bumper with the rush-hour crowd as it crawled slowly between the dull sea and the brown crumbly hills of fine shifting dust, forever dropping houses into the sea. This coastal region is quite inhospitable to man. What we have done is colonize the moon, and so are lunatic.

To amuse Mary-Ann, I acted out the entire plot of *Marriage Is a Private Affair.* She was very much amused, particularly when I quoted Parker Tyler to her. We both agreed that his explication of that paradigmatic wartime film is altogether wonderful.

Just as the red-smog sun was vanishing into the olive-drab sea, I turned casually into the private road of the Malibu Beach Colony, a number of opulent beach houses jammed together between road and sea; many are occupied by stars of the first and current (if that is not a contradiction!) magnitude.

"But this is where Miss Van Allen lives!" Until then, Mary-Ann had been indifferent to her surroundings, doubtless conducting some inner dialogue with Rusty even as I spoke of James Craig and the great days.

"Really? Where?" In fact, I did not know which was Letitia's house. Mary-Ann indicated a gray clapboard Provincetown-style house. "Then why don't we drop in and say hello?"

"Oh, no! I couldn't. Not after last time. Not after the way Rusty talked to her. I'd be too uncomfortable."

"Nonsense." I parked in front of the darkened house. The light from the sea was now very faint. "I'm sure she's forgiven him. She's used to artistic temperament. After all, that's her business."

"But he was so awful, and I looked so silly."

"Don't be a goose!" I took her hand and led her to the door and rang the bell. "Besides, this will be good for your career." To this argument, the only response was acquiescence.

From inside the house I could hear a Benny Goodman record (Letitia belongs in fact to the generation to which I belong in spirit). No one, however, answered the doorbell.

"She's out." Mary-Ann was relieved. "Let's go."

"But I hear music. Come on." I opened the front door and led the reluctant Mary-Ann into a large darkened room that looked onto the sea. Silhouetted against the last light of the day, two figures were dancing, intertwined.

According to plan, I switched on the light. Rusty and Letitia leapt apart; they wore bathing suits (marvelously reminiscent of Garfield and Crawford in *Humoresque*).

"What the hell!" exclaimed Letitia, simulating anger.

"Darling, I couldn't be sorrier!" I simulated alarm.

Both Rusty and Mary-Ann were genuinely shocked; but where she was hurt, he was truculent.

It was Mary-Ann who made the first move. "Where," she asked him in a quavering voice, "have you been?"

But Letitia did not allow him to answer. "Come on, children, let's all have a nice drink!" She crossed to the sanctuary of the bar at the end of the room opposite the plate-glass window, black now from the light within.

Rusty simply stared at Mary-Ann. Not once did he look at me. ". . . Then," said Letitia comfortably, "we can sit down and discuss this like adults." (Bette and Miriam in *Old Acquaintance*.) "Who wants what?" But no one answered her.

Then Mary-Ann repeated, "Where have you been all this time?"

To which Rusty responded in a clear hard voice, "What are you doing with *her*?" And he gave me a look of absolute hate.

"Myra's my friend." Mary-Ann's voice was faint.

Letitia gargled some Scotch and then said hoarsely, "Rusty's been staying here while I get him launched over at Fox with this new series. You sure you don't want a drink, honey? Or you, Myra?"

"Are you *living* with this woman?" Mary-Ann was still unable to comprehend the situation.

"Now, dear, don't get upset." Letitia was soothing. "Rusty and I do have a great deal in common but neither one of us would want to hurt you for the world." She gave Rusty a shot of whiskey which he gulped, eyes still on Mary-Ann. "In fact, he was all for telling you this morning but I thought we should wait. Anyway now that the cat's out of the bag . . ."

"It's all my fault, Letitia." I was humble. "The whole thing."

"No, dear. Don't blame yourself. It's probably for the best. Personally I like everything in the open. That's the way I am. And that's why I'm here to tell all the world that I'm proud to be in love with Rusty, and proud that he loves me!"

With a wail, Mary-Ann fled back to the car. When Rusty started to follow her, Letitia's arm darted out and held him back. "She'll be all right. She's got Myra." That stopped the young man. He made no further move to follow the girl.

Then Letitia crossed to me. She was thrilling, every inch of her a great actress on the order of Frances Dee or Ann Dvorak. She took my hands in hers and kissed my cheek. "Be kind to the girl."

"I will, Letitia. You know I will."

"When she's older, she'll understand how these things just happen and that we are all of us simply putty in the hands of the great potter." The metaphor was mixed, but the delivery was bravura. "Rusty and I need each other. That's all there is. A man, a woman . . . What else? It's Kismet." She let go my hands. "Good night, Myra."

I said good night and followed Mary-Ann into the darkness. She was in the car, weeping. I comforted her as best I could which was hardly at all since I am a nervous driver and need both hands on the wheel when driving through traffic, particularly along Sunset Boulevard at night.

Back at the apartment, Mary-Ann recovered sufficiently to finish the bottle of gin. But her mood did not improve. She is shattered. She cannot understand why Rusty has deserted her or what he sees in Letitia. This was of course my cue to point out that for an ambitious young man like Rusty to be taken up by Letitia is a sure way to stardom.

"But he *swore* he'd never do anything like that. He's just not that kind of a boy . . ."

"Apparently he is. I mean, let's face it, he is *living* with her." Since this brought on more tears, as I intended, I took her in my arms. She wept into my neck. Never in my life have I felt so entirely warm and contented.

"Forget him," I whispered into a soft pink ear that smelled of Lux toilet soap.

Suddenly she sat up and dried her eyes. "I could murder him!" Her voice had gone cello with rage.

"Now, now you mustn't be angry with the boy." I was supremely anodyne. "After all, that's the way he is. You can't change people. Just think how lucky you are to have learned all this *now* instead of after you were married, and had children."

"I'll never marry! I hate men." She got shakily to her feet (she was quite drunk), and made her way to the bedroom.

I helped her to undress—for once she really needed help. She was grateful for my attentions which I managed to make discreet, despite the turmoil caused in me whenever those marvelous breasts are unveiled. Then she threw herself onto the bed, and as I pulled off her stockings she pointed her feet like a ballerina. But before I could remove her panties, she pulled the sheet over herself and said, "I'm so tired. The room's spinning around. . . ." Her eyes shut.

I turned out the light and got into bed. Shyly, I put out my hand beneath the sheet and touched the nearer breast. She sighed in her tipsy sleep. "Oh,

Rusty . . ." That was chilling. I took the other breast in my hand, and she woke up. "Oh, Myra! You felt just like Rusty." But she pushed my hand away. "He's gentle, too."

"Gentle?" I recalled what Letitia had said. "I thought he was violent!"

"Whatever gave you that idea?" She mumbled, still half asleep. "It's because he was so gentle I loved him. He never grabs you like other boys. . . ."

If nothing else, I have changed at least one young man's sexual performance, and for the good—at least the good of Letitia. From now on Rusty will continue to take out his hatred of me on other women, never realizing to what extent he is really pleasing them. It is ironic what I have inadvertently accomplished. Wanting to tame for all time the archetypal male, I have created something ten times as masculine in the classic sense as what I started with. All in all, not the desired effect but perhaps, like Columbus, I have stumbled on a new world.

I caressed Mary-Ann's breasts, which she allowed . . . but only for a moment; then she turned away from me. "You are an angel, Myra, and I really love you, I do. But I just can't . . . you know . . ."

"Of course I know, dear." And I do; yet I am still profoundly hurt at being rejected.

"If only you were a man or there was a man like you, I'd really fall, I would—but not like this, even with you."

This froze me, turned me to stone.

But why should I care? After all, the silkiness of her body, the tautness of the skin, the firmness of the flesh is neither more nor less appetizing to me than Rusty's body since, in the final analysis (where I am now marooned), a girl is neither more nor less attractive than a boy and I have, God knows, possessed the boy. Yet taking all this into account, there is something about Mary-Ann's wholeness that excites me. There is a mystery to be plumbed, though whether or not it is in her or in myself or in us both I do not know. I did extract a certain pleasure from stroking the body that Rusty had loved, but that victory has already begun to pale. He no longer exists for me. Only the girl he loved matters.

Fortunately, she was compassionate enough to allow me to cradle her in my arms until she fell asleep. Then when she began softly to snore, obedient to her wishes, I got out of bed and returned to the living room where now I sit at the card table, drinking gin and tonic, writing these lines, too disturbed for sleep.

My head is spinning with fatigue. I must have Mary-Ann but only if she wants me, and that is impossible as things are now. I've just tried to ring Randolph but he gave instructions to the motel operator that he was not to be awakened until morning, the bastard! He knew that I would need to talk to him tonight. Obviously Disneyland was too much for him.

# 36

Buck's office. I sit at his desk. Randolph sits in the big chair beneath the portrait of Elvis Presley. Buck and his lawyer have gone into the next room to take a telephone call from New York.

As soon as they were out of the room, Randolph wanted to talk but I motioned for him to be quiet. The room is bugged, like everything out here. So Randolph now sits wheezing softly, chewing the stem of his pipe and staring out the window. I write these lines for something to do.

We've shaken them, no doubt of that. But I'm still not certain whether or not they will call our bluff.

Randolph presented them with a signed affidavit, duly notarized, swearing that he had witnessed my wedding to Myron in Monterrey, Mexico. Up until the very last moment I thought I would have trouble with Randolph. Fortunately his greed finally convinced him that he should do the right thing, despite the risk involved. Nevertheless, he is nervous as a cat. So am I.

Buck was true to form. "It was a real nice gesture of your'n, Doc, to come out here and help out this li'l ol' gal." More than ever was Buck, revoltingly, the Singin' Shootin' Cowboy, so inferior in every way to Hoot Gibson. "Naturally we want to do the right thing by her."

"Then cut the cackle," I said firmly, "and hand over the three hundred fifty G's which all of our lawyers now agree is my adjusted share of the property."

"Certainly, Mrs. Breckinridge," said Charlie Flagler Junior. "Just as soon as we get final word, any minute now, from our New York office which will like clear up one final detail, it's all yours because," he turned to Randolph, "we are not about to question the probity of such a well-known person and author like Dr. Montag."

"Thank you," I answered for Randolph, who looked gloomy as he always does when someone praises him (his father withheld all praise during Randolph's formative years and so today he can never accept any compliment without suspecting that it is loaded, as this one of course was).

"Right here," said Buck, holding up a check written on the Bank of America, Beverly Hills Branch, "I've got the check, all made out to you and everything."

Both Randolph and I felt a good deal better at the sight of the loot: three hundred and fifty thousand dollars is more than enough to finance me for the next few years while I finish Myron's work and begin my own. Yes, I have decided to make an investigation in *depth* of the problem of communication in the post-McLuhan world. Each day that I spend in the company of the students makes me more than ever aware that a new world is being born without a single reliable witness except me. I alone have the intuition as well as the profound grasp of philosophy and psychology to trace for man not only what he is but what he must become, once he has ceased to be confined to a single sexual role, to a single person . . . once he has become free to blend with others, to exchange personalities with both men and women, to play out the most elaborate of dreams in a world where there will soon be no limits to the human spirit's play. As I have been goddess, so others can be whatever they want in this vast theatre we call the world where all bodies and all minds will one day be at the disposal of everyone, and no one will read books for that is a solitary activity like going to the bathroom alone (it is the proliferation of private bathrooms, which has, more than anything else, created modern man's sense of alienation from others of his kind: our ancestors bathed and shat together and, all in all, relished the sharing of their common natural functions) or like making love alone if there are others available to share the body's pleasures. I see this new world whose prophetess I am as clearly as I see this page on which I scribble random notes while waiting for Buck and Charlie Flagler Junior to return from their telephoning in the next office.

I have made up my mind to continue teaching here, if Buck will have me . . . which I doubt. Yet I must make the effort to charm him, if it is not too late, for not only am I able to observe and learn from the students but they in turn profit from me. Without the Academy, I would have to invent an equivalent, a place in which to shape the minds of the young, particularly the boys who crave discipline. Yet, oddly enough, since that night of nights in the infirmary all my desires to dominate the male have been—if not satisfied—in abeyance, a true breakthrough, according to Randolph, though he still believes that I went too far and may have damaged Rusty's capacity to love women, to which I responded, "That is exactly what I wanted to do, to teach him fear."

"But why? Why not teach him love?" There are times when Randolph is singularly dense.

"Because only through a traumatic shock, through terrifying and humiliating him, could I hope to change his view of what is proper masculine behavior. To keep him from breeding, and so adding to the world's overpopulation, I was forced to violate everything he has been taught to regard as sacred, including the sanctity of his tiny back door. . . ."

Randolph looked suddenly queasy. "Please, Myra, you know how any *explicit* reference to the anal upsets me. The fault is mine, or weakness I should say," he added quickly, anticipating one of my sharp rejoinders. "But tell me, is there any evidence that your tormenting of him has had any effect at all, good or bad?"

"He quarreled with Mary-Ann . . ."

"A passing fit of ill-temper . . ."

"Not passing. He's left her for Letitia Van Allen." Candid as I always am with Randolph, I have not yet told him the entire story of my maneuvering to keep Rusty and Mary-Ann apart. There is evidence that Rusty is still in love with Mary-Ann. Fortunately she will not, in her present mood, have anything to do with him and I am certain that as long as she is with me I can prolong that mood for quite some time. Also, the fact that Mary-Ann is living with the woman who raped him will unconsciously identify her with me in Rusty's mind; if nothing else, this connection should help to maintain the current distance between the lovers. "And from what Letitia tells me, his lovemaking has been dramatically improved as a result of what I did to him."

"How would you know? He never made love to you."

"Mary-Ann has told me that he was always extremely gentle with her . . . she has a childhood trauma and cannot bear rough lovemaking and so, in time, will be drawn to women who are gentle. But with Letitia, he is a rampaging bull, knocking her about and otherwise getting back at me through her, to her delight of course."

"Interesting" was all that Randolph had to say on the subject. But I can tell that he is impressed at what I have accomplished even though, being a Jew and a dentist, he can never wholeheartedly accept my new order for the human race since the *fluidity* which I demand of the sexes is diametrically opposed to Mosaic solidity. Yet I am right, for it is demonstrably true that desire can take as many shapes as there are containers. Yet what one pours into those containers is always the same inchoate human passion, entirely lacking in definition until what holds it shapes it. So let us break the world's pots, and allow the stuff of desire to flow and intermingle in one great viscous sea. . . .

The door just opened. I keep my head down, continuing to write, pretending to be occupied and not at all eager. From the corner of my eye I can see two human sections approach. One section is brown (Buck) and one is blue (Charlie Flagler Junior). I don't look up. Buck says: "Myron Breckinridge is *not* dead."

**BUCK LONER REPORTS—**
Recording Disc No. 808—
1 April

Oh God I dont know if I can stand it dont know if I can go on its just not worth it reminder cancel masseuse for rest of week period paragraph they just left I dont know what to do not that theres anything I can do caught by the short hairs by the fickle finger of fate we thought we had them when this detective in New York came up with absolute proof that that fag nephew of mine was not dead because there never was any death certificate issued and New York City is a place where you cant screw around with that sort of thing unlike down old Mexico way well Myra who had been sitting at my desk pretending to write letters sat up real smart and said quote I say hes dead and that means hes dead to which statement Charlie Flagler Junior replies thinking he has got her over the barrel at last not knowing its his turn inside the barrel quote its not what you say Mrs Breckinridge its what the police and the city records say and they say your husband is alive and so his will cant be pro bated unquote well she smiled this funny smile and says quote the body was never found thats true but he was drowned while cruising the Staten Island ferry unquote there is says Flagler Junior not one iota of evidence he is dead so we are not paying you one single penny until your husband shows up to collect his share of Mrs Gertrude Percy Breckinridges estate unquote then Myra looks at that fat Jew doctor who is blowing ashes all over my brand new wall to wall carpeting and she says I quote Randolph I guess this is the moment of truth unquote and he nods and allows that maybe shes right and then so help me god she stands up and hikes up her dress and pulls down her goddam panties and shows us this scar where cock and balls should be and says quote Uncle Buck I am Myron Breckin ridge unquote period paragraph I like to have fainted at the sight not to mention the news Flagler Junior just stood there his mouth wide open then Myra or Myron says quote Randolph can testify to all this because he was my analyst before the operation which killed Myron and gave birth to me Myra unquote the Doc agreed saying I quote I should also add that I never approved of this operation but Myron was my friend as well as patient and so when I saw that there was nothing I could do to talk him out of this extreme gesture I arranged for the best surgeon in Copenhagen to perform the operation two years ago this spring unquote by then Flagler Junior had got back some of his cool I dont he said quote believe one word of this story so whoever you are you may have been a man once but how do we know that that man was Buck Loners nephew Myron question mark unquote well that bitch was ready for that one she opens her handbag with a smirk and says I quote we had two plans Uncle Buck one was to get you to accept me as Myrons widow the other was to prove to you that I used to be Myron here are Myrons fingerprints from the FBI when he was finger printed as a small boy while visiting the nations capital with a Boy Scout troop you are free at any time to check these prints with my own unquote well thats the ball game I said to Flagler Junior who still made noises about how did we know the prints were the same and not just another bluff so I said I accept the fact that this is my nephew Myron with his balls cut off like a year old steer God help us all end quote why Uncle Buck said that thing quote I am going to kiss you unquote and Buck Loner who has never been kissed by a man except by Leo Carrillo in a flick and is all male as the East West Home Massage Service can almost daily testify allowed himself to be kissed by that goddam thing that creep that capon oh screams Myron after he has got his goddam lipstick all over my ear I knew wed be great friends one day ever since I used to see every single picture you ever made and wrote you all those fan letters yes I said I sure remember those letters and I told Gertrude that you were obviously bright as they come so now Myron no no no it says to me Im Myra Myron is dead as a doornail why when I lost those ugly things it was like a ship losing its anchor and Ive been sailing ever since havent I Randolph free as a bird and perfectly happy in being the most extraordinary woman in the world unquote well what can you say to that question mark I said nothing but just handed her the check which she put in her handbag Ill cash it this afternoon he she said oh he she was bright as can be all smiles now that the moolah has been handed over but then on top of that she delivers the whammy quote you know Uncle Buck we make a wonderful team together you and I and so I thought if you didnt mind that Id just keep on teaching here for the rest of the year after all youve got to admit that Ive done well and now that Letitia Van Allen is my best girl friend I can help the students achieve real stardom end quote well I tried to be as polite as possible under the circum stances and so I said quote Myron Myra that is a wonderful thing of you to offer me your services here and theres no doubt about it but that youre a crackerjack teacher a little strict maybe and sometimes maybe a mite too sharp in what you say but all in all youve been a real asset to the Academy as I am the first to admit only thing is weve got two former teachers return ing who have like tenure and one wants to take over Posture and the other Empathy well she was not about to be conned I quote apparently what youre trying to say Myra said in this awful low voice she sometimes uses that now I recognize is a mans voice quote is that you dont want me here at all end quote now Myron Myra I said thats not true only with these two coming back but I was interrupted again when Myron came up to me and grabbed me by the collar that little bastard is strong as they come ball less or not listen Buck he says tough as nails quote if you dont give me a job I am going to announce to the world that Buck Loners nephew became his niece two years ago in Copenhagen and that will fix your wagon in this town unqoute thats blackmail says Flagler Junior but nobody paid him any mind OK Myra I said you win end quote then she was all smiles again I knew youd do the right thing Uncle Buck and I can help you I really can Jesus God what am I going to do now with this mad freak taking over my life and running the Academy that I built up on dreams and hopes which she believes in destroying by telling everybody whats wrong with him if I could get away with it I would kill her strike that period paragraph

# 37

Tomorrow is moving day. I have rented a house just above Santa Monica Canyon. A superb view of the Pacific Palisades somewhat compensates for the inevitable view of that despicable body of water, drowning the horizon to the west and all Asia.

So now I sit for the last time looking out upon the giant turning woman who holds her sombrero like a benediction over those who pass beneath her on the Strip.

I am not at all certain what to do about Mary-Ann. I know that I want her to live with me always. I know that I want to possess her entirely, body as well as mind; yet I puzzle myself, and Randolph has been no help at all. He has, incidentally, decided to stay on for one more week but of course that one week will become a lifetime. He is made for Hollywood and Hollywood is made for him, particularly now that he has discovered the Will Wright Ice Cream Parlors.

This morning Randolph again challenged my theory of sex. He maintains that the desire to possess another person's body simply as a means of achieving power is only one part of an infinitely complex response. To a point, I agree with him. It is of course true that, power aside, a certain amount of tenderness is necessary in human relations. Myron never understood this and it is possible that no man really can. Yet we women are instinctively tender, even when we are achieving total dominion. As a woman, I was touched by Rusty's tears. I even experienced a maternal warmth while tidying up his poor bloody bottom. That is woman's role, to make the wound and then to heal it. Not for nothing do the earliest of myths depict us as Fate itself, attending the male from swaddling clothes to winding sheet. But there has been nothing in my experience which has quite prepared me for Mary-Ann. Of course she is unique in her charm, her beauty, her womanliness. I have never known a girl who could arouse in me so many conflicting emotions. Even the uterine mysteries, so deplored by Myron, are now for me the be-all and end-all, the center to which one must return and not simply in search of Rusty's phallic track but for the sake of the journey itself to the very source of life.

We had dinner tonight with Letitia at Scandia, an excellent restaurant on the Strip where Scandinavian food is served to a most elegant clientele, among whom I counted four bona fide stars of the Forties.

It took me an entire day to talk Mary-Ann into having dinner with Letitia, whom she regards as "the other woman." She only agreed when I assured her that Letitia was the one being used by Rusty, not the other way around. Letitia and I had agreed on this approach when I saw her briefly this afternoon at the office. The poor woman's arm was in a sling but otherwise she was in splendid form. "*He* sprained it last night!" she exclaimed fondly. "I thought he was going to break every bone in my body!"

"And you really enjoy that?" It seemed to me incredible that a fellow goddess could endure such treatment from a mere man.

"I never knew what sex was until that little bastard moved in. Four, five times a night on the floor, on the beach, in the damned bathtub!" She looked misty at the recollection. My own experience of that small limp rose was obviously not the entire truth.

Then Letitia congratulated me on my appointment as co-director of the Academy. The announcement appeared in all the trade papers last Monday and so I am now, to my amusement, a figure in the world of show biz—which of course has only the most shadowy of connections with the world of mythic films.

"Yes, Uncle Buck and I seem to be getting on better." Buck has, in fact, completely surrendered and for the past week I have been running the Academy. As a result, morale is infinitely higher at every level. Even Dark Laughter found creative some of my suggestions for including Dionysian elements in his Atavistic Rhythm class. Morning, noon and night I am Rosalind Russell, efficient girl executive, and the students are the better for my constant brisk encouragement.

I came to the point. "As you know, Mary-Ann is living with me. Now don't smile like that, nothing dykey has happened or will. But I do feel responsible for the poor kid. And that's why I'd like to know just what Rusty is going to do about her."

"Not a damned thing if I can help it." Letitia was hard as nails. "I'm hanging on to that stud for as long as I can."

"That suits me. But what about him?"

"Mr. Martinson!" Letitia gave a laugh which started out to be tinkling but quickly became not unlike the minatory rattle of a leper's bell. I should have known that Letitia would be as clever as I. She, too, has Rusty by the balls. "We're on good terms, Mr. Martinson and I, and he thinks if anybody can make something of the boy it will be me."

"So if Rusty decides to stray . . ."

"Mr. Martinson will bring him back." Letitia sighed contentedly. Then she frowned. "But there's no doubt about it, he's still interested in Mary-Ann, even though he can't get over the fact that she's living with you. He absolutely hates you, darling. Why? He won't tell me."

"And never will." I daresay I looked as pleased as I felt. "Anyway, that's all in the past. Now I want you to have dinner with Mary-Ann and me and I want you to convince her that Rusty was just using you and that now he's off with someone else."

Letitia wondered if this was a wise tactic. I assured her that it was, and I was right. Our dinner at Scandia was a success. Mary-Ann got tiddly on snaps and, all in all, we were like three schoolgirls on the town. Mary-Ann soon forgave Letitia. "I understand what you must've felt. I mean, he's the most wonderful boy there is and I don't suppose any woman could resist him."

"I tried," said Letitia solemnly, stroking her sprained arm in its sling. "God knows I tried."

"I guess it was too much for me to hope to keep him." Mary-Ann was close to tears but we both did our best to cheer her up, assuring her of future boyfriends not to mention the prospect of stardom which Letitia dangled before our eyes, a dream made all the more palpable by the sudden appearance of a major television personality who embraced Letitia and complained, "You never call me!" Mary-Ann and I were duly impressed by this public display of Letitia's greatness, and flattered that we are now her friends.

After saying good night to Letitia, Mary-Ann and I came back to the apartment. We are both a little sad at the thought of leaving our first home together. But we are also excited at the thought of the new house, particularly the soundproofed music room where Mary-Ann will practice. She has become, suddenly, grimly ambitious. She means to be a major star and if she does not attain at least the magnitude of Susanna Foster my name is not Myra Breckinridge. In fact, according to Miss Cluff, there is a thrilling new quality to Mary-Ann's voice which "I'm sure staying with you and receiving a *woman's* love and guidance has given her." Miss Cluff giggled despite my coldness, for I do not want her—or anybody—to think that either of us is one of *les girls.* I must protect Mary-Ann. I must also protect myself since I can never rule out the possibility that some day I shall find that perfect man who will totally resist me and so win my love, and hand in marriage.

I find that lately I've been prone to the most sickening sentimental reveries, usually involving Mary-Ann though sometimes a faceless man is at my side and we live together in an enchanted cottage filled with the pitter-pat of little feet or I should say paws since I detest children but have lately come to adore dogs. First thing Monday, Mary-Ann and I are going to the kennel and buy two wirehaired terriers, "Hers" and "Hers"—in memory of Asta, that sweet dog who was in the *Thin Man* series with William Powell and Myrna Loy.

Tonight our love took on a new dimension. Mary-Ann now undresses in front of me. She then lies on the bed, eyes tight shut, lovely breasts fallen back upon themselves; and as I trace their contours with a finger, causing them to tighten visibly, she sighs with pleasure which is the signal for me to begin with my hand the exploration of that pale dimpled belly which curves its secret way to the blonde silky thatch so often penetrated by Rusty but still forbidden to me. In fact, every time my hand approaches that secret and for me so beautifully enticing and *central* reality, the cave of origin, she turns away and whispers, "No."

But tonight she was subtly changed. I don't know whether it was the snaps at Scandia or the cold bright charm of the powerful Letitia or the knowledge that Rusty would never be hers again but whatever it was, she allowed my hand to rest a long moment on the entrance to the last fantasy which is of course the first reality. Ecstatically, I fingered the lovely shape whose secret I must know or die, whose maze I must thread as best I can or go mad for if I am to prevail I must soon come face to face with the Minotaur of dreams and confound him in his charneled lair, and in our heroic coupling know the last mystery: total power achieved not over man, not over woman but over the heraldic beast, the devouring monster, the maw of creation itself that spews us forth and sucks us back into the black oblivion where stars are made and energy waits to be born in order to begin once more the cycle of destruction and creation at whose apex now I stand, once man, now woman, and soon to be privy to what lies beyond the uterine door, the mystery of creation that I mean to shatter with the fierce thrust of a will that alone separates me from the nothing of eternity; and as I have conquered the male, absorbed and been absorbed by the female, I am at last outside the human scale, and so may render impotent even familiar banal ubiquitous death whose mouth I see smiling at me with moist coral lips between the legs of my beloved girl who is the unwitting instrument of victory, and the beautiful fact of my life's vision made all too perfect flesh.

When at last she pulled away from me, she seemed almost reluctant, as though she wanted me to continue and achieve for her that orgasm which tonight I could sense was near. "Myra, don't. It spoils it."

"Darling, whatever you want." I have learned restraint, unlike Myron who could not be deterred from the object of his lust by even a teeth-rattling fist in his poor face. But Myron was tortured by having been attached to those male genitals which are linked to a power outside the man who sports them or, to be precise, they sport the man for they are peculiarly willful and separate and it is not for nothing that the simple boy so often says of his erection, partly as a joke but partly as a frightening fact, "He's got a head of his own." Indeed *he* has a head of his own and twice I have punished that head. Once by a literal decapitation, killing Myron so that Myra might be born and then, symbolically, by torturing and mocking Rusty's sex in order to avenge Myron for the countless times that he had been made victim by that mitred one-eyed beast, forever battering blindly at any orifice, seeking to scatter wide the dreaded seed that has already so filled up the world with superfluous people that our end is now at hand: through war and famine and the physical decadence of a race whose extinction is not only inevitable but, to my mind, desirable . . . for after me what new turn can the human take? Once I have comprehended the last mystery I shall be free to go without protest, full of wisdom, into night, happy in the knowledge that, above all men, I existed totally. Let the dust take me when the adventure's done and I shall make that dust glitter for all eternity with my marvelous fury. Meanwhile, I must change the last generation of man. I must bring back Eden. And I can, I am certain, for if there is a god in the human scale, I am she.

And so, unlike Myron, I am able to be loving and gentle. I am able to hold Mary-Ann in my arms as a mother cradles a child or as I hold a fox terrier puppy who has taken my fancy.

"I love being with you—like this," she said tonight, eyes shut, smiling.

"I love it, too." I was simple. "It's all I want, making you happy." I squeezed her bare shoulders; our breasts touched, teasingly. Mine are even larger than hers, filled with silicone, the result of a new process discovered in France and not always successful in its application (recently a French stripper died when the silicone was injected by mistake into an artery). I was fortunate, however, and no one, not even a trained physician, can tell that my beautiful firm breasts are not the real thing.

Shyly, Mary-Ann once said, "They're just super, Myra! I bet the boys were really after you in high school." An amusing thought since, in those days, it was I who was after the boys. At fourteen Myron vowed that he would, in one way or another, extract the essence of every good-looking boy in school and he succeeded in one hundred and one cases over a three-year period, a time in his life which he used to refer to as the Scheherazade phase, the hundred and one nights—or possibly "flights" is the better word to describe what he did with those birdlike objects whose thrust so fascinated him but so disgusts me, for I have got past that crude *obvious* instrument of procreation to the deep center where all is veiled, and purest magic.

But Mary-Ann is making progress; her admiration of my body is not entirely aesthetic . . . but then the body in question is, if I may say so, unusually lovely, the result of the most dedicated of plastic surgeons who allowed me, at my request, to remain conscious during all stages of my transformation, even though I was warned that I might be seriously traumatized in the process.

But I was not. Quite the contrary. I was enthralled, delighted, fascinated (of course the anesthetic had a somewhat intoxicating effect). And when, with one swift movement of the scalpel, the surgeon freed me from the detested penis, I amazed everyone by beginning to sing, I don't know why,

"I'll be seeing you" . . . hardly a fitting song since the point to the exercise is that I would *not* be seeing it or any of its equivalents, except for that of the tortured Rusty, ever again; at least not in the way Myron saw such things.

Nevertheless, I was elated, and have not for one moment regretted my decision to be unique. That my plans have lately gone somewhat awry is the sort of risk one must take if life is to be superb. For instance, I had always believed that between the operation, on the one hand, and the rape of someone like Rusty on the other, I would become Woman Triumphant, exercising total power over men as men once exerted that same power over Myron and still do over the usual woman. But the very literalness of my victory deprived me of the anticipated glory. To my astonishment, I have now lost all interest in men. I have simply gone past them, as if I were a new creation, a mutant diverging from original stock to become something quite unlike its former self or any self known to the race. All that I want now in the way of human power is to make Mary-Ann love me so that I might continue to love her—even without possessing her—to the end of my days.

Imagine my consternation when, once again, she said what she truly felt (and what I have known all along but refused to let myself admit even to myself): "If you were only a man, Myra, I would love you so!"

Of course the shock of the anticipated is always more intense than that of the unexpected. I let her go, as though her cool body had turned suddenly to flame. "Love is not always a matter of sex," I said weakly.

"Oh, I know. And I do love you, as you are. I even like it when you touch me, up to a point," she added judiciously, "but it's really only with a boy I can let myself go. That's the way I am."

"Rusty?"

She shut her eyes, frowning with recollected pain. "No. That's finished. But someone like him." She sighed. "And there aren't many."

"Not many!" I was tactless, and harsh. "The garages of America are crowded with Rustys."

She shook her head. "No. He *is* special. Most boys grab. He doesn't. He's so sweet in bed, and that's what I like. I can't stand the other. I never could. That first boy almost turned me off for good, in high school. He was like a maniac, all over me!" She shuddered at the memory. "In a funny way," she said, "you remind me of Rusty, the way you touch me."

As I write these lines at the card table, facing the Château Marmont and the solemnly turning chorine, I feel the tears rising. What am I to do?

Randolph has been useless. This morning I met him at Will Wright's on the Strip, near Larue's. He was already halfway through a double chocolate burnt-almond and pistachio sundae, gaining the sort of oral gratification that, were he not a puritan Jew, a cock might have provided, with far fewer calories. But he is hopeless. His first and only marriage ended after one year and though he has not confided in me what went wrong, I suspect that he was inadequate if not impotent. Since then, as far as I know, only the theory of sex interests him; the real thing causes him a profound distress which he relieves with food.

"You must tell her everything, if you love her," was his profound advice, as he munched on three maraschino cherries.

"I can't."

"Why not? You wish to exert power over her . . ."

"Only that she may exert it over me . . ."

"So power is intrasitive as well as transitive? Then you are clearly moving into a new phase."

"Whatever the phase, I don't know what to do. If I tell her that I used to be Myron, I destroy Myra . . ."

"Not a bad idea."

I was furious. "You always preferred Myron to me, didn't you?" I let him have it. "And I know why. You were in love with him, you God-damned closet-queen!"

But in my fury I had misplayed my hand for this is exactly the sort of scene Randolph delights in. Carefully he put down his spoon, licked his chops and said, "That's very interesting, what you say. Now tell me exactly: why do you feel that friendship must invariably have an *overt* sexual connotation when your own experience . . ."

"Darling Randolph, why don't you go fuck yourself? It would be an act of some mercy, and therapeutic, too."

There is nothing more satisfactory than to be at last entirely free of one's analyst, and I am rid of mine. The end occurred when I found myself deeply resenting having to pay him forty-two thousand five hundred dollars for perjuring himself when, as things turned out, I didn't need his help at all.

Unfortunately Randolph chooses to interpret my harsh dismissal as a new symptom of neurosis. "We're making splendid progress," he exclaimed, pig's eyes gleaming with excitement. "Now let's go back a moment. The emotional trigger, as usual, is your fear that I preferred Myron to you . . ."

"Look, I couldn't care less who or what you prefer. Your feelings are your own problem. My only concern in this world is not you and your gluttony (a sex life must be ruled out), but Mary-Ann . . ."

"Wonderful! This is the big breakthrough we've been waiting for! By saying that I have no sex life . . ."

". . . is apt to leave me if she knows that I used to be a man . . ."

". . . you must be able to visualize . . ."

". . . and I couldn't bear that. Yet if I don't tell her . . ."

". . . me having sexual relations with Myron. Now then, how exactly do you see me in the act? Active or passive . . ."

". . . I'll lose her to the first light-fingered stud who comes her way . . ."

". . . would I be oral in my desires or anal or . . ."

"From the way you eat, oral! Randolph, you disgust me, you really do!" Like all analysts, Radolph is interested only in himself. In fact, I have often thought that the analyst should pay the patient for allowing himself to be used as a captive looking-glass. "I take it all back," I said curtly. "I didn't mean a word of it."

"*Consciously* this may be true, but to have made the accusation you did reveals . . ."

I left him and crossed the street to where my car was parked, nearly getting myself run over by one of those maniac drivers who make walking so perilous in the Greater Los Angeles area. But then the pedestrian is not favored hereabouts. In fact, the police are quick to stop and question anyone found on foot in a residential district since it is a part of California folklore that only the queer or criminal walk; the good drive cars that fill the air with the foul odor of burning fossils, and so day by day our lungs fill up with the stuff of great ferns and dinosaurs who thus revenge themselves upon their successors, causing us to wither and die prematurely, as did they.

As I watch the Las Vegas chorine turn and turn, I find myself thinking, not unnaturally, of *Turnabout* (1937), with Adolphe Menjou, Carole Landis and adorable John Hubbard; and I ponder that brilliant plot in which husband and wife exchange personalities through the magic of the talking film (he speaks with her voice, she with his) and, as Parker Tyler puts it so well, we have, as a result, "a realization of ancient magical belief in the guise of modern make-believe, and the same ambiguity and ambivalence of spiritual essences are revealed that modern psychology, especially psychoanalysis, has uncovered in present-day civilization."

My worn copy of Tyler's *Magic and Myth of the Movies* is always open before me when I write, and I constantly search the familiar text for guidance. But tonight I can find nothing more comforting than Tyler's suggestion (referring to *Turnabout* and the Warsaw Art Players' film *The Dybbuk,* which also deals with the idea of possession) "that by *imitating* the female the male believes that he *becomes* the female, thus automatically and unconsciously practicing the imitative variety of sympathetic magic." Of course magic is involved at the beginning of my quest. But I have since crossed the shadow line, made magic real, created myself. But to what end? For what true purpose have I smashed the male principle only to become entrapped by the female? Something must soon be done or I am no longer triumphant, no longer the all-conquering Myra Breckinridge . . . whisper her name! Sympathetic magic must be made. But how?

## 38

I must record my situation exactly. They say that I am under sedation. That means I have been drugged. They are holding me against my will. But I shall outwit them.

The one who calls himself Dr. Mengers has already fallen into my trap. When I asked for this notebook, he granted my wish. "Excellent therapy," he said, assuming a bedside manner that even a child could detect was false. He is with the CIA. They all are. He pretended to take my pulse. "Much better today. Very much better. It was touch and go for a while, you know. But you've pulled through with flying colors!"

I played my part with magnificent cunning. I fell in with the game, pretended that I had been ill, made my voice even weaker than it is. "Tell me, Doctor," I quavered, "how long have I been here, like this?"

"Ten days. Out cold," he said with all-too-obvious satisfaction.

For ten days they have held me captive! But now for reasons of their own, they are bringing me around, and that is their mistake for when it comes to a contest of wills, I am bound to win, even in my present hallucinated condition.

"When can I get up?" I whispered.

"Not for a week at least. As you see, you are in a plaster cast from neck to ankles. But your arms are free." He pinched me hard above the elbow. "Does that hurt?"

He is a sadist, too. I refused to give him the satisfaction of crying out. "Certainly not," I said, and he frowned and made a note in a little black code book. Obviously I am a tougher nut to crack than he thought. Yet what I fear is not torture but the various drugs and serums that they have obviously been giving me from the look of my arms, which are blue, black and yellow with bruises and punctures. Not even a woman as brave and unique as I can hope to withstand an all-out chemical assault upon the brain and nervous system.

What have I told them? Did I reveal the secret of human destiny to the enemy? I pray not. But only a careful questioning of my captors will be able to set my mind at rest. If I *have* told all, then there is no hope for the coming breakthrough. They will do to me what they did to Mossadegh in Iran and Arbenz in Guatemala.

We were then joined by the "nurse." Even for the CIA she was a poor actress, obviously recruited at the last minute, assuming that she is not the mistress of some Pentagon bureaucrat. She approached me with a thermometer as though she were uncertain as to how to go about placing the object in question in my mouth. She was plainly nervous and ill at ease. But then the thermometer was drugged and it is possible that she was experiencing a momentary twinge of conscience, quickly dispelled by the "doctor," who had been watching her with ill-disguised irritation.

"Go on, take the temperature. Please," he said in an irritable voice.

"But he bit my finger last time," she said plaintively, as I allowed the thermometer to be placed beneath my tongue.

"But Mr. Breckinridge was delirious at the time. Now he's quite normal."

"What do you mean *Mr.* Breckinridge?" I asked, suddenly aware of the shift in sex, and nearly swallowing the thermometer in the process. They exchanged a conspiratorial look, much like the one Oswald gave Ruby on television seconds before he was struck down by his supposed friend and accomplice.

"Of course, *Miss* Breckinridge," said the "doctor" soothingly, readjusting the thermometer. I made no further complaint although I prefer the honorific title of Mrs., to which my uniqueness entitles me.

"I still have an ugly scar," said the "nurse," holding up a bandaged hand in an effort to engage the "doctor's" sympathy. I was pleased with myself: apparently I had fought hard to retain my mind's integrity so rudely violated by these drug-administering agents of imperialism.

"Now, Nurse, we must try and understand what he . . . what she has had to go through these last few days."

"What *we've* had to go through," grumbled the "nurse," at the very least the mistress of an Assistant Secretary of Defense, so cheeky is she.

Her superior was coldly unsympathetic (obviously a division in their ranks; one that I shall exploit). "I suggest we tend to our job, Nurse, and take the rough with the smooth."

"Yes, Doctor." She tried to sound chastened but failed. Then she withdrew the thermometer and said, "Normal," and looked disappointed. It is quite evident that they want me to die of what appear to be natural causes. Fortunately, my body will no more surrender to their poison than my mind has. I shall outwit them all, and prevail! If they mean to kill me they will have to take direct action, and so leave clues.

"Good news!" The charlatan beamed, writing in his code book. "We've passed the danger mark and I'm pleased as all get-out!"

Get out, I thought, smiling bravely, like . . . what's her name in . . . my memory seems to have left me. The drugs must have been enormously powerful. Or did they use electroshock treatments? That would explain my condition like who was it in . . . I can't recall that film's title either. Whole sections of memory are missing. But I shall regain them: it is simply a matter of will. Meanwhile, they are certain that I can find no way of getting a message to the outside world but in this, as in everything, they underestimate me.

They are gone now. I am sitting up in a metal bed placed at the center of a small cell disguised as a hospital room. There is even the awful odor of disinfectant to lend verisimilitude to the otherwise ridiculous decor. Any fool can see that this is a prison, not a hospital. Why else are the venetian blinds shut?

I am encased in what appears to be plaster of Paris from neck to ankle. Inside this carapace I can hardly move. My legs feel as if they had just been asleep and now, tingling, are coming to life again. I can wiggle my feet: that is something, and my poor arms, though discolored, are intact and I suppose, in time, I shall be able to peel off this plaster straitjacket . . . unless of course they keep such careful watch over me that any attempt at freeing myself will be thwarted. For the moment, it is my intelligence upon which I must rely.

I cannot recall the name of Lana Turner's first film! Something *has* been done to my brain. I know that I am Myra Breckinridge whom no man may possess, but what else? Film titles are lost to me. The past is a jumble. I must not panic.

What's the last thing I can recall before they captured me? This is difficult. Santa Monica. The mesa? No. Not mesa. A word like it. Canyon. The Santa Monica Canyon. A winding road. Sun in my eyes as I drive. Alone? Yes, alone. No one is in the car. A dog? Yes, a wirehaired fox terrier puppy. Sitting on my lap. Sun in my eyes. That means it was late afternoon and I am coming *from* Hollywood to the sea—oh, the mind of Myra Breckinridge can never be broken or too long deranged, even by the CIA!

I park the car in front of a small house, green with white shutters, overlooking the ugly ocean. Fortress? Canal? Pilings? Palisades . . . that's it: Pacific Palisades are visible. It's our house. Ours? Who else? No. I'm going too fast now and my head is throbbing. Sodium pentothal obviously.

I park the car on the main road. I get out of the car. I stand and wait for the dog to jump out. The dog does. He runs up the driveway. He stops at the door of the house. I start to follow then

## 39

Struck by a hit-and-run automobile, I have been unconscious for ten days. I sustained twelve broken ribs, one cracked femur, one fractured shin, a dozen torn and bruised ligaments, as well as a concussion of the brain. Only my powerful *physical* organism was able to save me, according to Dr. Mengers, who has been an absolute saint during my ordeal.

"Frankly we didn't think you were going to make it," he said earlier this evening. "But the first moment I saw you I said to myself: that one's going to put up a good fight, and you did. The night nurse is still home, convalescing."

"Night nurse? What did I do?"

"Bit her arm to the bone."

We had a merry laugh about that. Then I spoke seriously. "I'm worried about my memory, Doctor. For instance, I can recall the stars of *The Uninvited* (Ray Milland, Ruth Hussey, Donald Crisp) and I know that Charles Brackett produced the film for Paramount in 1944 but who . . . *who* was the director?"

"Lewis Allen." He did not pause to think.

I was momentarily distracted from my own problems at finding a doctor who knew so much about movies. Apparently he too had seen every film made between 1931 and 1947. He was even, for a short time, Roland Young's physician. We exchanged movie lore excitedly, and as we did, I found myself recalling more and more details which I had thought were forever lost to me. But not until I listed every film that Edith Head had worked on did Dr. Mengers show his delight. "You see? You *can* remember. It's just a matter of practice. Nothing serious has happened to your mind. With the sort of concussion you sustained, it is like having the wind knocked out of you . . . takes time to catch your breath. Don't worry. You're doing fine."

I was relieved, to say the least. I have every confidence in this marvelous doctor who is to me now more friend than physician. So close do I feel to him that I am able to confide in him. I did this evening, though not without a degree of embarrassment.

"Dr. Mengers, I realize I'm not looking my best, what with this turban which is not exactly flattering to my delicate features, and being all bruised, but there is one thing that does alarm me. I seem to be . . ." I could hardly get the words out. "I seem to be growing a beard."

He became immediately evasive. Why? In the vaguest of terms, he told me not to worry; he even suggested that I *shave*! To which I responded, rather sharply, that a woman who takes a razor to her face may as well say farewell to her femininity. "What I plainly need," I said, coming to the point, "is a massive shot of female hormones."

"I'm afraid that's out of the question in your present condition. Such an injection would interfere seriously with the healing process. Later, perhaps." But though he was soothing, I detect something very odd in his manner. Is it possible that my first impression was correct? That there is indeed a plot against me? I must be on my guard at all times and not allow myself to be lulled into a sense of false security by a man who *claims* to be a doctor but knows altogether too much about films.

Apparently Mary-Ann has been trying to see me. She comes to the hospital every day, the adorable girl! I told Dr. Mengers to tell her that I love her dearly and when I am looking less ghastly I will see her. Meanwhile, I talk to her twice a day on the telephone.

"You don't know what I've been through!" she exclaimed when she first heard my voice, and promptly burst into tears of joy. I'm afraid I wept, too, at the sound of my darling's voice. In any case, all is well at the house. The dogs are almost housebroken though there are still occasional accidents, particularly on the new curtains in the living room. Mary-Ann continues her singing lessons and attends the Academy where I am much missed. Buck inquires daily about my health and Dr. Montag is coming to see me tomorrow.

The driver of the car that struck me has not yet been apprehended. The police hope for me to give them some clue but I cannot. I have no memory of anything once the dog ran up the garden walk. Apparently I was struck from behind.

Was it an accident, or was it . . . who? Rusty? Buck? I am suddenly filled with suspicion. Two weeks ago I was almost run over in front of Larue's. A coincidence? Well, if either of those sons-of-bitches did this to me I will have his God-damned head or my name is not Myron Breckinridge!

## 40

The room is filled with the smell of Randolph's pipe. Across the floor, burnt-out cinders indicate his various maneuvers. He was in good form. So am I, despite constant headaches and the odd sensation that my legs are filled with burning pins. Fortunately the cast will be removed tomorrow.

To my surprise, Randolph did not think me paranoid when I told him my suspicions.

"It crossed my mind, too," he said, sucking at his pipe. "It could very well have been Rusty's revenge."

"Or Buck Loner's. He would do anything to remove me from the Academy. Even murder."

Yet as I gave voice to my suspicions I cannot, in my heart of hearts, really believe that anyone in his right mind could wish to remove me from a world so desperately in need of me. I prefer to have faith in my fellow-man. I must even have a certain tenderness for him if I am to change, through example as well as teaching, his attitude toward sex. There was a time in our evolution when hate alone was motor to our deeds. But that age is ending, for I mean to bring to the world love of the sort that I have learned from Mary-Ann, a love which, despite its intensity, is mere prelude to something else again, to a new dimension which I alone am able to perceive, if dimly. Once I have formulated it, the true mission will begin. But for now I must be cryptic and declare that nothing is what it seems and what nothing seems is false.

"I would suspect Rusty more than Buck," said Randolph, plunging his thick paws into the huge get-well basket of fruit sent me "with love" from Uncle Buck and Bobbie Dean Loner. Randolph crushed a peach against his jaws. I looked away. "The motive in the case of Rusty is more profound psychologically." Randolph's teeth struck the peach's pit with a grating sound that sent shivers along my spine.

"Well, it's done and past. And I'm willing to forgive whoever it was."

"Are you really?" Randolph sounded surprised, not prepared for the new me.

"Of course. Suffering ennobles, doesn't it?" I had no desire to confide in Randolph, particularly now when I am assembling an entirely new personality with which to take the world by storm. "But I do wish you'd talk to Dr. Mengers and ask him to give me a hormone cocktail. I'm sprouting hair in all directions."

Randolph wiped his lips free of peach juice with a banana which he then unpeeled. "Yes, he told me about your request. Unfortunately, it's medically dangerous at the moment."

"But I can't let Mary-Ann see me like this."

"I'm sure she'll understand."

Before I could remonstrate with Randolph, he was launched upon one of his monologues whose subject, as usual, was Randolph Spenser Montag.

". . . office in Brentwood, a quiet neighborhood. Many of my patients live nearby which makes things easy for them if not for me. I've already made the down payment on the house, which is Spanish-style ranch-type, and so I should be ready for business in a few weeks. Culturally the Los Angeles area is far richer than I had dreamed, with many extremely stimulating people . . ."

I was spared Randolph's rationalizations by the sudden opening of the door and the nurse shouting, "Surprise, surprise!"

The surprise was an incline board on wheels which the nurse rolled backwards into the room, to my amazement. Was I expected to get on it and be wheeled about like a sacred relic or Pharaonic mummy? The mystery was solved when, with a flourish, the nurse spun the thing around to reveal Letitia Van Allen in a neck brace, strapped to the board.

"Darling!" Letitia was exuberant, despite the strangeness of her position. "Thank God, you're conscious! We were so worried!"

"I'm Dr. Montag," said Randolph gravely, never one to be kept for long out of a conversation. I made the introductions.

"Sorry I can't shake hands." Letitia was intrepid. "My neck is fractured and two spinal discs have fused. Otherwise I'm in a great shape."

The nurse agreed. Obviously she worships Letitia. "Miss Van Allen is just *bursting* with energy. It's all we could do to keep her in traction."

"How long have you been here?" I asked, suspecting what had happened.

"Two days after your accident, I took a header on the stairs at Malibu, and here I am, getting the first real rest I've had in twenty years."

"Except she's a naughty girl and not resting at all." The nurse was adoring. "She has moved her whole office into the hospital. You should see her room. It's a madhouse!"

"Sweetie, will you mix us a nice martini? Beefeater gin, no vermouth, on the rocks, with just the tiniest dash of rock salt."

"Oh, Miss Van Allen, you know hospital rules . . ."

"And a glass of champagne for yourself. Hurry up now! Letitia is parched."

The nurse departed. Letitia beamed at us. Then she frowned. "Angel, what's wrong with your face? It looks like you're . . ."

". . . growing a beard." I sighed. "Well, I am. A result of some sort of hormonal imbalance caused by the accident. Isn't that right, Doctor?"

Randolph blew sparks at Letitia and agreed, at convincing quasi-scientific length. All the while, Letitia was studying me with a thoughtful look. I cursed myself for not having used a thick foundation makeup.

"You know," said Letitia, when Randolph had wheezed into silence, "you would make a marvelous-looking man. Really, Myra, I mean it."

"Don't be silly!" I grew hot with anxiety, as well as rage at Dr. Mengers for not having done more to prevent this dreadful, if temporary, reversion to my original state.

"Darling, I didn't mean it as an insult! Quite the contrary. In fact . . ." Letitia apologized at length as we drank the martinis the nurse brought us and watched Randolph break open a large pineapple and tear at its tallowy flesh.

After what seemed an age of small talk, Randolph finished the pineapple and, with many a puff and wheeze and groan, got to his feet and said good-bye.

The moment the door shut behind him, Letitia flew across the room on her incline board, coming to a full stop beside my bed. "It was perfection!" She roared happily. "Total perfection! I have never in my life known such absolute and complete happiness. Such a . . . no, there are no words to describe what I went through. All I know is that I am now *entirely* fulfilled.

I have lived and I have loved to the fullest! I can at last give up sex because anything more would be anticlimax."

"Not to mention fatal." I must say Letitia's happiness depressed me mortally. "Just what did Rusty do to you this time?"

"What did he *not* do!" Her eyes became glazed with memory and gin. "It all happened the day he signed the contract at Fox. You know I got him the lead in that series with top money, special billing, participation, the works. Anyway, after the signing, we went back to Malibu to celebrate." Her voice was dreamy. "It began upstairs when he tore my clothes off in the closet. Then he raped me standing up with a metal clothes hanger twisted around my neck, choking me. I could hardly breathe. It was exquisite! Then one thing led to another. Those small attentions a girl like me cherishes . . . a lighted cigarette stubbed out on my derriere, a complete beating with his great thick heavy leather belt, a series of ravenous bites up and down the inner thighs, drawing blood. All the usual fun things, except that this time he went beyond anything he had ever tried before. This time he dragged me to the head of the stairs and raped me from behind, all the while beating me with his boot. Then, just as I was about to reach the big O, shrieking with pleasure, he hurled me down the stairs, so that my orgasm and the final crash with the banister occurred simultaneously. I fainted with joy! Without a doubt, it was the completion of my life."

"And here you are, half paralyzed." I could not resist being sour.

"Only temporarily. But I agree, one more go and I'll be dead, which is why we've agreed not to see each other again, except in a business way."

"He no longer needs you, so he drops you."

"You are a case, Myra!" Letitia tolled a great bronze laugh. "Actually the opposite is true. Since he's going to be a star he'll need me more than ever, in the business way. No, these things run their course. Frankly I don't think I shall ever again need sex. Once you have known the kind of perfection that I obtained at the moment of collision with that banister, anything else is too second-rate to be endured. I am a fulfilled woman, perhaps the only one in the world."

I must say I can only admire (and perhaps envy) Letitia. Not since the early Betty Hutton films has female masochism been so beautifully served. But I have my own problems. I came straight to the point. "Will Rusty go back to Mary-Ann?"

"Never. He's playing the field now. He's taking a bachelor pad with that young stud who was just let go by Universal—John Edward Jane."

"So you think he'll settle down to a life of promiscuity." I was relieved.

"After me, where can he go? Don't worry. He's lost all interest in your girlfriend."

This was said gaily. Even so, I felt shame, not so much for myself as for Mary-Ann.

"She's *not* my girlfriend. She has a horror of Lesbianism."

"That you don't share. Oh, come off it, Myra. You can tell your pal Letitia. Why, we've all gone that route one time or another—it can be a lot of laughs, two girls and one dildo."

Nevertheless, I continued to protest our innocence, while Letitia, getting more and more drunk on gin, described in some detail how, many years before, she had been seduced by Buck Loner's wife Bobbie Dean who then, no doubt filled with remorse, got religion one day while buying Belgian endives at the Farmers Market and gave up dyking on the spot to become a Jehovah's Witness. The story is not without its inspirational side.

But I am more concerned with Mary-Ann's reputation, and our relationship which means more to me than anything in this world.

I talked to Mary-Ann a few minutes ago, shortly after the dead-drunk Letitia was wheeled back to her room. Mary-Ann sounded happy. She can't wait for me to come home. I told her what the doctor told me just now: the cast comes off tomorrow and I will be able to go home by the end of the week. Unfortunately he refuses to give me a hormonal injection and my face looks a fright, with strange patches of beard. I also dread the removal of the bandage since, according to the nurse, all my lovely hair has been cut off. I hope Mary-Ann can bear the gruesome sight. I hope I can.

## 41

Where are my breasts? *Where are my breasts?*

## 42

What an extraordinary document! I have spent all morning reading this notebook and I can hardly believe that I was ever the person who wrote those demented pages. I've been debating whether or not to show them to my wife but I think, all in all, it's better to let the dead past bury its dead. As it is, neither of us ever mentions the period in which I was a woman and except for my agent, Miss Van Allen, we deliberately avoid seeing anyone who knew me in those days.

For over three years now we have been living in the San Fernando Valley on what they call a ranch but is actually just a few acres of avocado and lemon trees. The house is modern with every convenience and I have just built an outdoor barbecue pit which is much admired by the neighbors, many of whom are personalities in show business or otherwise work in some capacity or another in the Industry. Ours is a friendly community, with many fine people to share interests with.

At present I am writing a series, currently in its second year on ABC. I would of course like very much to do feature films but they are not that easy to come by. Miss Van Allen, however, keeps submitting my name so who knows when lightning will strike? Meanwhile, the series is a good credit and I make good money.

While cleaning out the attic, I came across this notebook along with all the manuscripts I wrote back in New York. Frankly I can't make head or tail of them. I certainly went through a pretentious phase! Luckily everything is now stabilized for me and I have just about the best wife and marriage I know of. Mary-Ann still sings professionally from time to time as well as appearing locally on television with her own children's program five days a week in the early A.M. She is quite a celebrity with the small fry in the Valley.

It's been a long time since I've seen Buck Loner but he's doing O.K. with the Academy, I gather, and every now and then one of the students actually gets a job in show business. So my work wasn't entirely in vain. The most famous alumnus is Ace Mann who used to be Rusty Godowski. After mopping up in that television series, he promptly inked a multiple nonexclusive contract with Universal and is now the Number Four Box Office Star in the World, according to *Film Daily.* He is also, I'm sorry to learn, a complete homosexual, for which I feel a certain degree of responsibility and guilt. But Dr. Montag, whom I ran into last week outside Will Wright's on Santa Monica Boulevard, said he thought it was probably always in the cards for Rusty and what I did to him just brought his true nature to the surface. I hope he's right.

Dr. Montag seems happy, although he now weighs over three hundred pounds and at first I didn't recognize him, but then he didn't recognize me either. Well, none of us is getting any younger. I am now almost entirely bald, which I compensate for by wearing a rather dashing R.A.F.–style moustache. Needless to say, it is a constant sadness that Mary-Ann and I can never have children. But ever since we both became Christian Scientists we tend to believe that what happens in this life is for the best. Although I nearly lost my mind and tried to kill myself when I learned that my breasts had been removed (Dr. Mengers had been forced to take this step because my life was endangered by the silicone which, as a result of the accident, threatened to enter the bloodstream), I now realize that it was the best thing that ever happened to me if only because once Mary-Ann realized that I was really *Myron* Breckinridge, her attitude toward me changed completely. Two weeks after I left the hospital where I spent my long convalescence and rehabilitation, we were married in Vegas, and so were able at last to settle down and live a happy and normal life, raising dogs and working for Planned Parenthood.

Incidentally, I noticed a quotation scribbled in one of the margins of the notebook. Something she (I hate to say "I"!) copied from some book about Jean-Jacques Rousseau. I don't suppose it's giving away any secrets to say that like so many would-be intellectuals back East Myra never actually read books, only books about books. Anyway the quotation still sort of appeals to me. It is about how humanity would have been a lot happier if it had kept to "the middle ground between the indolence of the primitive state and the questing activity to which we are prompted by our self-esteem." I think that is a very fine statement and one which, all in all, I'm ready to buy, since it is a proven fact that happiness, like the proverbial bluebird, is to be found in your own backyard if you just know where to look.

# *DULUTH*

A SATIRIC PARODY of television soaps, romance novels, post-structualist theories, racial prejudice, gender simplicities, police brutality, and American politics—among other things—*Duluth* might best be understood less in terms of plot than of tone, structure, and imagery. The narrative is imagistically and thematically associative, as if the reader were surfing a large number of television channels, all of which are different nonsynchronous versions of the same show. The overriding images are the city of Duluth itself and the spaceship that has arrived in its environs, the significance of which the citizens of Duluth (and the reader) cannot fathom until the end of the novel. Explicitly self-referential, the author-narrator of *Duluth* creates other authors within the narrative (who may or may not actually be writing *Duluth*) and frequently comments, seriously and parodically, on the creative process. Among the novel's targets are book critics and literary theoreticians. *Myra Breckinridge* focused a satiric lens on repressive aspects of American culture in the 1960s. *Duluth,* which was published in 1983, extends the view to include what Vidal sees as new follies in literature and life. The book is not politically correct, and it infuriated those for whom the objects of Vidal's satire are sacred or at least popular icons; it also offended some of those who share Vidal's criticism of American popular and political culture but found the terms of his criticism offensive. For example, the strip-search scene in the following excerpt satirizes and parodies both police brutality and the machismo (connected to Hispanic ethnicity and the Aztec Terrorist Society) of the criminals. In Vidal's view neither victimizer nor victim, nothing in fact that is human, warrants protection or exclusion from the satirist's vision.

# From *Duluth*

## I

*Duluth! Love it or loathe it, you can never leave it or lose it.* Those words—in bright multicolored neon-blaze from atop the McKinley Communication Center Tower, the highest point in busy downtown present-day Duluth.

If, as it has been so often said, every society gets the Duluth that it deserves, the United States of America in the last but one decade of the twentieth century has come up with a knockout.

From the rows of palm trees on Duluth's languorous lake front to the elegantly better homes and gardens on Garfield Heights to the tall obsidian towers of McKinley Center, two million human beings have their being in a dynamo of city where their nonbeing is provided for in a superbly landscaped cemetery, known as Lincoln Groves.

All appetites are catered for in Duluth. From casual lake-front sex to warm meaningful relationships in the ethnic barrios at the glittering desert's edge, there is something—if not someone—for everyone. There is also gambling at The Dude Ranch at the end of brothel-lined Gilder Road as well as social climbing and contract bridge at any number of private clubs of which the most exclusive is The Eucalyptus, set on a high hill overlooking the Duluth Woods, at whose verdant heart there is a swamp known to insect-lovers the world over as a unique macrocosm of insect life, vermiforous and otherwise. Duluth's proud claim to be the bug capital of the world is no idle boast.

Small wonder then that Tulsa-born and -bred Beryl Hoover has a sense of being home at last as she plumps herself, dolphinlike, beside Edna

Herridge in Edna's reliable old station wagon with the legend "Herridge Realtor" on its dusty door.

"Mrs. Hoover . . ." Edna begins, starting up her jalopy.

"Beryl . . ."

"Beryl . . . Edna."

"Edna?"

"I am Ms. *Edna* Herridge."

"So you are. My mind was elsewhere." Beryl's mind is indeed elsewhere. She has just observed through the frosted glass of the car window—the month is chill February and though it is only noon, the lights of the aurora borealis fill the entire southern sky like the long cold fingers of some great metaphor—a number of white men slowly hoist from the frozen ground a black man with a rope that has been slung over the branch of a tree. As the white men all pull together, the black man slowly leaves the ground for whatever afterlife the Supreme Author may be writing for him.

"I believe, Edna, that a Negro is being lynched."

"You'll love Duluth. I can tell." Edna revs up her jalopy's motor. "We have excellent race relations here, as you can see. And numerous *nouvelle cuisine* restaurants." Edna swings into Main Street, glittering from the recent snowfall that has turned Duluth into a winter wonderland where cars skid, pelvises and femurs snap on the ice-slick pavements, and Edna's brother, the Mayor, appeals, yet again, for all-around good humor as opposed to the more expensive snow-removal units that City Hall cannot afford. Good humor he gets, certainly.

"You are from Tulsa, of course." Edna races through her third red light; then skids on two wheels at the corner of Garfield and Main. "This is Garfield Avenue. The promenade of Duluth's elite. Houses range from one hundred Gs to the chill mill. Bitter—that is, better—homes cost more."

"For me, the sky's *not* the limit," said Beryl, with a laugh. But, of course, it is. Beryl is a divorcée *cum* widow with money. A lot of it. The result of having taken oil-rich Mr. Hoover to the cleaners. At least that is the story that she has seen fit to bruit about Duluth, where face value is the universal currency and the one thing at which everything is taken.

A figure of some allure, Beryl is addicted to basic black, even when she goes to her Tulsa office where she personally keeps the books. From time to time, Pink Lady in hand, she can be seen at one or another of Tulsa's clandestine gambling casinos. She is something of a woman of mystery to the croupiers, because she never bets.

Beryl is free—except for Clive, her son, whom she adores despite the fact that he has a nose like a flattened baked potato. Beryl is guilty about that nose because Clive inherited it from her even though a year *before* Clive's birth, the greatest of all rhino plasticeurs in Century City, Los Angeles, replaced Beryl's baked potato with a tiny *pomme soufflée* of a nose that took by storm all Tulsa—and will do the same in Duluth *if* Clive does not show up in town, wearing her former nose, thereby giving the game away. He must undergo surgery first, she thinks. "This is no place for Clive," she murmurs, as the station wagon skids along a wide avenue lined with gracious oaks whose frozen Spanish moss resembles . . .

"What was that, Beryl dear?"

"What was . . . ? Oh, I said that this is really the place to be alive! To live it up!" Beryl looks down at the glittering downtown area. On top of the McKinley Communications Center Tower the huge neon sign proclaims: "Duluth! Love it or loathe it, you can never leave it or lose it." Beryl frowns. "Just what does that sign mean? About not being able to leave or lose Duluth?"

"I don't really know," says Edna, evasively. "It's always been there," she adds.

"Is is true, do you think?" Like so many practical people, Beryl likes to ask questions.

"You must ask my brother. He's the mayor of Duluth. And a real rotter." Edna turns off Garfield Avenue. "Here's gracious home number one!" The station wagon hurtles between a pair of Palladian plinths and into a huge snowdrift, where it comes to an abrupt halt.

"We are buried alive," says Beryl, grasping the point. "In a snowdrift."

" 'Spring,' " sings Edna, always the good sport, " 'will be a little late this year.' "

Right then and there, both girls know that they are going to become great chums in the days ahead, as they wait for the spring thaw.

"Rumor has it," says Edna, making conversation, "that you were seen at The Dude Ranch last night."

"Yes," says Beryl. "It is one of the finest gambling casinos that I have ever sipped a Pink Lady in. Personally, I don't gamble but I love the sense of drama that you get when a fortune rises or falls on the mere turn of a card or a throw of the dice."

"I suppose you know that no one knows who actually owns The Dude Ranch," says Edna, opening her window and poking the snow with a finger. The snow is packed absolutely solid. "But The Dude—as he is universally known—is numero uno behind the scenes here in Duluth."

"He is known as 'the will-o'-the-wisp,' " says Beryl, "back in Tulsa."

"Sometimes I think that I know who—if not exactly what—he is," says Edna, somewhat kittenishly, under the circumstances.

"Yes?" asks Beryl, pointedly. "Then tell me his—or her—name."

## 2

Captain Eddie Thurow of the Duluth Police Department—known to everyone as the DPD—is bewildered. He sits at his desk, holding the telephone to his ear with his arthritic shoulder, a painful business but Captain Eddie is into authenticity and since that is the way that the police chief in the new television series "Duluth" does it, that is the way that he is going to do it. Captain Eddie's speech last June on role models to the graduating class of Duluth's Huey Long High was all about role models—and a lot more, too. He is quite a guy, Captain Eddie, everyone agrees. In fact, many people think that he would make a swell mayor. As it happens, he is one of those many people.

Opposite Captain Eddie is a map of Greater Duluth, showing the winding Colorado River that empties into palm-lined Lake Erie as well as the primeval woods and the shimmering mirage-filled desert that begins just to the east of the city. At the point where the Colorado River intersects with the desert, there is a bright red thumbtack. This is where the spaceship landed on Christmas Day. It is now February and the spaceship is still there. To everyone's surprise, no one—or no thing—has ever come out of the spaceship. Worse, no one has been able to get inside the ship or even to make radio contact with the extraterrestrial aliens within. The thing just sits there in the desert, a block or so to the east of ethnic Kennedy Avenue where the barrios begin.

"You say, now I hope I got this straight." Captain Eddie's voice is deep. The police chief in "Duluth" can't pronounce his Rs. Captain Eddie can; and does. "That the FBI will not—repeat, will not—send a crew to determine what to do about this spacecraft filled with illegal aliens?"

As Captain Eddie listens to the voice from Washington, he squints his eyes the way that the well-known actor Ed Asner does on television.

In the chair opposite Captain Eddie sits Lieutenant "Chico" Jones of Homicide. He is black. A token black, some say. But not "Chico." He prefers the word "colored" to the word "black." "Chico" is old-fashioned. He has not only wife trouble but money trouble, too. He cannot meet his mortgage payments, thanks to the high interest rates. To make ends meet, "Chico," like most of the guys and gals in the DPD, sells key-rings, tourist mementoes of Duluth, and angel dust on the side. But competition is stiff. Ends never do quite meet—except with his buddy, the spectacularly beautiful blue-eyed blond goddess Lieutenant Darlene Ecks, Homicide.

As they drive aimlessly about Duluth, they are, each agrees, good for each other. At least once a week, Darlene handcuffs "Chico" to the steering wheel of their police car and abuses him verbally. He likes this. He also like it when she pounces on illegal Mexican workers in the kitchens of the better Duluth restaurants and strip-searches them, all the while thundering out her own version of "Gimme a pig's foot and a bottle of gin," which is "Gimme a piece of okra and a pair of prunes!" Darlene has great humor. It is her dream one day to open a boutique just across the border from Duluth in Mexico so that "Chico" could visit her on Sundays. They have been lovers for a year. "Chico's" wife suspects the truth. For what it is worth.

Captain Eddie slams the phone down. "No dice!" he snarls at "Chico." "This is our show, they say. Our spaceship."

"In that case, why not just forget about it, Captain Eddie?" "Chico" has a way with him, even Captain Eddie has to admit that.

"You mean . . . ?"

"I mean . . ."

"You mean just . . . ?"

"I mean just . . ."

"*Forget* about it?" Captain Eddie looks very thoughtful indeed. Then he gets up and goes over to the map and with his right thumbnail he pries the red thumbtack out of the map. "Good thinking, 'Chico.' How is Darlene?"

"Chasing wetbacks."

Captain Eddie looks at the red thumbtack that he is holding in his hand. "All we have to fear now," he says slowly and thoughtfully, "is Wayne Alexander of the *Duluth Blade.*"

*"Duluth Switch-Blade,"* snorts "Chico," scornfully. The DPD does not like the numerous exposés of police brutality that Wayne Alexander has written over the years for the city's one newspaper, which is, admittedly, read only for its want ads and department store sales. But then nobody has read much of anything in Duluth since the day that KDLM-TV broke into the big time as *the* ABC affiliate and flagship for the Great Lakes and Tijuana area. Overnight the *Six O'Clock News* out of the McKinley Communications Tower was able to achieve demographics so colossal that the *Blade* has all but folded.

The news team at *Six O'Clock News* consists of one Oriental female, one Occidental male and one paraplegic Polynesian—a first for the Greater Duluth area, particularly in sports, where Leo Lookaloney is popular not only as an interviewer in the dressing rooms of the Duluth Tigers but as an occasional first base at charity games. These three anchorpersons preside over a program of city fires, conflagrations and holocausts beyond anything known to the rest of the country. That many of the fires are secretly set by the news team is an open secret in Duluth, where not only are grateful landlords able to collect insurance *on prime time* but Captain Eddie Thurow is able to go on the *Morning Show* at least once a month for three minutes to discuss his department's ongoing investigations of the fires.

As Captain Eddie thinks of Wayne Alexander, he loses his nerve. He puts the thumbtack more or less back where it was on the map, originally.

Little do Captain Eddie and "Chico" suspect what extraordinary events have been set in train by Captain Eddie's removal—even for a moment—of the thumbtack representing the craft from outer space from the map of Greater Duluth.

## 3

Inside the snowbank on Garfield Heights, Beryl and Edna are hitting it off like two houses afire.

"I always knew that one day I'd make it here to Duluth." Beryl daintily mops her face with Kleenex. The air is beginning to get a bit close inside the station wagon due to the intense conversation of the two girls. They have already used up several thousand ccs of oxygen and yet neither has really got much beyond the getting-to-know-you stage.

"I'm sure we'll find you the right mansion, Beryl honey." Edna has figured out that she has latched onto what they call in the realtors' book "a live one."

"Nothing that is not tasteful . . ."

"Tasteful is Edna Herridge's maiden name . . ."

"A view of your glorious lake front . . ."

"Natch."

"Your palm trees, your cherry blossoms on the ridge above the primeval Duluth Woods . . ."

"Not to mention the gorgeous swamp that is a macrocosm of the higher insect life, the cerise spaceship . . ."

"The *what*?" Beryl has not counted on a spaceship as being part of the view from her manse high on Garfield Heights. She is not sure that she likes the notion. She says as much.

"Oh, it's a rather charming shade of cerise. I'm sure you'll like it, Beryl. We all do around here," Edna white-lies a bit. After all, she is a realtor.

"Well, I hope so." Beryl is dubious. "What does it look like?"

"Well, it's round. And—as I said—sort of red. It looks more like the head of a thumbtack than anything else."

"Maybe a trellis would hide it."

"So far nothing has come out of it."

"What's in it?"

"Aliens, I suppose."

"Mexicans?"

"Haitians. Boat people. Shriners. We're being destroyed from within, Beryl. You *are* a Republican, aren't you, sweetie?"

"There are no lefties in Tulsa, Edna."

"But you're not in Tulsa anymore." Edna is growing suspicious. It would be just her luck to be trapped in a snowdrift on fashionable Garfield Heights with a Communist from Oklahoma.

Beryl laughs a tinkling laugh. "No. I'm in Duluth. I'm single. I am—if I may say so—attractive."

"Good enough to eat," says Edna, sincerely. Since the death of Mr. Herridge—Edna's tyrannical father—not a day has passed that she has not thought of joining Duluth's Sapphic circle. But she wants to lose twelve pounds first and, so far, those twelve pounds continue to cling limpetlike to her slight frame. "I love your nose," says Edna.

Beryl flares her nostrils inadvertently, an effect not unlike that of a *pomme soufflée* getting its second wind. "Yes," she says, vaguely. Then she is purposeful. "Edna, I want to level with you. I also want your help. By this time next year I mean to be the social leader of Duluth."

There is a long moment as the two girls gasp for breath in the now almost airless station wagon. White snow crushes against the windows on every side. Everyone in Duluth knows that since the hedgehog's shadow froze in November, the winter will be a long one. Question: Will the girls last until the first thaw?

"Social leader?" wheezes Edna.

"*And* arbiter!" gasps Beryl. "I mean to replace Mrs. Bellamy Craig II with my own box at the opera. And a Eucalyptus Club lifetime membership."

"I must put my thinking cap on," says Edna. "You are asking for the moon, you know." Then Edna slumps across the wheel.

The air is now all gone save for one tiny cc of oxygen, which Beryl uses to repeat the magic name of the first lady of Duluth. "Mrs. Bellamy Craig II. Here I come!" But Beryl is not going anywhere in Duluth because The Supreme Eraser is now erasing her from *Duluth.* Bravely, she has fulfilled her function, which is exposition—something she hates. "But ours not to choose," is her motto, as she goes on to yet another tale. She has prepared the way for Clive—almost. As the eraser expunges the last fragment of her identity, Beryl Hoover realizes that she has been murdered by The Dude, who will try to murder her beloved Clive. She must warn him. But how can she? She is already in a different book, *Rogue Duke* by Rosemary Klein Kantor.

## 4

Wayne Alexander strides purposefully up the icy steps of the Craig mansion, high on Garfield Heights.

The new English butler ushers Wayne into the palatial living room of the

Craig home, where oates-colored drapes are shot through with golden threads and wall-to-wall tufted tourmaline fluffiness covers the floor, making not only for true elegance but for comfiness as well.

"Whom shall I say," asks the new English butler, "is calling she?" Wayne tells him his name and the new English butler goes.

As Wayne stands, looking out the picture window, he can see, just past the black towers of downtown Duluth, the sandy desert where the spaceship, like a cerise mole or beauty mark, is set.

Then Wayne feels two powerful arms embrace him from the back.

"Darling," he says, and turns—lips all puckered for that first kiss. But when he sees who it is, he gives a terrible cry.

Instead of Chloris, he finds, to his aghastment, the bearded face of Bellamy Craig II, whose own lips are puckered, all ready for *his* first kiss. As their eyes open and eye contact is duly made, four lips lose their pucker, four eyes their love-glow.

"Craig!"

"Wayne!"

"For God's sake, Craig, who did you think I was? I mean, I've got on a man's suit," says Wayne, looking down to make sure that that is what he is wearing, which it is.

"Evelyn, actually. We had a date. I'm sorry, old boy. Carry on. Silly mistake. Could happen to anyone. Chloris won't mind. Ours is an open marriage, as you know. Have a Lark cigarette from this Tiffany box. Here. I'll light it for you with my Dunhill. Some Asti Spumante? Beer? Byrrh? Canada Dry, maybe?" Bellamy is a good host who never overdoes it. But then good taste is sovereign on Garfield Heights. Or as they say in the local French patois, *bon ton,* a phrase that rhymes with a certain delicious Chinese soup.

Wayne puts him at ease. "That's O.K., Bellamy. I came to have a chat with Chloris."

"I know."

As they have now run out of big talk, they move, effortlessly, to small talk. "How do you think the Dodgers will do?" asks Wayne.

"They've got a good line. But that backfield . . ."

"Yes."

There is a pause. During this pause, a writer like Rosemary Klein Kantor would start hunting and pecking at the console of her word-processor, which is connected with a memory bank containing ten thousand popular novels. Rosemary only uses familiar types. She would take Bellamy, say, from an old best-seller classic like *Anthony Adverse.* Bellamy Craig II has a weak chin, which is entirely hidden by a beard that has been dyed black to take the place of the flaxen gold that mother nature originally intended for him. Bellamy is bald, with a skull full of interesting bumps, particularly over the ears. Bellamy's eyes are powder-blue, while his arms and legs work properly because he is not, as he likes to say, thank God, double-jointed, a condition much feared in Duluth, and for good reason. Bellamy's mother was once a Bohemian innkeeper in Key West, Florida, during the forties and fifties. Later, she started the first dinner theater in Duluth, the basis of the Craig fortune. It was at the dinner theater that she had the stroke that totally paralyzed her on the opening night of *The Bird Cage* by Arthur Laurents. She is now upstairs in the Craig mansion. She recognizes everyone who visits her, though no one does, actually.

Wayne Alexander is tall and Giacometti-fat. (Rosemary also draws on films for her characters: *her* Wayne would be like the late Dan Duryea in *The Little Foxes.*) The eyes are hazel, because he has seen a lot. In fact, he has seen it all. Before he joined the *Duluth Blade,* he was in Nam—or Viet Nam, as he prefers to call it. He was a grunt, or soldier, as he always says. He lost his right ear in an obscure engagement. He will tell no one how or when or why.

But the pause has now been broken by Bellamy, making conversation out of whole cloth. "What do you think is in the spaceship?"

"Beats me," says Wayne. "It could be empty."

"That would be funny, wouldn't it?"

"I've been doing an exposé of the space program. I think that they know exactly where it's from but they won't tell us."

"Why, Wayne?"

During this next pause Mrs. Bellamy Craig II—née Duluth des Bois and a direct descendant of the city's French founder—enters the room, shouting.

## 5

Just off ethnic Kennedy Avenue the barrios begin. Mile after mile of paper and plywood shacks give shelter—if that's the word—to almost one million illegal and legal Mexican aliens. Every night the barrios are alive with mariachi music and joyous laughter because illegal aliens are essentially life-enhancing, since their deepest feelings are all on the surface while their shallowest feelings are hidden deep down—unlike the cold Anglos of Garfield Heights who cannot relate to one another without using as an intermediary a wise psychiatrist who will break the ice for them so that Dad can finally kiss Junior. Should there ever be really real people, really warm loving people anywhere on earth, it is those one million or so Chicanos who live in the barrios off ethnic Kennedy Avenue in East Duluth.

But there is also a lot of rage in the barrios, much of it directed specifically against Lieutenant Darlene Ecks. In fact, at this very moment of time, ten of her victims are meeting at the back of a shanty where, in the front room, peasant women with age-old Aztec faces are ironing tacos, folding enchiladas, stitching tortillas by the light of a single kerosene lamp. Sometimes one of the women will break into song—a high eerie birdlike song first sung aeons ago by the ancient Sumacs.

In the back room, the male victims squat in a circle, broad-brimmed sombreros over their eyes. They are all young, vital, sleepy. They are planning their revenge.

"Three times she strip-searches me," say Manuel. "Three times she says . . ."

Together all ten imitate Darlene's bellow: "Gimme a piece of okra and a pair of prunes." They shudder—in unison.

"She must die," says Armando.

"Macho is what macho does," says their quondam leader Manuel, pulling a knife from his belt.

But it is Benito—the youngest—who asks, "Muchachos, what is okra?"

They tell him.

"What is prunes?"

They tell him.

Benito—who had not minded all that much the two-hour strip-search in the women's room of the Greyhound Bus Terminal—flushes with embarrassment and rage. "*Caramba!* She must die," he says, in Spanish. But then all the men are speaking Spanish to each other, as they are from Mexico.

## 6

Inside the station wagon, Beryl and Edna have long since breathed their last when Captain Eddie Thurow's Rescue Crew finally rescues them. As luck would have it, Lieutenant "Chico" Jones is in charge of this particular rescue. While the bodies of the two women are removed from the car and placed on stretchers, "Chico" bares his head in the falling snow. The other rescuers naturally follow suit.

"They are gone to a better world," says "Chico."

Actually, Edna has gone into "Duluth," the popular television series that is being filmed at Universal Studios for ABC, where she will play the part of a judge's alcoholic sister, while Beryl has been added to one of Rosemary Klein Kantor's Harlequin-style novels, set in Regency Hyatt England.

But "Chico"—who is all heart as well as all man—could not have known this. Nor can *we* ever know just what might have happened had Beryl Hoover ever confronted Chloris Craig and, *mano a mano,* fought with her for the social mastery of Duluth. That dream is over for Beryl. So, too, is her secret empire, which Clive—who is in mortal danger—will inherit.

Solemnly the rescue crew carry the two bodies, dusted now with snow like a pair of Mayflower doughnuts, between those two plinths, which are only, as luck yet again would have it, a stone's throw from the mansion of the Bellamy Craig IIs.

## *7*

Like most absolute laws, the fictive law of absolute uniqueness is relative. Although each character in any fiction—as in any life or nonfiction—is absolutely unique (even if you cannot tell one character from another), the actual truth of the matter is more complex.

When a fictive character dies or drops out of a narrative, he will then—promptly—reappear in a new narrative, as there are just so many characters—and plots—available at any given time. Corollary to the relative fictive law of absolute uniqueness is the *simultaneity effect,* which is to fiction what Miriam Heisenberg's law is to physics. It means that any character can appear, simultaneously, in as many fictions as the random may require. This corollary is unsettling and need not concern us other than to note, in passing, that each reader, like each writer, is, from different angles and at different times, in a finite number of different narratives where he is always the same yet always different. We call this *après* post-structuralism. The many studies that are currently being made of the *simultaneity effect* vividly demonstrate, as if demonstration is necessary! that although the English language may decline and dwindle, English studies are more than ever complex and rewarding.

The law of absolute uniqueness requires—except in those cases where it does not—the total loss of memory on the part of the character who has died or made only a brief appearance in a fictive narrative. Naturally, when the writing of the book is finished all the characters who are alive at the end are available to other writers for reentries, as it were. Sometimes this is called plagiarism but that is a harsh word when one considers how very little there is in the way of character and plot to go around. Ultimately, plagiarism is simply—in the words of Rosemary Klein Kantor herself—*creation by other means.*

The characters that are in any given book—though abandoned by their author when he writes *finis* to his *opus*—will still continue to go through their paces for anyone who happens to read the book. Hence, the proof—or a proof—of the *simultaneity effect.* Once this particular true fiction or fictive truth is concluded by the present author (one able to give, as it were, the worm's-eye view of this Duluth—thus, the reader is warned), the Bellamy Craig IIs, Darlene Ecks, Captain Eddie, the whole vivid living (for now) crew will drift off to new assignments, unknown to them or him. They will forget him. He will not recognize them—except in those cases of Outright Plagiarism when civil law will scrutinize the truth of a fictive text with a thoroughness unknown even at busy Yale.

At this instant—in midcomposition—all the characters are at hand except for the two that have just died. Due to an anomaly in the law of absolute uniqueness, Edna Herridge still remembers, from time to time, that she was once a realtor in quite a different Duluth from the series "Duluth," with a brother who is the mayor. On the other hand, Beryl Hoover has totally forgotten her previous existence in these pages for the excellent reason that the part of *Rogue Duke* in which she first appears was written *before* Beryl's brief appearance and disappearance in our Duluth. Later, as Rosemary pens further installments, Beryl Hoover will then recall *Duluth*—and some very exciting unfinished business that involves Clive. At this point—still in the future—Beryl will try to find a way to warn Clive that The Dude will try to kill him just as The Dude killed her.

## 8

"Hello, Wayne," shouts Chloris Craig. She is, very simply, beautiful. Then she stops when she sees her husband, Bellamy, standing beside her lover, Wayne. Chloris tries to frown but the plastic surgeons who created her matchless beauty had slyly snipped the frown muscles.

"I was just on my way, Chloris." Bellamy is apologetic.

"I should think so," says Chloris.

The two men shake hands. The husband goes. The lover remains. Thus it has always been in Duluth's higher circles.

Wayne takes Chloris in his toothpick arms. Throws her onto the sofa with the Porthault sheets. They tear at one another's clothes. They make love among the shreds of Valentino's finest gingham. No matter. Chloris is rich.

Finally, lust slaked and sated, they smoke Larks as a new moon rises behind the plate-glass window and the aurora borealis flares in the southern sky over Tijuana.

Gently, Wayne traces a circle where Chloris's navel used to be. When the last team of plastic surgeons took the last tuck in her abdomen, they eliminated, by mistake, her navel. Now whenever Chloris wears a bikini, she must always remember to paint on a navel—using Elizabeth Arden's Pink Dawn. But as Chloris has no secret from Wayne except for the ones that she has, she never puts on a navel for him.

Chloris lets her hand rove, appreciatively, over Wayne's turgid powers. She prefers them tumescent, of course. But turgid is all right, too, because Wayne turgid is better than Bellamy tumescent.

"Did you bring it, Wayne?"

"Yes, Chloris. It's over there. In the Gucci briefcase on that Swedish Knole what-not. Do you want a gander?"

"Later. How much did you bring me this time?"

"The marriage with Henry James. That's all done."

"Good. Can he sue?"

"No. What I've written is in good taste. I've also described *Mother Wore Tights.* The whole picture, every reel. Because that's where she first met Herbert Hoover, on the set . . ."

"And they fell head over heels in love!" Chloris sighs. "God, how I worship that woman! And what a book I am going to make of her star-crossed life!"

As well as being the first hostess of Duluth, Chloris Craig, under the name "Chloris Craig," is known to readers everywhere as a top-selling author. Six of Chloris's books have scored all around the world. In fact, everyone who likes to read sooner or later reads "Chloris Craig." This is because *she gets inside her characters,* according to Virginia Kirkus, the only woman to have read every book ever written and so is seldom seen socially at literary gatherings or even at Frank E. Campbell's regular get-togethers for the old-timers.

But Chloris has a secret. Two secrets, in fact—except that Wayne is on to one of them. The first secret is that Wayne Alexander writes the books for her, a secret that he knows, naturally, as it is hard not to know when you've written a book for someone. The second secret—the one that he does *not* know but is beginning to suspect—is that Chloris has never read a book by "Chloris Craig" or a book by anyone else either. Chloris can only read three-letter words if they are in big enough print. That is why she became a writer. To compensate, as Dr. Mengers, her ears, nose and throat doctor would say—and, in fact, does say.

But Chloris does do a lot of research, if the subject happens to be alive or has known a lot of people who are still alive. She has a tape recorder (Sony) which she works with marvelous precision. KDLM-TV's one-hour special on "Chloris Craig" caused more than one Duluth housewife to rush out and buy a tape recorder and then try to work it the way that Chloris worked it on television. But none has ever succeeded because "Talent is innate. Genius divine," as Chloris herself said at the end of the program when she was able to record, erase, re-rerecord, both forward *and* backward, simultaneously, on the same disk, one thousand Wayne-selected words.

"*Why* was Betty Grable murdered, Wayne?"

This is an old dialogue between the lovers, dating back to their first date on the Persian Paradise Houseboat in the Colorado River that glamorous summer a decade earlier. One look at Wayne and Chloris had felt his turgid powers through corduroy trousers while he had shuddered at the thought of her seething delta beneath the tulle that she wore with an extra fillip over her bikini. She wanted literary fame. He wanted money. She his turgid powers; he her delta. She the name of Betty Grable's assassin; he the motive. Not since Heloise and Abelard Schroeder of Winona has a couple been so exquisitely attuned, one to the other.

"Betty Grable, after she met Herbert Hoover, fell in love with him. But then most women did. He was like that, women tell me."

"I've seen his pictures, Wayne. And I can believe it. That wonderful stiff collar. They don't make them like that anymore."

"Now, as I have been piecing together the events leading up to the murder in 1973, a pattern begins to emerge. In fact, the more that I study this book of yours which I'm writing, the clearer it gets. First, was Betty Grable absolutely positive that Herbert Hoover was really Herbert Hoover?"

"I don't understand you," says Chloris, directly.

"Was the love of her life really Herbert Hoover?"

"But surely, Wayne, the last scrawled message, with the lipstick, on the glass-topped table, those two words—'Hoover love'—could mean only one thing . . ."

Thanks to Chloris's constant manipulation, Wayne's blood is swiftly being drained from his head to fill that tube which she cannot get enough of. But Wayne is now eager to tell her what he has found out before, as so often happens in their lovemaking, he faints dead away as he bestows—and captures—rapture. Wayne is now in a race with his own blood. Wayne can feel the crimson flood beginning to recede from his brain like the last of the bath water from a Carrara marble sunken tub. As everything starts to go black, he mounts her.

She cries out.

He blurts out, "The Hoover in lipstick was not . . ." Within the blazing magenta of her delta steams and seethes Wayne's purple tumescence. Ecstasy—and unconsciousness—is—or are—near.

"Who . . . ?" Although she is now yelping with esctasy, her steel-trap mind never ceases to try to trap info.

"It was . . . it was . . ."

Wayne comes. Chloris screams. Wayne faints. Chloris sleeps.

Through the picture window, one by one, the shy stars begin to fill up the blue-black sky, always careful to tip-toe 'round the shafts of light from the aurora borealis that makes Duluth by night so unique a wonderland.

## 9

While the *crème de la crème* disport themselves on Garfield Heights, Lieutenant Darlene Ecks, disguised as a virgin and carrying what look to be all her jewels and accessories in a string bag, is mincing through a mean part of the barrios just off ethnic Kennedy Avenue.

Suddenly a young would-be rapist comes up behind her, put a wiry arm about her neck and drags her into a deserted hovel on whose walls "Viva Castro" has been painted over and over again by agents of the Federal Bureau of Investigation in order to make it seem as if Castro is behind all the disorder in the barrios when, actually, it is the FBI itself that instigates most of the riots.

"Gringa!" snarls the alien youth from Mexico. He tears the string bag from her nerveless hand. He empties it on the floor. First, the loot. Then the rape. This order of events proves to be his undoing. While he is examining the loot, Darlene tears off her virgin's outfit—a black and white polka-dot dress surmounted by a small band-box hat—to reveal the sexy Ecks body clad in its blue Duluth Police Department uniform, designed years earlier by Mainbocher but never out of fashion as anything in good taste will never be.

Darlene then draws a gun on the unsuspecting rapist, who is now grinning happily at the small color TV that she has packed among the other enticing goodies in the string bag.

"O.K., wetback. Put 'em up. You're under arrest."

The would-be rapist's eyes narrow when he sees what he has taken to be a defenseless virgin transformed before his eyes into a police lieutenant with a gun in her hand. He lets the string bag drop to the floor.

"Oh," he says. He puts up his hands.

Darlene is delighted with her catch. He is her favorite type quarry. Thin macho moustache. Dark Latin Lover eyes. Thick greasy hair. He wears two overcoats. Illegal aliens hate the Duluth winters, which are so unlike the balmy weather of Mexico, a mere ten miles away, across the border.

"O.K., muchacho, this is a strip-search."

"What?" He has not understood her. But then his English is not really up to even Darlene's sort of snuff.

"Off!" Darlene snarls, pointing to the two scuffy highly pointed shoes that all illegal aliens wear.

"What?" Total incomprehension.

Expertly Darlene knocks him down and pulls off one of the pointy shoes. Then she motions for him to complete the job. Crouched on the floor of the hovel, he removes the other shoe and then, reluctantly, four pairs of socks to reveal on each little toe a corn, something that all illegal aliens have as the result of the too-tight shoes that they affect. At the sight of those corns, Darlene starts her ascent to seventh heaven.

## 10

Wayne has gone. Chloris lies in her round bed, staring at the television set on the ceiling. Idly, she uses her vibrator. Wayne has not really satisfied her. She told him so when he came to. Miffed, he departed without telling her who killed Betty Grable. Chloris thinks he is just stringing her along—taking her for a ride.

As Chloris switches on "Duluth," she wonders just how Wayne lost his right ear. Then she is caught up in "Duluth." An actor whom she has always liked—it is Lorne Greene?—is being warm and confiding as a judge named Claypoole. He is now in judge's chambers, wearing a black robe and holding a gavel. The gavel reminds Chloris that she is still holding the vibrator in her left hand. She puts it on high. This is more like it, she thinks.

A familiar-looking actress appears on the screen. Chloris frowns. I know her, she thinks.

The actress is appealing to the judge to go easy on her son who is also his nephew.

The judge is stern. "I'm sorry, Sis. But you know as well as I do that the law is the law. And if you bend it this way and that—well, there wouldn't be any justice left, now would there?"

Chloris does not like this sort of Communist rant on television—or in real life for that matter. She debates whether or not to switch to something else. But then the camera cuts to the familiar-looking woman's face.

"I know that woman!" says Chloris aloud.

"Of course you do," says the woman, speaking directly to Chloris as she lies on the Porthault sheets of her round bed.

"Of course I do *what*?" says the judge, with the puzzled look of an actor who has been thrown a wrong cue.

"Of course you know me. I'm Edna Herridge, Realtor."

"Edna! My God! I'm sorry I didn't go to the funeral."

"The flowers were nice . . ."

"What flowers?" The judge—it isn't Lorne Greene and Raymond Burr is dead, thinks Chloris, not that that makes any difference on television where just about everyone you see is dead, anyway, including Edna Herridge.

"I was on my way with a client to your house, a Beryl Hoover . . ."

That name, thinks Chloris, that magic name! "Any relation to Herbert?"

"When we got stuck in a snowdrift and died."

"A man died because of your son—in a snowdrift, was it?" The actor playing the judge is doing his best to get the show back on the road where it belongs.

"Then I was assigned to this soap opera. Beryl was really looking forward to getting to know you. You should look her up. Rumor has it that she's in the new novel by *your* Rosemary Klein Kantor. Not ours. 'Bye now." Edna goes back into the plot of "Duluth," very much aware that one more line *not* in the script and she can be had up on charges by Actors Equity. "He's my son," says Edna, weeping. "He's *your* nephew. He's going to be a fine doctor one day . . ."

The actor playing the judge looks relieved, hearing some dialogue from the script. "When I put on this black robe," he says gravely . . .

Chloris settles back to watch. The plot is beginning to thicken nicely. Chloris also makes a mental note to look for Rosemary Klein Kantor's latest novel. She is a little puzzled by the reference to "*your* Rosemary Klein Kantor. Not ours." Surely, there are not two Klein Kantors, she asks herself. But, of course, thanks to the *simultaneity effect,* there is the Klein Kantor creator of the series "Duluth," which is seen in *Duluth* but made in another continuum or alternative fiction, and so its Klein Kantor creatrix is entirely different from our Klein Kantor who has just published an installment of a novel called *Rogue Duke* in the latest issue of *Redbook,* a woman's magazine recently revived by the enemies of the Equal Rights Amendment of whom Chloris is one.

In principle, Chloris likes the idea of Rosemary Klein Kantor's tales of derring-do in Regency Hyatt England, and though she herself cannot read and hates being read to except when the book is her own, she likes nothing better than to be *told* about books. She must get Wayne to tell her about *Rogue Duke*—and Beryl Hoover, who may well be related, in some way, to the dark mystery at the heart of the Betty Grable Story.

## II

Meanwhile, in the hovel in the barrio, Darlene has now got to the part of strip-search that she most enjoys. In fact, her jockey shorts are beginning to moisten with excitement. She always wears men's jockey shorts on the job because they make her feel authoritative.

The illegal alien youth is now wearing nothing but a pair of dingy boxer shorts, a size too large for his slender frame. Only one of three original buttons remains at the point of closure in the front and that button hangs by but a thread. In the cold, the youth is beginning to turn blue, a shade that Darlene likes in her illegal aliens. She notes with satisfaction that the surprisingly sturdy legs are shivering while to the west and the east of the hairless chest two dark nipples have shrunk to a size no larger than that of any two bumps of surrounding gooseflesh. The sound of the illegal alien's teeth chattering is music to Darlene's ears.

"Drop those drawers, boy!" she booms.

"What?" This is his only word of English, as he stands, hands to his sides, narrow Aztec eyes wide with terror.

With a forefinger Darlene flicks the button, which detaches itself from the last thread of some long-forgotten Mexican summer. The alien youth gasps. The drawers open but do not fall, held in place by muscular thighs. A thick black bush of pubic hair is totally revealed. With a glad cry, Darlene pulls the drawers all the way down to the alien's corns. He gives a cry. Of shame. She gives a cry. Of surprise. The bush is bare. No okra. No prunes.

Modestly, he tries to cover nothing with his hands. "No you don't, muchacho!" Darlene drags away the hands; stares at the empty black bush. "What are you," she snarls, "some kind of transsexual?"

"What?" he gurgles.

"One of us is missing the whole point to strip-search," says Darlene, testily. "And it is not Lieutenant Ecks of Homicide."

Darlene pulls up a crate and sits on it in such a way that the area of most interest to her is now at eye level. Then, gingerly, she moves her fingers up the quavering and quivering left thigh to the point where the sturdy legs join the thin torso. Victory! Hidden in the wiry thicket are the two miniature prunes, removed from view by terror and cold.

"So you had them all along," she says, squeezing the prunes together. She is rewarded with a whimper. Next she removes her comb from her Mainbocher uniform pocket and, carefully, she parts the pubic bush in the middle. As she combs the hair to each side of the central parting, she is rewarded with a highly privileged close-up view of what proves to be easily the smallest and greenest—well, more bluish, she concedes—okra that she has yet found. It sticks straight out, the one eye shut tight with terror.

"For a rapist, boy, you're a nonstarter."

"What?"

On an impulse, Darlene pushed the okra back inside the alien, who screams. "Now you see it!" she shouts. "Now you don't!"

Little does Darlene Ecks dream that at this moment of her greatest triumph to date, she has just created the merciless chief of what will soon be known worldwide as the Aztec Terrorists Society, whose cry "The fire this time!" (in Spanish) will demoralize and destabilize Greater Duluth.

Yet, at heart, paradoxically, Darlene wants to be cherished and protected. If "Chico" were not so heavily married—and so seriously black—he could have been the answer to her prayers. But he is—and he is, seriously.

As compensation, Darlene's day-to-day life is nothing but strip-search, mixed with daydreaming. She is addicted to those glamorous romantic novels in which powerful masterful men, wearing cloaks, save shy heroines from terrible fates. Darlene particularly delights in Klein Kantor novels. In fact, so powerful is Darlene's need for beauty and tenderness that she is able, at the drop of an alien's drawers, to transport herself to the world of Regency Hyatt England and revel in the imaginings of her favorite authoress.

# RELIGION

# *JULIAN*

VIDAL'S SECOND HISTORICAL NOVEL (*A Search for the King,* 1950, was his first), *Julian* (1964) dramatizes the life of the fourth-century Roman emperor Julian, known after his death as "the Apostate" because of his rejection of Christianity. Julian's uncle, Constantine the Great, had become a Christian supporter after his victory over a rival at the Milvian Bridge, near Rome, in 312. Constantine was said to have had a vision of the Cross that inspired him. He founded a Christian empire and moved his capital to Constantinople. The emperor was baptized on his deathbed in 337 and was succeeded by his three sons, who ruled as Augusti.

A family bloodbath ensued, and Julian's father was brutally murdered by the Augusti. Julian was then only five years old, and since he did not appear to be a threat to his cousins, he was permitted to live and to travel widely and study with the great scholars and philosophers of the day. He was knowledgeable in both classical and Christian thought but was drawn most strongly to the teachings of the Greek philosopher Libanius, who rejected Christianity. Soon Julian too had rejected Christianity in favor of the pagan gods.

By 350 Constantine's second son, Constantius, ruled the empire alone. In 355, when Julian was twenty-three, he was named Caesar by Constantius, who desperately needed assistance in controlling the vast territory he had inherited. Unlikely as it seemed, the young scholar became an aggressive and successful general and secured the empire's western borders. Constantius was having less good fortune in the east, and he sent a message to Julian in Paris that he wanted reinforcements—more than half of Julian's army—to come to Persia. The soldiers refused to go. They mutinied and crowned Julian emperor. Before the two cousins came to blows, Constantius died of natural causes and Julian officially acceded to the throne. As emperor, Julian advocated a synthesis of pagan mystery cults and sun worship. A reluctant ruler and a fastidious advocate of personal liberty and public morality, he died in battle in 363, sixteen months after becoming emperor.

A novel of ideas as well as of historical pageantry, *Julian* draws on a variety of contemporary historical documents to provide an accurate presentation of life and politics in the fourth-century Roman world. Vidal creates his own imagined version of a memoir that Julian may actually have written but that no longer exists. In the novel, there is such a memoir, and seventeen years after Julian's death, Priscus and Libanius, his former teachers, exchange letters about what to do with this potentially dangerous work. Priscus sends a copy of the memoir to Libanius, who ponders writing a sympathetic biography of Julian. Thus Julian's first-person account of his own life is at the center of the novel, framed and interrupted by Libanius's and Priscus's inter- and extra-textual comments.

# From *Julian*

IT WAS MID-OCTOBER when I arrived in Milan. The weather was dry and the air so clear that one could see with perfect clarity those blue alps which separate civilization from barbarism, our world of sun from that melancholy green forest where dwells Rome's nemesis.

Just before the city's gate we were met by one of Constantius's eunuchs, a gorgeous fellow with many chins and an effortless sneer. He did not salute me as is proper, a bad omen. He gave the commander of my guard a letter from the Emperor. When I saw this, I began to recite the first of the passwords I should need when I arrived in the kingdom of the dead. But I was not to be dispatched just yet. Instead I was taken to a house in one of the suburbs. Here I was imprisoned.

Imprisonment exactly describes my state. I was under heavy guard. During the day, I was allowed to stroll in the atrium. But at night I was locked in my bedroom. No one could visit me, not that there was anyone in Milan I wanted to see or who wanted to see me, excepting the Empress Eusebia. Of my household, I was allowed to keep only two boys and two men. The rest were transferred to the imperial palace. There was no one I could talk to. That was the greatest hardship of all. I should have been pleased to have had even a eunuch for company!

Why was I treated this way? I have since pieced the story together. While I was in Athens, a general named Silvanus was proclaimed Augustus in Gaul. I am convinced that at heart he was innocent of any serious desire to take the purple, but the enmity of the court eunuchs drove him to rebellion.

As soon as this happened, Constantius arrested me because he was afraid that I might take advantage of the defection of Gaul to rise against him in Attica. As it turned out, before I reached Milan, Silvanus was dead at Cologne. Constantius's luck in civil war had proved itself again.

But the death of Silvanus did not solve the problem of Julian. While I was locked up in that suburban villa, the old debate was reopened. Eusebius wanted me put to death. Eusebia did not. Constantius kept his own counsel.

I prepared several letters to Eusebia, begging her to intercede with the Emperor that I might be allowed to return to Athens. But I finally decided not to send her any message, for Constantius's suspicions were easily aroused, to say the least, and any exchange between his wife and his heir presumptive would not only be known to him but would doubtless turn him against both of us. I did the wise thing.

At dawn, on the thirteenth day of my captivity, my life altered forever. I was awakened by a slave banging on the bedroom door. "Get up, Lord! Get up! A message from the Augustus!" Fully clothed, I leapt out of bed. I then reminded the slave that until someone unlocked the door I could hardly receive the imperial messenger.

The door flew open. The commander of my guard was beaming. I knew then that the divine will had begun its work. I was to be spared.

"A messenger, sir. The Emperor will receive you tonight."

I stepped into the atrium and got my first taste of what it is like to be in favor. The house was now full of strangers. Fat eunuchs in gaudy silk; clerks from various government offices; tailors; sandalmakers; barbers; youthful officers drawn to what might be a new sun and source of honor. It was dizzying.

The messenger from Constantius was no other than Arintheus, who serves with me now in Persia. He is remarkably beautiful, and the army loves him in that fervent way armies have of loving handsome officers. He is auburn-haired and blue-eyed, with a strong, supple body. He is completely uneducated, but brave and shrewd in warfare. His only vice is an excessive fondness for boys, a practice I usually find unseemly in generals. But the men are amused by his sensuality. Also, he is a cavalry man and among cavalry men pederasty is a tradition. I must say that day when Arintheus approached me, blue eyes flashing and ruddy face grinning, I nearly mistook him for Hermes himself, streaming glory from Olympus as he came to save his unworthy son. Arintheus saluted me briskly; then he read aloud the letter summoning me for audience. When he had finished reading (with some difficulty, for he has never found reading easy), he put the message away, gave me his most winning smile and said, "When you are Caesar, don't forget me. Take me with you. I prefer action." He patted his sword hilt. I dithered like a fool. He departed.

Then began a new struggle. My beard would have to go, also my student's clothes. I was now a prince, not a philosopher. So for the first time in my life my beard was shaved. It was like losing an arm. Two barbers worked on me while I sat in a chair in the center of the atrium as the morning sun shone on a spectacle which, looking back, was perfectly ludicrous. There was I, an awkward twenty-three-year-old philosophy student, late of the University of Athens, being turned into a courtier.

A slave girl trimmed my toenails and scrubbed my feet, to my embarrassment. Another worked on my hands, exclaiming at the inkiness of my fingers. The barber who shaved my beard also tried to shave my chest but I stopped him with an oath. We compromised by letting him trim the hair in my nostrils. When he was finished, he brought me a mirror. I was quite unable to recognize the youth who stared wide-eyed from the polished metal—and it was a youth, not a man as I had thought, for the beard had been deceptive, giving me an undeserved look of wisdom and age. Without it, I resembled any other youngster at court.

I was then bathed, oiled, perfumed and elaborately dressed. My flesh shrank from the lascivious touch of silk, which makes the body uncomfortably aware of itself. Today I never wear silk, preferring coarse linen or wool.

I have only a vague memory of the rest of that day. I was carried to the palace through crowded streets. The people stared at me curiously, uncertain whether or not it was right to applaud. I looked straight ahead as I had been instructed to do when on view. I tried not to hear conversations in the street. Desperately I tried to recall the eunuch's instructions.

At the edge of the city's main square the palace, gray and forbidding behind its Corinthian colonnade, rose before me like fate itself. Troops were drawn up in full dress on either side of the main door. When I stepped out of the litter, they saluted.

Several hundreds of the people of Milan drew close to examine me. In every city there is a special class whose only apparent function is to gather in public places and look at famous men. They are neither friendly nor unfriendly, merely interested. An elephant would have pleased them most, but since there was no elephant, the mysterious Prince Julian would have to do. Few of them could identify me. None was certain just what relation I was to the Emperor. It is amazing how little we are known to our subjects. I know of places on the boundaries of the empire where they believe Augustus himself still reigns, that he is a great magician who may not die. Of course, the fact each of us calls himself Augustus is a deliberate attempt to suggest that the continuity of power emanating from Rome is the one constant in a world of flux. Yet even in the cities where there is widespread literacy, the average citizen is often uncertain about who the ruler is. Several times already I have been addressed as Constantius by nervous delegations, while one old man actually thought I was Constantine and complimented me on how little I had changed since the battle at the Mulvian bridge!

Inside the palace, curiosity was mingled with excitement and anticipation. I was in favor. I read my good fortune in every face. In the vestibule they paid me homage. Heads bobbed; smiles flashed; my hand was wrung with warmth, kissed with hope. It was disgusting . . . in retrospect. At the time, it was marvelous proof that I was to live for a while longer.

I was delivered to the Master of the Offices, who gave me a final whispered briefing. Then, to the noise of horns, I entered the throne room.

Constantius wore the purple. The robe fell stiffly to his crimson shoes. In one hand he held an ivory staff, while the other rested on the arm of the throne, palm upward, holding the golden orb. As usual, he stared straight before him, unaware of anything except what was in his direct line of vision. He looked ill. His eyes were dark-circled, and his face was somewhat blotchy, as though from too much wine; yet he was abstemious. On a throne at floor level sat Eusebia, blazing with jewels. Though she too played statue, she managed to suggest sympathetic humanity. When she saw me, the sad mouth parted slightly.

To left and right, in full court dress, were the members of the Sacred Consistory. All stared at me as I slowly crossed to the throne, eyes downcast. October light streamed through high windows. The odor of incense was heavy in the room. I felt a child again, and this was Constantine. For a moment, the room swam before my eyes. Then Constantius spoke the first line of the ritual greeting. I answered, and prostrated myself at his feet. I kissed the purple, and was raised up. Like two actors we played our scene impersonally until it was done; then I was given a stool next to Eusebia.

I sat very still, looking straight ahead, aware of Eusebia next to me. I could smell the flowery scent of her robes. But neither of us looked at the other.

Ambassadors were received, generals appointed, titles bestowed. The audience ended when the emperor stood up. The rest of us dropped to our knees. Stiff-legged and swaying slightly from the weight of his robes and jewelry, Constantius marched off to the palace living quarters, followed by Eusebia. The moment the green bronze doors shut behind them, as though from a magician's spell, we were all set free.

Courtiers surrounded me and asked a thousand questions: Would I be made Caesar? Where would I live? Did I need any service? I had only to command. I answered as demurely and noncommittally as I could. Then my enemy Eusebius approached, his yellow moonface gravely respectful. Silk robes whispered as the heavy body bowed to me. "Lord, you are to dine with the sacred family." An excited whisper went through the court.

This was the highest recognition. I was exalted in all eyes. Though my own first reaction was: dinner means poison.

"I shall escort you to the sacred quarters." Eusebius led me to the bronze doors through which the imperial couple had just passed. We did not speak until we were alone in the corridor beyond.

"You should know, Lord, that I have always, in every way, assured the Augustus of your loyalty to him."

"I know that you have." I lied with equal dignity.

"There are those in the Sacred Consistory who are your enemies." He gestured for a guard to open a small oaken door. We passed through. "But I have always opposed them. As you know, I had hoped all along that you would take your rightful place here at court. And though there are some who think that the title Caesar should lapse because your brother . . ." He allowed that sentence to go unfinished. "I have urged his Eternity to make you Caesar."

"I do not seek such honor," I murmured, looking about me with some interest. The palace at Milan is a large rambling building. Originally it was a military governor's rather modest headquarters. In the last century when Rome ceased to be a practical center for the West, the palace was enlarged to become an imperial residence. Because of the German tribes, the emperors had to be close to the Alps. Also, the farther an emperor is from the city of Rome the longer his reign is apt to be, for the populace of that city is notoriously fickle and arrogant, with a long memory of the emperors it has overthrown. None of us stays for long at Rome if he can help it.

Constantine enlarged the palace in Milan, building the state rooms, while Constantius added the second-floor living quarters through which we now walked. These rooms look out on a large inner court. I personally prefer the old-fashioned form of architecture, with small private rooms arranged about an atrium, but Constantius was a modernist in architecture as well as in religion. I find such rooms too large, and of course ruinously expensive to heat.

Guards and eunuchs stood at every door, arrogant yet servile. A court is the most depressing place on earth. Wherever there is a throne, one may observe in rich detail every folly and wickedness of which man is capable, enameled with manners and gilded with hypocrisy. I keep court in the field. In residence, I keep as little as possible.

At the final door, Eusebius left me with a deep bow. Guards opened the door, and I stepped into the private dining room. Constantius reclined on one of the two couches within whose right angle was the table. Opposite him Eusebia sat in an ivory chair. I bowed low to both of them, intoning the proper formula.

Constantius mumbled his response. Then he waved me to the couch beside him.

"You look better without that damned beard."

I blushed as I took my place on the couch. Eusebia smiled encouragingly. "I rather liked the beard," she said.

"That's because you're an atheist, too."

My heart missed a beat. But it was only the Emperor's heavy wit.

"She likes these high-sounding, low-living Cynics." He indicated his wife with a knotty ringed hand. "She's always reading them. Not good for women to read." I said something agreeable, grateful to find him in a good mood. Constantius had removed his diadem and outer robes, and he looked almost human, quite unlike the statue he had appeared earlier.

Wine was brought me and though I seldom drink it full strength, this day I drank deep, to overcome nervousness.

"Who does he look like?" Constantius had been examining me curiously, like a new slave or horse. "Without that beard?"

Eusebia frowned, pretending to be thoughtful. One gives away nothing in dealing with a tyrant, even if the tyrant is one's husband.

The Emperor answered his own question. "Constans. You look just like him. Just like my brother." My heart sank. Constantius had always been thought to have had a hand in his brother's death. But there was no significance to this remark, either. Constantius, at his ease, tended to be literal and rather simple.

I said that I had been too young to recall what my late cousin had looked like.

"Much the best of the three of us. Tall. Like our father." Constantius was much concerned with his own shortness.

An elaborate dinner was served us, and I tasted everything, for to refuse any dish would show that one suspected the Emperor of treachery. It was an ordeal, and my stomach nearly rebelled.

Constantius led the conversation, as emperors are supposed to do—unless they are given to philosophic debate like me, in which case I must speak very fast at my own table to be heard.

I was asked about my studies at Athens. I described them, ending "I could spend the rest of my life there." As I said this, I noticed that Eusebia frowned imperceptibly: a signal that I was not to speak of student life.

But Constantius had not been listening. He lay now flat on his back, belching softly and kneading his barrel-like stomach with one hand. When he spoke, he did so with eyes shut.

"I am the first Augustus to reign alone since my father, who was himself the first to reign alone in this century. But he never intended for just one of us to rule. Any more than Diocletian intended for any one of *his* successors to govern alone." Constantius raised himself on one elbow and looked at me with those curiously mournful eyes which were his most attractive yet most puzzling feature. They were the eyes of a poet who had seen all the tragedy in this world and knows what is to come in the next. Yet the good effect of those eyes was entirely undone by a peevish mouth.

Who could ever know Constantius? I certainly did not. I hated him, but Eusebia loved him—I think—and she was a woman who would not have cared for what was evil. Like the rest of us, Constantius was many men in the body of one.

"The world is too big for one person to govern it." My heart beat faster for I knew now what was to come. "I cannot be everywhere. Yet the imperial power must be everywhere. Things have a habit of going wrong all at once. As soon as the German tribes get loose in the north, the Persians attack in the south. At times I think they must plan it. If I march to the East, I'm immediately threatened in the West. If one general rises up against me, then I must deal with at least two more traitors at the same time. The empire is big. Distances are great. Our enemies many." He tore off a roast duck's leg and chewed it, all the time looking at me with those melting eyes.

"I mean to hold the state together. I shall not sacrifice one city to the barbarians, one town, one field!" The high-pitched voice almost cracked. "I mean to hold the state for our family. We won it. We must maintain it. And that is why we must be loyal to one another." How that phrase from those cruel lips struck me! I dared not look at him.

"Julian," the voice was lower now. "I intend to make you Caesar, and my heir until such time as I have a son."

"Lord . . ." was all I could say. Tears unexpectedly filled my eyes. I shall never know if I *wanted* my fate. Yet when it came to me, a secret line snapped within and the perilous voyage began.

Eusebia congratulated me. I don't recall what was said. More wine was brought and Constantius, in a jovial mood, told me how the astrologists preferred 6 November to any other day in the month. He also insisted that I study military strategy, while assembling a household suitable to my new rank. I was to have a salary. It would not be large, he said, understating the matter considerably: if I had not had a small income from my mother's estate, I would have starved to death that first year. My cousin could never be accused of generosity.

Constantius almost smiled at me. "Now," he said, "I have a surprise for you." The surprise was his sister Helena. She entered the room with great dignity. I had never met her, though I had seen her at a distance during my first visit to Milan.

Helena was not an attractive woman. She was short, inclined to stoutness, with the short legs and long torso of Constantius. By one of those unlucky chances, her face was the face of her father Constantine the Great.

It was almost alarming: the same broad cheeks, the thin proud mouth, the large nose, the huge full jaw, an imperial portrait re-created in a middle-aged woman. Yet despite this unfortunate resemblance, she was otherwise most feminine with an agreeable soft voice. (I have always hated women with shrill voices.) She moved modestly, even shyly. At the time I knew nothing about her except that she was ten years older than I, and that she was Constantius's favorite sister.

After formally acknowledging our greetings, Helena took her place in the vacant chair. She was obviously under considerable strain. So was I, for I knew exactly what was going to happen next. I had always known that something like this was apt to be my fate, but I had put it as much as possible out of my mind. Now the moment was at hand.

"We do you the honor," said Constantius, "of bestowing our own beloved sister upon you as your wife and consort, a human and tangible link between our crowns." He had obviously prepared this sentence in advance. I wondered if he had spoken thus to Gallus when he gave him Constantia in marriage.

Helena looked at the floor. I am afraid I turned scarlet, Eusebia watched me, amused but guarded. She who had been my friend and ally could now quite easily become my enemy. I was aware of this, even then. Or do I write now with hindsight? In any case, it was perfectly plain that should Helena have a child and Eusebia remain barren, my child would be Constantius's heir. The four of us were now caught like flies in a spider's web.

I have no clear idea what I said to Constantius. I am sure that I stammered. Helena later said that I was most eloquent, though unable to look at her during my speech of acceptance. Doubtless I was thinking of my conjugal duties. Never did a woman attract me less. Yet we would have to have a child. This sort of burden is the usual fate of princes and I daresay it is a small price to pay for greatness, though at the time it seems larger than it ought.

Helena was a good woman but our moments of intimacy were rare, unsatisfactory, and somewhat pathetic, for I did want to please her. But it was never pleasant, making love to a bust of Constantine. Though I could not make her happy, I did not make her suffer, and I think we became friends.

The dinner ended when Constantius swung his short bowed legs to the floor, and stretched till his bones cracked. Then without a word to any of us, he left the room. Eusebia gave me a half-smile. She put her hand out to Helena and together the two women withdrew, leaving me staring at the pheasant's eggs which an artist-cook had arranged in a beautifully feathered nest as final course. It was an extraordinary moment. I had entered the room a proscribed student. I left it as Caesar and husband. The change was dizzying.

At dawn on the first of December I left Milan for Gaul. I said farewell to Helena, who was to join me later at Vienne. We both behaved according to the special protocol the eunuchs have devised governing a Caesar's farewell to his new wife as he goes to a beleaguered province. Then, accompanied by the newly arrived Oribasius, I went down to the courtyard of the palace to place myself at the head of my army.

Outside in the frosty air, some three hundred foot soldiers and a score of cavalry were drawn up. I took this to be my personal bodyguard. I was about to ask the whereabouts of the army of Gaul when I was joined by Eutherius. He was frowning. "I've just spoken to the Grand Chamberlain. There has been a last-minute change in plans. Your legions have been assigned to the Danube."

I indicated the men in the courtyard. "Is *this* my army?"

"I am afraid so, Caesar."

I have never in my life been so angry. Only the arrival of Constantius prevented me from saying the unsayable. I saluted the Emperor; gravely, he returned the salute. Then he mounted a black horse and I mounted a white one. His personal guard (twice the size of my "army") fell into place behind him. My troops and household brought up the rear. Thus the Augustus and his Caesar launched the power of Rome against the barbarians. It was ludicrous.

The few citizens who were up and around at this hour cheered us dutifully. We made a particularly fine impression at the vegetable market which is just inside the city gate. The farm women waved their carrots and turnips at us, and thought us a brave sight.

Neither Constantius nor I spoke until we were out on the main road, the high Alps visible to us across the Lombard Plain. He had agreed to escort me as far as the two columns which stand on either side of the road, midway between Lumello and Pavia. He had obviously decided this would give us sufficient time for a good talk. It did.

Constantius began with, "We have great confidence in Florentius, our praetorian prefect at Gaul." This was an announcement there was no invitation for me to comment.

Of course he has confidence in Florentius, I thought savagely, otherwise he would have had him murdered by now. But I said, "Yes, Augustus." And waited. We rode a few more yards. Occasionally our armored legs touched, metal striking metal, and each would shrink instinctively from the other. The touch of another man has always disturbed me; the touch of my father's murderer alarmed me.

We passed a number of carts containing poultry; they had pulled off the road at our approach. When the peasants saw the Emperor, they fell flat on their bellies, as though blinded by the sight of that sacred figure. Constantius ignored them.

"We are fond of our sister Helena." This was also launched upon the dry cool air in an oracular tone.

"She is dear to me, too, Augustus." I replied. I was afraid he was going to lecture me on my marital duties, but he made no further mention of Helena.

Constantius was constructing a case. His occasional flat sentences, suitable for carving in marble, were all part of an edifice created to contain me. I was to obey the praetorian prefect of Gaul, even though as Caesar I was his superior. I was to remember that Helena's first loyalty was to her brother and ruler, not to her husband. So far, I understood him clearly.

"We have heard from your military instructor that you show promise."

"I shall not fail you, Augustus. But it was my understanding that I was to go to Gaul with an army, not an escort."

Constantius ignored this. "You have come to soldiering late. I hope you are able to learn what you will need to know."

This was not optimistic, but not unnatural. There was no reason for anyone to suspect that a philosophy student should show *any* talent for war. Curiously enough, I had every confidence in myself because I knew that the gods would not desert me now they had raised me up. But my cousin had no way of knowing my feelings, or judging my capacity. He merely saw a young untried soldier about to go into battle against the fiercest fighters in the world.

"At all times remember that we are divine in the eyes of the people and sacred to heaven."

I took the "we" to mean Constantius and myself, though he may have been merely reminding me of his own rank. "I shall remember, Augustus." I always called him by his proper title, though he much preferred Lord, a title I despise and do not use for it means that one is the master of other men, rather than simply first among them.

"Control your generals." Though he still sounded as if he were repeating maxims, I could tell that now he was on the verge of actual advice, if not conversation. "No officer should be admitted to senatorial rank. All officers must be under strict civilian control. Any governor of any province outranks any general sent to him. No officer must be allowed to take part in civil affairs. Our praetorian prefects are set over all military and civil officials. That is why the administration of the empire runs as smoothly as it does."

Needless to say, I did not remark that the collapse of Gaul was hardly a sign of smooth administration. But in principle Constantius's advice was good and I tend still to follow it. There is no denying that he had a gift for administration.

"In matters of taxes, take whatever is owing us. Show no mercy to the cities and villages which are delinquent in meeting payments. It is their nature to complain. Assume that your taxgatherers are honest unless proved otherwise. They are *never* honest, but no one has yet found a way to correct their abuses. As long as they return to you the larger part of what they collect, be satisfied."

I was later to revise the system of taxation in Gaul, disproving everything he said. But all that in its proper place.

"Control the generals." He repeated this suddenly as if he'd forgotten he had already said it to me. Then he turned and looked at me for the first time that day. It was startling. No longer was he the sun god on his charger. This was my cousin, my enemy, my lord, source of my greatness and potential source of my death. "You must know what I mean," he said, sounding like a man, not an oracle. "You have seen the state disrupted. Our high place threatened. Provinces wrecked. Cities destroyed. Armies wasted. The barbarians seizing our lands, because we were too busy fighting one another to protect ourselves from the true enemy. Well, Caesar, remember this: allow no general sufficient power to raise an army against you. You have seen what I have had to suffer. Usurper after usurper has wasted our power. Be on your guard."

"I will, Augustus."

Then he said, very slowly, his eyes on mine, "As I am on my guard." He looked away when he saw that his meaning was quite clear. Then he added for good measure, "We have never yet lost so much as a foot of earth to any usurper, nor will we ever."

"As long as I live, Augustus, you shall have at least one arm to fight for you."

We rode until midday. Then at the two columns we stopped. It was a fine brisk noon and despite the chill in the air, the sun was hot and we were all sweating under our armor. A halt was ordered.

Constantius and I dismounted and he motioned for me to accompany him into a hard stubbled field. Except for our troops, no one was in sight. In every country peasants vanish when they see armed men coming; all soldiers are the enemy, I wish one could change that.

Constantius walked ahead of me toward a small ruined shrine to Hermes which stood at the edge of the field (a favorable omen, Hermes has always watched over me). Behind us, our men watered horses, rearranged armor, swore and chattered, pleased by the good weather. Just as Constantius entered the shrine, I broke a dead flower off its stalk. Then I followed him inside the shrine, which smelled of human excrement. Constantius was urinating on the floor. Even in this, he was grave and majestic.

"It is a pity," I heard myself saying, aware as I spoke that I was breaking protocol, "what has happened to these old temples."

"A pity? They should all be torn down." He rearranged his clothes. "I hate the sight of them."

"Of course," I muttered.

"I shall leave you here," he said. We stood facing one another. Though I deliberately stooped, I could not help but look down on him. He edged away from me, instinctively searching for higher ground.

"Whatever you need, you shall have. Call on me. Also, depend on our praetorian prefect. He represents us. You will find the legions of Vienne alert, ready for a spring campaign. So prepare yourself."

He handed me a thick document. "Instructions. To be read at your leisure." He paused. Then he remembered something. "The Empress has made you a gift. It is with your baggage. A library, I believe."

I was effusive in my gratitude. I said words but Constantius did not listen. He moved to the door. He paused; he turned; he tried to speak to me. I blushed. I wanted to reach out and take his hand and tell him not to fear me, but I did not dare. Neither of us was ever able to face the other.

When Constantius finally spoke, his voice broke with tension. "If this should come to you . . ." Awkwardly he gestured at himself to indicate the principate of the world, "Remember . . ." Then his voice stopped as if a strangler's thumb had blocked the windpipe. He could not go on. Words had failed him again, and me.

I have often wondered what it was he meant to say; what it was I should remember. That life is short? Dominion bitter? No. Constantius was not a profound man. I doubt if he had been about to offer me any startling insight. But as I think back on that scene in the ruined shrine (and I think of it often, I even dream of it), I suspect that all he meant to say was, "Remember me." If that is what you meant, cousin, then I have, in every sense, remembered you.

Constantius left the shrine. As soon as his back was to me, I placed the withered flower on the profaned floor and whispered a quick prayer to Hermes. Then I followed the Emperor across the field to the road.

Once mounted, we exchanged formal farewells, and Constantius rode back to Milan, the dragon banner streaming in the cool wind before him. We never saw one another again.

By the middle of August we were in the wild but beautiful valley of the Danube. Though the river is not as impressive to look at as the Rhine, it is far less treacherous to navigate. So I decided to make the rest of the journey by water.

At a village on the south bank, we halted and I ordered boats built.

While this was being done, I received the fealty of the local tribes. They were amazed to see a Roman emperor (even a not quite legitimate one!) so far north. When they discovered that I meant them no harm, they were most cooperative and offered to act as river pilots. They are a handsome, fair-skinned people, somewhat shy.

Meanwhile, messengers from Jovinus arrived, with good news. Milan had fallen. He also wrote me the latest news of Constantius. Sapor had advanced to the Tigris. Constantius had then withdrawn to Edessa, where he was now holed up, avoiding battle. I was amused to note that he had appointed Florentius praetorian prefect of Illyricum. I was obviously poor Florentius's nemesis. I had sent him out of Gaul; soon I would drive him from Illyricum. I believe of all those who hate me, he must hate me the most. He certainly has the best reason!

We sailed down the Danube through a golden country, rich with harvest. We paused at none of the towns or fortresses which became more numerous the farther south we went. There was no time to waste. If I took Sirmium, all these towns would be mine by right, but if I paused to lay siege to each I should never be done fighting. Most of the natives were well disposed toward us; but then none was put to the test.

In early October, at night, with the moon waning, we reached Bonmunster, nineteen miles north of Sirmium. It is a small town, with no garrison. Late as it was, I ordered all men ashore. We pitched camp on the bank of the river.

I do not know if it is common to all in my place, but it was my experience as a usurper (and one must call me by that blunt name) that everywhere I went well-wishers and informers flocked to me like bees to honey, until I was forced to devise a screening process to examine each would-be ally and determine if he could be used. Most proved to be sincere; but then I proved to be victorious!

Before the moon had set, I had learned that Count Lucillianus was at Sirmium, with a considerable army and orders to destroy me. However, Lucillianus did not expect me in the vicinity for another week, and so he slept now at Sirmium.

As soon as I had heard these reports, I sent for Dagalaif. I ordered him to go straight to Sirmium with a hundred men; he was to seize Lucillianus and bring him back. This was a considerable assignment, but I knew from spies that the city was no more than usually guarded and that the palace where Lucillianus was staying was close to the gate. At night our men would look no different from any other imperial troops; there would be no problem entering the city. For the rest, I counted on Dagalaif's boldness and ingenuity.

After Dagalaif had left, Oribasius and I strolled together on the river bank. It was a warm night. In the black sky a misshapen moon, like a worn marble head, made all the country silver. Behind us the fires and torches of the camp burned. The men were quiet; they had orders to make no unnecessary noise; only the horses occasionally disobeyed me, with sharp sudden whinnies. At the top of the river bank we stopped.

"I like this," I said, turning to Oribasius, who was seated now on a rock, staring at the bright diagonal the moonlight made across the slow deep water.

Oribasius looked up at me. The moon was so bright that I could make out his features. "This?" He frowned. "Do you mean the river? or war? or travel?"

"Life." I sat on the damp ground beside him and crossed my legs, muddying the purple I wore. "Not war. Nor travel. Just this. Right now." I sighed. "I can hardly believe we have crossed nearly half the world. I feel like the wind, without a body, invisible."

He laughed. "You are probably the most visible man on earth, and the most feared."

"Feared," I repeated, wondering if I would ever take satisfaction from the knowledge that men's lives and fortunes could be taken away from them at a nod of my head. No, I cannot enjoy that sort of power; it is not what I want.

"What do you want?" Oribasius had divined my mood, as he so often does.

"To restore the gods."

"But if they are real and do exist . . ."

"They are real! There is no 'if'! They do exist!" I was fierce.

His laughter stopped me. "Then they exist. But if they exist, they are always present, and so there's no need to 'restore' them."

"But we must worship what God tells us to."

"So the Christians say."

"Ah, but theirs is a false god, and I mean to destroy them."

Oribasius stiffened at my word "destroy." "*Kill* them?"

"No. I shall not allow them the pleasure of martyrdom. Besides, at the rate they kill one another, it would be gratuitous for me to intervene. No, I shall fight them with reason and example. I shall reopen the temples and reorganize the priesthood. We shall put Hellenism on such a footing that people will choose it of their own free will."

"I wonder." Oribasius was thoughtful. "They are rich, well-organized. Most important, they educate the children."

"We shall do the same!" I was thinking as I spoke; I had no plan. "Even better, we could take the schools away from them."

"If you could . . ."

"The Emperor can."

"It might work. Otherwise . . ."

"Otherwise?"

"You would have to reign as a bloody tyrant and even then you'd lose."

"I am not so pessimistic." But Oribasius had put an idea into my head, one which will save us all. Curiously enough, though we had often spoken of what it would be like when I became emperor, none of us had ever really considered in much detail what form the contest between Hellenism and the Galileans would take. We agreed that when I could I would publicly repudiate the Nazarene, but none of us had thought what the reaction might be, particularly from the common people of whom perhaps half are Galilean. Only the army is truly religious. The men worship Mithras. There are few Galileans in the ranks, through a third of the officers believe in the triple monster.

We talked until it was morning. Just as the sun appeared over the world's edge, like an omen, Dagalaif returned to camp with Count Lucillianus as prisoner.

I hurried to my tent. There on the ground in his nightclothes was Lucillianus, trussed like a chicken. He was terrified. For a moment I looked down on the shivering body, recalling that the last time I had seen him he had been my brother's jailer. Then I loosened his bonds and raised him to his feet. This friendly gesture somewhat relieved his anxiety. He is a large man, given to peculiar diets. For years he would eat only udder of sow; at least that is the story one hears.

"We are happy you could attend us on such short notice, Count." I was formal but agreeable.

"If only I had known, Caesar . . . I mean Augustus . . . I should have met you myself . . ."

"And put me to death, like Gallus?"

"Those were my orders, Augustus, but you may depend on my loyalty to you in this dispute. I have always been loyal. I have always preferred you to the Emp—to *him* at Antioch."

"We accept your loyalty, your troops, your city of Sirmium, and the prefecture of Illyricum."

He gasped but bowed. "Such is the will of Augustus. All these are yours."

"Thank you, Count." I was in an excellent mood. Lucillianus is the sort of man who does not think ahead—witness his failure to anticipate my arrival—and men who do not think ahead tend to accept what is; they never conspire.

I said, "Now swear your oath to me." He swore; and kissed the purple, getting a bit of Danube mud on his face. "You will retain your rank, Count, and serve in my army."

Lucillianus's recovery was swift. "If I may say so, Lord, it is a very rash thing you have done, coming here with such a small army in the midst of someone else's territory."

"Reserve, my dear Count, your wisdom for Constantius. I have given you my hand not to make you my counsellor but less afraid." I turned to Mamertinus. "Give the word to the army. We march to Sirmium."

Sirmium is a large city, highly suitable for an imperial capital, standing as it does upon the border between the prefecture of Illyricum and the diocese of Dacia—the westernmost country of the prefecture of the East. I was now at the beginning of the territory traditionally assigned to the Augustus of the East.

I had warned my officers that there might be incidents. I did not expect the city to surrender without token resistance, even though its commander was now with us, riding at my side.

But to my astonishment, we were met outside the gates by a vast crowd of men, women and children, carrying chains of flowers, boughs of trees and numerous sacred objects. I was hailed as Augustus with the most extraordinary enthusiasm.

I turned to Lucillianus and shouted to him above the din, "Did you arrange this?"

He shook his head. He was too stupid to lie. "No, Augustus. I don't know who arranged it . . ."

"Legend!" said Oribasius. "They know you'll win. They always do."

A large bouquet of flowers hit me in the face. Eyes stinging, I swept it aside; a blood-red poppy caught in my beard. Men and women kissed my robe, my legs, my horse. Thus was I escorted into the capital of Illyricum while the grapes were still green. It was the first great city ever to fall to me, twice the size of Strasbourg or Cologne or even Treves. The date was 3 October, 361.

I went straight to the palace, and to business. I received the senate of the city. I allayed their fears. They swore loyalty to me, as did the legions within the city. I ordered a week of chariot races next day to amuse the populace, one of the burdens the conquered invariably put upon the conqueror. With great pleasure, I received Nevitta who, true to his promise, arrived at Sirmium after a victorious passage through Raetia. The West was ours.

I called a staff meeting, and we discussed our next move. Some favored marching straight to Constantinople, two hundred miles distant. Dagalaif argued that with Constantius in Antioch, Constantinople would fall to us without a battle. Nevitta was not so certain. He was afraid that Constantius was probably already on the march from Antioch to the capital. If this were so, we were hardly a match for what was, in fact, the largest army on earth. I agreed with Nevitta. We would remain where we were for the winter.

I entrusted to Nevitta the defense of the Succi Pass, a narrow defile in the high mountains that separate Thrace from Illyricum. Whoever holds this pass is safe from attack by land. I then sent two of the Sirmium legions to Aquileia, to hold that important seaport for us. With the main part of the army I withdrew some fifty miles southeast to Nish (where Constantine was born); here I went into winter quarters.

The weeks at Nish were busy ones. Every night I dictated until dawn. I was determined to present my case against Constantius as clearly as possible for all to read and comprehend. I sent a lengthy message to the Roman senate. I also composed separate letters for the senates of Sparta, Corinth and Athens, explaining what I had done and what I intended to do. Heavily but justly, I placed the blame for all that had happened on Constantius. Then—though Oribasius warned me not to—I assured the various senates that I intended to restore the worship of the old gods, making the point that I personally imitated them in order that, by having the fewest possible needs, I might do good to the greatest possible number. These letters were read at every public gathering. They made a profound and favorable impression.

During this period I planned an amphibious attack on Constantinople to take place as soon as the winds favored us. We were in a good position militarily. At Succi we controlled the land approach to the West. At Aquileia we controlled the sea approach to northern Italy. I felt reasonably secure, and was confident that before civil war broke out, Constantius would come to terms with me. But my sense of security was rudely shattered when I learned that the two legions I had sent to Aquileia had promptly gone over to Constantius. The port was now his, and I was vulnerable to an attack by sea. Since I was not able to leave Nish and Nevitta could not leave Succi, my only hope was Jovinus, who was in Austria en route to Nish. I sent him a frantic message: proceed immediately to Aquileia. My situation was now most precarious. Constantius could at any time land an army at Aquileia and cut me off from Italy and Gaul. I was in despair, confident that the gods had deserted me. But they had not. At the last moment, they intervened.

On the night of 20 November I was working late. Lamps filled with cheap oil smoked abominably. The three night secretaries sat at a long table, mountains of parchment stacked in front of them. At a separate table I was writing a letter to my uncle Julian, trying to reassure him—and myself—that victory was certain. I had just finished the letter, with one of those postscripts even old friends say they cannot decipher, when I heard footsteps quickly approaching. Without ceremony the door flew open. The clerks and I leapt to our feet. One never knows if assassins are at hand. But it was Oribasius, out of breath, a letter in his hand.

"It's happened!" he gasped. Then he did something he had never done before. He dropped on his knees before me, offered me the letter. "This is for you . . . Augustus."

I read the first line. Then the words blurred together and I could read no more. "Constantius is dead." As I said those extraordinary words, the clerks one by one fell to their knees. Then, as in a dream, the room began to fill with people. All knew what had happened. All paid me silent homage for I had, miraculously, with the stopping of one man's breath, become sole Augustus, Emperor of Rome, Lord of the world. To my astonishment, I wept.

I am alone in my study. I have already put away Julian's papers. The thing is finished. The world Julian wanted to preserve and restore is gone . . . but I shall not write "forever," for who can know the future? Meanwhile, the barbarians are at the gate. Yet when they breach the wall, they will find nothing of value to seize, only empty relics. The spirit of what we were has fled. So be it.

I have been reading Plotinus all evening. He has the power to soothe me; and I find his sadness curiously comforting. Even when he writes: "Life here with the things of earth is a sinking, a defeat, a failing of the wing." The wing has indeed failed. One sinks. Defeat is certain. Even as I write these lines, the lamp wick sputters to an end, and the pool of light in which I sit contracts. Soon the room will be dark. One has always feared that death would be like this. But what else is there? With Julian, the light went, and now nothing remains but to let the darkness come, and hope for a new sun and another day, born of time's mystery and man's love of light.

# *CREATION*

RETROSPECTIVELY NARRATED in old age by a fictional fifth-century B.C. Persian diplomat, *Creation* (1981) is a novel of ideas and also of sweeping historical re-creation. In his blind old age, Cyrus Spitama, having spent his life traveling in Greece, Asia Minor, India, and China as a high-level representative of his government, finds himself on his last mission, compelled to serve as special ambassador to the quarrelsome, uncivilized Athenians. An eager adventurer as well as a diplomat, Cyrus has achieved some wisdom during his travels, particularly in his effort to answer the central cosmological questions associated with the history of religion: what is the nature of existence and is there a creator of all things? Cyrus is the grandson of Zoroaster and he has a passionate interest in the fundamental issues that the religions of the first half of the fifth century are grappling with.

As a novelist, historian, and cultural anthropologist, Vidal puts us into Cyrus's mind: we see the Persian–Greek hostilities from the Persian viewpoint; Cyrus's Zoroastrianism, vaguely anticipating some Christian doctrine, is the touchstone against which he measures Buddhism, Tao, and Confucism, the progenitors of all three of which Cyrus meets. In the end, it is Confucius's engagement with the ethical problems of this world (especially how to balance the interests of the individual and the community) that Cyrus finds most compelling. Vidal's fascination with the consequences of religious ideas makes *Creation* both pedagogic and entertaining. To some of its initial reviewers its depiction of the rivalries between ancient empires evoked similar post–World War II conflicts;

others emphasized the appostiveness of conveying information and religious philosophy within a compelling fictional narrative at a time when educational standards have declined and television increasingly crowds out serious reading.

# From *Creation*

## [Herodotus Gives a Reading at the Odeon in Athens]

### 1

I am blind. But I am not deaf. Because of the incompleteness of my misfortune, I was obliged yesterday to listen for nearly six hours to a self-styled historian whose account of what the Athenians like to call "the Persian Wars" was nonsense of a sort that were I less old and more privileged, I would have risen in my seat at the Odeon and scandalized all Athens by answering him.

But then, I know the origin of the *Greek* wars. He does not. How could he? How could any Greek? I spent most of my life at the court of Persia and even now, in my seventy-fifth year, I still serve the Great King as I did his father—my beloved friend Xerxes—and his father before him, a hero known even to the Greeks as Darius the Great.

When the painful reading finally ended—our "historian" has a thin monotonous voice made even less charming by a harsh Dorian accent—my eighteen-year-old nephew Democritus wanted to know if I would like to stay behind and speak to the traducer of Persia.

"You should," he said. "Because everyone is staring at you. They know you must be very angry." Democritus is studying philosophy here at Athens. This means that he delights in quarrels. Write that down, Democritus. After all, it is at your request that I am dictating this account of how and why the Greek wars began. I shall spare no one—including you. Where was I? the Odeon.

I smiled the poignant smile of the blind, as some unobservant poet characterized the expression of those of us who cannot see. Not that I ever paid much attention to blind men when I could see. On the other hand, I never expected to live long enough to be old, much less go blind, as I did three years ago when the white clouds that had been settling upon the retinas of my eyes became, suddenly, opaque.

The last thing that I ever saw was my own blurred face in a polished-silver mirror. This was at Susa, in the Great King's palace. At first I thought that the room was filling up with smoke. But it was summertime, and there was no fire. For an instant I saw myself in the mirror; then saw myself no longer; saw nothing else, ever again.

In Egypt the doctors perform an operation that is supposed to send the clouds scurrying. But I am too old to go to Egypt. Besides, I have seen quite enough. Have I not looked upon the holy fire, which is the face of Ahura Mazdah, the Wise Lord? I have also seen Persia and India and farthest Cathay. No other man alive has traveled in as many lands as I.

I am digressing. This is a habit of old men. My grandfather in *his* seventy-fifth year used to talk for hours without ever linking one subject to another. He was absolutely incoherent. But then, he was Zoroaster, the prophet of Truth; and just as the One God that he served is obliged to entertain, simultaneously, every aspect of all creation, so did His prophet Zoroaster. The result was inspiring if you could ever make sense of what he was saying.

Democritus wants me to record what happened as we were leaving the Odeon. Very well. It is your fingers that will grow tired. My voice never deserts me, nor does my memory . . . Thus far.

There was deafening applause when Herodotus of Halicarnassus finished his description of the Persian "defeat" at Salamis thirty-four years ago. By the way, the acoustics of the Odeon are dreadful. Apparently, I am not alone in finding the new music hall inadequate. Even the tone-deaf Athenians know that something is wrong with their precious Odeon, recently thrown together in record time by order of Pericles, who paid for it with money that had been collected from all the Greek cities for their common defense. The building itself is a copy in stone of the tent of the Great King Xerxes which somehow fell into Greek hands during the confusions of Persia's last campaign in Greece. They affect to despise us; then they imitate us.

As Democritus led me to the vestibule of the music hall, I heard on every side the phrase "The Persian ambassador!" The throaty syllables struck my ears like those potsherds on which Athenians periodically write the names of anyone who has happened to offend or bore them. The man who gets the most votes in this election—or rejection—is exiled from the city for a period of ten years. He is lucky.

I give a few of the remarks that I heard en route to the door.

"I'll bet he didn't like what he heard."

"He's a brother of Xerxes, isn't he?"

"No, he's a Magian."

"What's that?"

"A Persian priest. They eat snakes and dogs."

"And commit incest with their sisters and mothers and daughters."

"What about their brothers and fathers and sons?"

"You are insatiable, Glaucon."

"Magians are always blind. They have to be. Is that his grandson?"

"No. His lover."

"I don't think so. Persians are different from us."

"Yes. They lose battles. We don't."

"How would you know? You weren't even born when we sent Xerxes running home to Asia."

"That boy is very good-looking."

"He's Greek. He has to be. No barbarian could look like that."

"He's from Abdera. The grandson of Megacreon."

"A medizer! Scum of the earth."

"Rich scum. Megacreon owns half the silver mines in Thrace."

Of my two remaining and relatively unimpaired senses—touch and smell—I cannot report much of the first, other than the wiry arm of Democritus, which I clutched in my right hand, but as for the second! In summer Athenians do not bathe often. In winter—and we are now in the week that contains the shortest day of the year—they bathe not at all, while their diet appears to consist entirely of onions and preserved fish—preserved from the time of Homer.

I was jostled, breathed upon, insulted. I am of course aware that my position as the Great King's ambassador at Athens is not only a perilous one but highly ambiguous. It is perilous because at any moment these volatile people are apt to hold one of their assemblies in which every male citizen may speak his mind and, worst of all, vote. After listening to one of the city's many corrupt or demented demagogues, the citizens are quite capable of breaking a sacred treaty, which is what they did fourteen years ago when they sent out an expedition to conquer the Persian province of Egypt. They were roundly defeated. This adventure was doubly shameful because, sixteen years ago, an Athenian embassy had gone up to Susa with instructions to make a permanent peace with Persia. The chief ambassador was Callias, the richest man in Athens. In due course, a treaty was drafted. Athens acknowledged the Great King's sovereignty over the Greek cities of Asia Minor. In turn, the Great King agreed to keep the Persian fleet out of the Aegean Sea, and so on. The treaty was very long. In fact, I have often thought that during the composition of the Persian text, I permanently damaged my eyes. Certainly, the white clouds began to thicken during those months of negotiation when I was obliged to read every word of what the clerks had written.

After the Egyptian debacle, another embassy went up to Susa. The Great King was superb. He ignored the fact that the Athenians had broken the original treaty by invading his province of Egypt. Instead, he spoke warmly of his friendship for Sparta. The Athenians were terrified. Quite rightly, they fear Sparta. In a matter of days it was agreed that the treaty, which neither side could ever acknowledge, was once more in force, and as a proof of the Great King's faith in his Athenian slaves—so he calls them—he would send to Athens the friend closest to the bosom of his late father Xerxes, Cyrus Spitama, myself.

I cannot say that I was entirely pleased. I never thought that the last years of my life would be spent in this cold and windy city amongst a people as cold and windy as the place itself. On the other hand, and what I say is for your ears alone, Democritus—in fact, this commentary is largely for your benefit, to be used in any way you like once I am dead . . . a matter of days, I should think, considering the fever that now burns me up and the fits of coughing that must make this dictation as tiring for you as it is for me . . . I have lost my train of thought.

On the other hand . . . Yes. Since the murder of my beloved friend Xerxes and the accession of his son Artaxerxes, my position at Susa has been less than comfortable. Although the Great King is kind to me, I am too much associated with the previous reign to be entirely trusted by the new people at court. What little influence that I still exert derives from an accident of birth. I am the last living grandson in the male line of Zoroaster, the prophet of the One God, Ahura Mazdah—in Greek, the Wise Lord. Since the Great King Darius converted to Zoroastrianism a half-century ago, the royal family has always treated our family with reverence, which makes me feel something of an impostor. After all, one cannot choose one's grandfather.

At the door of the Odeon, I was stopped by Thucydides, a somber middle-aged man who has led the conservative party at Athens since the death of his famous father-in-law Cimon three years ago. As a result, he is the only serious rival to Pericles, the leader of the democratic party.

Political designations hereabouts are imprecise. The leaders of both factions are aristocrats. But certain nobles—like the late Cimon—favor the wealthy landowning class, while others—like Pericles—play to the city mob whose notorious assembly he has strengthened, continuing the work of *his* political mentor Ephialtes, a radical leader who was mysteriously murdered a dozen years ago. Naturally, the conservatives were blamed for the murder. If responsible, they should be congratulated. No mob can govern a city, much less an empire.

Certainly, if my father had been Greek and my mother Persian—instead of the other way around, I would have been a member of the conservative party, even though that party can never resist using the idea of Persia to frighten the people. Despite Cimon's love of Sparta and hatred of us, I would like to have known him. Everyone here says that his sister Elpinice resembles him in character. She is a marvelous woman, and a loyal friend to me.

Democritus reminds me, courteously, that I am again off the subject. I remind *him* that after listening all those hours to Herodotus, I can no longer move with any logic from one point to the next. He writes the way a grasshopper hops. I imitate him.

Thucydides spoke to me in the vestibule of the Odeon. "I suppose that a copy of what we've just heard will be sent on to Susa."

"Why not?" I was both bland and dull, the perfect ambassador. "The Great King enjoys wondrous tales. He has a taste for the fabulous."

Apparently I was insufficiently dull. I could sense the displeasure of Thucydides and the group of conservatives who were in attendance. Party leaders in Athens seldom walk out alone for fear of murder. Democritus tells me that whenever one sees a large group of noisy men at whose center looms either a helmeted onion or a scarlet moon, the first is bound to be Pericles, the second Thucydides. Between onion and autumnal moon the city is irritably divided.

Today was the day of the scarlet moon. For some reason the helmeted onion had not attended the reading in the Odeon. Could it be that Pericles is ashamed of the acoustics in *his* building? But I forget. Shame is not an emotion known to the Athenians.

Currently Pericles and his cabal of artists and builders are constructing a temple to Athena on the Acropolis, a grandiose replacement for the shabby temple that the Persion army burned to the ground thirty-four years ago, a fact that Herodotus tends not to dwell on.

"Do you mean, Ambassador, that the account we have just heard is untrue?" Thucydides was insolent. I daresay he was drunk. Although we Persians are accused of heavy drinking because of our ritual use of haoma, I have never seen a Persian as drunk as certain Athenians and, to be fair, no Athenian could ever be as drunk as a Spartan. My old friend King Demaratus of Sparta used to say that the Spartans never took wine without water until the northern nomads sent Sparta an embassy shortly after Darius laid waste their native Scythia. According to Demaratus, the Scythians taught the Spartans to drink wine without water. I don't believe this story.

"What we have heard, my dear young man, is only a version of events that took place before you were born and, I suspect, before the birth of the historian."

"There are still many of us left who remember well the day the Persians came to Marathon." An old voice sounded at my elbow. Democritus did not recognize its owner. But one hears that sort of old voice often enough. All over Greece, strangers of a certain age will greet one another with the questions, "And where were you and what did you do when Xerxes came to Marathon?" Then they exchange lies.

"Yes," I said. "There are those who still remember the ancient days. I am, alas, one. In fact, the Great King Xerxes and I are exactly the same age. If he were alive today, he would be seventy-five years old. When he came to the throne, he was thirty-four—the prime of life. Yet your historian has just finished telling us that Xerxes was a rash *boy* when he succeeded Darius."

"A small detail," Thucydides began.

"But typical of a work that will give as much delight at Susa as that play of Aeschylus called *The Persians,* which I myself translated for the Great King, who found delightful the author's Attic wit." None of this was true, of course; Xerxes would have gone into a rage had he ever known to what extent he and his mother had been travestied for the amusement of the Athenian mob.

I have made it a policy never to show distress when insulted by barbarians. Fortunately, I am spared their worst insults. These they save for one another. It is a lucky thing for the rest of the world that Greeks dislike one another far more than they do us outlanders.

A perfect example: When the once applauded dramatist Aeschylus lost a prize to the currently applauded Sophocles, he was so enraged that he left Athens for Sicily, where he came to a most satisfying end. An eagle, looking for a hard surface on which to break up the turtle that he held in his claws, mistook the bald head of the author of the *The Persians* for a rock and let slip the turtle, with fatal accuracy.

Thucydides was about to continue what looked to be the beginning of a most ugly scene, when young Democritus suddenly propelled me forward with the cry, "Way for the ambassador of the Great King!" And way was made.

Fortunately, my litter was waiting just outside the portico.

I have had the good luck to be able to rent a house built before we burned down Athens. It is somewhat more comfortable if less pretentious than the houses currently being built by wealthy Athenians. There is nothing like having your native city burned to the ground to inspire ambitious architects. Sardis is now far more splendid after the great fire than ever it was in the time of Croesus. Although I never saw the old Athens—and cannot of course see the new Athens—I am told that private houses are still built of mud brick, that the streets are seldom straight and never wide, that the new public buildings are splendid if makeshift—like the Odeon.

At present, most of the building is taking place on the Acropolis, a lion-colored lump of rock, Democritus' poetic phrase, that overhangs not only most of the city but this house. As a result, in winter—right now—we get less than an hour of sun a day.

But the rock has its charms. Democritus and I often stroll there. I touch ruined walls. Listen to the clatter of the masons. Ponder that splendid family of tyrants who used to live on the Acropolis before they were driven out of the city, as everyone truly noble is driven out sooner or later. I knew the last tyrant, the gentle Hippias. He was often at the court of Susa when I was young.

Today the principal feature of the Acropolis is the houses or temples that contain the images of the gods which the people pretend to worship. I say pretend because it is my view that despite the basic conservatism of the Athenian people when it comes to maintaining the *forms* of old things, the essential spirit of these people is atheistic—or as a Greek cousin of mine pointed out not long ago, with dangerous pride, man is the measure of all things. I think that in their hearts the Athenians truly believe this to be true. As a result, paradoxically, they are uncommonly superstitious and strictly punish those who are thought to have committed impiety.

## 2

Democritus was not prepared for some of the things that I said last night at dinner. Not only has he now asked me for a true account of the Greek wars but, more important, he wants me to record my memories of India and Cathay, and of the wise men that I met at the east—and at the east of the east. He has offered to write down everything that I remember. My guests at dinner were equally urgent. But I suspect that they were simply polite.

We are seated now in the courtyard of the house. It is the hour when we get the sun. The day is cool but not cold and I can feel the sun's warmth on my face. I am comfortable, because I am dressed in the Persian fashion. All parts of the body are covered except the face. Even the hands in repose are covered by sleeves. Naturally, I wear trousers—an article of clothing that always disturbs the Greeks.

Our notions of modesty greatly amuse the Greeks, who are never so happy as when they are watching naked youths play games. Blindness spares me the sight not only of Athens' romping youths but of those lecherous men who watch them. Yet the Athenians are modest when it comes to their women. Women here are swathed from head to toe like Persian ladies—but without color, ornament, style.

I dictate in Greek because I have always spoken Ionian Greek with ease. My mother, Lais, is a Greek from Abdera. She is a daughter of Megacreon, the great-grandfather of Democritus. Since Megacreon owned rich silver mines and you are descended from him in the male line, you are far rich than I. Yes, write that down. You are a part of this narrative, young and insignificant as you are. After all, you have stirred my memory.

Last night I gave dinner to the torchbearer Callias and to the sophist Anaxagoras. Democritus spends many hours a day with Anaxagoras, being talked at. This is known as education. In my time and country, education meant memorizing sacred texts, studying mathematics, practicing music, and archery . . .

"To ride, to draw the bow, to tell the truth." That is Persian education in a proverbial phrase. Democritus reminds me that Greek education is much the same—except for telling the truth. He knows by heart the Ionian Homer, another blind man. This may be true but in recent years traditional methods of education have been abandoned—Democritus says supplemented—by a new class of men who call themselves sophists. In theory, a sophist is supposed to be skilled in one or another of the arts. In practice, many local sophists have no single subject or competence. They are simply sly with words and it is hard to determine what, specifically, they mean to teach, since they question all things, except money. They see to it that they are well paid by the young men of the town.

Anaxagoras is the best of a bad lot. He speaks simply. He writes good Ionian Greek. Democritus read me his book *Physics.* Although I did not understand a lot of it, I marvel at the man's audacity. He has attempted to explain all things through a close observation of the visible world. I can follow him when he describes the visible but when it comes to the invisible, he loses me. He believes that *there is no nothing.* He believes that all space is filled with something, even if we cannot see it—the wind, for instance. He is most interesting (and atheistic!) about birth and death.

"The Greeks," he has written, "have a wrong conception of becoming and perishing. Nothing comes to be or perishes, but there is mixture and separation of things that exist. Thus they ought properly to speak of generation as mixture, and extinction as separation." This is acceptable. But what are these "things"? What makes them come together and go apart? How and when and why were they created? By whom? For me, there is only one subject worth pondering—creation.

In answer, Anaxagoras has come up with the word mind. "Originally, from the infinitely small to the infinitely large, all things were at rest. Then mind set them in order." Then those things (*what* are they? *where* are they? *why* are they?) started to rotate.

One of the largest things is a hot stone that we call the sun. When

Anaxagoras was very young, he predicted that sooner or later a piece of the sun would break off and fall to earth. Twenty years ago, he was proved right. The whole world saw a fragment of the sun fall in a fiery arc through the sky, landing near Aegospotami in Thrace. When the fiery fragment cooled, it proved to be nothing more than a chunk of brown rock. Overnight Anaxagoras was famous. Today his book is read everywhere. You can buy a secondhand-copy in the Agora for a drachma.

Pericles invited Anaxagoras to Athens and gave him a small pension, which currently supports the sophist and his family. Needless to say, conservatives hate him almost as much as they do Pericles. Whenever they wish to embarrass Pericles politically, they accuse his friend Anaxagoras of blasphemy and impiety and all the usual nonsense . . . no, not nonsense for Anaxagoras is as much an atheist as all the other Greeks, but unlike the rest he is not a hypocrite. He is a serious man. He thinks hard about the nature of the universe, and without a knowledge of the Wise Lord you must think very hard indeed for otherwise nothing will ever make sense.

Anaxagoras is about fifty years old. He is an Ionian Greek from a town called Clazomenae. He is small and fat, or so I am told by Democritus. He comes from a wealthy family. When his father died, he refused to administer the ancestral estate or hold political office. He was interested only in observing the natural world. Finally he turned over all his property to distant relatives and left home. When asked whether or not his native land concerned him at all, Anaxagoras said, "Oh, yes, my native land very much concerns me." And he pointed to the sky. I forgive him this characteristic Greek gesture. They do like to show off.

During the first table, as we dined on fresh rather than preserved fish, Anaxagoras was curious to know my reaction to the tales of Herodotus. I tried several times to answer him, but old Callias did most of the talking. I must indulge Callias because our invisible peace treaty is by no means popular with the Athenians. In fact, there is always a danger that our agreement will one day be renounced and I shall be obliged to move on, assuming that my ambassadorial status is recognized and I am not put to death. The Greeks do not honor ambassadors. Meanwhile, as co-author of the treaty, Callias is my protector.

Callias described yet again the battle of Marathon. I am very tired of the Greek version of this incident. Needless to say, Callias fought with the bravery of Hercules. "Not that I was obliged to. I mean, I'm hereditary torchbearer. I serve the mysteries of Demeter, the Great Goddess. At Eleusis. But you know all about that, don't you?"

"Indeed I do, Callias. We have that in common. Remember? I am also hereditary . . . torchbearer."

"*You* are?" Callias has not much memory for recent information. "Oh, yes. Of course. *Fire*-worship. Yes, very interesting, all that. You must let us watch one of your ceremonies. I'm told it's quite a sight. Particularly the part where the Arch-Magian eats the fire. That's you, isn't it?"

"Yes." I no longer bother to explain to Greeks the difference between Zoroastrians and Magians. "But we don't *eat* the fire. We tend it. The fire is the messenger between us and the Wise Lord. The fire also reminds us of the day of judgment when each of us must pass through a seal of molten metal—rather like the real sun, if Anaxagoras' theory is true."

"But then what happens?" Although Callias is an hereditary priest, he is most superstitious. I find this odd. Hereditary priests usually tend to atheism. They know too much.

I answered him, traditionally: "If you have served the Truth and rejected the Lie, you will not feel the boiling metal. You will—"

"I see." Callias' mind, such as it is, flits about like a threatened bird. "We have something like that, too. Anyway, I want to watch you eat fire one of these days. Naturally, I can't return the favor. Our mysteries are very deep, you know. I can't tell you a thing about them. Except that you'll be reborn once you've got through the whole lot. *If* you get through them. And when you're dead, you'll be able to avoid—" Callias stopped; the bird settled upon a bow. "Anyway, I fought at Marathon, even though I was obliged to wear these priestly robes that I must always wear, as you can see. Well, no, you can't see them, of course. But priest or not, I killed my share of Persians that day—"

"—and found your gold in a ditch." Anaxagoras finds Callias as exasperating as I do. Unlike me, he does not have to endure him.

"That story has been much distorted in the telling." Callias was suddenly precise. "I happened to take a prisoner who thought I was some sort of general or king because I wear this fillet around my head, which you can't see. Since he spoke only Persian and I spoke only Greek, there was no way to sort the matter out. I couldn't tell him that I was of no importance at all, outside of being torchbearer. Also, since I was only seventeen or eighteen, he should have figured out that I wasn't important. But he didn't. He showed me a riverbank—*not a ditch*—where he had hidden this chest of gold. Naturally, I took it. Spoils of war."

"And what happened to the owner?" Like everyone in Athens, Anaxagoras knew that Callias had promptly killed the Persian. Then, thanks to that chest of gold, Callias was able to invest in wine and oil and shipping. Today he is the richest man in Athens. He is deeply envied. But then, at Athens everyone is envied for something—even if it be nothing more than the absence of any enviable quality.

"I set him free. Naturally." Callias lied easily. Behind his back he is known as rich-ditch Callias. "The gold was by way of ransom. Normal sort of thing in battle. Happens every day between Greeks and Persians—or used to. That's all over now, thanks to us, Cyrus Spitama. The whole world owes me and you eternal gratitude."

"I will be quite happy with a year or two of gratitude."

Between the removal of the first tables and the arrival of the second tables, Elpinice joined us. She is the only Athenian lady who dines with men whenever she chooses. She is privileged because she is wife to the rich Callias and sister to the splendid Cimon—sister and true widow, too. Before she married Callias, she and her brother lived together as man and wife, scandalizing the Athenians. It is a sign of the essential crudity of the Greeks that they do not yet understand that a great family is made even greater when brother marries sister. After all, each is a half of the same entity. Combine the two in marriage and each is doubly formidable.

It is also said that Elpinice, not Cimon, actually ruled the conservative party. At the moment, she has great influence with her nephew Thucydides. She is admired and feared. She is good company. Tall as a man, Elpinice is handsome in a ravaged way—my informant is Democritus, who at the age of eighteen regards anyone with so much as a single gray hair as an unlawful fugitive from the tomb. She speaks with that soft Ionian accent which I like as much as I dislike the hard Dorian accent. But I learned my Greek from an Ionian mother.

"I am a scandal. I know it. I can't help it. I dine with men. Unattended. Unashamed. Like a Milesian companion—except I'm not musical." Hereabouts, the elegant prostitutes are called companions.

Although women have few rights in any Greek city, there are barbarous anomalies. The first time that I attended the games in one of the Ionian Greek cities of Asia Minor, I was startled to note that although the unmarried girls were encouraged to attend the games and examine potential husbands in the nude, the married ladies were forbidden to watch, on the no doubt sensible ground that any alternative to a lawful husband must not be viewed. In conservative Athens, wives and maidens are seldom allowed to leave their quarters, much less attend games. Except for Elpinice.

I could hear the great lady as she settled herself—like a man—on a couch instead of sitting modestly in a chair or on a stool, the way Greek ladies are supposed to do on those rare occasions when they dine with men. But Elpinice ignores custom. She does as she pleases and no one dares complain . . . to her face. As sister of Cimon, wife of Callias, aunt of Thucydides, she is the greatest lady in Athens. She is often tactless, and seldom bothers to disguise the contempt she has for Callias, who admires her inordinately.

I can never decide whether or not Callias is stupid. I daresay it takes a kind of cleverness to make money with or without a treasure found in a ditch. But his shrewdness in business matters is undone by his silliness in all other aspects of life. When his cousin the noble, the honest, the selfless (for an Athenian) statesman Aristides was living in poverty, Callias was much criticized for not helping him and his family.

When Callias realized that he was getting a reputation for meanness, he begged Aristides to tell the assembly how often he had refused to take money from Callias. The noble Aristides told the assembly exactly what Callias wanted him to say. Callias thanked him, and gave him no money. As a result Callias is now regarded not only as a miser but as a perfect hypocrite. Aristides is known as the just. I am not sure why. There are great blanks in my knowledge of this city and its political history.

Last night one blank was promptly filled by Elpinice. "*She* has had a son. Early this morning. *He* is delighted." *She* and *he* pronounced with a certain emphasis always mean the companion Aspasia and her lover, General Pericles.

The conservative Callias was much amused. "Then the boy will have to be sold into slavery. That's the law."

"That is not the law," said Anaxagoras. "The boy is freeborn because his parents are freeborn."

"Not according to that new law Pericles got the assembly to vote for. The law's very clear. If your mother is foreign. Or your father is foreign. I mean Athenian . . ." Callias was muddled.

Anaxagoras set him right. "To be a citizen of Athens, both parents must be Athenian. Since Aspasia is a Milesian by birth, her son by Pericles can never be a citizen or hold office. But he is not a slave, any more than his mother is—or the rest of us foreigners."

"You're right. Callias is wrong." Elpinice is brisk and to the point. She reminds me of Xerxes' mother, the old Queen Atossa. "Even so, I take some pleasure in the fact that it was Pericles who forced that law through the assembly. Now his own law will forever exclude his own son from citizenship."

"But Pericles has other sons. By his *lawful* wife." Callias still resents deeply, or so he maintains, the fact that many years ago the wife of his eldest son left her husband in order to marry Pericles, thus making two families wretched instead of one.

"Bad laws are made to entrap those who make them," said Elpinice, as if quoting some familiar proverb.

"Did Solon say that?" I asked. Solon is a legendary wise man, often quoted by Athenians.

"No," said Elpinice. "I said it. I like to quote myself. I am not modest. Now, who will be the king of our dinner party?"

As soon as the second tables are taken away, it is the Athenian custom for the company to elect a leader who will then decide, first, how much water should be mixed with the wine—too little obviously means a frivolous evening—and, second, to choose the topic of conversation. The king then guides, more or less, the discussion.

We elected Elpinice queen. She ordered three parts water to one of wine. A serious discussion was intended. And there was indeed a very serious discussion about the nature of the universe. I say very serious because there is a local law—what a place for laws!—which forbids not only the practice of astronomy but any sort of speculation as to the nature of the sky and the stars, the sun and the moon, creation.

The old religion maintains that the two largest celestial shapes are deities called, respectively, Apollo and Diana. Whenever Anaxagoras suggests that the sun and moon are simply great fiery stones rotating in the heavens, he runs a very real risk of being denounced for impiety. Needless to say, the liveliest of the Athenians speculate on these matters all the time. But there is the constant danger that some enemy will bring a charge of impiety against you in the assembly, and if you happen to be unpopular that week, you can be condemned to death. Athenians never cease to astonish me.

But before we got to dangerous matters, I was quizzed by Elpinice about Herodotus' performance at the Odeon. I was careful not to defend the Great King Xerxes' policy toward the Greeks—how could I? But I did mention with what horror I had heard Herodotus slander our queen mother. Amestris does not in the least resemble the bloodthirsty virago that Herodotus saw fit to invent for his audience. When he said that she had recently buried alive some Persian youths, the audience shuddered with delight. But the true story is quite different. After Xerxes was murdered, certain families went into rebellion. When order was restored, the sons of those families were executed in the normal manner. Magian ritual requires the exposure of the dead to the elements. As a good Zoroastrian, Amestris defied the Magians and ordered the dead youths buried. This was a calculated political gesture, demonstrating once again the victory of Zoroaster over the devil-worshipers.

I told them of Amestris' perfect loyalty to her husband the Great King. Of her heroic behavior at the time of his murder. Of the hard intelligence which she demonstrated in securing for her second son the throne.

Elpinice was delighted. "I should have been a Persian lady. Obviously I am wasted in Athens."

Callias was shocked. "You are far too free as it is. I'm also certain that not even in Persia is a lady allowed to lie on a couch, swilling wine with men and talking blasphemy. You'd be locked up in a harem."

"No, I'd be leading armies like what's-her-name from Halicarnassus. Artemisia? You must," Elpinice said to me, "prepare an answer to Herodotus."

"And tell us all about your travels," said Callias. "About all those eastern places you've seen. The trade routes . . . That would be really useful. I mean, just *how* does one get to India or Cathay?"

"But more important than trade routes are the notions about creation that you've encountered." Anaxagoras' dislike of trade and politics sets him apart from other Greeks. "And you must put into writing the message of your grandfather Zoroaster. I have heard of Zoroaster all my life, but no one has ever made clear to me who he was or what he actually believed to be the nature of the universe."

I leave to Democritus the recording of the serious discussion that followed. I note that Callias was predictable; he believes in all the gods, he says. How else was he able to win three times the chariot race at Olympia? But then, he is torchbearer of the mysteries of Demeter at Eleusis.

Elpinice was skeptical. She likes evidence. That means a well-made argument. For Greeks, the only evidence that matters is words. They are masters of making the fantastic sound plausible.

As always, Anaxagoras was modest; he speaks as one "who is simply curious." Although that stone which fell from the sky proved his theory about the nature of the sun, he is more than ever modest, since "there is so much else to know."

Democritus asked him about those famous *things* of his: the things that are everywhere all the time and cannot be seen.

"Nothing," Anaxagoras said, after his third cup of Elpinice's highly diluted wine, "is either generated or destroyed. It is simply mixed and separated from existing things."

"But surely," I said, "nothing is no thing and so has no existence at all."

"The word nothing will not do? Then let us try everything. Think of everything as an infinite number of small seeds that contain everything that there is. Therefore, everything is in everything else."

"This is a lot harder to believe than the passion of holy Demeter after her daughter went down into Hades," said Callias, "taking the spring and the summer with her, an *observable* fact." Callias then muttered a prayer, as befitted a high priest of the Eleusinian mysteries.

"I made no comparison, Callias." Anaxagoras is always tactful. "But you will admit that a bowl of lentils has no hair in it."

"At least we hope not," said Elpinice.

"Or fingernail parings? Or bits of bone?"

"I agree with my wife. I mean, I hope that none of these things gets mixed in with the lentils."

"Good. So do I. We also agree that no matter how closely you observe a lentil bean, it does not contain anything but bean. That is, there are no human hairs in it or bones or blood or skin."

"Certainly not. Personally, I don't like beans of any kind."

"That's because Callias is really a Pythagorean," said Elpinice. Pythagoras forbade members of his sect to eat beans because they contain transmigrating human souls. This is an Indian notion that somehow got taken up by Pythagoras.

"No, because I am really a victim of flatulence." Callias thought this amusing.

Anaxagoras made his point. "On a diet of nothing but lentils and invisible water, a man will grow hair, nails, bone, sinew, blood. Therefore, all the constituents of a human body are somehow present in the bean."

Democritus will record for himself but not for me the rest of our dinner party, which was pleasant and instructive.

Callias and Elpinice left first. Then Anaxagoras came over to my couch and said, "I may not be able to visit you for some time. I know you will understand."

"Medism?" This is what Athenians call those Greeks who favor the Persians and their brother-race the Medes.

"Yes."

I was more exasperated than alarmed. "These people are not sane on that subject. If the Great King didn't want peace, I wouldn't be ambassador at Athens. I would be military governor." This was unwise—the wine's effect.

"Pericles is popular. I am his friend. I also come from a city that was once subject to the Great King. So, sooner or later, I shall be charged with medism. For Pericles' sake, I hope it is later." As a very young man Anaxagoras fought at Marathon on *our* side. Neither of us has ever alluded to this episode in his life. Unlike me, he has no interest at all in politics. Therefore, he is bound to be used by the conservatives as a means of striking at General Pericles.

"Let us hope that you are never charged," I said. "If they find you guilty, they'll put you to death."

Anaxagoras gave a soft sigh which might have been a laugh. "The descent into Hades," he said, "is the same no matter where or when you start."

I then asked the grimmest of Greek questions, first phrased by the insufficiently hard-headed author of *The Persians,* " 'Is it not better for a man never to have been born?' "

"Certainly not." The response was brisk. "Just to be able to study the sky is reason enough to be alive."

"Unfortunately, I can't see the sky."

"Then listen to music." Anaxagoras is always to the point. "Anyway, Pericles is convinced that the Spartans are behind the rebellion of Euboea. So this season Sparta is the enemy, not Persia." Anaxagoras lowered his voice to a whisper. "When I told the general that I was coming here to dinner, he asked me to apologize to you. He has wanted to receive you for some time. But he is always watched."

"So much for Athenian freedom."

"There are worse cities, Cyrus Spitama."

As Anaxagoras was taking his leave I asked, "Where was all this infinitesimal matter *before* it was set in motion by mind?"

"Everywhere."

"No real answer."

"Perhaps no real question."

I laughed. "You remind me of a wise man that I met in the east. When I asked him how this world began, he made a nonsensical answer. When I told him that his answer made no sense, he said, 'Impossible questions require impossible answers.' "

"A wise man," said Anaxagoras, without conviction.

"But *why* was it that mind set creation in motion?"

"Because that is the nature of mind."

"Is this demonstrable?"

"It has been demonstrated that the sun is a rock which rotates so quickly that it has caught fire. Well, the sun must have been at rest at some point or it would have burned out by now, the way its fragment did when it fell to earth."

"Then why won't you agree with me that the mind which set all these seeds in motion was that of the Wise Lord, whose prophet was Zoroaster?"

"You must tell me more about the Wise Lord, and what he said to your grandfather. Perhaps the Wise Lord *is* mind. Who knows? I don't. You must instruct me."

I find Anaxagoras agreeable. He does not push himself forward like most sophists. I think of my kinsman Protagoras. Young men pay him to teach them something called morality. He is the wealthiest sophist in the Greek world, according to the other sophists—who should know.

Many years ago I met Protagoras in Abdera. He came one day to my grandfather's house to deliver wood. He was young, charming, quick-witted. Later, somehow, he became educated. I don't think that my grandfather helped him, though he was a very rich man. Protagoras has not been in Athens for several years. He is said to be teaching in Corinth, a city filled with wealthy, idle, impious youths, according to the Athenians. Democritus admires our kinsman and has offered to read me one of his many books. I have declined this pleasure. On the other hand, I should not mind meeting him again. Protagoras is another favorite of Pericles'.

Except for one brief public meeting with General Pericles at government house, I have not come within half a city of him. But then, as Anaxagoras said last night, Pericles is always watched. Although he is, in effect, the ruler of Athens, he can still be charged in the assembly with medism or atheism—or even the murder of his political mentor Ephialtes.

Democritus finds the great man dull. On the other hand, the boy admires Aspasia. Lately, he has had the run of her house, where a half-dozen charming girls from Miletus are permanently in residence.

Since Democritus is taking dictation, I cannot give my views on the ideal behavior of a young man in society. He assures me that Aspasia is still good-looking despite her advanced age—she is about twenty-five—and recent motherhood. She is also fearless, which is a good thing, since there is much to fear in this turbulent city; particularly, for a metic—the local word for foreigner—who happens to be the mistress of a man hated by the old aristocracy and their numerous hangers-on. She also surrounds herself with brilliant men who do not believe in the gods.

Currently, a mad soothsayer is threatening to charge Aspasia with impiety. If he does, she could be in real danger. But according to Democritus, she laughs at the mention of the soothsayer's name. Pours the wine. Instructs the musicians. Listens to the talkers. Attends to Pericles; and to their new son.

## [Persia]

### 3

At the beginning there was fire. All creation seemed to be aflame. We had drunk the sacred haoma and the world to be as ethereal and as luminous as the fire itself that blazed upon the altar.

This was in Bactra. I was seven years old. I stood next to my grandfather Zoroaster. In one hand I held the ritual bundle of sticks and watched . . .

## [India]

### 11

This is what I think I know about the Buddha. At the time that I met him—more than a half-century ago—he was about seventy-two or -three years old. He was born in the Shakya republic, which is located in the foothills of the Himalayas. He came from a warrior family called Gotama. At birth, he was named Siddhartha. He was brought up in the capital city of Kapila-vastru. At one time Gotama's father held high office in the republic, but he was hardly a king, as certain snobs at Shravasti and Rajagriha still like to pretend.

Siddhartha married. He had one son, Rahula—which means link or bond. I suspect that the child must have begun life with another name, but I never found out what it was. He certainly proved to be a bond with that world which the Buddha was to eliminate—for himself.

At the age of twenty-nine Siddhartha embarked upon what he called the noble quest. Because he was acutely conscious that he was "liable to birth because of self, and knowing the peril in whatever is liable to birth, he sought the uttermost security from this world's bonds—nirvana."

Siddhartha's quest took seven years. He lived in the forest. He mortified the flesh. He meditated. In due course, through his own efforts—or simply because he had evolved in the course of all his previous incarnations?—he understood not only the cause of pain but its cure. He saw all that was and all that will ever be. In a magical contest he defeated the evil god Mara, who is lord of this world.

Siddhartha became the enlightened one or the Buddha. Since he had eliminated not only himself but the tangible world as well, he is higher than all the gods: they are still evolving and he is not. They continue to exist within a world that he has entirely dissolved. Since enlightenment is an end in itself—*the* great end, the now-eliminated world ought not to have concerned the Buddha. But the world that he had awakened from returned to him, as it were, when the high god Brahma came down from heaven and begged him to show others the way. But the Buddha was not interested. Why speak, he said, of what cannot be described? But Brahma was so insistent that the Buddha agreed to go to Varanasi and set in motion the wheel of the doctrine. He expounded the four truths; and he revealed the eightfold path. Yet at the same time, paradoxically, the entire exercise was—is—pointless because he had abolished this world and all other worlds, too.

"Everything subject to causation," the Buddha said, "is like a mirage." For him, human personality is something like a bad dream—to be got rid of, preferably, by waking up to . . . nothing? There is a point beyond which I cannot follow the Buddha. But then, he is enlightened and I am not.

In every way, the Buddha's teaching is opposed to that of the Wise Lord. For Buddhists and Jains, the world deteriorates; therefore, extinction is the goal of the wise. For Zoroaster, each man must make his way either toward the Truth or the Lie, and in eternity he will be judged for what he did or did not do in the course of only one life. Finally, after a time in heaven or hell, all human souls will share in the Wise Lord's victory over Ahriman, and we shall achieve a perfect state of being that is not so different from the Buddha's sunyata, or shining void—if that is the right translation of a word which explains so precisely the inexplicable.

For the Indians, all creatures are subject to constant reincarnation. Punishment and rewards in any given life are the result of previous deeds, in previous lives. One is totally subject to one's karma, or destiny. For us, there is suffering or joy in time of the long dominion and, finally, union with Ahura Mazdah in eternal time. For them, there is endless death and rebirth, only broken for a very few by nirvana, which is nothing, and sunyata, which is what it is if it is.

Democritus thinks that the two attitudes are not so far apart. I *know* that they are entirely unlike. Admittedly, there is something luminous if slippery about the Buddha's conception of sunyata; in fact, the more I think of his truths, the more I feel that I am trying to catch with two clumsy hands one of those swift eels that writhe at night in hot southern seas, ablaze with cold light. At the core of the Buddhist system there is an empty space which is not just the sought-after nirvana. It is perfect atheism.

To my knowledge, the Buddha never discussed any of the gods except in the most offhand way. He never denied them; he simply ignored them. But despite his formidable conceit, he did not set himself in place of the gods because, by the time he had set in motion the wheel of his doctrine, he himself had ceased to be, which is the ultimate stage of evolution. But while he still inhabited Gotama's flesh, he allowed others to create the sangha in order to alleviate for the chosen few some of life's pain.

At first only men could be admitted to the order. But then Ananda persuaded the Buddha that women should be admitted too. They would live in their own communities, and follow the eightfold path. Although the Buddha was complaisant, he did make a joke, much quoted by misogynists. "Had the order been made up only of men, Ananda, it would have lasted a thousand years. Now that women have been included, it will last only five hundred years." In either case, I suspect he was unduly optimistic.

Toward the end of the rainy season I accompanied Prince Jeta to the park which he may or may not have sold to the merchant Anathapindika for the Buddha's use. Here live a thousand monks, disciples, admirers. Many ascetics sleep out of doors, while pilgrims live in guesthouses and members of the order are quartered in a large building with a thatched roof.

Not far from this monastery, a wooden hut had been erected on a low platform. Here on a mat sat the Buddha. Since the hut was built without walls, he lived in full view of the world.

Sariputra welcomed us to the monastery. He moved like a boy, with a skipping step. He did not carry a parasol. The warm rain seemed never to bother him. "You're in luck. Tathagata is in a mood to talk. We're so glad for you. Since the full moon, he's been silent. But not today." Sariputra patted my arm. "I told him who you were."

If he expected me to ask him what the Buddha had had to say about the Persian ambassador, he was disappointed. I was ceremonious. "I look forward to our meeting." I used the word upanishad, which means not just a meeting but a serious discussion about spiritual matters.

Sariputra escorted Prince Jeta and me to the pavilion that had been built on a platform approached by eight shallow steps—one for each part of the eightfold way? At the first step, a tall heavyset yellow man greeted Sariputra, who then introduced him to us. "This is Fan Ch'ih," said Sariputra. "He has come from Cathay to learn from the Buddha."

"It is not possible *not* to learn from the Buddha." Fan Ch'ih spoke the Koshalan dialect even better than I, despite an accent that was rather worse.

Since Fan Ch'ih and I were to become close friends, I will only note here that he had not come to India to learn from the Buddha; he was on a trade mission from a small nation in southeast Cathay. Later he told me that he had come to the park that day in order to meet the Persian ambassador. He was as fascinated by Persia as I was by Cathay.

We followed Sariputra up the steps and into the hut, where all of those who had been seated rose to greet us except for the Buddha, who remained seated on his mat. I could see why he was called the golden one. He was as yellow as any native of Cathay. Not only was he not Aryan, he was not Dravidian either. Obviously, some tribe from Cathay had crossed the Himalayas to sire the Gotama clan.

The Buddha was small, slender, supple. He sat very straight, legs crossed beneath him. The slanted eyes were so narrow that one could not tell if they were open or shut. Someone described the Buddha's eyes as being as luminous as the night sky in summer. I would not know. I never actually saw them. Pale arched eyebrows grew together in such a way that there was a tuft of hair at the juncture. In India this is considered a mark of divinity.

The old man's flesh was wrinkled but glowing with good health, and the bare skull shone like yellow alabaster. There was a scent of sandalwood about him that struck me as less than ascetic. During the time I was with him, he seldom moved either his head or his body. Occasionally he would gesture with the right hand. The Buddha's voice was low and agreeable, and seemed to cost him no breath. In fact, in some mysterious way, he seemed not to breathe at all.

I bowed low. He motioned for me to sit. I made a set speech. When I was finished, the Buddha smiled. That was all. He did not bother to answer me. There was an awkward moment.

Then a young man suddenly asked, "O Tathagata, is it your view that the world is eternal and all other views false?"

"No, child, I do not hold the view that the world is eternal and all other views false."

"Then, is it your view that the world is *not* eternal and all other views are false?"

"No, child, I do not hold the view that the world is not eternal, and all other views are false."

The young man then asked the Buddha if the cosmos was finite or infinite, if the body was similar or not similar to the soul, if a holy man exists or does not exist after death, and so on. To each question the Buddha gave the youth the same answer or non-answer that he had given to the question whether or not the world was eternal. Finally the young man asked, "What objection, then, does Tathagata perceive to each of these theories that he has not adopted any one of them?"

"Because, child, the theory that the world is eternal, is a jungle, a wilderness, a puppet show, a writhing, and a chain forever attached to misery, pain, despair and agony—this view does not contribute to aversion, absence of desire, cessation, quiescence, knowledge, supreme wisdom and nirvana."

"Is this Tathagata's answer to each question?"

The Buddha nodded. "This is the objection I perceive to these apparently conflicting theories, and that is why I have not adopted any one of them."

"But has Tathagata any theory of his own?"

There was a pause. I must confess that the blood was suddenly high in my cheeks, and I felt as if I had the fever. I wanted, desperately, to know the answer or non-answer.

"The Buddha is free from all theories." The voice was mild. The eyes seemed to be looking not at us but upon some world or non-world that we could not comprehend. "There are things, of course, that I know. I know the nature of matter. I know how things come into being and I know how they perish. I know the nature of sensation. I know how it is that sensation comes, and how it goes. I know how perception begins and ends. How consciousness starts, only to stop. Since I *know* these things, I have been able to free myself from all attachment. The self is gone, given up, relinquished."

"But Tathagata, are you . . . is the priest who is in such a state as yours, is he reborn?"

"To say that he is reborn does not fit the case."

"Does that mean he is not reborn?"

"That does not fit the case either."

"Then is he both reborn and not reborn?"

"No. Simultaneity does not fit the case."

"I am confused, Tathagata. Either he is the one thing or the other or even both things at the same time, yet—"

"Enough, child. You are confused because very often it is not possible to see what is right in front of you because you happen to be looking in the wrong direction. Let me ask you a question. If a fire was burning in front of you, would you notice it?"

"Yes, Tathagata."

"If the fire went out, would you notice that?"

"Yes, Tathagata."

"Now, then, when the fire goes out, where does it go? to the east? the west? the north? the south?"

"But the question is to no point, Tathagata. When a fire goes out for lack of fuel to burn, it is . . . well, it is gone, extinct."

"You have now answered your own question as to whether or not a holy man is reborn or not reborn. The question is to no point. Like the fire that goes out for lack of fuel to burn, he is gone, extinct."

"I see," said the young man. "I understand."

"Perhaps you *begin* to understand."

The Buddha looked in my direction. I cannot say that he ever looked *at* me. "We often hold this discussion," he said. "And I always use the image of the fire because it seems easy to understand."

There was a long silence.

Suddenly Sariputra announced, "Everything subject to causation is a mirage." There was another silence. By then I had forgotten every question that I had meant to ask. Like the proverbial fire, my mind had gone out.

Prince Jeta spoke for me. "Tathagata, the ambassador from the Great King of Persia is curious to know how the world was created."

The Buddha turned those strange blind eyes toward me. Then he smiled. "Perhaps," he said, "you would like to tell me." The Buddha's bared teeth were mottled and yellow, disconcertingly suggestive of fangs.

I don't know what I said. I suppose I described for him the simultaneous creation of good and evil. Repeated my grandfather's doctrines. Observed those narrow eyes which were aimed—there is no other verb—in my direction.

When I had finished, the Buddha made a polite response. "Since no one can ever know for certain whether or not his own view of creation is the correct one, it is absolutely impossible for him to know if someone else's is the wrong one." Then he dropped the only important subject that there is.

The next silence was the longest of all. I listened to the sound of the rain upon the thatched roof, of the wind in the trees, of the monks chanting in the nearby monastery.

Finally I remembered one of the many questions that I had intended to ask him: "Tell me, Buddha, if the life of this world is an evil, why then *is* the world?"

The Buddha stared at me. I think that this time he might actually have seen me, even though the light inside the hut was now as dim and as green as pond water when one opens one's eyes below the surface.

"The world is full of pain, suffering and evil. That is the first truth," he said. "Comprehend that first truth, and the other truths will be evident. Follow the eightfold way and—"

"—and nirvana may or may not extinguish the self." There was a slight gasp from those present. I had interrupted the Buddha. Nevertheless, I persisted in my rudeness. "But my question is: Who or what made a world whose only point, according to you, is that it causes pain to no purpose?"

The Buddha was benign. "My child, let us say that you have been fighting in a battle. You have been struck by a poisoned arrow. You are in pain. You are feverish. You fear death—and the next incarnation. I am nearby. I am a skilled surgeon. You come to me. What will you ask me to do?"

"Take out the arrow."

"Right away?"

"Right away."

"You would not want to know whose bow fired the arrow?"

"I would be curious, of course." I saw the direction that he was taking.

"But would you want to know *before* I took out the arrow whether or not the archer was tall or short, a warrior or a slave, handsome or ill-favored?"

"No, but—"

"Then, that is all that the eightfold way can offer you. A freedom from the arrow's pain and an antidote to the poison, which is this world."

"But once the arrow has been removed and I am cured, I might still want to know whose arrow struck me."

"If you have truly followed the way, the question will be immaterial. You will have seen that this life is a dream, a mirage, something produced by the self. And when the self goes, it goes."

"You are Tathagata—the one who has come and gone and come again. When you are here, you are here. But when you go, where do you go?"

"Where the fire goes when it's gone out. My child, no words can define nirvana. Make no attempt to catch in a net of familiar phrases that which is and is not. Finally, even to contemplate the idea of nirvana is a proof that one is still on the near-side of the river. Those who have achieved that state do not try to name what is nameless. Meanwhile, let us take out the arrow. Let us heal the flesh. Let us take a ride, if we can, on the ferryboat that goes to the far side. Thus we follow the middle way. Is this the right way?" The Buddha's smile was barely visible in the twilight. Then he said, "As the space of the universe is filled with countless wheels of fiery stars, the wisdom that transcends this life is abysmally profound."

"And difficult to comprehend, Tathagata," said Sariputra, "even for those who are awake."

"Which is why, Sariputra, no one can ever comprehend it *through* awakening."

The two old men burst out laughing at what was obviously a familiar joke.

I remember nothing more of that meeting with the Buddha. I think that before we left the park, we visited the monastery. I believe that I first met Ananda then. He was a small man whose life work was to learn by heart everything that the Buddha was reported to have said and done.

I do remember asking Prince Jeta if the Buddha had said anything to me that he had not said a thousand times before.

"No. He uses the same images over and over again. The only new thing—to me—was the paradox about awakening."

"But it was not new to Sariputra."

"Well, Sariputra sees him more than anyone else, and they tell each other complicated jokes. They laugh a good deal together. I don't know at what. Although I am sufficiently advanced that I can smile at this world, I cannot laugh at it just yet."

"But why is he so indifferent to the idea of creation?"

"Because he thinks it, literally, immaterial. The ultimate human task is to dematerialize the self. In his own case, he has succeeded. Now he has set up the wheel of the doctrine for others to turn as best they can. He himself is come—and he is gone."

Democritus finds these ideas easier to comprehend than I do. I can accept the notion that all creation is in flux and that what we take to be the real world is a kind of shifting dream, perceived by each of us in a way that differs from that of everyone else, as well as from the thing itself. But the absence of deity, of origin and of terminus, of good in conflict with evil . . . The absence of purpose, finally, makes the Buddha's truths too strange for me to accept.

. . .

## [Cathay]

### 2

Master Li led us across a narrow stone bridge to a charming pavilion on a limestone crag whose base was circled by a narrow, swift, white-foaming stream. I must say that I have never seen anything quite as strange or lovely as the Cathayan countryside, at least that region between the two great rivers. The hills are of every fantastic shape imaginable, while the trees are quite unlike anything to be found in the west. Also, wherever one travels, there are unexpected waterfalls, gorges, vistas whose cool blue-green depths are as magically inviting as they are perilous, for Cathay is a haunted land of dragons and ghosts and outlaws. Although I saw neither ghost nor dragon, I did see many brigands. Cathay's beautiful, seemingly empty landscape is a hazardous place for the traveler. But then, wherever one goes on this earth, all things are spoiled by men.

The pavilion was made of yellow brick with a steep tile roof. Moss grew in every fissure, and bats hung from beams wreathed in cobwebs. The old servant who prepared our meal treated Master Li as an equal; and ignored us. We did not care. Hungrily we devoured fresh fish to the soothing sound of fast water striking rocks.

As we knelt on rustic mats, Master Li discussed the meaning—or a meaning—of Tao. "Literally," he said, "Tao means a road or a way. Like a highway. Or a *low* way." I noticed that Master Li's hands looked as if they were made of fragile alabaster, and I realized then how much older he was than I had first thought. Later I learned that he was more than a century old.

"Where," I asked, "does the way—*your* way, that is—begin?"

"*My* way would begin with me. But I don't have a way. I am part of the Way."

"Which is what?"

The duke of Sheh began to hum contentedly, and pick his teeth. He enjoyed this sort of discourse.

"Which is what is. The primal unity of all creation. The first step that a man can take along the Way is to be in harmony with the laws of the universe, with what we call the always-so."

"How is this done?"

"Think of the Way as water. Water always takes the low ground, and permeates all things." I had the uneasy sense that I was again in the Gangetic plain, where complex things are expressed so simply that they become utterly mysterious.

To my astonishment, Master Li saw into my mind. "My dear barbarian, you think me deliberately obscure. But I can't help myself. After all, the doctrine of the Way is known as the *wordless* doctrine. Therefore, whatever I say is pointless. You can no more know what I know to be the Way than I can feel the pain in your left knee, which you keep shifting on the mat because you are not yet used to our way of sitting."

"But you perceive my discomfort without actually feeling it. So perhaps I can perceive the Way without following it, as you do."

"Very good," said the duke, and belched to show his satisfaction not only with the meal but with us. The Cathayans regard the belch as the mind-stomach's sincerest utterance.

"Then think of the Way as a condition in which there are no opposites or differences. Nothing is hot. Nothing is cold. Nothing is longer. Nothing is short. Such concepts are meaningless except in regard to other things. To the Way, they are all one."

"But to us they are many."

"So they seem. Yes, there are no *real* differences between things. In essence, there is only the dust that makes us up, a dust which takes temporary forms, yet never ceases to be dust. It is important to know this. Just as it is important to know that it is not possible to rebel against the fact of nature. Life and death are the same. Without the one, there cannot be the other. And without the other, there cannot be the one. But, finally, neither exists except in relationship to the other. There is nothing but the always-so."

Although I found this conception of a primal unity acceptable, I could not overlook those differences which Master Li so blithely drowned in his sea of the always-so. "But surely," I said, "a man must be judged for his actions. There are good actions and bad. The Truth and the Lie . . ." I spoke as the grandson of Zoroaster. When I had finished, Master Li answered me with a curious parable.

"You speak wisely." The old man bowed his head courteously. "Naturally, in the relative conduct of a given life there are seemly actions and unseemly ones, and I am sure that we would agree as to what is proper and what is not. But the Way transcends such things. Let me give you an example. Suppose you were a maker of bronze—"

"Actually, he is a smelter of iron, Master Li, a useful art which the barbarians have mastered." The duke looked at me as if he himself had invented me, out of primal unified dust.

Master Li ignored the duke's aside. "You are a maker of bronze. You want to cast a bell, and you have prepared a crucible for the molten metal. But when you pour out the fiery metal, the bronze refuses to flow. It says, 'No, I don't want to be a bell. I want to be a sword, like the flawless sword of Wu.' As a bronzemaker, you would be most distressed with this naughty metal, wouldn't you?"

"Yes. But metal may not choose its mold. The smelter has that choice."

"No." The softly spoken no was as chilling in its effect as Gosala's thrown string. "You may not rebel against the Way, any more than your hand can rebel against your arm or the metal against the mold. All things are a part of the universe, which is the always-so."

"What are the fundamental laws? And who was their creator?"

"The universe is the unity of all things, and to accept the Way is to accept the fact of this unity. Alive or dead, you are forever a part of the always-so, whose laws are simply the laws of becoming. When life comes, it is time. When life goes, this is natural, too. To accept with tranquillity whatever happens is to put oneself beyond sorrow or joy. That is how you follow the Way, by achieving wu-wei."

I was again puzzled by that phrase, which means, literally, do nothing.

"But how is our world to function if one is entirely passive? Someone must cast bronze so that we may have bells, swords."

"When we say do nothing, we mean do nothing that is not natural or spontaneous. You are an archer?"

"Yes. I was trained as a warrior."

"So was I." Master Li looked as unlike a warrior as it is possible to look. "Have you noticed how easy it is to hit the mark when you are idly practicing on your own?"

"Yes."

"But when you are in a contest with others, when there is a golden prize, don't you find it more difficult to hit the mark than when you are alone or not in competition?"

"Yes."

"When you try too hard, you become tense. When you are tense, you are not at your best. Well, to avoid that sort of tension is what we mean by wu-wei. Or to put it another way, cease to be self-conscious in what you do. Be natural. Have you ever cut up an animal for food?"

"Yes."

"Do you find it difficult to separate the parts of the body?"

"Yes. But I'm not a butcher or a Magian—I mean a priest."

"Neither am I. But I've observed butchers at work. They are always swift, always accurate. What is hard for us to do is simple for them. Why? Well, I once asked the lonely one's chief butcher how it was that he could dismember an ox in the time it would take me to clean a small fish. 'I don't really know,' he said. 'My senses seem to stand still, and my spirit—or whatever—takes over.' That's what we mean by wu-wei. Do nothing that is not natural, that is not in harmony with the principles of nature. The four seasons come and go without anxiety because they follow the Way. The wise man contemplates this order, and begins to understand the harmony implicit in the universe."

"I agree that it is wise to accept the natural world. But even the wisest man must do all he can to support what is good and to defy what is evil . . ."

"Oh, my dear barbarian, this idea of doing is what makes all the trouble. Don't *do*! That's the best doing. Rest in the position of doing nothing. Cast yourself into the ocean of existence. Forget what you take to be good, evil. Since neither exists except in relation to the other, forget the relationship. Let things take care of themselves. Free your own spirit. Make yourself as serene as a flower, as a tree. Because all true things return to their root, without knowing that they do so. Those things—that butterfly, that tree—which lack knowledge never leave the state of primal simplicity. But should they become conscious, like us, they would lose their naturalness. They would lose the Way. For a man, perfection is possible only in the womb. Then he is like the uncarved block before the sculptor shapes him, and in so doing spoils the block. In this life, he who needs others is forever shackled. He who is needed by others is forever sad."

But I could not accept the passivity of Master Li's doctrine of the Way any more than I could comprehend the desirability of the Buddha's nirvana.

I asked Master Li about the real world—or the world of things since the word real is apt to inspire the Taoist sage to pose a series of self-satisfied questions as to the nature of the real. "What you say, I understand. Or *begin* to understand," I added hastily. "I may not follow the Way, but you have given me a glimpse of it. I am in your debt. Now let us speak practically. States must be governed. How is this to be done if the ruler practices wu-wei?"

"Is there such a perfect ruler?" Master Li sighed. "The busy-ness of the world of things tends to preclude absorption with the Way."

"We dukes may only glimpse the road that you wise men take." The duke of Sheh looked very pleased with himself, and somewhat drowsy. "Yet we honor your journey. Deplore our own high busy place. Wait for you to tell us how to govern our people."

"Ideally, Lord Duke, the prince-sage who governs ought to empty the minds of the people while filling their bellies. He must weaken their will while strengthening their bones. If the people lack knowledge, they will lack desire. If they lack desire, they will do nothing but what is natural for men to do. Then good will be universal."

As statecraft, this did not differ too much from the precepts of the brutal Huan. "But"—I was most respectful—"if a man should acquire knowledge and if he should then desire to change his lot—or even change the state itself—how would the prince-sage respond to such a man?"

"Oh, the prince should kill him." Master Li smiled. Between two long incisors, there was only dark gum. He suddenly resembled one of the sleeping bats overhead.

"Then those who follow the Way have no feeling against taking human life?"

"Why should they? Death is as natural as life. Besides, the one who dies is not lost. No. Quite the contrary. Once gone, he is beyond all harm."

"Will his spirit be born again?"

"The dust will reassemble, certainly. But that is not, perhaps, what you mean by rebirth."

"When the spirits of the dead go to the Yellow Springs," I asked, "what happens?" In Cathay, when someone dies, the common people say that he has gone to the Yellow Springs. But should you ask them where and what that place is, answers tend to be confusing. From what I could gather, the notion of the Yellow Springs is very old; it seems to be a kind of eternal limbo, like the Greek Hades. There is no day of judgment. The good and the bad share the same fate.

"It would seem to me that the Yellow Springs are everywhere." Master Li stroked his right hand with his left. A magical gesture? "If they are everywhere, then no one can go there, since he is already there. But, of course; man is born, lives, dies. Although he is a part of the whole, the fact of his brief existence inclines him to resist wholeness. Well, we follow the Way in order not to resist the whole. Now, it is plain to all, or nearly all"—he bowed to me—"that when the body decomposes, the mind"—he patted his stomach—"vanished with the body. Those who have not experienced the Way find this deplorable, even frightening. We are not frightened. Since we identify with the cosmic process, we do not resist the always-so. In the face of both life and death, the perfect man does nothing, just as the true sage originates nothing. He merely contemplates the universe until he becomes the universe. This is what we call the mysterious absorption."

"To do nothing—" I began.

"—is an immense spiritual labor," ended Master Li. "The wise man has no ambitions. Therefore, he has no failures. He who never fails always succeeds. And he who always succeeds is all-powerful."

"There is," I said "no answer to that, Master Li." I was already used to the circular argument which is to the Athenians what the wheel of the doctrine is to Buddhists.

To my surprise, the duke challenged Master Li on the subject of how best to govern. "Surely," he said, "those who follow the Way have always opposed the death penalty on the ground that no man has the right to pronounce such an awful judgment upon another. To do so is the very opposite of wu-wei."

"Many followers of the Way agree with you, Lord Duke. Personally, I find the matter of no consequence. After all, nature is ruthless. Floods drown us. Famine starves us. Pestilence kills us. Nature is indifferent. Should man be unlike nature? Or course not. Nevertheless, I find sympathetic the notion that it might be better to let our world go its own way and not try to govern it at all, since truly good government is not possible. Everyone knows that the more good laws the ruler makes, the more thieves and bandits will be created in order to break those laws. And everyone knows that when the ruler takes too much for himself in taxes, the people will starve. Yet he always does; and they always do. So let us live in perfect harmony with the universe. Let us make no laws of any kind, and be happy."

"Without law, there can be no happiness." I was firm.

"Probably not." Master Li was blithe.

"I am sure that there must be a right way to govern," I said. "Certainly, we are well acquainted with all the wrong ways."

"No doubt. But, finally, who knows?" He bent like a reed to every argument.

I was growing impatient. "What," I asked, "*can* a man know?"

The answer was swift. "He can know that to be at one with the Way is to be like heaven, and so impenetrable. He can know that if he possesses the Way, though his body ceases to exist, he is not destroyed. The Way is like a cup which is never empty, which never needs to be filled. All complexities are reduced to simplicity. All opposites are blended, all contrasts harmonized. The Way is as calm as eternity itself. *Only cling to the unity.*" Master Li stopped. That was that.

The duke sat very straight, head held high; he was sound asleep and snoring softly. Below us the water sounded like a seashell held close to the ear.

"Tell me, Master Li," I asked, "who created the Way?"

The old man looked down at his now folded hands. "I do not know whose child it is."

## 3

. . .

In the mornings, Confucius would talk to anyone who came to see him. As a result, in no time at all, the inner court of the house became so full of young and not-so-young men that the master was often obliged to take the whole lot of them into the mulberry grove near the rain altars.

In the afternoons, Confucius received his friends or disciples. The two were the same because he was never not the teacher and the friends were never not disciples. Questions were constantly put to him about politics and religion, good and evil, life and death, music and ritual. He usually answered a question with a quotation, often from Duke Tan. Then, if pressed sufficiently, he would adapt the quotation to the question at hand.

I remember vividly my first visit to his house. I stood at the back of the inner courtyard. Between the sage and me a hundred students squatted on the ground. As I have already said, Confucius took little or no money from these young men. But presents were acceptable if they were modest. He liked to say, "No one who wants instruction from me has ever been denied it, no matter how poor he is—even if all he can bring is some dried meat." But there was a corollary to this. He did not waste his time on the stupid. "I only teach someone who's bubbling with eagerness, with excitement, who wants to know what I know." He called both students and disciples "little ones," as if they were children.

Since I had only the vaguest knowledge of the texts that Confucius quoted, I was not exactly an ideal, bubbling, excited student. Yet when the master spoke in his slow, rather high voice. I found myself listening carefully, even though I only half understood what he was quoting. But when he chose to interpret an ancient text, he was as clear as the waters of the Choaspes River.

I remember one question that he was asked by a definitely bubbling and overexcited youth: "If our Lord Duke should ask Master K'ung to serve in his government, what would Master K'ung do?"

Fan Ch'ih whispered in my ear, "This may be a clue."

Confucius looked at the youth for a moment. Then he quoted some old maxim. " 'When wanted, then go; when set aside, then hide.' "

Fan Ch'ih was delighted at this elegant evasion. I was not much impressed. Everyone knew that Confucius had spent his life trying to find a ruler who would, at best, let him govern the state; at worst, listen carefully to his advice. Even at seventy, the old man's ambition to rule was as strong as ever.

"Would you interpret that quotation, Master?" The young man was nervous. I wondered if Baron K'ang had told him to ask the question. "It is believed by many that you have been sent for in order to guide the state."

Confucius smiled; he had most of his teeth. "Little one, I know you think that there is something that I'm keeping from you, some secret or other. Believe me, I have no secrets. If I did, I would not be me."

"Excellent," whispered Fan Ch'ih in my ear.

I remember only one more exchange from that morning. An earnest, dull youth said, "In my village they say that you are known to be very learned, but they wonder why you've never actually done anything in the world or made a real name for yourself."

The other students gasped. Fan Ch'ih stiffened. Confucius laughed. He was genuinely amused. "Your friends are absolutely right. I've never really excelled at anything. But it's never too late, is it? So I shall start practicing. Today. But what? Archery? Chariot-racing? Chariot-racing! Yes, I shall enter the races as soon as I am ready." Everyone laughed with relief.

That afternoon I again joined Confucius. This time only a dozen of his closest friends were present. He seemed not to mind my presence. I remember thinking that perhaps it was true what he had said about having no secrets. But if there were secrets, it was my task to discover them and report to Baron K'ang.

Confucius sat on a mat in the guest hall. He was flanked by his oldest disciple, Tzu-lu, and by his most beloved disciple, the youthful but sickly Yen Hui. In the background lurked the prematurely aged son; in the foreground was *his* son Tze-ssu. Confucius treated the grandson as if he were the son, and the son as if he were an acquaintance, because the son was a fool. That seems to be a law of families. Whatsoever the father is, the son is not.

The disciples speculated, openly, about Baron K'ang's plans for Confucius. So did the master: "I came home because I was assured that I was needed, and to be needed is to serve the state, in any capacity."

Yen Hui shook his head. "Why should the master waste his valuable time on the business of office?" When Yen Hui spoke, his voice was so low that we all had to lean forward, ears cupped. "Isn't it best that you talk to us, to the young knights who come to see you, to the officers of state who consult you? Why should you burden yourself with the ministry of police when you alone can explain to men the way of the ancestors and so lead them to goodness?"

Tzu-lu answered Yen Hui. "You've heard the master say ten thousand times, 'He who holds no rank in a state does not discuss its policies.' Well, Baron K'ang has sent for Confucius. That means he needs him. That means that that harmonious state of affairs which we have dreamed of since the time of the Chou is close at hand."

There was then a lengthy argument between the two points of view. Confucius listened to each speaker as if he expected to hear words of shattering wisdom. That he was plainly not shattered by what he heard seemed in no way to surprise him. Tzu-lu was a fierce old man, not at all the sort of person, one would have thought, to attach himself to a wise man—unlike Yen Hui, who was gentle, contemplative, withdrawn.

Fan Ch'ih spoke of the high esteem that Baron K'ang had for Confucius; in fact, just recently, the prime minister had mentioned the possibility of appointing Confucius chief justice. Most of the others thought that this would be a suitable honor. All chose to ignore the fact that since Confucius was only a knight, he could not hold *any* of the great offices.

Finally, when Confucius spoke, he did not address himself directly to the issue. "You know, when I was fifteen I set my heart upon learning. At thirty, I had my feet planted firmly in the ground. At forty, I no longer suffered from . . . perplexities. At fifty, I knew what were the biddings of heaven. At sixty, I submitted to them. Now I am in my seventieth year." The master looked at the edge of the mat on which he was seated. Carefully, he smoothed out a wrinkle that was imperceptible to us. Then he looked up. "I am in my seventieth year," he repeated. "I can follow the dictates of my own heart because what I desire no longer oversteps the boundaries of what is right."

No one quite knew how to interpret this. As it turned out, no one was obliged to because at that moment Jan Ch'iu entered the room with the news that "Our lord would like for the master to attend him at the palace."

The Tzu-lu faction were delighted. They were positive that Confucius was to be given office. Yen Hui looked sad. But then everyone looked sad when Jan Ch'iu added, "I mean our lord, Duke Ai."

Confucius smiled at his disciples, aware of their disappointment. "Little ones," he said softly, "if out of the entire *Book of Songs* I had to take one phrase to cover all my teaching, I would say 'Let there be no evil in your thoughts.' "

I seldom saw Baron K'ang in private. Since the victory against Key had exhausted the national treasury, the prime minister's days were spent devising new and ingenious taxes which the equally ingenious citizens of Lu usually managed to avoid paying. I was reminded of the ruinous cost of the Greek wars that had forced Darius to levy such high taxes that Egypt had gone into rebellion.

Finally, after several meetings with Confucius, I reported directly to Baron K'ang at the Long Treasury. I found him seated at the head of a large table covered with bamboo strips, on which were listed the state's accounts. At a second table, clerks arranged and rearranged other strips; made notations; added and subtracted. Behind the baron, the statue of Duke Tan stared at the ceiling.

"Forgive me," said the baron, not rising. "This is the day that we check the state's inventories. A time of discouragement, I fear."

In Cathay, as in India, each state maintains reserves of grain. When grain is in short supply, the reserves are sold off at a small profit. In times of plenty, the grain is kept off the market. Weapons, farm implements, cloth, wagons, bullocks and horses are also maintained by the state not only as commodities to be sold when necessary but as reserves to be used in bad or interesting times. It was no secret that everything was now in short supply at Lu, including the coinage which was being not too subtly clipped.

As I advanced on tiptoe, shoulders hunched, head wagging with feigned humility and incredulity—the usual approach to a high official—the baron motioned for me to sit beside him on a low stool.

"Honored guest, your days are not too wretched, I pray, in this unworthy city." Cathayans can talk like this by the hour. Fortunately, Baron K'ang never made these conventional sounds for more than a moment at a time; usually he was all business. He was not unlike Darius—Darius the huckster, that is. Not Darius the Great King.

"You have seen Confucius four times."

I nodded, not at all surprised that I'd been spied on.

"Duke Ai has received him a number of times, which is highly appropriate."

"But *you* have not received him, Lord Baron." I put the question in the form of a statement, a useful Persian art as yet unknown in the Middle Kingdom.

"The war." The baron gestured at the clerks at the other long table. This meant that he had not yet spoken in private to Confucius.

"It is my impression that he thinks you sent for him in order to use him."

"That is my impression, too." Baron K'ang looked very solemn, a sure sign that he as amused. During my three years in Lu, I got so that I could read his face with the greatest of ease. At the end, we seldom exchanged words. We did not need to. We understood each other perfectly. I was also led to understand, from the beginning, that I was going to have to work very hard indeed for my release from his charming cage.

I made my report. I repeated everything of interest that Confucius had said, and almost everything that Fan Ch'ih had said on the subject of the master. When I was done, the baron said, "You must interest him."

"I am not sure that that is possible." I allowed myself a forbidden smile. In the presence of a superior the courtier must always look humble and apprehensive—by no means a difficult task at any of the volatile Cathayan courts.

It was the genius of the Chou dynasty to mitigate man's destructive nature through intricate rituals, observances, manners and music. A man of the court must know and act upon three hundred rules of major ritual. The mat he sits on must be straight, bedclothes must be exactly one and a half times the length of the sleeper, actual names of the recent dead must not be mentioned, and so on. In addition to the three hundred major observances, the true gentleman must also know and be able to practice three thousand minor ones. To spend one's time with a truly punctilious Cathayan gentleman is a most disturbing experience for a foreigner. Your companion is forever making mysterious hand gestures while looking up to heaven or down to earth, not to mention rolling his eyes from side to side, whispering prayers, assisting you when no help is needed while allowing you to flounder entirely when a degree of help might be useful. Even Baron K'ang's silences, cryptic utterances, uses or nonuses of the facial muscles were all a part of the nobleman's code, somewhat modified for a foreigner's benefit. Yet when men of power are together—anywhere on earth—they tend to disregard many of the niceties which they show to the public. Darius always spat in private; and laughed like a soldier.

"You must interest him." Thus, the baron ordered me to spy directly on Confucius.

"What subjects should I bring up in order to . . . interest him?" Thus, I accepted the commission.

"You are the grandson of a divine sage. That will interest him." After a long and boring list of so-called interesting subjects, the baron came to the point. "The subject of Key is deeply interesting to him, and to me. I believe that very soon we shall have unusual news from Key. When it comes, I have no idea what his response will be. After all, he is close to Duke Chien. He was often in the company of the warden of Pi . . ."

"The traitor!" I was properly outraged.

"To give him his proper name, yes. I am also aware that the warden offered to make Confucius prime minister of Lu if Confucius would help him betray his native land."

I was, for the first time, intrigued. "Did Confucius agree?"

"That is for you to discover. Certainly, the warden made a strong case for the return, as he would put it, of all power to the duke of Lu, who has never—as we know—lost one scintilla of that true power given to him by the celestial ancestors." The conviction that the hereditary ruler is all-powerful is central to the gentleman's thirty-three hundred ritual observances. Everything that the dictator did he did in the name of Duke Ai.

"Was that the reason for the war? The restoration, as they falsely call it, of the duke."

"Yes. The warden persuaded Duke Chien that now was the time to attack. Naturally, Key would like to diminish us, even absorb us. But then, over a year ago, Confucius crossed the Yellow River and settled in Wei. I don't know why. I would like to know why. Had he fallen out with the warden, as he tends to fall out with everyone? Or was it a ruse to make us think that he had no connection with our enemies in Key or with the recent war?"

I had never heard the baron speak quite so directly. I was equally direct. "You think that Confucius is a secret agent of the warden?"

"Or of Duke Chien. Now, even if he were, it would be of no importance except for the fact"—the baron looked me straight in the eye, something a Cathayan gentleman ought never to do—"that his disciples occupy positions in every ministry of our government. My own best general is a devoted Confucian. Your good friend and my second steward, Fan Ch'ih, would give his life for the master. Well, I would prefer that no lives be given. Do you understand me?"

"Yes, Lord Baron."

It was Baron K'ang's fear that the Confucians in his own government combined with the forces of Duke Chien might bring him down, particularly now that he lacked the resources to fight a second war. The baron had brought Confucius home not only to keep an eye on him but to neutralize him should there be a new war. In a sense, I was an ideal agent for the baron. I was a barbarian: I had no allegiance to anyone but the baron, who alone had the power to send me home. Although he did not trust me any more than I trusted him, neither of us had much choice in the matter. I accepted the commission in good faith. I would make myself interesting to Confucius—not the easiest of endeavors, since the world outside the four seas is of no concern to Cathayans. Fortunately, Confucius proved to be unique. He was fascinated by the world of the four barbarians: that is, those who lived north, south, east and west of the Middle Kingdom. In fact, whenever he grew discouraged, he would say, "I think I shall just get aboard a raft and float out to sea." This is the Cathayan formula for going native in some wild and uncivilized part of the world.

"How," I asked Baron K'ang, "am I to get him all to myself?"

"Take him fishing," said the baron, going back to the gloomy task of trying to salvage a state close to financial collapse.

As usual, the baron was right. Confucius had a passion for fishing. I cannot remember exactly how I got him to join me at the stream that runs through the willow grove just north of the rain altars, but one bright morning in early summer there we were, just the two of us, each equipped with bamboo pole, silken line, bronze hook, wicker basket. Confucius never fished with a net. "What pleasure can there be in that?" he would ask. "Unless your livelihood depends upon catching as many fish as you can."

Wearing an old quilted robe, Confucius sat cross-legged on the damp green riverbank. I sat next to him on a rock. I still remember how the silver surface of the slow river reflected the sun's light. I still remember that the white spring sky that day contained not only a hazy sun but a half-moon, like a ghost's skull.

We had the river to ourselves. Incidentally, this was the first time that I was able to observe the master without his disciples. I found him most agreeable, and not at all priestly. In fact, he was disagreeable only when someone powerful behaved in an unseemly way.

Confucius proved to be a master angler. Once a fish had taken the hook, he would ever so delicately shift the line this way and that; it was as if the line was moved not by a human hand but by the river's own current. Then, at precisely the right moment, he would strike.

After one long silence he said, "If only one could go on and on just like this, day after day."

"Fishing, Master?"

The old man smiled. "That, too, honored guest. But I was referring to the river, which never stops, which always is."

"Master Li would say that everything is already a part of the always-so." There is no better way of getting a man to let down his guard than to mention his rivals. But Confucius was not to be drawn out on the subject of Master Li. Instead, he asked me about the Wise Lord. I answered at my customary length. He listened noncommittally. I did get the impression that he was more interested in the day-to-day life of a good Zoroastrian than in the war between the Truth and the Lie. He was also curious about the various systems of government that I had encountered in my travels. I told him what I could.

I found Confucius to be a most impressive man in spite of the fact that I could not begin to appreciate the vast learning for which he was honored in the Middle Kingdom. Since I knew nothing of the rituals, the odes, the histories that he had committed to memory, I could not delight in the ease with which he quoted from these ancient works. In fact, I could not always tell when he was quoting and when he was extrapolating from an old text. As a rule he spoke quite simply, unlike so many of the Greeks who make simple matters difficult with syntax and then, triumphantly, clarify what they have managed to obscure with even more complex syntax.

I was startled to find how often this traditionalist sage was at odds with received opinion. For instance, when I asked him what the latest tortoise-shell auguries had foretold, he said, "The shell asked to be reunited with the tortoise."

"Is that a proverb, Master?"

"No, honored guest, a joke." And he showed the length of his two front teeth in a smile. Like so many people whose teeth are distorted, he suffered from stomach trouble—for which he was greatly admired. In Cathay, constant loud disturbances in that region of the body signify a superior mind forever at work.

Confucius discussed the poverty of the state. "Only yesterday Duke Ai asked me what he should do. So I asked him if the state had collected all of this year's tithes and he said yes, but the war had cost so much that there was nothing left."

"All the tithes will have to be increased," I said, recalling the glum figure of the baron at work in the Long Treasury.

"But that would be most unwise," said Confucius, "and unfair. After all, if in good times the ruler is willing to share in the plenty, then in bad times he should be willing to accept the fact that he is not going to have as much to spend as he would like to have."

I reported this comment to the baron because I thought that it might mean that Confucius was eager to weaken the state in the event of an attack from Key. The baron thought this possible but unlikely. "He has always taken that view. He thinks the people owe the state a fixed part of their income and no more; and he is angry whenever a government alters what he regards as a sacred contract."

Confucius told me of a wise man whom he had known in his youth. Apparently this statesman—he was the prime minister of one of the least powerful duchies—assembled and conformed all the laws of the Middle Kingdom and had them inscribed on bronze, much the way Darius did when he gave us our law code. The sage—Tzu-Ch'an by name—also worked out a new series of economic arrangements, to the horror of the conservatives. But his reforms proved to be so effective that today he is one of the most admired of modern Cathayans. Certainly, Confucius was generous in his praise of his mentor. "Tzu-Ch'an had the four virtues of the perfect gentleman." A fish tugged at the master's line. Delicately he flicked his pole downstream; then, more sharply, upstream. "He's hooked," he said happily.

"What are the four virtues?" I asked. Everything is numbered east of the Indus River.

As Confucius cautiously pulled in his line he listed these precious qualities: "The perfect gentleman is courteous in private life. He is punctilious in his dealings with the prince. He gives the common people not only their due but more. Finally, he is entirely just in dealing with those who serve him, and the state."

"Tzu-Ch'an sounds like a divine sage." I was polite. Actually, the wise man sounded to me like one of those masters of the commonplace who are always quoted at such length by the dull.

Confucius let the fish weary itself at the river's edge. "I doubt if we shall ever see a divine sage in our time. But we can always hope to find a perfect gentleman."

"You are considered to be that, Master. If not more." I spoke to him as if to a ruler.

But Confucius seemed not to take himself for granted in quite the same way that most eminent men do. "What I am considered to be and what I am are two different things. Like the fish, which is one thing in the water and another on the plate. I am a teacher because no one will allow me to conduct the affairs of a state. I'm like the bitter gourd: they hang me on the wall as a decoration, but I am not used." He said this without any apparent bitterness. Then he landed the fish, a sizable perch. With swift gestures he unhooked the fish, threw it into the wicker basket, prepared the hook once more with bait and cast his line—all this in the time it takes an ordinary person to phrase the response to a question whose answer he knows.

When I complimented Confucius on his expertness as a fisherman, he laughed and said, "I don't hold high office. That's why I have so many skills."

"It is said that the duke of Key offered you high office."

"That was the old duke. And that was many years ago. Lately, I have talked to his son. Duke Chien is a serious man. But I have no influence in Key."

"That is plain, Master." I began to fulfill Baron K'ang's commission. Simultaneously, I hooked a fish.

"Why is that so plain, honored guest?" Confucius was one of the few wise men who actually asked questions in order to find out what he did not know. As a rule, this world's sages prefer to bait the listener with carefully constructed questions in order to elicit answers that will reflect the wise man's immutable views. This is a very easy thing to do, as you observed the other day, Democritus, when I obliged Socrates to answer *my* questions. In this darkness, where I perpetually sit, I can *hear* you smile. Well, you'll see that I'm right one day. Wisdom did not begin in Attica, though it may yet end here.

"Because of the recent war, Master, which you would have opposed."

"I was not in Key when the war began." Confucius looked at my taut line. "Downstream, but easily," he advised. I moved the pole but not easily; and lost the fish. "Too bad," he said. "It takes the lightest touch. But then, I've fished this river all my life. I know the current. I'm surprised that anyone would think that I might have encouraged the war." Confucius knew exactly what *I* was fishing for. One could not fool him on his own ground, and I did not try.

I was to the point. "It is thought that you wanted the warden of Castle Pi to restore the duke to power."

Confucius nodded; and let out his line. "It's quite true that I've spoken to the warden. It's true that he offered me office. It's true that I said no. He is an adventurer, and not serious." The old man looked at me suddenly. The eyes were paler than those of most Cathayans. "It is also true that there shall never be a proper balance between heaven and earth until we restore the old ceremonies, music, manners and dynasty. We live in evil times because we are not good. Tell that to Baron K'ang." It did not disturb him that I had been assigned to spy on him. In fact, he used me as a means of communicating with the prime minister.

"What is goodness, Master?"

"Whoever submits himself to ritual is good." A cloud of gnats gathered about us. "Don't stir," he said. "They'll move on." We sat very still. They did not move on. I found myself breathing in gnats. But the master was oblivious to them. "A gentleman or a ruler"—Confucius again showed his front teeth in a smile—"the two can be the same, you know—must do nothing in defiance of ritual. He should treat everyone in the same courteous way. He should never do anything to anyone that he would not like them to do to him."

"But surely, when a ruler puts a man to death for a crime he is doing something that he would not like anyone to do to him."

"Presumably, the man who is put to death has defied ritual. He has committed evil in the eyes of heaven."

"But suppose he is serving his country in a war?" By now both Confucius and I were fighting off the gnats. He used his fan; I used my wide-brimmed straw hat. Finally the gnats began to depart in groups, like military units.

"War involves a different set of rituals. It is when a nation is at peace that the good ruler must be on his guard, must avoid the four ugly things."

Again the numbers! Since I was expected to ask what these four ugly things were, I did. Meanwhile, the last of the definitely ugly gnats had moved on.

"First, putting a man to death without having taught him what is right; that is called savagery. Second, to expect a task to be completed at a certain date without having given the worker warning; that is oppression. Third, to be vague in the orders you give while expecting absolute punctiliousness; that is being a tormentor. Finally, to give someone his due in a grudging way; that is contemptible and petty."

Since one could hardly deny the ugliness of these things, I made no comment. He expected none. "What exactly do you mean by ritual, Master?" The word for ritual is constantly used in Cathay and means much more than mere religious observance.

"The ancient rites of Chou purify us while the sacrifice to the ancestors binds earth to heaven in perfect harmony *if* the ruler is good and the rites are accurately performed."

"At Loyang I watched the ancestral ceremonies. I'm afraid that I found them confusing."

Confucius had hooked another fish. The bamboo pole bent in an arc. The fish was heavy but the angler's hand was light. "Anyone who understood all of the ancestral sacrifices could deal with everything under heaven as easily as I . . . catch—" With a powerful jerk, Confucius flipped the pole upward and a fat bream sailed over our heads. We both laughed with pleasure. It is always agreeable to see something done marvelously well. "—this fish." As Confucius completed the sentence the fish fell into a lilac bush. I retrieved it for the master, who said, "All the ancestral ceremonies are a bit like catching fish. Too hard a tug and you break your line or pole. Too soft a tug and you'll lose the fish—the pole, too."

"So to be good is to act in accordance with heaven's will."

"Of course." The old man put away his latest conquest.

"What," I asked, "is heaven?"

Confucius took rather longer than usual in baiting his hook. He did not answer until the line was once again cast. I noticed that the daytime moon had vanished. The sun was now aslant in the white sky.

"Heaven is the dispenser of life and death, good fortune and bad." He was aware that he had not answered my question. I said nothing. He continued, "Heaven is where the original ancestor dwells. When we make sacrifice to heaven, we make sacrifice to him."

I caught an eel. I thought that my wriggling eel was an excellent representation of Confucius on the subject of heaven. He was not specific—for the excellent reason that he did not believe in heaven any more than he believed in the so-called supreme ancestor.

Confucius was an atheist. I am certain of that. But he believed in the power of ritual and ceremony as conceived by the long-dead Chou dynasty because he was devoted to order, balance, harmony in human affairs. Since the common people believe in all sorts of star gods and since the ruling class believe in their direct descent from a series of celestial ancestors who watch them closely from heaven, Confucius strove to use these ancient beliefs in order to create a harmonious society. He emphasized the Chou dynasty because—aside from the charm of Duke Tan's admonitions—the last son of heaven was a Chou. Therefore, to create a united Middle Kingdom, it was necessary to find a new son of heaven, preferably from that family. But since Confucius rightly feared the emergence of the wrong sort of ruler, he constantly emphasized what he claimed to be the virtues of the old dynasty. Although I am fairly certain that he made up a good deal of what he said, Fan Ch'ih swore to me that Confucius did nothing but interpret actual texts. To which I answered, "Then he interprets them only to suit present occasions." Fan Ch'ih saw nothing wrong with that.

When I told him Confucius' joke about the tortoise shell, he frowned. "That was unseemly."

"Why?"

"The art of divination originates with the ancestors. They also gave us *The Book of Changes,* which the master venerates."

"Yet he smiled."

Fan Ch'ih looked unhappy. "It is no secret that the master is not as interested in divination as he ought to be. In fact, he is said to have said that a man makes his own fortune by complying with the laws of heaven."

"Which he does not believe exists."

Fan Ch'ih was shocked. "If you think that, you've not understood him. Of course, you're a barbarian." He grinned. "You serve that very peculiar god who created evil so that he would have an excuse to torture his other creations."

I did not dignify this blasphemy with an answer.

As far as I know, Confucius was the only Cathayan who had no interest at all in ghosts or demons or the spirit world. One might almost think that he did not believe in them. I questioned him several times on the subject, but never got a very satisfactory answer.

I do remember that just as I was trying to get the eel off my hook, I asked Confucius, "What of the dead? Where do they go? Are they judged? Do they rise again? Or are they born again?" The eel's twisting made it impossible for me to get the hook out of its jaw. "Is there not *some* merit in doing good which will be rewarded in heaven? And if not, then why—"

"You'd better let me unhook that eel," said the master. With a skilled gesture, the old man flipped the eel from the line to the basket. Then he dried his hands on the grass. "How well," he asked, "do you know life?"

"I'm not sure I know what you mean. I know my own life. I've traveled in strange lands, met all sorts of people . . ."

"But you've not met all races, all men?"

"Of course not."

"Then, honored guest, since you do not yet understand life, how can you understand death?"

"Do you understand life, Master?"

"Of course not. I know a few things. I love learning. I have tried to understand this world. I listen to everyone. I put to one side what seems doubtful and I'm cautious about the rest."

"You do not believe in divine revelation?"

"Such as?"

I told him of the time that I heard the voice of the Wise Lord. I also described the vision of Pythagoras, the enlightenment of the Buddha, the other-worldly experiences of our own Magians—admittedly haoma-induced, but still true vision. The old man listened, and smiled—or gave that impression: the tips of the two front teeth were always visible. As a result, Confucius' usual expression was one of gentle amusement.

When I finished, Confucius drew in his line and neatly put away his tackle. I did the same, less neatly. For a moment I thought he had forgotten what we had been talking about. But as he got to his feet, with some help from me—he had brittle joints—the master said, most casually, "I've heard many stories like the ones you've told me and I used to be tremendously impressed by them. So much so that I, finally, decided that the time had come for me to try meditation. I spent a whole day without food, a whole night without sleep. I was entirely concentrated. And then what do you think happened?" For the first time he addressed me informally. I had been accepted.

"I don't know, Master."

"Nothing. Absolutely nothing. My mind was a perfect blank. I saw nothing at all. I understood nothing at all. That is why I think it is better to study real things in a real world."

We walked slowly through the trees just back of the altars. Confucius was recognized and saluted by all the passers-by; he responded benignly, courteously, distantly.

In front of the altars a loutish knight suddenly appeared. "Master!" He greeted Confucius rapturously.

"Tzu-Kung." The master's greetings were correct; but no more.

"I have great news!"

"Tell us."

"You remember when I asked you if there was any one precept that I could and should act upon all day and every day?"

Confucius nodded. "I remember, yes. I told you, 'Never do to others what you would not like them to do to you.' "

"That was more than a month ago and now, thanks to you, Master, what I do not want others to do to me I have no desire—believe me!—no desire at all to do to them!"

"My dear," said Confucius, patting Tzu-Kung's arm, "you have not quite got to that point yet."

# *LIVE FROM GOLGOTHA*

NARRATED BY Saint Timothy (who allegedly died about A.D. 100 and is known from the two New Testament letters addressed to him and supposedly written by St. Paul), *Live from Golgotha* (1992) is a satirical invention whose main target is Christianity past and present. It also vigorously attacks what Vidal sees as other late-twentieth-century hypocrisies and depradations, among them homophobia, Zionism, the modern TV mentality, and the worldwide economic dominance of Asia. Born after the death of Jesus, Timothy is converted to Christianity by Paul. In Vidal's version, Timothy, Paul's boyfriend and traveling companion, recollects toward the end of his life his conversion and missionary experiences: his circumcision (and other pains and pleasures of the flesh), his view of the conflict between those followers of Jesus who want to remain Jewish and those who want to distinguish themselves from Judaism, and Paul's special role in the creation of Christianity as a new religion. A bisexual master pitchman, Paul has created and sold a new religion to serve the interests of its founders and proprietors. But Timothy's recollections, late in the first century, are interrupted and altered by some strange goings-on: messages and artifacts from the late twentieth century appear, including a Sony television set, computer-age concepts and technology, and representatives of American network television. Timothy gets a Vidalian education and additional information about Jesus and Paul. He learns that it was not Jesus who died on the cross but Judas. Jesus is alive in the twentieth century as a Zionist computer hacker/genius plotting to redo the crucifixion, substituting himself for Judas. He is rewriting (or erasing) much of the New Testament, and plans to create an early-twenty-first-century nuclear holocaust that will bring the real Jesus and Zionism into control of the Kingdom of the Earth. The television networks, under the control of the modern Japanese economic empire, want to use the computer and television time-machine equipment to go back to the day of the crucifixion in order to televise it as a high-ratings spectacular. At the end, "Jesus' " revisionist plot fails and the television spectacular wins an Emmy.

# From *Live from Golgotha*

## CHAPTER 1

In the beginning was the nightmare, and the knife was with Saint Paul, and the circumcision was a Jewish notion and definitely not mine.

I am Timothy, son of Eunice the Jewess and George the Greek. I am fifteen. I am in the kitchen of my family's home in Lystra. I am lying stark naked on a wooden table. I have golden hyacinthine curls and cornflower-blue, forget-me-not eyes and the largest dick in our part of Asia Minor.

The nightmare always begins the way that it did in actual life. I am surrounded by Jews except for my father, George, and Saint, as I called Saul of Tarsus, better known to the Roman world of which he was born a citizen as Paul. Of course Saint was a Jew to start with, but he ended up as the second- or third-ranking Christian in those days, and by those days I mean some fifty years after the birth of Our Savior, which was—for those who are counting—seventeen years after He was crucified, with a promise to be back in a few days, maybe a week at the outside.

So I was born a couple of years after Our Lord's first departure high atop old Golgotha in suburban Jerusalem. My father converted early to Christianity and then I did, too; it sounded kind of fun and, besides, what else is there to do in a small town like Lystra on a Sunday?

Little did I realize when I became a Christian and met Saint and his friends, that my body—specifically, my whang—was to be a battleground between two warring factions within the infant Christian Church.

It had been Saint's inspired notion that Jesus had come as the messiah for everyone, Gentiles as well as Jews. Most Jews still don't accept this, and of course we pray for them, morning, noon, and night. But the Jews in Jerusalem—like the oily James, kid-brother-of-Our-Lord, and Peter, known as "The Rock" because of the absolute thickness of his head—finally accepted Saint's notion that although the Gentiles were unclean, Jesus was probably too big an enterprise for just the one tribe, and so they allowed Paul to take the Message—"the good news," as we call it—to the Gentiles. Thanks largely to Saint's persuasive preaching and inspired fund-raising, a lot of Gentiles couldn't wait to convert, like my father, George the Greek.

So Saint went sashaying around Asia Minor, setting up churches and generally putting on a great show, aided by the cousins Barnaby and John Mark. But although the Jerusalem Jews liked the money that Saint kept sending back to headquarters, they still couldn't, in their heart of hearts, stomach the Gentiles, and so they refused to eat at the same table with us, since our huge uncut cocks were always on their minds. Finally, things came to a head when Saint took a shine to a young convert and stud named Titus and took him down to Jerusalem for a long weekend of fun. After having drunk too much Babylonian beer, Titus took a leak up against the wall of Fort Antonia, where the Roman troops were stationed. As luck would have it, his snakelike foreskin was duly noted with horror by some loitering Jews, who reported to the rabbinate the presence of a Gentile on the premises a stone's throw from the Temple. The central office then leaned on James, an employee of the Temple, and James told Saint that in the future those goyim who became converted to Jesus must be circumcised. That tore it.

When Saint threatened, there and then, to retire as apostle and fund-raiser, the subject was dropped by the Jerusalem Christians—or Jesists, as they liked to be called—because they were now hooked on the revenues from Asia Minor. Even so, they still kept the heat on Saint personally to show that he had his heart in the right, or kosher, place.

Finally, Saint suggested to John Mark that he undergo a public circumcision in order to convince Jerusalem that Saint was in no way an apostate or self-hating Jew. John Mark split, leaving an opening not only in Saint's office staff but sack, too. As an all-Greek Greek boy who wanted to see the world, I figured that Saint's fussing around with my bod was a small price to pay, or so I thought when I signed on. It wasn't as if there wasn't plenty of me left over for the girls of Lystra. Also, as secretary and gofer, I was pretty good, if not in John Mark's league. The work was never dull. And what a learning experience!

Then came the shock. Saint was denounced by the pillars of the church in Jerusalem: He ate with goyim. He christened goyim. He was having carnal knowledge of a teenage Greek with two centimeters of rose-velvety foreskin, me. This last was only whispered, but it would have been quite enough to get Saint stoned to death by a quorum of Jews anywhere on earth if James were to give the word.

That explains why I am in the nightmare that I can never get out of once it starts. Only this last time when I dreamed it, something unusual happened just before I woke up.

The dream's always the same. I am on my back. The room is chilly. I have goose bumps. All around me are Jews, wearing funny hats. Saint stands beside the table, my joint resting lightly in his hand. Needless to say, between the cold and the approaching mutilation, my fabled weenie has shrunk considerably.

"Let it be reported by all who presently bear witness that Timothy, our youthful brother in Christ, has now, of his own free will, undertaken to join the elect of the elect through the act of circumcision."

At this point I shut my eyes in the dream, an odd thing to do, since a dreamer's eyes are shut to begin with, but then dreams have their own funny laws. Anyway, I can no longer see Saint's huge staring black eyes set in that round bald head with its fringe of dyed black curls, but I can hear Saint's deep voice as he says, "Mohel, do thy business!"

A rough hand seizes my organ of generation. I feel a sharp pull. Then a burning, the knife . . . I scream, and wake up.

But last night I did not wake up as I always do at this point in the dream. Instead, cock afire, voices mumbling all round me in the dark, I had the sense that something was *really* going wrong. For one thing, I was not back in my bed in the bishop's bungalow here in Thessalonika where I am bishop of all Macedonia as well as sometime titular bishop of Ephesus. I was still lying on the kitchen table in my family's house in Lystra. I slowly open my eyes. Salt tears burn the lids.

The room is empty now. I look down at my naked body—my *teenage* body, which means I am still in the dream. My aching joint is swathed in linen like an Egyptian mummy. I am sweating like a horse. I sit up. I swing my legs over the table. I am dizzy. Where is everybody?

Saint is suddenly beside me. "Timmy"—he bats his eyes at me—"how do you feel?"

"Awful," I say. "Why hasn't the dream ended, like it's supposed to?"

"Dream?" He pretends not to know that we're in a dream. He acts as if now—my *now* in Thessalonika—is really and truly *then* in Lystra, our common memories unmediated by sleep and time and all the rest, and I am just coming to, per usual, on the kitchen table.

Carefully, I swing my legs back and forth, aware of the dull ache at the center of my everything. On the window sill, my mother, Eunice, has left the half-skinned remains of a rabbit, a nice touch dream-wise. Flies are devouring the rabbit. Eunice is terrible in the kitchen. I feel sick.

Sitting on the edge of the table, I am as mad as I must have been back then at what had been done to me just so Saint could stay in good with the Jerusalem pillars of salt of the church. Historically, as well as theologically, he should have made a clean break with the Jews then and there, using the preservation of my perfect dong as a perfect pretext. Then he should have preached *only* to the goyim. But I'm afraid that all those years working as a secret agent for Mossad had made Saint even more devious than the Big Fella in the sky had made him in the first place.

"Well, yes, honey bun, this is a dream, natch." Whenever Saint sounds as if he's just gargled in chicken fat, I am immediately on guard. Even at fifteen I knew I was dealing with a con man. "A *recurring* dream, to be precise . . ."

"No." I am nasty. "It is a recurring *nightmare*. . . ."

Since Saint's eyebrows meet in a straight line when he frowns, one black furry eyebrow seems to be humping the other like a couple of black caterpillars. I must write that down in the book of similes that I am keeping since succumbing to the lure of authorship in first-century A.D. vernacular Greek.

Saint frowns. Caterpillars make love. "Now, Timmy dearest, all of this happened long ago, though it seems like it was only moments ago that you were cut up for God. . . ." Aware he is off and running in the wrong direction, Saint changes course; he poses saintlike before the window. "I am dead and gone to glory." Black transcendent gaze is aimed at dead rabbit.

"When this is a nightmare, yes, you are long since dead, and the nightmare is supposed to end when I wake up in my bed, with Atalanta, my better half. . . ."

"Hallelujah!" Saint cries. "This is no nightmare, Timmy! We're in the big league now. *This is a vision.* There has been a *dispensation.* At last I've been allowed to channel into your recurring nightmare, darling boy, to see how you are—in the pink, obviously, in your rosy teenage succulent pink." He reaches for my right titty. I slap his hand. As a stud, I never had the slightest gender confusion. Anyway, Saint's hand turns out to be just air, though in the nightmare proper it is real enough. Something's going wrong, all right.

"I think I'm going to wake up." I begin to hear Atalanta's heavy breathing beside me in the bed where the nightmare—or vision—is taking place.

"First, a message from our sponsor." Saint is sonorous. "From God in the three sections. Timmy, these are the times that are about to try your soul. Yes, I am now in Heaven on the left-hand side of God, about twenty souls from The Elbow. But I am also, simultaneously, back here in your recurring nightmare—now promoted to vision—with a message. . . . A message," he repeats. He seems to be programmed, and I ponder for a moment if this is really Saint and not some sort of diabolic vision.

"So what's the message?" The sight of the dead rabbit and all the flies is making me really sick.

"There has been a systematic erasure of the Good News as recorded in the New Testament, which John Mark and the others so carefully assembled in order to record once and for all the Greatest Story Ever Told that *was* told but now is being *un*told thanks to this virus which has attacked the memory banks of every computer on earth as well as in Heaven and limbo, too. We know that it is the work of a single cyberpunk, or Hacker, as he will be known in the future, but why and how Satan has so disposed this man or woman to eliminate the Gospels—my own special good news, too—is a mystery as of this dream."

For me, this was, literally, *non*sense. "I hear you, Saint. But I don't understand a word you're saying. I mean, *what's* being erased. Let's start with that, OK?"

"The story of Our Lord Jesus Christ as told in the three Synoptic Gospels as well as by that creep John." Saint never liked John, who was very much a part of the Jerusalem crowd and close to James.

"How do you 'erase' all those books?" I ask, wondering, first, what's a computer? second, a memory bank? third, a virus?

"This is how." Saint's noncorporeal hand appears to seize my throbbing linen-swathed joint. "Suppose I had channeled in an hour ago, and suppose I had stopped the mohel from circumcising you in what is, for the purposes of the nightmare, your fifteenth year, which always occurs in the fiftieth year since the birth of Our Lord at Las Vegas . . ."

*"Where?"*

"At Bethlehem, state of Israel. I misspoke, I fear."

Saint starts to gabble, always a sign he's up to something. Glossolalia—speaking in tongues—was very big back then, particularly when you had nothing to say. "During this vision, I could easily have stopped the circumcision, thus changing my relationship with the Jews and the Greatest Story Now Being Untold. If your foreskin had not been cut off, *they* would have cut me off, as of 50 A.D., and then there would have been no Christian story worth telling, no Crusades, Lourdes, Oral Roberts, Wojtyla. But let us not get sidetracked into what *might* have been when we are stuck with what is happening this very minute in the future. The Gospels are being garbled, those that haven't already vanished, like John Mark's, a wonderful secretary, I still say, loyal as I am to you, with those glorious buns . . ."

"Shut up, Saint!" I am simultaneously both fifteen-year-old village lout and aging bishop in the midst of a vision-nightmare. "Why is the Hacker garbling the texts and, even if he does, how can all those books vanish?"

"The *why* is as unclear as the *who.* But there is now chaos in the Christian message. Just now, when I misspoke, I was repeating the latest Hacker-inspired blasphemy about Our Lord's birth in Las Vegas, and about his connection with the mob to which former Nevada Senator Laxalt does not—repeat *not*—belong only . . ."

I am getting a headache. My loins throb. I stand up. My head swims, and the kitchen seems to be going round.

"I'm losing you!" Saint cries. "Before you fade to black, and I to light, remember this: *You* must now tell the Greatest Story Ever to Be Told—by you, alone—Timothy, disciple of me, Saint Paul, and yourself titular bishop of Ephesus and *de facto* bishop of Macedonia, to be martyred in the reign of President Bush, I mean the emperor Domitian—or was it Nerva?—when Greater Israel is in flames. . . . Write it all down, Timmy, because you are the only witness that the virus cannot get to. You are immune, which means that long after Matt, Mark, Lu-lu, and John-John are just folk memories, there will be only one absolutely true gospel, and that will be according to Saint Timothy! You're all we've got, darling. Because everything written about Our Lord before 96 A.D.—you'll die, my angel, in 97—has been erased or distorted by the computer virus that rushes, nay, implodes the channels of human memory like the myriad photons of Satan, losing quarks to Hell and, worse, to the ultimate black star, that counterforce where all is mirror-reverse and the unknown Hacker at work in the computer is Satan, and Satan's God and you me, Yummy you, Tummy, Timmy, Me . . . Beware Marvin Wasserstein of General Electric."

During this dreadful spiel, I slowly dissolved out of that kitchen of nearly a half century ago and into my own bed where Atalanta, my helpmeet, has met me, post-nightmare, so many times now in the course of a quarter century of warm mature Christian marriage between two equal-in-Christ, if not in bed, human beings.

I opened my eyes. Atalanta was standing over me, a dishrag in her hand, which she promptly mopped my face with. "You were having a nightmare," she announced. "The usual?"

Heart racing, I took the rag from her and dried the cold sweat from my neck. "The usual," I said. "Only this time Saint came to me in the dream, at the end. . . ."

"How was he?" Atalanta had already lost interest in my nightmare. She was now at the window, looking down on the back courtyard where the maid was hanging up the laundry. Another bright clear day in Macedonia.

"He's put on weight." As usual when I dream of my mutilation, I was aroused. In the old days, I would fall upon my helpmeet, but now I save what is left of my once extraordinary potency for fun and games at the New Star Baths, which, as bishop, I have vowed to shut down as a center of impurity. Happily, our proconsul has shares in the syndicate that owns all the baths in Thessalonika and so, once again, Caesar and Christ must accommodate each other, and I go regularly to the baths for the steam and of course the concerts in season. "He says I am to write down everything because all the Gospels have been destroyed except mine, which isn't written yet."

"Praise God!" Atalanta never listens but then she is, like me, a natural blonde. Of course, she *hears* everything. "How were they all destroyed?"

"A computer virus."

"Oh, yes." Atalanta looked sad. "Yes. I've always been afraid that would happen. Some hacker, just for fun, no doubt, has punched his way into the memory banks and typed out all the secret code numbers and then—presto! no more tapes, Jesus, us. We are such stuff as fax are made on and our little tapes are rounded with a thermal sleep due to Cascade or Fish 6."

"You are talking in tongues again." But, as I always do when she does, I wrote down, phonetically, the strange words that she had just said.

Lately, Atalanta seems not to know whether or not she has left the everyday world for some waking dream of her own. When I have my nonsense visions—if they are nonsense—I'm asleep, as I was just now with Saint. But, wide awake and out of nowhere, Atalanta suddenly talks of computer viruses as if she knew what they were.

Now that I am at my desk in the upstairs rumpus room, and Atalanta is off preparing her celebrity auction at the proconsul's palace, I shall follow Saint's advice and begin the Gospel According to Myself with, as we usually do, the Word, after first recording last night's nightmare and this morning's weird message from Atalanta, the house glossolalist.

I shall put in Jesus's genealogy later. Although many gospel writers like to begin with His family, I have always thought genealogy a great bore even when it's one's own. Saint only threw it in because the Jews liked knowing that Jesus came from one of their better families, but, as I once pointed out to Saint, if He really came from God then He wasn't related to anybody human except maybe His mother's extended family. Saint finessed that by saying Jesus was related to *everyone* human as we are all in God's image since we are His children and so on and so forth.

Anyway, I shall skip the begats—Mark did, and his book is far more popular than Matthew's if *Publishers Weekly* in Alexandria is to be trusted. Actually, sales figures are often rigged by rival Christian publishing firms. For instance . . .

"The men have arrived with the television set." Those were the exact words that the maid said to me as I was sitting at this desk, about to describe Saint Paul's first meeting with our Lord on the eastbound Jerusalem–Damascus freeway.

## CHAPTER 2

The most confusing week of my life had come and gone. But not forever. What with rewind and fast forward, *nothing* is ever gone. All you have to do is know how to work the machine.

The machine is here beside my desk. It was delivered by two strange men. At first I thought that they were Scythians, since they were wearing trousers instead of the all-purpose tunic or cocktail dress that we wear under a cloak or, if you're high ranking, a toga. But if they were Scythians, they had the gift of tongues, for they spoke without accent of any kind. The television set is called Sony, the name, I seem to recall, of a German god of thunder—or was it metaphysics? The workmen didn't know what the name signified.

"Mr. Claypoole sent us" was the only information I could get out of them. They kept staring at me, the furniture, the view from the rumpus room window of downtown Thessalonika on a fine autumn day in 96 A.D. They were scared shitless.

"Where is your electrical outlet?" was the first and only question they put to me.

"I don't know what you mean." Then, remembering that I am a bishop, I said, "I assume that although you are not from this diocese you are both brothers in Christ."

"I'm Jewish," said one of the men, a curious thing to say since it is hardly possible in such a matter to be "ish." Either one is a Jew or not, a hacker or not. They put the black shining box on a chest against the wall. Then they adjusted some metal rods on top of the set.

"That should do it," said the hacker-ish one, pressing a button. That indeed *did* it. The screen was filled with the CNN financial news report, and what appears to be the usual ongoing bad news for the dollar. "The set is now working on a battery. Guaranteed for one thousand hours of constant viewing pleasure." Then, very simply, they vanished.

For a week now, I've been unable to stop watching television. Like a madman, I switch from channel to channel. I cannot get enough of the astonishing electronic world of the future as glimpsed through that small black window. The sickening yellows and the atrocious pulsing reds are like a never-ending, always-changing yet ever-the-same nightmare. I can now say, in life, that I have gazed on Hell, and it is even busier than one had feared.

Atalanta is less hooked on the Sony than I, but she is very partial to Twentieth Century—twenty centuries have gone by since now!—Fox musical comedies, as well as to the *Sunday Hour of Power and Prayer* program where a sort of Christianity is preached by a painted man with false hair, and choir.

For some reason, only we can see or hear anything on the set. When we ask visitors to our home if they can see pictures on the tube, they look surprised, and congratulate us on what they take to be a particularly valuable chunk of obsidian, polished to a high gloss.

Since I assume that Saint is behind all this, I do my best to make sense of these weird reports from close to two thousand years in the future—everything seems to be dated from the year of the birth of Jesus, a dicey business since it is well known that Our Lord was constantly knocking years off His age in order to appear youthful and with it.

"After forty there is no salvation," He used to say, or so Saint said He said. But then Saint lies about everything. Maybe Our Lord said, "After thirty-three," the accepted age for His first return to His Father in Heaven as well as to the famous, if theologically disputed, three-in-one of Father, Son, Holy Ghost, which is Satan's 666 divided by 222. But who is counting? I suppose I am, if I have to write the Sacred Story from scratch.

Question: Is Saint lying now? Have the Gospels really been lost except for this one that I can't seem to get started because of all the interruptions? Thus far, facts are few. I list them. In order.

First, Saint enters my recurrent nightmare. Tells me the bad news about the "computer virus." Although I don't know what the phrase means, I get the general drift. The Gospels are being physically erased from books and "tapes." But will they also be erased from the memory of those who still remember them? I address this question to the God Sony. He is silent.

Second, the Sony arrives from the future. No one saw how the men who brought it arrived. More to the point, who sent it and why?

Third, Saint always said that we were being monitored by people from the future. On principle, I never believed anything he said. Of course there was the one encounter at Philippi, which I'll get to. But except for that mildly weird business, I thought that Saint was just sounding off. Now I know that we have all been watched by a million eyes from the very beginning of the Greatest Story. I also know that, up ahead, in future time, there are going to be all sorts of ways to visit the past, which is us.

One way is "channeling," which is how Saint got into my last nightmare. I don't know *how* it's done but it is obviously easy to do, at least for someone as pushy as Saint is—you can't say *was* anymore since all of time is just a flat round plate. No, I don't know what that means either, but that's what a spokesperson for the Foundation for Inner Peace said on a talk-show program.

I cling to what sanity I have as I do my best to cope with the invasion—no other word—from the future, which entered a new phase this morning just after the CNN *Hollywood Minute,* a favorite of mine, despite *longeurs,* when a rosy-faced young man in what is known as a three-piece suit of polyester stepped out of the television set.

How does a fully grown man step out of a black shining Sony a tenth his size? The same way that Jesus raised the dead, I suppose. In any case, where the program was, there was Chester W. Claypoole, on the screen. Then, as he stepped out of the television set, he grew larger and larger until he was normal size. Behind him, the picture on the set went black.

"Good morning," he said, warmly. "I'm Chester W. Claypoole. I'm vice president in charge of Creative Programming at NBC."

"Welcome," I said, remembering my ecumenical manners, "to my humble bishop's bungalow." I help out my hand with the bishop's ring in such a way that he had the option of kissing the ring like a true believer or shaking my hand like a sport. He did neither.

"Call me Chet," he said. "I hope you're enjoying the TV set I sent you?" He sat on a stool opposite my chair, and smiled at me the way everyone always smiles on television. I suppose they all smile so much because, for some reason, they have perfect teeth. Back here in 96 A.D. those of us who still have a few teeth don't usually like to show them, which is why there isn't a lot of smiling going on—not that there is much to smile about, what with high taxes and the crazy Zionists threatening an intifada against the Romans who are, like it or not, the masters of the world, as the Jews learned twenty years ago when the Romans tore down the Temple in Jerusalem and wiped out the entire Zionist movement except for the Irgun terrorist gang, now going strong, setting fire to hotel lobbies.

"It was very kind of you, of course." I could be as cool as he. "Though I'm still not quite sure why you are so eager to clue me into late-twentieth-century A.D. television programming without first providing me with a satellite dish for Sky Channel viewing, the *sine qua non* of ultimate viewing pleasure, not that I am complaining."

"The dish won't work back here. But we've wired you into our classic broadcasting menu. You get NBC, natch, CBS, ABC and CNN. . . ."

Suddenly, Chet frowned. He pointed to the set. "You were to get a special GE set, and this is a Sony. . . . Funny. Well, where was I? Visitors. Yes. You see, I'm on the lookout for a certain . . . hacker?" He looked to see if I was at sea or not.

Since I was at sea, I asked him what a hacker was or is. Chet then reminded me of what Saint had told me in the dream, which proves that Saint and Chet are working together to restore the Christian message through me. Naturally, I cannot rule out that they are not who they seem to be but agents of Satan.

"We still don't know who *the* Hacker is but our resident genius, Dr. Cutler, at General Electric—NBC is a subsidiary of GE—came up with a

Super Sam Intercept which protects this tape from even the most brilliant hacker or cyberpunk."

"But not visitors, I see."

"If anybody from my time frame should drop in on you, I'd appreciate it if you'd give me a buzz on the Z Channel. I'll show you how. If I'm out, speak after you hear the electronic blip and I'll get the message."

Chet lit a cigarette. There was smoke but I could not smell it. Then he showed me what to push to get the Z Channel, as well as the intercom phone to NBC and Chet's direct line. Although I only understood half of what he was saying, I let him go on. Eventually, things tend to make sense. After all, I've been in religion a long time now.

"Your gospel is all-important to Christianity. On the other hand, creative programming is all-important to General Electric and its subsidiary, NBC. Now we are getting ready for a big technical breakthrough in software. Any day now we'll be able to get a camera crew back here, and when we do we'll be able to tape all sorts of historical events live—as of then anyway. Which is where you come in."

I chuckled, a noise that I do rather well. "Shouldn't I first get a lawyer?"

Chet gave me a sick smile. I had struck pay dirt. "It's a bit soon to be talking deal. But here's the big plan. We're going to be the first network to go back to Golgotha, where we will shoot the actual Crucifixion, Resurrection, the whole ball of wax, *live*! Now, because viewer identification is the name of the game, that will mean lots of in-depth interviews not only with the various notables present but with your average man in the street. Naturally, I don't want to get your hopes up, but for anchorperson, *you're* the front-runner. So that's one reason we've got an eye on you—Prime Time on the Big Time, Tim-san."

"Then I assume, Chester . . ."

"Call me Chet."

"I assume, Mr. Claypoole, that I'll be having other visits from the other networks and CNN, too—making me the same offer. Since this is what we in the church call a competitive situation."

Chester whistled. "And they think you saints are all rubes!"

"What's a rube?"

"A holy man." Chester was smooth. But, of course, I don't trust him. "Yes, you may have other offers but I doubt it. For technological know-how, GE is ahead of everyone else in the field. Dr. Cutler is the greatest genius since Mr. Moto invented television."

So the cat was out of the bag, and the deal was on the table. Should I accept the assignment as anchor for *Live from Golgotha*? So much would depend, I now know, on the ancillary rights, specifically videocassette. I must get an unscrupulous lawyer on the case. I jollied Chet along. "Let me mull it over. Meanwhile, tell me this. Saint Paul was always aware of your presence—or at least that of other Chesters. So why didn't you—or they—bring *him* a TV set?"

"The state of the art was still very new when he was alive. . . ."

"Sorry, Chet. That won't do. To you, we are both equally defunct. But you are now able to pay me a call, which means you can drop in on him, too—a while back of course. So why not just press the old rewind? Why not—what's the verb? Sony back to him, too?"

"Why do you torment me like this?" Chet stubbed out his cigarette in the last of Eunice's red and white Corinthian salad plates. But there was no ash—like Chet, the cigarette is an illusion. "We're not supposed to tell you *anything* and here you are working out the most advanced technology there is . . ."

"*You* came to *me,* my son." I was warmly ecclesiastical. "Come. Make a complete confession. In my hands lies salvation."

Chet groaned. "OK. There are these other tapes of your life. Lots and lots of them. I spliced into this one because if is hacker-proof. I never got through to Saint Paul because by the time Dr. Cutler had worked out the technology, the Hacker had eliminated the Saint Paul tapes."

"You must have had tapes of Our Lord as well."

"They were the first to go. But not before a foreign network got through to him—by remote, of course—and the interviewer *nearly* talked Him into giving up all that Zionist crap of His and emigrating to Palm Springs where there's this reformed temple with His name on it, along with a brand-new condo thrown in as a highly desirable extra."

*"Jesus was tempted?"*

"I'll say He was tempted! But, thank Moroni, there's still no way of transporting you folks fast forward to TV-land, while here, in your frame of time, there's no Palm Springs, hard to believe. But even so, if we had really convinced Him to retire in mid-messiahhood, He could have moved on to Cyprus, say, and the quiet life and then there would've been no Golgotha, no Saint Paul, no Christianity. Oh, it was a near miss, let me tell you."

Suddenly a great light dawned in my head. I had always been puzzled by that story of Jesus in the Gethsemane Botanical Gardens where He had been tempted to give up the whole thing, or so He said later. Well, now we know just who and what tempted Him. It was not Satan but a TV anchorperson from an unscrupulous foreign network, which rules out Murdoch, I suppose. Suddenly a lot of things are beginning to fall into place. I need Chester, Chet . . .

I picked up this scroll from my desk. "Thanks to the dream, I've been making some notes about my life with Saint Paul, and so on."

"That's why I'm here."

"I thought you were here to make me a firm offer to be the anchorperson during your exclusive *Live from Golgotha* program."

"That, too. That's the sweetener. But it's the Gospel According to Saint Timothy that we're really after. Look at this."

Chet showed me a photograph of a hole in the ground with a lot of broken bits of marble and a ton of dirt off to one side.

"What's that?"

"That's your cathedral here in Thessalonika, as of now. My now, that is. Archaeologists have been digging it up for several years and they've just detected—with sonar—a room beneath the high altar."

I nodded. "We keep our cleaning equipment there. Mops, brooms, buckets—and a couple of tombs, of course."

"At the moment, there's no particular hurry because they've run out of money for the digging. So there's plenty of time for you to write your book and plant it. Your time, that is, is our time." He hummed.

"I am to plant the . . ."

". . . manuscript of the life of Saint Paul and of Jesus, too, of course, as told to Timothy. It would be the discovery of the millennium! I see an initial print-run of King-size millions while the first-serial rights alone . . ."

"What good will this do me back here? Or the church?" I remembered to add.

"You will save Christianity. What greater good is there? I say that as a Mormon who, Moroni forgive me, smokes. Yours will be the only version the future will ever know—of how Jesus is the one child of the Sun . . . uh, One God."

Chet crossed to the TV. He switched to the Z Channel. "This is where I catch the last train to Westport." He gave me a wink. But there was no train to be seen on the TV, only a paper-walled room where a girl in a kimono was ceremonially pouring cups of tea.

"Why," I asked, "don't you just take the manuscript back with you on your next visit?"

"We can't take anything *from* here because we're not really real back here. Let's say we're A.C. and you're D.C. We can get stuff to you on *rewind* but not on *fast forward.* Feel." Chet held out his arm. I grabbed him by the wrist—just air, like Saint in the dream.

"You see? I'm what they call a hologram. A sort of three-dimensional picture of myself. Dr. Cutler hasn't figured out how to get a person back here without fatally scrambling the molecules. TV sets are less complicated. Bye now." Chet faded into the set. Then as the girl offered him a cup of tea, a commercial took their place.

I have a hunch that Jesus may have got it right the first time around, back in the Gethsemane Botanical Gardens, when He said that all these electronic visions—whether cable *or* network—are equally the work of the Devil.

Now I must return to the Gospel According to Saint Timothy as told to . . . why did I just write "as told to" when I am telling or, rather, writing the story as I recall it? I must remain in full control of myself on this tape. Kibitzers are everywhere.

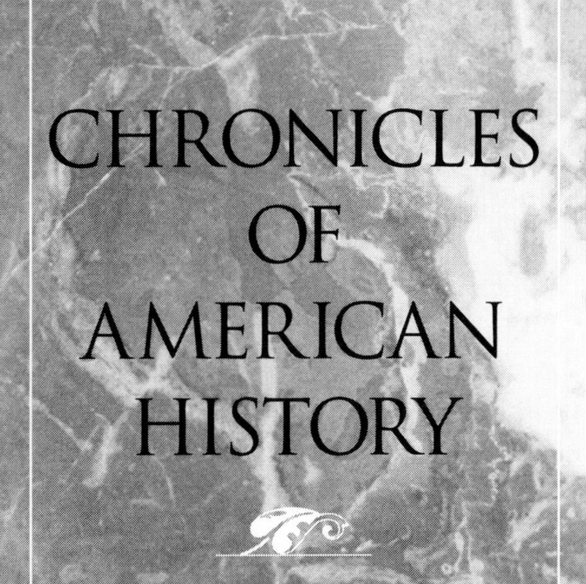
CHRONICLES
OF
AMERICAN
HISTORY

SEVERAL YEARS after he wrote *Washington, D.C.* (1967), Vidal envisioned a connected series of novels that would demonstrate his view of American history through a combination of historical re-creation and fictional invention. The series, which begins with *Burr* (1973) and ends with *Washington, D.C.,* has multiple plots and a large cast of real and invented characters. There are six distinct novels, woven together, more or less, by recurring characters and their descendants and by Vidal's interpretation of the panorama of American history. *Lincoln* (1984) is less directly linked to the series then the other books, although John Hay, its narrator, is an important character in *Empire* (1987), in which the nation that he has observed Lincoln forge from separate sovereign states becomes, under William McKinley and Theodore Roosevelt, an imperial world power. The dominant connecting pattern for the series is created through the use of a fictional journalist-historian, Charles Schermerhorn Schuyler, and his descendants. Their lives are interwoven with those of well-known historical figures.

In *Burr,* Schuyler provides us with a narrative of his young manhood (1833–40) that alternates with sections from Aaron Burr's journal of the Revolutionary War period, which the elderly Burr (1756–1836) gives him to read. As a journalist, Schuyler is assigned to learn all he can about Burr, and his increasingly obsessive investigation leads him to the fact that Burr is his father.

In *Lincoln,* which takes place between 1861 and 1867, the two dominant characters are Lincoln and John Hay. The narrative dramatizes the last four years of Lincoln's life through Hay's eyes; the connection with what precedes and follows in the series is mostly thematic. Charles Schuyler appears at the end, when Hay, who has become the first secretary to the American minister to France, is introduced to him and his daughter Emma, who was born in Italy in 1841, where Schuyler had married after going abroad to serve in the diplomatic service. He has not been back to America since. *Lincoln* is a dramatization of Vidal's understanding of the evolution of the nation from a republic of sovereign states to an empire with international economic and political power. For Vidal, it is Lincoln who is the architect of the transformation.

The next novel in the series, *1876* (1976), begins with Schuyler and Emma sailing into the port of New York in late 1875. A famous elderly historian who now feels like Rip Van Winkle, Schuyler has come to cover the election of 1876, to advance his own fortunes, and to reestablish his connection with his native country. He and his daughter become minor celebrities in New York social circles, and Emma soon falls in love with the wealthy, married William Sanford, whose wife dies giving birth to Blaise Delacroix Sanford. Three months later, when Emma and William marry, the rumors that they have had something to do with Sanford's wife's death compel them to leave for France to start a new life. Emma's father, who suspects that his daughter *has* done something questionable, stays on in New York, where he dies in 1877, having experienced the Revolutionary War via Burr, the Civil War via Lincoln and Hay, and survived until just after the Republic's one hundreth birthday.

The main character of *Empire* (1987), which begins precisely on the day when the Spanish-American War is over and twenty-one years after *1876* ends, is Caroline Sanford, Emma and William's daughter, Charles Schuyler's granddaughter, and Blaise Sanford's half sister. The young Caroline is in England, visiting the American ambassador John Hay, among whose famous guests are his friends Henry Adams and Henry James. Hay is about to be invited by President McKinley to become Secretary of State. Caroline soon moves to Washington, escapes her engagement to marry Del Hay, John Hay's son, and successfully thwarts her half-brother's attempt to deprive her of her part of their inheritance. She becomes the proprietor of an increasingly powerful Washington newspaper, competing with William Randolph Hearst and Blaise, Hearst's protégé, as the marriage of image-makers and power brokers solidifies the transformation of the Republic into a modern empire.

*Hollywood* (1990) begins in 1917 with Hearst at the White House and America about to enter World War I. Much of the book, which was initially conceived as the final part of *Empire,* concerns Caroline's life in Washington and then California, within the context of American history from 1917 to 1928. Woodrow Wilson and Warren Harding both make substantial appearances, and Senator Thomas P. Gore, Vidal's grandfather, appears as himself. An important new invented character, Senator James Burden Day, an up-and-coming political figure who has much in common with Senator Gore, is Caroline's married lover. He is also a friend of Caroline's half-brother Blaise, who is now an influential Washington newspaper publisher and political operative with designs on the presidency. Burden Day's history, sensibility, and political life are important elements in the novel. When Caroline moves to California and becomes a star of the silent screen, the worlds of Hollywood and Washington are united. A border-state Southerner, Senator Day carries one of the heavy weights of American history, the North-South antagonism, which is still very much alive. It is embodied for him in his constant awareness that his father, who had fought and died for the Confederacy, would strongly disapprove of his son's politics. Caroline fades from his life and then from the series.

The elderly Burden Day and the Blaise Sanford family (Blaise, his daughter Enid, and son Peter) are the most important characters in *Washington, D.C.,* the final novel in the series, although it was written first. It becomes the culminating narrative, and though the focus is on Burden's personal life and political ambitions, the themes are the same as in the other books in the series. The setting is the capital of the country for the ten-year or so period that surrounds World War II. Franklin Roosevelt, Burden's political nemesis (as he was Senator Gore's), is a hovering, pervasive shadow as well as a real presence. Burden's story is one of personal and political defeat. His defeat is also, secondarily, at the hands of the new generation, represented by his assistant and then successor, Clay Overbury, a John F. Kennedy figure. It is clear that Overbury will be not only senator but president. He marries Blaise Sanford's daughter, Enid, and although Blaise opposed the marriage, he becomes Overbury's intimate ally and supporter. Indeed, the willful, promiscuous, and explosive Enid (partly modeled after Vidal's mother) is institutionalized by Blaise and Overbury to advance Overbury's career. Blaise's son Peter, Enid's brother, whose growth and education into manhood and political awareness is one of the important strands of the novel, cannot save her, though he can save himself by becoming independent of his father and molding his literary and moral sensibility into a post–World War II career that maintains his integrity. Peter Sanford is about the same age as the author. Toward the end of the novel, Burden Day dies and is thus united with his father, who appears to him in the form of a young, wounded Confederate corporal in his Civil War uniform. "With a cry he flung himself upon the youth who was his father, plunged the handkerchief into the wound, lost his balance, fell against the beloved, was taken into those long-dead arms, and like impatient lovers, they embraced and together fell."

# From *Burr*

## 1833

"Charlie, this is not for the *Evening Post*!" Leggett looked at me with—well, amused scorn, as the English novelists say.

"Too long?" I had given him a straightforward two-page description of the wedding [of Aaron Burr and Madame Jumel] scribbled on the ride back to New York. The newly wed couple had departed at dawn in Madame's yellow coach with six horses to visit the Colonel's nephew, Governor Edwards, at Hartford, Connecticut. Yes, I am trying to be a journalist, mentioning all facts.

Leggett sighed. "We are interested in destroying Mr. Biddle's bank, in promoting free trade, in the gradual abolition of slavery, in workers' unions. We are not interested in a retired whore's wedding to a traitor."

Although I am used to Leggett's furious style, I was obliged to defend the Colonel, or at least my version of his nuptials. "Aaron Burr is not a traitor, as far as we know. Madame Jumel is not a whore but a respectable and rich widow no matter what she might have been years ago. And this is damned interesting. The two most notorious people in New York have got married."

Leggett gave a long wheeze, to signify disgust. At thirty-two (seven years older than I), he looks like my father. We met when I was still at Columbia and he was writing theatre reviews for the *Mirror,* and trying to become an actor like his friend Edwin Forrest. He failed on the stage. Yet of course he *is* an actor, with a stage more important than that of the Bowery Theatre. As a journalist he has taken all politics and literature for his field, and is famous.

The curtain-raiser to Leggett's continuing drama occurred when he was cashiered from the navy for fighting a duel. At the court-martial he insulted his commanding officer with a tirade of quotations from Shakespeare. Then he set out to take New York by storm. Although he failed as an actor, he succeeded as an author with a book called *The Rifle;* he then published his own magazine *Critic* which failed. Now he is an editor of the *Evening Post* and a power in the city. Feared by everyone for his pen, not to mention his duelling pistols or, more precisely, the Malacca cane with which he has whipped at least one rival editor. Yet he is plainly dying: a once solid frame shattered first by yellow fever in the navy, then consumption.

When I was seventeen I thought Leggett a god. Now he annoys more than he charms me. Annoys himself, too. But I continue to see him and he continues to encourage (as well as annoy) me. He knows I am not happy with the law, that I want to free myself somehow to write. Unfortunately, only political journalists are well-paid for writing, and I am not interested in politics (but then neither was Leggett until recently). So I dream of a career like Washington Irving's; and write short pieces that were sometimes published here and there but were almost never paid for until last month when Leggett proposed that I do an occasional piece for the *Evening Post.* Also: "You should use your relationship with Aaron Burr."

"In what way?"

But Leggett would say nothing beyond "Take notes. Keep a record. Assay his wickedness . . ."

The story of Colonel Burr's marriage was, I thought, exactly what Leggett had in mind. Apparently, I was wrong.

"All right, Charlie, I'll take it in to Mr. Bryant. He'll decide. I won't." Leggett went into the next office. I could hear the low murmur of talk. Then Leggett returned, shutting the door behind him. "Your prose will have Mr. Bryant's full attention."

"Thank you. Thank you." I tried to sound sardonic, like Colonel Burr.

Leggett put his feet on the table, dislodging papers and books. With a dirty handkerchief, he rubbed the ink from the middle finger of his right hand. "Charlie, are you still leading your dissolute life?"

"I am studying law, yes."

"Good answer. I trained you well." He grinned; then coughed for a long bad moment into the inky handkerchief and I looked away, not wanting to see what I suspected would be there, the bright arterial blood.

Coughing stopped, handsome haggard face gray and beaded with sweat, Leggett spoke in a low tired voice. "I meant, of course, Mrs. Townsend's establishment."

"Once a week. No more. I have put away boyish things."

"In order to spend, to *die* alone!" Eyes shone with amusement and fever. "Tell me of Mrs. Townsend's latest wards."

"There are three very young Irish girls, only just arrived, positively dewy . . ."

"No more! I am married, Charlie. That's enough."

"You asked."

"Like Odysseus then, I must stop my ears. Sing to me no more siren songs of my youth. Of those fair Hibernian charms I once . . ."

We were joined by Mr. Bryant. A remote man with carved lips and full face whiskers, [William Cullen Bryant] looks to be in his forties; he has the New English manner which effectively disguises whatever pleasure he takes in his reputation as America's First Poet (Leggett likes to think of himself as the Second Poet, particularly when Fitz-Greene Halleck is in the room). But Mr. Bryant has yet to mention anything so trivial as verse in my presence. Each time we meet, he is very much the assistant editor of the *Evening Post,* decorously devoted to radical politics. Incidentally, he is probably the only man in New York who still writes with a quill pen. Even Colonel Burr prefers modern steel to classic feather.

"Most interesting, Mr. Schuyler." I was on my feet. Since Mr. Bryant made no move for me to sit, a short interview was indicated. "Naturally we will record the . . . happy event. We are a *news*paper. But to serve the news—and our public—one sentence will suffice."

"You see?" Leggett was pleased at my failure.

I was angry. "I have obviously been misled. I thought that you were interested in Colonel Burr."

"Mr. Leggett is perhaps more interested than I." The two editors exchanged an uneasy look.

I persevered. "At Leggett's suggestion, I described a wedding which is, you must agree, of some interest."

Mr. Bryant was conciliatory. "I agree that Aaron Burr is one of the most interesting people in the city, in the United States . . ."

"And if only Charlie could get him to talk freely, candidly about his life, about his connections, particularly today."

"I doubt if the Colonel would be candid." Mr. Bryant's view of Burr is the traditional one.

Leggett, however, had something else in mind. "As you know, Charlie, we support President Jackson. The Vice-President, however, is a puzzling figure . . ."

"*I* do not find him puzzling." Mr. Bryant was sharp.

"Well, I do. I think him a trimmer. Without principle. And I'd like to know what everyone would like to know: the relationship between Vice-President Van Buren and Aaron Burr."

"Naturally, it is the *political* relation which interest Mr. Leggett and me." Mr. Bryant gave Leggett a warning look that was ignored on principle.

"No!" Leggett was on fire. "The *whole* relationship." He turned to me. "I had a good reason for asking you to take notes, to ask the Colonel questions. It is important for us to know how close the two men are."

"The Colonel admires Van Buren." I tried to recall what, if anything, Burr had said of the Vice-President. "But I would not say they are 'close.' "

Leggett was decisive. "Well they are, whether you know it or not. Twenty years ago when Burr came back from Europe, he went straight to Albany, straight to Van Buren, and stayed with him in his house. Stayed with a leader of the Albany regency. Yet Aaron Burr was still under indictment out west for treason. Still charged by the state of New Jersey for the killing of Hamilton . . ."

None of this is quite true but Leggett feels that to be excitingly right in general is better than to be dully accurate in particular. That is why he is such an effective journalist. "Now the question to be answered is: why did the careful, clever Martin Van Buren befriend such a dangerous, such a compromising man?"

"Naturally, there has always been a political affinity between the two." Mr. Bryant's elevated dullness makes a nice contrast to the vividness of his young colleague. "Colonel Burr was a founder of Tammany Hall. Martin Van Buren is now, in effect, a master of Tammany. They share the same . . . uh, ideals."

"Ideals!" Leggett threw wide his arms as though for a crucifixion. "Neither man has any ideals. Power is all that either ever wanted. Burr of course no longer matters. He's history. But Matty Van, now there's our target. The little wizard. Our own Merlin who's led General Jackson through one term as president and is now leading him through a second and as sure as there is corruption in Albany, will try to succeed him in 'thirty-six if we don't stop him."

"Why should we? Most of the positions he has taken . . ."

But Mr. Bryant is no match for Leggett when he is afire with what, I suppose, is moral passion.

"Positions be damned! Matty will do what he has to do to be nominated and win. He is the perfect politician. On the surface. But I tell you, beneath Matty's pink-blond Dutch exterior, behind that seraphic smile, there lurks something very odd, very rotten, very Aaron Burrish."

I had no idea what Leggett was talking about. "Surely you don't think a man should be denied the presidency simply because he befriended Colonel Burr."

"I don't think that that is precisely what Mr. Leggett has in mind." Mr. Bryant looked more than ever like an Old Testament prophet. "Now, if you'll forgive me, Mr. Schuyler." He was gone.

"Charlie." Leggett assumed his special schoolmaster's voice. "I shall now corrupt your innocence. Martin Van Buren is the illegitimate son of Aaron Burr."

I was stunned. "I don't believe it. And anyway, *how* would anyone know?"

"It is known that Colonel Burr used to stay at the Van Buren tavern in Kinderhook up the Hudson. It is widely suspected that he got with child the tavernkeeper's wife Mary, crowning with splendid antlers her husband Abraham."

" 'Widely suspected.' " I was scornful.

"As well as suspicion, there was a good deal of evidence of the circumstantial variety. Colonel Burr constantly befriended the entire family, particularly young Matty, short, subtle, large-eyed, high-browed Matty—sound familiar?"

It is true that there is a physical resemblance between the two, except "Van Buren is fair, Burr dark . . ."

"He had a mother." Airily Leggett set to one side contrary evidence. "Now all of this may be simply gossip. Or may be not. Certainly it's true that at a very young age Matty left Kinderhook, came to New York and promptly went to work in the law office of one of Burr's associates . . ."

"But suppose Burr is his father. What's the point?"

Leggett condescended to explain. "Think of the possibility. For *you.* A pamphlet—no, a book proving that Martin Van Buren is the son of Aaron Burr, why, that would make your fortune."

"Proof in law," I began, but Leggett was not listening.

"Even more important than your fortune, Charlie, is the fate of this republic. Jackson has begun great reforms. We are beginning to tend toward democracy. Van Buren will reverse that trend. Therefore let us prevent him from becoming president."

"By proving him to be a bastard?"

"Americans are a moral people. But even more damaging than his bastardy is his *political* connection with Burr, particularly in recent years. If we can prove secret meetings, dark plots, unholy combinations—then, by Heaven, Van Buren will not be chosen to succeed General Jackson."

"Does that mean you want Henry Clay for president?"

"No. I want the other senator from Kentucky, Richard Johnson. Despite his *penchant* for black ladies, Johnson will continue Jackson's reforms. Van Buren won't." Leggett became conspiratorial. "You've probably observed that Mr. Bryant and I are in disagreement. He trusts Van Buren. I don't. I like Johnson. He doesn't."

I have never seen Leggett so worked up. Eyes glassy with excitement; cheeks a dull red. A moment of silence, broken finally by a clam-seller singing his wares below in Pine Street:

*"Here's your fine clams*
*As white as snow*
*On Rockaway these clams do grow!"*

(I record all the songs I hear—for a possible article.)

I was tentative. "First, I don't think Colonel Burr is apt to tell me the truth . . ."

"You see him every day. He's fond of you."

"My father was a friend of his but that's hardly . . ."

"Burr's old. He lives in the past."

"In the *past*? At this very moment he's planning to settle Texas with Germans."

"Good God!" Leggett was impressed. "Anyway, you're the only one in a position to find out. And didn't you tell me he was writing the story of his life?"

"So he says. But I doubt it. Occasionally he speaks of dictating to me but . . ."

"So encourage him! Get him to talk about old times, about Kinderhook, about the days when he was in the Assembly and impregnating Mrs. Van Buren . . ."

"I'm afraid he's more interested in telling the 'true' story of the Revolution."

"Have you no guile?"

"You don't know Colonel Burr. And even if I did get the truth from him—which is doubtful—he can always prevent me from using it. He's the best lawyer in the state, and there is such a thing as libel."

Leggett was brisk. "We have three years before the next elections. He's bound to be dead by then, and under New York law you cannot libel the dead."

"What about Van Buren?"

"It is not libel to prove that a man is a bastard." Leggett was on his feet. "Charlie, we may have found a way to keep Matty Van out of the White House, and democratic principles in."

I rose, too. "The *Evening Post* will print the story?"

Leggett laughed and coughed simultaneously. "Certainly not! But don't worry. I'll have a publisher for you." He shambled along beside me to the door, loose as a wired skeleton. "I'm serious, Charlie." He took my hand in his hot dry one. "How often do you get a chance to alter the history of your country?"

Leggett had managed the wrong appeal. It was my turn to be condescending. "I'll tell *that* to Colonel Burr. Just by living and breathing he has altered the lives of every American a number of times, and I can't see that it has done him much good."

"Let *me* reflect ironically, dear Charlie. *You* change history."

Do I betray the Colonel? In a small way, yes. Do I hurt him? No. An anonymous pamphlet maintaining that he was the devil would distress him not at all. Much worse has been written about him by such supremely non-anonymous figures as Jefferson and Hamilton. Also, if he is consistent, he could hardly complain if the world were to know he is the father of Van Buren. The Colonel often says, "Whenever a woman does me the honour of saying that I am father to her child, I gracefully acknowledge the compliment and disguise any suspicion that I might have to the contrary."

On the other hand, the Colonel would be most distressed if Van Buren were to lose the election because of the Burr relationship. Well, I have no choice. Leggett has offered me a way out of drudgery; a means to support myself by writing. I shall take it. Also, there is—I confess—a certain joy in tricking the slyest trickster of our time. I'm fond of the Colonel; but fonder still of survival.

When I mention to Colonel Burr how much I enjoyed his account of the invasion of Canada, he looks at me as though not knowing to what I refer; pokes the coals in the grate (yes, in midsummer he often has a fire). "I am always cold," he likes to say. "It is the fault of General Washington." When Burr smiles he looks like the bust of Voltaire in Leggett's office. "He disliked me and saw to it that I was always assigned to swampy and malignant places."

Finally, "Oh, yes. My scribbling about those days. I still make notes from time to time. Pointless activity, I suppose. No one likes truth. For instance, we are now told that Benedict Arnold was a bad general because he was a bad man. But of course he was one of our best commanders. Superior certainly to Washington."

"That's not the impression one gets from your account."

Burr is surprised. "But Arnold was *splendid*! It was Montgomery who made the fatal error at Quebec. Arnold favoured my strategy, which I think was sound. Certainly Montgomery's plan to attack the Lower Town was not. Arnold's judgement in the field was excellent."

Nelson Chase interrupts us with a message from Madame. The Colonel takes it and frowns. He is much distracted these days. Things go badly at the mansion. He has promised to show me his notes on Washington, but every time I ask for them he says he cannot remember where he last put them.

I have grown lazy in the heat. August is nearly over. Colonel Burr is absent for days at a time. Sometimes he is at the mansion. Other times in Jersey City. I think he may have gone at least once to his old school Princeton College (his father was its president when it was called The College of New Jersey).

Although he is more than usually secretive, I gather that the Texas land leases may be invalid, and if they are, he has lost his (Madame's) entire investment.

Nelson Chase tells me that "There are terrible rows up there on the Heights!" Chase has also taken to questioning me about the Colonel's private life, an unbecoming subject considering how recently the Colonel married Chase's aunt or whatever she is to him. I say nothing. After all, I *know* nothing except that I have posted a number of letters from Burr to a certain Jane McManus in Jersey City. But *honi soit qui mal y pense.*

Yesterday Burr spent all afternoon with a Mrs. Tompkins and a five-year-old girl who was plainly his daughter though not, I should think, but the elderly Mrs. Tompkins.

Burr is marvellously patient with all children. Talks to them as though they were adult. Teaches them. Plays with them by the hour. Particularly with little girls, for "Women have souls, Charlie! They really do."

This evening, at five o'clock, I finally receive the Colonel's notes on George Washington. "It is a continuation of what you have already read. With some new marginal notes. It is a nice portrait, I think, but I am sure you will find it unrecognisable."

Burr looks pale and fragile today. This morning in court the judge saw fit to harangue for an hour the murderer of Alexander Hamilton. When at last the judge gave out of breath, the Colonel said with great mildness, "I am sorry that Your Honour is not feeling well today."

## *George Washington*

In the early spring of 1776, I decided that Colonel Arnold was mad. For days on end, he would march our shattered contingent back and forth before the walls of Quebec. Periodically, he would amuse the British with a demand for surrender. Asked to deliver one of these documents, I refused point-blank.

When it came time for me to go, Arnold forbade it. I told him that he could keep me only by force. He did not try to do that.

The middle of June, I arrived at General Washington's headquarters in the Mortier mansion at Richmond Hill, some two miles north of New York City.

I had never seen a house so fine. It commanded a superb view of the

Hudson River. Gardens, pavilions, ponds, a stream (the Minetta which I was later to dam and make a small lake of). A perfect paradise, I thought, as I rode up to the front porch where a dozen officers stood, waiting for admittance.

Above the main door, on the second balcony, the Lady Washington sat with her needlework. She had a benign if somewhat wintry smile and a quiet manner. The face was ordinary—what you could see of it because she was addicted to large hats, usually some years out of fashion. She had been the richest widow in Virginia when the poor but ambitious squire Washington married her.

As I entered the high-ceilinged main hall, I never dreamed—well, perhaps *imagined* for an instant—that I would one day own Richmond Hill.

I was shown by a staff captain into the side parlour where a half-dozen officers were waiting to see the General, who daily held court in an upstairs bedroom (which I was to make into a library, exorcizing, as best I could, that stern mediocre ghost).

Among the officers unknown to me in the parlour was Captain Alexander Hamilton of the New York artillery. We did not actually meet, however, until the end of June. "But I knew right away it was you," he told me later. "We all did. And I was filled with envy!" When Hamilton chose, his manner could be enormously charming. "There you were, the hero of Quebec, looking like a child while I was just another officer!" As a youth, Hamilton was physically most attractive with red-gold hair, bright if somewhat watery blue eyes and a small but strong body. It was our peculiar tragedy—or glory—to be of an age and quality at a time and place certain to make rivals of us. Yet from the beginning we had a personal liking for one another. We were like brothers (yes, Cain and Abel come to mind with the difference that each was part-Cain, part-Abel). At first meeting I knew Hamilton straight through. I suspect that he knew me as well, and could not endure the knowledge that of the two of us I alone had the means and talent to be what he most wanted to be, the president. He came to hate not only my capacity but my opportunity. Yet I wonder if he knew all along that I would fail, saw the flaw in me as I saw the one in him? Speculation is idle now. Like brothers, yes; but unlike, too. He was envious. I am not. Thwarted ambition never turned me sour as it did Hamilton, who at the end could not endure the American world I was helping to make and so, quite irrationally, made me out to be that hideous reality incarnate. Curious to think that we would almost certainly have been friends had we not been two young "heroes" at the beginning of a new nation, each aware that at the summit there is a place for only one. As it turned out, neither of us was to reach the highest place. I hurled Hamilton from the mountain-side, and myself fell.

General Washington stood beside his desk as I entered. In response to my salute, he gave me his gravest stare. He was a master of solemnity.

"Major Burr, you are welcome to stay here in the house until you find yourself a proper billet."

"Thank you, General, I am most sensible of the honour . . ." I was about to ask, as tactfully as possible, for a command in the field when Washington began to speak, formally, somewhat hesitantly. Conversation was not easy for him with anyone.

"We have heard excellent reports of you, Major Burr. From every source except Colonel Arnold."

"Colonel Arnold and I had but one disagreement. I thought it pointless to continue to send insulting messages to the British governor when we were in no position to do him the slightest damage."

"Why did we not take Quebec?"

"May I speak candidly?"

His answer came smoothly, from much practice. "I have always laid it down as a maxim to represent facts freely and impartially."

"We failed, General, because my plan was not followed." I saw no reason not to go down firing.

"*Your* plan, Sir?" The small dull eyes in their vast sockets stared at me with wonder.

I told him in detail my strategy for scaling Cap Diamond. He was not impressed. "Wiser heads no doubt prevailed."

"One of those wiser heads, Sir, was shot off. I was at General Montgomery's side when he was killed. The other wise head now commands a depleted and broken force."

"You are most certain, Major, of your military gift."

"No, Sir. But it is a fact that the other strategy failed. I had hoped only to imitate the same tactic King Frederick set in motion during the siege of Dresden." Young and opinionated, I hoped to impress my commander not only with my own military prowess but with my wide knowledge of modern warfare. Like so many young officers in those days, I had studied closely the campaigns of Frederick the Great.

General Washington, however, did not read books; he knew as little of Frederick as I did of tobacco farming, a business in which he had only recently failed. The wealth of his wife notwithstanding, Washington was in some financial difficulty when he took command of the army. He had not done well farming despite all sorts of theories about river mud being the best of manures (it is not), and the invention of a plough (shades of Jefferson!) which proved to be so heavy that two horses could not budge it even in moist earth.

Although Washington was always short of money, he lived grandly.

Later in the war, we were all startled and amused when his mother put it about that son George had robbed her of everything and so, being destitute, she was forced to apply to the Virginia Assembly for a pension. I am reasonably certain that Washington was innocent in this matter. He was, apparently, a dutiful son and the mother a source of much distress to him. When word came of her son's "victory" at Trenton, the virago was quoted as saying, "Here is too much flattery." It is plain she always disliked her son and he must, finally, have hated her. How odd not to like one's own mother! I always thought I would have adored mine, who saw fit to die before we could properly meet.

General Washington rang a bell. A staff colonel entered.

"Please instruct Major Burr in his duties. He will stay here, until billetted in the town." The General turned to me. "I shall want a full report of what happened at Quebec."

Interview ended, the General crossed to a long table covered with papers and began, at random I rather think, to read. From the back his heroic figure was only somewhat disfigured by a huge rump. Neither of us knew that even as we spoke, Montreal had been recaptured by the British, and our Canadian adventure was a failure.

Longing for military glory, I found myself seated at a desk for ten hours a day copying out letters from Washington to the Congress. Although defective in grammar and spelling, owing to a poor education, the General was uncommonly shrewd in the way he flattered congressmen. But then he had not spent fifteen years as a burgess in the Virginia Assembly without learning something of politics. Ultimately, I think, he must be judged as an excellent politician who had no gift for warfare. History, as usual, has got it all backward.

After ten days in which my most useful work was the examination of several bales of under-sized blankets from France, I was happy to receive from John Hancock an appointment as aide to General Israel Putnam . . . yes, I had gone over General Washington's head to the president of Congress. I had no choice if I was to serve usefully in the war. In fact, as I pointed out to Hancock, I would rather be out of the army than clerk to a Virginia land-surveyor.

There are of course many legends about my relations with Washington during those two weeks I spent at Richmond Hill. He is supposed to have been shocked by my licentiousness. I daresay he would have been had he known how I and a number of other young officers conducted ourselves on those rare occasions when we were free to visit New York City. But he knew nothing of such matters. It is true, however, that he was most puritanical.

Soon after I arrived a soldier named Hickey had been hanged for treason, to the delight of 20,000 New Yorkers. I was not present at the execution but I did read with amusement Washington's statement to the troops. According to our commander, the English-born Hickey had gone over to the British not for money but because *he was a life-long prey to lewd women*! It was a sermon worthy of my grandfather. Incidentally, the private soldiers disliked Washington as much as he disdained them. On the other hand, the young officers (with at least one exception) adored their commander, and it is the young officer not the private soldier who eventually decides what is history.

I have never known New York so gay—despite the British fleet which materialised in the harbour June 29. The Battery was regularly subjected to bombardments that did no damage. The girls, however, enjoyed squealing with excitement and rushing for protection to our strong arms.

On July 3, the British army under General Howe disembarked on Station Island, a Tory stronghold. Although our position was perilous, everyone had confidence in Washington. A confidence that was to evaporate when presently he contrived to lose both Long Island and New York City.

As I have already noted, Washington had had very little experience of actual war before 1776. Years before he had been involved in a few disastrous skirmishes with the French and their Indian allies on the Ohio. His first fame was the result of a despatch he sent to the Virginia governor in which he referred to the sound of the bullets that whistled past his head as "charming." Strange word. Strange young man.

In my view had Gates or Lee been placed in command of the army the war would have ended at least three years sooner. Each was brilliant. Each understood the enemy (Lee, in fact, knew personally the British commanders). Each won true victories in the field against the British, something Washington was never able to do. But though Washington could not defeat the enemy in battle, he had a fine talent for defeating rival generals in the Congress. At the end he alone was at the pinnacle, as he intended from the beginning.

Washington did have a most unexpected *penchant* for espionage. Our intelligence was almost always better than that of the British. Unfortunately Washington's judgement sometimes disallowed facts. For instance, despite every possible warning, he never believed that the British would attack New York Island when and where they did. Yet he must be given credit for tenacity. Although the war dragged on year after year due to his eerie incompetence, I suspect that the kind of victory he did achieve could only have been the work of a man who combined resolute courage with a total absence of imagination.

I fear that I did not properly appreciate being an aide to Washington. I did not enjoy copying out letters asking Congress for money that was seldom forthcoming: the American soldier was as mercenary as any Hessian.

No money, no battle. Nor did I much enjoy listening to the worshipful talk of the other aides who flattered Washington monstrously, to his obvious pleasure. I, on the other hand, was prone to question his judgement although I had been advised by everyone that independence of mind was not a quality he demanded of subordinates. We were happy to be rid of one another.

I was to have a better time of it with my good, old General Israel Putnam whose headquarters I joined in July 1776 at the corner of the Battery and the Broad Way. A former tavern-keeper, Putnam had the amiability of that class as well as a good if crude intelligence. His only fault was a tendency to repeat himself. Whenever the enemy drew close, he would invariably instruct the men not to shoot "till you see the whites of their eyes!" Having made the line famous at Bunker Hill, he tended to plagiarize himself, to the amusement of everyone except those officers who thought the firing ought to begin long *before* the whites became apparent to some of our myopic riflemen.

On July 9, I took the salute at General Putnam's side in the Bowling Green. Then at the request of the Continental Congress, our adjutant read aloud to the troops a document newly received from Philadelphia.

I confess to not having listened to a word of the Declaration of Independence. At the time I barely knew the name of the author of this sublime document. I do remember hearing someone comment that since Mr. Jefferson had seen fit to pledge so eloquently our lives to the cause of independence, he might at least join us in the army. But wise Tom preferred the safety of Virginia and the excitement of local politics to the discomforts and dangers of war.

Living at Putnam's house was a pretty girl of about thirteen whom I have been accused of having seduced. Margaret Moncrieffe was the daughter of a major with the British army; she was also a cousin of General Montgomery (how tangled our personal relationships were in those days!). Since her father had been a friend of Putnam, the General took her in. If nothing else, the girl had spirit. I was present when she baited General Washington himself at Putnam's table.

As dinner ended, a toast was proposed to liberty or victory or some such sentiment. All drank but Margaret.

"You do not drink your wine." Washington gave the child that cold dull serpent's glance he usually reserved for those private soldiers who were about to be flogged on The Horse ("Discipline is the soul of an army" was his favourite maxim). A disagreeable child, Margaret was not without courage. She raised her glass. "The toast is—the British Commander General Howe."

Washington's face went red in blotches. "You mock us, Miss Moncrieffe . . ." Washington began and then stopped, unable as usual to organize a sentence that contained a new thought.

The good Putnam came to everyone's aid. "What a child says, General, should amuse not offend us."

Washington regained his usual serenity of expression. With an elephantine attempt at gallantry, he said, "Well, Miss, I will overlook your indiscretion on condition that you drink my health or General Putnam's when you next dine with Sir William Howe, on the other side of the water."

I did not like the girl at all. Thought her precocious and sly. When I discovered that she spent hours on the roof with a telescope, looking across to the British encampment, I cautioned General Putnam but he took no notice. She then began a series of flower paintings to be sent as presents to her father. Watching the girl at work one day, I said, "Do you believe there is such a thing as a language of flowers?"

Margaret blushed prettily (she was full-bosomed at thirteen) and stammered. "Yes. I mean no. Not really." Suddenly I was aware of a true alarm that had nothing of the flirtatious in it. Obviously the language of flowers could communicate troop positions. The girl was a spy.

With some effort, I convinced General Putnam that she would be safer and happier farther removed from the potential line of battle (I suspect the good general of having *known* the child best of all).

Margaret was removed to Kingsbridge. Later she was returned to the British. Her subsequent life has been romantic and untidy. She lives now in London. For some years she was the paramour of the King's minister Charles James Fox. I am told she gives to me the honour of having been the first to take her virginity. But I do not think that would have been possible.

By the end of August 1776, General Howe had assembled on Staten Island some 34,000 men. It was his intention to seize New York City, take command of the Hudson and split the colonies in two. May I say, what he intended to do, he proceeded easily to do.

Immediately after the arrival of the British, I was sent by Putnam to every one of our outposts from the Brooklyn Heights to the Haarlem Heights. I had never seen men less prepared for a battle with anyone, much less with fresh modern European troops. Junior though I was to the great commanders, I took seriously my task which was to assess our situation as accurately as I could. My gloomy written report to General Putnam was sent on to the commanding general.

Two days later I encountered His Excellency on the Battery. A sulphurous New York August day. Tempers were short. Sweat mixed with the chalk the General used to powder his hair trickled down cheeks fiery from heat and bad temper. His mood was not improved by the sight of the

British fleet making complicated manoeuvres just opposite us, cannon beautifully polished, white sails pretty beneath a leaden sky.

"What, Sir, do you think the result will be should the enemy begin an assault?" I was taken by surprise: Washington seldom asked such questions of senior officers; never of junior officers.

"Why, Sir, we shall be routed," I said with stupid honesty.

"Never!" The "never" was from a permanent member of the chorus of worshippers that was to follow Washington throughout the Revolution . . . nay, throughout his long life, even to the grave! No man was ever so much praised and fortified by those about him.

I continued. "It is my belief, Sir, that the wisest course would be the one you have so far pursued with such success since Cambridge." Yes, I was a courtier, too.

"What, Sir, do you think that to be?" Our suspicious war-lord suspected even then that I was not entirely in thrall to his legend which, quite mysteriously, continued to grow from month to month no matter whether he won or lost or, as was more usual, did nothing.

"To imitate Fabius Cunctator. To avoid meeting head-on a superior enemy. To draw him away from his supplies. To draw him deeper and deeper into the continent where the advantage is ours not his. Sir, I would abandon New York City today. Give General Howe the sea-coast. He will take it anyway. But by withdrawing now, we keep intact the army, such as it is . . ."

I had gone too far. One of the aides reprimanded me. "The best troops of the colonies are here, Major Burr. The best commanders . . ."

"You under-estimate us, Major." Washington was unexpectedly mild. With a lace handkerchief, he mopped his chalk-streaked face; the pits from the small pox were particularly deep about the mouth.

"You have asked for my report, Sir."

"Yes." Washington turned his back to the port and gazed at the sooty old fort that used to dominate what was still a small Dutch town with rose brick houses and slender church-spires. But then John Jacob Astor was still a butcher boy in Waldorf, Germany.

"We shall defend the city." Washington's mistakes were always proclaimed with the sort of finality that made one feel any criticism was to deface a tablet newly brought down from Sinai.

"Sir, I would burn the city to the ground tomorrow and withdraw into Jersey."

"Thank you, Major. My compliments to General Putnam. Good day, Sir."

In defence of Washington, I must note that at the time very few of us knew much about the powerful secret force at work upon him. There is evidence that he would have liked to destroy the city but was stopped by the local merchants (to a man pro-British) and by the Congress at Philadelphia which, eventually, *ordered* him under no circumstances to fire the city. Yet it was his decision—and no one else's—to confront the enemy with all his forces at Brooklyn in Long Island. This was to be Washington's first set battle; it was very nearly the last. Even today's hagiographers admit his sole responsibility for the disaster.

Right off, Washington split into two parts an army which, entire, was not capable at that time of stopping a British brigade. Then he chose personally to respond to a dazzling series of British and Hessian feints: in a matter of hours, he was out-manned and out-generaled.

Thrown back to his main line of defence, the Brooklyn Heights, Washington was faced with the loss of his entire army if he remained on Long Island or humiliating defeat if he chose to give up the Heights and withdraw to New York Island. He chose humiliation.

On the unseasonably cold and foggy night of August 29, I stood in a water-melon patch near the slip of the Brookyn ferry and watched the evacuation of the army. All night boats went back and forth between New York and Brooklyn. Low dark shapes appearing and disappearing into a strange soft fog. The only sounds the soft moans of the wounded, the whispered commands of officers, the jangle of General Washington's bridle as he presided over the *débâcle* he had devised for us.

On September 15, 1776, the British fleet appeared at Kip's Bay about four miles north of the Battery. As usual, we were surprised. A powerful bombardment began at 11:00 A.M. Then the British and Hessians disembarked. Our troops promptly fled, despite the presence of Washington himself who shrieked at his own men like a man demented, broke his stick over a brigadier's head, cut a sergeant with his sword—to no avail. Raging and weeping, he was dragged away to the sound of British bugles mocking him with the fox-hunter's "View, halloo! Fox on the run!"

Washington retreated up the island to the Morris mansion on the Haarlem Heights (now the home of Colonel and Mrs. Aaron Burr *ci-devant Jumel*) which was to be his headquarters for the rest of September. This must have been the lowest point of his career; worse, in some ways, than the winter at Valley Forge.

I sit now in what was his office, as I amend these notes, and think of him more than a half-century ago, scribbling those long, ungrammatical, disingenuous letters to the Congress, trying to explain how he managed at such cost to lose Long Island and New York City.

During this period I saw General Washington only once at the Morris mansion. It was September 22, and I had accompanied General Putnam to a meeting of the senior officers. There was a good deal to talk about. The previous night almost a third of New York City had gone up in flames.

"Someone has done us a good turn." Washington stood at the foot of the stairs with his plump favourite young Colonel Knox. Before General Putnam could say anything, Washington turned to me and I received for the first and only time his bleak dark-toothed smile. "I would not, Sir, have put it past you to have done this thing."

"Only at your order, Your Excellency."

General Putnam and Colonel Knox had no idea what we were talking about.

Charlie, I shall burrow into my trunks and find you more of these notes—assuming that you are not too much ennuied by such old matters.

The other night as I wooed Madame on those very same stairs, I thought of Washington. For an instant I could *see* him, just next to Madame, with his dark smile, and the inevitable sprinkle of hair-powder on the shoulders of his buff and blue uniform.

Oh, there are ghosts among us! But then what are memories but shadows of objects gone to dust? Or in this case a smile that is no doubt preserved not only in my vivid if failing memory but actually on display somewhere, in the grisly form of a set of false teeth stained black with Madeira. . . .

At exactly six o'clock, I knocked on the front door of 3 Bridge Street. I was even more nervous than I thought I would be when Leggett told me that he had made the appointment.

A large woman opened the door. Without asking my name, she simply said, "*He's* in the front parlour." And vanished, into the back of the house where I could hear women laughing. There was also a pounding noise from upstairs, as though children were holding a foot-race. For a bachelor the great man was hardly lonely in his New York residence.

Standing at the fireplace, beneath a drawing of a Moorish-looking palace (the Alhambra?), was Washington Irving. In the books I read at school he is portrayed as a dreamy-looking, slender youth. No longer. He is now very stout and elderly, with a crooked but pleasing smile. The eyes are guarded, watchful; and he does take you in, every inch, the way painters do at the preliminary sketch. He affects to be shy. At first the voice was so low that I got only an occasional word. "So happy . . . Mr. Leggett . . . to Washington City soon . . . not used to . . . please . . . sit down . . . too warm?"

Mr. Irving sat us down face to face in the two wing chairs before the fire, our knees almost touching. A sharp wind made draughts in the room. He gave me another long look. "Schuyler. Which Schuyler?"

"*No* Schuyler." Invited to give my familiar demur, I lost some of my nervousness. I explained to him that my father had kept a tavern in Greenwich Village and was in no way connected with the glorious Schuylers.

"I am partial to the Dutch." Irving overcame his disappointment, finding what solace he would in the unmistakable physical fact of my Dutchness. With yellow hair and blue eyes, I look like every caricature ever drawn of a Dutch lout. I take after my late mother, a Schermerhorn; no, not the rich Schermerhorns, the others.

Irving tried speaking to me in Dutch and was disappointed when I did not understand. "The old talk is being forgotten. We're all of us the same now. Early this month I was at Kinderhook with . . ." The pause was marvellous. The whole world knows that he was visiting Vice-President Van Buren. ". . . with an old friend, of the Dutch stock. And we looked in vain for so many landmarks we used to know when we were young. The Dutch are like everyone else now. The colour goes." Irving's habitual tone seems to be melancholy, and his sentences tend to terminate in the dying fall.

"Is the Van Buren tavern still at Kinderhook?" I moved too swiftly.

"Yes, yes. Do you know it?" Polite interest, nothing more.

"I have heard so much about it from Colonel Burr. I am in his law office."

"Aaron Burr." Irving said the name softly and with some feeling. But precisely what emotion I could not determine. Certainly there is no hostility. Perhaps wonder. Regret. "Yes, Mr. Leggett said you were interested in Colonel Burr's career. My brother once edited a newspaper for Colonel Burr, a long time ago." The eyes shut. "*Morning Chronicle* it was called. Most political, my brother Peter was—and is. A dedicated Burrite. Colonel Burr was the vice-president when I first published my"—the eyes open wide—"*little* things in his paper. Over thirty years ago."

I told him that when I was in school I read his Jonathan Oldstyle letters. Apparently even then people were looking back to the "good days" of old New York. As much as I admire Irving's work, I do not share his delight in Dutch quaintness. I like nothing about being Dutch, including all the jokes about us.

"It is curious that one of the last of the *little* pieces I wrote for the paper was an attack upon the practice of duelling. That was just two years before . . ." Irving gestured. Eyes evaded mine; settled on the Moorish castle above the fireplace.

From upstairs came a terrible shriek. Irving gave a start; looked alarmed; sighed. "Children," he said, and for a moment lost his usual sweetness of manner. He is plainly not used to family life. But then he has been living a bachelor's life for the last twenty years in Spain and England. As a result, he is now more like an Englishman—of the polite kind—than an American. He could step on the stage of the Park Theatre tonight and play with the greatest of ease man-servant to a duke.

"You must have seen Colonel Burr at Richmond Hill?"

Irving smiled. "Oh, yes. But I was not one of The Little Band. That was what the Colonel's admirers called themselves. A most devoted group, and with good reason. Colonel Burr was New York's Maecenas. He loved artists. Liked to help them. No good artist who asked him for money was ever disappointed. Both he and Theodosia . . ."

"Mrs. Burr?"

"No, she was dead by then. I mean Theodosia his daughter. The most extraordinary woman I ever met." Irving seemed genuinely moved; the round eyes glazed over. "She was small, dark and splendid, with the Grecian profile. She spoke a half-dozen languages. Knew every science. Read Voltaire. Corresponded with Jeremy Bentham. Yet was womanly and loving . . ."

From all accounts Theodosia was indeed a paragon but for mysterious reasons of his own I have the impression that Irving exaggerates his passion for the long-dead beauty, expressing his adoration in complex complete sentences as a single tear rolls slowly down his cheek into the fortress of that tall starched stock there to splash in darkness from chin to chin like. . . . I am beginning to parody his style.

"Was Mr. Van Buren often at Richmond Hill?"

A silk handkerchief was used to remove the saline track the tear had made on the smooth plump cheek (I cannot forget that this is the man who wrote the favourite stories of my childhood). "I think not." Irving was cautious. "Their friendship has been made too much of."

"But didn't Colonel Burr stay with Mr. Van Buren at Albany when he came back from Europe . . ."

"Mr. Van Buren was once a friend. Therefore he will always be—amiable. But there is no *political* connection." This was said sharply. Irving is often mentioned as a possible secretary of state in a Van Buren cabinet. After all, he is an experienced diplomat who was for some time chargé d'affaires at the American legation in London. In fact, he was there last year when Van Buren arrived as minister, appointed by President Jackson and then, humiliatingly, rejected by the Senate as a result of Vice-President Calhoun's malice. The subtle Irving, however, was most kind to the discredited ambassador and managed for him to be received by the King and made much of by London society.

Irving is also supposed to have told Van Buren that his rejection by the Senate would be the making of him. "For," Irving is reported to have said, "there is such a thing in politics as killing a man too dead. You will now be Jackson's next vice-president, and that will be the end of Calhoun."

The unworldly Irving proved to be as good a political prophet as he was a friend. No wonder the two men take trips together up the Hudson and moon about Dutch ruins. Rip Van Winkle has indeed waked up and returned to us, with a future president in tow.

"I am not so certain that I can be of any use to you, Mr. Schuyler." I was aware now of the diplomat on guard. "I do agree that a study of Colonel Burr's career would be fascinating to read. But don't you think it is—perhaps—too soon? So many people still alive . . ."

"Like Mr. Van Buren?"

"It is also *said* that President Jackson was even more deeply involved with Colonel Burr." There was a definite sharp edge to the melodious voice. "So was Senator Clay who—"

We were interrupted by a powerfully built blond youth. "Mr. Irving! Oh, I am sorry. You are not alone." The boy hesitated in the doorway. I got to my feet.

"This is John Schell, Mr. Schuyler." The boy's handclasp was bone-crushing. "I met John on the ship coming from London. He is staying here while he gets the feel of our new country."

"Excuse me, Sirs." The German accent was heavy. The boy bowed stiffly and left us.

Irving continued: "I was about to say that when I saw Senator Clay at the Park Theatre last night—"

"Last night? But Colonel Burr was there, too."

"I know." Irving smiled. "Did he tell you what happened?"

I shook my head.

"Henry Clay came in at about nine o'clock. Almost everyone stood. And cheered. A most tumultuous welcome." A delicate crooked smile. "I *somehow* kept my seat during this Whiggish display. Then, at the interval, as I was crossing the foyer, what do I see but Colonel Burr suddenly—by accident, I should think—face to face with Mr. Clay. The one lean and mad-eyed with that awful mouth like a carp, the other like some dark imp from the lower regions. The imp put out his hand and Mr. Clay *reeled*—there is no other word for the backward falling movement he made. Then well-wishers bore him away. I don't suppose a dozen people standing there recognised Colonel Burr and of those who did hardly one was aware how, years ago, Clay, a very ambitious young lawyer in Kentucky, successfully defended Aaron Burr against a charge of treason—and very nearly nipped his own political career in the bud. Oh, your Aaron Burr is the sprightly skeleton in many a celebrated closet!"

"Including the President's?"

"I think—don't you?—that their involvement was explained at the time in a most satisfactory way by General Jackson." The response was stiff, to say the least. But then Irving's friend cannot be our next president unless the current president chooses to promote him; therefore Andrew Jackson must be above suspicion. They all must. Yet there are those who believe that the whole lot were once involved in treason, Burr, Jackson, Clay. How many secrets there are! and Washington Irving is willing to betray none.

A clatter from the kitchen beneath reminded us that the family supper was almost ready. I rose. "You never see Colonel Burr?"

Heavily, Irving got to his feet. Our knees for an instant struck.

"I *saw* him last night. But we do not speak. What would be the point? Of course he was once most admirable. But I do think—all in all—that he does himself—all of us—a disservice by . . ." The tentative crooked smile again, the voice suddenly, deliberately soft. ". . . well, by *living* so very, very long—so *unnaturally* long—a continuous reminder of things best forgotten."

"I think it splendid that he is still among us. Able to tell us the way things really were."

" 'Really were'? Perhaps. Yet isn't it better that we make our own *useful* version of our history and put away—in the attic, as it were—the sadder, less edifying details?"

Irving walked me to the front door, now blockaded by a child's hobby-horse. Together we lifted it out of the way.

"My compliments to Mr. Leggett. If you see him, say that I shall meet him Wednesday for our weekly *tête-à-tête* at the Washington Hotel. You must join us." The hand resting on my shoulder gave a sudden pinch, like a corpse's fingers going into *rigor.*

"I am sorry to be so little help to you." The hand and arm dropped to his side. "I do have the notes I made during the treason trial at Richmond. If you like, I shall have a copy made for you."

. . .

*Monmouth Court House*

Although I tend to think of the Revolution as a time of bitter cold, my own disaster took place on one of the hottest days in the history of a long life, June 28, 1778. What the cold could not accomplish the brutal heat very nearly did. My health was lost to me for five years and any effectiveness I may have had as an officer in the field ended at the battle of Monmouth Court House.

There was a considerable celebration in early May at Valley Forge. Not only had the army survived the winter (and Washington outwitted the cabals against him) but word came to us that the French government had officially recognised the United States of America; best of all, not only were the French sending out a fleet to help us but their navy had already begun a blockade of the English Channel. We were certain now that we would win.

On a fine May morning Washington reviewed the troops, read the news from France, fired thirteen rounds of precious powder, arranged a good deal of food under a bower, gave a gill of rum to every man, and generally created the impression that all things were at last possible for us, not least victory.

General Lee was on hand, recently exchanged for a British general. Some time before Lee had been mysteriously captured while visiting a lady in a tavern: mysteriously because some suspected Washington of having arranged the capture to remove a rival. Lee was brilliant, vain, fascinating, and we soon became good friends. It is significant that the only general officer I was ever close to was the only one to be court-martialled and broken. I plainly lacked Wilkinson's doggedness in pursuing those commanders who might help me up in the world. Yet for all of Jamie's adroitness, he finally managed to get himself involved in so many plots and counterplots at Valley Forge that General Gates eventually threatened him with a duel while Washington, whose nose for intriguers was keen, appointed him clothier-general to the army and sent him away. In this occupation Jamie was able to steal money in small quantities which was to be expected; unfortunately, he neglected to clothe the army and was let go.

I use the word "dogged" to describe Wilkinson's pursuit of honour—no, *place*—through the cultivation of important men. But Wilkinson was positively desultory in this occupation compared to Hamilton who wanted honour for itself alone, as did the best of us.

"I have often thought what a difficult time Hamilton must have had, forced to serve a man whose mind he despised. Certainly they were an incongruous pair. The solemn slow general waddling with dignity through the camp, while like a ginger terrier at his heel frisked the young impertinent aide. Washington plainly adored Hamilton, and must never have realized to what extent the beloved youth disliked him. But then Washington was not in the habit of friendship with men or women (I have known well many of those who were close to him and I have heard of no women in his life except the wife of a neighbour in Virginia who was, according to Jemmy Madison, more spiritual sister than inamorata). What affections he might have had were tightly reined in. The decorous relationship with his wife Martha was simply an alliance between properties, and typical of Washington's ambition, of his cold serpent's nature.

Also, from the age of forty-three Washington was forced not only to play but to *be* the god of America. This meant that he could have no friends among his contemporaries, for any one of them might have proved to be a rival. As a result, his affections tended to centre on young men who were no threat to his eminence. Watching him, however, with a contemporary and equal like Charles Lee was a marvellously droll spectacle. The usually majestic Washington would become the clumsy courtier: diffident, halting, given to sudden blushes, and then, at the right moment, a knife would flash in the dark and another rival would be stunned to discover that the dull, obsequious Virginia gentleman had effectively done for him.

If Washington's passion for Hamilton was plainly unrequited, it was more than compensated for by the adoration proffered him by that vivacious young Frenchman the Marquis de Lafayette, who joined our Revolution at Valley Forge. Lafayette was one of a number of glory-minded Europeans who came to help us battle tyranny. Of these foreigners, only Von Steuben had military talent. A marvellous liar who had put it about that he was lieutenant-general to Frederick the Great when the highest rank he ever held was captain, Von Steuben proved to be equally marvellous at training men.

As for Lafayette, he was all youthful enthusiasm and charm and silliness. Incidentally, he had the most unusual head I have ever seen; it came to a point at the top like a pineapple. He worshipped Washington, who was so overwhelmed by the young man's ardour that he allowed him nearly to lose us the battle of Monmouth Court House.

Thinking back, we must have been a strange-looking assembly. Although Washington was in full immaculate uniform, the rest of us were in rags except Lafayette and some of the foreigners. I should note that Benedict Arnold had arrived on the scene; he was constantly hobbling along at Washington's side, talking into his ear. Arnold had recently been passed over for promotion, which did his native bad temper no good. Gates was there, too, much chastened since the collapse of the conspiracy. And of course the burly Lord Stirling who was always attended by his aide James Monroe, whose principal task during the Revolution was to keep His Lordship's cup filled until it was time to put him to bed. What a small group it was that fought the Revolution, founded the republic, and governed the better part of a continent for a quarter-century! And so many of the future governors were present at Valley Forge, drinking rum and water in a bower of green branches, and toasting the king of France.

When the celebration was done, I joined General Lee and several of his admirers in a farm-house. Dishevelled, ill-shaven, eyes a-glitter, Lee sat with feet on the fire fender, a Pomeranian dog (rather resembling him) at his feet, and regaled us with tales of his captivity at Philadelphia. "Most civil the British were to me. Particularly the senior officers. Good fellows mostly. And how they hate this war! Blame it all on their politicians. Every night we'd drink together and toast the end of the war and the hanging of the politicians; of *all* the politicians in the world except His Excellency."

Lee winked. He had a special way of saying "His Excellency" that conveyed in each respectful syllable absolute contempt.

"General Clinton wants to give up Philadelphia. Move back to New York. He's trying to persuade the ministry in London either to abandon the colonies altogether, which is not likely, or settle for holding New York indefinitely. He's sick of the war. They all are. If he does move out of Philadelphia, I told His Excellency that we should do nothing to stop him. Quite the contrary. Build the British a bridge of gold, I said. Throw flowers in their path because we've won. It's all over. The French have decided the war in our favour and the day their fleet appears off Long Island the British will go home. Unhappily, His Excellency hungers for a victory in the field. I think he has grown tired of exaggerating what happened during that skirmish at Trenton. Although he now believes that he ranks with Marlborough and Frederick, he also knows that when people speak of American *victories* they speak of mine and Gates's and never, never of his. So I predict that as the British withdraw he will attempt a set battle with the British. I also predict that no matter how great our initial advantage, he will fail as he always does." If nothing else, Lee was a good prophet.

In June the British under General Clinton evacuated Philadelphia and began the long trek to New York City.

I attended the staff meeting where Washington presented his plan for attacking the enemy while they were in train. As usual, he elicited agreement from nearly everyone. Only Lee made his case for allowing the British to withdraw. As much as I respected Lee, I think Washington's strategy, in theory, was sound. But in execution it was, as always with our famous commander, a disaster—or in this case a near-disaster.

Washington made his error at the very beginning. Overwhelmed by the exuberant Lafayette's passion for renown (not to mention for his commander's august legend), Washington first proposed that the French youth lead the assault with *General Lee's* troops. Lee was rightfully angry. So Washington patched together, as only he could, a fatally divided command. If Lafayette attacked the enemy first, Lee would stand aside while he earned glory. Should Lafayette *not* have seized a hero's laurels by the time Lee appeared on the scene, then Lee would take command. It was the sort of stupid compromise that works marvellously well in a congress but not at all on the field of battle. Final idiocy, Washington at the last moment re-arranged a number of companies in such a way that many of the division commanders had no idea whom they were commanding.

So much for the grand design.

Although not a general, I was given command of a brigade that included my own regiment and parts of two other Pennsylvania regiments. I had an excellent second-in-command, Lieutenant-Colonel Bunner, and, all in all, I was content. Yet by the morning of July 27, as I mounted my horse in a rain which was, without too much exaggeration, scalding, I began to sense disaster. Soldiers often do. Some electrical quality in the air communicates hours in advance victory, defeat, pain, death.

I was part of Lord Stirling's division that commanded the American left, to the west of Monmouth Court House where the British army was entrenched. On orders from Stirling we spent the entire day and night of the 27th in the open, under a tropical sun that did us more damage than British guns. We were all light in the head. Many fainted; and some suffered paroxysms from the stroke. We were also prey to clouds of Jersey mosquitoes, the world's largest and most resourceful.

Before the sun was up on the 28th I was leading my brigade along a sandy lane to the west and south of Monmouth Court House. There was a constant ringing in my head. Yet I was lucid, and can recall to this day the look of the spindly heat-withered pines that edged the road—trail, rather; can recall how the sergeant just behind me kept whistling over and over again the same two bars of "The World Turn'd Upside Down," a song popular with the British army.

By noon we were on the high ground just west of a certain ravine on whose opposite side the advance troops of our wing of the army were supposed to make their first attack. I ordered a halt, to await orders.

Beneath us was a mosquito-whining swamp crossed by a narrow footbridge. On the far side, a forest and, somewhere, the enemy. I ordered the men into battle position. This was not easy, for every few minutes someone fainted. Colonel Bunner's thermometer registered ninety-four degrees.

I exhorted the men not to drink too much water but since I could not be everywhere, dozens of bellies were soon swollen and cramped from guzzling. I, too, was inconvenienced by a diarrhoea that was to remain with me for the next five years, despite an invalid's diet.

Shortly after noon we heard the first loud hollow blast of cannon. In all there were five reports from the direction of the court-house. Then silence. Another hour passed. Alarmed, I despatched a lieutenant to Lord Stirling with a request for orders.

At about three in the afternoon when the sun burned like a flaming cannon-ball above the pine-wood, battle was joined. Off to our right, but out of sight, we could hear the clatter of musketry fire; the whiz and thud of artillery. The Lafayette-Lee division after a long mysterious delay had begun to fight.

Suddenly I saw a flash of scarlet in the woods opposite. Simultaneously, scouts reported that a British detachment was now advancing through the woods, hoping to outflank General Lee's advance position.

I gave the order for attack. Indian file, the men started to cross the bridge while I maintained a covering fire. In a matter of minutes the entire brigade would have been safely across the bridge and under cover. But fate intervened.

One of Washington's aides materialised. "Stop those men, Colonel!" Wild eyes met mine.

I thought him mad. "I can't stop them. They're moving to take cover before the British get our range."

"Stop them! Recall them! It is General Washington's order."

I swung my horse in such a way that it looked as if he had shied from the sound of bullets. Pretending to have heard nothing, I rode to the bridge. Something like a third of the brigade was now on the other side. Behind a row of pines the British were getting our range.

The aide followed me. "Colonel, I order you in the name of the commanding general to withdraw those men." Sick from heat, the aide was interpreting, literally, an order based on Washington's ignorance of the terrain, not to mention terror at the thought of yet another defeat: unknown to us at the edge of the swamp, General Lee had abruptly withdrawn from the advance position and many of his troops had interpreted the command to withdraw to mean retreat; and for the American soldier retreat is best done through flight.

Washington himself stopped the rout and ordered General Lee back to his post with a series of violent oaths. Then, after some hesitation, Washington decided to remain where he was and to stop the rest of us from advancing. Thus we lost, fatally, the initiative, thanks to Lee's abrupt withdrawal and to Washington's refusal to do more than make a perfunctory feint at the British position. What might have been a clear-cut victory for us was no more than a skirmish, ultimately beneficial to the outnumbered British who ought, in the normal course, to have been destroyed.

"These men will be murdered!" I shouted at the aide but he was adamant: right or wrong, Washington must be obeyed.

I stopped the crossing of the bridge. Safe in the woods, the enemy was now able to pick off one by one our men.

As I rode up and down our side of the swamp, shouting at the men to take cover, to return the enemy's fire, I suddenly found myself flung like a stone through the air. The whole world had indeed gone upside down, I remember thinking as pine-trees upended around me.

I fell with a crash onto a sandy bank, winded but not hurt; my horse killed.

As I got to my feet, I saw Colonel Bunner being shot dead at the bridge. One third of the brigade was now dead; as many wounded.

The night was as hot as day. A copper moon illuminated the pine-wood where exhausted men slept; where the wounded moaned, gasped for breath, trying to live, to die.

I nursed the wounded until shortly before dawn when I collapsed in a field and did not awaken until the sun was well up. As a result I was dried out like an Egyptian mummy which I somewhat resembled. I had also been bled while I slept by a thousand mosquitoes. I could hardly walk.

In this highly debilitated state I learned to my disgust if not surprise that (unknown as usual to Washington, who had spent the night sleeping at the side of Lafayette on a mantel beneath the stars) the British army had departed, and were now safely on their way to Staten Island. The plan to intercept them had entirely failed; and we had sustained heavy casualties for nothing. Such was the "victory" for George Washington at Monmouth Court House.

When awakened by the news that the British army had escaped, Washington's response was characteristic. He arrested General Lee for disobedience, and ordered a court-martial. I openly supported Lee, as did many others. Washington took note of us all, and few of Lee's admirers were to earn promotion.

I even corresponded at some length with Lee while he was under arrest. At one point he wrote me that regardless of whatever sentence was imposed (a year's suspension from duty, as it turned out), he intended to quit the army and "retire to Virginia, and learn to hoe tobacco, which I find is the best school to form a consummate general."

I should note that two curious pieces of information that I was given in London by a permanent clerk at the war ministry. I do not vouch for their authenticity. The first was that when Charles Lee was captured by the British, they threatened to hang him for a deserter from the British army. To save his neck he persuaded them to let him go on condition that he persuade Washington not to interfere with their withdrawal to New York. When he failed to persuade Washington, he ordered the disastrous retreat at Monmouth Court House, saving the British army. The other information I find easier to believe: that during the Adams administration Alexander Hamilton was British Agent Seven, and paid for by London. Jefferson suspected this, but then Jefferson suspected all his enemies of treason and I never took his charges seriously.

With the breaking of Lee, Washington reigned supreme as military genius in the eyes of the states. Although Washington was never to defeat an English army, he had now won a far more important war—the one with his rivals.

"What was Washington's most notable trait?" I once asked Hamilton when we were working together on a law case. The quick smile flashed in that bright face, the malicious blue eyes shone. "Oh, Burr, self-love! Self-love! What else makes a god?"

## *West Point*

I sent two days' sick-leave near Paramus, at the Hermitage, with my future wife Theodosia Prevost. Then, ill as I was, I accepted Washington's appointment as a sort of spy to try and discover whatever possible about the enemy's shipping.

With a small group of men we ranged up and down the North River from Weehawk to Bergen, collecting gossip, some of it useful.

I was then given the task of escorting by barge a number of wealthy Tories from Fishkill to British-held New York City. This might have been enjoyable duty had I not been suffering from debilitating headaches as well as diarrhoea.

In October I asked to be given sick-leave *without* pay. I wanted to be under no obligation to Washington who granted the leave but insisted that I take full pay. Since this was unacceptable, I felt obliged to rejoin my regiment at West Point where I was promptly mistaken by a local farmer for Colonel Burr's *son.*

This section breaks off.

## *The Westchester Line*

January 13, 1779, I arrived at White Plains to take command of the Westchester Line that stretched some fourteen miles between the Hudson River and Long Island Sound. Below the line was New York City, the British army, and their friends the American Tories.

It was my task to regulate the passage of traffic between Tory New York and Whig Westchester. As it turned out, my actual work was to stop the plundering of the civilians who lived in the area. Stealing was the chief occupation not only of the troops under my command but of their officers as well. In fact, plunder was the principal occupation of what seemed to be half the population of Westchester. Those who stole from the Tories and the British were called Skinners. Those who stole from us were called Cowboys. By the spring of 1779, Skinners and Cowboys had been largely done away with; my health, too.

On March 10, I sent my resignation to General Washington who accepted it with the polite sentiment that he "not only regretted the loss of a good officer, but the cause which made his resignation necessary."

# 1834

The Colonel is unusually nervous today. "I feel like an actor who does not know his lines." He has been sitting with a packet of letters and some old newspaper cuttings on the table in front of him. Also, an open much-marked copy of *The Life of Alexander Hamilton,* recently published by Hamilton's son, John.

"For once, Charlie, I wish that I had sired a proper son. There is a good deal to be said for filial piety, no matter how infelicitous. Naturally, I assume that any son of mine would write better than this boy who sounds like a combination of his father at his most windy, and his grandfather Schuyler at his most confused. Well, I shall be my own son—with your help."

The Colonel puts his feet up on the grate; shuts his eyes as if he expects some inner curtain to rise upon past spectacles. "You asked me about Hamilton." I had asked him about Van Buren. "Let me recall a scene or two for you." He closes his throat. "It is November . . ."

The eyes open for a moment and he glances at a newspaper cutting. "November 25, 1783. I have just come to New York City from Albany, with my wife and daughter. The American states have made peace with England. The British are about to depart. General Washington is to make his triumphant entry into the city."

I record now the Colonel's recollections—not as he dictated them to me but as they currently exist after a number of revisions in his own hand.

## *Memoirs of Aaron Burr—One*

At about noon, I arrived with my wife Theodosia at Cape's Tavern in the Broad Way. The streets were filled with veterans, many drunk, all happy. New York City was a small place in those days but the people, despite a certain Dutchness, were as lively than as now.

The assembly-room of the tavern was crowded with former officers wearing cockades of black and white, as well as sprigs of laurel to attest to our gallantry and patriotism. I knew most of the officers, though not their wives. I particularly recall General McDougall; between the stammer and the Scots burr he was quite incoherent with joy.

Theodosia hung back, intimated by so many strangers. But then Elizabeth Hamilton took her firmly by the hand, in that effective Schuyler way, and presented her to various ladies. Elizabeth was uncommonly handsome as a girl, if too square-jawed. I have been told that Hamilton used to discuss his infidelities with her. If he did, they must have had a good deal to talk about.

My old friend Troup greeted me; he was now a lawyer like me (after two weeks in the city I had more business than I could handle).

"A great day!" we both agreed and of course it was, despite the fact that the war had been over for some time. Today's ceremony was a tribute to the dilatoriness of Sir Guy Carleton, the British commander in New York. He kept finding excuses not to go home: the weather was bad, the ships in disrepair, His Excellency indisposed. But now it was finally ended.

As we waited in the tavern, Sir Guy's troops were slowly embarking from the Battery. At last General Washington could make his "triumphal" entry into the city that he had lost to the British seven years earlier and never, by arms, regained.

Hamilton hurried into the long room, cheeks bright with excitement. He greeted Troup and me warmly. Though rival lawyers, each intent on being first in the town, we were all of us friends that day.

What a vivid, bright, pretty little man Hamilton was! And oh, what a gift he had for making a *moral* point while destroying the reputation of an adversary. The malice in him was as spontaneous as the brilliance. "*He's* in Chatham Street, at the Tea Water Pump!" We knew who *he* was. "Governor Clinton will escort *him* here."

We congratulated one another on our good luck in so soon having the glorious Washington amongst us. But human pageantry is peculiarly vulnerable to the ridiculous. The only time I saw the Emperor Napoleon he was proceeding up the marble stairs of a Paris theatre, moving with all that sombre elegance he had learned from the actor Talma. But then, at the very top of the stairs, as all of us bowed reverently, he shrilly broke wind.

Today's comedy had been prepared by two British soldiers who had slyly greased the flag pole on the Battery. When our flag and its attendant tried to mount the pole, flag and attendant dropped in a heap to the ground, deeply mortifying General Washington.

Colonel (now Brevet-General) Malcolm joined us. Like so many senior officers who have not seen combat, this good man wanted to discuss the war. But the young men—and Hamilton, Troup and I thought we had invented youth—spoke only of the present and the future.

I twitted Hamilton. "How are your rich and well-born friends?" Hamilton was representing half the wealthy Tories in New York.

"They suffer, too."

"I wish they would suffer me." Troup wanted clients.

"I shall send you an occasional rich widow." Hamilton's passion for the rich and the well-born was, doubtless, the result of having been born poor and illegitimate.

Although the Constitution and the federal government would not be invented for another five years, the division in our ruling class was already apparent. The Tories who had opposed the Revolution now had no choice but to accept a new American order. But though the army of their king was no longer installed on the Battery, the principles of British government were still very much installed in their minds. They believed that we must have a government in which the privileges of the rulers are as well-defined as are the obligations of the ruled. In order words, we must recreate the British system. Hamilton was so devoted to all things English that if I had been he, I would have set sail for England that afternoon with Sir Guy, gone into British politics, and become prime minister. But Hamilton chose to stay and fight not only the pernicious idea of democracy but the craftiest of all its proponents, Thomas Jefferson—soon to be American minister at Paris, a post to which the Congress hustled him in the wake of his disastrous governorship of Virginia.

The noise of cheering caused us to hurry to the windows. Washington the demigod—no, the god!—was dismounting. The crowd waved their hats. He raised his hat once and put it under his arm. Then accompanied by Governor Clinton His Mightiness entered the tavern. Incidentally, when Washington became president he wanted to be styled His Mightiness. The Senate was agreeable. The House of Representatives was not, and referred the other house to the Constitution which speaks of the chief executive as, simply, the president. In fact, the Speaker—the droll Mr. Muhlenberg—went so far as to suggest that perhaps the General would like to be known as "His High and Mightiness." Muhlenberg's mild pleasantry was not well received by the greatest man in the world who would very much have enjoyed, I suspect, being king had he not lacked a son, a prince of Virginia, to succeed him.

But that was in the future. At the moment it was quite enough that the most famous man on earth was in the assembly-room of Cape's Tavern.

We formed two lines. Washington walked slowly between the rows, turning from side to side, his cold slow gaze mitigated by a hesitant almost boyish smile when he chose to favour a particular aide.

He stopped when he came to Hamilton who was standing next to me. Suddenly the General looked positively merry, even animated; for an instant his face like a dull mirror reflected the bright intelligence of the other's image. "My boy." He was like a father.

"It is your day, General. Your country."

"*Our* day, Sir." Then the light went from his face as he turned to me and saw himself in a very different sort of mirror.

"Colonel Burr. You are recovered in your health, I trust?"

I said that I was and presented to him his old friend, my new wife. Theodosia curtsied, as to the King.

Washington smiled and lifted her up. "Colonel Burr like the rest of us is . . ." Words, as usual, failed him. I was embarrassed. Theodosia looked pale. Hamilton did the work Heaven had designed for him. "Bewitched by the mistress of the Hermitage."

"Just so." Washington moved on and Hamilton gave me an imperceptible wink—no, *flick* of his bright blue eyes. What did he really think of Washington? We come to that.

Colonel Burr is now delighted with our sessions, particularly when he re-reads his dictation and makes changes. "It is like preparing a brief—for the defence, of course!"

He is still reading and annotating his copy of *The Life of Alexander Hamilton.* The ancient rivalry is much on his mind. "You know, my friend Hamilton thought me 'equivocal' on the subject of the Constitution. For once in describing me he used the exact word. I was—I *am* equivocal. I have told you I did not think the Constitution in its original form would last fifty years. Nor has it. The habit of amendment continues to alter its nature—though not enough."

He opened a volume of Hamilton's works; riffled the pages. "No one can say that the Constitution was framed by innocent men. They were—and I knew most of them—as able a group of lawyers as ever argued a client from his rightful place on the gallows. They were most cynical. Listen to Hamilton." Burr read: " 'Men will pursue their interests. It is as easy to change human nature as to oppose the strong current of selfish passions. A wise legislator will gently divert the channel, and direct it, if possible, to the public good.' I like the 'if possible.' What does the wise legislator do if it is *not* possible? Feather his nest, I fear."

The Colonel laughed suddenly, and recalled "the time Hamilton made an election speech to a group of mechanics. Unfortunately Hamilton always addressed his inferiors as if they were his inferiors. This is never charming, and I fear the crowd made fun of him. Furious, exasperated, he shouted, 'You are your own worst enemy!' What would he think now when 'the beast,' as he used to call the generality, governs, or at least we flatter it into thinking that it governs."

He put down the book. Began the day's work.

## *Memoirs of Aaron Burr—Two*

In 1787, I took no part in the arguments for and against the Constitution. Like everybody else, I read Publius in the newspapers. Like everyone else, I soon worked out which Publius was Hamilton, which Jay, which Madison. Like everyone else, I knew Hobbes and his extraordinary belief (shared by Hamilton) that *any* form of government no matter how tyrannous is better than anarchy. I had also read Montesquieu whose work so influenced the three Publiuses. Yet at heart I was more pleased than not by the loose confederation of states that existed between 1783 and 1787. All in all, New York was agreeably governed by the Clinton faction. If certain of the other states were less well-governed, that was their affair; to be set right by them and not by a group of clever lawyers in Philadelphia. Yes, I was equivocal. A degree of anarchy is no bad thing.

Contrary to tradition, the movement for a strong Constitution and federal government began not with Hamilton but with General Washington. It is usual to picture him as a worthy, slow-witted man, a latter-day Cincinnatus only happy on his farm—trying to move that leaden plow he invented. He was of course worthy (if inordinately vain) and slow-witted in matters of the mind. But no man was cleverer when it came to business and to the promotion of his commercial interests. For very practical reasons, he wanted a strong central government with himself at its head. He was from the beginning a perfect federalist, and used Hamilton far more than Hamilton ever used him in order to make safe his investments in land.

Jefferson told me that for all of Washington's innumerable complaints about the exigencies of public life, he was actually bored to death after the Revolution. "They are making a damned tavern-keeper of me!" he used to swear when yet another party of curious guests descended upon him at Mount Vernon. It should be noted that at the time of Washington's election he was, as usual, short of cash and his first act as president was to get from the Treasury an advance on his salary.

I recollect only one private interview with Washington after the Revolution. It was in October of 1791, shortly after I arrived in Philadelphia as senator from New York. At the time I was most ambitious to write the true history of the Revolution. Each morning I would get up at five o'clock and go to the State Department, accompanied by a clerk. Together we would study and copy out documents until ten o'clock when I would attend the Senate.

Puzzled by certain military details, I requested an audience with His Mightiness. It was granted me so promptly that I ought to have been suspicious. Not only had I replaced Hamilton's father-in-law in the Senate, but the French Revolution was under way and I confess to having believed for a time that a new era in the world's history had begun. Later of course I realized that the same bad old era had simply shown us a new face whose smile would presently reveal bloody fangs. But in 1791 I was, like Jefferson, a devotee of the *other* Revolution and so anathema to the Federalist faction.

The President received me in his stately office. He had entirely redone the Morris House to make it resemble a royal palace. A diffident young secretary bowed me into the presence.

Washington stood before the fire, as though expecting to be painted. The altogether too famous sallow face was considerably aged. He was also in pain from carbuncles. He greeted me solemnly. Since he remained standing, we faced one another before the fire like ill-matched andirons.

I asked him questions about the Revolution; he made evasive answers. Both questions and answers are now lost. I do recall his cold benediction: "It is a most useful task, Senator Burr, that you are engaged upon." Plainly he was not happy with my line of questioning which seemed to stress unduly his defeats.

The secretary brought him despatches from the west; he glanced at them, then dismissed the secretary and bade me sit. Slowly, carefully, painfully, Washington arranged himself in a throne-like chair, favouring one huge buttock: the dread carbuncle had erupted in that sensitive fleshy quarter. I commiserated with him over the recent news from the west where his favourite General St. Clair had lost nearly a thousand men to the Indians.

Washington was cold and grim. "I shall presently send the Congress a report on this tragic matter. I firmly believe that if we do not destroy these warlike savage tribes, we shall lose the whole of our new lands west of the Ohio." He spoke the way one imagined a statue would speak.

But then he sat too far back in his chair. Gasping with pain, he swore mightily. Aware that he was now no longer royal in my eyes but simply a Virginia planter whose bottom hurt, he said, "I deteriorate before your eyes, do I not?"

"You seem most vigorous, Sir."

"I come from a short-lived family. I do not complain. That is fate. But I did not think that the last stages would be so humiliating." For the first and only time in our dealings with one another he was almost human—an extraordinary condescension considering that I was not a junior officer enamoured of him but an anti-Federalist senator detested by the beloved Hamilton.

"Glory is a good medicine, Sir."

"It is palliative." I caught a glimpse of the wintry dark-toothed smile. "But of course I shall not accept a second term." As we now know, all presidents talk in this fashion. But at the time none of us understood the nature of the executive disease; after all, we were at the beginning of the adventure.

"Colonel Burr, I dislike the spirit of faction. I cannot fathom why gentlemen of similar interest quarrel so bitterly with one another when they ought to unite in the face of the mob and its excesses." I was touched by his candour and—for him—ease of manner with someone he had no reason to trust and less to like.

"There are honest differences, Sir, on how best to govern . . ."

"It has come to my attention, Colonel Burr, that you admire much of what is presently happening in France."

"I think, Sir, that the reasons for their revolution are understandable and the principles they assert are admirable."

"Yet were it not for King Louis, the British might still be on this shore."

"I agree that their treatment of him is deplorable . . ."

Washington spoke through me, but not to cut me off: he was going deaf and did not hear half what was said to him. "When word came to me of the treasonous acts of a certain Captain Daniel Shays—a dirty fellow once known to me—it was apparent that we must have a strong government to protect our property. Mr. Hamilton concurred with me and we summoned a constitutional convention at which I, at great personal sacrifice, let me say, presided. I regard, Sir, that convention as the most important event of my own career. Because had we not invented this federal government, *they* would have taken away *everything.*"

The face was dark with sudden colour. The hands that were stretched to the fire trembled. "By now that Massachusetts rabble would have divided all property amongst the worthless classes. Not even your French have dared go so far. This is not natural, I said at the time. This must be stopped. We did not fight and win a war with a despot across the sea to be in turn tyrannized by a bloody mob whose contribution to our victory, if I may say so, was considerably less than that of those gentlemen who sacrificed all that they had in order that we be a separate nation. So what we won in that war we mean to keep, Colonel Burr. And I am sure that you agree with that sentiment."

Political theory was the last subject I ever expected to hear from General Washington. He did not read Hobbes or Montesquieu or Plato, or any book at all. But he could add and subtract sums in a ledger, survey a property, recognise with an eagle's eye the vermin that infest the crops—*his* crops—and like that eagle pounce and kill.

"I certainly did not support Captain Shays and I do not believe in a promiscuous division of property but . . ."

"I am relieved to hear you say that." I was being sounded out. Heaven knows what Hamilton had been telling His Mightiness about me.

"But I favour a looser federal structure."

"Yes. You are like my old friend Governor Clinton. Such *amicable* divisions are natural and healthy in a society."

The secretary slipped into the room, and whispered something in the General's good ear.

"Send them in." Washington heaved himself with a groan from his chair. Several liveried Negroes entered the room carrying trays of sample tableware. Washington indicated that the various knives, forks, plates be displayed on a table. "You may give us your opinion, Colonel Burr. I am told that you have redone Richmond Hill in a most splendid way."

"Yes, Sir, I have. But I must warn you that splendour is expensive."

"We are in sad accord."

So for half an hour the President and I examined tableware, trying to find a truly republican balance between too plain democratic ware and too rich royal plate.

I have never known a man so concerned with the trifles and show of wealth and position as Washington. But then it was his genius always to look the part he was called upon to play, and it is not possible to create a grand illusion without the most painstaking attention to detail. Much of his presidential day was occupied with designing monograms and liveries and stately carriages, not to mention inventing, with Hamilton's aid, elaborate court protocols.

Incidentally, at about this time, the Pennsylvania legislature passed a law that anyone moving into the state with full-grown Negro slaves must free them after six months. Although it was a moot point whether or not the President qualified as a Pennsylvanian simply because the capital was located in that state, Washington thought it best to whisk back to Virginia his personal slaves in order that they not get ideas about a freedom he had no intention of granting them. He was the total Virginian.

We parted on the most friendly terms. The next day when I went to the State Department to consult the archives, an embarrassed clerk told me that Secretary of State Jefferson was obliged to close the archives to me on the flimsy ground that since certain documents might involve current executive matters the constitutional separation between legislature and executive would be breached. Although Hamilton liked to take credit for my exclusion, Jefferson told me privately that it was actually President Washington who did not want me examining too closely his military record. Yet Washington had nothing to fear from me. Although I would have depicted him as the incompetent general he was, I would also have demonstrated how he was the supreme creator of this union; how his powerful will and serpentine cunning made of a loose confederation of sovereign states a strong federal government graven to this day in Washington's sombre Roman imperial image.

Some days later. Colonel Burr goes over what I have written. He makes corrections.

"How hungry for all credit, all glory, poor Hamilton was! Among his papers they found a note swearing that he had written more than sixty of the *Federalist* papers when, in fact, he had written at the most fifty. He made claim to some of Jemmy Madison's best efforts."

Burr blows three blue-white rings of smoke at me; becomes suddenly mischievous: "Now let us examine Mr. Jefferson. He is sometimes known as the Great Leveller of society. Actually, the only levelling he ever did was of me!" . . . .

Today the Colonel was in a most curious and excited mood. "If it amuses you, Charlie, we shall go to the Heights of Weehawk and I shall act out for you the duel of the century, when the infamous Burr slew the noble Hamilton, from behind a thistle—obviously a disparaging allusion to my small stature. Yet Hamilton was less than an inch taller than I though now he looms a giant of legend, with a statue to his divinity in the Merchants' Exchange, his temple. While for me no statue, no laurel, only thistle!"

I was delighted and somewhat embarrassed. Burr almost never speaks of the duel; and most people, unlike Leggett, are much too nervous of the subject ever to bring it up in his presence even though it is the one thing everyone in the world knows about Aaron Burr, and the one thing it is impossible *not* to think of upon first meeting him.

"*He* killed General Hamilton," my mother whispered to me when the elegant little old man first came into our Greenwich Village tavern, after his return from Europe. "Take a good look at him. He was a famous man once."

As I grew older, I realized that my family admired Burr more than not and that my mother was pleased when he took a fancy to me, gave me books to read, encouraged me to attend Columbia College and take up the law. But my first glimpse of him at a table close to the pump-room fire was of the devil himself, and I half-expected him to leave not by way of the door but up the chimney with the flames.

We walked to Middle Pier at the end of Duane Street. "I've ordered my young boatman to stand by."

The Colonel's eyes were bright at the prospect of such an unusual adventure—into past time rather than into that airy potential future time where he is most at home.

"It was a hot day like this—thirty years and one month ago. Yet I remember being most unseasonably cold. In fact, I ordered a fire the night of the tenth, and slept in my clothes on a sofa in the study. Slept very well, I might add. A detail to be added to your *heroic* portrait of me." An amused glance in my direction. "Around dawn, John Swartwout came to wake me up. I was then joined by Van Ness and Matt Davis. We embarked from Richmond Hill."

The tall young boatman was waiting for us at the deserted ship. The sun was fierce. We were the only people on the wharf: the whole town has gone away for August.

We got into the boat, and the young man began to row with slow regular strokes up-river to the high green Jersey shore opposite.

"On just such a morning . . ." He hummed to himself softly. Then: "My affairs were in order. I had set out six blue boxes, containing enough material for my biography, if anyone was minded to write such a thing. Those boxes now rest at the bottom of the sea." He was blithe even at this allusion to the beloved daughter: trailed his finger in the river; squinted at the sun. "What, I wonder, do the fishes make of my history?"

I tried to imagine him thirty years ago, with glossy dark hair, an unlined face, a steady hand—the Vice-President on an errand of honour. But I could not associate this tiny old man with that figure of legend.

"Love-letters to me were all discreetly filed, with instructions to be burned, to be returned to owners, to be read at my grave—whatever was fitting. My principal emotion that morning was relief. Everything was arranged. Everything was well-finished."

"Did you think you might be killed?"

The Colonel shook his head. "When I woke up on the sofa, saw dawn, I knew that I would live to see the sun set, that Hamilton would not." A sudden frown as he turned out of the bright sun; the face went into shadow. "You see, Hamilton *deserved* to die and at my hands."

I then asked the question I have wanted to ask since yesterday but Burr only shook his head. "I have no intention of repeating, ever, what it was that Hamilton said of me."

In silence, we watched the steamboat from Albany make its way down the centre channel of the river. On the decks women in bright summer finery twirl parasols; over the water their voices echo the gulls that follow in the ship's wake, waiting for food.

Apparently the Weehawk Heights "look just the same now as they did then." The Colonel skipped easily onto the rocky shore. While I helped our sailor drag his boat onto the beach, the Colonel walked briskly up a narrow footpath to a wooded ledge.

"Ideal for its purpose," Burr said when I joined him.

The ledge is about six feet wide and perhaps thirty or forty feet long with a steep cliff above and below it. At either end a green tangle of brush partly screens the view of the river.

The Colonel indicates the spires of New York City visible through the green foliage. "That is the last sight many a gentleman saw."

I notice that he is whispering; he notices, too, and laughs. "From habit. When duellists came here they were always very quiet for fear they'd wake an old man who lived in a hut near by. He was called the Captain and he hated duelling. If he heard you, he would rush onto the scene and thrust himself between the duellists and refuse to budge. Often to everyone's great relief."

Burr crosses to the marble obelisk at the centre of the ledge. "I have not seen this before." The monument is dedicated to the memory of Alexander Hamilton. Parts have been chipped away while the rest is scribbled over with lovers' names. The Colonel makes no comment.

Then he crosses slowly to a large cedar tree, pushing aside weeds, kicking pebbles from his path. At the base of the tree he stops and takes off his black jacket. He stares down at the river. I grow uneasy; cannot think why. I tell myself that there are no ghosts.

When Burr finally speaks his voice is matter-of-fact. "Just before seven o'clock Hamilton and his second Pendleton and the good Dr. Hosack—Hamilton was always fearful for his health—arrive. Just down there." Burr points. I look, half-expecting to see the dead disembark. But there is only river below us.

"Pendleton carries an umbrella. So does Van Ness. Which looks most peculiar on a summer morning but the umbrellas are to disguise our features. We are now about to break the law."

Burr leaves his post at the cedar tree, walks to the end of the ledge. "Now General Hamilton arrives, with his second."

For an instant I almost see the rust-coloured hair of Hamilton, shining in summer sun. I have the sense of being trapped in someone else's dream, caught in a constant circular unceasing present. It is a horrible sensation.

Burr bows. "Good morning, General. Mr. Pendleton, good morning." Burr turns and walks toward me. "Billy." I swear he now thinks me Van Ness. "You and Pendleton draw lots to see who has choice of position, and who will give the word to fire."

With blind eyes, the Colonel indicates for me to cross to the upper end of the ledge.

"Your principal has won both choices, Mr. Pendleton." A pause. "He wants to stand *there*?" A slight note of surprise in Burr's voice.

I realize suddenly that I am now standing where Hamilton stood. The sun is in my eyes; through green leaves water reflects brightness.

Burr has now taken up his position ten full paces opposite me. I think I am going to faint. Burr has the best position, facing the heights. I know that I am going to die. I want to scream, but dare not.

"I am ready." The Colonel seems to hold in his hand a heavy pistol. "What?" He looks at me, lowers the pistol. "You require your glasses? Of course, General. I shall wait."

"Is General Hamilton satisfied?" Burr then asks. "Good, I am ready, too."

I stand transfixed with terror as Burr takes aim, and shouts "Present!"

*And I am killed.*

Burr starts toward me, arms out-stretched. I feel my legs give way; feel the sting, the burning of the bullet in my belly; feel myself begin to die. Just in time Burr stops. He becomes his usual self, and so do I.

"Hamilton fired first. I fired an instant later. Hamilton's bullet broke a branch from this tree." Burr indicated the tall cedar. "My bullet pierced his liver and spine. He drew himself up on his toes. Like this." Burr rose like a dancer. "Then fell to a half-sitting position. Pendleton propped him up. 'I am a dead man,' Hamilton said. I started toward him but Van Ness stopped me. Dr. Hosack was coming. So we left.

"But . . . but I would've stayed and gone to you had it not been for what I saw in your face." Again the blind look in Burr's eyes. Again he sees me as Hamilton. And again I start to die, the bullet burns.

"I saw terror in your face, terror at the evil you had done me. And that is why I could not come to you or give you any comfort. Why I could do nothing but what I did. Aim to kill, and kill."

He sat down at the edge of the monument. Rubbed his eyes. The vision—or whatever this lunacy was—passed. In a quiet voice, he continued, "As usual with me, the world saw fit to believe a different story. The night before our meeting Hamilton wrote a letter to posterity; it was on the order of a penitent monk's last confession. He would reserve his first fire, he declared, and perhaps his second because, *morally,* he disapproved of duelling. Then of course he fired first. As for his disapproval of duelling, he had issued at least three challenges that I know of. But Hamilton realized better than anyone that the world—our American world at least—loves a canting hypocrite."

Burr got to his feet. Started toward the path. I followed dumbly.

"Hamilton lived for a day and a half. He was in character to the very last. He told Bishop Moore that he felt no ill-will toward me. That he had met me with a fixed resolution to do me no harm. What a contemptible thing to say!"

Burr started down the path. I staggered after him. At the river's edge he paused and looked across the slow water toward the flowery rise of Staten Island. "I had forgot how lovely this place was, if I had ever noticed."

We got into the boat. "You know, I made Hamilton a giant by killing him. If he had lived, he would have continued his decline. He would have been quite forgotten by now. Like me." This was said without emotion. "While that might have been *my* monument up there, all scribbled over."

# 1835

. . .

## *Memoirs of Aaron Burr—Twenty-one*

In the matter of treason, the Constitution is explicit: two persons must witness the traitor in the act of levying war against the United States or of adhering to their enemies, giving them aid and comfort. Since the place where I was supposed to have raised my "army" of insurrection was Blennerhassett's Island, in the month of December 1806, it was necessary for Jefferson to establish that I had indeed committed the crime he had told Congress I had committed.

Yet the facts were unimpressive. All that the prosecution could prove was that some thirty men associated with me stopped at the island on their way down the Ohio. They were not armed. They committed no acts of violence (unlike the local militia). They threatened no one. They said they were en route to the Washita River lands. But because General Wilkinson maintained that these unarmed men meant to seize New Orleans and revolutionize Mexico, they were accused of levying war against the United States *by construction,* and since I was thought to be responsible for their movements (even though I was in Kentucky at the time this "war" was levied against the United States in Virginia), I too was guilty of treason *by construction.*

May I say that the entire concept of *constructive treason* is unconstitutional and was known to be so by every lawyer in the United States, save Jefferson. But he was desperate. Although he had assembled nearly fifty witnesses to denounce me (of whom more than half perjured themselves), there was never any proof that I had levied war against the United States, or advised the thirty men on Blennerhassett's Island to levy such a war.

During the trial, the Governor of Virginia very nicely assigned me a three-room suite in the new penitentiary outside Richmond. I have seldom been so well looked after. The jailer received me most courteously, and hoped that I would be comfortable.

"I am certain to be," I said, graciously.

"I trust, Sir, it would not be disagreeable to you if I should bolt this door after dark?" He indicated the front door to my apartment.

"By no means, Sir. I should prefer it—to keep out intruders."

"It is also our custom, Sir, to extinguish all lights at nine o'clock."

"I fear, Sir, that that is not possible. I never go to bed before twelve, and always burn two candles." I did not add that I never go to bed but with regret, and by violence to myself.

"Just as you please, Sir. I should have been glad if it had been otherwise . . ." A sigh. "But as you please, Sir."

We became excellent friends, particularly when I shared with him the gifts that were hourly brought me by liveried servants—oranges, lemons, pineapples, raspberries, apricots, cream butter and even ice, a luxury in that equatorial zone.

On August 2, Theodosia and her husband arrived, and moved into Luther Martin's house. Theodosia swiftly became the queen of Richmond society, presiding at the Golden Eagle with such charm—despite ill health and natural anxiety—that Luther Martin said, "I must marry her, Colonel. I shall kill her unworthy husband, and then she will be mine, by right of conquest."

"You have my blessing." At that moment I confess that I should not in the least have minded anyone murdering my son-in-law who had all but denounced me in order to avoid being arrested by Jefferson. Alston was a man of weak character with but one interest—his wife and his son. For that shared passion, however, I forgave him everything.

Meanwhile, Blennerhassett had joined me. He, too, was under indictment, and somewhat out of sorts. Our first meeting was not harmonious, largely because he saw fit to pay a call upon me just as a lady of Richmond (a young widow, I hasten to add) was stealing from my presence, with the good jailer's assistance.

"I do not wish to criticise you, Colonel . . ."

"Then *indulge* your wish, my dear friend, and refrain from criticism."

"But immorality of any sort, *licence* of any sort . . ."

"Come now." I did my best to soothe the incestuous uncle.

". . . and in a *penitentiary*!"

"Ah, it is not *fitting*. I see what you mean."

"No, it is not." He then told me that he wanted back the money he had contributed to our venture. Since I was not able to oblige him, he most quixotically refused to hire a lawyer to defend himself. Fortunately my cohort of attorneys was willing to save him from the gallows.

The government had been led to believe that my son-in-law would testify in their behalf. But we undid them. On the day of the trial, August 3, Alston and I entered the court-room together, my arm through his.

It took us a week to assemble a jury from the usual panels. As it turned out, every prospective juror was of the opinion that I was guilty. We might still be at Richmond if Marshall had not ruled that an opinion of the defendant's guilt which was *lightly* held—as opposed to *deliberately* held—did not disqualify a juror. This exquisite decision pleased George Hay. But the wrangling continued.

Finally, I moved to pick any eight men from the existing panel, *if* the prosecution would accept them. Startled, Hay agreed. After all, the entire panel thought me guilty—and none appeared to hold their opinion with much lightness. Almost at random, I picked eight men, making the point that I was certain I could rely on the fairness of gentlemen. This proved to be an excellent move, and I won right off a convert or two, not that it much mattered. I knew that only the law could save me; the jury was irrelevant.

Next to Wilkinson, the government's most important witness was William Eaton, an adventurer who called himself "general" as a result of some interesting skirmishes in North Africa that had gained him a degree of celebrity, a fascinating costume inspired by the Berbers, and a long outstanding claim on the United States government for services supposedly rendered.

I had met Eaton in Washington, had mentioned something to him of my plans for Mexico. He had shown interest, and that was all. Now, suddenly, he had a marvellous tale to tell. Apparently I'd planned to seize the capital, murder the President, and so on. To forestall me, he told the court, he had gone to Jefferson and suggested that I be given a foreign embassy to remove me from the scene. Out of tact he forgot to mention to Jefferson that I intended to murder him.

In court I probed Eaton on the subject of his claim against the United States. Had it been paid? He tried not to answer. Finally, reluctantly, he admitted that shortly after my arrest the government suddenly saw virtue in his claim and he had received some ten thousand dollars.

The Morgan family also testified. Their reports of my conversation were sketchy, and self-contradictory. Nevertheless they, too, were rewarded by Jefferson, who saw to it that the government granted them the disputed Indiana land.

My chief of staff the good French Colonel de Pestre was secretly offered a commission in the American army if he would testify against me. He refused. Even Blennerhassett was approached by Jefferson's henchman, the editor Duane, and told that if he would fully incriminate me all charges would be dropped against him. Surprisingly, Blennerhassett refused. I suppose he thought that if I was hanged he would never see so much as a penny of the money he had lent me. The other witnesses for Jefferson made little impression.

Finally, Marshall asked Hay if he had any further "evidence" that Burr had been at Blennerhassett's Island on the famous December 10 when an act of "war" had been supposedly levied against the United States. Hay said that he had none.

John Wickham then moved that no further testimony be admitted. He also entranced the court for two days, making the point—and re-making it in a hundred subtle ways—that it was not possible to commit treason unless the traitor was himself present when war was levied against the United States. This argument was essential to my defence. Quite simply, I had not been at Blennerhassett's Island December 10. But the constitutional argument was even more important than my neck (which I would have, perhaps, denied at the time).

Wickham's target was the ancient notion of "constructive treason." In its purest sense this phrase means that anyone who might have wished well a potential traitor was as guilty as the traitor himself even though the well-wisher was miles away from the act of war. Wickham reminded the court that the Constitution is a unique document in which treason is exactly and narrowly defined. The traitor must actually be caught in the act of levying war against the United States. These absent figures who wish him well, who might even have inspired him, are nowhere mentioned in the Constitution, and so are not traitors.

This point had to be spelled out with great care because John Marshall had made a serious error in his earlier ruling on Bollman-Swartwout. Although Marshall had not found any evidence of any war of any kind being levied on Blennerhassett's Island, he did declare—no doubt wanting to impress Jefferson with the court's impartiality—that "it is not the intention of the court to say that no individual can be guilty of this crime who has not appeared in arms against his country. On the contrary, if war be actually levied, that is, if a body of men be actually assembled for the purpose of effecting, by force, a treasonable object, *all those who perform any part, however minute, or however remote from the scene of action, and who are actually leagued in the general conspiracy, are to be considered as traitors.*"

I am told that to the end of his days, Marshall regretted this extraordinary blunder, redolent of the medieval Star Chamber. As he himself was soon to recognise, if such a wide net is to be cast into the sea who cannot be caught in it if he has had the ill fortune to have said "God-speed" to a man who later levied war against the United States?

The prosecution was slow to use the weapon Marshall had forged for them. They were so intent on proving that I was on the island December 10 that when I was able, easily, to prove that I was elsewhere, their set-back made more of an impression on the jury than it ought. They would have been better advised to confine themselves to my *distant* leadership of the men on the island and to the treasonable words I was supposed so promiscuously to have said to the various perjurers Jefferson had paid to come to Richmond.

The task of the defence was now to modify Marshall's doctrine of "constructive treason." The Chief Justice, however, was moving in a different direction. He was going to evade as much as possible the trap he had set for himself by attending to the simpler issue of whether or not an act of war against the United States had indeed been levied December 10, and if it had could the government produce two witnesses to that act, as required by the Constitution?

Wickham's presentation proved so thorough and so masterly that the prosecution asked for a recess (which was granted); they also asked for more witnesses to be heard, and heard they were—to no avail.

Then the counter-attack began. William Wirt insinuated himself into the history of American prose if not of law by a splendid flowery description of Blennerhassett's Island as a perfect and innocent Eden to which Aaron Burr, the Devil himself, came as the sulphurous tempter of poor Blennerhassett (a monstrous composite of Adam and Eve), deliberately, cruelly changing to Hell a pristine island Paradise. I am told that this remarkable effusion is still taught in every school of the country as an example of—God knows what! I do suspect that my continuing dark fame in this republic is now almost entirely due to the fact that the only thing that three generations of American schoolchildren know of Aaron Burr they have learned while committing to memory William Wirt's oration. Not long ago I had the pleasure of listening to one of my wards proudly recite by rote Wirt's philippic against Aaron Burr, not realizing it was her kindly old Gamp she was denouncing in such rich, hyperbolic phrases.

Now on the defensive, George Hay not so delicately chose to threaten John Marshall, reminding him that for pre-judging a trial Justice Chase had been impeached. The defence made much of this threat. Wisely, Marshall made little. Luther Martin and Edmund Randolph then closed the case for the defence on Friday, August 29.

John Marshall spent Saturday and Sunday preparing his opinion. On August 31, he read it to us for three hours. From the legal and constitutional point of view, the opinion is often weak and contradictory. Having nearly undone himself (and the Constitution) with the Bollman-Swartwout ruling, he ignored, as best he could, his own previous statement that anyone who had contributed to the levying of war against the United States was as guilty as the actual leveller of war, and addressed himself to quite a different issue.

In order to prove treason, the government was obliged, first, to prove that an act of war had been levied against the United States and, second, to prove whether or not a given individual had been involved in that act. The case, in other words, had been presented backward. The government had arrested Aaron Burr for complicity in an act of war which had yet to be proved. Further, it was the government's contention that Burr was present when the as yet unproved act of war was levied. Marshall briskly dealt with that: the court was satisfied that Burr was elsewhere.

Then Marshall affected to deal with the prosecution's crucial point: had

Burr incited others to treason? and if he had was he guilty of treason? Marshall now edged with elephantine grace away from his own earlier position. He pointed out that Burr had been indicted for acts of war against the United States on a certain day and at a certain place. Now on that day Burr was not present in that place. Nevertheless, the question remained: was he guilty of inciting to treason those who were there? If he was, then the court must point out that the government had *not* indicted him of this crime for the excellent reason that incitement to treason was no crime under the Constitution. There was a murmur from the lawyers in the court as they saw which way our legal history was about to go.

"To advise or procure a treason," and Marshall's voice became suddenly loud and clear, "is in the nature of conspiracy or plotting treason . . ." He paused, no doubt aware that the obvious always sounds novel when stated with unexpected emphasis. Then he made his point, and took his place in history, "which is not treason in itself." With this formula, he undid his own decision of six months before.

As the murmuring increased in the court-room, Marshall patiently explained that no doubt there *ought* to be such a law, but since for the present it did not exist he would move on. Meanwhile, he was still not satisfied that "a secret furtive assemblage" on Blennerhassett's Island had ever been intended as an act of war but even if it had been so intended, the absence of Aaron Burr made him no party to it, and what advice he might have given the men there futively assembled could not be considered an act of war against the United States, as defined by the Constitution.

That was the end of the government's case. George Hay slammed down his papers on the prosecution's table for which diversion he was favoured with Marshall's full attention yet mildest tone.

"That this court dares not usurp power is most true." There was complete silence in the court. Everyone knew that Jefferson's wrath would now be focussed upon the Chief Justice. How would the Chief Justice respond? John Marshall was direct: "That this court dares not shrink from its duty is not less true." He spelled out as plain as any Martin Luther where he stood, and why he would not move, despite Jefferson's threats of impeachment and the breaking of the Supreme Court. On that note the jury was sent out to do its duty.

The next day, Tuesday, the jury found me "not proved to be guilty under this indictment by any evidence submitted to us." I was relieved; I was outraged. I was not to be hanged; I was also not to be exonerated. The jury had broken with all custom by refusing to answer simply "guilty" or "not guilty." Marshall chose to allow the jury's phrase to remain in the indictment while signifying that the court's record would be decorated with the usual, unadorned "not guilty."

The next day I was released from prison, on bail, and attended a dinner party given by John Wickham to celebrate our victory.

Theodosia was my consort for the evening, and we presided over the revels—and were happy except that I knew that my days in court were not yet finished while I was troubled by my daughter's health. I prayed it would not follow the same course as her mother's. Yet that evening she was witty, resplendent, triumphant.

. . .

# 1836

***September 14, 1836***

At 2:00 P.M. this afternoon, Aaron Burr died; aged eighty years and seven months.

I was at Leggett's house working on the first issue of the new paper when word was delivered me by a messenger from Mr. Bryant.

"You will write the obituary for us?" Leggett was cool.

"No, no. I must go see him." I was in an odd state of confusion.

"But he is not *there,*" said Leggett, "to be seen. Your old friend is gone."

"Even so, I have to go where he is." And I went across to Staten Island; found the parlour of Winant's Hotel crowded with friends and relations.

"You will want to go up," said Mr. Davis when he saw me. "I'll take you." Together we climbed the narrow stairs. "It was an easy death. He was conscious almost to the end. His last word was 'Madame.' "

I was startled. "His wife?"

Mr. Davis shrugged. "We don't know. I suspect it was addressed to the lady who was sitting with him, a Mrs. Keese. She is still with him."

In the pale evening light Mrs. Keese wept into both hands, making a silhouette framed by the sea-view. Beside her, head bowed, the Reverend Van Pelt prayed.

On the narrow bed lay the Colonel, a sheet to his chin. A single lamp overhead lit his face. Old people in death are supposed to look wondrously young. The Colonel looked exactly the way he did on my last visit except for bits of what I took to be lather in his side whiskers but proved to be plaster; the death-mask had already been taken. Although the face was as usual (he looked to be napping, with a slight frown), I could not help but notice in death what one was seldom conscious of in life: how very small he was—like a half-grown boy.

On the table beside the bed the portrait of Theodosia had been turned to the wall. Next to the portrait was an open book. *Tristram Shandy*? The Colonel's octagonal glasses marked his place.

Mr. Davis regarded the Colonel solemnly. "He will be buried at Princeton College on the sixteenth. It was his wish, and theirs."

Suddenly a deep voice filled the room. " 'The fashion of this world passeth away.' " It was the Reverend Van Pelt.

"Corinthians," sobbed Mrs. Keese. "Seven."

"All is vanity!" observed the holy man vainly.

"Did he die in the church?" I asked.

The Reverend Van Pelt shook his head. "No, he did not. I fear that I failed him. At the end he wanted . . ."

We were interrupted by Aaron Columbus Burr who burst into tears at the sight of his dead father. Rosary in hand, he dropped to his knees beside the bed. This so affected Mrs. Keese that she began to weep even more loudly than before while for the first time the Reverend Van Pelt looked as if he, too, might weep—at the popish display.

I ran from the room, hot-eyed, wishing that I had the Colonel to talk to one more time.

In the parlour, whiskey was being poured. Among the drinkers was Jane McManus, surprisingly calm. "I was with him only yesterday," she said to me. "The Colonel knew that he was going. 'It's like floating,' he says, 'on the river, on a barge, getting farther and farther from shore.' That was all he said. He talked very little the last days. There was no pain. At the end he just floated out too far, that's all, and left us."

I thought of a sled descending a snowy hill, cold wind in the face, a sense of falling, flying. All done.

Predictably, Sam Swartwout was the heart and soul of our wake. "Drink up, Charlie! He'd want us in a good mood, you know."

"But I don't think I am in a good mood."

"Well, this will make you laugh!" Swartwout withdrew a legal document from his pocket. "I swear to God it arrived an hour after he died. *It's his divorce.* Colonel Burr is no longer married to Liza Bowen. He's a free man, Charlie!"

## 1840

. . .

***December 8, 1840, at Amalfi;***
***in the Kingdom of the Two Sicilies***

At sundown I was on the terrace, wondering how to capture in words the exact way the sea below looks in winter light; the way the gradations of milky blue and green abruptly father darkest sapphire (no, no mention of jewels—that is cheating); give birth to a deep black-blue like . . . like the deep black-blue of the Mediterranean at the end of a sunny winter day. I have never been able to describe what I see every evening from the villa's terrace. Must make do with plain statements like the mist that signifies good weather eliminates the line between the sea and sky so that they look to be the same element and one has the sense of being at the centre of an opal's cool fire. Well, *one* jewel only. Washington Irving would have used a dozen.

I attempt this description for the hundredth time in order to give my pen something to do as I try to sort out what has happened to me since Pantaleone appeared on the terrace with the alarmed look he always has when an American comes to call and a barbarous name must be announced.

*"Signor Consul, c'è un americano, un colonello."* "Svaduz" was the name I heard. Since it is my job to be at home to American travellers—particularly colonels—I told Pantaleone to show the visitor onto the terrace.

I straightened my frock-coat. I was formally dressed, for today was the Feast of the Immaculate Conception and I was expected to represent the United States during the festivities in the piazza.

From the white arch that opens onto the sea terrace, a large slow figure stumbled into view. "Well, Charlie, if you're not glad to see me—and why should you be?—I'll turn right around and go down all those stairs I just climbed. I swear to God I've never seen so many steps that they call streets. Let me get my breath! Well, you've done all right by yourself, I'll say that. Look at your view!"

By the time all this had been said, Sam Swartwout had crossed to where I was standing. I stared at him like an idiot. What was I supposed to do? Send him away? Call for the police? As I stood, frozen to the spot, I was aware that I was not representing the glorious republic with much brilliance. What, I wondered desperately, would Washington Irving have done?

Like a large dog expecting to be hit, Sam tentatively extended a paw. Numbly I took it, to his relief.

"Haven't seen you for a long time, Charlie."

"A long time," I echoed stupidly. At least I did not repeat my own name.

Fortunately a few loud fireworks went off below us in the port of Amalfi, ending the first phase of our conversation. "What's that?" Sam leapt as though someone had fired at him.

"Fireworks. It's the beginning of the *festa.* There'll be a procession and . . ."

"I figured there was some kind of Fourth of July going on down there."

"Sit down." That was the best I could do. He praised the view. Who does not? The villa I have rented is next to the ruined watch-tower of the old mad queen of Naples. Below us is Amalfi wedged in its rocky ravine: white walls, red roofs, a Saracenic cathedral with a cupola of glazed green and yellow tiles. Above the town narrow terraces are bright with oranges and dark with wild laurel. In this setting Sam Swartwout is like a Fourth Avenue street-car in Arcady.

"I wasn't certain it was you who was consul till this American skipper in the port described you to me and I figured there just couldn't be two of the same name and looks. That's my boat." He pointed to a handsome sloop that I had noticed this morning when I made my consular round which consists mostly of visiting American ships and discussing with their captains how best to free the sailors arrested the previous night. I am a combination of justice of the peace and chaplain, obliged to carry about with me a greasy Bible for Americans to take their oath on—by kissing. I call it the perjurer's book.

"I've been here a year and a half . . ."

"I know. And before that you were at Antwerp. And just the other day I saw a copy of the book you wrote while you were there. Something about taking these little trips in the Lowlands."

"Something like that, yes." No one has ever been able to remember the title the publisher with such acumen chose for my first book.

"Have you been home since you got the job as consul in Antwerp?"

"Vice-consul. No. I haven't been back."

"Me, I left over a year ago."

"Yes. I know you did."

A rocket from the harbour slowly crossed the pale sickle of the new moon, and burst into white flames.

"You know, Charlie, I was caught in the depression of thirty-seven. It was really bad, as I guess you know. You see, I had everything tied up in England in these coal-mines. Good as gold, everyone said, and like always everyone was wrong. Well, I was wiped out. So I had to . . . I left."

In August 1839, Samuel Swartwout, collector of the port of New York, sailed for England. A few weeks later it was discovered that he had stolen from public funds one and a quarter million dollars: the most money ever stolen by an American official if not, very simply, the most money ever stolen by an American. Sam Swartwout will no doubt become a folk hero once the first wave of indignation ceases. Meanwhile, he has damaged the reputation of former President Jackson who was responsible for putting Sam in the way of being a thief on the largest scale. Worse, the scandal of his theft helped the Whig candidate William Henry Harrison defeat President Van Buren in the election last month. The poignant result of all this history is that there will be a new American consul at Amalfi next spring. As much as I am impressed by the extravagance of Sam's crime, I cannot say that I like losing my job because of it.

"There's been a lot of confusion back in New York." Sam stared at the smudge of smoke where the rocket had burst above the moon. "And a certain amount of misunderstanding over my . . . uh, affairs."

"I should think so."

"I travel a lot. Spain. France. We've been sailing down the coast of Italy for weeks now. After that North Africa. They tell me Algiers is a nice place."

My wife appeared on the terrace. Sam got to his feet. I made the introductions.

"An honour, Donna Carolina." Sam kissed Carolina's hand with some grace.

My wife apologized for not being able to speak English which is to say she will not speak it if she thinks she is apt to be bored. Actually, she is accomplished in English, German, French, and of course Italian; her father is the Swiss Baron Jost Josef de Traxler who was a chamberlain at the court of the last King of the Two Sicilies as was her mother's father (a Neapolitan of Spanish descent). I met the Traxler family when I was first presented to King Ferdinand at Caserta. After a year of bitter wrangling with her family over religion and property (they have a good deal of each while I have neither), we were married six months ago. Our first child will be born in June.

"Can we serve you coffee?" Carolina used her careful slow English voice.

"If you have no spirits."

After Carolina withdrew, Pantaleone brought Sam a bottle of brandy which he drank like tea. "I must tell you, Charlie, I'm home-sick. Never thought I'd be, what with all this." He waved toward the sea. As he did, a star fell. My consulship.

"I don't suppose you'll ever be able to go back." I wanted him to suffer a bit for what he had done to President Van Buren not to mention me.

"Well, now, I think once the *whole* story is known . . ." He mumbled into silence. I was grateful that he did not have an "explanation." Then he turned to me. "What about you, Charlie? When are you going to take your beautiful wife to live in God's country?"

"I think she prefers living in Pope's country."

"What about you?"

"I don't know." I was not about to tell Sam that Carolina has no desire ever to see America, that it is her dream one day to live near Stans in Unterwalden, Switzerland, where the Traxler castle is. Unfortunately, Switzerland is much too placid, too romantic for my present taste. I am no longer interested in roses and Moorish arches. Instead I am fascinated by the political situation at Naples (having found tedious the doings of Tammany!). I wait eagerly for the next round of revolution that is as certain to erupt as smoke-plumed Vesuvius. And when it does . . . what shall I do?

Run out and bark. That is plainly my nature. I am turning into Leggett as he turns to earth.

Swartwout was talking of Leggett. "You have to say one thing for Matty Van, he never holds a grudge. When that paper of Leggett's went out of business, Matty Van made him minister to Guatemala without even being asked."

"But Leggett always supported the President."

"Not always he didn't." Sam winked. Then drank deep; struck the maudlin note. "Poor fellow. He never got to Guatemala."

A year ago May, when Leggett died, I wrote the widow who answered me at length; unfortunately, the pouch containing her letter was dropped by mistake into the bay of Salerno and all the ink ran. I still do not know the details of Leggett's death but can guess.

"You're welcome to stay here," I said, realizing from the lights below in the piazza that the procession was beginning to form and I would soon be obliged to represent our nation.

"No, no. Thank you. I stay aboard the ship. I've got a good English crew. A fine captain—English, too, and partial to brandy and whist, like me."

"I must report for duty in the piazza," I said.

Sam got to his feet. "They seem like a cheerful people." Sam's interest in foreigners is slight.

Since Carolina had already gone down, Sam and I together descended the thousand steps from my villa to the main square of the town. A green sky touched a green sea, sharing the same stars, the sickle moon.

"What's become of your book about Colonel Burr?"

"I'm waiting for Mr. Davis to publish his biography first."

Two years ago Mr. Davis published the Colonel's journals, and though he bowdlerized a number of passages the result was still shocking to the American public and the Colonel's reputation is now more Satanic than before.

Swartwout paused. Took a deep breath. He was drunk. "He was most fond of you, the Colonel, most fond."

"I was fond of him." Not wanting to discuss the Colonel with Swartwout, I moved on ahead, said good evening to a family of peasants as they hurried past us, late for the *festa.*

"Yes, Sir, he liked you best of the whole lot . . . or almost best."

"I'm glad." I put my head down and hurried on.

Swartwout managed to keep up with me. "In fact, the Colonel wrote Matty Van about you . . . from Staten Island."

"Yes, I know he did."

"Asked him to look after you. Fact, he asked him to give you this job." Swartwout laughed. "Oh, the whole business tickled the Colonel. You know how things that shock most people always made him grin. 'Why shouldn't Matty look after young Charlie?' the Colonel said to me. 'After all, he's his big brother.' "

I stopped with a crash at a turn in the stairs. "What did you say?"

Swartwout came to an unsteady halt: a huge swaying figure in the twilight. "I'm sorry, Charlie. I thought you knew."

"I did not know."

"I'm sorry," Swartwout repeated.

In the piazza, we parted.

Coloured lights were strung from artificial trees. The crowd was packed in so tight that only with the aid of a carabiniere was I able to get through to the bottom of the cathedral stairs.

Hardly conscious of where I was, I walked up the steps to the wooden platform that had been built for various dignitaries. Here I was greeted by the Mayor, by the agent of the King, by my wife. In the narthex of the cathedral a uniformed band played marches. Fireworks exploded in the port. I was deafened, dazzled.

Although I bowed to this one and that, affected interest in the ceremonies, I could think of nothing but Colonel Burr and what we had not said to one another: he through tact and I through ignorance.

*"Ecco la Vergine!"* Carolina clapped her hands. A moaning from the crowd as the tall richly-clothed image of the Virgin was borne into the piazza on a high litter. Incense from censers swirled about the idol. A splendid bishop led the way.

Rockets exploding. Showers of white stars over the dark sea. A dazzle of red, yellow, green lights. Loud music. Cloying incense. The edge of the world suddenly began to recede from me. My eyes went in and out of focus. "Must not faint. Must not die," I said to myself, holding onto Carolina's arm and so, through an exercise of will, did not die, did not faint.

Silver robes flowing in the sea-wind, the crowned figure of the Virgin was now directly opposite us.

*"Ah, chiedi una grazia! Chiedi una grazia!"* Carolina spoke into my ear. "Make a wish. Quickly! She will grant it!"

But there was no wish that I could make that I have not already been granted by my father Aaron Burr.

# From *Lincoln*

THE SIDEWALK in front of Willard's Hotel seemed to hum and throb, and John Hay felt as if he were still on the cars as he made his way through the crowd of people—mostly colored, he noticed—who were on hand to get a look at Mr. Lincoln, who was not visible; unlike Mrs. Lincoln, who was, as well as the three Lincoln sons, the six lady relations of Mrs. Lincoln's, the two Lincoln secretaries John George Nicolay (born twenty-nine years ago in Bavaria; moved to Illinois as a child; grew up to edit a Pittsfield newspaper) and John Hay himself, aged twenty-two, a graduate of Brown who had been admitted to the Illinois bar exactly two weeks ago, thanks, in part, to the fact that his uncle was Springfield's leading lawyer and an old associate of Lincoln; thanks, again in part, to the fact that Hay had gone to school with Nicolay, Lincoln's secretary during the campaign for the presidency. Hay had been able to make himself so useful to Nicolay in the campaign that Nico had said to the President-elect, "Can't we take Johnny to Washington with us?" and although Lincoln had groaned and said, "We can't take all Illinois down with us to Washington," John Hay had been duly employed as a presidential secretary. Small, wiry, handsome, John Hay intended to enjoy as much as possible his sudden elevation in the world.

At Brown, Hay had wanted to be a poet; in fact, he was a poet who wrote verse that got published. But that was not exactly a career or a living. For a time, the pulpit had appealed to him—except for the business about God. Although the law had no great appeal to him, for a young man named Hay there was not much choice. He worked in his uncle's office, where he got to know his uncle's friend, Mr. Lincoln, a man whose ups-and-downs were much talked of in Springfield, particularly the downs. Mr. Lincoln was supposed to have gone mad for two weeks just before what was to have been his wedding day, which had to be postponed. He had gone into a decline after losing his seat in Congress and despite the campaigning that he had done for the new Whig President, Zachary Taylor, he was offered no government appointment other than the secretaryship of the Oregon territory, which Mrs. Lincoln had turned down for him. Home in Springfield, Lincoln practised law with the brilliant, hard-drinking William Herndon and let himself, many said, sink into apathy, while making a good deal of money as a railroad lawyer. When the great debate on slavery began, Mr. Lincoln found his voice, and after his challenge to Stephen Douglas, he had come to personify the new Republican Party and the new politics—whatever they were. Hay was never quite certain just where Mr. Lincoln meant to take the nation but he did know that wherever that was, he was going to go, too.

At the center of the lobby, the manager of Willard's was greeting Mrs. Lincoln, who was tired and not, Hay could see, in the best of moods. Nicolay and Hay had their code words for the great folk. Mary Todd Lincoln was known, depending on her mood, as either Madam or the Hellcat. Mr. Lincoln was either the Ancient or, in honor of the previous year's visit to Washington by the first ambassadors from that awesome Japanese official known as the Tycoon, the Tycoon.

The slender Nicolay was at the Hellcat's side, smiling grimly through his long, pointed, youthful beard. Although Hay could not hear what the Hellcat was saying, he suspected that a complaint was being duly registered. Suddenly, Hay found himself next to the oldest Lincoln son, Robert, a seventeen-year-old Harvard freshman who said, with pleasure, "Johnny!" as if they had not spent the last twelve days and nights cooped up together on the cars from Springfield, playing cards in the baggage car and, occasionally, taking a swig from a bottle that Lamon always carried, "just in case," he'd say, shoving it into the great side pocket that contained a slingshot, a pair of brass knuckles, a hunting knife and a derringer.

"I think Nicolay needs some help," said Hay, maneuvering himself through the crowd to Mrs. Lincoln's side just as her normal high color was beginning to take on that dusky glow which was the first sign of a Hellcat storm.

"Mrs. Lincoln!" Hay beamed, boyishly; but then with his youthful face he had no other way of looking, to his chagrin. Strange men often addressed him as Sonny; his cheek was often patted; he knew that he must, very soon, grow a moustache, if he could. "Your trunks are already in your rooms." This was a lie. But he knew Mrs. Lincoln's passionate attachment to her baggage and its integrity.

"Oh, Johnny! You do relieve my mind!" Mary Todd Lincoln's smile was, suddenly, winning and so Hay was won; she took his arm and they swept through the hotel lobby to the main staircase, as the manager and his outriders cleared a path for their considerable party.

Outside, the crowd dispersed. David and Annie were disappointed not to have seen the archfiend himself. "They say he's got whiskers now, so as no one will know him," said David, as they walked up Thirteenth Street.

"But once people get used to the whiskers, they'll know him after a while." Annie stopped in front of a raw-wood picket fence. Through the gap between two slats they could see a vacant lot where a number of young men were drilling with old rifles.

"Who are they?" asked David.

"The National Volunteers," Annie whispered, her breath white between them. "One of them is a friend of Brother Isaac."

"What are they drilling for?"

"Inauguration Day. Come on. Let's go. I don't want them to see me."

David and Annie hurried down the street. "They're crazy," he said, "to take on the whole U. S. Army."

In Parlor Suite Six at Willard's Hotel, it was agreed that the National Volunteers were indeed crazy but, potentially, dangerous: such was the intelligence already received by the suite's principal resident, the bewhiskered Abraham Lincoln, who now sat in a huge armchair in the parlor as his two youngest sons, Willie and Tad, climbed over him, and Hay smiled sweetly at this domestic scene. He had never hated two children more than these. Tad, at seven, could not be understood due to some sort of malformation of his palate, while the ruthlessly eloquent and intelligent Willie, at ten, could be understood all too well. Willie was a tendentious explainer, who regarded Johnny Hay as a somewhat dull-witted playmate.

While the children shouted and pummelled their father, Seward and Lamon discussed with Lincoln, as best they could, arrangements for his security. Mary had withdrawn to the bedroom to greet her—Hay prayed—not-mythical luggage.

Nicolay was at the door to the parlor, looking somewhat alarmed. Then Hay saw why. Behind Nicolay towered the unmistakable figure of Charles Sumner, senator from Massachusetts, heir to Daniel Webster, greatest of the Senate's scholars, an orator of such power that audiences had been known, after three hours of his burning-bush language, to beg for more of that incandescent flame, fuelled by a single passion—the conviction that there was no greater task on earth than to liberate the slaves, and punish their masters.

Lincoln positively jackknifed to his feet at the sight of Sumner, scattering his sons upon the flowered carpet. As the boys started to yell with indignation, Lincoln said, "John, you deliver the boys to their mother."

Hay grabbed Tad's hand and pulled him, squeaking, to his feet, while Willie ran into his mother's bedroom, shouting, "Mamma!"

Gracefully, Seward introduced Senator Sumner to the President-elect. Charles Sumner was not only remarkably handsome but, unlike most modern statesmen, he was cleanshaven. Hay had already sent out a curiously uninteresting story on the wire-service to the effect that Lincoln would be the first bearded president in American history. Face-hair was now respectable or *de rigueur,* as Hay's French-speaking Providence, Rhode Island muse, Mrs. Sarah Helen Whitman, would say. Since a brief engagement to Edgar Allan Poe, Mrs. Whitman had worn only white, like a shroud; she had also sprinkled herself with ether in order to suggest a terminal illness of the sort that had once ravished Poe; and entirely overwhelmed poetry-loving Brown undergraduates.

"I would've known you anywhere," said Lincoln. "From your pictures."

"I might *not* have known you, sir, with the beard of Abraham, you might say, so newly acquired." To Hay's ear Sumner sounded like so many of his fellow Boston Brahmins, more English than American. Even so, the voice was singularly beautiful in its way, thought Hay, the Westerner, as he slipped into the bedroom, where, to his delight, he found Madam and a colored maid opening a row of trunks. As Willie entered the adjoining bedroom, she said, "Take Tad with you."

"No," said Tad.

"Yes!" said the Hellcat with a sudden change of expression that everyone, including the remarkably spoiled Tad, understood and feared. Whimpering with self-pity, the child obeyed. "Oh, God, will this never end?" Madam appealed to Hay. "I feel seasick from the cars. I hate these trunks."

"Well, you'll soon be settled in the White House. Can I help?"

Madam was holding up a dress of blue velvet; she examined it carefully for signs of damage. "I am a martyr to moths," she said to herself, but spoke aloud, a curious habit to which Hay had got used during their days of confinement aboard the cars. When Mrs. Lincoln wanted to—or was able to (he could never tell whether her erratic behavior was calculated or simply uncontrolled)—she could charm anyone on earth, as she must have charmed the most ambitious young lawyer in Springfield, not that Lincoln would have needed much charming, for she was a Todd and lived with her sister whose house on the hill was the center of the town's social life and it was there that she had been courted by all the other ambitious lawyers, not to mention Judge Stephen Douglas; as a child in Lexington, Kentucky, she had known Henry Clay, the only American statesman, except for Parson Weems's Washington, that Lincoln had ever openly praised.

Madam gave the dress to the maid to hang up; turned to Hay with a sudden, almost girlish smile. "Between you and me, Mr. Hay, there is more to jest about in all of this than I might have suspected, for all the weariness as well."

"I've noticed that, too, Mrs. Lincoln."

But then the smile was gone. She had heard the sonorous voice in the next room. "Who is that with Mr. Lincoln?"

"Senator Sumner."

"Oh." Hay could see that she was torn between timidity and curiosity, which she resolved by going to the half-open door and looking into the parlor. "He's every bit as handsome as they say," she said in a low voice; this time to Hay and not to herself.

"He hasn't stopped talking since he arrived."

"At least he seems to have driven away Mr. Seward, that abolitionist sneak." Mary turned back into the room.

"Surely, Mr. Seward's no sneak—"

"Well, he was a rabid abolitionist once upon a time. Now, of course, he's gone and changed a few of his spots, but right or wrong, Mr. Sumner never changes. I do hope all these abolitionists never forget that Mr. Lincoln is *not* in favor of abolishing slavery. He simply does not want to extend it to the new territories. That is all; all!" In the last twelve days Hay had heard her say this so many times that he had ceased to hear the words. But then Mrs. Lincoln was in a difficult position. The Todds were a great slave-holding Kentucky family; worse, they were, many of them, secessionists, a source of much embarrassment to her, not to mention to the new president. "Find me Mrs. Ann Spriggs." This was unexpected.

"Who is that, Mrs. Lincoln?"

"She is a widow who has—or had—a boardinghouse on Capitol Hill. That's where we lived when Mr. Lincoln was in Congress. She's still alive, they say, and I'd dearly love to see her again and"—the girlish smile returned—"*and show off*!"

"For that," said Hay, again charmed by Madam, who had just taken over from the Hellcat, "I'll find her, Mrs. Lincoln."

With a wave, Madam dismissed him. She is going to be a very royal First Lady, he thought, as he returned to the parlor, hoping to escape the senatorial presence unremarked. But Hay's appearance stopped Sumner in midsentence. "Sir?"

"This is my secretary's secretary, Mr. Sumner. John Hay."

"Oh, yes." They shook hands. Hay felt a certain awe, seeing so famous a man up close. "I heard you speak, sir," he said. "Two years ago. In Providence. I was at Brown."

"I remember the speech." Sumner had lost interest. Hay looked at Lincoln: should he stay? The Tycoon raised his chin, which meant, no. "I'm curious to see which is taller, Mr. Sumner or myself, but when I suggested that we measure backs . . ."

"I said"—Sumner was not about to allow anyone to say his lines for him—"the time has come to unite our fronts and not our backs before the enemies of our country."

"Yes, that's *just* what you said." Lincoln turned to Hay, "Word for word," he added. With a low bow, Hay left the two statesmen to what, he suspected, was going to be a most disagreeable session. Sumner had supported Lincoln in the election; but now Sumner feared Seward's ascendancy over the new President. Sumner wanted Lincoln to abolish slavery in the seceded states. But Lincoln was not about to do that, not with Virginia and Maryland on the verge of secession, and half a dozen border-states, including Kentucky, ready to follow. On the train from Springfield, as Hay observed the large crowds that cheered the President-elect (everywhere except in New York City, where there was a powerful pro-secessionist movement), he had come to think of Lincoln as a beleaguered fortress, with cannons firing at him from every direction; a fortress waiting to be relieved by . . . But Hay did not know by what. No one knew what was in Lincoln's mind. Particularly not the boisterous young men crowded at the far end of Willard's bar, drinking cocktails at ten cents a glass.

Hay pushed through the swinging doors of the long bar just off the main parlor of the hotel, where ladies sat beneath a gilded dome, drinking tea and casting disapproving—when not envious—looks at the men as they entered and left the bibulous good fellowship of the smoky, long bar.

Hay found the smooth-faced—the boy could but would not grow whiskers—Robert Lincoln, talking to a short, bright-eyed young man who was already beginning to go bald. Robert introduced Hay to the young man, saying, "He graduated from Harvard the same year you graduated from Brown."

"Well, that's a bond, I guess," said Hay, ordering a brandy-smash.

The Harvard graduate was examining Hay curiously. "You're one of Mr. Lincoln's secretaries, aren't you?"

"Yes, sir."

"Everyone says Johnny's too young." Robert smiled shyly; but then he was shy; and a bit solemn. Two years earlier he had been uprooted by his father and sent east to enroll at Harvard. But since he had not been scholastically ready for that great university he had been obliged to spend a year in preparation at the Phillips Exeter Academy in New Hampshire. It was said that Mr. Lincoln wanted the best possible education for his oldest son just as he himself had had the very worst, which is to say practically none at all. After the debate with Douglas and the lost election, Lincoln decided to travel east to see how his son was getting on at Exeter. It was on this trip—coincidentally, hardly any claimed—that Mr. Lincoln was prevailed upon to speak third in a series at New York's Cooper Institute. He did so on February 27, 1860. The liberal editor of the New York *Evening Post,* William Cullen Bryant, chaired the meeting, while the city's most powerful editor, Horace Greeley, sat in the audience. The next day Lincoln was known to the entire nation. With the characteristic eloquence, he had accepted the slavery at the South, but he had opposed its extension elsewhere. This pleased a majority of the Republicans, while arousing great suspicion among Douglas's Northern Democrats, not to mention the Democrats of the South. After Lincoln's triumph at the Cooper Institute, he spoke elsewhere in the northeast, and in the course of this triumphal passage, he took the Republican nomination away from the powerful Seward as well as from that passionate anti-slavery man Salmon P. Chase of Ohio. "So if it hadn't been for you, Bob," Lincoln liked to say, "being up there at Exeter, I'd never have been nominated or elected." Robert appeared to believe this. Hay did not. From the beginning of his close association with Lincoln—less than a year but it seemed like a lifetime—he had been delightedly conscious of the Tycoon's endless cunning. There was nothing that Lincoln ever left to chance if he could help it. He was a master of guiding public opinion either directly through a set speech to a living audience or, indirectly, through an uncanny sense of how to use the press to his own ends. He was also the first politician to understand the importance and the influence of photography; no photographer was ever sent away unsatisfied. He had even grown a beard in order to soften his somewhat harsh features; and to make himself, at least in appearance, the nation's true Father Abraham. It was thus with characteristic forethought he had sent his son to New England to school so that with no other apparent end than ordinary paternal care, he might, when the time came, go east—and seize the crown.

"Hey, Johnny! Hasheesh Johnny Hay!" Hay turned and recognized the face but not the name of a fraternity brother from Brown. They made the fraternal handclasp of Theta Delta Chi. Since the young man was drunk, Hay pulled him to one side, out of range of Robert Lincoln, who was very much enjoying his anonymity, soon to end when the newspapers got through illustrating, one by one, the entire Lincoln family. Hay also did not want anyone to learn his college nickname.

"What're you doing in town?"

Hay recalled that the brother was Southern; was glad that the brother did not know of his appointment. "Oh, I'm just here for the inaugural." Hay was casual.

"If there is one!" The drunken youth scowled as darkly as such a foolish face could. "Me, I'm going home to Charleston to fight, if we have to. I guess you're for the Yankees, aren't you?"

"I guess so," said Hay.

"Well . . ." Words did not come easily to the soon-to-be-rebel. But a sheet of paper did materialize in his hand. "I take the boat in the morning. But as we're brothers, I leave you this. My richest legacy."

Hay looked at a neatly printed list of names and addresses; some were curiously cryptic, like The Haystack—his eye caught that at once—or The Blue Goose, The Devil's Own . . . After each name or title there was a number. "They've been numbered from one—which is the best—to five, which is pretty bad. Three of the brothers put this list together. Took more than a month to do. Now they've all gone South. Anyway, you can give copies of it to anybody you like, I guess. But they did say they'd prefer that only the Delts got the real good of it. 'Bye, Johnny."

It took Hay several days to figure out that he had been given what turned out to be a meticulously graded list of Washington's whorehouses. He was eternally grateful to the brother: at twenty-two, there was no finer gift one Theta Delt could have given another. A similar list had existed in the fraternity house at Providence and Hay had used it, from time to time, to while away what he liked to call "idle hours." One of the fraternity's most legendary idle hours occurred when Hay decided to imitate his idol Edgar Allan Poe. Although he could find no opium to eat, he did come across some hasheesh, which he and the brothers had smoked, with results still recalled in Providence as an idle hour that had expanded to what seemed to the smokers to be an idle eternity. Ever after, he was Hasheesh Johnny Hay.

Hay rejoined Robert and the bald young man, who turned out to be Henry, the son of Charles Francis Adams of Massachusetts, a Lincoln supporter. "I saw our senator on his way upstairs," said Henry. "I assumed he was on his way to Mr. Lincoln."

Hay nodded. "I left them together. I think Mr. Sumner was about to make a speech."

Henry sighed. "He is like a madman nowadays . . ."

"Well, he was knocked on the head with a stick, wasn't he? By that crazy Southerner?" Robert started to order another drink but Hay made a warning gesture; and Robert desisted. There were times when Hay had the sense that he had been hired not as a secretary to the president but as an elder brother to the boys.

"Oh, Mr. Sumner's recovered. Pretty much, anyway. But he seems to have conversed with God altogether too much during those three years that he was an invalid. When he came back to the Senate, he announced, 'I am in morals, not politics.' "

"That *is* chilling," said Hay.

"Much my own view," said Henry; and smiled for the first time. "I should think that the two are probably antithetical. My father disagrees, of course. I'm *his* secretary, by the way. He's in the Congress, you know."

"I know. I know. Mr. Lincoln thinks very highly of Mr. Adams."

"That's right," said Robert. "Fact, he said, maybe he was going to—"

"Robert!" Hay spoke warningly.

"All right, Johnny."

"Mr. Robert Lincoln . . ." Hay began.

"The Prince of Rails, as the press calls him. Oh, they'll enjoy *that* at Harvard," said Henry, whose smile, at best, was thin indeed.

"I'll never hear the end of it." Robert was glum. "At least they couldn't get me to make a speech on the back of the cars. I don't know how Father does it."

Henry turned to Robert. "I know my father's being considered for minister to England. Personally, I'd rather he stayed here."

"And miss out on London?" Hay betrayed his own youthful interest. For Hay, London was literature—Dickens, Thackeray and whoever wrote *Adam Bede,* and history. Washington was just old-shoe politics.

"I'd rather miss out on London than on Lincoln," said Henry.

"Why?" Hay was truly curious.

"Well, if he should fail, there will no longer be a country. And since my family believes that we invented the whole thing, I'd certainly like to see what becomes of the remains."

"I don't think he'll fail," said Hay, who thought that he would; as much as he prayed that somehow Lincoln might yet hold together what was now falling apart with such awful speed.

"In that case, if he succeeds, it will be even more interesting."

"How? It will be just as it was before."

"No, it won't. It can't be."

"What *will* it be?"

"No one knows. That's the excitement."

The day of the inaugural, March 4, David Herold was awake at dawn. Since this was not a day to be missed, he had slept in all his clothes, including the disintegrating shoes. As he slept on a bunk in a sort of larder off the kitchen, there were no creaking stairs to worry about. He could hear throughout the house the heavy breathing and restive movements of eight women, all flesh of his flesh. Unlike Chase, who was content to have a daughter who was like a son as well, the nineteen-year-old David still longed for a brother to do things with, like . . . well, go to the Capitol and watch Old Abe get shot.

The morning was misty; and not cold. The frozen mud had melted, yielding the first crocuses and snowdrops of the season. At the Capitol, a few streets from David's house, there was no crowd as yet; nor any sign of one. But there were troops everywhere. Some were in regulation blue; others were in dark green, with sharpshooter's rifles. They appeared to be searching for . . . wild boys? wondered David, happy to be a mere onloooker.

No one tried to stop David as he walked right up to the small wooden platform that had been built on the Capitol's east steps. The platform had a roof to it; presumably in order to keep anyone from shooting Lincoln from high up. Then David wandered over to the Capitol's north side, where, to his surprise, a pair of long wooden walls had been built between the plaza and the entrance to the Senate chamber. This meant that when Lincoln got out of his carriage, he would be shielded by two walls of planking as he made his way into the Capitol.

David still remembered the last inaugural vividly. He and the wild boys had had a marvelous time, whooping it up, cheering the President, Old Buck, and the beautiful lady got up as the Goddess of Liberty, as she stood on a moving float just in front of Old Buck's carriage while, back of him, there was a second float on which had been placed an entire warship filled with sailors. But today there were no signs of splendor. There were few flags in evidence and none of the red, white and blue bunting that was traditionally used to decorate the speaker's stand on Inaugural Day. On the other hand, he had never seen so many soldiers.

As David made his way up Pennsylvania Avenue to Fifteenth Street, the town was coming awake. The usual Negro population was being added to by the thousands of out-of-towners who had filled up the hotels. Early as it was, a crowd had gathered in front of Brown's Hotel, and as always, Willard's was the center of much activity. David stared up at the windows of Lincoln's suite. The presidential parlor was right over the main door, and an American flag had been attached to the window.

"Hello, David!" David turned and saw the round, cherubic face of Scipione Grillo, a professional musician, who had just opened a restaurant next to one of the town's most popular theaters.

"Hey, Skippy!" This was Mr. Grillo's universal nickname. "What're you doing up so early?"

"I go to the Center Market. I go buy food. We have a full house for every meal today."

"What's at the theater?"

"I don't notice. But whatever's there, we got good audiences." Skippy maintained that he could always tell what a play was like by what its audience drank at his bar. For instance, they drank wine or champagne before and after a good comedy, while good tragedy required champagne before and whiskey after. But if was an opera, there was little or no drinking because Americans know nothing of music, said Skippy; and that was why he was abandoning music for the food-and-drink business.

David knew every theater manager in the town. As a result, he could almost always get a seat in the gallery for nothing. If he brought Annie Surratt or some other girl, he was expected to pay for the one ticket. If he should have no money left after a performance at Ford's, Skippy would give him a free beer. In payment, David would do odd jobs for Skippy. He also worked for the various theater managements whenever an extra hand was needed to help load or unload scenery. He was besotted with the theater. In fact, had he been taller and his teeth less bucked, he would have been an actor; or perhaps, a theater manager.

"You going to watch the inaugural parade, Skippy?"

"How can I? I make dinner. Anyway, there's only the two bands. If there was the three, I'd be there. But I play violin tonight at the Union Ball. Mr. Scala needs me, he said. Marine Band's weak in the string section, he says."

"So you'll get to see the whole lot."

"All I look at is the sheet music. Oh, these new dances . . . !"

As Grillo crossed Lafayette Square, David presented himself at Thompson's Drug Store in Pennsylvania Avenue, close to Fifteenth Street. Although the store was not yet open for business, David knew that "William S. Thompson, Proprietor" was already busy at work, filling prescriptions and supervising the black woman who cleaned up.

David opened the door and took a deep breath. If nothing else, he had always like the smell of drugstores. In the last three years, he had worked first as a delivery boy and then as a prescription clerk for Mr. Thompson. Now he was about to enter, seriously, Mr. Thompson's employ. He was wretched at the thought; but he had no choice.

" 'Morning, Mr. Thompson. It's me, Davie." David blinked his eyes in the dim room, where one entire wall was occupied by a sort of wooden wardrobe containing a thousand small drawers while, parallel to the back wall, a highly polished wood counter supported two sets of scales and six huge china vases on whose sides gold Gothic script testified, in Latin, to their contents. David had picked up enough Latin in his last year at school to read a doctor's prescription; it was about the only thing that he had ever learned that had proved of the slightest use to him. Mrs. Herold had wept bitterly when he left school. But since there was no money in the family, there was no choice. He lived at home; worked when he needed money; enjoyed himself in ways that would have caused his mother distress, but then she was, as Sal always said, a saint; and saints suffer.

Mr. Thompson emerged from the back room. He was a cheery man who wore thick glasses with tiny metal frames. He had been related, somehow, to David's father. But then David was related to half the town: the lower half, Annie liked to say, as she thought of the Surratts of Surrattsville as being gentry, which they were not: just farm folk with a bit of money, in Mrs. Herold's phrase.

"Well, David, are you prepared to enter man's estate?" Mr. Thompson's concern in the past had been with David's entirely undisguised lack of seriousness about work of any kind.

"Yes, sir. I'm ready to go to work now, and settle down and everything." Even as David said this with perfect insincerity, he felt as if a prison door was swinging shut on him. He was only eighteen; he had never been anywhere, or done anything exciting; now he was to go to work as prescription clerk for the rest of his life in a shop just across Pennsylvania Avenue from the Treasury building and just around the corner from Willard's, where the grandees made love to their beautiful women and drank at the long bar and made fortunes at cards and dice and politics, unaware that just up the street David Herold, slave, was at work, filling prescriptions for them, nine hours a day, five-and-a-half days a week, with Sunday off to catch up on all that he had missed during the rest of the week. David felt the tears come to his eyes. Surely, something or someone would save him at the last minute. No young man in any play that he had ever seen had ended up like this.

"All right, Davie. We'll start you in today. You're to be here at seven o'clock every morning. I'll give you a key. Then you let Elvira in at seven-fifteen . . ." Elvira appeared from the back room. She grunted when she saw David; who grunted back. Elvira was not given to human speech.

"I wondered, sir, if I could start tomorrow? You see, I'm supposed to help out at the Union Ball tonight, as a waiter." David was a quick and adroit liar. He had learned how to lie partly from the actors whose work he had studied so carefully but mostly from his sisters on the subject of their beaux. Between what they said of the young men behind their backs and to their faces, there was a stunning gap. When David would taunt them, they would laugh at him; and tell him to mind his own business, which he was perfectly glad to do.

"Well, it is a *half* holiday today." Mr. Thompson was agreeable. "So you can work through the morning and then help me close up at noon, and still get to listen to Mr. Lincoln."

"I can't say that I care to all that much."

"Now, now, Davie. He's the President, after all."

"Jefferson Davis is *our* President."

Mr. Thompson frowned and smiled. "Now let's have no secesh talk in this shop. It does damage to my digestion—and business."

"But you ain't Union, Mr. Thompson. You're from Virginia, like us."

"What I may be in my heart of hearts, Davie"—Mr. Thompson was now solemn—"I keep to myself, and I suggest you do the same because of our numerous distinguished customers."

"Mr. Davis was one of your customers?"

"One of my *best* customers, poor man. I've never known anyone to suffer so much from that eye condition of his. He'll be blind by the summer, I said to Dr. Hardinge, if you don't change the prescription. But you can't tell Doctor Hardinge anything. On my own, I gave Mr. David belladonna to stop the pain—"

"So then he *is* your President."

"If I were in business in Montgomery, Alabama, yes, he would be. But I am here—with my loved ones—in a shop at Fifteenth and Pennsylvania Avenue, and I am the official unofficial pharmacist for the presidents of the United States and as I looked after Mr. Buchanan and Miss Lane—she'll never make old bones, I fear—I intend to look after the Lincoln family, a large one, for a change, and sickly, I should think, wonderfully sickly, from the glimpse I had of them yesterday." Mr. Thompson was smiling, without knowing it, thought David, who was aware that actors' tricks were not exclusive to actors, only the knowledge of them was.

"Well, you may not get your chance. There's talk he'll be shot today."

"Oh, the wild boys." David found disappointing Mr. Thompson's contemptuous dismissal of the dedicated young men of the National Volunteers. "General Scott will shoot the whole lot full of holes before the day's over. Which reminds me, fix a draft for his dropsy and take it straight across the road to the War Department, the new one up the street. The prescription's in the back."

As David entered the familiar back room, he felt as if he had left all life behind. What else could he do? As he mixed General Scott's prescription, he toyed with the idea of going south, to Montgomery, to join the army that Mr. Davis was supposed to be raising. But wasn't the army just another form of imprisonment? David wanted a world to conquer, any world, no matter how small. Idly, he wondered if he could seduce Annie; he decided that he could, but if he did, the greatest of all prison doors would then swing shut upon him: marriage, children and years of making up prescriptions for the likes of General Scott. It was too late to be General Scott when he grew up; you had to go to West Point for that, or serve a long time in the ranks. Were he better-looking, he might be an actor. After all, he could learn lines; and was a lot better at making believe than most of the touring-company players who came to town. But how was he ever to begin? A single warm tear was inadvertently added to General Scott's prescription.

While David Herold was enjoying a bearable amount of self-pity, John Hay was already at work in Parlor Suite One with Nicolay. Two large crates lay open on the floor and Hay was transferring folders filled with applications, affidavits, supplications, yellowed newspaper cuttings and fervent prayers from the room's wardrobe to the cases. "We have received, personally, nine hundred and twelve applications for jobs," said Hay, studying the last of the folders.

"It seems more like nine thousand," Nicolay still retained a slight German accent which Hay enjoyed imitating. Nicolay sat at a table, making a report to the President on which applications seemed promising.

"How much longer does this go on?"

"Until we leave office."

"I had no idea," said Hay, who had indeed had none. "I thought a few people might show up and he'd give them a postmaster's job and that was that. But we're going to have to deal with all thirty million Americans before we're through."

"Less the twelve million or so Mr. Davis has to find jobs for." In the distance, there was a premonitory roll of drums.

"Did you know Mr. Seward was thick as thieves with Mr. Davis, right up to a few weeks ago, when he left town and the Union?"

Nicolay nodded. "The Tycoon wanted the two of them to talk as much as possible."

Hay frowned. "Do you think Mr. Seward's really serious about taking himself out of the Cabinet?" Hay had been present in Lincoln's parlor when the Albany Plan had been revealed. The New York delegation, echoing Seward, had insisted that Lincoln exclude Chase from the Cabinet, which should be made up entirely of Whigs, instead of the four Democrats and three Whigs that Lincoln had in mind. When Lincoln had reminded the New Yorkers that he, too, was a Whig, which evened things, they had still been intransigent. They warned the Tycoon that Seward would not serve with Chase, to which Lincoln replied that he would be sorry to give up his first Cabinet slate in favor of a second list which he had prepared; but if that was the case, then he would appoint that good Whig Mr. Dayton as Secretary of State, while Mr. Seward could go as minister to London, a city that he had so recently taken by storm.

Alarmed, the New Yorkers withdrew; their Albany Plan a temporary failure.

Seward's rage when Lincoln's words were repeated to him resulted in a letter of withdrawal from the Cabinet. Lincoln had chosen not to accept Seward's defection; and had responded with a polite note, asking Seward to remain where he was. As Lincoln signed the letter, he said, half to himself, half to Hay, "I can't afford to let Seward take the first trick."

"Personally," said Nicolay, "I'd rather Seward stayed out. But . . ."

The door to the parlor opened, and the vast Lamon filled the doorway. "He wants to see you boys." Lamon lumbered out of view.

"What's Lamon going to be in the government?" asked Hay.

"Marshal of the District of Columbia, which means he can go on being a bodyguard."

"One of many, let's hope."

The city was filled with alarming reports. The President would be shot on his way to the Capitol. The President would be shot at the Capitol. The President would be kidnapped at the Inaugural Ball and taken across the Long Bridge to Virginia and held hostage. Of all the rumors this one struck Hay as a possibility. It had also enlivened General Scott, who had placed two sharpshooters in every window that looked upon the eastern portico of the Capitol, as well as sharpshooters all up and down Pennsylvania Avenue, not to mention plainclothesmen everywhere.

Lincoln himself seemed indifferent. For the last few days he had been preoccupied with the Virginians, who were holding a convention at Richmond to determine whether or not to secede. More than once, Hay had heard Lincoln pleading with one Virginian after another. Currently, the remaining Southerners in the Congress were particularly exercised by something called the Force Bill, which would give the President the right to call out the militia and accept volunteers into the armed forces. Lincoln had agreed, privately—and, Hay thought, cravenly—to reject the bill if that would satisfy Virginia. On Friday, acting on Lincoln's instructions, just before the Force Bill was to be voted on, Washburne had asked for an adjournment of the House. With this adjournment, the Thirty-sixth Congress expired. But not before, as a further gesture to the Southerners, Lincoln's party supported a measure, never, ever, to interfere with the institution of slavery in those states where slavery was legal. On that note of conciliation, the House of Representatives shut up shop on Monday, March 4, the day of Lincoln's inauguration. The Senate remained in session.

Nicolay and Hay proceeded down the police-lined corridor to Parlor Suite Six. Lincoln sat in his usual place behind the window, the light behind him, his glasses on his nose. Mrs. Lincoln, the three sons, the half-dozen female relations of Mrs. Lincoln quite filled the room.

Hay had never seen Mr. Lincoln so well turned out. He wore a new black suit that still fit him. But Hay knew that by the time that restless, angular body had finished pushing and prodding with knees and elbows, the suit would resemble all his others. For the present, the white of the shirtfront shone like snow, while beside his chair, next to the all-important grip-sack, was a new cane with a large gold knob. Hay could see that Mrs. Lincoln's expensive taste had prevailed.

"Gentlemen," Lincoln greeted his secretaries formally. "We are about to be joined by the Marshal-in-chief, who will put us in our carriages, show us our seats, give us our orders . . ." There was a sound of cheering outside the window. Then a fanfare of trumpets. Lincoln got to his feet; and peered out. "Well, if it's not the President himself, I'd say it's a very good likeness."

Mary had rushed to the window. "It's Mr. Buchanan! He's come to fetch you."

"In a sense." Lincoln smiled. "Now I shall want a lot of Illinois and"—he nodded to certain of Mrs. Todd's relatives—"Kentucky dignity."

With that, the Marshal-in-chief appeared in the doorway. For a moment, Hay feared that Lamon would not let him through. "Mr. Lincoln, the President," proclaimed the Marshal.

The aged Buchanan, as white of face as of hair, came forward to the center of the room. Lincoln crossed to him. They shook hands warmly. "I am here, sir," said the President, "to escort you to the Capitol."

"I am grateful, Mr. President, for your courtesy."

The two men left the room together. At the door Buchanan gestured for Lincoln to go first; but Lincoln stepped to one side, and the still-reigning President went through the door.

The Marshal-in-chief explained who was to go in what carriage. There would be individual marshals—each with a blue scarf and white rosette—assigned to Mrs. Lincoln, to the sons and to the ladies. Fortunately, Hay and Nicolay were allowed to follow Buchanan and Lincoln down the stairs to the lobby, where the police were holding back a considerable crowd. There was cheering at the sight of Lincoln. "Our applicants!" said Hay to Nicolay.

"Wait till we get outside," said Nicolay ominously.

Buchanan and Lincoln, now arm-in-arm, stood in Willard's doorway. A sudden storm of cheering—and of booing—was promptly drowned out by Major Scala's Marine Band, which struck up "Hail to the Chief" as President and President-elect proceeded to get into their open carriage. A nervous marshal then hustled Hay and Nicolay into a barouche, already filled with Washburne and Lamon.

Hay found Washburne edgy; and Lamon uncharacteristically relaxed. But then Lamon had turned his friend and charge over to the United States Army and if they could not protect him today, no one could. Washburne stared out of the window at the thin crowd along the brick sidewalk on the north side of Pennsylvania Avenue. There was no sidewalk or much of anything else on the south side, which, after a few blocks of houses and the Gothic red-brick Smithsonian Institution, turned into a marshland, the result of overflow from the canal that ended in the muddy waters of the Potomac River on whose banks poison ivy and oak grew in wreaths like sinister laurel.

"That is a dangerous crowd." Washburne stared out the window. They were now abreast the Kirkwood House. Thus far, there had been neither cheers nor boos for the two presidents up ahead.

"They're all secesh in this town," said Lamon, whose pronounced Virginia accent sounded somewhat incongruous to Hay.

"And spoiling for a fight," said Washburne.

"Watch the cavalry up ahead." Lamon pointed to the two rows of horsemen that flanked the presidential carriage. The men rode in such close order that anyone standing on the sidewalk would be unable to get more than a glimpse of the occupants of the carriage.

"Notice how the horses are sort of skittish?" Lamon gave a satisfied smile. "That was my idea. When you get horses pulling this way and that, it's going to be mighty hard for anyone with a gun to get himself a proper sight."

David Herold had exactly the same thought. With Annie on his arm, he stood in front of Woodward's and watched the strangely silent parade. "You can't see either of them," he complained.

"Well, we'll get to see them both pretty clear when they come out on the Capitol steps."

"And when they do," David began; but Annie pinched his arm, for silence.

There was only one float, drawn by four white horses; it represented the Republican Association. On top of the float, girls dressed in white represented each of the states in the Union that was no longer. The girls themselves were roundly cheered from the sidewalk; the Union was not.

David and Annie walked beside the float until they came to the plaza in front of the Capitol. Since noon, close to ten thousand people had been gathering. Boys sat in trees. A photographer had built himself a wooden platform where he was busily trying to get his camera in place while fighting off the boys and men who wanted to share the view with him.

Shoving and pushing, David and Annie were soon within a few yards of the speakers' platform, where a single row of troops held back the crowd. Above the platform, on the steps, the great folk of Washington were being led to their seats by ushers. David stared with awe at the foreign diplomats in uniforms that seemed made of pure gold or silver, while the ladies were resplendent in furs and velvet cloaks. The day had started to turn cold.

"My God," whispered Annie, "have you ever seen so many soldiers!" Soldiers were indeed everywhere; and under the eye of the commanding general himself, who sat in huge solitary splendor in his carriage on a nearby eminence. Winfield Scott had sworn a mighty oath that this president would take office, no matter what.

There was cheering from the north portico, which they could not see from where they were standing. "They're going inside the Senate now."

"I know," said Annie. "I read the same paper. Did you take the job with Mr. Thompson?"

"Yes."

"I'm glad."

"Why?"

"Everyone should work."

"You don't."

"I'm still at the seminary. But I'm going to be a music teacher when I graduate and then . . . oh, look! The Zouaves!"

In fire-red uniforms, a company of soldiers under the command of their uncommonly beautiful drillmaster, the curly-haired, twenty-three-year-old Elmer E. Ellsworth, a pet of the Lincoln family, began to divert the crowd with an intricate and somewhat eccentric close-order drill. David was ravished at the sight; and filled with a profound envy. Why wasn't he wearing that extraordinary uniform? And doing those extraordinary tricks? And making Annie and every girl in the crowd gasp with admiration while impressing even the wild boys who were scattered throughout the crowd, ready, as always, for violence, preferably impromptu.

Inside the Senate Chamber, John Hay had not the slightest envy of Hannibal Hamlin, the newly sworn-in Vice-President of the United States. On the other hand, from his seat in the crowded gallery, he quite liked the look of the Senate Chamber. They might never get a proper dome on the Capitol, but Congress had seen to it that the Senate and the House of Representatives were splendidly housed in chambers of marble, decorated in red and gold and bronze, to set off the solemn statesmen in their rusty black, each with his own armchair and desk, snuffbox and shining spittoon.

Hannibal Hamlin spoke well and to the point, and, for a moment, Hay actually looked and listened to the new Vice-President, who was so dark-complexioned that his predecessor sitting beside him on the high dais, John C. Breckinridge of Kentucky, had been quoted as having said that it was highly suitable that a radical government such as that of Mr. Lincoln should have for its Vice-President a mulatto. But mulatto or not, Hamlin was a former Democratic senator from Maine, who had helped found the Republican Party. Before the election, Lincoln and his running-mate Hamlin had never met. Hay was constantly surprised to learn how little these Northern men of state knew one another, as opposed to the Southerners, who seemed all to be brought up in the same crib.

After the election, Lincoln had invited his Vice-President-to-be to Chicago. They got on well, confounding the old Washington saw: there goes the Vice-President, with nothing on his mind but the President's health. Hamlin had introduced Lincoln to raw oysters; and Lincoln had said: "Well, I suppose I must deal with these, too." The two men had got on so well that Lincoln had told Hamlin that as he intended to place only one New Englander in the Cabinet, Hamlin could make the choice, which turned out to be a Connecticut newspaper editor named Gideon Welles. Somewhat reluctantly, Lincoln made him Secretary of the Navy.

Hay looked up at the presidential party. Buchanan and Lincoln were seated side by side in the center of the gallery. Lincoln was as dark as Buchanan was white. For all the talk of *Old* Abe, most people who met Lincoln were startled to find that, at fifty-two, he had not a gray hair in his black shock, which was, for the moment, contained by the barber's art and Mary Todd's firm brushwork. But once out of public view, the long fingers would start to stray through that haystack and, in no time at all, three cowlicks in opposition would make his head look like an Indian warbonnet.

Lincoln seemed distracted, thinking no doubt of his speech—which had been sent, secretly, to the Old Gentleman at Silver Spring, read and admired, and sent back. How close was Lincoln to old Mr. Blair? How close was he to anyone? Hay was still as new to Lincoln's relations with others as, presumably, they were. But Hay did wonder how on earth Lincoln would meet the present crisis, living in a Southern city, with a government that was more than half Southern, and a Cabinet filled with rivals. Plainly, Lincoln was equally bemused. There were times when he would simply drift off in the middle of a conversation, while the curiously heavy lidded left eye, always the indicator of his mood, would half shut, and he would no longer be present. But the eye was alert today, as far as Hay could tell from his end of the chamber, where the smell of men's cologne and ladies' perfume could not quite mask the stale odors of bodies imperfectly bathed. Hay's nose was sharp; his standards of hygiene high.

Hamlin was finished at last. He shook hands with the somber Breckinridge. Then the two Presidents rose, as the Marshal-in-chief came to escort them to the east portico.

Hay followed the black-robed justices of the Supreme Court onto the Capitol steps; he breathed the fresh air, gratefully. A sharp wind had started up, and Hay was suddenly terrified that Lincoln's speech would be blown from his hands. If it were, could the Tycoon remember it? No. The speech was so closely argued that if one word should be misplaced, a half-dozen more states would secede.

A justice's robe flapping in his face, Hay walked down the steps of the Capitol. Half the notables were already seated. The other half had packed the Senate Chamber. Members of the Congress, Supreme Court, Cabinet-to-be, as well as chiefs of foreign missions and high-ranking army and naval officers, each with family, assembled to participate in history. Hay took his seat next to Nicolay, just above the platform.

Nicolay pointed to the crowd. "Mr. Lincoln drew twice at many people as this just in Albany."

"Well, New York State voted for him," said Hay, "and these people didn't. There must be . . . what? ten thousand out there?"

"See the rifles?" Nicolay pointed to a boardinghouse across the Capitol plaza. Each window contained a man with a rifle.

"All trained on us," said Hay. He had always found the idea of assassination more exciting than not. But now he realized with a chill that had nothing to do with the March wind that he was seated just a row above the speakers' platform, with a thousand military rifles all aimed in his direction, not to mention who knew how many plug-uglies with hidden pistols and derringers and knives, ready to commit slaughter. He pulled his hat over his eyes, as if for protection.

The appearance of Lincoln and Buchanan had been greeted with unenthusiastic applause. Neither David nor Annie had so much as clapped a hand when the tall, dark-haired man took his seat behind a low table. David did notice how awkwardly Lincoln handled himself. He was no actor, David thought, scornfully, as he watched Lincoln take off his hat, and then hold it in the same hand as the cane to which he was plainly unused while, with the other hand, he removed his speech from an inside pocket and then was obliged to transfer the speech to the hand that held both hat and cane. Crazy and old as Edwin Forrest was, he could certainly give Lincoln lessons in how to move, thought David; and how to die.

David looked at the men in the trees but could not find a familiar face. Surely the National Volunteers had not given up. He would have bet his last penny, which was in his pocket, that they would make their attempt. At the moment he felt the same excitement that he did in the theater when the musical overture, dominated by drums, began.

When all the dignitaries were in place, a distinguished-looking old man rose and came down to the front of the platform; and in a voice that David approved of, full of baritone drama, and even better, with arms outstretched like Edwin Forrest's when between the acts of whatever play he did nowadays, he would come out and, to the audience's delight, with wondrous fury attack his wife, the old man proclaimed, "Fellow citizens, I introduce to you Abraham Lincoln, the President-elect of the United States!" Even David felt like applauding the old man, whoever he was. Meanwhile, Lincoln was having trouble with hat, cane, speech. He stood a moment, trying to manipulate the three, until a short, stocky man David recognized as Stephen Douglas, the defeated Democratic candidate, leaned forward and took the hat from Lincoln, who gave him a grateful smile. Lincoln then placed the cane on the table, put on his spectacles, moved to stage right of the table, which looked like a milking stool next to such a tall man, and began to read.

"Look," whispered Annie, "his hands are shaking."

"Wouldn't yours?"

Annie elbowed David in the ribs.

Hay was suffering stage fright for the Tycoon, who had never before sounded so tentative, even quavery of voice. Nevertheless, Hay knew that the high voice could be heard from one end of the plaza to the other. Lincoln was used to vast crowds in the open air. "Fellow citizens of the United States." The high voice was tremulous. "In compliance with a custom as old as the government itself, I appear before you to address you briefly, and to take, in your presence, the oath prescribed by the Constitution of the United States . . ." Hay was relieved that at the mention of the Constitution Lincoln's voice lost its quaver. He was now moving onto his own formidable high ground, as he made the case for the Union.

Back among the senators, Salmon P. Chase could not help but contrast how different his own speech on this day might have been. For one thing, he would *never* have read out that provision in the Constitution that slaves be returned to their lawful masters. Chase shuddered as Lincoln elaborated. "It is scarcely questioned that this provision was intended by those who wrote it, for the reclaiming of what we call fugitive slaves; and the intention of the law-giver is the law."

"Shameful," Chase muttered to Sumner, who sat very straight behind him. Sumner nodded, listening closely.

"All members of Congress swear their support to the whole Constitution—to this provision as much as to any other."

Sumner turned to Chase, "What he is doing is giving up the slaves in order to restore the Union."

"That is immoral."

"It is worse," said Sumner. "It is *impossible*."

For Mary the speech was the finest that she had ever heard; and she had heard Henry Clay and Judge Douglas; had heard her own husband proclaim that a house divided against itself cannot stand, losing thereby a Senate seat to Douglas while gaining the presidency for himself. She was also pleased that the new suit fitted him so well; and she was looking forward to showing off her own new wardrobe to the ladies of Washington, who had, thus far, refused to call on her because, she had read in the press, they disdained her as some uncouth westerner, unused to Washington's aristocratic ways. She, Mary Todd of the great Kentucky Todd family, First Lady of Springfield even before she was married, an invitation to whose mansion was the dream of every Illinois lady, if only to observe Mary preside over her witty and elegant court, known, far and wide, as the Coterie. Uncouth!

There was the sharp cracking sound of a gun being fired. Mary gasped. Lincoln stopped in his speech. All Mary could think was—has he been hit? But Lincoln was still standing, if mute. There was a murmur through the crowd. Hay craned forward to see if Lincoln was all right. Apparently, he was; but his face had gone chalk white.

David stood on tiptoe and looked off to the left, where the shot had come from. "Who did it?" whispered Annie. "Can you see?"

"Soldiers, I think." David watched as six soldiers converged on a tree. Then a soldier held up a thick branch. A dazed-looking man was brushing himself off. There was laughter.

"A branch broke off," said David sadly, "under some fellow's weight."

Annie was equally disappointed.

Lincoln resumed his speech. As he came to the coda, Seward leaned forward, eager to hear what Lincoln had cut from his own speech and what of Seward's paragraph he had used.

"You can have no conflict without being yourselves the aggressors. *You* have no oath registered in heaven to destroy the government . . ." Seward frowned: this was hard, too hard. ". . . while *I* shall have the most solemn one to 'preserve, protect and defend it.' "

Seward waited for the challenge. "With *you,* and not with *me,* is the solemn question, 'Shall it be peace, or a sword?' " To his great relief, Lincoln had cut this most dangerous question, and in its place came Seward's text, ruthlessly pruned of its richer blossoms. "I am loth to close. We are not enemies, but friends. We must not be enemies. Though passion may have strained, it must not break our bonds of affection. The mystic chords . . ."

Seward, eyes shut, chanted softly his own original phrase: "The majestic chords which, proceeding from so many battlefields and so many patriotic graves, pass through all the hearts and all the hearths . . ." Tears came to Seward's eyes whenever he declaimed this particular passage, first tried out many years ago at Utica. But Lincoln had changed the language. With some irritability, Seward heard the trumpet-voice intone the new "mystic chords of memory, stretching from every battlefield, and patriot grave, to every living heart and hearthstone, all over this broad land, will yet swell the chorus of the Union, when again touched, as surely they *will* be, by the better angels of our nature."

Lincoln stopped; took of his glasses; put the speech into his pocket. As Seward applauded politely, he could not help but think how odd it was that some men have a natural gift for elevated language while others have none at all. Lincoln had made a perfect hash of Seward's most splendid peroration. Since any one of Seward's speeches was apt to sell nearly one million copies, he had, suddenly, the sense of being jilted—worse, of being a great beauty abandoned at the altar by a plain and unworthy man. But Seward would prevail in time. The Albany Plan may have misfired but since the principle of it was still very much in his mind, he had taken back his letter of withdrawal. He would be Secretary of State; and prime minister yet.

Chase turned to Sumner. "What does he mean?"

Sumner was bemused. "He will take the South back—slaves and all. Anything, to preserve the Union."

"Thank God, they will not come."

"Thank God, they will not come, without a bloody war."

The speech was well enough received by the crowd in the plaza. Lincoln had now recovered his color, Hay noticed. The new President stood beside the small table waiting for the ancient Chief Justice to give him the oath of office.

At the age of eighty-three, Roger B. Taney was several years older than the Constitution, whose interpreter he had been for a quarter century, as the fifth Chief Justice of the United States. Seward was peculiarly aware of the irony of the present situation. Had the fragile, withered Chief Justice not said, in the course of a decision to return a slave to his master, that Congress had no right to ban slavery from any territory, Abraham Lincoln would not now be President. Lincoln looked down, gravely, at the little man who did not look up at him but looked only at the Bible in his right hand. In an inaudible voice, Taney administered the oath. Then Lincoln, hand on the Bible, turned from the Chief Justice to the crowd assembled and ignoring the slip of paper on which his response had been printed, declared in a voice that made even Chase's cold blood turn warm, "I, Abraham Lincoln, do solemnly swear that I will faithfully execute the office of President of the United States, and I will, to the best of my ability . . ."

Lincoln turned full-face to the crowd in the windswept plaza; and the famous war-trumpet of a voice, until now muted, sounded its declaration and what was meant to be its justification for all time, ". . . preserve, protect and . . . *defend* the Constitution of the United States!"

On the word "defend," as if by prearrangement, the first battery of artillery began to fire; then the second; then all guns fired their salute to the new President, who remained at attention throughout the bombardment.

"My God," said Hay to Nicolay, "it is going to be war!"

"I have known that for some time," said Nicolay. "The real question is how will it go for us?"

Lincoln stared at the painting of General Scott conquering Mexico while Seward stared at the painting of General Scott winning the War of 1812. General Scott stared at the bust of General Scott, executed in white marble by a student at Canova who had, in Seward's view, failed to matriculate.

General Scott's office was filled with all the usual sounds of the city, particularly the horsecars rattling up and down the Avenue, to which was added the thudding sound of troops marching, of drums beating the tattoo, of cavalry . . . In four days the empty, doleful city had filled up with troops; and the office-seekers were once more in evidence. Each train from the North brought more troops to the depot, while the telegraph in the

War Department had been restored and, at frequent intervals, the President was told of the success of his call for troops. To date, more than seventy-five thousand men had offered to fight, while the various state legislatures had contributed, thus far, millions of dollars to the Treasury for the defense of Washington; and for a successful prosecution of a war that everyone agreed would be brief but bloody.

Finally, Lincoln spoke to the youthful General Scott storming Chapultepec rather than to the ancient, mottled man who was propped up opposite him, one huge cylinder of a leg resting on a low table. "If the Maryland legislature meets as planned today, they are certain to vote an ordinance of secession."

"In the presence of General Butler?" Seward shook his head. "If they do such a thing, he has threatened to arrest the whole lot of them."

"To what end?" Lincoln shifted his eyes from the heights of Chapultepec; and looked at Seward. "The legislature of any state has the right to meet whenever they choose."

"Even if they plan to withdraw from the Union, which we hold to be not possible?" Seward was now lawyer for the prosecution.

Lincoln took the defense. "Until they actually meet and pass such an ordinance, we cannot presume to know what they will do."

"But, sir, if they do meet and they do secede?"

"We shall be in a worse fix, certainly. But put it this way, Mr. Seward. If we forbid the legislature to meet, which we have no right to do . . ."

"But we could stop them, sir." General Scott had not, as Seward thought, gone to sleep. The eyes were now so ringed with fat that it was hard to tell whether or not they were open, while the old man's breathing was that of a heavy sleeper.

"Oh, we can disperse them, General," said Lincoln. "We can lock them all up. But if we do, another legislature will convene somewhere else, and we'll be exactly where we are now. We can't keep shutting down legislatures from one end of the state to the other." Lincoln was now studying General Scott's winning of the War of 1812. "This morning we created the Military Department of Annapolis, with General Butler as its commander. I think Governor Hicks understands what I have done by making the capital of his state a *Federal* city, with a formidable garrison and a highly dramatic and bad-tempered commander."

"Governor Hicks may understand," said Seward, "but I don't. What is your intention?"

Lincoln slumped in his chair; and grabbed his knees in such a way that his chin could now rest comfortably upon them. The hair as usual resembled a stack of black hay after a wind. "I think the governor will take the hint, and guide the legislature in such a way that it will do nothing provocative for fear of our garrison."

"My informants," said General Scott, "tell me that he is planning to move the legislature out of the Department of Annapolis altogether."

Lincoln frowned. "That could be good for us. That could be bad for us."

"It would *look* good," said Seward. "We would not appear to be coercing them. But those fire-eating Baltimore secessionists are in the majority and once free of us . . ." Seward contemplated General Scott as if he were already a monument—to food if not to victory.

"I think we must run a certain risk in the eyes of the world." Lincoln's beard now resembled a bird's nest once the young had flown. "I've already instructed General Butler to let the legislature meet. But I have also given him orders to arrest anyone who takes up arms—or incites others to take up arms, against the Federal government."

"I assume that this comes under your 'inherent' powers?" Seward was always amused by Lincoln's solemn attempts to rationalize such illegalities as the removal of two million dollars from the Treasury or the confiscation of all of Western Union's files.

"An *inherent* power, Mr. Seward, is just as much a power as one that has been spelled out. But I realize now that I am going to have to stray a mite beyond our usual highly cautious interpretation of those peculiar powers." Lincoln gave Seward a look of such dreamy candor that Seward was immediately on guard.

"I thought, sir, that you'd strayed about as far from the usual as is possible."

"Well, there's always another stretch of field up ahead, as the farmer said." Lincoln turned to General Scott, who came to massive attention in his chair. "You are to instruct General Butler, in your capacity as general-in-chief, that he is to wait upon the legislature and if an ordinance of secession is passed, he is to interpret this as an incitement to take up arms against the United States, and those legislators—who would incite the people to take up arms against us, or attempt to seize Federal property, as they did when they occupied the Naval Academy—shall be promptly arrested and held in prison at the government's pleasure."

"I shall transmit this order gladly, sir. But what are the legal consequences? I mean, sir, with what are they to be charged?"

"I don't think we should be too specific. After all, if we were to put too fine a point on it, the charge would have to be treason, and such trails are endless, and very hard on the innocent, who might easily be rounded up along with the guilty."

Seward was too stunned to say anything. As for General Scott, although his legal training was a half-century in the past, he did understand treason trials. "You are right, sir, about the difficulty of proving treason. I myself testified at Richmond in the course of the trial of Colonel Aaron Burr, who was no more guilty—"

Seward interrupted the old man without even a show of courtesy. "Mr. Lincoln, you are willing to arrest and to hold men indefinitely without ever charging them with any offense?"

"That's about it, Mr. Seward." Lincoln's face was uncommonly serene.

"But on what authority?" Seward felt as if two millennia of law had been casually erased by this peculiar lazy-limbed figure, now twisted in his chair like an ebony German pretzel.

"On my authority, as Commander-in-Chief."

"But you have no authority to allow the military to arrest anyone they like and to hold them without due process of law."

"Plainly, I think that I do have that right because that is what I am about to do." Slowly, the coiled figure straightened out. Then Lincoln addressed General Scott. "Telegraph the order to General Butler."

"Yes, sir." Scott rang a bell. An orderly entered, received his instructions from Scott; and then departed with the order to overthrow the first rule of law—*habeas corpus.*

"The most ancient of all our liberties," said Seward, with some awe, "is the right of a man who has been detained to know what he is charged with and then to be brought, in due course, to trial . . ."

"Mr. Seward, the most ancient of all our human characteristics is survival. In order that this Union survive, I have found it necessary to suspend the privilege of the writ of *habeas corpus,* but only in the military zone."

Seward whistled, very loudly; something that he had not done in years. "No president has ever done this."

"No president has ever been in my situation."

"President Madison was driven from this city by the British, who then set fire to the Capitol and the Mansion. Yet Madison never dreamed of suspending *habeas corpus.*"

"The times are not comparable." Lincoln got to his feet. "Madison was faced with a foreign invasion that did not affect any but a small part of the country. I am faced with a war in which a third of the population has turned against the other two-thirds."

As Seward got to his feet, General Scott said, "You will forgive me, sir, if I do not rise."

"You are forgiven, General." Absently Lincoln patted the old man's epauleted shoulder.

Seward now stood next to the heroic bust of Scott; he looked up at Lincoln. "Will *you* be forgiven, sir, when the people learn of this?"

"Well, I don't plan to make a public announcement just yet—"

"But the word will spread."

"Mr. Seward, for the moment all that matters is to keep Maryland in the Union, and there is nothing that I will not do to accomplish that."

"Well, you have convinced me of that!" Although Seward chuckled, he was more alarmed than amused. "What happens when those hotheads in Baltimore find out?"

"Well, as we have a list of the worst of the lot, I reckon Ben Butler will lock them all up in Fort McHenry."

"What happens if the people of the city resist our troops?"

"We burn Baltimore to the ground. We are at war, Mr. Seward."

"Yes, sir." Seward wondered what precedents there were for the disposal of a mad president. Like so many other interesting matters, the Constitution had left the question unduly vague.

"Before you go, Mr. President," said General Scott, "what am I to do about the commissioning of General Butler and Governor Sprague? Each expects to be made major-general of volunteers. Each has made the point that he is a Democrat loyal to the Union and that you favor such men."

"That's true, of course. I must woo the Northern Democrats. Commission Butler. As for Governor Sprague . . ." Lincoln sighed. He turned to Seward. "Rhode Island is such a small state."

"And the governor is really such a small sort of Democrat."

Lincoln turned to General Scott. "If Governor Sprague pesters you, as he's been trying to pester me, offer him a brigadier-generalship. If he takes it, which I doubt, he can command his Rhode Islanders. But he'll have to resign as governor."

"Yes, sir."

As Lincoln and Seward stepped into Seventeenth Street, they were suddenly deafened by a military band playing "Columbia, the Gem of the Ocean."

"That's not the Marine Band," said Seward, whose ear for music was sharp, or so he liked to think—and always said.

"You're right. It's the New York Seventh's band. They're on the south lawn, giving a concert. Willie persuaded me that it was a good idea."

As they crossed the street, hats were raised to the President, who responded by raising his own hat and smiling, gravely.

"What was Willie's advice on *habeas corpus*?"

"Why, in those matters, I always turn to Tad, whose approach is singularly direct—like mine." An office-seeker stopped Lincoln at the White House gates.

"Mr. President, sir, I am a lifelong Republican from Dutchess County, New York . . ."

"But, sir, our party's only seven years old." Lincoln was amused.

"Exactly, sir, lifelong," the man repeated; and thrust a sheaf of documents at Lincoln. "The postmastership of Poughkeepsie is open . . ."

Politely, Lincoln stepped aside. "I'm not about to set up shop here in the street. You come during office hours." Lincoln strode through the White House gates; Seward behind him. At the gates, soldiers saluted smartly. When Seward's short legs had caught up with Lincoln's long ones, he asked, "What will Tad have to say when Congress impeaches you?"

"I reckon Tad will say, 'At least Paw saved the Capitol of the country, just so they'd have a nice place to impeach him in.' "

Seward was not prepared for so much blitheness; there was no other word. But Seward had also noticed that whenever Lincoln appeared to be vague and disturbed it was invariably before an important decision was made; after the decision was made, he acted as if he had not a care in the world, until the next crisis got him to brooding again.

At the portico, Lincoln paused. "I have high hopes for that railroad colonel, Burnside. He's a first-rate engineer who's invented something to do with the loading of guns. He's a trained military man, not like . . ." Lincoln paused and watched as a company from the New Jersey regiment marched past the gates of the Mansion. As the officer in charge shouted, "Eyes right!" and saluted the President, Lincoln lifted his hat.

"Not like Ben Butler," Seward supplied a name; then another, "or Governor Sprague."

"The governor has a plan to win the war quickly. I told him to put it in writing."

"That should take some time," said Seward wryly.

"That was the idea." Lincoln entered the Mansion, while Seward strolled across the shaggy lawn to the State Department building, which he had more than once compared to a brick privy in its close proximity to the vast stone palace of the Treasury.

Seward was having some difficulty in comprehending what he had just witnessed. Two lawyers and a professional general, who had been called in his day to the bar, had sat in a room and removed from an entire people their one inviolable right which had proved, upon test, to be as easily violable as a man transmitting a dozen or so words from a slip of paper to the telegraph wire. In six weeks, Congress would return. In six weeks, Seward was certain that an act of impeachment would be drawn up against the President. He wondered what his own line should be. After all, *he* was the advocate of the strong line; and certainly there was nothing stronger than what Lincoln had just done. Yet no Congress would ever allow the basic law of the land to be overthrown. Lincoln would be called to account. But could the country endure an impeachment and a trial of the President during a war? Perhaps Lincoln could be persuaded to resign.

Seward was smiling as he entered the office of the Secretary of State, where his son Frederick—the Assistant Secretary—sat in his shirt-sleeves at a table beneath a portrait of John Jay. The office was barely big enough for the two of them; yet, across the way, Chase sat alone in vast teakwood splendor, amidst crystal chandeliers, gilded cornices, velvet rugs.

If Lincoln were to go of his own free will, or otherwise, Hannibal Hamlin would be president; and Hamlin, Seward knew, was a modest man who would understand the need for a strong man from within the Cabinet to direct the war, a man who not only knew intimately how the nation functioned but had a vision, which all the others lacked. Seward's vision was simple: he wanted the entire western hemisphere to belong to the United States. Yet while Seward dreamed, splendidly and practically, of empire, the railroad lawyer in the White House wanted only to bring back into the Union a half-dozen or so rebellious mosquito-states—as Seward thought, contemptuously, of the Gulf states, so many irrelevant parcels of third-rate territory that would promptly revert to the Union once Mexico had come to accept American rule, much as the Cisalpine Gaul had come to accept that of Rome. There were times when Seward felt that Chase shared his imperial vision. But those times were few. Essentially, Chase was a man in thrall to a single cause—the abolition of slavery. It was a cause that tended, in Seward's view, to drive men quite mad, assuming that they were not already mad to begin with and so turned to the cause of abolition as a means of legitimizing the furies that drove them.

"Don't forget this evening, sir," said Frederick, putting down a month's worth of dispatches from London and Paris and Saint Petersburg.

"This evening?" Seward sat his desk, where a file labelled "Charles Francis Adams" had been set in front of him. Seward found Mr. Adams difficult; but able. Seward was also very much aware that he was seated at the desk of Mr. Adams's father, who had been eight years Secretary of State; and then President. Seward was also, glumly, aware that in eight years he himself would be either close to seventy years of age or dead; on the other hand, if President Lincoln did not seek reelection . . .

Frederick reminded his father that he had accepted an invitation to attend a reception at the Chases, in honor of Governor William Sprague IV. Seward sighed.

On the back porch of the Old Club House, Seward lay in a hammock, eyes shut, and ears attuned only to the chatter of birds in the flowering backyard, where huge roses in full bloom made the air heavy with their scent. Congress had dispersed three days earlier, and Seward felt like a free man again, no longer the target of Ben Wade the Bluff and all the other Jacobins who now held him totally responsible for the slowness of the war effort, not to mention the vile continuation of slavery everywhere on earth.

As Seward rocked slowly back and forth in the hammock, he thought, longingly, of sending a detachment of troops to surround the Capitol while Congress was in session. There would be a mass arrest. He himself would speak to the assembled members of the two houses—would they be chained to one another? He left that detail for a later daydream. But, for the present, he was seated in the Speaker's chair, and smoking a cigar as the terrified members of the Congress stood before him, guns trained on them from soldiers in the gallery. Naturally, he would address them pleasantly; he might even make a joke or two. Then he would explain how no state could support, in time of war, the luxury of such a large, unwieldy and often dangerously unpatriotic band of men. Therefore, it was with true sorrow that he was dissolving the legislative branch of the government. Most of the members would be allowed to return home. Unfortunately, there were a number who would be obliged to stand trial for treasonable activities. Senator Wade would, of course, be given every opportunity to defend himself before a military court. But should he and the other Jacobins be found guilty, they would, of course, be hanged—in front of the Capitol. Seward was debating whether or not the gallows should be placed at the east or the west end of the Capitol, when the servant announced, "Mr. Chase to see you, sir."

Seward opened his eyes; and there was Chase, in a white linen jacket, looking reasonably cool on such a hot day. "Forgive me for not stirring," said Seward.

"You are forgiven," Chase pulled up a chair and sat at the foot of the hammock—like a physician, thought Seward, motioning to the servant to light his cigar for him. "I've been enjoying the peace and the quiet, now that Congress has gone, and we've only the war to worry about."

Chase nodded. "They take up so much time, our old colleagues. I am told that Ben Wade has announced that the country is going to hell."

"I can only hope that he gets there first," said Seward.

"Things are coming to a climax, Mr. Seward." Chase stared at the small figure in the hammock so like, with its short legs and large nose, a parrot fallen from its perch.

"You mean with McClellan?" Seward knew what Chase meant: the freeing of the slaves was now a matter of great urgency. But *whose* slaves? That was the problem. Meanwhile, England and France were more than ever pro-rebel; each nation taking the high line that the Lincoln Administration was essentially indifferent to the fate of the black man, a subject of no particular interest to either power but a highly convenient rationale for supporting the South—and the breakup of the youthful American empire.

Currently, the radical Republicans were threatening to abandon the Republican Party and the Lincoln Administration. Some of the Jacobin firebrands in Congress—yes, he would have them chained to one another, and the executions would take place on the north side of the Capitol—were insisting that Seward, as Lincoln's evil genius of moderation, resign immediately and that the Joint Committee, together with Chase, free the slaves, sack McClellan and together prosecute the war. Seward was never entirely certain to what extent Chase was involved in these devious plots. He did know that Chase tended to agree with whatever any of the radicals had to say about the President or himself.

"I was not thinking of McClellan, though he is a part of the problem." Chase had come to detest the Young Napoleon. Ever since he himself had delivered Norfolk into the Union hands, Chase had lost all awe of the military. Some organizational ability, a degree of common sense—and courage—were all that was needed. McClellan had only the first. Chase had all the rest; and so did any number of civilian leaders. Even Lincoln was better equipped to conduct a military operation than McClellan, who had got within six miles of Richmond; and then had failed to take the city, though his army outnumbered the rebels at least five to one; and the rebel commander, Joe Johnston, had been seriously wounded at Seven Pines, one of the few real battles of the so-called Peninsula campaign. Johnston had been succeeded by Robert E. Lee, the friend of the Blairs.

During June and July, McClellan continued to ask for more troops. He claimed that Lee had two hundred thousand men, ready to crack the Union army. Actually, Chase had learned that Lee's army was closer to eighty-five thousand men. In desperation, Lincoln had slipped out of Washington and gone up the Hudson River to the military academy at West Point to confer with Winfield Scott. The result had been that Halleck was soon to arrive as general-in-chief while General John Pope—also from the Western army—was now the commander of a new Army of Virginia, to protect the capital and hold off the alarming "Stonewall" Jackson, who ranged at will up and down the nearby Shenandoah Valley. Finally, with Pope approaching Richmond from the west and McClellan from the east, the city was bound to fall.

McClellan's troops were still divided by the Chickahominy River; and the rains were falling, and the creeks were swollen. But then while everyone was predicting that with a single stroke McClellan could take Richmond, Lee attacked McClellan; and McClellan lost what little nerve he had. After denouncing the President and Stanton, the Young Napoleon retreated to the James River and set up a new headquarters at Harrison's Landing.

Since the Confederate government was now conscripting men, Lincoln sent Seward, secretly, to New York City to meet with the Northern governors and ask them to petition the President to call for more troops. As there was now no great general eagerness to enlist in the Union army, the day before Congress adjourned those men between the ages of eighteen and forty-five might be liable for military duty.

But Chase had not come to Seward's house to discuss McClellan. He had written off McClellan and he knew that Lincoln would, presently, replace him. Chase had total faith in John Pope, a dedicated abolitionist, who had made an excellent impression on the Joint Committee. The war would come to its predestined end. "But, Mr. Seward, we cannot remain silent any longer on the subject of slavery."

Chase got the full benefit of Seward's single, bright parrot's eye—the nose made it impossible for Chase to see both eyes at the same time of the recumbent Secretary of State.

"Silent? Mr. Chase, we chatter of nothing else. Even the President is beginning to sound like an abolitionist. I told him it would do no good to try to talk to those border-stage congressmen. But he thought he had to. So last week he told them he'd pay three hundred dollars a head for each of their Negroes; and they said no."

"They did not *all* say no." Chase had thought Lincoln more than usually feckless in the way that he had handled so difficult a business. Lincoln had appealed to their patriotism, which was irrelevant since they were all on the Union's side, more or less willingly. Lincoln had then made the curious point that as long as they maintained slavery within their borders, the states in rebellion would always feel that one day the border-states would join them; but should slavery be abolished and the slaveholders compensated, the rebel states would not continue to fight much longer. Like so many of Lincoln's attempts at logic, this essay had left Chase as cold as it had a majority of the border-men present. "But I suppose it is hard for the President to forget that he is a Kentuckian, and that Mrs. Lincoln's brothers are all at war against us."

"I think the President is peculiarly able to rise above his brothers-in-law," said Seward, swinging his hammock in a sort of semicircle, which made Chase dizzy to watch.

"I wish he would rise the entire way in this matter."

"You would free all of the slaves within the Union?"

"Yes, Mr. Seward, I would."

Seward was enjoying himself. "And in those states that are in rebellion?"

"I would have the military commanders free them, as each rebel state is brought to heel."

"The military commanders rather than the President?"

"I think," said Chase, judiciously, "that is the practical way."

"I see." Seward saw that for all of Chase's passion on the subject of abolition, he did not want the President to get any of the credit for so noble a deed. On the other hand, he would not object to Lincoln taking whatever blame might be handed around.

"I think, Mr. Seward, it is up to us guide the President in this matter. He will not act of his own accord . . ."

"You may be surprised, Mr. Chase."

Chase looked at Seward expectantly. "What form will the surprise take?"

"I think that Mr. Lincoln is thinking hard, and that means that he is about to make a move."

"You are in his confidence, of course." Chase was polite; but no more. He knew that if Seward had his way, nothing would be done until after the congressional elections in the fall. As Chase rose to go, Seward got out of his hammock with a surprisingly youthful spring.

"Would that we had a Cromwell!" Seward exclaimed, as he led Chase into the house.

"You?" asked Chase, who had often heard Seward go on in a similar vein.

"Or you. Or even Lincoln."

"I am sure *he* could never rise to the stern . . . necessity."

"Could you, Mr. Chase?"

Chase mopped his brow. The interior of the house was even warmer than the back porch.

"It is tempting, in a war, to give the leadership to one man. But once the war is over, he must, of course, be executed promptly."

"*I* would avoid that," said Seward, merrily.

*"Et tu, Brute?"* said Chase, thinking not of Shakespeare but of Scripture and of Christ's suffering on the cross that man might be redeemed through His blood. Now *that* would be a mighty, worthy fate.

Hay was at the window of Nicolay's office when the Secretary of the Treasury emerged from Seward's house. "They are plotting," he said to Nicolay. "Chase and Seward are up to something."

"We shall survive." Nicolay was on his feet. He was enroute to the cool wilds of Minnesota. Once Congress had gone home, half the secretary's work mysteriously ceased. Hay watched as Chase drove away in his carriage. Then the newest streetcar, an open affair for summer days, passed in all its cream-and-white splendor beneath the White House and a number of well-dressed gentlemen and ladies waved at the President, wherever he might be; and Hay waved back.

"I think," said Hay, half to himself and half to the busy Nicolay, "I shall call on Miss Kate."

"Isn't the boy-governor in town?"

"No. He's at Corinth, I think. He's asked the Tycoon to allow him to explain to Halleck how to wind up the war in the west."

"When does Halleck get here?" Nicolay's carpetbag was now filled up with papers.

"The twenty-third, he says. He keeps delaying. If I were to be general-in-chief, I'd come running." Hay sat at Nicolay's desk. "Miss Kate is more than usually agreeable this summer."

"Then beware. *She* is plotting."

Lincoln entered the office. "Well, Mr. Nicolay, you are off today, I see."

"Yes, sir."

"I hope you'll get a glimpse of Miss Therena Bates."

"If there is a chance, between the Chippewas and the Cheyennes, I will."

"Yes." Lincoln frowned. "You'll have your work cut out for you. As if we didn't have enough to do, we're about to have us an Indian war. Present my compliments to Chief Hole-in-the-Day."

"I will, sir."

"Offer him your scalp," added Hay, aware that Lincoln had drifted off. Absently, the President had walked over to the table strewn with newspapers. "It is ominous," he said, picking up the New York *Tribune,* "that I've not heard from Horace Greeley for a week."

"Perhaps," said Hay, "he is ill."

"Oh, we should have heard *that* news," said Lincoln, glancing at the editorial page. " 'A great man is fast sinking,' we'd read. Well, he favors last week's Confiscation Act, but he says it don't go far enough. How much further can Congress go than to say that the slaves of any person found guilty of treason are free?"

Both Nicolay and Hay realized that whenever Lincoln asked questions of a newspaper, he did not expect either of them to speak in the editor's place. Lincoln next addressed a number of ringing questions to James Gordon Bennett; and then threw down the *Herald.* "I ought not to read these people," he said; then added: "Anyway, our Railroad Bill seems popular."

"But the *New York Times,*" said Nicolay, "wonders how, in the middle of the most expensive war in history, you'll be able to pay for a railroad line from coast to coast."

"It's only from western Iowa to San Francisco . . ." Lincoln looked, for a moment, wistful. "You know, I really hope to take that train one day. I dearly want to see the Pacific Ocean. It is my last passion." He turned to Nicolay. "Have you a copy of General McClellan's letter to me, the one he gave me at Harrison's Landing?"

"Yes, sir." Nicolay touched the strongbox on his desk. "I keep it here, locked up."

"You keep it under lock and key, too, John," said the Ancient to Hay; then he bade Nicolay farewell; and returned to his own office, where Tad promptly started to bang a drum. "My son," they heard the President's mild voice from the corridor, "could you not manage to make less noise?"

"That boy's run wild since Mrs. Edwards went home." Hay had his own ideas about the way in which children should be brought up, and the Lincolns failed entirely to meet his standards. Tad was seen, was heard, was everywhere underfoot.

"I'd hoped she would stay longer," said Nicolay.

"Not even she can take the Hellcat."

"The scenes never stop." Nicolay shut his bag. "I don't envy you, Johnny."

"Do you think she's mad?" This was a recurring dialogue.

"She is certainly not like other people. She is two people . . ."

"She is Hell. She is Cat. And she is the Hellcat. That's *three* people." Since Willie's death, Hay had gone out of his way to be sympathetic and helpful, but nothing could allay Madam's suspicions, compounded, as always, by urgent demands for money. Since Watt continued, mysteriously, to work at the White House under a cloud rather larger than a President's message to Congress, she had turned more and more to the urbane Major French, whose urbanity with each passing month was more and more tested. Meanwhile, she was in darkest mourning. The Marine Band was no longer allowed to play on summer evenings in the President's Park, while the bedroom in which Willie had died was now off-limits for her as was the downstairs Green Room, where the boy had been embalmed. The President bore his own grief stoically—although Nico had told Hay that immediately after the Ancient had left the death-bed, he had come, in tears, to Nicolay's office and said, "Well, Nicolay, my boy is gone. He is actually gone. Gone," he repeated, as if he could not believe what had happened. But there it ended. After that, he shared his grief with no one, as far as Hay knew.

Nicolay was at the door, carpetbag in hand. "I shall think of you, Johnny, from time to time. Beware of fair Kate."

"Like the Medusa."

"You'll enjoy the coming surprise. I wish I were going to be here."

"Surprise?" Hay usually knew everything that Nicolay knew. But, lately, he had noticed that the Ancient and Nicolay were often alone together in the President's office; and that whenever he had entered the room, they would fall silent.

"You'll see. Now I must go. You have the key to the strongbox. All else is in order." Nicolay shook Hay's hand firmly; and left the room. Ten minutes later, Hay realized that Nicolay had forgotten to give him the key to the strongbox. Hay hurried downstairs, but Nicolay's carriage had already departed for the depot.

The surprise occurred at the Cabinet meeting on July 22. At first Hay feared that he would not be included, but the President, at the last moment, said that he would want notes of what the others said.

The room was bright; and the air hot. Flies buzzed in and out of the open windows. Lincoln had loosened his tie; and the corded brown neck looked as if it might have belonged to Chief Hole-in-the-Day. All the Cabinet was present save Blair. After a few bits of business, Lincoln removed a document from his pocket; and put on his glasses. But instead of looking at the pages in his hand, he stared at the gaslight fixtures that depended from the ceiling. "I think that we are, in many ways, about at the end of our rope on the plan of operations that we have been following—politically as well as militarily. We are to face a difficult election in November. There's a possibility we may lose Pennsylvania, Ohio and Indiana. Meanwhile, our French friends are busy across the border in Mexico, stirring up trouble, and our British friends are letting the rebels use their shipyards, in violation of our agreed-upon neutrality. In one year, Mr. Chase tells me the public debt has gone from ninety million dollars to a half billion dollars. Personally, I cannot visualize either sum. But I know that we cannot go on much longer as we are without victories in the field and in the world's political arena."

Lincoln glanced at the papers in his hand. Hay could not for the life of him guess what the Ancient was up to. But Seward knew; had indeed discussed the matter with the President. Chase suspected; and was now most uneasy. In a sense, he himself could—with a stroke of Lincoln's pen—lose his moral superiority to Lincoln. "As you know, I have said, more than once, if I could preserve the Union by freeing *all* of the slaves everywhere, I would do so. If I could preserve the Union by freeing *none* of the slaves, I would do so. If I could preserve the Union by freeing *some* of the slaves but not others, I would do so. Well, I have not the political power to do the first. I have not the inclination nor the need to do the second. So I shall now do the third, as a military necessity."

The silence in the room was made all the deeper by the buzzing of the flies—and the bluebottles that swept like artillery shells past Hay's face. The Ancient had at last seized the moment. Chase was very pale; and perturbed. Seward was in another, pleasanter world, gazing out the window. Stanton scowled. Wells sweated beneath his wig. Bates looked sorrowful. Smith looked indifferent. "I should tell you that I have myself prepared a proclamation of emancipation. I shall, in due course, publish it. And it will be the law. I have not asked you here for your advice, though once I have read you what I have written, you may certainly comment."

Lincoln then proceeded to read a most adroit document. To the slave-holding states within the Union, he promised to ask the Congress to provide some means of giving financial aid to those elements which favored the gradual abolishment of slavery. But for those states that were in rebellion against the Union, "I, as Commander-in-Chief of the army and navy of the United States, do order and declare that on the first day of January, in the year of our Lord one thousand eight hundred and sixty-three, all persons held as slaves within any State or States wherein the Constitutional authority of the United States shall not then be practically recognized, submitted to and maintained, shall then, thenceforward, and forever be free." The President put down the papers on the table; and removed his glasses; and rubbed his nose.

Blair entered the room, apologizing for being late. Lincoln indicated, silently, that he read the draft of the proclamation, which he did; not happily, thought Hay.

Lincoln turned not to Seward, as protocol required, but to Chase. "We all spoke yesterday, Mr. Chase, about a number of military orders that I have had in mind on the question of what is to be done with those Negroes from the rebel states who are now free of their masters, and I think we are all pretty much agreed that they may be employed by us as laborers, and so on. All of us supported the plan to colonize the Negroes in some tropical place except you."

"Yes, sir." Chase cleared his throat; he was suddenly aware that he was nervous, and he wondered why. "I have never taken to the idea that we simply remove three million Negroes from this continent, and send them to Central America or across the Atlantic to Africa. If nothing else, the cost of moving them would be prohibitive."

"Well, I have tabled the matter, at your insistence. On the other hand, I part company with some of you on the arming of former slaves. I think that this would have a most incendiary effect in the border-states, and not affect the rebels much one way or the other."

"There, sir, we differ." Chase looked to Seward for aid, but there was none; looked to Stanton, who was with him in this matter, but Stanton chose silence. "As for the proclamation that you have read to us, I would prefer that you leave to the various commanding generals the task of freeing—and arming—the slaves, as these Negroes come within their jurisdiction. But since you are averse to this, I give my entire support to the proclamation, in its place."

The President nodded. "Thank you, Mr. Chase." Then he turned to Montgomery Blair. "You missed yesterday's meeting, but you now know the gist of it; and you have read the proclamation."

"Yes, sir." Blair's naturally fierce face was made more ferocious by the bright sun that caused his eyes to shine like polished gray marble. "I think you know my views. I want all the slaves freed at the *end* of the war; and then I want every last Negro shipped off to Africa or New Granada or wherever we can find a country for them. The people, Mr. Chase"—Blair turned his glare on the bland Roman bust of the Secretary of the Treasury—"will find the money to transport them from this continent where they never should have been brought, which is why this war is the Judgment of God on us for bringing them here in the first place."

"That's very eloquent, Mr. Blair." Lincoln was dry. "And much my own view, but the issue at hand is the proclamation. What is your view of it?"

"My view, sir, is that if you publish it, we will lose the November election, and you will be faced with a Democratic Congress."

Lincoln seemed taken aback by Blair's directness. But before he could speak, Seward broke in. "I fully support the proclamation, which the President intends to publish in any case, and I think it will do us more good than ill, particularly in our relations with the European powers. But I would suggest, Mr. President, most respectfully, that as we are plainly *not* winning the war—and going bust in the process—that your postpone the proclamation until you can give it to the country supported by military success. Otherwise, the impression will be, in the light of so many reverses, of our last shriek on the retreat."

Lincoln stretched his arms, always, Hay knew, a sign that he was past the worst of some encounter. "I think that's eminently sound advice, Governor, which I shall take." Lincoln gave the pages to Hay. "Mr. Hay, put this away in the strongbox." Hay felt slightly ill. *Where* was the key? "We shall keep all of this a secret until such time as I am able to celebrate a victory. What news"—the Tycoon turned to Stanton—"of General McClellan?"

"The Great American Tortoise remains in place."

"He is consistent," said the President, wearily. "Well, soon we shall have General Halleck here as general-in-chief. At West Point, he is known as Old Brains, and he is, yet again, General Scott's choice. I've also been reading General Halleck's *Elements of Military Art and Science;* it is most serious, most serious."

The conversation turned to General Pope, who was everyone's idea of a fighting general. Chase had got very friendly with him; he had even shepherded the fiery general around the Capitol, where he had made an excellent impression on the abolitionists. Pope's father had been an Illinois district judge in whose court Lincoln had practised. But Lincoln had done nothing to promote him. Pope had succeeded quite on his own in the West, under Halleck. While Lincoln was with Scott at West Point, Stanton had summoned Pope to Washington and offered him the command of a new army, to be known as the Army of Virginia, with McDowell and Frémont and Banks under him. Pope had accepted the command. He was a magnificent-looking man with a vast beard. Unfortunately, he took an immediate dislike to McClellan, who reciprocated. As a result, the armies of Virginia and of the Potomac were now commanded by two rivals. Thus far, Lincoln chose not to notice the irritabilities of his commanders. But then after Hay had read the letter that McClellan gave Lincoln at Harrison's Landing, he had come to the conclusion that the Ancient was a saint. Unable to take Richmond, McClellan had had the audacity to present the President with a letter filled with political advice to the effect that the noble war to preserve the Union must not be fought against the Southern people or their property, which included slaves. It was plain to Hay that this document was intended to be the platform from which McClellan would run for president in 1864. It was also plain to Lincoln, who made no comment other than a wise smile when others made the same comment.

Chase thought *himself* a saint for concurring so wholeheartedly in Lincoln's plan to emancipate the slaves of the rebel states. Granted, he had no alternative, for the President had been uncharacteristically firm. Lincoln had assembled the Cabinet in order to tell them what he intended to do. Since Seward was plainly behind him, pulling the strings, Chase was outnumbered. More than ever, he was convinced that Seward was the mind of the Administration to the extent that such a haphazard and themeless government could be said to have a mind. Since he himself was not permitted to create grand strategy, he could at least continue to be the voice of conscience—seldom heeded, of course, by these conscienceless politicians.

As the conversation became desultory, Chase struck one of his themes. "In the matter of the currency . . ."

Lincoln gave a long sigh; and all the others save Stanton smiled.

The President's inability to cope with even the idea of the national finance was a sign, if nothing else, of his incompetence, thought Chase, who did understand the precarious nature of fiat money in general and of the so-called greenbacks in particular. "I know," said Lincoln, "that in the matter of the currency, we have, always, too much of it, which means too little of it. This is highly metaphysical, as my old partner, Billy Herndon, would say."

Hay had a sudden image of Herndon at Sal Austin's; and he wondered if the old man had married the young girl that he had been courting; and if he had, he wondered if Herndon had given up whiskey, as promised. He hoped so, for the Tycoon's sake.

"I did not mean to advert to the metaphysical," said Chase, with what he hoped was a polite smile. "I did not want to bring up again to the Cabinet my personal desire to have printed on our bank notes the same phrase that I devised for our coinage. I mean, of course, 'In God we Trust.' "

"Surely," said Bates, a constant antagonist in these matters, "the Constitutional separation of church and state makes such a phrase highly irregular if not illegal."

"Well," said Lincoln, getting to his feet, "if you are going to put a Biblical tag on the greenback, I would suggest that of Peter and John: 'Silver and gold have I none; but such as I have give I thee.' " In the ensuing laughter, the President withdrew to his office and Chase realized that, once again, he had not managed to get a straight answer from the President on an issue of signal importance to every God-fearing Unionist.

Seward put his arm through Chase's, a gesture that Chase deeply disliked but endured, as he did so much else, for his country. "The President is not the free-thinker you may suspect he is."

"I suspect nothing." Chase was aware of the smell of stale cigar smoke from the small figure at his side; also, a hint of port upon the breath.

"Well, you have your emancipation," said Seward comfortably, as the two men made their way down the crowded hallway. Every step or so, a petitioner or well-wisher stopped one or the other or both. Seward's responses were merrily elliptical. Chase's responses were gravely vague.

"It is not *my* emancipation. There are still the border-states. *I* would have freed all the slaves everywhere."

"Then I pity *your* poor Secretary of the Treasury, because he'd never sell another Treasury bond anywhere on earth."

Chase gave Seward what he hoped was a cold eye; certainly, it was an eye that was nearly blind in its central vision. On the other hand, the peripheral vision saw everything with fine clarity.

Saw Kate, radiant, in the front parlor, with the young Ohioan general who had just moved into the house for the summer. He sprang to his feet as Chase entered the room. He was tall, with blue eyes and a quantity of curling golden hair as well as an equally golden beard. When Kate had suggested that he had gilded at least the beard, he had cut off a lock, suitable, he said, for analysis or a locket or both. Kate had declined the trust on the ground that he must be as true as gold, if not steel, to his young wife, Lucretia, back in Hiram, Ohio. If only, Chase had thought more than once, William Sprague had half the charm and learning of James A. Garfield or, put another way, if only General Garfield had a tenth of Sprague's fortune, he would indeed, at the age of thirty and unmarried, be a suitable son-in-law. But nothing is ever as it should be. Garfield was married; and poor.

Kate presided over lemonade; asked her father what had happened at Cabinet; listened attentively to his report, which did not include the secret emancipation proclamation.

"I'm receiving today," said Kate, finally, as Chase drank deeply of the lemonade. "I said I'd be home to what's left of the town, now that Congress has gone."

"Well, there's the military left," said Chase.

"Worse luck," said Garfield. "Everything's beginning, at last, to happen and I'm here in the city—waiting."

"Well, it's nice for us, if not the war," said Kate.

"You won't wait long," said Chase. But he stopped speaking while the manservant dressed in a linen coat with gold braid and gold buttons—Kate's latest innovation—put out cakes on a tea-stand. When the man was out of earshot, Chase murmured, "I think I've got you the Florida command. But it's a secret."

"That's what I most want!" The youthful face was animated—Apollo, the ladies called General Garfield. "The war will be decided when the western troops join the eastern troops *below* Richmond."

"But, first we must wait for General Halleck to arrive. He'll make the final decision. Stanton likes him, and the President *thinks* that he will like him."

"Oh, he's first-rate, Old Brains. A born general-in-chief, if not a born field commander. Everything that we've won in the West was actually won by Grant . . ."

" . . . and Pope," said Chase.

"Your latest enthusiasm," said Kate.

"Pope, too," said Garfield, politely. "But I was with Grant at Shiloh, on the second day, the bloody day. I saw the way he was pounded and pounded . . ."

" . . . the way he killed and killed," said Kate, shuddering.

"Yes," said Garfield, "that is what we do in a war."

Kate's guests began to arrive; and Chase withdrew to his study, missing John Hay, who arrived just as the sun began, gloriously, to set.

Hay had seen Kate several times during the summer. They had gone three times to the theater, twice in the company of others. But the last time, the two of them had attended an operetta, followed by supper at Wormley's. Hay found Kate endlessly attractive in her person. He found less attractive the shrewd political mind that never ceased to plot, so reminiscent of the Tycoon if Herndon were to be believed; and certainly reminiscent of her father, who was constantly alert to his own advancement. Yet Hay liked the way that Kate would often ask him a direct question of the sort that no lady would but a politician might.

Hay now sat beside her, aware that the saffron light of the setting sun had turned each to gold. In the front parlor, the bebuttoned servant was lighting candles. "We must go riding Sunday," said Hay; he could feel the heat of her forearm on his left hand which now clutched, modestly, his right elbow.

"Oh, Atalanta's being shoed then, poor beast!" Kate looked at him and her ordinarily golden-hazel eyes were now like Spanish doubloons in the spectacular last light of day. "But during the week, if I haven't gone North . . ." As she raised her arm to indicate that Garfield should join them, the smooth skin touched Hay's finger for an instant and he felt an electrical shock to his system.

Garfield, all gold to begin with, looked somewhat brazen in the light. Hay found him amiable enough; but then Hay was also somewhat jealous. Of course, Garfield was older than he—thirty, at least; and married. But Garfield, who had been a state legislator, was now a distinguished general; and the President's second secretary felt very small in that glittering presence. Worse, Garfield possessed a most good-humored if highly generalized charm. "I know your uncle," he said to Hay's surprise. "I saw him last in Columbus, where we all used to live." He turned to Kate, who smiled at him as if, thought Hay, she were in love, always a sign, he now knew, that she was not. Kate Chase loved only her father; and, perhaps, herself.

"Some of us lived there more happily than others," she said. Kate turned to Hay. "If Atalanta's shoed in time, we could go riding in the afternoon."

"I'm always at your disposal," said Hay.

"The one man who is not." Garfield was amiable. "You keep late hours at the White House. I've seen your lights on at midnight—and after."

"The confusion never stops," said Hay, affecting a weariness that he only occasionally felt.

"How is Mrs. Lincoln?" asked Kate, with a worried frown that Hay had come to know meant that she was up to mischief.

"She's at the Soldiers' Home now, she and the boy."

"Still in deep mourning, they say." Garfield seemed genuinely sad.

"She speaks to the child." Kate's frown did not alter. "I know. I've met Mrs. Laury, the medium. Apparently, the boy is happy on the other side."

Garfield responded in Greek. The voice was musical; and the accent precise. But then he had been a professor of Greek and Latin literature before he went into politics.

"What is that?" asked Kate, not as "finished by school" as Hay had supposed.

"It is Achilles in the underworld," said Hay. "He is telling Odysseus he would rather be a serf among the living than king of all the dead."

"What paragons I know!" Kate was enchanted; and, thus, enchanting. But the golden evening light had gone. The candles were now lit. Through the windows fireflies flashed in the backyard. William Sanford presented himself to Kate, who smiled, and said, "We were speaking Greek, Captain Sanford."

"Well," said the rich young man, "that's Greek to me."

"Oh, three paragons!" Kate exclaimed; then leapt to her feet. "It is General Pope!" The hero of the hour was indeed in her parlor; but not to see her. Plainly a busy and preoccupied man, he greeted the guests en masse and disappeared into Chase's study. As the door closed, Garfield said, "There's the key to the lock. He is our best general—in the West, at least," he added with a politician's care.

"Better than Grant?" asked Hay, genuinely curious. He could not make up his mind which set of generals was worse—the West Pointers who had spent their careers making money in the railroad business or the politicians on horseback, looking for renown. Although Grant was a West Pointer, he had gone into the saddlery business, where he had attractively failed.

"He's a better all-round general than Grant. But Grant is best in the field. I know you disapprove, Miss Kate, of how he never lets up but that's the way it's done. The two sides lost more men at Shiloh than were ever before lost in a single day of modern warfare. That was because Grant would not retreat, even though the rebels had the advantage."

In Chase's study, Pope was saying the opposite. "Grant is hopeless. When not drunk, he is in a sort of stupor. At Shiloh, he was surprised by the enemy. He was unprepared. He barely survived. He is no general. But then McClellan's worse."

Chase nodded. "I have come to the conclusion, General—and this is just between the two of us—that McClellan has no intention of harming the South in any way. If possible, he would like them back in the Union by 'sixty-four, so that he could then get their votes as the Democratic candidate."

Pope combed his thick black beard with thick red fingers. "I would not be surprised if you are right. Certainly, he has acted curiously. Imagine being within six miles of Richmond, and not taking the city. I don't think he wants to fight at all, and your reason is the best I've heard—cowardice to one side. But *I* mean to fight. I've told the troops not to worry about lines of escape and all the rest of it. We shall see only *their* backs, I promise you, I said." Pope strode up and down the study, and Chase felt confidence at last—or at least for the first time since McDowell. He thanked Heaven yet again that the general who would defeat the South was a dedicated abolitionist; and partisan to him.

Pope wanted to know exactly where Lincoln stood on the matter of abolition. "I shall be inheriting thousands of black souls as I lead the Army of Virginia into Virginia. What am I to do with them?"

For an instant, Chase was tempted to tell him what he had sworn not to tell—about the Emancipation Proclamation. But that weak instant passed. "I would," said Chase, voice very low, "in the wake of victories—and I expect *you* to take Richmond with or without McClellan's aid—*I* would free the slaves on my own initiative and include them, if possible, in your army, even arm them if you choose. That is what *I* would do, of course. I concede that. It is not what Mr. Seward would do."

"Which means the President?"

"Which means the President." Chase nodded. The seed had now been planted. He prayed that it would take proper root and flourish. Lincoln's Emancipation Proclamation would then be a legislative afterthought to Pope's bold freeing of the slaves.

"I understand you, Mr. Chase."

"I think we understand each other, and what Heaven commands us to do. In my small way, I know what it is like to conquer an enemy city—as I did at Norfolk—and to see the black slaves all around me, beseeching me to strike their chains. But I had not the authority that day. You will. Your victories in the field will be your orders."

"I shall not disappoint you, Mr. Chase." Pope took Chase's hand in both of his. They were allies, committed to Heaven's work.

During their solemn pledge, William Sanford proposed to Kate in the front parlor. "I plan to leave the army the first of the year. We could go to France. There is a house there I've had my eye on since before the war. At St. Cloud, near Paris. We could have a wonderful life. I'd study music. You would be at court, if you wanted that."

Kate's eyes glowed in the candlelight. "You are good to ask me, Mr. Sanford. I am honored. I am touched. If there was no war, and if my father were not so deeply involved in public affairs, I cannot think of a happier life . . ."

"It is Governor Sprague, isn't it?" Sanford scowled; the rosy lips pouted.

"Oh, it's no one, I promise you, but my father and me," said Kate with, for once, perfect candor. Then General Pope swept through the room; and out into the night, and his destiny.

Hay was now at Kate's side. He had a fair notion of Sanford's conversation. The younger set in Washington was much aware of Sanford's passion for Kate. Some thought she should marry him; and never again worry about money for herself or her father. Others thought that she should settle for Sprague and *his* money, and remain with her father. Hay thought that she would make *him* an admirable consort, even though there was no money at all between them, and he was not certain that he had the knack of making it. "How do you like your new commander, Captain Sanford?" Hay asked Sanford the question but looked at Kate, who was staring, idly, at Garfield.

"General McDowell likes him well enough," said Sanford, who was still on McDowell's staff. "But General Frémont won't serve under an officer he outranks. So Frémont has quit."

"That's a bit of luck," said Hay, aware of his tactlessness; after all, the President had done everything in his power to keep content the absolutely incompetent but highly popular Frémont, who had been the first Republican candidate for president; thus, outranking, in a sense, the second candidate, Lincoln.

"That's what General McDowell thinks." Sanford continued to stare at Kate, who looked more than usually lovely and untouchable—but not untouching, for Hay could still feel on the back of his hand the smooth skin of her arm.

"What is the plan?" asked Kate. "Or is that secret?"

"We know very little," said Sanford, glancing at Hay. "The Army of Virginia will probably join up with the Army of the Potomac and together they'll occupy Richmond."

"I'm sure," said Kate, "that that is *not* what will happen. By design or plain incompetence something else is bound to take place, and the enemy already knows everything."

Mary sat at a round mahogany table. Across from her was the Roman emperor Constantine, in the plump form of Mrs. Laury of Georgetown. Constantine was Mrs. Laury's personal friend in the world of the dead, and if not otherwise engaged, he was wonderfully cooperative in delivering and transmitting messages between the world of light where he existed and that world of darkness and pain where the living are. "I saw Willie only this morning," said Constantine, whose deep voice was entirely different from Mrs. Laury's ordinary fluting tones. "He wants to know about his pony, and has Tad learned to ride it yet?"

"Oh, yes! Tad needs help, of course. But tell him the pony's fine, and every day Tad rides, with Mr. Watt next to him, to keep him from falling off. Did you ask Willie if he has seen little Eddie?"

Mrs. Laury-Constantine nodded gravely. By the light of the single candle on the table, Mrs. Laury looked very like a Roman emperor ought to look if he happened to be an elderly woman with dyed auburn hair. "At first they did not know each other. How could they? But in the world of light all things are clear at last and, suddenly, the two boys knew each other, and they were so excited and thrilled . . . Oh!" Mrs. Laury-Constantine's voice dropped to an even lower register. "There is danger."

"What danger?" Mary shuddered. "Danger to whom?"

"To the President. There is a dark cloud over him. A deep darkness. Danger."

As the two women sat in the small parlor of the stone house next to the Soldiers' Home, Lincoln was riding alone, toward the Soldiers' Home. In the bright moonlight, he was a perfect target, while Seventh Street was nothing more than a deserted country lane at this hour. As the horse—called Old Abe, too—trotted past a grove of willow trees, the wind suddenly stirred the moonlight branches. Menacing shadows danced. The horse shied. As Lincoln leaned forward to soothe the skittish horse, a shot rang out. Lincoln's hat was blown from his head. Reflexively, he lay forward atop the horse; and spurred him into a rolling canter. There was no second shot.

Both horse and Lincoln were breathing hard when they arrived at the stone cottage. The sergeant on duty helped the President dismount. "You've had a mighty good run, sir," said the man, somewhat disapprovingly: the horse's flanks were steaming in the moonlight.

"Yes. You'd better walk Old Abe around a bit, to cool him down." The President entered the cottage.

"Father!" Mary greeted him at the door to the parlor. "Where's your hat?"

"I seem to have mislaid it. Is that Mrs. Laury?"

"Yes. Come in. Sit down. Talk to her. Though it's actually the Emperor Constantine *I've* been talking to. He's been with Willie, who's met Eddie at last."

"Well, that must be nice for the codgers." Lincoln sat at the table.

"Oh!" Mary frowned. "He says that there's some sort of danger, involving you. There's a dark cloud over you. Isn't that right, Constantine?"

Mrs. Laury-Constantine nodded gravely. "There is a plot to take your life, Mr. President."

"I'm sure that there are quite a few, Emperor. I read about them every day in the papers. People like such sensations. But then you know how it is—or was, back in your day, too."

"Father! Don't joke. The Emperor has some very good advice, too. Don't you, sir?"

Mrs. Laury-Constantine spoke in a stern voice. "You must replace a general who will not fight. You must replace a member of the Cabinet who would be president. You must beware of a small man with a large nose . . ."

"Well, Mr. Chase is a large man with a small nose, so that rules him out . . ." Lincoln began.

But Mary stopped him, irritably. "It's Seward. Who else? And don't joke about these things. The Emperor Constantine thinks that Mr. Sumner would be a splendid secretary of state, and so do I."

"What about Mrs. Laury?"

"Mrs. Laury is in a trance, and she will remember nothing of what's been said between Constantine and us."

Ward Lamon was at the door to the parlor, holding the President's top hat. "Mr. President, I found your hat."

"Oh, good. Excuse me, Emperor." Lincoln joined Lamon in the entrance hall. "That hat fell off in the road, when the horse shied."

"No, sir," said Lamon, grimly. "It didn't fall off." Lamon held up the hat. From left side to right side, three inches above the brim, a bullet had made its way. "That bullet just barely missed you."

"Take the hat away, Ward," said Lincoln in a low voice. "Show it to no one. Tell no one."

"On one condition, sir. That you will never again ride out here, or anywhere else, without guards."

Lincoln nodded, gloomily. "I see now that I'll have to."

"Pinkerton says there are at least three plots against you."

"If Pinkerton says there are three that means one and a half. He doubles the enemy's numbers from habit." Lincoln put his forefinger through the bullet hole. "From the size of the hole, I'd say that's from one of our new rifles. The problem, Ward, is not my being killed. If that happens that happens and there's no way to stop it. I am a fatalist in this matter. But there is one recurring plot that I don't much care for, and that is being captured by the rebels and held for ranson."

"All the more reason for guards at all times, especially when people know in advance where you're going to be going."

Lincoln nodded. "I agree. If I could prevent the government from paying a ransom for me, I would. But I know what sentiment is at such times. They would go and pay no matter what *I* might want."

"How much, do you think, the rebels would ask for you?"

Lincoln smiled. "It's not how much, Ward. It's how many. They want their men back. The ones that we're holding prisoner. Sooner or later, they'll run out of men. Something we never will; and that's how we'll win. Well, to exchange one secondhand president for a hundred thousand soldiers, now that would be very tempting to Jeff Davis, or whoever decides such things at Richmond." Lincoln gave the hat to Lamon. "Funny how Old Abe—the horse, not me—knew that there was a rifle, trained on us. If he hadn't shied when he did . . ."

A platform had been built near the ruins of a farmhouse, and here the President took the salute of the troops. When they were again in formation, he made them a graceful little speech, something he always had difficulty in doing impromptu. Washburne, who was seated next to the President, noticed that Lincoln's hands trembled as he spoke. But the voice itself was as clear and firm as a tenor trumpet, each syllable as clearly pronounced as if it were chiselled on stone. Lincoln's best speeches were those that he had himself written and rewritten; sometimes he took weeks over a single paragraph. "My mind does not work quickly," he used to say to Washburne. Certainly, he had taken his time on the speeches that he had made in the course of the debates with Douglas. Those speeches were often learned by heart; certainly, each argument had been worked out in precise detail. At such times, Lincoln did seem to Washburne like a rail-splitter. The ax was his logic, going methodically and rhythmically to work on the subject's wood. "But I never go to make a speech that I wish it wasn't over," he had said to Washburne on more than one occasion. "Also, it is an agony for someone my height to stand by a table that comes up to my knee, trying to read a speech through glasses that are never much help, by the light of a candle that shines straight up into your eyes." Lincoln would shake his head comically. "It was no accident that the Little Giant was a better orator than me. He was built a lot closer to the folks—not to mention his text."

But Lincoln's words now flowed effortlessly in the bright October light. He paid homage to the bravery of the troops; and to the loyalty of the people of Frederick—a mild insincerity, Washburne thought, since many of the town's inhabitants had been delighted to welcome the Confederate army. As an election was approaching, Lincoln pointed out that it was not proper for him in his position to make a serious speech. But he felt obliged to say how proud he was of the army—there was no mention of its commander—and of the good citizens of Frederick "for their devotion to this glorious cause; and I say this with no malice in my heart for those who have done otherwise."

To three cheers from the army, the President and his suite departed for the next army corps. Washburne again rode beside Lincoln, who was relieved the speech was done. "After all, I don't want to appear to be electioneering."

"But you are. We all are now."

Lincoln frowned. "We don't have much choice. I'd hoped McClellan would do the campaigning for us. I'd hoped that between now and the election, he'd move against Lee. But he won't."

"He said he would."

"He won't. When I get back, I shall order him, officially, to cross the Potomac and give battle to the enemy."

"Then when he doesn't?"

Lincoln simply shook his head.

"Do we let the soldiers vote?" Congress had been arguing this matter all session. Republicans were eager that Republican soldiers vote; and Democrats were eager that Democratic soldiers vote. But the logistics of getting the men home was complex, to say the least, while many states refused to allow the soldiers to vote in the field.

"I don't see just what we can do." Lincoln was genuinely puzzled. "The only fair thing would be to send all the troops home. But then what happens to the war? Send the ones that we know are for us?" He shook his head; then he added, with a smile, "I will say that Mr. Stanton, although an ex-Democrat, is a dynamo for our cause. A week before the election, he's going to release just about everybody he and Seward and the generals have locked up."

"Just in time for them to vote Democratic?"

"Just in time to bring Horace Greeley into line. I'm afraid we're going to get a fair whipping in the press and at the polls, but Stanton says not to worry because of the border-states. He says that the army in those states will do what has to be done to get us the votes we need."

"By shooting all the Democrats?"

Lincoln chuckled. "Something along those lines. Stanton is a very determined man." The President reined in his horse. They were now opposite a large farmhouse on whose porch a dozen wounded men lay on pallets. Lincoln turned to his colonel-escort. "What's this, Colonel?"

"Confederate prisoners, sir. Wounded at Sharpsburg. We'll be sending them on to Washington once we've finished shipping our own wounded back."

"I think I'd like to take a look at these boys," said Lincoln. "And I'm sure that they'd like to take a look at me."

"No sir!" Lamon was firm.

"Yes, Ward." Lincoln was firmer. "You stand outside, with Mr. Pinkerton, while Mr. Washburne and I, two harmless Illinois politicians, pay these Southern boys a call."

Lamon cursed not entirely under his breath; but did as he was ordered. The colonel led Lincoln and Washburne up the steps and into the house, which consisted, at this level, of a single large room lined on both sides with cots. At least a hundred men and boys lay on the cots, some missing arms or legs or both. Some were dying; others were able to limp about. The smell of flesh corrupting was overpowering; and Washburne tried not to breathe. But Lincoln was oblivious of everything except the young men who were now aware that a stranger was in their midst. The low hum of talk suddenly ceased; and the only sound in the room was the moaning of the unconscious.

When the colonel started to call the men to attention, the President stopped him with a gesture. Then Lincoln walked the length of the room, very slowly, looking to left and right, with his dreamy smile. At the end of the room, he turned and faced the wounded men; then, slowly, he removed his hat. All eyes that could see now saw him, and recognized him.

When Lincoln spoke, the famous trumpet-voice was muted; even intimate. "I am Abraham Lincoln." There was a long collective sigh of wonder and of tension and of . . . ? Washburne had never heard a sound quite like it. "I know that you have fought gallantly for what you believe in, and for that I honor you, and for your wounds so honorably gained. I feel no anger in my heart toward you; and trust you feel none for me. That is why I am here. That is why I am willing to take the hand, in friendship, of any man among you."

The same long sigh, like a rising wind, began; and still no one spoke. Then a man on crutches approached the President and, in perfect silence, shook his hand. Others came forward, one by one; and each took Lincoln's hand; and to each he murmured something that the man alone could hear.

At the end, as Lincoln made his way between the beds, stopping to talk to those who could not move, half of the men were in tears, as was Washburne himself.

In the last bed by the door, a young officer turned his back on the President, who touched his shoulder, and murmured, "My son, we shall all be the same at the end." Then the President was gone.

The South's treasure was awake most of that night. He lay on the lounge in his office and received a series of callers. Hay was present when, toward midnight, Governor Curtin of Pennsylvania appeared. Curtin had come straight from Fredericksburg. Lincoln rose to greet him. Hay had never seen the Ancient so ancient and fragile and distraught.

As the excited Curtin paced the room, Lincoln half stood and half lay against the mantelpiece. Hay noted that in this position Lincoln's head and the portrait of Andrew Jackson were side by side; and they looked alike now—Old Abe every bit as old as Old Hickory.

"I saw our men torn to pieces before my eyes. Yet they kept on advancing. I've never seen such bravery. Or such butchery."

"I know. I know." Lincoln rubbed his eyes from weariness. "What are the casualties, thus far?"

Curtin removed a sheet of paper from his pocket. "I was given this by General Burnside's adjutant. These are the estimated losses for each of the grand divisions. General Sumner's. About five hundred men killed. About five thousand wounded . . ."

"Dear God! That is only *one* division?" Lincoln was now the color of the dead fire at his back.

"Some eight hundred missing." Curtin continued, "General Hooker's division. There are more than three hundred dead. And three thousand wounded. And eight hundred missing."

"This is too much, Governor. Far too much. The country cannot endure these losses. I cannot endure them. Oh, this was madness!" Lincoln struck the mantelpiece with his fist. "To attack." He struck it again. "In winter." And again. "Across a river. With the entire rebel army entrenched and waiting. It was a trap." Lincoln turned from the fireplace. "I see it all now. I did not see it then. Burnside insisted. You understand? So Halleck and Stanton and I gave way. You must give way to a general who fights . . ."

"Fights, sir, but does not think. The man is incompetent. Worse, he knows that he has not the competence to command a great army. He asked you, he told me himself, not to appoint him."

Lincoln was now walking about the room as if in search of some hitherto unseen door through which he might escape. Hay recalled Herndon's story of the time that Lincoln had been mad. Was there to be a repetition?

As Lincoln moved frantically along the wall, feeling his way like a blind man, Curtin continued his account of the dead and the wounded and the missing. Hay tried to divert him, with a gesture of "no." But Curtin ignored him. He too seemed to be on the verge of madness. "And so this defeat cost us, finally, sir, in dead and wounded and missing, roughly fifteen thousand men. I saw the wounded from one of our Pennsylvania regiments. I saw young boys of fifteen with their stomachs hanging out of them. I saw . . ."

"*You* saw, sir?" Lincoln opened and then shut the door to the Reception Room with a crash. "Think what *I* see! Think how I must watch as all this blood fills up this room and now is near to drowning me. You have no responsibility, sir, no oath registered in Heaven. Well, I do!" Lincoln's voice had gone so high that it broke on the word "do." Hay leapt to his feet. "Mr. President," he said in what he meant to be a soothing voice; but his own voice broke with emotion. Dumbly, the three men stood in a circle at the room's center.

Lincoln glared for a long moment at Curtin, who took a step backward, as if alarmed by what he saw in the President's eyes. "I am sorry, sir. To distress you like this. I only wanted to answer your question. I am overwrought, I fear. Because of what I saw. Certainly I would give anything to deliver you of this terrible war."

"Me?" Lincoln shook his head like a man who has suddenly awakened from a bad dream. "Oh, Governor, I don't matter. I am done for anyway. I was chosen to do a certain work, and I must do it, and then go. But I do need help. There's no doubt of that." The Ancient's face lightened; as did his mood. Hay saw that he was about to tell a story; and was deeply relieved. "This reminds me, Governor, of an old farmer out in Illinois, who had two mischievous boys called James and John. Or maybe John and James. Anyway, the farmer bought a mean-tempered prize hog, and penned him up, and told the boys they were to stay clear of the pen. Naturally, James let the hog out of his pen the next day and the hog went for the seat of James's trousers, and the only way the boy could save himself was by holding onto the hog's tail. So they went round and round a tree a number of times until the boy's courage began to fail, and he shouted to his brother, 'Come here quick and help me *let this hog go.*' " Lincoln chuckled. "Well, Governor, that is exactly my case. I wish someone would help me let this hog go." On that amiable and characteristic note, Lincoln bade Curtin, "Good-night."

After the governor had gone, Lincoln stood staring into the remains of the fire.

"Shall I have them make a new fire?" asked Hay.

"No, John. You go to bed now. Let Edward guard the fort. All is well now. That is, all *will* be well. Because, you see, it is like this. Should we lose the same number of men tomorrow as today, and they the same. And we the same the day after, and they the same. And so on, day after day after day, we shall have won. For we have more lives to give than they do, and we shall keep on giving these lives of ours until—yes, *all* of them, if need be—are dead."

Before Hay went to his room, he crossed into the living quarters, where Lamon sat at the door to the President's bedroom, armed to the teeth, and sound asleep. "Mr. Lamon," Hay whispered. Lamon raised first his derringer; then his eyelids. "Tell Mrs. Lincoln to get the President to bed. He's about at the end of his rope."

Lamon nodded. He rapped three times on the bedroom door. From within Madam's wide-awake voice sounded. "Yes, Mr. Lamon?"

"We think you should get the President to his bed."

"Yes," said the voice. Hay went into his own room, where Nicolay snored softly.

Mary opened the door to the President's office. Lincoln was stretched out on the lounge, reading a book. "Why, Mother, what are you doing up so late?"

From the sound of her husband's voice, she could tell that he was indeed at the edge of his strength. "You come to bed, Father. It's no good staying up all night."

"But they keep coming to me from Fredericksburg; and I must listen to them all."

"No, Father, you must not listen to them all. You've listened to too many, as it is. The battle is over. There is no more news tonight. Come on."

Lincoln got to his feet. He put down the book. "It is by Artemus Ward," he said. "Powerful funny."

"I know, Father." She took his arm; and led him into the dimly let hallway. Edward was at his desk. "You go home, Edward," said Mary.

"Yes," said Lincoln. "We're shutting up shop for the night."

"Good-night, Mr. President."

As Lincoln and Mary passed the guard on duty, he saluted the President and said, "Good-night, sir. Sleep well."

"Thank you. Thank you, my boy."

But once husband and wife were in their bedroom, Lincoln shook his head and said, "I'm better off awake tonight."

"Don't be foolish! You can hardly keep your eyes open, you are so tired."

"True. But I don't dare sleep."

"Are your dreams so bad?"

"Yes, Mother. They are so bad."

But, in the end, Lincoln slept; and it was Mary who stayed awake the night to comfort him, if need be. She knew the horror of dreams.

Hay sat with the Tycoon in the President's Office, waiting for Seward to usher in the latest delegation from New York. Lincoln sat on the window-sill, gold glasses on the end of his nose; and read from Artemus Ward: " 'Any gentleman living in Ireland who was never in this country, is not liable to the draft, nor are our forefathers.' " Lincoln chuckled, and looked at Hay over his glasses."That has the statesman's ring to it." Then he read on. " 'The term of enlistment is for three years, but any man who may have been drafted in two places has a right to go for six years. The only sons of a poor widow, whose husband is in California, are not exempt, but a man who owns stock in the Vermont Central Railway is.' " Lincoln threw back his head, and roared with laughter. Hay marvelled at the Tycoon's power of recovery. Whatever fire that kept this extraordinary engine going was plainly unquenchable if fuelled by laughter. " 'So also are incessant lunatics, habitual lecturers, persons born with wooden legs and false teeth, blind men, and people who deliberately voted for John Tyler.' " Hay and Lincoln were now both laughing, uncontrollably, as Edward opened the door and announced, solemnly, "The Secretary of State, Senator Morgan and Mr. Samuel J. Tilden of New York."

Seward had heard the laughter; saw the copy of Artemus Ward. "I shall want that next," he said to the President.

"It is a tonic, let me tell you. President Tyler died, didn't he?"

"A year ago January, in Richmond. He'd just been elected to the rebel congress. Mr. President, allow me to present Senator Morgan, whom you know, and Mr. Tilden, whom you don't."

Lincoln shook hands with each man; and to Tilden, a small, spare, cleanshaven man of about fifty, he said, "You were an associate of Martin Van Buren . . ."

"*He* died a year ago this month," interjected Seward, settling into his usual place at table.

"I know that, Governor." Lincoln turned to Tilden. "You worked with Mr. Van Buren?"

"I helped him as best I could during his presidency. I wrote many briefs for him." Tilden stifled a belch. Senator Morgan had assured Seward that although Mr. Tilden's acute and chronic dyspepsia had ruled him out as a candidate for office it did not prevent him from being an adroit manipulator behind the scenes.

"Well, I did not support Van Buren in 'forty-eight but he was plainly the best of the lot, as it turned out. And once upon a time he had favored Negro suffrage, too." Lincoln chuckled. "When I read that out to Judge Douglas, a Van Buren man through and through, I thought he'd have a fit.

'Where did he say that?' he asked in front of this huge crowd. So I gave him the book, open to the passage, and the Judge said, 'I want nothing to do with that damned book,' and threw it on the ground."

Seward allowed Lincoln a few more reminiscences; then he brought up the subject of the meeting. "We were able, Archbishop Hughes and I, to turn off the mob on the third day." Seward felt that he deserved full credit for having so bombarded the archbishop with telegrams that His Eminence had been obliged to summon the faithful to his house on Madison Avenue, where he had scolded and soothed a crowd of some five thousand men, mostly Irish. As a result, the city was tranquil—for the present.

"The danger now, Mr. President," said Senator Morgan, "is the reopening of the draft offices. Governor Seymour has done what he could to placate the immigrants, but they are in a devilish mood. He would like a clear statement from you that the draft will at least be postponed in the city."

"He will never get that, Senator. If you postpone the draft in one state, you will give other states the notion that they, too, can have postponements."

"But you do realize, sir, that the city will explode again if you try to impose conscription." Tilden watched Lincoln's face intently: one lawyer testing another.

"*I* do not impose conscription, Mr. Tilden. Congress does. The Conscription Act was much debated and thought out. It is not perfect. The Constitution is not perfect either. But at least the Conscription Act was passed almost unanimously. It is the law; and I must execute it." Seward thought that Lincoln must, presently and characteristically, soften his line. But, to Seward's surprise, Lincoln grew even more hard and legalistic. "To that end, ten thousand infantrymen are on their way to the city. Also, several artillery batteries."

"You will place the city under martial law?" Tilden probed.

"In effect, Mr. Tilden, the whole Union is under a kind of martial law; as it is wartime. Now I know that you and Governor Seymour and a number of other Democrats think that we have torn up the Constitution down here. But we are simply trying to salvage it, and the nation." To Seward's relief, Lincoln finally struck the conciliatory note. "Tell the governor that the principle to which I propose adhering is to proceed with the draft while, at the same time, applying"—Lincoln paused for a strong word; found one that Seward thought too strong—"*infallible* means to avoid any great wrongs."

"This," said Tilden, eyeing the bait, "is to be interpreted as giving a certain leeway to New York's conduct of the draft?"

"*I* did not say that. But I cannot control every interpretation put on my words."

"Yes," said Tilden, nodding. Seward was pleased. The two distinguished lawyers had understood each other.

But Senator Morgan had not got the point. "What do we say when demagogues cry out against the three-hundred-dollar exemption? 'Rich man's money against the poor man's blood,' they say. You know there is a lot of communist sentiment in the city; and all this just heats it up."

"To have an army, you must first have men," Lincoln was reasonable. "Ideally, they should be volunteers. Otherwise, we must have conscription. After all, other countries—republics as well as monarchies—have it. The exemption seems to me a fair enough thing. At least it brings money to the Treasury, which helps the war."

Senator Morgan was not pleased. "Why can't you wait until the Supreme Court has determined whether or not the Conscription Act is Constitutional?"

"Because I don't have the time, Senator. The war grows bloodier with each day. The rebels are conscripting every male who can walk; and they send them off to be slaughtered like cattle. Are we so degenerate that we cannot, with our greater numbers, raise an adequate army through a lawful draft?"

"Then you refuse, sir, to wait for the Supreme Court to rule?" Morgan was now very tense.

Seward looked at Lincoln, who, for no perceptible reason, was smiling. "Sir, I will not wait upon anyone. The time for argument is past. If this is not agreeable to you, then we shall just have to see who is the stronger."

Seward felt an involuntary shudder in his limbs. He was also ravished by the irony of the moment. For nearly three years, a thousand voices, including his own, had called for a Cromwell, a dictator, a despot; and in all that time, no one had suspected that there had been, from the beginning, a single-minded dictator in the White House, a Lord Protector of the Union by whose will alone the war had been prosecuted. For the first time, Seward understood the nature of Lincoln's political genius. He had been able to make himself absolute dictator without ever letting anyone suspect that he was anything more than a joking, timid backwoods lawyer, given to fits of humility in the presence of all the strutting military and political peacocks that flocked about him.

The two New Yorkers also appeared to have some inkling of who the man was that they were dealing with; or being dealt by. Senator Morgan fell silent, while Mr. Tilden belched softly. The President then read a page or two from Artemus Ward, lightening the mood.

As the meeting ended Tilden looked up at Lincoln and said, "Mr. Van Buren had the greatest respect for your tenacity and your general judgment in this war."

Lincoln could not resist the obvious joke. "My 'general' judgment has been on the whole pretty bad. But I am tenacious all right. I am glad he appreciated that."

"He was also much amused," said Tilden, ignoring the joke, "when he recollected an adjective you once used to describe *his* presidency."

Lincoln frowned. "What was that?"

" 'Monarchial,' Mr. President. He was much tickled by the word, as coming from you. In fact, at the end, Mr. Van Buren felt that you were bent on outdoing him."

Lincoln laughed, showing all his white teeth. "Well, if I am monarchial, it is the times that shoved the crown on my head. Anyway, when the war is won, I'll lose my crown fast enough, and probably my head, too. And, frankly, between us, I am heartily sick of both."

How *does* such a sovereign lay down his scepter? Seward wondered, as he walked down the main stairs of the Mansion, Senator Morgan to his left and Mr. Tilden to his right.

"Mr. Lincoln seems," said Tilden, thoughtfully, "a man of good will."

"Oh, Mr. Tilden!" Seward exclaimed, "I can testify to that! Mr. Lincoln's will is very good indeed. In fact, his will is all that we have here."

At the last moment, Madam decided that she could not leave Tad, who was still sick, while Stanton said that he must stay at the War Department in order to follow Grant's attack on Chattanooga. So, in the end, Seward and Blair and Usher were the only members of the Cabinet to accompany the President. The ubiquitous Lamon was, as always, at Lincoln's side, while, for once, Nicolay decided that he, too, would like an outing; so both secretaries attended the President at Gettysburg.

The morning of November 19, 1863, was warm and still. Indian summer had set in. The celebrated old orator Edward Everett had already sent the President a printed copy of his speech. "My God, John!" Lincoln had said, as he sat in the special railroad car. "He will speak for two hours." Lincoln had handed the thick pamphlet to Hay; and taken off his glasses.

"I suppose that is what he's always expected to do." Hay had decided not to read what he would be obliged to hear.

"A splendid old man." Lincoln had held in one hand a single sheet of White House notepaper on which he had written half of what would be, he said, "a short, short, short speech," dedicating the cemetery. "You know, I have heard of Everett all my life, and he has always been famous, and yet I never could find out why."

"Our greatest orator?"

"Greater than Clay or Webster?" Lincoln had smiled. "No, he is just famous, that's all. There are people like that in public life. They are there, and no one ever really knows why."

*They* were all there the next morning on Cemetery Hill. There were seven governors, among them Seymour and Curtin; many diplomats and members of Congress. A platform had been erected, with a tall flagpole next to it. In the warm stillness, the flag hung listlessly. A military band played. A crowd of some thirty thousand people had already gathered when, finally, at ten o'clock, the presidential procession came into view, and the military band struck up "Hail to the Chief."

Lincoln rode at the head of the ragged column of notables. He sat very straight on a sorrel horse too small for him. He was like some huge effigy, thought Hay, who rode with Nico behind him. It was odd that the biggest man in the country should also be among the very biggest—or at least tallest—of men. Seward looked sublimely sloppy at the Tycoon's side. Trousers pulled up to reveal thick, wrinkled gray stockings, the premier was blithely indifferent to how he or anyone else looked.

Earlier that morning, Nico had gone to the house where the President had spent the night; and he had stayed alone with the Tycoon for an hour. "What news?" asked Hay. The procession was now stopped by crowds singing, "We are coming, Father Abraham." Hay could see Lamon furiously shouting orders; but no one listened. The people wanted to see and touch the President.

"Tad is improved," said Nico.

"That is earth-shaking. What else?"

"A battle has begun at Chattanooga. Grant is attacking. Burnside is safe at Knoxville; he does not attack."

"How is the Tycoon?"

"He just finished rewording the speech an hour ago. He complains of dizziness."

Alarmed, Hay turned to Nico. "Oh, God! You know, in the train, he told me that he felt weak."

Nico nodded. "There's something wrong. I don't know what."

But if there was something wrong with the Ancient, there was nothing wrong with the Tycoon, who sat dutifully through Edward Everett's extended version of Pericles's commemoration of the Athenian dead. But where Pericles had been very much to the Attic point, Everett was to a myriad of New England points.

As the beautiful voice of Everett went on and on, Hay looked out over the battlefield. Trees had been smashed into matchwood by crossfire, while artillery shells had plowed up the muddy ground. Here and there, dead horses lay unburied; as they were not yet turned to neat bone, the smell of decomposing flesh intermingled with the odor of the crowd was mildly sickening. Now, in the noonday sun of an airless sort of day, Hay began to sweat.

When Everett sat down, Lincoln pulled out his sheet of paper; and put on his glasses. But there was a musical interval to be endured; and so he put away the paper. The Baltimore Glee Club intoned a hymn especially written for the occasion. A warm breeze started up, and the American flag began to snap like a whip cracking. Opposite the speaker's platform, a photographer had built a small platform so that his camera would be trained straight on the President when he spoke. He was constantly fiddling with his paraphernalia; raising and lowering the cloth hood at the back, and dusting his glass plates.

Finally, there was silence. Then Lamon stood up and bellowed, "The President of the United States!"

Lincoln rose, paper in hand; glasses perched on his nose. He was, Hay noted, a ghastly color, but the hand that held the paper did not tremble, always the orator's fear. There was a moment of warm—if slightly exhausted by Everett—applause.

Then the trumpet-voice sounded across the field of Gettysburg, and thirty thousand people fell silent. While Everett's voice had been like some deep rich cello, Lincoln's voice was like the sound that accompanies a sudden crack of summer lightning. "Fourscore and seven years ago," he lunged straight into his subject, "our fathers brought forth upon this continent a new nation, conceived in liberty and dedicated to the proposition that all men are created equal."

That will please the radicals, thought Hay. Then he noticed two odd things. First, the Tycoon did not consult the paper in his hand. He seemed, impossibly, to have memorized the text that had been put into final form only an hour or so earlier. Second, the Tycoon was speaking with unusual slowness. He seemed to be firing each word across the battlefield—a rifle salute to the dead?

"Now we are engaged in a great civil war, testing whether that nation—or any nation, so conceived and so dedicated—can long endure."

Seated just to the right of Lincoln, Seward began actually to listen. He had heard so many thousands of speeches in his life and he had himself given so many thousands that he could seldom actually listen to any speech, including his own. He, too, noted Lincoln's unusual deliberateness. It was as if the President was now trying to justify to the nation and to history and, thought Seward, to God, what he had done.

"We are met on a great battle-field of war. We are met to dedicate a portion of it as the final resting place of those who have given their lives that that nation might live." Seward nodded, inadvertently. Yes, that was the issue, the only issue. The preservation of this unique nation of states. Meanwhile, the photographer was trying to get the President in camera-frame.

"It is altogether fitting and proper that we should do this." Lincoln was now staring out over the heads of the crowd to a hill on which a row of wooden crosses had been newly set. For an instant, the hand that held the speech had dropped to his side. Then he recalled himself, and glanced at the text. "But, in a larger sense, we cannot dedicate, we cannot consecrate, we cannot hallow, this ground. The brave men, living and dead, who struggled here, have consecrated it, far above our power to add or to detract." Lincoln paused. There was a patter of applause; and then, to Seward's amazement, a shushing sound. The audience did not want to break into the music until it was done.

Seward studied the President with new—if entirely technical—interest. How had he accomplished this bit of magic with his singularly unmellifluous voice and harsh midwestern accent?

Lincoln was now staring off again, dreamily; this time at the sky. The photographer was under his hood, ready to take the picture.

"The world will very little note nor long remember what we say here; but it can never forget what they did here." The hand with the text again fell to his side. Hay knew that the Tycoon's eyes had turned inward. He was reading now from that marble tablet in his head; and he was reading a text written in nothing less than blood. "It is for us, the living, rather, to be dedicated, here, to the unfinished work that they have thus far so nobly carried on. It is rather for us to be here dedicated to the great task remaining before us; that from these honored dead we take increased devotion to that cause for which they here gave . . ." Hay was aware that the trumpet-voice had choked; and the gray eyes were suddenly aswim with uncharacteristic tears. But the Tycoon quickly recovered himself. ". . . the last full measure of devotion; that we here highly resolve," the voice was now that of a cavalry bugle calling for a charge, "that these dead shall not have died in vain; that the nation shall," he paused a moment then said, "under God . . ." Seward nodded—his advice had been taken.

Nico whispered to Hay, "He just added that. It's not in the text."

". . . have a new birth of freedom, and that government of the people, by the people, for the people, shall not perish from the earth."

Lincoln stood a moment, looking thoughtfully at the crowd, which stared back at him. Then he sat down. There was some applause. There was also laughter at the photographer, who was loudly cursing: he had failed to get any picture at all.

Lincoln turned to Seward and murmured, "Well, that fell on them like a wet blanket."

In the last of the presidential cars, Lincoln stood on the rear platform. He waved to the assembled crowd with his right hand while his left hand clutched Lamon's arm. Nicolay and Hay stood just back of the President. In the elaborately appointed car there were red-and-green plush armchairs with lace antimacassars, a long horsehair lounge and, everywhere, much inlaid wood and crystal and brass. A green Brussels carpet covered the floor, while the rows of brass spittoons shone like gold.

Politicians crowded the car, each eager to get the President's attention. Like a man in a dream, Lincoln had gone through a lunch with Governor Curtin, followed by a reception, followed by a sermon at the Presbyterian church. Then he had boarded the six-thirty evening cars to Washington. Now, as the train pulled out of the Gettysburg depot, Lincoln and Lamon stepped into the car. Sweat was streaming down Lincoln's pale yellow face; the eyes were out of focus; the wide mouth trembled. Lamon looked almost as ill, from fear. "Boys," he whispered to the secretaries, "get these people out of here. Don't let them near the President."

Lincoln said nothing. Propped up by Lamon, he stood swaying with the movement of the train. Nicolay led the disappointed Simon Cameron from the car while Hay asked Seward if he could persuade the others to go. The President had work to do, said Hay. There was news from Stanton. Seward got the point; had seen Lincoln's face. Exuberantly, he proposed to his fellow-politicians a banquet in the restaurant-car.

When the car was cleared, Lamon picked up Lincoln, who must have weighed no more than a farmer's scarecrow to such a powerful man, and carried the half-conscious President to the lounge, where he stretched him out. Nicolay fond a blanket and placed it over the shuddering form.

"What is it?" asked Nicolay.

Lamon shook his head. "I don't know. The fever, I think. Malaria?"

"But he has never had it," said Hay, a lifelong victim of that recurrent disease.

"Well, he can always catch it, I reckon," said Lamon.

Lincoln's eyes were now shut. Lamon found a towel, which he wetted from a water carafe; then he placed the towel on the Ancient's face. Suddenly, Lincoln said, in a clear voice, "Something has gone wrong." He took a deep breath and slept; or fainted.

On Tuesday, November 8, 1864, there was rain at Washington City. The President's Park was a sea of yellow mud. Only Welles and Bates had shown up that morning for a brief Cabinet meeting. Fessenden was in New York City, negotiating loans. Usher and Dennison were in their home states, voting. Seward was in New York, where he had been campaigning, while Stanton was in bed, seriously ill with the bilious fever. Mary had also taken to her bed with a headache that was midway between her usual nervous headache and The Headache. Tad, in the uniform of a colonel, had been sent off to Georgetown to the house of friends, whose sons were a part of his private regiment. Keckley hovered about the living quarters of the Mansion, ministering to Madam. The waiting room was empty. Edward was gone. Nicolay was in Illinois, getting out the vote. General Dix had helped him find a Negro to take his place in the army; there had been no newspaper scandal.

Only the Tycoon and Hay were stirring in the gloomy house on Election Day. There had been no visitors, save a Californian journalist that the Ancient had taken to; and Hay had taken against. What had to be done had been done, thought Hay, listing the states in a notebook. Later, as the returns came in, he would record the vote, district by district. He had put the states in alphabetical order, leaving out, he suddenly noticed, the eight-day-old state of Nevada.

Hay had already noted in his book the results of a preliminary election in October, involving Pennsylvania, Indiana and Ohio. The most doubtful of the three, Indiana, had been the most pro-Lincoln. Thanks to the confused efforts of Cameron and Stevens, Pennsylvania was a nearer thing. Fortunately, the Ohio and Pennsylvania soldiers in Washington's hospitals had been allowed to vote. The Ohians were ten to one for the Union. The Pennsylvanians less than three to one. The worst vote of all was from Carver Hospital, which Lincoln and Stanton passed each day. When the returns from Carver were read out, Stanton had fumed, and Lincoln had laughed. "That's pretty hard on us, Mars. They know us better than the others." Lincoln's own military guard voted for him, 63 to 11.

It was plain to everyone that the soldier vote would be the key to the election. In an extraordinary effort to secure every possible military vote, Stanton had so worn himself out that he was now seriously ill. Those states that allowed their men to vote in the field presented no difficulty. But Illinois—all-important to Lincoln—made no such allowance. Consequently, Grant's army was being stripped of every Illinois soldier; and the trains were crowded with furloughed soldiers, going home to vote for Lincoln.

Hay could not make up his mind why it was that these men were all so dedicated to Lincoln and to the Union. If he were a private in the field, he would be tempted to vote for McClellan and peace. In a curious way, Lincoln, privately, held the same view. He was certain that Illinois was lost, and he did not trust in the soldier vote, despite the evidence of October.

Just before seven in the evening, Hay had found Lincoln at his writing table. He, too, had made a list of the states in alphabetical order. He, too, had forgotten Nevada, which Hay pointed out to him. "It is only three electoral votes, but even so."

"Even so, I will need them," Lincoln agreed, writing in "Nevada." Then he showed Hay his prediction.

Hay whistled. "You think it is as close as that?"

Lincoln nodded. "In the electoral college the most I can get is 120 votes to 114 for McClellan."

Hay saw that, of the important states, Lincoln had given McClellan New York, Pennsylvania and Illinois. He gave himself New England and the West. "The the military vote will make all the difference," said Hay, handing back the paper.

"As they make the war," said the Ancient. "Well, let's go to the Telegraph Room, and learn our fate."

Together, with only Lamon in attendance, they crossed the dark empty street to the War Department. The steamy rain had let up for a moment and in the glare of gaslight the wet sidewalk shone like onyx, thought Hay, whose recent poems had been studded with precious and semiprecious stones. A guard in a rubber cloak saluted as the President bypassed the awkward turnstile which was supposed to control the traffic to and from Stanton's empire; and went instead to a side door, where a soaked and steaming sentinel saluted him; and opened the door.

A half-dozen orderlies came to brief attention. The Tycoon waved at them; and they went about their business. The business of one of them was to give the President the returns from Indianapolis—a majority of 8000 for Lincoln; since this was higher than that of the October vote, the Tycoon brightened. But he did not believe the next message from Forney. "You will carry Philadelphia by ten thousand votes." Lincoln shook his head. "I think he's a little on the excitable side."

They went upstairs to the Telegraph Room, where Lincoln made himself comfortable on a lounge. Originally, this large room had been a library, connected by a door to the office of the secretary of war. One of Stanton's first acts had been to move the army's telegraph headquarters from General McClellan's command to the War Department. Just off the Telegraph Room was a small office, where the military codes were kept. The man at the machine greeted the President, who asked for Major Eckert.

"Here he is," said the army's chief telegrapher. In the doorway stood the young major, covered with mud.

"Thank God Mr. Stanton can't see you, Eckert." The Tycoon shook his head with mock horror. "These things are progressive, you know. The first wallow in the mud is carefree, and joyous. But the next is less so. Finally, you cannot stop. Wherever there is mud, there you will be, Major, rolling and twisting and rooting like a hog!"

"I fell, sir. In the street. I was watching somebody up ahead who was slipping and sliding so comically that I started to laugh, and fell on my face." An orderly brought Eckert a towel. As he mopped up, the Tycoon told of the evening of the day that had decided the contest for Senate between him and Douglas. "It was a night like this. I'd read the returns, and knew I'd lost. So I started to go home, along a path worn hog-back and slippery. Then one of my feet slipped and kicked the other and I fell, but I landed on my feet anyway, and said to myself, 'Well, that was just a slip not a fall.' "

The next return was an estimate. Lincoln would carry the state of Maryland by 5000 votes; the city of Baltimore by 15,000. "That is a pleasant surprise, if true," he said.

Hay kept his notes. The California journalist Noah Brooks joined them. Previously, he had worked in Illinois, where the Tycoon had first known him. He flattered the President outrageously; and treated the President's secretaries with disdain. Nicolay was not only positive that Brooks was angling for the job of secretary in the second term, but "He is welcome to it," Nicolay had said.

The suspicious Lamon had reluctantly allowed a half-dozen highly partisan officers to keep the President company. Gideon Welles had also joined the long watch.

At nine o'clock the serious returns began. Although storms in the midwest interrupted and delayed the Illinois returns, by midnight it was clear that Lincoln had carried his home state. He immediately sent an orderly to the White House. "Tell Mrs. Lincoln. She's even more anxious than I am."

As Hay recorded the satisfactory returns from Massachusetts, Lincoln was telling Brooks, "I'm enough of a politician to know when things are pretty certain, like the Baltimore convention. But about this thing I'm far from certain."

"You should feel pretty confident now," said Brooks. The air of sycophancy was too much for Hay. He hoped it would be too much for the Tycoon during the second term, which seemed now to be at hand.

As New Jersey began to slip toward McClellan, the Tycoon grew philosophical. "It's strange about these elections I'm involved in. I don't think of myself as particularly vindictive or partisan man but every contest I've ever been involved in—except the first for Congress—has been marked by the greatest sort of bitterness and rancor. Can it be me, I wonder, that provokes all this, without knowing it?"

"I should think it was the times, not you, sir," said Brooks. "And lucky for us, you are there to mediate."

Hay decided that, for once, the Tycoon showed alarming bad taste in his companions. Was the second term to be one of vague complacencies and intrigue? Was the simple good Ancient that Hay knew, to be corrupted by youthful flatterers? Perhaps he himself should stay on. But then he thought of the Hellcat; and realized that he could not stay at the White House four more months, much less years. In fact, he had made up his mind that after the first of the year he would move to Willard's and then some time after the inaugural in March, he would go—as would Nicolay.

Seward arrived at midnight, in time for the supper that Major Eckert had had prepared in the War Department kitchen. The premier was in an exultant mood. He had returned on the so-called Owl Train from the North. "We shall take New York State by forty thousand votes," he announced.

"While McClellan sweeps the city. Have some fried oysters." Lincoln and an unknown general were helping fill up everyone's plate with food.

Eckert himself was now manning the telegraph machine. "Here comes New York," he said.

But Seward preferred to give his version of what was happening in that most imperial of all the states. "Governor Seymour threatened to call out the national guard, to scare away our people. So Butler promptly called out the army to scare off the national guard. He's been arresting Democratic agents all day." Seward poured himself champagne; and toasted Ben Butler.

Eckert reported: "McClellan has carried New York City by thirty-five thousand votes."

"That was pretty much my estimate," said the Tycoon, nibbling at a fried oyster.

"McClellan has also carried the state by four thousand votes," said Eckert.

"Not possible!" Seward nearly dropped his glass. "There is fraud here."

"That was *not* my estimate," said Lincoln, abandoning the rest of the oyster. "But I was certain that I would lose the state."

"Well, you have won the election," said Brooks.

"Not quite . . ."

Eckert announced that Kentucky seemed secure for McClellan. Hay began to add; and subtract. He was obliged to do on paper what the Tycoon could do in his head. Each state's electoral vote was on file in that swift, subtle but distinctly odd brain. Hay could not see how Lincoln could lose. Nevertheless, if New York's electoral votes were to go to McClellan, the margin of victory might resemble, more and more, the Ancient's original gloomy estimate.

Then Eckert, with a grin, announced: "Correction from New York. Lincoln not McClellan carried the state by four thousand votes, and Governor Horatio Seymour is defeated."

There was cheering in the room, and when Seward insisted that the Tycoon drink a glass of champagne, he did so. "Remember your hopes and dreams for Seymour this very night?" Seward teased Lincoln. "Just think, it might have been President Seymour, with you as his midwest manager."

"Fate has spared us," said Lincoln, demurely.

Eckert announced, "Steubenville, Ohio, the hometown of Mr. Stanton, has gone Republican."

"We are safe!" Lincoln exclaimed. Then, in wheezing imitation of Stanton, he said, "Let's give three cheers for Steubenville!"

When the cheering ceased, Seward observed, at large, "We owe Mr. Stanton a lot tonight. He got out the soldier vote, and they are the ones who have made all the difference."

Lincoln nodded, suddenly somber. "It is true," he said. "But I myself cannot see why they voted as they did—grateful as I am."

"They are loyal to you." Again Seward raised his glass. "They are also loyal to the army, to the Union, to themselves and to what they have done these last four years, and to all their dead."

"I will drink to that," said Lincoln; and finished the glass of champagne. "Certainly, I am honored that they have voted for me. Honored and surprised, with all the dead thus far." The voice trailed off.

"*They* would favor you, too, if they could vote," said Seward, expansively.

"The dead?" Lincoln sounded startled. Then he shook his head. "No, Governor. The dead would not vote for me, ever, in this—or any other—world."

On the evening of March 24, 1865, the *River Queen* cast anchor in the James River off City Point. On the deck stood the President, Mrs. Lincoln and Tad, who held a pistol in one hand and an American flag in the other. All around them ships of every size rode at anchor while the river bank was massed with arms and provisions. On a bluff, an improvised city of tents and huts and sheds was visible in the light of fires and kerosene lamps. From the main deck, Captain Robert Lincoln waved to his parents; then he hurried off.

"I expect he's going to fetch General Grant." Lincoln pointed to the bluff above the river port. "Grant's headquarters are up there."

"Is Robert a *real* captain?" asked Tad, aiming his revolver at the Commander-in-Chief.

"Of course, he is, Taddie," said Lincoln. "And don't aim guns at people like that."

In due course, General and Mrs. Grant and Robert were rowed alongside the *River Queen.* "How common she looks," murmured Mary.

"Now, Mother." Mary did not like the way that Lincoln had used exactly the same tone with her that he had used with Tad.

Mary embraced Robert while Tad climbed onto his shoulders. Grant shook hands with the President first; then with Mary. She noted that he did not look either of them in the eye. On the other hand, Julia Grant was not able to look anyone in the eye since one eye was permanently turned toward her aquiline nose while the other looked as if it would like to escape the wild gaze of its neighbor.

Lincoln led the Grants into the salon, where all the lamps had been lit. "We were poisoned by the ship's water on the way down," said Lincoln. "But we got us some decent water at Fortress Monroe."

"The water's foul here," said Grant. "We boil it." Mary wondered if Grant ever actually drank a substance so insipid. In the full light of the salon she studied him carefully. He *appeared* to be clear-eyed and sober. Of course, the presence of Mrs. Grant was known to be a guarantee of sobriety.

"Welcome to City Point, Mrs. Lincoln." Julia Grant was gracious in a way that Mary did not entirely like. It was as if City Point—and the army—were hers.

Mary smiled and bowed; and did not answer. Lincoln wanted to go ashore right then and there, and though Grant told him there was little to see at night, the President insisted.

Mary was then left alone with Mrs. Grant, who proceeded to make herself at home by sitting down on the only sofa in the salon. Mary said nothing; but she was certain that her glare was sufficient to convey to Mrs. Grant the enormity of her breach of etiquette. No one could sit, unbidden, in the presence of the First Lady. Slowly, and silently, Mary lowered herself onto the sofa. The two ladies were now so close to each other that their skirts overlapped.

Mary sat erect, looking straight ahead. After a moment's uneasy silence, Mrs. Grant moved from the sofa to a small chair opposite. "Did you have a pleasant journey?" asked Mrs. Grant.

"Yes," said Mary.

There was another, somewhat longer, silence; then Mrs. Grant said, "I believe General Sherman arrives tomorrow. He comes by sea from North Carolina. It will be the first that we have seen of him since he took Atlanta and Savannah."

"That will be nice for you," said Mary. But then she could not resist adding, "I hope he will explain why three months after he occupied Atlanta, he then burned the city down."

"He thought it was necessary, to protect his rear as he moved north."

"Obviously, he must have thought it necessary. But he has made negotiating a peace much more difficult for my husband."

"I do not think, Mrs. Lincoln, that there will be a negotiated peace now. The war will not end until my husband has taken Richmond."

"How often have we heard that!" Mary gave Julia Grant a wide smile; and blinked her eyes, to show what a good humor she was in. She was pleased to see Mrs. Grant grow somewhat red in the face. A highly satisfactory silence settled in the salon; and remained settled until Tad came rushing in to say he had been ashore. "But I came right back. We were stopped, Mr. Crook and me, by soldiers who said, 'Who goes there?' and 'What's the password?' and things like that. When I said, 'It's me,' they didn't know me. So I told Mr. Crook we better come back here before they shoot us."

"Such a . . . charming boy," said Mrs. Grant.

"Yes," said Mary, aware of the calculated hesitation before the adjective. "We have met *your* oldest boy," she added; and characterized that supremely plain child not at all.

Three days later Lincoln, Grant, Sherman and Admiral Porter met in the ship's salon while Mary took to her bed with certain preliminary signs of The Headache.

"I cannot tell you gentlemen what a pleasure it is to get away from Washington," said Lincoln.

"That's why I asked you, sir," said Grant. "I had a feeling you might want to take a trip, and get some rest."

"And what more restful place to be than at the front?" Lincoln smiled.

"We expect Sheridan any time now." Grant had placed a map of Virginia on a table. "He is making an arc from the valley here to Harrison's Landing there. At the moment he is crossing the James River just below us. Once he and his cavalry arrive, we should be able to take Petersburg—at last."

"At last," Lincoln repeated. He turned to Sherman. "Certainly, when your army joins that of General Grant, it will be all over."

"Yes, sir." Sherman was a slight wiry man, with uncombed wiry red hair and the pale eyes of, suitably, a bird of prey. "There's nothing left of the rebellion, except Johnston in North Carolina and Lee up here, and Lee can't have more than fifty thousand men."

"So we outnumber him three to one right now." Lincoln looked at Grant, who nodded. "Then there will be one more battle, at least."

Grant nodded, again.

"It would be good to avoid it, if we can. There's been so much bloodshed." Lincoln turned to Grant, "When Richmond falls, or even before, what is to prevent Lee and his army from getting on the cars and going south to North Carolina, and joining up with Johnston? They could live off the country down there and go on fighting us for years."

"For one thing, sir, they won't be able to take the cars." Sherman's voice was light but emphatic.

"What's to prevent them? They still control at least two railroad lines to the south and to the west."

"They don't control them where we have been, and we've been everywhere now except this last stretch from North Carolina to here."

"Yes," said Lincoln. "You have been there but you are now *not* there. You are here, or you soon will be. Well, the railroads are still where they were."

"Oh, the roads are still there," said Sherman, "but the rails are gone. We have torn them up. They can't be used."

"It's not hard to put the rails and the ties back down again. We did that at Annapolis when the war was new."

Sherman chuckled. "I don't think you understand my boys. What was wood they burned, and what was metal they put in the fire and made corkscrews of. There's not a railroad out of Virginia that Lee could ever use."

Lincoln whistled, comically. "You don't do things by halves, do you?"

"No, sir," said Sherman. "You remember when we first met four years ago?"

"Of course I do." Lincoln spoke somewhat too quickly. "With your brother Senator Sherman, wasn't it?"

Sherman ignored Lincoln's hesitancy. "I said to you then that this would be a long and terrible war, and you said you didn't think it would be all that long and, anyway, you supposed that even if it was, you'd manage somehow to keep house."

"Did I say that?" Lincoln shook his head with wonder. "Well, I am only a politician, you know, and we tend to say stupid things. What's worse, of course, is we do them, too. Well, you were the better prophet. So tell me, what do you prophesy next for us?"

"This time, sir, *you* are what the prophet must contemplate. Because once the fighting stops, the future is going to be what you make of it."

Grant stared hard at Lincoln. "Sherman's right. You'll have to decide everything. Like what do we do with the rebel armies? With the generals? With the politicians? What shall we do with Jefferson Davis?"

"Mr. Davis . . ." Lincoln's face lightened. "That reminds me of this man who took the temperance pledge. Then he went to the house of a drinking friend who tried to tempt him, but he would not be tempted. He asked for lemonade. So the lemonade was brought to him. Then the friend pointed to a bottle of brandy and said, 'Wouldn't it taste better with some of that in it?' and the temperance man said, 'Well, if it is added unbeknown to me, I wouldn't object.' "

The three men laughed. Admiral Porter said, "In other words, if Mr. Davis were to escape to another country you wouldn't mind?"

Lincoln merely smiled; then he said, "I am for getting the Union back to what it was as quickly and as painlessly as possible."

"You will have your problems with Congress," said Sherman, a senator's brother.

"Well, that is my job. I must say, Sherman, I'd feel safer if you were back in North Carolina with your army."

Sherman laughed. "I promise you it will not disintegrate that quickly."

Lincoln stretched his arms until there was a creaking sound from the vicinity of the shoulder blades. Then he said, suddenly, "Sherman, do you know why I took a shine to you and Grant?"

"I don't know, sir. I do know you have been kinder to me than I ever deserved."

"Well, it's because, unlike all the other generals, you never found fault with me." Lincoln rose. "At least not so that I ever heard."

Lincoln then took a long fire-ax from its bracket on the bulkhead. "Let's see if you fellows can do this." Lincoln grabbed the ax at the end of its haft and held it away from his body, arm outstretched and parallel to the deck. One by one, the others tried to do the same but, in each case, the weight was too great. "It is a sort of trick of balance," said Lincoln.

"And muscle," said Sherman.

The next day President and generals rode out to the main encampment of the Army of the James to witness a grand review. Mrs. Lincoln and Mrs. Grant followed in an ambulance, which kept to a corduroy road that had been set across a sea of red Virginia mud and swampland. Mary had never in her life known such discomfort, not to mention pain; a headache had now installed itself just back of her eyes and would not go away.

At the back of the swaying and lurching ambulance Mary and Julia Grant sat on a bench, side by side, when they were not thrown together. One of General Grant's aides sat opposite them, apologizing for the state of the road.

"It's never comfortable," said Mrs. Grant, clutching the wagon's side.

"We can endure the discomfort," said Mary regally. "But, surely," she addressed the officer, "we are going to be late for the review?"

"I think not," said the man. "Of course, the driver is deliberately slow."

"Then tell him we should like to go faster."

"But I don't think that's wise," said Julia Grant and the eye closest to Mary turned, impudently, away.

"But we *must* go faster!" Mary exclaimed. The officer gave the order to the driver, and the horses sprang forward just as flat marsh gave way to a section of corduroy road made up of trees of different sizes. The ambulance sprang into the air. The two ladies, as one, left their seat and would have departed the ambulance entirely had the back section not been roofed in. As it was, two large, splendidly decorated hats prevented the heads beneath from breaking open but at the cost of two miraculous examples of the milliner's craft, now crushed. As Mary fell back into the seat, she screamed, "Stop! Let me out! I shall walk!"

The ambulance stopped. The ornamental pheasant that had been the central decoration of Mrs. Grant's hat had slipped forward onto her forehead, and one glossy wing now pathetically caressed her round cheek. "Mrs. Lincoln, no! Please."

Mary was halfway out of the carriage, when the officer pulled her back in. "Madam," he said, soothingly, "the mud is three feet deep here. No one can walk."

"Oh, God!" shouted Mary, directly to the Deity, who did not answer her. As she sat back in the bench, head throbbing and eyes shut, she felt, one by one, the wax cherries that had made beautiful her hat come loose and fall to the ambulance floor exactly as the originals would have done when ripe.

But Mary had predicted correctly. They were late for the review. On a great muddy field, an army division was going through its paces. Mrs. Grant, helpfully, identified the commanding general in the distance, James Ord. Meanwhile, as the ambulance approached the review stand, a slender woman on a great horse cantered past them. "Who is that?" asked Mary. "I thought women were forbidden at the front."

"They are," said Julia Grant, "but that is General Griffin's wife. She has a special permit."

"From the President himself," said the aide, with a smile which was, for Mary, lasciviousness writ scarlet in the air. She responded with a scream; and was pleased to see some of the redness go from those hideous, mocking lips.

"*She* has had an interview with the President? Is that what you are hinting at? A *private* interview?" Mary could hear a mocking snigger from Mrs. Grant at her side. They were all in it together. "Yes, that is what you want people to believe. But no woman is ever alone with the President. So tell as many lies as you please . . ."

General Meade was now at the ambulance. Mary turned to him for alliance. As he helped her down, she said, most craftily, she thought, "General Meade, it has been suggested to me that that woman on the horse has received *special* permission to be at the front, given her by the President himself."

Meade said, "No, Mrs. Lincoln. Not by the President. Such permissions are given, and very rarely, by Mr. Stanton."

"See?" Mary wheeled on her tormentors. She addressed the corrupt officer. "General Meade is a gentleman, sir. It was not the President but the Secretary of War who gave permission to this slut." Mary savored her triumph. Fortunately, General Meade was very much a gentleman, from one of Philadelphia's finest old families; and so he acted as if nothing had happened as he escorted her to the reviewing stand. But Mary was conscious that her two mortal enemies were just behind her, heads together, whispering obscenities to each other. Well, she would bide her time.

As Mary took her seat facing an entire division drawn up at present arms, she saw the President, flanked by Generals Grant and Ord, begin his ride down the long dark-blue line of troops. As the President came to each regiment, the men would cheer him and he would remove his hat. Back of the three men, there were a dozen high-ranking officers, and a good-looking young woman on a horse.

"Who is that?" asked Mary.

Mrs. Grant said, "It is Mrs. Ord, the general's wife."

"She is riding next to my husband."

"She is actually," said Mrs. Grant, gently, "riding next to *her* husband, General Ord."

Mary turned to General Meade for assistance but he had moved away to the telegraph hut at the end of the reviewing stand. In his place, there was a solicitous colonel. "Sir, has that woman been riding with the President all during the review?" Mary watched his face very carefully; she knew that she could tell in an instant if he was lying; it was as if her eyes could see with perfect clarity straight past his dull face and deep into his brain.

"Why, yes," said the colonel.

"Actually, she is with *her* husband, Mrs. Lincoln . . ." began Julia Grant.

"I am quite capable of calculating the distance—look now!" Mrs. Ord was indeed alongside the President. "My God!" Mary exclaimed. "*She is pretending to be me!* They will think that that vile woman is me! Does she suppose that *he* wants *her* at his side like that?"

A young major rode up. The colonel said, quickly, "Here is Major Seward, the nephew of the Secretary of State . . ."

"Mrs. Lincoln." The Major saluted Mary.

"I know all about Mr. Seward," Mary began, noticing the young man's parrot's beak of a nose, so like that of his uncle, her enemy.

Major Seward was aware that they had been watching the President and Mrs. Ord, who were now riding side by side. "The President's horse is very gallant," said Major Seward, with all the corrupt insolence of his uncle. "He insists on riding by the side of Mrs. Ord's horse."

"What," Mary cried, pushed now to the very edge of public humiliation, "do you mean by that?"

Major Seward's response was an abrupt retreat. Meanwhile, President and generals had moved off the field toward the Petersburg front while Mrs. Ord rode toward the reviewing stand. Mary could not believe her eyes. The woman's insolence was beyond anything that she had ever had to endure in her life. The woman dismounted; and walked over to the reviewing stand. "Welcome, Mrs. Lincoln," she said.

Mary rose in her place. She felt exalted. At last, she could strike at her enemies a mortal blow. "You whore!" said Mary, delighted that she was able to control so well her voice. Then, word by word, sentence by sentence, effortlessly, she told the slut what she thought of her and of her behavior. Mary felt as if she were floating over the landscape like a cloud, a thundercloud, true, but a serene one. All that needed to be said to this now scarlet-faced woman was said. From high up, the cloudlike Mary saw the tears flow down the vicious face; saw the Colonel as he tried to divert her from her necessary task; saw Julia Grant as she dared to interrupt her.

In a way, Julia Grant was the worst, of course. Whores were whores everywhere and the good wife could always manage to shame them or, if they were truly shameless, to drive them away. But Mrs. Grant was a threat. Mrs. Grant was the wife of a hero—a butcher-hero, of course, but still a hero to the stupid public. Mrs. Grant was also insolent. She had sat unbidden in the presence of the First Lady. But then it was no secret that she was already scheming to be herself First Lady one day. "I suppose," said Mary, with incredible cunning and the kindliest of smiles, "that you think you'll get to the White House yourself, don't you?"

Mrs. Grant—whose eyes were as crossed and flawed as her character—dared to answer. "We are quite happy where we are, Mrs. Lincoln."

"Well, you had better take it if you can get it." Mary was delighted with her own subtlety. She was, however, somewhat taken aback by the sound of a woman screaming. Could it be Mrs. Ord? No, *she* was weeping silently. Mary wondered where the screaming was coming from as she said, coolly, "It's very nice, the White House." Then Mary saw the fiery nimbus around Julia Grant's head; and then Mary realized that the screaming that she heard was herself. Then Mary ceased to be conscious of where she was.

But it was not The Headache, because that same evening, aboard the *River Queen*, Mary was almost herself again. Naturally, she had been humiliated by Mrs. Ord in public view; and insulted by Mrs. Grant in private. But Mary presided at the dinner table with, she thought, admirable poise. She did find it disturbing that she could not recall how she had got from the reviewing stand back to the ship. In fact, as they sat at dinner with six staff officers—and Mrs. Grant to the President's right and General Grant to Mary's right, she was not entirely certain how the dinner had begun. But now that everything was going so smoothly, she felt that she could murmur to Grant, "I hope that you will, in future, control Mrs. Ord, whose exhibition today, in pursuit of my husband, caused so much unfavorable comment."

General Grant's response was not clear. But the President said, "Now, Mother, I hardly knew the lady was present."

"For no want of trying," Mary was regal. "Anyway, why should she, or any woman, be here?"

"Ord needs her," said Grant.

"The way General Grant needs me at times," said Mrs. Grant.

"Oh, we know all about *those* times," Mary began. But the President cut her off. "Mother, the army band is coming aboard after dinner. There will be dancing."

"We thought it might be gay," said Mrs. Grant. "In all this horror. To forget for a moment."

"I am glad if it makes you glad." Mary was consummately gracious. She turned to Lincoln. "Everyone seems agreed that General Ord is the principal reason why the Army of the James has been stopped here for so many, many months now." Mary felt that she had now outflanked the Grants. "If he were to be replaced might we not be able to win the war more quickly?"

"Now, Mother . . ." Lincoln seemed very distant from her at his end of the table. She had some difficulty in hearing his voice but she had no difficulty hearing General Grant, who said, "Ord is a fine officer. I cannot do without him."

As Mary explained to General Grant the urgent need to replace Ord, she felt a sudden swimming ecstasy that suffused her entire body and mind. Simultaneously, again like a cloud or, perhaps, the moon, she was floating far, far above the table. She was a little girl in Lexington again; and there were her dolls, far below, at a tea party.

The afternoon was clear and bright; and the spring flowers were already beginning to blossom, helter-skelter, where the military encampments had been at the foot of Washington's monument and in the grounds of the Smithsonian Institution, recently razed by fire. A cavalry detachment accompanied the carriage. Earlier that day, Lincoln and Stanton had argued, yet again, about protection. Lincoln thought that now, with the war over, he was of less interest to the assassin. Stanton said that now, more than ever, he was in danger. Lamon would have agreed; but he was in Richmond. Nevertheless, just before Lamon had gone South, he warned the President to stay away from the theater or any public place where his presence had been advertised in advance.

"Perhaps," Lincoln said, as the carriage swung down the less-peopled side of Pennsylvania Avenue, "we might stay at home tonight."

"But it's Laura Keene's last night; and she is counting on us." Mary frowned. "I cannot get over General Grant's rudeness. Yesterday he was coming with us, and today he is not."

"I suppose it is Mrs. Grant, wanting to get home to her children." The carriage paused as a line of ambulances passed in front of them. When Lincoln was recognized, the wounded cheered him. He removed his hat and held it in his hand until the last ambulance had passed.

Mary was concerned with Mrs. Grant. "I suspect that she does not dare to face me after the scene that she made at City Point. I have never seen anyone so out of control. She is an ambitious little thing. So is he, for that matter. I was watching from the window when he walked back to Willard's this morning. There was an enormous crowd all around him, as if he were you."

"Well, he isn't me but he *is* General Grant, Mother, and that's something very special."

The carriage proceeded down a side street toward the Navy Yard. "He is running for president. I can tell. I can always tell."

"So you can. So you can. And he's welcome to it. We've had our crack at it. So if he wants to take over, let him."

"Four years," said Mary. "When I was young that sounded like forever. Now it is nothing. Four weeks. Four days. Time rushes past us like the snowflake on the river."

"When it's all over," said Lincoln, "I want to go west. I want to see California and the Pacific Ocean."

"Well, *I* want to go to Europe. I must see Paris . . ."

"Certainly, a lot of Paris has already come your way, Molly. Fact, Paris clings to your person from shoes to hats."

"Oh, Father! I buy so little now. Keckley makes everything, anyway. Where will we live?"

"Springfield. Where else? I'll practice some law with Herndon . . ."

"If you do, I will divorce you." Mary was indignant. "Father, how could you live in Springfield now? Much less practice law with Billy."

"What else am I to do? I'll be sixty-one years old. I'll have to do something to make a living. So that means the law . . ."

"In Chicago then." Mary had already envisaged a fine new house on the lake-front, where palaces were now beginning to rise.

"If we can afford it. Well, today, I refuse to be worried about anything." Although gaunt, Lincoln's face was like that of a man who had just been let out of prison. "I have not been so happy in many years."

"Don't say that!" Mary was suddenly alarmed. She had heard him say these exact words once before; with ominous result.

"Why not? It is true."

"Because . . . the last time you said those same words was just before Eddie died."

Lincoln looked at her a moment; then he looked at the Capitol on its hill to their left. "I feel so personally—complete," he said, "now that the new lid is on. And I also feel so relieved that Congress has left town, and the place is empty."

After dinner that evening, Mary went to change her clothes for the theater while Lincoln sat in the upstairs oval parlor and gossiped with the new governor and the new senator from Illinois; he also treated them to a reading from Petroleum V. Nasby. Then Noah Brooks announced the Speaker of the House, Mr. Colfax, a man who never ceased smiling no matter what the occasion. "Sir, I must know"—he smiled radiantly, teeth yellow as maize—"if you intend to call a special session of the Congress in order to consider Mr. Stanton's proposals for reconstruction."

If Lincoln was taken aback by the reference to Stanton's supposedly private memorandum, he made no sign. "No, I shall not call a special session. After the superhuman labors of the last session, I believe Congress deserves its rest."

Colfax beamed his disappointment. "In that case, I shall make my long-deferred trip to the west."

Lincoln spoke with some interest of Colfax's proposed tour of the mountain states. Then Lincoln was reminded that when Senator Sumner was recently in Richmond, he had purloined the gavel of the speaker of the Confederate Congress. "Sumner is threatening to give it to Stanton. But I want you to have it, as proper custodian for this particular spoil of war."

Colfax's delight was hyenaish. "I should like nothing better."

"Well, you tell Sumner I said you're to have it."

Mary swept into the room; splendidly turned out for the theater. She was unanimously complimented.

"I think," said Brooks, looking at his watch, "that it is time to go."

"All in all," said Lincoln, collecting Mary's arm, "I would rather not go. But as the widow said to the preacher . . ."

"Oh, Father, not that one!" Bickering amiably, they proceeded downstairs to the waiting carriage, which contained the daughter of Senator Harris of New York and her fiancé, Major Rathbone, the best company that Hay could find at such short notice.

As Lincoln got into the carriage, he said to Cook, "Good-bye." Then an old friend from Chicago appeared in the driveway, waving his hat. "I'm sorry, Isaac, we're going to the theater. Come and see me tomorrow morning." Accompanied by one officer from the Metropolitan Police, the carriage pulled out into the avenue.

A long row of carriages blocked the entire east side of Tenth Street, except for the main entrance to the brightly illuminated theater where Mr. Ford's young brother was waiting. The play had already begun.

Although Eugénie, empress of the French, must have been about forty years of age, John Hay never ceased to find her as attractive as he found her husband, the Emperor Napoleon III, repellent. At the reception for the diplomatic corps on January 1, 1867, in the palace of the Tuileries, Hay kept to the splendid drawing room where Eugénie held court and avoided the statelier room where the emperor and his ministers stood, next to an elaborate, gilded throne in which the emperor never sat.

Eugénie's hair had been naturally dark red, and was still red; while her complexion had always been pale, and was still pale. The sad eyes were gray. She wore a ruby-red dress of velvet, cut low to reveal an explosion of diamond necklaces. Hay did his best not to stare, and could not take his eyes off her. But then he had spent four years in Washington, watching women imitate Eugénie; now he was able to look with awe upon the original herself. As the Spanish-born empress stood beneath a life-size portrait of her predecessor Marie-Louise, the wife of the real Napoleon, she used an ivory fan subtly to communicate with others. Hay regarded her with all the pleasure that he might have found in watching a splendid sunrise or, perhaps, considering the chronic fragility of the French political system, sunset.

All around the gold-encrusted room, gold-encrusted diplomats stood while members of the palace staff in violet uniforms tried, without success, to make themselves useful. At regular intervals, members of the emperor's personal guard were placed, at attention, like so many statues in blue and gold. Although it was still light outside, the chandeliers were ablaze; and wood fires burned in every marble fireplace. Hay was pleased to be conspicuous in plain black; but then he was more than ever a dedicated republican, not to mention implacable foe of despots, even a despot whose wife was a perfect sunset.

The outgoing American minister, John Bigelow, came toward Hay. Bigelow was accompanied by a stout, pink-cheeked old man and a beautiful young girl, definitely more sunrise than sunset. "Mr. Hay is my first secretary," said Bigelow to the old man and young girl, who turned out to be the American historian Charles Schermerhorn Schuyler and his daughter Emma, the Princesse d'Agrigente, a lady celebrated for her salon at which one never found her husband, the heir to the great Napoleon's marshal. Although Hay had never before met the splendid princess, he knew all about her unhappy marriage; and knew that absolutely no one was sorry for her in a city where unhappy marriages were the rule. The prince lived elsewhere with his mistress. The princess lived with her children, as if she were a wealthy widow; lived untouched by any scandal, which was not the rule in Paris.

But then Emma herself was rare, decided Hay, when she turned her dark eyes on him and said in softly accented English, "I am a true American, yet I have never set foot in the United States."

"It is my fault," said the amiable Mr. Schuyler. "I left New York in 'thirty-six, to be, like you, a diplomat. Only I went to Italy where I was married, and . . ."

". . . and you never went home," said Emma. "Well, I cannot wait to go."

"Nor can I," said Bigelow. "How I miss New York!"

"Where," asked Mr. Schuyler, "would you place Mr. Lincoln amongst the presidents of our country?"

"Oh, I would place him first."

"*Above* Washington?" Mr. Schuyler looked startled.

"Yes," said Hay, who had thought a good deal about the Tycoon's place in history. "Mr. Lincoln had a far greater and more difficult task than Washington's. You see, the Southern states had every Constitutional right to go out of the Union. But Lincoln said, no. Lincoln said, this Union can never be broken. Now that was a terrible responsibility for one man to take. But he took it, knowing he would be obliged to fight the greatest war in human history, which he did, and which he won. So he not only put the Union back together again, but he made an entirely new country, and all of it in his own image."

"You astonish me," said Mr. Schuyler.

"Mr. Lincoln astonished us all."

"I rather think," said Charles Schermerhorn Schuyler to his daughter, "that we should take a look at this new country, which plainly bears no resemblance to the one I left, in the quiet days of Martin Van Buren."

"Well, come soon," said Hay. "Because who knows what may happen next?"

"I have been writing, lately, about the German first minister." Mr. Schuyler was thoughtful. "In fact, I met him at Biarritz last summer when he came to see the emperor. Curiously enough, he has now done the same thing to Germany that you tell us Mr. Lincoln did to our country. Bismarck has made a single, centralized nation out of all the other German states."

Hay nodded; he, too, had noted the resemblance. "Bismarck would also give the vote to people who have never had it before."

"I think," said Mr. Schuyler to the princess, "we have here a subject—Lincoln and Bismarck, and new countries for old."

"It will be interesting to see how Herr Bismarck ends *his* career," said Hay, who was now more than ever convinced that Lincoln, in some mysterious fashion, had willed his own murder as a form of atonement for the great and terrible thing that he had done by giving so bloody and absolute a rebirth to his nation.

# From
# *1876*

THAT IS NEW YORK." I pointed to the waterfront just ahead as if the city were mine. Ships, barges, ferry boats, four-masted schooners were shoved like a child's toys against a confused jumble of buildings quite unfamiliar to me, a mingling of red brick and brownstone, of painted wood and dull granite, of church towers that I had never seen before and odd bulbous-domed creations of—cement? More suitable for the adornment of the Golden Horn than for my native city.

"At least I *think* it is New York. Perhaps it is Brooklyn. I am told that the new Brooklyn is marvellously exotic, with a thousand churches."

Gulls swooped and howled in our wake as the stewards on a lower deck threw overboard the remains of the large breakfast fed us at dawn.

"No," said Emma. "I've just left the captain. This is really New York. And how old, how very old it looks!" Emma's excitement gave me pleasure. Of late neither of us has had much to delight in, but now she looks a girl again, her dark eyes brilliant with that all-absorbed, grave, questioning look which all her life has meant: I must know what this new thing is and how best to use it. She responds to novelty and utility rather than to beauty. I am the opposite; thus father and daughter balance each other.

Grey clouds alternated with bands of bright blue sky; sharp wind from the northwest; sun directly in our eyes, which meant that we were facing due east from the North River, and so this was indeed the island of my birth and not Brooklyn to the south nor Jersey City at our back.

I took a deep breath of sea-salt air; smelt the city's fumes of burning anthracite mingled with the smell of fish not lately caught and lying like silver ingots in a passing barge.

"So old?" I had just realized what Emma had said.

"But yes." Emma's English is almost without accent, but occasionally she translates directly from the French, betraying her foreignness. But then I am the foreign one, the American who has lived most of his life in Europe while Emma has never until now left that old world where she was born thirty-five years ago in Italy, during a cyclone that uprooted half the trees in the garden of our villa and caused the frightened midwife nearly to strangle the newborn with the umbilical cord. Whenever I see trees falling before the wind, hear thunder, observe the sea furious, I think of that December day and the paleness of the mother's face in vivid contrast to the redness of her blood, that endless haemorrhaging of blood.

(I think that a little *mémoire* in the beautiful lyric style of the above might do very well for the *Atlantic Monthly.*)

Emma shivered in the wind. "Yes, old. Dingy. Like Liverpool."

"Waterfronts are the same everywhere. But there's nothing old here. I recognize nothing. Not even City Hall, which ought to be over there where that marble tomb is. See? With all the columns . . ."

"Perhaps you've forgotten. It's been so long."

"I feel like Rip Van Winkle." Already I could see the beginning of my first piece for the New York *Herald* (unless I can interest Mr. Bonner at the New York *Ledger;* he has been known to pay a thousand dollars for a single piece). "The New Rip Van Winkle, or How Charles Schermerhorn Schuyler Sailed to Europe Almost Half a Century Ago . . ." And stayed there (asleep?). Now he's come home, to report to President Martin Van Buren who sent him abroad on a diplomatic mission, to compare foreign notes with his friend Washington Irving (who invented him after all), to dine with the poet Fitz-Greene Halleck: only to find all of them, to his astonishment, long dead.

Must stop at this point.

These pages are to be a quarry, no more. A collection of day-to-day impressions of my *new* old country.

Titles: "The United States in the Year of the Centennial." "Traveller's Return." "Old New York: A Knickerbocker's Memories." "Recollections of the Age of Jackson and Van Buren . . ." Must try these out on publishers and lecture agents.

From a livery stable we hired a smart carriage to take us to Mrs. Astor's, and then to pick us up at midnight.

"That's the time you always have to leave, sir, from Mrs. Astor's." The concierge at the hotel who makes such arrangements did not for a moment betray his excitement at launching two of the hotel's guests to the very peak of Parnassus—if I have the right mountain. He also took quiet pleasure in showing us that he, too, was part of that great world, with a fair knowledge of who would and who would not be on the mountain's peak, as well as the exact hour that we would sit down at dinner (8:00 P.M.) and by whom the dinner would be catered, if the party happened to be too large for the chef to manage on his own.

Emma looked as if she had stepped down from a Winterhalter portrait at Schönbrunn: more Wittlesbach than Montijo empress. She wore the d'Agrigente diamonds, which are so cunningly reproduced in paste that only a jeweller with a magnifying glass could tell that they are false. I noticed with some pleasure that I am thinner than I was before the mysterious illness, and I think that we looked a most distinguished couple.

At first I was afraid that we might not know which of the two identical Astor houses belonged to our hostess, but as Emma pointed out, if the sisters-in-law were to give dinner parties on the same evening, Fifth Avenue would be impassable. Incidentally, when I said that I hoped she would not be bored by the provincialness of American society, she shook her head fiercely.

"Never bored, Papa. All that money is . . . well, like currents of electricity in those hideous rooms, and I am absolutely thrilled! I tingle all over. Your rich people here absolutely glow with money, like northern lights." At times Emma can be surprisingly literary, despite a rather vulgar taste in fiction.

As we were helped from the carriage by footmen in the Astor livery—dark-green plush coats, gold armorial buttons, red waistcoats, knee breeches and black silk stockings—a small crowd watched us, despite a light snow that had begun to fall. From the front door of 350 Fifth Avenue a red carpet had been prodigally flung down steps, across the sidewalk and into the gutter. We hurried inside.

What looked to be a court chamberlain directed the ladies to their retiring or repairing room, the gentlemen to a cloakroom. Then, properly retired and repaired, Emma and I made our way solemnly down a long corridor to the great staircase. The house is larger and more impressive inside than its thin wedge of chocolate-cake look from the street would indicate.

We passed through three enfiladed drawing rooms (two in blue, one in garnet) just as one did at the Tuileries. I was struck by the richness of everything and, in general, the good taste of the furnishings, though the pictures are not much good and the sculpture insipid. Nevertheless, the light from the splendid crystal chandeliers was reflected most magically in the many silver mirrors while everywhere there were fresh flowers—roses, orchids—and exotic plants, not to mention a proper conservatory just past the third drawing room. It is the perfect luxury to possess a complete tropical jungle in the midst of a freezing New York winter.

Mrs. William Backhouse Astor née Caroline Schermerhorn alias the Mystic Rose stood beneath a large bad portrait of herself, receiving guests. At her side was Ward McAllister, very much in his element, and slavishly devoted to the mysteries of his rather full-blown rose. Mrs. Astor is not young (forty, forty-five?) and her dead-black hair is not entirely her own, whilst the body she has decorated with chains of diamonds and pearl moonbursts and a stomacher of emeralds that the Great Mogul himself might envy is entirely her own (the word "body" is the subject of that last small verb: jewelled qualifying clauses now drip from my pen just as real jewels hung, fell, swayed, glittered not only from the tall stout erect figure of Mrs. Astor but from all the other ladies present).

Fifty ladies and gentlemen had been invited for this particular dinner party, Ward McAllister whispered in my ear, breath more foul with the violets that he'd been eating than the usual odour of port he wanted to disguise. "*All* New York that matters is under this roof tonight."

The Mystic Rose gave Emma a long look; then the eyes went straight to the replicas of the d'Agrigente diamonds. I feared for a moment that Mrs. Astor would suddenly produce not a lorgnette but a jeweller's magnifying glass, detect Emma's paste and order us to the door.

But Emma passed with colours that flew before the wind of our hostess's approbation like so many banners in a victory parade. "We've heard so much about you, Princess. We're so glad you could be with us tonight."

"You are most kind, Madame, to invite us." Emma's French accent was quite—deliberately?—noticeable.

"Mr. Schermerhorn Schuyler." Mrs. Astor allowed me to bow over her rather thick beringed fingers. "Mr. McAllister is confident that you and I are cousins. You see, I was born a Schermerhorn." The tone of her voice was reverent, as if she had been born a Plantagenet.

I deeply dislike McAllister's doubling of my name. In his ambition for us socially, he has managed to impose upon me a false persona, for I am connected with neither the grand Schermerhorns nor the grand Schuylers. My Schermerhorn mother was born on a poor upstate farm, one of eleven undistinguished children, all of whom had the misfortune to live while my father Schuyler kept a tavern in Greenwich Village—in those days a real village and not just a name to decorate a part of this never-ending city.

But I am willing to play whatever game is expected; and was complaisant. "Yes, my mother was a Schermerhorn, too. From Columbia County." All perfectly true. "Their place was near Claverack." Again perfectly honest.

"Ours is indeed a large family." Mrs. Astor gave me a gracious nod as if she were Queen Victoria and I one of a thousand German princely cousins to be suitably recognized.

Then we passed into the next drawing room, where everything was blue-green damask and rich malachite. McAllister remained beside his Rose, introducing her to people she for the most part appeared to know better than he, but then that is the task of the chamberlain in a royal household.

Emma caused some stir. Everyone knew of her. Several ladies had met her at one or another of Mrs. Mary Mason Jones's lunch parties, so she was well provided for with respectable companions of her own sex. The men eyed her most appreciatively—red-faced fat men, with eyes glazed from too many razzle-dazzles. Proudly they bear the great names of the New York that so bore me. But I am a beggar; may not choose.

"You have not been polite!" A woman's voice behind me. I turned and there was Mrs. William Sanford, as bright and cheerful as ever.

"How have I failed you?"

"You wouldn't join us for lunch at the Brunswick—"

"I was indisposed. No, really. Felled by Delmonico's splendid food—"

"—so the Princess said, but I thought you'd really dropped us."

We kept on in this vein. I was startled: Emma had not told me that she had accepted the Sanfords' invitation on the second day of my convalescence. I had been under the impression that she had retired, as usual, into Apgar-land.

"We had a charming time. I hope she did. The Belmonts were there and they took to her enormously, but then everyone does."

That explained the mysterious invitation from Mrs. August Belmont for dinner New Year's Eve. "I've not met them," I said to Emma when I saw the invitation.

"But I have," she said. "It's all right. They are charming. He's from our side of the Atlantic." Belmont—"the beautiful mountain"—was born with that name, but in German. As a Jew he occupies a somewhat equivocal place in the New York scheme of things. He is, however, a great magnate, for he represents the Rothschilds in America and since he possesses what McAllister calls true "tong," his palace and its entertainments almost rival those of the Mystic Rose.

"But Caroline won't have the Belmonts here. So narrow, I think." Mrs. Sanford was actually criticizing our hostess. I liked her more and more.

"But then I suppose she wants to draw the line somewhere," I said.

"Yes. And what she's doing is to draw the outer perimeter so as to contain the largest possible circle of bores that will fit comfortably into her dining room." This was a most unexpected announcement.

"Really, Mrs. Sanford, I think you are a revolutionary."

"You'll be one, too, if you stay too long in this city, revolving and revolving in the same orbit. Look at the gentlemen, will you!"

I said that I had already noticed them.

"Half drunk already. They leave their offices, drop in at the Hoffman bar or at their club, have a drink or two, come home, drink some more, quarrel with their wives. Then—well, here they are, thinking of food and drink like buffaloes heading for the watering hole."

"Surely Mr. Sanford does not qualify as a—buffalo."

I detected something odd in her manner, a slight turning away; the merriment ceased. "No, no. Bill is usually most abstemious. But he does love to go out, and I don't."

"Even now?"

"*You* are like a fresh Atlantic breeze in this hot-house, Mr. Schuyler."

I was perfectly flattered, and responded in kind until dinner was announced.

Ward McAllister, *in loco Astoris,* took in Emma first. I came in last with Mrs. Astor on my arm (McAllister had earlier sent me full verbal instructions as to protocol via the stately butler).

"Where is *Mr.* Astor?" I asked as the majestic figure beside me set the pace for our slow walk to the long dining room.

"In Florida." She said the name of the state as though it were something very strange and not quite nice. "He takes the boat. He has horses there. Do you like horses, Mr. Schermerhorn Schuyler?"

I did my best with that one. In fact, I did my best through the long luxurious dinner, for I was on Mrs. Astor's right—taking precedence as a sort of foreigner.

The motif of the dining room was of the purest, heaviest, most expensively wrought gold. Candelabra, epergnes, serving plates, all was gold, even the roses (mystical?) that decorated the table had a gold look to them.

But one works hard to sit in that high place, to eat that superb dinner. Conversation with Mrs. Astor is not easy, for she is swift to exclude whole subjects. As usual, I did not mention literature. That is for others to do if they are so minded. She was not so minded. She did not, she felt obliged to say, find much worth reading nowadays. But, graciously, she admitted to enjoying the illustrations to my article on the Empress Eugénie. On music she is better. She has seen and sometimes heard the second act of all the great operas. Painting and sculpture? No response except to praise her own things.

I moved boldly to grave matters. I told her that I was soon to go to Washington City. I would be dealing with the President. My hope of impressing her was stopped dead with an absolute exclusion. "*I* have never been to Washington myself."

"But why should you leave right here?" I babbled, implying, idiotically, that she remain forever seated at her own dinner table, while footmen filled golden goblets with Château Margaux.

"I go to Ferncliff." This was an announcement. It is the name of the house that her husband has built up the Hudson at Rhinebeck. "I also go to Newport. I have a cottage there. You and the Princess must visit us. One goes first by the cars to Boston. Then one changes to the cars of the Fall River line."

That, I think, gives the flavour of our conversation. At one point she did press me hard on the Schermerhorn connection; happily, I was able, without once lying, to convince her that we were indeed cousins.

Since the dinner lasted three hours, I feel now that I know Mrs. Astor as well as I shall ever want to. Alternate courses were a relief because I had Mrs. Sanford to my right. She knew exactly what I was going through without once making any reference to our hostess. I must say (as a result of the contrast?) she seems to me now a sort of angel of good sense and kindness; also, swift, oh, very swift to get the point to things. She is remarkably like Emma in that regard.

At about eleven Mrs. Astor rose from her place—in the middle of a sentence to me on the difficulties of finding footmen who would not drink up what was left in the bottles. With a marvellous silken, whispery, jingling sound, the ladies followed Mrs. Astor to the vast art gallery that runs parallel to the dining room. In the dining room the gentlemen huddled together, testing the port, the madeira.

I found myself joined on the one side by the solicitous McAllister: "*She* was enchanted by you. I can tell our Rose's every mood."

And on my other side was William Sanford, looking more glamourous than ever, and already breathing cigar smoke. "So how's the old tin oven, Mr. Schuyler?" This was meant to be jovial.

I responded with all the pomp of Mrs. Astor. "If I had a tin oven, Mr. Sanford, I would hope that it worked properly."

"You must pardon an old railroad man. That's one of our expressions." He went on for a while, spinning yet another identity for himself—a sort of diamond in the rough Commodore Vanderbilt type, straight-talking and mean as a snake. I found him tiring in this vein; happily, he is not slow to see what effect he is making and so changed entirely his manner.

"We enjoyed the Princess's company at lunch. As did the Belmonts."

"So Mrs. Sanford told me." I was deliberately flat; do not really care to encourage this peculiar acquaintance.

"I hope the Princess was amused."

"She has said nothing to me about what must have been something of a gala."

"Yes." The grey eyes were very round now; and calculating—what? How to win me? But I am hardly worth the effort. "We hope that you both will visit us at Newport, Rhode Island, in June."

"June is a long time away. Besides," I added, inspired, "we're committed to Mrs. Astor."

"Beechwood's uncomfortable."

I gathered that this was the name of the Astor cottage. "Besides I may have to be at the nominating conventions. Emma is eager to see St. Louis and Cincinnati, not to mention the god Demos in action." If Sanford believed a word of this, he would, as they say here, believe anything. But I laid it on.

"Of course." Sanford was mild. "Conkling's the man, you know."

"To be nominated for president?"

Sanford nodded, slowly, deliberately, as if he himself were kingmaker. "It's all been arranged by the Stalwarts, and in spite of all your reformers like Bristow and Schurz, Tom Murphy and Chet Arthur will decide who gets nominated. Of course there'll be a row."

"Is it true that General Grant would like a third term?"

"Mrs. Grant would dearly like it and I suppose he would, too. But this Babcock thing . . ." Sanford shook his head, affecting sadness. "Not to mention the constant fussing of your reformers, going on and on about Civil Service reform, like crazy fools."

I agreed that it was foolish to want to reform the Civil Service when it is plainly not possible under the present party system which requires that the incoming political party replace everyone in the departments of the government with their own supporters who are, to a man, every bit as undeserving and as unqualified as those whose places they have usurped. This has been going on all my life. Lately, examinations have been given to would-be government workers with, predictably, farcical results. Much quoted in the town is the reply of one of Collector Arthur's pets to the examiner's question, "By what process is a statute of the United States enacted?" To which the good Republican answered, "Never saw one erected and don't know the process."

"You have not met Senator Conkling, have you?"

I said that I had met him briefly last summer.

"An impressive man, a superb orator, vain as can be, of course. The ladies think the world of him."

"Yes. Particularly our friend Mrs. Sprague."

A look of interest was bestowed on me like a prize for deportment. "Well, now, you don't say?"

"So I do say. Mrs. Sprague has been living in Paris, you know. She has an apartment near the Madeleine, in the Rue Duphot." I piled on the details.

"An uncommonly handsome woman."

"She is indeed."

"I guess Kate Chase Sprague is the closest thing to a queen we've ever had in this country." Sanford lowered his voice. "Mustn't let McAllister hear me say that or he'll push one of the Mystic Rose's thorns my way. But Mrs. Astor is just New York, while Kate was queen of Washington, of politics, right until '73. Then it was all over. Funny thing. I warned Sprague that the Panic was on its way, but there was no talking to that man. There never is. When he's not drunk—which is rare—he's just plain eccentric. Of the two, Kate has the brains."

"But apparently those brains are now at the service of Senator Conkling and not of Senator Sprague." The most talked-of Washington liaison is that between Roscoe Conkling, the beautiful senator from New York and master of his state's Republican party, and Kate Chase Sprague, the beautiful daughter of the rather plain late Chief Justice and would-be president Salmon P. Chase, as well as wretched wife to the mad little senator from Rhode Island, William Sprague. Emma sees a good deal of Kate at Paris; finds her deeply embittered, resenting an exile not unlike that of our Empress but at least Kate has the good luck to be at Paris rather than at Chislehurst. Of all the Americans who have come our way in France, Emma took most to Kate, as she calls her, and I must say that despite the gloomy setting in the Rue Duphot the woman does have the curious gleam one notices in those who have been not only at a world's centre but for a time the focal point of that world's interest.

Kate has been in Paris for almost two years now; separated from her husband by an ocean—and a thousand bottles; from her lover Conkling by the force of society, not to mention that young man's ambition, for he is, as Sanford says, a contender for the presidency next year.

Sudden thought: This puts me in a curious dilemma. Should Conkling be the candidate and should I be at work for Tilden, what then ought my attitude be when the scandal of Kate and Conkling becomes a part of the ever-dingy electoral process? I shall have no attitude—and hope that the Republicans nominate Conkling's vigorous enemy the Speaker of the House of Representatives James G. Blaine.

Today has been both disturbing and splendid.

At noon Blaise Delacroix Sanford was baptized in the drawing room of the Sanford mansion by a Roman Catholic bishop with, as they say, the map of all Ireland writ large upon his red face.

Emma and I stood as godparents for the baby, who roared agreeably. Sanford was in an exuberant mood, made only slightly more distasteful than usual by a newfound religiosity. He has taken to exclaiming in a loud voice and at odd moments, "Praise God." He has not yet asked us to drop to our knees and pray with him, but I feel it is only a matter of time.

Some fifty people had been invited for dinner after the ceremony, amongst them Ward McAllister. "*She* could not come," he breathed into my ear. "But *she* has sent a most beautiful cup. So tragic, the loss of the beautiful Mrs. Sanford. He has taken it very hard, hasn't he?"

"Very hard. As we all have."

"So good of you and the Princess to stay with him. He has no family. She had Family, of course. But they are at the South, don't you know?"

Due to my gentle insistence, the Gilders (wife and sister as well as bookman) had been invited to the christening. I fear that I have taken to literary society in the biggest way. One day finds me at the Lotos Club, the next at the Century Club. I fawn relentlessly on publishers.

I now have, according to Gilder, "a truly princely offer from Scribner's. They will pay you five thousand dollars for the rights to your election book." Gilder was as pleased for me as I am for me. "Naturally, you'll let me publish as much as I can in *Scribner's Monthly.*"

"We *are* thrilled," said Jeanette Gilder, but whether by my sudden good fortune or by the Gilders' finding themselves in the same drawing room as the August Belmonts, I could not tell.

I now work every day on the book. Bigelow provides me with all sorts of information, and Tilden himself promises to give the final manuscript a careful reading.

I was well on my way to survival, until this afternoon, when my life was most unexpectedly changed.

After the guests had departed, I sat with Sanford and Emma in the pseudo-Renaissance library with its view of Fifth Avenue, bright and new-looking in the early April light. Sanford and I continued to drink champagne while Emma poured herself cup after cup of coffee from a massive Georgian silver pot.

"A good party!" Sanford lit a long cigar. "Praise God!" This last was addressed to the ceiling that, presumably, separates Sanford from his much-lauded Deity.

"I hope my literary *confrères* did not lower too much the 'tong.' "

"They give variety. Say, it sure was nice of Lina to send us that cup." Sanford has lately taken to referring to the Mystic Rose by her family nickname—no doubt, on the ground that the less he sees of her the greater the intimacy.

Then Emma put down her coffee cup and said, "Papa, William and I were married this morning."

"Praise God in Heaven!" Sanford addressed this prayer not to the ceiling but to me.

"My God!" I said, contaminated by so many celestial references.

"The Bishop married us, before anyone came." Emma was nervous . . . from too much coffee, I decided dumbly.

"Why didn't you tell me?" I heard my own voice, as if from far away; and noted that it was the querulous voice of an old man.

"Because—" Emma stopped.

"Because," said Sanford, "you might have objected. I mean it is . . . so soon . . . after—"

"Yes. It is *too* soon after." I was sharp. On the one hand (why deny it?), I am delighted that Emma has not only saved herself but released me from a burden that has been threatening to crush me entirely; yet, on the other hand, I cannot stop thinking of Denise, only three months dead. "Why couldn't you have waited a few more months?"

"The child," said Sanford. "He needs a mother. And I"—Sanford's small pretty mouth suddenly delivered a spontaneous if somewhat girlish, even coquettish smile—"*I* need Emma."

"The orchids," I said, not meaning to. But neither one of them was listening to me. They were looking at each other.

"We thought it the right thing to do, Papa." Emma shifted to rapid French, and I don't think Sanford was able to understand us. "William wants to get away. To go to Paris. As soon as possible. With the child. With me. Obviously, I can't travel with him unmarried. So last week we asked the Bishop, and he was most agreeable. He arranged it all."

"But it seems to me to be—and I'm not exactly punctilious in these matters—much too swift. Too . . . insulting to Denise."

"You will make me weep." Emma's eyes were indeed filled with tears.

"I'm sorry."

"*I* think Denise would have approved. She loved us both. William *and* me. And you, too, Papa. If you had been there, with us, you'd understand better what I've just done."

"No matter." I spoke again in English. "Well, congratulations, Sanford."

My son-in-law was on his feet. "Praise"—I fear he shouted—"God!" as he lunged forward to shake my hand.

I kissed Emma. She burst into tears. And so, on this lovely April day we at last buried the celebrated Princess d'Agrigente and attended the *accouchement* of the second Mrs. William Sanford, who will depart next week for France with her husband aboard his yacht.

I stay behind in the mansion, writing my book and living a life of perfect luxury. For the first time in years I am free. I feel the way a life-prisoner must when his heavy chains are suddenly, inexplicably, struck from him.

We parted this morning. My son-in-law shook my hand firmly; he looked surprised when Emma and I did not embrace. Emma gave me a long look; started to speak, and then thought better of it. She got into the waiting carriage. Two wagons were needed for the Sanfords' trunks.

"You'll join us soon. That's all agreed, isn't it?" At least Sanford does not call me Father.

"Yes. I'll join you soon. When the book is done."

"The Lord be praised."

Then they were gone, leaving the butler and me standing in the grey light of what promises to be a rainy day.

I have not a curious nature; do not read other people's letters; do not eavesdrop. Since I can usually imagine with the greatest ease the worst, I need not know it. In fact, I avoid confidences and hate all secrets. I assume that there are things even in the lives of those one loves that are dark, and I for one would rather not have them brought to light.

The greater the ascent, the longer the fall. Yes. All platitude is truth; all truth platitude. Unfortunately, it takes a long life to learn this, at the end.

I spent last night with Jamie, at his insistence. "I need company, Charlie. Because I hate everybody."

"That's normal."

"I can't wait to leave this city. It's bad luck for me."

We dined together at an obscure French restaurant back of Steinway Hall. Jamie will not go to any place where he might be recognized by the gentry. I had rather hoped that he would want to go on to the Chinese Pagoda, but like most people who hate everyone, he desperately needs company.

Although Jamie won't go to the new Delmonico's, he will go to shady places where the people are lively, and if he should meet any of the gentry there—well, they are fallen, too. He thinks of himself as Lucifer, and all because of a schoolboy tussle in the snow with young Mr. May.

My pen delays . . . Stops. Why write any of this? Why make a record? Answer: habit. To turn life to words is to make life yours to do with as you please, instead of the other way round. Words translate and transmute raw life, make bearable the unbearable. So at the end, as in the beginning, there is only The Word. I seem to be making a book of maxims.

Jamie took me to Madame Restell's house, where the usual charming women and eager men were gathered in her comfortable rich salons.

Jamie promptly went to the card room to gamble, leaving me with Madame Restell; she affected to be glad to see me once again. At her insistence I took brandy from a waiter, despite the bad effect it always has on my heart.

"We're neighbours." Madame grinned at me; her bright knowing eyes are like some quick flesh-eating bird's, forever on the lookout for provender.

"You do know everything."

"Well, I do see you coming and going from the Sanford house. But"—

she frowned—"I don't really know *every*thing. For instance, the charming Mrs. Sanford. I liked her so much."

"What about her?"

"Well . . . She is dead."

"Absolutely. And horribly so, for us."

"But why?"

"You tell me." I was hard. "*You* know. I don't. I do know that Denise wanted a child and that you told her that she could have one, safely, if she followed your regime. Well, she followed it, and she died."

Madame Restell was silent for some minutes. Past her shoulder I could see the gaming room. Handsome women stood back of the intent card players, no doubt giving signals to their partners.

Then Madame Restell said, "I saw Mrs. Sanford for the last time a year ago when she came here to ask me if she could ever have a child and I said, no, never. I was as blunt as I have ever been to anyone in my life because I liked her."

The room began to enlarge and contract. I thought I might faint or, better yet, die. "But last summer when my daughter came to see you, didn't you say . . ."

"I have never met your daughter, Mr. Schuyler."

I should have stopped right there, for I saw dawning in those old bright bird's eyes a truth that no one must ever know. But I could not stop myself. "The special nurse. She came from you, didn't she?"

"I sent no special nurse. And I have played no part at all in what has happened."

I have no memory of walking home. Although not drunk, I was not sane.

I went straight to Emma's room. She was reading in bed. She smiled; looked lovely.

"I've just come from Madame Restell."

Emma put down her book. She looked at me, and her face did not change expression.

I sat down in a chair because my legs had given way. I looked at Emma; saw her as she had been that evening in Philadelphia at the desk in Sanford's railway car. I saw two figures entwined in a summer gazebo and I knew exactly what had happened. I knew what Emma had done. Or thought I did.

Emma was to the point. "Madame Restell does not like failure, Papa. It is bad for business."

"Was she lying to me?"

Emma sighed; made a bookmark of her comb. "If it was only you, I wouldn't mind. You know the truth. You know I was devoted to Denise and that if I had had to choose between her and Sanford . . ." Emma stopped; took the comb out of the book and kept her place with one finger. "Anyway, to save her professional reputation Madame Restell is going to tell everyone in New York her terrible story. That's why we're running away to France."

"What did happen?"

"Nothing except what you already know. Madame Restell thought that Denise, with care, had a good chance of surviving—"

"Only a good chance?"

"Yes. Denise insisted that we pretend that there was no risk at all. But there was. That's why I begged her not to—go ahead. But she did."

"Madame Restell says that she never sent anyone to look after Denise."

"For a woman who does not exist, Madame Restell's assistant demanded a very large salary. She can be produced—though *I* never want to see her again."

"Madame Restell says that she has never met you."

Emma smiled. "Never having met people is Madame Restell's usual form of tact. Shall I describe the horrors of her drawing room?"

"No. I am relieved." I got to my feet. Emma kissed her hand to me, and as she did I saw between us, for a brief hallucinatory moment, a single white locust blossom spinning slowly, slowly, like a summer snowflake.

*"Bonne nuit, cher Papa."*

"Sleep well," I said, and meant it.

Emma opened her book and began to read.

I came back to this room.

I have just taken a double draught of laudanum.

I have moved into a pleasant room at the Buckingham Hotel (seventeen dollars a day, with excellent meals) across the avenue from St. Patrick's Cathedral. My room at the back looks out upon the large vegetable garden of a very pleasant farm just west of Fifth Avenue.

I work with Bigelow on the book. I write occasional articles for the *Post.* I dine out every night but, miraculously, I am losing rather than gaining weight and so I feel, at times, almost young again. Certainly the loss of excess flesh makes all the more intense, even rapturous, my cigarine interludes.

Bryant, I fear, is not long for this world, but then he is—what? eighty-two, no, eighty-three years old. I do worry what will happen to me when he is dead, since I have lost the *Herald* now that Jamie has turned Coriolanus and gone into exile whilst the young editors at the *Post* know me not.

Bryant has asked me to do an article on our old friend Fitz-Green Halleck. "Because I simply haven't the time. Besides, I've already paid him lengthy homage at the New-York Historical Society."

This morning—a fine May day—I was both journalist and memorialist, for I was called upon to say a few words at the unveiling of a statue to Halleck in the Central Park.

Bryant also spoke, as did that luminary, His Fraudulency himself, the President of the United States Rutherford B. Hayes, a true lover, to hear him tell it, of our home-grown American sweet-singers or warblers.

We sat on a wooden platform beside the bronze statue that looks not at all like the Halleck I knew, but then the best statues, unlike the best words, always lie.

I read my short, short speech, recalling the Shakespeare Tavern group of which Halleck was the presiding genius. On my feet, I was so much at ease that I am half convinced that I should attempt, at last, the lecture circuit once the book is finished.

I did not get a chance to talk to the President. Bryant had seen to it that no one could get at Mr. Hayes without first stepping over Bryant's long legs.

Hayes is an impressive-looking, rather stout man with a naturally fierce expression. I stared at him with some fascination, for he is, after all, my creation, a major character in the book that I am writing. It is not often that writers are actually able to see their fictional creatures made flesh.

*A Special Despatch to The New York Evening Post*
by William Cullen Bryant

It is with the greatest sorrow that I am obliged to record here the sudden death of Charles Schermerhorn Schuyler, a friend, a colleague, one of the last sharers with me of the old times in Knickerbocker's town.

I saw my old friend the morning of the day he died, May 16, 1877, in the Central Park, where we were both present at the unveiling of a statue commemorating our common long-dead friend the poet Fitz-Greene Halleck. In fact, Mr. Schuyler was writing a description for this newspaper of that memorial service when he died.

I find it peculiarly poignant, always, when a colleague of so many years dies. I had known Mr. Schuyler since he first wrote for the *Evening Post,* nearly half a century ago. But his true fame rests securely upon those valuable historical works that he composed during a lifetime spent for the most part in Europe. Perhaps the most exemplary of his works is that compelling and incisive study, *Paris Under the Communists.*

At the time of Mr. Schuyler's death, he was at work . . .

# From
# *Empire*

THE WAR ENDED last night, Caroline. Help me with these flowers." Elizabeth Cameron stood in the open French window, holding a large blue-and-white china vase filled with roses, somewhat showily past their prime. Caroline helped her hostess carry the heavy vase into the long cool dim drawing room.

At forty, Mrs. Cameron was, to Caroline's youthful eye, very old indeed; nevertheless, she was easily the handsomest of America's great ladies and certainly the most serenely efficient, able to arrange a platoon of flower vases before breakfast with the same ease and briskness that her uncle, General Sherman, had devastated Georgia.

"One must always be up at dawn in August." Mrs. Cameron sounded to Caroline rather like Julius Caesar, reporting home. "Servants—like flowers—tend to wilt. We shall be thirty-seven for lunch. Do you intend to marry Del?"

"I don't think I shall ever marry anyone." Caroline frowned with pleasure at Mrs. Cameron's directness. Although Caroline thought of herself as American, she had actually lived most of her life in Paris and so had had little contact with women like Elizabeth Sherman Cameron, the perfect modern American lady—thus, earth's latest, highest product, as Henry James had not too ironically proclaimed. When Del asked Caroline to join the house-party at Surrenden Dering, deep in the English countryside, she had not even pretended to give the matter thought. She had come straight on from Paris, with a single night at Brown's Hotel in London. That was Friday, and the United States and Spain had been at war for three exciting months. Now, apparently, the war was over. She tried to recall the date. Was it August 12 or August 13, 1898?

"Mr. Hay says that the President agreed to an armistice yesterday afternoon. Which was last night for us." She frowned. "Those roses look rather awful, don't they?"

"They're a bit . . . dusty. I suppose from all that heat."

"Heat!" Mrs. Cameron laughed, a fairly pleasant sound so unlike the stylized staccato screech of a Paris lady. "You should try Pennsylvania this time of year! My husband has two places. Each hotter than the other, with mosquitoes and gnats and something very small and vile that burrows like a mole under your skin and raises a welt. You would make a good wife for Del."

"But would he make a good husband for me?" Through the tall windows Caroline could see her co-host, Don Cameron, on the grassy lower terrace. He was driving a buggy, drawn by a pair of American trotting-horses. Senator Cameron was a red-faced, heavily moustached but modestly bearded man, older by a quarter century than his wife. As she could not abide him, she treated him with exquisite courtesy and deference; just as she treated in a rather cool and offhanded way Caroline's other co-host, the equally ancient Henry Adams, who entirely adored her as she entirely accepted him. According to Del, the trio had struck Henry James, who lived a few miles away at Rye, as "maddeningly romantic." When Del had repeated this to Caroline, both agreed that although antiquity might indeed be instructive, exotic, even touching, no couple so aged could ever be romantic, maddeningly or otherwise. But then the celebrated expatriate Mr. James was like some highly taut musical string of feline gut, constantly attuned to vibrations unheard by cruder ears.

Yet old as Mrs. Cameron was, Caroline could not help but admire the slender waist, which seemed unstayed; also, the heat had so flushed her cheeks that she looked—Caroline finally capitulated—beautiful, at least this morning, with naturally waved, old-gold hair, cat-like blue eyes, straight nose and straight mouth, framed by the square jaw of her celebrated uncle. Had Caroline not been so recently and so arduously finished at Mlle. Souvestre's Allenswood School she might have offered herself as an apprentice to Mrs. Cameron: "Because I want to live forever in America, now that Father's dead." Caroline heard herself say rather more than she had intended.

"Forever is a long time. But if I had forever to spend somewhere it wouldn't be there, let me tell you. It would be Paris."

"Well, since I've spent most of my life—so far—in Paris, home looks all the greener, I suppose."

In wicker chairs, placed side by side on the stone terrace, John Hay and Henry Adams presided over the Kentish Weald, as the summer light yielded, slowly, very slowly, to darkness.

"In Sweden, in summer, the sun shines all night long." Henry Adams lit a cigar. "One never thinks of England being almost as far to the north as Sweden. But look! It's after dinner, and it's light yet."

"I suppose we like to think of England as being closer to us than it really is." Carefully, John Hay pressed his lower back against the hard cushion that Clara had placed behind him. For some months the pain had been fairly constant, a dull aching that seemed to extend from the small of the back down into the pelvis, but, of course, ominously, the doctors said that it was the other way around. In some mysterious fashion the cushion stopped the pain from exploding into one of its sudden borealises, as Hay tended to think of those excruciating flare-ups when his whole body would be electrified by jolts of pain—originating in the atrophied—if not worse—prostate gland, whose dictatorship ordered his life, obliging him to pass water or, painfully, not to pass water, a dozen times during the night, accompanied by a burning sensation reminiscent of his youth when he had briefly contracted in war-time Washington a minor but highly popular venereal infection.

"Are you all right?" Although Adams was not looking at him, Hay knew that his old friend was highly attuned to his physical state.

"No, I'm not."

"Good. You're better. When you're really in pain, you boast of rude health. How pretty Del's girl is."

Hay looked across the terrace to the stone bench where his son and Caroline had combined to make a romantic picture, suitable for Gibson's pen, while the remaining houseguests—it was Monday—floated like subaquatic creatures in the watery half-light. The children had been removed, to Hay's delight, Adams's sorrow. "Do you recall her mother, Enrique?" Hay had a number of variations of Henry's name, playful tribute to his friend's absolute unprotean nature.

"The darkly beautiful Princesse d'Agrigente was not easy, once seen, ever to forget. I knew her back in the seventies, the beautiful decade, after our unbeautiful war was won. Did you know Sanford?"

Hay nodded. The pain which had started to radiate from the lumbar region suddenly surrendered to the pillow's pressure. "He was on McDowell's staff early in the war. I think he wanted to marry Kate Chase . . ."

"Surely he was not alone in this madness?" Hay sensed the Porcupine's smile beneath the beard, pale blue in the ghostly light.

"We were many, it's true. Kate was the Helen of Troy of E Street. But Sprague got her. And Sanford got Emma d'Agrigente."

"Money?"

"What else?" Hay thought of his own good luck. He had never thought that he could ever make a living. For a young man from Warsaw, Illinois, who liked to read and write, who had gone east to college, and graduated from Brown, there were only two careers. One was the law, which bored him; the other, the ministry, which intrigued him, despite a near-perfect absence of faith. Even so, he had been wooed by various ministers of a variety of denominations. But he had said no, finally, to the lot, for, as he wrote his lawyer uncle, Milton: "I would not do for a Methodist preacher, for I am a poor horseman. I would not suit the Baptists, for I would dislike water. I would fail as an Episcopalian, for I am no ladies' man." This last was disingenuous. Hay had always been more than usually susceptible to women and they to him. But as he had looked, at the age of twenty-two, no more than twelve years old, neither in Warsaw nor, later, in Springfield, was he in any great demand as a ladies' man.

Instead, Hay had grimly gone into his uncle's law office; got to know his uncle's friend, a railroad lawyer named Abraham Lincoln; helped Mr. Lincoln in the political campaign that made him president; and then boarded the train with the President-elect to go to Washington for five years, one month and two weeks. Hay had been present in the squalid boardinghouse when the murdered President had stopped breathing, on a mattress soaked with blood.

Hay had then gone to Paris, as secretary to the American legation. Later, he had served, as a diplomat, in Vienna and Madrid. He wrote verse, books of travel; was editor of the *New York Tribune.* He lectured on Lincoln. He wrote folksy poems, and his ballads of Pike County sold in the millions. But there was still no real money until the twenty-four-year-old Cleveland heiress Clara Stone asked him to marry her; and he had gratefully united himself with a woman nearly a head taller than he with an innate tendency to be as fat as it was his to be lean.

At thirty-six Hay was saved from poverty. He moved to Cleveland; worked for his father-in-law—railroads, mines, oil, Western Union Telegraph; found that he, too, had a gift for making money once he had money. He served, briefly, as assistant secretary of state; and wrote, anonymously, a best-selling novel, *The Bread-Winners,* in which he expressed his amiable creed that although men of property were the best situated to administer and regulate America's wealth and that labor agitators were a constant threat to the system, the ruling class of a city in the Western Reserve (Cleveland was never named) was hopelessly narrow, vulgar, opinionated. Henry Adams had called him a snob; he had agreed. Both agreed that it was a good idea that he had published the book anonymously; otherwise, the Major could not have offered him the all-important embassy at London. Had the Senate suspected that Hay did not admire all things American, he would not have been confirmed.

"Money makes the difference." Hay took a deep puff of his Havana cigar: what on earth, he suddenly wondered, were they to *do* with Cuba? Then, aware not only of the vapidity of what he had said but also of the thin blue smile beneath the thick blue beard in the chair beside him, he added, "Not that gilded porcupines would know—except by hearsay—what it is like to be poor and struggling."

"You wrench my heart." Adams was sardonic. "Also, my quills were not heavily gilded at birth. I have acquired just enough shekels to creep through life, serving the odd breakfast to a friend . . ."

"Perhaps you might have been less angelic if you'd had to throw yourself into . . ."

". . . wealthy matrimony?"

A spasm of pain forced Hay to cough. He pretended it was cigar smoke inhaled, as he maneuvered his spine against the pillow. "Into the real world. Business, which is actually rather easy. Politics, which, for us, is not."

"Well, you've done well, thanks to a rich wife. So has Whitelaw Reid. So has William Whitney. So, would have Clarence King had he had your luck—all right, good sense—to marry wealthily and well."

Below the terrace, in the dark woods, owls called to one another. Why, Hay wondered, was the Surrenden nightingale silent? "Why has he never married?" asked Hay: their constant question to one another. Of the three friends, King was the most brilliant, the handsomest, the best talker; also, athlete, explorer, geologist. In the eighties all three had been at Washington, and, thanks largely to King's brilliance, Adams's old house became the first salon, as the newspapers liked to say, of the republic.

"He has no luck," said Hay. "And we have had too much."

"Do you see it that way?" Adams turned his pale blue head toward Hay. The voice was suddenly cold. Inadvertently, Hay had approached the forbidden door. The only one in their long friendship to which Hay had not the key. In the thirteen years since Adams had found his dead wife on the floor, he had not mentioned her to Hay—or to anyone that Hay knew of. Adams had simply locked a door; and that was that.

But Hay was experiencing vivid pain; and so was less than his usual tactful self. "Compared to King, we have lived in Paradise, you and I."

A tall, tentative figure appeared on the terrace. Hay was relieved at the diversion. "Here I am, White," he called out to the embassy's first secretary, just arrived from London.

White pulled up a chair; refused a cigar. "I have a telegram," he said. "It's a bit crumpled. The paper is so flimsy." He gave the telegram to Hay, who said, "Am I expected, as a director of Western Union, to defend the quality of the paper we use?"

"Oh, no. No!" White frowned, and Hay was suddenly put on his guard by his colleague's nervousness: it was part of White's charm to laugh at pleasantries that were neither funny nor pleasant. "I can't read in the dark," said Hay. "Unlike the owl . . . and the porcupine." Adams had taken the telegram from Hay; now he held it very close to his eyes, deciphering it in the long day's waning light.

"My God," said Adams softly. He put down the telegram. He stared at Hay.

"The German fleet has opened fire in Cavite Bay." This had been Hay's fear ever since the fall of Manila.

"No, no." Adams gave the telegram to Hay, who put it in his pocket. "Perhaps you should go inside and read it. Alone."

"Who's it from?" Hay turned to White.

"The President, sir. He has appointed you . . . ah . . . has offered to appoint you . . ."

"Secretary of state," Adams finished. "*The* great office of state is now upon offer, to you."

"Everything comes to me either too late or too soon," said Hay. He was unprepared for his own response, which was closer to somber regret than joy. Certainly, he could not pretend to be surprised. He had known all along that the current secretary, Judge Day, was only a temporary appointment. The Judge wanted a judgeship and he had agreed to fill in, temporarily, at the State Department as a courtesy to his old friend the Major. Hay was also aware that the Major thought highly of his own performance, in which he had handled a number of delicate situations in a fashion that had enhanced the President's reputation. Now, in John Hay's sixtieth year, actual power was offered him, on a yellow sheet of Western Union's notoriously cheap paper.

Hay was conscious of the two men's intent gaze, like a pair of predatory night birds in the forest. "Well," said Hay, "late or soon, this is the bolt from the blue, isn't it?"

"Surely," said Adams, "you have something more memorable to say at such a time."

A sudden spasm of pain made Hay gasp the word "Yes." Then: "I could. But won't." But inside his head an aria began: Because, if I were to tell the truth I would have to confess that I have somehow managed to mislay my life. Through carelessness, I have lost track of time and now time is losing, rapidly, all track of me. Therefore, I cannot accept this longed-for honor because, oh, isn't it plain to all of you, my friends and foes, that I am dying?

White was speaking through Hay's pain: ". . . he would like you to be in Washington by the first of September so that Judge Day can then go to Paris for the peace conference with Spain."

"I see," said Hay distractedly. "Yes. Yes."

"*Is* it too late?" Adams had read his mind.

"Of course it's too late." Hay managed to laugh; he got to his feet. Suddenly, the pain was gone: an omen. "Well, White, we have work to do. When in doubt about anything, Mr. Lincoln always wrote two briefs, one in favor, one opposed. Then he'd compare the two and the better argument carried the day, or so we liked to think. Now we're going to write my refusal of this honor. Then we're going to write my acceptance."

Henry Adams stood up. "Remember," he said, "if you don't accept—and I think you shouldn't, considering your age—our age—and health, you will have to resign as ambassador."

"On the ground . . . ?" Hay knew what Adams would say.

And Adams said it. "If you were just an office-seeker, it would make no difference either way. But you are *in* office. You are a man of state; and you are serious. As such, you may not refuse the President. One cannot accept a favor and then, when truly needed, refuse a service."

Thus, the Adamses—and the old republic. Hay nodded; and went inside. All deaths are the same, he thought. But some are Roman; and virtuous.

The bronze busts of Henry James and William Dean Howells stared off into space, as did the earthly head of Henry Adams beside the fire. It was John Hay's turn to be host to his friend and neighbor, and from his armchair he surveyed the three heads with a pleasure he was quick to identify to himself as elderly. Each belonged to a friend. If nothing else, he had done very well when it came to friends. Although he was not the man-of-letters that James or Howells was, or the historian that Adams was, he felt extended through them beyond his natural talents. Had he wanted to turn round in his chair, he could have stared into Lincoln's bronze face, surprisingly life-like for a life-mask. But Hay seldom looked at the face that he had once known far better than his own. During the years that he and Nicolay were writing their enormous history of the President, Hay was amazed to find that he had lost all firsthand memory of Lincoln. The million words that they had written had had the effect of erasing Hay's own memory. Nowadays, when asked about the President, he could only remember what they had written, so dully he knew, of that odd astounding man. Hay and Adams often discussed whether or not a memoir might not have the same effect—a gradual erasing of oneself, bit by bit, with words. Adams thought that this would be ideal; Hay did not. He liked his own past, as symbolized by the two busts, one life-mask. He had always suspected, even in moods melancholy and hypochondriacal, that he would end his days in comfort, with abundant memories, seated at his fireside on a February night in the last year of the nineteenth century, in the company of a friend not yet bust-ed. Of course, he had not counted on being secretary of state at the end of the road, but he did not any longer object to the dull grind, which he had turned over to Adee, or to the battles with the Senate, which he allowed Senator Lodge to conduct for him, with considerable help from Lodge's old Harvard professor Henry Adams.

Now the old friends waited for Mrs. Hay, and the dinner guests and "the shrimps," as Hay addressed his children: two out of four were in the house. Alice and Helen were deeply involved in the capital's social life. Clarence was away at school. Del was in New York, perhaps studying law. Hay had always found it easy to talk to his own father; yet found it impossible to talk to his oldest son. Some bond of sympathy had, simply, not developed between them. But then Hay had been a country boy like Lincoln, with nothing but his wits—and a connection or two; while Del, like Lincoln's son Robert, was born to wealth. Lincoln father and Lincoln son had not got on well, either.

"Will Del marry the Sanford girl?" Adams often strayed into Hay's mind.

"I was just thinking of Del, as you must have known, with those otherworldly Adams psychic powers. I don't know. He doesn't confide in me. I know he sees her in New York, where she's set up for the winter."

"She's uncommonly clever," said Adams. "Of all the young girls I know . . ."

"The brigade of girls . . ."

"You make me sound like Tiberius. But of the lot, she is the only one I can't work out."

"Well, she's not like an American girl. That's one reason." Hay had found Caroline disturbingly direct in small matters and unfathomable when it came to those things that must be taken seriously, like marriage. There was also the problem, even mystery, of her father's will. "I think she's made a mistake, contesting the will. After all, when she's twenty-five, or whatever, she'll inherit. So why fuss?"

"Because at her age five years seems forever. I hope Del brings her into the family. I should like her for a niece."

"He threatens to bring her here, for a visit. But he hasn't."

The butler announced, "Senator Lodge, sir." Both Hay and Adams rose as the handsome, were it not for a pair of cavernous nostrils that always made Hay think, idly, of a bumblebee, patrician-politician glided into the room. "Mrs. Hay has got off with Nannie. Neither one can bear to hear me say another word about the treaty."

"Well, we want to hear nothing else." Hay did his best to be genial; and, as always, succeeded. The problem with Henry Cabot Lodge—aside from the disagreeable fact that he looked young enough to be Hay's son—was his serene conviction that he alone knew what the United States ought to do in foreign affairs, and from his high Republican Senate seat he drove the Administration like some reluctant ox, toward the annexation of, if possible, the entire world.

Worse, at a bureaucratic level, Lodge meddled so much with the State Department that even the patient Adee now found unbearable the Senator's constant demands for consulates, to reward right-thinking imperialist friends and allies. But the President wanted peace at any price with the Senate, and the price in Lodge's case was patronage. In exchange, however, Lodge had taken charge of getting the Administration's treaty with Spain through the Senate, a surprisingly difficult task because of the Constitution's unwise stipulation that no treaty could be enacted without the concurrence of two-thirds of the Senate, an august body filled with men of the most boundless conceit, as Adams had so neatly portrayed in an anonymous, highly satiric novel which even now no one, except the remaining Hearts, knew for certain that he had written.

Apparently, the Senators were, once again, running true to form, according to Lodge, whose British accent offended Hay's ears. But then Hay still spoke near-Indiana, and deeply loved England, while Lodge spoke like an Englishman, and hated England. La-di-da Lodge was one of the less unkind epithets for Massachusetts's junior senator, who was now denouncing his state's senior senator, the noble if misguided anti-imperialist George F. Hoar, who had told the nation that "no nation was ever created good enough to own another," a sly paraphrase of Lincoln. "Theodore writes me almost every day." Lodge stood, back to the fire, rocking from side to side on short legs. "He says that Hoar and the rest are little better than traitors."

Adams sighed. "I would think that Theodore would have quite enough to do up in Albany without worrying about the Senate."

"Well, he does think of the war as his war." Lodge smiled at Hay. "His *splendid* little war, as you put it. Now he wants to make sure we keep the Philippines."

"So do we all," said Hay. But this was not strictly true. Hay and Adams had thought, from the beginning, that a coaling station for the American fleet would be sufficient recompense for the splendors and miseries of the small war. This was also the view of several of the American commissioners at the Paris Peace Conference. In fact, one commissioner—a Delaware senator—had written Hay a curiously eloquent telegram to say that as the United States had fought Spain in order to free Spain's colonies from tyranny, the United States had no right to take Spain's place as tyrant, no matter how benign. We must, he said, stick to our word.

Hay had put the case to the President, but St. Louis, as it were, had inspired McKinley with a sense of mission. After ten days in the West,

McKinley returned to Washington, convinced that it was the will of the American people, and probably God, too, that the United States annex the entire Philippine archipelago. He instructed the commissioners to that effect; he also offered Spain twenty million dollars; and the Spanish agreed. Meanwhile, something called the Anti-Imperialist League was breathing fire, and an odd mixture they were, ranging from the last Democratic president, Grover Cleveland, to the millionaire Republican Andrew Carnegie, from Henry Adams's own brother, Charles Francis, a one-time president of the Union Pacific Railroad, to Mark Twain.

"I wish, Cabot, I could be as certain as you are . . ." said Adams.

"About everything?" Lodge was amused and slightly, thought Hay, patronizing. Hay had observed the phenomenon before: when the pupil has surpassed—or thinks he has—his teacher.

"No. I have *never* wished for senatorial certitude." Adams was dry. "That is beyond me. I'm always uncertain."

"You were certainly certain that the Spanish must be driven out of Cuba," began Lodge; to be stopped by Adams, who suddenly raised a pale small poodle-like paw.

"That was different. The only important contribution that my family ever made to the United States was the invention of the doctrine that is known by President Monroe's name. The Western Hemisphere must be free of European influence, and the Cuba Libre movement was the last act—the completion—of my grandfather's doctrine. Now, in the large sense, Spain is gone from our hemisphere, along with the French and for all intents and purposes, the British. The Caribbean is ours forever. But for us to end up with vast holdings in the Pacific, that strikes me as potentially dangerous, as more trouble than it's worth. I've sailed the South Seas . . ."

"Old gold," murmured Hay, the phrase Adams had used to describe the entrancing native women of Polynesia.

Adams affected not to hear. "Now you want us to take over a hostile population, made up of worthless Malay types, and Roman Catholics, as well. I thought you had enough of those in Boston without taking on another ten million or so."

Lodge was airy. "Well, unlike the ones in Boston, we won't let your worthless Malays vote, at least not in Massachusetts elections. And they're not hostile, at least not the ones who matter, the people of property, who want us to stay."

"Those are the tame cats, the ones who liked the Spanish. But all the rest follow this young man Aguinaldo, and they want independence." Adams tugged at his beard, which was a white version of Lodge's beard as Hay's beard was a grizzled compromise. Hay was touched that a relatively young politician should want to emulate his elders when modern politics now required clean-shaven men like McKinley and Hanna, or the moustachioed Roosevelt. What did beards imply? he wondered. The early Roman emperors, like the early presidents, were clean-shaven; then decadence—and beards; then Christianity and the clean-shaven Constantine. Was McKinley to be a religious leader, as well as imperial consolidator?

Hay gave the latest news of Emilio Aguinaldo, whose troops had fought with Admiral Dewey on condition that once the Spaniards were gone there would be an independent Philippine—or Vishayan—republic. But McKinley's change of heart had put an end to that dream. Now Aguinaldo's troops—mostly from the Tagal tribe—had occupied the Spanish forts. Aguinaldo had also occupied Iloilo, the capital of Panay province. Thus far, neither side had been eager to begin hostilities. "But this can't last much longer," said Hay, completing his tour of the archipelago's horizon as viewed from the State Department. Elsewhere in Mullett's wedding cake of a building, Hay knew that the War Department was contemplating games that he knew nothing of; and did not want to know about.

"Obviously some sort of incident now would get us our two-thirds vote." Lodge sat in the armchair opposite Adams and adopted the same meditative pose as his old professor—and editor. After Lodge had graduated from Harvard, Adams had hired his former student to be an assistant editor of the *North American Review,* with one standing instruction: when editing historians, strike out all superfluous words, particularly adjectives. Hay had always envied Adams's continence in the matter of English prose. Adams wrote like a Roman, with an urgent war to report; Hay's prose simply idled, waiting for a joke to turn up.

"We had—you had—the two-thirds vote two weeks ago." Adams scowled. "Then the whole thing was frittered away. How I wish Don Cameron was still in the Senate . . ."

"And La Dona across the square," Hay added. Without Lizzie Cameron, Adams was incomplete. But the Camerons were wintering in Paris; and Adams was more than usually irritable and restless in Washington.

For once, Lodge did not make an excuse or, rather, more characteristically, blame someone else for the erosion of support in a Senate where the Republicans not only had a majority but he himself was the guiding spirit of the Foreign Affairs Committee. "I've never seen so much pressure brought to bear, never heard senators give so many positively crazed reasons for not doing the obvious. Anyway, we now have help from Mr. Bryan. Or Colonel Bryan, as he calls himself . . ."

"And who does not, who can?" said Hay, himself a major in the Civil War, who had never fought because he was Lincoln's secretary. Then, the war won without his participation, he was brevetted lieutenant colonel; hence, always and forever, he was Colonel Hay just as the President was always Major McKinley. But the President had actually seen action under his mentor, Ohio's politician-general Rutherford B. Hayes, whose own mentor had been yet another politician-general, James Garfield, and Hay's dear friend, as well. When General Garfield, the golden, had been elected president, he had offered Colonel Hay the position of private secretary; but Hay had gently declined. He could not be in middle age what he had been in youth. Now, of course, all the political generals from Grant to Garfield were dead; the colonels were on the shelf; and the majors had come into their own. After them, no more military-titled politicians. Yet every American war had bred at least one president. Who, Hay wondered, would the splendid little war—oh, fatuous phrase!—bring forth? Adams favored General Miles, the brother-in-law of his beloved Lizzie Cameron. Lodge had already declared that Admiral Dewey's victory at Manila was equal to Nelson's at Aboukir. But of course Lodge would support McKinley, who would be reelected; and so there would be no splendid little war-hero president in the foreseeable future.

Hay caught himself daydreaming; and not listening. In his youth, he could do both. What *was* Lodge talking about? "He holds court in the Marble Room back of the Senate. They come in, one by one, to get their instructions. He's like the pope." Bryan. Colonel Bryan was in town to persuade the Democratic senators to support the treaty on patriotic grounds; then, the treaty passed, they would support a separate resolution to the effect that, in due course, the Philippines would be given their independence. Hay decided that Bryan was probably clever. If imperialism proved to be as popular as McKinley sensed it was in St. Louis, Bryan could enter the next presidential race as one who had joined the army and then favored the treaty and temporary annexation; but if imperialism, for some reason, should not be popular, he was on record as favoring the independence of the Philippines while the Major was now firmly for annexation. "He's also like the pope in that he is not a gentleman." Lodge could not resist the double thrust. Hay, who had not begun life as a gentleman by Lodge's standards, had become one; so much so, in fact, that he, unlike Lodge, never saw any need to use the dangerous word in any context. Politicians, no matter how patrician their birth, were a vulgar infantile lot. "We should be grateful to him, of course, wild man that he is. Because if the treaty passes . . ."

"No 'if,' please." Hay refused to envisage the treaty's failure.

"It's going to be close, Mr. Hay, very close. But Bryan's changing votes. I'm changing votes, I think, and . . ."

"And Mark Hanna's buying one or two," said Adams. "Such is the way of our world."

"A very good thing, too. Corruption in a good cause is a good thing. So who cares that a senator's been bought in the process?" Hay got to his feet, with some difficulty. Although the mortal ailment was, temporarily, in recession, he had lately developed an exciting new set of pains, both arthritic and sciatic; as a result, what felt like jolts of electric energy kept assaulting his nerve ends while odd tendons twitched quite on their own and joints, for no reason, would suddenly lock. "I've come around, Cabot. At first I thought it not only wrong but inconvenient to try to govern so many Catholic Malays. But time's running out on us. The Europeans are partitioning China. The Russians are in Port Arthur. The Germans are in Shantung . . ."

"I want us in Shanghai." Lodge's eyes gleamed at the prospect of yet more Asiatic victories.

"Well, I want us in Siberia," said Adams. "We have no future in the Pacific, but when Russia breaks up, as it must, there's our opportunity. Who controls the Siberian land-mass is the master of Europe and Asia."

Happily, Hay was spared an Adams meditation on the world's ever-shifting balance of power by the arrival of ladies. Hay greeted Mrs. Lodge, known as Sister Anne or Nannie, at the door, aware that her suspicious eye was on her husband. She did not entirely approve of Lodge when he was too much the senator; husband gave wife an innocent look. "Henry and I talk and talk about the treaty, while Cabot, who knows everything, just sits and listens, quiet as pussy," said Hay, maintaining peace in the Lodge family. "In fact, cat's got his tongue tonight."

"There is no cat," said Nannie Lodge, "large enough to get Cabot's silver tongue."

Meanwhile, Clara Hay and their two daughters quite filled the study, and Adams began to shine, as he always did when young women were present, while Lodge grew ever more courtly, and Sister Anne witty. Three of five Hearts in the same room: Hay was content. But contentment ceased in the midst of the bombe-glacée, Clara Hay's ongoing masterpiece. Although cooks came and went over the years, Clara, who could not, as they say, boil water, nevertheless was able to pass on the secret receipts to a number of all-important dishes of which the bombe-glacée was the quivering, delicate, mocha-flavored, creamy, filigree-sugared piece, as Hay called it, of least resistance.

Hay's fork was posed for a stab at this perfection when the butler appeared in the doorway to announce, "The President, sir. He would like you to go over to the mansion."

The dining room was silent. Lodge's dark eyes shone; and the bumblebee nose looked as if it scented pollen. Adams gave his old friend a mournful look. Clara was firm. "He can wait until we've finished dinner."

Hay had discovered a new and almost painless way of getting out of a chair; he used his relatively strong right arm rather than his relatively bad knees to get to his feet. Now he pushed hard against the arm of his chair; and was, almost painlessly, upright. "Henry, you be host. I'll be back—when I'm back."

"I can't think," said Clara, "what the Major is doing up at this hour. Over there, they go to bed with the chickens."

"A fox," said Lodge, "is loose in the chicken house."

At the foot of Hay's majestic staircase stood Mr. Eddy and a White House messenger. Hay's descent was cautious; the scarlet runner a magnificent peril. "What is it, Mr. Eddy?"

"I don't know, Mr. Secretary."

"I don't know either, sir," said the messenger.

"All I know, sir, is he wants you straightaway, sir."

"In mid-bomb," Hay murmured sadly, as the butler got him into his fur-lined coat.

Although February had been lethally cold, no snow had yet fallen, and the three men were able to walk across the avenue to the White House, where the offices in the east end were ominously lit up while the downstairs was dark.

In March Caroline had arrived at the outermost ring of the republic's circles, when she rented a small rose-red brick house in N Street, which ran through a part of dilapidated Georgetown, reminiscent of Aswan in Egypt, where she had once wintered with her father and his arthritis. There was hardly a white face to be seen; and the owner of the house, a commodore's widow of pronounced whiteness, hoped that she would not mind "the darkies." Caroline pronounced herself entranced; and hoped, she said, to hear tom-toms in the night. The widow said that as there were, happily, no Indians nearby, tom-toms would not sound; on the other hand, a good deal of voodoo was practiced between the Potomac River and the canal. She did not recommend it, in practice. The commodore's widow left behind her a large black woman, who would "help out." It was agreed that Caroline would take the house for at least one year. On the brick sidewalk in front of the house two vast shiny-leaved magnolia trees put the front rooms in deepest shadow, always desirable, Caroline had remarked, when living in the tropics. Predictably, Marguerite was stunned to find herself marooned in Africa, with an African in the kitchen.

From the outermost circle, Caroline moved to the innermost: the dining room of Henry Adams, where breakfast was served for six each mid-day and no one was ever invited; yet the table was never empty except for this particular morning, when Caroline ate Virginia smoked ham and biscuits made with buttermilk, and the host, more round than ever, discussed his departure the next day for New York; and then a tour of Sicily with Senator and Mrs. Lodge. "After that, I shall spend the summer in Paris, in the Boulevard Bois de Boulogne. The Camerons are there. *She* is there, at least. No more coffee, William," he said to the manservant, William Gray, who poured him more coffee, which he drank. "Do you know a young poet, an American, named Trumbull Stickney?"

Caroline said, accurately, that she knew very few Americans in Paris. "While we don't seem to know any French," said Adams, judiciously. "We go abroad to see one another. I gather that Mrs. Cameron is Mr. Stickney's muse this spring. If I were young, I would not be jealous. As it is, I writhe." But Adams seemed not to be writhing at all. "You must come over—or back in your case—and show us France."

"I don't know France at all." Caroline was again accurate. "But I know the French."

"Well, I can show you France. I tour the cathedrals yet again. I brood on the relics of the twelfth century."

"They are . . . energetic?"

Adams smiled, almost shyly. "You remembered? I'm flattered."

"I'd hoped for more instruction. But just as I move to Washington, you go away. I feel as if you had created me, a second Mrs. Lightfoot Lee, and then left me in mid-chapter." Caroline was now on forbidden territory. No one was ever supposed to suggest that Adams might be the author of the novel *Democracy,* whose heroine, a Mrs. Lightfoot Lee, settles in Washington in order to understand power in a democracy; and is duly appalled. Caroline had delighted in the book, almost as much as she did in its author. Of course, there were those who thought that John Hay had written the novel (he had been photographed holding a copy of the French edition and wearing a secret smile); others thought that the late Clover Adams, a born wit, was the author. But Caroline was certain that Adams himself had written his quintessential book of Hearts. He never, with her, denied—or affirmed—it. "The lesson of that amorality tale is—stay away from senators."

"That's not difficult."

"In Washington? They are like cardinals in Renaissance Rome. You can't avoid them. That's why I flee to the twelfth century, where there were only three classes: the priest, the warrior and the artist. Then the commercial sort took over, the money-lenders, the parasites. They create nothing; and they enslave everyone. They expropriated the priest—don't you like to hear all this at breakfast?"

"Only when there is honey in the comb," said Caroline, spreading the wax and honey over a piece of hot cornbread. "I can take quite a lot of priests expropriated. And the warriors . . . ?"

"Turned into wage-earning policemen, to defend the moneymen, while the artists make dresses or paint bad portraits, like Sargent . . ."

"Oh, I like him. He never tries to disguise how much his sitters bore him."

"That is our last revenge against money. See? I count myself an artist; but I am only a *rentier,* a parasite. Why Washington?"

Caroline was not certain how much she should confide in this brilliant old professional uncle. "My brother and I have disagreed . . ."

"Yes, we've heard all about that. There is nothing to do with money that we don't seem to hear about. We have lost our spirituality."

"Well, I may lose something far worse, my inheritance." Where was it that she had read that there was a certain honey that made one mad? She had just eaten it, plainly; she confided: "Blaise could control everything for five years. He worships Mr. Hearst, who loses money on a scale that makes me very nervous."

"The terrible Mr. Hearst could end up losing the Sanford money, too?"

As Caroline took more honey, she noted, in the comb, a tiny grub. Perversely, she ate it. "That's my fear. Anyway, while our lawyers duel, Blaise lives in New York and I have come here to Aswan, to observe democracy in action, like Mrs. Lee."

"Then," said Adams, pushing back from the table, and lighting a cigar, with a by-your-leave gesture, "there is Del."

"There is Del."

"He is next door, even as we speak. Are you tempted?"

"My teacher—"

"The formidable Mlle. Souvestre, now established at Wimbledon. She has advised you?"

"No. She gives no advice. That is her style. I mean no *practical* advice. But she is brilliant, and she has never married, and she is happy, teaching."

"You want to teach?"

"I have nothing to teach."

"Neither have I. Yet I run a school for statesmen, from Lodge to Hay. I am also Professor Adams, late of Harvard."

"I am not so ambitious. But I am curious what it would be like to remain single."

"With your—appearance?" Adams laughed; an appreciative bark. "You will not be allowed to stay single. The forces will be too great for you. Unlike you, your Grande Mademoiselle had neither beauty nor a fortune."

"In time, I shall lose the first, and in an even shorter time could lose the second. Besides, she is very handsome. She has had suitors."

"Perhaps," said Adams, "she prefers the company of serious ladies, like an abbess of the twelfth century."

Caroline flushed, not certain why. Mademoiselle had had a partner when the school first began at Les Ruches. There had been quarrels; they parted. Mademoiselle had reigned alone ever since. No, this was not what she herself would prefer in the way of a life alone. But then she had had no experience, of any kind. "I have not the vocation," she said, "of an abbess, even a worldly one."

The honey's power released her. Adams led her into the library, her favorite American room. The overall effect was meant to be medieval, Romanesque even, with windows so sited that one could ignore the White House across the square by looking slightly upward, to Heaven. The room's focal point was the fireplace, carved from a pale jade-green Mexican onyx shot through with scarlet threads; she had never seen anything like it before, but unlike so many things never seen before, the extraordinary silk-like stone fascinated her. On either side of the fireplace Italian *cinquecento* paintings were arranged, as well as a Turner view of the English countryside lit by hell-fire; best of all, there was a crude drawing by William Blake of Nebuchadnezzar, king of Babylon, on all fours, munching grass in his madness. "It is the portrait of my soul," Adams had said when he showed it to her for the first time. The room smelled of woodsmoke, narcissi and hyacinth. The leather chairs were low, built to suit Adams and no one else. They quite suited Caroline, who settled in one, and said, "You must tell me when I'm to go."

"I'm already packed." Adams groaned. "I hate travel. But I can never remain in one place." William announced Mr. Hay, who limped into the room. He was in pain, Caroline decided; and looked a decade older than he had in Kent.

"What are you doing here?" Adams pulled out his clock. "It's Thursday. Your day to receive the diplomatic corps."

"Not till three. Cinderella holds the fort."

"Cinderella?" asked Caroline.

Adams answered, "Mr. Hay's name for his assistant, Mr. Adee, who does all the work in the kitchen, and is never asked to the ball."

"You've settled in, Miss Sanford?" Hay took coffee from William, who knew his ways. Caroline said that she had. Hay nodded vaguely; then turned to Adams. "I think of you, Enricus Porcupinus, as a deserter. When I need you most, you and Lodge leave town."

"You have the Maj-ah." Adams was not in the least sentimental. "We've worked hard enough for you all winter. We got you your treaty. I long, now, to see La Dona—and the Don, too, of course."

"Tell her she may have her house back sooner than she thinks."

"What's wrong with the Vice-President?"

"Heart trouble. Doctor's ordered him out of town, indefinitely."

"Well, it is not as if his absence will be noted."

"Oh, Henry, you are so hard on us poor hacks! Mr. Hobart may not be much as vice-presidents go, but he is one of the best financial investors in the country. He invests money for the Maj-ah and me, and we all do well. Though I prefer real estate. I've been negotiating for a lot on Connecticut Avenue. It is my dream to build a many-spired apartment house. They are the coming thing in this town of transients . . ."

Caroline had hoped for, perhaps, more elevated conversation at Hearts' heart. But today the old men obviously did not inspire one another to breakfast brilliance, while her presence was now sufficiently familiar not to require any special exertion. In a way, she was relieved to be taken for granted. But that was by the old; she was, to the young Del, very much a wish ungranted. "I heard you were here," he said, as he entered the room.

Adams turned to Caroline: "Our kitchens correspond closely. From cook to cook. Our Maggie to their Flora."

"And I knew you'd be here, Mr. Adams, and Mr. Adee said Father was here, too. So I . . ."

"You were at the office?" Hay looked surprised.

"Why, yes. Then I went to the White House, where I had a meeting with the President. He's asked me to surprise you."

"Is such a thing possible? Is such a thing wise?"

"We'll soon see." Del took a deep breath. "I have just been appointed American consul general in Pretoria."

To Caroline's astonishment, Hay looked as if someone had struck him. He took a deep breath, apparently uncertain whether or not tremulous lungs could absorb so much scented Adams library air. "The . . . ?" He could not utter the literally magisterial noun.

Del nodded. "The President made the appointment himself. He wanted to surprise you. He certainly surprised me. He also didn't want people to think that I got the job because I am your son."

"Surely a republic ends," said Adams, "when the rule of nepotism—like the second law of thermodynamics—ceases to apply."

"I could not," said Hay, breath regained, "be more thrilled, as Helen used to say when we'd go inside the monkey house at the zoo." Caroline watched father and son with considerable interest. What she had always taken to be Anglo-Saxon lack of intimacy between males she now decided was antipathy on the part of the famously charming and affable father toward the equally affable and, in time, no doubt, equally charming son who had not, after all, been trained in the art of storytelling by the admitted master himself, Abraham Lincoln, who could make, it was said, a mule with a broken leg laugh.

"I thought you'd be." Del was impassive; he looked not unlike photographs of President McKinley. If this were Paris, Caroline would put the odd and the even numbers together and understand precisely the nature of the appointment. But Del had his father's eyes, mouth; and there was little chance, she decided, of Ohio, known as the mother of presidents, having produced, through unlikely presidential lust, a consul to Pretoria, which was—where? Australia? She had not liked the geography teacher at Allenswood.

"South Africa could be a turbulent post," said Adams; he, too, was gauging Hay's response to his son's abrupt elevation. "What *is* our policy, between the English and those Dutch lunatics?"

"Extreme benign neutrality," said Del, looking at his father. "In public, that is."

"Yes. Yes. Yes." Hay shook his head and smiled broadly. "Neutral on England's side. The great fun will be if there's a war down there . . ."

"Splendid, perhaps?" Adams smiled. "Little?"

"Little-ish. Hardly splendid. The fun will be how our own Irish Catholic voters will respond. They are for anyone who's against England, including these Dutchmen, these Boers, who are not only Protestant but refuse to allow the Catholics to practice their exciting rites. I predict Hibernian confusion hereabouts. I also predict that though it's only noon, and I must greet, soberly and responsibly, the Diplomatic Corps, there is champagne no farther than the flight of a porcupine's quill. We drink to Del!"

Adams and Caroline cheered; Del's forehead remained, as always, oddly pale, while his face turned to rose.

After champagne had been ceremoniously drunk to the new consul general, Caroline announced, "I can't think why *I* am celebrating. Now that I'm settled into N Street, Mr. Adams deserts me for Sicily, and Del for South Africa."

"You still have my wife and me," said Hay. "We're more than enough, I should say."

"And I don't go till fall," said Del. "The President still has some work for me to do, at the White House." Again Caroline noted the father's perplexed look.

"Then I have a few months of cousinhood if not unclehood." Caroline was pleased that Del should still be at hand. She must learn Washington at every level, and as quickly as possible. "One must be like Napoleon, Mlle. Souvestre always said, never without a plan."

"Even a woman must always have a plan?" Caroline had asked.

"Especially a woman. We don't often have much else. After all, they don't teach *us* artillery."

Caroline had indeed worked out a plan of action. John Apgar Sanford could not believe it when she told him. He begged her to think twice; to do nothing; to let the law take its course. But she was convinced that she could bring Blaise around in a more startling and satisfying fashion; assuming, of course, that she had Napoleonic luck as well as cunning. But the key to her future was here in a strange tropical city, among strangers. She needed Del. She needed all the help that she could get. John—as a cousin, she now called him by his first name—was more than willing to help her; but he was, by nature, timid. He was also, at last, a widower. One night at Delmonico's showy new restaurant, and with the witty Mrs. Fish at the next table, straining to hear every word (for once Caroline blessed Harry Lehr's never-failing laughter), John had lost his timidity and proposed that once his term of mourning was at an end, she take his hand in marriage. Caroline's eyes had filled with genuine tears. She had done her share of flirting in Paris and London, but aside from Del no one, as far as she could determine, had ever wanted to marry her; nor had she met anyone that she wanted to marry; hence, the comfortable image of herself alone, and in command—of her own life. Yet Caroline had been touched by John's declaration; she would, she had said, have to think it over very carefully, for was not marriage the most important step in a young woman's life? As she began to unfurl all the sentences that she had learned from Marguerite, the theater, novels, she started to laugh, while the tears continued to stream down her face.

"What are you laughing at?" John had looked hurt.

"Not you, dear John!" Mrs. Fish's not unpiscine face was now costive with attention. "At myself, in the world, like this."

Adams insisted that Caroline remain behind, as father and son departed together for the State Department across the street and what would doubtless be a very serious conversation indeed. "That," said Adams, when the Hays had gone, "was a bit of a shocker."

"Mr. Hay seemed unenthusiastic."

"You felt that?" Adams was curious. "What else did you feel?"

"That the father expects the son to fail in life, and that the son . . ." She stopped.

"The son . . . what?"

"The son has tricked him."

Adams nodded. "I think you're right. Of course, I know nothing of sons. Only daughters—or nieces, I should say. I can't think what it is that goes on or does not go on between fathers and sons. Cabot Lodge's son George is a poet. I would be proud, I suppose. Cabot is not."

"It is sad that you have no heir."

Adams glared at her, with wrath. Whether real or simulated, the effect was disconcerting. Then he gave his abrupt laugh. "It has been four generations since John Adams, my great-grandfather, wrote the constitution of the state of Massachusetts, and we entered the republic's history by launching, in effect, the republic. It's quite enough that Brooks and I now bring the Adamses to a close. We were born to sum up our ancestors and predict—if not design—the future for our, I suspect, humble descendants, I refer," he smiled mischievously, "not to any illicit issue that we have but to the sons of our brother Charles Francis."

"I cannot imagine humility ever devouring the Adamses, even in the fifth generation." Caroline enjoyed the old man. It was as if Paul Bourget had been wise as well as witty.

Adams now came to his point. "I am aware of your connection with Aaron Burr, and I seem to remember you mentioning, last summer, that you had some of his papers."

"I do. Or I *think* I do. Anyway, I don't have to share them with Blaise. They came to me from my mother. They are in leather cases. I've glanced at them, but that's all. It seems that Grandfather Schuyler persuaded Burr to write some fragments of memoir. Grandfather worked in Burr's law office, when Burr was very old. There is also a journal grandfather kept during the years that he knew Burr. There is also," she frowned, "a journal, which I've never looked at, because my mother, I think it was she, wrote on the cover, 'Burn.' But it is still in its case, and no one has ever burned it—or probably read it! At least I haven't and I don't think my father ever did."

"Clearly, your bump of curiosity is less than ordinary. It is not like my family, where everyone has been writing down everything for a hundred years, and if anyone were to write, 'Burn,' we would obey, with relief." Adams placed two small, highly polished shoes on the fender to the fireplace. "Some time ago I wrote a book about your ancestor Burr . . ."

"*Perhaps* my ancestor. Though I am absolutely certain that he was. He is romantic."

"I thought him, forgive me, a windbag."

Caroline was startled. "Compared to *Jefferson*!"

Adams's laugh was loud and genuine, no longer the stylized bark of approval. "Oh, you have me there! Do you read American history?"

"Only to find out about Burr."

"American history is deeply enervating. I can tell you that firsthand. I've spent my life reading and writing it. Enervating because there are no women in it."

"Perhaps we can change that." Caroline thought of Mlle. Souvestre's battles for women's suffrage.

"I hope you can. Anyway, I've done with our history. There's no pattern to it, that I can see, and that's all I ever cared about. I don't care *what* happened. I want to know *why* it happened."

"I think, in my ignorance, I am opposite. I've always thought that the only power was to know everything that has ever happened."

Adams gave her a sidelong glance. "Power? Is that what intrigues you?"

"Well, yes. One doesn't want to be a victim—because of not knowing." Caroline thought of Blaise and Mr. Houghteling; thought of her father, whom she had known too little about; thought of the dark woman painted in the style of Winterhalter, who was completely unknown to her, and always referred to, with a kind of awe, as "dark."

"I think you must come join your uncle in Paris. I give graduate courses to girls, too; girls, mind you, not women."

Caroline smiled. "I shall enroll." She rose to go. He stood; he was smaller than she. "I shall also let you read the Burr papers."

"I was going to ask you that. I destroy a good deal of what I write. Probably nowhere near enough. I have been considering adding my Burr manuscript to the ongoing bonfire."

"Why a windbag?" Caroline was curious. "After all, he never theorized, like the others."

"He was the founder of the Tammany Hall–style politics, and that is windbagging. But I am unfair. He made one prescient remark, which I like, when he said farewell to the Senate. 'If the Constitution is to perish, its dying agonies will be seen on this floor.' "

"Will it perish?"

"All things do." At the door Adams kissed her chastely on each cheek. She felt the prickling of his beard; smelled his cologne-water. "You must marry Del."

"And leave all this for Pretoria?"

Adams laughed. "Except for my unique, avuncular presence, I suspect that Washington and Pretoria are much the same."

Del thought not. Caroline and Helen Hay dined with Del at Wormley's, a small hotel with numerous dining rooms, both small and large, and, traditionally, the best food in Washington. Whenever the young Hays wanted to escape the medieval splendor of the joint house with Adams, they would cross Lafayette Square to the hotel at Fifteenth and H Streets, where the mulatto Mr. Wormley presided. As the senior Hays were committed that evening to the British embassy, Del and Helen invited Caroline to dinner, to celebrate Pretoria. They were joined in a small upstairs dining room by a lean young Westerner named James Burden Day. "He's the assistant comptroller of the United States, for the next few hours," said Del, as they took their seats in the low-ceilinged room with its view of the vast granite Treasury Building down the street.

"What do you assist at controlling?" asked Caroline.

"The currency, ma'am." The voice was softly Western. "Such as it is."

"He's a Democrat," said Del, "and so he's devoted to silver, sixteen to one."

"I," said Helen Hay, large and comfortable-looking, like her mother, with dimples like Del, "am devoted to shad-roe, which is coming in now, isn't it? Isn't it?" Helen had a habit of repeating phrases. The courtly black waiter, more family butler than mere restaurant worker, said that it was, *it was,* and proposed diamond terrapin, a house specialty, and, of course, canvasback duck, which would be served, Caroline knew, bloody and terrible. But she agreed to the menu. Del continued with the champagne, begun at Mr. Adams's breakfast.

"I should be giving the dinner," said Caroline. "In the consul general's honor."

"You must start to do things jointly." Helen Hay even sounded like her mother, the amiable voice, which always spoke a command. In a well-run world, what splendid generals Clara and Helen Hay would have made. During the shad course, Caroline decided that she could do a lot worse than marry Del; on the other hand, she could imagine nothing worse than a season (unless it be a year) in Pretoria. Plainly, her interest in him was less than romantic. She had often wondered what it was that other girls meant when they said that they were "in love," or deeply attracted or whatever adhesive verb a lady might politely use. Caroline found certain masculine types attractive, as types, quite apart from personality—the young man on her right, addressed by Del as Jim, was such a one. Del himself was too much, physically, created in his mother's baroque mould. But had she not always been taught that fineness of character is the best that any woman could hope for in a mate? And Del's was incomparably fine.

Thinking of Del's fineness, Caroline turned to the figure on her right; he was definitely not baroque, she decided. Gothic, in fact—slender, aspiring, lean; she tried to recall Henry Adam's other adjectives in praise of Gothic; and failed. Besides, the young man's hair was curly and its color was not gray stone but pale sand; yet the eyes were Chartres blue. Was—what *was* his name? there were three, of course, to indicate noble birth at the South: James Burden Day—was his character incomparably fine? She was tempted to ask him; but asked instead how a Democrat enjoyed working for a Republican administration. "I like it better than they do." He smiled; the incisors were oddly canine; would he bite? she hoped. "But it's just another job to them, and that's all government is—in this country, anyway. Jobs. Mine should belong to a Republican, and it will in September when I go home."

A few minutes after four o'clock in the afternoon of September 6, 1901, in the Temple of Music of the Pan-American Exposition at Buffalo, New York,

President McKinley stood before a large American flag, with potted plants to his left and right. An organ played Bach. The day was hot. The presidential collar had twice been changed. Mrs. McKinley was, as usual, ill; and bedded down in the International Hotel. The President was attended only by Cortelyou, and three agents of the Secret Service. Exposition police were also on hand, but when the President gave the order to throw open the doors, so that the people could come shake his hand, there was more than the usual confusion. For one thing, the line was not orderly and rapid, the way the President preferred: one citizen's hand succeeded rapidly by another, one pair of eyes deeply, if briefly, transfixed by the President's luminous stare. Instead, the citizens of the republic advanced slowly, hesitantly, singly, in couples, even in groups. There was no sorting them out.

A young, slight man approached the President with a bandaged right hand. Face to face, there was a moment of confusion. As McKinley's right arm outstretched automatically, he was presented with a problem. Did one shake a bandaged hand? or would its owner offer him his left hand? The young man solved the problem. He darted forward, pushing to one side the President's arm while, simultaneously, firing twice a pistol that he had been holding in the bandaged hand. The stunned President remained standing while guards threw the man to the floor; then, as they dragged him from the hall, a chair was brought for the President, who sat down and, dazedly, felt his waistcoat, where blood was oozing. But he seemed more interested in the assailant than in his wound, and he said to Cortelyou, most calmly, "Don't let them hurt him." Then, when he saw the blood on his fingers, he said, "Be careful, Cortelyou, how you tell my wife."

Eleven minutes later, the President was on the operating table of the Exposition's emergency hospital. One bullet had grazed his chest; the other had entered the vast paunch, and gone through the stomach. The surgeons were able to repair the points of entry and of exit; the bullet, however, was not found. Then the President was sewed up. No vital organs had been harmed; on the other hand, the wound was not drained, and there remained the possibility of infection, not to mention shock to a system that might not prove to be as strong as it appeared.

During the next few days, Vice-President, Cabinet, and Mark Hanna, as well as McKinley's sisters and brother, came to Buffalo. But after a feverish weekend, the President's temperature returned to normal; and he was pronounced out of danger. The Vice-President vanished into the Adirondacks, while the Cabinet dispersed. Meanwhile, Leon Czolgosz was closely questioned. When he confessed to an admiration for a leading anarchist named Emma Goldman, she was immediately arrested in Chicago; and declared the originator of the plot to kill the President.

But at Beverly Farms, news was slow in coming. Don Cameron relied on visitors to bring him day-old newspapers. As there was neither telephone nor telegraph office nearby, Caroline wondered if she should go back to Washington, to her command post at the *Tribune.* But Lizzie said, "There's no one in the government left in town. What news there is is at Buffalo, and who wants to go there?"

Kiki began to bark; visitors had appeared on the piazza of the house. Brooks Adams and his wife, Daisy, waved to the group on the lawn. Then Brooks shouted, "Teddy!"

"Teddy what?" responded Cameron, getting first to his knees; then, laboriously, onto his feet.

"Teddy Roosevelt," roared Brooks, as his wife, frowning, put her hands over her ears, "is president of the United States."

"Oh, God," murmured Cameron.

Caroline crossed herself. The poor good McKinley was now as vanished from the story as Del. Then to Kiki's delight, everyone ran toward the house.

"When—how?" asked Lizzie.

"Yesterday evening. Friday the thirteenth. Gangrene set in. At two-fifteen this morning, he died. Teddy was off in the woods, somewhere. But he should be in Buffalo by now, being sworn in. The Cabinet's all there except for Hay, who's in Washington, holding together the government. No one knows the extent of the conspiracy. The Spanish-Cubans are thought to be behind it, out of revenge, for what McKinley did—and did not do—in Cuba." Brooks spoke rapidly, without a pause for breath. Then, like a child, he began to jump up and down on the porch; and Kiki jumped alongside him. "Teddy's got it all now! Do you realize that he occupies a place greater than Trajan's at the high noon of the Roman empire?" Brooks, like his brother, never spoke when he could lecture. "There has never been so much power given a man at so propitious a time in history! He will have the opportunity—and the means—to subjugate all Asia, and so give America the hegemony of the earth, which is our destiny, written in stars! Also," Brooks came to earth with a crash, "today is a day of great importance to Daisy and me. It is our wedding anniversary."

"History does seem to have us by the throat," said Lizzie mildly. "Come inside."

"Champagne," said Cameron, brightening. "For your anniversary . . ."

"And for Theodore the Great, whose reign has, at last, begun."

"No period of mourning for Mr. McKinley?" asked Caroline, who felt, suddenly, an intense grief for Del, the Major and, not least, herself, bereft.

"The King is dead." Brooks was cold. "Long live the King."

Caroline was surprised at how few disagreements there were between herself and Blaise. The new publisher knew his job, if not Washington. Trimble continued to put out the paper. Caroline gladly surrendered to Blaise the task of wringing advertising money from their mutual relatives, and everyone else. He had gone twice to Mrs. Bingham's; and showed no great disdain. Although Frederika was helping him furnish the palace, he seemed to have no particular interest in her, or in anyone. He had become, in some mysterious way, a creature of Hearst. It was as if their close association had made it impossible for him to find anyone else interesting; yet Blaise did not much like Hearst personally. Obviously, this was a case of inadvertent fascination. Luckily, it was a very useful one for the *Tribune.* Blaise, was, by any standard, an excellent publisher.

As Marguerite helped Caroline dress for the Diplomatic Reception, she counted the number of days which would bring her to the magic, if not exactly joyous in itself, twenty-seventh birthday: fifty-two days, and she would be able to soar, on eagle-wings of gold. But soar where? What would change? other than the constant dull worry that money was in short supply. John had paid his debts; and remained, at her request, in New York. Jim seldom missed a Sunday; and she was reasonably content. But Marguerite, who was not always—as opposed to usually—wrong, was right when she said that so ridiculous a situation could not go on forever. Mrs. Belmont had made it possible, if not exactly fashionable, to divorce a husband and still remain within the world. That was progress. But divorce implied an alternative, in the form of yet another marriage, and except for Jim, there was no one who interested her; and Jim was beyond her reach, even if she had been so minded to reach out, which she was not. Still, it was now an absolute fact that Caroline had no more use for John Apgar Sanford; and he had none for her. Only Emma was satisfactory.

Blaise arrived in a motor car, with a handsome uniformed driver, who helped Caroline into the back seat, where Blaise was resplendent in white tie. "We are," Caroline observed, "a couple."

"For the purposes of Diplomatic Receptions, anyway." He was more relaxed with her now. The meeting on the river-boat had been their lowest moment. Relations could only improve, or break off entirely. They had improved. "Court will be unusually brilliant tonight." Caroline turned into the Society Lady. "Mr. Adams is not coming, but he is sending not only Henry James but Saint-Gaudens and John La Farge—literature, sculpture, painting will celebrate our sovereign and decorate his court."

"He is so full of himself."

"No more than Mr. Hearst."

"Hearst's an original. He's done something."

"Isn't the . . . the . . . the Panama Canal something?"

"Nothing compared to reporting . . ."

". . . and inventing . . ."

". . . news." This was an old debate between them, or, rather, discourse, since they were generally in agreement. To determine what people read and thought about each day was not only action but power of a kind no ruler could, with such regularity, exercise. Caroline often thought of the public as a great mass of shapeless modelling clay which she, in Washington, at least, could mould with what she chose to put in the columns of the *Tribune.* No wonder that Hearst, with eight newspapers, and a magazine or two, felt that he could—even should—be president. No wonder Theodore Roosevelt genuinely hated and feared him.

The East Room of the White House had been simplified to the point of brilliance, and the result was more royal than republican. Also, the Roosevelts had increased the number of military aides, their gold-braid loopings complementing the quantities of gold-and-silver braid worn by the diplomatic corps. The astonishing McKinley pumpkin seats, each fountaining a sickly palm, had long since vanished; the mustard rug was now only a memory of a time when the East Room was like the lobby of a Cleveland hotel. The floor was now shining parquet, the chandeliers were more elaborate then ever, while the sparse furniture was much gilded and marbled. Red silk ropes were everywhere, in order to control the public, which were allowed, at certain hours, to wander through their sovereign's palace.

The President and Mrs. Theodore Roosevelt stood at the room's center, shaking hands, as glittering aides discreetly moved the guests along. Theodore was more than ever stout, and hearty, and delighted with himself, while Edith Roosevelt was her usual calm self, ever ready to curb her volatile mate, whose self-love was curiously contagious.

"Very sound. *Very* sound on Japan, Mrs. Sanford," was his greeting to Caroline. "Things are about to happen." Then he looked very grim, as Cassini, dean of the diplomatic corps, approached, Marguerite in tow. Caroline exchanged amiable whispers with Edith Roosevelt, and moved on. President and Russian Ambassador had nothing to say to each other, and contrary to all diplomatic usage *said* nothing to each other. Marguerite looked worn. She had had a love affair that had gone wrong, and now the word was that Cassini was to be replaced. End of glory, thought Caroline, as Henry James, the embodiment of all literary glory, shook her hand warmly and said, "At last. At last."

"It has been almost seven years since Surrenden Dering," Caroline observed, with some not entirely banal wonder at the rapidity of time's passage.

"You never come to our side of the water, so I've come to yours." James lowered his voice in mock fear, as if Theodore might be listening. "Ours. *Ours!* What have I said? *Lèse majesté des États-Unis.*"

"I shall be on the other side this summer," said Caroline, as they crossed the room, for the most part filled with people that she knew. Washington was indeed a village still; and so a newcomer like Henry James was a mild sensation. Once the diplomatic reception was concluded, there would be a supper for the chosen few, among them James and Caroline but not Blaise.

They paused in an empty corner, as the Hays made their entrance. "Our Henry refuses to come," James observed with quiet satisfaction. "He was here earlier this month, and he has now declared that he has had his absolute fill of the sublime Theodore, whilst conceding how strenuous, vigorous and, yes, let us acknowledge it, *supple,* our sovereign is, the sun at the center of the sky, with us as . . . as . . ."

"Clouds," Caroline volunteered.

James frowned. "I once was obliged to let go an excellent typewriter-operator because whenever I paused for a word, she would offer me one, and always not simply the wrong word, but the very worst word."

"I'm sorry. But I quite like us as clouds."

"Why," asked James, "with the delicious exception of yourself, are there no beautiful women at court?"

"Well, there is Mrs. Cameron—if not Martha."

"Alas, not Martha. But Mrs. Cameron's a visitor. What I take to be the local ladies here are plainer than what one would find at a comparable—if anything in poor shabby London could be compared to this incomparability—reception."

Caroline repeated the Washington adage that the capital was filled with ambitious energetic men and the faded women that they had married in their green youth. James was amused. "The same doubtless applies to diplomats . . ."

They were joined by Jules Jusserand, the resplendent French ambassador, and the three lapsed into French, a language James spoke quite as melodiously as his own. "What did the President say to you?" asked Jusserand. "We were all watching the two of you, with fascination."

"He expressed his delight—the very word he used, as, apparently, he always does—at my—and his—election to something called the National Institute of Arts and Letters, which has, parthenogetically, given birth to an American Academy, a rustic version of your august French Academy, some half a hundred members whose souls if not achievements are held to be immortal."

"What," said Jusserand, "will you wear?"

"Ah, that vexes us tremendously. As the President and I tend to corpulence, I have proposed togas, on the Roman model, but our leader John Hay favors some sort of uniform like—Admiral Dewey's." James bowed low, as the hero passed by them. "He is my new friend. We have exchanged cards. I know," James swept the air with an extended arm, "*everyone* at last."

"You are a lion," said Caroline.

Supper was served in the new dining room, where a number of tables for ten had been set. Henry James was placed at the President's table, a Cabinet lady between them. Saint-Gaudens was also at the monarch's table, with Caroline to his right. Edith Roosevelt had come to depend upon Caroline for those occasions where the ability to talk French was necessary, not that the great American Dublin-born sculptor, despite his name, spoke much French. He lived in New Hampshire, not France. Of Lizzie Cameron, who had posed for the figure of Victory in Saint-Gaudens's equestrienne monument to her uncle General Sherman, he said, "She has the finest profile of any woman in the world."

"How satisfactory, to have such a thing, and to have *you* acknowledge it."

Unfortunately, a table of ten was, for the President, no place for the ritual dinner-party conversation: first course, partner to right; second course, partner to left; and so on. The table for ten was Theodore's pulpit, and they his congregation. "We must see more of Mr. James in his own country." Theodore's pince-nez glittered. As James opened his mouth to launch what would be a long but beautifully shaped response, the President spoke through him, and James, slowly, comically, shut his mouth as the torrent of sound, broken only by the clicking of teeth, swept over the table. "I cannot say that I very much like the idea of Mark Twain in our Academy." He looked at James, but spoke to the table. "Howells, yes. He's sound, much of the time. But Twain is like an old woman, ranting about imperialism. I've found there's usually a physical reason for such people. They are congenitally weak in the body, and this makes them weak in nerves, in courage, makes them fearful of war . . ."

"Surely," began James.

The President's shrill voice kept on. "Everyone knows that Twain ran away from the Civil War, a shameful thing to do . . ."

To Caroline's astonishment, James's deep baritone continued under the presidential tirade. The result was disconcerting but fascinating, a cello and a flute, simultaneously, playing separate melodies.

". . . Mr. Twain, or Clemens, as I prefer to call him . . ."

". . . testing of character and manhood. A forge . . ."

". . . much strength of arm as well as, let us say . . ."

". . . cannot flourish without the martial arts, or any civilization . . ."

". . . distinguished and peculiarly American genius . . ."

". . . desertion of the United States for a life abroad . . ."

". . . when Mr. Hay telephoned Mr. Clemens from the Century Club to . . ."

". . . without which the white race can no longer flourish, and prevail."

The President paused to drink soup. The table watched, and listened, as Henry James, master of so many millions of words, had the last. "And though I say—ah, tentatively, of course," the President glared at him over his soup spoon, "the sublimity of the greatest art may be beyond his method, his—what other word?" The entire table leaned forward, what *would* the word be? and on what, Caroline wondered, was James's astonishing self-confidence and authority, even majesty, based? "*Drollery,* that so often tires, and yet never entirely obscures for us the vision of that mighty river, so peculiarly august and ah—yes, yes? Yes! *American.*"

Before the President could again dominate the table, James turned to his post-soup partner, and Caroline turned to Saint-Gaudens, who said, "I can't wait to tell Henry. The reason he won't set foot ever again in this house is that he's never allowed to finish a sentence and no Adams likes to be interrupted."

"Mr. James is indeed a master."

"Of an art considerably higher than mere politics." Saint-Gaudens reminded Caroline of a bearded Puritan satyr, if such a creature was possible; he seemed very old in a way that the lively Adams, or the boyish if ill Hay, did not. "I wish I had read more in my life," he said, as a fish was offered up to them.

"You have time."

"No time." He smiled. "Hay was furious at Mark Twain, who wouldn't answer the telephone. We knew he was home, of course, but he didn't want to join us at the Century Club. What bees are swarming in that bonnet! Twain's latest bogey is Christian Science. He told me quite seriously, after only one Scotch sour, that in thirty years Christian Scientists will have taken over the government of the United States, and that they would then establish an absolute religious tyranny."

"Why are Americans so mad for religion?"

"In the absence of a civilization," Saint-Gaudens was direct, "what else have they?"

"Absence?" Caroline indicated James, who was smiling abstractedly at the President, who was again in the conversational saddle, but only at his end of the table. "And you. And Mr. Adams. And even the Sun King there."

"Mr. James is truly absent. Gone from us for good. Mr. Adams writes of Virgins and dynamos in France. I am nothing. The President—well . . ."

"So Christ Scientist . . ."

"Or Christ Dentist . . ."

"Sets the tone." Caroline never ceased to be amazed at the number of religious sects and societies the country spawned each year. Jim had told her that if he were to miss a Sunday service at the Methodist church in American City, he would not be reelected, while Kitty taught Sunday school, with true belief. If for nothing else, Caroline was grateful to Mlle. Souvestre for having dealt God so absolute a death blow that she had never again felt the slightest need for that highly American—or Americanized—commodity.

The voice of Theodore was again heard at table. "I stood in the Red Room, I remember, on election night, and I told the press that I would not be a candidate again. Two terms is enough for anyone, I said, and say again." Henry James stared dreamily at the President, as if by closely scrutinizing him he might distil his essence. "Politicians always stay on too long. Better to go at the top of your form, and give someone else a chance to measure up, which is what it is all about."

"Measure up," James murmured, with mysterious, to Caroline, approval. "Yes, yes, yes," he added to no one, as Theodore told them how he had invented, first, Panama, and then the canal. He did not lack for self-esteem. James kept repeating, softly, "*Measure* up. Measure *up.* Yes. Yes."

Caroline sat at the large marquetry table, said to have been the very one that the Duke had used when he was the controller of the royal revenues, and opened the two letter-boxes. The first contained fragments of Aaron Burr's autobiography, with a commentary by his law-clerk Charles Schemerhorn Schuyler. She glanced through the pages, and decided that Henry Adams, if no one else, would be fascinated. She skipped to the end of the book, written years after Burr's death, and read what she already knew, of her grandfather's accidental discovery that he was one of Burr's numerous illegitimate children.

The second leather box was a final journal by her grandfather, covering the year 1876. He had returned to New York for the first time since 1836, with his daughter, Emma, the Princesse d'Agrigente. This was the volume that she intended to read carefully.

Once the Hearst party had left, Caroline spent every moment that she could reading her grandfather's journal. She was charmed by his amusement at the strange American world, fascinated by his description of her mother's campaign to find a wealthy husband, the object of the visit, appalled at her grandfather's cynical complaisance. But then father and daughter were broke, and he was just able to support the two of them by writing for the magazines. Fortunately, Mrs. Astor took them up; and they were in demand socially, thanks to Emma's beauty, and her father's charm. At one point, Emma had almost married an Apgar cousin, for convenience, something her daughter had actually done.

As Caroline read on, she began to see something alter in Emma's character—alter or be revealed to the reader, Caroline, but not to the narrator, who seemed unable to understand the thrust of his own narrative. Sanford made his entrance, with wife Denise, who could not give birth without danger. As Denise and Emma became closer and closer friends, Caroline found that her fingers were suddenly so cold that she could hardly, clumsily, turn the pages. Caroline knew the end before the end. Emma persuaded Denise to give birth to Blaise. In effect, Emma murdered Denise in order to marry Sanford.

Emma's expiation was the long painful time she took to die after Caroline's birth. But did Emma feel guilt? Did she atone? Confess?

Caroline sent for Plon. It was late afternoon. She wanted to talk to Emma's oldest son while the—crime was still vivid in her mind. Plon sprawled handsomely on a sofa. Caroline told him what their mother had done. At the end, somewhat dramatically, she held up the journal and waved it in the air; told him of the murder. *"Brûlez,"* Plon read from the cover. "That's what you should have done, you idiot! Burn it. What difference does any of this make now?"

"You knew all along, didn't you?"

Plon shrugged. "I thought something had happened."

"Did she say anything?"

"Of course not."

"Did she seem tragic or sad or—dark?"

"She was adorable, as always, even at the end, when there was pain."

"Did she make confession, to a priest?"

"She was given the last rites. She was conscious. I suppose she did."

Plon lit a cigarette from a new gold case. "You know, when someone becomes emperor of the French, and conquers all Europe, he doesn't brood much about the people he killed."

"But she was a woman, and a mother, not emperor of the French . . ."

"You don't know how—*I* don't know how—she saw herself. She had to survive, and if the sad lady, her friend, Blaise's mother, must die, naturally, in childbirth, then she must."

The next morning, Caroline invited Blaise to breakfast in her wing of the chateau. He knew why. Plon had told him. They sat in an oval breakfast room, with du Barry dove-gray walls. "Now you know," he said, casually, "that your mother killed my mother for our father's money. I'm sure it happens all the time."

"Don't be—don't make a joke of it. Now I know why your grandmother was so insistent with me. I am to expiate . . ."

"You? Don't exaggerate your importance. You weren't even there. I, at least, was the direct cause of my mother's death."

"I think these things go on, into the next generation, and further, maybe."

"*You!* The atheist from Mlle. Souvestre's stable." Blaise laughed into his omelette.

"Atheists believe in character, and I certainly believe in cause and effect, and consequence."

"The consequence is that you and I are still fairly young by the standards of our world and very rich by any standard. This isn't the house of Artois."

"Arteus." She corrected him from force of habit. "Plon sounded as if he would have done the same."

"I doubt it. Men are never as cruel as women when it comes to this sort of thing. Look at your dismissal of John. That was very Emmaesque. I couldn't have done that."

Caroline felt a chill in the room, which turned out to be not a ghost but a sudden cold wind from the lake; a summer storm was on its way. Blaise closed the window. "You prove my point then," she said. "The old crime."

"Don't be carried away. Think of all the new crimes we can commit. Let poor Emma rest in peace. I have never, once, thought of Denise. Why should you think of Emma, who, according to Plon, except for one nicely executed murder, was delightful, as a woman, and admirable as a mother?"

"You are immoral, Blaise." Caroline wanted to be shocked; but felt nothing at all.

"I never said I wasn't. I'm indifferent. You remember our last night in New York, at Rector's? when you were so shocked by the way the whole room sang that song?—well, I was thrilled because I was just like the singers of that song."

Caroline shuddered at the memory. The latest Victor Herbert musical contained a highly minatory song called "I Want What I Want When I Want It." On the night that she and Blaise came, as it were, full circle, in their knowledge of each other, they had dined at Rector's, and when the singer from the musical comedy entered the restaurant, he boomed out, "I want . . ." and the entire restaurant took up the chorus, and on the word "want" everyone banged a fist on the table. It was like a war being conducted by very fat people against—the waiters? or everyone on earth who was not as fat or as rich as they? "So Emma was right, to want what she wanted?"

"You have only one chance sometimes. Anyway, what she wanted," Blaise brought down his fist on the table, and Caroline jumped in her chair, "she got, and that's what counts, and because she did, you're here."

So, in the end, Caroline, the successful American publisher, was not the acclimatized American that her brother, her appendage, was. She wished Mr. Adams was on hand, to delight in the irony.

John Hay sat in a rocking chair on the verandah of The Fells and stared across the green New Hampshire lawn to the gray New Hampshire mountains with Lake Winnepesaukee between, so much flat shining water that reflected the deep clear blue summer sky. Exhaustion did not describe his condition. He had returned on June 15, and after a day at Manhasset with Helen, he had gone on to Washington, despite firm instructions from the President to go home. For a week in the damp heat of the tropical capital, he had done the business of his department, and plotted with Theodore on how—and where—to get the Japanese and the Russians to sign a peace treaty. He had found Theodore more than ever regnant, and the mammoth Taft apparently indispensable. The last bit of business that they had set in motion was to put an end to the Chinese Exclusion Act, which earlier administrations had used to keep the Chinese from immigrating to the United States. With the rise of Japan, paradoxically, the Yellow Peril must be put to rest as a means for politicians to frighten the people.

The house in Washington was depressing, with white sheets over everything, closed shutters and windows, and a musty smell. Clarence, now grown and amiable if not brilliant, kept him company, and together they had left the city on June 24 for Newbury, on the overnight sleeper, where Hay had caught his inevitable sleeper-cold. Today he was better; but mortally tired. He had also developed a habit of falling asleep in the middle of a sentence, and dreaming vividly; then he'd wake up, disoriented, with the sensation, yet again, of being, simultaneously, in two places, even two epochs of time. But now Clarence sat beside him in a noisy rocker, made noisier by the instinct of the young to rock vigorously, while that of the old is to be rocked gently.

"Of course, I've been lucky." Hay stared at the sky. "There must be a kind of law. For every bit of bad luck Clarence King—for whom we named you—had, I got a prize. He wanted to make a fortune, and lost everything ten times over. I didn't care one way or another, and everything I did, just about, made me rich, even if I hadn't married an heiress." Hay wondered if this was entirely true. When he had worked for Amasa Stone, he had been drilled thoroughly in business. Of course, he had been an apt student, but without Stone's coaching he might have ended up as just another newspaper editor, earning extra money on the lecture-circuit.

"I've never really been sick till now, or, as old Shylock says, 'never felt it till now.' The family's turned out better than I ever had any right to hope." He turned and gazed at the attentive Clarence. "I'd go to law school, if I were you. Also, don't marry young. It's a mistake for a boy to tie himself up—or down—too young."

"I've no intention," said Clarence.

"Good boy. Poor Del." Hay's chest seemed to constrict a moment; and his breath stopped. But, for once, there was no sense of panic. Either he would breathe again, or he would not, and that was that. He breathed; he sighed. "But Del's life was splendid for someone so young. We got used to that, my generation, to dying young. Just about everybody I knew my age was killed in that terrible trouble. Name me a battle, and I can tell you which of my friends fell there, some never to rise again. Say Fredericksburg and I see Johnny Curtis of Springfield, his face blown away. Say . . ." But already Hay was beginning to forget both battles and youths. Things had begun to fade; past, present mingled.

"I thought I'd die young, and here I am. I thought I wouldn't amount to much and . . . I really believe that in all history, I never read of a man who has had so much—and such varied—success as I have had, with so little ability and so little power of sustained industry. Nothing to be proud of. Something to be grateful for." Hay looked at Clarence, thoughtfully, and was somewhat surprised—and mildly irritated—to find him reading a stack of letters.

"You're busy, I see." Hay struck the sardonic note.

"You should be, too." Clarence did not look up. As he finished reading a letter, he would let it fall to the floor of the verandah, in two piles. Obviously one pile was to be answered; the other not. Who used to do that? Hay wondered. Then he thought of himself again, soon to be no self at all, and he wondered why he had been he and not another, why he had been at all and not simply nothing. "I have had success beyond all the dreams of my boyhood," he proclaimed. But that was not true. The poet John Hay, heir to Milton and Poe, had come to nothing but a pair of very "Little Breeches." "My name is printed in the journals of the world without descriptive qualifications." Who had said that that was the only proof of fame, as opposed to notoriety? It sounded like Root, but Hay had forgotten.

Hay turned to Clarence, who was now on his feet. For the first time Hay noticed that the boy had grown a long pointed beard, not the style of the young these days. He must tell him, tactfully, that when the summer was over he must face the world clean-shaven.

"The President wants to see you," said Clarence.

Hay leapt—to his own amazement—to his feet, and crossed the crowded corridor to the President's office. Obviously he had been dreaming of New Hampshire while napping in the White House, awaiting Theodore's summons. The Japanese . . .

In the office, Hay found the President staring out the window at the Potomac, and blue Virginia beyond. The President was hunched over, and was unlike his usual exuberant noisy self. Over the fireplace, the portrait of Jackson glowered at the world.

"Sit down, John." The familiar high voice sounded deathly tired. "I'm sorry you've been sick."

"Thank you, Mr. President," and Hay realized that he had made a mistake in hurrying so quickly across the corridor. Exhausted, he sat in the special visitor's chair with all the maps of battle in full view, and a yellow curtain ready to cover them up, if the visitor was not to be trusted.

Abraham Lincoln turned from the window, and smiled. "You look pretty seedy, Johnny."

"You don't look too good yourself, if I may say so, sir."

"When did I ever?" Lincoln went to his pigeon-holed desk, and took out two letters. "I've got a couple of letters for you to answer. Nothing important." Lincoln gave Hay the letters; then he sat very low in the chair opposite, so that the small of his back would press against hard wood, while one long leg was slung over the chair's arm. Hay realized with some excitement that he had, at last, after so many years, been able to remember Lincoln's face from life as opposed to ubiquitous effigy. But what was he thinking? This *was* the President, he realized, on a Sunday afternoon, in summer. "I can't sleep," the Ancient was saying. "I *think* I'm sleeping but then I find I'm only day-dreaming and I wake up, and by the time it's morning, I am plumb worn out, or as the preacher said to his wife . . ."

Hay felt, suddenly, as one with the President, as the melancholy dark green walls, picked out with tiny golden stars, swirled all about the two of them like the first attack of sleep which always starts, no matter how restless one has been, with a nothingness out of which emerges, first, one image, then another, and, finally, made narratives unfold which take the place of the real world stolen now by sleep, unless sleep be the real world stolen by the day, for life.

Although William Randolph Hearst had been requested to enter the White House from the south side, where private visitors came and went, the great man ordered his chauffeur to drive up the main driveway to the north portico, to the general consternation of the police. Then, slowly, like some huge bear of the sort that the President liked to shoot in quantity while roaring about the necessity of the preservation of wildlife, Hearst entered the main hall of the house which he would never, short of an armed revolution, occupy. Apprehensively, the chief usher received him.

"Tell the President that I am here." Hearst did not bother to identify himself. He took off his coat, and let it fall, quite aware that someone would catch it before it touched the floor; and an usher did.

"Come this way, Mr. Hearst." The chief usher led Hearst to the west wing. When told to wait in the secretary's office, Hearst opened the door to the empty Cabinet room, and took his place at the head of the table. The secretary's shock was silent; but profound.

Hearst sat back in the chair of state, and shut his eyes, like a man exhausted in a noble cause. He was home. But not for long. As usual, noise preceded the Chief Magistrate. "Delighted you're here! Bully!" The President was now at the door to the Cabinet room. Hearst opened his eyes, and gravely nodded his head in greeting. For a moment, Roosevelt appeared uncertain what next to do. Then he shut the door behind him. There would be no witnesses to what might follow.

Slowly, majestically, Hearst got to his feet. As the two men shook hands, Hearst deliberately pulled Roosevelt toward him so that the President was obliged to stare straight up into the air at the taller man. "You wanted to see me?" Hearst inquired, as if bestowing a huge favor on a junior editor.

"Indeed. Indeed. We have so much to talk about." Although Hearst stood between the President and the presidential chair, the tubby but sturdy Roosevelt simply charged the chair, knocking Hearst to one side in the process. Most royally, Roosevelt seated himself; and said, with smooth condescension, "Sit there. On my right. Mr. Root's chair."

Hearst's smile was thinner than usual. "I'd fear some terrible contagion if I were to sit in the chair of so notorious a liar."

Roosevelt's face was now dark red; and the smile a snarl. "I've never known Mr. Root to lie."

"Then you've had a lot less experience with lawyers than I'd suspected." Hearst pulled an armchair from its place at center table, putting a considerable distance between himself and the President.

"Root spoke for me in Utica." Roosevelt was flat.

"Well, I didn't think he was speaking on oath to God. Of course, he spoke for you when he accused me of McKinley's murder."

The conversation was, plainly, not going where Roosevelt had intended. "Your press incited—incites—violence and class hatred. Do you deny that?"

"I don't deny or affirm anything. Do you understand that? I'm here at *your* request, Roosevelt. Personally, I have no wish to see you at all, anywhere, ever—unless, of course, we share the same quarters in hell. So I must warn you, no one says 'Do you deny' to me, in my country."

"*Your* country, is it?" Roosevelt's falsetto had deepened to a mellifluous alto. "When did you buy it?"

"In 1898, when I made war with Spain, and won it. All my doing, that was, and none of yours. Ever since then, the country's gone pretty much the way I've wanted it to go, and you've gone right along, too, because you had to."

"You exaggerate your importance, Mr. Hearst."

"You understand nothing, Mr. Roosevelt."

"I understand this much. You, the owner—no, no, the *father* of the country, couldn't get the Democrats to nominate you for president even in a year when there was no chance of their winning. How do you explain that?"

Hearst's pale close-set eyes were now directed straight at Roosevelt; the effect was cyclopean, intimidating. "First, I'd say it makes no difference at all who sits in that chair of yours. The country is run by the trusts, as you like to remind us. They've bought everything and everyone, including you. They can't buy me. I'm rich. So I'm free to do as I please, and you're not. In general, I go along with them, simply to keep the people docile, for now. I do that through the press. Now you're just an office-holder. Soon you'll move out of here, and that's the end of you. But I go on and on, describing the world we live in, which then becomes what I say it is. Long after no one knows the difference between you and Chester A. Arthur, I'll still be here." Hearst's smile was frosty. "But if they *do* remember who you are, it'll be because I've decided to remind them, by telling them, maybe, how I made you up in the first place, in Cuba."

"You have raised, Mr. Hearst, the Fourth Estate to a level quite unheard of in any time . . ."

"I know I have. And for once you've got it right. I have placed the press above everything else, except maybe money, and even when it comes to money, I can usually make the market rise or fall. When I made—invented, I should say—the war with Spain, all of it fiction to begin with, I saw to it that the war would be a real one at the end, and it was. For better or worse, we took over a real empire from the Caribbean to the shores of China. Now, in the process, a lot of small fry like you and Dewey benefitted. I'm afraid I couldn't control the thing once I set it in motion. No one could. I was also struck with the fact that once you start a war you have to have heroes. So you—of all people—came bustling along, and I told the editors, 'All right. Build him up.' So that's how a second-rate New York politician, wandering around Kettle Hill, blind as a bat and just about as effective, got turned into a war hero. But you sure knew how to cash in. I'll hand you that. Of all my inventions you certainly leapt off the page of the *Journal*, and into the White House. Not like poor dumb Dewey, who just stayed there in cold print until he ended up wrapped around the fish at Fulton's Market."

Hearst sat back in his chair, hands clasped behind his head. Eyes on the ceiling fan. "When I saw what my invention could do, I decided to get elected, too. I wanted to show how I could take on the people who own the country that I—yes, that I helped invent—and win. Well, I was obliged to pay the inventor's price. I was—I am—resented and feared by the rich, who love you. I could never get money out of Standard Oil the way you could. So in the long—no, short—run it's who pays the most who wins these silly elections. But you and your sort won't hold on forever. The future's with the common man, and there are a whole lot more of him than there are of you . . ."

"Or you." Roosevelt stared at the painting of Lincoln on the opposite wall, the melancholy face looking at something outside the frame. "Well, Mr. Hearst, I was aware of your pretentions as a publisher, but I never realized that you are the sole inventor of us all."

"Oh, I wouldn't put it so grandly." Hearst was mild. "I just make up this country pretty much as it happens to be at the moment. That's hardly major work, though *you* should thank me, since you're the principal beneficiary of what I've been doing."

Roosevelt arranged several statute books on the table. "What do you know about me and Mr. Archbold?"

"Standard Oil helped finance your last campaign. Everyone knows that."

"Have you any proof that *I* asked for the money?"

"The asking was done by Hanna, Quay, Penrose. You only hint."

"Mr. Archbold is an old friend of mine." Roosevelt started to say more; but then did not.

Hearst's voice was dreamy. "I am going to drive many men from public life. I am also going to expose you as the hypocrite you are."

Roosevelt's smile was gone; the high color had returned to normal; the voice was matter-of-fact. "You will have an easy time with the Sibleys and Haskells. You will have an impossible time with me."

"You fight the trusts?"

"As best I can."

"Have you ever objected to Standard Oil's numerous crimes against individuals, not to mention the public?"

"I have spoken out against them many times as malefactors of great wealth."

"But what," Hearst's voice was soft, "have you *done* to bring Standard Oil to heel? You've been here six years. What have you done, except rant in public, and take their money in secret?"

"You will see." Roosevelt was very calm indeed. "Next year, we bring suit against them in Indiana . . ."

"*Next* year!" Hearst slapped the table gleefully. "Who says this is not my country? I've forced *you,* of all people, to act against your own kind. Because of what I've revealed this year, you'll do something next year. But you don't ever really lead. You follow *my* lead, Roosevelt." Hearst was on his feet, but Roosevelt, not to be outdone, had done his special Jack-in-the-box rapid leap to the perpendicular so that, technically, the President had risen first, as protocol required, ending the audience.

At the door to the Cabinet room, Hearst got his hand on the doorknob first. "You're pretty safe, for now."

"I wonder," said Roosevelt, softly, "if you are."

"It's my story, isn't it? This country. The author's always safe. It's his characters who better watch out. Of course, there are surprises. Here's one. When you're out of a job, and need money to feed that family of yours, I'll hire you to write for me, the way Bryan does. I'll pay you whatever you want."

Roosevelt produced his most dazzling smile. "I may be a hypocrite, Mr. Hearst, but I'm not a scoundrel."

"I know," said Hearst, with mock sadness. "After all, I made you up, didn't I?"

"Mr. Hearst," said the President, "history invented me, not you."

"Well, if you really want to be highfalutin, then at this time and in this place, I am history—or at least the creator of the record."

"True history comes long after us. That's when it will be decided whether or not we measured up, and our greatness—or its lack—will be defined."

"True history," said Hearst, with a smile that was, for once, almost charming, "is the final fiction. I thought even you knew that." Then Hearst was gone, leaving the President alone in the Cabinet room, with its great table, leather armchairs, and the full-length painting of Abraham Lincoln, eyes fixed on some far distance beyond the viewer's range, a prospect unknown and unknowable to the mere observer, at sea in present time.

# From *Hollywood*

SLOWLY, WILLIAM RANDOLPH HEARST lowered his vast bear-like body into a handsome Biedermeier chair, all scrolls and lyres and marquetry. "Tell no one I'm in Washington," he commanded. Then, slowly, he blinked his pale blue eyes at Blaise Delacroix Sanford. Although Blaise was now forty-one and the publisher of the Washington *Tribune,* he was still awed by his former chief and mentor, gone gray in *his* fifty-fourth year, the most famous newspaper publisher in the world, owner of dozens of journals and magazines and, most curiously, the recent begetter of that worldwide sensation, a photo-play serial called *The Perils of Pauline.*

"I won't, of course." Blaise sat on the edge of his desk, flexing leg muscles. Unlike the Chief, Blaise was in excellent physical shape: he rode horseback every day, played squash in his own court, fought age.

"Millicent and I've been spending the winter at the Breakers. You know, Palm Beach." The Chief's face was Indian-brown from the sun. Just past Hearst's head, Blaise could see, through the window, a partial view of Fourteenth Street until, with a dry soft sigh, the Biedermeier chair crumpled in on itself like an accordion and Hearst and chair were suddenly as one with the thick Persian carpet, and the view of Fourteenth Street was now unobstructed.

Blaise leapt to his feet. "I'm sorry . . ."

But Hearst serenely ignored gravity's interruption of his thought. He remained where he was on the floor, holding in one hand a fragile wooden lyre that had been an armrest: the Orpheus of popular journalism, thought Blaise wildly, unnerved by the sight. "Anyway, what I sneaked into town for was to find out whether or not there's anything to this Zimmermann-telegram thing, and if there is, how are *you* going to play it? After all, you're the Washington publisher. I'm just New York."

"And everywhere else. Personally, I think it's a hoax. . . . Why don't you try another chair?"

Hearst put down his lyre. "You know, I bought a whole houseful of Biedermeier furniture when I was in Salzburg and I shipped it back to New York, where I never got around to uncrating it. Don't think I will now." As slowly as Hearst had sat so, majestically, he rose to his full height, at least two heads taller than Blaise. "Sorry I smashed that thing. Bill me for the damages."

"Forget it, Chief." In his nervousness, Blaise called Hearst the name that he was known by to all his employees but never to his equal, Blaise. As Hearst settled himself into a fortress-like leather armchair, Blaise picked up the so-called Zimmermann telegram. Blaise had received a copy from a reliable source at the White House and so, apparently, had Hearst. The telegram had been secretly transmitted from London to President Wilson on Saturday, February 24, 1917. It was now Monday and, later in the day, Woodrow Wilson would address a joint session of Congress on the subject of war or peace or continued neutrality or whatever with the Central Powers, specifically Germany, in their war against the Entente Cordiale, or France and England and Russia and, lately, Italy. If authentic, the telegram from the German foreign minister, Arthur Zimmermann, to the German ambassador in Mexico, a country for some time more or less at war with the United States, would end once and for all the neutrality of the United States. Blaise suspected that the telegram was the work of the British Foreign Office. The boldness of tone was the sort of thing that only a desperate country, losing a war, would concoct in order to frighten the United States into coming to its aid.

"My spies tell me that the telegram has been sitting around in London since last month, which means that that's where it was written, *if* it didn't start here first." Hearst withdrew his copy from a pocket; then he read in his high thin voice, " 'We intend to begin on the first of February unrestricted submarine warfare.' " He looked up. "Well, that part's true, the Germans are really giving it to us, sinking just about every ship in sight between here and Europe. Dumb of them, you know. Most Americans don't want war. I don't want war. Did you know Bernstorff was Mrs. Wilson's lover?"

The Chief had a disconcerting habit of moving from subject to subject with no discernible connection; yet there was often some mysterious link that connected his staccato musings. Blaise had indeed heard the rumor that the German ambassador and the widow Mrs. Galt, as the second Mrs.

Wilson had been styled a year earlier, had been lovers. But then Washington was not only Henry James's "city of conversation" but Hearst's city of fantastic gossip. "If they were lovers, I'm sure it was all over by the time she married the President."

"You never can tell unless you were in the room, as my mother keeps telling me. The money my mother has! And she's pro-English, too." Hearst began to read again. " 'We shall endeavor in spite of this to keep the United States of America neutral. In the event of this not succeeding we make Mexico a proposal of alliance on the following basis: Make war together, make peace together, generous financial support and an understanding on our part that Mexico is to reconquer the lost territory in Texas, New Mexico and Arizona.' " Hearst looked up. "At least whoever wrote this isn't promising them my place in California."

"Who do you think wrote this, if not Zimmermann?"

Hearst looked grim. "Thomas W. Gregory, the attorney general. That's what I hear. He's pushing Wilson harder and harder to go to war now. Luckily, the rest of the Cabinet want Wilson to hold out because," Hearst squinted at the telegram, "this part here is what this war is all about. I mean, Zimmermann or Gregory or the English or whoever wrote it suggests that the president of Mexico approach the Japanese and get them into the war against us. Well, that's the big danger!"

Blaise moved off his desk and into his chair. Back of him hung a life-size painting of himself, his half-sister and co-publisher Caroline, and their editor, Trimble. Blaise knew, everyone knew, that whenever Hearst was in need of a scare story for his newspapers, he would invoke the Yellow Peril. Although Blaise was neutral on the subject of Japanese expansion in China, others were not. On February 1 when Germany had delivered its ultimatum to the United States that all shipping from American ports to those of the Allied Powers would be fair game for German submarines, or U-boats as they were popularly known, the Cabinet had met, and though Gregory among others was eager for a declaration of war, the President, remembering that he had just been re-elected as "the man who kept us out of war," wanted only to sever relations between the two countries. He had been unexpectedly supported by his secretaries of war and Navy; each had made the case that the United States should allow Germany its head in Europe and then, at a future date, the entire white race would unite as one against the yellow hordes, led by Japan. Hearst had played this diversion for all that it was worth. Blaise had not.

Trimble entered the room, without knocking. He was an aging Southerner whose once red hair was now a disagreeable pink. "Mr. Hearst." Trimble bowed. Hearst inclined his head. Trimble said, "We've just got a report on what the President is going to say to Congress . . ."

"War?" Hearst sat up straight.

"No, sir. But he is going to ask for armed neutrality . . ."

"Preparedness. . . ." Hearst sighed. "Peace without victory. A world league of nations with Mr. Wilson in the chair. Self-determination for all."

"Well," said Trimble, "he doesn't say all that in this speech." Then Trimble withdrew.

Blaise repeated the week's Washington joke. "The President wants to declare war in confidence, so the Bryanites—the pacifists—in his party won't turn on him."

"Not to mention me. I'm still in politics, you know." Blaise knew; everyone knew. Hearst was preparing to run yet again for governor of New York or mayor of New York City or president in 1920. He still had a huge following, particularly among the so-called hyphenates, the German-Americans and the Irish-Americans, all enemies of England and her allies. "Did you see *The Perils of Pauline*?"

Blaise adjusted easily to the sudden shift of subject. The Chief's mind was a wondrous kaleidoscope, unshielded by any sort of consciousness. Like a child, whatever suddenly bubbled up in his brain, he said. There was no screening process except when he chose, as he often did, to be enigmatically silent. "Yes, I saw several of them. She's very handsome, Miss Pearl White, and always on the move."

"That's why we call them *moving* pictures." Hearst was tutorial. "She has to keep running away from danger or the audience will start to run out of the theater. You know, on this war thing, I'm for staying out just as you are for getting us in. But I'll say this—if the people really want a war, then I'll go along. After all, they're the ones who're going to have to fight it, not me. I'm going to ask for a national referendum, get a vote from everybody, you know? Do you want to fight for England and France against your own people, the Germans and the Irish?"

Blaise laughed. "I don't think they'll let you put the question like that."

Hearst grunted. "Well, you know what I mean. There's no real support out there. I know. I got eight newspapers from California to New York. But of course it's too late. This thing's gone too far. We'll get a war all right. Then England will cave in. Then the Germans will come over here, or try to. Have you thought about flags?"

"Flags?" This time the Chief's unconscious mind was ahead of Blaise.

Hearst pulled a copy of the New York *American* from his huge side pocket. On the front page there were red-white-and-blue flags as well as several stanzas from "The Star-Spangled Banner." "Looks nice, don't it?"

"Very patriotic."

"That's the idea. I'm getting tired of being called pro-German. Anyway I'm about to start a photo-play company, and I'd like you to come in with me."

Blaise adjusted to this new shift with, he thought, admirable coolness. "But I don't know anything about the movies."

"Nobody does. That's what's so wonderful. You know, while we're sitting here, all over the world illiterate Chinese and Hindus and . . . and Patagonians are watching my Pauline. You see, to watch a movie you don't need to know another language the way you have to when you read a paper because it's all there—up there, moving around. It's the only international thing there is. Anyway the point is that Mother, who's the rich one, won't lend me the money and I don't want to go to the banks."

At last Hearst had startled Blaise. It was true that Phoebe Apperson Hearst controlled the vast mining wealth of Hearst's late father, but Hearst's personal empire was more than enough to finance a photo-play company. Of course, Hearst lived more grandly than anyone in the United States on, it was said, five million dollars a year, much of which went for the acquisition of every spurious artwork for sale anywhere. "Well, let me think about it." Blaise was cautious.

"What about that sister of yours, Caroline?"

"Ask her."

"You don't want to sell me the *Tribune,* do you?"

"No."

Hearst rose. "That's what you always say. I've got my eye on the *Times* here. It's a lousy paper, but then so was this till Caroline bought it and fixed it up."

Blaise's sudden pang of envy was, he hoped, not visible to the other. Caroline had indeed bought and revived the moribund *Tribune;* then, and only then, had she allowed her half-brother to buy in. Now, jointly, amiably, they co-published.

Hearst stared down at Fourteenth Street. "Four," he said, "no, five movie theaters just on this one street. I've got my eye on a place up in Harlem, an old casino, where I can set up a studio." Idly, he kicked at the remains of the Biedermeier chair. "I have to stay in New York. Because of 1920. War or not, that's going to be the big political year. Whoever gets to be president then can . . ." Hearst tapped the Zimmermann telegram which lay on Blaise's desk. "I think it's a fake."

Blaise nodded. "So do I. It's too convenient. . . ."

Hearst shook Blaise's hand. "I'm heading back to Palm Beach now. We'll get this war anyway, like it or not. Remember my proposal. I'm only starting up in Harlem because New York is my base. But the place to be from now on is Hollywood. You got that?"

"No," said Blaise. Like a circus trainer, he led the great bear to the door. "But I'm sure *you've* . . . got it."

James Burden Day walked up the steps to the north portico of the White House, where he was greeted by an usher who led him across the entrance hall to the small electric elevator. "Mrs. Wilson will be waiting for you in the upstairs hall. The President's in bed. The chill stays with him."

Burden was struck by the calm of the White House. There was no sign of emergency. A few politicians could be seen, showing friends the state apartments. Of course, the executive offices were in a separate wing to the west of the mansion, and although telephones never ceased to ring in the offices, there was, as yet, none of that tension which he remembered from the days of McKinley and the Spanish war, not to mention the tremendous bustle of the Roosevelt era when children and their ponies were to be seen indoors as well as out, and the President gave the impression of presiding simultaneously in every room with a maximum of joyous noise.

The Wilson White House was like the President himself: scholarly, remote, and somewhat lady-like. The President had been entirely devoted to his first wife. Now he was besotted by her successor. He was easily the most uxorious of the recent presidents; he also had the fewest friends. Ill-at-ease with men, Wilson preferred the company of women, particularly of his three daughters, gracious replicas of himself, ranging from the sad plainness of the spinster Margaret, who wanted to be a singer, to the dim beauty of Eleanor, married to the secretary of the Treasury, William G. McAdoo, to the equine-featured Jessie, married to one Francis B. Sayre.

The elevator stopped. The glass-panelled door opened. Burden found himself in the familiar upstairs corridor that ran the length of the building from west to east. In the old days, the President's offices had been at the east end and the living quarters at the west, with the oval sitting room as a sort of no-man's-land at dead center. But Theodore Roosevelt's family had been big; ambitious, too. He had added the executive wing to the mansion, while converting the entire second floor for himself and his family: successors, too, of course.

The wife of the most despised of his two despised successors stood opposite the elevator, waiting for Burden. Edith Bolling Galt Wilson was a large, full-breasted woman whose wide face contained small regular features, reflecting the Indian blood that she had inherited, she claimed, from Pocahontas. The smile was truly charming. "Senator Day! Now tell me the absolute truth. Did the usher refer to me as Mrs. Wilson or as the First Lady?"

"I think he said 'Mrs. Wilson.' "

"Oh, good! I hate 'First Lady' so! It sounds like something out of vaudeville, with Weber and Fields and me as Lillie Langtry."

Burden was aware that she was the focal point of a heavy jasmine scent that ebbed and flowed in her wake as she led him to the end of the hall where a desk with two telephones had been placed beneath a great fanlight window that looked out on the executive offices to the west and the State War and Navy Building to the north. At the desk sat Edith's social secretary, Edith Benham, an admiral's daughter who had replaced the magnificent Belle Hagner, a queen of the Aboriginal City, and secretary to the first Mrs. Wilson as well as to Mrs. Roosevelt and Mrs. Taft. It had been suggested that as Edith Bolling Galt had never been included in Mrs. Hagner's list of those who were invitable to the White House, Miss Hagner herself was no longer to be found there with her lists, her files, her telephones at the desk below the fan window. Kitty had talked of nothing else for a week; and Burden had listened less than usual.

"I do hope Mrs. Day will come to tea April twelfth." This was Mrs. Benham's greeting.

Burden said that he hoped that she would, too. "Edith is a treasure," said Edith. "Of course, she's Navy. We're surrounded by Navy here. You know Admiral Grayson." A small trim handsome man in mufti had come out of the southwest suite. "Senator," he shook Burden's hand; another Southerner, Burden duly noticed, more amused than not that it had taken Virginia less than a half-century to reconquer the White House with Woodrow Wilson, who had, as a boy, actually gazed upon the sainted features of Robert E. Lee in the days of their common country's terrible ruin. Now the South had returned in triumph to its true home, city, nation; and the President was surrounded, as was proper, by Virginians. "He's doing very well, sir." Grayson spoke to Burden but looked at Edith. "Only don't tire him. He's strong as an ox but susceptible to strain. The digestive system . . ."

". . . is the first to record the disagreeable." Edith smiled, like a little girl, Burden noted; hence the President's famous nickname for her, "little girl," which had caused much mirth considering Edith's ship-like tonnage, inevitably decorated, festooned, bannered with orchids. "I was horrified when I first learned about Mr. Wilson's breakfast . . ."

"Two raw eggs in grape juice." Grayson was prompt. "It solved the dyspepsia as much as one can. Anyway, let him conduct the conversation." Grayson gave more instructions, to Burden's deep annoyance. He was perfectly capable of talking politics in his own way to what, after all, was just another politician, no matter how elevated and hedged round with state. Then Edith led him into the bedroom.

Woodrow Wilson was propped up by four pillows; he wore a plaid wool dressing gown; and his famous pince-nez. Beside the bed, on a chair, sat his brother-in-law Randolph. Between them, on the coverlet, there was a Ouija board, and each had a hand on top of the table-like contraption that moved as if of its own will over a wooden board on which had been drawn the alphabet, stopping, as the spirit dictated, at this or that letter, which

Randolph duly noted on a pad of paper. Wilson held a finger to his lips as Burden and Edith sat beside the bed, a huge affair of carved dark wood that Edith had had moved from the so-called Lincoln bedroom at the other end of the corridor. Actually, the "Lincoln bedroom" had been Lincoln's office while the bed, known reverently as *his* bed, was never used by him. All that anyone could recall was that Mrs. Lincoln had bought it for a guest room. In any case, Burden regarded the bed as singularly hideous despite its provenance; but then he disliked anything to do with the Civil War era. Red plush, horsehair stuffing, gas-lamps were mingled with his own memories of growing up poor in the Reconstruction South before his family had moved west.

While the two men played with the Ouija board, Edith whispered to Burden. "The place was—is—so run-down. You must ride herd on everyone here twenty-four hours a day, which poor Mrs. Wilson, being sick, couldn't do, and Mrs. Taft was too grand to do. Now, of course, all the money goes to Preparedness and so we just scrimp along."

But they scrimped most pleasantly, thought Burden. A fire burned in the fireplace, while above the mantel a splendid American landscape afforded some relief from all those replicas of dim politicians and their wives that gave the White House rooms a sense of being mere stage-sets for an audience of glum, peering ghosts. The window opposite Burden framed a wintry view of the becolumned State War and Navy Building, where lights were already burning. On a table, beneath the window-sill, the President's Hammond type-writer was set. It was said that not only could he type as well as any professional but he alone wrote those high-minded mellifluous speeches that had so entranced the country, including Burden, who was generally immune to the oratory of others.

Both Edith and Burden watched the President intently. But then he was most watchable, Burden decided. Roosevelt was always in motion, and so always the center of attention. But there was nothing of particular interest in T.R.'s chubby face or the rather jerky movements of his stout little body. On the other hand, Wilson was lean, large-headed, and nearly handsome. The long face ended in a lantern jaw; the pale gray eyes were watchful; the thin gray hair cut short; the sallow skin deeply lined. Grayson kept him physically active, particularly on the golf-course, where Edith often joined him; reputedly, she was the better player. At sixty, the twenty-eighth president of the United States, re-elected to a second term five months earlier, looked quite capable (in Virginia's interest?) of being elected to an unprecedented third term in 1920. Such was the nightmare of the professional politician; and Burden himself was nothing if not professional, and like the rest of the tribe, he too saw himself abed in this house, if not with a Ouija board. Mildly dismayed, he gazed upon what might yet be the first three-term president.

Randolph announced the message from the spirit world. "Use mines to sink German submarines. Signed Horatio Nelson."

"I wonder how Nelson knows about mines. Or submarines." The President's voice was resonant, and only an ear as sharp as Burden's could detect Virginia beneath the correct professorial diction. If Wilson had not written more books than his nemesis Theodore Roosevelt, he had written weightier ones—solemn histories that were used as university texts, which made him something of an anomaly. The historian suddenly torn from his study in order to make history for others to write about. Most politicians disliked him for this suspected—true?—doubleness. But Burden found it intriguing. The President seemed always to be observing himself and others as if he knew that sooner or later, he would be teaching himself—others, too.

The fact that there had never been a president quite like Wilson made him all the more difficult to assess. For one thing, did the professional historian, who preferred the British parliamentary system to the American executive system, inhibit the president in his duties? Certainly Wilson had begun his reign with a dramatic parliamentary gesture. Instead of sending a message to be read to the Congress like his predecessors, he himself went up to the Capitol and read his own message, the first president to do so since John Quincy Adams. He had behaved like a prime minister in the Congress, except no one there could ask him a question in that constitutionally separated place. He also enjoyed conferring directly with members of the press; thus, he could mitigate if not circumvent their publishers. Finally, as he could not alter the checks and balances of the Constitution, he was obliged to maintain his power through his adroit mastery of the Democratic Party, a delicate task for one who belonged to its minority eastern wing made up of Tammany Hall and Hearst and worse, while the party's majority was Southern and Western and far too long enamored of William Jennings Bryan.

Burden knew that he had been summoned to the White House because, with his elevation to the Senate, he was now leader of the Bryanite wing of the party, which hated war, England, the rich, and, by and large, Woodrow Wilson, too. Wilson's re-election had been a very close thing indeed, thanks to his own party's suspicion that he wanted to join the Allies in the war against Germany. Only the inspired slogan "He kept us out of war" had, finally, rallied the faithful. Now war was at hand. What to do?

Wilson motioned for Randolph to remove the Ouija board; and himself. Edith also took the hint. At the door she said, "Don't tire yourself."

"That's hardly possible, little girl, in a sickbed." She was gone. Then Wilson noted the elaborate bed, rather like a Neapolitan hearse that Burden had once seen at the base of Vesuvius. "Though I'm not so sure about *this* bed." Wilson removed a sheaf of papers from his bedside table, and placed them on the coverlet.

"Have you seen Mr. Bryan?"

Burden shook his head. "I think he's in Florida."

"The Speaker?" Wilson stared at Burden out of the corner of his eye, a disquieting effect. But then they were embarked upon a disquieting subject. The speaker of the House, Champ Clark, was the *de facto* heir of Bryan. He had opposed Wilson at every turn and he had been, in 1916, a serious candidate for the presidential nomination. Had it not been for the maneuvering of such Wilsonian Bryanites as Burden, Champ Clark might now be enjoying a chill in the Lincoln bed.

"The Speaker's Southern. Southerners—Southwesterners—tend to peace at any price—in Europe, anyway."

"I know. I'm one, too. That's why I'm far too proud to fight." Wryly, Wilson quoted himself. This single phrase had enraged every war-lover in the land, particularly the war-besotted Theodore Roosevelt, who sounded no longer sane. Wilson picked up the papers. "I tell you, Mr. Day, I have done everything a man could possibly do to stay out of this terrible business. I'd hoped Germany would be sufficiently intelligent not to force my hand—to allow us to go on as we are, neutral but helpful . . ."

"To England and France."

The President was not tolerant of interruptions. He had taught others for too many years: ladies at Bryn Mawr and gentlemen at Princeton; and at neither place had the students been encouraged to interrupt the inspired—and inspiring—lecturer. "England and France. But also there is—was—cotton to the Central Powers, at the insistence of the anti-war ten-cent cotton senators . . ."

"Of which I am one."

"Of which you are one." Although Wilson smiled, his mind was plainly on the set of papers which he kept distractedly shaking as if to dislodge their message. Burden noted that two of them were tagged with red seals. "It is curious that if I am impelled to go to war, it will give pleasure to the Republicans, our enemies, and pain to much of our party."

Burden was still enough of a lawyer to seize upon a key word. "Impelled," he repeated. "Who impels you?"

"Events." Wilson gazed vaguely out the window, toward a row of lights where his clerk-like secretary of state, Robert Lansing, was, no doubt, busy doing clerkly things, so unlike his predecessor, the Great Commoner, who was incapable of clerkdom or indeed of anything less mundane than Jovian thunderings for peace.

"I know that many of you thought I was . . . uh, striking a bargain during the last election. That you would get out the vote because I had kept us out of war, despite so much provocation. Well . . ." He had either lost his train of thought or he was preparing to indulge himself in the presidential privilege of abruptly abandoning a potentially dangerous line of argument. "Someone asked me the other day—an old colleague from Princeton—what was the worst thing about being president." Wilson looked directly at Burden, the face solemn but the eyes bright behind the pince-nez. "Luckily, he didn't ask me what the best thing was. I might never have thought of an answer to that one. Anyway I could answer what was the worst. All day long people tell you things that you already know, and you must act as if you were hearing their news for the first time. Now Senator Gore tells me," there was plainly a bridge from repetitions of the obvious to Oklahoma's blind senator, whose opposition to the war had set in motion a series of parliamentary maneuvers designed to smoke out the President's intentions, "that I owe my re-election entirely to his efforts for me in California."

"But you do owe your majority to California."

Wilson had gone to bed on election night thinking that his Republican opponent, Charles Evans Hughes, had been elected; so, indeed, had "President" Hughes. The next day the Far Western returns came in and Wilson was narrowly re-elected. Burden knew that this might not have happened if that professional spellbinder Gore had not been persuaded to leave his sulky seclusion in Oklahoma City and go to California and take the stump for Wilson. Gore had done so on condition that he could guarantee that Wilson would continue to keep, as he had kept, the peace. On election night Gore had wired Tumulty the exact figure by which Wilson would carry California.

Now Wilson was faced with his own less than courageous record. At various times, he had managed to be both war and peace candidate. This sort of thing never troubled the public, whose memory was short; but senators were constitutionally endowed with long memories and, often, mysterious constituencies as well. Some were obliged to follow the prejudices of their pro-German constituents. Others saw themselves as architects of a new and perfect republic, and their leader was La Follette of Wisconsin, far more dangerous in his idealism than any of the Bryanites, who were bound to be swayed by popular opinion, a highly volatile substance produced, often at whim, by William Randolph Hearst in his eight newspapers, not to mention all the other publishers, to a man for war. Thus far, Hearst was still the voice of the Germans and the Irish; and his papers in the great Northern cities played shamelessly to that city mob which he still counted on to make *him* president in 1920.

"I expected to be a reformer president." Wilson sounded wistful. "There was so much to do right here at home, and we did do so much, so fast."

Burden agreed, without reserve. The sort of reforms that Roosevelt had always spoken of with such transcendent passion Wilson had actually accomplished with gentle reason, combined with the subtle twisting of congressional arms. But then, as he liked to say, anyone who could master the Princeton faculty *and* the alumni association would find a mere Congress easy to deal with. Was it Senator Lodge who had said, "But he never did master them. That's why politics was his only escape"?

"What position will they—will *you* take if I were to ask for war?" Wilson had collected himself.

"It will depend on what your reasons are. I always thought you missed your chance—if war is what you want—when the Germans sank the *Lusitania,* and so many American lives were lost. The public was ready for war that day."

"But," Wilson was cool, "I was not. It was too soon. We were—we are—not prepared."

"Two weeks ago," Burden was enjoying the game, "when you sent Ambassador Bernstorff home, the people were ready, again. Now comes the Zimmermann business. . . ." Although Burden was most sensitive to Wilson's aversion to advice of any kind, he knew that he had been invited to the President's sickbed to give him a reading of the Senate's mood. He took the plunge. "The time has come. The thing is here. You can't wait much longer. The press is doing its work. Gallant little Belgium. Raped nuns. Devoured children. The Hun is the devil. If there is to be war, prepared or unprepared, now is the time."

Wilson stared at the papers in his hand; and waited.

Burden proceeded. "Isn't that why you've called a special session? To ask us to declare war?"

"If I do, how many would oppose me? And on what ground?" Wilson's usual Presbyterian moralizing and cloudy poetic images tended to evaporate when faced with a political problem. He was now very much the political manager, counting heads.

Burden named a dozen names, the leaders. "Actually, there is a clear but weak majority in each house that is against war, and nothing will stir them unless you have some new example of Hunnishness."

Wilson took off his pince-nez; rubbed the two indentations on either side of his nose—like red thumbprints. "I do believe that the Germans must be the stupidest people on earth. They provoke us. Sink our ships. Plot with Mexico against our territory. Then—now—they have done it." He held up the red-tagged papers. "Today three of our ships have been sunk. The *City of Memphis.* The *Illinois.* The *Vigilancia.*"

Burden experienced a chill as the names were read off. "I have tried—I *believe* with absolute sincerity, but who can tell the human heart? least of all one's own—to stay out of this incredibly stupid and wasteful war, which has so suddenly made us, thanks to England's bankruptcy, the richest nation on earth. Once we are armed, there is no power that can stop us. But once we arm, will we ever disarm? You see my—predicament, or what was a predicament until the Kaiser shoved me this morning." The President's face looked as if it had just been roughly brought forth, with chisel and mallet, from a chunk of gray granite.

"Why," asked Burden, "have you taken so long when it's been plain to so many that your heart has always been with England and the Allies?"

Wilson stared at Burden as if he were not there. "I was three years old," he said at last, "when Lincoln was elected and the Civil War began. My father was a clergyman in Staunton—then, later, we moved to Augusta, Georgia. I was eight years old when the war ended and Mr. Lincoln was killed. In Augusta my father's church was a . . . was *used* as a hospital for our troops. I remember all that. I remember Jefferson Davis being led a captive through the town. I remember how he . . . My family suffered very little. But what we saw around us, the bitterness of the losers in the war and the brutality of the winners . . . well, none of this was lost on me. I am not," a wintry close-lipped smile divided for an instant the rude stone face, "an enthusiast of war like Colonel Roosevelt, whose mentality is that of a child of six and whose imagination must be nonexistent. You see, I can *imagine* what this war will do to us. I pray I'm wrong. But I am deathly afraid that once you lead this people—and I know them well—into war, they'll forget there ever was such a thing as tolerance. Because to fight to win, you must be brutal and ruthless, and that spirit of ruthless brutality will enter into the very fibre of our national life. You—Congress—will be infected by it, too, and the police, and the average citizen. The whole lot. Then we shall win. But *what* shall we win? How do we help the South . . . I mean the Central Powers to return from a war-time to a peace-time basis? How do we help ourselves? We shall have become what we are fighting. We shall be trying to reconstruct a peace-time civilization with war-time standards. That's not possible, and since everyone will be involved, there'll be no bystanders with sufficient power to make a just peace. That's what I had wanted us to be. Too proud to fight in the mud, but ready to stand by, ready to mediate, ready to . . ." The voice stopped.

There was a long silence. If the sun had not set, it had long since vanished behind cold dense clouds; and the room was dark except for the single lamp beside Wilson's bed and the fading coals in the fireplace. Although Burden was used to the President's eloquence, he was not entirely immune to its potency. Wilson had the gift of going straight to the altogether too palpitating heart of the business.

"I am calling Congress back two weeks earlier. On April second. I shall . . ." He put the dangerous documents on the table beside the bed. "How ironic it is!" He shook his head in wonder. "After all the work we've done to control big business, guess what will happen now? They will be more firmly in the saddle than ever before. Because who else can arm us? they'll say. Who else can administer the war?"

"Who else?" Burden had had much the same thought. If ever anyone benefited from an American war it was the trusts, the cartels, the Wall Street speculators. "We shall revert to the age of Grant."

Wilson nodded bleakly. "Then, if the war should be a long one, and we be weakened, there is the true enemy waiting for us in the West. The yellow races, led by Japan, ready to overwhelm us through sheer numbers. . . ."

Kitty sat on a boulder overlooking Rock Creek, her eye on the baby, as it tottered ever closer to a clump of shiny poison ivy at the foot of an English walnut tree whose green fruit glowed in the summer sun. "Why not," said Kitty, "put the parlor here, over the creek, and our bedroom over there?"

"The road's too near." Burden had taken off his jacket and unbuttoned his shirt, and felt free of all things worldly except Kitty, who had become surprisingly pretty as she aged; she was no longer the somewhat hard-faced young woman that he had felt obliged to marry because her father was the master of the Democratic Party of their state. If nothing else, Caroline had taught him never to disguise his motives from himself. In early days, Caroline had shocked him. Now he shocked her whenever he chose to reveal just how the affairs of the republic were conducted. Admittedly, the shock to her system was not moral: rather, she appeared to resent the lack of form to American life, so unlike France, where everyone knew what to expect, including the exact nature of the almost always predictable unexpected.

On the other hand, Kitty was a natural politician, true heiress to her father, the legendary judge, not only as a political tactician but now as possessor of her late father's fortune soon to be transformed from abstract stocks and bonds into wood, brick, stone.

Burden himself had never been able to acquire money. Somehow or other the munificent seventy-five hundred dollars a year salary of a United States senator was hardly enough for them to live on, even though their large house in American City was always profitably rented. When it came time to go home to vote or to campaign, they would check into the Henry Clay Hotel across from the state capitol, and pretend that they had been living in town all year, just folks, with only the odd trip to Washington.

The first installment of Kitty's inheritance had gone to buy one and a half acres of Rock Creek Park, mostly wooded hills whose undergrowth was as green and thick as any jungle. In fact, the park was almost too much of a jungle for Burden's taste, as he seized his daughter's pinafore just as she was about to bury her face in a cluster of poison ivy which could, within hours, cover its victim with oozing itching blisters, torment for an adult, hell for a child.

"Diana!" Kitty's voice sounded too late. "What is it about poison ivy? Jim Junior had a dowsing rod for the stuff."

Burden settled himself on a fallen log opposite Kitty, Diana on his knee. Birds silently circled overhead, their singing-mating season past. Now they were solicitous parents and providers, as well as flight instructors to the young—and mourners for those who fell to earth.

"The architect says that *this* should be the parlor, facing south." Burden tried and failed to imagine a room where they were sitting. Jungle or not, he preferred the open. Unlike most boys brought up on a farm, he did not prefer the indoors, as long, of course, as he did not have to do chores. "She'll grow up here," he added, looking down at Diana, a grave as yet speechless child, who sighed.

Kitty took a crust of bread from her handbag. Then, bread in hand, she extended her arm. The miracle, as Burden always thought of it, occurred in a matter of seconds. A large thrush made several close passes in order to get a good look at Kitty before he settled on her wrist. Then he took the bread in his beak, shook it free of encumbering crumbs, and rose to a branch of the nearest tree, where he ate the crust and watched Kitty.

"How do you do it?"

"I've always done it." Kitty's relationship with the animal world was intimate, collusive, extra-human. All creatures came to her without fear; and she was there. As a girl, she had befriended a full-grown wolf, dying of hunger during a hard winter. The wolf had followed her about like a dog; then, according to the Judge, while she was at school, the wolf had attacked the hired man and the hired man had shot the beast in self-defense. To which Kitty had replied with a terminal coldness, "No, Father. You just had him killed." Father and daughter never spoke of the subject again but father and son-in-law did discuss the matter years later, and the Judge had said, with puzzled awe, "How did she know—how *could* she know that I killed the brute when there was no one there to see me?" It was decided then that Kitty was psychic, at least with animals and birds. She seemed less interested in people as opposed to voters. She knew as much of Burden's alliances and arrangements as he did; yet he was certain that she knew nothing of Caroline. He also suspected that if she did know, she would be indifferent. Odd, he thought, not to know your own wife as well as—a thrush did. When Jim Junior had died at six, it was Burden who had wept. Kitty had simply busied herself with the funeral arrangements; then she had quarrelled with her Negro cook over the refreshments for the wake, a bit of Romanism popular in their Protestant state. That was the end of their son.

Although a cool west breeze was rustling the branches of the taller trees, Burden was still uncomfortably hot. But then everyone said that this was the hottest summer in memory, the first war-time summer. "High ceilings." Kitty looked up at the tallest tree, an oak.

"The highest." Burden was knowledgeable. "A Norman facade. Gray stonework. A terrace. A pond. A porch to the side . . ."

"Let's hope the war won't interfere."

"Building goes on. Even if food doesn't." Burden moved from log to ground; and the inevitable grass stains on his trousers. "The President's fit to be tied over Section 23."

"You can't blame him." The animal psychic was now the political psychic, having skipped any sort of rapport with those human beings between the two poles of her life.

"They're trying to do to him what they did to Lincoln when they set up that joint congressional committee to oversee the war."

"Same thing." Kitty nodded. "And all tucked inside the food bill, which is sly. But you won't let it go through?"

"No. But there'll be a real fight. Can't you just hear the talk? Oh, the talk!" More than ever, the Senate encouraged personal oddity. Originally intended as a house of lords for the American patriciate or its assigns, the members of the upper house were selected by the various state legislators that were themselves paid for by the moneyed class. But since 1913, senators were now popularly elected. As a result, a new breed of lordly tribunes of the people had appeared in the sleepy chamber; and they delighted in tormenting the gentlemanly old guard of the patriciate. Also, since any senator who had got the floor to speak could speak as long as he was conscious, a great new age of filibuster had dawned, and a leather-lunged senator might, in the last hours before adjournment, talk to death a piece of legislation or threaten to do so in exchange for favors.

Even so, Burden was delighted to belong to so powerful a club, in which he had found his place as chief conciliator of his party's chief, the schoolmaster president, whose control over the Senate's Democratic majority was fragile at best. This meant constant work for Burden, who must placate—when not outright bribe—the Bryanites, the isolationists, the pro-Germanites and all the rest, who chose to reign in committee rather than serve their president.

"I wonder who she'll marry." Kitty gazed fondly at Diana, almost as if she were a plump raccoon arrived at the kitchen door for a handout.

"Isn't that tempting fate?" Burden felt a swift chill; and shuddered.

He had once speculated on Jim Junior's future and promptly lost him to diphtheria.

"No. She'll marry in this house, or from this house." Kitty had a sort of second sight. "I suppose she'll be happy, too."

"Yes." Burden was noncommittal. Kitty was fond of him; he of her; no more.

"Did your father like your mother?" This was sudden.

"That was so long ago. I don't recall." Burden had grown up on a farm in Alabama, surrounded by veterans of the lost war like his father. Burden had always been amazed at how Mark Twain had managed to make so idyllic that harsh crude muddy—always mud—world of mosquitoes and chiggers and wet-heat and poisonous snakes the color of the mud. Of course, Twain had been writing of an earlier generation before the war, but even so Burden had been aware all his childhood that this was not the way life was meant to be. There had been a very great fall, which his father, unlike so many veterans, was eager to explain and describe, the pale blue eyes fierce and crazy, as they must have been that day at Chickamauga when the bullet felled but did not kill him and he was taken prisoner. Later, among the ruins, Obadiah Day had begun his life all over in the delta mud. Of his children—seven, eight? Burden did not know the count—all but two had died of bloody flux, as the cholera was known. Burden did recall how much of his childhood seemed to have been spent in the local cemetery, watching small boxes being hidden under red dirt. He also recalled hours spent listening to his father speak of how They had ruined the South, corrupted the Negroes, foreclosed on the land of the best true stock of the country. *They* were a shifting entity composed of all Yankees and bankers and railroad men and, sometimes, of plain aliens, of whom Catholics and Jews were the worst. Curiously, the Negroes, no matter how out-of-hand, were never held directly responsible for their behavior. If a nigger went bad it was They who'd gone and turned him.

In time, the defeated Confederates turned to politics, the only weapon that they could use against Them. The political picnic and the under-canvas rally became the true church of those who had been dispossessed in their own land, and Obadiah was among those who had helped form the Party of the People in order to redress the people's wrongs, and the party flourished everywhere in the South, and Obadiah himself was elected to a series of small state offices. Then came the day when he heard the fourteen-year-old Burden speak at a rally, and joyously he had welcomed his son to the great struggle, much as the Baptist had received the Messiah on Jordan's shining bank. So, at Alabama's edge, James Burden Day had come into his kingdom to do his father's work and rout Them in the people's name.

For Caroline, love had always meant—if anything—separation. In the golden days of her affair with Burden, she was allowed to see him only on Sundays in Washington; with rare excursions elsewhere, to exotic river cities like St. Louis, and to the wonderful blankness of hotel rooms. She had not needed Burden—or anyone—every day. She had had a full life, beginning with her seven years' war against Blaise for her share of the Sanford inheritance. Although Blaise had won the war in the sense that she had received her capital when she was twenty-seven and not, as their father's will required, twenty-one, she had scored the greater victory by acquiring a moribund Washington newspaper and making a success of it, largely because Blaise had always wanted to be a publisher, like his friend and sometime employer Hearst. But it was Caroline not Blaise who had recreated the Washington *Tribune.* Finally, at a peace conference in exotic St. Louis, she had allowed him to buy into the paper while she kept control.

But control of what? she wondered, as she carefully crossed the icy sidewalk in front of Henry Adams's Romanesque villa across from the Byzantine-classical St. John's Church, whose gilded cupola mocked the demure primness of Lafayette Park. Whatever urge that she might have had for political power had been entirely extinguished by her years in Washington. Seen close to, the rulers of the country were no different from the ruled, or if they were, she could not tell the difference. Money mattered, and nothing else. For anyone who had been brought up in a nation whose most famous play was called *The Miser,* this was more agreeable than not, particularly if one had enough of what mattered. The problem now was what to do with what remained of her life. Tim, as she now somewhat self-consciously called Farrell, had entered her orderly life like a sudden high wind at a Newport picnic, and everything was in a state of disorder.

In Los Angeles, their days were spent in the surprisingly small barn-like buildings where photo-plays were created at a very rapid rate; and their nights at early "supper," as it was called in California, with the world-famous men and women who were the stars, each tinier than the other; only their large heads in proportion to their small bodies demonstrated some obscure Darwinian principle that when evolution required movie stars those best adapted to the screen—large heads atop small neat bodies—would be ready to make the journey to Southern California "because there's sun all year round," the town proclaimed. Actually, there was fog almost every morning and a thousand other places would have been more suitable except for one crucial detail—the Mexican border was only a hundred miles away. Since all the moving-picture makers in California were using equipment developed by that protean genius Edison, and since none acknowledged his patents, the village was filled with hard-eyed detectives, waiting to catch a glimpse of something called the Latham Loop, which, if found in use, could lead to gun-fire and endless lawsuits.

The President was standing in his open car. Edith sat beside him, clutching flowers. The President held his hat in his left hand, and waved with his right. The smile looked genuine; fatigue, too. Then the car with its Secret Service outriders pulled into a street lined with working-class people. As the President waved, they crossed their arms over their chests and looked away. Suddenly, one man held up a sign: "Release Political Prisoners." The President's hand dropped to his side. The smile vanished. Edith stared up at her husband, with a fixed awful smile, as the car, like a hearse, made its way through the sombre crowd.

The lights came on in the screening room. "Where was that?" asked Caroline, appropriately shaken.

"Seattle." Tim waved to the projectionist. "That's all. Thanks." Together they left the screening room and walked down the musty-smelling hall to the offices that Famous Players–Lasky had rented Traxler Productions, overlooking the corner of Vine and Selma. Soon they would have to decide whether or not they would buy or build a studio, or continue to rent.

"You can't use that." Caroline was firm.

"If I knew how, I would. But there's no story to go with it." Tim stared down at the row of pepper trees that bordered Vine Street. The Lasky studio, as everyone called it, occupied two city blocks. On Vine Street was the studio, a two-storied gray frame building, while just back of it, on Argyle Street, was the fenced-in back lot, filled with technicians' sheds, New York streets, French villages, English mansions—every sort of setting that a photo-play might require.

Caroline studied a stack of photographs of herself. In the nick of time, for her at least, a cameraman had discovered that if black maline silk was placed over the camera lens years would be subtracted from those photographed, thus adding years to the acting lives of elderly players, of which Emma Traxler was one. Lines vanished or were reduced to more platonic essences. At her worst, Emma simply looked faded but spiritual, and that was what the plot of *The Dangerous Years* called for: a widow with a fortune falls in love with her son's best friend at college, who wears knickerbockers to emphasize his youth. Although the actor was only a decade younger than Caroline, the new lens kept him a boy and Caroline a gamine in her late thirties. At the end, Caroline would commit suicide, something she very much looked forward to. Usually, she was to be seen at picture's end striding into the future during a long shot on a desolate moor, which was almost always the Burbank Golf Course after the mist-machine had disguised all the holes. Then a final close shot of her luminous face, transfigured, as Mr. Wurlitzer's organ played Tchaikovsky's Fourth Symphony, and the women in the audience wept. Somehow, mysteriously and without design, Caroline Sanford had become Emma Traxler if not for good then for the amount of time that she chose to spend in Hollywood with Tim, and that looked to be most of the year.

Tim had recovered from the fiasco of *The Strike-Breakers* through the simple expedient of rewriting the title cards to favor the railroad management and denounce the strikers. The result had been cheered in the popular press as a victory for capitalism; and no one had gone to see the movie. So, in the end, as Caroline observed, political integrity had been maintained.

"You've got to admit that that footage would make a swell ending to a story about the Wobblies. You know, the workers ignoring the President who had put so many of their leaders in jail."

"Why pick on poor Mr. Wilson?"

"Because he picked on poor Mr. Debs."

Caroline had made it a rule to ignore Tim's curious political line. "Philosophy" was too large a word to describe what seemed to her a perverse impulse to take the side of the unpopular and the weak. Since Americans only worshipped the strong and the bullying, she had at least convinced him that it was bad for his career to become too identified with the hated poor; yet, surprisingly, when she had suggested they make a film about Russia's October Revolution, he had not been interested. Plainly, he was more radical priest than revolutionary. She herself knew too much about politics to believe in anything other than the prevailing fact of force in human affairs. Henry Adams had been a thorough teacher.

When the secretary announced that Grace Kingsley of the Los Angeles *Times* had materialized, Tim left the office by a back door. Miss Kingsley's section on entertainment in the *Times* was read by everyone in Hollywood, and much reprinted elsewhere. The world could not get enough news about the movies, and Miss Kingsley was the principal conduit between the studios and public. A maiden lady, she was startlingly unprurient. She was not interested in love affairs or scandals, only photo-plays planned or in production or in release.

"Dear Miss Traxler." Miss Kingsley withdrew a long glove from a mottled hand and Caroline, though preferring the glove, shook the hand warmly. "It's so nice having you here close to home. My heart sinks when I have to go over to Burbank or that ultima Thule, Universal City. I feel like a pioneer, so much cactus, so many onions, and the Cahuenga Pass terrifies me."

Miss Kingsley made herself comfortable in a chintz-covered chair. "I've just come from Mr. Griffith. Thanks to Mr. Lasky, he's got financing again and he'll be able to finish *Scarlet Days,* certain to be a monument, I predict, to the western, which, if memory serves, he's never made before, at feature length. He also tells me—this is between us, of course, as I won't write it yet—that he's going back to the East when he finishes his contract with Artcraft here. But *then* another little bird has told me that he's just signed a three-picture deal with First National, and that will keep him here, I should think, for at least another halcyon year."

"Is his studio for sale?" Caroline revered Mr. Griffith, as did everyone; but she was far more interested in the studio that he had created at the juncture of Hollywood and Sunset boulevards: two sound-stages, a house whose owner had been moved out, and a laboratory where it was possible not only to experiment with special effects but to create an entire movie from the printing of the negative to the editing to the making of copies for the distributors.

In Griffith's case, the entire process seldom took more than a month. Once he had decided on a story, he would get his artist in residence to draw each scene, which he then gave to the art director, who would call in the studio's carpenters, plasterers and painters, and the sets would be built. Meanwhile, Griffith would be rehearsing his actors; for years, he himself had been a stock-company actor, constantly on tour, and he had learned, firsthand, what thrilled the mass public. Then, in a great burst of energy, sometimes in as little as eighteen days, he would film the photo-play in an atmosphere very like a war, according to Tim, who had been involved as a cameraman in two of Griffith's early films. Although Griffith himself was relentlessly polite, he also enjoyed creating unease and tension all about him. Tim had learned what he could from him; and quickly moved on.

"I suspect . . . I cannot be positive . . . that he *will* sell once he's finished up his commitments here and removed himself to Mamaroneck in the East, Heaven only knows why."

"We would like to increase our production, as you know. Mr. Lasky has been very gracious, but we're crowded here. Mr. Farrell has found a place on Poverty Row . . ."

Miss Kingsley shook her head and sighed. "No. No. Not for Traxler Productions. *You* are a hallmark of quality. Down the road there they make a movie in a week. *Vulgar* movies."

Caroline gazed out the window at Poverty Row, which was just visible on nearby Gower Street. The cheap studios resembled a row of barns or garages haphazardly assembled in what was still a large orange grove.

"We could build, I suppose."

"Do! Like Charlie Chaplin. Now there's a charming studio. How I enjoy going there! So English, with tea being served all the time, and of course it's where I like to think home is, *this* area, the true Hollywood and not the Valley or Culver City, in spite of dear Mr. Ince."

Chaplin's studio was on the east side of La Brea, below Santa Monica Boulevard, while two blocks west of La Brea, his fellow United Artist, Douglas Fairbanks, had built *his* studio. Here he would eventually be joined by Mary Pickford if she, a good Catholic, could ever get divorced from her alcoholic husband, a source of constant interest to the entire world if not to Caroline, who wanted nothing more than an inexpensive sound-stage of her own.

"You are," Miss Kingsley had opened her notebook, "contemplating a film about the Bolshevik terror in Russia."

"How did you know that?" Caroline was always surprised at how much the vague Miss Kingsley knew about everything that had to do with "home," the true Hollywood.

"One of my little birds. Now, you know that those Warner Brothers people spent fifty thousand dollars to buy Ambassador Gerard's book about Germany and the war, so there's now a serious trend, which I can detect, of doing real-life historical stories of a modern nature. Would you be working from a tome on the subject?"

Caroline was so thrilled to hear the word "tome" used in conversation that she said, without thinking, "Ah, yes. Yes! The tome will be *Ten Days That Shook the World,* if we can get the rights, of course."

Miss Kingsley's notebook nearly fell from her hand. "But that is a *pro*-Bolshevik tome, I am told."

"Oh, not the way we plan to do it."

"You will change the message the way you did in *The Strike-Breakers*?" Miss Kingsley was far from being the fool she seemed, and Caroline already regretted having spoken without a thought in her head.

"On that order, yes. Mr. Farrell is eager to alert all Americans to the dangers of communism, which is everywhere on the march. . . ."

Miss Kingsley hummed happily to herself and wrote and wrote as Caroline improvised and improvised. Then Emma Traxler was questioned about *her* plans as an actress. Emma Traxler had made five films since *Huns from Hell,* and though each had made money none had equalled her startling debut. Even so, Caroline was amazed that she was something of a cult whom producers wanted to use. The previous year, Fairbanks had asked her to play Queen Berengaria to his Richard the Lion-hearted; and she had said yes, eagerly. But so far, there were no plans to make the film. "Everyone thinks I'm too contemporary for costume pictures," he had apologized when they last met in the Dining Room of the Stars at the Hollywood Hotel, where, surprisingly, a few stars occasionally dined.

"I have plans—hopes, I should say—to play Mary Stuart before I'm too old." Caroline enjoyed using the one word that Hollywood did not acknowledge.

"Dear, dear, dear," murmured Miss Kingsley, as if Caroline had confessed to some incurable disease. "No, no, no," she then added. "Never *old.* Will Mr. Farrell direct you?"

"I don't think that's his sort of thing. I'd like to use that young German director, Mr. Lubitsch."

"I saw his *Madame Du Barry.*" Miss Kingsley looked stern. "It was very *continental,* if you know what I mean."

"But then so was Mary Stuart, and so," Caroline practiced a husky laugh like Bernhardt, "am I."

"You seem thoroughly American, Miss Traxler." After Miss Kingsley had bestowed her highest accolade, they discussed Caroline's current film, now in its second week of shooting. She was free today because the company was doing a garden-party scene to which her character had not been invited. Graciously, Miss Kingsley declined an invitation to visit the set.

Caroline then walked her to the main door of the studio, where, as always, a small crowd of innocent fans waited to see the stars come and go, not knowing what the less innocent fans knew, that the stars tended to enter from the Argyle Lot, a block away. Mr. Lasky himself greeted Miss Kingsley at the door, where a studio policeman stood guard. Lasky was a small plump cheerful gnome of a man. Of the Jewish producers, he was the only one to be born in the United States. Where his partner, Zukor, was imperious and harsh, Lasky was easy and charming, and it was only a matter of time, everyone agreed, before Lasky would be devoured by the great predator. Caroline studied the various movie magnates with all the fascinated zeal of an anthropologist.

"I've got Maurice Maeterlinck and Edward Knoblock and Somerset Maugham and Elinor Glyn." This was Lasky's greeting to Miss Kingsley, who responded with, "Hooray! When do they come?"

"January. I'm getting them all. You want one, Miss Traxler?"

"Yes. Bernard Shaw."

Lasky frowned. "He won't come. I guess he's holding out. But when he sees how we've gone and got every famous writer there is, he'll hightail it out here pretty fast, let me tell you."

Caroline left Mr. Lasky and Miss Kingsley together; and made her way through the building to the back lot, where the New York City row of brownstones always reminded her how much she would like to appear in Mrs. Wharton's *The House of Mirth.*

A film was being shot in the street. Two gunmen came out of a shop, firing at the camera. Caroline ducked behind the street, where a metal frame held up the facades, which were so realistic that one could not tell they were not real. Thanks to San Francisco's 1915 Exposition, Hollywood had acquired a number of first-rate Italian plasterers, brought over to build fake Renaissance exhibit halls. At one point, Griffith had hired the lot of them to build Babylon for *Intolerance,* a set still to be seen, slightly peeling—all trumpeting elephants and fertility goddesses—at the confluence of Hollywood and Sunset boulevards.

Burden and his blind neighbor, former Senator Thomas Gore, gazed upon the moonlit woods where Gore was building a house. Defeated in 1920 after three terms in the Senate, Gore was practicing law in Washington and for the first time making money. "The house will be just out of view, three hundred yards to the northwest of that hill." The blind man pointed accurately with his cane. Burden had always been delighted by the way that Gore would hold a manuscript in his hand when he spoke and, from time to time, would pretend to look at it, as if to check a statistic or the exact wording of a Latin quotation. Although two separate accidents had blinded him by the time he was ten, there was a legend that he had been elected Oklahoma's first senator by pretending not to be blind. Hence, the pretense of reading, of seeing.

During dinner the wives had talked, now the wives were talking in the living room and the men were enjoying the warm August night. Fireflies blinked in the dark woods. The moon was behind clouds. Burden shut his eyes to see what it was like not to see. Unbearable, he decided. They spoke of the investigation of Fall. "He's an old friend," said Gore. "I won't speculate on what he did or didn't do. But Sinclair and Doheny are hard to discourage once they've got you in their sights."

"Well, *you* turned them in." Some years earlier, Gore had created a sensation in the Senate by revealing that he had been offered a bribe by an oil company. No one had ever done that before and, privately, Gore's eccentricity was deplored in the cloakroom. "I'd *starve* if it wasn't for my friends!" a Southern statesman had declaimed.

"I wonder now if I would've done what I did if I'd been as broke as Fall is. You never can tell what you might do in a different situation."

"I don't think you or I would take a bribe, ever." Burden was firm.

"But then there are the contributions." Gore sighed. "That's where things can get right shadowy. You know, back in 1907, my first campaign, I had no money at all. Literally. Fact, I was in debt because instead of practicing law I'd been politicking, to get Oklahoma into the Union, and so on. Anyway, after I was nominated I was standing in front of the barber shop in Lawton, thinking what a fix I was in, when a stranger came up and said, 'Here, take this,' and gave me an envelope. Then he was gone. Well, inside that envelope was a thousand dollars." Gore laughed. "I love telling that story because I've never met anybody who believes it. But that's the way it happened."

"You plan to come back, don't you?"

Gore looked at him. In the moonlight his single glass eye shone, while the blind one was dull and reflected no light. "When I went down in the Harding sweep, I thought it was the end of the world. Then I pulled myself together and said to myself, Here you are, fifty years old, and you've been a senator since you were thirty-seven and never had a chance to make a penny. So take time off. Build a house in Rock Creek Park. Then go back. I wrote a note and hid it in the Senate chamber, saying I'd be back one day. Funny," he held his cane in front of him like a dowsing rod, "right after I hid that scrap of paper, I went into the cloakroom to collect my gear—this was the last day of the session—and suddenly I felt two arms around me and I was being given a bear-hug and I said, 'Who is it?' and this voice said, 'Just an old duffer, going off to be hung,' and it was Harding."

Burden recalled how radiant Harding had looked on his last day as a senator, gently teasing those senators who had taken all the credit for his election. Now he was sick in a hotel room in San Francisco. Officially he was supposed to have contracted ptomaine poisoning. But ptomaine poisoning was quick to pass, and the President had been ill for five days, and the balance of his tour was cancelled. There was talk of heart trouble. "He had so much luck for so long," Burden said. "Now the people are getting ready to turn on him."

"Sooner or later, they turn on everybody." Gore sighed. "I tell you, if there was any race other than the human race, I'd go join it."

Burden had forgotten how much he'd missed Gore's black wit. When forced to take a stand on Prohibition, a dangerous thing to do for a Bible Belt politician, Gore had said that he thought the Eighteenth Amendment was a very fine thing. "Because now the Drys have their law and the Wets have their whisky, and everybody's happy."

Kitty came out onto the porch. "The White House is calling. Mr. Christian's office."

"So late?" Burden went into the hall; he picked up the receiver. "This is Senator Day."

An unidentified voice said, "I'm sorry to bother you so late but Mr. Christian thinks you should know that the President is dead."

"Dead? What?" Burden sat down on top of the refectory table, something not allowed in Kitty's by-laws.

"Apoplexy, they say. Mr. Christian wanted you to know before the papers report it." Burden thanked the unknown man. Then he rang Lodge. Had he heard the news? Lodge had not. When Burden told him, Lodge exclaimed, "Oh, my God! This is terrible. *Unthinkable.*" He seemed truly shattered.

"Well, yes, it's pretty awful, at his age and everything. But I didn't know you two were so close."

"We weren't." Lodge's voice had regained its usual cold balance. "I'm upset because Calvin Coolidge is now the president. *Calvin Coolidge.* What a humiliation for the country, that dreadful little creature in his dreadful little two-family house."

In the living room, the Gores and Kitty responded more sympathetically. Kitty was not surprised. "You could tell he was getting sicker and sicker this last year. He was always a bad color, and so swollen-looking. I'm sure it was an old-fashioned stroke."

Gore thought that Harding was probably well out of it. "He was much too nice a man for the presidency."

Burden sat on a sofa, and drank Coca-Cola. "You know, he wasn't going to run again with Coolidge."

"Who did he want?" asked Mrs. Gore.

"Charlie Dawes. So Dawes told me. He couldn't stand Coolidge. Nobody can. In the Cabinet he just sits and stares."

"Now he has it all," said Gore. "You'll be running against him, I expect."

"If nominated . . ." Burden felt the familiar tide of ambition begin its rise. Who else was there? Cox would not be acceptable after his disastrous defeat in 1920. Franklin Roosevelt was a cripple from polio and would never walk—much less run for office—again. The governor of New York, Al Smith, was a Roman Catholic. Hearst was dead politically to all but himself. McAdoo had no following. James Burden Day against Calvin Coolidge seemed now to be inevitable, with the inevitable result. Burden shuddered with delight and fear; and thought of his father.

Caroline stood on the terrace of Laurel House and looked down at the river. "It is All Souls' Eve," she observed to no one but herself. Blaise and Frederika had decided to entertain everyone in Washington, and, somehow, they had picked the evening of November 1, when the souls of the dead were abroad or asleep or somewhere, waiting to be—what?—propitiated: she could not remember exactly what. Mlle. Souvestre had driven all religion out of her soul, including the attractive pagan.

The night was ominously warm, and a last summer storm was approaching the house. Time of equinox, she thought, time of change. But then *was* this the equinox? The science teacher had not been as successful in filling the niches in her mind which Mademoiselle had so ruthlessly emptied of their idols.

Tim had come out on the terrace. He wore evening dress; and looked older than he was. "Do they do nothing here but talk politics?"

"The gentry talk horses—and blood lines. Theirs and the horses. My father talked about music," she added, wondering how that curious man had suddenly slipped back into her memory. "All Souls," she said, in explanation to herself. "My father's spirit is abroad tonight. But I'd rather see my mother's."

"Your namesake."

"Partly. Emma de Traxler Schuyler d'Agrigente Sanford. It is too long for a marquee."

"What about for a life?"

"I don't think she thought so. But I don't know. I don't remember her."

From the lower terrace, a couple emerged from the darkness. Plainly, they had been at the pool house. "Young lovers," said Caroline tolerantly, holding up the lorgnette that was both a decoration and necessary to see with.

"Not so young," said Tim, whose far-sightedness complemented her myopia.

"Caroline," said Alice Longworth, with a bright smile. "What a lovely party. What a lovely place. What a lovely film star you are. Act for us."

"I *am* acting for you. I am smiling tolerantly, and recalling the fevers of my long-past youth. I am Marschallin at last."

Senator Borah found none of this amusing. He shook hands solemnly with Caroline and Tim. "We were looking over the place," he said. "I hadn't realized it was so big."

"The pool house is a great success," said Caroline. "It is All Souls' Night." She turned to Alice, handsome in blue and as happy as that restless creature could be.

"So it is. I think I've met them all by now. After all, everyone who's interesting is dead. We better go join them—in hell, I suppose."

"You do. I'm going inside." The Lion of Idaho opened the French door and stepped into the crowded drawing room.

"Do you find maternity rewarding?" asked Alice.

"My daughter's here tonight," was Caroline's non-answer.

"I remember when you had her, years and years ago. Have I missed anything?"

"A great deal of trouble."

"I'm almost forty." In the half-light from the drawing room, Alice looked pale, like a phantom, a restless soul.

"Well, it does wonders for your skin. But then you have perfect skin. So you need not . . . replicate."

"What a disgusting word," said Alice, and went inside.

"She's worried," Caroline observed.

"About getting pregnant? From Senator Walsh?"

"Borah. No. Oil. Her brothers Ted and Archie Roosevelt are involved with Mr. Sinclair. If he gets involved in the Teapot Dome hearings . . . Why do I talk about these things when I'm out of it?"

Tim's face was half in shadow and so he half smiled at her. Through the French windows the guests could be seen, moving about in what looked to be some hieratic dance. "I think you're more in it now than you ever were before. That's if we pull it off."

Caroline had not made the connection, but, of course, he was right. "Because now we'll be acting in the first place instead of reacting, the way the press usually has to do. Here comes our transmitter."

Will Hays stepped out onto the terrace. The light back of him made his huge ears glow pink as they stood out from his neat rodentine head. "My two favorite producers," he said, with a show of proprietary warmth.

"And our preferred candidate for president." Caroline laid it on with her ancient skill, more Sanford than Traxler.

Hays held up a curved rodentine paw. "Now, now, that's quite a ways down the road if it's there at all." The ears shone like rubies. "Say, I like that first photo-play of yours a whole lot, what I read, anyway, not that I know much about these things. But it's got a lot of heart, sort of Booth Tarkington stuff, which I really like, you know, small town, family life, kid growing up, the whole thing's very truthful . . ."

"Only," said Caroline, who could detect a demur in even the most enthusiastic panegyric.

"Only . . . well, I was thinking about what you said about how everything that goes on in this town of yours will be like what's going on in the country, only you'll sort of point up maybe what's wrong or not quite right. So I was thinking about this really serious problem we've got now with drugs and how you just might show how dope can kill young people . . ."

"Mr. Hays," it was Tim to the rescue, "the whole point to our sort of picture is not to melodramatize things. Drugs are a big problem in and around Hollywood Boulevard, but nobody would know where to find them in our town, and I don't think we should go and give the audience ideas."

Hays was still for a minute; then he nodded, "You've got a point there . . ."

"Besides," said Caroline, "the boy's experience with cigarettes, where he gets sick, is exactly the same thing as drug-taking only it's more typical."

Hays dropped the subject. "I also liked your old newspaper editor. Why, I've known that sort of man all my life. Somebody who's always trying to do good but it's always uphill work."

Both Caroline and Tim laughed. The old newspaper editor, who managed, always, to be so smugly in the wrong on every subject, had been carefully based on a year's observation of Will Hays in action. Through the window closest, Caroline could see her daughter Emma, haranguing a terrified-looking senator.

"When do you folks release your first picture, the one I read?"

"January 1924," said Tim. "The first Sanford-Farrell Studio movie will open at the Strand in New York, New Year's Day. We're calling it *Hometown.*"

"No more Traxler Productions?" Hays, like McAdoo before him, had taken mightily to the corporate end of movie-making.

"Emma Traxler died earlier this year," said Caroline, with quiet joy. "At Monte Carlo. She drank one glass of champagne too many and waltzed one time too often. She simply fell asleep and breathed her last, eyes shut."

"We'll sure miss her," said Hays, sincerely, as if of someone real. But then Emma Traxler had been very real to a great many people, including Caroline on certain mad days. "That's quite a big studio you're building yourselves out at Santa Monica."

Frederika was standing now in the doorway. "Everyone wants to talk to you, Mr. Hays, about Fatty Arbuckle. You must come in, and tell all."

"I hope they'll want to hear something more wholesome than that." Hays went inside. Frederika smiled at her sister-in-law. "Is it true that you two are getting married?"

"No," said Caroline. "It would give my daughter and Mr. Hays too much pleasure."

"Good. Then you need never divorce." Frederika returned to her party.

Caroline shivered. "All souls are chilly on their night out. Now I shall go get us some money for the studio." Before Tim could ask how, Caroline had gone inside.

Millicent Inverness, now Mrs. Daniel Truscott Carhart, greeted Caroline warmly. "I have given up drink," she said. "It is part of my new life."

"You look years younger," Caroline lied easily. Always punctilious, Millicent had waited until the Earl was safely dead before she remarried. Mr. Carhart was a dim New Englander connected in some way with the Smithsonian Institution, itself one of Washington's on-going mysteries that Caroline had never penetrated nor, indeed, tried to.

"I saw your daughter a moment ago. She appears to be divorced from that nice young man. I have some difficulty understanding her. She speaks so rapidly."

Emma had indeed been divorced. Now she was working with the Federal Bureau of Investigation, exposing those Communists who had managed to infiltrate the government. Mother and daughter met as seldom as possible. Emma refused to speak to Tim, on moral as well as political grounds. Emma had also found God and was a regular at mass, where Héloise encountered her, and got what news there was.

"She is trying to atone for her butterfly mother," said Caroline. "She is serious. I am frivolous."

"Oh, no, you're not, honey," said Millicent Carhart, settling into her new Americanism and very much the niece of a folksy—but which one?—president.

Blaise was seated in the wood-panelled study where hung the portrait of Aaron Burr, Caroline's ancestor not Blaise's; yet he was a significant icon to each. Blaise was talking to the aged Trimble, who seldom went out anymore.

"Here we three are," said Caroline. "The *Tribune* made flesh."

"I'm shucking mine off pretty damn soon," said Trimble glumly. "I hadn't realized that age was such a God-damned mess."

Caroline sat with her co-publishers. "Am I interrupting?"

Blaise shook his head. The handsome pony body had vanished beneath new flesh; he was definitely stout and the once-pale face was ruddy. He looked a clubman. She wondered about his private life. There must be someone; otherwise, he would not have accepted so easily Frederika's affair with Burden.

"It seems," said Blaise, "that last summer when our late President was in Kansas City, Mrs. Fall visited him secretly at the Muehlbach Hotel. No one knows what she told him but he was never the same again. Then, when he was in Alaska, he got a coded message from the White House, and this made him very agitated, according to Herbert Hoover, who was there. So he must have known a lot of what we're learning."

"Just known?" asked Caroline. "Or was he in on it?"

"The problem is how do you get all this to the public." Despite his age, Trimble never ceased to be an inquisitive editor. "Harding died one of the most popular presidents in history."

"The Senate hearings will change all that," said Blaise. "Forbes will go to jail. Fall, too. Maybe Daugherty, if half of what they say about him is true."

"Did he murder Jess Smith?" For Caroline, the Smith affair was the most intriguing of all.

"Daugherty was asleep in the White House when Smith was shot," said Trimble. "Of course, his deputy was with Smith in the apartment. Then Mr. Burns of the F.B.I. came upstairs and took the gun that killed him, and mislaid it, he says."

Frederika was at the door, splendid in white and gold. "Come out, you three. You do enough plotting at the office. The President's here." In the hallway, the small orchestra was playing "Hail to the Chief."

"Oh, God," said Blaise. The three stood up. "I'd rather spend an hour at the dentist than five minutes trying to talk to that man."

When Millicent Carhart had been placed next to the new President at dinner, she had said, "I've just made a ten-dollar bet that I can get you to say more than three words to me." The President had then turned his wizened-apple head toward her and, in his highly imitable Yankee voice, said, "You lose."

At the door to the library, Caroline pulled Blaise back. Trimble went on ahead into the hallway, where a crowd was gathering about the Coolidges.

"Do you still want to buy my share of the *Tribune*?"

Blaise gave her a long, curious look; then he nodded.

"Good. I'll tell my lawyer to talk to your lawyer. It will be like the old days."

"Why?"

"Why not? I've come to the end of this. That's all. Besides, I need the money for the Sanford-Farrell Studio."

"Are you really settling in out there?"

Caroline nodded. "After all, that's the only world there is now, what we invent."

"Invent or reflect?"

"What we invent others reflect, if we're ingenious enough, of course. Hearst showed us how to invent news, which we do, some of the time, for the best of reasons. But nothing we do ever goes very deep. We don't get into people's dreams, the way the movies do—or can do."

"The way you and Tim mean to do. Well, it must be very nice to be so . . . creative."

"Are you envious?"

"Yes."

"I *am* pleased."

Then Blaise went into the hallway to greet the President, who was, like some white knight—in the press, at least—purifying the nation's political life just as Will Hays was doing the same for Hollywood, only Coolidge had no secret advisers and Hays, unknown to him, did.

Comfortably, Caroline, now entirely herself, one person at last, stared into the fire and thought of all the souls that she had known and if they were indeed abroad tonight, they would be all fire and air, light and shadow so fixed upon her memory that she might, if she chose, transfer them to strips of film that the whole world could then forever imagine until reel's end.

# From *Washington, D.C.*

BENEATH A SUN like a bronze shield, the new Senate Office Building gleamed white in its setting of Capitoline green. As Burden approached the main door, several citizens of the Republic (at crucial moments he saw life as a Shakespeare play) stopped him to shake hands and he murmured his thanks in a voice less than audible but with an expression full of grace and mutual understanding.

Inside the building the guard, surprisingly, rose when he entered. "Nice day, Senator." Better and better, he thought, as he proceeded to the mahogany door with its simple legend "Mr. Day."

The outer office of his suite contained leather chairs, two desks, and two secretaries. Miss Perrine was young and plump, with uncontrollable hair; she was engaged to a man with a hearing aid who occasionally came to pick her up at the end of the day. Mrs. Blaine was old and in every way admirable, except for her voice. Because of a malformation of the palate, she had a tendency to honk. "The out-of-town press is *marvelous*!" She patted a pile of newspapers on the chair beside her desk. "You should read the editorials."

"I will. I will." Pushing past the swinging door of the protective balustrade, Burden glanced absently down into the savage tangle of Miss Perrine's hair, half expecting to see a family of birds poke their heads up to him, crying for Kitty to feed them. Then he went into his private office, one of the most desirable in the building, a tribute not only to his seniority but to his long membership in The Club. No one was ever quite sure who belonged to The Club since members denied its existence but everyone knew who did not belong. The Club was permanently closed to the outsize personality, to the firebrand tribune of the people, to the Senator running too crudely for President. Members of The Club preferred to do their work quietly and to get re-elected without fanfare. On principle they detested the President, and despite that magnate's power to loose and to bind, The Club ruled the Senate in its own way and for its own ends, usually contrary to those of the President.

Ever since Burden first arrived in Washington, he had belonged to The Club. They had known right off that he was one of them: subtle, easy-going, able to yield gracefully when it was necessary to yield. Though he was not yet forty when first elected, The Club took him in and showed him the machinery of power; even allowed him, occasionally, to manipulate the levers. They also saw to it that he was preferred over controversial men, and given his pick of useful committees. When rivals appeared back home, The Club did its best to see that he was able to take full credit for a dam, a road, a post office, those necessary gifts a Senator must bring back to the people to ensure their support.

Between tall windows his desk was placed, back to the view. On the wall opposite the desk hung a portrait of Jefferson. Elsewhere in the room there were gavels, plaques, signed photographs—all the usual memorabilia of a public man's life; the only unusual decoration was a life-size bust of Cicero on a wooden pedestal.

As always when alone, Burden saluted Cicero. The two republicans shared many secrets. One of the best was that nearly everyone in the Senate Office Building thought that the bust was a portrait of William Jennings Bryan.

Burden sent for Clay. While waiting, he glanced at the mail. In the last few days of the Court battle his mail had trebled, and most of it was favorable. He delighted in the praise, even though it was almost invariably followed by a request for aid: I feed your self-esteem, Senator, now you feed me.

Clay entered, carrying newspapers, eyes bright with pleasure. "That's where we're headed now." He indicated the barrier of green which hid the White House from observers on Capitol Hill.

Burden shook his head, not wanting to tempt fate. "A lot can happen in three years," he said, all on exhalation.

"Just keep the momentum going, and we're in. All we have to do is keep this thing alive."

"Keep it alive." Burden murmured approvingly, fingers feeling for his favorite talisman: the flattened bullet removed from his father's shoulder after the Battle of Shiloh and kept by that sardonic and violent man as a memento of a heroic time . . . except that to his father there was nothing in that struggle but discomfort and folly, whereas his son regarded the War of the Secession as the last true moment of virtue in a falling world. For sentimentalizing those days, his father had despised him. But then they had always hated one another. Now the Confederate corporal was dead and all that was left of him was this lump of metal, crumpled from having struck the no longer living bone.

"Keep the thing alive," Burden repeated, his forefinger gently feeling the fissures in the metal. Was it here that the flesh first felt the metal as it cut? Or here? Unbidden the furious face of his father materialized midway between Jefferson and the desk. For an instant he saw the tobacco-stained teeth, the mad gray eyes, the mottled red skin; and vivid in that incorporeal face was all his father's contempt for him. "You joined the bastards who cut us up. You're one of 'em, *Senator*!" How he had snorted the title the last time they met, shortly after Burden's election, shortly before the old man's cancerous death. Burden blinked hard; the face went.

Burden sat up abruptly; energy coursed through him. He gave Clay rapid instructions. Journalists to seek out. Editors to write to. Members of Congress to see. Money to be raised. He paused a moment at the thought of money.

"That's the worst of it. That's the one thing which can stop us."

Clay shook his head. "The fat cats love you."

"Today. But maybe not tomorrow. After all, no one can be conservative enough for them and . . ."

". . . and be elected President," Clay spoke almost too quickly. But he was right.

"And be elected President. But no one can be President . . . *I* can't be President . . . without their help. That's the problem. Well, at least we've got three years to raise the money . . ."

"And before then, you'll have spoken in every state." They planned; they plotted; they guessed; they hoped. But Burden knew that all too often political planning was nothing more than a form of mutual reassurance. The future was perfectly incalculable. Clay showed him telegrams of congratulations and invitations to speak. Mrs. Blaine interrupted them several times with news. The Supreme Court (unofficially of course) was delighted, and the Vice President would like to have a word with him if he could spare the time.

Accompanied by Clay, Burden took the elevator to the basement, where they boarded the ridiculous but useful subway car that connected the Senate Office Building to the Capitol. They rode with a new Senator and three of his constituents, who were delighted to meet Burden Day. Everyone is delighted to meet Burden Day, thought Burden Day, greeting the constituents warmly, aware that the other Senator was visibly enhanced in the eyes of his people because he was acquainted with the Defender of the Constitution. Burden made a mental note to cultivate the new man.

At the Capitol, they ascended back stairs. As always, Burden took pleasure in the subterranean corridors, which smelled of stone, harsh soap and, he was positive, woodwork burned by the British in 1814. Despite the rising heat outside, the inner depths of the Capitol remained cool all summer long.

At the level of the Senate floor, Burden avoided the tourists by slipping into the Senate washroom, a noble chamber with enormous urinals. While Clay washed his face and hands, Burden asked casually, "Can you come to the house for dinner tonight?"

Clay shook his head, face covered with soap. "I have a date."

Burden nodded. He dreaded collision, feared rebuff. Yet it was his duty as a father to net for his child the husband she wanted, and though Diana had never actually said as much it was apparent that she was in love, and helpless.

Clay dried his face until the pink skin glowed like the face of a child who has put a flashlight in its mouth to amaze bystanders in the night with the blood's luminosity. Yes, Clay was handsome. Burden experienced a momentary pang. *He* was not young, as Clay was young; not desirable, as Clay was desirable. Yet he lusted, too, and craved that response which is something more than complaisance; something more than tribute to solvency or to fame. A woman would burn at night for want of Clay. He became Diana, saw Clay as she saw him, and realized that she did not have a chance. Diana was plain to look at, shy but sharp, intelligent and good. How she could compete with softer beauties like . . .

". . . Enid Sanford asked me. It's at Chevy Chase. Some sort of dance for a friend of hers from New York. I said I'd go." Clay was placating. "Enid's a lovely girl." Obviously, Clay preferred Enid to Diana and there was nothing he could do about it. Burden arranged his hair so that the forelock would fall gracefully across the brow. In a moment, he would be on the floor of the Senate, and the gallery would recognize him and perhaps applaud. At least *that* was sweet. His mood improved as he set his mask.

". . . fascinating girl. But it's not easy keeping up with her. That's how I got this." Clay touched his thickened nose regretfully. "Keeping up with her at Warrenton, riding through those damned woods in the rain and getting thrown. And how she laughed. There I was bleeding like a pig and she laughed. I could have killed her."

Yes, thought Burden, he was hooked. "Rich girl," observed Burden. "All that Sanford money will be mighty useful to a young man who wants to serve his country in the highest councils of the state." Burden parodied his own somewhat ornate platform style.

Clay blushed and started toward the door. "She just wants a good time. That's all."

They went out into the corridor. "Well, come visit us one of these days. Diana hasn't seen much of you since she got back."

"I will. You know I will."

Duty is done, thought Burden, as he crossed the corridor to the door which led into the cloakroom. Clay was to wait for him in the gallery. At a certain agreed-upon gesture (placing of left hand against cheek) Clay would come and fetch him.

Squaring shoulders, breathing deeply (and wondering why his heart was beating so erratically), Burden nodded to the huge Capitol policeman who guarded the door and stepped into the world of the Senate.

The cloakroom, narrow as a corridor, ran the length of the Senate Chamber. Here, amid lockers, black leather sofas and writing tables, the Senators of his party gossiped and politicked. When Burden made his entrance, he was given a playful ovation. A Southerner in a Prince Albert gave out a Rebel yell and waved a small Confederate banner. Two New Dealers retreated to the far end of the cloakroom and pretended to study the day's legislation. Happy, Burden drank a glass of soda water and listened to praise.

"Best thing we've done in twenty years, and it's all your doing."

"President's sworn to have your neck if it's the last thing he ever does . . ."

". . . *will* be the last. Old Burden'll lick him every time . . ."

"Burden can lick the President in 1940. That's our year."

"Why spoil a good Senator by making a President out of him?"

Then they were joined by the senior Senator from Burden's state. Jesse Momberger was a lean man who wore hats that seemed like sombreros and built-up shoes that resembled boots. He liked to refer cryptically to famous Western outlaws, as though he knew more than he ever intended to say. "Well, pardner." He took Burden's hand in his own surprisingly soft one: the West had long since been won. "You're goin' to be the President. That's clear as a mule's ass at noon. Now I got some advice for you . . ."

Burden smiled and listened until a pale-faced page in knickerbockers came to tell him, "The Vice President is on the floor. He'd like a word with you, Senator."

Burden slipped away from his admirers. At the frosted glass doors to the Senate Chamber, he paused to straighten his tie, arrange hair. Then giving the swinging doors a somewhat stronger push than was necessary, he stepped onto the floor of the Senate, and was home.

Careful not to look at the gallery, Burden walked up the aisle to his seat, chin held high so that he would be recognized. He was. There was a patter of applause, quickly gaveled to silence by the chair. He took his seat and pretended to study the papers stacked in front of him. But in his excitement he could not read a word. Finally he sneaked a look at the gallery. There were several men in the press box, while the gallery itself was perhaps a third full, which was remarkable on a day when there was neither a debate nor a vote. Evidently the people had come to see him, and the Senate which had humbled the President.

Several Senators stopped to congratulate him, their gestures slightly larger than life: each aware of the hundreds of watching eyes.

Then Burden saw the Vice President. He was not in the chair but beside it, talking to a group of Senators. Burden waved to him and then, solemnly, he walked down into the well of the Chamber. The murmur from the galleries increased as the knowledgeable wondered what they would say to one another. The answer, of course, was nothing. At best, the Vice President's style was gnomic. In any case, Burden knew that the thing not spoken in politics is invariably the essential. Today the words exchanged were amiable, and seemingly direct. Details about the Court bill's progress in committee, nothing more. But what the exchange meant was plain to those who understood the workings of The Club. The tiny red-faced man with teeth like black pearls had allied himself with Burden Day. Power had been exerted, and as with fire on contiguous metal fragments, fusion had taken place. They were one, for the time being.

Delighted, Burden returned to the cloakroom, forgetting to signal Clay. This was better than he had hoped. With the Vice President's support in 1940, the thing was his.

Burden made his way briskly through a crowd of tourists who stopped him from time to time with fervent praise. He was halfway to the main door when Clay joined him. "What did the Vice President say?"

"He's with us. All the way." They spoke then of a committee meeting to be held that afternoon. Burden would not be there. Clay was to tell the appropriate Senator to take charge. "Where will you be?"

Burden shook his head. "Invisible. I want to think. Call me at home tonight."

Under the stone porte cochere of the Capitol, Burden waited for Henry, eyes shut against the glare. The heat was literally breathtaking. He ought to stay at the Capitol where it was cool but perversely he preferred to be alone with his triumph.

"Nice work, Senator." The voice was pleasant; the associations not.

Burden turned as a man, slender and cool in brown gabardine, approached him. Reflexively, Burden's right arm sprang from his side. He recalled it just in time, making an awkward circular gesture as though exercising a shoulder. "I am waiting for my car," said Burden irrelevantly.

"What else?" Mr. Nillson was amused, quite unaware of the effect he was making. "I saw you just now with the Vice President. He must have been pleased at what's happened."

Burden turned to look down the driveway for Henry and the Packard. But neither was in sight. The amiable voice continued. "In fact, everyone's pleased with you. Did you know that the Hearst papers are going to propose you for President?"

The man was cunning, no doubt about it. Burden was unable to disguise his interest. "How do you know?"

"I never disclose sources, Senator." Mr. Nillson grinned. "You'll find that's my best quality."

Burden grunted and started to turn away again, but Mr. Nillson's voice (was it Southern? Western?) recalled him. "But I *can* tell you that the Day for President campaign will begin with tomorrow's editorial, written by the old man himself."

"That's very interesting, Mr. Nillson."

"I think you would be a remarkable President. *I* would certainly vote for you."

"Mr. Nillson . . ."

"Sir?"

"Who the hell are you?"

"A friend."

"No, you are not a friend."

"Then I should like to be. After all, we choose our friends because they are not like ourselves. I shall never be a great statesman, like you." Irony, guile, truth in delicate balance. "You live a life that I might have wanted, but as there is not time for one person to be everything, I choose my friends so that through them I can be a politician, a journalist, an artist . . ."

"A criminal?"

"Yes, even a criminal."

"But *what* do you do?"

"I'm a businessman. Now I have spoken very directly to you, Senator. I have been completely honest."

"Yes, you have. And do you know the penalty for bribing . . . for attempting to bribe a member of Congress?"

"Among my many friends there are lawyers." Mr. Nillson was genuinely amused. Burden felt himself losing control again, anger beginning to rise, also bewilderment. "I know the law's penalties. Also the world's rewards. I wish you would think seriously about what I said to you the other day."

"There is nothing to think about. I don't take . . ." Burden found himself lowering his voice automatically even though no one was within earshot, "bribes."

"Others . . ."

"I don't care what others do."

"Is an investment in your career a bribe? A contribution to electing you President, is that a bribe? How do you think money is ever raised for a national campaign? Anyway, should I invest in your future, I shall demand a good deal less of you than, say, the CIO or the National Association of Manufacturers."

"I am not for sale, Mr. Nillson." The pomposity and hollowness of his words appalled him and he wondered desperately what had become of his celebrated gift for the single withering phrase. Speechless, he stood, head filled with copybook maxims, a portion of his brain paralyzed.

"I don't want to buy you, Senator." The easy voice was now as cold as his own. "I will *give* you the money that you need if you make it possible for me to buy what I want. That is a legitimate exchange. The word for what I propose may be strange to your ears. So I will say it to you slowly and carefully. The word is 'business.' "

Then Henry and the Packard arrived and Burden got in without a word. The car swung away from the starling-infested portico of the Capitol, gray as ash in the fiery noon.

"Where to, Senator?"

"Where to?" Burden recalled himself. "Cross to the Virginia side. Then we'll see."

Henry knew exactly where Burden wanted to go. Near Bull Run there was a field where Civil War earthworks twisted like a huge snake beneath tall grass. Here Burden liked to sit and brood about the days before his birth and wish that he had been born in time for that good war in which he might have died, like his uncle Aaron Hawkins, struck down before Atlanta at nineteen years of age, right leg shattered by a cannon ball; two days later, dead from gangrene. Thus did fate shear the balance of that boy's life.

Burden looked out the car window and watched those few abroad in the heat as they moved slowly, trying not to sweat; and simply to watch them from the relative coolness of the car made him hot. He reached in his pocket for a handkerchief and felt heavy metal; it was the bullet that had struck his father. He had no recollection of having taken it from the office. Delicately he touched the metal and wondered, as always, which part of the bullet struck the flesh.

At Chain Bridge they crossed the Potomac, narrowed by drought. On the Virginia side the woods were dense and almost cool. He rolled down the car window, breathed deeply, shut his eyes; dozed.

"Here we are, Senator." Burden awakened to find that they were parked in a country lane where the branches of trees met over head, filtering green the fierce sunlight. At the end of the lane was the field where the Confederates had built their earthworks.

"Stay in the car, Henry. I won't be long."

The field was bright with goldenrod and Queen Anne's lace, with sword grass that plucked at his trousers as he walked slowly to the place where two mounds of earth met at a right angle. With each step he was conscious of what lay beneath the ground, of the bones, the buttons, the belt buckles and misshapen bullets.

Burden was breathing hard when he finally reached his usual place atop the earthworks. Beneath green saplings, he took his seat upon a boulder streaked with lichen. From this perch he could survey the terrain where the first Battle of Bull Run had been fought. The seventy-sixth anniversary of that battle had occurred the day before, when he had won his own victory. The omen was good, except that of course the Confederates had then gone on to lose the war.

Across the field, pine woods broke the horizon, just as they had nearly a century before. A photograph made right after the battle showed these same woods burnt and splintered like so many matchsticks while in the foreground of the picture there lay what looked to be a pile of old clothes, until one saw a hand startlingly extended toward the sky, the sinewy brown fingers curved as though to seize a fallen rifle. Recalling that hand, Burden curved his own fingers in imitation of the dead soldier and as he did he realized suddenly that it was not for a rifle those fingers curved but for life, as though life was something literally to be seized and held. He shuddered and let his own hand fall to his lap, not wanting to know what it was the man had felt as the life left him.

Grass steamed in the sun. From damp earth, a haze rose. Weeds stirred in the hot breeze, leaves rustled, clouds of gnats moved erratically back and forth. At peace, drowsy, Burden balanced the bullet in his hand as he had done a thousand times before. Now, he told himself, he must think, plan for the future, devise a timetable extending from this very moment to that day in November of 1940 when he would be elected President. First he would talk to Blaise about money. Then he would go to William Randolph Hearst and make it perfectly clear that . . . His mind shifted stubbornly: despite the boldness of Mr. Nillson's offer (and the assumption behind it) he had never in his life taken a bribe. At worst, he had accepted campaign money with the vague understanding that he might some day be of use to the donor, a disagreeable procedure but the way things are done in the Republic. Mr. Nillson, however, had offered a straightforward bribe, which no honest man could accept. More to the point, to deprive the Indians of their land was both cruel and dishonorable.

But what was honor? The hand that held the bullet became a hard fist The usual answer: to do what one had to do regardless of personal consequences. But in practice that sort of piety was not much help. One could not always know what it was one ought to do. If the country was best served by the Presidency of James Burden Day and that Presidency could come about only as a result of taking Mr. Nillson's money, ought he not to take the money? After all, a defender of the Constitution who had taken a bribe was morally preferable to an unbribed President whose aim was to subvert the Republic. Then, finally, the familiar black question: What difference did any of it make? Recently he had been shown the plans for his tomb in the State Capitol. "There will be room," said the architect comfortably, "for four people in the crypt. Naturally, Mrs. Day will want to join you and perhaps your daughter will, too." In time no one would know or care which dust was Bill, which dust was Joe.

Half asleep in the sun, Burden once more reviewed the exchange in front of the Capitol and wondered again how Mr. Nillson could have been so certain that his victim would not bring charges against him. The only possible explanation was that the man Nillson was a born tempter, a bold provocateur whose instinct told him, rightly, that it was not in Burden's nature to make a fuss.

Had other Senators been approached? This was worth opening eyes to contemplate. But the sunlight blinded him and he quickly shut his eyes, returning to the dark rose night of his own blood. Senators seldom discussed such things. He recalled the embarrassment that they had all felt when a famous but poor member of The Club had died and his widow discovered eight hundred thousand dollars in currency in a safety deposit box. "Well," Burden had said to a colleague when this was mentioned over bean soup in the Senate dining room. "Well," the colleague had replied. Some did; some did not. He did not. He would not.

Burden opened his eyes just as a man came out of the woods carrying a long rifle. He was obviously a hunter who might at any moment decide that Burden, viewed from a distance, was a raccoon or a fox or whatever was then being shot in Virginia. To prevent an accident, Burden waved to the man who leaped back and took refuge behind a stump. Burden was alarmed. "Runaway Convict" made black headlines in his mind. But then Henry was nearby; and the man was more frightened than he. Burden waved again, smiling and nodding to show that he meant no harm.

Cautiously, the man approached. At the foot of the earthworks he stopped. "Where you from?" he asked. The accent was Carolinian and comforting to his ear. The man was young, dirty and bearded, with long hair that fell across his forehead in a wide tangle.

Burden said that he lived in Washington; the boy frowned. "Then you oughtn't to be here, sir." The manner was curiously grave.

"Why not?"

The youth was now so close that Burden could smell the sweat of his body, could examine close-to the curious costume he wore: shapeless jacket, torn trousers, boots with slits between sole and shoe through which black toes showed. He wondered if he would have the strength to call for Henry.

The boy held the rifle across his chest as though presenting arms. He grinned down at Burden. "Now you know why, sir. Don't make out you don't." He jerked his head toward the pine woods where he had come from and Burden saw that suddenly the woods were aflame. White smoke hid the sun. The sky was lurid. He tried to get to his feet but the man's body was in his way and he did not dare to touch him or ask him to move for fear of the long rifle he held.

Burden sat back against the boulder. "But there's fire," he said weakly. "The woods are on fire."

" 'Course there's fire."

Burden shrank back, trying not to breathe, not to smell the other's sweat, to avoid the oddly intimate look in the bright blood shot eyes. "Let me up," Burden whispered. "Let me go."

But the boy did not stir. Bearded lips grinned down at Burden who lay helpless on the ground, unable to move. Then suddenly the youth extended a sinewy brown hand in whose familiar curve Burden saw death remembered and death to come. He screamed and awakened just in time to keep from rolling down the earthworks to the stony field below. For a moment, he sprawled on the ground, heart beating wildly. Then carefully he touched grass, earth, stone, to make sure that he was still alive.

"You all right, Senator?" Henry stood at the edge of the field, like a black scarecrow.

"Yes, Henry!" He was surprised at the vigor of his own voice. Then he got up as rapidly as aging muscles would allow. "I'll be right with you. Go on back to the car."

When Henry was out of sight, Burden sat on the boulder and waited until his heart regained its usual slow beat. Apprehensively he looked across the field, half expecting to see the smoke and flame of that famous burning day. But the woods were green. There was no fire. It had all been a part of the mind's theatre, without significance. Yet the face of the Confederate soldier had been familiar: but then the face of death would hardly be that of a total stranger and it was indeed his own death that had raised the rifle against him. Shuddering at the nearness of his escape, he rose to go. As he did, he noticed, gleaming dully in the grass, the bullet which had struck his father. Stooping down, he dug a hole in the ground with his fingers. Then he placed the bullet in the hole and covered it up. Pleased at what he had done, he began the descent of the earthworks and the crossing of the field.

At a signal from the President's wife, the ladies rose. Led by Mrs. Roosevelt and the Queen, they left the men in possession of the State Dining Room.

As the usher shut the dining room door, Burden moved from his place just below the left curve of the horseshoe-shaped table toward the center where President and King sat. The empty chair on the King's left was swiftly filled by the Vice President, who exuberantly patted and prodded the little King, to the President's obvious annoyance and Burden's amusement. The knives were out between the President and his Constitutional if not political heir.

Brandy was served; cigars appeared. Burden sat down between Blaise Sanford and an Englishman whose name sounded like Lord Garbage. They complained of the heat.

"The President refuses to put in air conditioning." Blaise chewed his cigar. "Says it's bad for his sinus. Sinus, hell! What about the people that work here? What about us? Cardiac cases, that's what we'll be."

"Maybe he doesn't care." Like the others, Burden found it an effort not to stare at the President, who looked fit if somewhat overweight, the famous smile flashing on and off as though controlled by a master switch. Earlier, when Burden and Kitty had been presented, the President had given him the widest of smiles and then turned to the King and said in a stagy whisper, "He wants to live here, too!" The King looked faintly unsettled.

Later Burden discovered that the President had been making the same little joke about all his rivals, most of whom were present—Hull, Vandenberg, Farley, as well as the fragile Harry Hopkins, who had already maneuvered himself close to the magic center of the table. It would be a scrap but Burden was increasingly confident. According to the Gallup Poll, Hull was the party's first choice and he was the second choice, but since Hull was a Southerner and could not be nominated . . . Burden visualized himself at the head of the table; then he recalled his vow; no daydreaming. He tuned in on Blaise.

"Of course maybe he *wants* us to have heart attacks. Some of us anyway." Blaise chuckled.

Lord Garbage smiled and turned to Burden. "You must come here often, Senator."

"Never!" Blaise answered for Burden. "They hate each other," he said in a voice loud enough to be heard by the President, who did not hear because his full attention was concentrated upon the Vice President, now kneading the King's shoulder as though it were dough. The President's smile was set; the cold gray eyes glared. Full of bourbon and gay malice, the Vice President ignored that withering gaze.

It was explained to Lord Garbage (who seemed to have something to do with the Foreign Office) that although Burden belonged in the President's party they were political enemies. "I can't fathom your politics," said the Englishman.

"You should give it a try," said Blaise coldly, reflecting Burden's own irritation with those British who took pride in not knowing or, worse, pretending not to know how the American political system worked.

Lord Garbage was apologetic. "One ought to know of course. It's just that we're so used to party loyalty. I mean in Parliament you *have* to follow your party leader or you get out."

"We don't follow," said Burden, "and we never get out. Voluntarily."

"But sometimes we drop the party leader," said Blaise ominously, puffing blue smoke into Lord Garbage's face.

"It *is* hot," said the Englishman. On all sides Burden saw faces flushed with heat and wine. He was suddenly seized by a sense of unreality, recalling the other Presidents who had sat in this same room wining and dining the magnates of their day, all forgotten now. They come and they go, he thought, comforting himself. Nothing mattered but the moment. Then he noticed the newly carved motto just below the mantel on the main facing of the fireplace: the pious hope of John Adams that "None but Honest and Wise Men ever rule under This Roof." Of course it mattered who governed. He pulled himself together. The trick was to avoid being overwhelmed by the swift rushing moment; to act as if the future did exist, as if one might indeed by doing good affect the lives of the unborn. But watching the President at the head of the table, Burden saw only vanity in that conceited face; nothing else, certainly no trace of *virtus,* to use Cicero's word, that moral goodness which does not translate as "virtue."

Blaise and Lord Garbage were discussing friends in England. Lord Garbage (that *couldn't* be his name) was assuring Blaise that an old friend had not really gone insane. "He just doesn't like people, which is perfectly normal. He lives alone in the country. And reads Carlyle to the pig."

Burden gave this his full attention. "The pig?"

"Yes. He used to read Gibbon, but he didn't like the style."

"Your friend?"

"No, the pig. Actually our friend rather likes Gibbon, and I don't think he's at all keen on Carlyle, but the pig finds Carlyle soothing. So what can he do?"

Blaise laughed delightedly. "Burden, you must get to know the English. They're not like us."

"Fortunately for you," said Lord Garbage who might or might not have been making fun of them. Yet Burden did not at heart dislike the British, differing from many of his Senatorial colleagues who resented England's eminence. Southerners still recalled with bitterness England's betrayal of the Confederacy, while in the Northern cities any politician with not much to say could always count on the Irish to applaud if he threatened to punch King George in the snoot. Burden looked at King George's long distinguished snoot and felt protective. The King seemed so fragile, so distinguished, so perfectly undeserving of anything but courtesy. Burden decided that this year he must definitely go to Europe and in the course of his travels propose himself for an interview with Hitler. Hitler would receive him at Berchtesgaden and Burden would begin by saying that he was speaking not for the Senate but for himself, and for world peace. The Chancellor would be attentive as Burden outlined a course of action which would take into account Germany's *legitimate* interests while maintaining the good will of the Western powers. As Burden spoke, Hitler would take notes, muttering "Ja, ja," from time to time.

"I think there will be war this summer." Burden's reverie was shattered. He turned to the Englishman whose tone of voice had not changed at all; he might have been giving a review of the pig's reading list. Blaise frowned. "I don't think so."

Lord Garbage blew smoke out large curved nostrils. "Mid-July is our guess. The little man will do to Poland what he did to Czechoslovakia."

"And what will *you* do?" asked Burden.

"I rather think we'll fight, this time."

"How?" Blaise was scornful. "The Germans have ninety-five hundred planes ready for combat. How many does England have?"

"None, I should think. Part of the charm of being a democracy is that one's always unprepared." He smiled. "How many planes do you Yanks have?"

"We don't need any because we're not going to fight anybody." Blaise was firm.

"Yes, I read your newspaper. But Hitler has already said first France, then England, then America."

"He's just bluffing, and who wouldn't? The way you people give into him, he's be crazy not to try for more."

Burden stopped listening as the familiar arguments went back and forth. He knew them all. Essentially he was isolationist. He saw no reason for the New World to involve itself once again in the sheer bloodiness of the Old. But he also knew that it would be difficult to stay out, particularly with a President who had an itch to perform on the world stage. Like Wilson, thought Burden, looking toward the President who was now whispering something into the King's ear. Yes, that was how Roosevelt saw himself, whispering to monarchs, obscuring domestic failures with foreign pageants. It was all too plain.

There must be no war. If only because the President would then run for re-election, and who in the party could stop him? Burden looked about the room at his peers, not one of whom could defeat the President at a convention. All that they could do was pray that the Europeans would keep the peace until the next convention which was (he counted on his fingers) fourteen months away.

"No," he said, to reassure himself, "I agree with Blaise. Hitler's too smart to begin a war . . . This summer," he added, native caution not allowing his thinking ever to be entirely wishful.

"I hope you're both right," said Lord Garbage politely.

There was a commotion at the magnet's center. The President's son was wheeling his father away from the table and, as always, Burden was reminded with a shock that the enemy was a cripple whose emaciated legs were locked inside heavy metal braces. It was distressing to watch the President get up and sit down. Yet he himself seemed not to notice his infirmity. Only once had Burden seen the President diconcerted by it. As he was walking laboriously to the rostrum to accept a second nomination for the Presidency, someone accidentally knocked him off balance, and like a tower he fell almost to the ground before aides caught him, the pages of his speech fluttering in the air. As much as Burden despised the man, he did feel a certain pity for one who governed a powerful nation but could not walk unaided.

Burden sat at his desk in the Senate Chamber, holding in his hand H.R. 1776. The roll was being called. Voting on the bill had begun early. The galleries were packed. Just above him sat Kitty and Clay while Blaise Sanford presided imperially over the press box. Even the most frivolous of the Senators was aware that this was an important moment. Faces were grave, voices solemn as the "Ayes" and the "Nays" rang out in the green-lit Chamber.

It had been a discouraging month for the isolationists. One outspoken Senator had not helped the cause by accusing the President of wanting to "plow under every fourth American boy." On the other hand, the cause of intervention had not been much helped by the insouciant testimony of Wendell Willkie who, explaining his sudden conversion to aid for England, referred to his recent speeches denouncing the New Deal warmongers as "campaign oratory."

Nevertheless the bill which had been drafted at the Treasury and given to the majority leader of each House to introduce was certain to pass. Helplessly, the America First Committee raged. Important hostesses spoke bitterly of secret alliances between Roosevelt and the British. Catholic priests declared that Hitler was, after all, the last stout shield against Stalin, the Antichrist. But to no avail. The bill would pass.

"Mr. Clapper." They were approaching the "D's." Burden thought for a moment of the consternation in the Chamber were he to vote "Aye." He would make the headlines but lose the coming election, even though he suspected that at heart the citizens of his state were not so isolationist as their Congressional delegation. The people tended to be unreliable on issues they did not ordinarily think much about. Although they disliked Europe on principle, a few newspaper stories about the rape of Belgian nuns and they would want to stand up to the bully.

"Mr. Chavez."

No, Burden could not vote "Aye." He was too closely identified with the isolationists. Yet, in a way, he wanted the British to win and Hitler to fail—unlike certain of his colleagues who hated England and secretly supported Hitler for reasons that did not bear close scrutiny. At the most Burden had wanted to amend the bill, to limit the President's power to give away arms and materials. But his amendment had failed and he was conscious of having played no significant part in the great debate. A year ago, he was the President's conservative successor, courted by all. Now he was one of ninety-six Senators. Suddenly in need of solace, he looked up at Kitty who gave him a little wave.

But there was no disguising the fact that at a time when he should be leading the Senate, he was not. Of course, no one else was either. The day before the Bill was to be presented to Congress, he had gone to the White House with a group of Congressional leaders. Not once during the meeting was Burden consulted. Except for Senator Barkley, who talked political strategy, the others were as silent and acquiescent as he.

At the end of the meeting Burden shook the President's huge hand and said, "I had a splendid time in Chicago." The President looked at him blankly. Burden could not resist a twist to the screw. "Mr. Wallace was an excellent choice, not popular perhaps but I'm sure what you had in mind all along."

The President was saved by a Senator from Texas who made him vow solemnly that the battleship *Texas* would never be given to the British. The President so swore.

Burden had, of course, been outmaneuvered at Chicago by the President. Once the first shock had passed, he rather admired the way in which it had been done. In a private meeting at the White House, the President had been friendly, apparently candid, entirely plausible. In so many words he had said that taking into account the importance and restiveness of the conservative wing of the party, his running mate would almost certainly be a conservative. The President had mentioned several possible choices, of whom the first was Burden, who fell crashing into the sort of trap he himself was so expert at laying for others: seeming to promise favors he had no intention of bestowing in order to keep the would-be recipient in a cordial and optimistic frame of mind. Having left the meeting convinced that he would be selected Vice President, Burden had not pressed his own campaign for the Presidency. If he had, he might seriously have hurt the President at the convention and dramatized the split between Left and Right. But he had done nothing, just as the President wanted. Thinking of that day in the Blackstone Hotel when he had heard the news on the radio, Burden's blood pressure rose so that he could hardly breathe. Fortunately, at that instant the clerk called his name and he shouted "Nay," relieving the pressure in his throat and evoking, as reward for vehemence, applause from the gallery. A small recognition was better than none.

The final vote was sixty in favor of Lend-Lease to thirty-one opposed. The President had won again.

The day was bright but chilly. Spring was late. Ordinarily by March, daffodils and forsythia would be in bloom. But this year the winter had lasted longer than usual. The lawns and gardens of the Capitol were brown and bleak. With Clay beside him, Burden made his way to the Senate Office Building. The anti-Nazi, pro-British pickets had all gone home, and only the America First banners were still forlornly displayed by angry youths and well-dressed matrons in cloth coats.

"Pretty much what I predicted," said Burden.

"We never had a chance." Clay was perfunctory. Burden suspected him of wanting America to join the war. None of the young men knew what modern war was like. He did. As a new Senator, he had toured the battlefields of France and seen corpses rotting in the mud and dangling from barbed wire; he had heard shells whistle and explode; he had smelled poison gas. It was not like Shiloh where a man with a gun could fight for his honor on equal terms with another man so armed and so inspired. It was not the same thing now. Not at all.

An America Firster waved a placard angrily in Burden's face. "I'm Senator Day." Burden smiled pleasantly, hoping the youth would realize that they were allies.

"It's you Jew bastards who want a war!" shouted the zealot.

"Oh, dear." Burden hurried away, followed by the amused Clay. "Heaven protect us from our admirers."

Not until they were in Burden's inner office, with Mrs. Blaine as buffer between them and the mob of reporters wanting statements and partisans wanting comfort, did Burden at last summon up the nerve to say what he had wanted to say all week. Standing now at the bust of Cicero, holding the *New York Times* in his hands as though it contained notes for a speech, he said, "Is it true that Enid has left you?"

Clay's answer was prompt. "No. She's gone to New York for a few weeks, to visit friends. That's all."

Burden was relieved despite the fact that he knew he was not entirely above enjoying the misfortunes of those he loved. He put down the newspaper and turned from Cicero to Clay who now sat on the edge of the desk, balancing a letter opener as though it were a dagger. "I'm glad. But you should do something to stop the rumors."

"What are they?"

"That you . . ." Burden was embarrassed. He was not one to discuss sexual matters with anyone, particularly another man. ". . . are having an affair with a girl and that Enid caught you *flagrante delicto,* as it were."

Clay's expression was stony. "Who is the girl supposed to be?"

"A Brazilian, I believe. A diplomat's wife. Look, I'm only repeating what I've heard and if *I've* heard it everyone's heard it because I don't exactly move in . . . youthful circles, or amongst embassies." The "amongst" rather pleased him, suggested a courtly old-fashioned statesman with a face like Emerson and the habits of a saint.

"Well, it's not true." Clay paused, as though pondering what to say. Burden took it for granted that he was lying. "But that doesn't help, does it? Truth has nothing to do with reputation, and that's what we're talking about, isn't it?"

Burden nodded. "You're going to have a tough fight. If Enid wants to make trouble, she can lose you the election."

"Don't think I don't know that." Clay looked suddenly wretched, and young.

Burden, wanting to be compassionate, was harsh.

"The family is sacred out there on the hustings, particularly in your district with all those wild-eyed Baptists, wallowing in the thought of sin. You're going to have to run as a good clean family man."

"Is is worth it?" A cry from the heart, but the heart lies, too, thought Burden, who said, "Of course it's worth it. What about Blaise?"

"We *seem* to be on good terms. He even asked me to Laurel House for dinner."

"Did you talk to him about the election?"

Clay nodded. "He's interested. Or so he says."

"But if Enid should tell him about your indiscretion . . ."

"I think she has told him."

"And he's said nothing?"

"Not to me. For some reason, he seems angry at *her.*"

"A strange man. If I were you . . ." Burden paused. He was reluctant to give advice, particularly good advice, since this was the sort most resented. ". . . I should cultivate your father-in-law. And apologize to Enid."

"Apologize?" Clay looked at him coldly.

"You want her to divorce you?"

Clay did not answer.

"Of course you don't. Certainly not now when you're just beginning."

"I seem to be in a trap."

Burden managed not to say that the trap was of Clay's own devising. Any married man who brought a girl to his house was a fool. He wondered if perhaps he had overestimated Clay. But then, aware of the other's wretchedness, he was gentle. "When in doubt, do nothing. I'm sure if Blaise is on your side, Enid will come around. After all, there is the child." That was what one always said, thought Burden, who as a lawyer knew that the welfare of children was the first weapon and the last consideration in any power struggle between parents.

Then Burden gave Clay instructions: he was to meet a pair of constituents at Union Station and escort them to the house in Rock Creek Park, where Kitty would take over. He would join them no later than six o'clock. "Now I'm off to the doctor."

"Anything wrong?"

Burden, who had never felt better, could not resist an enigmatic smile. "Blood pressure, too much sugar, hardening arteries, nothing more than the usual pleasures of being sixty." He waved goodbye. As he left the office, he remembered ever so slightly to shuffle.

Once in the street, Burden walked briskly to the nearest taxi stand and gave the driver an address in Georgetown. He felt extraordinarily elated, thanks to the cool March day, the political hopes deferred but still alive, and the sense of a body still capable of taking and giving pleasure, even though his blood pressure *was* high and his arteries probably hardening.

Whistling tonelessly (he had no ear for music), Burden paid the driver, tipping him well. "Thanks, Senator." Usually he was pleased at being recognized, but not today. Nevertheless he tapped the man's arm affectionately, vowing to himself that next time he would give a different address and then walk to the house before which he now stood: eighteenth century rose-brick, with shutters and classic front door newly painted black. After looking first to left and right, Burden walked up the steps and rang the doorbell. A white-jacketed Negro butler admitted him, smiling broadly, happy to see Senator.

Burden followed the butler up the staircase to the second floor where he was shown into a paneled study whose shelves were filled with rather too many leather-bound books. A fire burned in the Adam fireplace. Before it, a table was set for tea. The effect was rich and careful; somewhat too careful for Burden's taste, used as he was to Kitty's haphazard arrangements.

She entered the room, slightly breathless, arms outstretched. "My dear!" she exclaimed in her careful voice from which almost all source of origin had been removed. "You are early. No, on time. On the dot. And I'm late." She kissed his cheek; he responded to the scent she wore. Yes, today everything would work properly. He was certain of that, aroused as always by her manner (attentive if careful) and her figure (well and carefully made).

Best of all, he liked her paleness. Either she wore no makeup or what she did wear was so discreetly applied that she seemed like . . . like a camellia, a word which unexpectedly conjured up the image of a bright pink flower. But of course there were also white camellias.

"Do sit down. Let's have our tea." Burden sat in his usual place on the sofa beside the fire. She sat next to him, poured tea and knew without asking one lump or two, milk or lemon. For a year they had known a perfect if occasional intimacy. Occasional because they thought it best only to meet when her husband was not in the city; though the husband was indifferent, Burden preferred to have his tea secure in the knowledge that they would not be interrupted.

They spoke fondly of the absent. "He's in Jersey City today. At the other emporium." She stressed each syllable of the word "emporium," simultaneously mocking and emphasizing the source of her considerable wealth. The husband was indeed a merchant prince, and Burden was impressed by him. Fortunately the prince worshiped the princess and allowed her every freedom, knowing that she would never compromise or embarrass him; and he was right. She was superbly shrewd. Only the most malicious of Washington ladies would have interpreted these occasional afternoon meetings in Georgetown as anything but an open friendship between a would-be lady of fashion and a famous Senator of known discretion. At worst their meetings might be thought political. It was a useful thing for a shopkeeper to be able, through his wife, to influence a Senator who rather carelessly governed the District of Columbia through a minor Senate committee of which he was, he admitted, without pride, the altogether too indolent chairman, much criticized by civic organizations. Happily, whenever they met at tea, no mention was ever made of such knotty problems as home rule for the District or the sales tax. Only great world issues were threshed out between the watercress sandwiches, carefully rolled, and the chocolate-covered leaves of pastry from Hubert's.

"What a blow it must have been to you, the final vote!" She looked at him tenderly, narrow eyes like an icon gleaming.

"I expected it. We never really had a chance. I was counting on being able to amend the bill, not give Franklin such a completely free hand to play at being Santa Claus. But . . ." he shrugged.

"On the other hand, I am glad, in a way, you know, about helping England." He adored her at that moment. Her diffidence was such a contrast to the usual Washington lady who made speeches when she disagreed with a Senator's politics. But not his mistress. *She* was apologetic. Quite suddenly he kissed her cheek, almost losing his balance for in moving toward her, he slipped into the trough between the thick cushions. Luckily the teacup did not spill.

"You are . . ." He wanted to give her a compliment but his heart was beating so rapidly from the narrow escape that he could think of nothing suitably elaborate and so he said, "looking so well today." Then, to compensate, he took her hand and kissed it, as earnest of what was to come. He was still amazed at having found so late in life something so profoundly satisfying. More to the point, at a time when he thought himself altogether free of the demands of the flesh, he had become like a boy again, or almost.

Lovingly, on cue, she recalled their first meeting. How he had impressed her! For his part, he could not recall when he first met her. It had seemed to him that she had always been very much around town. Then one day, shortly before the Chicago convention, she had asked him to tea. Tired as he was and distracted by all the confused maneuvering for the Vice Presidency, he had joined her in the rose garden at the back of the house and after drinking iced tea full of mint, they almost became lovers.

He frowned slightly, biting down very hard on a cucumber sandwich. At first he had been embarrassed. But her tactfulness had saved the day. She had been, in every sense, marvelous. Since then their encounters had been a bit like Russian roulette. Neither ever knew whether or not he would be capable of the act, but this uncertainty, instead of demoralizing him, added piquancy to the lovemaking. In any case, she was so good about everything; so sensitive; so entirely appreciative.

Thinking of lovemaking, Burden experienced a sharp tug of desire, all senses suddenly heightened. This was going to be a memorable encounter, he told himself. No doubt of it. He could hardly wait for her to lead him into the bedroom with its fourposter bed and the view from the window of a copper beech, one of whose branches occasionally tapped on the windowpane, reminding her that it needed pruning, reminding him of a world outside, well lost.

"And how is Clay?" She had first to go through the usual catechism of how was this one and have you seen that one. She was not to be rushed. He told her that Clay was in good spirits, but she frowned. "I wonder. I saw them the other night, at Laurel House."

Burden was astonished. He had the impression that she was not known to the Sanfords. "Were you *there*?" he asked, for once almost tactless.

"Yes, after dinner. For a moment. With friends. I do like Blaise, and of course the house! *Ma foi!*" Burden was always impressed and only a little put off by her occasional use of French phrases, acquired, she once said, during a summer in Paris, at a school for *jeunes filles.* Although Burden knew no French, his ear was good and he could tell by certain flatnesses and odd nasalities that her pronunciation was not precise. But he loved her ambition. So few Washington women made the effort to learn anything.

They drank hard, laughed loudly, knew all sorts of disreputable gossip about the great, and there it ended: village women inhabiting not a city but a supervillage.

"I had the impression that she . . . that Enid was somewhat in her cups."

"I can remember when women never drank in public." Burden pursued a tangent; a bad habit, he knew, a sure sign of age.

"*I* never drink." A quick careful smile kept smugness to a minimum.

Burden continued to recall early days in Washington. "Before the war, there was no such thing as the cocktail party. There were tea parties, and that was it. Some of the grand houses served wine, of course, and after dinner the men might drink but not the women. Enid was drunk, you say?"

"I don't know her well enough really to say but I *think* she was. There had obviously been some sort of trouble between her and Clay." She looked at him shrewdly, knowing that he knew.

"Trouble?" Native caution exerted itself, even with her.

"I've heard it said—you know how people will *say* anything—that Clay has been involved with a woman who's married, a South American."

"Oh, I doubt that." Burden wondered if Clay might not be, unexpectedly, a fool. No woman was worth the loss of a vote, much less a career.

"I was told that after I left Laurel House there was a dreadful scene and that Blaise struck Enid in front of everyone."

"Struck her? Oh, I doubt *that*!" Blaise was hot-tempered but he was also daughter-dazzled, like himself. Burden tried not to think of Billy Thorne; his blood pressure was already too high.

"But he did. People who were there saw it happen."

"People often exaggerate. What did Enid do?"

"She left with Clay. Most upsetting."

"I should think so." Suddenly exuberant, he put his arm around her, kissed lips, neck. She returned his embrace with so much fervor that a hairpin came loose in the sweep of hair that covered her right ear. But, uncannily, she knew it was loose and fixed it with one hand while she pushed the tea table away with the other.

Burden leaped to his feet, muscles unexpectedly supple. Sex *was* rejuvenating. Bernard Macfadden was right. He was light-headed with desire. "I can't wait," he said.

Her face went suddenly pale. As he reached out to take her, her eyes grew round with horror. She stepped back, as though in the presence of an executioner.

"What's wrong Irene?" His own voice sounded faint and far away. What *was* wrong? he asked himself as his face turned to ice and he fell slowly, leisurely toward the floor, catching at the cloth of the tea table on the way down and pulling the plates and saucers after him. For a long moment he lay at the bottom of a pit, with the not uncomfortable sensation that he was, literally, floating away on a vast tide. From far above him the white face shone and he heard a voice through the noise of the blood's surf. "Quick! It's the Senator. Call a doctor! He's fainted!" Perfectly at ease and not in the least alarmed, Burden floated away. If this was death, he thought languidly, it was easy.

The leisurely pace of prewar Washington was now replaced by a positively New York surge of people coming and going, particularly women hurrying to do manly jobs: their short skirts revealed knees, while mountainous hair fell to padded shoulders, despite urgent warnings that long hair, by getting into machinery, not only slowed down production thereby delaying America's inevitable victory over tyranny, but scalped its owner. The hair, however, was necessary to maintain a femininity compromised by so many hundreds of thousands of women fitting altogether too easily into the jobs of absent husbands and lovers. It was the army of women in the streets (the servicemen he took for granted) that most astonished Peter when he returned to the city on a warm June day, after intensive training as a rifleman in the swamps of Florida. Influence had saved him from a more active participation in the war. Now assigned to the Pentagon, he had every intention of surviving a war which so far had failed to interest him.

The taxicab stopped in front of a large house on Connecticut Avenue. Duffel bag slung over one shoulder, he entered the building, the property of a lady who had recently lost a husband who, unknown to her, had lost her fortune. But the lady believed in survival, too, and with Frederika's help she had converted her house into the District Club, a successful venture thanks to the excellence of the cook, the resolute exclusiveness of the board of directors, and the need for just such a place where the gentry of Washington could give discreet parties or simply have a quiet lunch while charting the course of a love affair or, more likely, threading the maze of government bureaus in pursuit of treasure.

Peter's duffel bag was taken by John, a butler long known to him. "You look mighty nice in your uniform, Mr. Peter," said John, perfunctorily playing the part of family retainer. It seemed as if all the butlers of his generation had gone to the same school where ante-bellum charm was applied to them like spar varnish. But when Peter asked how business was, John showed an unexpectedly commercial side.

"We turn 'em away at lunch," he said with some satisfaction, hiding Peter's duffel bag in a closet. "Then most every night there's at least a couple parties. Of course we get a lot of *new people.*" John betrayed his schooling by the pinched way in which he said "new people." Although the city's leaders were entirely the creation of the voters—at least to begin with—there had always been a division between "us" and the new people, who of course might be very nice but only time would decide whether or not "they" would translate to "we." Time of course was not on the new people's side. The voters were fickle. Many new people were forced to return to the provinces; while others moved on to New York and the big money. Yet of those rejected by the voters, an astonishing number remained in Washington to practice law, to lobby, to live the good life and eventually become "us," or "cliff-dwellers" as they were known to the prosperous class which existed to serve them as realtors and insurance salesmen, doctors and morticians.

"Mrs. Sanford isn't here yet." John showed him into the sitting room, empty at this time of day. Over the mantelpiece hung a portrait of the dead husband who had squandered the fortune. He looked as if he had enjoyed the going of the money. His widow's maid, an old German woman, put her head in the door to say how glad she was Mr. Peter was home from the war, and still alive. Peter, who had come no closer to the enemy than Tallahassee, Florida, did his best to look doomed but the poignancy of early death did not really interest anyone in a city concerned almost entirely with shortages. "Madam says we cannot stay in business this winter unless that *liebe* general who was here last night helps us get more oil!" She disappeared.

On an English hunt table, magazines were filled with photographs of the Battle of Midway, in which the Japanese fleet had received its "first defeat in three hundred fifty years." What, Peter wondered idly, had happened in 1592? There were also aerial photographs of Cologne burning, the result of a Royal Air Force raid in which a thousand bombers had done to Cologne what the Luftwaffe had done repeatedly to London. Obviously the Allies would win the war, but when? He saw himself putting pins in a map forever, a sergeant (clerk non-typist) for the rest of his life or certainly youth.

Happily the longest period of his life was over, and already half-forgotten. Basic training in Georgia, cretinous Southern non-coms, shouting commands in a non-language. *Missed the Saturday dance, heard they crowded the floor.* Jukeboxes blared in country stores converted to dance halls for the pleasure of a million recruits. Bright-eyed, long-haired girls danced together until they were cut in on. *Gonna buy a paper doll that I can call my own.* Then the furtive tugging and feeling in the warm night. *Only a paper moon.* Venereal disease films, in which diseased penises dangled from troubled youths as kindly but stern doctors explained the arcane workings of the foreskin and the necessity of prompt *post coitum* attention to the exposed glans and urethra, all in technicolor. *Don't sit under the apple tree with anyone else but me.* The jolting train rides with shades drawn. The betting: four to one it's New York. No, L.A. *Got* to be West

Coast. Why? Look, we got our suntans, right? Well, they can't send us to no place cold. Why not? Laughter. Troops in summer uniform had indeed been sent to winter while those with parkas and thick wool clothing had gone to summer. Situation normal, all fucked up. Peter applied to officers' candidate school, and was rejected: eyesight not good enough, though adequate to fire an M-1 rifle and remain in the infantry. Queen of battles. But he was found useful in Intelligence. Promoted to sergeant, he put pins in a map of Europe after reading Intelligence reports, based on dispatches from the *New York Times.* Germans now attacking Sevastopol. *Roll out the barrel.* Weak coffee in the mess halls. Food bad except for pork chops. He once ate twelve while on twenty-four hour K.P. which, despite the grease and the noise, was preferable to being night fireman and sleeping on a cement floor beside furnaces constantly in need of stoking. Again the small towns. The bars. The girls with too much hair and bold shiny eyes. *They're either too young or too old.* And as it must to every American fighting man, clap came to Peter Sanford, and the cure was by no means as disagreeable as the kindly but stern doctor in the film had said it would be.

"But you're thin!" With those welcome words, his mother embraced him. "You're not sick, are you? You look pale as a sheet!"

"Never felt better," was the usual response; and accurate, too. The old fullness of breasts and thighs had gone; he was hard to the touch. Waist: thirty inches. Height: six feet. Weight: One hundred seventy pounds. He would never be fat again.

They crossed Chain Bridge and turned left on the road toward Great Falls. It had been years since Burden had made this journey, and he found the countryside sadly altered. Wooden frameworks of new houses stood, their pale wood raw against dark trees while billboards advertised entire new communities where life could be lived on easy terms with every modern appliance, a mere twenty minutes from downtown Washington. Burden liked nothing that he saw. But he refused to be distressed by anything today. He would think of nothing but the cool woods that smelled of mushrooms and decay.

"That's the turnoff there, at the gas station."

"O.K.," said the chauffeur, a young Negro found for him by Henry who had gone to work for the government with Burden's reluctant blessing. To lose the somber Henry was like losing a brother but he could not refuse him the chance to become available for a government pension. Solemnly Henry had departed that summer, promising to reappear every Sunday to tend the roses, and in fact he did make an occasional appearance at the house to discuss politics with the Senator and spray a rose or two. He also spoke privately and at length with his replacement but so far he had yet to convince the young man that his employer should be addressed as "Sir." Passively, Burden disliked the new driver but the effort to find another was beyond him.

Nor was Kitty any help. She had no interests now except the birds, for whom she was currently building an elaborate sanctuary. In their twittering company her days were spent. Wearing a bathrobe and slippers, hair all undone, she seldom spoke to anyone, which was just as well, for with age her mind had filled with fantasies and instead of blurting out embarrassing truths she now revealed eccentric dreams that astonished and repelled even those who knew her best. But she was happy among her birds, and Burden envied her for having so completely escaped the human. There would be no pain for Kitty ever again, other than brief sorrow at a bird's fall, made instantly pleasurable by a burial service witnessed by trees. Now that he needed her, she was gone, which was fair enough, for in the days when she had needed him he had taken her for granted, had left her behind while he pursued the Presidency, year after year, back and forth across the continent. Now there would be no more journeys; he was home again but the girl he had married half a century before had ceased to exist and in her place an old woman with thin hair crumbled stale bread to feed birds.

"Where do I go now?" The voice combined hostility and petulance. Burden looked out the window. They were on an unfamiliar road with new houses to left and right, each with its high television antenna drawing from the air crude pictures and lying words. Oh, detestable age! he thought, hating all.

"It's straight ahead. Just keep on." He had recognized the patch of woods where Henry usually parked. At least the pine trees were unchanged, unspoiled.

"But what do you want me to do?" The black face looked at him, stupid in its self-absorption.

"I want you to wait," said Burden coldly; then he turned and walked toward the woods where North and South had met in deadly battle and, that day at least, the South, his South, had won.

Burrs stuck to his trousers as he made his way slowly through tall grass, but he did not pause to pick them off. He was intent on finding his hill. Everything depended on that now. Once he had achieved it, all would be well. He would be safe from attack, protected by that Southern victory, redolent of virtue, courage, honor. Like burrs the words stuck to his mind. And though he reminded himself that words meant only what one wanted them to mean, he also knew that, once invested with meaning, words became magic, and could destroy as well as sustain.

The field was the same. But upon the hill where he used to sit, trees had been cleared, a cellar dug, and in orderly piles cement block was stacked. The bullet would long since have been dug up by the bulldozer which had scooped out the cellar of the house-to-be.

"What're you doing here?" The voice belonged to a sad-faced man in blue jeans and windbreaker.

"I'm sorry." Burden was gracious. "I am Senator Day."

"I didn't ask who you were. I asked what are you doing here. This is private property."

Stung, Burden stepped back, away from the profaned hill. "I'm sorry. I didn't know anyone lived here. I used to visit . . ."

"I've got signs posted. I'm sure you can read."

"Yes. Very well. Thank you." In a rage, Burden turned his back on the man. He had said who he was and yet the man had persisted in his rudeness. So a world of honor ends.

Burden made his way back through the woods to the car, aware that the man in the field continued to watch him as if he might suddenly set the woods afire or in some other way diminish the value of the property.

Burden's driver had turned on the radio full volume. He was listening raptly, thick lips ajar, to the thunder of a lover's lament.

"Turn that damned thing off!" A long slow look as the young man absorbed the command. Then he switched off the radio and, slowly, opened the car door for Burden.

"Take the river road. I'll tell you when to stop." As the car started, Burden realized that he was shivering. He held his hands together and with all his strength forced each hand to steady the other. But tremors still went through his body. Obviously a delayed reaction to what Peter had told him. By deliberately refusing to address his mind to his own ruin, the body had been forced to absorb the shock the mind disowned.

He tried to imagine what the next few days would be like. The story would break on Thursday. He could anticipate the sneering tone. Lately Harold had taken to writing exposés of small (never great) corruptions in the Congress. Padded payrolls and illegal campaign contributions were the usual crimes, momentarily embarrassing to the legislator involved but seldom causing much damage. Americans had always believed that their representatives were corrupt since, given the same opportunity, they would be, too. As it was, the common folk daily cheated one another, misrepresenting the goods they sold and otherwise conducting themselves like their governors. If Clay Overbury was able to present himself as a war hero and be elected, why, then, they reckoned, more power to him. After all, he was no different from the used-car dealer who makes a profit on a car he knows will not run properly. Of course, "If you can't be good, be careful" was the national wisdom, and it was hardly wise to be caught. Yet Burden was by no means convinced that Clay, for one, would have been defeated even if he had not had a war to hide in. The people seemed genuinely uninterested in moral matters. What mattered was winning, and Clay had won. For that matter if he himself had become President in 1940, the taking of Nillson's money would have been regarded in retrospect as a brilliant necessity which in a sense it had been. Even now he regretted not so much the selling of his vote as the abandoning of his responsibility to the Indians.

Sweat clouded his face while cold arms and legs twitched as though they were on strings, manipulated by someone not himself. He must regain control. He recalled a visit recently made by him by one of the Indians whose land was sold to Nillson. "Best thing ever happened to us, selling off that land. No damn oil in it anyway, and if we had stayed there we'd gone right on the way we was, ignorant as all hell. Now I got my own business and . . ." Success story: a bad action with good results.

But Burden refused himself this easy comfort. He had all his life believed that one should behave in a certain way despite the example of others, and for most of his life he had been honest. Even as he sounded most royally all the depths and shoals of honor, he had made few compromises with his own sense of virtue. That others did not share his scrupulous niceness merely made him all the more pleased with himself. Now all that was at an end and he would be revealed as what he was, worse than the others because they at least never for a moment believed that it was better to be honest than dishonest, noble than ignoble, good than bad; no sophistry as to what was *truly* good could save him from himself, not to mention from the world's contempt once Harold's column had been printed. And to be truthful, it was the thought of what others would say that gave him the most pain. To know that they would laugh at him for being found out, take delight in the end of his career and then, easily, forget that he had ever existed, since what, after all, was he, but just another crooked politician who had had his day?

"Stop here."

The driver put on the brakes too quickly. Burden's bad shoulder struck against the side of the car. He cursed softly. Then before the fool could ask what he was supposed to do next, Burden told him that he was to wait. "I'm going to take a walk. You can play the radio if you like."

Trees without leaves descended a steep slope to the Potomac, whose brown waters swirled about sharp rocks that broke the river's flow, like so many stepping-stones set out for a giant's use.

A narrow path zigzagged among trees to which he clung as he hurried, like a boy, toward the river, nothing in his mind but a desire to escape entirely the present and the human.

Abruptly the path turned to reveal a ruined cabin with roof half gone, door sprung and windows broken in. He stopped and looked inside. The floor was strewn with yellow newspapers and ashes from old fires. He thought of the soul's dark cottage which, battered and decayed, let in new light, but only to reveal, on closer inspection, empty beer bottles, used contraceptives, and a man's shoe. He continued his descent through the cool woods, the roar of water upon rocks growing louder with each step.

The path ended at a narrow rocky beach. Between tall boulders worn smooth by the last glacier, his father stood, wearing a torn Confederate uniform and holding a rifle, just as he had that day in the field at Manassas when his son had failed to recognize him. But there was no mistaking him now. The blazing eyes of the furious boy he had never known were those of the man who had been his life's tormentor.

Burden spoke first. "You were right," he said. "It has all gone wrong. You should be pleased." He took a tentative step toward the Confederate corporal, who took a step back, revealing as he did the torn cloth of his tunic, bright with a new wound's blood.

"You're bleeding still!" The triumphant shout caused the boy to hold his rifle in such a way as to bar Burden's approach to him. But in his passion Burden was not to be put off by mere death. All life was now concentrated in that single gaping wound and all that needed doing in the world was the staunching of the blood.

With stiff fingers Burden removed a handkerchief from his pocket. Then he walked toward the wounded soldier, half expecting him to run away. But this was no ordinary youth; it was his father honorably struck by an enemy's bullet in the field of battle. The Confederate corporal did not flinch even when at last they were face to face.

For a long moment Burden stared into the blue eyes that perfectly reflected empty sky. Then slowly he extended the hand which held the handkerchief. Now only the rifle barred his way. He waited patiently until at last, marvelously, the rifle was lowered. With a cry he flung himself upon the youth who was his father, plunged the handkerchief into the wound, lost his balance, fell against the beloved, was taken into those long-dead arms, and like impatient lovers, they embraced and together fell.

# ESSAYS

WIDELY PRAISED AND HONORED for his essays, Vidal has published eleven volumes of his observations and ruminations on life, literature, and politics, a large number of which were collected in *United States, Essays 1952–1992* (1993), which won the National Book Award in 1993. *The Second American Revolution and Other Essays, 1976–1982* was awarded the National Book Critics Circle prize for criticism. Many of the essays have a strong personal element that connect them to his autobiographical books, particularly *Screening History* (1992) and *Palimpsest* (1995). All appeared initially in periodicals, usually *Esquire, The Nation,* or *The New York Review of Books,* or as prefaces to his own books. They are distinguished for their conversational tone. One of their early admirers, the critic Fred Dupee, remarked that Vidal, the essayist, writes like some great conversationalist lying relaxed in a hammock, talking about whatever comes into his head. The essays are, however, the artful presentation of wide reading and considerable thought. If Vidal has any one model it is Montaigne, to whom he has applied Emerson's fine observation that "in every work of genius we recognize our own rejected thoughts; they come back to us with a certain alienated majesty." That last phrase captures some of the tone and effect of Vidal's essays.

For the National Book Awards ceremony in 1993, Vidal provided his representative with a brief acceptance speech: "Unaccustomed as I am to winning prizes in my native land, I have not a set piece of the sort seasoned prizewinners are wont to give. Who can forget Faulkner's 'eternal truths and verities'?—that famed tautology so unlike my own bleak 'relative truth.' As you have already, I am sure, picked the wrong novelist and the wrong poet, I am not so vain as to think that you've got it right this time either. Incidentally, I did attend the first National Book Award forty years ago—that was also my last experience of book-prize giving. My date was Dylan Thomas, dead sober for a change and terrified of everyone. The winner in fiction was my old friend James Jones, for *From Here to Eternity.* His victory was somewhat marred by Jean Stafford, one of the judges, who moved slowly if unsurely about the room, stopping before each notable to announce in a loud voice, 'The decision was *not* unanimous.' But Jimmy won, and Dylan and I retired to a tavern in the Village, and the rest was biography. In any case, I am delighted that you have encouraged Random House to continue publishing three-and-a-half-pound books by elderly writers."

# At Home in Washington, D.C.

LIKE SO MANY blind people my grandfather was a passionate sightseer, not to mention a compulsive guide. One of my first memories is driving with him to a slum in southeast Washington. "All this," he said, pointing at the dilapidated red brick buildings, "was once our land." Since I saw only shabby buildings and could not imagine the land beneath, I was not impressed.

Years later I saw a map of how the District of Columbia had looked before the district's invention. Georgetown was a small community on the Potomac. The rest was farmland, owned by nineteen families. I seem to remember that the Gore land was next to that of the Notleys—a name that remains with me since my great-grandfather was called Thomas Notley Gore. (A kind reader tells me that the landowning Notleys were located elsewhere in Maryland.) Most of these families were what we continue to call—mistakenly—Scots-Irish. Actually, the Gores were Anglo-Irish from Donegal. They arrived in North America at the end of the seventeenth century and they tended to intermarry with other Anglo-Irish families—particularly in Virginia and Maryland.

George Washington not only presided over the war of separation from Great Britain (*revolution* is much too strong a word for that confused and confusing operation) but he also invented the federal republic whose original constitution reflected his powerful will to create the sort of government which would see to it that the rights of property will be forever revered. He was then congenial, if not controlling, party to the deal that moved the capital of the new republic from the city of Philadelphia to the wilderness not far from his own Virginia estate.

When a grateful nation saw fit to call the capital-to-be Washington City, the great man made no strenuous demur. Had he not already established his modesty and republican virtue by refusing the crown of the new Atlantic nation on the ground that to replace George III with George I did not sound entirely right? Also, and perhaps more to the point, Washington had no children. There would be no Prince of Virginia, ready to ascend the rustic throne at Washington City when the founder of the dynasty was translated to a higher sphere.

Although Washington himself did not have to sell or give up any of his own land, he did buy a couple of lots as speculation. Then he died a year before the city was occupied by its first president-in-residence, John Adams. The families that had been dispossessed to make way for the capital city did not do too badly. The Gores who remained sold lots, built houses and hotels, and became rich. The Gores who went away—my grandfather's branch—moved to the far west, in those days Mississippi. It was not until my grandfather was elected to the Senate in 1907 that he was able to come home again—never to leave until his death in 1949.

Although foreign diplomats enjoy maintaining that Washington is—or was—a hardship post, the British minister in 1809, one Francis James Jackson, had the good sense to observe: "I have procured two very good saddle horses, and Elizabeth and I have been riding in all directions round the place whenever the weather has been cool enough. The country has a beautifully picturesque appearance, and I have nowhere seen finer scenery than is composed by the Potomac and the woods and hills about it; yet it has a wild and desolated air from being so scantily and rudely cultivated, and from the want of population. . . . So you see we are not fallen into a wilderness,—so far from it that I am surprised no one should before have mentioned the great beauty of the neighborhood. The natives trouble themselves but little about it; their thoughts are chiefly of tobacco, flour, shingles, and the news of the day." *Plus ça change.*

Twenty years ago, that well-known wit and man-about-town, John F. Kennedy, said, "Washington perfectly combines southern efficiency with northern charm." I think that this was certainly true of the era when he and his knights of the Round Table were establishing Camelot amongst the local chiggers. By then too many glass buildings were going up. Too many old houses were being torn down or allowed to crumble. Too many slums were metastasizing around Capitol Hill. Also, the prewar decision to make an imperial Roman—literally, Roman—capital out of what had been originally a pleasant Frenchified southern city was, in retrospect, a mistake.

When such Roman palaces as the Commerce Department were being built, I can remember how we used to wonder, rather innocently, if these huge buildings could ever be filled up with people. But a city is an organism like any other and an organism knows its own encodement. Long before the American empire was a reality, the city was turning itself into New Rome. While the basilicas and porticoes were going up, one often had the sense that one was living not in a city that was being built but in a set of ruins. It is curious that even in those pre-nuclear days many of us could image the city devastated. Was this, perhaps, some memory of the War of 1812 when the British burned Capitol and White House? Or of the Civil War when southern troops invaded the city, coming down Seventh Street Road?

"At least they will make wonderful ruins," said my grandfather, turning his blind eyes on the Archives Building; he was never a man to spend public money on anything if he could help it. But those Piranesi blocks of marble eventually became real buildings that soon filled up with real bureaucrats, and by the end of the Second World War Washington had a real world empire to go with all those (to my eyes, at least) bogus-Roman sets.

Empires are dangerous possessions, as Pericles was among the first to point out. Since I recall pre-imperial Washington, I am a bit of an old Republican in the Ciceronian mode, given to decrying the corruption of the simpler, saner city of my youth. In the twenties and thirties, Washington was a small town where everyone knew everyone else. When school was out in June, boys took off their shoes and did not put them on again—at least outside the house—until September. The summer heat was—and is—Egyptian. In June, before Congress adjourned, I used to be sent with car and driver to pick up my grandfather at the Capitol and bring him home. In those casual days, there were few guards at the Capitol—and, again, everyone knew everyone else. I would wander on to the floor of the Senate, sit on my grandfather's desk if he wasn't ready to go, experiment with the snuff that was ritually allotted each senator; then I would lead him off the floor. On one occasion, I came down the aisle of the Senate wearing nothing but a bathing suit. This caused a good deal of amusement, to the blind man's bewilderment. Finally, the vice president, Mr. Garner—teeth like tiny black pearls and a breath that was all whisky—came down from the chair and said, "Senator, this boy is nekkid." Afterward I always wore a shirt on the Senate floor—but never shoes.

I date the end of the old republic and the birth of the empire to the invention, in the late thirties, of air-conditioning. Before air-conditioning, Washington was deserted from mid-June to September. The president—always Franklin Roosevelt—headed up the Hudson and all of Congress went home. The gentry withdrew to the northern resorts. Middle-income people flocked to Rehoboth Beach, Delaware or Virginia Beach, which was slightly more racy. But since air-conditioning and the Second World War arrived, more or less at the same time, Congress sits and sits while the presidents and their staffs never stop making mischief at the White House or in "Mr. Mullett's masterpiece," the splendid old State, War and Navy building, now totally absorbed by the minions of President Augustus. The Pentagon—a building everyone hated when it was being built—still gives us no great cause to love either its crude appearance or its function, so like that of a wasp's nest aswarm.

Now our Roman buildings are beginning to darken with time and pigeon droppings while the brutal glass towers of the late twentieth century tend to mask and dwarf them. But here and there in the city one still comes across shaded streets and houses; so many relics of lost time—when men wore white straw hats and suits in summer while huge hats decorated the ladies (hats always got larger just before a war) and one dined at Harvey's Restaurant, where the slow-turning ceiling-fans and tessellated floors made the hottest summer day seem cool even though the air of the street outside was ovenlike and smelled of jasmine and hot tar, while nearby Lafayette Park was a lush tropical jungle where one could see that Civil War hero, Mr. Justice Oliver Wendell Holmes, Jr., stroll, his white moustaches unfurled like fierce battle pennants. At the park's edge our entirely own and perfectly unique Henry Adams held court for decades in a house opposite to that Executive Mansion where grandfather and great-grandfather had reigned over a capital that was little more than a village down whose muddy main street ran a shallow creek that was known to some even then as—what else?—the Tiber.

*The New York Review of Books*
*April 29, 1982*

# On Flying

I WAS twice footnote to the history of aviation. On July 7, 1929, still on the sunny side of four years old, I flew in the first commercially scheduled airliner (a Ford trimotor) across the United States, from New York to Los Angeles in forty-eight hours. Aviation was now so safe that even a little child could fly in comfort. I remember only two things about the flight: the lurid flames from the exhaust through the window; then a sudden loss of altitude over Los Angeles, during which my eardrums burst. Always the trouper, I was later posed, smiling, for the rotogravure sections of the newspapers, blood trickling from tiny lobes. Among my supporting cast that day were my father, the assistant general manager of the company (Transcontinental Air Transport), his great and good friend, as the never great, never good *Time* magazine would say, Amelia Earhart, as well as Anne Morrow Lindbergh, whose husband Charles was my pilot.* Both Lindbergh and Amelia had been hired by the line's promoter, one C. M. Keys (not even a footnote now but then known as the czar of aviation), to publicize TAT, popularly known as "The Lindbergh Line."

My second moment of footnotehood occurred in the spring of 1936, when I was—significantly—on the sunny side of eleven. I was picked up at St. Albans School in Washington, D.C., by my father, Eugene L. Vidal,

*A recent investigation of a certain newspaper of record shows that, contrary to family tradition, I was *not* on the first flight. I made my first cross-country flight a few months later, at the age of four. In any case, I am still a triumphant footnote: the first child ever to cross the country by air-rail.

director of the Bureau of Air Commerce (an appointee of one Franklin D. Roosevelt, himself mere tinkling prelude to Reagan's heavenly choir). FDR wanted to have a ministry of aviation like the European powers; and so the Bureau of Air Commerce was created.

On hot spring mornings Washington's streets smelled of melting asphalt, and everything was a dull tropical green. The city was more like a Virginia county seat than a world capital. Instead of air conditioning, people used palmetto fans. As we got into my implausibly handsome father's plausible Plymouth, he was mysterious, while I was delighted to be liberated from school. I wore short trousers and polo shirt, the standard costume of those obliged to pretend that they were children a half-century ago. What was up? I asked. My father said, You'll see. Since we were now on the familiar road to Bolling Field, I knew that whatever was up, it was probably going to be us. Ever since my father—known to all as Gene—had become director in 1933, we used to fly together nearly every weekend in the director's Stinson monoplane. Occasionally he'd let me take the controls. Otherwise, I was navigator. With a filling-station road map on my bony knees, I would look out the window for familiar landmarks. When in doubt, you followed a railroad line or a main highway. Period joke: A dumb pilot was told to follow the Super Chief no matter what; when the train entered a tunnel, so did the pilot. End of joke.

At Bolling Field, I recognized the so-called Hammond flivver plane. Gene had recently told the press that a plane had been developed so safe that anyone could fly it and so practical that anyone who could afford a flivver car could buy it—in mass production, that is. At present, there was only the prototype. But it was my father's dream to put everyone in the air, just as Henry Ford had put everyone on the road. Since 1933, miles of newsprint and celluloid had been devoted to Gene Vidal's dream—or was it folly?

We had been up in the Hammond plane before, and I suppose it really was almost "foolproof," as my father claimed. I forget the plane's range and speed but the speed was probably less than a hundred miles an hour. (One pleasure of flying then: sliding the window open and sticking out your hand, and feeling the wind smash against it.) As a boy, the actual flying of a plane was a lot simpler for me than building one of those model planes that the other lads were so adept at making and I all thumbs in the presence of balsa wood, paper, and glue—the Dionysiac properties of glue were hardly known then. But those were Depression years, and we Americans a serious people. That is how we beat Hitler, Mussolini, and Tojo.

Next to the Hammond, there was a Pathé newsreel crew, presided over by the familiar figure of Floyd Gibbons, a dark patch covering the vacancy in his florid face where once there had been an eye that he had lost—it was rumored—as a correspondent in the war to make the world safe for democracy. Since my father appeared regularly in newsreels and *The March of Time,* a newsreel crew was no novelty. At age seven, when asked what my father did, I said, He's in the newsreels. But now, since I had been taken so mysteriously out of class, could it be . . . ? I felt a premonitory chill.

As we drove on to the runway (no nonsense in those days when the director came calling), Gene said, "Well, you want to be a movie actor. So here's your chance." He was, if nothing else, a superb salesman. Jaded when it came to flying, I was overwhelmed by the movies. Ever since Mickey Rooney played Puck in *A Midsummer Night's Dream,* I had wanted to be a star, too. What could Rooney do that I couldn't? Why was I at St. Albans, starting Latin, when I might be darting about the world, unconfined by either gravity or the director's Stinson? "I'll put a girdle round about the earth in forty minutes!" Rooney had croaked. Now I was about to do the same.

As we parked, Gene explained that I was to take off, circle the field once, and land. After I got out of the plane, I would have to do some acting. Floyd Gibbons would ask me what it was like to fly the flivver plane, and I was to say it was just like driving a bicycle. I told Gene that it was a lot harder than riding a bicycle. He told me to keep to the script.

My earlier footnotehood was clear-cut. I was indeed the first child to cross the country by air. But now I was a challenger. In 1927, one Jack Chapman, aged eleven, had soloed. Since there had been so much public complaint (suppose he had gone and killed a cow?), my father's predecessor had made it the law that no one under sixteen years of age could solo. Now here I was a few months younger than Chapman had been in 1927, ready to break the prepubescent record. But the law said that I could not fly unattended. Ordinarily, my father—true pioneer—would have ignored this sort of law. But the director of Air Commerce could not—at least in front of *Pathé News of the Week*—break a law that he was sworn to uphold.

As I stood by the door to the plane, staring glassy-eyed at the cobra-camera, a long discussion took place. How was I to solo (thus proving that the Hammond flivver was if not foolproof boyproof) and yet not break the 1927 law? Floyd Gibbons proposed that my father sit behind me. But Gene said, no. He was already so familiar a figure in the Trans-Luxes of the Republic that the audience would think that he had done the flying. Finally, Fred Geisse, an official of the bureau (and, like me, a nonpilot), got in first and crouched behind the pilot's seat. The cameras started to turn. With a slight but lovable Rooneyesque swagger, I climbed aboard.

. . .

Recently, I saw some footage from the newsreel. As I fasten my seat belt, I stare serenely off into space, not unlike Lindbergh-Earhart. I even looked a bit like the god and goddess of flight who, in turn, looked spookily like each other. I start up the engine. I am still serene. But as I watched the ancient footage, I recalled suddenly the terror that I was actually feeling. Terror not of flying but of the camera. This was my big chance to replace Mickey Rooney. But where was my script? My director? My talent? Thinking only of stardom, I took off. With Geisse behind me kindly suggesting that I keep into the wind (that is, opposite to the way that the lady's stocking on the flagpole was blowing), I circled the field not once but twice and landed with the sort of jolt with which today's jet cowboys bring to earth their DC-10s.

The real terror began when I got out of the plane and stood, one hand on the door knob, staring into the camera. Gibbons asked me about the flight. I said, Oh, it wasn't much, and it wasn't, either. But I was now suffering from terminal stage fright. As my voice box began to shut down, the fingers on the door knob appeared to have a life of their own. I stammered incoherently. Finally, I gave what I thought was a puckish Rooneyesque grin which exploded on to the screen with all the sinister force of Peter Lorre's *M.* In that final ghastly frame, suddenly broken off as if edited by someone's teeth in the cutting room, my career as boy film star ended and my career as boy aviator was launched. I watched the newsreel twice in the Belasco Theater, built on the site of William Seward's Old Club House. Each time, I shuddered with horror at that demented leer which had cost me stardom. Yet, leer notwithstanding, I was summer-famous; and my contemporaries knew loathing. The young Streckfus Persons (a.k.a. Truman Capote) knew of my exploit. "Among other things," Harper Lee writes of the boy she based on Capote, "he had been up in a mail plane seventeen times, he had been to Nova Scotia, he had seen an elephant, etc." In the sixties, when I introduced Norman Mailer to my father, I was amazed how much Mailer knew of Gene's pioneering.

I record this trivia not to try to regain my forever-lost feetnotehood but to try to recall the spirit of the early days of aviation, a spirit itself now footnote to the vast air and aerospace industries of today. In Anthony Sampson's *Empires of the Sky,* only a dozen pages are devoted to the first quarter-century of American aviation. There are also three times as many references to something called Freddie Laker as there are to Lindbergh. Well, *sic transit* was always the name of the game, even now when the focus is on space itself. Finally, I am put in mind of all this by a number of recent books on aviation, of which the most intriguing and original is *The Winged Gospel* by Joseph J. Corn, in which the author recalls the quasi-religious fervor that Americans experienced when men took to the air and how, for a time, there was "a gospel of flight," and Gene Vidal was its "high priest."* Flight would make men near-angels, it was believed; and a peaceful world one.

## 2

Ever since the development of the balloon in eighteenth-century France, so-called "lighter-than-air craft" were a reality. Heavier-than-air craft were considered mad inventors' dreams until the brothers Orville and Wilbur Wright created the first heavier-than-air plane and flew it at Kitty Hawk, North Carolina, on December 17, 1903. Curiously enough, it took five years before the press could figure out exactly *what* it was that they had done. At that time the world was full of inventors like the Wright brothers; but the others were either inventing lighter-than-air craft such as the dirigible, or experimenting with gliders. Only a few certified nuts believed in the practicality of heavier-than-air craft. One of these "crackpots" was Henry Adams's friend at the Smithsonian Institution, Dr. S. P. Langley, and he was on much the same theoretical tack as the Wright brothers. But they left earth first.

It was not until Orville Wright flew a plane at Fort Myer outside Washington in the presence of five thousand people that the world realized that man had indeed kicked gravity and that the sky was only the beginning of no known limit. Like so many of the early airship makers, the Wright brothers were bicycle mechanics. But then the bicycle itself had been a revolutionary machine, adding an inch or two to the world's population by making it possible for boys to wheel over to faraway villages where taller (or shorter) girls might be found. At least in the days when eugenics was a science that was the story. Other bicycle manufacturers soon got into the act, notably Glenn H. Curtiss, who was to be a major manufacturer of aircraft.

Although the first generation of flyers believed that airplanes would eventually make war unthinkable, the 1914–18 war did develop a new glamorous sort of warfare, with Gary Cooper gallantly dueling Von Stroheim across the bright heavens. By 1918 the American government had an airmail service. In 1927 the twenty-five-year-old Lindbergh flew the Atlantic and became, overnight, the most famous man on earth, the air age beautifully incarnate. In 1928 Amelia Earhart flew the Atlantic and took her place in the heavens as yin to Lindbergh's yang.

*Joseph J. Corn, *The Winged Gospel: America's Romance with Aviation, 1900–1950* (London: Oxford University Press, 1984).

. . .

It is hard to describe to later generations what it was like to live in a world dominated by two such shining youthful deities. Neither could appear in public without worshipers—no other word—storming them. Yet each was obliged to spend a lot of time not only publicizing and selling aircraft but encouraging air transport. Of the two, Lindbergh was the better paid. But, as a deity, the commercial aspect was nothing to him, he claimed, and the religion all. On the other hand, Earhart's husband, the publisher and publicist George Palmer Putnam (known as G.P.), worked her very hard indeed. The icons of the air age were big business.

*Time* magazine, September 28, 1931:

> To Charles Townsend Ludington, socialite of Philadelphia, $8,000 might be the price of a small cabin cruiser such as he sails on Biscayne Bay. . . . But the $8,073.61 profit which showed on a balance sheet upon [his] desk last week was as exciting to him as a great fortune. It was the first year's net earning of the Ludington Line, plane-per-hour passenger service between New York, Philadelphia and Washington.
>
> As practically sole financiers of the company [Nicholas and Charles Townsend] Ludington might well be proud. But they would be the first to insist that all credit go to two young men who sold them the plan and then made it work: brawny, handsome Gene Vidal, West Point halfback of 1916–20, one-time Army flyer; and squint-eyed, leathery Paul ("Dog") Collins, war pilot, old-time air-mail pilot.

*Time* style still exerts its old magic, while *Time* checkers are, as always, a bit off—my father graduated from West Point in 1918. An all-American halfback, he also played quarterback. But he *was* one of the first army flyers and the first instructor in aeronautics at West Point. Bored with peacetime army life and excited by aviation, he quit the army in 1926. Already married to the "beauteous" (*Time* epithet) Nina Gore, daughter of "blind solon" (ditto) Senator T. P. Gore, he had a year-old son for whom *Time* had yet to mint any of those Lucite epithets that, in time (where "All things shall come to pass," Ecclesiastes), they would.

New airliners were cropping up all over the country. After 1918, anyone who could nail down a contract from the postmaster general to fly the mail was in business. Since this was the good old United States, there was corruption. Unkind gossips thought that an army flyer whose father-in-law was a senator would be well placed to get such a contract. But during the last years of President Hoover, Senator Gore was a Democrat; and during the first term of President Roosevelt, he was an enemy of the New Deal. Gore was no help at all to Gene. But anyone who could fly was automatically in demand at one or another of the small airlines that carried (or did not carry) the mail.

In 1929, C. M. Keys combined a couple of airlines and started Transcontinental Air Transport, or TAT. For a quarter million dollars cash, Keys hired, as a sort of consultant, Charles Lindbergh; he also gave the Lone Eagle shrewd advice on how to avoid income tax. Thus, TAT was dubbed "The Lindbergh Line." Keys was perhaps the first true hustler or robber baron in American aviation: "He had been an editor of *The Wall Street Journal* and had worked with Walter Hines Page on the old *World's Work;* Keys was also an important aviation promoter. He got into the manufacturing end of the industry during the war and eventually won control of Curtiss Aeroplane & Motor Company. . . ." In other words, a businessman who "got control" of companies; who bought and sold them. TAT also acquired ex–airmail flyer Paul Collins and Gene Vidal.

Like most of the early airlines, TAT was a combined air-rail service. Passenger planes did not fly at night or over the turbulent Alleghenys. On a TAT transcontinental flight, the passengers left New York by rail in the evening; then, in Columbus, Ohio, they boarded a Ford trimotor (eight passengers maximum) and flew to Waynoka, Oklahoma. Here they transferred to the Santa Fe railroad for an overnight haul to Clovis, New Mexico, where another plane flew them into Los Angeles—or Burbank, to be precise. It is a tribute to the faith of the air-gospellers that they truly believed that this grueling two-day journey would, in time, be preferable to the comforts of a Pullman car. Interestingly enough, many descendants of the original railroad barons were immediately attracted to aviation, and names like Harriman and Whitney and Vanderbilt crop up on the boards of directors. These young men were prescient. By the end of the Second War, the railroads that had dominated American life since the Civil War, buying not only politicians but whole states, would be almost entirely superseded by civil aviation and the Teamsters union. But the railroad lords suffered not at all; they simply became airlords.

The transition was hardly overnight. In TAT's eighteen months of service, the line lost $2,750,000. There were simply not enough customers at sixteen cents a mile; also, more important, there was no mail contract.

TAT's headquarters were at St. Louis, and my only memory of the summer of 1929 (other than bleeding eardrums) was of city lights, as seen from a downtown hotel window. For anyone interested in period detail, there were almost no colored lights then. So, on a hot airless night in St. Louis, the city had a weird white arctic glow. Also, little did I suspect as I stared out over the tropical city with its icy blinking signs, that a stone's throw away, a youth of eighteen, as yet unknown to me and to the world, Thomas Lanier Williams, was typing, typing, typing into the night, while across the dark fields of the Republic . . .

Paul Collins describes the end of TAT (*Tales of an Old Air-Faring Man*):

> About Christmastime 1929 all the St. Louis executives were called to a meeting in New York including Joseph Magee, the general manager; Gene Vidal, his assistant; Luke Harris, Jack Herlihy, and me. We were introduced in Mr. Keye's [*sic*] office to one Jack Maddux, President of Maddux Airlines, an operation that flew from Los Angeles to San Francisco. . . . Mr. Keyes [*sic*] stated that a merger had been effected between TAT and Maddux.

The ineffable Keys then waited until the assembled management of TAT had returned to St. Louis, where they were all fired.

Simultaneously, the Great Depression began. Small airlines either merged or died. Since a contract to fly the mail was the key to survival, the postmaster general, one Walter F. Brown, was, in effect, the most powerful single figure in aviation. He was also a political spoilsman of considerable energy. In principle, he wanted fewer airlines; and those beholden to him. As of 1930, United Air Lines carried all transcontinental mail. But Brown decided that, in this case, there should be two transcontinental carriers: one would have the central New York–Los Angeles route; the second the southern Atlanta–Dallas–Los Angeles route. As befitted a Herbert Hoover socialist, Brown did not believe in competitive bidding. The southern route would go to Brown-favored American Airlines and the central route to an airline yet to be created but already titled Transcontinental and Western Air, today's Trans World Airlines.

Brown then forced a merger between TAT (willing) and Western Air Express (unwilling). But as neither flew the mail, Brown's promise of a federal contract for the combined operation did the trick. Since Brown was not above corporate troilism, a third airline, a shy mouse of a company called Pittsburgh Aviation Industries Corporation (PAIC), became a member of the wedding. How on earth did such a mouse get involved with two working airlines? Well, there were three Mellons on PAIC's board of directors, of whom the most active was Richard, nephew of Andrew, former secretary of the treasury. The nobles missed few tricks in the early days of aviation. As it turned out, the first real boss of TWA was a PAIC man, Richard W. Robbins. And so, on August 25, 1930, TWA was awarded the central airmail route even though its competitor, United, had made a lower bid. There was outcry, but nothing more. After all, the chief radio engineer for TWA was the president's twenty-eight-year-old son, Herbert Hoover,

Jr. In those days, Hoover socialism was total; and it was not until his successor, Franklin D. Roosevelt, that old-fashioned capitalism was restored.

During all this, Gene Vidal had retreated to Senator Gore's house in Rock Creek Park, Washington, D.C. Certain that he had learned enough about the airline business to start one, he convinced the brothers Ludington that a regular New York–Philadelphia–Washington service was practical. He also came up with the revolutionary notion that the planes would fly "every hour on the hour": New York to Washington round trip was twenty-three dollars. When the Ludingtons insisted that costs be kept to a minimum, Gene, ever ingenious, said, "We'll operate at forty cents a mile, taking only a livable salary. Anything under forty cents, we'll agree to take in stock." The Ludingtons were charmed.

In September 1930, the Ludington Line began regular service. Tickets were sold in railway terminals. Gene personally built the first counter in Washington, using two crates with a board across. Everything was ad hoc. On one occasion, in Philadelphia, passengers from New York to Washington were stretching their legs while passengers from Washington to New York were doing the same. Then each group was shepherded into the wrong plane and the passengers to Washington went back to New York and those to New York back to Washington.

What to serve for lunch? My mother, always dieting, decided that consommé was bound to be popular. Fortunately, in those less litigious times, the first batch of badly scalded passengers gallantly did not sue. Later, hard-boiled eggs and saltine crackers made the sort of lunch that stayed down longest. As the passengers dined, and the plane lurched, and the smell of exhaust filled the cabin, cylindrical cardboard ice-cream containers were tactfully passed around. The fact that what was supposed to contain ice cream was used, instead, for vomit was my first metaphysical experience, an intimation of the skull beneath the skin. During the Second War, as first mate of an army ship in the Aleutians, I would grimly stuff our shaky passengers with crackers and hard-boiled eggs; and it is true: They do stay down longest.

At the end of the first year, the Ludington Line showed the profit duly noted by *Time.* As organizer and general manager, my father persuaded Amelia Earhart to become a vice president; he also hired Felix Du Pont to be the agent in Washington. He persuaded Herbert Hoover to light up the Washington monument at dusk because, sooner or later, a plane was bound to hit it. On the other hand, he ignored the mandatory fire drills at the Washington terminal on the sensible ground that "We have a real fire," as one of his mechanics put it, "most every day." Between New York and Washington, he put up twenty-four billboards. Slowpoke passengers on the Pennsylvania railroad could read, at regular intervals, "If you'd flown Ludington, you'd have been there." Were it not for Hoover socialism, so successful and busy a passenger airline would have got a mail contract. But Postmaster General Brown chose to give the franchise to Eastern Air Transport, who were eager to carry the mail at eighty-nine cents a mile versus Ludington's twenty-five cents. But that has always been the American way; who dares question it? The Ludingtons lost heart; and in February 1933 they sold out to Eastern—even though Hoover socialism had been rejected at the polls and there was now a new president, eager to restore prosperity with classic capitalistic measures.

Franklin Roosevelt was something of an aviation freak and, thanks in part to some backstage maneuvering on the part of Amelia Earhart and her friend Eleanor Roosevelt, Eugene L. Vidal became the director of the Bureau of Air Commerce at the age of thirty-eight. He was a popular figure not only in aviation circles but with the press. Henry Ladd Smith wrote: "Gene Vidal had fared so badly at the hands of Postmaster General Brown and the Republican administration that there was a certain poetic justice in his appointment. . . ." But Smith felt that there was more honor than power in the job. The bureau was divided into three parts and Vidal "had all the responsibilities that go with the title, but few of the powers. Unhappy Mr. Vidal took all the blame for mistakes, but he had to share credit with his two colleagues. . . ." I don't think Gene felt all that powerless, although he certainly took a good deal of blame. Mainly he was concerned with, in Mr. Corn's words,

> the dream of wings for all . . . in November 1933 [he] announced that the government would soon spend half a million dollars to produce a "poor man's airplane." The machine would sell for $700. . . . He planned to launch the project with a grant from Harold Ickes's Public Works Administration (PWA), one of the numerous government agencies established in the depression to battle unemployment.

Although a lot of out-of-work engineers and craftsmen would be employed, Ickes saw nothing public in private planes, and Gene was obliged to use his power to buy planes for the bureau's inspectors. He ordered five experimental prototypes. The results were certainly unusual. There was one plane whose wings could be folded up; you could then drive it like an automobile. Although nothing came of this hybrid, its overhead rotor was the precursor of the helicopter, still worshiped as a god by the Vietnamese. Finally, there was the Hammond Y-1, which I was to fly.

Along with the glamor of flight, there was the grim fact that planes often crashed and that the bodies of the passengers tended to be unpretty, whether charred or simply in pieces strewn across the landscape. Knute Rockne, Grace Moore, Carole Lombard died; and at least half of the people I used to see in my childhood would, suddenly, one day, not be there. "Crashed" was the word; nothing more was said. As director, Gene was obliged to visit the scenes of every major accident, and he had gruesome tales to report. One survivor sued the bureau because the doctor at the scene of the accident refused to replace in his scrotal sac the testicles that lay nearby.

In 1934 the Democratic senator Hugo Black chaired a Senate committee to investigate the former Republican postmaster general Brown's dealings with the airlines. Black's highly partisan committee painted Brown even darker than he was. Yes, he had played favorites in awarding mail contracts but no one could prove that he—or the Grand Old Party—had in any specific way profited. Nevertheless, Jim Farley, the new postmaster general, charged Brown with "conspiracy and collusion" while the president, himself a man of truly superhuman vindictiveness, decided to punish Brown, the Republican party, and the colluded-with airlines.

What could be more punitive—and dramatic—than the cancellation of all U.S. airmail contracts with private companies? Since the army had flown the mail back in 1918, let them fly the mail now. The president consulted the director of Air Commerce, who told him that army flyers did not have the sort of skills needed to fly the mail. After all, he should know; he was one. Undeterred, the president turned to General Benjamin D. Foulois, the chief of the air corps, who lusted for appropriations as all air corps chiefs do; and the general said, of course, the air corps could fly the mail.

On February 9, 1934, by executive order, the president canceled all airmail contracts; and the Army flew the mail. At the end of the first week, five army pilots were dead, six critically injured, eight planes wrecked. One evening in mid-March, my father was called to the White House. As Gene pushed the president's wheelchair along the upstairs corridor, the president, his usual airy self, said, "Well, Brother Vidal, we seem to have a bit of a mess on our hands." Gene always said, "I found that 'we' pretty funny." But good soldiers covered up for their superiors. What, FDR wondered, should they do? Although my father had a deep and lifelong contempt for politicians in general ("They tell lies," he used to say with wonder, "even when they don't have to") and for Roosevelt's cheerful mendacities in particular, he did admire the president's resilience: "He was always ready to try something new. He was like a good athlete. Never worry about the last play. Only the next one." Unfortunately, before they could extricate the administration from the mess, Charles Lindbergh attacked the president; publicly, the Lone Eagle held FDR responsible for the dead and injured army pilots.

Roosevelt never forgave Lindbergh. "After that," said Gene, "he would always refer to Slim as 'this man Lindbergh,' in that condescending voice of his. Or he'd say '*your* friend Lindbergh,' which was worse." Although Roosevelt was convinced that Lindbergh's statement was entirely inspired by the airlines who wanted to get back their airmail contracts, he was too shrewd a politician to get in a shooting match with the world's most popular hero. Abruptly, on April 20, 1934, Postmaster General Farley let the airlines know that the Post Office was open to bids for mail contracts because, come May, the army would no longer fly the mail. It was, as one thoughtful observer put it, the same old crap game, with Farley not Brown as spoilsman.

In 1935, "lifelong bachelor" (as *Time* would say) Senator Bronson Cutting was killed in an air crash. He was a popular senator (survived to this day by his estimable niece, Iris Origo) and the Senate promptly investigated. My father was grilled at length.

> The bureau was accused of wasting time and money in a futile effort to develop a "flivver plane" for the masses. . . . Vidal himself did not fare so badly. The committee rebuked him mildly and reported that he appeared "lacking in iron," but since Vidal was hardly in the position to enforce orders, perhaps even this accusation was unfair.

My father's affection for politicians was not increased by the Senate hearings. But the real prince of darkness had now entered his life, Juan Trippe, and a lifelong struggle began. Even after I was grown, at the Maidstone Club in East Hampton, I used to observe the two men, who never exactly *not* spoke to each other and yet never did speak.

Juan Trippe was a smooth-looking man with very dark eyes. Grandson of a bank robber, as Gene liked to recall, Trippe had gone to Yale; got into the airline business in 1926, backed by two Yale friends, C. V. Whitney and William Rockefeller (what on earth do the rich *do* nowadays?). While Lindbergh was officially associated with my father and the Ludington Line, Slim was also being wooed by Trippe, who had acquired a small Florida—Cuba airline called Pan American. By 1931, Trippe had replaced Keys as the principal robber baron of the airways. Unlike Keys, he was wonderfully well connected socially and politically. For Pan American's original board, he managed to collect not only a Whitney but a Mellon son-in-law, David Bruce, and Robert Lehman. During Black's investigation of Brown, Trippe had been caught disguising his profits in what is now standard conglomerate procedure but in those sweet days was fraud; worse, Trippe was a Republican. But smoothness is all, and, in due course, Trippe charmed Farley and Gene; and, for a time, the sly president.

Trippe's ambitions for Pan American were worldwide. He already had

South America; he now wanted the Pacific and China, the Atlantic and Europe. But he would need considerable help from the administration to get the routes nailed securely down. Smoothly, he invited the director of the Bureau of Air Commerce to tour South America. A good time was had by all and, en route, Gene collected a number of exotic decorations from various exotic presidents. Then, back in Washington, Trippe presented Gene with a long list of requests: The guileless director explained to his recent host that the law required *competitive* bidding and that the United States, unlike old Europe, did not have "chosen instruments." Naturally, if Pan American wanted to enter in competition with other airlines . . .

Trippe took his revenge. He went to his friend William Randolph Hearst—no longer a Roosevelt enthusiast—and together they orchestrated a press campaign against Gene Vidal, Jim Farley, and FDR—in that order. It is my impression that Lindbergh may have sided with Trippe. There is a curious photograph in *The Chosen Instrument.** My father is at the center, speaking into a microphone. Trippe is smoothly obsequious to his right, while Igor Sikorsky and Lindbergh are also present. The caption: "Attending the delivery of the Sikorsky S-42 in May 1934," followed by the names of all those present except for the director, whose endorsement was the point to the photograph. Thanks in part to Trippe's inspired press campaign, Gene quit the government in 1937, and the bureau was broken up. The Civil Aeronautics Board was then created; on January 1, 1985, it, too, ended, a victim of Reaganism.

Although Trippe got most of the world, he never forgave Gene. Some years later, when my father was put up for membership in Philadelphia's Racquet Club, Trippe tried to blackball him because Gene's father's name was Felix. "A *Jewish* name," said Juan, smoothly. Those were racist days. When my father pointed out that in our section of *Romano-Rhaetia,* Felix is a common Christian name, he inadvertently revealed the family's darkest secret. Upon arrival (1848) in the Great Protestant Republic, the Roman Catholic Vidals had promptly turned Protestant. Obviously, during the Republic's high noon, no mass was worth exclusion from the Racquet Club, against whose windows were pressed so many wistful Kennedy and Lee (born Levy) noses. Recently, a journalist told me that while interviewing Trippe, he noticed the old man was reading one of my books. When the journalist told him that the author was Gene Vidal's son, Trippe shook his head with wonder. "My, my," he said. "Hard to believe, isn't it?" Oh, there were real shits in those days.

*Marylin Bender and Selig Altschul, *The Chosen Instrument* (New York: Simon and Schuster, 1982).

## 3

I have no memory of Lindbergh. But Amelia Earhart was very much a part of my life. She wrote poetry and encouraged me to write, too. She had a beautiful speaking voice, which I am sure I would have recognized during the war if she had really been, as certain fabulists believe, Tokyo Rose, a captive of the Japanese. Since she usually dressed as a boy, it was assumed that she had what were then called Sapphic tendencies. I have no idea whether or not she did but I do know that she wore trousers because she thought her legs were ugly; and if she were truly Sapphic, I doubt that she would have been so much in love with my father. She had milk-white eyelashes.

In the fall of 1936, Amelia, Gene, and I went to the Army–Navy game at West Point. On the way back, as her fans peered excitedly into our train compartment, she described how she planned to fly around the world, following, more or less, the equator. I asked her what part of the flight worried her the most. "Africa," she said. "If you got forced down in those jungles, they'd never find you." I said that the Pacific looked pretty large and wet to me. "Oh, there are always islands," she said. Then she asked Gene: "Wouldn't it be wonderful to just go off and live on a desert island?" He rather doubted it. Then they discussed just *how* you could survive; and what would you do if there was no water? and if there was no water, you would have to make a sun-still and extract salt from sea water and how was that done? As we approached Grand Central Station, I suddenly decided that I wanted a souvenir of Amelia. Shortly before she left on her flight around the world, she sent me the blue-and-white checked leather belt that she often wore. She gave my father her old watch. She also made a new will, as she usually did before a dangerous flight. She left Gene her California house, on condition that if he didn't want it (he didn't), he would give it to her mother, something she did not trust G.P., her husband, to do.*

Although my father was as fond of conspiracy theories as any other good American, he rejected most of the notions that still circulate about Amelia's last flight. Of course, he was at a disadvantage: He knew something about it. When Amelia's plane vanished on July 2, 1937, somewhere between Lae, New Guinea, and Howland Island in the Pacific—where there are all those islands—the president sent the navy to look for her. He also asked Gene to help out and act as a sort of coordinator. If Amelia had been on a spy mission for the American government, as is still believed in

*G.P. managed to suppress Amelia's final will; my father didn't inherit the California property. I don't know what became of Amelia's mother.

many quarters,* the commander in chief hadn't been told about it. Years later, Eleanor Roosevelt used to talk a lot about Amelia. When I asked her if she had ever been able to find out anything, she said no. More to the point, since Mrs. Roosevelt had been devoted to Amelia, if there *had* been a secret mission, Mrs. Roosevelt would have certainly revealed it after the war and demanded all sorts of posthumous recognition for her friend. But Mrs. Roosevelt was certain that there had been no spy mission; on the other hand, she—like my father—thought there *was* something fishy about the whole business.

Shortly before Amelia left the States, she told my father that since she would have to take a navigator with her, she was going to hire Fred Noonan, formerly Pan American's chief navigator. Gene was alarmed: Noonan was a drunk. "Take anyone but Noonan," he said. "All right then," said Amelia, "why not you?" To Gene's surprise she wasn't joking. Although Gene had recently divorced my mother and G.P. was simply Amelia's manager, Gene's affection for Amelia was not equal to her love for him. "I'm not that good a navigator," he said. She then hired Noonan, who swore he was forever off the sauce. The flight began.

From India, Amelia rang G.P. and Gene together. She reported "personnel trouble": code for Noonan's drinking. Gene advised her to stop the flight. But she chose to keep on. Amelia rang again; this time from New Guinea. "Personnel trouble" had delayed her next hop—to Howland Island. This time both Gene and G.P. told her to abandon the flight. But she thought "personnel" might be improving. She was wrong. The night before they left Lae, Noonan was drunk; worse, he had had only forty-five minutes' sleep. When they took off, he was still drunk.

Gene's theory of what happened is this: Amelia was going through a disagreeable early menopause; she deeply disliked her husband; she hated the publicness of her life and she was, at some romantic level, quite serious about withdrawing to a desert island—symbolically if not literally. Years earlier, she had made a number of conditions when she allowed G.P. to marry her. The marriage was to be, as they called it then, "open." Also, "I may have to keep some place where I can go to be by myself now and then, for I cannot guarantee to endure at all times the confinements of even an attractive cage." Finally, Gene thought it unlikely that even a navy so sublimely incompetent that, four years later, it would allow most of its fleet to be sunk at Pearl Harbor, would ever have engaged such a nervy lady to spy

*For a gorgeously off-the-wall "search" for Amelia, read *Amelia Earhart Lives,* by Joe Klaas (New York: McGraw-Hill, 1970). Apparently, in the sixties, she was alive and well and living in New Bedford; she who had so deeply hated Rye.

on Japan, while *she* would have pointed out that a pioneer circumnavigation of the globe was quite enough for one outing.

According to Gene, there were only two mysteries. One of Amelia's last radio messages was, "742 from KHAQQ: We must be on you but we cannot see you. Gas is running low. Been unable to reach you by radio. Flying at one thousand feet. One half-hour's gas left." Gene said that this was not a true report. She had a good deal more than a half-hour's gas left. Why did she lie? The second mystery was that of the radio frequency. Amelia's last message was at 8:46 A.M.; after that, some fourteen minutes passed with her frequency still coming in strong at what is known as "maximum 5." "Then," said Gene, "the frequency didn't break off, the way it does when you crash. Someone switched it off." So what happened? It was Gene's hunch that she had indeed found an island—and landed. "But what about Fred Noonan?" I asked. "He sounds even worse than G.P." Gene's response was grim: "If Amelia wanted to get rid of him, she'd have got rid of him. Hit him over the head with one of his bottles. She was like that."

Over the years, there were many stories of a white woman sighted on this or that island. The only intriguing one, according to G.P., was from a Russian sailor whose ship had passed a small island on which a white woman signaled them; she was wearing nothing except a man's drawers. "The funny thing is," said G.P. to my father, "she always wore my shorts when she flew, but I wore boxer shorts, and the sailor said this woman was wearing those new jockey shorts." Gene never told G.P. that for some years Amelia had been wearing Gene's "new jockey shorts." In any event, the ship had not stopped; and no one ever followed up.

Four years before Amelia's last flight, she and Gene started what became Northeast Airlines, with Paul Collins as president. Although Gene was never very active in the airline, he remained a director to the end of his life. According to Mr. Corn, Vidal never gave up his dream "of mass-produced personal planes, and in private life began experiments with molded plywood, a material he thought appropriate for the purpose." This is true enough, except that he also experimented, more successfully, with fiberglass. But by the time he died in 1969, the world was far too full of people even to dream of filling the skies with private planes in competition with military aircraft and the planes of those airlines, three of which he had had a hand in founding. I do know that he found modern civil aviation deeply boring; and though he shared the general ecstasy when a man got to the moon, the gospel of flight that he and Lindbergh and Earhart preached was by then a blurred footnote to the space age, where technology is all and, to the extent that there is a human aspect to space, it involves team players with the right stuff. Neil Armstrong first stepped on the moon but it was Werner von Braun and a cast of thousands who put him there. Mr. Armstrong did not fly to the moon; and for all his personal pluck and luck, he is already perceived as a footnote, a name for Trivial Pursuit.

It was different on December 17, 1934, when my father asked all the nation's pilots "to take off at 10.30 in the morning and to stay in the air for half an hour. They would thus be aloft at the precise time at which, thirty-one years earlier, Orville Wright had also been airborne. The response to Vidal's call was impressive . . . an estimated 8,000 aircraft participated in the ritual."*

Today it is marvelous indeed to watch on television the rings of Saturn close and to speculate on what we may yet find at galaxy's edge. But in the process, we have lost the human element; not to mention the high hope of those quaint days when flight would create "one world." Instead of one world, we have "star wars," and a future in which dumb, dented human toys will drift mindlessly about the cosmos long after our small planet's dead.

***The New York Review of Books***
***January 17, 1985***

*Corn, *The Winged Gospel,* p. 64.

# West Point

ON THE TABLE at which I write is a small silver mug with a square handle; it is inscribed to *Eugene L. Vidal, Jr., October 3, 1925*—a gift from the West Point football team to its mascot, which that year was not a mule but me. I drank milk from the cup for a good many years and from the look of the rim did a bit of teething on it, too.

I have no early memory of West Point. Apparently I was born in the cadet hospital on a Saturday morning because my mother had decided to stay on the post and go to a football game. I was delivered not by an obstetrician but by one Major Howard Snyder who happened to be officer of the day at the cadet hospital. Later, as surgeon general of the army, he looked after President Eisenhower ("Just indigestion, Mamie," he was reported to have said when she rang him in the middle of the night with news of the Great Golfer's first tussle with the Reaper. "Give him some bicarbonate"). More than thirty years later I visited General Snyder at his office in the basement of the White House. He recalled my birth; was still angry at my mother for not having gone to a civilian hospital; was most protective of his old friend the President. "Tough South German peasant. There's nothing at all wrong with him, you know, except this really nasty temper. That's what'll kill him." Then the inevitable question, "Why didn't *you* go to the Point?" A member of a West Point family had chosen *not* to join the Long Gray Line. Something wrong there.

At the time of my birth Eugene L. Vidal, *Sr.,* was known as Gene Vidal to the world of jocks—and to just about everybody else in the country, for in those days college athletes were like rock stars (Scott Fitzgerald's apostrophe to Princeton's Hobe Baker is plainly tribute to a god). Class of 1918 at West Point, G.V. was an All-American quarterback; he is still regarded as the best all-around athlete in the history of the Academy, moving with equal ease from track to basketball to football to rugby (learned in one afternoon); a master of every sport except the one invented by Abner Doubleday (West Point 1842). "Baseball is the favorite American sport because it's so slow," G.V. used to say. "Any idiot can follow it. And just about any idiot can play it." After graduation, he came back to the Point as football coach; he was also the first instructor in aeronautics.

Shortly after I was born, G.V. resigned from the army (he found it boring) and went into civil aviation. But, as with most West Pointers of his generation, the links between him and the Academy proved to be unbreakable. Although his disposition was ironic, his style deflationary, his eye for the idiocies of the military sharp, he took some pride in being not only a part of the history of the Point but also a sort of icon for those graduates who came to prominence in the Second War.

The Eisenhowers, Groveses, Stratemeyers, Ridgways and Taylors created the American world empire; they also gave us the peacetime draft, a garrison state, and the current military debacle in Southeast Asia. With the best will in the world (and with the blessing of their civilian masters to whom the cold war was good business), these paladins have in the quarter century since Hiroshima wasted lives and money while treating with contempt the institutions of the republic. Now the game is changing—the army, too. Currently the West Pointers are fighting for a permanent draft. Otherwise, they tell us, we will have an "unrepresentative" (i.e., black) military establishment. But these same officers never objected to the prewar army, which was redneck and every bit as dumb as the coming black army because nobody smart (black or white) is going to be an enlisted man in the American army if he can help it.

I was less than a year old when my parents moved into the Washington house of my mother's father, Senator T. P. Gore (where I was put to bed in a bureau drawer). Like a number of high-powered cadets Gene Vidal was hypergamous. Yet, as a boy growing up in Madison, South Dakota, he was not particularly ambitious, as far as one can tell—which is not much: he had no memory for the past, his own or that of the family. He was so vague, in fact, that he was not certain if his middle initial "L" stood for Louis, as he put on my birth certificate, or for Luther. It was Luther. At fourteen I settled the confusion by taking my grandfather's name Gore.

As it turned out, the congressman from South Dakota was ambitious enough for two. After watching G.V. play football at the University of South Dakota, the congressman said, "How would you like an appointment to West Point?" "And where," answered my father with his usual charm and inability to dissemble, "is West Point? And what is there?" He was promptly appointed; thus ended his dream of becoming a barber because barbers seemed to have a lot of free time. Apparently in a town like Madison there was no one very interesting to emulate. Certainly G.V.'s father Felix was no model. Felix had been an engineer on whatever railroad it is that goes through South Dakota; for reasons unknown, he got off at Madison one day and went into the coal business.

Felix's father had been born in Feldkirch, Austria, of Romanic stock (descendants of the Roman legionnaires who settled Rhaetia in the first century).* A hypergamous adventurer and phony MD, Eugen Fidel Vidal married Emma de Traxler Hartmann of Lucerne, Switzerland—an heiress until she married him and got herself disinherited. "A *real* countess," my aunt used to say with wonder. In 1848 the unhappy couple came to Wisconsin where the Gräfin was promptly deserted by her husband. She brought up five children by translating American news stories for German, French, and Italian newspapers. She had every reason to be bitter; and was bitter. I go into all this family history because it has a good deal to do with the kind of men who went to West Point in those days.

Athlete. Lapsed Roman Catholic. The meager prairie background, somewhat confused by a family tradition of exciting wars (the Traxlers and Hartmanns had been professional soldiers for several hundred years). Then West Point and the companionship of men like himself. In the class three years ahead of G.V. were Bradley and Eisenhower (Ike was known as the "Swedish Jew"—my father as "Tony the Wop"); while in the class of 1918 were Mark Clark, Leslie Groves, and Lucius Clay (who once persuaded me to write a speech for his friend President Eisenhower on the virtues—if any—of integration: the speech was not delivered). Among those my father taught was the grand architect of our empire's Syracusan adventure in Southeast Asia, the Alcibiades of counterinsurgency, Maxwell Taylor.

These men had a good deal in common even before they were put into the pressure cooker on the Hudson. Most came from rural backgrounds; from lower-middle-class families; certainly they were not representative of the country's ruling class. In this century our nobles have not encouraged their sons to go to West Point. There were also no blacks at the Academy and few, if any, Jews or Roman Catholics. West Point was a very special sort of place.

According to K. Bruce Galloway and Robert Bowie Johnson, Jr. (*West*

*A certain venerable vendor of American book-chat thought it preposterous that I should claim descent from the Romans. But the Romanic Vidals were originally called Vitalis and from Trieste north to Friuli and to Vorarlberg, Roman monuments bear witness to our ubiquitousness.

*Point: America's Power Fraternity*),* "The Military Academy offers an ideology, not an education, and because of this and the uniform, the graduates find themselves anointed with access to America's ruling elite." The authors take a dark view of the Academy and its graduates, and they tend to see conspiracy where there is often only coincidence. For instance:

> By 1933 President Roosevelt had created the position of Director of Aeronautics . . . and appointed Eugene L. Vidal (W.P. 1918) as first director. Vidal had to deal immediately with the controversy over the place of aviation in—where else?—military affairs. He survived that problem, only to be faced with the airmail scandals of 1933 and 1934. . . . In the years following, West Point control of civil aeronautics lapsed only temporarily.

Galloway and Johnson would be more nearly right if they simply said that all West Pointers tend to look out for one another. In 1943 (aged seventeen) I enlisted as a private in the army and was assigned to a much publicized Training Program, which promptly collapsed. Aware that I was about to be shunted off to an infantry outfit that was soon to contribute a number of half-trained eighteen-year-olds to be butchered on the Rhine, I signaled to the nonexistent but very real West Point Protective Association. I was promptly transferred to the Air Force. I do not in the least regret this use of privilege and would do it again; but privilege comes from the Latin words meaning "private law," and even in a would-be canting democracy like ours there ought to be only public laws.

*Duty, Honor, Country.* That is the motto of West Point. It is curious that no one until recently seems to have made much of an ominous precedence that makes the nation the third loyalty of our military elite. Duty comes first. But duty to what? Galloway and Johnson are plain: the officer class. Or as a veteran instructor at the Point puts it, "In my system of values West Point comes first, the Army second, and the country comes third."

Honor. Galloway and Johnson are particularly interesting on the origins of West Point's honor system. The Academy's true founding father, Sylvanus Thayer, was a passionate admirer of Bonaparte; he also found good things in the Prussian system. Although the United States did not seem to have much need for an officer caste when he took charge of the Academy in 1817 (of course the British had burned down Washington a few years earlier but that sort of thing doesn't happen very often), Thayer set about creating a four-year hell for the young men sent to him from all over the country. They were kept constantly busy; treated like robots; given an honor system which, simply put, required them to spy on one another.

*Simon and Schuster, 1973.

This sort of system is always diabolic and usually effective, particularly in an environment like West Point where, according to Colonel L. C. West of the Judge Advocate General Corps, "at a tender age, the West Point Cadet learns that military rules are sacred and in time readily accepts them as a substitute for integrity. As he progresses through his military career, the rules remain uppermost in his code of honor. In fact, his 'honor' is entwined with the rules and so long as he obeys the rules, whatever their content, or whatever manner of man or fool may have written them, his honor is sound." This explains the ease with which these self-regarding young men whose honor is, officially, not to lie, cheat or steal (or go to the bars in Highland Falls) can with such ease cover up a massacre like My Lai or, like General Lavelle, falsify bombing reports, invent military victories in order to help one another get decorations and promotions—not to mention take bribes from those large corporations whose manufacture of expensive weaponry absorbs so much of the military budget.

Country. To the West Pointer loyalty to the United States comes after loyalty to the Academy and to himself. Over the years this lack of patriotism has not gone entirely unnoticed. In fact, ever since the Academy was founded there have been critics of Thayer's military elite and its separateness from the rest of the country. According to the third superintendent, Alden Partridge (W.P. 1806), the Academy was "monarchial, corrupt and corrupting . . . a palpable violation of the constitution and laws of the country, and its direct tendency to introduce and build up a privileged order of the very worst class—a military aristocracy—in the United States."

In 1830 Tennessee's show-biz congressman Davy Crockett introduced a bill to shut down the Academy while in 1863 another bill in Congress also proposed abolition. Speaking for the later measure, the radical Republican Senator B. F. Wade of Ohio declared: "I do not believe that there can be found on the whole face of the earth . . . any institution that has turned out as many false, ungrateful men as have emanated from this institution."

For more than a century West Pointers have returned the compliment. They do not like civilians, while their contempt for politicians is as nearly perfect as their ignorance of the institutions of the country that they are required to serve—after duty, that is; after honor. Specifically, my father's generation—the empire-makers—disliked Jews, regarded blacks as low comedy relief, politicians as corrupt, Filipinos as sly . . . still fresh in everyone's memory was the slaughter by the American army of several hundred thousand Filipinos at the beginning of the century: the largest experiment in genocide the world was to know until Hitler. The West Pointers regard only one another with true reverence.

The authors of *West Point* are particularly interesting when they discuss what goes on nowadays in the classrooms at the Academy. One of the authors graduated in 1965 and no doubt writes from personal experience. Since the teachers tend to be graduates, they often have no special knowledge of the subject they teach—nor do they need to have because each day's lesson is already prepared for them in "blocs." But then, according to General George A. Lincoln, the Academy's academic guru (and Nixon adviser): "West Point is an under-graduate scholarship school without many scholars or any great motivation for learning as far as a material proportion of each class is concerned." He seems rather pleased by this. Galloway and Johnson are not. They believe that the cadets are taught "the ability to think and reason without really being able to do so."

Boys who go to West Point today do so for a variety of reasons, none having much to do with learning. There is the romantic appeal of the Long Gray Line. There is the cozy appeal of a life in which all important decisions will be made by others. There is the attractive lure of retirement at an early age—not to mention translation to the upper echelons of those corporations which do business with the Pentagon. Simply by stepping on an escalator, the West Pointer can have the sense of duty done, of honor upheld, of country served—and self, too. It is an irresistible package. Yet an instructor at the Academy recently commented (anonymously), "The cadets at West Point are fifth rate." To which the answer must be: they are fifth-rate because that is what the system requires of them. Since they are not different from other American boys their age, their intellectual torpor is due to a system that requires loyalty and obedience above all else—two qualities that flourish most luxuriantly in the ignorant; most dangerously in the fanatic.

It is no surprise that the military elite was delighted by the anticommunist line of their civilian masters. The Truman-Acheson, Eisenhower-Dulles, Kennedy-Johnson-Rusk, Nixon-Kissinger war on commies at home and abroad was thrilling to the military. For one thing the ideals of socialism are anathema to them even though, paradoxically, the West Pointer is entirely cared for by the state from his birth in any army hospital (if he is born into a military family) to taps at government expense in a federal boneyard. Yet the West Pointer takes this coddling as his due and does not believe that a steel worker, say, ought to enjoy privileges that belong rightfully to the military elite. Retired officers are particularly articulate on this point, and their passionate letters supporting the AMA's stand against socialized medicine are often as not written from government-paid private rooms at Walter Reed.

The cold war also meant vast military appropriations for weapons. One of the few American traditions (almost as venerable as the Warner Brothers Christmas layoff) is the secretary of defense's annual warning to Congress at budget time. Since his last request for money, the diabolical Reds are once again about to pass us—or have passed us—in atomic warheads, cutlery, missiles, saddles, disposable tissues. Distraught, Congress immediately responds to this threat with as many billions of dollars as the military feel they need to defend freedom and human dignity for all men everywhere regardless of color or creed—with the small proviso that important military installations and contracts be located in those areas whose representatives enjoy seniority in Congress.

In this fashion, two thirds of the nation's federal income has been spent for more than a generation in order that the congressmen who give the generals the money they ask for will then be re-elected with money given *them* by the corporations that were awarded federal money by generals who, when they retire, will go to work for those same corporations. Beautifully, both nation and self are served because the commies are rats, aren't they? Particularly the home-grown ones.

Just before the Second War, I listened several times to Air Force generals discuss with a humor that soon turned into obsession the ease with which the White House could be seized, the Congress sent home, and the nation kept out of the war that the Jew Franklin D. Rosenfeld was trying to start against Hitler. Although Hitler was a miserable joker (and probably a crypto-Jew), he was doing our work for us by killing commies. I do not think this sort of thinking is by any means dead today. I once asked Fletcher Knebel what gave him the idea for his *Seven Days in May,* a lively and popular thriller about the possibility of a military coup in Washington. "Talking to Admiral Radford," he told me. "He scared me to death. I could just see the Joint Chiefs kicking Kennedy out."

The United States has now been a garrison state for thirty-two years. To justify all those billions of dollars spent, the military likes to have a small war going on somewhere in the world. Or as General Van Fleet (W.P. 1915) said with some satisfaction, "Korea has been a blessing. There has to be a Korea either here or some place in the world." And so these blessings continued to shower upon us until August 15. Has peace at last come to our restless empire? Well, several weeks ago the new secretary of defense warned Congress that the Soviet's iron fist is still powerful within that velvet glove. If this striking image does not get the money out of Congress, a military crisis in the Middle East, or a small war in Chile, say, ought to keep the money flowing in the right direction.

Galloway and Johnson are, I think, too hard on the individual shortcomings of the West Pointers. After all, if we didn't want them to be the way they are (militantly anti-communist, anti-politician, anti-dissenter) they would be different. A class of this sort is made not born. I have known a good many West Pointers of the imperial generation and found them to be men of considerable virtue though none had, I should say, much sense of the civilian world. But then how could they? Their education was fifth-rate; their lives remote from everyday cares; their duty and honor directed not toward the republic but toward one another.

For a half century now West Pointers have been taught that communism is America's number one enemy without ever being told what communism is. Paradoxically, fascist-minded Americans tend to admire the communist societies once they actually visit them. The Nixons and the Agnews particularly delight in the absence of dissent; not to mention the finality of all social arrangements. Certainly the world of Mao (less some of his subtler thoughts) is nothing but the civilian world as West Point would like it to be. And if Mao is not an admirer of elites—well, neither (officially) were the founders of the American republic, and just look what we have created. Anomalies are the stuff of political systems.

Certainly the West Pointers would approve the puritanism of the communist societies. Galloway and Johnson give a grim picture of the sexual deprivation of the cadets which, they maintain, makes for a lifetime of uneasy relations with women—not to mention "the entire company [that] once masturbated together in the showers." Life on the Hudson was even more austere in my father's day. But there were occasional mavericks. Although G.V. never much liked Eisenhower ("a sour cuss, always on the make"), he did give Ike credit for having managed, under the most perilous conditions, to lay the wife of the post dentist. Obviously *supreme* commanders are made early.

The military–industrial–West Point complex is more than a century old. One of the first functions of the Academy was to supply engineers to the nation. West Pointers built the first railroads as well as many roads and dams. Working as engineers for the early tycoons, West Pointers were brought into close contact with the business elite of the country and the result has been a long and happy marriage.

The military was also used to protect American business interests overseas. On at least one occasion the business interests tried to get the military to overthrow a president. In 1933 the Liberty League secretly approached Major General Smedley Butler and asked him to help them remove President Roosevelt. Butler turned them down flat. He also launched the most devastating attack ever made on American capitalism. Of his thirty-three years in the Marine Corps, he declared,

> I spent most of my time being a high-class muscle-man for Big Business, for Wall Street, and for the Bankers. In short, I was a racketeer, a gangster for capitalism . . . Like all members of the military profession, I never had an original thought until I left the service. . . . I helped make Mexico—and especially Tampico—safe for American

> oil interests in 1914. I decided to make Haiti and Cuba a decent place for the National City Bank boys to collect revenues in. . . .

He also lists among his fields of operations Nicaragua, the Dominican Republic, China (where the Marines protected Standard Oil's interests in 1927). Butler summed up, "Looking back on it, I feel that I might have given Al Capone a few hints. The best he could do was operate his racket in three districts. I operated on three continents."

Our military today operates on all five continents with results that no longer please anyone except those businesses that make weapons and pay for presidential elections. The final irony is that despite all the money we pour into our military establishment it probably could not win a war against anyone—except perhaps the American people. The disaster in Vietnam showed that the services could not fight a war in a primitive country against a "highly motivated" enemy. Naturally, the West Pointers blame this defeat on the commie-weirdo-fags (and/or politicians) who forced them in the President's elegant phrase, "to fight with one arm tied behind them." Whatever that meant: after all, the military were given a half-million American troops and more than 100 billion dollars to play with. Admittedly there were a few targets they were told not to bomb, like hospitals in Hanoi—or Peking or Moscow—but secretly president and generals bombed pretty much whatever they wanted to. Perhaps the generals felt betrayed because they could not use hydrogen bombs on the jungles and dikes of North Vietnam, or attack China. Yet even the bloodthirstiest of the Pentagon hawks did not want another go 'round with Chinese ground troops after the rout we suffered in Korea.

It should be noted that the American fighting man has been pretty lousy from the beginning of the republic, and more power to him. He has no desire to kill strangers or get hurt himself. He does not like to be told what to do. For him, there is neither duty nor honor; his country is his skin. This does not make for a world conqueror. In fact, according to a 1968 study of American performance in World War II and Korea, "the US side never won unless it had a 2-to-1 superiority of forces over the other side."* Shades of George Washington, who disliked taking on the British unless he was certain to outnumber them, preferably five to one. Even then, Washington's troops were usually beaten. Like the Italians, we Americans are killers for personal profit or revenge; the large-scale stuff doesn't really grip us.

Stuart H. Loory's *Defeated: Inside America's Military Machine* is an

*From "Ideology and Primary Group," a paper delivered by John Helmer to the annual meeting of the American Sociological Association on August 27, 1973.

analysis of the state of the armed forces today. If his report is true, let us hope that the Soviet military machine is in just as big a mess as ours. Loory begins with the usual but always staggering statistics. Between 1946 and 1972 five million citizens of a free republic were drafted into the "peace-time" [*sic*] armed forces. Year in, year out, two thirds of the federal budget goes to the military. Of all military expenditures by every nation in the world, the United States accounts for 27.6 percent. The army's PX system is America's third largest retailer. The Defense Department owns land equivalent in area to the state of Ohio. And so on.

But what are we getting in exchange for all this money spent? A fifth-rate "ticket punching" officer corps, according to Loory. Apparently no officer is allowed to stay in any job long enough to learn to do anything well. In order to be promoted, he must get his ticket punched: a brief time in the field, then to command school, to the Pentagon, etc. This moving about ("personnel turbulence" is the army's nice phrase) has resulted in what appears to be a near-total demoralization of the basic units of the army. Officers are shipped out just as they get to know the names of the men in their outfits, while the problems of drugs and race occupy most of the time of the commanders, particularly in Europe. Even the nuclear forces of SAC, forever guarding the free world, are in disarray. Obviously the second law of thermodynamics is in operation, and irreversible.

Mr. Loory contrasts American troops in Germany unfavorably to the soldiers of the Bundwehr. Apparently American troops are assigned to broken-down barracks and constantly oppressed with that mindless chicken shit which so appeals to the traditional "West Point mind": if you have nothing to do, police the area. The Germans, on the other hand, have modern barracks, interesting training, a good deal of freedom, and of course a stronger currency. In a nice reversal of history, the Americans are now the Prussians—in a sloppy sort of way—while the Prussians behave as if the private soldier is actually an intelligent member of the same race as his officers.

In the wake of the defeat of the American military machine in Asia and the resulting shocks to our institutions at home, a good many questions are bound to be asked about what sort of a country we want. Fatigue and lack of resources have stopped the long march from the Atlantic to the borders of China. The West Point elite have not served us well even though they have never disguised the fact that we are number three on their list of priorities. Yet even when they try to work peacefully for the country, they are often a menace. The Army Corps of Engineers has made such an ecological mess of our rivers and lakes that Justice Douglas has termed them "public enemy number one."

Not unnaturally, the West Pointers are most successful at creating miniature West Points, particularly in Latin American (though Ethiopia and several other exotic countries have been seeded with Duty, Honor, Country academies). All around the world West Pointers are turning out military elites trained to fight not wars but those who would extend democracy at home. Galloway and Johnson have a particularly fascinating chapter on the links between West Pointers and their opposite numbers in Latin America, particularly with the dictator of Nicaragua, Tachito Somoza (W.P. 1946).

Galloway and Johnson favor placing the Academy's four regiments in four different cities, making them closer to the grass roots of, say, Harlem or of San Francisco. They feel that this would in some way acquaint the cadet corps with their third loyalty. I doubt it. I agree with Davy Crockett and Senator Wade: an aristocratic military elite is deeply contrary to the idea of this republic and its constitution. Since the next great war will be fought by computers and by highly trained technicians, we have no need of a peacetime army of two million or even of two hundred thousand. Certainly a large army controlled by the West Point elite will continue, as it has done for nearly a quarter century, to squander money and create wars.

Forgetting the morality of a republic trying to be an empire, we now lack the material resources to carry on in the old way (LBJ ran out of bombs one afternoon downstairs in his war room; later, Nixon was to run out of kerosene for his bombers). What money we have would be better used for internal improvements, in Henry Clay's phrase. After all, the two most successful nations in the world today are Japan and Germany—and neither has much of a military establishment. This simple lesson ought to be plain to America's capitalists; yet many of our magnates are as bemused by military grandeur as any plebe, misty-eyed at the thought of the Long Gray Line and by the resonant self-aggrandizing rhetoric the late Douglas MacArthur used so successfully to peddle.

Self-delusion is a constant in human affairs. Certainly without self-delusion on the grandest scale we could never have got into our present situation; and West Point has certainly made its contribution. But reality has never been West Point's bag. According to George A. Custer (W.P. 1861), "The Army is the Indian's best friend." While according to West Point's current version of what happened in Vietnam, "The War . . . ended in August of 1968 when sorely battered Communist troops were unable to engage the allied war machine." With historians like that who needs generals?

There is also mounting evidence that today's soldier will not endure much longer West Point's traditional oppression. John Helmer's thesis in "Ideology and Primary Group" makes this pretty plain. According to Helmer, the division between the West Point officer class and today's working-class soldier is now almost unbridgeable. Since middle-class men were able to stay out of the worst of the Vietnam war, the working class provided the combat troops. They quickly got the point that "in the search and destroy tactics most commonly used [the infantryman] was, strictly speaking, the bait to catch the enemy. According to the plan he was intended to be a target, a sitting duck for the other side to attack at its ultimate cost."

The same cynical use of men is at work in Europe, where working-class American troops are, if not exactly bait, political hostages to ensure a "proper" American response in case of a Soviet strike. These men don't have to be good soldiers; they don't have to be anything but on the spot. It does not take great prescience, however, to know that should a Soviet army ever occupy Paris, the United States would abandon its own troops as swiftly as it would its allies. The American empire is not about to lose a single of its cities to save all Europe—much less three hundred thousand fuck-ups (in the eyes of the West Point elite) with their drugs, their brawling, their fragging of officers whom they regard as an alien and hostile class.

Today the first order of business in the United States is the dismantling of the military machine. Obviously, we must continue to make it disagreeable for anyone who might decide to attack us (this could be done of course by not provoking other nations but that is too much to ask). Nevertheless the military budget must be cut by two thirds; and the service academies phased out.

What to do with the officer corps? That is a delicate point. West Pointers are now more and more into politics and, as always, they are on the side of reaction. Their web of connections with the military academies they have created in Latin America, Asia, and Africa makes them truly international. Also their creations may give them dangerous ideas. It is not inconceivable that a coup of the sort that General Butler refused to lead might one day prove attractive to a group of the Honor, Duty, Country boys. Let us hope that Richard Nixon never asks General Haig (W.P. 1947) to send home Congress and Supreme Court so that the sovereign might get on with the country's true business, which is the making of armaments and small wars. Finding suitable employment for our officer caste will be, as they say, a challenge.

I look guiltily at the silver cup, and think of the generals who gave it to me. On a bright day in May four years ago I stood beside my uncle, General F. L. Vidal (W.P. 1933), at the edge of an Air Force runway near Washington, D.C. Awkwardly, my uncle held what looked to be a shoebox. "It's *heavy,*" he muttered in my ear. I shuddered. Like the contents of the box (my father's ashes), I am a lifelong thanatophobe. Behind us stood a dozen of G.V.'s classmates. Among them the solemn, pompous, haggard Leslie

Groves—himself to die a few months later; and that handsome figure of the right wing, General Wedemeyer.

After the helicopter departed on its mission, the old generals of the empire commiserated with one another. The icon of their generation, the lovely athlete of a half century before, was now entirely gone, ashes settling upon the Virginia countryside. The generals looked dazed; not so much with grief as with a sense of hurt at what time does to men, and to their particular innocence. Although I have always found poignant (yes, even honorable) the loyalty of West Pointers to one another, I could not help thinking as I walked away from them for the last time that the harm they have done to this republic and to the world elsewhere far outweighs their personal excellence, their duty, their honor. But then the country that they never understood was always last in their affections and so the first of their loyalties to be betrayed.

*The New York Review of Books*
*October 18, 1973*

# The Twelve Caesars

TIBERIUS, CAPRI. Pool of water. Small children . . . So far so good. One's laborious translation was making awful sense. Then . . . Fish. Fish? The erotic mental image became surreal. Another victory for the Loeb Library's sly translator, J. C. Rolfe, who, correctly anticipating the prurience of schoolboy readers, left Suetonius' gaudier passages in the hard original. One failed to crack those intriguing footnotes not because the syntax was so difficult (though it was not easy for students drilled in military rather than civilian Latin) but because the range of vice revealed was considerably beyond the imagination of even the most depraved schoolboy. There was a point at which one rejected one's own translation. Tiberius and the little fish, for instance.

Happily, we now have a full translation of the text, the work of Mr. Robert Graves, who, under the spell of his Triple Goddess, has lately been retranslating the classics. One of his first tributes to her was a fine rendering of *The Golden Ass;* then Lucan's *Pharsalia;* then the *Greek Myths,* a collation aimed at rearranging the hierarchy of Olympus to afford his Goddess (the female principle) a central position at the expense of the male. (Beware Apollo's wrath, Graves: the "godling" is more than front man for the "Ninefold Muse-Goddess.") Now, as a diversion, Mr. Graves has given us *The Twelve Caesars* of Suetonius in a good, dry, no-nonsense style; and, pleasantly enough, the Ancient Mother of Us All is remarkable only by her absence, perhaps a subtle criticism of an intensely masculine period in history.

Gaius Suetonius Tranquillus—lawyer and author of a dozen books, among them *Lives of Famous Whores* and *The Physical Defects of Mankind* (What was that about?)—worked for a time as private secretary to the Emperor Hadrian. Presumably it was during this period that he had access to the imperial archives, where he got the material for *The Twelve Caesars,* the only complete book of his to survive. Suetonius was born in A.D. 69, the year of the three Caesars Galba, Otho, Vitellius; and he grew up under the Flavians: Vespasian, Titus, Domitian, whom he deals with as contemporaries. He was also close enough in time to the first six Caesars to have known men who knew them intimately, at least from Tiberius on, and it is this place in time which gives such immediacy to his history.

Suetonius saw the world's history from 49 B.C. to A.D. 96 as the intimate narrative of twelve men wielding absolute power. With impressive curiosity he tracked down anecdotes, recording them dispassionately, despite a somewhat stylized reactionary bias. Like his fellow historians from Livy to the stuffy but interesting Dion Cassius, Suetonius was a political reactionary to whom the old Republic was the time of virtue and the Empire, implicitly, was not. But it is not for his political convictions that we read Suetonius. Rather, it is his gift for telling us what we want to know. I am delighted to read that Augustus was under five feet seven, blond, wore lifts in his sandals to appear taller, had seven birthmarks and weak eyes; that he softened the hairs of his legs with hot walnut shells, and liked to gamble. Or to learn that the droll Vespasian's last words were: "Dear me, I must be turning into a god." ("Dear me" being Graves for *"Vae."*) The stories, true or not, are entertaining, and when they deal with sex, startling, even to a post-Kinseyan.

Gibbon, in his stately way, mourned that of the twelve Caesars only Claudius was sexually "regular." From the sexual opportunism of Julius Caesar to the sadism of Nero to the doddering pederasty of Galba, the sexual lives of the Caesars encompassed every aspect of what our post-medieval time has termed "sexual abnormality." It would be wrong, however, to dismiss, as so many commentators have, the wide variety of Caesarean sensuality as simply the viciousness of twelve abnormal men. They were, after all, a fairly representative lot. They differed from us—and their contemporaries—only in the fact of power, which made it possible for each to act out his most recondite sexual fantasies. This is the psychological fascination of Suetonius. What will men so placed do? The answer, apparently, is anything and everything. Alfred Whitehead once remarked that one got the essence of a culture not by those things which were said at the time but by those things which were *not* said, the underlying assumptions of the society, too obvious to be stated. Now, it is an underlying assumption of twentieth-century America that human beings are either heterosexual or, through some arresting of normal psychic growth, homosexual, with very little traffic back and forth. To us, the norm is heterosexual; the family is central; all else is deviation, pleasing or not depending on one's own tastes and moral preoccupations. Suetonius reveals a very different world. His underlying assumption is that man is bisexual and that given complete freedom to love—or, perhaps more to the point in the case of the Caesars, to violate—others, he will do so, going blithely from male to female as fancy dictates. Nor is Suetonius alone in this assumption of man's variousness. From Plato to the rise of Pauline Christianity, which tried to put the lid on sex, it is explicit in classical writing. Yet to this day Christian, Freudian and Marxian commentators have all decreed or ignored this fact of nature in the interest each of a patented approach to the Kingdom of Heaven. It is an odd experience for a contemporary to read of Nero's simultaneous passion for both a man and a woman. Something seems wrong. It must be one or the other, not both. And yet this sexual eclecticism recurs again and again. And though some of the Caesars quite obviously preferred women to men (Augustus had a particular penchant for Nabokovian nymphets), their sexual crisscrossing is extraordinary in its lack of pattern. And one suspects that despite the stern moral legislation of our own time other human beings are no different. If nothing else, Dr. Kinsey revealed in his dogged, arithmetical way that we are all a good deal less predictable and bland than anyone had suspected.

One of the few engaging aspects of the Julio-Claudians was authorship. They all wrote; some wrote well. Julius Caesar, in addition to his account of that famed crusade in Gaul, wrote an *Oedipus.* Augustus wrote an *Ajax,* with some difficulty. When asked by a friend what his *Ajax* had been up to lately, Augustus sighed: "He has fallen not on his sword, but wiped himself out on my sponge." Tiberius wrote an *Elegy on the Death of Julius Caesar.* The scatterbrained Claudius, a charmingly dim prince, was a devoted pedant who tried to reform the alphabet. He was also among the first to have a serious go at Etruscan history. Nero of course is remembered as a poet. Julius Caesar and Augustus were distinguished prose writers; each preferred plain old-fashioned Latin. Augustus particularly disliked what he called the "Asiatic" style, favored by, among others, his rival Marc Antony, whose speeches he found imprecise and "stinking of farfetched phrases."

Other than the fact of power, the twelve Caesars as men had little in common with one another. But that little was significant: a fear of the knife in the dark. Of the twelve, eight (perhaps nine) were murdered. As Domitian remarked not long before he himself was struck down: "Emperors are necessarily wretched men since only their assassination can convince the public that the conspiracies against their lives are real." In an understandable attempt to outguess destiny, they studied omens, cast horoscopes, and analyzed dreams (they were ingenious symbolists, anticipating Dr. Freud, himself a Roman buff). The view of life from Palatine Hill was not comforting, and though none of the Caesars was religious in our sense of the word, all inclined to the Stoic. It was Tiberius, with characteristic bleakness, who underscored their dangerous estate when he declared that it was Fate, not the gods, which ordered the lives of men.

Yet what, finally, was the effect of absolute power on twelve representative men? Suetonius makes it quite plain: disastrous. Caligula was certifiably mad. Nero, who started well, became progressively irrational. Even the stern Tiberius' character weakened. In fact, Tacitus, in covering the same period as Suetonius, observes: "Even after his enormous experience of public affairs, Tiberius was ruined and transformed by the violent influence of absolute power." Caligula gave the game away when he told a critic, "Bear in mind that I can treat anyone exactly as I please." And that cruelty which is innate in human beings, now given the opportunity to use others as toys, flowered monstrously in the Caesars. Suetonius' case history (and it is precisely that) of Domitian is particularly fascinating. An intelligent man of some charm, trained to govern, Domitian upon succeeding to the Principate at first contented himself with tearing the wings off flies, an infantile pastime which gradually palled until, inevitably, for flies he substituted men. His favorite game was to talk gently of mercy to a nervous victim; then, once all fears had been allayed, execute him. Nor were the Caesars entirely unobjective about their bizarre position. There is an oddly revealing letter of Tiberius to the Senate which had offered to ensure in advance ratification of all his future deeds. Tiberius declined the offer: "So long as my wits do not fail me, you can count on the consistency of my behavior; but I should not like you to set the precedent of binding yourselves to approve a man's every action; for what if something happened to alter that man's character?" In terror of their lives, haunted by dreams and omens, giddy with dominion, it is no wonder that actual insanity was often the Caesarean refuge from a reality so intoxicating.

The unifying *Leitmotiv* in these lives is Alexander the Great. The Caesars were fascinated by him. The young Julius Caesar sighed enviously at his tomb. Augustus had the tomb opened and stared long at the conqueror's face. Caligula stole the breastplate from the corpse and wore it. Nero called his guard the "Phalanx of Alexander the Great." And the significance of this fascination? Power for the sake of power. Conquest for the sake of conquest. Earthly dominion as an end in itself: no Utopian vision, no dissembling, no hypocrisy. I knock you down; now *I* am king of the castle. Why should young Julius Caesar be envious of Alexander? It does not occur to Suetonius to explain. He assumes that *any* young man would like to conquer the world. And why did Julius Caesar, a man of first-rate mind, want the world? Simply, to have it. Even the resulting Pax Romana was not a calculated policy but a fortunate accident. Caesar and Augustus, the makers of the Principate, represent the naked will to power for its own sake. And though our own society has not much changed from the Roman (we may point with somber pride to Hitler and Stalin), we have, nevertheless, got so into the habit of dissembling motives, of denying certain dark constants of human behavior, that it is difficult to find a reputable American historian who will acknowledge the crude fact that a Franklin Roosevelt, say, wanted to be President merely to wield power, to be famed and to be feared. To learn this simple fact one must wade through a sea of evasions: history as sociology, leaders as teachers, bland benevolence as a motive force, when finally, power *is* an end to itself, and the instinctive urge to prevail the most important single human trait, the necessary force without which no city was built, no city destroyed. Yet many contemporary sociologists and religionists turned historians will propose, quite seriously: If there had not been a Julius Caesar then the *Zeitgeist* would have provided another like him, even though it is quite evident that had this particular Caesar not existed no one would have dared invent him. World events are the work of individuals whose motives are often frivolous, even casual. Had Claudius not wanted an easy conquest so that he might celebrate a triumph at Rome, Britain would not have been conquered in A.D. 44. If Britain had not been colonized in the first century . . . the chain of causality is plain.

One understands of course why the role of the individual in history is instinctively played down by a would-be egalitarian society. We are, quite naturally, afraid of being victimized by reckless adventurers. To avoid this we have created the myth of the ineluctable mass ("other-directedness") which governs all. Science, we are told, is not a matter of individual inquiry but of collective effort. Even the surface storminess of our elections disguises a fundamental indifference to human personality: if not this man, then that one; it's all the same; life will go on. Up to a point there is some virtue in this; and though none can deny that there is a prevailing grayness in our placid land, it is certainly better to be non-ruled by mediocrities than enslaved by Caesars. But to deny the dark nature of human personality is not only fatuous but dangerous. For in our insistence on the surrender of private will ("inner-directedness") to a conception of the human race as some sort of virus in the stream of time, unaffected by individual deeds, we have been made vulnerable not only to boredom, to that sense of meaninglessness which more than anything else is characteristic of our age, but vulnerable to the first messiah who offers the young and bored some splendid prospect, some Caesarean certainty. That is the political danger, and it is a real one.

. . .

Most of the world today is governed by Caesars. Men are more and more treated as things. Torture is ubiquitous. And, as Sartre wrote in his preface to Henri Alleg's chilling book about Algeria, "Anybody, at any time, may equally find himself victim or executioner." Suetonius, in holding up a mirror to those Caesars of diverting legend, reflects not only them but ourselves: half-tamed creatures, whose great moral task it is to hold in balance the angel and the monster within—for we are both, and to ignore this duality is to invite disaster.

*1952*
*(published in* **The Nation**, *1959)*

# The Birds and the Bees

RECENTLY, while assembling forty years of bookchat, I noted with some alarm—even guilt—that I had never really explained sex. True, I have demonstrated that sex is politics and I have noted that the dumb neologisms, homo-sexual and hetero-sexual, are adjectives that describe acts but never people. Even so, I haven't spelled the whole thing out. So now, before reading skills further atrophy, let me set the record straight, as it were.

First, the bad news: Men and women are *not* alike. They have different sexual roles to perform. Despite the best efforts of theologians and philosophers to disguise our condition, there is no point to us, or to any species, except proliferation and survival. This is hardly glamorous, and so to give Meaning to Life, we have invented some of the most bizarre religions that . . . alas, we have nothing to compare ourselves to. We are biped mammals filled with red sea water (reminder of our oceanic origin), and we exist to reproduce until we are eventually done in by the planet's changing weather or a stray meteor.

Men and women are dispensable carriers, respectively, of seeds and eggs; programmed to mate and die, mate and die, mate and die. One can see why "love" was invented by some artist who found depressing the dull mechanics of our mindless mission to be fruitful and multiply.

Apparently, the first human societies were tribal—extended families. Then the prenuclear family was invented. Skygods were put in place—jealous ones, too. The monotheistic religions from which we continue to suffer are fiercely grounded on the only fact that we can be certain of: Man plus Woman equals Baby. This, for many, is *the* Natural Law. Inevitably, if unnaturally, natural lawyers thought up marriage and monogamy and then, faced with the actual nature of the male and the female, they created numerous sexual taboos in order to keep the population in line so that the senior partners in the earthly firm could keep the rest of us busy building expensive pyramids to the glory of the Great Lawyer in the Sky.

But as a certain Viennese novelist and classics buff, Sigmund ("It's all in the vagina, dear") Freud, noted, all those fierce do's and don'ts have created discontents, not to mention asthma and date rape. In fact, everything that the Book (from which come Judaism, Christianity, Islam) has to say about sex is wrong. Of course, practically everything the Book has to say about everything else, including real estate, is wrong too, but today's lesson is sex.

The male's function is to shoot semen as often as possible into as many women (or attractive surrogates) as possible, while the female's function is to be shot briefly by a male in order to fertilize an egg, which she will lay nine months later. Although there is nothing anywhere in the male psyche that finds monogamy natural or normal (the scientific search for monogamous, exclusively heterosexual mammals has been sadly given up, while our feathery friends—those loving doves, too—have let the natural lawyers down), the monogamous concept is drilled into the male's head from birth because, in the absence of those original tribal support systems that we discarded for the Book, someone must help the woman during gravidity and the early years of baby rearing.

If one starts with the anatomical difference, which even a patriarchal Viennese novelist was able to see was destiny, then one begins to understand why men and women don't get on very well within marriage, or indeed in any exclusive sort of long-range sexual relationship. *He* is designed to make as many babies as possible with as many different women as he can get his hands on, while *she* is designed to take time off from her busy schedule as astronaut and role model to lay an egg and bring up the result. Male and female are on different sexual tracks, and that cannot be changed by the Book or any book. Since all our natural instincts are carefully perverted from birth, it is no wonder that we tend to be, if not all of us serial killers, killers of our own true nature.

It is a fact that, like any species, our only function is replication. It is a fact that even the dullest and most superstitious of us now suspects that we may have overdone the replicating. Five and a half billion people now clutter a small planet built for two. Simply to maintain the breeders in the United States we have managed to poison all our water. Yes, *all* of it. When I was told this by a member of the Sierra Club, I asked, so what do we drink? And he said, well, some of it's less poisoned than the rest. Despite the fulminations of the Sky Lawyer's earthly representatives, some effort is being made to limit population. But the true damage is already done, and I would not bet the farm on our species continuing in rude health too far into the next century. Those who would outlaw abortion, contraception and same-sex while extolling the family and breeding are themselves the active agents of the destruction of our species. I would be angrier if I had a high opinion of the species, but I don't, and so I regard with serenity Pope and Ayatollah as the somehow preprogrammed agents of our demise, the fate of every species. Hordes of furious lemmings are loose among us; and who would stay them, particularly if they have the Book to throw?

But while we are still here, I suggest a change in attitude among those few capable of rational thought. Let us accept the demonstrable fact that the male has no exclusive object in his desire to shoot. Instead of hysteria, when he wants to shoot with another shootist, he should be encouraged in an activity that will not add another consumer to the population. The woman who decides not to lay that egg should be encouraged, if so minded, to mate with another woman. As it is, a considerable portion of the population, despite horrendous persecution, does just that, and they should be considered benefactors by everyone, while the breeders must be discouraged though, of course, not persecuted.

*The Day America Told the Truth* is a recent book in which a cross section of the population expressed its ignorance on many issues and confessed to some of its most dreadful deeds and reveries. Since 91 percent of the population admit to telling lies habitually, I can't think why the authors should take too seriously the lies new-minted for them; but then lies often illustrate inadvertent truths. A majority of men and women like oral sex (as the passive partner, presumably). Next in popularity was sex with a famous person. Plainly being blown by George or Barbara Bush would be the ultimate trip for our huddled masses.

Although the authors list twenty-three sexual fantasies (such as sex in a public—pubic?—place), they do not ask about same-sex fantasies, which tells us where they are, as we say in pollster land, coming from. But in what people do do, they report that 17 percent of the men and 11 percent of the women practice same-sex. This strikes me as low—even mendacious. It is true that in the age of AIDS both sexes are very nervous about same-sex or even other-sex, but not, surely, in experimental youth. In the prewar Southern town of Washington, D.C., it was common for boys to have sex with one another. It was called "messing around," and it was no big deal. If the boy became a man who kept on messing around, it was thought a bit queer—sexual exclusivity *is* odd and suggests obsession—but no big deal as long as he kept it quiet. If he didn't, our natural lawyers would do their best to deprive him of his inalienable rights. In any case, I don't think the folks have changed all that much since 1948, when 37 percent of the men told Dr. Kinsey that they had messed around in those years.

Certainly, women today are more candid about their preference for other women. Although this "preference" has been noted for millenniums, it was thought by shootists to be simply a coming together of two unhappy wives for mutual solace. Instead, there seems to have been a strong sexual element all along. But then a pair of egg-layers will have more in common (including a common genetic programming for nurturing) than they will ever have with a shootist, who wants to move on the second he's done his planting—no nurturing for him, no warm, mature, caring relationship. He isn't built for it. His teats may have a perky charm but they are not connected to a dairy. He can fake a caring relationship, of course, but at great cost to his own nature, not to mention battered wife and abused little ones. The fact that couples may live together harmoniously for decades is indeed a fact, but such relationships are demonstrations not of sexuality but of human comity—I dare not use the word "love," because the 91 percent who habitually lie do so about love.

Unfortunately, the propaganda to conform is unrelenting. In a charming fable of a movie, *Moonstruck,* a middle-aged woman discovers that her husband is having an affair with another woman. As the wife is a loving, caring, warm, mature person in love with her husband, why on earth would he stray from her ancient body, which is ever-ready to receive his even greater wreck of a biped? Why do men chase women? Why do they want more than one woman? She asks everyone in sight and no one can think of an answer until she herself does: *Men fear death,* she says—something that, apparently, women never do. Confronted with this profound insight, the husband stops seeing the other woman. Whether or not he loses the fear of death is unclear. This is really loony. It is true that sex/death are complementary: No sex, no birth for the unlucky nonamoeba; once born, death—that's our ticket. Meanwhile, fire at will.

When people were few and the environment was hostile, it is understandable that we should have put together a Book about a Skygod that we had created in our own image—a breathtaking bit of solipsism, but why not? The notion is comforting, and there were no Book reviewers at the time of publication, while later ones, if they wrote bad Book reviews, were regularly condemned to death by natural lawyers employing earthly hit men, as Salman Rushdie can testify. Then our Skygod told us to multiply in a world that he had put together just for us, with dominion over every living thing. Hence the solemn wrecking of a planet that, in time, will do to us what we have done to it.

Meanwhile, "the heterosexual dictatorship," to use Isherwood's irritable phrase, goes on its merry way, adding unwanted children to a dusty planet while persecuting the virtuous nonbreeders. Actually, the percentage of the population that is deeply enthusiastic about other-sex is probably not much larger than those exclusively devoted to same-sex—something like 10 percent in either case. The remaining 80 percent does this, does that, does nothing; settles into an acceptable if dull social role where the husband dreams of Barbara Bush while pounding the old wife, who lies there, eyes shut, dreaming of Barbara too. Yes, the whole thing is a perfect mess, but my conscience is clear. I have just done something more rare than people suspect—stated the obvious.

***The Nation***
***October 28, 1991***

# Women's Liberation: Feminism and Its Discontents

EVERY SCHOOLBOY has a pretty good idea of what the situation was down at Sodom but what went on in Gomorrah is as mysterious to us as the name Achilles took when he went among women. Or was. Thanks to Eva Figes, author of *Patriarchal Attitudes,* we now know what Gomorrheans are up to. Miss Figes quotes from an eighth-century Palestinian midrash which tries to explain the real reason for the Flood (one of the better jokes in the Old Testament). Apparently passage on the Ark was highly restricted. "Some authorities say that according to God's orders, if the male lorded it over the female of his own kind, both were admitted but not otherwise."

The Founding Father had strong views on the position of woman (under the man) and one of the few mistakes he ever admitted to was the creation of Lilith as a mate for Adam. Using the same dust as his earthly replica . . . but let us hear it in his own words, rabbinically divined in the fifth century.

> Adam and Lilith never found peace together; for when he wished to lie with her, she took offense at the recumbent posture he demanded. "Why must I lie beneath you?" she asked. "I also was made from dust, and am therefore your equal." Because Adam tried to compel her obedience by force, Lilith, in a rage, uttered the magic name of God, rose into the air and left him.

The outcast Lilith is still hanging about the *Zeitgeist,* we are told, causing babies to strangle in their sleep, men to have wet dreams, and Kate Millett, Betty Friedan, Germaine Greer, and Eva Figes to write books.

The response to *Sexual Politics, Feminine Mystique,* etcetera, has been as interesting as anything that has happened in our time, with the possible exception of Richard Nixon's political career. The hatred these girls have inspired is to me convincing proof that their central argument is valid. Men do hate women (or as Germaine Greer puts it: "Women have very little idea of how much men hate them") and dream of torture, murder, flight.

It is no accident that in the United States the phrase "sex and violence" is used as one word to describe acts of equal wickedness, equal fun, equal danger to that law and order our masters would impose upon us. Yet equating sex with violence does change the nature of each (words govern us more than anatomy), and it is quite plain that those who fear what they call permissiveness do so because they know that if sex is truly freed of taboo it will lead to torture and murder because that is what *they* dream of or, as Norman Mailer puts it, "Murder offers us the promise of vast relief. It is never unsexual."

There has been from Henry Miller to Norman Mailer to Phyllis Schlafly a logical progression. The Patriarchalists have been conditioned to think of women as, at best, breeders of sons; at worst, objects to be poked, humiliated, killed. Needless to say, their reaction to Women's Liberation has been one of panic. They believe that if women are allowed parity with men they will treat men the way men have treated women and that, even they will agree, has not been very well or, as Cato the Censor observed, if woman be made man's equal she will swiftly become his master.

Patriarchalists know that women are dangerously different from men, and not as intelligent (though they have their competencies: needlework, child-care, detective stories). When a woman does show herself to be superior at, say, engineering, Freud finessed that anomaly by reminding us that since she is a bisexual, like everyone else, her engineering skill simply means that she's got a bit too much of the tomboy in her, as W. C. Fields once remarked to Grady Sutton on a similar occasion.

Women are not going to make it until the Patriarchalists reform, and that is going to take a long time. Meanwhile the current phase of the battle is intense and illuminating. Men are on the defensive, shouting names; they think that to scream "dyke" is enough to make the girls burst into tears, but so far they have played it cool. Some have even admitted to a bit of dyking now and then along with warm mature heterosexual relationships of the deeply meaningful fruitful kind that bring much-needed children into the world ("Good fucks make good babies"—N. Mailer). I love you Marion and I love you too, Marvin. The women are responding with a series of books and position papers that range from shrill to literature. In the last category one must place Eva Figes who, of the lot, is the only one whose work can be set beside John Stuart Mill's celebrated review of the subject and not seem shoddy or self-serving.

In effect, the girls are all writing the same book. Each does a quick biological tour of the human body, takes on Moses and St. Paul, congratulates Mill, savages Freud (that mistake about vaginal orgasm has cost him glory), sighs over Marx, roughs up the Patriarchalists, and concludes with pleas for child-care centers, free abortions, equal pay, and—in most cases—an end to marriage. These things seem to be well worth accomplishing. And even the enemy are now saying that of course women should be paid the same as men for the same work. On that point alone Women's Lib has already won an important battle because, until recently, the enemy was damned if a woman was going to be paid as much as he for the same job.

Figes begins her short, elegant work with an attempt to define masculine and feminine. Is there any real difference between male and female other than sexual gear? Figes admits to the systematic fluctuation of progesterone levels during the woman's menstrual cycle and pregnancy, and these fluctuations make for "moods," which stop with menopause. Yet Figes makes a most telling point when she observes that although there is little or no hormonal difference between girls and boys before puberty, by the age of four or five boys are acting in a very different manner from girls. Since there is no hormonal explanation for this, the answer is plainly one of indoctrination.

What Figes is saying and what anyone who has ever thought with any seriousness about the human estate knows is that we are, or try to be, what our society wants us to be. There is nothing innate in us that can be called masculine or feminine. We have certain common drives involving survival. Yet our drive toward procreation, oddly enough, is not as powerful as our present-day obsession with sex would lead us to believe.

Of all mammals, man is the only one who must be taught how to mate. In open societies this is accomplished through observation but in a veiled, minatory, Puritan society, sex is a dirty secret, the body shameful, and making love a guilty business, often made dreadful through plain ignorance of what to do. Yet the peripheral male and female roles are carefully taught us. A little girl is given a doll instead of a chemistry set. That she might not like dolls, might prefer a chemistry set, will be the start of a nice neurosis for her, a sense of guilt that she is not playing the part society wants her to play. This arbitrary and brutal shaping of men and women has filled the madhouses of the West, particularly today when the kind of society we still prepare children for (man outside at work, woman at home with children) is no longer the only possibility for a restless generation.

Figes quotes Lévi-Strauss. "Men do not act as members of a group, in accordance with what each feels as an individual; each man feels as a function of the way in which he is permitted or obliged to act. Customs are given as external norms before giving rise to internal sentiments, and these non-sentiment norms determine the sentiments of individuals as well as the circumstances in which they may, or must, be displayed." One sees this in our society's emphasis on what Hemingway called "grace under pressure," or that plain old-fashioned patriotism which so often means nothing more than persuading a man to kill a man he does not know. To get him to do this the society must with its full weight pervert the normal human instinct not to kill a stranger against whom he has no grudge.

This kind of conditioning is necessary for the maintenance of that acquisitive, warrior society to which we belong, a society which now appears to be cracking up in the United States, to the despair of the Patriarchalists, not to mention those financial interests whose profits depend upon the exploitation and conquest of distant lands and markets. Concentrating on social pressures, Figes has written a book concerned with those external norms "which give rise to internal sentiments, with the organization of emotions into sentiments."

For those who like to remind the girls that no woman wrote anything in the same class as *Paradise Lost* or painted anything like the Sistine Chapel or composed *Don Carlos* (in the novel the girls hold their own), Figes observes that women were not expected to do that sort of thing and so did not. It is easy for a talented boy to be a sculptor because there are other males whom he can identify with and learn from. But society does everything to discourage a girl from making the attempt; and so she stifles as best she can whatever secret yearning she might have to shape stone, and gets on with the dishes.

In recent years, however, women have begun to invade fields traditionally assigned to men. Eventually, the boys will have to face the fact that the arts and sciences are not masculine or feminine activities, but simply human ones. Incidentally, all the girls have a go at one Otto Weininger, a nineteenth-century *philosophe* who at twenty-three wrote a book to prove that women were incapable of genius, then killed himself. The girls tend unkindly to cackle over that.

Figes does the obligatory chapters on Moses and St. Paul, those proud misogynists whose words have caused so much misery down the millennia. The hatred of women that courses through both Old and New Testaments is either lunatic or a mask for something else. What were the Patriarchs so afraid of? Is Robert Graves right after all? Was there really a Great Mother cult the Patriarchs destroyed? Were the attacks on woman political in origin? to discredit the Great Mother and her priestesses? We shall never know.

Perhaps it is simply guilt. People don't like their slaves very much. Women were—and in some cases still are—slaves to men, and attempts to free slaves must be put down. Also, as Figes puts it, "Human beings have always been particularly slow to accept ideas that diminish their own absolute supremacy and importance." For men, "like all people who are privileged by birth and long tradition, the idea of sharing could only mean giving up."

According to Figes, "The rise of capitalism is the root cause of the modern social and economic discrimination against women, which came to a peak in the last century." She remarks upon the degree of equality women enjoyed in Tudor times. From Portia to Rosalind, women existed as people in their own right. But with the simultaneous rise of Puritanism and industry, woman was more and more confined to the home—when she was not exploited in the factories as a cheap source of labor. Also, the Puritan tide (now only beginning to ebb) served to remind man that woman was unclean, sinful, less than he, and the cause of his fall. It was in those years that Patriarchalism was born, emigrated to America, killed Indians, enslaved blacks, conned women with sonorous good manners to get them into the wilderness, then tried to dominate them but never quite succeeded: a woman in a covered wagon with a rifle on her lap is going to be a formidable opponent, as the American woman has proved to be, from Daisy Miller to Kate Millett (a name James would have savored, weakly changing "i" to "a").

What does the American woman want? is the plaintive cry. Doesn't she kill off her husbands with mantis-abandon, inherit the money, become a Mom to Attis-like sons, dominate primary education (most American men are "feminized" in what they would regard as the worst sense of that word by being brought up almost entirely by women and made to conform to American female values which are every bit as twisted as American male values)?

Yet the American woman who seems to have so much is still very much a victim of patriarchal attitudes—after all, she is made to believe that marriage is the most important thing in life, a sentiment peculiarly necessary to a capitalist society in which marriage is still the employer's best means of controlling the employee. The young man with a child and pregnant wife is going to do as he is told. The young man or woman on his own might not be so tractable. Now that organized religion is of little social significance, the great corporations through advertising (remember "Togetherness"?) and hiring policies favor the married, while looking with great suspicion on the bachelor who might be a Commie Weirdo Fag or a Pro-Crypto Dyke. As long as marriage (and Betty Friedan's *Feminine Mystique*) are central to our capitalism (and to its depressing Soviet counterpart) neither man nor woman can be regarded as free to be human.

"In a society where men have an overriding interest in the acquisition of wealth, and where women themselves have become a form of property, the link between sexuality and money becomes inextricable." This is grim truth. Most men buy their wives, though neither party would admit to the nature of the transaction, preferring such euphemisms as Marvin is a good provider and Marion is built. Then Marion divorces Marvin and takes him to the cleaners, and he buys with whatever is left a younger model. It is money, not sex, that Puritans want. After all, the English word for "coming" used to be "spending": you spend your seed in the woman's bank and, if the moon is right, nine months later you will get an eight-pound dividend.

Needless to say, if you buy a woman you don't want anyone else using her. To assure your rights, you must uphold all the taboos against any form of sex outside marriage. Figes draws an interesting parallel between our own society and the Mainus, as reported by Margaret Mead.

> There was such a close tie between women and property that adultery was always a threat to the economic system. These people devalued sex, were prudish, and tended to equate the sex act with the excretory functions and, perhaps most significant of all, had commercial prostitution which is rare in primitive societies.

Rousseau is briskly dealt with by the girls: his rights of man were just that, for men. He believed women "should reign in the home as a minister reigns in the state, by contriving to be ordered to do what she wants." Darwin? According to Figes, "Darwin was typically a creature of his age in seeing the class and economic struggles as a continuation of the evolutionary one." In this struggle woman was *hors de combat.* "The chief distinction in the intellectual powers of the two sexes is shown by man attaining to a higher eminence, in whatever he takes up, than woman can attain, etc." Schopenhauer found woman "in every respect backward, lacking in reason and true morality . . . a kind of middle step between the child and the man, who is the true human being."

Figes finds a link between anti-feminism and anti-Semitism. It is called Nietzsche. "Man should be trained for war and woman for the recreation of the warrior: all else is folly." Like the effeminate Jews, women subvert the warrior ideal, demanding sympathy for the poor and the weak. Hitler's reaction to this rousing philosophy has not gone unnoticed.

Like her fellow polemicists, Figes is at her most glittering with Freud . . . one almost wrote "poor Freud," as Millett calls him. Apparently Freud's gravest limitation was an inability to question the status quo of the society into which he was born. Politically, he felt that "it is just as impossible to do without control of the mass by a minority as it is to dispense with coercion in the work of civilization. For the masses are lazy and unintelligent."

To Freud, civilization meant a Spartan denial of pleasure in the present in order to enjoy solvency and power in middle age. Unhappily, the main line of Freudian psychoanalysis has served well the status quo by insisting that if one is not happy with one's lot, a better adjustment to society must be made because society is an unalterable fact, not to be trifled with or changed. Now, of course, every assumption about the rights of society as opposed to those of the individual is in question, and Freud's complacency seems almost as odd to us as his wild notion that clitoral excitement was a wicked (immature) thing in a grown woman, and the longer she resisted making the transfer from the tiny pseudo-penis to the heavenly inner space of the vagina (Erik Erikson is not in the girls' good books either) the sicker she would become.

One would like to have been a fly on the wall of that Vienna study as one woman after another tearfully admitted to an itch that would not go away, despite the kindly patriarch's attempts to get to the root of the problem. It is a nice irony that the man who said that anatomy is destiny took no trouble to learn woman's anatomy. He did *know* that the penis was the essential symbol and fact of power and primacy; otherwise (and his reasoning was circular) why would girls envy boys' having penises? Why would little boys suffer from fears of castration if they did not instinctively know that the penis is a priceless sign of God the Father, which an envious teeth-lined cunt might want to snap off? Figes's response to Freud's circle is reasonable.

> In a society not sexually repressive little boys would be unlikely to develop castration fears; in a society where all the material rewards did not go to those endowed with penises there would be no natural envy of that regalia.

The Patriarchs' counterattack is only now gathering momentum. So far Figes appears to be unknown to United Statesmen, but Millett has been attacked hereabouts with a ferocity usually reserved for major novelists. She should feel important. The two principal spokesmen to weigh in so far are Norman Mailer and Irving Howe. Mailer's answer to Millett ("The Prisoner of Sex" in *Harper's*) gave the impression of being longer than her book *Sexual Politics.* Part of this is due to a style which now resembles H. P. Lovecraft rather more than the interesting, modest Mailer of better days. Or as Emma Cockburn (excellent name for a Women's Libber) pointed out, Mailer's thoughts on sex read like three days of menstrual flow.

Mailer begins by reminding the reader who he is. This is cunning and necessary in a country with no past. We learn of marriages, children, prizes (the Nobel is almost at hand), the great novel he will one day write, the rejection of *Time*'s offer to put him on the cover which Millett then gets for, among other things, attacking him. His credits given, he counterattacks, says she writes like a tough faggot, a literary Mafiosa, calls her comrade and commissar. He then makes some excellent points on her disingenuous use of quotations from Miller and Lawrence (she has a tendency to replace those qualifying phrases which make the Patriarchs seem human with three dots).

But Mailer's essential argument boils down to the following points. Masturbation is bad and so is contraception because the whole point to sex between man and woman is conception. Well, that's what the Bible says, too. He links homosexuality with evil. The man who gives in to his homosexual drives is consorting with the enemy. Worse, not only does he betray moral weakness by not fighting those drives but he is a coward for not daring to enter into competition with other Alpha males for toothsome females. This is dizzy but at least a new thought. One of the many compliments Mailer has tendered the Patriarchs over the years is never having succumbed to whatever homosexual urges they might have had. Now, to his shock, instead of getting at least a Congressional Medal of Honor for heroism, he sees slowly descending upon his brow an unmistakable dunce cap. All that hanging about boxers, to no good end!

Finally, Mailer's attitude toward woman is pretty much that of any VFW commander in heartland America. He can never understand that a woman is not simply a creature to be used for breeding (his "awe" at the thought of her procreative function is blarney), that she is as human as he is, and that he is dangerous to her since did not the Lord thy God say, "In sorrow thou shalt bring forth children. And thy desire shall be thy husband. And he shall rule over thee." Which brings us to Figes's remark, "We cannot be iconoclasts, we cannot relinquish the old gods because so much has been sacrificed to them."

Irving Howe's tone is apoplectic. He *knows* what the relations between men and women ought to be and no Millett is going to change his mind or pervert other women if he can do anything about it—which is to write a great deal on the subject in a magazine piece called "The Middle Class Mind of Kate Millett." Astonishingly enough, the phrase "middle class" is used in a pejorative sense, not the most tactful thing to do in a middle-class country. Particularly when one is not only middle class oneself but possessed of a brow that is just this side of high.

Anyway, Howe was aroused enough to address to her a series of *ad hominem* (*ad hysteram*?) insults that are startling even by the vicious and mindless standards of New York bookchat writing. Millett is "squalid," "feckless," "morally shameful," a failed scholar, a female impersonator, and so on. But Howe is never able to take on the essential argument of the girls. Men have enslaved women, made them second-rate citizens, made them hate themselves (this to me is the worst of all . . . I'm a man's woman, says the beauty complacently, I don't like other women; meaning, I don't like myself), and now that woman is beginning to come alive, to see herself as the equal of man, Rabbi Howe is going to strike her down for impertinence, just as the good Christian knows that "it is shameful for women to speak in church."

Howe has always had an agreeable gift for literary demolition and his mind, though hardly of the first quality, is certainly good by American academic standards. But now watch him tie himself in a knot. Millett makes the point, as Figes does, that the Nazis were anti-woman and pro-family. Woman was breeder, man was warrior. Now Irving doesn't want the Nazis to be so "sensible," so much like himself. He writes:

> The comedy of all this is that Miss Millett prints, at one point, a footnote quoting from a book by Joseph Folsom. "The Nazis have always wanted to strengthen the family as an instrument of the state. *State interest is always paramount.* Germany does not hesitate to turn a husband against a wife or children against parents when political loyalty is involved." (Emphasis added.) Miss Millett prints this footnote but clearly does not understand it: otherwise she would recognize how completely it undermines her claim that in the totalitarian countries the "sexual counterrevolution" consisted in the reinforcement of the family.

This passage would make a good test question for a class in logic. Find where Howe misses or distorts the point to the Folsom footnote. Point one: the Nazis strengthened the family yet put the state first. All agreed? What does this mean? It means that, on occasion, Nazis would try to turn members of a family against one another *"when political loyalty is involved."* (Emphasis added.) O.K.? Well, class, how many people are politically subversive in any country at any time? Not many, alas; therefore Millett's point still stands that the Nazis celebrated old-time family virtues except in cases of suspected subversion.

Howe's piece is full of this sort of thing and I can only assume that his usually logical mind has been unhinged by all these unnatural girls. Howe ends with a celebration of the values of his immigrant parents in the Depression years. Apparently his mother was no more a drudge than his father (but why in a good society should either be a drudge?), and they were happy in the old-time Mosaic, St. Pauline, Freudian way, and . . . well, this hymn to tribal values was rather better sung by the judge in the movie version of *Little Murders.*

Those who have been treated cruelly will treat others cruelly. This seems to be a fact of our condition. The Patriarchs have every reason to be fearful of woman's revenge should she achieve equality. He is also faced with the nightmare (for him) of being used as a sexual object or, worse, being ignored (the menacing cloud in the middle distance is presently no larger than a vibrator). He is fighting back on every front.

Take pornography. Though female nudes have been usually acceptable in our Puritan culture, until recently the male nude was unacceptable to the Patriarchs. After all, the male—any male—is a stand-in for God, and God wears a suit at all times, or at least jockey shorts. Now, thanks to randy Lilith, the male can be shown entirely nude but, say the American censors, never with an erection. The holy of holies, the totem of our race, the symbol of the Patriarchs' victory over the Great Mother, must be respected. Also, as psychologists point out, though women are not as prone to stimulus through looking at pictures as men (is this innate or the result of conditioning?), they are more excited by pictures of the male erect than of the male at ease. And excitement of course is bad for them, gives them ideas, makes them insatiable; even the ancient Greeks, though freer in sexual matters than we, took marriage seriously. As a result, only unmarried girls could watch naked young men play because young girls ought to be able to look over a field which married women had better not know about.

Today we are witnessing the breakup of patterns thousands of years old. The patriarchal response is predictable: if man on top of woman has been the pattern for all our known history, it must be right. This of course was the same argument he made when the institution of slavery was challenged. After all, slavery was quite as old an institution as marriage. With the rejection of the idea of ownership of one person by another at the time of our Civil War, Women's Lib truly began. If you could not own a black man, you could not own a woman either. So the war began. Needless to say, the forces of reaction are very much in the saddle (in every sense), and women must fight for their equality in a system which wants to keep them in manageable family groups, buying consumer goods, raising future consumers, until the end of time—or the world's raw resources, which is rather closer at hand.

Curiously enough, not even Figes senses what is behind this new restiveness, this new desire to exist not as male or female but as human. It is very simple: we are breeding ourselves into extinction. We cannot feed the people now alive. In thirty-seven years the world's population will double unless we have the "good luck" to experience on the grandest scale famine, plague, war. To survive we must stop making babies at the current rate, and this can only be accomplished by breaking the ancient stereotypes of man the warrior, woman the breeder. The patriarchal roar is that of our tribal past, quite unsuitable, as the old Stalinists used to say, to new necessities.

Figes feels that a change in the economic system will free women (and men) from unwanted roles. I have another idea. Free the sexes first and the system will have to change. There will be no housewife to be conned into buying things she does not need. But all this is in the future. The present is the battleground, and the next voice you hear will be that of a patriarch, defending his attitudes—on a stack of Bibles.

*The New York Review of Books*
*July 22, 1971*

# Pink Triangle and Yellow Star

A FEW YEARS AGO on a trip to Paris, I read an intriguing review in *Le Monde* of a book called *Comme un Frère, Comme un Amant,* a study of "Male Homosexuality in the American Novel and Theatre from Herman Melville to James Baldwin," the work of one Georges-Michel Sarotte, a Sorbonne graduate and a visiting professor at the University of Massachusetts. I read the book, found it interesting; met the author, found him interesting. He told me that he was looking forward to the publication of his book in the United States by Anchor Press/Doubleday. What sort of response did I think he would have? I was touched by so much innocent good faith. There will be no reaction, I said, because no one outside of the so-called gay press will review your book. He was shocked. Wasn't the book serious? scholarly? with an extensive bibliography? I agreed that it was all those things; unfortunately, scholarly studies having to do with fags do not get reviewed in the United States (this was before the breakthrough of Yale's John Boswell, whose ferociously learned *Christianity, Social Tolerance and Homosexuality* obliged even the "homophobic" *New York Times* to review it intelligently). If Sarotte had written about the agony and wonder of being female and/or Jewish and/or divorced, he would have been extensively reviewed. Even a study of black literature might have got attention (Sarotte is beige), although blacks are currently something of a nonsubject in these last days of empire.

I don't think that Professor Sarotte believed me. I have not seen him since. I also have never seen a review of his book or of Roger Austen's *Playing the Game* (a remarkably detailed account of American writing on homosexuality) or of *The Homosexual as Hero in Contemporary Fiction* by Stephen Adams, reviewed at much length in England and ignored here, or of a dozen other books that have been sent to me by writers who seem not to understand why an activity of more than casual interest to more than one-third of the male population of the United States warrants no serious discussion. That is to say, no serious *benign* discussion. All-out attacks on faggots are perennially fashionable in our better periodicals.

I am certain that the novel *Tricks* by Renaud Camus (recently translated for St. Martin's Press by Richard Howard, with a preface by Roland Barthes) will receive a perfunctory and hostile response out there in bookchat land. Yet in France, the book was treated as if it were actually literature, admittedly a somewhat moot activity nowadays. So I shall review *Tricks.* But first I think it worth bringing out in the open certain curious facts of our social and cultural life.

The American passion for categorizing has now managed to create two nonexistent categories—gay and straight. Either you are one or you are the other. But since everyone is a mixture of inclinations, the categories keep breaking down; and when they break down, the irrational takes over. You *have* to be one or the other. Although our mental therapists and writers for the better journals usually agree that those who prefer same-sex sex are not exactly criminals (in most of our states and under most circumstances they still are) or sinful or, officially, sick in the head, they must be, somehow, evil or inadequate or dangerous. The Roman Empire fell, didn't it? because of the fags?

Our therapists, journalists, and clergy are seldom very learned. They seem not to realize that most military societies on the rise tend to encourage same-sex activities for reasons that should be obvious to anyone who has not grown up ass-backward, as most Americans have. In the centuries of Rome's great military and political success, there was no differentiation between same-sexers and other-sexers; there was also a lot of crossing back and forth of the sort that those Americans who *do* enjoy inhabiting category-gay or category-straight find hard to deal with. Of the first twelve Roman emperors, only one was exclusively heterosexual. Since these twelve men were pretty tough cookies, rigorously trained as warriors, perhaps our sexual categories and stereotypes are—can it really be?—false. It was not until the sixth century of the empire that same-sex sex was proscribed by church and state. By then, of course, the barbarians were within the gates and the glory had fled.

Today, American evangelical Christians are busy trying to impose on the population at large their superstitions about sex and the sexes and the creation of the world. Given enough turbulence in the land, these natural fascists can be counted on to assist some sort of authoritarian—but never,

never totalitarian—political movement. Divines from Santa Clara to Falls Church are particularly fearful of what they describe as the gay liberation movement's attempt to gain "special rights and privileges" when all that the same-sexers want is to be included, which they are not by law and custom, within the framework of the Fourteenth Amendment. The divine in Santa Clara believes that same-sexers should be killed. The divine in Falls Church believes that they should be denied equal rights under the law. Meanwhile, the redneck divines have been joined by a group of New York Jewish publicists who belong to what they proudly call "the new class" (*né arrivistes*), and these lively hucksters have now managed to raise fag-baiting to a level undreamed of in Falls Church—or even in Moscow.

In a letter to a friend, George Orwell wrote, "It is impossible to mention Jews in print, either favorably or unfavorably, without getting into trouble." But there are times when trouble had better be got into before mere trouble turns into catastrophe. Jews, blacks, and homosexualists are despised by the Christian and Communist majorities of East and West. Also, as a result of the invention of Israel, Jews can now count on the hatred of the Islamic world. Since our own Christian majority looks to be getting ready for great adventures at home and abroad, I would suggest that the three despised minorities join forces in order not to be destroyed. This seems an obvious thing to do. Unfortunately, most Jews refuse to see any similarity between their special situation and that of the same-sexers. At one level, the Jews are perfectly correct. A racial or religious or tribal identity is a kind of fact. Although sexual preference is an even more powerful fact, it is not one that creates any particular social or cultural or religious bond between those so-minded. Although Jews would doubtless be Jews if there was no anti-Semitism, same-sexers would think little or nothing at all about their preference if society ignored it. So there *is* a difference between the two estates. But there is no difference in the degree of hatred felt by the Christian majority for Christ-killers and Sodomites. In the German concentration camps, Jews wore yellow stars while homosexualists wore pink triangles. I was present when Christopher Isherwood tried to make this point to a young Jewish movie producer. "After all," said Isherwood, "Hitler killed six hundred thousand homosexuals." The young man was not impressed. "But Hitler killed six *million* Jews," he said sternly. "What are you?" asked Isherwood. "In real estate?"

Like it or not, Jews and homosexualists are in the same fragile boat, and one would have to be pretty obtuse not to see the common danger. But obtuseness is the name of the game among New York's new class. Elsewhere, I have described the shrill fag-baiting of Joseph Epstein, Norman Podhoretz, Alfred Kazin, and the Hilton Kramer Hotel. *Harper's* magazine and *Commentary* usually publish these pieces, though other periodicals are not above printing the odd exposé of the latest homosexual conspiracy to turn the United States over to the Soviet Union or to structuralism or to Christian Dior. Although the new class's thoughts are never much in themselves, and they themselves are no more than spear carriers in the political and cultural life of the West, their prejudices and superstitions do register in a subliminal way, making mephitic the air of Manhattan if not of the Republic.

A case in point is that of Mrs. Norman Podhoretz, also known as Midge Decter (like Martha Ivers, *whisper* her name). In September of last year, Decter published a piece called "The Boys on the Beach" in her husband's magazine, *Commentary.* It is well worth examining in some detail because she has managed not only to come up with every known prejudice and superstition about same-sexers but also to make up some brand-new ones. For sheer vim and vigor, "The Boys on the Beach" outdoes its implicit model, *The Protocols of the Elders of Zion.*

Decter notes that when the "homosexual-rights movement first burst upon the scene," she was "more than a little astonished." Like so many new-class persons, she writes a stilted sort of genteel-gentile prose not unlike—but not very like, either—*The New Yorker* house style of the 1940s and 50s. She also writes with the authority and easy confidence of someone who knows that she is very well known indeed to those few who know her.

Decter tells us that twenty years ago, she got to know a lot of pansies at a resort called Fire Island Pines, where she and a number of other new-class persons used to make it during the summers. She estimates that 40 percent of the summer people were heterosexual; the rest were not. Yet the "denizens, homosexual and heterosexual alike, were predominantly professionals and people in soft marginal businesses—lawyers, advertising executives, psychotherapists, actors, editors, writers, publishers, etc." Keep this in mind. Our authoress does not.

Decter goes on to tell us that she is now amazed at the recent changes in the boys on the beach. Why have they become so politically militant—and so ill groomed? "What indeed has happened to the homosexual community I used to know—they who only a few short years ago [as opposed to those manly 370-day years] were characterized by nothing so much as a sweet, vain, pouting, girlish attention to the youth and beauty of their bodies?" Decter wrestles with this problem. She tells us how, in the old days, she did her very best to come to terms with her own normal dislike for these half-men—and half-women, too: "There were also homosexual women at the Pines, but they were, or seemed to be, far fewer in number. Nor, except for a marked tendency to hang out in the company of large and ferocious dogs, were they instantly recognizable as the men were." Well, if I were a dyke and a pair of Podhoretzes came waddling toward me on the beach, copies of Leviticus and Freud in hand, I'd get in touch with the nearest Alsatian dealer pronto.

Decter was disturbed by "the slender, seamless, elegant and utterly chic" clothes of the fairies. She also found it "a constant source of wonder" that when the fairies took off their clothes, "the largest number of homosexuals had hairless bodies. Chests, backs, arms, even legs were smooth and silky. . . . We were never able to determine just why there should be so definite a connection between what is nowadays called their sexual preference [previously known to right-thinking Jews as an abomination against Jehovah] and their smooth feminine skin. Was it a matter of hormones?" Here Decter betrays her essential modesty and lack of experience. In the no doubt privileged environment of her Midwestern youth, she could not have seen very many gentile males without their clothes on. If she had, she would have discovered that gentile men tend to be less hairy than Jews except, of course, when they are not. Because the Jews killed our Lord, they are forever marked with hair on their shoulders—something that no gentile man has on *his* shoulders except for John Travolta and a handful of other Italian-Americans from the Englewood, New Jersey, area.

It is startling that Decter has not yet learned that there is no hormonal difference between men who like sex with other men and those who like sex with women. She notes, "There is also such a thing as characteristic homosexual speech . . . it is something of an accent redolent of small towns in the Midwest whence so many homosexuals seemed to have migrated to the big city." Here one detects the disdain of the self-made New Yorker for the rural or small-town American. "Midwest" is often a code word for the fly-overs, for the millions who do not really matter. But she is right in the sense that when a group chooses to live and work together, they do tend to sound and look alike. No matter how crowded and noisy a room, one can always detect the new-class person's nasal whine.

Every now and then, Decter does wonder if, perhaps, she is generalizing and whether this will "no doubt in itself seem to many of the uninitiated a bigoted formulation." Well, Midge, it does. But the spirit is upon her, and she cannot stop because "one cannot even begin to get at the truth about homosexuals without this kind of generalization. They are a group so readily distinguishable." Except of course, when they are not. It is one thing for a group of queens, in "soft, marginal" jobs, to "cavort," as she puts it, in a summer place and be "easily distinguishable" to her cold eye just as Jewish members of the new class are equally noticeable to the cold gentile eye. But it is quite another thing for those men and women who prefer same-sex sex to other-sex sex yet do not choose to be identified—and so are not. To begin to get at the truth about homosexuals, one must realize that the majority of those millions of Americans who prefer same-sex sex to other-sex sex are obliged, sometimes willingly and happily but often not, to marry and have children and to conform to the guidelines set down by the heterosexual dictatorship.

Decter would know nothing of this because in her "soft, marginal" world, she is not meant to know. She does remark upon the fairies at the Pines who did have wives and children: "They were for the most part charming and amusing fathers, rather like favorite uncles. And their wives . . . drank." This dramatic ellipsis is most Decterian.

She ticks off Susan Sontag for omitting to mention in the course of an essay on camp "that camp is of the essence of homosexual style, invented by homosexuals, and serving the purpose of domination by ridicule." The word "domination" is a characteristic new-class touch. The powerless are always obsessed by power. Decter seems unaware that all despised minorities are quick to make rather good jokes about themselves before the hostile majority does. Certainly Jewish humor, from the Book of Job (a laff-riot) to pre-*auteur* Woody Allen, is based on this.

Decter next does the ritual attack on Edward Albee and Tennessee Williams for presenting "what could only have been homosexual relationships as the deeper truth about love in our time." This is about as true as the late Maria Callas's conviction that you could always tell a Jew because he had a hump at the back of his neck—something Callas herself had in dromedarian spades.

Decter makes much of what she assumes to be the fags' mockery of the heterosexual men at the Pines: "Homosexuality paints them [heterosexuals] with the color of sheer entrapment," while the fags' "smooth and elegant exteriors, unmussed by traffic with the detritus of modern family existence, constituted a kind of sniggering reproach to their striving and harried straight brothers." Although I have never visited the Pines, I am pretty sure that I know the "soft marginal" types, both hetero and homo, that hung out there in the 1960s. One of the most noticeable characteristics of the self-ghettoized same-sexer is his perfect indifference to the world of the other-sexers. Although Decter's blood was always at the boil when contemplating these unnatural and immature half-men, they were, I would suspect, serenely unaware of her and her new-class cronies, solemnly worshiping at the shrine of The Family.

To hear Decter tell it, fags had nothing to complain of then, and they have nothing to complain of now: "Just to name the professions and industries in which they had, and still have, a significant presence is to define the boundaries of a certain kind of privilege: theatre, music, letters, dance, design, architecture, the visual arts, fashion at every level—from head, as it were, to foot, and from inception to retail—advertising, journalism, interior decoration, antique dealing, publishing . . . the list could go on." Yes. But these are all pretty "soft, marginal" occupations. And none is "dominated" by fags. Most male same-sexers are laborers, farmers, mechanics, small businessmen, schoolteachers, firemen, policemen, soldiers, sailors. Most female same-sexers are wives and mothers. In other words, they are like the rest of the population. But then it is hard for the new-class person to realize that Manhattan is not the world. Or as a somewhat alarmed Philip Rahv said to me after he had taken a drive across the United States, "My God! There are so many of them!" In theory, Rahv had always known that there were a couple of hundred million gentiles out there, but to see them, in the flesh, unnerved him. I told him that I was unnerved, too, particularly when they start showering in the Blood of the Lamb.

Decter does concede that homosexualists have probably not "established much of a presence in basic industry or government service or in such classic [new-classy?] professions as doctoring and lawyering but then for anyone acquainted with them as a group the thought suggests itself that few of them have ever made much effort in these directions." Plainly, the silly billies are too busy dressing up and dancing the hully-gully to argue a case in court. Decter will be relieved to know that the percentage of same-sexers in the "classic" activities is almost as high, proportionately, as that of Jews. But a homosexualist in a key position at, let us say, the Department of Labor will be married and living under a good deal of strain because he could be fired if it is known that he likes to have sex with other men.

Decter knows that there have always been homosexual teachers, and she thinks that they should keep quiet about it. But if they keep quiet, they can be blackmailed or fired. Also, a point that would really distress her, a teacher known to be a same-sexer would be a splendid role model for those same-sexers that he—or she—is teaching. Decter would think this an unmitigated evil because men and women were created to breed; but, of course, it would be a perfect good because we have more babies than we know what to do with while we lack, notoriously, useful citizens at ease with themselves. That is what the row over the schools is all about.

Like most members of the new class, Decter accepts without question Freud's line (*Introductory Lectures on Psychoanalysis*) that "we actually describe a sexual activity as perverse if it has given up the aim of reproduction and pursues the attainment of pleasure as an aim independent of it." For Freud, perversion was any sexual activity involving "the abandonment of the reproductive function." Freud also deplored masturbation as a dangerous "primal affliction." So did Moses. But then it was Freud's curious task to try to create a rational, quasi-scientific basis for Mosaic law. The result has been not unlike the accomplishments of Freud's great contemporary, the ineffable and inexorable Mary Baker Eddy, whose First

Church of Christ Scientist he was able to match with *his* First Temple of Moses Scientist.

Decter says that once faggots have "ensconced" themselves in certain professions or arts, "they themselves have engaged in a good deal of discriminatory practices against others. There are businesses and professions [which ones? She is congenitally short of data] in which it is less than easy for a straight, unless he makes the requisite gesture of propitiation to the homosexual in power, to get ahead." This, of course, was Hitler's original line about the Jews: they had taken over German medicine, teaching, law, journalism. Ruthlessly, they kept out gentiles; lecherously, they demanded sexual favors. "I simply want to reduce their numbers in these fields," Hitler told Prince Philip of Hesse. "I want them proportionate to their overall number in the population." This was the early solution; the final solution followed with equal logic.

In the 1950s, it was an article of faith in new-class circles that television had been taken over by the fags. Now I happen to have known most of the leading producers of that time and, of a dozen, the two who were interested in same-sex activities were both married to women who . . . did not drink. Neither man dared mix sex with business. Every now and then an actor would say that he had not got work because he had refused to put out for a faggot producer, but I doubt very much if there was ever any truth to what was to become a bright jack-o'-lantern in the McCarthy *Walpurgisnacht.*

When I was several thousand words into Decter's tirade, I suddenly realized that she does not know what homosexuality is. At some level she may have stumbled, by accident, on a truth that she would never have been able to comprehend in a rational way. Although to have sexual relations with a member of one's own sex is a common and natural activity (currently disapproved of by certain elements in this culture), there is no such thing as a homosexualist any more than there is such a thing as a heterosexualist. That is one of the reasons there has been so much difficulty with nomenclature. Despite John Boswell's attempts to give legitimacy to the word "gay," it is still a ridiculous word to use as a common identification for Frederick the Great, Franklin Pangborn and Eleanor Roosevelt. What makes some people prefer same-sex sex derives from whatever impulse or conditioning makes some people prefer other-sex sex. This is so plain that it seems impossible that our Mosaic-Pauline-Freudian society has not yet figured it out. But to ignore the absence of evidence is the basis of true faith.

Decter seems to think that yesteryear's chic and silly boys on the beach and today's socially militant fags are simply, to use her verb, "adopting" what she calls, in her tastefully appointed English, a lifestyle. On the other hand, "whatever disciplines it might entail, heterosexuality is not something adopted but something accepted. Its woes—and they have of course nowhere been more exaggerated than in those areas of the culture consciously or unconsciously influenced by the propaganda of homosexuals—are experienced as the woes of life."

"Propaganda"—another key word. "Power." "Propitiation." "Domination." What *does* the new class dream of?

Decter now moves in the big artillery. Not only are fags silly and a nuisance but they are, in their unrelenting hatred of heterosexualists, given to depicting them in their plays and films and books as a bunch of klutzes, thereby causing truly good men and women to falter—even question—that warm, mature heterosexuality that is so necessary to keeping this country great while allowing new-class persons to make it materially.

Decter is in full cry. Fags are really imitation women. Decter persists in thinking that same-sexers are effeminate, swishy, girlish. It is true that a small percentage of homosexualists are indeed effeminate, just as there are effeminate heterosexualists. I don't know why this is so. No one knows why. Except Decter. She believes that this sort "of female imitation pointed neither to sympathy with nor flattery of the female principle." Yet queens of the sort she is writing about tend to get on very well with women. But Decter can only cope with two stereotypes: the boys on the beach, mincing about, and the drab political radicals of gay liberation. The millions of ordinary masculine types are unknown to her because they are not identifiable by voice or walk and, most important, because they have nothing in common with one another except the desire to have same-sex relations. Or, put the other way around, since Lyndon Johnson and Bertrand Russell were both heterosexualists, what character traits did *they* have in common? I should think none at all. So it is with the invisible millions—now becoming less invisible—of same-sexers.

But Decter knows her Freud, and reality may not intrude: "The desire to escape from the sexual reminder of birth and death, with its threat of paternity—that is, the displacement of oneself by others—was the main underlying desire that sent those Fire Island homosexuals into the arms of other men. Had it been the opposite desire—that is, the positive attraction to the manly—at least half the boutiques, etc.," would have closed. Decter should take a stroll down San Francisco's Castro Street, where members of the present generation of fags look like off-duty policemen or construction workers. They have embraced the manly. But Freud has spoken. Fags are fags because they adored their mothers and hated their poor, hard-working daddies. It is amazing the credence still given this unproven, unprovable thesis.

Curiously enough, as I was writing these lines, expressing yet again the unacceptable obvious, I ran across Ralph Blumenthal's article in *The New York Times* (August 25), which used "unpublished letters and growing research into the hidden life of Sigmund Freud" to examine "Freud's reversal of his theory attributing neurosis in adults to sexual seduction in childhood." Despite the evidence given by his patients, Freud decided that their memories of molestation were "phantasies." He then appropriated from the high culture (a real act of hubris) Oedipus the King, and made him a complex. Freud was much criticized for this theory at the time—particularly by Sandor Ferenczi. Now, as we learn more about Freud (not to mention about the sexual habits of Victorian Vienna as reported in police records), his theory is again under attack. Drs. Milton Klein and David Tribich have written a paper titled "On Freud's Blindness." They have studied his case histories and observed how he ignored evidence, how "he looked to the child and only to the child, in uncovering the causes of psychopathology." Dr. Karl Menninger wrote Dr. Klein about these findings: "Why oh why couldn't Freud believe his own ears?" Dr. Menninger then noted, "Seventy-five per cent of the girls we accept at the Villages have been molested in childhood by an adult. And that's today in Kansas! I don't think Vienna in 1900 was any less sophisticated."

In the same week as Blumenthal's report on the discrediting of the Oedipus complex, researchers at the Kinsey Institute reported (*The Observer,* August 30) that after studying 979 homosexualists ("the largest sample of homosexuals—black and white, male and female—ever questioned in an academic study") and 477 heterosexualists, they came to the conclusion that family life has nothing to do with sexual preference. Apparently, "homosexuality is deep-rooted in childhood, may be biological in origin, and simply shows in more and more important ways as a child grows older. It is not a condition which therapy can reverse." Also, "homosexual feelings begin as much as three years before any sort of homosexual act, undermining theories that homosexuality is learned through experience." There goes the teacher-as-seducer-and-perverter myth. Finally, "Psychoanalysts' theories about smothering mum and absent dad do not stand investigation. Patients may tend to believe that they are true because therapists subtly coach them in the appropriate memories of their family life."

Some years ago, gay activists came to *Harper's,* where Decter was an editor, to demonstrate against an article by Joseph Epstein, who had announced, "If I had the power to do so, I would wish homosexuality off the face of the earth." Well, that's what Hitler had the power to do in Germany, and did—or tried to do. The confrontation at *Harper's* now provides Decter with her theme. She tells us that one of the demonstrators asked, "Are you aware of how many suicides you may be responsible for in the homosexual community?" I suspect that she is leaving out the context of this somewhat left-field *cri de coeur.* After all, homosexualists have more to fear from murder than suicide. I am sure that the actual conversation had to do with the sort of mischievous effect that Epstein's Hitlerian piece might have had on those fag-baiters who read it.

But Decter slyly zeroes in on the word "suicide." She then develops a most unusual thesis. Homosexualists hate themselves to such an extent that they wish to become extinct either through inviting murder or committing suicide. She notes that in a survey of San Francisco's homosexual men, half of them "claimed to have had sex with at least five hundred people." This "bespeaks the obliteration of all experience, if not, indeed, of oneself." Plainly Decter has a Mosaic paradigm forever in mind and any variation on it is abominable. Most men—homo or hetero—given the opportunity to have sex with 500 different people would do so, gladly; but most men are not going to be given the opportunity by a society that wants them safely married so that they will be docile workers and loyal consumers. It does not suit our rulers to have the proles tomcatting around the way that our rulers do. I can assure Decter that the thirty-fifth president went to bed with more than 500 women and that the well-known . . . but I must not give away the secrets of the old class or the newly-middle-class new class will go into shock.

Meanwhile, according to Decter, "many homosexuals are nowadays engaged in efforts at self-obliteration . . . there is the appalling rate of suicide among them." But the rate is not appreciably higher than that for the rest of the population. In any case, most who do commit—or contemplate—suicide do so because they cannot cope in a world where they are, to say the least, second-class citizens. But Decter is now entering uncharted country. She also has a point to make: "What is undeniable is the increasing longing among the homosexuals to do away with themselves—if not in the actual physical sense then at least spiritually—a longing whose chief emblem, among others, is the leather bars."

So Epstein will not be obliged to press that button in order to get rid of the fags. They will do it themselves. Decter ought to be pleased by this, but it is not in her nature to be pleased by anything that the same-sexers do. If they get married and have children and swear fealty to the family gods of the new class, their wives will . . . drink. If they live openly with one another, they have fled from woman and real life. If they pursue careers in the arts, heteros will have to be on guard against vicious covert assaults on heterosexual values. If they congregate in the fashion business the way that Jews do in psychiatry, they will employ only those heterosexuals who will put out for them.

Decter is appalled by the fag "takeover" of San Francisco. She tells us about the "ever deepening resentment of the San Francisco straight community at the homosexuals' defiant displays and power ['power'!] over this city," but five paragraphs later she contradicts herself: "Having to a very great extent overcome revulsion of common opinion, are they left with some kind of unappeased hunger that only their own feelings of hatefulness can now satisfy?"

There it is. *They are hateful.* They know it. That is why they want to eliminate themselves. "One thing is certain." Decter finds a lot of certainty around. "To become homosexual is a weighty act." She still has not got the point that one does not choose to have same-sex impulses; one simply has them, as everyone has, to a greater or lesser degree, other-sex impulses. To deny giving physical expression to those desires may be pleasing to Moses and Saint Paul and Freud, but these three rabbis are aberrant figures whose nomadic values are not those of the thousands of other tribes that live or have lived on the planet. Women's and gay liberation are simply small efforts to free men and women from this trio.

Decter writes, "Taking oneself out of the tides of ordinary mortal existence is not something one does from any longing to think oneself ordinary (but only following a different 'life-style')." I don't quite grasp this sentence. Let us move on to the next: "Gay Lib has been an effort to set the weight of that act at naught, to define homosexuality as nothing more than a casual option among options." Gay lib has done just the opposite. After all, people are what they are sexually not through "adoption" but because that is the way they are structured. Some people do shift about in the course of a life. Also, most of those with same-sex drives do indeed "adopt" the heterosexual life-style because they don't want to go to prison or to the madhouse or become unemployable. Obviously, there *is* an option but it is a hard one that ought not to be forced on any human being. After all, homosexuality is only important when made so by irrational opponents. In this, as in so much else, the Jewish situation is precisely the same.

Decter now gives us not a final solution so much as a final conclusion: "In accepting the movement's terms [hardly anyone has, by the way], heterosexuals have only raised to a nearly intolerable height the costs of the homosexuals' flight from normality." The flight, apparently, is deliberate, a matter of perverse choice, a misunderstanding of daddy, a passion for mummy, a fear of responsibility. Decter threads her clichés like Teclas on a string: "Faced with the accelerating round of drugs, S-M and suicide, can either the movement or its heterosexual sympathizers imagine they have done anyone a kindness?"

Although the kindness of strangers is much sought after, gay liberation has not got much support from anyone. Natural allies like the Jews are often virulent in their attacks. Blacks in their ghettos, Chicanos in their barrios, and rednecks in their pulpits also have been influenced by the same tribal taboos. That Jews and blacks and Chicanos and rednecks all contribute to the ranks of the same-sexers only increases the madness. But the world of the Decters is a world of perfect illogic.

Herewith the burden of "The Boys on the Beach": since homosexualists choose to be the way they are out of idle hatefulness, it has been a mistake to allow them to come out of the closet to the extent that they have, but now that they are out (which most are not), they will have no choice but to face up to their essential hatefulness and abnormality and so be driven to kill themselves with promiscuity, drugs, S-M and suicide. Not even the authors of *The Protocols of the Elders of Zion* ever suggested that the Jews, who were so hateful to them, were also hateful to themselves. So Decter has managed to go one step further than the *Protocols'* authors; she is indeed a virtuoso of hate, and thus do pogroms begin.

*Tricks* is the story of an author—Renaud Camus himself—who has twenty-five sexual encounters in the course of six months. Each of these encounters involves a pick-up. Extrapolating from Camus's sexual vigor at the age of 35, I would suspect that he has already passed the 500 mark and so is completely obliterated as a human being. If he is, he still writes very well indeed. He seems to be having a good time, and he shows no sign of wanting to kill himself, but then that may be a front he's keeping up. I am sure that Decter will be able to tell just how close he is to OD'ing.

From his photograph, Camus appears to have a lot of hair on his chest. I don't know about the shoulders, as they are covered, modestly, with a shirt. Perhaps he is Jewish. Roland Barthes wrote an introduction to *Tricks.* For a time, Barthes was much admired in American academe. But then, a few years ago, Barthes began to write about his same-sexual activities; he is now mentioned a bit less than he was in the days before he came out, as they say.

Barthes notes that Camus's book is a "text that belongs to literature." It is not pornographic. It is also not a Homosexual Novel in that there are no deep, anguished chats about homosexuality. In fact, the subject is never mentioned; it just is. Barthes remarks, "Homosexuality shocks less [well, he is—or was—French], but continues to be interesting; it is still at that stage of excitation where it provokes what might be called feats of discourse [see "The Boys on the Beach," no mean feat!]. Speaking of homosexuality permits those who aren't to show how open, liberal, and modern they are; and those who are to bear witness, to assume responsibility, to militate. Everyone gets busy, in different ways, whipping it up." You can say that again! And Barthes does. But with a nice variation. He makes the point that you are never allowed *not* to be categorized. But then, "say 'I am' and you will be socially saved." Hence the passion for the either/or.

Camus does not set out to give a panoramic view of homosexuality. He comments, in *his* preface, on the variety of homosexual expressions. Although there is no stigma attached to homosexuality in the French intellectual world where, presumably, there is no equivalent of the new class, the feeling among the lower classes is still intense, a memento of the now exhausted (in France) Roman Catholic Church's old dirty work ("I don't understand the French Catholics," said John Paul II). As a result, many "refuse to grant their tastes because they live in such circumstances, in such circles, that their desires are not only for themselves inadmissible but inconceivable, unspeakable."

It is hard to describe a book that is itself a description, and that is what *Tricks* is—a flat, matter-of-fact description of how the narrator meets the tricks, what each says to the other, where they go, how the rooms are furnished, and what the men do. One of the tricks is nuts; a number are very hairy—the narrator has a Decterian passion for the furry; there is a lot of anal and banal sex as well as oral and floral sex. *Frottage* flows. Most of the encounters take place in France, but there is one in Washington, D.C., with a black man. There is a good deal of comedy, in the Raymond Roussel manner.

*Tricks* will give ammunition to those new-class persons and redneck divines who find promiscuity every bit as abominable as same-sex relations. But that is the way men are when they are given freedom to go about their business unmolested. One current Arab ruler boasts of having ten sexual encounters a day, usually with different women. A diplomat who knows him says that he exaggerates, but not much. Of course, he is a Moslem.

The family, as we know it, is an economic, not a biological, unit. I realize that this is startling news in this culture and at a time when the economies of both East and West require that the nuclear family be, simply, God. But our ancestors did not live as we do. They lived in packs for hundreds of millennia before "history" began, a mere 5,000 years ago. Whatever social arrangements human society may come up with in the future, it will have to be acknowledged that those children who are needed should be rather more thoughtfully brought up than they are today and that those adults who do not care to be fathers or mothers should be let off the hook. This is beginning, slowly, to dawn. Hence, the rising hysteria in the land. Hence, the concerted effort to deny the human ordinariness of same-sexualists. A recent attempt to portray such a person sympathetically on television was abandoned when the Christers rose up in arms.

Although I would never suggest that Truman Capote's bright wit and sweet charm as a television performer would not have easily achieved for him his present stardom had he been a *hetero*sexualist, I do know that if he had not existed in his present form, another would have been run up on the old sewing machine because that sort of *persona* must be, for a whole nation, the stereotype of what a fag is. Should some macho film star like Clint Eastwood, say, decide to confess on television that he is really into same-sex sex, the cathode tube would blow a fuse. That could never be allowed. That is all wrong. That is how the Roman Empire fell.

There is not much *angst* in *Tricks.* No one commits suicide—but there is one sad story. A militant leftist friend of Camus's was a teacher in the south of France. He taught 14-year-old members of that oldest of all the classes, the exploited laborer. One of his pupils saw him in a fag bar and spread the word. The students began to torment what had been a favorite teacher. "These are little proles," he tells Camus, "and Mediterranean besides—which means they're obsessed by every possible macho myth, and by homosexuality as well. It's all they can think about." One of the boys, an Arab, followed him down the street, screaming "Faggot!" "It was as if he had finally found someone onto whom he could project his resentment, someone he could hold in contempt with complete peace of mind."

This might explain the ferocity of the new class on the subject. They know that should the bad times return, the Jews will be singled out yet again. Meanwhile, like so many Max Naumanns (Naumann was a German Jew who embraced Nazism), the new class passionately supports our ruling class—from the Chase Manhattan Bank to the Pentagon to the Op-Ed page of *The Wall Street Journal*—while holding in fierce contempt faggots, blacks (see Norman Podhoretz's "My Negro Problem and Ours," *Commentary,* February 1963), and the poor (see Midge Decter's "Looting and Liberal Racism," *Commentary,* September 1977). Since these Neo-Naumannites are going to be in the same gas chambers as the blacks and the faggots, I would suggest a cease-fire and a common front against the common enemy, whose kindly voice is that of Ronald Reagan and whose less than kindly mind is elsewhere in the boardrooms of the Republic.

***The Nation***
***November 14, 1981***

# Drugs

It is possible to stop most drug addiction in the United States within a very short time. Simply make all drugs available and sell them at cost. Label each drug with a precise description of what effect—good and bad—the drug will have on the taker. This will require heroic honesty. Don't say that marijuana is addictive or dangerous when it is neither, as millions of people know—unlike "speed," which kills most unpleasantly, or heroin, which is addictive and difficult to kick.

For the record, I have tried—once—almost every drug and liked none, disproving the popular Fu Manchu theory that a single whiff of opium will enslave the mind. Nevertheless many drugs are bad for certain people to take and they should be told why in a sensible way.

Along with exhortation and warning, it might be good for our citizens to recall (or learn for the first time) that the United States was the creation of men who believed that each man has the right to do what he wants with his own life as long as he does not interfere with his neighbor's pursuit of happiness (that his neighbor's idea of happiness is persecuting others does confuse matters a bit).

This is a startling notion to the current generation of Americans. They reflect a system of public education which has made the Bill of Rights, literally, unacceptable to a majority of high school graduates (see the annual Purdue reports) who now form the "silent majority"—a phrase which that underestimated wit Richard Nixon took from Homer who used it to describe the dead.

Now one can hear the warning rumble begin: if everyone is allowed to take drugs everyone will and the GNP will decrease, the Commies will stop us from making everyone free, and we shall end up a race of Zombies, passively murmuring "groovie" to one another. Alarming thought. Yet it seems most unlikely that any reasonably sane person will become a drug addict if he knows in advance what addiction is going to be like.

Is everyone reasonably sane? No. Some people will always become drug addicts just as some people will always become alcoholics, and it is just too bad. Every man, however, has the power (and should have the legal right) to kill himself if he chooses. But since most men don't, they won't be mainliners either. Nevertheless, forbidding people things they like or think they might enjoy only makes them want those things all the more. This psychological insight is, for some mysterious reason, perennially denied our governors.

It is a lucky thing for the American moralist that our country has always existed in a kind of time-vacuum: we have no public memory of anything that happened before last Tuesday. No one in Washington today recalls what happened during the years alcohol was forbidden to the people by a Congress that thought it had a divine mission to stamp out Demon Rum—launching, in the process, the greatest crime wave in the country's history, causing thousands of deaths from bad alcohol, and creating a general (and persisting) contempt among the citizenry for the laws of the United States.

The same thing is happening today. But the government has learned nothing from past attempts at prohibition, not to mention repression.

Last year when the supply of Mexican marijuana was slightly curtailed by the Feds, the pushers got the kids hooked on heroin and deaths increased dramatically, particularly in New York. Whose fault? Evil men like the Mafiosi? Permissive Dr. Spock? Wild-eyed Dr. Leary? No.

The Government of the United States was responsible for those deaths. The bureaucratic machine has a vested interest in playing cops and robbers. Both the Bureau of Narcotics and the Mafia want strong laws against the sale and use of drugs because if drugs are sold at cost there would be no money in it for anyone.

If there was no money in it for the Mafia, there would be no friendly playground pushers, and addicts would not commit crimes to pay for the next fix. Finally, if there was no money in it, the Bureau of Narcotics would wither away, something they are not about to do without a struggle.

Will anything sensible be done? Of course not. The American people are as devoted to the idea of sin and its punishment as they are to making money—and fighting drugs is nearly as big a business as pushing them. Since the combination of sin and money is irresistible (particularly to the professional politician), the situation will only grow worse.

***The New York Times***
***September 26, 1970***

# The Day the American Empire Ran Out of Gas

On September 16, 1985, when the Commerce Department announced that the United States had become a debtor nation, the American Empire died. The empire was seventy-one years old and had been in ill health since 1968. Like most modern empires, ours rested not so much on military prowess as on economic primacy.*

After the French Revolution, the world money power shifted from Paris to London. For three generations, the British maintained an old-fashioned colonial empire, as well as a modern empire based on London's primacy in the money markets. Then, in 1914, New York replaced London as the world's financial capital. Before 1914, the United States had been a developing country, dependent on outside investment. But with the shift of the money power from Old World to New, what had been a debtor nation became a creditor nation and central motor to the world's economy. All in all, the English were well pleased to have us take their place. They were too few in number for so big a task. As early as the turn of the century, they were eager for us not only to help them out financially but to continue, in their behalf, the destiny of the Anglo-Saxon race: to bear with courage the white man's burden, as Rudyard Kipling not so tactfully put it. Were we not—English and Americans—all Anglo-Saxons, united by common blood, laws, language? Well, no, we were not. But our differences were

*In *The Guardian* (November 20, 1987) Frank Kermode wrote: "I happened to hear Vidal expound this thesis in a New York theater, to a highly ribald and incredulous, though doubtless very ignorant audience. . . ." Since then, my thesis has been repeated by others so many times that it is now conventional wisdom.

not so apparent then. In any case, we took on the job. We would supervise and civilize the lesser breeds. We would make money.

By the end of the Second World War, we were the most powerful and least damaged of the great nations. We also had most of the money. America's hegemony lasted exactly five years. Then the cold and hot wars began. Our masters would have us believe that all our problems are the fault of the Evil Empire of the East, with its satanic and atheistic religion, ever ready to destroy us in the night. This nonsense began at a time when we had atomic weapons and the Russians did not. They had lost twenty million of their people in the war, and eight million of them before the war, thanks to their neoconservative Mongolian political system. Most important, there was never any chance, then or now, of the money power shifting from New York to Moscow. What was—and is—the reason for the big scare? Well, the Second War made prosperous the United States, which had been undergoing a depression for a dozen years, and made very rich those magnates and their managers who govern the republic, with many a wink, in the people's name. In order to maintain a general prosperity (and enormous wealth for the few) they decided that we would become the world's policeman, perennial shield against the Mongol hordes. We shall have an arms race, said one of the high priests, John Foster Dulles, and we shall win it because the Russians will go broke first. We were then put on a permanent wartime economy, which is why close to two thirds of the government's revenues are constantly being siphoned off to pay for what is euphemistically called defense.

As early as 1950, Albert Einstein understood the nature of the rip-off. He said, "The men who possess real power in this country have no intention of ending the cold war." Thirty-five years later, they are still at it, making money while the nation itself declines to eleventh place in world per capita income, to forty-sixth in literacy and so on, until last summer (not suddenly, I fear) we found ourselves close to two trillion dollars in debt. Then, in the fall, the money power shifted from New York to Tokyo, and that was the end of our empire. Now the long-feared Asiatic colossus takes its turn as world leader, and we—the white race—have become the yellow man's burden. Let us hope that he will treat us more kindly than we treated him.* In any case, if the foreseeable future is not nuclear, it will be Asiatic, some combination of Japan's advanced technology with China's resourceful landmass. Europe and the United States will then be, simply, irrelevant to the world that matters, and so we come full circle: Europe began as the relatively empty uncivilized Wild West of Asia; then the Western Hemi-

*Believe it or not, this plain observation was interpreted as a racist invocation of "the Yellow Peril"!

sphere became the Wild West of Europe. Now the sun has set in our West and risen once more in the East.

The British used to say that their empire was obtained in a fit of absent-mindedness. They exaggerate, of course. On the other hand, our modern empire was carefully thought out by four men. In 1890 a U.S. Navy captain, Alfred Thayer Mahan, wrote the blueprint for the American imperium, *The Influence of Sea Power Upon History, 1660–1783*. Then Mahan's friend, the historian-geopolitician Brooks Adams, younger brother of Henry, came up with the following formula: "All civilization is centralization. All centralization is economy." He applied the formula in the following syllogism: "Under economical centralization, Asia is cheaper than Europe. The world tends to economic centralization. Therefore, Asia tends to survive and Europe to perish." Ultimately, *that* is why we were in Vietnam. The amateur historian and professional politician Theodore Roosevelt was much under the influence of Adams and Mahan; he was also their political instrument, most active not so much during his presidency as during the crucial war with Spain, where he can take a good deal of credit for our seizure of the Philippines, which made us a world empire. Finally, Senator Henry Cabot Lodge, Roosevelt's closest friend, kept in line a Congress that had a tendency to forget our holy mission—our manifest destiny—and ask, rather wistfully, for internal improvements.

From the beginning of our republic we have had imperial longings. We took care—as we continue to take care—of the indigenous population. We maintained slavery a bit too long even by a cynical world's tolerant standards. Then, in 1846, we produced our first conquistador, President James K. Polk. After acquiring Texas, Polk deliberately started a war with Mexico because, as he later told the historian George Bancroft, we had to acquire California. Thanks to Polk, we did. And that is why to this day the Mexicans refer to our southwestern states as "the occupied lands," which Hispanics are now, quite sensibly, filling up.

The case against empire began as early as 1847. Representative Abraham Lincoln did not think much of Polk's war, while Lieutenant Ulysses S. Grant, who fought at Veracruz, said in his memoirs, "The war was an instance of a republic following the bad example of European monarchies, in not considering justice in their desire to acquire additional territory." He went on to make a causal link, something not usual in our politics then and completely unknown now: "The Southern rebellion was largely the outgrowth of the Mexican War. Nations, like individuals, are punished for their transgressions. We got our punishment in the most sanguinary and expensive war of modern times."

But the empire has always had more supporters than opponents. By 1895 we had filled up our section of North America. We had tried twice—

and failed—to conquer Canada. We had taken everything that we wanted from Mexico. Where next? Well, there was the Caribbean at our front door and the vast Pacific at our back. Enter the Four Horsemen—Mahan, Adams, Roosevelt, and Lodge.

The original republic was thought out carefully, and openly, in *The Federalist Papers*: We were not going to have a monarchy and we were not going to have a democracy. And to this day we have had neither. For two hundred years we have had an oligarchical system in which men of property can do well and the others are on their own. Or, as Brooks Adams put it, the sole problem of our ruling class is whether to coerce or to bribe the powerless majority. The so-called Great Society bribed; today coercion is very much in the air. Happily, our neoconservative Mongoloids favor only authoritarian and never totalitarian means of coercion.

Unlike the republic, the empire was worked out largely in secret. Captain Mahan, in a series of lectures delivered at the Naval War College, compared the United States with England. Each was essentially an island state that could prevail in the world only through sea power. England had already proved his thesis. Now the United States must do the same. We must build a great navy in order to acquire overseas possessions. Since great navies are expensive, the wealth of new colonies must be used to pay for our fleets. In fact, the more colonies acquired, the more ships; the more ships, the more empire. Mahan's thesis is agreeably circular. He showed how small England had ended up with most of Africa and all of southern Asia, thanks to sea power. He thought that we should do the same. The Caribbean was our first and easiest target. Then on to the Pacific Ocean, with all its islands. And, finally, to China, which was breaking up as a political entity.

Theodore Roosevelt and Brooks Adams were tremendously excited by this prospect. At the time Roosevelt was a mere police commissioner in New York City, but he had dreams of imperial glory. "He wants to be," snarled Henry Adams, "our Dutch-American Napoleon." Roosevelt began to maneuver his way toward the heart of power, sea power. With Lodge's help, he got himself appointed assistant secretary of the navy, under a weak secretary and a mild president. Now he was in place to modernize the fleet and to acquire colonies. Hawaii was annexed. Then a part of Samoa. Finally, colonial Cuba, somehow, had to be liberated from Spain's tyranny. At the Naval War College, Roosevelt declared, "To prepare for war is the most effectual means to promote peace." How familiar that sounds! But since the United States had no enemies as of June 1897, a contemporary might have remarked that since we were already at peace with everyone, why prepare for war? Today, of course, we are what he dreamed we would be, a nation armed to the teeth and hostile to everyone.

But what with Roosevelt was a design to acquire an empire is for us a means to transfer money from the Treasury to the various defense industries, which in turn pay for the elections of Congress and president.

Our turn-of-the-century imperialists may have been wrong, and I think they were. But they were intelligent men with a plan, and the plan worked. Aided by Lodge in the Senate, Brooks Adams in the press, Admiral Mahan at the Naval War College, the young assistant secretary of the navy began to build up the fleet and look for enemies. After all, as Brooks Adams proclaimed, "war is the solvent." But war with whom? And for what? And where? At one point England seemed a likely enemy. There was a boundary dispute over Venezuela, which meant that we could invoke the all-purpose Monroe Doctrine (the invention of John Quincy Adams, Brooks's grandfather). But as we might have lost such a war, nothing happened. Nevertheless, Roosevelt kept on beating his drum: "No triumph of peace," he shouted, "can equal the armed triumph of war." Also: "We must take Hawaii in the interests of the white race." Even Henry Adams, who found T.R. tiresome and Brooks, his own brother, brilliant but mad, suddenly declared, "In another fifty years . . . the white race will have to reconquer the tropics by war and nomadic invasion, or be shut up north of the 50th parallel." And so at century's end, our most distinguished ancestral voices were not prophesying but praying for war.

An American warship, the *Maine,* blew up in Havana harbor. We held Spain responsible; thus, we got what John Hay called "a splendid little war." We would liberate Cuba, drive Spain from the Caribbean. As for the Pacific, even before the *Maine* was sunk, Roosevelt had ordered Commodore Dewey and his fleet to the Spanish Philippines—just in case. Spain promptly collapsed, and we inherited its Pacific and Caribbean colonies. Admiral Mahan's plan was working triumphantly.

In time we allowed Cuba the appearance of freedom while holding on to Puerto Rico. Then President William McKinley, after an in-depth talk with God, decided that we should also keep the Philippines, in order, he said, to Christianize them. When reminded that the Filipinos were Roman Catholics, the president said, Exactly. We must Christianize them. Although Philippine nationalists had been our allies against Spain, we promptly betrayed them and their leader, Emilio Aguinaldo. As a result it took us several years to conquer the Philippines, and tens—some say hundreds—of thousands of Filipinos died that our empire might grow.

The war was the making of Theodore Roosevelt. Surrounded by the flower of the American press, he led a group of so-called Rough Riders up a very small hill in Cuba. As a result of this proto–photo opportunity he became a national hero, governor of New York, McKinley's running mate and, when McKinley was killed in 1901, president.

Not everyone liked the new empire. After Manila, Mark Twain thought that the stars and bars of the American flag should be replaced by a skull and crossbones. He also said, "We cannot maintain an empire in the Orient and maintain a republic in America." He was right, of course. But as he was only a writer who said funny things, he was ignored. The compulsively vigorous Roosevelt defended our war against the Philippine population, and he attacked the likes of Twain. "Every argument that can be made for the Filipinos could be made for the Apaches," he explained, with his lovely gift for analogy. "And every word that can be said for Aguinaldo could be said for Sitting Bull. As peace, order and prosperity followed our expansion over the land of the Indians, so they will follow us in the Philippines."

Despite the criticism of the few, the Four Horsemen had pulled it off. The United States was a world empire. And one of the horsemen not only got to be president, but for his pious meddling in the Russo-Japanese conflict our greatest apostle of war was awarded the Nobel Peace Prize. One must never underestimate Scandinavian wit.

Empires are restless organisms. They must constantly renew themselves; should an empire start leaking energy, it will die. Not for nothing were the Adams brothers fascinated by entropy. By energy. By force. Brooks Adams, as usual, said the unsayable. "Laws are a necessity," he declared. "Laws are made by the strongest, and they must and shall be obeyed." Oliver Wendell Holmes, Jr., thought this a wonderful observation, while the philosopher William James came to a similar conclusion, which can also be detected, like an invisible dynamo, at the heart of the novels of his brother Henry.

According to Brooks Adams, "The most difficult problem of modern times is unquestionably how to protect property under popular governments." The Four Horsemen fretted a lot about this. They need not have. We have never had a popular government in the sense that they feared, nor are we in any danger now. Our only political party has two right wings, one called Republican, the other Democratic. But Henry Adams figured all that out back in the 1890s. "We have a single system," he wrote, and "in that system the only question is the price at which the proletariat is to be bought and sold, the bread and circuses." But none of this was for public consumption. Publicly, the Four Horsemen and their outriders spoke of the American mission to bring to all the world freedom and peace, through slavery and war if necessary. Privately, their constant fear was that the weak masses might combine one day against the strong few, their natural leaders, and take away their money. As early as the election of 1876 socialism had been targeted as a vast evil that must never be allowed to corrupt simple American persons. When Christianity was invoked as the natural enemy of those who might limit the rich and their games, the combination of cross and dollar sign proved—and proves—irresistible.

During the first decade of our disagreeable century, the great world fact was the internal collapse of China. Who could pick up the pieces? Britain grabbed Kowloon; Russia was busy in the north; the Kaiser's fleet prowled the China coast; Japan was modernizing itself and biding its time. Although Theodore Roosevelt lived and died a dedicated racist, the Japanese puzzled him. After they sank the Russian fleet, Roosevelt decided that they were to be respected and feared even though they were our racial inferiors. For those Americans who served in the Second World War, it was an article of faith—as of 1941 anyway—that the Japanese could never win a modern war. Because of their slant eyes, they would not be able to master aircraft. Then they sank our fleet at Pearl Harbor.

Jingoism aside, Brooks Adams was a good analyst. In the 1890s he wrote: "Russia, to survive, must undergo a social revolution internally and/or expand externally. She will try to move into Shansi Province, richest prize in the world. Should Russia and Germany combine . . ." That was the nightmare of the Four Horsemen. At a time when simpler folk feared the rise of Germany alone, Brooks Adams saw the world ultimately polarized between Russia and the United States, with China as the common prize. American maritime power versus Russia's landmass. That is why, quite seriously, he wanted to extend the Monroe Doctrine to the Pacific Ocean. For him, "war [was] the ultimate form of economic competition."

We are now at the end of the twentieth century. England, France, and Germany have all disappeared from the imperial stage. China is now reassembling itself, and Confucius, greatest of political thinkers, is again at the center of the Middle Kingdom. Japan has the world money power and wants a landmass; China now seems ready to go into business with its ancient enemy. Wars of the sort that the Four Horsemen enjoyed are, if no longer possible, no longer practical. Today's conquests are shifts of currency by computer and the manufacture of those things that people everywhere are willing to buy.

I have said very little about writers because writers have figured very little in our imperial story. The founders of both republic and empire wrote well: Jefferson and Hamilton, Lincoln and Grant, T.R. and the Adamses. Today public figures can no longer write their own speeches or books, and there is some evidence that they can't read them either.

Yet at the dawn of the empire, for a brief instant, our *professional* writers tried to make a difference. Upton Sinclair and company attacked the excesses of the ruling class. Theodore Roosevelt coined the word "muckraking" to describe what they were doing. He did not mean the word as praise. Since then a few of our writers have written on public themes, but as they were not taken seriously, they have ended by not taking themselves seriously, at least as citizens of a republic. After all, most writers are paid by universities, and it is not wise to be thought critical of a garrison state which spends so much money on so many campuses.

When Confucius was asked what would be the first thing that he would do if he were to lead the state—his never-to-be-fulfilled dream—he said *rectify the language.* This is wise. This is subtle. As societies grow decadent, the language grows decadent, too. Words are used to disguise, not to illuminate, action: You liberate a city by destroying it. Words are used to confuse, so that at election time people will solemnly vote against their own interests. Finally, words must be so twisted as to justify an empire that has now ceased to exist, much less make sense. Is rectification of our system possible for us? Henry Adams thought not. In 1910 he wrote: "The whole fabric of society will go to wrack if we really lay hands of reform on our rotten institutions." Then he added, "From top to bottom the whole system is a fraud, all of us know it, laborers and capitalists alike, and all of us are consenting parties to it." Since then, consent has grown frayed; and we have become poor, and our people sullen.

To maintain a thirty-five-year arms race it is necessary to have a fearsome enemy. Not since the invention of the Wizard of Oz have American publicists created anything quite so demented as the idea that the Soviet Union is a monolithic, omnipotent empire with tentacles everywhere on earth, intent on our destruction, which will surely take place unless we constantly imitate it with our war machine and secret services.

In actual fact, the Soviet Union is a Second World country with a First World military capacity. Frighten the Russians sufficiently and they might blow us up. By the same token, as our republic now begins to crack under the vast expense of maintaining a mindless imperial force, we might try to blow them up. Particularly if we had a president who really was a twice-born Christian and believed that the good folks would all go to heaven (where they were headed anyway) and the bad folks would go where *they* belong.

Even worse than the not-very-likely prospect of a nuclear war—deliberate or by accident—is the economic collapse of our society because too many of our resources have been wasted on the military. The Pentagon is like a black hole; what goes in is forever lost to us, and no new wealth is created. Hence, our cities, whose centers are unlivable; our crime rate, the highest in the Western world; a public education system that has given up . . . you know the litany.

There is now only one way out. The time has come for the United States to make common cause with the Soviet Union. The bringing together of the Soviet landmass (with all its natural resources) and our island empire (with all its technological resources) would be of great benefit to each society, not to mention the world. Also, to recall the wisdom of the Four

Horsemen who gave us our empire, the Soviet Union and our section of North America combined would be a match, industrially and technologically, for the Sino-Japanese axis that will dominate the future just as Japan dominates world trade today. But where the horsemen thought of war as the supreme solvent, we now know that war is worse than useless. Therefore, the alliance of the two great powers of the Northern Hemisphere will double the strength of each and give us, working together, an opportunity to survive, economically, in a highly centralized Asiatic world.

*The Nation*
*January 11, 1986*

# Bad History

SHORTLY AFTER the publication of David McCullough's prizewinning biography *Truman,* an ad hoc committee of concerned historians was formed to ponder how any historian, no matter how amiably "in the grain," could write at such length about so crucial a President and reveal absolutely nothing of his actual politics, whose effects still resonate in the permanent garrison state and economy he bequeathed us. Since this question has many answers, we continue to meet—in secrecy: Tenure is at stake in some cases, while prizes, grants, fellowships, hang in a balance that can go swiftly crashing if any of us dares question openly the image of America the beauteous on its hill, so envied by all that it is subject to attacks by terrorists who cannot bear so much sheer goodness to triumph in a world that belongs to *their* master, the son of morning himself, Satan.

As we discuss in increasing detail the various American history departments, a large portrait of Comer Vann Woodward beams down on us; he is the acknowledged premier conductor of that joyous, glory-bound gravy train. In due course, we plan to give a Vann Woodward Prize to the historian who has shown what biologists term "absolute maze-brightness," that is, the ability to get ahead of the pack to the scrumptious cheese at a complex labyrinth's end. Comer's own Pulitzer Prize (bestowed for his having edited the perhaps questionable diary of Mary Chesnut) was the result of a lifetime of successful maze-threading, which ended with a friend, John Blum, awarding him the prime cheddar for what is hardly history writing in our committee's strict sense. To be fair, Comer did deserve an honorable mention back in 1955 for *The Strange Career of Jim Crow.* Our committee tends to agree that prize-giving is largely a racket in which self-serving schoolteachers look after one another. We shall, in due course, address this interesting if ancillary subject.

Meanwhile, we debate whether or not to create a vulgar splash and give an annual prize to the worst American historian of the year. But the first nominations are coming in so thick and fast that none of us really can, in a single life, read all the evidence—and graduate students are forbidden to do our work for us. So we have tentatively abandoned that notion. Instead, we have been surveying current publications, applying our strict standards to the works of an eclectic group that has only one thing in common (badness aside): the public approbation of like-minded toilers in the field.

Our criteria: First, the book must be badly written. Since this is as true, alas, of some of our best historians, we do not dwell too much on aesthetics. Gibbon and Macaulay and Carlyle knew that history was an important aspect of literature and so made literature; but this secret seems to have got lost by the end of the last century. Even our own wise hero, Edmund Wilson, didn't really write all that good himself. Second, the book in question must be composed in perfect bad faith. This is much easier for us to judge than literary value and very satisfying, particularly when one can figure where the writer is, as they say, coming from. Naturally, our own tastes condition our responses. Most of us are not enthusiasts of the National Security State of 1950 *et seq.* And we suspect that the empire, now spinning out of control, was a bad idea. After all, the federal government must borrow heavily every single day to keep it humming along. But anyone who can make a good case for Truman's invention of the National Security State does not necessarily, on the ground of our own political incorrectness, earn a place in the crowded *galère.* Only if he or she denies that there is such a thing as an American empire (an act of bad faith, since that is the line those who endow universities want taken) will inclusion occur.

In the matter of race, the opportunities for bad faith are beyond mere counting. Even so, our committee has just voted *unanimously* that the worst of the books currently in print is *America in Black and White: One Nation, Indivisible, Race in America,* by Stephan Thernstrom and Abigail Thernstrom. The two nervous subtitles betray unease, just as rapid eye-blinking, behaviorists tell us, signifies a liar in full flood. In presenting the Thernstroms' work as the first of a series of bad histories we do not want to create in them a sense of pride or, indeed, of uniqueness. There are many, many others in their league and, from time to time, they too will be revealed in these pages.

The Thernstroms are a husband-and-wife team: He is a Harvard professor, she a self-proclaimed liberal because, she said to me, she wrote once for

*The Economist.* The hearty laughter you now hear from across the Atlantic is that of Evelyn Rothschild, that splendid conservative paper's splendidly conservative proprietor.

The Thernstroms are crude writers, but then if they were not, they would not be so honored here. What they have perfected—much appreciated by their natural constituency, the anti-blacks—is what we call the Reverse Angle Shot in the matter of race. In the movies a reverse angle is exactly what it sounds like. You shoot a scene one way; then you switch about and shoot it from the exact opposite point of view. In debate, however, the Thernstrom Reverse Angle is supposed to take the place of the master shot: that is, the wide-angle look at the whole scene. Their argument is simple. Affirmative action for minorities is wrong, particularly in the case of African-Americans, because such action takes it for granted that they are by nature inferior to whites and so require more financial aid (and slacker educational standards) than canny whites or those eerily look-alike, overly numerate Asians. This is inspired. Now the Therns can maintain that the true racist is one who believes in affirmative action, because he is anti-black, while *Economist*-reading Therns believe that blacks can stand on their own two feet alongside the best of whites if only evil liberals, in their condescending racism, would not try to help them out of ghettos of their own feckless making.

To "prove" this, the Thernstroms have come up with a blizzard of statistics reminiscent of the late Robert Benchley's "Treasurer's Report" in order to make the case that blacks were really getting their act together from 1945 until the sixties, when affirmative action, welfare and other liberal deviltries so spoiled them that they took to drugs and murder while, most tragic of all, not living up to "our" S.A.T. norms.

One of the hallmarks of the truly bad historian is not so much the routine manipulation of the stats as the glee with which it is done, sad and sober though he tries to appear, crocodile tear forever clinging to nose-tip. The Therns' Introduction is high comedy. Quotations routinely turn reality upside down. A state court strikes down a blacks-only scholarship program at the University of Maryland: " 'Of all the criteria by which men and women can be judged,' the court intoned, 'the most pernicious is that of race.' " Therefore, special blacks-only scholarships are racist.

But like so many zealots, the Therns cannot control that Strangelovian arm forever going rigid with a life of its own as it rises in salute. A few lines after establishing the overt racism of affirmative action, they up the rhetoric: "What do we owe those who arrive on our shores in 1619 and remained members of an oppressed caste for more than three centuries?" I like that "our shores." After three centuries surely these are African-American shores, too, not to mention the shores of the indigenous Mongol population, which needs quite as much affirmative action these days as do "our" involuntary African visitors. Certainly the Therns themselves are hardly in the "our" business; they did not, as idle gossip has it, hit shore with Leif Ericson. Rather, theirs is the disdain, even rage, of recent arrivals against those who preceded them but did less well. Racism, after all, is a complex matter beyond the competence of a pair of publicists for the shrinking white majority and its institutions, among them the Manhattan Institute, where Abigail is "a senior fellow," as well as the John M. Olin Foundation and the Bradley, Richardson, Earhart and Carthage generators of light, fueled by corporate money. Joel Pulliam, one of the Therns' undergraduate helots, "worked for us part-time throughout his college career." The Pulliam family are—or were—newspaper proprietors of great malignity. (Our committee is now taking cognizance of these un-American covens and shall, in due course, work to remove their tax exemptions on the ground that they are political activists.)

Now the argument again: Everything was getting better for the blacks until *Brown v. Board of Education,* affirmative action, etc., destroyed their moral fiber. Result: "Today's typical black twelfth-grader scores no better on a reading test than the average white in the eighth grade, and is 5.4 years behind the typical white in science." Our committee is still examining all Thernstrom figures that "prove" blacks have never been better off than now, or were better off before anyone did anything to be of use to them, or aren't really worth bothering with as they are demonstrably inferior. After all, "the proportion of blacks in poverty is still triple that of whites. The unemployment rate for black males is double the white rate, the rate of death from homicide" . . . and so on. Then the horror, the horror: "Blacks from families earning over $70,000 a year have lower average SAT scores than whites from families taking in less than $10,000." So even if they make money (dealing drugs, entertaining or playing games), they are still awfully dumb. Curiously, no Thern has questioned the value of the S.A.T. score or, indeed, the value of the curriculum that is taught in "our" high schools or available in universities. "G.V." was so bored at one of the country's best prep schools (prewar) that he made no effort to do more than pass dull courses. Could it be that African-American culture might not be satisfied with what passes for education today? Even—or especially, when one considers the Therns' polemics—at Harvard?

For the Therns, the political activism of the sixties is the wrong road taken. Apparently, "three of four Southern whites . . . were ready to concede that racial integration was bound to come," presumably when the bird of dawning singeth all night long. But Americans rightly deplored "brutal tactics"—i.e., demonstrations. The Therns produce an ancient cold war gloss on the matter of race: "Surveys disclosed a pervasive and bizarre skepticism about whether the civil rights movement reflected the true feelings of typical African-Americans." As of a 1963 poll, a quarter of the white population suspected the Commies of egging on listless African-Americans. The F.B.I. bugging of Martin Luther King Jr. on the suspicion that he was in with the Commies is justified "in the context of the deadly struggle between the United States and Soviet totalitarianism." Thus the Great Red Herring once again makes an obligatory appearance, in a footnote.

"G.V." must now confess that he met the Therns in 1991. He had come to Harvard to deliver the Massey lectures, which are sponsored by a small, suitably obscure department known, he recalls, as "American Civilization," then headed by Professor Thern. "G.V." met them at a dinner, which was, he now realizes, a day of apotheosis, particularly for Mrs. Thern, an adorable elfin minx. The Los Angeles Police Department had just beaten Rodney King to a pulp and a video of cops clobbering his fallen figure had been playing on television all day. Abigail was firmly on the side of the police. "Their work is so dangerous, so unappreciated." Her panegyric to the L.A.P.D. stunned the dinner party. She speculated on Rodney King's as yet unrevealed crimes and shuddered at the thought of his ebon-dark associates, lying in wait for pink porker cops. Professor Thern gave a secret smile as his helpmeet's aria grew more and more rich and strange.

Now, somewhat sated by numbing stats, the Therns go on attacking blacks in what they appear to think is a sound and sympathetic way. They quote angry citizens like the young black man who says, after King's attackers were let off by a Simi Valley jury, "Is there a conspiracy to allow and condone the destruction of black people?" Needless to say, there is nothing a Thern likes as much as a conspiracy theory to pooh-pooh. "That these charges have been repeated so often and so vehemently does not make them true. The issue is complicated." The Therns conclude that blacks are locked up more often than whites because they commit more crimes, and to try to help them is useless, as the sixties proved.

As one reads this curiously insistent racist tract, one begins to sense that there is some sort of demonic spirit on the scene, unacknowledged but ever-present, as the Therns make their endless case. Reading Thern-prose, somewhat more demure than Abbey's table-rant, I was put in uneasy mind of kindly old Dr. Maimonides. In Book III, chapter 51 of his *Guide for the Perplexed* (copyright 1190 C.E.), the revered codifier of the Talmud lists those who cannot begin to acknowledge, much less worship, the true God. Among those nonhumans are "some of the Turks [he means Mongols] and the nomads in the North and the Blacks and the nomads in the South, and those who resemble them in our climates. And their nature is like the nature of mute animals, and according to my opinion they are not on the level of human beings, and their level among existing things is below that of a man and above that of a monkey, because they have the image and the resemblance of a man more than a monkey does." When this celebrated book was translated into English early this century, the translators were embarrassed, as well they should have been, by the racism. So instead of using the word "black" or "Negro," they went back to the Hebrew word for blacks—Kushim, which they transliterated as Kushites—a previously unknown and unidentifiable tribe for Anglophones and so easily despised.

There was an eccentric English duke who, according to legend, spoke only once a year. His remarks were treasured. At the time of the abdication of Edward VIII, he suddenly said at a Sunday dinner, "If there is any trouble anywhere, look for an archbishop." Change "archbishop" to "monotheist" and one understands the powerful engine that drives Therns to write bad history. Also, in fairness, it must be noted that Judaism's two dreary spinoffs, Christianity and Islam, have given even wider range to the notion of the true godless folk as "white man's burden," "cursed infidels" and "lesser breeds" so much less human than those whipped up in the true God's bookish image.

Finally, a bad historian is one who dares not say what he means. He must count on his "evidence"—those stats—to bring us round to his often hidden-in-plain-sight point of view. At the conclusion of their screed, the Therns produce such tautologies as "the issue of group differences is actually enormously complicated." This extraordinary insight appears as late as page 541. "The complexities of the matter become evident when we notice that the socioeconomic gap between Jews and Christians today is greater than the gap between blacks and whites. Jewish per capita incomes are nearly double those of non-Jews, a bigger difference than the black-white income gap. Although Jews make up less than 3 percent of the population, they constitute more than a quarter of the people on the *Forbes* magazine list of the richest four hundred Americans. . . . Asian Americans similarly outrank whites on most measures." We are also told that Scots are highly educated but don't make all that much money, because they are drawn to "the ministry and teaching." Cajuns? Forget it. "What explains why some of these groups have done so much better than others is very hard to say." Actually, it is quite easy for a Thern to say, but perhaps a bit dangerous. So at the end of their long book, the matter of race is both a reality and a chimera. In short, *complicated*; yet, to the Therns' credit, we know exactly what they mean.

Perhaps the only literary form perfected by late-twentieth-century United Statespersons is the blurb for the dust jacket. It is for us what the haiku was for the medieval Japanese. Of all the varieties of blurb, the Academic Courtesy is the most exquisite in its balances and reticences and encodements. Now, there was one blurb that the Therns knew that they dare not publish without: that of the chairman of Harvard's Department of Afro-American Studies. Would this elusive, allusive—illusive?—figure misread the text as hoped or, worse for them, would he actually read it for what it is? Great risk either way. One can picture the Therns agonizing over how best to rope him in. He was their White Whale, nay, their Cinque of Sierra Leone. Night after night, Therns and their ilk flitted about Harvard Yard, suitably hooded against the night air. Meanwhile, the beleaguered chairman, quite aware of their plot, was careful to take the Underground Railroad when crossing the Yard. But in the end, he broke. He gathered loved ones around him. "I can no longer live like this, in terror of the Therns. I'm going out." Loved ones keened, "But not *tonight.* The moon's full. *This is Thern weather.*"

But the chairman said, "I fear not. My blurb will protect me from all harm." Blurb? Had he perjured himself? No, he had not, he declared; and so, casting aside fear, he entered the Yard, where a posse of howling Therns promptly held him for ransom in the form of what proved to be the very paradigm of all Harvard blurbs: "This book is essential reading for anyone wishing to understand the state of race relations at the end of the great American century." Thus, he tricked his pursuers and freed graduate students as yet unborn from, at the very least, a hoisting by the Thern petard.

*The Nation*
*April 20, 1998*

# President and Mrs. U. S. Grant

SOME YEARS AGO a friend remarked to a brand-new President's wife (a woman of unique charm, wit, sensibility, and good grooming) that there was no phrase in our language which so sets the teeth on edge as "First Lady."

"Oh, how true!" said that lady, after the tiniest of pauses. "I keep telling the operators at the White House not to call me that, but they just love saying 'First Lady.' And of course Mrs. E+++++++++r always insisted on being called that."

According to one Ralph Geoffrey Newman, in a note to the recently published *The Personal Memoirs of Julia Dent Grant,* "the term 'First Lady' became a popular one after the *Lady in the Land* . . . December 4, 1911." The phrase was in use, however, as early as the Ladyhood of Mrs. Rutherford B. ("Lemonade Lucy") Hayes.

Martha Washington contented herself with the unofficial (hence seldom omitted) title "Lady" Washington. Mrs. James Monroe took a crack at regal status, receiving guests on a dais with something suspiciously like a coronet in her tousled hair. When twenty-four-year-old Miss Julia Gardiner of Gardiners Island became the doting wife of senior citizen John Tyler, she insisted that his tottering arrivals and departures be accompanied by the martial chords of "Hail to the Chief." Mary Todd Lincoln often gave the impression that she thought she was Marie Antoinette.

It is curious that a Johnny-come-fairly-lately republic like the United States should so much want to envelop in majesty those for the most part seedy political hacks quadrennially "chosen" by the people to rule over them. As the world's royalties take to their bicycles—or to their heels—the world's presidents from Giscard to Leone to our own dear sovereign affect the most splendid state.

It would seem to be a rule of history that as the actual power of a state declines, the pageantry increases. Certainly the last days of the Byzantine empire were marked by a court protocol so elaborate and time-consuming that the arrival of the Turks must have been a relief to everyone. Now, as our own imperial republic moves gorgeously into its terminal phase, it is pleasant and useful to contemplate two centuries of American court life, to examine those personages who have lived in the White House and borne those two simple but awful titles "The President," "The First Lady" and, finally, to meditate on that peculiarly American religion, President-worship.

The Eighteenth President Ulysses Simpson Grant and his First Lady Julia Dent Grant are almost at dead center of that solemn cavalcade which has brought us from Washington to Ford, and in the process made a monkey of Darwin. Since 1885 we have had Grant's own memoirs to study; unfortunately, they end with the Civil War and do not deal with his presidency. Now Julia Dent Grant's memoirs have been published for the first time and, as that ubiquitous clone of Parson Weems Mr. Bruce Catton says in his introduction, she comes through these pages as a most "likeable" woman. "No longer is she just Mrs. Grant. Now she has three dimensions."

From her own account Julia Dent Grant does seem to have been a likeable, rather silly woman, enamored of First Ladyhood (and why not?), with a passion for clothes. If photographs are to be trusted (and why should they be when our Parson Weemses never accept as a fact anything that might obscure those figures illuminated by the high noon of Demos?), Julia was short and dumpy, with quite astonishingly crossed eyes. As divinity in the form of First Ladyhood approached, Julia wanted to correct with surgery nature's error but her husband very nicely said that since he had married her with crossed eyes he preferred her to stay the way she was. In any case, whatever the number of Julia's dimensions, she is never anything but Mrs. Grant and one reads her only to find out more about that strange enigmatic figure who proved to be one of our country's best generals and worst presidents.

Grant was as much a puzzle to contemporaries as he is to us now. To Henry Adams, Grant was "pre-intellectual, archaic, and would have seemed so even to the cave-dwellers." Henry Adams's brother had served with Grant in the war and saw him in a somewhat different light. "He is a man of the most exquisite judgment and tact," wrote Charles Francis Adams. But "he might pass well enough for a dumpy and slouchy little subaltern, very fond of smoking." C. F. Adams saw Grant at his best, in the field; H. Adams saw him at his worst, in the White House.

During Grant's first forty years of relative failure, he took to the bottle. When given command in the war, he seems to have pretty much given up the booze (though there was a bad tumble not only off the wagon but off his horse at New Orleans). According to Mr. Bruce Catton, "It was widely believed that [Grant], especially during his career as a soldier, was much too fond of whiskey, and that the cure consisted in bringing Mrs. Grant to camp; in her presence, it was held, he instantly became a teetotaler. . . . This contains hardly a wisp of truth." It never does out there in Parson Weems land where all our presidents were good and some were great and none ever served out his term without visibly growing in the office. One has only to listen to Rabbi Korff to know that this was true even of Richard M. Nixon. Yet there is every evidence that General Grant not only did not grow in office but dramatically shrank.

The last year of Grant's life was the noblest, and the most terrible. Dying of cancer, wiped out financially by a speculator, he was obliged to do what he had always said he had no intention of doing: write his memoirs in order to provide for his widow. He succeeded admirably. The two volumes entitled *Personal Memoirs of U. S. Grant* earned $450,000; and Julia Grant was able to live in comfort for the seventeen years that she survived her husband. Now for the first time we can compare Grant's memoirs with those of his wife.

With the instinct of one who knows what the public wants (or ought to get), Grant devoted only thirty-one pages to his humble youth in Ohio. The prose is Roman—lean, rather flat, and, cumulatively, impressive. Even the condescending Matthew Arnold allowed that Grant had "the high merit of saying clearly in the fewest possible words what had to be said, and saying it, frequently, with shrewd and unexpected turns of expression." There is even a quiet wit that Grant's contemporaries were not often allowed to see: "Boys enjoy the misery of their contemporaries, at least village boys in that day did" (this is known as the Eisenhower qualification: is it taught at West Point? in order to confuse the press?), "and in later life I have found that all adults are not free from this peculiarity."

The next 161 pages are devoted to West Point and to Grant's early career as a professional army officer. Grant's eyes did not fill with tears at the thought of his school days on the banks of the Hudson. In fact, he hated the Academy: "Early in the session of the Congress which met in December, 1839, a bill was discussed abolishing the Military Academy. I saw this as an honorable way to obtain a discharge . . . for I was selfish enough to favor the bill." But the Academy remained, as it does today, impregnable to any Congress.

On graduation, Second Lieutenant Grant was posted to Jefferson Barracks, St. Louis, where, he noted, "too many of the older officers, when they came to command posts, made it a study to think what orders they could publish to annoy their subordinates and render them uncomfortable."

Grant also tells us, rather casually, that "At West Point I had a classmate . . . F. T. Dent, whose family resides some five miles west of Jefferson Barracks. . . ." The sister of the classmate was Julia Dent, aged seventeen. According to Grant, visits to the Dent household were "enjoyable." "We could often take long walks, or go on horseback to visit the neighbors. . . . Sometimes one of the brothers would accompany us, sometimes one of the younger sisters."

In May 1844, when it came time to move on (the administration was preparing an interdiction or incursion of Mexico), Grant writes: "before separating [from Julia] it was definitely understood that at a convenient time we would join our fortunes. . . ." Then Grant went off to his first war. Offhandedly, he gives us what I take to be the key if not to his character to his success: "One of my superstitions had always been when I started to go any where, or to do anything, not to turn back, or stop until the thing intended was accomplished." This defines not only a certain sort of military genius but explains field-commander Grant who would throw wave after wave of troops into battle, counting on superior numbers to shatter the enemy while himself ignoring losses.

When Henry Adams met Grant at the White House, he came away appalled by the torpor, the dullness of the sort of man "always needing stimulants, but for whom action was the highest stimulant—the instinct of fight. Such men were forces of nature, energies of the prime. . . ." This was of course only partly true of Grant. Unlike so many American jingoes, Grant did not like war for its own bloody self or conquest for conquest's sake. Of the administration's chicanery leading up to the invasion of Mexico, he wrote with hard clarity, "I was bitterly opposed to the measure, and to this day regard the war, which resulted, as one of the most unjust ever waged by a stronger against a weaker nation. . . . It was an instance of a republic following the bad example of European monarchies, in not considering justice in their desire to acquire additional territory."

Grant also had a causal sense of history that would have astonished Henry Adams had he got to know the taciturn and corrupted, if not corrupt, president. Of the conquest of Mexico and the annexation of Texas, Grant wrote, "To us it was an empire and of incalculable value; but it might have been obtained by other means. The Southern rebellion was largely the outgrowth of the Mexican War. Nations, like individuals, are punished for their transgressions. We got our punishment in the most sanguinary and expensive war of modern times." If Grant's law still obtains, then the only hope for today's American is emigration.

The Grant of those youthful years seems most engaging (but then we are reading his own account). He says firmly, "I do not believe that I ever would have the courage to fight a duel." He was probably unique among military commanders in disliking dirty stories while "I am not aware of ever having used a profane expletive in my life; but I would have the charity to excuse those who may have done so, if they were in charge of a train of Mexican pack mules. . . ."

Grant saw right through the Mexican war, which "was a political war, and the administration conducting it desired to make party capital of it." Grant was also very much on to the head of the army General Scott, who was "known to have political aspirations, and nothing so popularizes a candidate for high civil positions as military victories." It takes one, as they say, to know another.

Mark Twain published Grant's memoirs posthumously, and one wonders if he might have added a joke or two. Some possible Twainisms: "My regiment lost four commissioned officers, all senior to me, by steamboat explosions during the Mexican war. The Mexicans were not so discriminating. They sometimes picked off my juniors." The cadence of those sentences reveals an expert sense of music-hall timing. When a Mexican priest refused to let Grant use his church during an engagement, Grant threatened the priest with arrest. Immediately, the man "began to see his duty in the same light that I did, and opened the door, though he did not look as if it gave him any special pleasure to do so." But whether or not Twain helped with the jokes, it must be remembered that the glum, often silent, always self-pitying president was capable, when he chose, of the sharp remark. Told that the brilliant but inordinately vain *littérateur* Senator Charles Sumner did not believe in the Bible, Grant said, "That's only because he didn't write it."

The Mexican war ended, and "On the twenty-second of August, 1848, I was married to Miss Julia Dent Grant, the lady of whom I have before spoken." With that Caesarian line, the lady appears no more in the two volumes dedicated to the fighting of the Civil War. Now Julia's memoirs redress the balance.

In old age, Julia put pen to paper and gave her own version of her life and marriage, but for one reason or another she could never get the book published. Now, at last, her memoirs are available, suitably loaded with a plangent introduction by Mr. Catton ("they shared one of the great, romantic, beautiful loves of all American history"), a note by R. G. Newman on "The First Lady as an Author," and a foreword and notes by J. Y. Simon. The notes are excellent and instructive.

In her last years Julia was not above hawking her manuscript to millionaire acquaintances; at one point she offered the manuscript to book-lover Andrew Carnegie for $125,000. Just why the book was never published is obscure. I suspect Julia wanted too much money for it; also, as she wrote in a letter, the first readers of the text thought it "*too* near, *too* close to the private life of the Genl for the public, and I thought this was just what was wanted." Julia was right; and her artless narrative does give a new dimension (if not entirely the third) to one of the most mysterious (because so simple?) figures in our history.

"My first recollections in life reach back a long way, more than three-score years, and ten now. We, my gentle mother and two little brothers, were on the south end of the front piazza at our old home, White Haven." Julia sets us down firmly in Margaret Mitchell country. "Life seemed one long summer of sunshine, flowers, and smiles to me and to all at that happy home." Mamma came from "a large eastern city," and did not find it easy being "a western pioneer's wife." The darkies were happy as can be (this was slave-holding Missouri) and "I think our people were very happy. At least they were in mamma's time, though the young ones became somewhat demoralized about the beginning of the Rebellion, when all the comforts of slavery passed away forever."

Julia was obviously much indulged. "Coming as I did to the family after the fourth great boy, I was necessarily something of a pet. . . . It was always 'Will little daughter like to do this?' 'No!' Then little daughter did not do it." I suspect that little daughter's alarmingly crossed eyes may have made the family overprotective. She herself seems unaware of any flaw: "Imagine what a pet I was with my three, brave, handsome brothers." She was also indulged in school where she was good in philosophy (what could that have been?), mythology, and history, but "in every other branch I was below the standard, and, worse still, my indifference was very exasperating." Although Julia enjoys referring to herself as "poor little me," she sounds like a pretty tough customer.

Enter Lieutenant Grant. Julia's description of their time together is considerably richer than that of the great commander. "Such delightful rides we all used to take!" So far her account tallies with his. But then, I fear, Julia falls victim to prurience: "As we sat on the piazza alone, he took his class ring from his finger and asked me if I would not wear it. . . . I declined, saying, 'Oh, no, mamma would not approve . . . !' " "I, child that I was, never for a moment thought of him as a lover." He goes. "Oh! how lonely it was without him." "I remember he was kind enough to make a nice little coffin for my canary bird and he painted it yellow. About eight officers attended the funeral of my little pet." When Grant came back to visit, Julia told him "that I had named one of my new bedstead posts for him." Surely the good taste of the editor might have spared us this pre-Freudian pornography. In any case, after this shocker, Julia was obliged to marry Grant . . . or "Ulys" as she called him.

"Our station at Detroit is one pleasant memory . . . gay parties and dinners, the fêtes champêtres. . . . Our house was very snug and convenient: two sitting rooms, dining room, bedroom, and kitchen all on the first floor." (And all of this on a captain's pay.) Julia's especial friend that winter was the wife of Major John H. Gore. Together they gave a fancy dress ball on a Sunday, invoking the wrath of the Sabbatarians. But the girls persisted and Mrs. Gore came as the Sultana of Turkey while "I, after much consideration, decided upon the costume of the ideal tambourine girl. . . . Ulys called me 'Tambourina' for a long time afterwards."

But then Grant left the army; and the descent began. "I was now to commence," he wrote, "at the age of thirty-two, a new struggle for our support." Like most professional army men Grant was fitted for no work of any kind save the presidency and that was not yet in the cards. "My wife had a farm near St. Louis, to which we went, but I had no means to stock it." Nevertheless, "I managed to keep along very well until 1858, when I was attacked by fever and ague." Perhaps he was; he was also attacked by acute alcoholism.

But the innumerable clones of Parson Weems tend to ignore any blemish on our national heroes. And Julia does her part, too. She writes, "I have been both indignant and grieved over the statement of pretended personal acquaintances of Captain Grant at this time to the effect that he was dejected, low-spirited, badly dressed, and even slovenly." "Low-spirited" is a nice euphemism for full of spirits. Julia had the Southern woman's loyalty to kin: protect at all costs and ignore the unpleasant. She even goes beyond her husband's dour record, declaring, "Ulys was really very successful at farming . . . and I was a splendid farmer's wife."

Julia's family loyalty did not extend to Ulys's folks. Although Ulys and the Dent family could do no wrong, the Grants were generally exempted from her benign policy. In fact, Julia loathed them. "I was joyous at the thought of not going to Kentucky, for the Captain's family, with the exception of his mother, did not like me. . . . we were brought up in different schools. They considered me unpardonably extravagant, and I considered them inexcusably the other way and may, unintentionally, have shown my feelings." There were also political disagreements between the two families as the Civil War approached. The Dents were essentially Southern, and Julia "was a Democrat at that time (because my father was). . . . I was very much disturbed in my political sentiments, feeling that the states had a right to go out of the Union if they wished to." But she also thought that the Union should be preserved. "Ulys was much amused at my enthusiasm and said I was a little inconsistent when I talked of states' rights."

With the coming of the Civil War, the lives of the Grants were never again to be private. Rapidly he rose from Illinois colonel (they had moved to Galena) to lieutenant general in command of the Union forces. The victories were splendid. Julia had anxious moments, not to mention innumerable prophetic dreams which she solemnly records.

At one point, separated from the General, "I wept like a deserted child . . . Only once again in my life—when I left the White House—did this feeling of desertion come over me." There were also those unremitting base rumors. Why, "The report went out," on some crucial occasion, "that General Grant was not in the field, that he was at some dance house. The idea! Dear Ulys! so earnest and serious; he never went to a party of any kind, except to take me." Julia's usual euphemism for the drunken bouts was "he was ill." And she always helped him get well.

Grant was not above making fun of her. Julia: "Ulys, I don't like standing stationary washstands, do you?" Ulys: "Yes, I do; why don't you?" Julia: "Well, I don't know." Ulys: "I'll tell you why. You have to go to the stand. It cannot be brought to you."

Midway through the war, some Southern friends were talking of "the Constitution, telling me the action of the government was unconstitutional. Well, I did not know a thing about this dreadful Constitution and told them so. . . . I would not know where to look for it even if I wished to read it. . . . I was dreadfully puzzled about the horrid old Constitution." She even asked her father: "Why don't they make a new Constitution since this is such an enigma—one to suit the time." I suspect Julia was pretty much reflecting her husband's lifelong contempt for a Constitution that he saw put aside in the most casual way by Abraham Lincoln, who found habeas corpus incompatible with national security. But although neither Grant nor Julia was very strong on the Bill of Rights, she at least had a good PR sense. When "General Grant wrote that obnoxious order expelling the Jews from his lines for which he was so severely reprimanded by the federal Congress—the General said deservedly so, as he had no right to make an order against any special sect."

In triumph, Julia came east after Ulys assumed command of the armies. Julia was enchanted by the White House and President Lincoln, in that order. Mrs. Lincoln appears to have been on her worst behavior and Julia has a hard time glossing over a number of difficult moments. On one occasion, Julia plumped herself down beside the First Lady. Outraged, Mrs. Lincoln is alleged to have said, "How dare you be seated, until I invite you?" Julia denies that this ever happened. But she does describe a day in the field when Mrs. Lincoln was upset by a mounted lady who seemed to be trying to ride beside President Lincoln. As one reads, in the vast spaces between the lines of Julia's narrative, it would seem that Mrs. Lincoln went absolutely bananas, "growing more and more indignant and not being able to control her wrath. . . ." But, fortunately, Julia was masterful—"I quietly placed my hand on hers"—and was soothing.

Later, when the presidential yacht was in the James River, close to

Grant's headquarters, Julia confesses that "I saw very little of the presidential party now, as Mrs. Lincoln had a good deal of company and seemed to have forgotten us. I felt this deeply and could not understand it. . . . Richmond had fallen; so had Petersburg. All of these places were visited by the President and party, and I, not a hundred yards from them, was not invited to join them."

Despite the dresses, the dreams, the self-serving silly-little-me talk, Julia has a sharp eye for detail; describing Richmond, the last capital of the Confederacy, she writes: "I remember that all the streets near the public buildings were covered with papers—public documents and letters, I suppose. So many of these papers lay on the ground that they reminded me of the forest leaves when summer is gone."

Although Grant ignores such details he is shrewd not only about his colleagues but about his former colleagues, the West Pointers who led the Confederate army. He writes of Jefferson Davis with whom he had served in Mexico: "Mr. Davis had an exalted opinion of his own military genius. . . . On several occasions during the war he came to the relief of the Union army by means of his superior *military genius.*" Grant also makes the Cromwellian assertion: "It is men who wait to be selected, and not those who seek, from whom we may always expect the most efficient service."

Although never a Lincoln man in politics, Grant came to like the President, and would listen respectfully to Lincoln's strategic proposals, refraining from pointing out their glaring flaws. Grant also took seriously Secretary of War Stanton's injunction never to tell Lincoln his plans in advance because the President is "so kind-hearted, so averse to refusing anything asked of him, that some friend would be sure to get from him all he knew." Lincoln was plainly aware of this defect because he "told me he did not want to know what I proposed to do."

At about this time the press that was to be Grant's constant, lifelong *bête noire* began to get on his nerves. *The New York Times* was a particular offender; grimly, Grant remarked on that portion of the press which "always magnified rebel successes and belittled ours." In fact, "the press was free up to the point of treason."

Grant had great respect for the Confederate army, and in retrospect lauded the Fabian tactics of General J. E. Johnston on the ground that "anything that could have prolonged the war a year beyond the time that it did finally close, would probably have exhausted the North to such an extent that they might then have abandoned the contest and agreed to a separation." Because "the South was a military camp, controlled absolutely by the government with soldiers to back it . . . the war could have been protracted, no matter to what extent the discontent reached. . . ." One suspects that if Grant had been the president, he would have shut down the press, sent Congress home, and made the North an armed camp.

Grant had much the same lifelong problem with the "horrid old Constitution" that Julia had. Magisterially, he writes, "The Constitution was not framed with a view to any such rebellion as that of 1861–5. While it did not authorize rebellion it made no provision against it. Yet the right to resist or suppress rebellion is as inherent as the right of self defense. . . ." Accepting this peculiar view of that intricate document, Grant noted with some satisfaction that "the Constitution was therefore in abeyance for the time being, so far as it in any way affected the progress and termination of the war." During Grant's presidency, the Constitution was simply an annoyance to be circumvented whenever possible. Or as he used to say when he found himself, as president, blocked by mere law: "Let the law be executed."

On that day when lilacs in the dooryard bloomed, Julia was in Washington preparing to go with Grant to Philadelphia. At noon, a peculiar-looking man rapped on her door. " 'Mrs. Lincoln sends me, Madam, with her compliments, to say she will call for you at exactly eight o'clock to go to the theater.' To this, I replied with some feeling (not liking either the looks of the messenger or the message, thinking the former savored of discourtesy and the latter seemed like a command), 'You may return with my compliments to Mrs. Lincoln and say I regret that as General Grant and I intend leaving the city this afternoon, we will not, therefore, be here. . . .' "

It is nice to speculate that if Mrs. Lincoln had asked Julia aboard the yacht that day in the James River, there might never have been a Grant administration. Julia has her own speculation: "I am perfectly sure that he [the messenger], with three others, one of them [John Wilkes] Booth himself, sat opposite me and my party at luncheon."

That night in Philadelphia they heard the news. "I asked, 'This will make Andy Johnson President, will it not?' 'Yes,' the General said, 'and for some reason, I dread the change.' " Nobly, Julia did her duty: "With my heart full of sorrow, I went many times to call on dear heart-broken Mrs. Lincoln, but she could not see me."

After commanding the armies in peacetime and behaving not too well during that impasse between President Johnson and Secretary of War Stanton which led to Johnson's impeachment, Grant was himself elected president. Although, unhappily, Grant's own memoirs stop with the war, Julia's continue gaily, haphazardly, and sometimes nervously through that gilded age at whose center these two odd little creatures presided.

Until our own colorful period, nothing quite like the Grant administration had ever happened to the imperial republic. In eight years almost everyone around Grant was found to be corrupt from his first vice president Colfax to his brother-in-law to his private secretary to his secretary of war to his minister to Great Britain; the list is endless. Yet the people forgave the solemn little man who had preserved the Union and then proposed himself to a grateful nation with the phrase "Let us have peace."

Grant was re-elected president in 1872, despite a split in the Republican party: the so-called Liberal Republicans supported Horace Greeley as did the regular Democrats. Although the second term was even more scandalous than the first, the Grants were eager for yet a third term. But the country was finally fed up with Grantism. In the centennial summer of 1876, at the Philadelphia exhibition, President Grant had the rare experience of being booed in public. Julia does not mention the booing. But she does remember that the Empress of Brazil was asked to start the famous Corliss engine, while "I, the wife of the President of the United States—I, the wife of General Grant—was there and was not invited to assist at this little ceremony. . . . Of this I am quite sure: if General Grant had known of this intended slight to his wife, the engine never would have moved with his assistance."

Nevertheless, after four years out of office General and Mrs. Grant were again eager to return to the White House, to "the dear old house. . . . Eight happy years I spent there," wrote Julia, "so happy! It still seems as much like home to me as the old farm in Missouri, White Haven." But it looked rather different from the farm or, for that matter, from the way the White House has usually looked. By the time Mrs. Grant had finished her refurbishments, the East Room was divided into three columned sections and filled with furniture of ebony and gold. Julia was highly pleased with her creation; in fact, "I have visited many courts and, I am proud to say, I saw none that excelled in brilliancy the receptions of President Grant."

Except for a disingenuous account of the secretary of war's impeachment (his wife "Puss" Belknap was a favorite of Julia's), the First Lady herself hardly alludes to the scandals of those years. On the other hand, Julia describes in rapturous detail her trip around the world with Ulys. In London dinner was given them by the Duke of Wellington at Apsley House. "This great house was presented to Wellington by the government for the single [*sic*] victory at Waterloo, along with wealth and a noble title which will descend throughout his line. As I sat there, I thought, 'How would it have been if General Grant had been an Englishman—I wonder, I wonder?' "

So did Grant. Constantly. In fact, he became obsessed by the generosity of England to Marlborough and to Wellington and by the niggardliness of the United States to its unique savior. It is possible that Grant's corruption in office stems from this resentment; certainly, he felt that he had every right to take expensive presents from men who gained thereby favors. Until ruined by a speculator-friend of his son, Grant seems to have acquired a fortune; although nowhere near as large as that of the master-criminal Lyndon Johnson, it was probably larger than that of another receiver of rich men's gifts, General Eisenhower.

Circling the globe, the vigorous Grant enjoyed sightseeing and Julia enjoyed shopping. There was culture, too: at Heidelberg "we remained there all night and listened with pleasure to Wagner or Liszt—I cannot remember which—who performed several of his own delightful pieces of music for us." (It was Wagner.) "Of course, we visited the Taj and admired it as everyone does. . . . Everyone says it is the most beautiful building in the world, and I suppose it is. Only I think that everyone has not seen the Capitol at Washington!" It is no accident that General Grant's favorite book was *Innocents Abroad.* After nearly two years, Maggie and Jiggs completed the grand tour, and came home with every hope of returning to the "dear old house" in Washington.

A triumphal progress across the States began on the West Coast (it was Grant's misfortune never to have become what he had wanted to be ever since his early years in the army, a Californian). Then they returned to their last official home, Galena, Illinois, "To Galena, dear Galena, where we were at home again in reality," writes Julia. Then "after a week's rest, we went to Chicago." The Grants were effete Easterners now, and Galena was no more than a place from which to regain the heights. "We were at Galena when the Republican Convention met at Chicago . . . I did not feel that General Grant would be nominated. . . . The General would not believe, but I saw it plainly." Julia was right, and James A. Garfield was nominated and elected.

Galena was promptly abandoned for a handsome house in New York City's East 66th Street. The Grants' days were halcyon until that grim moment when Grant cried out while eating a peach: he thought that something had stung him in the throat. It was cancer. The Grants were broke, and now the General was dying. Happily, various magnates like the Drexels and the Vanderbilts were willing to help out. But Grant was too proud for overt charity. Instead he accepted Mark Twain's offer to write his memoirs. And so, "General Grant, commander-in-chief of 1,000,000 men, General Grant, eight years President of the United States, was writing, writing of his own grand deeds, recording them that he might leave a home and independence to his family." On July 19, 1885, Grant finished the book, "and on the morning of July the twenty-third, he, my beloved, my all, passed away, and I was alone, alone."

In *Patriotic Gore* Edmund Wilson writes: "It was the age of the audacious confidence man, and Grant was the incurable sucker. He easily fell victim to their [*sic*] trickery and allowed them to betray him into compromising his office because he could not believe that such people existed."

This strikes me as all wrong. I think Grant knew exactly what was going on. For instance, when Grant's private secretary General Babcock was indicted for his part in the Whisky Ring, the President, with Nixonian zeal, gave a false deposition attesting to Babcock's character. Then Grant saw to it that the witnesses for the prosecution would not, as originally agreed, be granted exemption for testifying. When this did not inhibit the United States Attorney handling the suit, Grant fired him in mid-case: obstruction of justice in spades.

More to the point, it is simply not possible to read Grant's memoirs without realizing that the author is a man of first-rate intelligence. As president, he made it his policy to be cryptic and taciturn, partly in order not to be bored by the politicians (and from the preening Charles Sumner to the atrocious Roscoe Conkling it was an age of insufferable megalomaniacs, so nicely described by Henry Adams in *Democracy*) and partly not to give the game away. After all, everyone was on the take. Since an ungrateful nation had neglected to give him a Blenheim palace, Grant felt perfectly justified in consorting with such crooks as Jim Fisk and Jay Gould, and profiting from their crimes.

Neither in war nor in peace did Grant respect the "horrid old Constitution." This disrespect led to such bizarre shenanigans as Babcock's deal to buy and annex to the United States the unhappy island of Santo Domingo, the Treasury's money to be divvied up between Babcock and the Dominican president (and, perhaps, Grant, too). Fortunately, Grant was saved from this folly by cabinet and Congress. Later, in his memoirs, he loftily justifies the caper by saying that Santo Domingo would have been a nice place to put the former slaves.

Between Lincoln and Grant the original American republic of states united in free association was jettisoned. From the many states they forged one union, a centralized nation-state devoted to the acquisition of wealth and territory by any means. Piously, they spoke of the need to eliminate slavery but, as Grant remarked to Prince Bismarck, the real struggle *"in the beginning"* was to preserve the Union, and slavery was a secondary issue. It is no accident that although Lincoln was swift to go to war for the Union, he was downright lackadaisical when it came to Emancipation. Much of the sympathy for the South among enlightened Europeans of that day was due to the fierce arbitrariness of Lincoln's policy to deny the states their constitutional rights while refusing to take a firm stand on the moral issue of slavery.

In the last thirty-four years, the republic has become, in many ways, the sort of armed camp that Grant so much esteemed in the South. For both Lincoln and Grant it was *e pluribus unum* no matter what the price in blood or constitutional rights. Now those centripetal forces they helped to release a century ago are running down and a countervailing force is being felt: *ex uno plures.*

But enough. In this bicentennial year, as the benign spirit of Walt Disney ranges up and down the land, let us look only to what was good in Ulysses S. Grant. Let us forget the corrupted little president and remember only the great general, the kind and exquisitely tactful leader, the Roman figure who, when dying, did his duty and made the last years of his beloved goose of a wife comfortable and happy.

***The New York Review of Books***
***September 18, 1975***

# Theodore Roosevelt: An American Sissy

IN WASHINGTON, D.C., there is—or was—a place where Rock Creek crosses the main road and makes a ford which horses and, later, cars could cross if the creek was not in flood. Half a hundred years ago, I lived with my grandparents on a wooded hill not far from the ford. On summer days, my grandmother and I would walk down to the creek, careful to avoid the poison ivy that grew so luxuriously amid the crowded laurel. We would then walk beside the creek, looking out for crayfish and salamanders. When we came to the ford, I would ask her to tell me, yet again, what happened when the old President Roosevelt—not the current President Roosevelt—had come riding out of the woods on a huge horse just as two ladies on slow nags had begun a slow crossing of the ford.

"Well, suddenly, Mr. Roosevelt screamed at them, 'Out of my way!' " My grandmother imitated the president's harsh falsetto. "Stand to one side, women. *I am the President.*" What happened next? I'd ask, delighted. "Oh, they were both soaked to the skin by his horse's splashing all over them. But then, the very next year," she would say with some satisfaction, "*nice* Mr. Taft was the president." Plainly, there was a link in her mind between the Event at the Ford and the change in the presidency. Perhaps there was. In those stately pre-personal days you did not call ladies women.

The attic of the Rock Creek house was filled with thousands of books on undusted shelves while newspapers, clippings, copies of the *Congressional Record* were strewn about the floor. My grandmother was not a zealous housekeeper. There was never a time when rolled-up Persian rugs did not lie at the edge of the drawing room, like crocodiles dozing. In 1907, the last year but one of Theodore Roosevelt's administration, my grandfather came to the Senate. I don't think that they had much to do with each other. I found only one reference to TR—as he was always known—on the attic floor. In 1908, when Senator Gore nominated William Jennings Bryan for president, he made an alliterative aside, "I much prefer the strenuosity of Roosevelt to the sinuosity of Taft."

Years later I asked him why he had supported Bryan, a man who had never, in my grandfather's own words, "developed. He was too famous too young. He just stopped in his thirties." So why had he nominated Bryan for president? Well, at the time there were reasons: he was vague. Then, suddenly, the pale face grew mischievous and the thin, straight Roman mouth broke into a crooked grin. "After I nominated him at Denver, we rode back to the hotel in the same carriage and he turned to me and said, 'You know, I base my political success on just three things.' " The old man paused for dramatic effect. What were they? I asked. "I've completely forgotten," he said. "But I do remember wondering why he thought he was a success."

In 1936, Theodore Roosevelt's sinuous cousin Franklin brought an end to my grandfather's career in the Senate. But the old man stayed on in Rock Creek Park and lived to a Nestorian age, convinced that FDR, as he was always known, was our republic's Caesar while his wife, Eleanor, Theodore's niece, was a revolutionary. The old man despised the whole family except Theodore's daughter Alice Longworth.

Alice gave pleasure to three generations of our family. She was as witty—and as reactionary—as Senator Gore; she was also deeply resentful of her distant cousin Franklin's success while the canonization of her own first cousin Eleanor filled her with horror. "Isn't Eleanor no-ble," she would say, breaking the word into two syllables, each hummed reverently. "So very, *very* good!" Then she would imitate Eleanor's buck teeth which were not so very unlike her own quite prominent choppers. But Alice did have occasional, rare fits of fairness. She realized that what she felt for her cousins was "Simply envy. *We* were the President Roosevelt family. But then along came the Feather Duster," as she habitually referred to Franklin, "and we were forgotten." But she was exaggerating, as a number of new books attest, not to mention that once beautiful Dakota cliff defaced by the somber Gutzon Borglum with the faces of dead pols.

It is hard for Americans today to realize what a power the Roosevelts exerted not only in our politics but in the public's imagination. There had been nothing like them since the entirely different Adamses and there has been nothing like them since—the sad story of the Kennedys bears about as much resemblance to the Roosevelts as the admittedly entertaining and cautionary television series *Dallas* does to Shakespeare's chronicle plays.

From the moment in 1898 when TR raced up Kettle Hill (incorrectly known as San Juan) to April 12, 1945, when Franklin Roosevelt died, the Roosevelts were at the republic's center stage. Also, for nearly half that fifty-year period, a Roosevelt had been president. Then, as poignant coda, Eleanor Roosevelt, now quite alone, acted for seventeen years as conscience to a world very different from that of her uncle TR or even of FDR, her cousin-husband.

In the age of the condominium and fast foods, the family has declined not only as a fact but as a concept. Although there are, presumably, just as many Roosevelts alive today as there were a century ago, they are now like everyone else, scattered about, no longer tribal or even all of the same class. Americans can now change class almost as fast—downward, at least—as they shift from city to city or job to job. A century ago, a member of the patriciate was not allowed to drop out of his class no matter how little money he had. He might be allowed to retire from the world, like TR's alcoholic brother Elliott, in order to cultivate his vices, but even Elliott remained very much a part of the family until death—not his own kind—declassed him.

As a descendant of Theodore Roosevelt said to David McCullough, author of *Mornings on Horseback,* "No writer seems to have understood the degree to which [TR] was part of a clan." A clan that was on the rise, socially and financially, in nineteenth-century New York City. In three generations the Roosevelts had gone from hardware to plate glass to land development and banking (Chemical). By and large, the Roosevelts of that era were a solemn, hardworking, uninspired lot who, according to the *New York World,* had a tendency "to cling to the fixed and the venerable." Then, suddenly, out of this clan of solid burghers erupted the restless Theodore and his interesting siblings. How did this happen? *Cherchez la mère* is the usual key to the unexpected—for good or ill—in a family's history.

During Winston Churchill's last government, a minister found him in the Cabinet room, staring at a newspaper headline: one of his daughters had been arrested, yet again, for drunkenness. The minister said something consoling. Churchill grunted. The minister was then inspired to ask: "How is it possible that a Churchill could end up like this?" To which the old man replied: "Do you realize just *what* there was between the first Duke of Marlborough and *me*?" Plainly, a genetic disaster area had been altered, in Winston's case, by an American mother, Jennie Jerome, and in Theodore Roosevelt's case by a southern mother, named Mittie Bulloch, a beautiful, somewhat eccentric woman whom everyone delighted in even though she was not, to say the least, old New York. Rather, she was proudly southern and told her sons exciting stories of what their swashbuckling southern kin had done on land and sea. In later life, everyone agreed that Theodore was more Bulloch than Roosevelt just as his cousin Franklin was more Delano—or at least *Sara* Delano—than Roosevelt.

Mr. McCullough's book belongs to a new and welcome genre: the biographical sketch. Edmund Wilson in *Patriotic Gore* and Richard Hofstadter in *The American Political Tradition* were somewhat specialized practitioners of this art but, by and large, from Plutarch to Strachey, it has been more of a European than an American genre. Lately, American biography has fallen more and more into the hands not of writers but of academics. That some academics write very well indeed is, of course, perfectly true and, of course, perfectly rare. When it comes to any one of the glorious founders of our imperial republic, the ten-volume hagiography is now the rule. Under the direction of a tenured Capo, squads of graduate students spend years assembling every known fact, legend, statistic. The Capo then factors everything into the text, like sand into a cement mixer. The result is, literally, monumental, and unreadable. Even such minor figures as Ernest Hemingway and Sinclair Lewis have been accorded huge volumes in which every letter, telegram, drunken quarrel is memorialized at random. "Would *you* read this sort of book?" I asked Mark Schorer, holding up his thick life of Sinclair Lewis. He blinked, slightly startled by my bad manners. "Well," he said mildly, politely, "I must say I never really *liked* Lewis's work all that much."

Now, as bright footnotes to the academic texts, we are offered such books as Otto Friedrich's *Clover* and Jean Strouse's *Alice James.* These sketches seem to me to belong to literature in a way that Schorer's *Sinclair Lewis* or Dumas Malone's *Jefferson and His Time* do not—the first simply a journeyman compilation, the second a banal hagiography (with, admittedly, extremely valuable footnotes). In a sense, the reader of Malone et al. is obliged to make his own text out of the unshaped raw material while the reader of Strouse or Friedrich is given a finished work of literature that supplies the reader with an idiosyncratic view of the subject. To this genre *Mornings on Horseback* belongs: a sketch of Theodore Roosevelt's parents, brothers and sisters, wife, and self until the age of twenty-eight. Mr. McCullough has done a good swift job of sketching this family group.

Unfortunately, he follows in the wake not of the usual dull, ten-volume academic biography of the twenty-sixth president but of the first volume of Edmund Morris's *The Rise of Theodore Roosevelt.* This is bad luck for Mr. McCullough. Morris's work is not only splendid but covers the same period as Mr. McCullough, ending some years later with the death of McKinley. Where Mr. McCullough scores is in the portrait of the family, particularly during Theodore's youth. Fortunately, there can never be too much of a good thing. Since Morris's work has a different, longer rhythm, he does not examine at all closely those lesser lives which shaped—and explain, somewhat—the principal character.

Theodore Roosevelt, Senior, was a man of good works; unlike his wife Mittie. "She played no part in his good works, and those speculations on life in the hereafter or the status of one's soul, speculations that appear in Theodore's correspondence . . . are not to be found in what she wrote. She was not an agnostic exactly," writes McCullough, but at a time when the church was central to organized society she seems more than slightly indifferent or, as her own mother wrote, "If she was only a Christian, I think I could feel more satisfied."

Mittie's lack of religion was to have a lasting effect on her granddaughter Eleanor, the future Mrs. Franklin Delano Roosevelt. In 1870 Mittie placed her eldest child, Anna—known as Bamie—in Les Ruches, a girls' school at Fontainebleau. The school's creator was Mlle. Marie Souvestre, "a woman of singular poise and great culture, but also an outspoken agnostic . . . as brief as Bamie's time there would be, Mlle. Souvestre's influence would carry far." Indeed it did. In the next generation Bamie's niece Eleanor was also sent to school with Mlle. Souvestre, now removed to Allenwood in England. One of Mlle. Souvestre's teachers was Dorothy Bussy, a sister of Lytton Strachey and the pseudonymous as well as eponymous author of *Olivia* by Olivia, a story of *amitiés particulières* in a girls' school.

Bamie was not to marry until she was forty, while Eleanor's dislike of heterosexuality was lifelong ("*They* think of nothing else," she once said to me, grimly—and somewhat vaguely, for she never really said exactly who "they" were); it would seem that Mlle. Souvestre and her school deserve a proper study—before M. Roger Peyrefitte gets to it. Certainly, Eleanor had learned Mlle. Souvestre's lesson well: this world is the one that we must deal with and, if possible, improve. Eleanor had no patience with the other-worldly. Neither had her uncle TR. In a letter to Bamie, the future president says that he is marrying for a second time—the first wife had died. As a highly moral man, he is disgusted with himself. So much so that "were I sure there were a heaven my one prayer would be I might never go there, lest I should meet those I loved on earth who are dead."

A recurrent theme in this family chronicle is ill health. Bamie had a disfiguring curvature of the spine. Elliott had what sounds like epileptic fits. Then, at thirty-four, he was dead of alcoholism, in West 102nd Street, looked after by a mistress. Theodore Junior's general physical fragility was made intolerable by asthma. Mr. McCullough has done a good deal of research into asthma, that most debilitating and frightening of nervous afflictions. "Asthma is repeatedly described as a 'suppressed cry for the mother'—a cry of rage as well as a cry for help." Asthmatics live in constant terror of the next attack, which will always seem to be—if indeed it is not—terminal.

Parenthetically, I ran into the Wise Hack not long ago—in the lobby of the Beverly Hills Hotel. Where else? He is now very old, very rich: he owns a lot of Encino. Although he will no longer watch a movie made after 1945, he still keeps an eye on "the product." He knows all the deals. "One funny thing," he said, wheezing from emphysema—not asthma. "You know, all these hotshot young directors they got now? Well, every last one of them is a fat sissy who likes guns. And every last one of them has those thick glasses and the asthma." But before I could get him to give me the essential data, as Mrs. Wharton used to say, he had been swept into the Polo Lounge by the former managing editor of *Liberty.*

I must say that I thought of the Wise Hack's gnomic words as I read Mr. McCullough's account of TR's asthma attacks, which usually took place on a Sunday "which in the Victorian era was still the Lord's day . . . the one day of the week when the head of the household was home from work. . . ." Sunday also involved getting dressed up and going to church, something TR did not like. On the other hand, he enjoyed everyone's attention once the attacks had ended. Eventually, father and son came under the spell of a Dr. Salter, who had written that "organs are made for action, not existence; they are made to *work,* not to be; and when they *work* well, they can *be* well." You must change your life, said Rilke's Apollo. And that is what the young TR did: he went to a gymnasium, became an outdoorsman, built up his fragile body. At Harvard he was five foot eight inches tall and weighed one hundred twenty-five pounds. In later life, he was no taller but he came to weigh more than two hundred pounds; he was definitely a butterball type, though a vigorous one. He also wore thick glasses; liked guns.

Unlike the sissies who now make violent movies celebrating those who kill others, Theodore was a sissy who did not know that he was one until he was able to do something about it. For one thing, none of the Roosevelt children was sent to school. They were tutored at home. The boys seemed not to have had a great deal to do with other boys outside their own tribe. When Theodore went to Harvard, he was on his own for the first time in his life. But even at Harvard, Mittie would not allow him to room with other boys. He had an apartment in a private house; and a manservant. At first, he was probably surprised to find that he was unpopular with the other students; but then he was not used to dealing with those he did not know. He was very much a prig. "I had a headache," he writes in his diary, aged eleven, "and Conie and Ellie made a tremendous noise playing at my expense and rather laughed when I remonstrated."

At Harvard, he was very conscious of who was and who was not a gentleman. "I stand 19th in the class. . . . Only one gentleman stands ahead of me." He did not smoke; he got drunk on only one occasion—when he joined the Porcellian Club; he remained "pure" sexually. He was a lively, energetic youth who spoke rapidly, biting off his words as if afraid there would not be enough breath for him to say what he wanted to say. Properly bespectacled and gunned since the age of thirteen, he shot and killed every bird and animal that he could; he was also a fair taxidermist. Toward the end of his Harvard career, he was accepted as what he was, a not unattractive New York noble who was also rich; his income was $8,000 a year, about $80,000 in today's money. In his last two years at Harvard "clothes and club dues . . . added up to $2,400, a sum the average American family could have lived on for six years."

In later years, Theodore was remembered by a classmate as "a joke . . . active and enthusiastic and that was all," while a girl of his generation said "he was not the sort to appeal at first." Harvard's President Eliot, who prided himself on knowing no one, remembered Theodore as "feeble" and rather shallow. According to Mr. McCullough, he made "no lasting male friendships" at Harvard, but then, like so many men of power, he had few attachments outside his own family. During the early part of his life he had only one friend—Henry Cabot (known as La-de-dah) Lodge, a Boston aristo-sissy much like himself.

The death of his father was a shattering experience; and the family grew even closer to one another than before. Then Theodore fell in love and added a new member to the clan. When TR met Alice Lee, she was seventeen and he was nineteen. "See that girl," he said to Mrs. Robert Bacon at a party. "I am going to marry her. She won't have me, but I am going to have *her.*" Have her he did. "Alice," said Mrs. Bacon years later, "did not want to marry him, but she did." They were married October 27, 1880, on Theodore's twenty-second birthday. They lived happily ever after—for four years. Alice died of Bright's disease, shortly after giving birth to their daughter; a few hours earlier, in the same house, Mittie had died of typhoid fever. The double blow entirely changed Theodore's life. He went west to become a rancher, leaving little Alice with his sister Bamie. That same year Elliott also became a father when his wife, Anna Hall, gave birth to Eleanor.

In 1876, as General Grant's second administration fell apart in a storm of scandal and the winds of reform gathered force, New York State's great lord of corruption, Senator Roscoe Conkling, observed with characteristic sour wit: "When Dr. Johnson defined patriotism as the last refuge of a scoundrel, he ignored the enormous possibilities of the word reform." Since good Republicans like Theodore Roosevelt, Senior, could not endure what was happening to their party and country, they joined together to cleanse party, country.

As a member of the New York delegation to the Republican convention at Cincinnati, Theodore, Senior, helped deny both Conkling and James G. Blaine, another lord of corruption, the nomination for president. After a good deal of confusion the dim but blameless Rutherford B. Hayes was nominated. Although Hayes was not exactly *elected* president, he became the president as a result of the Republican Party's continued mastery of corruption at every level of the republic.

The new president then offered Theodore, Senior, the Collectorship of the Port of New York, a powerhouse of patronage and loot that had been for some years within Conkling's gift. And so it remained: thanks to Conkling's efforts in the Senate, Theodore, Senior, was denied the Collectorship. A week after this rejection, he wrote his son at Harvard to say that, all in all, he was relieved that he was not to be obliged to "purify our Customhouse." Nevertheless, he was glad that he had fought the good fight against the "machine politicians" who "think of nothing higher than their own interests. I fear for your future. We cannot stand so corrupt a government for any great length of time." This was the last letter from father to son. Two months later Theodore, Senior, was dead of cancer, at the age of forty-six.

Although TR worshipped his father, he does not seem to have been particularly interested in the politics of reform. During the Collectorship battle, he had wanted to be a naturalist; later he thought of writing, and began to compose what proved to be, or so one is told, a magisterial study of the early years of the American navy, *The Naval War of 1812*. He also attended Columbia Law School until 1881, when he got himself elected to the New York State Assembly. He was twenty-three years old; as lively and bumptious as ever.

Much has been made of what a startling and original and noble thing it was for a rich young aristo to enter the sordid politics of New York State. Actually, quite a number of young men of the ruling class were going into politics, often inspired by fathers who had felt, like Theodore, Senior, that the republic could not survive so much corruption. In fact, no less a grandee than the young William Waldorf Astor had been elected to the Assembly (1877) while, right in the family, TR's Uncle Rob had served in Congress, as a Democrat. There is no evidence that Theodore went into politics with any other notion than to have an exciting time and to rise to the top. He had no theory of government. He was, simply, loyal to his class—or what he called, approvingly, "our kind." He found the Tammany politicians repellent on physical and social as well as political grounds.

To TR's credit, he made no effort at all to be one of the boys; quite the contrary. He played the city dude to the hilt. In Albany, he arrived at his first Republican caucus, according to an eyewitness, "as if he had been ejected by a catapult. He had on an enormous great ulster . . . and he pulled off his coat; he was dressed in full dress, he had been to dinner somewhere. . . ." Even then, his high-pitched voice and upper-class accent proved to be a joy for imitators, just as his niece Eleanor's voice—so very like his—was a staple of mimics for fifty years. To the press, he was known, variously, as a "Jane-Dandy," "his Lordship," "Oscar Wilde," "the exquisite Mr. Roosevelt." He sailed above these epithets. He was in a hurry to . . . do what?

Mr. McCullough quotes Henry James's description of a similar character in *The Bostonians* (published five years after Theodore's entry into politics): "He was full of purpose to live . . . and with a high success; to become great, in order not to be obscure, and powerful not to be useless." In politics, it is character rather than ideas that makes for success; and the right sort of character combined with high energy can be fairly irresistible. Although TR was the most literary of our post–Civil War presidents, he had a mind that was more alert to fact than to theory. Like his father, he was against corruption and machine politicians, and that was pretty much that—until he met Samuel Gompers, a rising young trade unionist. Gompers took the dude around the tenements of New York City; showed him how immigrants were forced to live, doing such sweated labor as making cigars for wealthy firms. TR had planned to oppose a bill that the Cigar-maker's Union had sponsored, outlawing the manufacture of cigars "at home." After all, TR was a laissez-faire man; he had already opposed a minimum wage of $2.00 a day for municipal workers. But the tour of the tenements so shocked the dude that he supported the Cigar Bill.

TR also began to understand just how the United States was governed. Predictably, he found the unsavory Jay Gould at the center of a web that involved not only financiers but judges and newspaper proprietors and, to his horror, people that he knew socially. He describes how a kindly friend of the family, someone whom he referred to as a "member of a prominent law firm," explained the facts of life to him. Since *everyone,* more or less openly, did business with the likes of Jay Gould, TR was advised to give up "the reform play" and settle down as a representative member of the city's ruling—as opposed to governing—class. This was the sort of advice that was guaranteed to set him furiously in motion. He had found, at last, the Horatio-at-the-bridge role that he had been looking for. He took on the powers that be; and he coined a famous phrase, "the wealthy criminal class." Needless to say, he got nowhere in this particular battle, but by the time he was twenty-six he had made a national name for himself, the object of the exercise. He had also proven yet again that he could take it, was no sissy, had what Mark Sullivan was to call "a trait of ruthless righteousness."

In 1884, TR was a delegate to the Republican convention where, once again, James G. Blaine was a candidate. Like his father before him, TR joined the reformers; and together they fought to eliminate Blaine; but this time the gorgeous old trickster finally got the nomination, only to lose the election to Grover Cleveland. But by the time Cleveland was elected, the young widower and ex-assemblyman was playing cowboy in the Dakota Badlands. Just before TR disappeared into the wilderness, he made what was to be the most important decision of his career. In 1884 the reform Republicans deserted Blaine much as the antiwar Democrats were to abandon Hubert Humphrey in 1968. But TR had already made up his mind that he was going to have a major political career and so, cold-bloodedly, he endorsed Blaine: "I have been called a reformer but I am a Republican." For this show of solidarity with the Grand Old Party, he lost the decent opinion of the reformers and gained the presidency. He might have achieved both, but that would have required moral courage, something he had not been told about.

Give a sissy a gun and he will kill everything in sight. TR's slaughter of the animals in the Badlands outdoes in spades the butcheries of that sissy of a later era, Ernest Hemingway. Elks, grizzly bears, blacktail bucks are killed joyously while a bear cub is shot, TR reports proudly, "clean through . . . from end to end" (the Teddy bear was yet to be invented). "By Godfrey, but this is fun!" TR was still very much the prig, at least in speech: "He immortalized himself along the Little Missouri by calling to one of his cowboys, 'Hasten forward quickly here!' " Years later he wrote: "There were all kinds of things of which I was afraid at first, ranging from grizzly bears to 'mean' horses and gunfighters; but by acting as if I was not afraid I gradually ceased to be afraid."

There is something strangely infantile in this obsession with dice-loaded physical courage when the only courage that matters in political or even "real" life is moral. Although TR was often reckless and always domineering in politics, he never showed much real courage, and despite some trust-busting, he never took on the great ring of corruption that ruled and rules in this republic. But then, he was born a part of it. At best, he was just a dude with the reform play. Fortunately, foreign affairs would bring him glory. As Lincoln was the Bismarck of the American states, Theodore Roosevelt was the Kaiser Wilhelm II, a more fortunate and intelligent figure than the Kaiser but every bit as bellicose and conceited. Edith Wharton described with what pride TR showed her a photograph of himself and the Kaiser with the Kaiser's inscription: "President Roosevelt shows the Emperor of Germany how to command an attack."

I once asked Alice Longworth just why her father was such a war-lover. She denied that he was. I quoted her father's dictum: "No triumph of peace is quite as great as the supreme triumph of war." A sentiment to be echoed by yet another sissy in the next generation: *"Meglio un giorno da leone che cento anni da pecora."* "Oh, well," she said, "that's the way they all sounded in those days." But they did not all sound that way. Certainly Theodore, Senior, would have been appalled, and I doubt if Eleanor really approved of Uncle Teddy's war-mongering.

As president, TR spoke loudly and carried a fair-sized stick. When Colombia wouldn't give him the land that he needed for a canal, he helped invent Panama out of a piece of Colombia; and got his canal. He also installed the United States as the policeman of the Western Hemisphere. In order to establish an American hegemony in the Pacific, TR presided over the tail-end of the slaughter of more than half a million Filipinos who had been under the illusion that after the Spanish-American War they would be free to set up an independent republic under the leadership of Emilio Aguinaldo. But TR had other plans for the Philippines. Nice Mr. Taft was made the governor-general and one thousand American teachers of English were sent to the islands to teach the natives the sovereign's language.

Meanwhile, in the aftermath of the Boxer Rebellion, TR's "open-door policy" to China had its ups and downs. In 1905 the Chinese boycotted American goods because of American immigration policies, but the United States was still able to establish the sort of beachhead on the mainland of Asia that was bound to lead to what TR would have regarded as a bully fine war with Japan. Those of us who were involved in that war did not like it all that much.

In 1905, the world-famous Henry James came, in triumph, to Washington. He was a friend of Secretary of State John Hay and of Henry Adams. "Theodore Rex," as James called the president, felt obliged to invite the Master to the White House even though TR had denounced James as "effete" and a "miserable little snob"—it takes one to know one—while James thought of TR as "a dangerous and ominous Jingo." But the dinner was a success. James described the president as a "wonderful little machine . . . quite exciting to see. But it's really like something behind a great plate-glass window on Broadway." TR continued to loathe "the tone of satirical cynicism" of Henry James and Henry Adams while the Master finally dismissed the president as "the mere monstrous embodiment of unprecedented and resounding noise."

Alice Longworth used to boast that she and her father's viceroy Taft were the last Westerners to be received by the Dowager Empress of China. "We went to Peking. To the Forbidden City. And there we were taken to see this strange little old lady standing at the end of a room. Well, there was no bowing or scraping for us. So we marched down the room just behind the chamberlain, a eunuch, like one of those in that book of yours, *Justinian,* who slithered on his belly toward her. After he had announced us, she gave him a kick and he rolled over like a dog and slithered out." What had they talked about? She couldn't recall. I had my impression that she rather liked the way the empress treated her officials.

In the years before World War II, Alice was to be part of a marital rectangle. The heart having its reasons, Alice saw fit to conduct a long affair with the corrupt Senator William Borah, the so-called lion of Idaho, who had once roared, "I'd rather be right than president," causing my grandfather to murmur, "Of course, he was neither." In 1940, when the poor and supposedly virtuous Borah died, several hundred thousand dollars were found in his safety deposit box. Where had the money come from? asked the press. "He was my friend," said Senator Gore, for public consumption, "I do not speculate." But when I asked him who had paid off Borah, the answer was blunt. "The Nazis. To keep us out of the war." Meanwhile, Alice's husband, the Speaker of the House Nicholas Longworth, was happily involved with Mrs. Tracy (another Alice) Dows.

Rather late in life, Alice Longworth gave birth to her only child. In *The Making of Nicholas Longworth,* by Longworth's sister Clara de Chambrun, there is a touching photograph of Longworth holding in his arms a child whose features are unmistakably those of a lion's cub. "I should have been a grandmother, not a mother," Alice used to say of her daughter. But then, she had as little maternal instinct toward her only child as TR had had paternal instinct for her. When Nicholas Longworth died in 1931, Alice Dows told me how well Alice Longworth had behaved. "She asked me to go with her in the private train that took Nick back to Ohio. Oh, it was very moving. Particularly the way Alice treated me, as if *I* was the widow, which I suppose I was." She paused; then the handsome, square-jawed face broke into a smile and she used the Edwardian phrase: "Too killing."

When Alice Dows died she left me a number of her books. Among them was *The Making of Nicholas Longworth,* which I have just read. It is a loving, quite uninteresting account of what must have been a charming, not very interesting man. On the page where Alice Dows makes her appearance "one evening at Mrs. Tracy Dows's home . . . ," she had placed a four-leaf clover—now quite faded: nice emblem for a lucky lot.

In the electronic era, letter-writing has declined while diaries are kept only by those ill-educated, crazed, lone killers who feel obliged to report, in clinical detail, just how crazed and solitary they are as they prepare to assassinate political leaders. Except for Christopher Isherwood, I can think of no contemporary literary figure who has kept, for most of a lifetime, a journal. *The Diaries of Anaïs Nin* were, of course, her fiction. Fortunately, the pre-electronic Roosevelts and their friends wrote countless letters and journals and books, and Mr. McCullough has done a good job of selection; one is particularly grateful for excerpts from the writings of Elliott Roosevelt, a rather more natural and engaging writer than his industrious but not always felicitous older brother. Mr. McCullough's own style is easy to the point of incoherence. "The horse he rode so hard day after day that he all but ruined it," sounds more like idle dictation than written English. But, all in all, he has succeeded in showing us how a certain world, now lost, shaped the young Theodore Roosevelt. I think it worth noting that Simon and Schuster has managed to produce the worst set of bound galleys that I have ever read. There are so many misspellings that one has no sense of TR's own hit-or-miss approach to spelling, while two pages are entirely blank.

Now that war is once more thinkable among the thoughtless, Theodore Roosevelt should enjoy a revival. Certainly, the New Right will find his jingoism appealing, though his trust-busting will give less pleasure to the Honorable Society of the Invisible Hand. The figure that emerges from the texts of both Mr. McCullough and Mr. Morris is both fascinating and repellent. Theodore Roosevelt was a classic American sissy who overcame—or appeared to overcome—his physical fragility through "manly" activities of which the most exciting and ennobling was war.

As a politician-writer, Theodore Roosevelt most closely resembles Winston Churchill and Benito Mussolini. Each was as much a journalist as a politician. Each was a sissy turned showoff. The not unwitty Churchill—the most engaging of the lot—once confessed that if no one had been watching him he could quite easily have run away during a skirmish in the Boer War. Each was a romantic, in love with the nineteenth-century notion of earthly glory, best personified by Napoleon Bonaparte, whose eagerness to do in *his* biological superiors led to such a slaughter of alpha-males that the average French soldier of 1914 was markedly shorter than the soldier of 1800—pretty good going for a fat little fellow, five foot four inches tall—with, to be fair, no history of asthma.

As our dismal century draws to a close, it is fairly safe to say that no matter what tricks and torments are in store for us, we shall not see *their* like again. Faceless computer analysts and mindless cue-card readers will preside over our bright noisy terminus.

*The New York Review of Books*
*August 13, 1981*

# Eleanor Roosevelt

NICHOLAS AND ALEXANDRA. Now *Eleanor and Franklin.* Who's next for the tandem treatment? *Dick and Pat*? *J. Edgar and Clyde*? Obviously there is a large public curious as to what goes on in the bedrooms of Winter Palace and White House, not to mention who passed whom in the corridors of power. All in all, this kind of voyeurism is not a bad thing in a country where, like snakes, the people shed their past each year ("Today nobody even remembers there *was* a Depression!" Eleanor Roosevelt exclaimed to me in 1960, shaking her head at the dullness of an audience we had been jointly trying to inspire). But though Americans dislike history, they do like soap operas about the sexual misbehavior and the illnesses—particularly the illnesses—of real people in high places: "Will handsome, ambitious Franklin ever regain the use of his legs? Tune in tomorrow."

The man responsible for the latest peek at our masters, off-duty and on, is Joseph Lash. A journalist by trade, a political activist by inclination, an old friend of Eleanor Roosevelt as luck would have it (hers as well as his), Mr. Lash has written a very long book. Were it shorter, it would have a smaller sale but more readers. Unfortunately, Mr. Lash has not been able to resist the current fashion in popular biography: he puts in everything. The Wastebasket School leaves to the reader the task of arranging the mess the author has collected. Bank balances, invitations to parties, funerals, vastations in the Galerie d'Apollon—all are presented in a cool democratic way. Nothing is more important than anything else. At worst the result is "scholarly" narrative; at best, lively soap opera. No more does prophet laurel flower in the abandoned Delphi of Plutarch, Johnson, Carlyle, Strachey: Ph.D. mills have polluted the sacred waters.

Objections duly noted, I confess that I found *Eleanor and Franklin* completely fascinating. Although Mr. Lash is writing principally about Eleanor Roosevelt, someone I knew and admired, I still think it impossible for anyone to read his narrative without being as moved as I was. After all, Eleanor Roosevelt was a last (*the* last? the *only*?) flower of that thorny Puritan American conscience which was, when it was good, very, very good, and now it's quite gone things are horrid.

A dozen years ago, Mrs. Roosevelt asked me to come see her at Hyde Park. I drove down to Val-Kill cottage from where I lived on the Hudson. With some difficulty, I found the house. The front door was open. I went inside. "Anybody home?" No answer. I opened the nearest door. A bathroom. To my horror, there in front of the toilet bowl, stood Eleanor Roosevelt. She gave a startled squeak. "Oh, *dear*!" Then, resignedly, "Well, now you know *everything.*" And she stepped aside, revealing a dozen gladiolas she had been arranging in the toilet bowl. "It does keep them fresh." So began our political and personal acquaintance.

I found her remarkably candid about herself and others. So much so that I occasionally made notes, proud that I alone knew the truth about this or that. Needless to say, just about every "confidence" she bestowed on me appears in Mr. Lash's book and I can testify that he is a remarkably accurate recorder of both her substance and style. In fact, reading him is like having her alive again, hearing that odd, fluting yet precise voice with its careful emphases, its nervous glissade of giggles, the great smile which was calculated not only to avert wrath but warn potential enemies that here was a lioness quite capable of making a meal of anyone.

Then there were those shrewd, gray-blue eyes which stared and stared at you when you were not looking at her. When you did catch her at it, she would blush—even in her seventies the delicate gray skin would grow pink—giggle, and look away. When she was not interested in someone she would ask a polite question; then remove her glasses, which contained a hearing aid, and nod pleasantly—assuming she did not drop into one of her thirty-second catnaps.

The growing up of Eleanor Roosevelt is as interesting to read about as it was, no doubt, hard to have lived through. Born plain. Daughter of an alcoholic father whom she adored. Brought up by a sternly religious maternal grandmother in a house at Tivoli, New York, some thirty miles north of Hyde Park, where her cousin Franklin was also growing up, a fatherless little boy spoiled by his mother, the dread Sara Delano, for forty years the constant never-to-be-slain dragon in Eleanor's life.

Long after the death of Mrs. James (as Sara Delano Roosevelt was known to the Valley), Eleanor would speak of her with a kind of wonder and a slight distention of the knotty veins at her temples. "Only once did I ever *openly* quarrel with Mrs. James. I had come back to Hyde Park to find that she had allowed the children to run wild. Nothing I'd wanted done for them had been done. 'Mama,' I said" (accent on the second syllable, incidentally, in the French fashion), " 'you are *impossible*!' " "And what did she say?" I asked. "Why nothing." Mrs. Roosevelt looked at me with some surprise. "You see, she was a grande dame. She never noticed *anything* unpleasant. By the next day she'd quite forgotten it. But of course I couldn't. I forgive . . ." One of her favorite lines, which often cropped up in her conversation as well as—now—in the pages of Mr. Lash's book, "but I *never* forget."

But if Mrs. James was to be for Eleanor a life's antagonist, her father was to be the good—if unlikely—angel, a continuing spur to greatness, loved all the better after death. Elliott Roosevelt was charming and talented (many of his letters are remarkably vivid and well-written) and adored by everyone, including his older brother Theodore, the President-to-be. Elliott had everything, as they say; unfortunately, he was an alcoholic. When his drinking finally got out of control, the family sent him south; kept him away from Eleanor and her young brother Hall (himself to be an alcoholic). During these long absences, father and daughter exchanged what were, in effect, love letters, usually full of plans to meet. But when those rare meetings did take place, he was apt to vanish and leave her sitting alone at his club until, hours later, someone remembered she was there and took her home.

Yet in his letters, if not in his life, Elliott was a Puritan moralist—with charm. He wanted his daughter, simply, to be good. It is hard now to imagine what being good is, but to that generation there was not much ambiguity about the word. As Eleanor wrote in 1927, in a plainly autobiographical sketch,

> She was an ugly little thing, keenly conscious of her deficiencies, and her father, the only person who really cared for her, was away much of the time; but he never criticized her or blamed her, instead he wrote her letters and stories, telling her how he dreamed of her growing up and what they would do together in the future, but she must be truthful, loyal, brave, well-educated, or the woman he dreamed of would not be there when the wonderful day came for them to fare forth together. The child was full of fears and because of them lying was easy; she had no intellectual stimulus at that time and *yet she made herself as the years went on into a fairly good copy of the picture he painted.*

As it turned out, Eleanor did not fare forth with her father Elliott but with his cousin Franklin, and she was indeed all the things her father had wanted her to be, which made her marriage difficult and her life work great.

In 1894, Elliott died at 313 West 102nd Street, attended by a mistress. The ten-year-old Eleanor continued to live in the somber house at Tivoli, her character forming in a way to suggest that something unusual was at work. The sort of world she was living in could hardly have inspired her to write, as she did at fourteen:

> Those who are ambitious & make a place & a name in the great world for themselves are nearly always despised & laughed at by lesser souls who could not do as well & all they do for the good of men is construed into wrong & yet they do the good and they leave their mark upon the ages & if they had had no ambition would they have ever made a mark?

This was written in the era of Ward McAllister, when the best circles were still intent on gilding the age with bright excess. Eleanor was already unlike others of her class and time.

The turning point—the turning on—of her life occurred at Allenswood, an English school run by the formidable Mlle. Souvestre, a free-thinker (doubtless shocking to Eleanor, who remained a believing Christian to the end of her days) and a political liberal. Readers of *Olivia* know the school through the eyes of its author, Dorothy Bussy—a sister of Lytton Strachey. Allenswood was a perfect atmosphere in which to form a character and "furnish a mind." The awkward withdrawn American girl bloomed, even became popular. Some of Eleanor's essays from this period are very good. On literature:

"The greatest men often write very badly and all the better for them. It is not in them that we look for perfect style but in the secondary writers (Horace, La Bruyère)—one must know the masters by heart, adore them, try to think as they do and then leave them forever. For technical instruction there is little of profit to draw from the learned and polished men of genius."

So exactly did Flaubert speak of Balzac (but it is unlikely that Eleanor could have read that report of dinner Chez Magny). She perfected her French, learned Italian and German, and became civilized, according to the day's best standards.

Nearly eighteen, Eleanor returned to America. It was 1902: a time of great hope for the Republic. Uncle Theodore was the youngest President in history. A reformer (up to a point), he was a bright example of the "right" kind of ambition. But Tivoli was no more cheerful than before. In fact, life there was downright dangerous because of Uncle Vallie, a splendid alcoholic huntsman who enjoyed placing himself at an upstairs window and then, as the family gathered on the lawn, opening fire with a shotgun, forcing them to duck behind trees (in the forties there was a young critic who solemnly assured us that America could never have a proper literature because the country lacked a rich and complex class system!). It is no wonder that Eleanor thought the Volstead Act a fine thing and refused to serve drink at home for many years.

Eleanor came out, as was expected, and suffered from what she considered her ungainly appearance. Yet she was much liked, particularly by her cousin Franklin (known to *their* cousin Alice as "The Feather Duster": "You know, the sort of person you wouldn't ask to dinner, but for afterward"). During this period, Eleanor's social conscience was stirring. She worked at a settlement house where she not only saw how the poor lived but met a generation of women reformers, many of them also active in the suffragette movement. Eleanor was a slow convert to women's rights. But a convert she became. Just as she was able to change her prejudices against Jews and blacks (she was once attacked by the NAACP for referring to the colored, as they were then known, as "darkies").

Franklin began to court her. The letters he wrote her she destroyed—no doubt, a symbolic act when she found him out in adultery. But her letters remain. They are serious (she had been nicknamed "Granny"); they are also ambitious. For a young man who had made up his mind that he would rise to the top of the world she was a perfect mate. It is a sign of Franklin's genius—if that is the word—that even in his spoiled and callow youth he had sense enough to realize what Eleanor was all about.

The marriage ceremony was fine comedy. The bride and groom were entirely overshadowed by Uncle Ted. Eleanor was amused, Franklin not. Mr. Lash misses—or omits—one important factor in the marriage. For all of Eleanor's virtues (not immediately apparent to the great world which Franklin always rather liked) she was a catch for one excellent reason: she was the President's niece, and not just your average run-of-the-mill President but a unique political phenomenon who had roused the country in a way no other President had since Jackson. I suspect this weighed heavily with Franklin. Certainly when it came time for him to run for office as a Democrat, many Republicans voted for him simply because his name was Roosevelt and he was married to the paladin's niece.

As the world knows, Franklin and Eleanor were a powerful political partnership. But at the personal level, the marriage must never have been happy. For one thing, Eleanor did not like sex, as she confided in later years to her daughter. Franklin obviously did. Then there was his mother. The lives of the young couple were largely managed by Mrs. James, who remained mistress of the house at Hyde Park until she died. It is poignant to read a note from Eleanor to Franklin after the old lady's death in 1941, asking permission to move furniture around—permission generally not granted, for the place was to remain, as long as Franklin lived (and as it is now), the way his mother wanted it—and the most God-awful Victorian taste it is. But surroundings never meant much to any of the family, although Mrs. Roosevelt once told me how "Mr. Truman showed me around the White House, which he'd just redone, and he was so proud of the upstairs which looked to me *exactly* like a Sheraton Hotel!"

Franklin went to the State Senate. Eleanor learned to make speeches—not an easy matter because her voice was high, with a tendency to get out of control. Finally, she went to a voice coach. "You must tell President Kennedy. The exercises did wonders for my voice." A giggle. "Yes, I know, I don't sound *very* good but I was certainly a lot worse before, and Mr. Kennedy does need help because he talks much too fast and too high for the average person to understand him."

I remarked that in the television age it was quite enough to watch the speaker. She was not convinced. One spoke to the people in order to *educate* them. That was what politics was all about, as she was among the last to believe.

It is startling how much is known at the time about the private lives of the great. My grandfather Senator Gore's political career ended in 1936 after a collision with President Roosevelt ("This is the last relief check you'll get if Gore is reelected" was the nice tactic in Oklahoma), but in earlier times they were both in the liberal wing of the Democratic party and when Franklin came to Washington as Assistant Secretary of the Navy under Wilson, he was on friendly terms with the Senator. Washington was a small town then and everyone knew all about everyone else's private life. Not long ago Alice Longworth managed to startle even me by announcing, at a dinner party: "Daisy Harriman told me that every time she was alone with Senator Gore he would pounce on her. I could never understand why he liked her. After all, he was *blind*. But then Daisy always smelled nice."*

Meanwhile, the Gores were keeping track of the Roosevelts. Franklin fell in love with Eleanor's young secretary, Lucy Mercer, and they conducted an intense affair (known to everyone in Washington except Eleanor who discovered the truth in the tried-and-true soap opera way: innocently going through her husband's mail when he was ill). Senator Gore used to say, "What a trial Eleanor must be! She waits up all night in the vestibule until he comes home." I never knew exactly what this meant. Now Mr. Lash tells us "the vestibule story." Angry at her husband's attentions to

*My sister responded to this story by reminding Mrs. Longworth of a certain peculiar episode in the Governor's office at Albany between TR and a lady. Mrs. Longworth was not amused.

Lucy at a party, Eleanor went home alone but because Franklin had the keys, she spent much of the night sitting on the stoop.

Later, confronted with proof of Franklin's adultery, Eleanor acted decisively. She would give him a divorce but, she pointed out, she had five children and Lucy would have to bring them up. Lucy, a Catholic, and Franklin, a politician-on-the-make, agreed to cool it. But toward the end of his life they began to see each other again. He died with Lucy in the room at Warm Springs and Eleanor far away. Eleanor knew none of this until the day of her husband's death. From what she later wrote about that day, a certain amount of normal grief seems not to have been present.

When Franklin got polio in 1921, Eleanor came into her own. On his behalf, she joined committees, kept an eye on the political situation, pursued her own good works. When the determined couple finally arrived at the White House, Eleanor became a national figure in her own right. She had her own radio program. She wrote a syndicated column for the newspapers. She gave regular press conferences. At last she was loved, and on the grandest scale. She was also hated. But at fourteen she had anticipated everything ("It is better to be ambitious & do something than to be unambitious & do nothing").

Much of what Mr. Lash writes is new to me (or known and forgotten), particularly Eleanor's sponsorship of Arthurdale, an attempt to create a community in West Virginia where out-of-work miners could each own a house, a bit of land to grow things on, and work for decent wages at a nearby factory. This was a fine dream and a bureaucratic catastrophe. The houses were haphazardly designed, while the factory was not forthcoming (for years any industrialist who wanted to be invited to the White House had only to suggest to Eleanor that he might bring industry to Arthurdale). The right wing of course howled about socialism.

The right wing in America has always believed that those who have money are good people and those who lack it are bad people. At a deeper level, our conservatives are true Darwinians and think that the weak and the poor ought to die off, leaving the spoils to the fit. Certainly a do-gooder is the worst thing anyone can be, a societal pervert who would alter with government subsidy nature's harsh but necessary way with the weak. Eleanor always understood the nature of the enemy: she was a Puritan, too. But since she was Christian and not Manichaean, she felt obliged to work on behalf of those dealt a bad hand at birth. Needless to say, Franklin was quite happy to let her go about her business, increasing his majorities.

"Eleanor has this state trooper she lives with in a cottage near Hyde Park." I never believed that one but, by God, here the trooper is in the pages of Mr. Lash. Sergeant Earl R. Miller was first assigned to the Roosevelts in

Albany days. Then he became Eleanor's friend. For many years she mothered him, was nice to his girlfriends and wives, all perfectly innocent—to anyone but a Republican. It is a curious fact of American political life that the right wing is enamored of the sexual smear. Eleanor to me: "There are actually people in Hyde Park who knew Franklin all his life and said that he did not have polio but the sort of disease you get from not living the *right* sort of life."

The left wing plays dirty pool, too, but I have no recollection of their having organized whispering campaigns of a sexual nature against Nixon, say, the way the right so often does against liberal figures. Knowing Eleanor's active dislike of sex as a subject and, on the evidence of her daughter, as a fact, I think it most unlikely she ever had an affair with anyone. But she did crave affection, and jealously held on to her friends, helped them, protected them—often unwisely. Mr. Lash describes most poignantly Eleanor's grief when she realized that *her* friend Harry Hopkins had cold-bloodedly shifted his allegiance to Franklin.

Eleanor was also faced with the President's secretary and *de facto* wife Missy Le Hand ("Everybody knows the old man's been living with her for years," said one of the Roosevelt sons to my father who had just joined the subcabinet. My father, an innocent West Pointer, from that moment on regarded the Roosevelt family arrangements as not unlike those of Ibn Saud). Yet when Missy was dying, it was Eleanor who would ring her up. Franklin simply dropped her. But then Missy was probably not surprised. She once told Fulton Oursler that the President "was really incapable of a personal friendship with anyone."

Mr. Lash writes a good deal about Eleanor's long friendship with two tweedy ladies, Marion Dickerman and Nancy Cook. For years Eleanor shared Val-Kill cottage with them; jointly they ran a furniture factory and the Todhunter School, where Eleanor taught until she went to the White House. The relationship of the three women seems unusually tangled, and Mr. Lash cannot do much with it. Things ended badly with an exchange of letters, filled with uncharacteristic bitterness on Eleanor's side. If only the author of *Olivia* could have had a go at that subject.

In a sense Eleanor had no personal life after the White House years began. She was forever on the go (and did not cease motion during the long widowhood). She suffered many disappointments from friends and family. I remember her amused description of Caroline Kennedy and what a good thing it was that the two Kennedy children would still be very young when they left the White House because, she frowned and shook her head, "It is a terrible place for young people to grown up in, continually flattered and—*used.*"

I was with her the day the news broke that a son had married yet again. While we were talking, he rang her and she smiled and murmured, over and over, "Yes, dear . . . yes, I'm very happy." Then when she hung up, her face set like stone. "You would think that he might have told his mother *first,* before the press." But that was a rare weakness. Her usual line was "people are what they are, you can't change them." Since she had obviously begun life as the sort of Puritan who thought people not only could but must be changed, this later tolerance was doubtless achieved at some cost.

When I was selected as Democratic-Liberal candidate for Congress, Eleanor (I called her Mrs. R) was at first cool to the idea—I had known her slightly all my life (she had liked my father, detested my grandfather). But as the campaign got going and I began to move up in the polls and it suddenly looked as if, wonder of wonders, Dutchess County might go Democratic in a congressional election for the first time in fifty years (since Franklin's senatorial race, in fact), she became more and more excited. She joined me at a number of meetings. She gave a tea at Val-Kill for the women workers in the campaign. Just as the women were leaving, the telephone rang. She spoke a few minutes in a low voice, hung up, said good-by to the last of the ladies, took me aside for some political counsel, was exactly as always except that the tears were streaming down her face. Driving home, I heard on the radio that her favorite granddaughter had just been killed.

In later years, though Eleanor would talk—if asked—about the past, she was not given to strolls down memory lane. In fact, she was contemptuous of old people who lived in the past, particularly those politicians prone to the Ciceronian vice of exaggerating their contribution to history, a category in which she firmly placed that quaint Don Quixote of the cold war, Dean Acheson. She was also indifferent to her own death. "I remember Queen Wilhelmina when she came to visit during the war" (good democrat that she was, nothing royal was alien to Eleanor) "and she would sit under a tree on the lawn and commune with the dead. She would even try to get *me* interested in spiritualism but I always said: Since we're going to be dead such a long time anyway it's rather a waste of time chatting with all of them *before* we get there."

Although a marvelous friend and conscience to the world, she was, I suspect, a somewhat unsatisfactory parent. Descendants and their connections often look rather hard and hurt at the mention of her. For those well-placed by birth to do humanity's work, she had no patience if they were—ultimate sin—unhappy. A woman I know went to discuss with her a disastrous marriage; she came away chilled to the bone. These things were to be borne.

What did Eleanor feel about Franklin? That is an enigma, and perhaps she herself never sorted it out. He was complex and cold and cruel (so many of her stories of life with him would end, "And then I *fled* from the table in tears!"). He liked telling her the latest "Eleanor stories"; his sense of fun was heavy. A romantic, Mr. Lash thinks she kept right on loving him to the end (a favorite poem of the two was E. B. Browning's "Unless you can swear, 'For life, for death,'/Oh, fear to call it loving!"). But I wonder. Certainly he hurt her mortally in their private relationship; worse, he often let her down in their public partnership. Yet she respected his cunning even when she deplored his tactics.

I wonder, too, how well she understood him. One day Eleanor told me about something in his will that had surprised her. He wanted one side of his coffin to be left open. "Well, we hadn't seen the will when he was buried and of course it was too late when we did read it. But what *could* he have meant?" I knew and told her: "He wanted, physically, to get back into circulation as quickly as possible, in the rose garden." She looked at me as if this were the maddest thing she had ever heard.

I suspect the best years of Eleanor's life were the widowhood. She was on her own, no longer an adjunct to his career. In this regard, I offer Mr. Lash an anecdote. We were four at table: Mrs. Tracy Dows, Mrs. Roosevelt, her uncle David Gray (our wartime Ambassador to Ireland), and myself. Eleanor began: "When Mr. Joe Kennedy came back from London, during the war . . ." David Gray interrupted her. "Damned coward, Joe Kennedy! Terrified they were going to drop a bomb on him." Eleanor merely grinned and continued. "Anyway he came back to Boston and gave that *unfortunate* interview in which he was . . . well, somewhat *critical* of us."

She gave me her teacher's smile, and an aside. "You see, it's a very funny thing but whatever people say about us we almost always hear. I don't know *how* this happens but it does." David Gray scowled. "Unpleasant fellow, that Joe. Thought he knew everything. Damned coward." I said nothing, since I was trying to persuade Eleanor to support the wicked Joe's son at the Democratic convention; something she could not, finally, bring herself to do.

"Well, *my* Franklin said, 'We better have him down here'—we were at Hyde Park—'and see what he has to say.' So Mr. Kennedy arrived at Rhinecliff on the train and I met him and took him straight to Franklin. Well, ten minutes later one of the aides came and said, 'The President wants to see you right away.' This was unheard of. So I *rushed* into the office and there was Franklin, white as a sheet. He asked Mr. Kennedy to step outside and then he said, and his voice was *shaking,* 'I never want to see that man again as long as I live.' " David Gray nodded: "Wanted us to make a deal with Hitler." But Eleanor was not going to get into that. "Whatever it was, it was *very* bad. Then Franklin said, 'Get him out of here,' and I said, 'But, dear, you've invited him for the weekend, and we've got guests for lunch and the train doesn't leave until two,' and Franklin said, 'Then you drive him around Hyde Park and put him on that train,' and I did and it was the most dreadful four hours of my life!" She laughed.

Then, seriously: "I wonder if the *true* story of Joe Kennedy will ever be known."

To read Mr. Lash's book is to relive not only the hopeful period in American life (1933–40) but the brief time of world triumph (1941–45). The book stops, mercifully, with the President's death and the end of Eleanor and Franklin (Mr. Lash is correct to put her name first; of the two she was greater). Also, the end of . . . what? American innocence? Optimism? From 1950 on, our story has been progressively more and more squalid. Nor can one say it is a lack of the good and the great in high places: they are always there when needed. Rather the corruption of empire has etiolated the words themselves. Now we live in a society which none of us much likes, all would like to change, but no one knows how. Most ominous of all, there is now a sense that what has gone wrong for us may be irreversible. The empire will not liquidate itself. The lakes and rivers and seas will not become fresh again. The arms race will not stop. Land ruined by insecticides and fertilizers will not be restored. The smash-up will come.

To read of Eleanor and Franklin is to weep at what we have lost. Gone is the ancient American sense that whatever is wrong with human society can be put right by human action. Eleanor never stopped believing this. A simple faith, no doubt simplistic—but it gave her a stoic serenity. On the funeral train from Georgia to Washington: "I lay in my berth all night with the window shade up, looking out at the countryside he had loved and watching the faces of the people at stations, and even at the crossroads, who came to pay their last tribute all through the night. The only recollection I clearly have is thinking about 'The Lonesome Train,' the musical poem about Lincoln's death. ('A lonesome train on a lonesome track/Seven coaches painted black/A slow train, a quiet train/Carrying Lincoln home again . . .') I had always liked it so well—and now this was so much like it."

I had other thoughts in 1962 at Hyde Park as I stood alongside the thirty-third, the thirty-fourth, the thirty-fifth, and the thirty-sixth Presidents of the United States, not to mention all the remaining figures of the Roosevelt era who had assembled for her funeral (unlike the golden figures in Proust's last chapter, they all looked if not smaller than life smaller than legend—so many shrunken March of Time dolls soon to be put away). Whether or not one thought of Eleanor Roosevelt as a world ombudsman or as a chronic explainer or as a scourge of the selfish, she was like no one else in her usefulness. As the box containing her went past me, I thought, well, that's that. We're really on our own now.

***The New York Review of Books***
***November 18, 1971***

# The Holy Family

FROM THE BEGINNING of the Republic, Americans have enjoyed accusing the first magistrate of kingly ambition. Sometimes seriously but more often derisively, the president is denounced as a would-be king, subverting the Constitution for personal ends. From General Washington to the present incumbent, the wielder of power has usually been regarded with suspicion, a disagreeable but not unhealthy state of affairs for both governor and governed. Few presidents, however, have been accused of wanting to establish family dynasties, if only because most presidents have found it impossible to select a successor of any sort, much less promote a relative. Each of the Adamses and the Harrisons reigned at an interval of not less than a political generation from the other, while the two Roosevelts were close neither in blood nor in politics. But now something new is happening in the Republic, and as the Chinese say, we are living "in interesting times."

In 1960, with the election of the thirty-fifth President, the famous ambition of Joseph P. Kennedy seemed at last fulfilled. He himself had come a long way from obscurity to great wealth and prominence; now his eldest surviving son, according to primogeniture, had gone the full distance and become president. It was a triumph for the patriarch. It was also a splendid moment for at least half the nation. What doubts one may have had about the Kennedys were obscured by the charm and intelligence of John F. Kennedy. He appeared to be beautifully on to himself; he was also on to us; there is even evidence that he was on to the family, too. As a result, there were few intellectuals in 1960 who were not beguiled by the spectacle of a president who seemed always to be standing at a certain remove from himself, watching with amusement his own performance. He was an ironist in a profession where the prize usually goes to the apparent cornball. With such a man as chief of state, all things were possible. He would "get America moving again."

But then mysteriously the thing went wrong. Despite fine rhetoric and wise commentary, despite the glamor of his presence, we did not move, and if historians are correct when they tell us that presidents are "made" in their first eighteen months in office, then one can assume that the Kennedy administration would never have fulfilled our hopes, much less his own. Kennedy was of course ill-fated from the beginning. The Bay of Pigs used up much of his credit in the bank of public opinion, while his attempts at social legislation were resolutely blocked by a more than usually obstructive Congress. In foreign affairs he was overwhelmed by the masterful Khrushchev and not until the Cuban missile crisis did he achieve tactical parity with that sly gambler. His administration's one achievement was the test-ban treaty, an encouraging footnote to the cold war.

Yet today Kennedy dead has infinitely more force than Kennedy living. Though his administration was not a success, he himself has become an exemplar of political excellence. Part of this phenomenon is attributable to the race's need for heroes, even in deflationary times. But mostly the legend is the deliberate creation of the Kennedy family and its clients. Wanting to regain power, it is now necessary to show that once upon a time there was indeed a Camelot beside the Potomac, a golden age forever lost unless a second Kennedy should become the president. And so, to insure the restoration of that lovely time, the past must be transformed, dull facts transcended, and the dead hero extolled in films, through memorials, and in the pages of books.

The most notorious of the books has been William Manchester's *The Death of a President.* Hoping to stop Jim Bishop from writing one of his ghoulish *The Day They Shot* sagas, the Kennedys decided to "hire" Mr. Manchester to write their version of what happened at Dallas. Unfortunately, they have never understood that treason is the natural business of clerks. Mr. Manchester's use of Mrs. Kennedy's taped recollections did not please the family. The famous comedy of errors that ensued not only insured the book's success but also made current certain intimate details which the family preferred for the electorate not to know, such as the President's selection of Mrs. Kennedy's dress on that last day in order, as he put it, "to show up those cheap Texas broads," a remark not calculated to give pleasure to the clients of Neiman-Marcus. Also, the family's irrational dislike of President Johnson came through all too plainly, creating an unexpected amount of sympathy for that least sympathetic of magistrates.

Aware of what was at stake, Mrs. Kennedy tried to alter a book which neither she nor her brothers-in-law had read. Not since Mary Todd Lincoln has a president's widow been so fiercely engaged with legend if not history.

But then, legend-making is necessary to the Kennedy future. As a result, most of the recent books about the late president are not so much political in approach as religious. There is the ritual beginning of the book which is the end: the death at Dallas. Then the witness goes back in time to the moment when he first met the Kennedys. He finds them strenuous but fun. Along with riotous good times, there is the constant question: How are we to elect Jack president? This sort of talk was in the open after 1956, but as long ago as 1943, according to *The Pleasure of His Company,* Paul B. Fay, Jr., made a bet that one day Jack would be JFK.

From the beginning the godhead shone for those who had the eyes to see. The witness then gives us his synoptic version of the making of the President. Once again we visit cold Wisconsin and dangerous West Virginia (can a young Catholic war hero defeat a Protestant accused of being a draft dodger in a poor mining state where primary votes are bought and sold?). From triumph to triumph the hero proceeds to the convention at Los Angeles, where the god is recognized. The only shadow upon that perfect day is cast, significantly, by Lyndon B. Johnson. Like Lucifer he challenged the god at the convention, and was struck down only to be raised again as son of morning. The deal to make Johnson vice-president still causes violent argument among the new theologians. Pierre Salinger in *With Kennedy* quotes JFK as observing glumly, "The whole story will never be known, and it's just as well that it won't be." Then the campaign itself. The great television debates (Quemoy and Matsu) in which Nixon's obvious lack of class, as classy Jack duly noted, did him in—barely. The narrowness of the electoral victory was swiftly erased by the splendor of the inaugural ("It all began in the cold": Arthur M. Schlesinger, Jr., *A Thousand Days*). From this point on, the thousand days unfold in familiar sequence and, though details differ from gospel to gospel, the story already possesses the quality of a passion play: disaster at Cuba One, triumph at Cuba Two; the eloquent speeches; the fine pageantry; and always the crowds and the glory, ending at Dallas.

With Lucifer now rampant upon the heights, the surviving Kennedys are again at work to regain the lost paradise, which means that books must be written not only about the new incarnation of the Kennedy godhead but the old. For it is the dead hero's magic that makes legitimate the family's pretensions. As an Osiris-Adonis-Christ figure, JFK is already the subject of a cult that may persist, through the machinery of publicity, long after all memory of his administration has been absorbed by the golden myth now being created in a thousand books to the single end of maintaining in power our extraordinary holy family.

The most recent batch of books about JFK, though hagiographies, at times cannot help but illuminate the three themes which dominate any telling of the sacred story: money, image-making, family. That is the trinity without which nothing. Mr. Salinger, the late President's press secretary, is necessarily concerned with the second theme, though he touches on the other two. Paul B. Fay, Jr., (a wartime buddy of JFK and Under Secretary of the Navy) is interesting on every count, and since he seems not to know what he is saying, his book is the least calculated and the most lifelike of the ones so far published. Other books at hand are Richard J. Whalen's *The Founding Father* (particularly good on money and family) and Evelyn Lincoln's *My Twelve Years with John F. Kennedy,* which in its simple way tells us a good deal about those who are drawn to the Kennedys.

While on the clerical staff of a Georgia Congressman, Mrs. Lincoln decided in 1952 that she wanted to work for "someone in Congress who seemed to have what it takes to be President"; after a careful canvass, she picked the Representative from the Massachusetts Eleventh District. Like the other witnesses under review, she never says *why* she wants to work for a future president; it is taken for granted that anyone would, an interesting commentary on all the witnesses from Schlesinger (whose *A Thousand Days* is the best political novel since *Coningsby*) to Theodore Sorensen's dour *Kennedy.* Needless to say, in all the books there is not only love and awe for the fallen hero who was, in most cases, the witness's single claim to public attention, but there are also a remarkable number of tributes to the holy family. From Jacqueline (Isis-Aphrodite-Madonna) to Bobby (Ares and perhaps Christ-to-be) the Kennedys appear at the very least as demigods, larger than life. Bobby's hard-working staff seldom complained, as Mr. Salinger put it, "because we all knew that Bob was working just a little harder than we were." For the same reason "we could accept without complaint [JFK's] bristling temper, his cold sarcasm, and his demands for always higher standards of excellence because we knew he was driving himself harder than he was driving us—despite great and persistent physical pain and personal tragedy." Mrs. Lincoln surprisingly finds the late President "humble"—doubtless since the popular wisdom requires all great men to be humble. She refers often to his "deep low voice" [*sic*], "his proud head held high, his eyes fixed firmly on the goals—sometimes seemingly impossible goals—he set for himself and all those around him." Mr. Schlesinger's moving threnody at the close of *his* gospel makes it plain that we will not see JFK's like again, at least not until the administration of Kennedy II.

Of the lot, only Mr. Fay seems not to be writing a book with an eye to holding office in the next Kennedy administration. He is garrulous and indiscreet (the Kennedys are still displeased with his memoirs even though thousands of words were cut from the manuscript on the narrow theological ground that since certain things he witnessed fail to enhance the image, they must be apocryphal). On the subject of the Kennedys and money, Mr. Fay tells a most revealing story. In December, 1959, the family was assembled at Palm Beach; someone mentioned money, "causing Mr. [Joseph] Kennedy to plunge in, fire blazing from his eyes. 'I don't know what is going to happen to this family when I die,' Mr. Kennedy said. 'There is no one in the entire family, except Joan and Teddy, who is living within their means. No one appears to have the slightest concern for how much they spend.' " The tirade ended with a Kennedy sister running from the room in tears, her extravagance condemned in open family session. Characteristically, Jack deflected the progenitor's wrath with the comment that the only "solution is to have Dad work harder." A story which contradicts, incidentally, Mr. Salinger's pious "Despite his great wealth and his generosity in contributing all of his salaries as Congressman, Senator and President to charities, the President was not a man to waste pennies."

But for all the founding father's grumbling, the children's attitude toward money—like so much else—is pretty much what he wanted it to be. It is now a familiar part of the sacred story of how Zeus made each of the nine Olympians individually wealthy, creating trust funds which now total some ten million dollars per god or goddess. Also at the disposal of the celestials is the great fortune itself, estimated at a hundred, two hundred, three hundred, or whatever hundred millions of dollars, administered from an office on Park Avenue, to which the Kennedys send their bills, for we are told in *The Founding Father,* "the childhood habit of dependence persisted in adult life. As grown men and women the younger Kennedys still look to their father's staff of accountants to keep track of their expenditures and see to their personal finances." There are, of course, obvious limitations to not understanding the role of money in the lives of the majority. The late President was aware of this limitation and he was forever asking his working friends how much money they made. On occasion, he was at a disadvantage because he did not understand the trader's mentality. He missed the point to Khrushchev at Vienna and took offense at what, after all, was simply the boorishness of the marketplace. His father, an old hand in Hollywood, would have understood better the mogul's bluffing.

It will probably never be known how much money Joe Kennedy has spent for the political promotion of his sons. At the moment, an estimated million dollars a year is being spent on Bobby's behalf, and this sum can be matched year after year until 1972, and longer. Needless to say, the sons are sensitive to the charge that their elections are bought. As JFK said of his 1952 election to the Senate, "People say 'Kennedy bought the election. Kennedy could never have been elected if his father hadn't been a millionaire.' Well, it wasn't the Kennedy name and the Kennedy money that won that election. I beat Lodge because I hustled for three years" (quoted in *The Founding Father*). But of course without the Kennedy name and the Kennedy money, he would not even have been a contender. Not only was a vast amount of money spent for his election in the usual ways, but a great deal was spent in not so usual ways. For instance, according to Richard J. Whalen, right after the pro-Lodge Boston *Post* unexpectedly endorsed Jack Kennedy for the Senate, Joe Kennedy loaned the paper's publisher $500,000.

But the most expensive legitimate item in today's politics is the making of the image. Highly paid technicians are able to determine with alarming accuracy just what sort of characteristics the public desires at any given moment in a national figure, and with adroit handling a personable candidate can be made to seem whatever the times require. The Kennedys are not of course responsible for applying to politics the techniques of advertising (the two have always gone hand in hand), but of contemporary politicians (the Rockefellers excepted) the Kennedys alone possess the money to maintain one of the most remarkable self-publicizing machines in the history of advertising, a machine which for a time had the resources of the Federal government at its disposal.

It is in describing the activities of a chief press officer at the White House that Mr. Salinger is most interesting. A talented image maker, he was responsible, among other things, for the televised press conferences in which the President was seen at his best, responding to simple questions with careful and often charming answers. That these press conferences were not very informative was hardly the fault of Mr. Salinger or the President. If it is true that the medium is the message and television is the coolest of all media and to be cool is desirable, then the televised thirty-fifth President was positively glacial in his effectiveness. He was a natural for this time and place, largely because of his obsession with the appearance of things. In fact, much of his political timidity was the result of a quite uncanny ability to sense how others would respond to what he said or did, and if he foresaw a negative response, he was apt to avoid action altogether. There were times, however, when his superb sense of occasion led him astray. In the course of a speech to the Cuban refugees in Miami, he was so overwhelmed by the drama of the situation that he practically launched on the spot a second invasion of that beleaguered island. Yet generally he was cool. He enjoyed the game of pleasing others, which is the actor's art.

He was also aware that vanity is perhaps the strongest of human emotions, particularly the closer one comes to the top of the slippery pole. Mrs. Kennedy once told me that the last thing Mrs. Eisenhower had done before leaving the White House was to hang a portrait of herself in the entrance hall. The first thing Mrs. Kennedy had done on moving in was to put the portrait in the basement, on aesthetic, not political grounds. Overhearing this, the President told an usher to restore the painting to its original place. "The Eisenhowers are coming to lunch tomorrow," he explained patiently to his wife, "and that's the first thing she'll look for." Mrs. Lincoln records that before the new Cabinet met, the President and Bobby were about to enter the Cabinet room when the President "said to his brother, 'Why don't you go through the other door?' The President waited until the Attorney General entered the Cabinet room from the hall door, and then he walked into the room from my office."

In its relaxed way Mr. Fay's book illuminates the actual man much better than the other books if only because he was a friend to the President, and not just an employee. He is particularly interesting on the early days when Jack could discuss openly the uses to which he was being put by his father's ambition. Early in 1945 the future President told Mr. Fay how much he envied Fay his postwar life in sunny California while "I'll be back here with Dad trying to parlay a lost PT boat and a bad back into a political advantage. I tell you, Dad is ready right now and can't understand why Johnny boy isn't 'all engines full ahead.' " Yet the exploitation of son by father had begun long before the war. In 1940 a thesis written by Jack at Harvard was published under the title *Why England Slept,* with a foreword by longtime, balding family friend Henry Luce. The book became a best seller and (Richard J. Whalen tells us) as Joe wrote at the time in a letter to his son, "You would be surprised how a book that really makes the grade with high-class people stands you in good stead for years to come."

Joe was right of course and bookmaking is now an important part of the holy family's home industry. As Mrs. Lincoln observed, when JFK's collection of political sketches "won the Pulitzer prize for biography in 1957, the Senator's prominence as a scholar and statesman grew. As his book continued to be a best seller, he climbed higher up on public-opinion polls and moved into a leading position among Presidential possibilities for 1960." Later Bobby would "write" a book about how he almost nailed Jimmy Hoffa; and so great was the impact of this work that many people had the impression that Bobby had indeed put an end to the career of that turbulent figure.

Most interesting of all the myth-making was the creation of Jack the war hero. John Hersey first described for *The New Yorker* how Jack's Navy boat was wrecked after colliding with a Japanese ship; in the course of a long swim, the young skipper saved the life of a crewman, an admirable thing to do. Later they were all rescued. Since the officer who survived was Ambassador Kennedy's son, the story was deliberately told and retold as an example of heroism unequaled in war's history. Through constant repetition the simple facts of the story merged into a blurred impression that somehow at some point a unique act of heroism had been committed by Jack Kennedy. The last telling of the story was a film starring Cliff Robertson as JFK (the President had wanted Warren Beatty for the part, but the producer thought Beatty's image was "too mixed up").

So the image was created early: the high-class book that made the grade; the much-publicized heroism at war; the election to the House of Representatives in 1946. From that point on, the publicity was constant and though the Congressman's record of service was unimpressive, he himself was photogenic and appealing. Then came the Senate, the marriage, the illnesses, the second high-class book, and the rest is history. But though it was Joe Kennedy who paid the bills and to a certain extent managed the politics, the recipient of all this attention was meanwhile developing into a shrewd psychologist. Mr. Fay quotes a letter written him by the new Senator in 1953. The tone is jocular (part of the charm of Mr. Fay's book is that it captures as no one else has the preppish side to JFK's character; he was droll, particularly about himself, in a splendid W. C. Fields way): "I gave everything a good deal of thought. I am getting married this fall. This means the end of a promising political career, as it has been based up to now almost completely on the old sex appeal." After a few more sentences in this vein the groom-to-be comes straight to the point. "Let me know the general reaction to this in the Bay area." He did indeed want to know, like a romantic film star, what effect marriage would have on his career. But then most of his life was governed, as Mrs. Lincoln wrote of the year 1959, "by the public-opinion polls. We were not unlike the people who check their horoscope each day before venturing out." And when they did venture out, it was always to create an illusion. As Mrs. Lincoln remarks in her guileless way: after Senator Kennedy returned to Washington from a four-week tour of Europe, "it was obvious that his stature as a Senator had grown, for he came back as an authority on the current situation in Poland."

It is not to denigrate the late President or the writers of his gospel that neither he nor they ever seemed at all concerned by the bland phoniness of so much of what he did and said. Of course politicians have been pretty much the same since the beginning of history, and part of the game is creating illusion. In fact, the late President himself shortly after Cuba Two summed up what might very well have been not only his political philosophy but that of the age in which we live. When asked whether or not the Soviet's placement of missiles in Cuba would have actually shifted the balance of world power, he indicated that he thought not. "But it would have politically changed the balance of power. It would have appeared to, and appearances contribute to reality."

From the beginning, the holy family has tried to make itself appear to be what it thinks people want rather than what the realities of any situation might require. Since Bobby is thought by some to be ruthless, he must therefore be photographed as often as possible with children, smiling and happy and athletic, in every way a boy's ideal man. Politically, he must *seem* to be at odds with the present administration without ever actually taking any important position that President Johnson does not already hold. Bobby's Vietnamese war dance was particularly illustrative of the technique. A step to the Left (let's talk to the Viet Cong), followed by two steps to the Right, simultaneously giving "the beards"—as he calls them—the sense that he is for peace in Vietnam while maintaining his brother's war policy. Characteristically, the world at large believes that if JFK were alive there would be no war in Vietnam. The mythmakers have obscured the fact that it was JFK who began our active participation in the war when, in 1961, he added to the six hundred American observers the first of a gradual buildup of American troops, which reached twenty thousand at the time of his assassination. And there is no evidence that he would not have persisted in that war, for, as he said to a friend shortly before he died, "I have to go all the way with this one." He could not suffer a second Cuba and hope to maintain the appearance of Defender of the Free World at the ballot box in 1964.

The authors of the latest Kennedy books are usually at their most interesting when they write about themselves. They are cautious, of course (except for the jaunty Mr. Fay), and most are thinking ahead to Kennedy II. Yet despite a hope of future preferment, Mr. Salinger's self-portrait is a most curious one. He veers between a coarse unawareness of what it was all about (he never, for instance, expresses an opinion of the war in Vietnam), and a solemn bogusness that is most putting off. Like an after-dinner speaker, he characterizes everyone ("Clark Clifford, the brilliant Washington lawyer"); he pays heavy tribute to his office staff; he praises Rusk and the State Department, remarking that "JFK had more effective liaison with the State Department than any President in history," which would have come as news to the late President. Firmly Mr. Salinger puts Arthur Schlesinger, Jr., in his place, saying that he himself never heard the President express a lack of confidence in Rusk. Mr. Salinger also remarks that though Schlesinger was "a strong friend" of the President (something Mr. Salinger, incidentally, was not), "JFK occasionally was impatient with their [Schlesinger's memoranda] length and frequency." Mrs. Lincoln also weighs in on the subject of the historian-in-residence. Apparently JFK's "relationship with Schlesinger was never that close. He admired Schlesinger's brilliant mind, his enormous store of information . . . but Schlesinger was never more than an ally and assistant."

It is a tribute to Kennedy's gift for compartmentalizing the people in his life that none knew to what extent he saw the others. Mr. Fay was an after-hours buddy. Mrs. Lincoln was the girl in the office. Mr. Salinger was a technician and not a part of the President's social or private or even, as Mr. Salinger himself admits, political life. Contrasting his role with that of James Hagerty, Mr. Salinger writes, "My only policy duties were in the information field. While Jim had a voice in deciding what the administration would do, I was responsible only for presenting that decision to the public in a way and at a time that would generate the best possible reception." His book is valuable only when he discusses the relations between press and government. And of course when he writes about himself. His 1964 campaign for the Senate is nicely told and it is good to know that he lost because he came out firmly for fair housing on the ground that "morally I had no choice—not after sweating out Birmingham and Oxford with John F. Kennedy." This is splendid but it might have made his present book more interesting had he told us something about that crucial period of sweating out. Although he devotes a chapter to telling how he did not take a fifty-mile hike, he never discusses Birmingham, Oxford, or the black revolution.

All in all, his book is pretty much what one might expect of a PR man. He papers over personalities with the reflexive and usually inaccurate phrase (Eisenhower and Kennedy "had deep respect for each other"; Mrs. Kennedy has "a keen understanding of the problems which beset mankind"). Yet for all his gift at creating images for others, Mr. Salinger seems not to have found his own. Uneasily he plays at being U.S. Senator, fat boy at court, thoughtful emissary to Khrushchev. Lately there has been a report in the press that he is contemplating writing a novel. If he does, Harold Robbins may be in the sort of danger that George Murphy never was. The evidence at hand shows that he has the gift. Describing his divorce from "Nancy, my wife of eight years," Mr. Salinger manages in a few lines to say everything. "An extremely artistic woman, she was determined to live a quieter life in which she could pursue her skills as a ceramicist. And we both knew that I could not be happy unless I was on the move. It was this difference in philosophies, not a lack of respect, that led to our decision to obtain a divorce. But a vacation in Palm Springs, as Frank Sinatra's guest, did much to revive my spirits."

Mr. Fay emerges as very much his own man, and it is apparent that he amused the President at a level which was more that of a playmate escorting the actress Angie Dickinson to the Inaugural than as serious companion to the prince. Unlike the other witnesses, Mr. Fay has no pretensions about himself. He tells how "the President then began showing us the new paintings on the wall. 'Those two are Renoirs and that's a Cézanne,' he told us. Knowing next to nothing about painters or paintings, I asked, 'Who are they?' The President's response was predictable, 'My God, if you ask a question like that, do it in a whisper or wait till we get outside. We're trying to give this administration a semblance of class.' " The President saw the joke; he also saw the image which must at all times be projected. Parenthetically, a majority of the recorded anecdotes about Kennedy involve keeping up appearances; he was compulsively given to emphasizing, often with great charm, the division between how things must be made to seem, as opposed to the way they are. This division is noticeable, even in the censored version of Mr. Manchester's *The Death of a President.* The author records that when Kennedy spoke at Houston's coliseum, Jack Valenti, crouched below the lectern, was able to observe the extraordinary tremor of the President's hands, and the artful way in which he managed to conceal them from the audience. This tension between the serene appearance and that taut reality add to the poignancy of the true legend, so unlike the Parson Weems version Mrs. Kennedy would like the world to accept.

Money, image, family: the three are extraordinarily intertwined. The origin of the Kennedy sense of family is the holy land of Ireland, priest-ridden, superstitious, clannish. While most of the West in the nineteenth century was industrialized and urbanized, Ireland remained a famine-ridden agrarian country, in thrall to politicians, homegrown and British, priest and lay. In 1848, the first Kennedy set up shop in Boston, where the Irish were exploited and patronized by the Wasps; not unnaturally, the Irish grew bitter and vengeful and finally asserted themselves at the ballot box. But the old resentment remained as late as Joe Kennedy's generation and with it flourished a powerful sense that the family is the only unit that could withstand the enemy, as long as each member remained loyal to the others, "regarding life as a joint venture between one generation and the next." In *The Fruitful Bough,* a privately printed cluster of tributes to the Elder Kennedy (collected by Edward M. Kennedy) we are told, in Bobby's words, that to Joe Kennedy "the most important thing . . . was the advancement of his children . . . except for his influence and encouragement, my brother Jack might not have run for the Senate in 1952." (So much for JFK's comment that it was his own "hustling" that got him Lodge's seat.)

The father is of course a far more interesting figure than any of his sons if only because his will to impose himself upon a society which he felt had snubbed him has been in the most extraordinary way fulfilled. He drove his sons to "win, win, win." But never at any point did he pause to ask himself or them just what it was they were supposed to win. He taught them to regard life as a game of Monopoly (a family favorite): you put up as many hotels as you can on Ventnor Avenue and win. Consequently, some of the failure of his son's administration can be ascribed to the family philosophy. All his life Jack Kennedy was driven by his father and then by himself to be first in politics, which meant to be the president. But once that goal had been achieved, he had no future, no place else to go. This absence of any sense of the whole emerged in the famous exchange between him and James Reston, who asked the newly elected President what his philosophy was, what vision did he have of the good life. Mr. Reston got a blank stare for answer. Kennedy apologists are quick to use this exchange as proof of their man's essentially pragmatic nature ("pragmatic" was a favorite word of the era, even though its political meaning is opportunist). As they saw it: give the President a specific problem and he will solve it through intelligence and expertise. A "philosophy" was simply of no use to a man of action. For a time, actual philosophers were charmed by the thought of an intelligent young empiricist fashioning a New Frontier.

Not until the second year of his administration did it become plain that Kennedy was not about to do much of anything. Since his concern was so much with the appearance of things, he was at his worst when confronted with those issues where a moral commitment might have informed his political response not only with passion but with shrewdness. Had he challenged the Congress in the Truman manner on such bills as Medicare and Civil Rights, he might at least have inspired the country, if not the Congress, to follow his lead. But he was reluctant to rock the boat, and it is significant that he often quoted Hotspur on summoning spirits from the deep: any man can summon, but will the spirits come? JFK never found out; he would not take the chance. His excuse in private for his lack of force, particularly in dealing with the Congress, was the narrow electoral victory of 1960. The second term, he declared, would be the one in which all things might be accomplished. With a solid majority behind him, he could work wonders. But knowing his character, it is doubtful that the second term would have been much more useful than the first. After all, he would have been constitutionally a lame duck president, interested in holding the franchise for his brother. The family, finally, was his only commitment and it colored all his deeds and judgment.

In 1960, after listening to him denounce Eleanor Roosevelt at some length, I asked him why he thought she was so much opposed to his candidacy. The answer was quick: "She hated my father and she can't stand it that his children turned out so much better than hers." I was startled at how little he understood Mrs. Roosevelt, who, to be fair, did not at all understand him, though at the end she was won by his personal charm. Yet it was significant that he could not take seriously any of her political objections to him (e.g., his attitude to McCarthyism); he merely assumed that she, like himself, was essentially concerned with family and, envying the father, would want to thwart the son. He was, finally, very much his father's son even though, as all the witnesses are at pains to remind us, he did not share that magnate's political philosophy—which goes without saying, since anyone who did could not be elected to anything except possibly the Chamber of Commerce. But the Founding Father's confidence in his own wisdom ("I know more about Europe than anybody else in this country," he said in 1940, "because I've been closer to it longer") and the assumption that he alone knew the absolute inside story about everything is a trait inherited by the sons, particularly Bobby, whose principal objection to the "talking liberals" is that they never know what's really going on, as he in his privileged place does but may not tell. The Kennedy children have always observed our world from the heights.

The distinguished jurist Francis Morrissey tells in *The Fruitful Bough* a most revealing story of life upon Olympus. "During the Lodge campaign, the Ambassador told [Jack and me] clearly that the campaign . . . would be the toughest fight he could think of, but there was no question that Lodge would be beaten, and if that should come to pass Jack would be nominated and elected President. . . . In that clear and commanding voice of his he said to Jack, 'I will work out the plans to elect you President. It will not be any more difficult for you to be elected President than it will be to win the Lodge fight . . . you will need to get about twenty key men in the country to get the nomination for it is these men who will control the convention. . . .' "

One of the most fascinating aspects of politician-watching is trying to determine to what extent any politician believes what he says. Most of course never do, regarding public statements as necessary noises to soothe the electorate or deflect the wrath of the passionate, who are forever mucking things up for the man who wants decently and normally to rise. Yet there are cases of politicians who have swayed themselves by their own speeches. Take a man of conservative disposition and force him to give liberal speeches for a few years in order to be elected and he will, often as not, come to believe himself. There is evidence that JFK often spellbound himself. Bobby is something else again. Andrew Kopkind in *The New Republic* once described Bobby's career as a series of "happenings": the McCarthy friend and fellow traveler of one year emerges as an intense New York liberal in another, and between these two happenings there is no thread at all to give a clue as to what the man actually thinks or who he really is. That consistency which liberals so furiously demanded of the hapless Nixon need not apply to any Kennedy.

After all, as the recent gospels point out, JFK himself was slow to become a liberal, to the extent he ever was (in our society no working politician can be radical). As JFK said to James MacGregor Burns, "Some people have their liberalism 'made' by the time they reach their late twenties. I didn't. I was caught in crosscurrents and eddies. It was only later that I got into the stream of things." His comment made liberalism sound rather like something run up by a tailor, a necessary garment which he regrets that he never had time in his youth to be fitted for. Elsewhere (in William Manchester's *Portrait of a President*) he explains those "currents and eddies." Of his somewhat reactionary career in the House of Representatives he said, "I'd just come out of my father's house at the time, and these were the things I knew." It is of course a truism that character is formed in one's father's house. Ideas may change but the attitude toward others does not. A father who teaches his sons that the only thing that matters is to be first, not second, not third, is obviously (should his example be followed) going to be rewarded with energetic sons. Yet it is hardly surprising that to date one cannot determine where the junior Senator from New York stands on such a straightforward issue (morally if not politically) as the American adventure in Vietnam. Differing with the President as to which cities ought to be bombed in the North does not constitute an alternative policy. His sophisticated liberal admirers, however, do not seem in the least distressed by his lack of a position; instead they delight in the *uses* to which he has put the war in Vietnam in order to embarrass the usurper in the White House.

The cold-blooded jauntiness of the Kennedys in politics has a remarkable appeal for those who also want to rise and who find annoying—to the extent they are aware of it at all—the moral sense. Also, the success of the three Kennedy brothers nicely makes hash of the old American belief that by working hard and being good one will deserve (and if fortunate, receive) promotion. A mediocre Representative, an absentee Senator, through wealth and family connections, becomes the president while his youngest brother inherits the Senate seat. Now Bobby is about to become RFK because he is Bobby. It is as if the United States had suddenly reverted to the eighteenth century, when the politics of many states were family affairs. In those days, if one wanted a political career in New York one had best be born a Livingston, a Clinton, or a Schuyler; failing that, one must marry into the family, as Alexander Hamilton did, or go to work for them. In a way, the whole Kennedy episode is a fascinating throwback to an earlier phase of civilization. Because the Irish maintained the ancient village sense of the family longer than most places in the West and to the extent that the sons of Joe Kennedy reflect those values and prejudices, they are an anachronism in an urbanized nonfamily-minded society. Yet the fact that they are so plainly not of this time makes them fascinating; their family story is a glamorous continuing soap opera whose appeal few can resist, including the liberals, who, though they may suspect that the Kennedys are not with them at heart, believe that the two boys are educable. At this very moment beside the river Charles a thousand Aristotles dream of their young Alexanders, and the coming heady conquest of the earth.

Meanwhile, the source of the holy family's power is the legend of the dead brother, who did not much resemble the hero of the books under review. Yet the myth that JFK was a philosopher-king will continue as long as the Kennedys remain in politics. And much of the power they exert over the national imagination is a direct result of the ghastliness of what happened at Dallas. But though the world's grief and shock were genuine, they were not entirely for JFK himself. The death of a young leader necessarily strikes an atavistic chord. For thousands of years the man-god was sacrificed to ensure with blood the harvest, and there is always an element of ecstasy as well as awe in our collective grief. Also, Jack Kennedy was a television star, more seen by most people than their friends or relatives. His death in public was all the more stunning because he was not an abstraction called The President, but a man the people thought they knew. At the risk of *lèse-divinité,* however, the assassination of President Nixon at, let us say, Cambridge by what at first was thought to be a member of the ADA but later turned out to be a dotty Bircher would have occasioned quite as much national horror, mourning, and even hagiography. But in time the terrible deed would have been forgotten, for there are no Nixon heirs.

Beyond what one thinks of the Kennedys themselves, there remains the large question: What sort of men ought we to be governed by in the coming years? With the high cost of politics and image-making, it is plain that only the very wealthy or those allied with the very wealthy can afford the top prizes. And among the rich, only those who are able to please the people on television are Presidential. With the decline of the religions, the moral sense has become confused, to say the least, and intellectual or political commitments that go beyond the merely expedient are regarded with cheerful contempt not only by the great operators themselves but also by their admirers and, perhaps, by the electorate itself. Also, to be fair, politicians working within a system like ours can never be much more than what the system will allow. Hypocrisy and self-deception are the traditional characteristics of the middle class in any place and time, and the United States today is the paradigmatic middle-class society. Therefore we can hardly blame our political gamesmen for being, literally, representative. Any public man has every right to try and trick us, not only for his own good but, if he is honorable, for ours as well. However, if he himself is not aware of what he is doing or to what end he is playing the game, then to entrust him with the first magistracy of what may be the last empire on earth is to endanger us all. One does not necessarily demand of our leaders passion (Hitler supplied the age with quite enough for this century) or reforming zeal (Mao Tse-tung is incomparable), but one does insist that they possess a sense of community larger than simply personal power for its own sake, being first because it's fun. Finally, in an age of supercommunications, one must have a clear sense of the way things are, as opposed to the way they have been made to seem. Since the politics of the Kennedys are so often the work of publicists, it is necessary to keep trying to find out just who they are and what they really mean. If only because should *they* be confused as to the realities of Cuba, say, or Vietnam, then the world's end is at hand.

At one time in the United States, the popular wisdom maintained that there was no better work for a man to do than to set in motion some idea whose time had not yet arrived, even at the risk of becoming as unpopular as those politicians JFK so much admired in print and so little emulated in life. It may well be that it is now impossible for such men to rise to the top in our present system. If so, this is a tragedy. Meanwhile, in their unimaginative fierce way, the Kennedys continue to play successfully the game as they found it. They create illusions and call them facts, and between what they are said to be and what they are falls the shadow of all the useful words not spoken, of all the actual deeds not done. But if it is true that in a rough way nations deserve the leadership they get, then a frivolous and apathetic electorate combined with a vain and greedy intellectual establishment will most certainly restore to power the illusion-making Kennedys. Holy family and bedazzled nation, in their faults at least, are well matched. In any case, the age of the commune in which we have lived since the time of Jackson is drawing to a close and if historical analogies are at all relevant, the rise of the *signori* is about to begin, and we may soon find ourselves enjoying a strange new era in which all our lives and dreams are presided over by smiling, interchangeable, initialed gods.

***Esquire***
***April 1967***

# Ronnie and Nancy: A Life in Pictures

## I

I first saw Ronnie and Nancy Reagan at the Republican convention of 1964 in San Francisco's Cow Palace. Ronnie and Nancy (they are called by these names throughout Laurence Leamer's book *Make-Believe: The Story of Nancy and Ronald Reagan*) were seated in a box to one side of the central area where the cows—the delegates, that is—were whooping it up. Barry Goldwater was about to be nominated for president. Nelson Rockefeller was being booed not only for his communism but for his indecently unclos-eted heterosexuality. Who present that famous day can ever forget those women with blue-rinsed hair and leathery faces and large costume jewelry and pastel-tinted dresses with tasteful matching accessories as they screamed "Lover!" at Nelson? It was like a TV rerun of *The Bacchae,* with Nelson as Pentheus.

I felt sorry for Nelson. I felt sorry for David Brinkley when a number of seriously overweight Sunbelt Goldwaterites chased him through the kitchens of the Mark Hopkins Hotel. I felt sorry for myself when I, too, had to ward off their righteous wrath: I was there as a television commen-tator for Westinghouse. I felt sorry for the entire media that day as fists were actually shaken at the anchorpersons high up in the eaves of the hall. I felt particularly sorry for the media when a former president named Eisenhower, reading a speech with his usual sense of discovery, attacked the press, and the convention hall went mad. At last Ike was giving it to those commie-weirdo-Jew-fags who did not believe in the real America of humming electric chairs, well-packed prisons, and kitchens filled with every electrical device that a small brown person of extranational prove-nance might successfully operate at a fraction of the legal minimum wage.

. . .

As luck would have it, I stood leaning on the metal railing that enclosed the boxed-in open place where, side by side, Ronnie and Nancy were seated watching Ike. Suddenly, I was fascinated by them. First, there was her furious glare when someone created a diversion during Ike's aria. She turned, lip curled with Bacchantish rage, huge unblinking eyes afire with a passion to kill the enemy so palpably at hand—or so it looked to me. For all I know she might have been trying out new contact lenses. In any case, I had barely heard of Nancy then. Even so, I said to myself: There is a lot of rage in this little lady. I turned then to Ronnie. I had seen him in the flesh for a decade or so as each of us earned his mite in the Hollyjungle. Ronnie was already notorious for his speeches for General Electric, excoriating communists who were, apparently, everywhere. I had never actually spoken to him at a party because I knew—as who did not?—that although he was the soul of amiability when not excoriating the international monolithic menace of atheistic godless communism, he was, far and away, Hollywood's most grinding bore—Chester Chatterbox, in fact. Ronnie never stopped talking, even though he never had anything to say except what he had just read in the *Reader's Digest,* which he studied the way that Jefferson did Montesquieu. He also told show-biz stories of the sort that overexcites civilians in awe of old movie stars, but causes other toilers in the industry to stampede.

I had heard that Reagan might be involved in the coming campaign. So I studied him with some care. He was slumped in a folding chair, one hand holding up his chins; he was totally concentrated on Eisenhower. I remember thinking that I had made the right choice in 1959 when we were casting *The Best Man,* a play that I had written about a presidential convention. An agent had suggested Ronald Reagan for the lead. We all had a good laugh. He is by no means a bad actor, but he would hardly be convincing, I said with that eerie prescience which has earned me the title the American Nostradamus, as a presidential candidate. So I cast Melvyn Douglas, who could have made a splendid president in real life had his career not been rejuvenated by the play's success, while the actor whom I had rejected had no choice but to get himself elected president. I do remember being struck by the intensity with which Reagan studied Eisenhower. I had seen that sort of concentration a thousand times in half-darkened theatres during rehearsals or Saturday matinees: The understudy examines the star's performance and tries to figure how it is done. An actor prepares, I said to myself: Mr. Reagan is planning to go into politics. With his crude charm, I was reasonably certain that he could be elected mayor of Beverly Hills.

In time all things converge. The campaign biography and the movie star's biography are now interchangeable. The carefully packaged persona of the old-time movie star resembles nothing so much as the carefully packaged persona of today's politician. Was it not inevitable that the two would at last coincide in one person? That that person should have been Ronald Reagan is a curiosity of more than minor interest. George Murphy had broken the ice, as it were, by getting elected to the Senate from California.

Since Mr. Leamer is as little interested in politics and history as his two subjects, he is in some ways an ideal chronicler. He loves the kind of gossip that ordinary folks—his subjects and their friends—love. He takes an O'Haran delight in brand names while the "proper" names that are most often seen in syndicated columns ravish him. On the other hand, he is not very interested in the actual way politics, even as practiced by Ronnie, works. Although Reagan's eight years as governor of California are of some interest, Leamer gets through the-time-in-Sacramento as quickly as possible, with only one reference to Bob Moretti, the Democratic speaker of the assembly who, in effect, ran the state while Ronnie made his speeches around state, country, world on the dangers of communism. When in town, Ronnie played with his electric trains (something omitted by Mr. Leamer). On the other hand, there are twenty-four references to "wardrobe" in the index. So, perhaps, Mr. Leamer has got his priorities right after all. In any case, he never promised us a Rosebud.

Leamer begins with the inaugural of the fortieth president. First sentence: "On a gilded California day, Ronald and Nancy Reagan left their home for the last time." That is *echt Photoplay* and there is much, much more to come. Such lines as: "She had begun dating him when he thought he would never love again." You know, I think I will have some of those Hydrox cookies after all. "Unlike many of his backers, Ronnie was no snob. He believed that everybody should have his shot at this great golden honeypot of American free enterprise." The Golden Horde now arrives in Washington for the inaugural. "Ostentatious," growled that old meanie Barry Goldwater, nose out of joint because the man who got started in politics by giving The Speech for him in 1964 kept on giving The Speech for himself, and so, sixteen years and four wonderful presidents later, got elected Numero Uno.

Leamer tells us about their wardrobes for the great day. Also, "as a teenager and a young woman, [Nancy] had had her weight problems, but now at fifty-nine [Leamer finks on Nancy: Long ago she sliced two years off her age] she was a perfect size six. Her high cheekbones, huge eyes, delicate features and extraordinary attention to appearance made her lovelier than she had ever been." According to the testimony of the numerous ill-reproduced photographs in the book, this is quite true. The adventures simply of Nancy's nose down the years is an odyssey that we *Photoplay* fans would like to know a lot more about. At first there is a bulb on the tip;

then the bulb vanishes but there is a certain thickness around the ridge; then, suddenly, retroussé triumph!

The inaugural turns out to be a long and beautiful commercial to Adolfo, Blass, Saint Laurent, Galanos, De la Renta, and Halston. At one point, Ronnie reads a poem his mother had written; there were "tears in his eyes." During the ceremonies, Ronnie said later, "It was so hard not to cry during the whole thing." But then Ronnie had been discovered, groomed, and coiffed by the brothers Warner, who knew how to produce tears on cue with Max Steiner's ineffable musical scores. So overwhelming was Maestro Steiner that at one point, halfway up the stairs to die nobly in *Dark Victory,* Bette Davis suddenly stopped and looked down at the weeping director and crew and said, "Tell me now. Just who is going up these goddamned stairs to die? Me or Max Steiner?" She thought the teary music a bit hard on her thespian talents. No, I don't like the Oreos as much as the Hydrox but if that's all there is . . .

"As her husband spoke . . . her eyes gleamed with tears," while "the Mormon Tabernacle choir brought tears to his eyes." Tears, size sixes, Edwards-Lowell furs, Jimmy and Gloria Stewart, Roy Rogers and Dale Evans, new noses and old ideas, with charity toward none . . . then a final phone call to one of Nancy's oldest friends, who says: "Oh, Nancy, you aren't a movie star now, not the biggest movie star. You're the star of the whole world. The biggest star of all." To which Nancy answers, "Yes, I know, and it scares me to death." To which, halfway around the world, at Windsor Castle, an erect small woman of a certain age somewhat less than that of Nancy is heard to mutter, "What is all this shit?"

Mr. Leamer's book is nicely organized. After "A Gilded Dawn," he flashes back to tell us Nancy's story up until she meets Ronnie (who thought he would never love again); then Mr. Leamer flashes back and tells us Ronnie's story up until that momentous meeting. Then it is side by side into history. Curiously enough Nancy's story is more interesting than Ronnie's because she is more explicable and Mr. Leamer can get a grip on her. Ronnie is as mysterious a figure as ever appeared on the American political stage.

Nancy's mother was Edith Luckett, an actress from Washington, D.C. She worked in films and on the stage: "Edith's just been divorced from a rich playboy who's not worth the powder to blow him up." There is a lot of fine period dialogue in *Make-Believe.* Edith's father was a Virginian who worked for the old Adams Express Company where, thirty-one years earlier, John Surratt had worked; as you will recall, Surratt was one of the conspirators in the Abraham Lincoln murder case. Mr. Leamer tactfully omits this ominous detail.

Edith's marriage to Ken Robbins, "a handsome stage-door johnny . . .

from a far better family than Edith's," is skimpily, even mysteriously, described by Mr. Leamer. Where did they meet? When and where were they married? Where did they live? All we are told is that "when Ken entered the service in 1917, he and Edith were newlyweds. But he had his duties and she had her career. . . . Ken had been released from the army in January 1919. Edith had tried to keep the marriage going with her twenty-three-year-old husband [with her career? his duties?], but all she had to show for it was a baby, born on July 6, 1921, in New York City. Ken hadn't even been there." After two years of dragging Nancy around with her ("using trunks as cradles," what else?) Edith parked baby with her older sister, Virginia, in Maryland, while Ken went to live with his mother in New Jersey. So when were Edith and Ken divorced? It does not help that Mr. Leamer constantly refers to Ken as Nancy's "natural father."

Nancy was well looked after by her aunt; she was sent to Sidwell Friends School in Washington, some four years before I went there. Mr. Sidwell was an ancient Quaker whose elephantine ears were filled with hair while numerous liver spots made piebald his kindly bald head. I used to talk to him occasionally: *Never once did he mention Nancy Robbins.*

Meanwhile, Edith had found Mr. Right, Loyal Davis, M.D., F.A.C.S., a brain surgeon of pronounced reactionary politics and a loathing of the lesser breeds, particularly those of a dusky hue. The marriage of Edith and Loyal (I feel I know them, thanks to Mr. Leamer) seems to have been happy and, at fourteen, Nancy got herself adopted by Mr. Davis and took his name. Nancy Davis now "traveled at the top of Chicago's social world." She was a school leader. Yearbook: "Nancy's social perfection is a constant source of amazement. She is invariably becomingly and suitably dressed. She can talk, and even better listen intelligently . . ." Thus was child begetter of the woman and First Lady-to-be. Destiny was to unite her with a man who has not stopped talking, according to his associates and relatives, for threescore years at least.

Nancy went to Smith and to deb parties. She herself had a tea-dance debut in Chicago. She had beaux. She was a bit overweight, while her nose was still a Platonic essence waiting to happen. A friend of her mother's, ZaSu Pitts, gave Nancy a small part in a play that she was bringing to Broadway. From an early age, Nancy had greasepaint in her eyes. The play opened on Broadway unsuccessfully but Nancy stayed on. She modeled, looked for work (found it in *Lute Song*), dated famous family friends, among them Clark Gable, who after a few drinks would loosen his false teeth, which were on some sort of peg, and then shake his head until they rattled like dice. I wonder if he ever did that for Nancy. Can we ever really and truly know *anyone*? The Oreos are stale.

Hollywood came Nancy's way in the form of Benny Thau, a vice president of MGM. Nancy had a "blind date" with him. In 1949 Thau was a great power at the greatest studio. He got Nancy a screen test, and a contract. By now Nancy was, as Mr. Leamer puts it,

> dating Benny Thau. Barbara, the pretty teen-age receptionist, saw Nancy frequently. Many years later she remembered that she had orders that on Sunday morning Nancy was to be sent directly into Benny Thau's suite. Barbara nodded to Miss Davis as she walked into the vice-president's office; nodded again when she left later.

No wonder Nancy thinks the ERA is just plain silly.

Now Mr. Leamer cuts to the career of Ronnie ("Dutch") Reagan. This story has been told so much that it now makes no sense at all. Dixon, Illinois. Father drank (Irish Catholic). Mother stern (Protestant Scots-Irish); also, a fundamentalist Christian, a Disciple of Christ. Brother Neil is Catholic. Ronnie is Protestant. Sunday School teacher. Lifeguard. Eureka College. Drama department. Debating society. Lousy grades. Lousy football player but eager to be a successful jock (like Nixon and Ike *et al.* . . . What would happen if someone who could really play football got elected President?). Imitates radio sportscasters. Incessantly. Told to stop. Gets on everyone's nerves. Has the last laugh. Got a job as . . . sportscaster. At twenty-two. Midst of depression. Gets better job. Goes west. Meets agent. Gets hired by Warner Brothers as an actor. Becomes, in his own words, "the Errol Flynn of the B's."

Mr. Leamer bats out this stuff rather the way the studio press departments used to do. He seems to have done no firsthand research. Dutch is a dreamer, quiet (except that he talks all the time, from puberty on), unread and incurious about the world beyond the road ahead, which was in his case a thrilling one for a boy at that time; sportscaster at twenty-two and then film actor and movie star.

Mr. Leamer might have done well to talk to some of the California journalists who covered Reagan as governor. I was chatting with one last year, backstage in an Orange County auditorium. When I said something to the effect how odd it was that a klutz like Reagan should ever have been elected president, the journalist then proceeded to give an analysis of Reagan that was far more interesting than Mr. Leamer's mosaic of *Photoplay* tidbits. "He's not stupid at all. He's ignorant, which is another thing. He's also lazy, so what he doesn't know by now, which is a lot, he'll never know. That's the way he is. But he's a perfect politician. He knows exactly how to make the thing work for him."

I made some objections, pointed to errors along the way, not to mention the storms now gathering over the republic. "You can't look at it like that.

You see, he's not interested in politics as such. He's only interested in himself. Consider this. Here is a fairly handsome ordinary young man with a pleasant speaking voice who first gets to be what he wants to be and everybody else then wanted to be, a radio announcer [equivalent to an anchorperson nowadays]. Then he gets to be a movie star in the Golden Age of the movies. Then he gets credit for being in the Second World War while never leaving L.A. Then he gets in at the start of television as an actor and host. Then he picks up a lot of rich friends who underwrite him politically and personally and get him elected governor twice of the biggest state in the union and then they get him elected president, and if he survives he'll be reelected. The point is that here is the only man I've ever heard of who got everything that he ever wanted. That's no accident."

I must say that as I stepped out onto the stage to make my speech, I could not help but think that though there may not be a God there is quite possibly a devil, and we are now trapped in the era of the Dixon, Illinois, Faust.

One thing that Mr. Leamer quickly picks up on is Ronnie's freedom with facts. Apparently this began quite early. "Dutch had been brought up to tell the truth; but to him, facts had become flat little balloons that had to be blown up if they were to be seen and sufficiently appreciated." In Hollywood he began a lifelong habit of exaggerating not only his own past but those stories that he read in the *Reader's Digest* and other right-wing publications. No wonder his aides worry every time he opens his mouth without a script on the TelePrompTer to be read through those contact lenses that he used, idly, to take out at dinner parties and suck on.

By 1938 Ronnie was a featured player in *Brother Rat.* He was and still is an excellent film actor. The notion that he was just another Jon Hall is nonsense. For a time he was, in popularity with the fans, one of the top five actors in the country. If his range is limited that is because what he was called on to do was limited. You were a type in those days, and you didn't change your type if you wanted to be a star. But he did marry an actress who was an exception to the rule. Jane Wyman did graduate from brash blonde wisecracker to "dramatic" actress (as Mr. Leamer would say). After the war, she was the bigger star. The marriage fell apart. Natural daughter Maureen and adopted son Michael could not hold them together. Plainly, Jane could not follow Ronnie's sage advice. "We'll lead an ideal life if you'll just avoid doing one thing: Don't think." Never has there been such a perfect prescription for success in late-twentieth-century American political life.

But war clouds were now gathering over the Hollywood Hills. Five months after Pearl Harbor was attacked, Ronnie, though extremely nearsighted, was available for "limited service." To much weeping and gorge-rising, Ronnie went not overseas but over to Culver City where he made training films for the rest of the war. *Modern Screen* headline: BUT WHEN RONNIE WENT RIDING OFF TO BATTLE, HE LEFT HIS HEART BEHIND HIM! *Photoplay:* I WON'T BE DOING THESE PICTURES. UNCLE SAM HAS CALLED ME . . . AND I'M OFF TO THE WAR.

Ronnie was now known for two important roles, one as the doomed "Gipper" in *Knute Rockne, All American* and the other as the playboy whose legs are sawed off ("Where's the rest of me?") in *Kings Row.* As Ronnie's films moved once again B-ward, he moved toward politics. Originally, he had been a New Deal liberal, or something. Actually his real political activity was with the Screen Actors Guild where, by and large, in those days at least, first-rate working actors were seldom to be found giving much time to meetings, much less to becoming its president, as Reagan did.

When the McCarthy era broke upon America, Ronnie took a stern anti-commie line within his own union. In 1951 in *Fortnight,* he wrote that "several members of Congress are known Communists," and as one whose reviews had not been so good lately, he went on to add that though good American newspapers were attacking "dirty Reds" their publishers didn't know that they were employing "drama and book critics who . . . were praising the creative efforts of their little 'Red Brothers' while panning the work of all non-Communists."

Ronnie then went to work vetting (or, as it was called then, "clearing") people in the movies who might be tainted with communism. This was done through the Motion Picture Industry Council. The witch hunt was on, and many careers were duly ruined. Ronnie believed that no commie should be allowed to work in the movies and that anyone who did not cooperate with his council or the House Committee on Un-American Activities (in other words, refused to allow the committee to ask impertinent questions about political beliefs) should walk the plank. To this day, he takes the line that there was never a blacklist in Hollywood except for the one that commies within the industry drew up in order to exclude good Americans from jobs. Ronnie has always been a very sincere sort of liar.

As luck would have it, Nancy Davis cropped up on one of the nonexistent blacklists. Apparently there was another possibly pinker actress named Nancy Davis in lotusland. She asked a producer what to do; he said that Reagan could clear her. Thus, they met . . . not so cute, as the Wise Hack would say. It was the end of 1949. They "dated" for two years. Plainly, she loved this bona fide movie star who never stopped talking just as she could never stop appearing to listen (what her stepfather Dr. Davis must have been like at the breakfast table can only be imagined). But the woman who had launched the marriage of Ronnie and Janie, Louella Parson, the Saint Simon of San Simeon as well as of all movieland, could not understand why that idyllic couple had split up. She described in her column how "one of the lovely girls Ronnie seemed interested in for a while told me he recently said to her, 'Sure, I like you. I like you fine. But I think I've forgotten how to fall in love.' I wonder—do those embers of the once perfect love they shared still burn deep with haunting memories that won't let them forget?" If the popcorn isn't too old, we can pop it. But no salt and use oleomargarine.

Apparently, the embers had turned to ash. After two years, thirty-year-old Nancy married the forty-one-year-old Ronnie in the company of glamorous Mr. and Mrs. William Holden who posed, beaming, beside their new best friends at a time when they were their own new worst friends, for, according to Mr. Leamer, as they posed side by side with the Reagans, "The Holdens weren't even talking to one another."

Nancy's career is now one of wifedom and motherhood and, of course, listening. Also, in due course, social climbing. She was born with a silver ladder in her hand, just like the rest of us who went to Sidwell Friends School. Naturally, there were problems with Ronnie's first set of children. Ronnie seems not to have been a particularly attentive father, while Nancy was an overattentive mother to her own two children. But she took a dim view of Ronnie's first litter. The Reagans settled on Pacific Palisades. Ronnie's movie career was grinding to an end; he was obliged to go to Las Vegas to be a gambling casino "emcee." As there were no commies working for the trade papers by then, the reviews were good.

## 2

The year 1952 is crucial in Reagan's life. The Hollywood unions had always taken the position that no talent agency could go into production on a regular basis since the resulting conflict of interest would screw agency clients. Eventually, federal law forbade this anomaly. But thirty years ago there was a tacit agreement between agencies and unions that, on a case-by-case basis, an occasional movie might be produced by an agency. The Music Corporation of America represented actor Ronald Reagan. Within that vast agency, one Taft Schreiber looked after Ronald Reagan's declining career. At the end of Reagan's term as president of the Screen Actors Guild, he did something unprecedented.

> On July 3, 1952, after a series of meeting, Ronnie sent a letter to MCA granting the agency the blanket right to produce films.

> Within a few years, MCA was a dominant force in show business. In television, the forty or so shows that Revue Productions produced each week far surpassed the output of other programming suppliers.

Now for the payoff:

> Later that year [1954], Taft Schreiber . . . told Ronnie about a possible role introducing a new weekly television anthology series, "The GE Theater" . . . Schreiber owed his position as head of MCA's new Revue Productions to a SAG decision in which Ronnie played an instrumental role,

and so on.

For eight years, Ronnie was GE's host and occasional actor; he also became the corporate voice for General Electric's conservative viewpoint. During Reagan's tours of the country, he gave The Speech in the name of General Electric in particular and free enterprise in general. Gradually, Reagan became more and more right wing. But then if his principal reading matter told him that the Russians were not only coming but that their little Red brothers were entrenched in Congress and the school libraries and the reservoirs (fluoride at the ready), he must speak out. Finally, all this nonsense began to alarm even GE. When he started to attack socialism's masterpiece, the TVA (a GE client worth 50 million a year to the firm), he was told to start cooling it, which he did. Then, "In 1962, pleading bad ratings, GE canceled the program."

During this period, Reagan was not only getting deeper and deeper into the politics of the far right, but he and Nancy were getting to know some of the new-rich Hollywood folk outside show biz. Car dealers such as Holmes Tuttle and other wheeler-dealers became friends. The wives were into conspicuous consumption while the husbands were into money and, marginally, conservative politics which would enable them to make more money, pay less tax, and punish the poor. Thanks to Ronnie's brother Neil, then with an advertising agency that peddled Borax, the future leader of Righteous Christendom became host to Borax's television series, *Death Valley Days.* That same year Ronnie attended the Cow Palace investiture of Barry Goldwater.

"In late October, Goldwater was unable to speak at the big $1,000-a-plate fund raiser at the Ambassador Hotel in Los Angeles. . . . Holmes Tuttle asked Ronnie to pinch-hit." Tuttle sat next to wealthy Henry Salvatori, Goldwater's finance chairman. Tuttle suggested that they run Ronnie for governor of California in 1966. Salvatori didn't think you could run an actor against an old political pro like the Democratic incumbent Pat

Brown. But when Ronnie went national with The Speech on television, Ronnie was in business as a politician, and his friends decided to finance a Reagan race. To these new-rich Sunbelters, "Politicians and candidates, even Ronnie, were an inferior breed. 'Reagan doesn't have great depth,' Salvatori admits, 'but I don't know any politician who does. He's not the most intelligent man who ever was, but I've never met a politician with great depth. I don't know of any politician who would be smart enough to run my business, but Reagan just might.' " There it all is in one nut's shell.

The rest is beginning now to be history. "In the spring of 1965, forty-one rich businessmen formed 'The Friends of Ronald Reagan.' " For fifty thousand dollars a year, they hired a public-relations firm that specialized in political campaigns to groom Ronnie. California politics were carefully explained to him and he was given a crash course in the state's geography, which he may have flunked. He often had no idea where he was, or, as a supporter remarked to Leamer, "once, he didn't know a goddamn canal and where it went. Another time, he was standing in the Eagle River and didn't know where the hell he was," etc. But he had his dream of the city on the hill and he had The Speech and he had such insights as: the graduated income tax was "spawned by Marx as the prime essential of the socialistic state."

Alas, Mr. Leamer is not interested in Reagan's two terms as governor. He is more interested in Nancy's good grooming and circle of "best dressed" friends; also, in the way her past was falsified: "Nancy Davis Reagan was born in Chicago, the only daughter of Dr. and Mrs. Loyal Davis," said a campaign biography. Although Nancy had denied seeing her "natural" father after her adoption, she had indeed kept in touch for a time; but when he was dying in 1972 and her natural cousin tried to get through to her, there was no response. Mr. Leamer goes on rather too much about Nancy's wealthy girlfriends and their clothes as well as her wealthy *cavaliere servente* Jerome Zipkin who has known everyone from my mother to W. Somerset Maugham. "Maugham's biographer, Ted Morgan, thinks the British author may have patterned Eliott Templeton, a snobbish character in *The Razor's Edge,* on his American friend." Since *The Razor's Edge* was published in 1944, when Mr. Zipkin was still under thirty, it is most unlikely that that exquisite Anglophile American snob (and anti-Semite) could have been based on the charming Mr. Zipkin. Actually, for those interested in such trivia, the character was based on Henry de Courcey May, a monocled figure of my youth, much visible at Bailey's Beach in Newport, Rhode Island; although this exquisite was adored by our mothers, we little lads were under orders never to be alone with nice Mr. May—or not-so-nice Mr. Maugham for that matter. But once, on the train from Providence, Mr. May . . . But that is for Mr. Leamer's next book.

In a bored way, Mr. Leamer rushes through the governorship, using familiar Reagan boiler plate: the highest taxes in the state's history, and so on. He skirts around the most interesting caper of all, the ranch that Reagan was able to acquire through the good offices of MCA. When some details of this transaction were reported in the press, I was at a health spa near San Diego where Jules Stein and his wife (lifelong friends, as Mr. Leamer would say) were also taking the waters. When I asked Jules about the ranch caper, he got very nervous indeed. "What exactly did they print?" he asked. I told him. "Well," he said, "I didn't know anything about that. It was Schreiber who looked after Ronnie." By then Schreiber was dead.

Mr. Leamer tells us more than we want to know about the Reagan children. There seems to be a good deal of bitterness in a family that is closer to that of the Louds than to Judge Hardy's. But this is par for the course in the families of celebrities in general, and of politicians in particular. A ballet-dancer son with his mother's nose did not go down well. A daughter who decided to run for the Senate (and support the ERA) did not go down well either. So in 1982 Ronnie and his brother, Neil, helped to defeat Maureen, which was a pity since she would have been a more honorable public servant than her father. Apparently he has now had second thoughts or something; he has appointed her consultant "to improve his image among women." The family seems a lot creepier than it probably is simply because Reagan, a divorced men, has always put himself forward as the champion of prayer in the schools, and monogamy, and God, and a foe of abortion and smut and pot and the poor.

Mr. Leamer races through the political life: Ronnie sets out to replace Ford as president but instead is defeated in the primaries of 1976. Mr. Leamer finds Ronnie a pretty cold fish despite the professional appearance of warmth. When one of Ronnie's aides, Mike Deaver, lost out in a power struggle within the Reagan campaign, he was banished; and Ronnie never even telephoned him to say, "How are tricks?"

> As he did in his own family, Ronnie stood above the squabble. Indeed four years before, when Ronnie had been choking on a peanut, Deaver had saved his life.

For God's sake, Leamer, dramatize! as Henry James always told us to do. When and how did that peanut get into his windpipe? Where were they? Was it the Heimlich maneuver Deaver used?

In 1980 Reagan took the nomination from Bush, whom he genuinely dislikes, if Mr. Leamer is correct. Reagan then wins the presidency though it might be more accurate to say that Carter lost it. Nancy woos Washington's old guard, the Bright Old Things as they are dubbed, who were at first mildly charmed and then more and more bemused by this curious couple who have no interest at all in talking about what Washington's BOT have always talked about: power and politics and history and even, shades of Henry Adams and John Hay, literature and art. Henry James was not entirely ironic when he called Washington "the city of conversation." Ronnie simply bends their ears with stories about Jack Warner while Nancy discusses pretty things.

Mr. Leamer gets quickly through the politics to the drama: the shooting of Ronnie, who was more gravely injured than anyone admitted at the time. By now, Mr. Leamer is racing along: "Unknown to [Nancy's] staff . . . she was accepting dresses and gowns from major designers as well as jewels from Bulgari and Harry Winston." Seven pages later: "Unknown to Nancy's staff, much of this jewelry didn't belong to her; it had been 'borrowed' for an unspecified period from the exclusive jeweler to be part of a White House collection." Nancy wriggled out of all this as best she could, proposing to give her dresses to a museum while suggesting a permanent White House collection of crown jewels for future first ladies. Conspicuous consumption at the White House has not been so visible since Mrs. Lincoln's day. But at least old Abe paid out of his own pocket for his wife's "flub dubs."

The most disturbing aspect of *Make-Believe* is that Ronnie not only is still the president but could probably be reelected. Almost as an afterthought, Mr. Leamer suddenly reveals, in the last pages of his book, the true Reagan problem, which is now a world problem:

> What was so extraordinary was Ronnie's apparent psychic distance from the burden of the presidency. He sat in cabinet meetings doodling. Unless held to a rigid agenda, he would start telling Hollywood stories or talk about football in Dixon. Often in one-on-one conversations Ronnie seemed distracted or withdrawn: "He has a habit now," his brother, Neil, said. "You might be talking to him, and it's like he's picking his fingernails, but he's not. And you know then he's talking to himself."
>
> "If people knew about him living in his own reality, they wouldn't believe it," said one White House aide. "There are only ten to fifteen people who know the extent, and until they leave and begin talking, no one will believe it."

Of all our presidents, Reagan most resembles Warren Harding. He is handsome, amiable, ignorant; he has an ambitious wife (Mrs. Harding was known as the Duchess). But in the year 1983 who keeps what brooch from Bulgari is supremely unimportant. What is important is that in a dangerous world, the United States, thanks to a worn-out political system, has not a president but an indolent cue-card reader, whose writers seem eager for us to be, as soon as possible, at war. To the extent that Reagan is aware of what is happening, he probably concurs. But then what actor, no matter how old, could resist playing the part of a wartime president? even though war is now the last worst hope of earth; and hardly make-believe.

Mr. Leamer's *Make-Believe* will be criticized because it is largely a compendium of trivia about personalities. Unfortunately, there is no other book for him to write—unless it be an updated version of *Who Owns America?*

***The New York Review of Books***
***September 29, 1983***

# Remembering Orson Welles

ALTHOUGH ORSON WELLES was only ten years my senior, he had been famous for most of my life. I was thirteen when he made his famous Martians-are-coming radio broadcast. Then, three years later, when Welles was twenty-six, there was, suddenly, *Citizen Kane.* I was particularly susceptible to *Citizen Kane* because I was brought up among politicians and often saw more of my own father in newsreels than in life, particularly *The March of Time,* whose deep-toned thundering narrator—the voice of history itself—Welles was to evoke in his first film, whose cunning surface is so close to that of newsreel-real life that one felt, literally, at home in a way that one never did in such works of more gorgeous cinematic art as *All This and Heaven Too.*

Five years later, at the Beverly Hills Hotel, I first beheld the relatively lean Orson Welles. ("Note," Mercury Player Joseph Cotten once told me, "how Orson either never smiles on camera, or, if he has to, how he sucks in his cheeks so as not to look like a Halloween pumpkin.") On his arm was Rita Hayworth, his wife. He has it all, I remember thinking in a state of perfect awe untouched by pity. Little did I know—did he know?—that just as I was observing him in triumph, the great career was already going off the rails while the Gilda of all our dreams was being supplanted by the even more beautiful Dolores del Rio. Well, Rita never had any luck. As for Welles . . .

For the television generation he is remembered as an enormously fat and garrulous man with a booming voice, seen most often on talk shows and in commercials where he somberly assured us that a certain wine would not be sold "before its time," whatever that meant. But Welles himself was on sale, as it were, long before *his* time in the sense that he was an astonishing prodigy, as Frank Brady records in *Citizen Welles,* a long biography which, blessedly, emphasises the films in detail rather than the set of conflicting humours that made up the man.

Born in Kenosha, Wisconsin, on May 6, 1915, Welles was much indulged by a well-to-do, somewhat arty family. He was a born actor, artist, writer, magician. At fifteen, he ended his schooling. At sixteen, he was acting, successfully, grown-up parts for Dublin's Gate Theatre. At eighteen, he co-edited and illustrated three Shakespeare plays and a commercial textbook. *Everybody's Shakespeare.* At nineteen, he appeared on Broadway as Chorus and Tybalt in *Romeo and Juliet.* At twenty-two, he founded his own acting company, The Mercury Theater, whose greatest success was a modern-dress *Julius Caesar* with Welles as Brutus. The Mercury Theater then took radio by storm, dramatising novels and stories, among them H. G. Wells's *War of the Worlds,* done in a realistic radio way, using the medium to report, moment by moment, the arrival of Martians in New Jersey. The subsequent national panic augurs ill for that inevitable day when some evil Panamanian tyrant drops his Señor Buén Muchacho mask and nukes Miami.

In due course RKO gave Welles a free hand, if a limited budget, to write, direct, and star in his first film. *Citizen Kane* began a new era in the movies. For those given to making lists, *Citizen Kane* still remains on everyone's list of the ten best films; often as the best film ever made. But for Welles himself things started to fall apart almost immediately. The Hearst newspapers declared war on him for his supposed travesty of Hearst's personal life. On Kane's deathbed, he whispers the word "Rosebud." This is thought to be the key, somehow, to his life. In the film it turns out to be a boy's sled, which Mr. Steven Spielberg recently bought for $55,000. In actual life, Rosebud was what Hearst called his friend Marion Davies's clitoris, the sort of item that producers of children's films tend not to collect. Although the next film, *The Magnificent Ambersons* (1942), might have been even better than *Citizen Kane,* there was trouble with the editing—largely because Welles was in South America, failing to make a film.

For the rest of his life Welles moved restlessly around the world, acting on stage, in movies, on television. As director-actor, he managed to make *Macbeth, Othello, Chimes at Midnight* (the world from Falstaff's point of view). He also invented, as much as anyone did, the so-called film noir with *Journey into Fear* (1943), *The Lady from Shanghai* (1948), *Touch of Evil* (1958).

Everything that Welles touched as a director has a degree of brilliance, here and there, but he was always running out of money not to mention leading ladies, who kept mysteriously changing in his films, because he was often obliged to shut down for long periods of time, and then, when he started again, actors would be unavailable. In *Othello* Desdemona, finally, is a most expressive blonde wig. Meanwhile, Welles took every acting job he could to finance his own films and pay American taxes. We got to know each other in the Sixties, a period which Mr. Brady regards as "the nadir" of Welles's acting career. Well, all I can say is that there was an awful lot of nadir going around in those days. In fact, Welles acted in a nadir film that I had written called *Is Paris Burning?**

In later years we appeared on television together. "You see, I have to do the talk shows to keep my lecture price up at the universities." Orson always acted as if he were broke and, I suppose, relative to the Business, he was. He seemed to live in Spain as well as Hollywood and Las Vegas, "where I am near the airport," he would say mysteriously. "Also there are no death duties in Nevada unlike, shall we say, Haiti."

Orson's conversation was often surreal and always cryptic. Either you picked up on it or you were left out. At one point, he asked me to intervene on his behalf with Johnny Carson because there had been a "misunderstanding" between them and he was no longer asked to go on *The Tonight Show* and his lecture fees had, presumably, plummeted. I intervened. Carson was astonished. There was no problem that he knew of. I reported this to Orson in the course of one of our regular lunches at a French restaurant in Hollywood where Orson always sat in a vast chair to the right of the door. There was a smaller chair for a totally unprincipled small black poodle called Kiki.

"There is more to this than Johnny will ever tell you," he rumbled. "Much, much more. Why," he turned to the waiter with cold eyes, "do you keep bringing me a menu when you know what I must eat? Grilled fish." The voice boomed throughout the room. "And iced tea. How I hate grilled fish! But doctor's orders. I've lost twenty pounds. No one ever believes this. But then no one ever believes I hardly eat anything." He was close to four hundred pounds at the time of our last lunch in 1982. He wore bifurcated tents to which, rather idly, lapels, pocket flaps, buttons were attached in order to suggest a conventional suit. He hated the fat jokes that he was

*I was astonished to read in Frank Brady's *Citizen Welles* that Orson was offered the starring role in *Caligula,* "but when he read the Gore Vidal script and found it to be a mixture of hard-core pornography and violence, he peremptorily turned it down on moral grounds." Since Brady also gets the plot to *The Big Brass Ring* wrong, I assumed that he was wrong about Caligula, a part Orson could not have played even if my script for the picture had been used as written. But now, suddenly, I recalled Kenneth Tynan telling me that Orson had been upset by my original script. "You must never forget what a Puritan he is when it comes to sex."

obliged to listen to—on television at least—with a merry smile and an insouciant retort or two, carefully honed in advance. When I asked him why he didn't have the operation that vacuums the fat out of the body, he was gleeful. "Because I have seen the results of liposuction *when the operation goes wrong.* It happened to a woman I know. First, they insert the catheter in the abdomen, subcutaneously." Orson was up on every medical procedure. "The suction begins and the fat—it looks like yellow chicken fat. You must try the chicken here. But then the fat—hers not the chicken's—came out unevenly. And so where once had been a Rubenesque torso, there was now something all hideously rippled and valleyed and canyoned like the moon." He chuckled and, as always, the blood rose in his face, slowly, from lower lip to forehead until the eyes vanished in a scarlet cloud, and I wondered, as always, what I'd do were he to drop dead of a stroke.

We talked mostly of politics and literature. At our last lunch, I was running in the Democratic primary for Senate. Orson approved. "I too had political ambitions, particularly back in the FDR days. I used to help him with speeches and I like to think I was useful to him. I know he thought I should have a serious go at politics some day. Well, some day came. They wanted me to run for the Senate in my home state of Wisconsin, against Joe McCarthy. Then I let them—another 'them'—convince me that I could never win because," and the chuckle began again, "I was an actor—hence, frivolous. And divorced—hence, immoral. And now Ronnie Reagan, who is both, is president." Eyes drowned in the red sea; laughter tolled; then, out of who knows what depths of moral nullity, Kiki bit a waiter's sleeve.

When I observed that acting—particularly old-time movie acting—was the worst possible preparation for the presidency because the movie actor must be entirely passive so that he can do and say exactly what others tell him to do and say, Orson agreed that although this might be true in general (we both excluded *him* from any generality), he had known two movie actors who would have been good presidents. One was Melvyn Douglas. The other was Gregory Peck. "Of course," he was thoughtful, "Greg isn't much as an actor, which may explain why he has so good a character."

During the last year of our occasional meetings, Orson and I were much preoccupied with Rudy Vallee. The popular singer of yesteryear was living in the mansion "Silvertip" high atop that Hollywood hill halfway up which I sometimes live. When the maestro heard that I was his neighbor, he sent me a copy of his memoirs *Let The Chips Fall* . . . Like a pair of Talmudic scholars, Orson and I constantly studied this astonishing book. Parts of it we memorized:

> Somehow I have never inspired confidence. I don't think it is due to any weakness particularly evident in my face, but there is something about me, possibly a quiet reserve or shyness, that gives most people the impression that I can't do anything very well.

Each of us had his favorite moments. Mine was the telegram (reproduced) that Rudy sent the relatively unknown radio announcer, Arthur Godfrey, in 1940, to show what a keen eye and ear Rudy had for talent (for a time Vallee ran a talent agency). Orson preferred the highly detailed indictment of Rudy's protégé, "The Ungreatfulcholy Dane," Victor Borge, complete with reproductions of inter-office memoranda, telegrams sent and received, culminating in two newspaper cuttings. One headline: VICTOR BORGE SUED FOR $750,000; the other: BORGE SUED BY THE IRS.

As professional storytellers, we were duly awed by Rudy's handling of The Grapefruit Incident, which begins, so causally, at Yale.

> Ironically, the dean was the father of the boy who, nine years later, was to hurl a grapefruit at me in a Boston theater and almost kill me.

Then the story is dropped. Pages pass. Years pass. Then the grapefruit motif is reintroduced. Rudy and his band have played for the dean; afterward, when they are given ice cream, Rudy asks, "Is this all we're having . . ."

> Apparently one of [the dean's] sons noticed my rather uncivil question . . . and resolved that some day he would avenge this slight. What he actually did later at a Boston theater might have put him in the electric chair and me in my grave but fortunately his aim was bad. But of that more later.

Orson thought this masterful. Appetites whetted, we read on until the now inevitable rendezvous of hero and grapefruit in a Boston theatre where, as Rudy is singing—"Oh, Give Me Something to Remember You By,"

> a large yellow grapefruit came hurtling from the balcony. With a tremendous crash it struck the drummer's cymbal . . . [but] if it had struck the gooseneck of my sax squarely where it curves into the mouth it might have driven it back through the vertebra in the back of my neck.

Of this passage, the ecstatic Orson whispered, "Conrad"—what might have been *if* Lord Jim had remained on watch.

Finally, in a scene reminiscent of Saint-Simon's last evocation of the Duchess of Burgundy, Vallee tells us how he had got the Chairman of the Board himself to come see his house and its rooms of memorabilia. Frank Sinatra dutifully toured room after room of artifacts relating to the master.

Although an offending journalist gave "the impression that most of the pictures portrayed my likeness, actually, one third of the pictures are of neutral subjects or of personalities other than myself." Even so, "as Frank Sinatra rather snidely put it as we left this particular corridor, 'You would never guess who lived here.' "*

In literary matters, Orson was encyclopedic, with an actor's memory for poetry. I have known few American writers who have had much or, indeed, any enthusiasm for literature. Writers who teach tend to prefer literary theory to literature and tenure to all else. Writers who do not teach prefer the contemplation of Careers to art of any kind. On the other hand, those actors who do read are often most learned, even passionate, when it comes to literature. I think that this unusual taste comes from a thorough grounding in Shakespeare combined with all that time waiting around on movie-sets.

When we had finished with politics and literature and the broiled fish, Orson told me a hilarious story of a sexual intrigue in Yugoslavia during the shooting of Kafka's *The Trial.* How was Orson to maneuver a willing young woman away from her escort in a bar that was connected by a dark and creaking staircase to Orson's room, and then . . . ? Each detail of this labyrinthine tale was lovingly recounted right up until the final victory in the wrong bed or room—or something. Orson was a superb dramatizer. As an actor, he was limited by his unique physical presence and that great booming conman's voice. But when it came to storytelling, he was as exciting at a corner table, talking, as he was on the screen itself in a work all his own. But the tragedy of Welles ("How," I can hear him say, eyes theatrically narrowed to slits in that great round pudding of a face, "do you define tragedy?") is that more time was spent evoking movies at corner tables than in a studio. Yet he was always seriously at work on a number of projects that he could never get the financing for.

"This time I've written a political script. Rather your kind of thing." He puffed on a cigar. He looked like Harry Lime. "You know Paul Newman. Can you put in a word for him? Because if I don't have one of the Six Bankable Boys, there's no financing. What one has to go through." He patted his stomach as if it were his dog. He looked like Falstaff. "They always ask me, aren't you glad, *cher maître,* that the old studio system is finished,

*Rudy Vallee scholars will search in vain for the adverb "snidely" in *Let the Chips Fall* . . . I have taken the liberty of using an earlier version of the Sinatra visit as recorded in *My Time Is Your Time* (1962). Even though Rudy Vallee always wrote the same book, he was given to subtle changes, particularly in his use or omission of adverbs, reminiscent, in their mastery, of the grace notes in Bach. A synoptic edition of Vallee's three memoirs is long overdue, as well as a meticulous concordance.

that there are no more vulgar furriers controlling your films? And I say, my God, how I miss them! Even Harry Cohn. When you make fifty-two pictures a year on an assembly-line basis there is always room for an Orson Welles film. But now there is no room anywhere." He smoothed the dog's fur as if it were his stomach. Then he chuckled. "I have made an art form of the interview. The French are the best interviewers, despite their addiction to the triad, like all Cartesians." I took this well: triad = trinity, but *versus,* I would have thought, Descartes.

Orson was now in full flow. "They also have the gift of the unexpected letdown. The ultimate Zinger. 'There are only three great directors in the history of the film,' they will announce. I smile shyly." Orson smiled. Cotten was right. Though he doesn't seem to be sucking in his cheeks, the corners of his mouth are drawn not up but down. "There is D. W. Griffith. I roll my eyes toward Heaven in an ecstasy of agreement. There is Orson Welles. I lower my lids, all modesty—little me? Then," his voice drops, basso profundissimo, "there is—Nicholas Ray!" Orson erupts in laughter. We meditate on the interview as art form as well as necessity for Orson, "because I don't lecture anymore."

"Then why," I asked, "did you ask me to ask Carson to get you back on *The Tonight Show* so that you could get more lecture dates when you've given up lecturing?" He looked at me in true surprise. "Surely I told you I've stopped lecturing because I can't walk from the airport terminal to the gate." "You can use a wheelchair," I said. "But that would be the end of me as an actor. Word would spread I was terminally ill. Besides there is no wheelchair large enough unless I bring my own, which would make a truly bad impression."

Orson never knew that I knew how, the previous week, Orson's driver had delivered him to the restaurant's parking lot, only to find that Orson was so tightly wedged in the front seat that the car had to be taken apart so that he could get out.

"If not Newman, there's Nicholson or Beatty. Warren has consented to give me an audience. But Nicholson would be better. The story's called *The Big Brass Ring,* about a senator who's just been defeated by Reagan for president—two years from now, of course. Really right down your alley . . ."

Three years after our last lunch, Orson died at the age of seventy. He had not been able to get one of the Bankable Boys to agree to do *The Big Brass Ring* and so it is now just one more cloudy trophy to provoke one's imagination. What would Welles's Don Quixote have been like if he had been able to finish it? But then it is pleasurable to imagine what he might have done with any theme because he was, literally, a magician, fascinated by legerdemain, tricks of eye, forgeries, labyrinths, mirrors reflecting mirrors. He was a master of finding new ways of seeing things that others saw not at all.

Happily, I now know something about *The Big Brass Ring,* which was published obscurely in 1987 as "an original screen-play by Orson Welles with Oja Kodar." Wellesian mysteries begin to swirl. Who is Oja Kodar? The dust jacket identifies her as Welles's "companion and collaborator (as actress and screenwriter, among other capacities) over the last twenty years of his life. She is a Yugoslav sculptor who has had one-woman shows in both Europe and the US. The lead actress in *F for Fake* [which I've never seen] and *The Other Side of the Wind* [unreleased], she collaborated on the scripts of both films as well as many other Welles projects" . . . all unmade.

Orson never mentioned her. But then, come to think of it, except for bizarre dreamlike adventures, he never spoke of his private life. In all the years I knew him, I never set foot in any place where he was living, or met his wife, Paola Mori, who died a year after he did. I invited Orson several times to the house where I lived within megaphone distance of the Rudy Vallee shrine and he always accepted, with delight. Then the phone calls would start. "I know that it is the height of rudeness to ask who will be there, so my rudeness is of the loftiest sort. Who will be there?" I would tell him and he'd be pleased to see so many old friends; finally, an hour before the party began, he'd ring. "I have an early call tomorrow. For a commercial. Dog food, I think it is this time. No, I do not have to eat from the can on camera but I *celebrate* the contents. Yes, I have fallen so low."

Further mysteries: there is an afterword published to the script by Jonathan Rosenbaum, who tells us that Welles left two estates, "one of them controlled by his wife Paola Mori and daughter Beatrice, . . . the other controlled by Kodar." Now the two estates appear to be in equilibrium; hence, "the publication of *The Big Brass Ring* represents a major step forward in the clarification of the invisible Orson Welles, even though it comprises only a piece of the iceberg (or jigsaw puzzle, if one prefers)." I prefer jigsaw puzzle. And now, for me, an essential piece is at hand: the screenplay, which is purest Welles. He is plainly at the top of his glittering form, which was as deeply literary as it was visual.

What, precisely, is "purest Welles"? Although every line sounds like Welles, we are told that he based some of the story on an autobiographical sketch by Kodar. Thus, they collaborated. But the germ of the story, one of Welles's few "originals" (a word in this context never to be let out of quotes), was first expressed by Welles in a conversation with the film director Henry Jaglom. Welles said that there was a story that "he'd been thinking about for years, about an old political adviser to Roosevelt who was homosexual, and whose lover had gotten crippled in the Spanish Civil War fighting the fascists. Now he was in an African kingdom, advising the murderous leader—and back in the US, a young senator who'd been his protégé was going to run against Reagan in 1984, as the Democratic nominee." So far so Wellesian. The fascination with politics, particularly the New Deal; with homosexuality to the extent that it involves masks and revelation; and, finally, with the relationship between the teacher and the taught.

The action is swift. A series of images—fading campaign posters: the defeated presidential candidate, Pellarin, walks through a restaurant where he is recognised and cheered: he is a combination of Texas Good-Ole-Boy and Harvard Law School. The wife, Diana, is edgy, long-suffering, rich. Then we are aboard a yacht. Pellarin is bored. Diana plays backgammon with a woman friend. Pellarin goes into their bedroom and finds a girl—a manicurist—stealing his wife's emerald necklace. To his own amazement, he tells her, "Keep it." With this Gidean *acte gratuit* the story takes off. When a shipwide search for the necklace begins, Pellarin realizes that it will be found on the girl; so he makes her give him the jewels; then he promises her that he will turn them over to a fence at the next port, which is Tangiers.

At Tangiers, Pellarin books a flight to the African country where his old mentor, Kimball Menaker, is advising the local Idi Amin. At the airport, he is ambushed by Cela Brandini, a superb portrait of the dread Oriana Fallaci in the terminal throes of requited self-love. "I am Cela Brandini," she declares with all the authority of a bush afire. "Of course you are," he says, mildly. Brandini: "And I have never asked you for an interview." Pellarin: "Guess I'm just plain lucky." Now Welles can use his second art form, the interview with tape recorder. Brandini has just interviewed Menaker, a figure that Pellarin must never see again because . . . The plot of the emerald necklace crosses with that of the search for Menaker, to be played by Welles at his most oracular, not to mention polymathematical.

As they wait in the airport lounge, Brandini plays for him some of Menaker's dialogue on her recorder, a nice narrative device. Menaker: "A message? Do I wish to send a message to the Senator from Texas? ex-chairman of the Foreign Affairs Committee? former vedette of the Hasty Pudding Club Review, our future President, and my former friend?" Brandini has interviewed Menaker as background for a piece she wants to do on Pellarin. She is aware that Menaker is the skeleton in Pellarin's closet. Had they been lovers? What glorious scandal! Brandini: "The way he speaks of you—he seems to think he's your [father]." Pellarin is pleased. She strikes, "And yet, politically—he almost killed you off." Pellarin demurs: "He didn't quite do that, you know—He killed himself." Mysteries within mysteries. A quest. Nothing now is what it seems. Pellarin, pilgrim.

Pellarin finds Menaker in the Batunga Hilton; he is in bed with a sick monkey while two naked black women play backgammon as they keep guard over him. Although the scene is about finding a fence for the emeralds (Menaker is the author of *The Criminal Underworld Considered as a Primitive Culture—An Anthropological View*: "I'm an authority on everything," he says), the subtext concerns a woman, Pellarin's lost love, a Cambodian beauty, last seen by Menaker in Paris.

Pellarin departs with the sick monkey knotted about his neck, hiding the emeralds. He joins the yacht at Barcelona. Brandini is also there. She declaims: "I'm an anarchist." Pellarin: "I wish you were a veterinarian." Brandini: "I do not think that monkey has very long to live." Pellarin: "Neither do I." Brandini: "Interesting," Pellarin: "Death? The subject doesn't capture my imagination." Brandini: "I know something about it, Pellarin. I've seen it in Vietnam, Central America—in Greece." Pellarin: "I know. There's a lot of that stuff going around." Back on the yacht, Pellarin tries to get the monkey off his neck; it falls into the sea, the emeralds clutched in its fist. How is Pellarin to get the money he "owes" the girl?

Meanwhile, Menaker is out of Africa and again in the clutches of Brandini. A reference is made to Menaker's Harvard rival, Henry Kissinger, "chief brown-noser to the Rockefellers." Menaker is concerned about Kissinger because: "He *is* getting *shorter*—Have you noticed that? He's positively *dwindling* with thwarted ambition: Metternich as the incredible shrinking man. They ought to give poor shrinking Henry one last go at State. As a foreigner, there's no higher he can go—and who knows how much smaller he can get." They speak of Menaker's influence on Pellarin. Menaker seems to him triumphant despite their association, not to mention that of Harvard. These are only minor limitations. Brandini: "You've spoken of his limitations—What are yours?" Menaker: "I'm an old man, Miss Brandini—and a faggot. I couldn't use another limitation."

Pellarin and Menaker meet. Menaker says not to worry about the emeralds: they are false. Diana sold the originals to help get Pellarin elected to Congress. She has worn paste copies ever since. So Pellarin must cash a cheque in order to give money to the girl for the worthless jewels that she stole and Pellarin lost. This is exquisite Welles. And he brings it off with Wildean panache.

Now the story of the emeralds again crosses the story of the lost love in Paris. Apparently, she is in Madrid. She wants to see Pellarin. Menaker will take him to her. Meanwhile they meditate upon identity. Menaker: "Even the great ones must have sometimes felt uncomfortable in their own skins. Caesar must have dreamt of Alexander, and Napoleon of Caesar." Pellarin: "Shit, Professor—I couldn't make their weight." Menaker: "Then think of poor Dick Nixon—mincing about inside his fortress in the Oval Room, all bristling with bugs—hoping a playback would eventually inform him who he was . . . He told us often what he *wasn't,* but he never really got it figured out." Pellarin: "Neither have I . . . You sly old son of a bitch, so *that's* what you've been getting at." Menaker: "In a perfect world, all of us should be allowed some short vacations from our own identities. Last week you were Bulldog Drummond, gentleman jewel thief. Soon you'll be hoping to sneak down that rabbit hole again to where it's always Paris in the spring." Orson Welles, who was known to all the world as Orson Welles, could never be anyone else in life but, in art, he could saw a lady in half, pull a rabbit from a hat, arrange shadows on celluloid in such a way as to be any number of entirely other selves.

Menaker leads Pellarin to "The Old Dark House." A *feria* is in progress; fireworks. Only Pellarin goes inside the house: "The scene is strange, almost surreal . . . (the action must be given in synopsis . . . The climax of this sequence is strongly erotic: to spell out its specific details would be to risk pornography) . . . A man searching and searching—up and down, from floor to floor, from room to room of an empty house, comes to discover (in a lightning flash of fireworks breaking through a shuttered window) that all along there has been someone watching him:—naked, in a shadowed chair." This is much the same scene that Orson told me at our last lunch as having happened to him. Did it? Or was he trying out the scene on me? She is found; they speak in French; make love; then she vanishes. Although the film was to be shot in black and white, Orson intended the fireworks to be in colour; at the scene's end "The colored lights fall into darkness."

Pellarin faces Menaker in the street. Menaker never delivered the letter that Pellarin had written asking the girl to marry him. Menaker did not deliver it because he wants Pellarin to go to glory. Pellarin: "Screw Pennsylvania Avenue." Menaker: "Boysie—There's nowhere else for you to go." Later, the ubiquitous Brandini strikes. She tells Pellarin that "during his sexual fantasizing about you—Dr. Menaker would masturbate into a handkerchief . . . Then, when it was stiff with his dried semen, he mailed it to his crippled friend, as . . . I don't know what: a sentimental souvenir." I must say that even at the lively fun-court of Tiberius and of his heir, Caligula, neither Suetonius nor I ever came up with anything quite so—dare I use so punitive a word?—icky. But Orson needed an emotional trigger for a nightmare flight through the city and an encounter with a blind beggar who menaces Pellarin and whom he kills. Let it come down. The police suspect; but cover for him.

Pellarin re-enters the world. A speech must be given in Brussels. Menaker is on the train, which Brandini satisfactorily misses—"dressed as usual: semi-safari with a strong hint of battle fatigues." They sing, jointly, Menaker's "hit number from the Hasty Pudding Show of nineteen twenty-nine." Then Orson adds, with his usual flourish: "If you want a happy ending, that depends, of course, on where you stop your story."

In a statement to Henry Jaglom (May 20, 1982), Orson wrote of Pellarin.

> He is a great man—like all great men he is never satisfied that he has chosen the right path in life. Even being President, he feels, may somehow not be right. He is a man who has within him the devil of self-destruction that lives in every genius . . . There is this foolish, romantic side of us all . . . That is what the *circumstances* of the film are about—the theft of the necklace, the situation with the monkey, etc. All these idiotic events that one's romantic nature leads one into.

But of course Orson is describing Menaker, not Pellarin, and, again of course, Orson is describing his own "romantic nature" which led him down so many odd roads, to our enduring delight if not always his.

I have a recurring fantasy that if one were to dial the telephone number of someone in the past, one would hear again a familiar voice, and time would instantly rewind from now to then. I still have Orson's telephone number in my book (213-851-8458). Do I dare ring him and talk to him back in 1982, where he is busy trying to convince Jack Nicholson to play Pellarin for two not four million dollars? Should I tell him that he'll not get the picture made? No. That would be too harsh. I'll pretend that I have somehow got a copy of it, and that I think it marvelous though perhaps the handkerchief was, from so prudish a master, a bit much? Even incredible.

"Incredible?" The voice booms in my ear. "How could it be incredible when I stole it from *Othello*? But now I have a real treat for you. Standing here is your neighbor . . . Rudy! Overcome 'that quiet reserve or shyness.' *Sing.*"

From out of the past, I hear "My time is your time," in that reedy highly imitable voice. The after-life's only a dial tone away. "What makes you think that this is the after-life?" Orson chuckles. "This is a recording." Stop story here.

***The New York Review of Books***
***June 1, 1989***

# Who Makes the Movies?

FORTY-NINE YEARS AGO last October, Al Jolson not only filled with hideous song the sound track of a film called *The Jazz Singer,* he also spoke. With the words "You ain't heard nothin' yet" (surely the most menacing line in the history of world drama), the age of the screen director came to an end and the age of the screenwriter began.

Until 1927, the director was king, turning out by the mile his "molds of light" (André Bazin's nice phrase). But once the movies talked, the director as creator became secondary to the writer. Even now, except for an occasional director-writer like Ingmar Bergman,* the director tends to be the one interchangeable (if not entirely expendable) element in the making of a film. After all, there are thousands of movie technicians who can do what a director is supposed to do because, in fact, collectively (and sometimes individually) they actually do do his work behind the camera and in the cutter's room. On the other hand, there is no film without a written script.

In the Fifties when I came to MGM as a contract writer and took my place at the Writers' Table in the commissary, the Wise Hack used to tell us newcomers, "The director is the brother-in-law." Apparently the ambitious man became a producer (that's where the power was). The talented man became a writer (that's where the creation was). The pretty man became a star.

*Questions I am advised to anticipate: What about such true *auteurs du cinéma* as Truffaut? Well, *Jules et Jim* was a novel by Henri-Pierre Roché. Did Truffaut adapt the screenplay by himself? No, he worked with Jean Gruault. Did Buñuel create *The Exterminating Angel*? No, it was "suggested" by an unpublished play by José Bergamin. Did Buñuel take it from there? No, he had as co-author Luis Alcorisa. So it goes.

Even before Jolson spoke, the director had begun to give way to the producer. Director Lewis Milestone saw the writing on the screen as early as 1923 when "baby producer" Irving Thalberg fired the legendary director Erich von Stroheim from his film *Merry Go Round.* "That," wrote Milestone somberly in *New Theater and Film* (March 1937), "was the beginning of the storm and the end of the reign of the director. . . ." Even as late as 1950 the star Dick Powell assured the film cutter Robert Parrish that "anybody can direct a movie, even I could do it. I'd rather not because it would take too much time. I can make more money acting, selling real estate and playing the market." That was pretty much the way the director was viewed in the Thirties and Forties, the so-called classic age of the talking movie.

Although the essential creator of the classic Hollywood film was the writer, the actual master of the film was the producer, as Scott Fitzgerald recognized when he took as protagonist for his last novel Irving Thalberg. Although Thalberg himself was a lousy movie-maker, he was the head of production at MGM; and in those days MGM was a kind of Vatican where the chief of production was Pope, holding in his fists the golden keys of Schenck. The staff producers were the College of Cardinals. The movie stars were holy and valuable objects to be bought, borrowed, stolen. Like icons, they were moved from sound stage to sound stage, studio to studio, film to film, bringing in their wake good fortune and gold.

With certain exceptions (Alfred Hitchcock, for one), the directors were, at worst, brothers-in-law; at best, bright technicians. All in all, they were a cheery, unpretentious lot, and if anyone had told them that they were *auteurs du cinéma,* few could have coped with the concept, much less the French. They were technicians; proud commercialities, happy to serve what was optimistically known as The Industry.

This state of affairs lasted until television replaced the movies as America's principal dispenser of mass entertainment. Overnight the producers lost control of what was left of The Industry and, unexpectedly, the icons took charge. Apparently, during all those years when we thought the icons nothing more than beautiful painted images of all our dreams and lusts, they had been not only alive but secretly greedy for power and gold.

"The lunatics are running the asylum," moaned the Wise Hack at the Writers' Table, but soldiered on. Meanwhile, the icons started to produce, direct, even write. For a time, they were able to ignore the fact that with television on the rise, no movie star could outdraw *The $64,000 Question.* During this transitional decade, the director was still the brother-in-law. But instead of marrying himself off to a producer, he shacked up, as it were, with an icon. For a time each icon had his or her favorite director and The Industry was soon on the rocks.

Then out of France came the dreadful news: all those brothers-in-law of the classic era were really autonomous and original artists. Apparently each had his own style that impressed itself on every frame of any film he worked on. Proof? Since the director was the same person from film to film, each image of his *oeuvre* must then be stamped with his authorship. The argument was circular but no less overwhelming in its implications. Much quoted was Giraudoux's solemn inanity: "There are no works, there are only *auteurs.*"

The often wise André Bazin eventually ridiculed this notion in *La Politique des Auteurs,* but the damage was done in the pages of the magazine he founded, *Cahiers du cinéma.* The fact that, regardless of director, every Warner Brothers film during the classic age had a dark look owing to the Brothers' passion for saving money in electricity and set-dressing cut no ice with ambitious critics on the prowl for high art in a field once thought entirely low.

In 1948, Bazin's disciple Alexandre Astruc wrote the challenging "*La Caméra-stylo.*" This manifesto advanced the notion that the director is—or should be—the true and solitary creator of a movie, "penning" his film on celluloid. Astruc thought that *caméra-stylo* could

> tackle any subject, any genre. . . . I will even go so far as to say that contemporary ideas and philosophies of life are such that only the cinema can do justice to them. Maurice Nadeau wrote in an article in the newspaper *Combat:* "If Descartes lived today, he would write novels." With all due respect to Nadeau, a Descartes of today would already have shut himself up in his bedroom with a 16mm camera and some film, and would be writing his philosophy on film: for his *Discours de la Méthode* would today be of such a kind that only the cinema could express it satisfactorily.

With all due respect to Astruc, the cinema has many charming possibilities but it cannot convey complex ideas through words or even, paradoxically, dialogue in the Socratic sense. *Le Genou de Claire* is about as close as we shall ever come to dialectic in a film and though Rohmer's work has its delights, the ghost of Descartes is not very apt to abandon the marshaling of words on a page for the flickering shadows of talking heads. In any case, the Descartes of Astruc's period did not make a film; he wrote the novel *La Nausée.*

But the would-be camera-writers are not interested in philosophy or history or literature. They want only to acquire for the cinema the prestige of ancient forms without having first to crack the code. "Let's face it," writes Astruc:

> between the pure cinema of the 1920s and filmed theater, there is plenty of room for a different and individual kind of film-making.

> This of course implies that the scriptwriter directs his own scripts; or rather, that the scriptwriter ceases to exist, for in this kind of film-making the distinction between author and director loses all meaning. Direction is no longer a means of illustrating or presenting a scene, but a true act of writing.

It is curious that despite Astruc's fierce will to eliminate the scriptwriter (and perhaps literature itself), he is forced to use terms from the art form he would like to supersede. For him the film director uses a *pen* with which he *writes* in order to become—highest praise—an *author.*

As the French theories made their way across the Atlantic, bemused brothers-in-law found themselves being courted by odd-looking French youths with tape recorders. Details of long-forgotten Westerns were recalled and explicated. Every halting word from the *auteur*'s lips was taken down and reverently examined. The despised brothers-in-law of the Thirties were now Artists. With newfound confidence, directors started inking major pacts to meg superstar thesps whom the meggers could control as hyphenates: that is, as director-producers or even as writer-director-producers. Although the icons continued to be worshiped and overpaid, the truly big deals were now made by directors. To them, also, went the glory. For all practical purposes the producer has either vanished from the scene (the "package" is now put together by a "talent" agency) or merged with the director. Meanwhile, the screenwriter continues to be the prime creator of the talking film, and though he is generally paid very well and his name is listed right after that of the director in the movie reviews of *Time,* he is entirely in the shadow of the director just as the director was once in the shadow of the producer and the star.

What do directors actually do? What do screenwriters do? This is difficult to explain to those who have never been involved in the making of a film. It is particularly difficult when French theoreticians add to the confusion by devising false hypotheses (studio director as *auteur* in the Thirties) on which to build irrelevant and misleading theories. Actually, if Astruc and Bazin had wanted to be truly perverse (and almost accurate), they would have declared that the cameraman is the *auteur* of any film. They could then have ranked James Wong Howe with Dante, Braque, and Gandhi. Cameramen do tend to have styles in a way that the best writers do but most directors don't—style as opposed to preoccupation. Gregg Toland's camera work is a vivid fact from film to film, linking *Citizen Kane* to Wyler's *The Best Years of Our Lives* in a way that one cannot link *Citizen Kane* to, say, Welles's *Confidential Report.* Certainly the cameraman is usually more important than the director in the day-to-day making of a film as opposed to the preparation of a film. Once the film is shot the editor becomes the principal interpreter of the writer's invention.

Since there are few reliable accounts of the making of any of the classic talking movies, Pauline Kael's book on the making of *Citizen Kane* is a valuable document. In considerable detail she establishes the primacy in that enterprise of the screenwriter Herman Mankiewicz. The story of how Orson Welles saw to it that Mankiewicz became, officially, the noncreator of his own film is grimly fascinating and highly typical of the way so many director-hustlers acquire for themselves the writer's creation.* Few directors in this area possess the modesty of Kurosawa, who said, recently, "With a very good script, even a second-class director may make a first-class film. But with a bad script even a first-class director cannot make a really first-class film."

A useful if necessarily superficial look at the way movies were written in the classic era can be found in the pages of *Some Time in the Sun.* The author, Mr. Tom Dardis, examines the movie careers of five celebrated writers who took jobs as movie-writers. They are Scott Fitzgerald, Aldous Huxley, William Faulkner, Nathanael West, and James Agee.

Mr. Dardis's approach to his writers and to the movies is that of a deeply serious and highly concerned lowbrow, a type now heavily tenured in American Academe. He writes of "literate" dialogue, "massive" biographies. Magisterially, he misquotes Henry James on the subject of gold. More seriously, *he misquotes Joan Crawford.* She did not say to Fitzgerald, "Work hard, Mr. Fitzgerald, work hard!" when he was preparing a film for her. She said "*Write* hard. . . ." There are many small inaccuracies that set on edge the film buff's teeth. For instance, Mr. Dardis thinks that the hotel on Sunset Boulevard known, gorgeously, as The Garden of Allah is "now demolished and reduced to the status of a large parking lot. . . ." Well, it is not a parking lot. Hollywood has its own peculiar reverence for the past. The Garden of Allah was replaced by a bank that subtly suggests in glass and metal the mock-Saracen façade of the hotel that once housed Scott Fitzgerald. Mr. Dardis also thinks that the hotel was "demolished" during World War II. I stayed there in the late Fifties, right next door to fun-loving, bibulous Errol Flynn.

Errors and starry-eyed vulgarity to one side, Mr. Dardis has done a good deal of interesting research on how films were written and made in those days. For one thing, he catches the ambivalence felt by the writers who had descended (but only temporarily) from literature's Parnassus to the swampy marketplace of the movies. There was a tendency to play Lucifer. One was thought to have sold out. "Better to reign in hell than to

*Peter Bogdanovich maintains that Kael's version of the making of *Citizen Kane* is not only inaccurate but highly unfair to Orson Welles, a master whom I revere.

serve in heaven," was more than once quoted—well, paraphrased—at the Writers' Table. We knew we smelled of sulphur. Needless to say, most of the time it was a lot of fun if the booze didn't get you.

For the Parnassian writer the movies were not just a means of making easy money; even under the worst conditions, movies were genuinely interesting to write. Mr. Dardis is at his best when he shows his writers taking seriously their various "assignments." The instinct to do good work is hard to eradicate.

Faulkner was the luckiest (and the most cynical) of Mr. Dardis's five. For one thing, he usually worked with Howard Hawks, a director who might actually qualify as an *auteur.* Hawks was himself a writer and he had a strong sense of how to manipulate those clichés that he could handle best. Together Faulkner and Hawks created a pair of satisfying movies, *To Have and Have Not* and *The Big Sleep.* But who did what? Apparently there is not enough remaining evidence (at least available to Mr. Dardis) to sort out authorship. Also, Faulkner's public line was pretty much: I'm just a hired hand who does what he's told.

Nunnally Johnson (as quoted by Mr. Dardis) found Hawks's professional relationship with Faulkner mysterious. "It may be that he simply wanted his name attached to Faulkner's. Or since Hawks liked to write it was easy to do it with Faulkner, for Bill didn't care much one way or the other. . . . We shall probably never know just how much Bill cared about any of the scripts he worked on with Hawks." Yet it is interesting to note that Johnson takes it entirely for granted that the director wants—and must get—*all* credit for a film.

Problem for the director: how to get a script without its author? Partial solution: of all writers, the one who does not mind anonymity is the one most apt to appeal to an ambitious director. When the studio producer was king, he used to minimize the writer's role by assigning a dozen writers to a script. No director today has the resources of the old studios. But he can hire a writer who doesn't "care much one way or the other." He can also put his name on the screen as co-author (standard procedure in Italy and France). Even the noble Jean Renoir played this game when he came to direct *The Southerner.* Faulkner not only wrote the script, he liked the project. The picture's star Zachary Scott has said that the script was entirely Faulkner's. But then, other hands were engaged and "the whole problem," according to Mr. Dardis, "of who did what was neatly solved by Renoir's giving himself sole credit for the screenplay—the best way possible for an *auteur* director to label his films."

Unlike Faulkner, Scott Fitzgerald cared deeply about movies; he wanted to make a success of movie-writing and, all in all, if Mr. Dardis is to be believed (and for what it may be worth, his account of Fitzgerald's time in the sun tallies with what one used to hear), he had a far better and more healthy time of it in Hollywood than is generally suspected.

Of a methodical nature, Fitzgerald ran a lot of films at the studio. (Unlike Faulkner, who affected to respond only to Mickey Mouse and Pathé News.) Fitzgerald made notes. He also did what an ambitious writer must do if he wants to write the sort of movie he himself might want to see: he made friends with the producers. Rather censoriously, Mr. Dardis notes Fitzgerald's "clearly stated intention to work with film producers rather than with film directors, here downgraded to the rank of 'collaborators.' Actually, Fitzgerald seems to have had no use whatsoever for directors as such." But neither did anyone else.

During much of this time Howard Hawks, say, was a low-budget director known for the neatness and efficiency of his work. Not until the French beatified him twenty years later did he appear to anyone as an original artist instead of just another hired technician. It is true that Hawks was allowed to work with writers, but then, he was at Warner Brothers, a frontier outpost facing upon barbarous Burbank. At MGM, the holy capital, writers and directors did not get much chance to work together. It was the producer who worked with the writer, and Scott Fitzgerald was an MGM writer. Even as late as my own years at MGM (1956–1958), the final script was the writer's creation (under the producer's supervision). The writer even pre-empted the director's most important function by describing each camera shot: Long, Medium, Close, and the director was expected faithfully to follow the writer's score.

One of the most successful directors at MGM during this period was George Cukor. In an essay on "The Director" (1938), Cukor reveals the game as it used to be played. "In most cases," he writes, "the director makes his appearance very early in the life story of a motion picture." I am sure that this was often the case with Cukor but the fact that he thinks it necessary to mention "early" participation is significant.

> There are times when the whole idea for a film may come from [the director], but in a more usual case he makes his entry when he is summoned by a producer and it is suggested that he should be the director of a proposed story.

Not only was this the most usual way but, very often, the director left the producer's presence with the finished script under his arm. Cukor does describe his own experience working with writers but Cukor was something of a star at the studio. Most directors were "summoned" by the producer and told what to do. It is curious, incidentally, how entirely the idea of the working producer has vanished. He is no longer remembered except as the butt of familiar stories: fragile artist treated cruelly by insensitive cigar-smoking producer—or Fitzgerald savaged yet again by Joe Mankiewicz.

Of Mr. Dardis's five writers, James Agee is, to say the least, the lightest in literary weight. But he was a passionate film-goer and critic. He was a child of the movies just as Huxley was a child of Meredith and Peacock. Given a different temperament, luck, birth-date, Agee might have been the first American cinema *auteur*: a writer who wrote screenplays in such a way that, like the score of a symphony, they needed nothing more than a conductor's interpretation . . . an interpretation he could have provided himself and perhaps would have provided if he had lived.

Agee's screenplays were remarkably detailed. "All the shots," writes Mr. Dardis, "were set down with extreme precision in a way that no other screenwriter had ever set things down before. . . ." This is exaggerated. Most screenwriters of the classic period wrote highly detailed scripts in order to direct the director but, certainly, the examples Mr. Dardis gives of Agee's screenplays show them to be remarkably visual. Most of us hear stories. He saw them, too. But I am not so sure that what he saw was the reflection of a living reality in his head. As with many of today's young directors, Agee's memory was crowded with memories not of life but of old films. For Agee, rain falling was not a memory of April at Exeter but a scene recalled from Eisenstein. This is particularly noticeable in the adaptation Agee made of Stephen Crane's *The Blue Hotel,* which, Mr. Dardis tells us, no "film director has yet taken on, although it has been televised twice, each time with a different director and cast and with the Agee script cut to the bone, being used only as a guidepost to the story." This is nonsense. In 1954, CBS hired me to adapt *The Blue Hotel.* I worked directly from Stephen Crane and did not know that James Agee had ever adapted it until I read *Some Time in the Sun.*

At the mention of any director's name, the Wise Hack at the Writers' Table would bark out a percentage, representing how much, in his estimate, a given director would subtract from the potential 100 percent of the script he was directing. The thought that a director might *add* something worthwhile never crossed the good gray Hack's mind. Certainly he would have found hilarious David Thomson's *A Biographical Dictionary of Film,* whose haphazard pages are studded with tributes to directors.

Mr. Thomson has his own pleasantly eccentric pantheon in which writers figure hardly at all. A column is devoted to the dim Micheline Presle but the finest of all screenwriters, Jacques Prévert, is ignored. There is a long silly tribute to Arthur Penn; yet there is no biography of Penn's contemporary at NBC television, Paddy Chayefsky, whose films in the Fifties and early Sixties were far more interesting than anything Penn has done. Possibly Chayefsky was excluded because not only did he write his own films, he would then hire a director rather the way one would employ a plumber—or a cameraman. For a time, Chayefsky was the only American *auteur,* and his pencil was the director. Certainly Chayefsky's early career in films perfectly disproves Nicholas Ray's dictum (approvingly quoted by Mr. Thomson): "If it were all in the script, why make the film?" If it is not all in the script, there is no film to make.

Twenty years ago at the Writers' Table we all agreed with the Wise Hack that William Wyler subtracted no more than 10 percent from a script. Some of the most attractive and sensible of Bazin's pages are devoted to Wyler's work in the Forties. On the other hand, Mr. Thomson does not like him at all (because Wyler lacks those redundant faults that create the illusion of a Style?). Yet whatever was in a script, Wyler rendered faithfully: when he was given a bad script, he would make not only a bad movie, but the script's particular kind of badness would be revealed in a way that could altogether too easily boomerang on the too skillful director. But when the script was good (of its kind, *of its kind!*), *The Letter,* say, or *The Little Foxes,* there was no better interpreter.

At MGM, I worked exclusively with the producer Sam Zimbalist. He was a remarkably good and decent man in a business where such qualities are rare. He was also a producer of the old-fashioned sort. This meant that the script was prepared for him and with him. Once the script was ready, the director was summoned; he would then have the chance to say, yes, he would direct the script or, no, he wouldn't. Few changes were made in the script after the director was assigned. But this was not to be the case in Zimbalist's last film.

For several years MGM had been planning a remake of *Ben-Hur,* the studio's most successful silent film. A Contract Writer wrote a script; it was discarded. Then Zimbalist offered me the job. I said no, and went on suspension. During the next year or two S. N. Behrman and Maxwell Anderson, among others, added many yards of portentous dialogue to a script which kept growing and changing. The result was not happy. By 1958 MGM was going bust. Suddenly the remake of *Ben-Hur* seemed like a last chance to regain the mass audience lost to television. Zimbalist again asked me if I would take on the job. I said that if the studio released me from the remainder of my contract, I would go to Rome for two or three months and rewrite the script. The studio agreed. Meanwhile, Wyler had been signed to direct.

On a chilly March day Wyler, Zimbalist, and I took an overnight flight from New York. On the plane Wyler read for the first time the latest of the many scripts. As we drove together into Rome from the airport, Wyler looked gray and rather frightened. "This is awful," he said, indicating the huge script that I had placed between us on the back seat. "I know," I said. "What are we going to do?"

Wyler groaned: "These Romans. . . . Do you know anything about them?" I said, yes, I had done my reading. Wyler stared at me. "Well," he said, "when a Roman sits down and relaxes, what does he unbuckle?"

That spring I rewrote more than half the script (and Wyler studied every "Roman" film ever made). When I was finished with a scene, I would give it to Zimbalist. We would go over it. Then the scene would be passed on to Wyler. Normally, Wyler is slow and deliberately indecisive; but first-century Jerusalem had been built at enormous expense; the first day of shooting was approaching; the studio was nervous. As a result, I did not often hear Wyler's famous cry, as he would hand you back your script, "If I knew what was wrong with it, I'd fix it myself."

The plot of *Ben-Hur* is, basically, absurd and any attempt to make sense of it would destroy the story's awful integrity. But for a film to be watchable the characters must make some kind of psychological sense. We were stuck with the following: the Jew Ben-Hur and the Roman Messala were friends in childhood. Then they were separated. Now the adult Messala returns to Jerusalem; meets Ben-Hur; asks him to help with the Romanization of Judea. Ben-Hur refuses; there is a quarrel; they part and vengeance is sworn. This one scene is the sole motor that must propel a very long story until Jesus Christ suddenly and pointlessly drifts onto the scene, automatically untying some of the cruder knots in the plot. Wyler and I agreed that a single political quarrel would not turn into a lifelong vendetta.

I thought of a solution, which I delivered into Wyler's good ear. "As boys they were lovers. Now Messala wants to continue the affair. Ben-Hur rejects him. Messala is furious. *Chagrin d'amour,* the classic motivation for murder."

Wyler looked at me as if I had gone mad. "But we can't do *that*! I mean this is Ben-Hur! My God. . . ."

"We won't really do it. We just suggest it. I'll write the scenes so that they will make sense to those who are tuned in. Those who aren't will still feel that Messala's rage is somehow emotionally logical."

I don't think Wyler particularly liked my solution but he agreed that "anything is better than what we've got. So let's try it."

I broke the original scene into two parts. Charlton Heston (Ben-Hur) and Stephen Boyd (Messala) read them for us in Zimbalist's office. Wyler knew his actors. He warned me: "Don't ever tell Chuck what it's all about, or he'll fall apart." I suspect that Heston does not know to this day what luridness we managed to contrive around him. But Boyd knew: every time he looked at Ben-Hur it was like a starving man getting a glimpse of dinner through a pane of glass. And so, among the thundering hooves and clichés of the last (to date) *Ben-Hur,* there is something odd and authentic in one unstated relationship.

As agreed, I left in early summer and Christopher Fry wrote the rest of the script. Before the picture ended, Zimbalist died of a heart attack. Later, when it came time to credit the writers of the film, Wyler proposed that Fry be given screen credit. Then Fry insisted that I be given credit with him, since I had written the first half of the picture. Wyler was in a quandary. Only Zimbalist (and Fry and myself—two interested parties) knew who had written what, and Zimbalist was dead. The matter was given to the Screenwriters Guild for arbitration and they, mysteriously, awarded the credit to the Contract Writer whose script was separated from ours by at least two other discarded scripts. The film was released in 1959 and saved MGM from financial collapse.

I have recorded in some detail this unimportant business to show the near-impossibility of determining how a movie is actually created. Had *Ben-Hur* been taken seriously by, let us say, those French critics who admire *Johnny Guitar,* then Wyler would have been credited with the unusually subtle relationship between Ben-Hur and Messala. No credit would ever have gone to me because my name was not on the screen, nor would credit have gone to the official scriptwriter because, according to the *auteuri* theory, every aspect of a film is the creation of the director.

The twenty-year interregnum when the producer was supreme is now a memory. The ascendancy of the movie stars was brief. The directors have now regained their original primacy, and Milestone's storm is only an echo. Today the marquees of movie houses feature the names of directors and journalists ("*A work of art,*" J. Crist); the other collaborators are in fine print.

This situation might be more acceptable if the film directors had become true *auteurs.* But most of them are further than ever away from art—not to mention life. The majority are simply technicians. A few have come from the theatre; many began as editors, cameramen, makers of television series, and commercials; in recent years, ominously, a majority have been graduates of film schools. In principle, there is nothing wrong with a profound understanding of the technical means by which an image is impressed upon celluloid. But movies are not just molds of light any more than a novel is just inked-over paper. A movie is a response to reality in a certain way and that way must first be found by a writer. Unfortunately, no contemporary film director can bear to be thought a mere interpreter. He must be sole creator. As a result, he is more often than not a plagiarist, telling stories that are not his.

Over the years a number of writers have become directors, but except for such rare figures as Cocteau and Bergman, the writers who have gone in for directing were generally not much better at writing than they proved to be at directing. Even in commercial terms, for every Joe Mankiewicz or Preston Sturges there are a dozen Xs and Ys, not to mention the depressing Z.

Today's films are more than ever artifacts of light. Cars chase one another mindlessly along irrelevant freeways. Violence seems rooted in a notion about what ought to happen next on the screen to help the images move rather than in any human situation anterior to those images. In fact, the human situation has been eliminated not through any intentional philosophic design but because those who have spent too much time with cameras and machines seldom have much apprehension of that living world without whose presence there is no art.

I suspect that the time has now come to take Astruc seriously . . . after first rearranging his thesis. Astruc's *caméra-stylo* requires that "the script writer ceases to exist. . . . The filmmaker/author writes with his camera as a writer writes with his pen." Good. But let us eliminate not the screenwriter but that technician-hustler—the director (a.k.a. *auteur du cinéma*). Not until he has been replaced by those who can use a pen to write from life for the screen is there going to be much of anything worth seeing. Nor does it take a genius of a writer to achieve great effects in film. Compared to the works of his nineteenth-century mentors, the writing of Ingmar Bergman is second-rate. But when he writes straight through the page and onto the screen itself his talent is transformed and the result is often first-rate.

As a poet, Jacques Prévert is not in the same literary class as Valéry, but Prévert's films *Les Enfants du Paradis* and *Lumière d'été* are extraordinary achievements. They were also disdained by the French theoreticians of the Forties who knew perfectly well that the directors Carné and Grémillon were inferior to their script-writer; but since the Theory requires that only a director can create a film, any film that is plainly a writer's work cannot be true cinema. This attitude has given rise to some highly comic critical musings. Recently a movie critic could not figure out why there had been such a dramatic change in the quality of the work of the director Joseph Losey after he moved to England. Was it a difference in the culture? the light? the water? Or could it—and the critic faltered—could it be that perhaps Losey's films changed when he . . . when he—oh, dear!—got Harold Pinter to write screenplays for him? The critic promptly dismissed the notion. Mr. Thomson prints no biography of Pinter in his *Dictionary.*

I have never much liked the films of Pier Paolo Pasolini, but I find most interesting the ease with which he turned to film after some twenty years as poet and novelist. He could not have been a film-maker in America because the costs are too high; also, the technician-hustlers are in total charge. But in Italy, during the Fifties, it was possible for an actual *auteur* to use for a pen the camera (having first composed rather than stolen the narrative to be illuminated).

Since the talking movie is closest in form to the novel ("the novel is a narrative that organizes itself in the world, while the cinema is a world that organizes itself into a narrative"—Jean Mitry), it strikes me that the rising literary generation might think of the movies as, peculiarly, their kind of novel, to be created by them in collaboration with technicians but without the interference of The Director, that hustler-plagiarist who has for twenty years dominated and exploited and (occasionally) enhanced an art form still in search of its true authors.

*The New York Review of Books*
*November 25, 1976*

# French Letters: Theories of the New Novel

TO SAY THAT NO ONE now much likes novels is to exaggerate very little. The large public which used to find pleasure in prose fictions prefers movies, television, journalism, and books of "fact." But then, Americans have never been enthusiastic readers. According to Dr. Gallup, only five percent of our population can be regarded as habitual readers. This five percent is probably a constant minority from generation to generation, despite the fact that at the end of the nineteenth century there were as many bookstores in the United States as there are today. It is true that novels in paperback often reach a very large audience. But that public is hardly serious, if one is to believe a recent *New York Times* symposium on paperback publishing. Apparently novels sell not according to who wrote them but according to how they are presented, which means that *Boys and Girls Together* will outsell *Pale Fire,* something it did not do in hard cover. Except for a handful of entertainers like the late Ian Fleming, the mass audience knows nothing of authors. They buy titles, and most of those titles are not of novels but of nonfiction: books about the Kennedys, doctors, and vivid murders are preferred to the work of anyone's imagination no matter how agreeably debased.

In this, if nothing else, the large public resembles the clerks, one of whom, Norman Podhoretz, observed nine years ago that "A feeling of dissatisfaction and impatience, irritation and boredom with contemporary serious fiction is very widespread," and he made the point that the magazine article is preferred to the novel because the article is useful, specific, relevant—something that most novels are not. This liking for fact may explain why some of our best-known novelists are read with attention only when they comment on literary or social matters. In the highest intellectual circles, a new novel by James Baldwin or William Gass or Norman Mailer—to name at random three celebrated novelists—is apt to be regarded with a certain embarrassment, hostage to a fortune often too crudely gained, and bearing little relation to its author's distinguished commentaries.

An even odder situation exists in the academy. At a time when the works of living writers are used promiscuously as classroom texts, the students themselves do little voluntary reading. "I hate to read," said a Harvard senior to a *New York Times* reporter, "and I never buy any paperbacks." The undergraduates' dislike of reading novels is partly due to the laborious way in which novels are taught: the slow killing of the work through a close textual analysis. Between the work and the reader comes the explication, and the explicator is prone to regard the object of analysis as being somehow inferior to the analysis itself.

In fact, according to Saul Bellow, "Critics and professors have declared themselves the true heirs and successors of the modern classic authors." And so, in order to maintain their usurped dignity, they are given "to redescribing everything downward, blackening the present age and denying creative scope to their contemporaries." Although Mr. Bellow overstates the case, the fact remains that the novel as currently practiced does not appeal to the intellectuals any more than it does to the large public, and it may well be that the form will become extinct now that we have entered the age which Professor Marshall McLuhan has termed post-Gutenberg. Whether or not the Professor's engaging generalities are true (that linear type, for centuries a shaper of our thought, has been superseded by electronic devices), it is a fact that the generation now in college is the first to be brought up entirely within the tradition of television and differs significantly from its predecessors. Quick to learn through sight and sound, today's student often experiences difficulty in reading and writing. Linear type's warm glow, so comforting to Gutenberg man, makes his successors uncomfortably hot. Needless to say, that bright minority which continues the literary culture exists as always, but it is no secret that even they prefer watching movies to reading novels. John Barth ought to interest them more than Antonioni, but he doesn't.

For the serious novelist, however, the loss of the audience should not be disturbing. "I write," declared one of them serenely. "Let the reader learn to read." And contrary to Whitman, great audiences are not necessary for the creation of a high literature. The last fifty years have been a particularly good time for poetry in English, but even that public which can read intelligently knows very little of what has been done. Ideally, the writer needs no audience other than the few who understand. It is immodest and greedy to want more. Unhappily, the novelist, by the very nature of his coarse art, is greedy and immodest; unless he is read by everyone, he cannot delight, instruct, reform, destroy a world he wants, at the least, to be different for his having lived in it. Writers as various as Dickens and Joyce, as George Eliot and Proust, have suffered from this madness. It is the nature of the beast. But now the beast is caged, confined by old forms that have ceased to attract. And so the question is: can those forms be changed, and the beast set free?

Since the Second World War, Alain Robbe-Grillet, Nathalie Sarraute, Michel Butor, Claude Simon, and Robert Pinget, among others, have attempted to change not only the form of the novel but the relationship between book and reader, and though their experiments are taken most seriously on the Continent, they are still too little known and thought about in those countries the late General de Gaulle believed to be largely populated by Anglo-Saxons. Among American commentators, only Susan Sontag in *Against Interpretation, and Other Essays,* published in 1966, has made a sustained effort to understand what the French are doing, and her occasional essays on their work are well worth reading, not only as reflections of an interesting and interested mind but also because she shares with the New Novelists (as they loosely describe themselves) a desire for the novel to become "what it is not in England and America, with rare and unrelated exceptions: a form of art which people with serious and sophisticated [*sic*] taste in the other arts can take seriously." Certainly Miss Sontag finds nothing adventurous or serious in "the work of the American writers most admired today: for example, Saul Bellow, Norman Mailer, James Baldwin, William Styron, Philip Roth, Bernard Malamud." They are "essentially unconcerned with the problems of the novel as an art form. Their main concern is with their 'subjects.' " And because of this, she finds them "essentially unserious and unambitious." By this criterion, to be serious and ambitious in the novel, the writer must create works of prose comparable to those experiments in painting which have brought us to Pop and Op art and in music to the strategic silences of John Cage. Whether or not these experiments succeed or fail is irrelevant. It is enough, if the artist is serious, to attempt new forms; certainly he must not repeat old ones.

The two chief theorists of the New Novel are Alain Robbe-Grillet and Nathalie Sarraute. As novelists, their works do not much resemble one another or, for that matter, conform to each other's strictures. But it is as theorists not as novelists that they shall concern us here. Of the two, Alain Robbe-Grillet has done the most to explain what he thinks the New Novel is and is not, in *Snapshots* and *For a New Novel,* translated by Richard Howard (1965). To begin with, he believes that any attempt at controlling the world by assigning it a meaning (the accepted task of the traditional novelist) is no longer possible. At best, meaning was

> an illusory simplification; and far from becoming clearer and clearer because of it, the world has only, little by little, lost all its life. Since it is chiefly in its presence that the world's reality resides, our task is now to create a literature which takes that presence into account.

He then attacks the idea of psychological "depth" as a myth. From the Comtesse de La Fayette to Gide, the novelist's role was to burrow "deeper and deeper to reach some ever more intimate strata." Since then, however, "something" has been "changing totally, definitively in our relations with the universe." Though he does not define that ominous "something," its principal effect is that "we no longer consider the world as our own, our private property, designed according to our needs and readily domesticated." Consequently:

> the novel of characters belongs entirely to the past; it describes a period: and that which marked the apogee of the individual. Perhaps this is not an advance, but it is evident that the present period is rather one of administrative numbers. The world's destiny has ceased, for us, to be identified with the rise or fall of certain men, of certain families.

Nathalie Sarraute is also concerned with the idea of man the administrative number in *Tropisms* and in *The Age of Suspicion,* translated by Maria Jolas (1964). She quotes Claude-Edmonde Magny: "Modern man, overwhelmed by mechanical civilization, is reduced to the triple determinism of hunger, sexuality and social status: Freud, Marx and Pavlov." (Surely in the wrong order.) She, too, rejects the idea of human depth: "The deep uncovered by Proust's analyses had already proved to be nothing but a surface."

Like Robbe-Grillet, she sees the modern novel as an evolution from Dostoevsky-Flaubert to Proust-Kafka; and each agrees (in essays written by her in 1947 and by him in 1958) that one of its principal touchstones is Camus's *The Stranger,* a work which she feels "came at the appointed time," when the old psychological novel was bankrupt because, paradoxically, psychology itself, having gone deeper than ever before, "inspired doubts as to the ultimate value of all methods of research." *Homo absurdus,* therefore, was Noah's dove, the messenger of deliverance. Camus's stranger is shown entirely from the inside, "all sentiment or thought whatsoever appears to have been completely abolished." He has been created without psychology or memory; he exists in a perpetual present. Robbe-Grillet goes even further in his analysis:

> It is no exaggeration to claim that it is things quite specifically which ultimately lead this man to crime: the sun, the sea, the brilliant sand, the gleaming knife, the spring among the rocks, the revolver . . . as, of course, among these things, the leading role is taken by Nature.

Only the absolute presence of things can be recorded; certainly the depiction of human character is no longer possible. In fact, Miss Sarraute believes that for both author and reader, character is "the converging point of their mutual distrust," and she makes of Stendhal's "The genius of suspicion has appeared on the scene" a leitmotiv for an age in which "the reader has grown wary of practically everything. The reason being that for some time now he has been learning too many things and he is unable to forget entirely all he had learned." Perhaps the most vivid thing he has learned (or at least it was vivid when she was writing in 1947) is the fact of genocide in the concentration camps:

> Beyond these furthermost limits to which Kafka did not follow them but to where he had the superhuman courage to precede them, all feeling disappears, even contempt and hatred; there remains only vast, empty stupefaction, definitive total, don't understand.
>
> To remain at the point where he left off or to attempt to go on from there are equally impossible. Those who live in a world of human beings can only retrace their steps.

The proof that human life can be as perfectly meaningless in the scale of a human society as it is in eternity stunned a generation, and the shock of this knowledge, more than anything else (certainly more than the discoveries of the mental therapists or the new techniques of industrial automation), caused a dislocation of human values which in turn made something like the New Novel inevitable.

Although Nathalie Sarraute and Alain Robbe-Grillet are formidable theorists, neither is entirely free of those rhetorical plangencies the French so often revert to when their best aperçus are about to slip the net of logic. Each is very much a part of that French intellectual tradition so wickedly described in *Tristes Tropiques* by Lévi-Strauss (1964, translated by John Russell):

> First you establish the traditional "two views" of the question. You then put forward a common-sensical justification of the one, only to refute it by the other. Finally, you send them both packing by the use of a third interpretation, in which both the others are shown to be equally unsatisfactory. Certain verbal maneuvers enable you, that is, to line up the traditional "antitheses" as complementary aspects of a single reality: form and substance, content and con-

> tainer, appearance and reality, essence and existence, continuity and discontinuity, and so on. Before long the exercise becomes the merest verbalizing, reflection gives place to a kind of superior punning, and the "accomplished philosopher" may be recognized by the ingenuity with which he makes ever-bolder play with assonance, ambiguity, and the use of those words which sound alike and yet bear quite different meanings.

Miss Sarraute is not above this sort of juggling, particularly when she redefines literary categories, maintaining that the traditional novelists are formalists, while the New Novelists, by eschewing old forms, are the true realists because

> their works, which seek to break away from all that is prescribed, conventional and dead, to turn towards what is free, sincere and alive, will necessarily, sooner or later, become ferments of emancipation and progress.

This fine demagoguery does not obscure the fact that she is obsessed with form in a way that the traditional writer seldom is. It is she, not he, who dreams

> of a technique that might succeed in plunging the reader into the stream of those subterranean dreams of which Proust only had time to obtain a rapid aerial view, and concerning which he observed and reproduced nothing but the broad motionless lines. This technique would give the reader the illusion of repeating these actions himself, in a more clearly aware, more orderly, distinct and forceful manner than he can do in life, without their losing that element of indetermination, of opacity and mystery, that one's own actions always have for the one who lives them.

This is perilously close to fine lady-writing (Miss Sarraute is addicted to the triad, particularly of adjectives), but despite all protestations, she is totally absorbed with form; and though she dislikes being called a formalist, she can hardly hope to avoid the label, since she has set herself the superb task of continuing consciously those prose experiments that made the early part of the twentieth century one of the great ages of the novel.

In regard to the modern masters, both Robbe-Grillet and Miss Sarraute remark with a certain wonder that there have been no true heirs to Proust, Joyce, and Kafka; the main line of the realistic novel simply resumed as though they had never existed. Yet, as Robbe-Grillet remarks:

> Flaubert wrote the new novel of 1860, Proust the new novel of 1910. The writer must proudly consent to bear his own date, knowing

> that there are no masterpieces in eternity, but only works in history, and that they have survived only to the degree that they have left the past behind them and heralded the future.

Here, as so often in Robbe-Grillet's theorizing, one is offered a sensible statement, followed by a dubious observation about survival (many conventional, even reactionary works have survived nicely), ending with a look-to-the-dawn-of-a-new-age chord, played fortissimo. Yet the desire to continue the modern tradition is perfectly valid. And even if the New Novelists do not succeed (in science most experiments fail), they are at least "really serious," as Miss Sontag would say.

There is, however, something very odd about a literary movement so radical in its pronouncements yet so traditional in its references. Both Miss Sarraute and Robbe-Grillet continually relate themselves to great predecessors, giving rise to the suspicion that, like Saul Bellow's literary usurpers, they are assuming for themselves the accomplishments of Dostoevsky, Flaubert, Proust, Joyce, and Beckett. In this, at least, they are significantly more modest than their heroes. One cannot imagine the Joyce of *Finnegans Wake* acknowledging a literary debt to anyone or Flaubert admitting—as Robbe-Grillet does—that his work is "merely pursuing a constant evolution of a genre." Curiously enough, the writers whom Robbe-Grillet and Miss Sarraute most resemble wrote books which were described by Arthur Symons for the *Encyclopaedia Britannica* as being

> made up of an infinite number of details, set side by side, every detail equally prominent. . . . [the authors] do not search further than "the physical basis of life," and they find everything that can be known of that unknown force written visibly upon the sudden faces of little incidents, little expressive movements. . . . It is their distinction—the finest of their inventions—that, in order to render new sensations, a new vision of things, they invented a new language.

*They,* of course, are the presently unfashionable brothers Edmond and Jules de Goncourt, whose collaboration ended in 1870.

In attacking the traditional novel, both Robbe-Grillet and Miss Sarraute are on safe ground. Miss Sarraute is particularly effective when she observes that even the least aware of the traditionalists seems "unable to escape a certain feeling of uneasiness as regards dialogue." She remarks upon the self-conscious way in which contemporary writers sprinkle their pages with "he saids" and "she replieds," and she makes gentle fun of Henry Green's hopeful comment that perhaps the novel of the future will be largely composed in dialogue since, as she quotes him, people don't write letters any more: they use the telephone.

But the dialogue novel does not appeal to her, for it brings "the novel dangerously near the domain of the theater, where it is bound to be in a position of inferiority"—on the ground that the nuances of dialogue in the theater are supplied by actors while in the novel the writer himself must provide, somehow, the sub-conversation which is the true meaning. Opposed to the dialogue novel is the one of Proustian analysis. Miss Sarraute finds much fault with this method (no meaningful depths left to plumb in the wake of Freud), but concedes that "In spite of the rather serious charges that may be brought against analysis, it is difficult to turn from it today without turning one's back on progress."

"Progress," "*New* Novel," "permanent creation of tomorrow's world," "the discovery of reality will continue only if we abandon outward forms," "general evolution of the genre" . . . again and again one is reminded in reading the manifestos of these two explorers that we are living (one might even say that we are trapped) in the age of science. Miss Sarraute particularly delights in using quasi-scientific references. She refers to her first collection of pieces as "Tropisms." (According to authority, a tropism is "the turning of an organism, or part of one, in a particular direction in response to some special external stimulus.") She is also addicted to words like "larval" and "magma," and her analogies are often clinical: "Suspicion, which is by way of destroying the character and the entire outmoded mechanism that guaranteed its force, is one of the morbid reactions by which an organism defends itself and seeks another equilibrium. . . ."

Yet she does not like to be called a "laboratory novelist" any more than she likes to be called a formalist. One wonders why. For it is obvious that both she and Robbe-Grillet see themselves in white smocks working out new formulas for a new fiction. Underlying all their theories is the assumption that if scientists can break the atom with an equation, a dedicated writer ought to be able to find a new form in which to redefine the "unchanging human heart," as Bouvard might have said to Pécuchet. Since the old formulas have lost their efficacy, the novel, if it is to survive, must become something new; and so, to create that something new, they believe that writers must resort to calculated invention and bold experiment.

It is an interesting comment on the age that both Miss Sarraute and Robbe-Grillet take for granted that the highest literature has always been made by self-conscious avant-gardists. Although this was certainly true of Flaubert, whose letters show him in the laboratory, agonizing over that double genitive which nearly soured the recipe for *Madame Bovary,* and of Joyce, who spent a third of his life making a language for the night, Dostoevsky, Conrad, and Tolstoi—to name three novelists quite as great—were not much concerned with laboratory experiments. Their interest was in what Miss Sontag calls "the subject"; and though it is true they did not leave the form of the novel as they found it, their art was not the product of calculated experiments with form so much as it was the result of their ability, by virtue of what they were, to transmute the familiar and make it rare. They were men of genius unobsessed by what Goethe once referred to as "an eccentric desire for originality." Or as Saul Bellow puts it: "Genius is always, without strain, avant-garde. Its departure from tradition is not the result of caprice or of policy but of an inner necessity."

Absorbed by his subject, the genius is a natural innovator—a fact which must be maddening to the ordinary writer, who, because he is merely ambitious, is forced to approach literature from the outside, hoping by the study of a masterpiece's form and by an analysis of its content to reconstruct the principle of its composition in order that he may create either simulacra or, if he is furiously ambitious, by rearranging the component parts, something "new." This approach from the outside is of course the natural way of the critic, and it is significant that the New Novelists tend to blur the boundary between critic and novelist. "Critical preoccupation," writes Robbe-Grillet, "far from sterilizing creation, can on the contrary serve it as a driving force."

In the present age the methods of the scientist, who deals only in what can be measured, demonstrated and proved, are central. Consequently, anything as unverifiable as a novel is suspect. Or, as Miss Sarraute quotes Paul Tournier:

> There is nobody left who is willing to admit that he invents. The only thing that matters is the document, which must be precise, dated, proven, authentic. Works of the imagination are banned, because they are invented. . . . The public, in order to believe what it is told, must be convinced that it is not being "taken in." All that counts now is the "true fact."

This may explain why so many contemporary novelists feel they must apologize for effects which seem unduly extravagant or made up ("but that's the way it really happened!"). Nor is it to make a scandal to observe that most "serious" American novels are autobiographies, usually composed to pay off grudges. But then the novelist can hardly be held responsible for the society he reflects. After all, much of the world's reading consists of those weekly news magazines in which actual people are dealt with in fictional terms. It is the spirit of the age to believe that any fact, no matter how suspect, is superior to any imaginative exercise, no matter how true. The result of this attitude has been particularly harrowing in the universities, where English departments now do their best to pretend that they are every bit as fact-minded as the physical scientists (to whom the largest appropriations go). Doggedly, English teachers do research, publish learned findings, make breakthroughs in F. Scott Fitzgerald and, in their search for facts, behave as if no work of literature can be called complete until each character has been satisfactorily identified as someone who actually lived and had a history known to the author. It is no wonder that the ambitious writer is tempted to re-create the novel along what he believes to be scientific lines. With admiration, Miss Sontag quotes William Burroughs:

> I think there's going to be more and more merging of art and science. Scientists are already studying the creative process, and I think that the whole line between art and science will break down and that scientists, I hope, will become more creative and writers more scientific.

Recently in France the matter of science and the novel was much debated. In an essay called *Nouvelle Critique ou Nouvelle Imposture,* Raymond Picard attacked the new critic Roland Barthes, who promptly defended himself on the ground that a concern with form is only natural since structure precedes creation (an insight appropriated from anthropology, a discipline recently become fashionable). Picard then returned to the attack, mocking those writers who pretend to be scientists, pointing out that they

> improperly apply to the literary domain methods which have proved fruitful elsewhere but which here lose their efficiency and rigor. . . . These critical approaches have a scientific air to them, but the resemblance is pure caricature. The new critics use science roughly as someone ignorant of electricity might use electronics. What they're after is its prestige: in other respects they are at opposite poles to the scientific spirit. Their statements generally sound more like oracles than useful hypotheses: categorical, unverifiable, unilluminating.

Picard is perhaps too harsh, but no one can deny that Robbe-Grillet and Nathalie Sarraute often appropriate the language of science without understanding its spirit—for instance, one can verify the law of physics which states that there is no action without reaction, but how to prove the critical assertion that things in themselves are what caused Camus's creature to kill? Yet if to revive a moribund art form writers find it helpful to pretend to be physicists, then one ought not to tease them unduly for donning so solemnly mask and rubber gloves. After all, Count Tolstoi thought he was a philosopher. But whether pseudo-scientists or original thinkers, neither Robbe-Grillet nor Miss Sarraute finds it easy to put theory into practice. As Robbe-Grillet says disarmingly: "It is easier to indicate a new form than to follow it without failure." And he must be said to fail a good deal of the time: is there anything more incantatory than the repetition of the word *"lugubre"* in *Last Year at Marienbad*? Or more visceral than the repetition of the killing of the centipede in *Jealousy*? While Miss Sarraute finds that her later essays are "far removed from the conception and composition of my first book"—which, nevertheless, she includes in the same volume as the essays, with the somewhat puzzling comment that "this first book contains *in nuce* all the raw material that I have continued to develop in my later works."

For Robbe-Grillet, the problem of the novel is—obviously—the problem of man in relation to his environment, a relationship which he believes has changed radically in the last fifty years. In the past, man attempted to personalize the universe. In prose, this is revealed by metaphor: "majestic peaks," "huddled villages," "pitiless sun." "These anthropomorphic analogies are repeated too insistently, too coherently, not to reveal an entire metaphysical system." And he attacks what he holds to be the humanistic view: "On the pretext that man can achieve only a subjective knowledge of the world, humanism decides to elect man the justification of everything." In fact, he believes that humanists will go so far as to maintain that "it is not enough to show man where he is: it must further be proclaimed that man is everywhere." Quite shrewdly he observes: "If I say 'the world is man,' I shall always gain absolution; while if I say things are things, and man is only man, I am immediately charged with a crime against humanity."

It is this desire to remove the falsely human from the nature of things that is at the basis of Robbe-Grillet's theory. He is arguing not so much against what Ruskin called "the pathetic fallacy," as against our race's tendency to console itself by making human what is plainly nonhuman. To those who accuse him of trying to dehumanize the novel, he replies that since any book is written by a man "animated by torments and passion," it cannot help but be human. Nevertheless, "suppose the eyes of this man rest on things without indulgence, insistently: he sees them but he refuses to appropriate them." Finally, "man looks at the world but the world does not look back at him, and so, if he rejects communion, he also rejects tragedy." Inconsistently, he later quotes with admiration Joé Bousquet's "We watch things pass by in order to forget that they are watching us die."

Do those things watch or not? At times Miss Sarraute writes as if she thought they did. Her *Tropisms* are full of things invested with human response ("The crouched houses standing watch all along the gray streets"), but then she is not so strict as Robbe-Grillet in her apprehension of reality. She will accept "those analogies which are limited to the instinctive irresistible nature of the movements . . . produced in us by the presence of others, or by objects from the outside world." For Robbe-Grillet, however, "All analogies are dangerous."

Man's consciousness has now been separated from his environment. He lives in a perpetual present. He possesses memory but it is not chronological. Therefore the best that the writer can hope to do is to impart a precise sense of man's being in the present. To achieve this immediacy, Miss Sarraute favors "some precise dramatic action shown in slow motion"; a world in which "time was no longer the time of real life but a hugely amplified present." While Robbe-Grillet, in commenting upon his film *Last Year at Marienbad,* declares:

> The Universe in which the entire film occurs is, characteristically, in a perpetual present which makes all recourse to memory impossible. This is a world without a past, a world which is self-sufficient at every moment and which obliterates itself as it proceeds.

To him, the film is a ninety-minute fact without antecedents. "The only important 'character' is the spectator. In his mind unfolds the whole story which is precisely imagined by him." The verb "imagine" is of course incorrect, while the adverb means nothing. The spectator is *not* imagining the film; he is watching a creation which was made in a precise historic past by a writer, a director, actors, cameramen, etc. Yet to have the spectator or reader involve himself directly and temporally in the act of creation continues to be Robbe-Grillet's goal. He wants "a present which constantly invents itself" with "the reader's creative assistance," participating "in a creation, to invent in his turn the work—and the world—and thus to learn to invent his own life." This is most ambitious. But the ingredients of the formula keep varying. For instance, in praising Raymond Roussel, Robbe-Grillet admires the author's "*investigation* which destroys, in the writing itself, its own object." Elsewhere: "The work must seem necessary but necessary for nothing; its architecture is without use; its strength is untried." And again: "The genuine writer has nothing to say. He has only a way of speaking. He must create a world but starting from nothing, from the dust. . . ." It would not seem to be possible, on the one hand, to invent a world that would cause the reader to "invent his own life" while, on the other hand, the world in question is being destroyed as it is being created. Perhaps he means for the reader to turn to dust, gradually, page by page: not the worst of solutions.

No doubt there are those who regard the contradictions in Robbe-Grillet's critical writing as the point to them—rather in the way that the boredom of certain plays or the incompetence of certain pictures are, we are assured, their achievement. Yet it is worrisome to be told that a man can create a world from nothing when that is the one thing he cannot begin to do, simply because, no matter how hard he tries, he cannot dispose of himself. Even if what he writes is no more than nouns and adjectives, who and what he is will subconsciously dictate order. Nothing human is random and it is nonsense to say:

> Art is based on no truth that exists before it; and one may say that it expresses nothing but itself. It creates its own equilibrium and its own meaning. It stands all by itself . . . or else it fails.

Which reminds us of Professor Herzog's plaintive response to the philosophic proposition that modern man at a given moment fell into the quotidian: so where was he standing before the fall? In any case, how can something unique, in Robbe-Grillet's sense, rise or fall or be anything except itself? As for reflecting "no truth that existed before it," this is not possible. The fact that the author is a man "filled with torments and passion" means that all sorts of "truths" are going to occur in the course of the writing. The act of composing prose is a demonstration not only of human will but of the desire to reflect truth—particularly if one's instinct is messianic, and Robbe-Grillet is very much in that tradition. Not only does he want man "to invent his own life" (by reading Robbe-Grillet), but he proposes that today's art is "a way of living in the present world, and of participating in the permanent creation of tomorrow's world." It also seems odd that a theory of the novel which demands total existence in a self-devouring present should be concerned at all with the idea of future time since man exists, demonstrably, only in the present—the future tense is a human conceit, on the order of "majestic peaks." As for the use of the adjective "permanent," one suspects that rhetoric, not thought, forced this unfortunate word from the author's unconscious mind.

The ideal work, according to Robbe-Grillet, is

> A text both "dense and irreducible"; so perfect that it does not seem "to have touched," an object so perfect that it would obliterate our tracks. . . . Do we not recognize here the highest ambition of every writer?

Further, the only meaning for the novel is the invention of the world. "In dreams, in memory, as in the sense of sight, our imagination is the organizing force of our life, of *our* world. Each man, in his turn, must reinvent the things around him." Yet, referring to things, he writes a few pages later,

> They refer to no other world. They are the sign of nothing but themselves. And the only contact man can make with them is to imagine them.

But how is one to be loyal to the actual fact of things if they must be reinvented? Either they are *there* or they are not. In any case, by filtering them through the imagination (reinvention), true objectivity is lost, as he himself admits in a further snarling of his argument: "Objectivity in the ordinary sense of the word—total impersonality of observation—is all too obviously an illusion. But freedom of observation should be possible and yet it is not"—because a "continuous fringe of culture (psychology, ethics, metaphysics, etc.) is added to things, giving them a less alien aspect." But he believes that "humanizing" can be kept to a minimum, if we try "to construct a world both more solid and more immediate. Let it be first of all by their presence that objects and gestures establish themselves and let this presence continue to prevail over the subjective." Consequently, the task of the New Novel is nothing less than to seek

> new forms for the novel . . . forms capable of expressing (or of creating) new relations between man and the world, to all those who have determined to invent the novel, in other words, to invent man. Such writers know that the systematic repetition of the forms of the past is not only absurd and futile, but that it can even become harmful: blinding us to our real situation in the world today, it keeps us, ultimately, from constructing the world and man of tomorrow.

With the change of a noun or two, this could easily be the coda of an address on American foreign policy, delivered by Professor Arthur Schlesinger, Jr., to the ADA.

Like Robbe-Grillet, Nathalie Sarraute regards Camus's *The Stranger* as a point of departure. She sees the book's immediate predecessors as "The promising art of the cinema" and "the wholesome simplicity of the new American novel." Incidentally, she is quite amusing when she describes just what the effect of these "wholesome" novels was upon the French during the years immediately after the war:

> By transporting the French reader into a foreign universe in which he had no foothold, [they] lulled his wariness, aroused in him the kind of credulous curiosity that travel books inspire, and gave him a delightful impression of escape into an unknown world.

It is reassuring to learn that these works were not regarded with any great seriousness by the French and that Horace McCoy was not finally the master they once hailed him. Apparently the American novel was simply a vigorous tonic for an old literature gone stale. Miss Sarraute is, however, sincerely admiring of Faulkner's ability to involve the reader in his own world. To her the most necessary thing of all is "to dispossess the reader and entice him, at all costs, into the author's territory. To achieve this the device that consists in referring to the leading characters as 'I' constitutes a means." The use of the first person seems to her to be the emblem of modern art. ("Since Impressionism all pictures have been painted in the first person.") And so, just as photography drove painters away from representing nature (ending such ancient arts as that of the miniaturist and the maker of portrait busts), the cinema "garners and perfects what is left of it by the novel." The novel must now go where the camera may not follow. In this new country the reader has been aided by such modern writers as Proust and Joyce; they have so awakened his sensibilities that he is now able to respond to what is beneath the interior monologue, that "immense profusion of sensations, images, sentiments, memories, impulses, little larval actions that no inner language can convey." For her, emphasis falls upon what she calls the sub-conversation, that which is sensed and not said, the hidden counterpoint to the stated theme (obviously a very difficult thing to suggest, much less write, since "no inner language can convey it").

"Bosquet's universe—ours—is a universe of signs," writes Robbe-Grillet. "Everything in it is a sign; and not the sign of something else, something more perfect, situated out of reach, but a sign of itself, of that reality which asks only to be revealed." This answer to Baudelaire's *The Salon of 1859* is reasonable (although it is anthropomorphic to suggest that reality *asks* to be revealed). Robbe-Grillet is equally reasonable in his desire for things to be shown, as much as possible, as they are.

> In the future universe of the novel, gestures and objects will be there before being *something;* and they will still be there afterwards, hard, unalterably, eternally present, mocking their own "meaning," that meaning which vainly tries to reduce them to the role of precarious tools, etc.

One agrees with him that the integrity of the nonhuman world should be honored. But what does he mean (that proscribed verb!) when he says that the objects will be *there,* after meaning has attempted to rape them? Does he mean that they will still exist on the page, in someway inviolate in their thing-ness? If he does, surely he is mistaken. What exists on the page is ink; or, if one wishes to give the ink designs their agreed-upon human meaning, letters have been formed to make words in order to suggest things not present. What is on the page are not real things but their word-shadows. Yet even if the things were there, it is most unlikely that they would be so human as to "mock their own meaning." In an eerie way, Robbe-Grillet's highly rhetorical style has a tendency to destroy his arguments even as he makes them; critically, this technique complements ideally the self-obliterating anecdote.

On the question of how to establish the separateness, the autonomy of things, Robbe-Grillet and Miss Sarraute part company. In contemplating her method, she ceases altogether to be "scientific." Instead she alarmingly intones a hymn to words—all words—for they "possess the qualities needed to seize upon, protect and bring out into the open those subterranean movements that are at once impatient and afraid." (Are those subterranean movements really "impatient and afraid"?) For her, words possess suppleness, freedom, iridescent richness of shading, and by their nature they are protected "from suspicion and from minute examination." (In an age of suspicion, to let words off scot-free is an act of singular trust.) Consequently, once words have entered the other person, they swell, explode, and "by virtue of this game of actions and reactions . . . they constitute a most valuable tool for the novelist." Which, as the French say, goes without saying.

But of course words are not at all what she believes they are. All words lie. Or as Professor Frank Kermode put it in *Literary Fiction and Reality*: "Words, thoughts, patterns of word and thought, are enemies of truth, if you identify that with what may be had by phenomenological reductions." Nevertheless, Miss Sarraute likes to think that subterranean movements (tropisms) can be captured by words, which might explain why her attitude toward things is so much more conventional than that of Robbe-Grillet, who writes:

> Perhaps Kafka's staircases lead *elsewhere,* but they are *there,* and we look at them step by step following the details of the banisters and the risers.

This is untrue. First, we do not look at the staircases; we look at a number of words arranged upon a page by a conscious human intelligence which would like us to consider, among a thousand other things, the fact of those staircases. Since a primary concern of the human mind is cause and effect, the reader is bound to speculate upon why those staircases have been shown him; also, since staircases are usually built to connect one man-made level with another, the mind will naturally speculate as to what those two levels are like. Only a far-gone schizophrenic (or an LSD tripper) would find entirely absorbing the description of a banister.

Perhaps the most naïve aspect of Robbe-Grillet's theory of fiction is his assumption that words can ever describe with absolute precision anything. At no point does he acknowledge that words are simply fiat for real things; by their nature, words are imprecise and layered with meanings—the signs of things, not the things themselves. Therefore, even if Robbe-Grillet's goal of achieving a total reality for the world of things was desirable, it would not be possible to do it with language, since the author (that man full of torments and passions) is bound to betray his attitude to the sequence of signs he offered us; he has an "interest" in the matter, or else he would not write. Certainly if he means to reinvent man, then he will want to find a way of defining man through human (yes, psychological) relations as well as through a catalogue of things observed and gestures coolly noted. Wanting to play God, ambition is bound to dictate the order of words, and so the subjective will prevail just as it does in the traditional novel. To follow Robbe-Grillet's theory to its logical terminus, the only sort of book which might be said to be *not* a collection of signs of absent things but the actual things themselves would be a collection of ink, paper, cardboard, glue, and typeface, to be assembled or not by the reader-spectator. If this be too heavy a joke, then the ambitious writer must devise a new language which might give the appearance of maintaining the autonomy of things, since the words, new-minted, will possess a minimum of associations of a subjective or anthropomorphic sort. No existing language will be of any use to him, unless it be that of the Trobriand Islanders: those happy people have no words for "why" or "because"; for them, things just happen. Needless to say, they do not write novels or speculate on the nature of things.

The philosophic origins of the New Novel can be found (like most things French) in Descartes, whose dualism was the reflection of a split between the subjective and the objective, between the irrational and the rational, between the physical and the metaphysical. In the last century Auguste Comte, accepting this dualism, conceived of a logical empiricism which would emphasize the "purely" objective at the expense of the subjective or metaphysical. An optimist who believed in human progress, Comte saw history as an evolution toward a better society. For him the age of religion and metaphysics ended with the French Revolution. Since that time the human race was living in what he termed "the age of science," and he was confident that the methods of the positive sciences would enrich and transform human life. At last things were coming into their own. But not until the twentieth century did the methods of science entirely overwhelm the arts of the traditional humanists. To the scientific-minded, all things, including human personality, must in time yield their secrets to orderly experiment. Meanwhile, only that which is verifiable is to be taken seriously; emotive meaning must yield to cognitive meaning. Since the opacity of human character has so far defeated all objective attempts at illumination, the New Novelists prefer, as much as possible, to replace the human with objects closely observed and simple gestures noted but not explained.

In many ways, the New Novel appears to be approaching the "pure" state of music. In fact, there are many like Miss Sontag who look forward to "a kind of total structuring" of the novel, analogous to music. This is an old dream of the novelist. Nearly half a century ago, Joyce wrote (in a letter to his brother), "Why should not a modern literature be as unsparing and as direct as song?" Why not indeed? And again, why? The answer to the second "why" is easy enough. In the age of science, the objective is preferred to the subjective. Since human behavior is notoriously irrational and mysterious, it can be demonstrated only in the most impressionistic and unscientific way; it yields few secrets to objective analysis. Mathematics, on the other hand, is rational and verifiable, and music is a form of mathematics. Therefore, if one were to eliminate as much as possible the human from the novel, one might, through "a kind of total restructuring," come close to the state of mathematics or music—in short, achieve that perfect irreducible artifact Robbe-Grillet dreams of.

The dates of Miss Sarraute's essays range from 1947 to 1956, those of Robbe-Grillet from 1955 to 1963. To categorize in the French manner, it might be said that their views are particularly representative of the 50s, a period in which the traditional-minded (among whom they must be counted) still believed it possible to salvage the novel—or anything—by new techniques. With a certain grimness, they experimented. But though some of their books are good (even very good) and some are bad, they did not make a "new" novel, if only because art forms do not evolve—in literature at least—from the top down. Despite Robbe-Grillet's tendency to self-congratulation ("Although these descriptions—motionless arguments or fragments of scene—have acted on the readers in a satisfactory fashion, the judgment many specialists make of them remains pejorative"), there is not much in what he has so far written that will interest anyone except the specialist. It is, however, a convention of the avant-garde that to be in advance of the majority is to be "right." But the New Novelists are not in advance of anyone. Their works derive from what they believe to be a need for experiment and the imposition of certain of the methods of science upon the making of novels. Fair enough. Yet in this they resemble everyone, since to have a liking for the new is to be with the dull majority. In the arts, the obviously experimental is almost never denounced *because* it is new: if anything, our taste-makers tend to be altogether too permissive in the presence of what looks to be an experiment, as anyone who reads New York art criticism knows. There is not much likelihood that Robbe-Grillet will be able to reinvent man as a result of his exercises in prose. Rather he himself is in the process of being reinvented (along with the rest of us) by the new world in which we are living.

At the moment, advance culture scouts are reporting with a certain awe that those men and women who were brought up as television-watchers respond, predictably, to pictures that move and talk but not at all to prose fictions; and though fashion might dictate the presence of an occasional irreducible artifact in a room, no one is about to be reinvented by it. Yet the old avant-garde continues worriedly to putter with form.

Surveying the literary output for 1965, Miss Sontag found it "hard to think of any one book [in English] that exemplifies in a *central* way the possibilities for enlarging and complicating the forms of prose literature." This desire to "enlarge" and "complicate" the novel has an air of madness to it. Why not minimize and simplify? One suspects that out of desperation she is picking verbs at random. But then, like so many at present, she has a taste for the random. Referring to William Burroughs's resolutely random work *The Soft Machine,* she writes: "In the end, the voices come together and sound what is to my mind the most serious, urgent and original voice in American letters to be heard for many years." It is, however, the point to Mr. Burroughs's method that the voices *don't* come together: he is essentially a sport who is (blessedly) not serious, not urgent, and original only in the sense that no other American writer has been so relentlessly ill-humored in his send-up of the serious. He is the Grand Guy Grand of American letters. But whether or not Miss Sontag is right or wrong in her analyses of specific works and general trends, there is something old-fashioned and touching in her assumption (shared with the New Novelists) that if only we all try hard enough in a "really serious" way, we can come up with the better novel. This attitude reflects not so much the spirit of art as it does that of Detroit.

No one today can predict what games post-Gutenberg man will want to play. The only certainty is that his mind will work differently from ours; just as ours works differently from that of pre-Gutenberg man, as Miss Frances Yates demonstrated so dramatically in *The Art of Memory.* Perhaps there will be more Happenings in the future. Perhaps the random will take the place of the calculated. Perhaps the ephemeral will be preferred to the permanent: we stop in time, so why should works of art endure? Also, as the shadow of atomic catastrophe continues to fall across our merry games, the ephemeral will necessarily be valued to the extent it gives pleasure in the present and makes no pretense of having a future life. Since nothing will survive the firewind, the ashes of one thing will be very like those of another, and so what matters excellence?

One interesting result of today's passion for the immediate and the casual has been the decline, in all the arts, of the idea of technical virtuosity as being in any way desirable. The culture (*kitsch* as well as camp) enjoys singers who sing no better than the average listener, actors who do not act yet are, in Andy Warhol's happy phrase, "super-stars," painters whose effects are too easily achieved, writers whose swift flow of words across the page is not submitted to the rigors of grammar or shaped by conscious thought. There is a general Zen-ish sense of why bother? If a natural fall of pebbles can "say" as much as any shaping of paint on canvas or cutting of stone, why go to the trouble of recording what is there for all to see? In any case, if the world should become, as predicted, a village united by an electronic buzzing, our ideas of what is art will seem as curious to those gregarious villagers as the works of what we used to call the Dark Ages appear to us.

Regardless of what games men in the future will want to play, the matter of fiction seems to be closed. Reading skills—as the educationalists say—continue to decline with each new generation. Novel reading is not a pastime of the young now being educated, nor, for that matter, is it a preoccupation of any but a very few of those who came of age in the last warm years of linear type's hegemony. It is possible that fashion may from time to time bring back a book or produce a book which arouses something like general interest (Miss Sontag darkly suspects that "the nineteenth-century novel has a much better chance for a comeback than verse drama, the sonnet, or landscape painting"). Yet it is literature itself which seems on the verge of obsolescence, and not so much because the new people will prefer watching to reading as because the language in which books are written has become corrupt from misuse.

In fact, George Steiner believes that there is a definite possibility that "The political inhumanity of the twentieth century and certain elements in the technological mass-society which has followed on the erosion of European bourgeois values have done injury to language. . . ." He even goes so far as to suggest that for now at least silence may be a virtue for the writer—when

> language simply ceases, and the motion of spirit gives no further outward manifestation of its being. The poet enters into silence. Here the word borders not on radiance or music, but on night.

Although Mr. Steiner does not himself take this romantic position ("I am not saying that writers should stop writing. This would be fatuous"), he does propose silence as a proud alternative for those who have lived at the time of Belsen and of Vietnam, and have witnessed the perversion of so many words by publicists and political clowns. The credibility gap is now an abyss, separating even the most honorable words from their ancient meanings. Fortunately, ways of communication are now changing, and though none of us understands exactly what is happening, language is bound to be affected.

But no matter what happens to language, the novel is not apt to be revived by electronics. The portentous theorizings of the New Novelists are of no more use to us than the self-conscious avant-gardism of those who are forever trying to figure out what the next "really serious" thing will be when it is plain that there is not going to be a next serious thing in the novel. Our lovely vulgar and most human art is at an end, if not the end. Yet that is no reason not to want to practice it, or even to read it. In any case, rather like priests who have forgotten the meaning of the prayers they chant, we shall go on for quite a long time talking of books and writing books, pretending all the while not to notice that the church is empty and the parishioners have gone elsewhere to attend other gods, perhaps in silence or with new words.

***Encounter***
***December 1967***

# Edmund Wilson: This Critic and This Gin and These Shoes

ON FEBRUARY 2, 1821, gin-drinker Lord Byron wrote in his Ravenna Journal: "I have been considering what can be the reason why I always wake at a certain hour in the morning, and always in very bad spirits—I may say, in actual despair and despondency, in all respects—even of that which pleased me overnight. . . . In England, five years ago, I had the same kind of hypochondria, but accompanied with so violent a thirst that I have drank as many as fifteen bottles of soda-water in one night, after going to bed, and been still thirsty. . . . What is it?—liver?"

In Edmund Wilson's journal, published as *Upstate,* he wrote, in 1955: "One evening (August 13, Saturday) I drank a whole bottle of champagne and what was left of a bottle of old Grand-Dad and started on a bottle of red wine—I was eating Limburger cheese and gingersnaps. This began about five in the afternoon—I fell asleep in my chair, but woke up when Beverly came, thinking it was the next morning. I decided to skip supper; and felt queasy for the next twenty-four hours." The sixty-year-old Wilson does not ask, what is it? as Byron did. Wilson knows. "This kind of life," he writes, rather demurely, "in the long run, does, however, get rather unhealthy."

About the time that Wilson was munching on those gingersnaps and Limburger cheese, washed down with fiery waters, I received a letter from Upton Sinclair (whom I had never met), asking me about something. Then, obsessively, from left field, as it were, Sinclair denounced John Barleycorn. In the course of a long life, practically every writer Sinclair had known had died of drink, starting with his friend Jack London. Needless to say, this was not the sort of unsolicited letter that one likes to read while starting on one's fifteenth bottle of soda water, or to be precise and up-to-date, Coca-Cola, Georgia's sole gift to a nation whose first century was recently described in a book titled *The Alcoholic Republic* . . . of letters, I remember adding to myself when I first saw the book.

In this century, it would be safe to say that a significant percent of American writers are to a greater or lesser degree alcoholics and why this should be the case I leave to the medicine men. Alcoholism ended the careers of Hemingway, Fitzgerald, and Faulkner, to name three fashionable novelists of our mid-century. Out of charity toward the descendants and keepers of the still flickering flames of once glorious literary figures, I shall name no other names. Heavy drinking stopped Hemingway from writing anything of value in his later years; killed Fitzgerald at forty-four; turned the William Faulkner of *As I Lay Dying* into a fable.

Meanwhile, the contemporary of these three blasted stars, Edmund Wilson, outlived and outworked them all; he also outdrank them. Well into his seventies, Wilson would totter into the Princeton Club and order a half dozen martinis, to be prepared not sequentially but simultaneously—six shining glasses in a bright row, down which Wilson would work, all the while talking and thinking at a rapid pace. To the end of a long life, he kept on making the only thing he thought worth making: sense, a quality almost entirely lacking in American literature where stupidity—if sufficiently sincere and authentic—is deeply revered, and easily achieved. Although this *was* a rather unhealthy life in the long run, Wilson had a very long run indeed. But then, he was perfect proof of the proposition that the more the mind is used and fed the less apt it is to devour itself. When he died, at seventy-seven, he was busy stuffing his head with irregular Hungarian verbs. Plainly, he had a brain to match his liver.

Edmund Wilson was the last of a leisurely educated generation who were not obliged, if they were intellectually minded, to join the hicks and hacks of Academe. Wilson supported himself almost entirely by literary journalism, something not possible today if only because, for all practical purposes, literary journalism of the sort that he practiced no longer exists. Instead, book-chat is now dominated either by academic bureaucrats, crudely pursuing bureaucratic careers, or by journalists whose "leprous jealousy" (Flaubert's pretty phrase) has made mephitic the air of our alcoholic literary republic. But then, Flaubert thought that "critics write criticism because they are unable to be artists, just as a man unfit to bear arms becomes a police spy." Wilson would have challenged this romantic notion. Certainly, he would have made the point that to write essays is as much an aspect of the literary artist's temperament as the ability to evoke an alien sensibility on a page while sweating to avoid a double genitive. In any case, Wilson himself wrote stories, plays, novels. He knew how such things were made even if he was not entirely a master of any of these forms.

Of what, then, was Edmund Wilson a master? That is a question in need of an answer, or answers; and there are clues in the book at hand, *The Thirties: From Notebooks and Diaries of the Period.* At the time of Wilson's death, eight years ago, he was editing the notebooks that dealt with the Twenties. He had already finished *Upstate,* a chronicle of his works and days from the early Fifties to 1970. *Upstate* is a highly satisfactory Wilsonian book, filled with sharp personal details, long scholarly asides on those things or people or notions (like New York religions) that had caught his fancy. Although he had planned to rework his earlier records, he soon realized that he might not live long enough to complete them. He then designated, in his will, that Professor Leon Edel edit the remains, with the injunction that the text be published the way he wrote it, except for straightening out "misspellings and faulty punctuations" (but not, apparently, faulty grammar: Wilson often "feels badly"—it *is* liver). With *The Thirties,* Professor Edel had his work cut out for him because, he writes, "It is clear from the condition of the typescript that [Wilson] intended to do much more work on this book." That is understatement.

At the beginning of the Thirties, Wilson completed *Axel's Castle*; at the end, he had finished *To the Finland Station.* He wrote for *The New Republic,* supported, briefly, the American Communist party, visited the Soviet Union, Detroit, Appalachia, Scotsboro, and tried a season of teaching at the University of Chicago. The decade, in a sense, was the making of him as critic and triple thinker. Emotionally, it was shattering: in 1930 he married Margaret Canby; in 1932 she died. He also conducted a wide range of affairs, many on the raunchy side.

Professor Edel rather flinches at Wilson's "record of his own copulations" in general and the notes about his marriage in particular (so unlike the home life of our own dear Master): "some readers may be startled by this intimate candid record of a marriage." But Professor Edel is quick to remind us that this is all part of "the notebooks of a chronicler, a way of tidying the mind for his craft of criticism. . . . He tries, rather, to be a camera, for this is what he finds most comfortable." Well, yes and no.

In 1930 Edmund Wilson was thirty-five. He was a member of the minor Eastern gentry, a Princeton graduate, a World War I overseas noncombatant. In the Twenties, he had lived the life of the roaring boy but unlike the other lads that light-footed it over the greensward, he never stopped reading and writing and thinking. Thanks, in large part, to the Christers who had managed to prohibit the legal sale of spirits, alcohol was as much a curse to that generation as Gin Lane had been to the poor of eighteenth-century London. I suspect that a great deal of the grimness of this volume is a result of hangover and its concomitant despairs. At the same time, it is the record of an astonishing constitution: Wilson would write while he was drinking—something I should not have thought possible for anyone, even his doomed friend Scott Fitzgerald.

From thirty-five to forty-five men go from relative youth to middle age. The transit is often rocky. As a man's life settles into a rut, in mindless rut the man is apt to go. Certainly, this was true of Wilson, as readers of *Memoirs of Hecate County* might have suspected and as readers of *The Thirties* will now know for certain. During the so-called "ignoble" decade, despite constant drinking, Wilson was sexually very active. He enjoyed trade in the form of the Slavic Anna, a working-class woman whose proletarian ways fascinated him. He had sex with a number of those women who used to hang about writers, as well as with ladies at the edge of the great world. He bedded no Oriane but he knew at least one Guermantes *before* her translation to the aristocracy.

Although Wilson's bedmates are sometimes masked by initials, he enjoys writing detailed descriptions of what Professor Edel calls his "copulations." These descriptions are mechanistic, to say the least. Since they are not connected with character, they are about as erotic as a *Popular Mechanics* blueprint of the sort that is said to appeal to the growing boy. I am not sure just why Wilson felt that he should write so much about cock and cunt except that in those days it was a very daring thing to do, as Henry Miller had discovered when his books were burned and as Wilson was to discover when his own novel, *Memoirs of Hecate County,* was banned.

In literature, sexual revelation is a matter of tact and occasion. Whether or not such candor is of interest to a reader depends a good deal on the revealer's attitude. James Boswell is enchanting to read on sex because he is by self, as well as by sex, enchanted and possessed. The author of *My Secret Life* (if for real) is engaging because he is only interested in getting laid as often as possible in as many different ways and combinations. We also don't know what he looks like—an important aid to masturbation. Frank Harris (not for real) has the exuberance of a natural liar and so moves the reader toward fiction.

The list now starts to get short. The recently published (in English) letters of Flaubert are interesting because he has interesting things to say about what he sees and does in the brothels and baths of North Africa. Also, tactfully, mercifully, he never tells us what he feels or Feels. The sex that Flaubert has with women and men, with boys and girls, is fascinating to read about (even though we know exactly how *he* looks). This is due, partly, to the fact that his experiences are, literally, exotic as well as erotic and, partly, to that famous tone of voice. Today one is never quite certain why memoirists are so eager to tell us what they do in bed. Unless the autobiographer has a case to be argued, I suspect that future readers will skip those sexual details that our writers have so generously shared with us in order to get to the gossip and the jokes.

In Wilson's notebooks, he liked to describe sex in the same way that he liked "doing" landscapes. "It is certainly very hard," he concedes, "to write about sex in English without making it unattractive. *Come* is a horrible word to apply to something ecstatic." Finally, he did neither sex scenes nor landscapes very well. But in sexual matters, he has no real case to make, unlike, let us say, the committed homosexualist who thinks, incorrectly, that candor will so rend the veil that light will be shed upon what the society considers an abominable act and in a blaze of clarity and charity all will be forgiven. This is naïve, as Wilson himself demonstrates in these pages. He was very much an American of his time and class and the notebooks are filled with innumerable references to "fairies" that range from derisive to nervous; yet Wilson also admits to occasional homosexual reveries which he thought "were a way of living in the grip of the vise, getting away into a different world where those values that pressed me did not function."

Nevertheless, it is disquieting to find Wilson, in the Thirties (having admired Proust and Gide), quite unable to accept the fact that a fairy could be a major artist. In *Axel's Castle,* he has great trouble admitting, or not admitting, the sexual source of Proust's jealousy.

On the other hand, he made a curious and admirable exception in the case of Thornton Wilder.

During the Twenties and Thirties, Wilder was one of the most celebrated and successful American novelists. He was also one of the few first-rate writers the United States has produced. Fortunately for Wilder's early reputation, he was able to keep his private life relatively secret. As a result, he was very much a hero in book-chat land. In *The Twenties* Wilson describes a meeting with Wilder. He was startled to find Wilder "a person of such positive and even peppery opinions." Wilson had not read any of Wilder's novels because he thought that "they must be rather on the fragile and precious side" (what else can a fairy write?). As it turned out, each had been reading the new installment of Proust's novel and Wilson was delighted to find that Wilder thought Saint Loup's homosexuality unjustified. Over the years, Wilson was to review Wilder seriously and well. When Wilder was the victim of a celebrated Marxist attack, Wilson came to Wilder's defense—not to mention literature's. But the word was out and Thornton Wilder's reputation never recovered; to this day, he is a literary nonperson. Nevertheless, it is to Wilson's credit that he was able to overcome his horror of fairydom in order to do justice to a remarkable contemporary.

Of a certain Victorian Englishman it was said that no lady's shoe, unescorted, was safe in his company. It could be said of Edmund Wilson that, like Cecil B. DeMille, "he never met a woman's foot he didn't like." Is there any reader of Wilson's novel *I Thought of Daisy* who does not recall Wilson's description of a girl's feet as being like "moist cream cheeses"? But Wilson's podophilia did not stop there: he could have made a fortune in women's footwear. From *The Thirties:* ". . . shoes, blue with silver straps, that arched her insteps very high . . . ," "Katy's little green socks and untied gray moccasins . . . ," "young Scotch girl M.P. [with] large feet bulging out of black shoes. . . ," ". . . silver open-work shoes that disclosed her reddened toenails, such a combination as only she could wear. . . ." In *The Thirties,* I counted twenty-four references to shoes and feet; each, let me quickly say, belonging to a woman. When it came to shoes, Wilson was sternly heterosexual—not for him the stud's boot or the little lad's Ked. But, to be absolutely precise, there is one very odd reference. Wilson is struck by the number of Chicago men who wear spats. Reverie: "Excuse me, sir. But a hook is loose on your left spat. As chance would have it, I have with me a spats-hook. If you'll allow me, sir. . . ." Whenever Wilson strikes the Florsheim note, he is in rut.

As a lover, Wilson is proud of his "large pink prong." (Surely, Anaïs Nin said it was "short and puce"—or was that Henry Miller's thumb?) In action, "My penis went in and out so beautifully sensitively, caressing (me) each time so sweet-smoothly (silkily). . . ." Yet he refers, clinically, to his "all too fat and debauched face" not to mention belly. He was a stubby little man who drank a lot. But his sexual energy matched his intellectual energy; so much for Freud's theory of sublimation.

The section called "The Death of Margaret" is fascinating, and quite unlike anything else he was ever to write. He started scribbling in a notebook aboard an airliner in 1932, en route to California where his wife of two years had just died of a fall. A compulsive writer, Wilson felt, instinctively, that by a close running description of what he saw from the plane window and in the air terminals he could get control of the fact of death and loss, or at least neutralize the shock in the act of re-creation. He writes a good many impressionistic pages of the trip before he gets to Margaret. Some very odd items: "—touching fellow passenger's thigh, moving over to keep away from it, did he move, too?—shutting eyes and homosexual fantasies, losing in vivid reality from Provincetown, gray, abstract, unreal sexual stimulus—also thought about coming back with Jean Gorman on train as situation that promises possibilities; but couldn't stomach it—young man too big, not my type—" Then impressions of his time together with Margaret: "I felt for the first time how she'd given me all my self-confidence, the courage that I hadn't had before to say what I thought. . . ."

In Santa Barbara, he stays with her family. "At Mrs. Waterman's house [Margaret's mother], when I began to cry, she said, I've never broken down. . . ." "Second night: homosexual wet dream, figures still rather dim, a boy. Third night: nightmare—the trolls were in the dark part of the cellar. . . ." Finally, the inevitable epitaph; "After she was dead, I loved her." That is the story of every life—and death. For the next decade, Wilson dreams of Margaret and writes down the dreams. In these dreams he usually knows that she is dead but, somehow, they can overcome this obstacle. They don't; even in dreams. Eurydice always stays put: It is the blight man was born for.

During the Thirties, Wilson's interests were more political than literary. The Depression, the New Deal, the Soviet experiment absorbed him. Wilson is at his most attractive and, I should think, characteristic when he describes going to Russia. He wanted to think well of communism, and, to a point, he was enthralled by the "classless" society and by the way that one man, Lenin, "has stamped his thought and his language on a whole people." This is not the treason but the very nature of the true clerk: the word as absolute can be motor to behavior and to governance. Gradually, Wilson is disillusioned about Stalin and the state he was making.

But what is fascinating to read today is not Wilson's account of what he saw and did but the way that he goes about taking on a subject, a language, a world. This is what sets him apart from all other American critics. He has to get to the root of things. He will learn Hebrew to unravel the Dead Sea scrolls. Read a thousand windy texts to figure out the Civil War. Learn Russian to get past the barrier of Constance Garnett's prose. He was the perfect autodidact. He wanted to know it all. Or, as he wrote, after he had a nervous breakdown in the Thirties, "I usually know exactly what I want to do, and it has only been when I could not make up my mind that I have really gone to pieces."

Early in *The Thirties,* Wilson is a fellow traveler of the American communists' *faute de mieux.* He can see no other way out of the Depression than an overthrow of the form of capitalism that had caused it. Before the election of 1932, he wrote: "Hoover stands frankly for the interests of the class who live on profits as against the wage-earning classes. Franklin Roosevelt, though he speaks as a Democrat in the name of the small businessmen and farmers and is likely to be elected by them in the expectation that he can do something for them, can hardly be imagined effecting any very drastic changes in the system which has allowed him to get into office. Whatever amiable gestures he may make, he will be largely controlled by the profit-squeezing class just as Hoover is." This is prescient. Apropos the fireside chats: "Roosevelt's unsatisfactory way of emphasizing his sentences, fairyish, or as if there weren't real conviction behind him—in spite of his clearness and neatness—but regular radio announcers, I noticed later, did the same thing. (The remoteness of the speaker from his audience.)" It is a pity that Wilson, who was on the fringes of the New Deal, never got to know the president. "Roosevelt is reported to have answered when someone had said to him that he would either be the best president the country had ever had or the most hated: No—that he would either be the most popular or the last."

Wilson often traveled to Washington in the Thirties and he had a sense of the place (derived from Henry Adams?) that makes him sound like one of us cliff-dwellers: "Washington is really a hollow shell which holds the liberalism of the New Deal as easily as the crooks and thugs of the Harding Administration—no trouble to clean it out every night and put something else in the past Administration's place."

Wilson goes to see one Martha Blair—"a rather appealing mouth and slim arms, though pale thyroid eyes: pink flowered print dress, with sleeves that gave a glimpse of her upper arms . . . she complained of the small town character of Washington—if you said you had another engagement, people asked you what it was—when she had said she was going to Virginia for the weekend they had asked her where in Virginia." It is odd to see this old formidable "socialite" of my childhood (she was then in her early thirties) as viewed from a totally different angle. Martha Blair kept company in those days with Arthur Krock of *The New York Times*. They were known as Martha'n'Artha. Wilson thinks they were married in 1934. I don't. At about that time, I remember there was a great row between my mother and her husband over whether or not the unmarried couple Martha and Arthur could stay overnight at our house in Virginia—where she was so often headed. My mother won that round. They were often at Merrywood, and Arthur Krock was the first Jew that I ever met. Anti-semitism was in full boisterous American flower in the Thirties, and Wilson's record of conversations and attitudes haunt a survivor in much the same way that the background of a Thirties movie will reverse time, making it possible to see again a *People's Drug* store (golden lettering), straw hats, squared-off cars, and the actual light that encompassed one as a child, the very same light that all those who are now dead saw then.

Wilson notes, rather perfunctorily, friends and contemporaries. Scott Fitzgerald makes his usual appearances, and in his usual state. Once again we get the Hemingway-Wilson-Fitzgerald evening. "When Scott was lying in the corner on the floor, Hemingway said, Scott thinks that his penis is too small. (John Bishop had told me this and said that Scott was in the habit of making this assertion to anybody he met—to the lady who sat next to him at dinner and who might be meeting him for the first time.) I explained to him, Hemingway continued, that it only seemed to him small because he looked at it from above. You have to look at it in the mirror. (I did not understand this.)" I have never understood what Hemingway meant either. For one thing, Fitzgerald had obviously studied his diminutive part in a mirror. Even so, he would still be looking down at it unless, like a boy that I went to school with, he could so bend himself as to have an eye to eye, as it were, exchange with the Great American (Male) Obsession.

"Scott Fitzgerald at this time [1934] had the habit of insulting people, and then saying, if the victim came back at him: 'Can't take it, huh?' (I learned years later from Morley Callaghan that this was a habit of Hemingway's, from whom Scott had undoubtedly acquired it.)" There is altogether too little about Wilson's friend Dawn Powell, one of the wittiest of our novelists, and the most resolutely overlooked. But then American society, literary or lay, tends to be humorless. What other culture could have produced someone like Hemingway and *not* seen the joke?

Wilson's glimpses of people are always to the point. But they are brief. He is far more interested in writing descriptions of landscapes. I cannot think where the terrible habit began. Since Fitzgerald did the same thing in his notebooks, I suppose someone at Princeton (Professor Gauss? Project for a scholar-squirrel) must have told them that a writer must constantly describe things as a form of finger-exercise. The result is not unlike those watercolors Victorian girls were encouraged to turn out. Just as Wilson is about to tell us something quite interesting about e. e. cummings, he feels that he must devote a page or two to the deeply boring waterfront at Provincetown. A backdrop with no action in front of it is to no point at all.

There were trolls in the cellar of Wilson's psyche, and they tended to come upstairs "When I was suffering from the bad nerves of a hangover. . . ." There is also an echo of Mrs. Dalloway's vastation in the following passage: "Getting out of an elevator in some office building—I must have been nervously exhausted—I saw a man in a darkened hall—he was in his shirt sleeves with open neck, had evidently been working around the building—his eyes were wide open, and there seemed to be no expression on his face: he looked, not like an ape, but like some kind of primitive man—and his staring face, as I stared at him, appalled me: humanity was still an animal, still glaring out of its dark caves, not yet having mastered the world, not even comprehending what he saw. I was frightened—at him, at us all. *The horrible look of the human race.*"

As a critic, Wilson was not always at his best when it came to the design or pattern of a text—what used to be called aesthetics. He liked data, language. He did not have much sympathy for the New Critics with their emphasis on text *qua* text. After all, nothing human exists in limbo; nothing human is without connection. Wilson's particular genius lay in his ability to make rather more connections than any other critic of his time. As Diderot said of Voltaire: "He knows a great deal and our young poets are ignorant. The work of Voltaire is full of things; their works are empty."

But Wilson was quite aware that "things" in themselves are not enough. Professor Edel quotes from Wilson's Princeton lecture: "no matter how thoroughly and searchingly we may have scrutinized works of literature from the historical and biographical point of view . . . we must be able to tell the good from the bad, the first-rate from the second-rate. We shall not otherwise write literary criticism at all."

We do not, of course, write literary criticism at all now. Academe has won the battle in which Wilson fought so fiercely on the other side. Ambitious English teachers now invent systems that have nothing to do with literature or life but everything to do with those games that must be played in order for them to rise in the academic bureaucracy. Their works are empty indeed. But then, their works are not meant to be full. They are to be taught, not read. The long dialogue has broken down. Fortunately, as Flaubert pointed out, the worst thing about the present is the future. One day there will be no. . . . But I have been asked not to give the game away. Meanwhile, I shall drop a single hint: Only construct!

*The New York Review of Books*
*September 25, 1980*

# Montaigne

"IN EVERY WORK OF GENIUS," wrote Emerson, "we recognize our own rejected thoughts; they come back to us with a certain alienated majesty." After four centuries, Montaigne's curious genius still has that effect on his readers and, time and again, one finds in his self-portrait one's own most brilliant *aperçus* (the ones that somehow we forgot to write down and so forgot) restored to us in his essays—attempts—to assay—value—himself in his own time as well as, if he was on the subject, all time, if there is such a thing.

For thirty years I have kept Donald M. Frame's translation of *The Complete Works of Montaigne* at, if not bedside, hand. There are numerous interlocking Olympic circles on the maroon binding where glasses were set after I had written some no longer decipherable commentary in the margin or, simply, "How true!" I never actually read all of *The Complete Works,* but I did read here and there, and I reread favourite essays rather more than I ever tried to read the famous "Apology for Raymond Sebond," who needed, I used to think, neither apology nor indeed memorial. But the generation of the twenty-first century is now in place, and to celebrate its entry into the greenhouse there is a new translation of *The Complete Essays of Montaigne* by M. A. Screech who, years ago, so ably—even sternly—led me through Rabelais.

It has taken me one month to read every one of the 1,269 pages. (Montaigne, III 8: "I have just read through at one go Tacitus's *History* [something which rarely happens to me, it is twenty years since I spent one full hour at a time on a book]. . . .") I enjoyed comparing Screech with Frame.

Where Frame is sonorous and euphemistic, Screech is sharp and up-to-date, as readers of his *Montaigne and Melancholy* (1983) might suspect. Although my nature inclines me to enrol Montaigne in the relativist school of Lucretius and the Epicureans, thus making him proto-Enlightenment, Screech firmly nails Montaigne within the Roman Catholic Church of his day, beleaguered as it was by the Reformation, which took the form of civil war in France between Catholics and Protestants, an ideological, that is pointless, war of the crude sort that has entertained us for so much of our own science-ridden century.

Michel Eyquem was born in 1533 at his father's estate, Montaigne, east of Bordeaux. A family of fish and wine merchants, the Eyquems were minimally ennobled by the acquisition of Montaigne, which gave them their "de." The mother's family were Spanish Jewish, presumably long since converted. When schism came, Michel, his parents, two brothers and a sister remained Catholic, while one brother and two sisters became Protestant. By the 1560s, there was an out-and-out civil war that continued to Michel's death in 1592. The Montaigne family remained on amiable terms not only with the Catholic court at Paris but with that Protestant sovereign of nearby Navarre who so proverbially celebrated a Mass in order to become King Henry IV of France.

Montaigne's education was odd but useful. As his tutor spoke no French, Latin became his first language, spoken and written, until he was six. Then he went on to spend seven years at a Latin school, where he was immersed in the Roman classics; but little Greek. He also learned the agreed-upon French of the day, as well as Gascon dialect. He was more or less trained to be a soldier, a lawyer, an estate manager and what used to be called a "gentleman," a category that no longer exists in our specialized time. As such, Montaigne naturally hated lying, and it was his essay on the subject that first drew me to him years ago. "Lying is an accursed vice. It is only our words which bind us together and make us human. If we realized the horror and weight of lying, we would see that it is more worthy of the stake than other crimes. . . . Once let the tongue acquire the habit of lying and it is astonishing how impossible it is to make it give it up" (I 8). As one who has been obliged to spend a lifetime in diverse liar-worlds (worlds where the liar is often most honoured when he is known to be lying and getting away with it), I find Montaigne consoling.

Montaigne's father became Mayor of Bordeaux, while his son spent thirteen years in the city's legal council. It was during this period that he met a fellow public servant, Etienne de La Boëtie. Each was to become the other's other self. "If you press me to say why I loved him, I feel that it can only be expressed by replying 'Because it was him: because it was me.' . . . We were seeking each other before we set eyes on each other . . ." (I 28).

Their relationship was an intense dialogue on every possible subject. De La Boëtie inclined to stoicism. He had written against tyranny. He died young.

Montaigne's letter to his father on de La Boëtie's last days is rather like that of Ammianus Marcellinus on the death of the Emperor Julian, something of a hero to Montaigne if not to the Holy Office. (Letter to father: "He gave up the ghost at about three o'clock on the Wednesday morning, August 18th, 1563, after living 32 years, nine months, and 17 days. . . .")

Certainly, we are all in poor de La Boëtie's debt for dying, because Montaigne was never to find another soulmate and so, in due course, after marriage, children, the inheritance of the estate, "In the year of Christ 1571, at the age of thirty-eight, on the last day of February, his birthday, Michel de Montaigne, long weary of the servitude of the court and of public employment . . .", retired to Montaigne, where he then began to make attempts at understanding everything, which meant, principally, the unknowable (so Socrates thought) self. In the absence of a friend to talk to or an Atticus to write to, Montaigne started writing to himself about himself and about what he had been reading which became himself. He made many attempts to try—*essayer*—to find his form. "If I had somebody to write to I would readily have chosen it as the means of publishing my chatter. . . . Unless I deceive myself my achievement then would have been greater" (I 40). At first, he wrote short memoranda—how to invest a city, or what one is to make of a certain line of Seneca. Later, he settled for the long essay that could be read in an hour. He did a lot of free-associating, as "all subjects are linked to each other" (III 5). Essentially, he wrote as a man of action, involved in the world both locally and nationally. He was personally esteemed by Catherine de Medici, Henry III, Marguerite de Valois and Henry of Navarre, who twice visited him at Montaigne and would, as King of France, have made him a counsellor had the essayist not made one final attempt to understand death—life by dying.

The greatest action of this man of action was to withdraw to his library in order to read and think and write notes to himself that eventually became books for the world:

> At home I slip off to my library (it is on the third storey of a tower); it is easy for me to oversee my household from there. I am above my gateway and have a view of my garden, my chicken-run, my backyard and most parts of my house. There I can turn over the leaves of this book or that, a bit at a time without order or design. Sometimes my mind wanders off, at others I walk to and fro, noting down and dictating these whims of mine. . . . My library is round in shape, squared off only for the needs of my table and chair: as it curves round, it

offers me at a glance every one of my books ranged on five shelves all the way along. It has three splendid and unhampered views and a circle of free space sixteen yards in diameter (III 3).

Montaigne seems to have read every Latin author extant; he was also much intrigued with contemporary stories of the Americas and other exotic places where cannibals and realms of gold coexisted. Much of his writing starts with a quotation that sets him to ruminating on his own, buttressed by more quotations, making a sort of palimpsest. If nothing else, he was a superb arranger of other men's flowers. He was particularly drawn to biographical anecdote, and it was lucky for him that not long after he settled in his tower room, Bishop Jacques Amyot published a French translation of Plutarch, who quickly became Montaigne's most useful source and touchstone. In fact, one wonders what the essays would have been like without Plutarch. Would Montaigne have found so attractive those human titans, Alexander and Caesar? Or those paradigms of human virtue, Epaminondas and Cato the Younger?

Among the thousand books on the five shelves, Montaigne returns most often to Lucretius and Seneca. He reveres Homer, but he is happiest with those two worldly writers who appeal to his own worldliness. The first because of his sense of the diversity—even relativity—of things, the second as a wise counsellor, not only in the conduct of a life at home but at a dangerous court. He turns often to Cicero, but he is vaguely disapproving of the vanity of that politician, ever avid, especially in retirement, for glory. Cicero "said he wanted to use his withdrawal and his repose from affairs of state to gain life ever-lasting through his writings" (I 39). Then Montaigne, slyly, quotes Persius: "Does *knowing* mean nothing to you, unless somebody else knows that you know it?"

I thought of a chat with Robert Lowell at my Hudson river house forty years ago. Somehow, we had got on to the subject of Julius Caesar's character. I mentioned Cicero's letter to Atticus on how unnerving it was to have Caesar as a house guest. "But," said Lowell, "remember how pleased Cicero was when Caesar praised his consulship." Of course, each of us wanted the other to know that *he* had read the letter and that, if nothing else, we held, in common, a small part of the classical heritage—so etiolated! so testeronish! so Eurocentric!—that Montaigne had spent his life in communion with. I wonder what a poet and a novelist would have in common to talk about nowadays. After all, a shared knowledge of old books was probably the largest part of the "loving friendship" between Étienne and Montaigne. Today they would share—what? Robert Altman's films?

Montaigne disliked pedants. He notes that in his local dialect they are called *Lettreferits*—word-struck. He himself is after other game than words or "words about words": "scribbling seems to be one of the symptoms of an age of excess" (III 9). "We work merely to fill the memory, leaving the understanding and the sense of right and wrong. . . . Off I go, rummaging about in books for sayings which please me—not so as to store them up (for I have no storehouses) but so as to carry them back to the book, where they are no more mine than they were in their original place. We only know, I believe, what we know now: 'knowing' no more consists in what we once knew than in what we shall know in the future" (I 24). He frets about his poor memory. "I am so outstanding a forgetter that, along with all the rest, I forget even my own works and writings. People are constantly quoting me to me without my realising it" (II 17). This is a bit swank. But writers often forget what they have written, since the act of writing is a letting go of a piece of one's mind, and so an erasure. Montaigne's first two volumes of essays were published in 1580: he was forty-seven. Eight years later, he revised the first two volumes and published a third. From the beginning, he was accepted as a classic in the Roman sense, or as a writer *utile-doux,* as the French styled the great works.

Montaigne was much concerned with his body and believed Sebond's proposition that man is a marriage between soul and body. He hated doctors, a family tradition to which he not only adhered but attributed the long lives in the male line (he himself was dead at sixty, rather younger than father and grandfather). He feared kidney stones, which tortured his father and, finally, himself. To cure "the stone," he visited spas everywhere and took the baths: "I reckon that bathing in general is salubrious and I believe that our health has suffered . . . since we lost the habit. . . . we are all the worst for having our limbs encrusted and our pores blocked up with filth" (II 37). Of himself, "my build is a little below the average. This defect is not only ugly but unbecoming, especially in those who hold commands . . ." (II 17), but "my build is tough and thick-set, my face is not fat but full, my complexion is between the jovial and the melancholic. . . . Skill and agility I have never had . . . except at running (at which I was among the average)."

He records without despair or even pride that he has almost no gifts for music, dancing, tennis, wrestling, and none at all for swimming, fencing, vaulting and jumping.

> My hand is so clumsy that I cannot even read my own writing, so that I prefer to write things over again rather than to give myself the trouble of disentangling my scribbles. . . . That apart, I am quite a good scholar! I can never fold up a letter neatly, never sharpen a pen, never carve passably at table, nor put harness on horse, nor bear a hawk properly nor release it, nor address hounds, birds or horses. My bod-

ily endowments are, in brief, in close harmony with my soul's. There is no agility, merely a full firm vigour, but I can stick things out.

Like his father, he wore mostly black and white. "Whether riding or walking I have always been used to burdening my hand with a cane or stick, even affecting an air of elegance by leaning on it with a distinguished look on my face" (II 25).

He deplored the codpieces of the previous generation, which drew attention to and exaggerated the unmentionables. He had had sex at so early an age that he could not recall just when. Like Abraham Lincoln, he contracted syphilis ("a couple of light anticipatory doses") (III 3). For this vileness, American universities would erase him from the canon, if they could, since no great man has ever had syphilis or engaged in same-sexuality. On Greek love, Montaigne understood exactly what Achilles and Patroclus were up to in the sack and he found their activities "rightly abhorrent to our manners" on the novel ground that what was not equal in body-mind could not be love, much less "perfect love." The man chose not another man but a boy for his looks. It was Montaigne's view that true love, sexual or not, meant the congruence of two men as equals. This was the highest form of human relationship. He does note that "male and female are cast in the same mould: save for education and custom the difference between them is not great" (III 6). Theoretically, if a woman was educated as a man and met her male equal, this could be the "perfect love": but he gives no examples. Odd, since Plutarch had filled him in on Aspasia and Pericles. But then he did not place Pericles very high; thought him a tricky orator. Of course, he had not read Thucydides.

On "Some Lines of Virgil," he has a good time with sex, as both necessity and madness. "The genital activities of mankind are so natural, so necessary and so right: what have they done to make us never dare to mention them without embarrassment . . . ? We are not afraid to utter the words 'kill,' 'thief,' or 'betray' " (III 5). Yet "The whole movement of the world tends and leads towards copulation. It is a substance infused through everything; it is the centre—towards which all things turn." He comments on the uncontrollability—and unreliability—of the male member. "Every man knows . . . that he has a part of his body which often stirs, erects, and lies down again without his leave. Now such passive movements which only touch our outside cannot be called ours" (II 6). (Screech thinks that Montaigne never read Augustine's *Confessions.*) Montaigne notes priapic cults in other lands and times. Finally, all in all, he favours arranged marriages: "A good marriage (if there be such a thing) rejects the company and conditions of Cupid; it strives to reproduce those of loving friendship" (III 5). Incidentally, nowhere does Montaigne mention his wife. There is one reference to his daughter Léonor, and a mysterious panegyric to a sort of adopted daughter that, Screech thinks, may have been written by herself in a posthumous edition, which gives rise to the agreeable notion that there may have been some sort of Ibsen plot unfolding in old Périgord. Rousseau thought that Montaigne ought to have told us a lot more about his private life, but then Rousseau was no gentleman.

On politics, Montaigne was deeply but not dully conservative. That is, he did not, figuratively or literally, believe in witches:

> I abhor novelty, no matter what visage it presents, and am right to do so, for I have seen some of its disastrous effects. That novelty (the wars of religion) which has for so many years beset us is not solely responsible, but one can say with every likelihood that it has incidentally caused and given birth to them all. . . . Those who shake the State are easily the first to be engulfed in its destruction. The fruits of dissension are not gathered by the one who began it: he stirs and troubles the water for other men to fish in (I 23).

A nice presage of France's revolution two centuries later, though not particularly applicable to the American adventure that actually turned the whole world upside down. But in the midst of a civil war over religion, the absolutist must appear more than usually monstrous: "There is a great deal of self-love and arrogance in judging so highly of your opinions that you are obliged to disturb the public peace in order to establish them" (I 23). Plainly, he was not the sort of conservative who would have admired that radical British prime minister who, for a decade, so strenuously disturbed the death-like peace of those sunnily arid North Sea islands.

Montaigne was very much school of the-devil-we-know: "Not as a matter of opinion but of truth, the best and most excellent polity for each nation is the one under which it has been sustained. Its form and its essential advantages depend upon custom. It is easy for us to be displeased with its present condition; I nevertheless hold that to yearn for an oligarchy in a democracy or for another form of government in a monarchy is wrong and insane" (III 9). He regarded any fundamental change as "the cure of illness by death. . . . My own contemporaries here in France could tell you a thing or two about that!"

Since I want Montaigne on my side in the great task of reworking my own country's broken-down political system, I must invoke him—like Scripture—in another context. "The most desirable laws are those which are fewest, simplest and most general. I think moreover that it would be better to have none at all than to have them in the profusion as we do now. . . . When King Ferdinand sent colonies of immigrants to the Indies he made the wise stipulation that no one should be included who had studied jurisprudence, lest law suits should pullulate in the New World" (III 13), causing endless faction and altercation. Since *our* New World is entirely paralysed by lawyers hired by pullulating polluters of politics as well as of environment and put in place to undo many thousands of laws made by other lawyers, I cannot think Montaigne would be so cruel as *not* to want us to rid ourselves of such a government, but I suppose he would echo, mockingly, his young contemporary Shakespeare's final solution for lawyers, while suggesting that it might do us Americans a world of good if each took a course or two in torts and malfeasances since, from the beginning, we were intended to be a lawyerly republic and must not change.

Common sense is a phrase, if not a quality, much revered in the bright island of the North Sea. Montaigne is often accused of possessing this rare quality, but what most strikes me in his meanderings is the *un*commonness of his sense. He turns a subject round and round and suddenly sees something that others had not noticed. He is also inclined to humour, usually of the dead-pan sort: "Herodotus tells us of a certain district of Libya where men lie with women indiscriminately, but where, once a child can toddle, it recognizes its own father out of the crowd, natural instinct guiding its first footsteps. There are frequent mistakes, I believe . . ." (II 8).

Of literary style, he wrote: "I want things to dominate, so filling the thoughts of the hearer that he does not even remember the words. I like the kind of speech which is simple and natural, the same on paper as on the lip; speech which is rich in matter, sinewy, brief and short" (I 26). As for "the French authors of our time. They are bold enough and proud enough not to follow the common road; but their want of invention and their power of selection destroy them. All we can see is some wretched affectation of novelty, cold and absurd fictions which instead of elevating their subject batter it down" (III 5). He delighted in Boccaccio, Rabelais and the *Basia* of Johannes Secundus. Of poets, he put Virgil highest, especially the *Georgics;* then Lucretius, Catullus and Horace. He finds Aesop interestingly complex. "Seneca is full of pithy phrases and sallies; Plutarch is full of matter. Seneca inflames you and stirs you: Plutarch is more satisfying and repays you more. Plutarch leads us: Seneca drives us" (II 10). He seems to be looking ahead at our own scribbling time when he writes, "There are so many ways of taking anything, that it is hard for a clever mind *not* to find in almost any subject something or other which appears to serve his point, directly or indirectly. That explains why an opaque, ambiguous style has been so long in vogue" (II 12).

From 1581 to 1585, Montaigne served as Mayor of Bordeaux: "People say that my period of office passed without trace or mark. Good!" In 1582, the Pope dealt him a grievous blow by replacing the Julian calendar with the

Gregorian, which lopped eleven days off everyone's life. "Since I cannot stand novelty even when corrective, I am constrained to be a bit of a heretic in this case" (III 10). He enjoyed his fame as a writer but noted "that in my own climate of Gascony they find it funny to see me in print; I am valued the more, the farther from home knowledge of me has spread . . ." (III 2). In the Frame translation, there is a "How true" in the margin next to what could be the mark of a tear, if it did not still smell of whisky. In a variation on Aesop, he notes, "A hundred times a day when we go mocking our neighbour we are really mocking ourselves; we abominate in others those faults which are most manifestly our own, and with a miraculous lack of shame and perspicacity, are astonished by them" (III 8). Perhaps this universal failing is why "I study myself more than any other subject. That is my metaphysics; that is my physics" (III 13).

In a comment on Montaigne's most celebrated essay, "On the Education of Children," Sainte-Beuve remarked that "he goes too far, like a child of Aristippus who forgets Adam's fall." He is "*simply* Nature . . . Nature in all its Grace-less completeness." The clarity—charity, too—with which he saw his world has made him seem a precursor of the age of Enlightenment, even that of Wordsworth. But Screech does not allow us so easily to appropriate him to our secular ends, and Montaigne's Epicurean stoicism is more than balanced by his non-questioning—indeed defence—of the traditional faith. For him, his translation of the *Theologia Naturalis* of Raymond Sebond was to be regarded as a prophylactic against the dread Luther.

Incidentally, Screech's own translation is as little ambiguous as possible; it is also demotic. Where Frame writes "ruminating," Screech writes "chewing over," "frenzied" becomes "raging mad," "loose-boweled" becomes "squittering," a word that I was obliged to look up—"to void thin excrement." We are all in Screech's debt for giving us back a word so entirely useful that no critic's portmanteau should ever again be without it. On the other hand, Frame's "this bundle of so many disparate pieces is being composed" becomes the perhaps less happy phrase "all the various pieces of this faggot are being bundled together . . ."

"The writer's function is not without arduous duties. By definition, he cannot serve those who make history; he must serve those who are subject to it." Montaigne would not have agreed with Albert Camus. In a sense, Montaigne is writing for the rulers (Henry IV was particularly taken by his essay "On High Rank as a Disadvantage"). Educate the rulers, and they will not torment their subjects. But Montaigne's political interests are aside from his main point, the exploration of self. Once he had lost Étienne, he was all he had; so he wrote a book about himself. "I am most ignorant about myself. I marvel at the assurance and confidence everyone has about himself, whereas there is virtually nothing that I *know* I know. . . . I think that I am an ordinary sort of man, except in considering myself to be one. . . . That I find my own work pardonable is not so much for itself or its true worth as from a comparison with others' writings which are worse—things which I can see people taking seriously" (II 17).

Vanity of any sort amuses him. Even the great Julius Caesar is ticked off: "Observe how Caesar spreads himself when he tells us about his ingenuity in building bridges and siege-machines; in comparison, he is quite cramped when he talks of his professional soldiering, his valour or the way he conducts his wars. His exploits are sufficient proof that he was an outstanding general: he wants to be known as something else rather different: a good engineer" (I 17).

Montaigne begins his essays (first thought of as *rhapsodies*—confused medleys) with a pro forma bow to Cicero–Plato: "Cicero says that philosophizing is nothing other than getting ready to die. That is because study and contemplation draw our souls somewhat outside ourselves keeping them occupied away from the body, a state which both resembles death and which forms a kind of apprenticeship for it; or perhaps it is because all the wisdom and argument in the world eventually come down to one conclusion which is to teach us not to be afraid of dying" (I 20). In this way "all the labour of reason must be to make us live well."

Montaigne's reigning humour may have been melancholic, but he is hardly morbid in his musings on that good life which leads to a good death. He is a true stoic, despite occasional obeisance to the Holy Spirit, a post-Platonic novelty now running down. He is even a bit sardonic: "Everybody goes out as though he had just come in. Moreover, however decrepit a man may be, he thinks he still has another twenty years." But "I have adopted the practice of always having death not only in my mind but on my lips. There is nothing I inquire about more readily than how men have died: what did they say? How did they look?" Like me, when he read a biography, he first skipped to the end to see how its subject died. As his book—and life—proceed, he is more than ever aware of the diversity within the unity of things and the inability to know very much of what came before us because, "Great heroes lived before Agamemnon. Many there were: yet none is lamented, being swept away unknown into the long night."

After the arrival of kidney stones, Montaigne occasionally strikes a bleak note: "I am on the way out: I would readily leave to one who comes later whatever wisdom I have learnt about dealing with the world. . . . At the finish of every task the ending makes itself known. My world is over: my mould has been emptied; I belong entirely to the past" (III 10). But before self-pity could spread her great fluffy wings, he then makes a joke about being cruelly robbed of eleven days of life by the Pope's new calendar. Meanwhile, "Time and custom condition us to anything strange: nevertheless, the more I haunt myself and know myself the more my misshapenness amazes me and the less I understand myself" (III 11). Finally, "We confuse life with worries about death, and death with worries about life. One torments us; the other terrifies us" (III 12). Yet,

> If we have not known how to live, it is not right to teach us how to die, making the form of the end incongruous with the whole. If we have known how to live steadfastly and calmly we shall know how to die the same way. . . . death is indeed the ending of life, but not therefore its end: it puts an end to it, it is its ultimate point: but it is not its objective. Life must be its own objective, its own purpose. . . . Numbered among its other duties included under the general and principal heading, *How to Live,* there is the sub-section, *How to Die.*

Thus, Montaigne firmly reverses the Cicero–Plato notion that "to philosophize is to learn how to die" and enjoins us to meditate not on unknowable, irrelevant death but on life which can be known, at least in part. Sixteen years of observing himself and reading and rereading the thousand books in the round library had convinced him not only that life was all there is but that "Each man bears the entire form of man's estate" (III 2). At the end, Montaigne had met himself at last; and everyone else, too. On September 13, 1592, he died in bed while listening to Mass. What one would give to know what he said, how he looked, just before he, too, entered the long night.

Meanwhile, Screech now replaces Frame at my bedside. Anglophones of the next century will be deeply in his debt. Despite his insistence on the Catholicism of Montaigne, the good Screech does note that Montaigne uses the word Fortune—in the sense of fate—350 times. That is satisfying.

***The Times Literary Supplement***
***June 26, 1992***

# Thomas Love Peacock: The Novel of Ideas

WHAT IS A NOVEL FOR? To be read is the simple answer. But since fewer and fewer people want to read novels (as opposed to what the conglomerate-publishers call "category fiction"), it might be a good idea to take a look at what is being written, and why; at what is being read, and why.

In *Ideas and the Novel* Mary McCarthy notes that since the time of Henry James, the serious novel has dealt in a more and more concentrated—if not refined—way with the moral relations of characters who resemble rather closely the writer and his putative reader. It is not, she says, that people actually write Jamesian novels; rather, "The Jamesian model remains a standard, an archetype, against which contemporary impurities and laxities are measured." In addition, for Americans, sincerity if not authenticity is all-important; and requires a minimum of invention.

During the last fifty years, the main line of the Serious American Novel has been almost exclusively concerned with the doings and feelings, often erotic, of white middle-class Americans, often schoolteachers, as they confront what they take to be life. It should be noted that these problems seldom have much or anything to do with politics, with theories of education, with the nature of the good. It should also be noted that the tone of the Serious Novel is always solemn and often vatic. Irony and wit are unknown while the preferred view of the human estate is standard American, which is to say positive. For some reason, dialogue tends to be minimal and flat.

Virginia Woolf thought that the Victorian novelists "created their characters mainly through dialogue." Then, somehow, "the sense of an audience" was lost. "*Middlemarch* I should say is the transition novel: Mr. Brooke done directly by dialogue: Dorothea indirectly. Hence its great interest—the first modern novel. Henry James of course receded further and further from the spoken word, and finally I think only used dialogue when he wanted a very high light."

Today's Serious Novel is not well lit. The characters do, say, and think ordinary things, as they confront those problems that the serious writer must face in his everyday life. Since the serious novel is written by middle-class, middlebrow whites, political activists, intellectuals, members of the ruling classes, blacks seldom make appearances in these books, except as the odd flasher.

Predictably, despite the reflexive support of old-fashioned editors and book-reviewers, the Serious Novel is of no actual interest to anyone, including the sort of people who write them: they are apt to read Agatha Christie, if they read at all. But then, this is an old story. In 1859, Nathaniel Hawthorne, having just perpetrated that "moonshiny Romance" (his own phrase) *The Marble Faun,* wrote to his publishers: "It is odd enough, moreover, that my own individual taste is for quite another class of works than those which I myself am able to write." Sensible man, he preferred Trollope to himself. Nevertheless, in a sort of void, Serious Novels continue to be published and praised, but they are not much read.

What is a novel for, if it is *not* to be read? Since the rise of modernism a century ago—is there anything quite as old or as little changed as modern literature?—the notion of the artist as saint and martyr, reviled and ignored in his own time, has had a powerful appeal to many writers and teachers. Echoing Stendhal, the ambitious artist will write not for the people of his own day but for the residents of the next century—on the peculiar ground that the sort of reader who preferred Paul de Kock to Stendhal in the nineteenth century and Barbara Cartland to Iris Murdoch in our own will have developed an exquisite sensibility by the year 2080. These innocents seem not to understand that posterity is a permanent darkness where no whistle sounds. It is reasonable to assume that, by and large, what is not read now will not be read, ever. It is also reasonable to assume that practically nothing that is read now will be read later. Finally, it is not too farfetched to imagine a future in which novels are not read at all. But, for the present, if a Serious Novel is not going to be read, it can always be taught—if it is so made as to be more teacherly than readerly. Further, if the serious student keeps on going to school and acquiring degrees, he will find that not only is his life enhanced by the possession of tools with which to crack the code of rich arcane texts but he will also be able to earn a living by teaching others to teach books written to be taught. Admittedly, none of this has much to do with literature but, as a way of life, it is a lot easier than many other—phrase? Service-oriented Fields.

Although there is no reason why the universities should not take over the Serious Novel and manufacture it right on campus, there are signs that the magistri ludi of Academe are now after more glorious game. Suddenly, simultaneously, on many campuses and in many states, a terrible truth has become self-evident. *The true study of English studies is English studies.* If this truth is true, then the novel can be dispensed with. As our teachers begin to compose their so-called "charters," setting forth powerful new theories of English studies, complete with graphs and startling neologisms, the dream of the truly ambitious schoolteacher will be fulfilled and the interpreter-theorist will replace the creator as culture hero.

Meanwhile, in the real world—take the elevator to the mezzanine, and turn left; you can't miss it—what sort of novels are still read, *voluntarily,* by people who will not be graded on what they have read?

Conglomerate-publishers are a good consumer guide, catering, as they do, to a number of different, not always contiguous publics: Gothic stories, spy thrillers, Harlequin romances . . . each genre has its measurable public. Occasionally, books are written which appear to fit a genre but transcend it because they are works of the imagination, dealing with the past or the future; with alternative worlds. Although these books cannot be truly serious because they are not, literally, *true,* there is no serious American novelist who can write as well or as originally (not a recommendation, perhaps) as John Fowles or William Golding, two English writers whose works are often read outside institutions. Yet neither Fowles nor Golding is taken with any great seriousness by American schoolteachers. Fowles is regarded as a sort of Daphne du Maurier with grammar while Golding is known as the author of a book that the young once fancied—and so was taught in the lower grades. For reasons that have to do with the origins of the United States, Americans will never accept any literature that does not plainly support the prejudices and aspirations of a powerful and bigoted middle class which is now supplementing its powerful churches with equally powerful universities where what is said and thought and imagined is homogenized to a degree that teachers and students do not begin to suspect because they have never set foot outside the cage that they were born in. Like the gorilla who was taught to draw, they keep drawing the bars of their cage; and think it the world.

Historical novels and political novels can never be taken seriously because true history and disturbing politics are not acceptable subjects. Works of high imagination cause unease: if it didn't really happen, how can your story be really *sincere* . . . ? The imaginative writer can never be serious unless, like Mr. Thomas Pynchon, he makes it clear that he is writing about Entropy and the Second Law of Thermodynamics and a number of other subjects that he picked up in his freshman year at Cornell. English teachers without science like this sort of thing while physicists are tempted to write excited letters to literary journals. Thus, the Snow-called gap between the two cultures looks to be bridged, while nothing at all has been disturbed in the way that the society obliges us to see ourselves.

One of the great losses to world literature has been the novel of ideas. Or the symposium-novel. Or the dialogue-novel. Or the. . . . One has to search for some sort of hyphenate even to describe what one has in mind. Mary McCarthy calls it the "conversation novel."

From Aristophanes to Petronius to Lucian to Rabelais to Swift to Voltaire to Thomas Love Peacock, there has been a brilliant line of satirical narratives and had it not been for certain events at the beginning of the nineteenth century in England, this useful form might still be with us, assuming that those who have been brought up on sincere simple Serious Novels would appreciate—or even recognize—any play of wit at the expense of dearly held serious superstitions. Where the True is worshiped, truth is alien. But then to be middle class is to be, by definition, frightened of losing one's place. Traditionally, the virtuous member of the middle class is encouraged to cultivate sincerity and its twin, hypocrisy. The sort of harsh truth-telling that one gets in Aristophanes, say, is not possible in a highly organized zoo like the United States where the best cuts are flung to those who never question the zoo's management. The satirist breaks with his origins; looks at things with a cold eye; says what he means, and mocks those who do not know what *they* mean.

It is significant that the only American writer who might have taken his place in the glittering line was, finally, scared off. Since Mark Twain was not about to lose his audience, he told dumb jokes in public while writing, in private, all sorts of earth-shattering notions. Twain thought that if there was a God, He was evil. Twain's poignant invention, Huck, is a boy who wants to get his ass out of the serious, simple, sincere, bigoted world on whose fringe he was born. He is a lovely, true evocation. But he is in flight; can't cope; knows something is wrong. There is a world elsewhere, he suspects; but there are practically no people in it—it is the territory.

Every quarter century, like clockwork, there is a Peacock revival. The great tail feathers unfurl in all their Pavonian splendor, and like-minded folk delight in the display; and that's the end of that for the next twenty-five years. Although it is now too late in history to revive either Peacock or the conversation novel, Marilyn Butler in *Peacock Displayed* has written an admirable book about a valuable writer.

Thomas Love Peacock was born in 1785; he died in 1866. He was well read in Greek, Latin, French, and Italian literature; he was an early and knowledgeable devotee of opera, particularly Mozart, Rossini, Bellini. Since he did not go to school after the age of twelve, he was able to teach himself what he wanted to know, which was a lot. In 1819, he was taken on by the East India Company where he worked until his retirement in 1856. He associated at India House with James and John Stuart Mill; he was a lifelong friend of Jeremy Bentham and of Byron's friend John Cam Hobhouse. For three years, he was close to Shelley; and got him to read the classics. Peacock's wife went mad while his daughter Mary Ellen married a bearded, dyspeptic, cigarette-smoker—three demerits in Peacock's eyes. George Meredith was less than an ideal son-in-law, particularly at table. Some of Mary Ellen's recipes survive. Ingredients for Athenian Eel and Sauce: "Half a pint of good Stock. One tablespoon of Mushroom Ketchup. One mustard-spoonful of Mustard. One dessert spoonful of Shalot Vinegar. One dessert spoonful of Anchovy Sauce. One dessert spoonful of Worcester Sauce. Marjoram and Parsley." That was just the sauce. Meanwhile, cut the eels in pieces. . . . When Mary Ellen deserted Meredith for the painter Henry Wallis, Meredith's digestive tract must have known a certain relief. Later he memorialized his father-in-law as Dr. Middleton in *The Egoist.* Mary Ellen died young. Despite the deaths of children and a wife's madness, one has the sense that Peacock's long life was happy; but then he was a true Epicurean.

Peacock began as a poet in the didactic Augustan style. He was much interested in politics, as were most of the English writers of the late eighteenth and early nineteenth centuries. Butler is particularly good in setting Peacock firmly in a world of political faction and theorizing. By the time Peacock was of age, the American and French revolutions had happened. The ideas of Rousseau and Paine were everywhere talked of, and writers wrote in order to change society. As a result, what was written was considered more important than who wrote it—or even read it. The writer as his own text was unknown because it was unthinkable, while the writer as sacred monster was not to emerge until mid-century. Ironically, Peacock's idealistic friend Shelley was to be Sacred Monster Number Two. Number One was Byron (who figures as Mr. Cypress in Peacock's *Nightmare Abbey*).

In the first quarter of the century, British intellectual life was mostly Scottish. The *Edinburgh Review*'s chief critic was Francis Jeffrey, a liberal Whig who tended to utilitarianism: to what social end does the work in question contribute? Will it or won't it *do*? This was Jeffrey's narrow but, obviously, useful approach to literature. Peacock was also a utilitarian; and subscribed to his friend Bentham's dictum: "the greatest good of the greatest number." But Peacock regarded the *Edinburgh Review* ("that shallow and dishonest publication") as much too Whiggish and class-bound. Peacock seems always to have known that in England the Whig-versus-Tory debate was essentially hollow because "though there is no censorship of the press, there is an influence widely diffused and mighty in its operation that is almost equivalent to it. The whole scheme of our government is based on influence, and the immense number of genteel persons, who are maintained by the taxes, gives this influence an extent and complication from which few persons are free. They shrink from truth, for it shews those dangers which they dare not face." Thus, in our own day, *The New York Times* reflects the will of the administration at Washington which in turn reflects the will of the moneyed interests. Should a contemporary American writer point out this connection, he will either be ignored or, worse, found guilty of Bad Taste, something that middle-class people are taught at birth forever to eschew.

The debate that helped to shape Peacock (and the century) was between Shelley's father-in-law William Godwin and the Reverend Thomas Malthus. The anarchist Godwin believed in progress; thought human nature perfectible. He believed society could be so ordered that the need for any man to work might be reduced to an hour or two a day. Godwin's *Political Justice* and *The Enquirer* inspired Malthus to write *An Essay on the Principle of Population,* published in 1798. Everyone knows Malthus's great proposition: "Population, when unchecked, increases in a geometrical ratio. Subsistence increases only in arithmetical ratio. A slight acquaintance with numbers will show the immensity of the first power in comparison with the second." This proposition is still being argued, as it was for at least two millennia before Malthus. At the time of Confucious, China was underpopulated; yet all ills were ascribed to overpopulation: "When men were few and things were many," went an already ancient saying, "there was a golden age; but now men are many and things are few and misery is man's lot."

In a series of dialogue-novels, Peacock enlarged upon the debate. *Headlong Hall* appeared in 1816. As Butler notes: "Peacock's satires are all centered on a recent controversy large in its ideological implications but also amusingly rich in personality and detail. For its full effect, the satire requires the reader to be in the know." This explains why the form is not apt to be very popular. At any given moment too few people are in the know about much of anything. As time passes, the urgencies of how best to landscape a park—a debate in *Headlong Hall*—quite fades even though the various points of view from romantic to utilitarian are eternal.

Aristophanes made jokes about people who were sitting in the audience at the theatre of Dionysos. When we do know what's being sent up—Socrates' style, say—the bright savagery is exciting. But who is Glaucon? And what did he steal? Happily, most of Peacock's characters (based on Shelley, Byron, Coleridge, Malthus, et al.) are still well enough known to some readers for the jokes to work. More important, the tone of Peacock's sentences is highly pleasing. He writes a stately, balanced prose that moves, always, toward unexpected judgment or revelation.

Peacock begins a review of Thomas Moore's novel *The Epicurean* with: "This volume will, no doubt, be infinitely acceptable to the ladies 'who make the fortune of new books.' Love, very intense; mystery, somewhat recondite; piety, very profound; and philosophy, sufficiently shallow. . . . In the reign of the emperor Valerian, a young Epicurean philosopher is elected chief of that school in the beginning of his twenty-fourth year, a circumstance, the author says, without precedent, and we conceive without probability."

*Melincourt* was published in 1817, starring a truly noble savage, a monkey called Sir Oran Haut-ton. Malthus makes an appearance as Mr. Fax. Sir Oran, though he cannot speak, is elected to Parliament. *Nightmare Abbey* (1818) is a take-off on the cult of melancholy affected, in one way, by Byron (Mr. Cypress) and, in another, by Coleridge (Mr. Flosky). Shelley appears as Scythrop, though Butler makes the point that neither Shelley nor Peacock ever admitted to the likeness. Mr. Cypress has quarreled with his wife; he sees only darkness and misery as man's estate. Peacock works in actual lines from *Childe Harold* to mock if not Byron Byronism, while Mr. Flosky's dialogue is filled with metaphysical conceits that even he cannot unravel. Scythrop is not practical.

Peacock's next two works, *Maid Marian* (1818) and *The Misfortunes of Elphin* (1829), are set, respectively, in the late twelfth century and the sixth century. But Robin Hood's England is used to illuminate Peacock's dim view of the Holy Alliance of his own day while sixth-century Wales is used to savage Wellington's current Tory administration. *Crotchet Castle* (1831) is like the early books in form: culture is the theme. One of the characters is Dr. Folliott, a philistine Tory who mocks those who would improve man's lot. Since Dr. Folliott has been thought to be a voice for his creator, serious critics have tended to dismiss Peacock as a crotchety, unserious hedonist whose tastes are antiquarian and whose political views are irrelevant. Butler takes exception to this; she thinks that Folliott's likeness to his creator "cannot in fact survive a close reading." On education, Folliott advances opinions that were not Peacock's:

> I hold that there is every variety of natural capacity from the idiot to Newton and Shakespeare; the mass of mankind, midway between these extremes, being blockheads of different degrees; education leaving them pretty nearly as it found them, with this single difference, that it gives a fixed direction to their stupidity, a sort of incurable wry neck to the thing they call their understanding.

I rather suspect that Peacock, in a certain mood, felt exactly as Dr. Folliott did. He also possessed negative capability to a high degree. In this instance, he may well be saying what he thinks at the moment, perfectly aware that he will think its opposite in relation to a different formulation on the order, say, of certain observations in Jefferson's memoirs which he reviewed in 1830. Peacock was absolutely bowled over by the mellifluous old faker's announcement that between "a government without newspapers, or newspapers without a government" he would choose the latter. This is, surely, one of the silliest statements ever made by a politician; yet it is perennially attractive to—yes, journalists. In any case, Jefferson was sufficiently sly to add, immediately, a line that is seldom quoted by those who love the sentiment: "But I should mean that every man should receive those papers, and be capable of reading them." The last phrase nicely cancels all that has gone before. Jefferson was no leveler.

In any case, the endlessly interesting controversy of who should be taught what and how and why is joined in this bright set of dialogues and every position is advanced. We get the Tory view, as published by the Rev. E. W. Grinfield; he thought that the masses need nothing more than to have religion and morals instilled in them: "We inculcate a strong attachment to the constitution, *such as it now is;* we teach them to love and revere our establishments in Church and State, even *with all their real or supposed imperfections;* and we are far more anxious to make them good and contented citizens, than to fit them for noisy patriots, who would perhaps destroy the constitution whilst pretending to correct it." There, in one sentence, is the principle on which American public education is based (*vide* Frances FitzGerald's *America Revised*).

In opposition to Grinfield is John Stuart Mill:

> I thought, that while the higher and richer classes held the power of government, the instruction and improvement of the mass of the people were contrary to the self-interest of those classes, because tending to render the people more powerful for throwing off the yoke; but if the democracy obtained a large, and perhaps the principal share, in the governing power, it would become the interest of the opulent classes to promote their education, in order to ward off really mischievous errors, and especially those which would lead to unjust violations of property.

This has proven to be idealistic. Neither Washington nor Moscow thinks it worthwhile to teach their citizens to address themselves to "real or supposed imperfections" in the system. Rather, to keep the citizens "good and contented" is the perennial aim of powerful governing classes or, as one of Peacock's Tory characters puts it: "Discontent increases with the increase of information."

Five years before Peacock's death at eighty-one, he published the most satisfying of his works (I still don't know what to call them: they are not novels as novels were written then or now, and they are not theatre pieces even though many pages are set up like a playscript), *Gryll Grange.* The subject is everything in general, the uses of the classics in particular. The form is resolutely Pavonian. Each character represents a viewpoint; each makes his argument.

Here is an example of Peacock when he slips into dialogue.

LORD CURRYFIN: Well, then, what say you to the electric telegraph, by which you converse at the distance of thousands of miles? Even across the Atlantic, as no doubt we shall do yet.

MR. GRYLL: Some of us have already heard the Doctor's opinion on the subject.

THE REVEREND DOCTOR OPIMIAN: I have no wish to expedite communication with the Americans. If we could apply the power of electrical repulsion to preserve us from ever hearing anything more of them, I should think that we had for once derived a benefit from science.

MR. GRYLL: Your love for the Americans, Doctor, seems something like that of Cicero's friend Marius for the Greeks. He would not take the nearest road to his villa, because it was called the Greek-road. Perhaps if your nearest way home were called the American-road, you would make a circuit to avoid it.

THE REVEREND DOCTOR OPIMIAN: I am happy to say that I am not put to the test. Magnetism, galvanism, electricity, are "one form of many names." Without magnetism, we should never have discovered America; to which we are indebted for nothing but evil; diseases in the worst form that can afflict humanity, and slavery in the worst form in which slavery can exist. The Old World had the sugarcane and the cotton-plant, though it did not so misuse them. Then, what good have we got from America? What good of any kind, from the whole continent and its islands, from the Esquimaux to Patagonia?

MR. GRYLL: Newfoundland salt fish, Doctor.

THE REVEREND DOCTOR OPIMIAN: That is something, but it does not turn the scale.

MR. GRYLL: If they have given us no good, we have given them none.

THE REVEREND DOCTOR OPIMIAN: We have given them wine and classical literature; but I am afraid Bacchus and Minerva have equally "Scattered their bounty upon barren ground." On the other hand, we have given the red men rum, which has been the chief instrument of their perdition. On the whole, our intercourse with America has been little else than interchange of vices and diseases.

LORD CURRYFIN: Do you count it nothing to have substituted civilized for savage men?

THE REVEREND DOCTOR OPIMIAN: Civilized. The word requires definition. But looking into futurity, it seems to me that the ultimate tendency of the change is to substitute the worse for the better race; the Negro for the Red Indian. The Red Indian will not work for a master. No ill-usage will make him. Herein, he is the noblest specimen of humanity that ever walked the earth. Therefore, the white men exterminate his race. But the time will come, when, by mere force of numbers, the black race will predominate, and exterminate the white.

Mr. Falconer remonstrates that "the white slavery of our [English] factories is not worse than the black slavery of America. We have done so much to amend it, and shall do more. Still much remains to be done." Opimian responds: "And will be done, I hope and believe. The Americans do nothing to amend their system." When Lord Curryfin remarks that he has met many good Americans who think as Doctor Opimian does, the response is serene: "Of that I have no doubt. But I look to public acts and public men."

In the half century between Peacock's first work and his last, the novel was transformed by Dickens and the comedy of character replaced the comedy of ideas. In fact, character—the more prodigious the better—was the novel. In the year of *Gryll Grange* (1860), the novel was about to undergo yet another change with the publication of *The Mill on the Floss.* In the everyday world of George Eliot's characters the play of intelligence is quite unlike that of Peacock, since the only vivid intelligence in an Eliot novel is that of the author or, as Mary McCarthy writes: ". . . the kind of questions her characters put to themselves and to each other, though sometimes lofty, never question basic principles such as the notion of betterment or the inviolability of the moral law."

Elsewhere in *Ideas and the Novel,* McCarthy contrasts Peacock with James. Where James managed to exclude almost everything in the way of ideas from the novel in order to concentrate on getting all the way 'round, as it were (oh, *as it were*!), his made-up characters, "consider Thomas Love Peacock," she writes. "There the ordinary stuff of life is swept away to make room for abstract speculation. That, and just that, is the joke. . . . In hearty, plain-man style (which is partly a simulation), Peacock treats the brain's sickly products as the end-result of the general disease of modishness for which the remedy would be prolonged exposure to common, garden reality." But that was written of *Nightmare Abbey:* common, garden reality flourishes during the debates in *Gryll Grange,* a book which Butler believes "occupies the same position in Peacock's oeuvre as *The Clouds* in that of Aristophanes: both seem less directly political than usual because the author's approach is oblique and fantastic, almost surreal."

It is fitting that in *Gryll Grange* the characters are composing a comedy in the Aristophanic manner while the book itself is a variation on Old Comedy. Although the tone of this old man's work is highly genial, he still strikes with youthful vigor the negative. He still says no to Romanticism which had, by then, entirely triumphed, and which, not much changed, continues to dominate our own culture.

In a review of C. O. Müller's *A History of the Literature of Ancient Greece,* Peacock explains the value of the negative: "there is much justice in the comparison of Lucian and Voltaire. The view is not only just, it is also eminently liberal. That 'the results of the efforts of both against false religion and false philosophy were merely negative'; that they had 'nothing tangible to substitute for what they destroyed,' is open to observation." Indeed it is. After all, this is the constant complaint of those who support the crimes and injustices of the status quo. Peacock proceeds to observe, "To clear the ground of falsehood is to leave room for the introduction of truth. Lucian decidedly held that moral certainty, a complete code of duty founded on reason, existed in the writings of Epicurus; and Voltaire's theism, the belief in a pervading spirit of good, was clear and consistent throughout. The main object of both was, by sweeping away false dogmas, to teach toleration. Voltaire warred against opinions which sustained themselves by persecution."

Needless to say, there is no more certain way of achieving perfect unpopularity in any society than to speak against the reigning pieties and agreed-upon mendacities. The official line never varies: To be negative is to be bad; to be positive is to be good. In fact, that is even more the rule in our society than it was in Peacock's smaller world where the means to destroy dissent through censorship or ridicule or silence were not as institutionalized as they are now.

Even so, Peacock himself was forced to play a very sly game when he dealt with the Christian dictatorship of England. After giving an admiring account of Epicurus' "favorite dogma of the mortality of the soul," he remarks, "In England, we all believe in the immortality of the soul" because "the truth of the Christian Religion is too clearly established amongst us to admit of dispute." In his novels, he treated Christianity with great caution. What he really thought of a religion that was the negation of all that *he* held positive only came to light posthumously.

In 1862, a year after Mary Ellen's death, he sent to the printers a poem he had written in Greek on Jesus' exuberantly vicious tirade (Matthew 10:34): "Think not that I am come to send peace on earth: I came not to send peace, but a sword." The executors of Peacock's estate suppressed the poem; and only the last lines survive in translation. A pagan appears to be exhorting a crowd to "come now in a body and dash in pieces" this armed enemy, Jesus. "Break in pieces, hurl down him who is a seller of marvels, him who is hostile to the Graces, and him who is abominable to Aphrodite, the hater of the marriage bed, this mischievous wonder-worker, this destroyer of the world, CHRIST." There are times when positive capability must masquerade as negative.

Butler is at her most interesting when she relates Peacock to our own time where "students of literature are taught to think more highly of introspection than of objectivity, to isolate works of art from their social context, and to give them a high and special kind of value." She ascribes this to "the early nineteenth century irrationalist reaction—Romanticism—[which] is a current movement still. . . . In England at the close of the Napoleonic Wars, Romanticism was perceived to encourage indifference to contemporary politics, or to offer outright aid to illiberal governments. A literature that is concerned with style, and with feeling, rather than with intellect and reason, may be merely decorative; in relation to practical affairs, it will almost certainly be passive."

One can understand the emphasis that our universities continue to place on the necessary separation of literature from ideas. "We are stunned," writes Butler, "by reiteration into believing that what the world wants is positive thinking. Peacock makes out a case, illustrated by Voltaire, for negative thinking, and its attendant virtues of challenge, self-doubt, mutual acceptance, and toleration." Finally, "Since Coleridge we have been fond of the artist-prophet, and the art-work which is monologue, or confession, or even opium dream. Peacock, whose art is based on the dialogue, has waited a long time for his turn to be heard."

I don't know how these things are being arranged in Butler's England but the passive yea-sayer who has no ideas at all about politics, religion, ethics, history is absolutely central to our syllabus and his only competition is the artist as advertiser of sweet self alone. The culture would not have it otherwise and so, as McCarthy puts it, "in the place of ideas, images still rule the roost, and Balzac's distinction between the *roman idée* and the *roman imagé* appears to have been prophetic, though his order of preference is reversed."

In *Ideas and the Novel,* McCarthy joins in the battle (assuming that this is not just a skirmish in a byway where the mirror lies shattered). Although McCarthy takes the Pavonian side, she moves beyond Peacock's satiric dialogue-novels to those formidable nineteenth-century novelists to whom ideas are essential and, for her, it is James not Coleridge who is terminus to this line. "When you think of James in the light of his predecessors," she writes, "you are suddenly conscious of what is not there: battles, riots, tempests, sunrises, the sewers of Paris, crime, hunger, the plague, the scaffold, the clergy, but also minute particulars such as you find in Jane Austen—poor Miss Bates's twice-baked apples."

McCarthy is particularly interesting when she examines Victor Hugo, a great novelist doomed to be forever unknown to Americans. She examines Hugo's curious way of staying outside his characters whose "emotions are inferred for us by Victor Hugo and reported in summary form." Hugo deals with ideas on every subject from capital punishment to argot. He is also possessed by an Idea: "The manifest destiny of France to lead and inspire was identified by Hugo with his own mission to the nation as seer and epic novelist." McCarthy's survey of this sort of, admittedly, rare master (Tolstoi, Dostoevsky, Manzoni, Balzac, Stendhal, George Eliot) is illuminating, particularly when she discusses "the ambition to get everything in, to make this book *the* Book," a passion still to be found post-James in Proust and Joyce "Though public spirit as an animating force was no longer evident (in fact the reverse) . . . the ambition to produce a single compendious sacred writing survived, and we may even find it today in an author like Pynchon (*Gravity's Rainbow*)."

It is usual in discussion of the novel (what is it for? what is it?) to point to the displacement that occurred when the film took the novel's place at the center of our culture. What James had removed from the novel in the way of vulgar life, film seized upon: "It was not until the invention of the moving-picture," writes McCarthy, "that the novel lost its supremacy as purveyor of irreality to a multitude composed of solitary units." McCarthy goes on to make the point that "unlike the novel, the moving-picture, at least in my belief, cannot be an idea-spreader; its images are too enigmatic, e.g., Eisenstein's baby carriage bouncing down those stairs in *Potemkin.* A film cannot have a spokesman or chorus character to point the moral as in a stage play; that function is assumed by the camera, which is inarticulate. And the absence of spokesmen in the films we remember shows rather eerily that with the cinema, for the first time, humanity has found a narrative medium that is incapable of thought."

If McCarthy's startling insight is true (I *think* it is), the curious invention by the French of the auteur-theory begins to make a degree of sense. Aware that something was missing in films (a unifying intelligence), M. Bazin and his friends decided that the camera's lens was nothing but a surrogate for the director who held it or guided it or aimed it, just as the painter deploys his brush. For M. Bazin *et cie.,* the director is the unifying intelligence who controls the image and makes sense of the piece: he is The Creator. Needless to say, this perfect misapprehension of the way movies were made in Hollywood's Golden Age has been a source of mirth to those who were there.

The movie-goer is passive, unlike the reader; and one does not hear a creator's voice while watching a movie. Yet, curiously enough, the kind of satire that was practiced by Aristophanes might just find its way onto the screen. As I watched *Airplane!,* I kept hoping that its three auteurs (bright show-biz kids) would open up the farce. Include President Carter and his dread family; show how each would respond to the near-disaster. Add Reagan, Cronkite, the Polish Pope. But the auteurs stuck to the only thing that show-biz people ever know about—other movies and television commercials. Although the result is highly enjoyable, a chance was missed to send up a whole society in a satire of the Old Comedy sort.

At the end of McCarthy's notes on the novel, she looks about for new ways of salvaging a form that has lost its traditional content. She thinks that it might be possible, simply, to go back in time: "If because of ideas and other unfashionable components your novel is going to seem dated, don't be alarmed—date it." She mentions several recent examples of quasi-historical novels; she also notes that "in the U.S.A., a special license has always been granted to the Jewish novel, which is free to juggle ideas in full public; Bellow, Malamud, Philip Roth still avail themselves of the right, which is never conceded to us goys." With all due respect to three interesting writers, they don't use their "concession" with any more skill than we mindless goys. The reason that they sometimes appear to be dealing in ideas is that they arrived post-James. Jewish writers over forty do—or did—comprise a new, not quite American class, more closely connected with ideological, argumentative Europe (and Talmudic studies) than with those of us whose ancestors killed Indians, pursued the white whale, suffered, in varying degrees, etiolation as a result of overexposure to the Master's lesson. In any case, today's young Jewish writers are every bit as lacking in ideas as the goyim.

McCarthy admires Robert Pirsig's *Zen and the Art of Motorcycle Maintenance,* "an American story of a cross-country trip with philosophical interludes." She believes that "if the novel is to be revitalized, maybe more such emergency strategies will have to be employed to disarm and disorient reviewers and teachers of literature, who, as always, are the reader's main foe." They are not the writer's ally either—unless he conforms to their kitsch romantic notions of what writing ought to be or, more to the point, what it must never be.

Although I suspect that it is far too late for emergency strategies, one final tactic that *might* work is to infiltrate the genre forms. To fill them up, stealthily, with ideas, wit, subversive notions: an Agatha Christie plot with well-cut cardboard characters that demonstrated, among other bright subjects, the rise and fall of monetarism in England would be attractive to all sorts of readers and highly useful.

In any case, write what you know will always be excellent advice for those who ought not to write at all. Write what you think, what you imagine, what you suspect: that is the only way out of the dead end of the Serious Novel which so many ambitious people want to write and no one on earth—or even on campus—wants to read.

***The New York Review of Books***
***December 4, 1980***

# The Bookchat of Henry James

On the evening of January 12, 1905, President and Mrs. Theodore Roosevelt held a reception for the diplomatic corps. After the reception, a limited number of grandees were given a dinner; among those so distinguished was Henry James, who was staying across the street at the house of Henry Adams. The reception had been boycotted by Adams himself, who found it impossible to finish a sentence once the voluble president was wound up. But Adams sent over his houseguests, James, John La Farge, and Augustus Saint-Gaudens.

The confrontation between Master and Sovereign contained all the elements of high comedy. Each detested the other. James regarded Roosevelt as "a dangerous and ominous jingo" as well as "the mere monstrous embodiment of unprecedented and resounding noise" while Theodore Rex, as the Adams circle dubbed him, regarded the novelist as "a miserable little snob" and, worse, "effete." As it turned out, snob and jingo were each on his best behavior that night, and James, in a letter to Mary Cadwalader Jones, noted that the president was "a really extraordinary creature for native intensity, veracity and *bonhomie.*" What TR thought of his guest on that occasion is not recorded, but he could never have been approving of James, who had settled in England, had never roughed it, had never ridden, roughly, up Kettle Hill (to be renamed San Juan, since no one could be the hero of anything so homely as a kettle).

But the true high comedy of that January evening was that the two great men were meeting not as literary lion and president but as book reviewer and author reviewed. Seven years earlier, James had given Roosevelt (an indefatigable writer of echoing banality) a very bad review in the English paper *Literature.* Although reviews were not signed in those days, concerned authors could almost always find out who had done them in, and if the wielder of the axe were a writer of James's fame, the secret could never have been kept for long.

James begins, blandly,

> Mr. Theodore Roosevelt appears to propose [the first verb is a hint of fun to come]—in *American Ideals and Other Essays Social and Political*—to tighten the screws of the national consciousness as they have never been tightened before. The national consciousness for Mr. Theodore Roosevelt is, moreover, at the best a very fierce affair.

James then suggests that this approach is not only overwrought but vague.

> It is "purely as an American," he constantly reminds us, that each of us must live and breathe. Breathing, indeed, is a trifle; it is purely as Americans that we must think, and all that is wanting to the author's demonstration is that he shall give us a receipt for the process. He labours, however . . . under the drollest confusion of mind.

All in all, TR was saintly to put such an un-American reviewer at his dinner table, separated from his own intensely American self by a single (American) lady. Of course, in April 1898, James could not have known that the author, a mere assistant secretary of the Navy, was glory-bound. Yet if he had, the Jamesian irony (so like that of his friends John Hay and Henry Adams, and so deeply deplored, in retrospect, by the president) could not resist serving up such quotes as,

> "The politician who cheats or swindles, or the newspaperman who lies in any form, should be made to feel that he is an object of scorn for all honest men." That is luminous; but, none the less, "an educated man must not go into politics as such; he must go in simply as an American . . . or he will be upset by some other American with no education at all . . ." A better way perhaps than to barbarize the upset—already, surely, sufficiently unfortunate—would be to civilize the upsetter.

For James, whatever useful insights that politician Roosevelt might have are undone "by the puerility of his simplifications."

The Library of America has seen fit to publish in one volume all of James's book reviews on American and English writers, as well as a number of other meditations on literature. To read the book straight through (1413 pages of highly uneven bookchat) is to get to know Henry James in a way that no biographer, not even the estimable Leon Edel, the present editor, can ever capture. Here one can study the evolution of James's taste and mind.

As a critic, James began far too young. From age twenty-three to twenty-five, he was reviewing everything that came to hand for the *North American Review* and *The Nation.* He was still an American resident: He did not set out from the territory for old Europe until John Hay, then at the *New York Tribune,* sent him to Paris as a general correspondent (1875–1876). By 1878 he was settled in England, his domicile to the end.

In London, he wrote *French Poets and Novelists,* and a long study of Hawthorne. In 1878, "I had ceased to 'notice' books—that faculty seemed to diminish for me, perversely, as my acquaintance with books grew." Fortunately for the readers of this volume, in 1898 James became a householder. In need of money, he went back to book reviewing for a year or two and produced some of his most interesting pieces. Finally, in 1914, he wrote *The New Novel,* in which he threaded his way, as best he could, among the young Turks—H. G. Wells and Arnold Bennett and (they meet at last! the great tradition) D. H. Lawrence, whose *Sons and Lovers* James remarks "hang(s) in the dusty rear of Wells and Bennett."

There is a lifelong prejudice in James against the slice-of-life novel as opposed to the consciously shaped work of art. (Yet, paradoxically, he is enthralled by Balzac, on whom he was lecturing in 1905.) In that sense, he is the snob that Theodore Rex called him. Although he is most comfortably at home in fairly high society, his true subject is displaced, classless, innocent Americans with money, at sea in old Europe which, at the beginning of his career, he saw as beguiling and dangerous and, at the end, quite the reverse: Old Europe was no match for young America's furious energy and ruthless, mindless exertion of force. But the milieu of *Sons and Lovers* depressed him, as did that of Thomas Hardy, whose village oafs he quotes at length in a review of *Far from the Madding Crowd.*

James, justifiably, hated dialect novels, American or English. Hardy's "inexhaustible faculty for spinning smart dialogue makes him forget that dialogue in a story is after all but episode. . . ." The book "is inordinately diffuse, and, as a piece of narrative, singularly inartistic. The author has little sense of proportion, and almost none of composition." Worse, the book is much too long (this from James the First not yet Old Pretender), thanks to the tradition of the three-volume novel. "Mr. Hardy has gone astray very cleverly, and his superficial novel is a really curious imitation of something better."

Yet with George Eliot, whom he admires, he notes of *Silas Marner,* "Here, as in all George Eliot's books, there is a middle life and a low life;

and here, as usual, I prefer the low life." This is James, aged twenty-three, indicating that Eliot does not feel quite at home in middle life much less high life. But twenty years later, a wiser James sums up the great novelist:

> What *is* remarkable, extraordinary—and the process remains inscrutable and mysterious—is that this quiet, anxious, sedentary, serious, invalidical English lady, without animal spirits, without adventures or sensations, should have made us believe that nothing in the world was alien to her; should have produced such rich, deep, masterly pictures of the multiform life of man.

In the notorious case of Walt Whitman one can observe James's evolution from disdainful, supercilious, but observant youth to mystified, awed admirer. Of *Drum-Taps* he writes (1865),

> It has been a melancholy task to read this book; and it is a still more melancholy one to write about it. . . . It exhibits the effort of an essentially prosaic mind [and] frequent capitals are the only marks of verse in Mr. Whitman's writing . . . As a general principle, we know of no circumstance more likely to impugn a writer's earnestness than the adoption of an anomalous style. He must have something very original to say if none of the old vehicles will carry his thoughts. Of course, he *may* be surprisingly original. Still, presumption is against him. . . . This volume is an offense against art.

He scolds Whitman for crowning himself the national poet: "You cannot entertain and exhibit ideas; but, as we have seen, you are prepared to incarnate them." This was the point, of course, to Whitman; but young James can only groan, "What would be bald nonsense, and dreary platitudes in anyone else becomes sublimity in you." A quarter century later, Whitman has become "the good Walt." Of *Calamus* (Whitman's highly adhesive letters to the working-class lad Pete Doyle): "There is not even by accident a line with a hint of style—it is all flat, familiar, affectionate, illiterate colloquy" yet "the record remains, by a mysterious marvel, a thing positively delightful. If we can ever find out why, it must be another time. The riddle meanwhile is a neat one for the sphinx of democracy to offer." When the riddle was "solved" by Dr. Kinsey in 1948, the Republic had a nervous breakdown, which continues to this day.

One is constantly surprised by the spaciousness of James's sympathies as he got older. In time, the vulgarity of Whitman was seen for what it is, the nation itself made flesh. Edith Wharton in *A Backward Glance* writes,

> It was a joy to me to discover that James thought [Whitman] the greatest of American poets. *Leaves of Grass* was put into his hands,

> and all that evening we sat rapt while he wandered from "The Song of Myself" to "When Lilacs Last in the Dooryard Bloom'd."

On the other hand, no sentiment was ever exempt from his critical irony, and James could not resist exclaiming, at the reading's end, "Oh, yes, a great genius; undoubtedly a very great genius! Only one cannot help deploring his too-extensive acquaintance with foreign languages." Like the late Tennessee Williams, Whitman loved foreign phrases and usually got them wrong.

The fact that one is never told just how James's heroes make their money was neither coyness nor disdain: It was simply a blank, as he confessed in 1898: "Those who know [business] are not the men to paint it; those who might attempt it are not the men who know it." One wonders what his friend the author of *The Rise of Silas Lapham* thought of the alleged absence in our literature of the businessman—of "the magnificent theme *en disponibilité.*"

James was very much interested in "the real world"; and not without a certain shrewdness in political matters. Surprisingly, he reviews in *The Nation* (1875) Charles Nordhoff's *The Communistic Societies of the United States, from Personal Visit and Observation, Etc.*, a book once again in print. Nordhoff was a Prussian-born American journalist who covered the Civil War for the *New York Herald.* In the 1870s, he decided to investigate applied communism in the United States, as demonstrated by the Oneida, Amana, Mount Lebanon, and Shaker groups. "Hitherto," Nordhoff writes, "very little, indeed almost nothing definite and precise, has been made known concerning these societies; and Communism remains loudly but very vaguely spoken of, by friends as well as enemies, and is commonly either a word of terror or contempt in the public prints." *Tout ça change,* as the good Walt might have said.

For over a century, communism has been the necessary enemy of our republic's ruling oligarchy. Yet before 1917, communism was not associated with totalitarianism or Russian imperialism or the iron rule of a *nomenklatura.* Communism was simply an economic theory, having to do with greater efficiency in production as a result of making those who did the work the owners. James grasps this principle rather better than most of his contemporaries, and he commends Nordhoff for his ability to show us

> communistic life from the point of view of an adversary to trades-unions, and to see whether in the United States, with their vast area for free experiments in this line, it might not offer a better promise to workingmen than mere coalitions to increase wages and shorten the hours of labor.

Although he thinks Nordhoff (probably a closet German socialist) tends to "dip his pen into rose-color," James is intrigued by the material efficiency of the societies. He is also appalled by their social customs: Some are celibate, some swap mates. "One is struck, throughout Mr. Nordhoff's book, with the existence in human nature of lurking and unsuspected strata, as it were, of asceticism, of the capacity for taking a grim satisfaction in dreariness." Then James adds with characteristic sly irony: "Remember that there are in America many domestic circles in which, as compared with the dreariness of private life, the dreariness of Shakerism seems like boisterous gaiety."

Predictably, James deplores the "attempt to organize and glorify the detestable tendency toward the complete effacement of privacy in life and thought everywhere so rampant with us nowadays." Would that he could move among us today and revel in our government's call for obligatory blood and urine tests. "But [lack of privacy] is the worst fact chronicled in Mr. Nordhoff's volume, which, for the rest, seems to establish fairly that, under certain conditions and with strictly rational hopes, communism in America may be a paying experiment." Now that I have revived these lines, James, already banned in certain public libraries for pornography (*The Turn of the Screw,* what else?), can now be banned as a communist. A small price, all in all, to pay for freedom.

As the complete Henry James is to be republished in the Library of America, it is amusing to read what he has to say of the other novelists in the series, also, more to the point, what he does *not* have to say. For instance, there is no mention of Jack London, whose best work was done before James died in 1916. Although the inner life of a dog in the Arctic Circle might not have appealed to the Master, James might have found a good deal to ponder in *The Sea Wolf* and *The Iron Heel.* Stephen Crane appears in his letters (and his life; he liked him, not her) but there is no reference to Crane anywhere in the flow, the torrent, of names like Alger, Bazley, Channing, Fletcher, Gannett, Sedley, Spofford, Whitney . . .

James's study of Hawthorne is famous; it is also full of evasive high praise: James did not care for romance; yet Hawthorne's one "real" novel, *The Blithedale Romance,* which is not, to me, a romance at all, is to James notable for its "absence of satire . . . of its not aiming in the least at satire." I thought the whole thing a splendid send-up of Brook Farm, and Zenobia a truly comic character. In any case, Hawthorne is the only American novelist to whom James pays full homage.

He does do justice to his friend Howells. He certainly applauds Howells's ability for "definite notation"; yet he doesn't much care for Howells's ladies. But Howells is not writing about the drawing room; he writes about men, work, business. Bartley Hubbard is a splendid invention—the newspaperman as inventor—while the story of Silas Lapham does for the paint business what Balzac so magically did for paper. James (writing for lady readers?) looks elsewhere.

Fenimore Cooper is mentioned, blandly, twice, while Melville is dismissed in the following line: "the charming *Putnam* [magazine] of faraway years—the early fifties . . . the prose, as mild and easy as an Indian summer in the woods, of Herman Melville, of George William Curtis and 'Ik Marvel.' "

Mark Twain, with whom Henry James was forced so titanically to contest in the pages of Van Wyck Brooks (James lost), is mentioned only once: "In the day of Mark Twain there is no harm in being reminded that the absence of drollery may, at a stretch, be compensated by the presence of sublimity." So much for the Redskin Chief from the Paleface Prince. Finally, James praises his friend Mrs. Wharton, with the no longer acceptable but perfectly apt characterization: "of the masculine conclusion tending to crown the feminine observation."

James is on happier ground when dealing with English and French writers. As for the Russians, except for Turgenev, whom he knew, they seem to have made no impression. There is a perfunctory nod to Tolstoi (1914) in a survey of the new novel. Tolstoi is "the great Russian" whose influence can be detected in the world of Wells and Bennett. The name Dostoevsky is added to a list of deliberately disparate writers. Admittedly, by then (1897) James had ceased to be a working reviewer as opposed to being an occasional writer of "London Notes" for *Harper's,* with a tendency "to pass judgment in parenthesis," something he maintained that the critic by him admired, Matthew Arnold, never did.

Henry James's admiration of the never entirely fashionable and often despised Balzac is to his eternal credit as a critic. On the other hand, his attitude to Flaubert, whom he knew, is very odd indeed. He thought that Flaubert (whom he could see all 'round, he once declared) had produced a single masterpiece; and that was that. He seems not to have got the point to *Sentimental Education,* the first truly "modern novel," which demonstrated for the first time in literature the fact that life is simply drift and though *Bouvard and Pécuchet* is unfinished, the notion is still splendid if droll (James, who was, in life, the essence of drollery, did not much care for levity in the novel, *tant pis*).

It is always easy to make fun of book reviewers, and what we take now to be, in our superior future time, their mistakes. But he *is* wrongheaded when he writes (1876): "Putting aside Mme. Sand, it is hard to see who among the French purveyors of more or less ingenious fiction, is more accomplished than [M. Octave Feuillet]. There are writers who began with better things—Flaubert, Gustave Droz, and Victor Cherbuliez—but they have lately done worse, whereas Mr. Feuillet never falls below himself." Flaubert had been lately doing such "worse" things as publishing *Sentimental Education* (1869) and *The Temptation of Saint Anthony* (1874), while *Three Tales* would be published the next year. James had read one of them:

> Gustave Flaubert has written a story about the devotion of a servant-girl to a parrot, and the production, highly finished as it is, cannot, on the whole, be called a success. We are perfectly free to call it flat, but I think it might have been interesting; and I, for my part, am extremely glad he should have written it; it is a contribution to our knowledge of what can be done—or what cannot. Ivan Turgenev has written a tale about a deaf and dumb serf and a lap-dog, and the thing is touching, loving, a little masterpiece. He struck the note of life where Flaubert missed it—he flew in the face of a presumption and achieved a victory.

James is never on thinner ice than when he goes on about "presumptions," as if the lovely art was nothing but constant presuming. In *The Art of Fiction* (1884), he is more open: "There is no impression of life, no manner of seeing it and feeling it, to which the plan of the novel may not offer a place; you have only to remember that talents so dissimilar as those of Alexander Dumas and Jane Austen, Charles Dickens and Gustave Flaubert have worked in this field with equal glory." *Equal* is not the right word; but *glory* is.

The usually generous James cannot entirely accept Flaubert, the one contemporary writer whose dedication to his art was comparable to his own. Although James goes on and on about the greatness of *Madame Bovary,* he cannot, simultaneously, resist undermining it.

> Nothing will ever prevent Flaubert's heroine from having been an extremely minor specimen, even of the possibilities of her own type, a twopenny lady, in truth, of an experience so limited that some of her chords, it is clear, can never be sounded at all. It is a mistake, in other words, to speak of any feminine nature as consummately exhibited, that is exhibited in so small a number of its possible relations. Give it three or four others, we feel moved to say—"then we can talk."

Plainly, Flaubert's version of a "twopenny lady" is not the portrait of a lady of the sort that James could happily "talk" about. I suspect, finally, that James not only did not like Flaubert's writing but that he had serious moral reservations about French literature in general: "There are other subjects," he wrote plaintively, "than those of the eternal triangle of the husband, the wife and the lover." Among critics, James is hardly a master; rather, he is a master of the novel who makes asides that are, often, luminous; as often, not.

In the spring of 1948, I was received in Paris by André Gide at 1 *bis* rue Vaneau. I spent a pleasant hour with the Master and John Lehmann, my English publisher. We talked of literature, of national differences, of changing fashions, of James. Then Gide (the proud translator of Conrad) asked, "What is it that you Americans—and English—see in Henry James?" I could only stammer idiocies in my schoolboy French. Ironically, now, nearly forty years later, I find myself explaining to the young that there was once a famous French writer named André Gide. Fashions change but, as George Santayana remarked, "it would be insufferable if they did not." Each generation has its own likes and dislikes and ignorances.

In our postliterary time, it is hard to believe that once upon a time a life could be devoted to the perfecting of an art form, and that of all the art forms the novel was the most—exigent, to use a modest word. Today the novel is either a commodity that anyone can put together, or it is an artifact, which means nothing or anything or everything, depending on one's literary theory. No longer can it be said of a writer, as James said of Hawthorne in 1905: "The grand sign of being a classic is that when you have 'passed,' as they say at examinations, you have passed; you have become one once for all; you have taken your degree and may be left to the light and the ages." In our exciting world the only light cast is cast by the cathode-ray tube; and the idea of "the ages" is, at best, moot—mute?

***The New York Review of Books***
***November 6, 1986***

# William Dean Howells

## I

On May 1, 1886, American workers in general and Chicago's workers in particular decided that the eight-hour workday was an idea whose time had come. Workers demonstrated, and a number of factories were struck. Management responded in kind. At McCormick Reaper strikers were replaced by "scabs." On May 3, when the scabs left the factory at the end of a long traditional workday, they were mobbed by the strikers. Chicago's police promptly opened fire and America's gilded age looked to be cracking open.

The next night, in Haymarket Square, the anarchists held a meeting presided over by the mayor of Chicago. A thousand workers listened to many thousands of highly incendiary words. But all was orderly until His Honor went home; then the police "dispersed" the meeting with that tact which has ever marked Hog City's law-enforcement officers. At one point, someone (never identified) threw a bomb; a number of policemen and workers were killed or wounded. Subsequently, there were numerous arrests and in-depth grillings.

Finally, more or less at random, eight men were indicted for "conspiracy to murder." There was no hard evidence of any kind. One man was not even in town that day while another was home playing cards. By and large, the great conservative Republic felt no compassion for anarchists, even the ones who had taken up the revolutionary game of bridge; worse, an eight-hour workday would drive a stake through the economy's heart.

On August 20, a prejudiced judge and jury found seven of the eight men guilty of murder in the first degree; the eighth man (who had not been in town that night) got fifteen years in the slammer because he had a big mouth. The anarchists' counsel, Judge Roger A. Pryor, then appealed the verdict to the Supreme Court.

During the short hot summer of 1886, the case was much discussed. The peculiar arbitrariness of condemning to death men whom no one had seen commit a crime but who had been heard, at one time or another, to use "incendiary and seditious language" was duly noted in bookish circles. Yet no intellectual of the slightest national importance spoke up. Of America's famous men of letters, Mark Twain maintained his habitual silence on any issue where he might, even for an instant, lose the love of the folks. Henry James was in London, somewhat shaken by the recent failure of not only *The Bostonians* but *The Princess Casamassima.* The sad young man of *The Princess Casamassima* is an anarchist, who has had, like James himself that year, "more news of life than he knew what to do with." Although Henry Adams's education was being conducted that summer in Japan, he had made, the previous year, an interesting comment on the American political system—or lack of one:

> Where no real principle divides us . . . some queer mechanical balance holds the two parties even, so that changes of great numbers of voters leave no trace in the sum total. I suspect the law will someday be formulated that in democratic societies, parties tend to an equilibrium.

As the original entropy man, Adams had to explain, somehow, the election of the Democrat Grover Cleveland in 1884, after a quarter-century of Republican abolitionist virtue and exuberant greed.

Of the Republic's major literary and intellectual figures (the division was not so clearly drawn then between town, as it were, and gown), only one took a public stand. At forty-nine, William Dean Howells was the author of that year's charming "realistic" novel, *Indian Summer;* he was also easily the busiest and smoothest of America's men of letters. Years before, he had come out of Ohio to conquer the world of literature; and had succeeded. He had been the first outlander to be editor of the *Atlantic Monthly.* In the year of the Haymarket Square riot, he had shifted the literary capital of the country from Boston to New York when he took over *Harper's Monthly,* for which he wrote a column called "The Editor's Study"; and a thousand other things as well. That summer Howells had been reading Tolstoi. In fact, Tolstoi was making a socialist out of him; and Howells was appalled by Chicago's judge, jury, and press. He was also turning out his column, a hasty affair by his own best standards but positively lapidary by ours.

In the September 1886 issue of *Harper's,* Howells, who had done so much to bring Turgenev and Tolstoi to the attention of American readers, decided to do the same for Dostoevsky, whose *Crime and Punishment* was then available only in a French translation. Since Howells had left school at fifteen, he had been able to become very learned indeed. He had taught himself Latin and Greek; learned Spanish, German, Italian, and French. He read many books in many languages, and he knew many things. He also wrote many books; and many of those books are of the first rank. He was different from us. Look at Dean run! Look at Dean read! Look-say what Dean writes!

While the Haymarket Square riots were causing Howells to question the basis of the American "democracy," he was describing a Russian writer who had been arrested for what he had written and sent off to Siberia where he was taken out to be shot but not shot—the kind of fun still to be found to this very day south of our borders where the dominoes roam. As Howells proceeded most shrewdly to explain Dostoevsky to American readers, he rather absently dynamited his own reputation for the next century. Although he admired Dostoevsky's art, he could find little similarity between the officially happy, shadowless United States and the dark Byzantine cruelties of czarist Russia:

> It is one of the reflections suggested by Dostoevsky's book that whoever struck a note so profoundly tragic in American fiction would do a false and mistaken thing. . . . Whatever their deserts, very few American novelists have been led out to be shot, or finally expelled to the rigors of a winter at Duluth. . . . We invite our novelists, therefore, to concern themselves with the more smiling aspects of life, which are the more American, and to seek the universal in the individual rather than the social interests. It is worth while even at the risk of being called commonplace, to be true to our well-to-do actualities.

This was meant to be a plea for realism. But it sounded like an invitation to ignore the sort of thing that was happening in Chicago. Ironists are often inadvertent victims of their own irony.

On November 2, 1887, the Supreme Court denied the anarchists' appeal. On November 4, Howells canvassed his literary peers. What to do? The dedicated abolitionist of thirty years earlier, George William Curtis, whose lecture *Political Infidelity* was a touchstone of political virtue, and the noble John Greenleaf Whittier agreed that something must be done; but they were damned if they were going to do it. So the belletrist who had just enjoined the nation's scribblers to address themselves to the smiling aspects of a near-perfect land hurled his own grenade at the courts.

In an open letter to the *New York Tribune* (published with deep reluctance by the ineffable Whitelaw Reid) Howells addressed all right-thinking persons to join with him in petitioning the governor of Illinois to commute the sentences. No respectable American man of letters had taken on the American system since Thomas Paine, who was neither American nor respectable. Of the Supreme Court, Howells wrote, it "simply affirmed the legality of the forms under which the Chicago court proceeded; it did not affirm the propriety of trying for murder men fairly indictable for conspiracy alone . . ." The men had been originally convicted of "constructive conspiracy to commit murder," a star-chamberish offense, based on their fiery language, and never proved to be relevant to the actual events in Haymarket Square. In any case, he made the point that the Supreme Court

> by no means approved the principle of punishing them because of their frantic opinions, for a crime which they were not shown to have committed. The justice or injustice of their sentence was not before the highest tribunal of our law, and unhappily could not be got there. That question must remain for history, which judges the judgment of courts, to deal with; and I, for one, cannot doubt what the decision of history will be.

Howells said that the remaining few days before the men were executed should be used to persuade the governor to show mercy. In the course of the next week the national press attacked Howells, which is what the American system has a national press for.

On November 11, four of the men, wearing what looked like surgical gowns, were hanged. Of the others, one had committed suicide and two had had their sentences commuted. On November 12, Howells, undaunted by the national hysteria now directed as much against him as against the enemies of property, wrote another public letter:

> It seems of course almost a pity to mix a note of regret with the hymn of thanksgiving for blood growing up from thousands of newspapers all over the land this morning; but I reflect that though I write amidst this joyful noise, my letter cannot reach the public before Monday at the earliest, and cannot therefore be regarded as an indecent interruption of the Te Deum.
>
> By that time journalism will not have ceased, but history will have at least begun. All over the world where civilized men can think and feel, they are even now asking themselves, For what, really, did those four men die so bravely? Why did one other die so miserably? Next week the journalistic theory that they died so because they were desperate murderers will have grown even more insufficient than it is now for the minds and hearts of dispassionate inquirers, and history will make the answer to which she must adhere for all time, *They died in the prime of the first Republic the world has ever known, for their opinions' sake* [original emphasis].

Howells then proceeds to make the case against the state's attorney general and the judge and the shrieking press. It is a devastating attack: "I have wished to deal with facts. One of these is that we had a political execution in Chicago yesterday. The sooner we realize this, the better for us." As polemic, Howells's letter is more devastating and eloquent than Emile Zola's *J'accuse*; as a defense of the right to express unpopular opinions, it is the equal of what we mistakenly take to be the thrust of Milton's *Areopagitica.*

Unfortunately, the letter was not published in the year 1887. Eventually, the manuscript was found in an envelope addressed to Whitelaw Reid. The piece had been revised three times. It is possible that a copy had been sent to Reid who had not published it; it is possible that Howells had had second thoughts about the possibilities of libel actions from judge and state's attorney general; it is possible that he was scared off by the general outcry against him. After all, he had not only a great career to worry about but an ill wife and a dying daughter. Whatever the reason, Howells let his great moment slip by. Even so, the letter-not-sent reveals a powerful mind affronted by "one of those spasms of paroxysmal righteousness to which our Anglo-Saxon race is peculiarly subject . . ." He also grimly notes that this "trial by passion, by terror, by prejudice, by hate, by newspaper" had ended with a result that has won "the approval of the entire nation."

I suspect that the cautious lifetime careerist advised the Tolstoian socialist to cool it. Howells was in enough trouble already. After all, he was the most successful magazine editor in the country; he was a best-selling novelist. He could not afford to lose a public made up mostly of ladies. So he was heard no more on the subject. But at least he, alone of the country's writers, had asked, publicly, on November 4, 1887, that justice be done.

Howells, a master of irony, would no doubt have found ironic in the extreme his subsequent reputation as a synonym for middle-brow pusillanimity. After all, it was he who was the spiritual father of Dreiser (whom he did nothing for, curiously enough) and of Stephen Crane and Harold Frederic and Frank Norris, for whom he did a very great deal. He managed to be the friend and confidant of both Henry James and Mark Twain, quite a trick. He himself wrote a half-dozen of the Republic's best novels. He was learned, witty, and generous.

Howells lived far too long. Shortly before his death at the age of eighty-four, he wrote his old friend Henry James: "I am comparatively a dead cult with my statues cut down and the grass growing over me in the pale moonlight." By then he had been dismissed by the likes of Sinclair Lewis as a dully beaming happy writer. But then Lewis knew as little of the American literary near-past as today's writers know, say, of Lewis. If Lewis had read Howells at all, he would have detected in the work of this American realist a darkness sufficiently sable for even the most lost-and-found of literary generations or, as Howells wrote James two years after the Haymarket Square riots: "After fifty years of optimistic content with 'civilization' and its ability to come out all right in the end, I now abhor it, and feel that it is coming out all wrong in the end unless it bases itself on a real equality." What that last phrase means is anyone's guess. He is a spiritual rather than a practical socialist. It is interesting that the letter was written in the same year that Edward Bellamy's *Looking Backward: 2000–1887* was published. The ideas of Robert Owen that Howells had absorbed from his father (later a Swedenborgian like Henry James, Sr.) were now commingled with the theories of Henry George, the tracts of William Morris, and, always, Tolstoi. Howells thought that there must be a path through the political jungle of a republic that had just hanged four men for their opinions; he never found it. But as a novelist he was making a path for himself and for others, and he called it realism.

## 2

On Thanksgiving Day 1858, the twenty-one-year-old Howells was received at the court of the nineteen-year-old first lady of Ohio, Kate Chase, a handsome ambitious motherless girl who acted as hostess to her father the governor, Salmon P. Chase, a handsome ambitious wifeless man who was, in Abraham Lincoln's thoughtful phrase, "on the subject of the Presidency, a little insane."

Howells had grown up in Ohio; his father was an itinerant newspaper editor and publisher. He himself was a trained printer as well as an ambitious but not insane poet. Under the influence of Heine, he wrote a number of poems; one was published in the *Atlantic Monthly.* He was big in Cleveland. Howells and Kate got on well; she teased him for his social awkwardness; he charmed her as he charmed almost everyone. Although he wrote about the doings of the Ohio legislature for the Cincinnati *Gazette,* he preferred the company of cultivated ladies to that of politicians. A passionate autodidact, he tended to prefer the company of books to people. But through Kate he met future presidents and was served at table by his first butler.

In a sense the Chase connection was the making of Howells. When Lincoln won the Republican presidential nomination in 1860, Howells was chosen, somewhat improbably, to write a campaign biography of the candidate. Characteristically, Howells sent a friend to Springfield to chat with the subject of his book; he himself never met Lincoln. He then cobbled together a book that Lincoln did not think too bad. One suspects that he did not think it too good, either. Shortly before the president was shot, he withdrew the book for the second time from the Library of Congress: nice that he did not have a copy of it on the coffee table in the Blue Room, but then Lincoln was so unlike, in so many ways, our own recent sovereigns.

Once Lincoln was president, Chase became secretary of the treasury. Chase proposed that the campaign biographer be rewarded with a consulate. But nothing happened until Howells himself went to Washington where he found an ally in Lincoln's very young and highly literary second secretary, John Hay, who, with the first secretary, John Nicolay, finally got Howells the consulate at Venice.

It is odd to think that a writer as curiously American as Howells should have been shaped by the Most Serene Republic at a bad moment in that ancient polity's history—the Austrian occupation—rather than by the United States at the most dramatic moment in that polity's history: the Civil War. Odd, also, that Howells managed, like the other two major writers of his generation, to stay out of the war. Neither Mark Twain nor Henry James rushed to the colors.

Since Howells had practically no official work to do, he learned Italian and perfected his German and French. He turned out poems that did not get printed in the *Atlantic.* "Not one of the MSS you have sent us," wrote the editor, "swims our seas." So Howells went off the deep end, into prose. He wrote Venetian sketches of great charm; he was always to be a good—even original—travel writer. Where the previous generation of Irving and Hawthorne had tended to love far too dearly a ruined castle wall, Howells gave the reader not only the accustomed romantic wall but the laundry drying on it, too. The Boston *Advertiser* published him.

Then came the turning point, as Howells termed it, in his life. He had acquired a charming if garrulous wife, who talked even more than Mark Twain's wife, or as Twain put it, when Elinor Howells entered a room "dialogue ceased and monologue inherited its assets and continued the business at the old stand." Howells wrote a serious study of the Italian theater called "Recent Italian Comedy," which he sent to the *North American Review,* the most prestigious of American papers, coedited by his friend James Russell Lowell and Charles Eliot Norton. At the time, Boston and Cambridge were in the throes of advanced Italophilia. Longfellow was translating Dante; and all the ladies spoke of Michelangelo. Lowell accepted the essay. Howells was now on his way, as a *serious* writer.

After nearly four years in Venice, which he did not much care for, Howells returned to New York. With a book of sketches called *Venetian Life* at the printers, he went job hunting. He was promptly hired by E. L. Godkin to help edit *The Nation.* Not long after, he was hired by the *Atlantic*

*Monthly* as assistant to the editor; then from 1871 to 1881 he was editor in chief. In Boston, Howells was now at the heart of an American literary establishment which had no way of knowing that what looked to be eternal noon was actually Indian summer—for New England.

Just before Howells had gone to Venice, he had made the rounds of New England's literary personages. He had met Holmes and Hawthorne whom he had liked; and Emerson whom he had not. Now, at the *Atlantic*, every distinguished writer came his editorial way; and soon he himself would be one of them. But what sort of writer was he to be? Poetry was plainly not his métier. Journalism was always easy for him, but he was ambitious. That left the novel, an art form which was not yet entirely "right." The American product of the 1860s was even less "aesthetic" than the English and neither was up to the French, who were, alas, sexually vicious, or to the Russians, who were still largely untranslated except for the Paris-based Turgenev. At this interesting moment, Howells had one advantage denied his contemporaries, always excepting Henry James. He could read—and he had read—the new Europeans in the original. He went to school to Zola and Flaubert. Realism was in the European air, but how much reality could Americans endure? Out of the tension between the adventurousness of Flaubert and the edgy reticence of Hawthorne came the novels of William Dean Howells.

From Heine, Howells had learned the power of the plain style. Mark Twain had also learned the same lesson—from life. Whereas the previous generation of Melville and Hawthorne had inclined to elevated, even "poetic" prose, Twain and Howells and James the First were relatively straightforward in their prose and quotidian in their effects—no fauns with pointed ears need apply. In fact, when Howells first met Hawthorne, he shyly pointed to a copy of *The Blithedale Romance* and told the great man that that was his own favorite of the master's works. Hawthorne appeared pleased; and said, "The Germans like it, too."

But realism, for Howells, had its limits. He had grown up in a happy if somewhat uncertain environment: His father was constantly changing jobs, houses, religions. For a writer, Howells himself was more than usually a dedicated hypochondriac whose adolescence was shadowed by the certainty that he had contracted rabies which would surface in time to kill him at sixteen. Like most serious hypochondriacs, he enjoyed full rude health until he was eighty. But there were nervous collapses. Also, early in life, Howells had developed a deep aversion to sexual irregularity, which meant any form of sexuality outside marriage. When his mother befriended a knocked-up seamstress, the twelve-year-old Howells refused to pass her so much as the salt at table.

In Venice he could not get over the fact that there could be no social intercourse of any kind with unmarried girls (unlike the fun to be had with The American Girl, soon to be celebrated not only by Henry James but by Howells himself), while every married woman seemed bent on flinging even the purest of young bachelors into the sack. Doubtless, he kept himself chaste until marriage. But he railed a good deal against European decadence, to the amusement of the instinctively more worldly, if perhaps less operative Henry ("Oh, my aching back!") James, who used to tease him about the latest descriptions of whorehouses to be found in French fiction. Nevertheless, for a writer who was to remain an influence well into the twentieth century, an aversion to irregular sexuality was not apt to endear him to a later generation which, once it could put sex into the novel, proceeded to leave out almost everything else. Where the late-nineteenth-century realistic novel might be said to deal with social climbing, the twentieth-century novel has dealt with sexual climbing, an activity rather easier to do than to write about.

The Library of America now brings us four of Howells's novels written between 1875 and 1886. Before the publications of these four novels, Howells had already published his first novel *Their Wedding Journey* (1871); his second novel *A Chance Acquaintance* (1873); as well as sketches of Italy, people, and yet another personage. Elinor Mead Howells was a cousin of President Rutherford (known to all good Democrats as Rather-fraud) B. Hayes. So the campaign biographer of Lincoln, duly and dutifully and dully, wrote a book called *Sketch of the Life and Character of Rutherford B. Hayes* (1876). Thanks to Cousin Hayes, Howells was now able to reward those who had helped him. James Russell Lowell was sent to London as American ambassador.

Of the books written before *A Foregone Conclusion* (the first of the four now reissued), the ever-polite but never fraudulent Turgenev wrote Howells in 1874:

> Accept my best thanks for the gracious gift of your delightful book *Their Wedding Journey,* which I have read with the same pleasure experienced before in reading *A Chance Acquaintance* and *Venetian Life.* Your literary physiognomy is a most sympathetic one; it is natural, simple and clear—and in the same time—it is full of unobtrusive poetry and fine humor. Then—I feel the peculiar American stamp on it—and that is not one of the least causes of my relishing so much your works.

This was written in English. In a sense, Turgenev is responding to Howells's championing of his own work (Howells had reviewed *Lisa* and *Rudin*) but he is also responding to a sympathetic confrere, a young writer whom he has influenced though not so much as has "the peculiar American stamp." Unfortunately, Turgenev never lived to read the later books. It would be interesting to see what he might have made of *A Modern Instance,* a book as dark and, at times, as melodramatic as a novel by Zola whose *L'Assommoir* Turgenev disliked.

*A Foregone Conclusion* (1875) has, as protagonist, the—what else?—American consul at Venice. The consul is a painter (young writers almost always make their protagonists artists who practice the one art that they themselves know nothing about: It's the light, you see, in Cimabue). The consul attracts a young priest, Don Ippolito, who wants to emigrate to America and become an inventor. It is no accident that practically the first building in Washington to be completed in imperial marble splendor was the Patent Office. Don Ippolito is a sort of Italian Major Hoople. The inventions don't really work but he keeps on because "Heaven only knows what kind of inventor's Utopia our poor, patent-ridden country appeared to him in those dreams of his, and I can but dimly figure it to myself." Here the auctorial "I" masquerades as the "I" of the consul, Ferris, who is otherwise presented in the objective third person. Howells has not entirely learned Turgenev's lesson: stay out of the narrative. Let the characters move the narration and the reader. Howells's native American garrulousness—and tendentiousness—occasionally breaks in.

Enter, inexorably, middle-aged American lady and daughter—Mrs. Vervain and Florida. This was four years before Howells's friend sicked *Daisy Miller* on to a ravished world. But then The American Girl was to be a Howells theme, just as it was to be James's and, later, and in a much tougher way, Mrs. Wharton's. As every writer then knew, the readers of novels were mostly women, and they liked to read about the vicissitudes of young women, preferably ladies. But while James would eventually transmute his American girls into something that Euripides himself might find homely (e.g., Maggie Verver), Howells tends, gently, to mock. Incidentally, I do not believe that it has ever before been noted that the portrait of Florida is uncannily like Kate Chase.

It is a foregone conclusion that American girl and American mother ("the most extraordinary combination of perfect fool and perfect lady I ever saw") will miss the point to Don Ippolito and Venice and Europe, and that he will miss the point to them. Don Ippolito falls in love with Florida. The Americans are horrified. How can a priest sworn to celibacy . . . ? Since they are Protestants, the enormity of his fall from Roman Catholic grace is all the greater. Although Don Ippolito is perfectly happy to give up the Church, they will not let him. Mother and daughter flee. As for Ferris, he has misunderstood not only Don Ippolito but Florida's response to him. Don Ippolito dies—with the comment to Ferris, "You would never see me as I was."

The consul goes home to the States and joins the army. Like so many other characters in the works of those writers who managed to stay out of the Civil War, Ferris has a splendid war: "Ferris's regiment was sent to a part of the southwest where he saw a good deal of fighting and fever and ague" (probably a lot easier than trying to get a job at the *Atlantic*). "At the end of two years, spent alternately in the field and the hospital, he was riding out near the camp one morning in unusual spirits, when two men in butternut fired at him: one had the mortification to miss him; the bullet of the other struck him in the arm. There was talk of amputation at first . . ." Pre-dictaphone and word processor, it was every writer's nightmare that he lose his writing arm. But, worse, Ferris is a painter: *he can never crosshatch again.* Broke, at a loose end, he shows an old picture at an exhibition. Florida sees the picture. They are reunited. Mrs. Vervain is dead. Florida is rich. Ferris is poor. What is to be done?

It is here that the avant-garde realism of Howells shoves forward the whole art of the popular American novel: "It was fortunate for Ferris, since he could not work, that she had money; in exalted moments he had thought this a barrier to their marriage; yet he could not recall anyone who had refused the hand of a beautiful girl because of the accident of her wealth, and in the end, he silenced his scruples." This is highly satisfying.

Then Howells, perhaps a bit nervous at just how far he has gone in the direction of realism, tosses a bone of marzipan to the lady-reader: "It might be said that in many other ways he was not her equal; but one ought to reflect how very few men are worthy of their wives in any sense." Sighs of relief from many a hammock and boudoir! How well he knows the human heart.

Howells smiles at the end; but the smile is aslant, while the point to the tragedy (not Ferris's for he had none, but that of Don Ippolito) is that, during the subsequent years of Ferris's marriage, Don Ippolito "has at last ceased to be even the memory of a man with a passionate love and a mortal sorrow. Perhaps this final effect in the mind of him who has realized the happiness of which the poor priest vainly dreamed is not the least tragic phase of the tragedy of Don Ippolito."

This coda is unexpectedly harsh—and not at all smiling. A priest ought not to fall in love. It is a foregone conclusion that if you violate the rules governing sexuality, society will get you, as Mrs. Wharton would demonstrate so much more subtly in *The Age of Innocence*; and Henry James would subtly deny since he knew, in a way that Howells did not, that the forbidden cake could be both safely eaten and kept. It is an odd irony that the donnée on which James based *The Ambassadors* was a remark that the fifty-seven-year-old Howells made to a friend in Paris: No matter what, one ought to have one's life; that it was too late for him, personally, but for someone young . . . "Don't, at any rate, make *my* mistake," Howells said. "Live!"

Kenneth S. Lynn has put the case, persuasively to my mind, that the "happy endings" of so many of Howells's novels are deliberately "hollow or ironic." After all, it was Howells who had fashioned the, to Edith Wharton, "lapidary phrase": Americans want tragedies with happy endings. There are times when Howells's conclusion—let's end with a marriage and live happily ever after—carry more formidable weight than the sometimes too-lacquered tragic codas of James: "We shall never be again as we were." The fact is that people are almost always exactly as they were and they will be so again and again, given half a chance.

At forty-four, the highly experienced man of letters began his most ambitious novel, *A Modern Instance.* Although the story starts in a New England village, the drama is acted out in the Boston of Howells's professional life, and the very unusual protagonist is a newspaperman on the make who charms everyone and hoodwinks a few; he also puts on too much weight, steals another man's story, and makes suffer the innocent young village heiress whom he marries. In a sense, Howells is sending himself up; or some dark side of himself. Although Bartley Hubbard is nowhere in Howells's class as a writer, much less standard-bearer for Western civilization, he is a man who gets what he wants through personal charm, hard work, and the ability to write recklessly and scandalously for newspapers in a way that the young William Randolph Hearst would capitalize on at century's end, thus making possible today's antipodean "popular" press, currently best exemplified by London's giggly newspapers.

Unlike Howells, or the Howells that we think we know, Bartley is sexually active; he is not about to make the Howells-Strether mistake. He *lives* until he is murdered by a man whom he may have libeled in a western newspaper. It would have been more convincing if an angry husband had been responsible for doing him in, but there were conventions that Howells felt obliged to observe, as his detractors, among them Leslie Fielder, like to remind us. Mr. Fielder writes in *Love and Death in the American Novel* (1975):

> Only in *A Modern Instance,* written in 1882 [*sic*: 1881], does Howells deal for once with a radically unhappy marriage; and here he adapts the genteel-sentimental pattern which had substituted the bad husband (his Bartley Hubbard has "no more moral nature than a baseball") for the Seducer, the long-suffering wife for the Persecuted Maiden or fallen woman.

Mr. Fiedler, of course, is—or was in 1960—deeply into "the reality of dream and nightmare, fantasy and fear," and for him Howells is "the author of flawlessly polite, high-minded, well-written studies of untragic, essentially eventless life in New England—the antiseptic upper-middle-brow romance. Yet his forty books [*sic:* he means novels, of which Howells wrote thirty-five; there are close to one hundred books], in which there are no seductions and only rare moments of violence, are too restrictedly 'realistic', too . . . ," *et cetera.*

Mr. Fiedler gets himself a bit off the hook by putting those quotes around the word realistic. After all, Howells had developed an aesthetic of the novel: and if he preferred to shoot Bartley offstage, why not? The classic tragedians did the same. He also inclined to Turgenev's view that the real drama is in the usual. Obviously, this is not the way of the romantic writer but it is a no less valid way of apprehending reality than that of Melville or Faulkner, two writers Howells would have called "romancers," about as much a term of compliment with him as "too unrestrictedly 'realistic' " is to Mr. Fiedler. Without rehashing the tired Redskin versus Paleface debate of the 1940s, it should be noted that there is something wrong with a critical bias that insists upon, above all else, "dream and nightmare, fantasy and fear" but then when faced with the genuine article in, say, the books of William Burroughs or James Purdy or Paul Bowles starts to back off, nervously, lighting candles to The Family and all the other life-enhancing if unsmiling aspects of American life that do *not* cause AIDS or social unrest.

Whatever our romantic critics may say, Bartley Hubbard is an archetypal American figure, caught for the first time by Howells: the amiable, easy-going bastard, who thinks nothing of taking what belongs to another. Certainly Mark Twain experienced the shock of recognition when he read the book: "You didn't intend Bartley for me but he *is* me just the same . . ." James, more literary, thought the character derived from Tito, in the one (to me) close-to-bad novel of George Eliot, *Romola.* In later years Howells said that he himself was the model. Who was what makes no difference. There is only one Bartley Hubbard, and he appears for the first time in the pages of a remarkable novel that opened the way to Dreiser and to all those other realists who were to see the United States plain. The fact that there are no overt sexual scenes in Howells ("no palpitating divans," as he put it) does not mean that sexual passion is not a powerful motor to many of the situations, as in life. On the other hand, the fact that there are other motors—ambition, greed, love of power—simply extends the author's range and makes him more interesting to read than most writers.

In this novel, Howells is interesting on the rise of journalism as a "serious" occupation. "There had not yet begun to be that talk of journalism as a profession which has since prevailed with our collegians . . ." There is also a crucial drunk scene in which Bartley blots his copybook with Boston; not to mention with his wife. It is curious how often Howells shows a protagonist who gets disastrously drunk and starts then to fall. Mark Twain had a dark suspicion that Howells always had *him* in mind when he wrote these scenes. But for Mr. Fiedler, "drunkenness is used as a chief symbol for the husband's betrayal of the wife." Arguably, it would have been better (and certainly more manly) if Bartley had cornholed the Irish maid in full view of wife and child, but would a scene so powerful, even *existential,* add in any way to the delicate moral balances that Howells is trying to make?

After all, Howells is illuminating a new character in American fiction, if not life, who, as "he wrote more than ever in the paper . . . discovered in himself that dual life, of which every one who sins or sorrows is sooner or later aware: that strange separation of the intellectual activity from the suffering of the soul, by which the mind toils on in a sort of ironical indifference to the pangs that wring the heart; the realization that in some ways his brain can get on perfectly well without his conscience." This is worthy of the author of *Sentimental Education*; it is also the kind of insight about post-Christian man that Flaubert so often adverted to, indirectly, in his own novels and head-on in his letters.

*The Rise of Silas Lapham* (1885) begins with Bartley Hubbard brought back to life. It is, obviously, some years earlier than the end of *A Modern Instance.* Bartley is interviewing a self-made man called Silas Lapham who has made a fortune out of paint. Lapham is the familiar diamond in the rough, New England Jonathan style. He has two pretty daughters, a sensible wife, a comfortable house; and a growing fortune, faced with all the usual hazards. Howells makes the paint business quite as interesting as Balzac made paper making. This is not entirely a full-hearted compliment to either; nevertheless, each is a novelist fascinated by the way the real world works; and each makes it interesting to read about.

In a sense, Silas Lapham's rise is not unlike that of William Dean Howells: from a small town to Boston back street to Beacon Street on the Back Bay. But en route to the great address there are many lesser houses and Howells is at his best when he goes house hunting—and building. In fact, one suspects that, like Edith Wharton later, he would have made a splendid architect and interior decorator. In a fine comic scene, a tactful architect (plainly the author himself) guides Lapham to Good Taste. " 'Of course,' resumed the architect, 'I know there has been a great craze for black walnut. But it's an ugly wood . . .' " All over the United States there must have been feminine gasps as stricken eyes were raised from the page to focus on the middle distance where quantities of once-beauteous black shone dully by gaslight; but worse was to come: " '. . . and for a drawing room there is really nothing like white paint. We should want to introduce a little gold here and there. Perhaps we might run a painted frieze round under the cornice—garlands of roses on a gold ground; it would tell wonderfully in a white room.' " From that moment on, no more was black walnut seen again in the parlors of the Republic, while the sale of white paint soared; gold, too.

The rise of Lapham's house on Beacon Hill is, in a sense, the plot of the book, as well as the obvious symbol of worldly success. Howells makes us see and feel and smell the house as it slowly takes shape. Simultaneously, a young man called Tom Corey wants to work for Lapham. Since Corey belongs to the old patriciate, Lapham finds it hard to believe Corey is serious. But the young man is sincere; he really likes the old man. He must also work to live. There are romantic exchanges between him and the two daughters; there is an amiable mix-up. Finally, Tom says that it is Penelope not her sister whom he wants to marry. Mr. and Mrs. Lapham are bemused. In the world of the Coreys they are a proto–Maggie and Jiggs couple.

Corey takes Lapham to a grand dinner party where the old man gets drunk and chats rather too much. It is the same scene, in a sense, as Bartley's fall in the earlier novel, but where Bartley could not have minded less the impression he made, Lapham is deeply humiliated; and the fall begins. He loses his money; the new house burns down; by then, the house is an even more poignant character than Lapham, and the reader mourns the white-and-gold drawing room gone to ash. But there is a happy enough ending. Maggie and Jiggs return to the Vermont village of their origin (which they should never have left?) while Corey marries Penelope.

> It would be easy to point out traits in Penelope's character which finally reconciled all her husband's family and endeared her to them. These things continually happen in novels; and the Coreys, as they had always promised themselves to do, made the best, and not the worst, of Tom's marriage. . . . But the differences remained uneffaced, if not uneffaceable, between the Coreys and Tom Corey's wife.

The young couple move from Boston. Then Howells shifts from the specific to the general:

> It is certain that our manners and customs go for more in life than our qualities. The price that we pay for civilization is the fine yet impassable differentiation of these. Perhaps we pay too much; but it will not be possible to persuade those who have the difference in their

> favor that this is so. They may be right; and at any rate the blank misgiving, the recurring sense of disappointment to which the young people's departure left the Coreys is to be considered. That was the end of their son and brother for them; they felt that; and they were not mean or unamiable people.

This strikes me as a subtle and wise reading of the world—no, not *a* world but *the* world; and quite the equal of James or Hardy.

Whether or not this sort of careful social reading is still of interest to the few people who read novels voluntarily is not really relevant. But then today's "serious" novel, when it is not reinventing itself as an artifact of words and signs, seldom deals with the world at all. One is no longer shown a businessman making money or his wife climbing up or down the social ladder. As most of our novelists now teach school, they tend to tell us what it is like to be a schoolteacher, and since schoolteachers have been taught to teach others to write only about what they know, they tell us what they know about, too, which is next to nothing about the way the rest of the population of the Republic lives.

In a sense, if they are realists, they are acting in good faith. If you don't know something about the paint business you had better not choose a protagonist who manufactures paint. Today, if the son of an Ohio newspaper editor would like to be a novelist, he would not quit school at fifteen to become a printer, and then learn six languages and do his best to read all the great literary figures of the present as well as of the past so that he could introduce, say, Barthes or Gadda to the American public while writing his own novels based on a close scrutiny of as many classes of society as he can get to know. Rather, he would graduate from high school; go on to a university and take a creative writing course; get an M.A. for having submitted a novel (about the son of an Ohio editor who grew up in a small town *and found out about sex* and wants to be a writer and so goes to a university where he submits, etc.).

Then, if he is truly serious about a truly serious literary career, he will become a teacher. With luck, he will obtain tenure. In the summers and on sabbatical, he will write novels that others like himself will want to teach just as he, obligingly, teaches their novels. He will visit other campuses as a lecturer and he will talk about his books and about those books written by other teachers to an audience made up of ambitious young people who intend to write novels to be taught by one another to the rising generation and so on and on. What tends to be left out of these works is the world. World gone, no voluntary readers. No voluntary readers, no literature—only creative writing courses and English studies, activities marginal (to put it tactfully) to civilization.

## 3

Civilization was very much on Howells's mind when he came to write *Indian Summer* (1886). He deals, once more, with Americans in Italy. But this time there are no Don Ippolitos. The principals are all Americans in Florence. A middle-aged man, Theodore Colville, meets, again, Mrs. Bowen, a lady who once did not marry him when he wanted to marry her. She married a congressman. She has a young daughter, Effie. She is a widow.

Colville started life as an architect, a suitable occupation for a Howells character; then he shifted to newspaper publishing, an equally suitable profession. In Des Vaches, Indiana, he published, successfully, the *Democrat-Republican* newspaper. Although he lost a race for Congress, he has received from former political opponents "fulsome" praise. Like most American writers Howells never learned the meaning of the word *fulsome.* Colville then sold his newspaper and went to Europe because "he wanted to get away, to get far away, and with the abrupt and total change in his humor he reverted to a period in his life when journalism and politics and the ambition of Congress were things undreamed of." He had been young in Italy, with a Ruskinian interest in architecture; he had loved and been rejected by Evelina—now the widow Bowen. He looks at Florence: "It is a city superficially so well known that it affects one somewhat like a collection of views of itself: they are from the most striking points, of course, but one has examined them before, and is disposed to be critical of them." The same goes for people one has known when young.

Mrs. Bowen has a beautiful young friend named Imogene. Colville decides that he is in love with Imogene, and they drift toward marriage. There are numerous misunderstandings. Finally, it is Mrs. Bowen not Imogene who is in love with Colville. The drama of the three of them (a shadowy young clergyman named Morton is an undelineated fourth) is rendered beautifully. There are many unanticipated turns to what could easily have been a simpleminded romantic novella.

When Colville is confronted with the thought of his own great age (forty-one), he is told by a very old American expatriate:

> At forty, one has still a great part of youth before him—perhaps the richest and sweetest part. By that time the turmoil of ideas and sensations is over; we see clearly and feel consciously. We are in a sort of quiet in which we peacefully enjoy. We have enlarged our perspective sufficiently to perceive things in their true proportion and relation; we are no longer tormented with the lurking fear of death, which darkens and imbitters our earlier years; we have got into the habit of life; we have often been ailing and we have not died . . .

Finally, "we are put into the world to be of it." Thus, Howells strikes the Tolstoian note. Yes, he is also smiling. But even as *Indian Summer* was being published, its author was attacking the state of Illinois for the murder of four workmen. He also sends himself up in the pages of his own novel. A Mrs. Amsden finds Colville and Imogene and Effie together after an emotional storm. Mrs. Amsden remarks that they form an interesting, even dramatic group:

> "Oh, call us a passage from a modern novel," suggested Colville, "if you're in a romantic mood. One of Mr. James's."
>
> "Don't you think we ought to be rather more of the great world for that? I hardly feel up to Mr. James. I should have said Howells. Only nothing happens in that case."

For this beguiling modesty Howells no doubt dug even deeper the grave for his reputation. How can an American novelist who is ironic about himself ever be great? In a nation that has developed to a high art advertising, the creator who refuses to advertise himself is immediately suspected of having no product worth selling. Actually, Howells is fascinated with the interior drama of his characters, and quite a lot happens—to the reader as well as to the characters who are, finally, suitably paired: Imogene and Mr. Morton, Colville and Mrs. Bowen.

The Library of America has served William Dean Howells well. Although the spiritual father of the library, Edmund Wilson, did not want this project ever to fall into the hands of the Modern Language Association, all four of the novels in the present volume bear the proud emblem of that association. One can only assume that there are now fewer scholars outside academe's groves than within. I found no misprints; but there are eccentricities.

In *A Modern Instance* (p. 474) we read of "the presidential canvas of the summer"; then (p. 485) we read "But the political canvass . . ." Now a tent is made of canvas and an election is a canvass of votes. It is true that the secondary spelling of "canvass" is "canvas" and so allowable; nevertheless, it is disturbing to find the same word spelled two ways within eleven pages. On page 3 the variant spelling "ancles" is used for "ankles." On page 747 Howells writes "party-colored statues" when, surely, "parti-colored" was nineteenth-century common usage as opposed to the Chaucerian English "party." Of course, as the editors tell us, "In nineteenth-century writings, for example, a word might be spelled in more than one way, even in the same work, and such variations might be carried into print."

Anyway, none of this is serious. There are no disfiguring footnotes. The notes at the back are for the most part helpful translations of foreign phrases in the text. The chronology of Howells's life is faultless but perhaps, skimpy. For those who are obliged for career reasons to read Howells, this is a useful book. For those who are still able to read novels for pleasure, this is a marvelous book.

For some years I have been haunted by a story of Howells and that most civilized of all our presidents, James A. Garfield. In the early 1870s Howells and his father paid a call on Garfield. As they sat on Garfield's veranda, young Howells began to talk about poetry and about the poets that he had met in Boston and New York. Suddenly, Garfield told him to stop. Then Garfield went to the edge of the veranda and shouted to his Ohio neighbors. "Come over here! He's telling about Holmes, and Longfellow, and Lowell, and Whittier!" So the neighbors gathered around in the dusk; then Garfield said to Howells, "Now go on."

Today we take it for granted that no living president will ever have heard the name of any living poet. This is not, necessarily, an unbearable loss. But it is unbearable to have lost those Ohio neighbors who actually read books of poetry and wanted to know about the poets.

For thirty years bookchat writers have accused me of having written that the novel is dead. I wrote no such thing but bookchat writers have the same difficulty extracting meaning from writing as presidents do. What I wrote was, "After some three hundred years the novel in English has lost the general reader (or rather the general reader has lost the novel), and I propose that he will not again recover his old enthusiasm." Since 1956, the audience for the serious (or whatever this year's adjective is) novel has continued to shrink. Arguably, the readers that are left are for the most part involuntary ones, obliged by the schools to read novels that they often have little taste for. The fact that a novelist like Howells—or even Bellow—is probably no longer accessible to much of anyone would be bearable if one felt that the sense of alternative worlds or visions or—all right, Leslie—nightmares, fantasies, fears could be obtained in some other way. But movies are no substitute while television is, literally, narcotizing: The human eye was not designed to stare at a light for any length of time. Popular prose fictions are still marketed with TV and movie tie-ins, but even the writers or word-processors of these books find it harder and harder to write simply enough for people who don't really know how to read.

Obviously, there is a great deal wrong with our educational system, as President Reagan recently, and rather gratuitously, noted. After all, an educated electorate would not have elected him president. It is generally agreed that things started to go wrong with the schools after the First World War. The past was taught less and less, and Latin and Greek ceased to be compulsory. Languages were either not taught or taught so badly that they might just as well not have been taught at all, while American history books grew more and more mendacious, as Frances FitzGerald so nicely described (*America Revised,* 1979), and even basic geography is now a nonsubject. Yet the average "educated" American has been made to believe that, somehow, the United States must lead the world even though hardly anyone has any information at all about those countries we are meant to lead. Worse, we have very little information about our own country and its past. That is why it is not really possible to compare a writer like Howells with any living American writer because Howells thought that it was a good thing to know as much as possible about his own country as well as other countries while our writers today, in common with the presidents and paint manufacturers, live in a present without past among signs whose meanings are uninterpretable.

Edmund Wilson's practical response was to come up with the idea of making readily available the better part of American literature; hence, the Library of America. It is a step in the right direction. But will this library attract voluntary readers? Ultimately—and paradoxically—that will depend on the schools.

Since no one quite knows what a university ought to do, perhaps *that* should be the subject of our educational system. What variety of things should *all* educated people know? What is it that we don't know that we need to know? Naturally, there is a certain risk in holding up a mirror to the system itself (something the realistic novelist always used to do) because one is apt to see, glaring back, the face of Caliban or, worse, plain glass reflecting glass. But something must now be done because Herzen's terrible truth is absolutely true: "The end of each generation is itself."

***The New York Review of Books***
***October 27, 1983***

# Calvino's Death

On the morning of Friday, September 20, 1985, the first equinoctial storm of the year broke over the city of Rome. I awoke to thunder and lightning; and thought I was, yet again, in the Second World War. Shortly before noon, a car and driver arrived to take me up the Mediterranean coast to a small town on the sea called Castiglion della Pescáia where, at one o'clock, Italo Calvino, who had died the day before, would be buried in the village cemetery.

Calvino had had a cerebral hemorrhage two weeks earlier while sitting in the garden of his house at Pineta di Roccamare, where he had spent the summer working on the Charles Eliot Norton lectures that he planned to give during the fall and winter at Harvard. I last saw him in May. I commended him on his bravery: He planned to give the lectures in English, a language that he read easily but spoke hesitantly, unlike French and Spanish, which he spoke perfectly; but then he had been born in Cuba, son of two Italian agronomists; and had lived for many years in Paris.

It was night. We were on the terrace of my apartment in Rome; an overhead light made his deep-set eyes look even darker than usual. Italo gave me his either-this-or-that frown; then he smiled, and when he smiled, suddenly, the face would become like that of an enormously bright child who has just worked out the unified field theory. "At Harvard, I shall stammer," he said. "But then I stammer in every language."

Unlike the United States, Italy has both an educational system (good or bad is immaterial) and a common culture, both good and bad. In recent years Calvino had become the central figure in Italy's culture. Italians were proud that they had produced a world writer whose American reputation began, if I may say so, since no one else has, when I described all of his novels as of May 30, 1974, in *The New York Review of Books.* By 1985, except for England, Calvino was read wherever books are read. I even found a Calvino coven in Moscow's literary bureaucracy, and I think that I may have convinced the state publishers to translate more of him. Curiously, the fact that he had slipped away from the Italian Communist party in 1957 disturbed no one.

Three weeks short of Calvino's sixty-second birthday, he died; and Italy went into mourning, as if a beloved prince had died. For an American, the contrast between them and us is striking. When an American writer dies, there will be, if he's a celebrity (fame is no longer possible for any of us), a picture below the fold on the front page; later, a short appreciation on the newspaper's book page (if there is one), usually the work of a journalist or other near-writer who has not actually read any of the dead author's work but is at home with the arcana of gossipy "Page Six"; and that would be that.

In Calvino's case, the American newspaper obituaries were perfunctory and incompetent: The circuits between the English departments, where our tablets of literary reputation are now kept, and the world of journalism are more than ever fragile and the reception is always bad. Surprisingly, *Time* and *Newsweek,* though each put him on the "book page," were not bad, though one thought him "surrealist" and the other a "master of fantasy"; he was, of course, a true realist, who believed "that only a certain prosaic solidity can give birth to creativity: fantasy is like jam; you have to spread it on a solid slice of bread. If not, it remains a shapeless thing, like jam, out of which you can't make anything." This homely analogy is from an Italian television interview, shown after his death.

*The New York Times,* to show how well regarded Calvino is in these parts, quoted John Updike, our literature's perennial apostle to the middlebrows* (this is not meant, entirely, unkindly), as well as Margaret Atwood (a name new to me), Ursula K. Le Guin (an estimable sci-fi writer, but what is she doing, giving, as it were, a last word on one of the most complex of modern writers?), Michael Wood, whose comment was pretty good, and, finally, the excellent Anthony Burgess, who was not up to his usual par on this occasion. Elsewhere, Mr. Herbert Mitgang again quoted Mr. Updike as well as John Gardner, late apostle to the lowbrows, a sort of Christian evangelical who saw Heaven as a paradigmatic American university.

*Although the three estates, high-, middle-, and lowbrow, are as dead as Dwight Macdonald, their most vigorous deployer, something about today's literary scene, combined with Calvino's death, impels me to resurrect the terms. Presently, I shall demonstrate.

Europe regarded Calvino's death as a calamity for culture. A literary critic, as opposed to theorist, wrote at length in *Le Monde,* while in Italy itself, each day for two weeks, bulletins from the hospital at Siena were published, and the whole country was suddenly united in its esteem not only for a great writer but for someone who reached not only primary schoolchildren through his collections of folk and fairy tales but, at one time or another, everyone else who reads.

After the first hemorrhage, there was a surgical intervention that lasted many hours. Calvino came out of coma. He was disoriented: He thought that one of the medical attendants was a policeman; then he wondered if he'd had open-heart surgery. Meanwhile, the surgeon had become optimistic, even garrulous. He told the press that he'd never seen a brain structure of such delicacy and complexity as that of Calvino. I thought immediately of the smallest brain ever recorded, that of Anatole France. The surgeon told the press that he had been obliged to do his very best. After all, he and his sons had read and argued over *Marcovaldo* last winter. The brain that could so puzzle them must be kept alive in all its rarity. One can imagine a comparable surgeon in America: Only last Saturday she had kept me and my sons in stitches; now I could hardly believe that I was actually gazing into the fabulous brain of Joan Rivers! On the other hand, the admirer of Joan Rivers might have saved Calvino; except that there was no real hope, ever. In June he had had what he thought was a bad headache; it was the first stroke. Also, he came from a family with a history of arterial weakness. Or so it was said in the newspapers. The press coverage of Calvino's final days resembled nothing so much as that of the recent operation on the ancient actor that our masters have hired to impersonate a president, the sort of subject that used to delight Calvino—the Acting President, that is.

As we drove north through the rain, I read Calvino's last novel, *Palomar.* He had given it to me on November 28, 1983. I was chilled—and guilty—to read for the first time the inscription: "For Gore, these last meditations about Nature, Italo." *Last* is a word artists should not easily use. What did this "last" mean? Latest? Or his last attempt to write about the phenomenal world? Or did he know, somehow, that he was in the process of "Learning to be dead," the title of the book's last chapter?

I read the book. It is very short. A number of meditations on different subjects by one Mr. Palomar, who is Calvino himself. The settings are, variously, the beach at Castiglion della Pescáia, the nearby house in the woods at Roccamare, the flat in Rome with its terrace, a food specialty shop in Paris. This is not the occasion to review the book. But I made some observations and marked certain passages that seemed to me to illuminate the prospect.

Palomar is on the beach at Castiglion: he is trying to figure out the nature of waves. Is it possible to follow just one? Or do they all become one? *E pluribus unum* and its reverse might well sum up Calvino's approach to our condition. Are we a part of the universe? Or is the universe, simply, us thinking that there is such a thing? Calvino often writes like the scientist that his parents were. He observes, precisely, the minutiae of nature: stars, waves, lizards, turtles, a woman's breast exposed on the beach. In the process, he vacillates between macro and micro. The whole and the part. Also, tricks of eye. The book is written in the present tense, like a scientist making reports on that ongoing experiment, the examined life.

The waves provide him with suggestions but no answers: Viewed in a certain way, they seem to come not from the horizon but from the shore itself. "Is this perhaps the real result that Mr. Palomar is about to achieve? To make the waves run in the opposite direction, to overturn time, to perceive the true substance of the world beyond sensory and mental habits?" But it doesn't quite work, and he cannot extend "this knowledge to the entire universe." He notes during his evening swim that "the sun's reflection becomes a shining sword on the water stretching from shore to him. Mr. Palomar swims in that sword . . ." But then so does everyone else at that time of day, each in the same sword which is everywhere and nowhere. "The sword is imposed equally on the eye of each swimmer; there is no avoiding it. 'Is what we have in common precisely what is given to each of us as something exclusively his?' " As Palomar floats he wonders if he exists. He drifts now toward solipsism: "If no eye except the glassy eye of the dead were to open again on the surface of the terraqueous globe, the sword would not gleam any more." He develops this, floating on his back. "Perhaps it was not the birth of the eye that caused the birth of the sword, but vice versa, because the sword had to have an eye to observe it at its climax." But the day is ending, the windsurfers are all beached, and Palomar comes back to land: "He has become convinced that the sword will exist even without him."

In the garden at Roccamare, Palomar observes the exotic mating of turtles; he ponders the blackbird's whistle, so like that of a human being that it might well be the same sort of communication. "Here a prospect that is very promising for Mr. Palomar's thinking opens out; for him the discrepancy between human behavior and the rest of the universe has always been a source of anguish. The equal whistle of man and blackbird now seems to him a bridge thrown over the abyss." But his attempts to communicate with them through a similar whistling leads to "puzzlement" on both sides. Then, contemplating the horrors of his lawn and its constituent parts, among them weeds, he precisely names and numbers what he sees until "he no longer thinks of the lawn: he thinks of the universe. He is trying to apply to the universe everything he has thought about the lawn. The universe as regular and ordered cosmos or as chaotic proliferation." The analogy, as always with Calvino, then takes off (the jam on the bread) and the answer is again the many within the one, or "collections of collections."

Observations and meditations continue. He notes, "Nobody looks at the moon in the afternoon, and this is the moment when it would most require our attention, since its existence is still in doubt." As night comes on, he wonders if the moon's bright splendor is "due to the slow retreat of the sky, which, as it moves away, sinks deeper and deeper into darkness or whether, on the contrary it is the moon that is coming forward, collecting the previously scattered light and depriving the sky of it, concentrating it all in the round mouth of its funnel." One begins now to see the method of a Calvino meditation. He looks; he describes; he has a scientist's respect for data (the opposite of the surrealist or fantasist). He wants us to see not only what he sees but what we may have missed by not looking with sufficient attention. It is no wonder that Galileo crops up in his writing. The received opinion of mankind over the centuries (which is what middlebrow is all about) was certain that the sun moved around the earth but to a divergent highbrow's mind, Galileo's or Calvino's, it is plainly the other way around. Galileo applied the scientific methods of his day; Calvino used his imagination. Each either got it right or assembled the data so that others could understand the phenomenon.

In April 1982, while I was speaking to a Los Angeles audience with George McGovern, Eugene McCarthy, and the dread physical therapist Ms. Fonda-Hayden, "the three 'external' planets, visible to the naked eye . . . are all three 'in opposition' and therefore visible for the whole night." Needless to say, "Mr. Palomar rushes out on to the terrace." Between Calvino's stars and mine, he had the better of it; yet he wrote a good deal of political commentary for newspapers. But after he left the Communist party, he tended more to describe politics and its delusions than take up causes. "In a time and in a country where everyone goes out of his way to announce opinions or hand down judgments, Mr. Palomar has made a habit of biting his tongue three times before asserting anything. After the bite, if he is still convinced of what he was going to say, he says it." But then, "having had the correct view is nothing meritorious; statistically, it is almost inevitable that among the many cockeyed, confused or banal ideas that come into his mind, there should also be some perspicacious ideas, even ideas of genius; and as they occurred to him, they can surely have occurred also to somebody else." As he was a writer of literature and not a theorist, so he was an observer of politics and not a politician.

. . .

Calvino was as inspired by the inhabitants of zoos as by those of cities. "At this point Mr. Palomar's little girl, who has long since tired of watching the giraffes, pulls him toward the penguins' cave. Mr. Palomar, in whom penguins inspire anguish, follows her reluctantly and asks himself why he is so interested in giraffes. Perhaps because the world around him moves in an unharmonious way, and he hopes always to find some pattern to it, a constant. Perhaps because he himself feels that his own advance is impelled by uncoordinated movements of the mind, which seem to have nothing to do with one another and are increasingly difficult to fit into any pattern of inner harmony."

Palomar is drawn to the evil-smelling reptile house. "Beyond the glass of every cage, there is the world as it was before man, or after, to show that the world of man is not eternal and is not unique." The crocodiles, in their stillness, horrify him. "What are they waiting for, or what have they given up waiting for? In what time are they immersed? . . . The thought of a time outside our existence is intolerable." Palomar flees to the albino gorilla, "sole exemplar in the world of a form not chosen, not loved." The gorilla, in his boredom, plays with a rubber tire; he presses it to his bosom by the hour. The image haunts Palomar. " 'Just as the gorilla has his tire, which serves as tangible support for a raving, wordless speech,' he thinks, 'so I have this image of a great white ape. We all turn in our hands an old, empty tire through which we would like to reach the final meaning, at which words do not arrive.' " This is the ultimate of writers' images; that indescribable state where words are absent not because they are stopped by the iron bars of a cage at the zoo but by the limitations of that bone-covered binary electrical system which, in Calvino's case, broke down on September 19, 1985.

Suddenly, up ahead, on a hill overlooking the sea, is Castiglion della Pescáia. To my left is the beach where Palomar saw but sees no longer the sword of light. The sea has turned an odd disagreeable purple color, more suitable to the Caribbean of Calvino's birth than the Mediterranean. The sky is overcast. The air is hot, humid, windless (the headline of today's newspaper, which has devoted six pages to Calvino's life and work: CATACLISMA IN MESSICO). I am forty minutes early.

The cemetery is on a hill back of the town which is on a lower hill. We park next to a piece of medieval wall and a broken tower. I walk up to the cemetery which is surrounded by a high cement wall. I am reminded of Calvino's deep dislike of cement. In one of his early books, *La Speculazione Edilizia,* he described how the building trade had managed, in the 1950s, to bury the Italian Riviera, his native Liguria, under a sea of "horrible reinforced cement"; *"il boom,"* it was called. To the right of the cemetery entrance a large section of wall has been papered over with the same small funeral notice, repeated several hundred times. The name "Italo Calvino," the name of Castiglion della Pescáia, "the town of Palomar," the sign says proudly; then the homage of mayor and city council and populace.

Inside the cemetery there are several walled-off areas. The first is a sort of atrium, whose walls are filled with drawers containing the dead, stacked one above the other, each with a photograph of the occupant, taken rather too late in life to arouse much pity as opposed to awe. There are plastic flowers everywhere and a few real flowers. There are occasional small chapels, the final repository of wealthy or noble families. I have a sense of panic: They aren't going to put Italo in a drawer, are they? But then to the right, at the end of the atrium, in the open air, against a low wall, I see a row of vast floral wreaths, suitable for an American or Neapolitan gangster, and not a drawer but a new grave, the size of a bathtub in a moderately luxurious hotel. On one of the wreaths, I can make out the words *Senato* and *Communist . . .* , the homage of the Communist delegation in the Italian Senate. Parenthetically, since Italy is a country of many political parties and few ideologies, the level of the ordinary parliamentarian is apt to be higher than his American or English counterpart. Moravia sits in the European Parliament. Sciascia was in the chamber of deputies. Every party tries to put on its electoral list a number of celebrated intellectual names. The current mayor of Florence was, until recently, the head of the Paris Opéra: According to popular wisdom, anyone who could handle that can of worms can probably deal with Florence.

Over the wall, the purple sea and red-tiled whitewashed houses are visible. As I gaze, moderately melancholy, at Palomar country, I am recognized by a journalist from Naples. I am a neighbor, after all; I live at nearby Ravello. Among the tombs, I am interviewed. How had I met Calvino? A few drops of warm rain fall. A cameraman appears from behind a family chapel and takes my picture. The state television crew is arriving. Eleven years ago, I say, I wrote a piece about his work. Had you met him *before* that? Logrolling is even more noticeable in a small country like Italy than it is in our own dear *New York Times.* No, I had not met him when I wrote the piece. I had just read him, admired him; described (the critic's only task) his work for those who were able to read me (the critic's single aim). Did you meet him later? Yes, he wrote me a letter about the piece. In Italian or English? Italian, I say. What did he say? What do you think he said? I am getting irritable. He said he liked what I'd written.

Actually, Calvino's letter had been, characteristically, interesting and tangential. I had ended my description with "Reading Calvino, I had the unnerving sense that I was also writing what he had written; thus does his art prove his case as writer and reader become one, or One." This caught his attention. Politely, he began by saying that he had always been attracted by my "mordant irony," and so forth, but he particularly liked what I had written about him for two reasons. The first, "One feels that you have written this essay for the pleasure of writing it, alternating warm praise and criticism and reserve with an absolute sincerity, with freedom, and continuous humor, and this sensation of pleasure is irresistibly communicated to the reader. Second, I have always thought it would be difficult to extract a unifying theme from my books, each so different from the other. Now you—exploring my works as it should be done, that is, by going at it in an unsystematic way, stopping here and there; sometimes aimed directly without straying aside; other times, wandering like a vagabond—have succeeded in giving a general sense to all I have written, almost a philosophy—'the whole and the many,' etc.—and it makes me very happy when someone is able to find a philosophy from the productions of my mind which has little philosophy." Then Calvino comes to the point. "The ending of your essay contains an affirmation of what seems to me important in an absolute sense. I don't know if it really refers to me, but it is true of an ideal literature for each one of us: the end being that every one of us must be, that the writer and reader become one, or One. And to close all of my discourse and yours in a perfect circle, let us say that this One is All." In a sense, the later Palomar was the gathering together of the strands of a philosophy or philosophies; hence, the inscription "my last meditations on Nature."

I let slip not a word of this to the young journalist. But I do tell him that soon after the letter I had met Calvino and his wife, Chichita, at the house of an American publisher, and though assured that there would be no writers there but us, I found a room ablaze with American literary genius. Fearful of becoming prematurely One with them, I split into the night.

Two years ago, when I was made an honorary citizen of Ravello, Calvino accepted the town's invitation to participate in the ceremony, where he delivered a splendid discourse on my work in general and on *Duluth* in particular. Also, since Calvino's Roman flat was on the same street as mine (we were separated by—oh, the beauty of the random symbol!—the Pantheon), we saw each other occasionally.

For the last year, Calvino had been looking forward to his fall and winter at Harvard. He even began to bone up on "literary theory." He knew perfectly well what a mephitic kindergarten our English departments have become, and I cannot wait to see what he has to say in the five lectures that he did write. I had planned to arm him with a wonderfully silly bit of lowbrow criticism (from *Partisan Review*) on why people just don't like to read much anymore. John Gardner is quoted with admiration: " 'In nearly all good fiction, the basic—all but inescapable—plot form is this: a central character wants something, goes after it despite opposition (perhaps including his own doubts), and so arrives at a win, lose or draw.' " For those still curious about high-, middle-, and lowbrow, this last is the Excelsior of lowbrow commercialities, written in letters of gold in the halls of the Thalberg Building at MGM but never to be found in, say, the original *Partisan Review* of Rahv and Dupee, Trilling and Chase. The *PR* "critic" then quotes "a reviewer" in *The New York Times* who is trying to figure out why Calvino is popular. "If love fails, they begin again; their lives are a series of new beginnings, where complications have not yet begun to show themselves. Unlike the great Russian and French novelists [this is pure middlebrow: *Which* novelists, dummy? Name names, make your case, *describe*], who follow their characters through the long and winding caverns [!] of their lives, Calvino just turns off the set after the easy beginning and switches to another channel." This sort of writing has given American bookchat a permanently bad name. But our *PR* critic, a woman, this year's favored minority (*sic*), states, sternly, that all this "indeterminacy" is not the kind of stuff real folks want to read. "And Calvino is popular, if at all, among theorists, consumers of 'texts' rather than of novels and stories." I shall now never have the chance to laugh with Calvino over this latest report from the land to which Bouvard and Pécuchet emigrated.

At the foot of cemetery hill, a van filled with police arrives. Crowds are anticipated. The day before, the president of the republic had come to the Siena hospital to say farewell. One can imagine a similar scene in the United States. High atop the Tulsa Tower Hospital, the Reverend Oral Roberts enters the hushed room. "Mr. President, it's all over. *He* has crossed the shining river." A tear gleams in the Acting President's eye. "The last roundup," he murmurs. The tiny figure at his side, huge lidless eyes aswim with tears, whispers, "Does this mean, no more Harlequin novels?" The Acting President holds her close. "There will always be Harlequins, Mommie," he says. "But they won't be the same. Not without Louis L'Amour."

Now several hundred friends of Calvino, writers, editors, publishers, press, local dignitaries fill up the cemetery. I hold Chichita's hand a long moment; she has had, someone said, two weeks of coming to terms not so much with death as with the nightmare of dying.

The last chapter of *Palomar* begins, "Mr. Palomar decides that from now on he will act as if he were dead, to see how the world gets along without him." So far, not too good, I thought. Mexico City has fallen down and his daughter is late to the burial. On the plus side, there is no priest, no service, no words. Suddenly, as a dozen television cameras switch on, the dark shiny wooden box, containing Calvino, appears in the atrium. How small the box is, I think. Was he smaller than I remember? Or has he shrunk? Of course, he is dead but, as he wrote, "First of all, you must not confuse being dead with not being, a condition that occupies the vast expanse of time before birth, apparently symmetrical with the other, equally vast expanse that follows death. In fact, before birth we are part of the infinite possibilities that may or may not be fulfilled; whereas, once dead, we cannot fulfill ourselves either in the past (to which we now belong entirely but on which we can no longer have any influence) or in the future (which, even if influenced by us, remains forbidden to us)."

With a crash, the pallbearers drop the box into the shallow bathtub. Palomar's nose is now about four inches beneath the earth he used to examine so minutely. Then tiles are casually arranged over the coffin; and the box is seen no more. As we wait for the daughter to arrive, the heat is disagreeable. We look at one another as though we are at a party that has refused to take off. I recognize Natalia Ginzburg. I see someone who looks as if he ought to be Umberto Eco, and is. "A person's life consists of a collection of events, the last of which could also change the meaning of the whole . . ." I notice, in the crowd, several dozen young schoolchildren. They are fans of Calvino's fairy tales; plainly, precocious consumers of "texts" and proto-theorists. Then daughter and buckets of cement arrive simultaneously. One of the masons pours cement over the tiles; expertly, he smooths the viscous surface with a trowel. Horrible cement. "Therefore Palomar prepares to become a grouchy dead man, reluctant to submit to the sentence to remain exactly as he is; but he is unwilling to give up anything of himself, even if it is a burden." Finally, the cement is flush with the ground; and that's that.

I am standing behind Chichita, who is very still. Finally, I look up from the gray oblong of fresh cement and there, staring straight at me, is Calvino. He looks anguished, odd, not quite right. But it is unmistakably Mr. Palomar, witnessing his own funeral. For one brief mad moment we stare at each other; then he looks down at the coffin that contains not himself but Italo. The man I thought was Italo is his younger brother, Floriano.

I move away, before the others. On the drive back to Rome, the sun is bright and hot; yet rain starts to fall. Devil is beating his wife, as they say in the South. Then a rainbow covers the entire eastern sky. For the Romans and the Etruscans, earlier inhabitants of the countryside through which we are driving, the rainbow was an ominous herald of coming change in human affairs, death of kings, cities, world. I make a gesture to ward off the evil eye. Time can now end. But " 'If time has to end, it can be described, instant by instant,' Palomar thinks, 'and each instant, when described, expands so that its end can no longer be seen.' He decides that he will set himself to describing every instant of his life, and until he has described them all he will no longer think of being dead. At that moment he dies." So end "my last meditations on Nature," as Calvino and Nature are now one, or One.

***The New York Review of Books***
***November 21, 1985***

# Some Memories of the Glorious Bird and an Earlier Self

"I PARTICULARLY LIKE New York on hot summer nights when all the . . . uh, superfluous people are off the streets." Those were, I think, the first words Tennessee addressed to me; then the foggy blue eyes blinked, and a nervous chuckle filled the moment's silence before I said whatever I said.

Curtain rising. The place: an apartment at the American Academy in Rome. Occasion: a party for some newly arrived Americans, among them Frederic Prokosch, Samuel Barber. The month: March 1948. The day: glittering. What else could a March day be in the golden age?

I am pleased that I can remember so clearly my first meeting with the Glorious Bird, as I almost immediately called him for reasons long since forgotten (premonition, perhaps, of the eventual take-off and flight of youth's sweet bird?). Usually, I forget first meetings, excepting always those solemn audiences granted by the old and famous when I was young and green. I recall vividly every detail of André Gide's conversation and appearance, including the dark velvet beret he wore in his study at 1 *bis* rue Vaneau. I recall even more vividly my visits to George Santayana in his cell at the Convent of the Blue Nuns. All these audiences, meetings, introductions took place in that *anno mirabilis* 1948, a year that proved to be the exact midpoint between the end of the Second World War and the beginning of what looks to be a permanent cold war. At the time, of course, none of us knew where history had placed us.

At that first meeting I thought Tennessee every bit as ancient as Gide and Santayana. After all, I was twenty-two. He was thirty-seven; but claimed to be thirty-three on the sensible ground that the four years he had spent working for a shoe company did not count. Now he was the most celebrated American playwright. *A Streetcar Named Desire* was still running in New York when we met that evening in a flat overlooking what was, in those days, a quiet city where hardly anyone was superfluous unless it was us, the first group of American writers and artists to arrive in Rome after the war.

In 1946 and 1947 Europe was still out-of-bounds for foreigners. But by 1948 the Italians had begun to pull themselves together, demonstrating once more their astonishing ability to cope with disaster which is so perfectly balanced by their absolute inability to deal with success.

Rome was strange to all of us. For one thing, Italy had been sealed off not only by war but by Fascism. Since the early thirties few English or American artists knew Italy well. Those who did included mad Ezra, gentle Max, spurious B.B. and, of course, the Anglo-American historian Harold (now Sir Harold) Acton, in stately residence at Florence. By 1948 Acton had written supremely well about both the Bourbons of Naples and the later Medici of Florence; unfortunately, he was—is—prone to the writing of memoirs. And so, wanting no doubt to flesh out yet another chapter in the ongoing story of a long and marvelously uninteresting life, Acton came down to Rome to look at the new invaders. What he believed he saw and heard, he subsequently published in a little volume called *More Memoirs of an Aesthete,* a work to be cherished for its quite remarkable number of unaesthetic misprints and mispellings.

"After the First World War American writers and artists had emigrated to Paris; now they pitched upon Rome." So Acton begins. "According to Stendhal, the climate was enough to gladden anybody, but this was not the reason: one of them explained to me that it was the facility of finding taxis, and very little of Rome can be seen from a taxi. Classical and Romantic Rome was no more to them than a picturesque background. Tennessee Williams, Victor [he means Frederic] Prokosch and Gore Vidal created a bohemian annexe to the American Academy. . . ." Liking Rome for its many taxis is splendid stuff and I wish I had said it. Certainly whoever did was putting Acton on, since the charm of Rome—1948—was the lack of automobiles of any kind. But Acton is just getting into stride. More to come.

Toward the end of March Tennessee gave a party to inaugurate his new flat in the Via Aurora (in the golden age even the street names were apt). Somehow or other, Acton got himself invited to the party. I remember him floating like some large pale fish through the crowded room; from time to time, he would make a sudden lunge at this or that promising bit of bait while Tennessee, he tells us, "wandered as a lost soul among the guests he assembled in an apartment which might have been in New York. . . . Neither he nor any of the group I met with him spoke Italian, yet he had a typically Neapolitan protégé who could speak no English."

At this time Tennessee and I had been in Rome for only a few weeks and French, not Italian, was the second language of the reasonably well-educated American of that era. On the other hand, Prokosch knew Italian, German, and French; he also bore with becoming grace the heavy weight of a Yale doctorate in Middle English. But to Acton the author of *The Asiatics,* the translator of Hölderlin and Louise Labé was just another barbarian whose works "fell short of his perfervid imagination, [he] had the dark good looks of an advertiser of razor blades. . . ." Happily, "Gore Vidal, the youngest in age, aggressively handsome in a clean-limbed sophomore style, had success written all over him. . . . His candour was engaging but he was slightly on the defensive, as if he anticipated an attack on his writings or his virtue." Well, the young G.V. wasn't so dumb: seeing the old one-two plainly in the middle distance, he kept sensibly out of reach.

"A pudgy, taciturn, moustached little man without any obvious distinction." Thus Acton describes Tennessee. He then zeroes in on the "protégé" from Naples, a young man whom Acton calls "Pierino." Acton tells us that Pierino had many complaints about Tennessee and his friends, mostly due to the language barrier. The boy was also eager to go to America. Acton tried to discourage him. Even so, Pierino was enthralled. " 'You are the first *galantuomo* who has spoken to me this evening.' " After making a date to see the *galantuomo* later on that evening, Pierino split. Acton then told Tennessee, "as tactfully as I could, that his young protégé felt neglected. . . . [Tennessee] rubbed his chin thoughtfully and said nothing, a little perplexed. There was something innocently childish about his expression." It does not occur to the memoirist that Tennessee might have been alarmed at his strange guest's bad manners. "Evidently he was not aware that Pierino wanted to be taken to America and I have wondered since whether he took him there, for that was my last meeting with Tennessee Williams." It must be said that Acton managed to extract quite a lot of copy out of a single meeting. To put his mind at rest, Tennessee did take Pierino to America and Pierino is now a married man and doing, as they say, well.

"This trifling episode illustrated the casual yet condescending attitude of certain foreigners towards the young Italians they cultivated on account of their Latin charm without any interest in their character, aspirations or desires." This sentiment or sentimentality could be put just as well the other way around and with far more accuracy. Italian trade has never had much interest in the character, aspirations or desires of those to whom they rent their ass. When Acton meditates upon The Italian Boy, a sweet and sickly hypocrisy clouds his usually sharp prose and we are in E. M.

Forsterland where the lower orders (male) are worshiped, and entirely misunderstood. But magnum of sour grapes to one side, Acton is by no means inaccurate. Certainly he got right Tennessee's indifference to place, art, history. The Bird seldom reads a book and the only history he knows is his own; he depends, finally, on a romantic genius to get him through life. Above all, he is a survivor, never more so than now in what he calls his "crocodile years."

I picked up Tennessee's *Memoirs* with a certain apprehension. I looked myself up in the Index; read the entries and found some errors, none grave. I started to read; was startled by the technique he had chosen. Some years ago, Tennessee told me that he had been reading (that is to say, looking at) my "memoir in the form of a novel" *Two Sisters.* In this book I alternated sections describing certain events in 1948 with my everyday life while writing the book. Memory sections I called *Then.* The day-by-day descriptions I called *Now.* At the time Tennessee found *Two Sisters* interesting because he figured in it. He must also have found it technically interesting because he has serenely appropriated my form and has now no doubt forgotten just how the idea first came to him to describe the day-to-day life of a famous beleaguered playwright acting in an off-Broadway production of the failing play *Small Craft Warnings* while, in alternating sections, he recalls the early days not only of Tennessee Williams but of one Thomas Lanier Williams, who bears only a faint resemblance to the playwright we all know from a thousand and one altogether too candid interviews.

There is a foreword and, like all forewords, it is meant to disarm. Unfortunately, it armed me to the teeth. During the 1973 tryout of a play in New Haven, Tennessee was asked to address some Yale drama students. Incidentally, the style of the foreword is unusually seductive, the old master at his most beguiling: self-pity and self-serving kept in exquisite balance by the finest comic style since S. L. Clemens.

"I found myself entering (through a door marked EXIT) an auditorium considerably smaller than the Shubert but containing a more than proportionately small audience. I would say roughly about two-score and ten, not including a large black dog which was resting in the lap of a male student in the front row. . . . The young faces before me were uniformly inexpressive of any kind of emotional reaction to my entrance. . . ." I am surprised that Tennessee was surprised. The arrogance and self-satisfaction of drama students throughout Academe are among the few constants in a changing world. Any student who has read Sophocles in translation is, demonstrably, superior to Tennessee Williams in the untidy flesh. These dummies reflect of course the proud mediocrity of their teachers, who range, magisterially, through something called "world drama" where evolution works only backward. Teachers and taught are to be avoided.

"I am not much good at disguising my feelings, and after a few moments I abandoned all pretense of feeling less dejection than I felt." The jokes did not work. So "I heard myself describing an encounter, then quite recent, with a fellow playwright in the Oak Room Bar at Manhattan's Plaza Hotel." It was with "my old friend Gore Vidal. I had embraced him warmly. However, Mr. Vidal is not a gentleman to be disarmed by a cordial embrace, and when, in response to his perfunctory inquiries about the progress of rehearsals . . . I told him . . . all seemed a dream come true after many precedent nightmares, he smiled at me with a sort of rueful benevolence and said 'Well, Bird, it won't do much good, I'm afraid, you've had too much bad personal exposure for anything to help you much anymore.'

"Well, then, for the first time, I could see a flicker of interest in the young faces before me. It may have been the magic word Vidal or it may have been his prophecy of my professional doom." Asked if the prognosis was accurate, Tennessee looked at the black dog and said, "Ask the dog."

An unsettling anecdote. I have no memory of the Plaza meeting. I am also prone, when dining late, to suffer from what Dorothy Parker used grimly to refer to as "the frankies," or straight talk for the other person's good like frankly-that-child-would-not-have-been-born-mongoloid-if-you-hadn't. . . . An eyewitness, however, assures me that I did not say what Tennessee attributes to me. Yet his paranoia always has some basis in reality. I have an uncomfortable feeling that I was probably thinking what I did not say and what he later thought I did say. When it comes to something unspoken, the Bird has a sharp ear.

It is hard now to realize what a bad time of it Tennessee used to have from the American press. During the forties and fifties the anti-fag battalions were everywhere on the march. From the high lands of *Partisan Review* to the middle ground of *Time* magazine, envenomed attacks on real or suspected fags never let up. A *Time* cover story on Auden was killed when the managing editor of the day was told that Auden was a fag. From 1945 to 1961 *Time* attacked with unusual ferocity everything produced or published by Tennessee Williams. "Fetid swamp" was the phrase most used to describe his work. But, in *Time,* as well as in time, all things will come to pass. The Bird is now a beloved institution.

Today, at sixty-four, Tennessee has the same voracious appetite for work and for applause that he had at twenty-four. More so, I would suspect, since glory is a drug more addictive than any other as heroes have known from Achilles on (Donald Windham's *roman à clef* about Tennessee bore the apt title *The Hero Continues*). But fashions in the theater change. The superstar of the forties and fifties fell on bad times, and that is the burden of these memoirs. In sharp detail we are told how the hero came into being.

Less sharply, Tennessee describes the bad days when the booze and the pills caused him to hallucinate; to slip out of a world quite bad enough as it is into nightmare land. "I said to my friend Gore, 'I slept through the sixties,' and he said, 'You didn't miss a thing.' " Tennessee often quotes this exchange. But he leaves out the accompanying caveat: "If you missed the sixties, Bird, God knows what you are going to do with the seventies."

But of course life is not divided into good and bad decades; it is simply living. For a writer, life is, again simply, writing and in these memoirs the old magician can still create a world. But since it is hardly news to the Bird that we are for the night, the world he shows us is no longer the Romantic's lost Eden but Prospero's island where, at sunset, magicians often enjoy revealing the sources of their rude magic, the tricks of a trade.

Not that a magician is honor-bound to tell the whole truth. For instance: "I want to admit to you that I undertook this memoir for mercenary reasons. It is actually the first piece of work, in the line of writing, that I have undertaken for material profit." The sniffy tone is very much that of St. Theresa scrubbing floors. Actually, Tennessee is one of the richest of living writers. After all, a successful play will earn its author a million or more dollars and Tennessee has written quite a few successful plays. Also, thirteen of his works have been made into films.

Why the poor-mouthing? Because it has always been the Bird's tactic to appear in public flapping what looks to be a pathetically broken wing. By arousing universal pity, he hopes to escape predators. In the old days before a play opened on Broadway, the author would be asked to write a piece for the Sunday *New York Times* drama section. Tennessee's pieces were always thrilling; sometimes horrendous. He would reveal how that very morning he had coughed up blood with his sputum. But, valiantly, he had gone on writing, knowing the new play would be his last work, ever . . . By the time the Bird had finished working us over, only Louis Kronenberger at *Time* had the heart to attack him.

But now that Tennessee's physical and mental health are good (he would deny this instantly; "I have had, in recent days, a series of palpitations of the variety known as terminal"), only the cry of poverty will, he thinks, act as lightning conductor and insure him a good press for the *Memoirs.* Certainly he did not write this book for the $50,000 advance. As always, fame is the spur. Incidentally, he has forgotten that in the past he *did* write for money when he was under contract to MGM and worked on a film called *Marriage Is a Private Affair,* starring Lana Turner and James Craig (unless of course Tennessee now sees in this movie that awesome moral grandeur first detected by the film critic Myra Breckinridge).

The *Memoirs* start briskly. Tennessee is a guest at a country house in Wiltshire near Stonehenge. On the grounds of the estate is a "stone which didn't quite make it to Henge." He looks himself up in *Who's Who.* Broods on his past; shifts back and forth in time. *Now* and *Then.* The early days are fascinating to read about even though the Williams family is already known to every playgoer not only from *The Glass Menagerie* but also from the many other plays and stories in which appear, inexorably, Rose the Sister, Edwina the Mother, Dakin the Brother, Cornelius the Father, Reverend Dakin the Grandfather, as well as various other relatives now identified for the first time. He also tells us how he was hooked by the theater when some St. Louis amateurs put on a play he had written. "I knew that writing was my life, and its failure would be my death. . . ."

I have never known any writer with the exception of the artistically gifted and humanly appalling Carson McCullers who cared so much about the opinion of those condemned to write for newspapers. Uneasily confronting a truly remarkable hunger for absolute praise and total notice, Tennessee admits that, when being interviewed, he instinctively "hams it up in order to provide 'good copy.' The reason? I guess a need to convince the world that I do indeed still exist and to make this fact a matter of public interest and amusement." Fair enough, Bird. But leave your old friends out.

"This book is a sort of catharsis of puritanical guilt feelings, I suppose. 'All good art is an indiscretion.' Well, I can't assure you that this book will be art, but it is bound to be an indiscretion, since it deals with my adult life. . . .

"Of course I could devote this whole book to a discussion of the art of drama, but wouldn't that be a bore?

"It would bore me to extinction, I'm afraid, and it would be a very, very short book, about three sentences to the page with extremely wide margins. The plays speak for themselves."

A wise choice: the plays do speak for themselves and Tennessee's mind is not, to say the least, at home with theory. Most beautifully, the plays speak for themselves. Not only does Tennessee have a marvelous comedic sense but his gloriously outrageous dramatic effects can be enormously satisfying. He makes poetic (without quotes) the speech of those half-educated would-be genteel folk who still maintain their babble in his head. Only on those rare occasions when he tries to depict educated or upper-class people does he falter. Somewhat reproachfully, he told me that he had been forced several times to use a dictionary while reading *Two Sisters.*

What, I asked, was one of the words you had to look up? "Solipsistic," he said. Tennessee's vocabulary has never been large (I note that he still thinks "eclectic" means "esoteric"). But then he is not the sort of writer who sees words on the page; rather he hears them in his head and when he is plugged into the right character, the wrong word never sounds.

"Life that winter in Rome: a golden dream, and I don't just mean Raffaello [Acton's 'Pierino'] and the mimosa and total freedom of life. Stop there: What I do mean is the total freedom of life and Raffaello and the mimosa. . . ." That season we were, all of us, symbolically, out of jail. Free of poverty and hack work, Tennessee had metamorphosed into the Glorious Bird while I had left behind me three years in the wartime army and a near-fatal bout with hepatitis. So it was, at the beginning of that golden dream, we met.

Tennessee's version: "[Gore] had just published a best-seller, called *The City and the Pillar,* which was one of the first homosexual novels of consequence. I had not read it but I knew that it had made the best-seller lists and that it dealt with a 'forbidden subject.' " Later, Tennessee actually read the book (the only novel of mine he has ever been able to get through) and said, "You know you spoiled it with that ending. You didn't know what a good book you had." Fair comment.

"Gore was a handsome kid, about twenty-four [*sic*], and I was quite taken by his wit as well as his appearance." Incidentally, I am mesmerized by the tributes to my beauty that keep cropping up in the memoirs of the period. At the time nobody reliable thought to tell me. In fact, it was my impression that I was not making out as well as most people because, with characteristic malice, Nature had allowed Guy Madison and not me to look like Guy Madison.

"We found that we had interests in common and we spent a lot of time together. Please don't imagine that I am suggesting that there was a romance." I don't remember whether or not I ever told Tennessee that I had actually seen but not met him the previous year. He was following me up Fifth Avenue while I, in turn, was stalking yet another quarry. I recognized him: he wore a blue bow tie with white polka dots. In no mood for literary encounters, I gave him a scowl and he abandoned the chase just north of Rockefeller Center. I don't recall how my own pursuit ended. We walked a lot in the golden age.

"I believe we also went to Florence that season and were entertained by that marvelous old aesthete Berenson." No, that was someone else. "And then one afternoon Gore took me to the Convent of the Blue Nuns to meet the great philosopher and essayist, by then an octogenarian and semi-invalid, Santayana." I had to drag Tennessee to meet Santayana. Neither had heard of the other. But Tennessee did stare at the old man with great interest. Afterward, the Bird remarked, "Did you notice how he said 'in the days when I had secretaries, *young men*?' "

In the *Memoirs* Tennessee tells us a great deal about his sex life, which is one way of saying nothing about oneself. Details of this body and that body tend to blur on the page as they do in life. Tennessee did not get around to his first homosexual affair until he was well into his twenties, by which time he had achieved several mature as well as sexually meaningful and life-enhancing heterosexual relationships. Except he wasn't really all that enhanced by these "mature" relationships. Lust for the male set his nerves to jangling. Why was he such a late-developer? Well, this was close to half a century ago, and Tennessee was the product of that Southern puritan environment where all sex was sin and unnatural sex was peculiarly horrible.

I think that the marked difference between my attitude toward sex and that of Tennessee made each of us somewhat startling to the other. I never had the slightest guilt or anxiety about what I always took to be a normal human appetite. He was—and is—guilt-ridden, and although he tells us that he believes in no afterlife, he is still too much the puritan not to believe in sin. At some deep level Tennessee truly believes that the homosexualist is wrong and that the heterosexualist is right. Given this all-pervading sense of guilt, he is drawn in both life and work to the idea of expiation, of death.

Tennessee tells of his affair with a dancer named Kip. But Kip left him; got married; died young. Then Tennessee was drawn to a pseudonymous lover in New Orleans; that affair ended in drink and violence. For a number of years Tennessee lived with an Italo-American, Frank Merlo. Eventually they fell out. They were reunited when Frank was dying of cancer. Frank's last days were sufficiently horrifying to satisfy any puritan's uneasy conscience while, simultaneously, justifying the romantic's extreme vision of the world: "I shall but love thee better after death."

The other line running through Tennessee's emotional life is what I call the Monster Women. Surrogate mothers one might say if Tennessee's own mother, Miss Edwina, were not so implacably in this world, even as I write these lines. Currently convinced that the blacks signal to one another during the long St. Louis nights by clanging the lids of the trash cans, Miss Edwina is every inch the Amanda of *The Glass Menagerie.* In fact, so powerful is Tennessee's creation that in the presence of Miss Edwina one does not listen to her but only to what he has made of her.

"I had forty gentlemen callers that day," she says complacently. We are having dinner in the restaurant of the Robert Clay Hotel in Miami. Delicately she holds a fork with a shrimp on it. Fork and shrimp proceed slowly to her mouth while Tennessee and I stare, hypnotized not only by the constant flow of conversation but by the never-eaten shrimp for just as she is about to take the first bite, yet another anecdote wells up from deep inside her . . . ah, *solipsistic* brain and the fork returns to the plate, the shrimp untouched. "Tom, remember when that little dog took the hat with the plume and ran all 'round the yard . . . ?" This is also from *The Glass*

*Menagerie.* Tennessee nervously clears his throat. Again the shrimp slowly rises to the wide straight mouth which resembles nothing so much as the opening to a miniature letter box—one designed for engraved invitations only. But once again the shrimp does not arrive. "Tom, do you remember . . . ?"

Tennessee clears his throat again. *"Mother, eat your shrimp."*

"Why," counters Miss Edwina, "do you keep making that funny sound in your throat?"

"Because, Mother, when you destroy someone's life you must expect certain nervous disabilities."

Yet Tennessee went on adding even more grotesque ladies than Miss Edwina to his life. I could never take any of them from Carson McCullers to Jane Bowles to Anna Magnani. Yes, yes, yes, they were superb talents all. Part of the artistic heritage of the twentieth century. I concede their talent, their glory, their charm—for Tennessee but not for me. Carson spoke only of her work. Of its greatness. The lugubrious Southern singsong voice never stopped: "Did ya see muh lovely play? Did ya lahk muh lovely play? Am Ah gonna win the Pew-litzuh prahzz?" Jane ("the finest writer of fiction we have in the States") Bowles was more original. She thought and talked a good deal about food and made powerful scenes in restaurants. The best that one could say of Magnani was that she liked dogs. When Marlon Brando agreed to act with her in the film of Tennessee's *Orpheus Descending,* he warned, "When I do a scene with her, I'm going to carry a rock in each hand."

I don't know what Tennessee gets from the Monster Women, but if they give him solace nothing else matters. Certainly he has a huge appetite for the grotesque not only in art but in life. In fact, he is dogged by the grotesque. Once, in the airport at Miami, we were stopped by a plump middle-aged man who had known Tennessee whom he called Tom from the old days in St. Louis. The man seemed perfectly ordinary. He talked to Tennessee about friends they had in common. Then I noticed that the man was carrying a large string bag containing two roast turkeys and a half dozen loaves of bread. "What," I asked, "is that?" The man gave us a knowing wink. "Well, I got me two roast turkeys in there. And also these loaves of bread *because you know about the food in Miami."* Then he was gone. It would seem that the true artist need never search for a subject; the subject always knows where to find him.

It is curious how friends actually regard one another—or think they do—when memoir-time rolls around, and the boneyard beckons. A figure of some consequence in our far-off golden age was the composer-novelist Paul Bowles. From time to time over the years, Tennessee has bestowed a number of Walter Winchellish Orchids on Paul as well as on Jane (I fear that a lifetime on Broadway has somewhat corrupted the Bird's everyday speech and prose although nothing, happily, can affect the authenticity of those voices in his head). Certainly Bowles was an early hero of Tennessee's.

But now let us see what Bowles makes of Tennessee in *his* memoir *Without Stopping.* "One morning when we were getting ready to leave for the beach" (this was Acapulco, 1940), "someone arrived at the door and asked to see me. It was a round-faced, sun-burned young man in a big floppy sombrero and a striped sailor sweater, who said his name was Tennessee Williams, that he was a playwright, and that Lawrence Langner of the Theatre Guild had told him to look me up. I asked him to come in and installed him in a hammock, explaining that we had to hurry to the beach with friends. I brought him books and magazines and rum and coke, and told him to ask the servants for sandwiches if he got hungry. Then we left. Seven hours later we got back to the house and found our visitor lying contentedly in the hammock, reading. We saw him again each day until he left."

Paul Bowles used to quote Virgil Thomson's advice to a young music critic: Never intrude your personal opinions when you write music criticism. "The words that you use to describe what you've heard will be the criticism." Bowles on Tennessee demonstrates a mastery of the unsaid. Needless to say, Tennessee read what Bowles had written about him. Now watch the Bird as he strikes . . .

"It was there in Acapulco that summer that I first met Jane and Paul Bowles. They were staying at a pension in town and Paul was, as ever, upset about the diet and his stomach. The one evening that we spent together that summer was given over almost entirely to the question of what he could eat in Acapulco that he could digest, and poor little Janie kept saying, 'Oh, Bubbles, if you'd just stick to cornflakes and fresh fruit!' and so on and so on. None of her suggestions relieved his dyspeptic humor.

"I thought them a very odd and charming couple." I think I give Tennessee that round, on points. But Bowles's prose still remains the perfect model for judgment by indirection even though, like Tennessee, he occasionally gets the facts wrong. Bowles writes: "Gore had just played a practical joke on Tennessee and Truman Capote which he recounted to me in dialect, as it were. He had called Tennessee on the telephone and, being a stupendous mimic, had made himself into Truman for the occasion. Then, complete with a snigger, he induced Tennessee to make uncomplimentary remarks about Gore's writing."

This is a curious variation on the actual story. A number of times I would ring Tennessee, using Capote's voice. The game was to see how long it would take him to figure out that it was not Capote. One day I rang and spoke to what I thought was Tennessee. But it was Frank Merlo, newly installed in the flat. I had not got beyond my imitable whine, "This is *Truman*," when Frank began to attack Tennessee. I broke the connection. Frank never knew whether or not I had repeated his complaints to Tennessee. I did not. But years later I did tell Bowles the story.

Back to 1948: "In those days Truman was about the best companion you could want," writes Tennessee. "He had not turned bitchy. Well, he had not turned *maliciously* bitchy. But he was full of fantasies and mischief." That summer Capote arrived in Paris where Tennessee and I were staying at the Hôtel de l'Université ("A raffish hotel but it suited Gore and me perfectly as there was no objection to young callers"), and Capote would keep us entranced with mischievous fantasies about the great. Apparently, the very sight of him was enough to cause lifelong heterosexual men to tumble out of unsuspected closets. When Capote refused to surrender his virtue to the drunken Errol Flynn, "Errol threw *all* my suitcases out of the window of the Beverly Wilshire Hotel!" I should note here that the young Capote was no less attractive in his person then than he is today.

When Tennessee and I would exchange glances during these stories, Capote would redouble his efforts. Did we know that Albert Camus was in love with him? Yes, Camus! Madly in love. Recently Capote's biographer told me that the Capote-Camus connection might well prove to be a key chapter. No doubt it will also provide a startling footnote to the life story of Camus, a man known until now as a womanizer. Then Capote showed us a gold and amethyst ring. "From André Gide," he sighed. Happily, I was able to check that one out. A few days later I called on Gide in the company of my English publisher. "How," I asked in my best Phillips Exeter French, "did you find Truman Capote?" "Who?" Gide asked. I suspect that it was then, in the fabulous summer of '48, that the nonfiction novel was born.

To return again to 1948, I have a bit more to report on that season.

"Frankie and I had been out late one evening and when we returned to the apartment the transom on the front door was open and from within came the voice of Truman Capote, shrill with agitation. . . . In the apartment were Truman, Gore Vidal, and a female policeman. . . . It seemed that Truman and Gore, still on friendly terms at this point, had got a bit drunk together and had climbed in through the transom of the apartment to wait for me and Frankie."

Before this story petrifies into literary history, let me amend the record. Tennessee, an actress, and I came back to Tennessee's flat to find Capote and a friend in the clutches of the law. They had indeed been caught entering the flat. But by the time we arrived, Capote had matters well under control. Plainclotheswoman and plainclothesman were listening bug-eyed to Capote, who was telling them *every*thing about the private lives of Mr. and Mrs. Charles Chaplin.

Tennessee's asides on the various personages who have come his way are often amusing, sometimes revelatory. He describes a hilarious dinner with the Russian performer Yevtushenko, who saw fit to lecture Tennessee on commercialism, sexual perversion, and the responsibilities of art while swilling expensive wine. Tennessee admired Dylan Thomas until he actually met him and received "this put-down: 'How does it feel to make all that Hollywood money?' " There was also the snub from Sartre. Tennessee gave a party at the Hôtel de l'Université, hoping that Sartre would come. Instead the Master sat a few blocks away at a café, and for several hours he made a point of *not* coming to the party despite the pleas of various emissaries.

Tennessee omits to mention a splendid lunch given us at the Grand Véfour by Jean Cocteau, who wanted the French rights to *A Streetcar Named Desire* for Jean Marais to act in. I came along as translator. Marais looked beautiful but sleepy. Cocteau was characteristically brilliant. He spoke no English but since he could manage an occasional "the" sound as well as the final "g," he often gave the impression that he was speaking English. Tennessee knew no French. He also had no clear idea just who Cocteau was, while Cocteau knew nothing about Tennessee except that he had written a popular American play with a splendid part in it for his lover Marais. Between Tennessee's solemn analysis of the play and Cocteau's rhetoric about theater (the long arms flailed like semaphores denoting some dangerous last junction), no one made any sense at all except Marais who broke his long silence to ask, apropos the character Stanley Kowalski, "Will I have to use a Polish accent?"

Although Marais and Cocteau broke up soon afterward, Cocteau did the play without Marais. Cocteau's adaptation was, apparently, a gorgeous mess. Naked black youths writhed through beaded curtains while Arletty, miscast as Blanche, struck attitudes among peacock feathers.

The situation of a practicing playwright in the United States is not a happy one, to understate the matter. Broadway is more and more an abandoned parcel of real estate. Except for a native farce or two and a handful of "serious" plays imported from the British Isles, Broadway is noted chiefly for large and usually bad musicals. During the theater season of 1947–48 there were 43 straight plays running on Broadway. In 1974–75 there were 18, mostly imported. Adventurous plays are now done off-Broadway and sometimes off-off . . . where our memoirist ended up as a performer in *Small Craft Warnings.*

Unique among writers, the American playwright must depend upon the praise of journalists who seldom know very much about anything save the prejudices of their employers. With the collapse of a half dozen newspapers in the last third of the century, the success of a play now depends almost entirely upon the good will of the critic for *The New York Times.* The current reviewer is an amiable and enthusiastic Englishman who knows a good deal about ballet but not so much about the social and political nuances of his adopted land. Yet at sixty-four Tennessee Williams is still trying to curry favor with the press. Of *Small Craft Warnings,* "Clive Barnes" (in *The New York Times*) "was cautiously respectful. With the exception of Leonard Harris, I disregard TV reviews. I suppose they were generally negative."

Then Tennessee has second thoughts. And a new paragraph: "To say that I disregard TV reviews is hardly the total truth. How could I disregard any review which determines the life or death of a production?" How indeed? Yet after thirty years of meaningless praise and equally meaningless abuse, it is no wonder that Tennessee is a bit batty. On those rare occasions when Tennessee's literary peers have got around to looking at his work, the result has been depressing: witness, Mary McCarthy's piece "A Streetcar Named Success."

There have been complaints that these *Memoirs* tell us too much about Tennessee's sex life and too little about his art. Personally, I find the candor about his sex life interesting if not illuminating. At the worst, it will feed that homophobia which is too much a part of the national psyche. Yet perhaps it is better to write this sort of thing oneself rather than leave it to others to invent.

Recently that venerable vendor of book-chat Alfred Kazin wrote, "Vidal gets more literary mileage out of his sex life than anyone since Oscar Wilde and Jean Cocteau." This struck me as breathtakingly wrong. First, neither Wilde nor Cocteau ever exploited his sex life for "mileage." Each was reticent in public. Eventually the law revealed the private life of the first, while friends (and an ambiguous sort of unsigned memoir) revealed the life of the second. The book-chat writer does mention the admittedly too many interviews I've lately given to magazines like *Playboy* where sex is always a Solemn and Sacred subject and where I, too, am Solemn but never personal. As evidence of my seeking mileage he quotes the rather lame " 'In youth I never missed a trick . . . I tried everything . . . I could no more go to bed with somebody whose work I admired than I could . . . well, make love to a mirror. Fame in others switches off desire.' " Not, I would say, the most prurient of giveaway lines. Except in *Two Sisters,* a memoir done with mirrors, I have not used myself as a subject for private analysis on the ground that since we live in a time where the personality of the writer is everything and what he writes is nothing, only a fool would aid the enemy by helping to trivialize life, work.

A columnist reports that Tennessee was obliged to cut his *Memoirs* in half because of the "filth." I hope that we are given that other half one day; and I doubt that there will be much "filth," only indiscretions which ought to be interesting. After all, Tennessee has known or come across a great many of our time's movers and shakers. I say "come across" because for a long period he was . . . well, inattentive. Sometimes the stupefying combination of Nembutal and vodka (now abandoned) addled him. I was present when Edna Ferber (yes, Edna Ferber) came over to our table at a restaurant and introduced herself. With considerable charm, she told Tennessee how much she admired him. He listened to her with eyes that had narrowed to what Miss Ferber would have described as "mere slits." As she walked away, the Bird hissed, "Why is that woman attacking me?"

Tennessee is the sort of writer who does not develop; he simply continues. By the time he was an adolescent he had his themes. Constantly he plays and replays the same small but brilliant set of cards. I am not aware that any new information (or feeling?) has got through to him in the twenty-eight years since our Roman spring. In consequence, we have drifted apart. "Gore no longer receives me," said the Bird to one of his innumerable interviewers; and he put this down to my allegedly glamorous social life. But the reason for the drifting apart is nothing more than difference of temperament. I am a compulsive learner of new things while the Bird's occasional and sporadic responses to the world outside the proscenium arch have not been fortunate. "Castro was, after all, a gentleman," he announced after an amiable meeting with the dictator. Tell that to the proscribed fags of Cuba.

Tennessee's much publicized conversion to Roman Catholicism took place during the time of his great confusion. Shortly after the Bird was received into the arms of Mother Church, a Jesuit priest rang him up and asked if he would like an audience with the Pope? a meeting with the head of the Jesuit order? Oh yes. Yes! Tennessee was delighted. The next morning the priest arrived to take Tennessee to the Vatican where, presumably, the Pope was waiting on tenderhooks to examine the Church's latest haul. Unfortunately, Tennessee had forgotten all about the audience. He would have to beg off, he said; he was just not up to the Pope that day. The priest was stunned. The Pope's reaction has not been recorded.

The Jesuits, however, are made of tougher material. The secretary of the Black Pope rang to say that since a cocktail party had been arranged, Mr. Williams was going to be there, or else. The Bird was present. Almost immediately, he began to ham it up about God. Now if there is anything a Jesuit likes less than chat of God, it is having to listen to the religious enthusiasm of a layman. Trying to deflect Tennessee from what was fast turning into a Billy Graham exhortation about God and goodness, one of the Jesuits asked, "How do you start to write a play, Mr. Williams?" The Bird barely paused in his glorious ascent. "I start," he said sharply, "with a sentence." He then told the assembled members of the Society of Jesus that ever since becoming a Roman Catholic, he had felt a divine presence constantly with him. The Jesuits shifted uneasily at this. Like the old trouper he is, the Bird then paused abruptly in midflight in order to see just what effect he was having. After a moment of embarrassed silence, one of the Jesuits asked, timidly, "Is this presence a *warm* presence?"

"There is," said the Bird firmly, "no temperature."

But despite the "conversion," Tennessee now writes, "I am unable to believe that there is anything but permanent oblivion after death. . . . For me, what is there but to feel beneath me the steadily rising current of mortality and to summon from my blood whatever courage is native to it, and once there was a great deal." As he ends the *Memoirs,* he thinks back upon Hart Crane, whose legend has always haunted him. But though a romantic, Tennessee is no Crane. For one thing, it is too late to choose an abrupt death at sea. For another, art is too beguiling and difficult: "life is made up of moment-to-moment occurrences in the nerves and the perceptions, and try as you may, you can't commit them to the actualities of your own history."

But Tennessee continues to try. Now he has invited the world to take a close look at him, more or less as he is (the lighting of course has been carefully arranged, and he is not one to confuse an Entrance with an Exit). The result should be gratifying. The Glorious Bird is not only recognized but applauded in the streets. When he came to sign copies of the *Memoirs* in a large Manhattan bookstore, nearly a thousand copies were sold and the store had to be shut because of overcrowding. The resemblance to the latter days of Judy Garland would be disquieting were it not for the happy fact that since Tennessee cannot now die young he will probably not die at all (his grandfather lived for almost a century). In any case, artists who continue to find exhilarating the puzzles art proposes never grow bored and so have no need of death.

As for life? Well, that is a hard matter. But it was always a hard matter for those of us born with a sense of the transiency of these borrowed atoms that make up our corporeal being.

"I need," Tennessee writes with sudden poignancy, "somebody to laugh with." Well, don't we all, Bird? Anyway, be happy that your art has proved to be one of those stones that really did make it to Henge, enabling future magicians to gauge from its crafty placement not only the dour winter solstice of our last days but the summer solstice, too—the golden dream, the mimosa, the total freedom, and all that lovely time unspent now spent.

*The New York Review of Books*
*February 5, 1976*

# Chronology

**1925** Born Eugene Luther Vidal, Jr., at West Point Military Academy, October 3, the only child of Eugene Luther Vidal (1895–1969) and Nina Gore Vidal (1903–1978). His father was an instructor of aeronautics at the academy. The Vidal family, which was probably of Sephardic origin, had been successful apothecaries for six centuries in Northern Italy and Austria. They immigrated to the American Midwest in 1848. Nina Gore Vidal was the daughter of Thomas Pryor Gore (1870–1949), the senator (1907–21, 1931–37) from Oklahoma. The Anglo-Irish Gore family had immigrated to Maryland, probably in the early seventeenth century. Farmers, lawyers, doctors, and Methodist ministers, the line that produced Thomas Pryor Gore settled in Virginia, South Carolina, Alabama, Mississippi, and then the Oklahoma territory. T. P. Gore helped organize Oklahoma into a state and became its first United States senator. Eugene Vidal and Nina Gore married in Washington, D.C., in January 1922.

**1925–33** Eugene Vidal resigns his commission and the family moves to Washington, D.C., in late 1925. They live at Senator Gore's home in Rock Creek Park, though at other addresses also. Vidal helps found and run TAT, a forerunner of TWA, and the Ludington Airline, the forerunner of Eastern Airlines. The marriage is increasingly stormy; Vidal travels frequently; he and his wife have overlapping but separate social lives. In 1933, he is appointed director of aeronautics in the Commerce

Department. Eugene, Jr., spends long periods with his Gore grandparents. He attends Potomac School and Landon School briefly, develops a lifelong passion for reading, and is conscripted to read aloud to his grandfather Senator Gore, who has been blind since the age of ten.

**1934–39** Attends Sidwell Friends School in Washington, D.C., for two years (1934–36). In May 1935, the Vidals divorce. In October 1935, Nina marries Hugh D. Auchincloss, a wealthy Washington investment broker with whom she is to have a daughter and a son. She moves with Eugene, Jr., to Merrywood, a Virginia estate on the Potomac. Vidal attends St. Albans School in Washington from 1936 to 1939. He is an erratic, nearsighted student who does well only in what interests him. He plays tennis but declines to participate in team sports. He develops an intimate friendship with a classmate, Jimmie Trimble, a star athelete. In 1937, his father, forced out of his government position, becomes a pioneer inventor in plastics and molded wood; he attempts to apply these products to aviation and various industrial uses with minimal commercial success. Vidal is baptised in order to be confirmed in February 1939 at Washington Cathedral as Eugene Luther Gore Vidal. During the summer of 1939, he travels to England, France, and Italy with a group of St. Albans School students and teachers. In June 1939, Nina Vidal removes Eugene, against his wishes, from St. Albans school and enrolls him in the Los Alamos Ranch School in New Mexico, which he attends from 1939–40. In December 1939, Eugene Vidal marries twenty-year-old Katharine Roberts, with whom he is to have two children.

**1940–43** Enrolls for the 1940 summer session at Phillips Exeter Academy. He spends much of his time reading, and writing poems, essays, short stories, and a novel. He also draws and sculpts enthusiastically. A prominent student debater, he is much influenced in his political opinions by his anti-Roosevelt, anti–New Deal isolationist grandfather, in whose honor he informally drops Eugene Luther from his name. In 1941 his mother and Hugh Auchincloss are divorced. In July 1943, after graduation, Vidal enlists as a private in the army. He is too young for active service, and is sent for three months to an engineering program at Virginia Military Institute.

**1943–45** Unable to qualify because of poor eyesight for officer's training or for West Point, Vidal becomes a junior-grade warrant officer in the army's sea transport service. He serves from December 1944 to March 1945 as first mate on a freight supply ship in the Aleutian Islands, off the Alaskan coast in the Bering Sea. On various leaves, he spends time in Los Angeles, where his mother now lives, and in New York. In Alaska he contracts rheumatoid arthritis and is hospitalized in Van Nuys, California, then is transferred to Camp Gordon Johnson in Florida, where he finishes a novel, *Williwaw.* In late 1945 he is employed in New York as an associate editor by E. P. Dutton, which has agreed to publish his novel. Meets Anaïs Nin in late 1945.

**1946–49** Officially discharged from the army in February 1946. Lives at his father's Manhattan apartment and works daily at E. P. Dutton. Continues to write and circulate poems for publication. Resigns from Dutton in spring 1946 in order to write full-time. *Williwaw,* published June 1946, is a success, and in the next few years Vidal becomes a part of New York literary and cultural life. In 1946, he buys a writing retreat in Antigua, Guatemala, where Anaïs Nin visits him. He writes *In a Yellow Wood* (1947) and the controversial *The City and the Pillar* (1948), dedicated to J.T. (Jimmie Trimble). In March 1948, Vidal meets Tennessee Williams in Rome. He also meets Santayana, Frederic Prokosch, and Samuel Barber. Williams and Vidal travel together in southern Italy; they stay in Naples and Amalfi and visit Ravello. In April, Vidal visits Cairo. Meets Gide and Cocteau in Paris. Also Christopher Isherwood, with whom, as with Bowles and Williams, he develops a lifelong friendship. In London and Cambridge, Isherwood and John Lehmann, his British publisher, introduce him to the remnants of the Bloomsbury world and to early post–World War II British literary and social life. In early 1949, he publishes *The Season of Comfort,* dedicated to his father. In March 1949, Senator Gore dies.

**1950–54** Conceives and helps edit Victor Weybright's paperback anthology *New World Writing.* Publishes *Dark Green, Bright Red* (1950). In July, with the encouragement of a new friend, Alice Astor, he buys a run-down Federal-period house, Edgewater, on the Hudson near Rhinebeck, New York. Labor Day 1950 he meets Howard Austen, who becomes his closest friend and a regular visitor at Edgewater. Gradually Austen assumes responsibility for many domestic aspects of Vidal's life. At Edgewater, he works on a novel, *The Judgment of Paris,* which is published in 1952. When this book and his next novel, *Messiah* (1954), dedicated to Williams, are not commercially successful, he turns to live television drama.

**1954–56** Creates about thirty original scripts and adaptations for television and soon stabilizes his finances. The most successful scripts are *Dark Possession* (1954), *Summer Pavilion* (1955), *A Sense of Justice* (1955), *The Death of Billy the Kid* (1955), *Visit* *to a Small Planet* (1955), *Honor* (1956), and *The Indestructible Mr. Gore* (1959). In 1955 he signs a five-year contract to write scripts for MGM. They will include *The Catered Affair, I Accuse, The Scapegoat,* and a portion of the script of *Ben-Hur,* for which he is not credited. In 1950 he meets Joanne Woodward; in 1954, Paul Newman, who stars in *The Death of Billy the Kid* and its movie version, *The Left-Handed Gun* (not written by Vidal). At the Chateau Marmont in 1955, his residence in Los Angeles, the three become close friends. In 1956 Zero Press publishes *A Thirsty Evil: Seven Short Stories,* several of them with homosexual themes.

**1957–59** In early 1957 he adapts his television script *Visit to a Small Planet* into a stage play that has a successful Broadway run of 338 performances. That summer he shares a Malibu house with Newman, Woodward, and Austen. In London, in early 1958, he rents a flat at Chesham Place, where he is joined by Austen and by his mother. After a bitter row, he never sees her again. In January 1958 he works at MGM studios in London on a filmscript of *The Scapegoat.* In New York, he again meets Jacqueline Bouvier (whose mother had married Hugh Auchincloss) and becomes friendly with the Kennedys. In Rhinebeck, he regularly sees the Bard College group and their associates, Mary McCarthy, Saul Bellow, Ralph Ellison, Dwight McDonald, Philip Rahv, Richard Rovere, and especially Fred and Barbara (Andy) Dupee. During the winter of 1958–59 he writes the film adaptation of *Suddenly Last Summer.* By the end of the 1950s he is writing frequent drama reviews for *The Reporter* and on literary and political topics for *The Nation* and *Esquire*.

**1959–61** In 1959 he writes *The Best Man*; the next year it has a successful Broadway run of 520 performances. He becomes a regular guest on a number of TV talk shows, particularly David Susskind's. In early 1960 Vidal accepts the Democratic Party's nomination for Congress from his Dutchess County district. Eleanor Roosevelt becomes a patron and friend. In July he is a delegate to the Democratic National Convention in Los Angeles that nominates John F. Kennedy for president. In November he runs far ahead of the Democratic national ticket in his heavily Republican district but loses nonetheless. The success of *Visit to a Small Planet* and *The Best Man* on Broadway and his income from movie scripts make him financially independent. At the beginning of 1961 he returns full-time to writing fiction. In 1961 he writes two unpublished essays, "On Campaigning" and "Pederasty, Plato, and Mr. Barrett," the latter a cultural defense of homosexuality. Increasingly prominent as an essayist, in 1961 he attacks Barry Goldwater in "A Liberal Meets Mr. Conservative" (*Life,* June 9, 1961) and the reactionary right in "The Wrath of the Radical Right" (*Esquire,* December 1961).

**1962–64** His play *Romulus* opens January 1962 at the Music Box Theatre and runs for 69 performances. Little, Brown brings out his first collection of essays, *Rocking the Boat: A Political, Literary and Theatrical Commentary.* Heinemann in London brings out *Three Plays* (*Visit to a Small Planet, On the March to the Sea, The Best Man*). Early in 1962 he seriously considers and then decides against accepting the New York Democratic nomination for the Senate. In January 1963 Vidal and Austen depart for Italy; they take an apartment on Via Giulia in Rome, where he works on *Julian.* Completes his break with the Kennedys with the publication of "The Best Man, 1968" (*Esquire,* March 1963), a severe attack on Robert Kennedy, whom he predicts the Kennedy family is grooming to succeed John Kennedy in 1968. *The New York Review of Books* is founded in mid-1963, and Vidal writes for the first issue. He continues to publish essays there regularly. In August–September 1963 he is in Hollywood for the filming of *The Best Man,* starring Henry Fonda. In late fall he finishes *Julian.*

**1964–65** In May 1964, *Julian* is published and becomes a number one bestseller. In August 1964, Vidal covers the Republican National Convention in San Francisco on television; appears widely on political and entertainment talk shows. In the fall, Vidal supports the incumbent Republican New York senator, Kenneth Keating, for reelection in a race against Robert Kennedy. Vidal is co-chairman of a Democrats for Keating committee. In November, 1.7 million New York Democrats vote against Kennedy, who nevertheless wins in the Lyndon Johnson landslide. The film version of *The Best Man* opens. Writes the play *Drawing Room Comedy.* Rewrites *The City and the Pillar* with changed ending. Begins writing a long-contemplated Washington novel.

**1966–68** In June 1966 Vidal moves to a penthouse apartment in "a crumbling palazzo" at 21, Via di Torre Argentina, his Roman residence until 1993. Works on *Washington, D.C.* throughout the year and finishes a nearly final draft in September. Little, Brown publishes *Washington, D.C.,* dedicated to the Dupees. In Rome in April–May 1967 he writes *Myra Breckinridge,* dedicated to Christopher Isherwood; in July he sends completed manuscript to Little, Brown. Writes a political play, *Weekend,* which opens in New Haven in February 1968, then at the National Theatre, Washington, where it breaks house attendance records. After bad reviews in New York it has a disappointing 22-performance Broadway run in late March–early April. *Myra Breckinridge,* published in January 1968, becomes an immediate bestseller. Works on a screenplay of *Myra.* Attends the Republican and Democratic National Conventions in August 1968, during which he appears on ABC television paired with William F. Buckley. Discussions are philosphically, politically, and personally acrimonious and lead to a dramatic on-camera confrontation on August 28. After the convention he joins with other Eugene McCarthy supporters to create the New Party.

**1969–70** Early 1969 he visits Los Angeles to see his father, who has cancer. Eugene Vidal dies on February 2. Vidal's new book of essays, *Reflections Upon a Sinking Ship,* is published by Little, Brown in April. He takes a five-year lease on a vacation apartment in Klosters, Switzerland where various literary and film-world figures, including Greta Garbo, are his neighbors. Spends August in Klosters and works on a new novel, *Two Sisters: A Memoir in the Form of a Novel,* which he finishes in October. In late December he sells Edgewater. *Two Sisters* is published in June 1970. It is not a critical or commercial success. Encouraged by his friend Jason Epstein, he leaves Little, Brown for Random House, where Epstein becomes his editor.

**1971–72** In Los Angeles May 1971 he works on a film and begins to write *Burr.* In the fall Austen locates through a newspaper advertisement a cliffside villa in Ravello which Vidal purchases for a summer residence. February–March 1972, Vidal is in New York attending rehearsals of *An Evening with Richard Nixon,* which opens on April 30 at the Shubert Theatre; it runs for 13 performances. A regular guest on the Jack Paar show in the early 1960s, he becomes in the 1970s and for the next twenty years a regular guest on *The Tonight Show* with Johnny Carson. In June 1972, Vidal and Austen take possession of La Rondinaia, the run-down villa in Ravello that they gradually renovate into a comfortable home capable of year-round occupancy. In the fall Random House publishes *Homage to Daniel Shays: Collected Essays, 1952–1972.* In Rome, fall–winter 1972, he works on *Burr.*

**1973–76** Works at Ravello for much of winter–spring 1973 on revisions of *Burr,* which is published by Random House on November 1; it becomes a number one bestseller. Works on *Myron,* a sequel to *Myra Breckinridge,* for much of 1973. Works on *1876* throughout the second half of the year. *Myron* is published by Random House in November 1974, and *1876* a year and a half later. Vidal appears on the cover of *Time.* Works on *Gore Vidal's*

*Caligula,* then withdraws entirely from the project. Buys 2562 Outpost Drive, a house in the Hollywood Hills.

**1977–80** Random House publishes *Matters of Fact and of Fiction: Essays, 1971–1976,* in March 1977. Vidal writes and extensively rewrites *Kalki* throughout 1977. In early April 1978 Nina Gore Olds, whom he has not seen since 1958, dies in New York of lung cancer and emphysema. He spends winter 1978–79 in Los Angeles, working on *Creation,* and returns to Italy in March. Continues to work on *Creation* and writes a screenplay, *Dress Gray.* Agrees to write a script for a television miniseries based on the life of Lincoln. *Views from a Window: Conversations with Gore Vidal,* a collection of interviews, is published in spring 1980.

**1981–83** Random House publishes *Creation* in March 1981. That summer, Jason Epstein encourages him to transform his miniseries scripts and his projected stage play based on the life of Lincoln into a novel. In November *The Nation* publishes "Pink Triangle and Yellow Star," in which Vidal compares the minority position of homosexuals with that of Jews and calls for an alliance between them. In March 1982, he becomes a candidate for the Democratic nomination for senator from California. In April Random House publishes *The Second American Revolution and Other Essays, 1976–1982*; it wins the National Book Critics Circle award for criticism. Campaigns vigorously March–June 1982, mostly through personal appearances, on an anti-military-budget platform and with a call for additional money for education and social services. Loses to Governor Jerry Brown in the June primary, getting approximately a half million votes; he comes in second in a field of nine candidates. In August he visits Moscow and then Mongolia to write an article about threats to the environment; spends a week in Bangkok. In late fall he begins writing the novel about Lincoln. In May Random House publishes *Duluth.* In a ceremony at the beginning of October 1983, Vidal is made an honorary citizen of Ravello. His friend and admirer Italo Calvino gives the main speech.

**1984–85** In June 1984 Random House publishes *Lincoln*; it becomes an immense bestseller. By August he has begun the next volume in the American history series, "Manifest Destiny," which will later be published as *Empire.* In November 1984 he writes an autobiographical essay, "On Flying." At the invitation of Norman Mailer and on the same program with Mailer, in November 1985 he speaks in New York at a benefit for PEN. His subject is "The Day the American Empire Ran Out of Gas."

**1986–87** Vidal's criticism of America's role in the Cold War and its support of hard-line Israeli positions against the Palestinians leads to accusations of anti-Semitism. Engages in an ongoing debate (his contributions appear mostly in *The Nation*) with American neoconservatives. Mid-August 1986 he finishes *Empire.* In February 1987 he attends a conference organized by Mikhail Gorbachev at the Kremlin in Moscow, where he gives a speech on the origins of the Cold War. In June *Empire* is published. At the request of the historian William Appleman Williams, he speaks on the Cold War in Eugene, Oregon. In October *The Best Man* has a brief revival at the Ahmanson Theatre in Los Angeles. Visits Brown University, where he is the subject of a three-day symposium and awarded an honorary degree. In November a *South Bank Show* on the BBC is devoted to Vidal. During the last two weeks of November 1987 he is in England for the British publication of *Empire,* a volume of essays (*Armageddon? Essays, 1983–1987*), and a single-volume reissue of *Myra/Myron*. In November *The New York Review of Books* publishes his essay on Dawn Powell, which precipitates a revival of the work of the forgotten novelist.

**1988–90** In Rome and at Ravello for much of the winter. April 1988, ABC airs a miniseries based on *Lincoln*. Vidal responds to criticism by some scholars of his depiction of Lincoln; addresses the National Press Club in Washington on the national security state. Spends much of the spring and summer at Ravello, working on *Hollywood* and writing essays. In November, Random House publishes *At Home: Essays 1982–1988.* He writes *Gore Vidal's Billy the Kid* for TNT cable network. Finishes *Hollywood* in the late summer. Begins writing *Live from Golgotha*. Works on a film script of *Kalki* and writes the screenplay for *To Forget Palermo,* directed by Francesco Rosi. In Paris in July he participates in a television panel on the occasion of the bicentennial of the Rights of Man. In August 1989 a day is devoted to honoring him at the Edinburgh Festival. February 1990, Random House publishes *Hollywood.* In May he attends the annual Gore family reunion, this one in Houston, Mississippi, where he is filmed for a BBC program, *Gore Vidal's Gore Vidal.* During the summer he writes a movie script for Martin Scorsese based on the lives of Theodora and Justinian. In September he presides over the annual film festival in Venice. In the autumn he works on *Live from Golgotha.*

**1991–93** Writes a script for ABC for a two-hour television movie adaptation of *Burr.* Gives the Massey lectures in the History of

American Civilization at Harvard, April 1–3, 1991. In November Vidal lectures at East Anglia University and spends two weeks as a fellow at Dartmouth. Addresses the National Press Club in Washington in December. Publishes *A View from the Diners Club: Essays 1987–1991* in Britain. In April 1992, he gives the Lowell lecture at Harvard on monotheism and its discontents. In August he plays the role of a United States senator in the film *Bob Roberts.* Harvard University Press publishes the Massey lectures under the title *Screening History. Live from Golgotha* is published and becomes a bestseller. In February 1993 Random House publishes *United States: Essays 1952–1992,* which wins the National Book Award. Works on a memoir in winter–spring 1993. In April he and Austen give up their Rome apartment for year-round residency at La Rondinaia. In Washington, D.C., he speaks at the Folger Library, in conjunction with screenings at the Kennedy Center of the films discussed in *Screening History.* Spends two weeks in Chicago, acting in the film *With Honors.* In July, he lectures in seven German cities and in Norway and Austria. In October 1993 he lectures at the Cheltenham Literary Festival in Britain.

**1994–98** In March 1994 he is in Washington being filmed for two documentaries. Early in 1995 he lectures at Oxford and a few months later goes to Richmond, Virginia, to appear in a film and then to Washington for further filming. *The City and the Pillar and Seven Early Stories* is published, followed by *Palimpsest,* which appears on October 3, his seventieth birthday. The British-made two-hour BBC television documentary on his life is aired in the United States to coincide with this occasion. In January 1996 in London he records for British television a three-part program on the history of the American presidency. *The Smithsonian Institution* is published in March 1998. It becomes a bestseller.

# Bibliography

*At Home: Essays 1982–1988.* New York: Random House, 1988.
*Armageddon? Essays, 1983–1987.* London: André Deutsch, 1987.
*The Best Man: A Play of Politics.* Boston: Little, Brown, 1960.
*Burr.* New York: Random House, 1973.
*The City and the Pillar.* New York: E. P. Dutton, 1948. Rev. ed., New York: E. P. Dutton, 1965.
*The City and the Pillar and Seven Early Stories.* New York: Random House, 1995.
*Creation.* New York: Random House, 1981.
*Dark Green, Bright Red.* New York: E. P. Dutton, 1950. Rev. ed., New York: New American Library, 1968.
*Duluth.* New York: Random House, 1983.
*1876.* New York: Random House, 1976.
*Empire.* New York: Random House, 1987.
*An Evening with Richard Nixon.* New York: Random House, 1972.
*Hollywood.* New York: Random House, 1990.
*Homage to Daniel Shays: Collected Essays, 1952–1972.* New York: Random House, 1972. London: William Heinemann, 1974.
*In a Yellow Wood.* New York: E. P. Dutton, 1947.
*The Judgment of Paris.* New York: E. P. Dutton, 1952. Rev. ed., Boston: Little, Brown, 1965.
*Julian.* Boston: Little, Brown, 1964.
*Kalki.* New York: Random House, 1978.
*Lincoln.* New York: Random House, 1984.

*Live from Golgotha.* New York: Random House, 1992.
*Matters of Fact and of Fiction: Essays, 1973–1976.* New York: Random House, 1977.
*Messiah.* New York: E. P. Dutton, 1954. Rev. ed., Boston: Little, Brown, 1965.
*Myra Breckinridge.* Boston: Little, Brown, 1968.
*Myron.* New York: Random House, 1974.
*On the March to the Sea: A Southron Tragedy.* Evergreen Playscript Series. New York: Grove Press, n.d.
*Palimpsest: A Memoir.* New York: Random House, 1995.
*Reflections Upon a Sinking Ship.* Boston: Little, Brown, 1969.
*Rocking the Boat.* Boston: Little, Brown, 1962.
*Romulus: A New Comedy, Adapted from a Play by Friedrich Dürrenmatt.* New York: Dramatists Play Service, 1962.
*Screening History.* Cambridge, Mass.: Harvard University Press, 1992.
*A Search for the King: A Twelfth-Century Legend.* New York: E. P. Dutton, 1950.
*The Season of Comfort.* New York: E. P. Dutton, 1949.
*The Second American Revolution and Other Essays, 1976–1982.* New York: Random House, 1982.
*Sex, Death and Money.* New York: Bantam Books, 1968.
*The Smithsonian Institution.* New York: Random House, 1998.
*A Thirsty Evil: Seven Short Stories.* New York: Zero Press, 1956.
*Three: Williwaw, A Thirsty Evil, Julian the Apostate.* New York: New American Library, 1962.
*Three Plays.* London: William Heinemann, 1962.
*Two Sisters: A Memoir in the Form of a Novel.* Boston: Little, Brown, 1970.
*United States: Essays 1952–1992.* New York: Random House, 1993.
*A View from the Diners Club: Essays 1987–1991.* London: André Deutsch, 1991.
*Views from a Window: Conversations with Gore Vidal.* Edited by Robert J. Stanton and Gore Vidal. Secaucus, N.J.: Lyle Stuart, 1980.
*Virgin Islands: Essays 1992–1997.* London: André Deutsch, 1997.
*Visit to a Small Planet: A Comedy Akin to a Vaudeville* [Broadway Version]. Boston: Little, Brown, 1957.
*Visit to a Small Planet and Other Television Plays.* Boston: Little, Brown, 1956.
*Washington, D.C.* Boston: Little, Brown, 1967.
*Weekend: A Comedy in Two Acts.* New York: Dramatists Play Service, 1968.
*Williwaw.* New York: E. P. Dutton, 1946.

# ABOUT THE EDITOR

FRED KAPLAN is Distinguished Professor of English at Queens College and the Graduate Center of the City University of New York. He is the author of three biographies: *Thomas Carlyle* (1983), which was nominated for the National Book Critics' Circle Award and was a jury-nominated finalist for the Pulitzer Prize; *Charles Dickens* (1988); and *Henry James, The Imagination of Genius* (1992). He is also the author of three studies of Romantic and Victorian British literature and culture: *Miracles of Rare Device: The Poet's Sense of Self in Nineteenth-Century Poetry* (1972), *Dickens and Mesmerism: The Hidden Springs of Fiction* (1975), and *Sacred Tears: Sentimentality in Victorian Literature* (1987). He is the editor of *Dickens' Book of Memoranda* (1981), an annotated edition of *Oliver Twist* (1993), and *Traveling in Italy with Henry James* (1994). He has held Guggenheim and National Endowment for the Humanities Fellowships and been a Fellow of the National Humanities Center, the Huntington Library, and the Rockefeller Study Center at Bellagio. He is at work on a biography of Gore Vidal.

# ABOUT THE TYPE

This book was set in Times Roman, a typeface designed by Stanley Morison specifically for *The Times* of London. Times Roman was introduced in the newspaper in 1932. It had its greatest success in the United States as a book and commercial typeface, rather than one used in newspapers.